Handbook of Research Methods in Early Childhood Education

Review of Research Methodologies

Volume I

A volume in
Contemporary Perspectives in Early Childhood Education
Olivia N. Saracho, *Series Editor*

Handbook of Research Methods in Early Childhood Education

Review of Research Methodologies

Volume I

edited by
Olivia N. Saracho
University of Maryland

INFORMATION AGE PUBLISHING, INC.
Charlotte, NC • www.infoagepub.com

Library of Congress Cataloging-in-Publication Data

Handbook of research methods in early childhood education : research methodologies / edited by Olivia N. Saracho, University of Maryland.
    pages cm.
  ISBN 978-1-62396-610-2 (pbk.) – ISBN 978-1-62396-611-9 (hardcover) – ISBN 978-1-62396-612-6 (e-book) 1. Early childhood education–Research. I. Saracho, Olivia N.
  LB1139.225.H36 2014
  372.21–dc23
                                                                  2014002397

Copyright © 2015 Information Age Publishing Inc.

All rights reserved. No part of this publication may be reproduced, stored in a retrieval system, or transmitted, in any form or by any means, electronic, mechanical, photocopying, microfilming, recording or otherwise, without written permission from the publisher.

Printed in the United States of America

EDITORIAL ADVISORY BOARD

Bernard Spodek
University of Illinois
Champaign-Urbana, IL

Doris Bergen
Miami University
Oxford, OH

Roy Evans
Brunel University
Twickenham, Middlesex, UK

Joe Frost
University of Texas at Austin
Austin, TX

Eugene García
Arizona State University
Tempe, AZ

Celia Genishi
Teachers College, Columbia University
New York, NY

Amos Hatch
University of Tennessee
Knoxville, TN

Mary Renck Jalongo
Indiana University of Pennsylvania
Indiana, Pennsylvania

Michaelene M. Ostrosky
University of Illinois at
Urbana-Champaign
Champaign IL

Kelvin Seifert
University of Manitoba
Winnipeg, MB, Canada

CONSULTING EDITORS

Volume I

Debbie Albon
Lisa S. Badanes
Sara Baker
John Barker
Barbara R Beatty
Aaron Bodle
Heather A. Bower
Steven R. Brown
Antony Bryant
Lee D. Butterfield
Andrade Chittaranjan
Antonius H Cillessen
Elena Commodari
Catherine Compton-Lilly
Susan Danby
Christine S. Davis
Sarah Eagle
Caroline Eick
Montserrat Fargas-Malet
Barbara Finkelstein
Maria Assunção Folque
Jackie Goodway
Dwayne D. Gremler

Frances Hancock
Blythe F. Hinitz
James Hoot
Diane Jass Ketelhut
Burke R. Johnson
Victoria-Maria MacDonald
Glenda MacNaughton
Joseph McCaleb
Judith Lynne McConnell-Farmer
Robert Mikecz
Reidar Mosvold
Amanda L. Nolen
Germán Posada
Joann L. Robinson
Tonette S. Rocco
Wendy Schiller
Ali Fuad Selvi
Wayne H. Slater
Dorothy Sluss
Spyros Spyrou
Christine Stephen
Andrew Stremmel
Ronan Van Rossem

CONTENTS

1 Research Methodologies for Studying Young Children 1
   Olivia N. Saracho

PART I
SYSTEMATIC RESEARCH METHODOLOGIES

2 Using Peer Sociometrics and Behavioral Nominations With
   Young Children 27
   Heidi Gazelle, Richard A. Faldowski, and Divya Peter

3 Sociometric Measures for Peer Relations Research With Young
   Children 71
   Rosanne Burton Smith

4 Using Q Methodology in Conducting Research With Young
   Children 147
   Aesha John, Diane Montgomery, and Amy L. Halliburton Tate

5 Q-Methodology and Q-sorting as Tools for Addressing
   Research Questions in Educational Settings: Historical
   Overview and Illustrations Using Three Standardized Q-Sets 175
   Brian E. Vaughn, António J. Santos, and Gabrielle Coppola

viii ▪ Contents

    6 The Delphi Process 203
         Ian P. Sinha and Olivia N. Saracho

    7 Using the Critical Incident Technique in Early Childhood
        Research 225
         Beth S. Rous

    8 Utility of Implementation and Intervention Performance
        Checklists for Conducting Research in Early Childhood
        Education 247
         Carl J. Dunst, Carol M. Trivette, and Melinda Raab

    9 Ethical, Narrative, and Projective Processes in Research
        Interviews With Young Children 277
         Helen L. Cameron

  10 Story Completion Play Narrative Methods for Preschool
        Children 323
         Shira Yuval-Adler and David Oppenheim

  11 Using Mixed Methods in Research With Young Children
        Across Cultures and Contexts 383
         Linda Liebenberg and Michael Ungar

PART II

QUALITATIVE RESEARCH METHODOLOGIES

  12 Grounded Theory 405
         Robert Thornberg, Lisa M. Perhamus, and Kathy Charmaz

  13 Conducting Early Childhood Qualitative Research in the
        Twenty-First Century 441
         J. Amos Hatch and Chonika Coleman-King

  14 Innovative Qualitative Research Methods With Children
        Aged 4–7 Years 479
         Karen Winter

  15 Case Study Research: The Child in Context 523
         Susan Hill and Ngaire Millar

  16 Action Research With Children 547
         Kylie Smith

17 Microethnographic Research in Early Childhood Education 577
   John A. Sutterby

18 Preschoolers' Selective Learning From Adults: Lessons
   for Research Methods in Early Childhood Education 601
   Kathleen H. Corriveau and Julie Dwyer

19 Conducting Historical Research in Early Childhood Education 645
   Sue C. Wortham

20 Past As Prologue: Doing Historical Research in Early
   Childhood Education 667
   Edna Runnels Ranck

PART III

THE RESEARCH PROCESS:
FROM CONCEPTUALIZATION TO PUBLICATION

21 Methods for Developing Scientific Education: Research-Based
   Development of Practices, Pedagogies, Programs, and Policies 717
   Douglas H. Clements and Julie Sarama

22 Re-Examining the Literature Review: Purposes, Approaches,
   and Issues 753
   Mary Renck Jalongo and Kelly Heider

23 Reading and Interpreting Early Childhood Research 783
   Angela C. Baum and Paula McMurray-Schwarz

24 Elements in Writing Scientific Research Publications 801
   Olivia N. Saracho

25 Writing for Publication on Research with Young Children 819
   Nancy Dixon

   About the Contributors 853

CHAPTER 1

RESEARCH METHODOLOGIES FOR STUDYING YOUNG CHILDREN

Olivia N. Saracho

For several decades early childhood education programs have expanded throughout the world. Various countries faced many difficulties and trepidations with these programs. In the United States, society has recognized the importance of young children's learning. This is apparent in the growth in enrollments in early childhood education programs. Despite the present economy, enrollment in early childhood education programs has rapidly increased during the previous decade, and quality standards continue to increase in several states in spite of various declines in funding. In 2011–2012 enrollment in early childhood education programs continued to increase at a remarkable high rate (Barnett, Carolan, Fitzgerald, & Squires, 2012). In the year 2020–2021, it is projected that this population will increase to 37.4 million students (Aud et al., 2011).

The increase in enrollment has lead to the expansion of early childhood teacher education programs at the community college and university levels. Similar to this growth is the increase in knowledge in early childhood education that may be due to the broad-spectrum knowledge outburst in our

Handbook of Research Methods in Early Childhood Education, pages 1–23
Copyright © 2015 by Information Age Publishing
All rights of reproduction in any form reserved.

society and throughout the world. This development has led to an increase of early childhood education research studies, research journals, research associations (Spodek & Saracho, 2003), and government funding.

This sudden increase of knowledge and related research outcomes in early childhood education requires that researchers contribute to this knowledge. Such requirement motivated the development and publication of the *Handbook of Research Methods in Early Childhood Education*. The *Handbook* can be an important guide to researchers who conduct studies in the early childhood education field.

RESEARCH AND THE KNOWLEDGE BASE IN EARLY CHILDHOOD EDUCATION

Knowledge in early childhood education derives from theory, research, and practice. Although these areas usually give the impression to be isolated from each other, they are interrelated. The process of generating knowledge is *cyclical*, instead of being deductive (top down) or linear (one step continuously go after the other). All forms intersect. The process typically is initiated with a problem or issue that must be investigated through research, which is motivated by theory and practice. The outcomes also affect theory and practice, which then offer guidelines for forthcoming research studies. Saracho and Spodek (2012) use Figure 1.1[1] to illustrate this cyclical process.

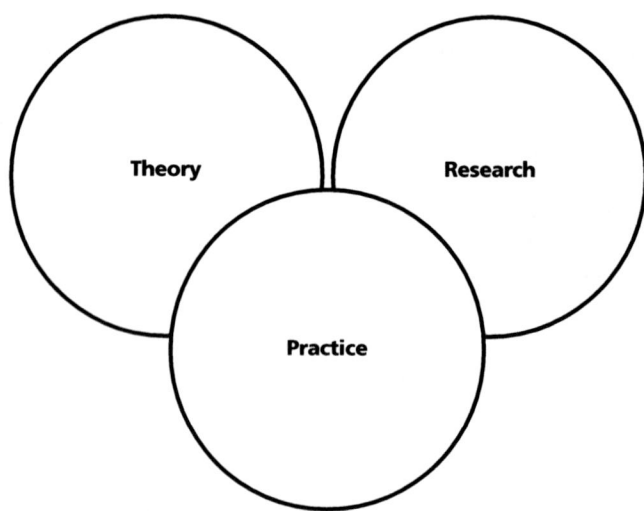

Figure 1.1 Interaction process.

This *Handbook* focuses on research techniques that can be used to conduct studies that will contribute to the knowledge of the early childhood education field. Published research outcomes in early childhood education contribute to the field's knowledge, theory, and practice. They also guide future early childhood education research studies. The research techniques in the *Handbook* are examples of the ones that are available and will be a good beginning for novice researchers. The editor acknowledges that research is only possible because of the theoretical work and the research studies that have been conducted in the past. As researchers, we very much "stand on the shoulders of giants" (Spodek & Saracho, 2003). However, in the early childhood education field, there has been a considerable amount of new theory building as well as the development and use of new research paradigms to conduct research in early childhood education. These are acknowledged here.

Present social and historical situations have also stimulated a more energetic focal point on the prospective for practical effects of the methodical investigation of early childhood education. These conditions have guided numerous early childhood education researchers to take action by concentrating their research on practical problems, such as developing teaching strategies and increasing the children's educational and intellectual development. Empirical examinations in these problem areas have influenced both theoretical and practical foundations. Drawing on previous knowledge and integrating it with contemporary knowledge can provide a better understanding of early childhood education and help the researchers, teachers and children who participate in it.

ENVIRONMENTS THAT ENCOURAGE EARLY CHILDHOOD EDUCATION RESEARCH

Scientists interact to form a scientific community, which consists of numerous "subcommunities" that conduct research in specific scientific areas within institutions. They also engage in interdisciplinary and cross-institutional research experiences. Several environments in early childhood education promote research. These environments:

1. Make it possible for research studies to flourish.
2. Nurture and or allocate ways for research to develop.
3. Provide financial support for research to be conducted.
4. Facilitate the dissemination of research to help researchers communicate and share their work with others (e.g., researchers, practitioners, administrators, policy makers).

5. Motivate a cadre of well-trained researchers who are knowledgeable of their field to form a scientific community.

Universities lead most of the research in the United States. After World War II numerous state teachers colleges became multiuse colleges and ultimately full-fledged universities. As a result, in this period several paths were generated where the output of research increased and flourished in many disciplines except in early childhood education.

Since early childhood education was a small field well into the 1960s, there were no public kindergartens in the southeast or the central areas of the United States. In addition, only a small number of teacher preparation programs in colleges, universities, or community colleges were available. At the beginning of 1970, kindergarten education and the whole field of early childhood education expanded, which established and increased early childhood education programs in colleges and universities. Simultaneously there was an increase in early childhood education doctoral programs and PhDs who were prepared to conduct research to complete the dissertation requirement. Furthermore, the majority of the universities require that their faculty conduct and publish research.

While the development of research in early childhood education expanded in the United States, there were restricted means for disseminating that research. During the previous years, several professional American organizations started to support research journals. The *Early Childhood Research Quarterly* began its publication in 1986. It was sponsored by the National Association for the Education of Young Children (NAEYC) and initially published by Ablex, but it is presently published by Elsevier. Concurrently, the *Journal of Research in Childhood Education* was originally published by the Association of Childhood Education International (ACEI) and is presently published by Taylor and Francis/Routledge. Over the years other research journals in early childhood education were established. These journals included *Early Child Development and Care* published by Taylor and Francis/Routledge, *Early Education and Development* published by Taylor and Francis/Routledge, and *Early Childhood Education* published by Springer Verlag. These journals have become more scholarly and research oriented.

The Society for Research in Child Development (SRCD) and the American Educational Research Association (AERA) are two other professional organizations that assist early childhood education researchers to disseminate their research in early childhood education. The Society for Research in Child Development is a professional organization that concentrates predominantly on child development research. In recent years, SRCD has included early childhood education research in both its journal and its conference programs. SRCD publishes a research journal, *Child Development*, and has a biennial research conference. The American Educational

Research Association sponsors several journals and has an annual conference. AERA is divided into divisions (e.g., Curriculum Studies, History & Historiography, Measurement & Research Methodology, Research, Evaluation, & Assessment in Schools, Social Context of Education) and Special Interest Groups (SIGs) (e.g., Critical Perspectives on Early Childhood Education, Early Education and Child Development, Action Research, Advanced Studies of National Databases). Both the division and SIG groups establish the content of the AERA conference. In the AERA organization, numerous early childhood studies are presented in sessions sponsored by Divisions B (Curriculum Studies) and C (Learning and Instruction). AERA has two special interest groups (SIGs) that focus exclusively on early childhood education research: the Early Education and Child Development SIG and the Critical Perspectives in Early Childhood Education SIG. Additionally, the conference of the National Association for the Education of Young Children integrates a research path. Thus, several opportunities are available to report research and these have expanded recently.

At the same time as the production and dissemination of research in early childhood education has expanded considerably in recent years in the United States, it has also increased to a large extent in other parts of the world. The European Early Childhood Education Research Association with its annual research conference and journal, the *European Journal of Research in Early Childhood Education*, as well as the Pacific Early Childhood Education Research Association with its annual research conference and journal, the *Asia-Pacific Journal of Research in Early Childhood Education*, provide verification of this growth.

The *Handbook of Research Methods in Early Childhood Education* is developed to bring together in one source research techniques that researchers can use to collect data in early childhood education. These studies can then contribute to the knowledge in early childhood education. To conduct valid and reliable studies, researchers need to be knowledgeable about numerous research methodologies. The *Handbook* primarily addresses the researchers, scholars, and graduate or advanced undergraduate students who are preparing to conduct research in early childhood education. It provides them with the intellectual resources that will help them join the cadre of early childhood education researchers and scholars. The purpose of the *Handbook* is to prepare and guide researchers to achieve a high level of competence and sophistication, to avoid past mistakes, and to benefit from the best researchers. This *Handbook* is also useful to professors of education who conduct research and prepare teachers in early childhood education. It aims to improve the researchers' conceptual and methodological abilities in early childhood education. Thus, the *Handbook* can be used as a guide that focuses on important contemporary research methodologies in early childhood education and describes them to offer researchers the necessary information to use these methodologies appropriately.

ORGANIZATION OF THE CURRENT VOLUME

This handbook is organized into three sections:

1. Systematic Research Methodologies
2. Qualitative Research Methodologies
3. The Research Process: From Conceptualization to Publication

Although there are many research methodologies, it is impossible to include them all. However, enough research methodologies are included to help researchers in their studies. Some of the chapters cover the same areas of research but in a different context. The chapters within each section are described below.

Systematic Research Method ologies

Early childhood education researchers need to have a repertoire of methodologies to study complex educational issues and contribute knowledge to the field. Present society requires researchers to go beyond experiments or surveys to address research hypotheses or research questions. Research methodology alternatives have changed dramatically during the past decade or so. Some of the new methodologies have been developed as a result of new, more complex issues being studied, such as the need to study for integrated early childhood services. Some research methodologies have been developed as a result of new paradigms, such as postpositivist, constructivist, critical/feminist, and poststructuralist epistemologies. In addition, more traditional methodologies have expanded to embrace new views of what is research and what is researchable. Educational researchers need a repertoire of methodologies to study complex educational issues such as the children's social behavior.

The children's classmates can provide a unique and valuable source of information about children's social behavior and social relationships among peers. They offer an "inside" perception of the children's perceptions, appraisals, interactions, and relationships with one another. The next two chapters describe how researchers can gather data using peer informants. In the first chapter titled, "*Using Peer Sociometrics and Behavioral Nominations With Young Children,*" Heidi Gazelle, Richard A. Faldowski, and Divya Peter provide an overview of current peer report methodology appropriate for young children from three to seven years of age, including peer sociometrics as well as peer reports of peer treatment, friendship, and child behavior. The chapter opens with a discussion of the value of peer reports relative to other sources of information about children's peer relations and social behavior and a brief historical overview of peer report methodology. Subsequent sections review peer report content; administration procedures; validity, reliability, and stability measures; methods of statistical analysis and interpretation; and ethical considerations. These topics are discussed with consideration of issues specific to children from three to seven years of age. Contemporary methodological practices are distinguished from older approaches. Likewise, the chapter features a discussion of innovative approaches to the statistical analysis of peer report data. Rosanne Burton Smith also describes this methodology in similar and different ways. In her chapter titled, "*Sociometric Measures for Peer Relations Research With Young Children,*" Rosanne Burton Smith offers essential information for researchers using sociometric assessments with young children. She focuses on investigators who are developing their own sociometric instruments as well as those using existing sociometric methods. It covers the two aspects of children's peer relationships assessed by sociometric methods—friendship and peer group status—detailing with how the different approaches to measuring these aspects can be carried out as well as their limitations and advantages for assessing young children. Methods of estimating the validity and reliability of different sociometric approaches are discussed, along with caveats for the application of sociometric measurement to young children. Sociometric classification is explained with details of how different schemes can be developed. Their validity and reliability estimates are discussed, along with suggestions on how investigators can evaluate the meaning and stability of different sociometric categories in young children. Ethical considerations for the participation of young children in sociometric research are described.

Early childhood educators and researchers confront a wide-range of assessment challenges in developing and improving curricula and learning environments that are developmentally appropriate and meet the young children's needs and interests. They also need to assess the value of the curricula and monitor the young children's progress. Therefore, they need to select reliable and valid measures to determine the young children's progress and the worth of the curriculum. These two domains suggest different research questions (e.g., a direct focus on child performance within a school setting *vs.* a focus setting conditions characteristic of different education settings that may interact directly or indirectly with children's abilities and other attributes to affect their academic performance). These research questions may require assessments that are more "subjective" (or qualitative) measures that are not readily standardized across different school settings and the results of analysis for these types of data may be more descriptive.

The next two chapters describe the type of methodology that can be used for subjective data, although objective (quantitative) data may also be used. A research methodology to use for these research questions may be Q-Methodology, which is a research method used in psychology and other social sciences to study people's "subjectivity"—that is, their point of view. Q-Methodology, also referred to as Q-sort is a ranking of variables that are usually presented as statements that are printed on small cards. In the chapter titled, "*Using Q-Methodology in Conducting Research With Young Children,*" Aesha John, Diane Montgomery, and Amy L. Halliburton Tate describe the relevance of Q-methodology to the field of early childhood research, with a special focus on participatory research. First, the chapter outlines the various steps involved in carrying a Q study. Specifically, it provides detailed directions for constructing a concourse, developing a Q-set, and conducting Q-sorts. The various steps are substantiated with examples from past Q studies in the early childhood field. Second, the chapter includes reviews of past Q studies to demonstrate the potential of Q-methodology to address a diverse set of early childhood research questions. Third, the chapter discusses how Q-methodology presents opportunities to early childhood researchers to keep pace with the emerging trends. The chapter concludes with key issues relevant to Q-methodology such as variations within Q-methodology, methodological limitations, and the potential place of Q-methodology in the research toolkit. In the following chapter titled, "*Q-Methodology and Q-Sorting as Tools for Addressing Research Questions in Educational Settings: Historical Overview and Illustrations Using Three Standardized Q-Sets,*" Brian E. Vaughn, António J. Santos, and Gabrielle Coppola present a brief overview of Q-methodology and Q-sorting as tools for answering research questions in educational settings. The Q-method was originally intended as a means to represent subjective realities of persons but has been extended by behavioral and developmental scientists to provide objective descriptions of persons and other entities. Following the overview of the methodology and techniques, illustrative examples are provided from published and unpublished data to show how these techniques might be used in educational settings.

Several researchers have used the Delphi technique to elicit and refine the combined opinion and expertise of a panel of experts to reach a consensus, which indicates how effective decisions are made in situations where there is inconsistent or scarce information. Consensus is achieved through brainstorming, nominal group technique, and the "Delphi" survey technique, which is a systematic method to acquire the opinions and, preferably a consensus from a panel of experts on a specific issue. The Delphi technique is a method of ascertaining the opinions of a group of experts to reach consensus around areas of uncertainty. The Delphi is a research technique that has been extensively applied to a broad range of problems in a variety of areas. Since the technique was established in the early 1950s at the Rand Corporation, many deviations of the Delphi have emerged to guide researchers to examine their unique research problems. In the chapter titled, "*The Delphi Process*," Ian P. Sinha and Olivia N. Saracho define the Delphi technique as well as discuss consensus development methods, the use of the Delphi as a research technique, steps in designing a Delphi research study (including validity and reliability), important methodological considerations for researchers, and highlight potential pitfalls. The chapter concludes with recommendations for the reporting of studies that utilize the Delphi technique, such that people reading the report will be able to comprehensively understand and critique the methods and results. The chapter deals mainly with the use of the Delphi technique for reaching consensus in order to formulate a "list," as this is the manner in which it is most likely to be used, but the methodological recommendations also pertain to studies that use the technique for other purposes. This chapter does not deal with the development and validation of questionnaires, which are covered elsewhere in this book.

A research technique that is used to observe human behaviors and identify the subjects' perceptions is termed critical incidents. Flanagan (1954) defines critical incidents as:

> any observable human activity that is sufficiently complete in itself to permit inferences and predictions to be made about the person performing the act. To be critical, an incident must occur in a situation where the purpose or intent of the act seems fairly clear to the observer and where its consequences are sufficiently definite to leave little doubt concerning its effects. (p. 327)

Presently, researchers continue to use the Critical Incident Technique (CIT) as a research method across a variety of fields, including education, psychology, medicine, and business. The CIT method has been used since 1954 in the study of human behavior, specifically related to job practices. In the chapter titled, "*Using the Critical Incident Technique in Early Childhood Research*," Beth S. Rous provides an overview of the development and processes used to implement research in the field of early care and education using the Critical Incident Technique (CIT). The CIT method presents a five step process flexible enough to be modified across settings and can be implemented using a variety of data collection methods (i.e., observation, interview, and questionnaire). It is widely used across a number of professional fields, such as nursing, social work, and business. Through the CIT process, participants provide rich descriptions of critical events that allow the researcher to understand why specific decisions were made and explore the outcomes of the event as a way to identify effective behaviors and practices.

A checklist is a list of items, as names or tasks, for comparison, verification, or other checking purposes. It helps individuals ensure consistency and completeness in carrying out a task. A basic example is the "to do list." However, researchers also develop checklists to conduct research. Checklists in research can take on different formats (yes/no, Likert scales, etc.) and can be used to assess adoption and use of practices constituting the focus of investigation. In the chapter titled, *"Utility of Implementation and Intervention Performance Checklists for Conducting Research in Early Childhood Education,"* Carl J. Dunst, Carol M. Trivette, and Melinda Raab describe a process for developing performance checklists and measuring the dependability of use of early childhood practices using checklists. An implementation of the sciences' framework is used for differentiating between implementation practices and intervention practices and hypothesizing the manner in which the two practices are related and would be expected to influence outcomes of interest. The two types of practices are the ones used by early childhood teachers to promote and enhance child learning and development (e.g., Bennett-Armistead, Duke, & Moses, 2005; National Association for the Education of Young Children, 2005; Sandall, Hemmeter, Smith, & McLean, 2005) and the ones used by professional development staff to promote early childhood teachers use of research-based or recommended early childhood practices (e.g., Neuman & Kamil, 2010; Skiffington, Washburn, & Elliott, 2011). An evidence-based approach to developing checklist indicators is described. In addition, findings from a study of both implementation and intervention practices in Head Start classrooms is used to illustrate the applicability of checklists for research in early childhood education.

Interviewing young children for research is a pleasant and valuable experience. Some researchers enjoy engaging young children in research. According to Irwin and Johnson (2005), children as young as four years "can provide important insights into their daily lives and health experiences" (p. 822). Consequently, more researchers are conducting research with young children. Researchers used to consider young children to be unreliable and incomplete objects to be studied. However, their belief has shifted. Presently they consider young children as social agents or "experts" of their own lives (De Jong & Berg, 2008). In the chapter titled, *"Ethical, Narrative and Projective Processes in Research Interviews With Young Children,"* Helen Cameron focuses on individual research interviews with children between three and eight years of age who have some verbal capacity. The ethical management of the relationship between the child and researcher includes confidentiality and consent or assent and mandated reporting. The recording of interviews to gather data for further analysis is discussed. In conducting the interview, the chapter emphasizes the establishment of rapport, adaptation of the physical setting for the interview, and discussion of some ground rules in conversing with the young child. The child's free conversation is seen as encouraged through a range of nonverbal, empathic, and narrative responses. A description of a range of projective activities, applied to enhance individual research interviews, includes the application of drawing, painting, dolls, and other more modern devices. The appropriateness of applying measures of validity and reliability on qualitative data gained from interviews is critiqued. The range of recorded data and the researchers' observations and reflections in research journals are discussed. A description of procedures for analyzing qualitative data is included. Content analysis and an interpretive approach, particularly applicable in qualitative research, is described especially in reference to honoring the intended meaning from the child's actions and accompanying narrative. A related methodology is described next. It has some similarities and differences.

Most of the research involving the socioemotional development of young children and their adjustment relies on adult reports or observations, and much less research relies on children's perspectives. Shira Yuval-Adler and David Oppenheim address this gap in their chapter, *"Story Completionm Play Narrative Methods for Preschool Children."* They describe the story completion play narrative method. Shira Yuval-Adler and David Oppenheim begin by describing the historical roots of story completion methods and proceed to describe three story-completion methods that have accumulated the most research findings: The MacArthur Story Stem Battery (Bretherton, Oppenheim, Buchsbaum, Emde, & the MacArthur Narrative Group, 1990), the Attachment Story Completion Task (Bretherton, Ridgeway, & Cassidy, 1990) and the Manchester Child Attachment Story Task (Green, Stanley, Smith, & Goldwyn, 2000). Next Shira Yuval-Adler and David Oppenheim provide a general overview of the different dimensions on the way children's story completions are coded. Then they summarize empirical evidence regarding the associations between story completion tasks and six domains of child and family functioning: children's attachment, parents' attachment, parenting, children's socioemotional development, measures reflecting the child's family environment, and children's clinical diagnoses. In addition, Shira Yuval-Adler and David Oppenheim provide guidelines for researchers who are interested in using story completion methods. Then they conclude with a methodological critique of the methodology and offer directions for future research.

The past two decades have seen increased attention to both the experiences of children and the resilience processes that facilitate their well-being and positive outcomes. Understanding the nuances in the similarities and differences of these processes across contexts and cultures is imperative to the researchers' inquiries, because it influences their approach to research design. The inclusion of children in research as both collaborators and participants presents exciting opportunities to identify the obscured and unnamed processes that reinforce their positive outcomes. In the chapter titled, "*Using Mixed Methods in Research With Young Children Across Cultures and Contexts,*" Linda Liebenberg and Michael Ungar discuss the use of mixed methods when conducting research with young children across cultures and contexts. They focus specifically on an iterative approach that integrates community comments into the design to be able to enhance contextual relevance. Special focus is given to the integration of children's perspectives in this process. Linda Liebenberg and Michael Ungar draw on the experiences of studies conducted at the Resilience Research Centre to illustrate the proposed process. A large amount of their own work explores the use of available qualitative and quantitative research tools and methods in ways that includes the children's cultural experiences, while simultaneously achieving rigorous, valid, and reliable data sets (Liebenberg, 2009; Liebenberg, Didkowsky, & Ungar, 2012; Ungar & Liebenberg, 2011). As resilience researchers, Linda Liebenberg and Michael Ungar are continuously challenged to explore ways to understand how young children who are encountering persistent risks in their lives navigate through these obstacles and make use of the resources that facilitate their well-being (Ungar & Liebenberg, 2011). They focus on the young children's experiences and their cultural contexts. They recommend that researchers take into account in child development research the multiple factors impacting the young children's experiences including their culture, internal family dynamics, and socioeconomic positioning of the family. This is imperative in child development research as it influences the research design.

Qualitative Research Methodologies

Qualitative studies provide unique insights into the lived realities of young children, their families, and the adults who work with and on behalf of them. They offer conceptual productivity and contextualized understandings that go beyond research based on statistical analyses of rigorously controlled variables. Qualitative research methodologies assist researchers to discover how things actually work for real individuals in actual settings.

A variety of approaches and terms are used in reference to qualitative research. For example, field research is frequently used interchangeably with qualitative research to describe systematic observations of social behavior with no predetermined hypotheses to be tested (Rubin & Babbie, 2011). Researchers develop hypotheses based on their observation and interpretation of human behavior, which usually evolve into more observations and the generation of new hypotheses for exploration. Qualitative researchers use an inductive process to develop themes and categories through analysis of data collected by such techniques as interviews, observations, videotapes, and case studies. Qualitative research typically has small samples that are usually purposively selected. Qualitative researchers record detailed descriptions from the participants' point of view to explore particular issues and problems. Presently, qualitative research methodology has achieved acceptance in the research community. Its methods have gained recognition among researchers. Researchers believe that qualitative methodologies use systematic inquiry to provide them with information and insights that bring knowledge and understanding to the important work of early childhood educators at all levels that are unavailable from other sources. Qualitative inquiry has the distinct ability to explore the lived realities of young children and the adults who work with them, which makes it an invaluable research tool. Early childhood qualitative research is well positioned to provide data-based findings that can structure contemporary early childhood theory, research, policy, and practice. This section has nine different chapters that describe several qualitative research approaches that are frequently used. Some methodologies have some similarities while others are very different. One methodology is grounded theory.

Grounded theory is a method that structures the research process while freeing the researcher to explore the data and develop fresh theoretical analyses from them. The tools of grounded theory provide the researcher a structured approach to sorting through data that, in turn, free the researchers to fully immerse into the data, explore the events in the data and discover the analytic stories the data convey. Like early childhood education itself, grounded theory is an approach to data analysis that honors process over product (committed to the process of conducting research rather than being preoccupied with producing a particular result) and that works in that exciting tension area between structure and freedom, routine and playfulness, consistency and surprise. In the chapter titled, "*Grounded Theory,*" Robert Thornberg, Lisa M. Perhamus, and Kathy Charmaz introduce and explain the grounded theory method and illustrate how to use it for research in early childhood education. The method begins with inductive data collection and analysis but also employs logical reasoning, in which the researcher forms and tests hypotheses to account for surprising findings. Robert Thornberg, Lisa M. Perhamus, and Kathy Charmaz describe the basic strategies of the grounded theory method including coding data for what is happening in the setting, constructing categories, filling out and checking these categories, and writing analytic memos about them. Worked examples from the authors' research in early childhood education demonstrate how grounded theory strategies work in research practice. They review the arguments about the role and place of the literature review in grounded theory and support treating the literature with theoretical agnosticism but not ignoring it or claiming to begin inquiry as a *tabula rasa*. In keeping with grounded theory logic of focusing the literature review after completing the analysis, Robert Thornberg, Lisa M. Perhamus, and Kathy

Charmaz summarize recent works in grounded theory research in early childhood education and conclude with a discussion of quality in grounded theory studies.

In the next chapter titled, *"Conducting Early Childhood Qualitative Research in the Twenty-First Century,"* J. Amos Hatch and Chonika Coleman-King provide an overview of the state of the art in early childhood qualitative research in the second decade of the twenty-first century. They define early childhood qualitative research, then discuss the following characteristics of early childhood qualitative studies: natural settings, researcher as data collection instrument, flexible design, inductive data processing, participant perspectives, complexity, extended first-hand engagement, and meaning. They also present key considerations for conducting early childhood qualitative studies, including descriptions of six elements directly related to the design and implementation of high-quality qualitative studies in early childhood contexts: theory, research questions, research contexts and participants, data collection, data analysis, and findings. Then J. Amos Hatch and Chonika Coleman-King discuss each element is discussed and provide specific guidance for applying these elements in conducting early childhood qualitative studies. Next, they identify several types of contemporary early childhood qualitative research that they found in their analysis of recently published work. Each type of study (i.e., case studies, interviews, focus groups, ethnography, microethnography, ethnomethodology, grounded theory and action research) is described and an example from the current literature is utilized to demonstrate applications to early childhood inquiry. J. Amos Hatch and Chonika Coleman-King conclude their chapter with a discussion of issues in conducting early childhood qualitative research.

There is a growing body of knowledge that uses innovative qualitative methods to support and facilitate the involvement of young children, aged seven years and under, in the research process. Across several fields of study the recent growth in research that engages with young children stands in sharp contrast with the situation just a few years ago where there was a dearth of activity and knowledge in this area. Designed to seek their views, experiences, and perspectives the range of methods is now burgeoning. In the chapter titled, *"Innovative Qualitative Research Methods With Children Aged 4–7 Years,"* Karen Winter explores reasons for the growth in the use of innovative qualitative methods, the underlying principles through which the engagement of young children has been achieved and the different types of methods with detailed case examples. For each method the main critical issues regarding their effectiveness are identified and discussed in further detail. The latter sections of the chapter focus on contemporary issues regarding the use of innovative methods. Highlighted, in particular, are some of the common concerns and criticisms with regards to the trustworthiness, reliability, validity, and generalizability of the data that are collated using innovative qualitative methods.

Case study research in early childhood has a rich and very influential history that can be traced back to well know theorists such as Piaget, Freud, and Darwin who used case study approaches to explore and to understand children's learning and development in the early years. Case studies have been used in medical research and psychology to understand the development of young children and how children respond in different contexts (Mukherji & Albon, 2010). Case study in early childhood research foregrounds the importance of the child in context. The case is a bounded unit—a person, a group, an institution, or an organization and involves interactions, communications, relationships, and practices between the case and the broader context. The case study researcher employs multiple data collection methods to develop a detailed description of the case. In the chapter titled, *"Case Study Research: The Child in Context,"* Susan Hill and Ngaire Millar consider the big picture of what a case study is and what a case study is not. Their chapter then explores the similarities and differences between case study research and ethnography, different approaches to case study research and types of case studies. Following this, they provide a discussion about the importance of framing the research questions in case studies and then the range of data collection methods that particularly relate to early childhood case study research. The next section includes ways data may be analyzed and this leads into sections about triangulation, validity, and reliability. Susan Hill and Ngaire Millar conclude their chapter with explanations of the various roles of the case study researcher and suggestions for organizing and writing case study reports.

Action research is about inducing change in individuals as well as changing the culture of a group. It can support the questioning of taken for granted knowledge to help rethink what is "known," "spoken," and "practiced." The participatory model of action research methodology is a powerful tool for bringing about changes in theory and practice as it lends its support at the local level. With the influence of children's rights and sociology of childhood, researchers are increasingly drawn to participatory research methodologies that recognize children's agency and children as current (rather than future) citizens in the world and researched *with* rather than researched on children. In the chapter titled, *"Action Research with Children,"* Kylie Smith discusses action research as a methodology to conduct research *with* children. Then she identifies the processes, characteristics, possibilities, and limitations of this methodology. Throughout the chapter, Kylie Smith provides examples that were drawn from an Australian doctoral research study. These examples demonstrate the methodology in practice through her first venture into action research.

Microethnography is a research methodology that has been used to explore early childhood environments with both children and adults. This methodology surfaced in the 1960s and 1970s. Microethnography was derived from ethnography and adapted its methodology from the fields of anthropology, psychology, and sociology. The fundamental focus of microethnography is on communicative interactions in specific settings (LeBaron, 2006). In the chapter titled, *"Microethnographic Research in Early Childhood Education,"* John A. Sutterby describes the process of the microethnography research methodology. He provides a concept of microethnography based on his own research experience. His chapter situates microethnography within the larger field of ethnography. According to John A. Sutterby, microethnography is used to examine a particular setting in a much focused way. The methodology usually relies on some type of audio or video recording of naturalistic interactions, which are microanalyzed through repeated viewing or listening. He also discusses the ethics of microethnography and the ethics of research with young children. In the final section, John A. Sutterby reviews studies in early education settings that have used microethnography as a research methodology. The most common areas of research in early childhood education using microethnography as a method have focused on two areas, school-family interactions and cross-cultural interactions among children.

Young children often rely on the adults around them to learn important information about their world. In fact, most educational settings are based on the premise that children will automatically take in and learn from what the adults around them say. However, there is evidence that preschoolers are surprisingly discerning in their trust in the veracity of information from adult informants. In the chapter titled, *"Preschoolers' Selective Learning from Adults: Lessons for Research Methods in Early Childhood Education,"* Kathleen H. Corriveau and Julie Dwyer describe the findings from studies and their methodologies used in a body of literature investigating preschooler's selective learning from informants. First, they provide an overview of outcomes regarding children's selective trust in the adults around them and begin to delve into methodologies appropriate for this area of study. Next, they include a description of children's use of accuracy and inaccuracy responses when monitoring informants, with a specific focus on studying developmental differences between three- and four-year-olds. Then Kathleen H. Corriveau and Julie Dwyer discuss how children use social group cues when monitoring informants for accuracy, including methods and findings investigating children's use of informant familiarity, syntax, accent, and position in a group consensus. Finally, they provide general suggestions for early childhood educators and researchers regarding methods of study and practical implications from this field of study.

The next two chapters focus on historical research as a research methodology. A basic purpose for studying history is to understand trends and issues on a topic over a period of time. Early childhood education programs and services in the United States are critically important in the twenty-first century, not just for young children, but also for society itself. To understand how the education and care programs for young children have been organized throughout the past centuries, the historical record must be enhanced and expanded. Early childhood education research conducted in the present must, as in the past, align with political, economic, social, and historical contexts. Examples of historiographical general, educational, and early childhood educational sources describe aspects of the past. Historical research in early childhood can be cumulative or revisionist. Historical content is presented as a range of documents and processes that include the use of style manuals; primary sources available in archives, libraries, historical societies, and independent, often unknown, locations; secondary sources including books, journals, and oral and film recordings; and tertiary sources composed of documentary histories, encyclopedias, and dictionaries. In the chapter titled, *"Conducting Historical Research in Early Childhood Education,"* Sue C. Wortham introduces a basic framework for conducting historical research in early childhood education. The focus of her chapter is how to conduct historical research in early childhood education in the United States. She describes how data are collected to support ongoing influences in early childhood education (cumulative) or how trends and issues have changed history over time (revisionist). The same principles of historical research are applicable to many types of research. An important element in locating historical data is to use both primary and secondary resources, although primary research is preferred. Sue C. Wortham's framework for research incorporates a sequence of strategies from determining the purpose or question for the research, collecting relevant data, taking notes, organizing and evaluating sources, and preparing the final written report. She discusses that the length of the report should be compatible with the extent of the research and the amount of data collected; therefore, careful planning on the scope of the project ensures a quality product that thoroughly examines the information that is appropriate. In the next chapter titled, *"Past as Prologue: Doing Historical Research in Early Childhood Education,"* Edna Runnels Ranck discusses lessons learned from previous historiography, offers guidelines for conducting historical research, and suggests future research studies. She also provides appendices that address the detailed steps involved in writing historical publications, confronting and addressing conflicting source data, recognizing characteristics of historians, and considering caveats for early childhood education historians.

The Research Process: From Conceptualization to Publication

Researchers need to know the meaning of a scientific publication. According to Day and Sakaduski (2011), a scientific paper is "a *written* and *published* report describing *original* research results." Scientific publications are determined based on *how* the paper is written and published, which suggest that the process, content, style, and development of the publication are equally important. A scientific publication is published in an appropriate research journal (e.g., peer-reviewed journal in the appropriate field). On the other hand, a research study that is published elsewhere (e.g., newspaper, conference proceedings, government reports, institutional bulletins, newsletters, conference reports, internal reports, newspapers) fails to meet the criteria of a scientific publication (Day & Sakaduski, 2011). The Council of Biology Editors developed the following definition for scientific publication (Council of Biology Editors, 1968), which is included in most contemporary publication guidelines:

> An acceptable primary scientific publication must be the first disclosure containing sufficient information to enable peers (1) to assess observations, (2) to repeat experiments, and (3) to evaluate intellectual processes; moreover, it must be susceptible to sensory perception, essentially permanent, available to the scientific community without restriction, and available for regular screening by one or more of the major recognized secondary services [such as educational abstracts, databases, and indices]. (Council of Biology Editors Newsletter, November 1968, pp. 1–2)

A recent ad hoc committee, whose responsibility was to develop a definition for scientific publication, examined the definition that was in the 1968 newsletter. The ad hoc committee was impressed with both the prescience and the precision of the definition that it accepted it (Stegemann & Gastel, 2009) as a current definition of a scientific research publication. The next five chapters focus on the publication of scientific research articles. Since scientific publications are based on *how* the paper is written and published including the writing process, content, style, and development of the publication. The chapters in this section consist of scientific education, writing literature reviews, being able to read research articles, and publishing research studies.

Many types of studies contribute to the field of education. However, too few directly address the core of the educational enterprise—developing and evaluating scientifically-based practices, pedagogies, programs, and policies. In the chapter titled, *"Methods for Developing Scientific Education: Research-Based Development of Practices, Pedagogies, Programs, and Policies,"* Douglas H. Clements and Julie Sarama discuss why this type of research-and-development program should take precedence in early childhood education.

They present a framework for the construction of research-based education, which includes a comprehensive and organized structure of multiple research methods. Such a coherent structure for development and evaluation synthesizes useful but separate methods and techniques, replacing inadequate, traditional strategies such as research-to-practice models.

The ability to complete a competent review of the literature is an essential skill for scholars at all levels in their professional development. Expectations for literature reviews are constantly evolving and are influenced by advances in technology. Although there is a tendency for those beyond the novice level to presume that they "already know" how to review the literature, reviewing has many different purposes, categories, and pitfalls. In the current context, locating information is less of a challenge than analyzing, synthesizing, and evaluating information in ways that advance knowledge in the field of early childhood education. Reviewers of literature need to avail themselves of both human and technological resources, produce reviews with publication potential, and be aware of recent developments that affect the quality of the reviews produced by scholars as they progress from the master's level to the doctoral level and beyond. Effective literature reviews are rooted in the higher order thinking skills that are part of the cognitive domain in Bloom's (1956, 1984) taxonomy of educational objectives. In the chapter titled, *"Re-Examining the Literature Review: Purposes, Approaches, and Issues,"* Mary Renck Jalongo and Kelly Heider review what the field offers in terms of guidelines for researchers who work with teachers. They guide the reader through the review process—from conceptualization to writing—and offer research-based recommendations on improving the quality of literature reviews. They describe necessary conditions and issues for working effectively with teachers who are gatekeepers and who are participating in research themselves. In addition, they examine the researchers' role when conducting collaborative research with teachers as partners. Themes found throughout their review focus on the time, commitment, and interpersonal skills of the researcher necessary for building relationships with teachers that increase their comfort and functioning as a research participant. Additionally, researchers must become well versed in the contexts within which teachers work. Mary Renck Jalongo and Kelly Heider conclude with the presentation of reflective essays from researchers, who provide lessons learned from their work.

Reading research is an important activity that offers benefits to a variety of professionals in the field of early childhood education, including researchers, practitioners, policymakers, and teacher educators. For some, however, the task of reading published research may be a challenging undertaking. In the chapter titled, *"Reading and Interpreting Early Childhood Research,"* Angela C. Baum and Paula McMurray-Schwarz guide researchers on how to make the experience of reading research more manageable. They delineate the sections of a typical research manuscript, describe the purpose of each section, and identify practical strategies for developing clear interpretations and understandings of the research. In addition, Angela C. Baum and Paula McMurray-Schwarz aim to support readers as they become wise consumers of research, preparing them to engage in basic evaluation by identifying important points and questions to consider while reading research studies.

Expectations to publish developed from scholarly, scientific, and ethical philosophies concerning the value of disseminating knowledge. Researchers are required to publish their studies. Many of them encounter several obstacles in writing and getting a manuscript published. Writing publishable research articles requires a high level of writing skills and researchers find that the publication demands require them to learn strategies on how to become productive writers. The next two chapters focus on the publication process. In the chapter titled, *"Elements in Writing Scientific Research Publications,"* Olivia N. Saracho guides researchers to develop their completed studies into a scientific research publication. She provides researchers introductory fundamental concerns, components in a research publication, and guidelines to structure and develop scientific research manuscripts. Olivia N. Saracho specifically describes steps in the development process with examples in manuscript preparation to guide novice and experienced researchers to write a coherent scientific research publication. In addition, she identifies the most widely used research journals in early childhood education.

Researchers need to publish their work in professional journals to share their findings, contribute to advancing knowledge about the effectiveness of research methods, and identify areas for further research. In the chapter titled, *"Writing for Publication on Research With Young Children,"* Nancy Dixon describes a structured approach on how to write for publication and gives practical techniques to help researchers select a journal to submit a paper, clarify authorship, understand journal requirements for an article, decide on and develop the content of a paper, plan the time needed to do the writing work, check and edit drafts of a paper, and anticipate how reviewers might evaluate a paper. She also describes the writing and journal submission processes and suggests steps on preparing a scientific research article in early childhood education.

CONCLUSION

Research and practice in early childhood education are informed by and related to child development research. There are trends and issues in early childhood educational research just like in early childhood educational practices and policies. Being knowledgeable about the nature of the research process and its methodologies in educational research is important to both researchers and educators. Thus, the chapters in this volume describe different types of research methodologies such as quantitative, qualitative, historical, and several others including the ever-increasing use of technology.

The development of any book forces hard choices that must be made such as what to include and exclude. It is impossible to include all research methodologies in one volume. Thus, the authors were forced to cautiously select what to include and, as editor, I had to make similar choices. It is important to note that other important research methodologies were excluded. Most of those selected were based on what seemed to be of critical importance in contributing to the knowledge in the field at this time. If this *Handbook* had been developed at a different time, another set of research methodologies might have been included. For example, in the 1960s, more quantitative research methodologies and statistical analyses would have been the focus of the volume. Presently, a variety of research methodologies are being implemented according to the various theoretical foundations, research needs, and more action-oriented research.

This *Handbook* is designed to be used by students of early childhood education at all levels of professional development as well as mature scholars who want to conduct research in areas needing more in-depth study. It is hoped that this *Handbook of Research Methods* will serve the needs of many in the research community. Scholars seeking the current state of research knowledge in various areas should find this volume useful. Similarly, practitioners who are trying to seek knowledge of research and its practical implications should find this volume helpful as well. This *Handbook* with its individual chapters presents several research methodologies to address a variety of hypotheses or research questions that will contribute to the knowledge of the field in early childhood education.

NOTE

1. From Saracho, O. N., & Spodek, B. (2012). Introduction: A contemporary researcher's vade mecum (redux). In O. N. Saracho & B. Spodek (Eds.), *Handbook of research on the education of young children* (3rd ed., pp. 1–15). New York, NY: Routledge.

REFERENCES

Aud, S., Hussar, W., Kena, G., Bianco, K., Frohlich, L., Kemp, J., & Tahan, K. (2011). *The condition of education 2011* (NCES 2011-033). U.S. Department of Education, National Center for Education Statistics. Washington, DC: U.S. Government Printing Office.

Barnett, W. S., Carolan, M. E., Fitzgerald, J., & Squires, J. H. (2012). *The state of preschool 2012: State preschool yearbook.* New Brunswick, NJ: National Institute for Early Education Research.

Bennett-Armistead, V. S., Duke, N. K., & Moses, A. M. (2005). *Literacy and the youngest learner: Best practices for educators of children from birth to 5.* New York, NY: Scholastic.

Bloom, B. S. (1956). *Taxonomy of educational objectives: Handbook I, The cognitive domain.* New York, NY: David McKay & Co.

Bloom, B. S. (1956/1984). *Taxonomy of educational objectives.* Boston, MA: Allyn & Bacon. (originally published in 1956).

Bretherton, I., Oppenheim, D., Buchsbaum, H., Emde, R. N., & the MacArthur Narrative Group (1990). *MacArthur Story-Stem Battery.* Unpublished manual.

Bretherton, I., Ridgeway, D., & Cassidy, J. (1990). Assessing internal working models of attachment relationship: An attachment story completion task for 3-year-olds. In M. T. Greenberg, D. Cicchetti, & E. M. Cummings (Eds.), *Attachment in the preschool years: Theory, research, and intervention* (pp. 273–308). Chicago: University of Chicago Press.

Council of Biology Editors (November, 1968). Proposed definition of a primary publication. *Council of Biology Editors Newsletter,* 1–2.

Day, R., & Sakaduski, N. (2011). *How to write and publish a scientific paper.* Westport, CT.: Greenwood Press.

De Jong, P., & Berg, I., K. (2008). *Interviewing for solutions.* Belmont, CA: Thomson/Brooks/Cole.

Flanagan, J. C. (1954). The critical incident technique. *Psychological Bulletin, 51*(4), 327–358.

Green, J., Stanley, C., Smith, V., & Goldwyn, R. (2000). A new method of evaluating attachment representations in young school-age children: The Manchester child attachment story task. *Attachment & Human Development, 2*(1), 48–70.

Irwin, L., & Johnson, J. (2005). Interviewing young children: Explicating our practices and dilemmas. *Qualitative Health Research, 15*(6) 821–831.

LeBaron, C. (2006). Microethnography. In V. Jupp (Ed.) *The Sage dictionary of social research methods* (pp. 177–179). Thousand Oaks, CA: Sage Publications.

Liebenberg, L. (2009). The visual image as discussion point: Increasing validity in boundary crossing research. *Qualitative Research, 9*(4), 441–467.

Liebenberg, L., Didkowsky, N., & Ungar, M. (2012). Analyzing visual data using grounded theory: An exemplar of the Negotiating Resilience Project. *Visual Studies, 27*(1), 59–74.

Mukherji, P., & Albon, D. (2010). *Research methods in early childhood: An introductory guide.* Thousand Oaks, CA: Sage.

National Association for the Education of Young Children. (2005). *NAEYC early childhood program standards and accreditation criteria: The mark of quality in early childhood.* Washington, DC: Author.

Neuman, S. B., & Kamil, M. L. (2010). *Preparing teachers for the early childhood classroom: Proven models and key principles.* Baltimore, MD: Brookes.

Rubin, A., & Babbie, E. R. (2011). *Research methods for social work.* Belmont, CA: Brooks/Cole. Cengage Learning.

Sandall, S., Hemmeter, M. L., Smith, B. J., & McLean, M. E. (2005). *DEC recommended practices: A comprehensive guide for practical application in early intervention/ early childhood special education.* Longmont, CA: Sopris West.

Saracho, O. N., & Spodek, B. (2012). Introduction: A contemporary researcher's vade mecum (redux). In O. N. Saracho & B. Spodek (Eds.), *Handbook of research on the education of young children*/3rd (pp. 1–15). New York, NY: Routledge/Taylor and Francis Group.

Skiffington, S., Washburn, S., & Elliott, K. (2011). Instructional coaching: Helping preschool teachers reach their full potential. *Young Children, 66*(3), 12–19.

Spodek, B., & Saracho, O. N. (2003). On the Shoulders of Giants: Exploring the Traditions of Early Childhood Education. *Early Childhood Education Journal, 31*(1), 3–10.

Stegemann, S., & Gastel, B. (2009). Council Classics: What constitutes primary publication? *Science Editor, 32*(2), 57–58

Ungar, M., & Liebenberg, L., (2011). Assessing Resilience across Cultures Using Mixed-Methods: Construction of the Child and Youth Resilience Measure-28. *Journal of Mixed-Methods Research, 5*(2), 126–149.

PART I

SYSTEMATIC RESEARCH METHODOLOGIES

CHAPTER 2

USING PEER SOCIOMETRICS AND BEHAVIORAL NOMINATIONS WITH YOUNG CHILDREN

Heidi Gazelle, Richard A. Faldowski, and Divya Peter

Peer reports are a unique and valuable source of information about children's social behavior and social relations among peers. They provide an "inside" or participant's view of children's perceptions, appraisals, interactions and relationships with one another. Peer informants are typically children's same-age classmates in school or child-care settings. Classmates spend a great deal of time together, observe each other's behavior and peer interactions across multiple contexts at school or child care (classroom, recess, lunchtime), are aware of each other's interactions and relationships with classmates, and the roles each child typically assumes in the classroom.

Although adult informants, chiefly teachers and parents, provide important information on children's social behavior and social relations among peers, they lack this inside perspective and access to the multiple contexts in children's lives (Achenbach, McConaughy, & Howell, 1987; Foster,

Bell-Dolan, & Berler, 1986; Spangler & Gazelle, 2009). For instance, parents' typically have limited time to directly observe their child's peer interactions at school and child care. Teachers have greater opportunity to observe children's peer interactions in these contexts, but may be more aware of child behavior in the classroom than at recess where interactions of particular interest are more likely to occur (e.g., peer victimization). Additionally, both parent and teacher perspectives are colored somewhat by their respective roles. Parents' special investment in their child may color their perspective and they may vary widely in their awareness of age-appropriate norms. Teachers typically perceive behaviors that are disruptive to their teaching goals as salient (aggressive, hyperactive, and noncompliant behaviors), whereas nondisruptive behaviors (e.g., social withdrawal) may appear less salient.

Moreover, information from these adult informants is often influenced by single-rater bias (a variety of factors that influence an individual's perception in idiosyncratic ways, Pronin, Lin, & Ross, 2002), whereas peer reports benefit from multiple raters. This multi-informant nature of peer reports is known to enhance their reliability (Coie, Dodge, & Kupersmidt, 1990). For instance, the views of any individual peer that may be idiosyncratic or not representative of broader peer views will not substantially bias peer reports, because this individual's ratings will contribute only a fraction to a score which results from summing, averaging, or proportionalizing information from all participating classmates. Thus, due to both their inside cross-context view and their reliable multi-informant nature, peer reports are particularly valuable sources of information about children's social behavior, interactions, and relationships with peers.

A BRIEF HISTORY

Peer report methodology dates back to the 1930s and the work of Jacob Moreno (Moreno, 1934). The 1980s were the "hay days" of peer report methodology—most methods currently in use were developed in this period. More recent work reflects subsequent refinement of both administration procedures and item content. This reflects both the increasing methodological and analytic sophistication in social science broadly speaking, and the conceptual evolution of knowledge about childhood social behavior, relationships, and their development. For instance, in the 80s many investigations focused on social status groups (e.g., rejected and popular children) and examined their behavioral correlates. In more recent times peer relations researchers have made finer distinctions among social behaviors (e.g., physical versus relational aggression, anxious solitude versus unsociability) and peer treatment (e.g., physical victimization versus relational victimization and exclusion). In contemporary research, indices of peer relations are more often framed as processes than as means of group identification.

The field of peer relations continues to thrive today and is a focus of research for investigators in multiple disciplines including developmental and clinical psychology and education. Peer report methodology is particularly widely used in middle childhood (especially in the last half of elementary school or third through fifth or sixth grade), because in this age range, standard peer-report methodology is well-suited to both children's social cognitive and communicative capacities and school structure (i.e., children largely spend their time with one set of classmates each year). At other ages, adaptations have been developed to make peer report methodology appropriate to children's capacities and the peer contexts which they inhabit. For instance, in early adolescence peer informants are typically drawn from members of youth's middle school teams in order to account for the variety of classmates they encounter as they attend various classes with different sets of classmates across the school day. In early childhood, the focus of the current chapter, adaptations to methodology have focused primarily on children's social cognitive and communicative capacities. The purpose of this chapter is to describe peer-report methods appropriate for use in young children, and to review the current state of knowledge about practices likely to yield valid and reliable peer reports in this age-range. In regard to the analysis of peer report data, we also discuss both traditional and more recent innovative approaches that may improve future research practices. This chapter's primary intended audience is graduate students and other researchers new to peer-report methods, but even experienced peer relations researchers may find our discussion of recent advances in the analysis of peer report data to be of interest.

AGE RANGE: THREE TO SEVEN YEARS OF AGE

Although the focus of the volume of which this chapter is a part is on methodology appropriate for children from birth though age eight, in this chapter we review peer report methodology for children from three to seven years of age. This is the most appropriate age-range for a chapter on peer-report methodology in young children for several reasons. First, our review of the literature indicated that many investigations have used peer report methodology with children three years of age and older, but not with younger children. Second and third, by three years of age children have the social cognitive and verbal capacity to reliably report on the social behaviors, interactions, and relationships among their classmates when appropriate methodology is used; whereas younger children may not have well-enough formed concepts related to their classmates' social behaviors, interactions, and relationships and the communicative capacity to reliably communicate these concepts to others (whether through gestures or verbalizations). As an anecdotal example of the presence of enduring social behavioral impressions of peers in children in the three year age-range, at the time of the writing of this chapter, the first author has a son in a preschool classroom for three-year old children. He has spontaneously reported on several different occasions that a specific schoolmate is "naughty." He had not repeatedly and consistently remarked on differentiated, enduring behavioral qualities of peers prior to three years of age. Rather, at two years he would describe many individuals he encountered as "nice" in a relatively undifferentiated manner. Also, on a more practical note, he can immediately recognize and name each of his classmates when shown their photographs—a capacity that is essential to peer report methodology with young children. When asked to name his classmates he also spontaneously comments that he likes each of them, with the exception of the child he reports is naughty.

ASSESSMENT PROCEDURES AND COMMUNICATIVE CAPACITY

We cover peer-report procedures through seven years of age because administration procedures change substantially at eight years of age (i.e., in third grade). At eight years and thereafter, peer-report interviews are typically administered in a group setting (e.g., to all children in a classroom at once) and children record their responses to questions read aloud by a research assistant (e.g., Who do you like to play with?) by circling the names of participating classmates on a printed roster.

However, from three to seven years of age this procedure is adapted to simplify the cognitive and communicative demands of the task in several ways (Asher, Singleton, Tinsley, & Hymel, 1979; McCandless & Marshall, 1957). First, the interview is conducted one-on-one with the researcher reading questions aloud and recording the child's responses. Second, children choose photographs (typically via pointing or placing photos into different boxes) of their classmates rather than circling written names. This is not only more appropriate given the limited reading abilities and concrete nature of thinking of children in this age-range, but also increases confidence that children are assigning nominations or ratings to the correct individual. We consider variations in peer-report administration methods (e.g., nominations versus ratings) and current evidence as to whether such variations impact the psychometric properties of resulting data below. However, because we anticipate that researchers may want to consider whether peer report methodology is appropriate for particular content areas of interest prior to considering methodology, we first describe major content areas most often assessed with peer reports in young children.

CONTENT DESCRIPTION OF ASSESSMENTS

Peer report methods can be used to assess peer attitudes (e.g., liking), peer relationships (e.g., friendships), peer treatment (e.g., victimization), and child behavior (e.g., aggression, withdrawal, prosocial behavior) in young children. For each of these major types of peer reports, the conceptualization of constructs and corresponding item content are described below.

Peer Acceptance, Rejection, and Status

Peer acceptance, rejection, social preference, and social status are attitudinal variables that indicate peers' like or dislike of specific children at a group level. It is important to note that liking and disliking are often not inversely related (e.g., $r = .03$, *ns*, Asher, et al., 1979; Olson & Lifgren, 1988; Wasik, 1987). For example, some children are both liked and disliked by many classmates, as detailed in the controversial peer status type description below. Additionally, these attitudinal variables should not be confounded with peer treatment. The relation between attitudes and behavior (i.e., peer treatment) are complex. For instance, a child may dislike a peer, but this does not mean that the child will necessarily victimize that peer. In order to assess peer treatment, children must be directly asked to report on peer treatment as specified in a following section.

Acceptance
Peer acceptance indicates the number or proportion of peers out of those participating that like a specific child. Nomination questions used to assess acceptance are "Who do you...like to play with," "...like most," or "...especially like." These are sometimes referred to as "positive nominations." A single question/item is typically used to assess acceptance. Acceptance scores can be employed as a continuous dimension for the purposes of data analysis.

Rejection
Peer rejection indicates the number or proportion of peers out of those participating that dislike a specific child. Nomination questions used to assess rejection are "Who do you...not like to play with," "...like least," or "...don't especially like." A single question/item is typically used to assess

rejection. These are sometimes referred to as "negative nominations." Similar to acceptance, rejection scores can be employed as a continuous dimension for the purposes of data analysis.

Social Preference

In order to consider information from acceptance and rejection scores simultaneously, researchers sometimes compute social preference scores by subtracting negative from positive nominations. Social preference indicates the number or proportion of peers that like a child after subtracting the number or proportion children that dislike the child. Thus, positive raw scores would indicate that more children like than dislike a child, whereas negative raw scores would indicate that more children dislike than like a child. Social preference scores can be employed as a continuous dimension for the purposes of data analysis. Social preference scores, in conjunction with social impact scores, are also used to identify social status types (i.e., groups of children).

Social Impact

Social impact scores indicate the number or proportion of peers that nominate a child as liked or disliked, regardless of the valence of the nomination. Impact scores are calculated by summing the number or proportion of positive and negative nominations. As described below under social status types, there are some children who receive many nominations of both types, and other children who receive few nominations of either type.

Status Types: Popular, Rejected, Controversial, Average, Neglected

Children can be classified into social status groups according to their social preference, social impact, and additional reference to positive and negative scores (Coie, Dodge, & Coppotelli, 1982). Group membership is determined as follows: *popular:* high social preference (SP) with below average negative nominations (LL or liked least) and above average positive (LM or liked most) nominations (SP > 1 SD, LL < 0 SD, LM > 0 SD); *rejected:* low social preference with above average negative nominations and below average positive nominations (SP < –1 SD, LL > 0 SD, LM < 0 SD); *controversial:* high social impact with above average negative and positive nominations (SI > 1 SD, LL > 0 SD, LM > 0 SD); *neglected:* low social impact and no positive nominations (SI < –1 SD, LM = 0); *average:* moderate social preference (SP > –0.5 SD & < 0.5 SD).

The Coie and colleagues or "CDC" method (Coie et al., 1982) is most widely used to form status groups, but two alternative methods of forming similar status groups have also been developed. The Newcomb and Bukowski or "NB" (Newcomb & Bukowski, 1984) method also employs negative and positive nominations, but probabilities are used instead of standard deviation cutoffs. For instance, rejected children are identified by a lower than chance negative nomination score and a positive nomination score at or less than the mean. Also, average children are identified as those not belonging to other groups, so the average group is somewhat more heterogeneous. However, this method of identifying average children also confers the benefit of classifying all children in status groups. The Asher and Dodge or "AD" (Asher & Dodge, 1986) method avoids the usage of negative nominations scores by employing positive nominations but substituting the lowest sociometric rating scores ("children you don't like to play with") for negative nominations in the CDC group identification formulas. This feature makes the AD method ideal if schools or parents object to the use of negative nominations. However, research evidence indicates that negative nominations do not influence children's play behavior or otherwise negatively impact children (see ethical considerations section at the end of this chapter). The AD method also has a somewhat stricter definition of the average group by requiring moderate scores (> -0.5 SD & < 0.5 SD) for social impact as well as social preference, thus yielding the most homogenous average group. Both the AD and NB methods also differ slightly from the CDC method in requiring that neglected children score below the mean for both negative and positive nominations, in addition to scoring low (< -1 SD) for social impact.

Overall, when the CDC method is compared with the NB and AD methods a high percentage of children (88%–91%) are classified in the same group (for a review see Cillessen, Bukowski, & Haselager, 2000). However, the CDC and AD methods are somewhat more discrepant with younger versus older children, probably because the AD method is more stable with young children and this difference in stability disappears with older children. In particular, the AD system yields higher stability for rejected and popular preschool-aged children (Vaughn & Mize, 1991). Thus, in studies with young children, if there is a desire to maximize stability of sociometric continua and groups, use of sociometric ratings and the AD classification system would be ideal. However, the other methods also yield acceptable psychometrics in young children.

Friendship Quantity

Whereas acceptance, rejection, and social status indicate peer attitudes towards a child at a group-level, friendship nominations assess the presence and quantity of reciprocal dyadic relationships. A reciprocal friendship is identified when both a child and their peer independently identify each other as a friend. Quantity of unreciprocated friendship bids made and received can also be analyzed as continuous data and be informative (Gazelle, 2008).

When examining longitudinal patterns of friendship quantity from early to later childhood, it is important to keep in mind that children's definitions of friendship change over the course of development. Young children define friendship based on shared play activity—even on a single occasion—whereas older children increasingly define friendship as involving a shared history of repeated interaction and the establishment of mutual trust and loyalty (Hartup & Abecassis, 2004). As children develop they also increasingly refer to friends' psychological characteristics (e.g., kind, funny) when explaining who makes a good friend. Thus, any investigation of continuity of friendship quantity from early to later childhood would be examining heterotypic continuity, or continuity of a phenomenon that has a changing nature over the course of development.

Assessment of friendship quality requires follow-up self-report questionnaire or interview procedures in which each participant in a reciprocated friendship (that was previously identified via peer-report methods) reports on specific qualities of that friendship (The Friendship Quality Questioinnaire, FQQ, Parker & Asher, 1993). However, existing friendship quality questionnaires were designed for children eight years of age and up. We are not aware of child-report methods for assessment of friendship quality in young children, probably because this concept is too sophisticated for young children. However, reliable methods exist for assessing the interaction patterns of young friends via behavioral observation (Gazelle & Spangler, 2007) and the friendship quality of young children via maternal report (Engle, McElwain, & Lasky, 2011). These methods yield individual differences in friends' interaction patterns and friendship quality in young children. Thus, individual differences in friendships exist in young children, but children may not be the best informants of these differences in early childhood.

Peer Treatment

There are several peer interviews that contain questions intended to assess a broad range of peer treatment and child behavior. The most widely used is the Revised Class Play (RCP, Masten, Morison, & Pellegrini, 1985) and, after that, the Peer Evaluation Inventory (Pekarik, Prinz, Liebert, Weintraub, & Neale, 1976). Although these interviews were initially designed for children age eight and up (3rd grade and up), many of these items have successfully been used with children as young as four years. If administering these items to three-year-olds, as with all young children, care should be taken to insure that language is understood. The peer-report composites used to assess constructs range from demonstrating moderate to high psychometric indices, although insufficient information is available about the psychometrics of some constructs in young children, as detailed in the following sections. Some questions from these inventories remain widely used today, but much contemporary work also employs questions that have been refined to assess distinctions that were not commonly made at the time these inventories were developed (e.g., physical vs. relational victimization and exclusion, physical vs. relational aggression, anxious withdrawal vs. unsociability), as detailed below.

Physical Victimization

Physical victimization indicates the number or proportion of peers that perceive that a child is a target of physical aggression by peers. Nominations that have been used with young children include: "Other children start fights with this child; Gets hit, kicked, or punched by other children; Other children push this child out of the way to get something they want" (Nelson, Robinson, & Hart, 2005). These items have demonstrated factor loadings ranging from .52 to .65 in young children (Nelson, Robinson, Hart, Albano, & Marshall, 2010).

Exclusion/ Relational Victimization

Peer exclusion indicates the number or proportion of peers that perceive that a child is left out of their peers' activities. Peer exclusion nominations have been successfully used with young children (1st grade, Younger & Daniels, 1992). Items used include "Someone who . . . is often left out" and ". . . can't get others to listen" (Younger & Daniels, 1992). Both of these are from the RCP (Masten, et al., 1985). Additionally, Nelson and colleagues have developed a set of items to assess relational victimization (actions intended to harm a child's peer relationships) which are similar: "When others are mad or angry at this child they tell their friends not to play with him or her; Gets told by others that they cannot be their friend anymore; Gets told 'You can't play with us unless you do what we want you to do'; When others are mad or angry they will not listen to this child (may even cover their ears)" (Nelson, et al., 2010). These items have demonstrated factor loadings ranging from .43 to .60 in young children (Nelson, et al., 2010).

In young children, exclusion and relational victimization can be construed to be identical phenomena. However, in older children, relational victimization takes multiple forms, such as being the target of negative rumors, not all of which would qualify as exclusion (although that may be the ultimate goal of such actions). Additionally, it is important to note that by age eight (3rd grade) most exclusion has been observed to occur in a passive (i.e., peers do not approach a child at recess) rather than an active manner (i.e., peers say "you can't play with us," Shell & Gazelle, 2014), without an apparent organizer. Active exclusion may be more common in young children and similar observational work is needed with young children to examine this possibility.

Behavioral Nominations

Physical Aggression

Peer reports of physical and direct verbal aggression have been used successfully with young children. Items used to assess physical aggression include "Someone who...hits, kicks, or punches other children; starts physical fights with other children; pushes other children out of the way to get something they want; grabs toys or things away from other children?" (Leflot, van Lier, Verschueren, Onghena, & Colpin, 2011; Nelson, et al., 2005; Nelson, et al., 2010; Wasik, 1987). The internal consistency of physical aggression composites in young children is generally good (.85 with the Kudar Richardson Formula, Cillessen, et al., 2000, factor loadings ranging from .57 to .75, Nelson, et al., 2010).

Relational Aggression

Relational aggression nominations are used to identify children who often attempt to hurt a peer's relationships (Crick & Grotpeter, 1995). With young children this would typically involve attempts to exclude a child from playing with peers and withdrawing one's own friendship (Nelson, et al., 2005). Nominations that have been used with young children include: "Someone who...says 'Don't play with that kid' or 'You can't play with us' when mad or angry;...tells other children they can't play unless they do what everyone wants them to do;"...says 'I'm not going be your friend anymore' when mad or angry; won't listen to someone if they are mad at them (they may even cover their ears) (Nelson, et al., 2005; Nelson, et al., 2010). These items demonstrated factor loadings ranging from .41 to .69 (Nelson, et al., 2010).

Anxious Withdrawal

Anxious withdrawal nominations identify children who play alone at school or child care at a relatively high rate due to social anxiety. One nomination that has been used with young children is: "Someone who...is very shy" (1st grade) (Masten, et al., 1985; Younger & Daniels, 1992). Other items that have been used to assess social withdrawal from the RCP (Masten, et al., 1985) and PEI (Pekarik, et al., 1976) are heterogeneous, with various items employing concepts consistent with unsociability, exclusion, sensitivity, and sadness. Consequently, we do not recommend these items. Items with better face validity have been developed more recently: "Who...is shy and plays alone a lot?; watches other kids play but plays by themselves?; and is shy and doesn't have much to say to other kids" (Spangler & Gazelle, 2009). These items have demonstrated good internal consistency ($\alpha = .81$) for children 8 years of age and older (Spangler & Gazelle, 2009). Although they are yet to be tested with children under 8 years of age, they do not appear to be more complex linguistically than other items used with young children. Whether young children perceive anxious solitude as a salient characteristic in peers is a more difficult question, but evidence indicates that 5 year-old children have well-developed concepts of fearful shyness (Crozier & Burnham, 1990). This issue is discussed further below in the sections on reliability and validity.

Unsociability

Unsociable nominations indicate the number or proportion of peers who nominate a child as playing alone at school or child care due to social disinterest. Nominations that have been used with young children include "Someone who would rather play alone than with others" (1st grade) (Masten, et al., 1985; Younger & Daniels, 1992). A variation that is linguistically simpler and thus likely more appropriate for young children is "likes to be alone and does not like to play with other children"(Wasik, 1987). However, we would suggest modifying this item because some scholars conceptualize unsociable children as liking to play alone but not as disliking to play with other children (Coplan & Armer, 2007). Similar to anxious solitude, research is needed to establish the psychometrics of peer assessments of unsociability in young children.

Sociability

Sociability nominations indicate the number or proportion of peers who perceive a child as enjoying social interaction with peers. Nominations that have been used with young children include "Is fun to talk to; Is fun to do pretend things with; Has many friends" (Nelson, et al., 2005; Nelson, et al., 2010). The factor loadings for these items ranged from .47 to .64 (Nelson, et al., 2010). Although the labels "sociability" and "unsociability" suggest that these composites are opposite ends of the same spectrum, and we would expect the two composites to be negatively correlated, we were unable to find studies that reported correlations among these composites for young children.

Prosocial Behavior

Prosocial nominations indicate the number or proportion of peers who perceive a child as helpful and considerate towards peers. Nominations that have been used with young children include "Who takes turns and shares?" (Nelson, et al., 2005) and "Someone who follows directions, helps other people, shares" (Wasik, 1987). Because studies of young children typically include single peer report items for prosocial behavior, little information on the psychometrics of peer assessments of this construct are available.

Other Constructs

There are a variety of other social behavioral constructs that could be assessed in young children, including disruptiveness, leadership, and obedience (Wasik, 1987); however, use of peer reports of such constructs has been limited to date and available measures have not shown strong psychometric properties. Although it may be possible to obtain valid and reliable peer assessments of these constructs in young children, further methodological work would be needed to insure such assessments would demonstrate acceptable psychometric properties.

Peer Sociometric and Behavioral Nomination Procedures and Measurement Issues Nomination, Rating, and Paired Comparison Administration Methods

Three alternative methods have been used to administer peer report questions to young children: nomination, rating, and paired comparison methods. Each yields data with acceptable validity and reliability when used to assess acceptance and rejection (for information on other peer report content see below), but the choice between methods involves tradeoffs between speed of administration (with nominations demanding less time than ratings and paired comparisons requiring the most time) and reliability (with most studies indicating greater reliability and stability for ratings when compared to nominations; Asher, et al., 1979; Maassen, Steenbeek, & Van Geert, 2004; Olson & Lifgren, 1988).

As mentioned above, photographs of peers are used to administer peer report questions to children below 8 years of age. Such "picture" sociometric nomination techniques are based on methods originally developed by McCandless and Marshall (1957) and subsequently adapted by Asher et al. (1979). The researcher interviews each child individually. At the beginning of the interview the child is shown a poster board on which photographs of all participating peers in his or her class are mounted. Children are asked to identify themselves, and to name each classmate. They are next asked to point to the pictures of peers they most like to play with and peers they least like to play with at preschool. Continuous acceptance and rejection nomination scores are created by summing or proportionalizing the "votes" each child receives for each nomination (see the section above on content descriptions of peer report methods for further information). This method can be used with both limited nominations in which the child is asked to choose a specific number of peers (most often 3) and with unlimited nominations in which the child can choose as may peers as they'd like.

In the rating scale method described by Asher et al. (1979), children are asked to assign pictures of each classmate to one of the three boxes, which depict either a happy face ("children you like to play with a lot"), a neutral face ("children you 'kinda' like to play with"), or a sad face ("children you don't like to play with"). In contrast to the acceptance and rejection nomination method described above, this rating method yields information on every child in the class by all participating classmates. Other investigations that have employed this rating method include Olson & Lifgren, 1988; Vaughn, Colvin, Azria, Caya, & Krzysik, 2001; Wasik, 1987; Wu, Hart, Draper, & Olsen, 2001.

In the paired-comparison method (A. S. Cohen & Van Tassel, 1978), stimulus cards displaying photographs of all pairs of participating children in the class are prepared, with each child's photograph appearing on the left- or right-hand side of the cards an equal number of times. The order of presentation is such that no child is seen twice before all other children are seen once. Cards are presented one at a time and the child is asked, "Which of these two children do you especially like?" The goal of this method is to simplify the task of ranking children from most to least liked. Similar to the rating task, participating children receive information from all participating peers. However, in this method each child receives a unique rank from each peer nominator. In contrast, multiple children can receive the same score with nomination and ranking methods. Other investigations that have employed this paired-comparison method include Szewczyk-Sokolowski, Bost, & Wainwright, 2005; Vaughn et al., 2009.

Unlimited Versus Limited Nominations

In studies using peer nominations, it was common practice for many years to allow children to nominate up to three classmates for each question—or to use "limited" nominations. Alternatively, children can be allowed to choose as many peers as they like—"unlimited" nominations. The relative advantages of limited versus unlimited nominations have been the subject of debate (Terry, 2000). Unlimited nominations have the advantage of insuring that there is no artificial barrier to children expressing their preferences for and perceptions of peers (e.g., a child may like more than three of their classmates) and thus potentially result in more complete information about affiliation patterns. Unlimited nominations also avoid the implicit suggestion that children should have three nominations for every question (e.g., a child may like fewer than three classmates). However, limited nominations may have some advantage in regard to shortening administration time (i.e., because no child will require time to make a large number of nominations) and forcing children to be more discerning (e.g., pick the three children they like best). In older children, unlimited nominations have been shown to have superior psychometric properties (Terry, 2000), but this has not been explicitly tested in younger children. Nonetheless, when Nelson et al. (2010) allowed up to five peer nominations per question, the majority of five-year old children chose three nominations and only 1%–2% of children chose more than three, suggesting that both techniques would yield close to equivalent results at this age. Taken together, unlimited versus limited nominations are likely to provide more complete information, making them more like rating and paired-comparison methods. Thus we return to a familiar theme: there is a tradeoff between administration time and completeness and potential reliability of data.

In the past peer nominations were also sometimes limited to same-sex peers, but this practice is no longer common or recommended. Three-year old children often affiliate with children of both sexes, although this pattern decreases with age and four- and five-year-old children typically demonstrate clear same-sex preferences (Diamond, Furgy, & Blass, 1993; Ramsey, 1995). Thus, limiting friendship nominations to same-sex peers would differentially bias younger children's friendship data. If the researcher is interested in sex-linked nomination patterns, nominations unrestricted by sex can be gathered and then later analyzed by the sex of the nominator and nominee. Despite the increasing same-sex affiliation patterns across early childhood, young children have knowledge about the behaviors of peers of both sexes (Ramsey, 1995). Thus, for many of the same reasons mentioned above, the most reliable data should be obtained with nominations that are unlimited by sex or number.

Number of Items Administered and Administration Time

In the majority of studies that have employed peer report methodology with young children it is reported that one to three questions were administered and these were combinations of acceptance and rejection nominations and/or sociometric ratings. Administration time varies with the number of questions, number of participating classmates, age of children, and administration method, but most studies with young children report peer report administration times of 10 to 15 minutes. However, two 15 minute sessions per child are typical to administer one paired comparison question (A. S. Cohen & Van Tassel, 1978). There are also examples of studies that employ many behavioral nominations with young children (Nelson, et al., 2005; Nelson, et al., 2010; Wasik, 1987), as is more typical with older children who are able to participate in more time-efficient group-administration procedures involving circling names on rosters instead of pointing to pictures. When administering peer report interviews with young children, it is always recommended that if the child appears distracted or his or her attention appears to wander, the interview be continued at another time (Vaughn, et al., 2001). Thus administering many questions or using time-intensive techniques can be feasible across multiple sessions.

VALIDITY

When peer reports are employed, as with any other methodology, researchers should be confident that their assessments are valid. In other words, researchers should be confident that they have measured the construct they intended to measure. Therefore, when using peer report methodology, evidence of validity should be reported. When using well-established measures, it is acceptable to refer to previous research which established the measures' validity. However, when new measures are developed, researchers have the responsibility for establishing their validity.

Face Validity

Face validity indicates that the content of items used to assess a construct match the conceptual definition of that construct. This is a conceptual rather than an empirical judgment. However, if the face validity of a construct is poor, it may well be that it displays poor psychometrics (i.e., empirical evidence of validity or reliability) as a consequence. For example, as discussed above, composites used to assess social withdrawal in the past were composed of diverse items (e.g., Younger, Schwartzman, & Ledingham, 1985, 1986) that are now recognized as describing the separate constructs of anxious solitude, unsociability, and exclusion (Spangler & Gazelle, 2009). Incidentally, previous incarnations of such social withdrawal composites demonstrated poor psychometrics with young children, perhaps at least as a partial consequence.

Convergent and Divergent Validity

One method of demonstrating that an assessment is measuring what it is supposed to measure is via demonstrating convergent and divergent validity. Providing evidence of convergent validity involves demonstrating that the measure is positively correlated with constructs with similar content at the same point in time. Conversely, evidence of divergent validity indicates that a measure is uncorrelated or negatively correlated with distinct constructs at the same point in time. Moderate convergent and divergent validity coefficients for sociometric ratings and nominations have been demonstrated with 4–5 year olds: sociometric ratings correlated with acceptance ($r = .48$) and rejection ($r = -.43$) (Olson & Lifgren, 1988). Importantly, the convergent validity of sociometric ratings and nominations has been found to be higher for 4 year olds ($r = .37-.54$) than 3 year olds ($r = .16-.19$, for a review see Hymel, 1983). This may be because the task of rating each classmate is relatively straight-forward for 3 year olds, but picking the three most or least liked classmates is more challenging (e.g., requiring the child to consider all classmates pictured at once, mentally rank them as most or least liked, and select the top three). This task likely becomes less challenging with age. Also, paired-comparison scores have been found to correlate highly with positive sociometric nominations ($r = .82$) in children 3–6 years of age (Szewczyk-Sokolowski, et al., 2005). These results indicate that sociometric measures used with preschool children demonstrate moderate to high convergent validity, and when available, divergent validity.

Alastair Younger and colleagues provide evidence to suggest that peer reports of both acceptance and aggression demonstrate good convergent and divergent validity at age 6 (1st grade, the youngest age at which they assessed children; see also Epkins, 1995; Leflot, et al., 2011; Philips, Driscoll, & Hooe, 2002; Younger, et al., 1985), but social withdrawal demonstrates relatively poor convergent and divergent validity at age six. Nonetheless, these psychometric qualities of peer-reported social withdrawal improved from age 6 to 9 (4th grade) and 12 (7th grade; Younger, et al., 1985, 1986). These authors propose that the low reliability and validity of peer reports of social withdrawal in young children is due to the relatively low salience of these behaviors in this developmental period. In contrast, aggressive behaviors are both highly salient and concrete for children in this age range—hence, their greater reliability and validity. However, it is possible that the poor psychometrics obtained for peer reports of social withdrawal are due, at least in part, to the use of items which assess different types of withdrawal—anxious solitude vs. unsociability—or assess constructs that are not part of the definition of withdrawal (e.g., general sensitivity "someone whose feelings get hurt easily", Masten, et al., 1985; Younger & Daniels, 1992). Consequently, items with greater face validity might result in better psychometrics in early childhood. Indeed, in 8-year-old children (3rd grade), a peer-reported anxious solitude composite demonstrated acceptable convergent validity with multiple informants (observers, teachers, parents, self) and divergence with the constructs of peer exclusion, and to a lesser extent, unsociability (Spangler & Gazelle, 2009). Similar research is needed in young children.

RELIABILITY

When peer reports are employed, as with any other methodology, researchers should be confident that their assessments are reliable, or in other words, that their measurements would demonstrate consistency (or "repeatability") over short periods of time (test–retest reliability) and among items comprising multi-item composites (internal reliability). Therefore, when using peer report methodology, evidence of reliability should be reported. When using well-established measures, it is acceptable to refer to previous research which established the measures' test–retest reliability. However, even when using well-established measures, it is common practice to report their internal reliability for the sample that is the focus of the investigation. Although single questionnaire items are often not reliable with single-informants (e.g., teacher and parent reports), even single-item peer reports (e.g., acceptance, rejection) are often reliable due to their multi-informant nature (Coie, et al., 1990).

Test–Retest Reliability

One method of demonstrating that an assessment is reliable is by obtaining a substantial positive correlation between repeated identical assessments administered a short time apart (typically a few weeks apart). Such evidence indicates that the assessment captures a phenomenon that endures over short periods of time.

Several studies have demonstrated that sociometric ratings have somewhat higher test–retest reliability than sociometric nominations with preschool children (Asher, et al., 1979; Olson & Lifgren, 1988; Wasik, 1987). For example, in samples of 3–6 year-old children, sociometric rating scores showed higher test–retest reliability ($r = .64–.81$) over 3–8 week intervals than sociometric nomination scores (acceptance $r = .38–.56$, rejection $r = .42–.48$, Asher, et al., 1979; Olson & Lifgren, 1988; Wu, et al., 2001; for 30–65 day test–retest rating reliability see also Maassen, et al., 2004). The superior reliability of ratings is likely due the more complete information they provide about each child by all participating classmates (not just those who consider the child to be among their three most or least liked classmates). Consequently, minor fluctuations in peer liking rankings would be less detrimental to reliability estimates when using rating than nomination methods (e.g., a child might assign "liked" ratings to a particular peer at two closely-spaced successive time points but select this peer as among the top three most liked at only one time point as their peer liking ranking fluctuates somewhat from week to week).

Internal Reliability

When multi-item child behavior and peer treatment composites are employed, evidence of internal reliability (symbolized by an alpha or α or reported as factor loadings) should be reported. Internal reliability indicates the extent to which multiple items which are construed to tap the same construct correspond with one another (or in the case of factor analysis, the extent to which items contribute to the same latent construct). In this sense, both test–retest reliability and internal reliability are indices of the "repeatability" of the data, but test–retest reliability assesses repeatability over short periods of time whereas internal reliability assesses repeatability over multiple items within a composite at the same point in time. In the studies we reviewed, the internal reliability of peer treatment and child behavior composites was found to be moderate to high in young children (see α and factor loading data reported throughout the content description sections above). Overall, this indicates that a variety of peer treatment and child behaviors can be reliably accessed via peer report in young children. However, little information was available on the psychometrics of peer-reported anxious solitude and unsociability in young children. Further research is needed to establish the psychometrics of assessments of these constructs in young children.

STABILITY

The stability of a continuous attribute is usually defined as the correlation between repeated measurements of the same sample on two or more occasions which are typically spaced at least several months apart. The stability of peer sociometric scores over time has long been a subject of interest. For instance, it is necessary to examine stability to determine if children who are rejected by their peers in preschool continue to experience peer rejection over the course of middle childhood. There is particular reason to be cognizant of the stability of peer reports in young children, as young children's peer affiliations are both more quickly formed and dissolved than those of older children (Hartup & Abecassis, 2004). This occurs in part because young children's playmate preferences can fluctuate frequently as a function of reactions to specific events (e.g., fighting over a toy) or moods (Hymel, 1983). Additionally, young children's playmate preferences may be influenced by immediate factors such as a specific child's availability or broader developmental patterns such as diminished preference for opposite-sex peers over time (Ramsey, 1995).

Sociometric Nominations Versus Ratings

Jiang and Cillessen (2005) conducted a meta-analytic review of 77 studies reporting the short-term and long-term stability of four continuous dimensions of sociometric status—acceptance, rejection, social preference, and peer ratings—for children 5 to 11 years of age. The average long-term stability coefficients (rs) for acceptance, rejection, social preference scores (all based on nominations), and liking ratings for the entire 5 to 11 year age range were .53, .52, .58, and .52, respectively. For the 5 to 7 year age-range relevant to this report stability coefficients were approximately .54–.56, .38–.46, .60–.68, and .64, respectively, as estimated based on Jiang and Cillessen's (2005) figure displaying age effects. These are large effect sizes according to conventional standards (large $r > .40$, J. Cohen, 1977). Regression analysis revealed that long-term stability was influenced by the length of stability intervals. Not surprisingly, shorter intervals resulted in higher stability. The stability correlation was reduced approximately .01 to .04 for every 1-month increase of the test–retest interval. Most importantly, results indicated that long-term stability coefficients for nominations, but not ratings, were influenced by age. Sociometric nominations were more stable for older children than younger children. This pattern is compatible with earlier studies that had found that ratings ($r = .80$) are somewhat more stable over a 5-month period than nominations (acceptance $r = .57$; rejection $r = .76$) in young children (Wasik, 1987). Jiang and Cillessen (2005) argue that age-effects in the stability of sociometric nominations but not ratings should not occur because sociometric nominations and ratings should assess the same underlying conceptual dimension. However, most authors argue that the ratings demonstrate more stability in young children because they simplify the cognitive task of evaluating all peers and produce more refined information because each child is rated by all peers (Maassen, et al., 2004).

Sociometric Status Groups

Cillessen and colleagues (Cillessen et al., 2000) analyzed the findings of 29 studies that reported the stability of sociometric status groups. Of these studies, 5 were based on samples which included children below 8 years of age. These studies examined stability of repeated sociometric group classifications over time intervals varying from 5–12 months. Some studies reported stability as percentage of children classified in the same group at a later date, whereas others reported stability kappas (which correct for chance levels of reclassification in the same group). For those studies focusing on young children, stability of group membership ranged from 48%–58% for popular groups, 32%–69% for rejected groups, 29%–54% for neglected groups, 18%–28% for controversial groups, and 33%–52% for average groups. For the rejected group, Cohen's kappas demonstrated large effect sizes for two out of the four studies reported ($k = .13–.57$), followed the popular group which demonstrated a large effect size for one of the three studies reported ($k = .04–.43$). All other status groups had $k < 40$ indicating low stability. It may be that the controversial group demonstrated particularly low stability because controversial status is in part an artifact of limited sociometric nominations. Few children are classified as having controversial status when unlimited nominations are employed. The limited stability of sociometric groups overall may be in part be a disadvantage of extreme-group approaches to sociometric status (e.g., slight variations around an arbitrary cutoff can create apparent instability in group classification over time), and in part reflect true instability in sociometric status in young children.

ANALYZING PEER REPORT DATA

As noted above, the most common forms of peer report sociometric data can generally be classified into nominations or ratings. Peer nomination data typically results from each classmate judging whether he or she "likes" each class peer, "dislikes" each class peer, or whether each peer possesses a particular characteristic (e.g., "is very shy") or not. For example, when performing judgments of peer "liking," each classmate would be asked to point to the photographs of their class peers that they "like" (McCandless & Marshall, 1957). Each child would be assigned values based on whether they were selected ($= 1$) or not ($= 0$) by a particular classmate, and then scores from all classmates would be aggregated. Rating data is similar, but rather than requesting a binary judgment, raters are asked about the *degree* to which the description fits each class peer. For example, raters from a kindergarten classroom might be asked, by pointing to photographs of classmates, how much they liked each classmate on a scale ranging from "none" ($= 0$) to "a little" ($= 1$) to "a lot" ($= 2$). Note that nominations can be considered a special type of rating data with only two response options: not selected ($= 0$) and selected ($= 1$).

Regardless of whether the judgments are nominations or ratings, the structure of raw peer report data is a matrix, tabulated separately by classroom and characteristic. The left side of Table 2.1 illustrates what a nomination table might look like for a classroom of seven children, out of which five provided judgments. In the table, unique children are designated by letters (A, B, ... G). The shaded cells, which represent children's judgments about

Using Peer Sociometrics and Behavioral Nominations With Young Children ▪ 47

TABLE 2.1   Example Nominations of "Liked" Peers Within a Classroom by 4 Peer Judges

Child	Judge A	B	C	E	G	Num Judges	Count (Sum)	Proportion (Average)	Z-Score
Question: Which peers does Judge "Like"?									
A		1	0	1	0	4	2	0.5	−0.1062
B	1		0	0	1	4	2	0.5	−0.1062
C	1	1		1	1	4	4	1.0	1.3806
D	1	0	1	0	1	4	3	0.75	0.6372
E	0	1	0		0	4	1	0.25	−0.8496
F	0	0	0	0	0	4	0	0.0	−1.5930
G	1	0	1	1		4	3	0.75	0.6372

Note: Letters designate unique children. Children D and F did not provide peer reports, but they were available to be chosen (nominated) by the other children in their classroom. Calculations for the summary measures—Count (Sum), Proportion (Average), and Z-Score—are described in the text below.

themselves, are excluded. Note that children D and F were unavailable to provide ratings on the day that other children from the classroom were assessed, so although they were available for nomination, they did not contribute to the judgments of their class peers.

If rating data had been obtained, cells in the left side of the table would contain ratings, indicating degrees of liking instead of binary indicators of liked versus not. In general, analysis challenges associated with rating data are less severe than the challenges associated with nomination data. Specifically, compared to nomination data, rating data tend to be less affected by group size, have less skewed distributions that are more nearly normal, and manifest higher reliability and validity coefficients (Connolly, 1983; Hops & Lewin, 1984; McConnell & Odom, 1986). Also, as mentioned above, a recent meta-analysis indicates that ratings versus nominations were more stable for young children, but the stability of nominations increased with age (Jiang & Cillessen, 2005).

Standardization

The right side of the Table 2.1 shows common descriptive statistics for the nominations (or ratings) that may be computed for each child. Each column is labeled with the descriptive statistic that pertains to nominations; whereas the corresponding descriptive statistics for ratings data is in parentheses. The most basic descriptive statistic for nominations is the total count, and for ratings is the sum. In the table, the nomination counts indicate that child C was universally liked by all raters, Child F was universally not liked (not nominated as liked, but not necessarily disliked) by all raters; and the other children fall in between.

Raw counts and sums, however, have a serious limitation—they cannot be directly compared across classrooms that differ in class size or the numbers of peer judges. For example, with raw nomination data on likability, each child in a larger class has a greater chance of *appearing* more likable (receiving more nominations) simply because he or she is rated by more peers. Thus, a count of 5 nominations implies a completely different degree of likability in a class of 6 students than it does in a class of 21 students.

In order to create peer report scores that are comparable across classrooms, the nomination counts (or sums of ratings) must be standardized to remove the influence of class size. The simplest type of standardization is nomination proportion (or average rating), created by dividing each child's nomination count (ratings sum) by the number of judges in the classroom. In the case of nomination data, the average score will equal the proportion of nominations received, out of the total number of judges in the classroom. In Table 2.1, this is shown as the *Proportion (Average)* column.

Although averaging adjusts nomination counts (or rating sums) for differences in classroom size, it does not account for classroom-level heterogeneity in nomination counts (or ratings). Specifically, classrooms may vary in the proportion of children who receive nominations for particular items. This type of heterogeneity can be adjusted through conversion of the nomination proportions (or average ratings) into "standard" or "z-scores" (Asher & Dodge, 1986; Coie & Dodge, 1983; Coie, et al., 1982; Terry & Coie, 1991). Z-score standardization calibrates the scores of children from different classrooms into a common metric. In the calculation of social status composites (i.e., social preference and social impact), it also insures that positive and negative nominations are weighted equally (Bukowski, Sippola, Hoza, & Newcomb, 2000, Note 3).

Based on normal distribution theory, z-scores for each student are calculated by taking the deviation of each student's nomination count (or rating sum) from the classroom mean, and then divided by the class standard deviation. The classroom mean nomination count, $\overline{Count}$, is the sum of the individual children's nomination counts divided by the number of children in the class. For the nomination data in Table 2.1, it equals 2.143; while classroom mean proportions, which are similarly defined, equal .538. The class standard deviation in nomination counts is defined as the square root of the sum of squared deviations of each child's nomination count from the classroom average divided by the number of classmates minus one. More precisely, it is: $\sigma_{Count} = Count_i - Count_{2n-1}$. For the Table 2.1 data, $\hat{\sigma}_{Count}$ equals 1.345 and, $\hat{\sigma}_{Proportion}$, which is defined comparably, equals .336. The z-score for the *i*th child in Table 2.1, then may be calculated as:

$$z_i = \frac{\text{Count}_i - \overline{\text{Count}}}{\hat{\sigma}_{\text{Count}}} = \frac{\text{Proportion}_i - \overline{\text{Proportion}}}{\hat{\sigma}_{\text{Proportion}}}$$

Because z-scores are invariant with respect to linear transformations, it does not matter if they are calculated on student nomination counts or proportions. Likewise, z-scores based on rating sums and average ratings are also equivalent.

An alternative procedure for identifying extreme children, based on the binomial distribution has also been proposed (Newcomb & Bukowski, 1984); however, as the number of judges per classroom increases, z-score-based and binomial probability-based classifications become asymptotically equivalent (Hays, 1994), suggesting that the same children should generally be identified as extreme under both systems. High degrees of congruence between the classifications under the Coie and Dodge and the Bukowski systems empirically validate this expectation; although other differences between the categorization methods lead to less than perfect agreement (Bukowski, et al., 2000; Terry & Coie, 1991).

Recent work by Faldowski et al. (2012) evaluated the statistical consequences of ignoring the distributional properties of peer nominations and the multilevel structure of longitudinal data collected from children nested within classrooms that changed annually. They found that, compared to longitudinal Poisson models of children's nomination counts, analyses of children's nomination z-scores or proportion scores resulted in grossly distorted estimates of relations between child and classroom characteristics, even when the multilevel, cross-classified structure of the data was correctly taken into account. Moreover, the Poisson models were more sensitive for detecting smaller magnitudes of child and classroom effects, suggesting greater statistical power. The overall conclusion of Faldowski and colleagues was that distributional irregularities of z-score or proportion score analyses of peer nominations were sufficiently insensitive to small effects and introduced sufficiently high risks of modeling errors that they cannot be recommended.[1]

Poisson Models for Count Data

Although standard score methods have been widely and productively employed to statistically identify children who receive high ratings or large numbers of nominations, or to classify students into status typologies, recent interest has shifted toward understanding the personal, familial, classroom, and other social processes that may influence children's functioning among their peers. In these types of analyses, peer ratings or counts often serve as dependent variables and accounting for their key features and distributional properties becomes important for protecting the validity of statistical inference. Advantages

50 ■ H. GAZELLE, R. A. FALDOWSKI, and D. PETER

and limitations in the use of sum (nomination count) scores, averaging (nomination proportion), and z-score standardization were appreciated even as early as the 1930s and 1940s (for a review see Veldman & Sheffield, 1979; Kane & Lawler, 1978). In particular, as illustrated in Figures 2.1a and 2.1b, z-scores do not alter the general shape of a distribution, although they change the zero point of the distribution and uniformly stretch or shrink it. If the original nomination count distribution was skewed, then the distribution of z-scores will remain skewed. If the original nominations distribution had a large preponderance of children who received 0 nominations, then the z-score distribution will have a large spike of values at the z-score corresponding to 0 nominations. This is confirmed in the tables below Figures 2.1a and 2.1b, which report the one-to-one correspondence between nomination count values and specific z-score values between the tables. The same inability of z-score transformations to alter

(a)

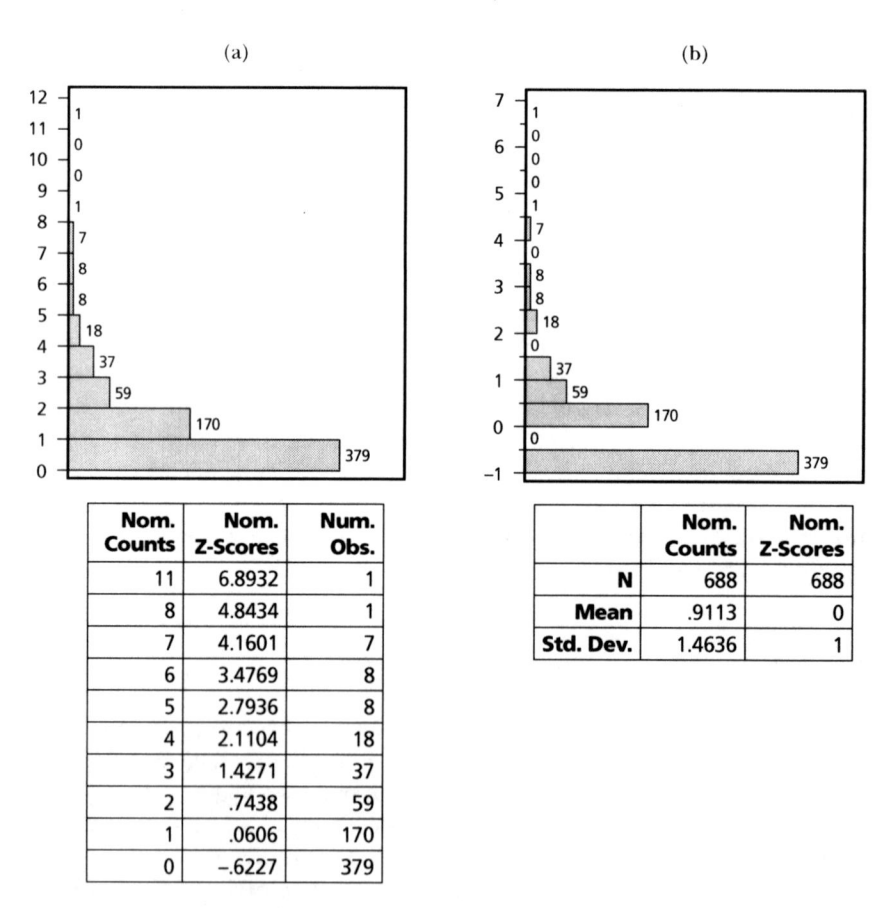

(b)

Nom. Counts	Nom. Z-Scores	Num. Obs.
11	6.8932	1
8	4.8434	1
7	4.1601	7
6	3.4769	8
5	2.7936	8
4	2.1104	18
3	1.4271	37
2	.7438	59
1	.0606	170
0	−.6227	379

	Nom. Counts	Nom. Z-Scores
N	688	688
Mean	.9113	0
Std. Dev.	1.4636	1

Figure 2.1 (a) Overall distribution of nomination counts across classrooms; (b) Distribution of nomination count z-scores across classrooms.

the shapes of source distributions will hold regardless of whether z-scores are calculated in the sample as a whole or within classrooms.

Compared to peer nomination count data, ratings data tend to be more normally distributed than nominations (Hops & Lewin, 1984) and, even when not, it is more amenable to transformations such that standard assumptions on the error structure (conditional normality, homoscedasticity, and independence of errors) of ordinary least squares models will hold (Atkinson, 1985; Chatterjee & Hadi, 2006; J. Cohen, Cohen, West, & Aiken, 2003; Draper & Smith, 1998). In the discussion below, therefore, the focus is on innovative methods for the analysis of nomination counts because of the greater analytic challenges associated with them, as well as the prevalence of this type of data.

Nomination count data have several key characteristics that distinguish it from more continuous, more normally-distributed rating data. Figure 2.1a illustrates the overall distribution of nomination counts for the characteristic "likes to play alone" across 46 third-grade classrooms (688 students) without regard for classroom size (which varies from 9 to 22 students). Figure 2.2 describes representative nomination count distributions for the same characteristic among six individual third grade classrooms out of the 46. In the figures, note that distributions of counts comprise positive integer values bounded by minimum values of zero. They tend to be skewed, especially for characteristics on which most children in a class receive few nominations. Moreover, because class means of count data tend to be heavily influenced by the few children who receive more nominations than others in the class, the classroom variance of nomination counts tends to increase in direct proportion to its estimated mean. This characteristic is shown in Figure 2.3 for the set of 46 classrooms, where the variance increases in direct proportions of about 2:1 with classroom means. Lastly, nomination data, especially for young children, tend to be collected within classrooms or preschool groups, which introduces statistical "cluster" effects (or nonindependence) that must be addressed in analyses (Hox, 2010; Raudenbush & Bryk, 2002; Snijders & Bosker, 2012). All of these characteristics can lead to biased parameter estimates, biased standard errors of parameter estimates, and biased tests of significance when peer nomination counts are naively included as outcomes in analyses like analysis of variance, analysis of covariance, multiple regression, or traditional (non-Poisson and non-Bernouli) hierarchical linear growth curve analysis.

Poisson regression directly addresses the challenges associated with analyzing count data. Although the method is well-known in the biological, biostatistical, econometric, and other social science literatures (Coxe, West, & Aiken, 2009; Dobson & Barnett, 2008; Gardner, Mulvey, & Shaw, 1995; McCullagh & Nelder, 1989), it is underutilized for analyzing peer nomination data (however, for a recent longitudinal application see

52 ■ H. GAZELLE, R. A. FALDOWSKI, and D. PETER

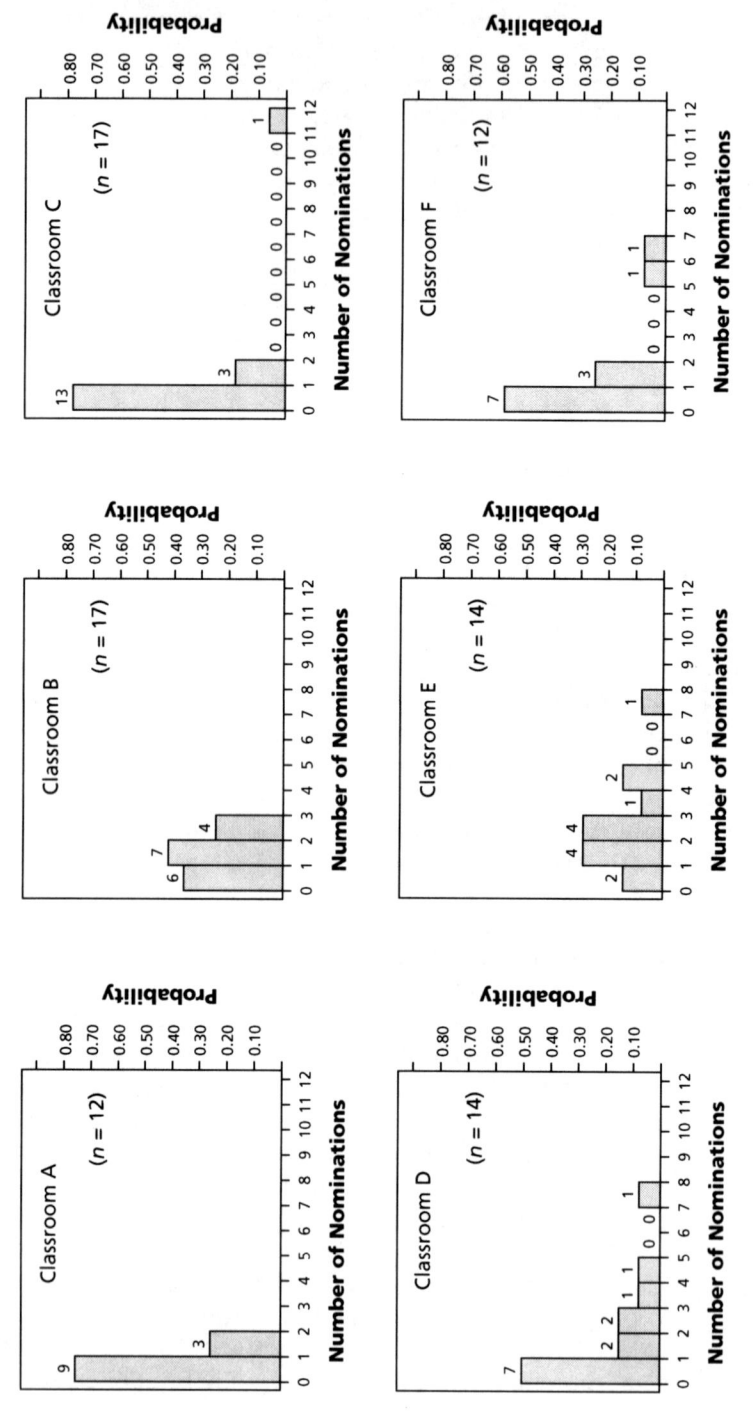

Figure 2.2 Variations on distributions of nomination counts within classrooms.

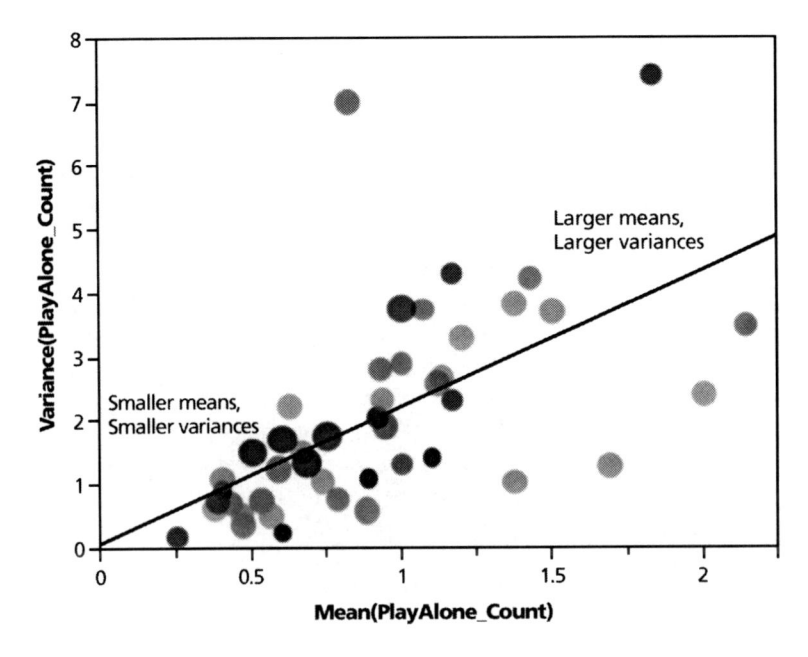

[Figure: scatter plot of Variance(PlayAlone_Count) vs Mean(PlayAlone_Count), with annotations "Smaller means, Smaller variances" and "Larger means, Larger variances"]

Figure 2.3 Classroom nomination count variances versus classroom nomination count means among 46 classrooms. On average, classroom variances roughly double for each unit increase in average number of classroom nominations. The size of the dots are directly proportional to the size of classrooms, which vary from 9 to 22 students.

Spangler Avant, Gazelle, & Faldowski, 2011). Essentially, Poisson regression is a straightforward generalization of ordinary multiple regression that models the number nominations each child receives, while accounting for varying numbers of students per class and (when applicable) varying numbers of items in peer report composites. It does this by transforming each child's nomination count into a rate based on their *exposure* or total possibility of receiving nominations i.e.,

$$\text{rate}_i = \frac{\text{Count}_i}{\text{Exposure}_i}.$$

Exposures are typically a child's number of peer judges or, for composites, the product of the number of peer judges and the number of items in the composite. Next, the zero-bounded, skewed, heteroscedastic properties of nomination count distributions are addressed by taking the natural logarithm (ln) of the rates, which linearizes the regression relationship and stabilizes the model's error structure so that maximum likelihood estimation methods may be applied (Dobson & Barnett, 2008; McCullagh & Nelder, 1989).

A Poisson regression model for a child's predicted counts, $\widehat{\text{Count}}_{ij}$, can be expressed as: $\widehat{\text{Count}}_{ij} = \text{Expos}_{ij} \hat{\lambda}_{ij}$ with $\ln(\hat{\lambda}_{ij}) = b_0 + b_1 x_1 + b_2 x_2 + \cdots + b_r X_r$. In this pair of equations, the predicted count for a particular child in a particular classroom (the ith child in the jth classroom) is the product of their exposure, Expos_{ij}, and their estimated rate of receiving nominations, $\hat{\lambda}_{ij}$. Their estimated rate of receiving nominations, in turn, is linked to the hypothesized set of predictors specified in a regression equation. Predicted values in the log metric, $\hat{\lambda}_{ij}$, and unstandardized regression coefficients, $(b_0 \ldots b_r)$, behave and are tested, interpreted, and plotted in exactly the same ways as their counterparts in ordinary linear regression analyses (Atkinson, 1985; Chatterjee & Hadi, 2006; J. Cohen, et al., 2003; Draper & Smith, 1998). The original nomination counts, however, are nonlinearly related to parameters of the Poisson regression model through a multiplicative, exponential function.

$$\hat{\lambda}_{ij} = e^{b_0 + b_1 X_1 + b_2 X_2 + \cdots + b_r X_r} = e^{b_0} e^{b_1 X_1} e^{b_2 X_2} \cdots e^{b_r X_r}$$

$$\widehat{\text{Count}}_{ij} = (\text{Expos}_{ij}) \hat{\lambda}_{ij} = (\text{Expos}_{ij}) e^{b_0} e^{b_1 X_1} e^{b_2 X_2} \cdots e^{b_r X_r}$$

In the second equation, it is clear that predicted counts can never become less than zero and each regression term has a multiplicative effect on the predicted numbers of nominations received. However, figures and graphs of model effects based on the second equation are notoriously difficult to interpret correctly. For this reason, Spangler Avant et.al. (2011), as well as Coxe et al. (2009), strongly recommended presenting and interpreting the model in the logarithmic metric (i.e., in terms of $[\hat{\lambda}_{ij}]$).

Challenges and Extensions to Poisson Models

The simplicity of Poisson-regression models is accompanied by a restrictive assumption about the distribution of errors (ie., deviations of observed data from model predicted values). Specifically, Poisson models assume that variances are directly proportional to the magnitude of model predicted values, and more specifically, that they increase in a 1:1 ratio with the predicted values. In practice it is common for this assumption to be violated (Cameron & Trivedi, 1998; Dobson & Barnett, 2008; Hilbe, 2007; Long, 1997). In Figure 2.3, for example, on average, classroom variances increased at a rate approximately twice the size of classroom means. If the data were exactly Poisson-distributed, classroom variances would increase in a one-to-one ratio with the classroom means. This situation, where Poisson model variances exceed their means (or predicted values), is called *overdispersion*. It has long been recognized as a common condition in Poisson regression models that can result in invalid statistical tests of model parameters. Most statistical software for Poisson modeling now allows for incorporation of an estimated over-dispersion scale factor into analyses, along with a statistical test of its significance (i.e., whether the degree of over-dispersion is equal to 1 or not). If over-dispersion is present, Poisson models with the estimated scale factor correctly adjust all statistical tests of parameters for the extra variability, resulting in correct inferential conclusions.

A couple of alternative approaches to modeling over-dispersed Poisson data are also available. The first, called "zero-inflated" Poisson models (Lambert, 1992) was developed to account for Poisson data containing an over-abundance of zeros (ie. more zeros then predicted under a standard Poisson model). Zero-inflated Poisson models assume that, in addition to the process that generates standard Poisson-distributed data, a second process works to generate the excessive number of zeros. Although zero-inflated Poisson models can fit overdispersed Poisson data well, for sociometric nomination data we find its assumption that a second process is generating the overabundance of zeros uncompelling. Specifically, in sociometric nomination data, an abundance of zeros typically occurs simply because an attribute does not apply to many children. Therefore invoking a second process in order statistically account for the "extra" zeros is theoretically unappealing (cf. Allison, 2012).

An alternative, more theoretically compelling approach to overdispersed Poisson data is called negative binomial regression (Hilbe, 2007). It is a model very similar to the Poisson, but includes an extra parameter which allows the model to accommodate data containing greater numbers of small values—including zeros—than predicted under a standard Poisson model. Unfortunately, negative binomial regression is not widely incorporated into extant multilevel modeling software packages for the types of innovative approaches we describe below (e.g., cross-classified models). In the future, as this changes, negative binomial regression is likely to become the preferred method for modeling over-dispersed peer nomination data, but all of the considerations and approaches described should remain applicable to it, as well.

In Poisson models, the degree of overdispersion seems particularly sensitive to the presence of small numbers of cases with unusually large counts, which is especially germane for peer nomination data. Hilbe (2007) reported simulation results for a large data set (10,000 observations) in which contamination by one-tenth of one percent (1 observation in a thousand) of all observations (10 observations out of 10,000) with values 2.5 and 5 times higher than the group mean were sufficient to induce over-dispersion rates of 6% and 30%, respectively. By contrast, one child with 8 nominations in a 20 student class where the average student receives 2 nominations, can be considered a "contamination" rate (in Hilbe's terminology) of 5% (1 student out of 20) with a mean value 4 times higher than the class average. If Hilbe's results hold for small datasets, it suggests that researchers should *always* anticipate and allow for overdispersion when modeling peer nomination data. It also suggests that classrooms may be heterogeneous in their manifestations of overdispersion, depending on the presence of small numbers of children who receive unusually large numbers of nominations for particular items.

As noted earlier, peer nominations from young children are typically collected on and from intact groups such as classrooms. Whenever data is collected from members of social groups (schools, classrooms, families, churches,...) the statistical assumption of independence between observations is likely to be violated (Hox, 2010; Raudenbush & Bryk, 2002; Snijders & Bosker, 2012). In other words, if the ratings or nominations of two children from the same classroom are more similar than the ratings or nominations of two children from different classrooms, then the data collected from children within classrooms cannot be considered independent. In statistical modeling, lack of independence between children in groups yields biased statistical tests of parameters, often making them appear statistically significant when they really are not. A family of statistical methods, called multilevel models, has been developed specifically to address the challenges associated with nested data (Goldstein, 2003; Hox, 2010; Raudenbush & Bryk, 2002; Snijders & Bosker, 2012), and a number of high-level software packages, such as SAS/STAT (SAS_Institute, 2011), HLM (Raudenbush, Bryk, Cheong, Congdon, & du Toit, 2011), MPlus (Muthén & Muthén, 1998–2010), and MLWin (Rasbash, Charlton, Browne, Healy, & Cameron, 2009), now allow multilevel versions of Poisson regression analyses.

Besides questions about how the personal characteristics of individual children (behavioral style, sex, race, poverty status...) are related to the numbers of nominations received, researchers are increasingly posing questions about how classroom, teacher, or other contextual characteristics influence peer ratings or nominations in classrooms. For example, can especially warm and supportive teachers foster classroom environments where socially anxious children are more included in group activities, leading them to be judged as less isolated than anxious solitary children in other classrooms? Multilevel Poisson models, like multilevel linear models, naturally accommodate these types of questions by formulating two related regression equations: a Level 1 (individual-level) Poisson model relates individual children's characteristics to the number of nominations they receive in their classroom; and a Level 2 (group-level) model that relates classroom level characteristics to the parameters of the individual-level model. When both levels are combined and estimated as a single multilevel

Poisson regression model, the simultaneous assessment of the influence of both individual-level and group-level predictors on the rates at which children receive nominations is achieved (Hox, 2010; Raudenbush & Bryk, 2002; Raudenbush, et al., 2011; Snijders & Bosker, 2012).

Further generalizations of the multilevel Poisson analytic framework to accommodate multilevel modeling of peer nominations over time were proposed by Spangler Avant, Gazelle, and Faldowski (2011). In their study, peer nominations were obtained from elementary school children each fall and spring semester from third through fifth grades. A longitudinal Poisson model of change over grades (Raudenbush, et al., 2011) was formulated, along with a coding system that allowed for assessment of changing fall to spring variations in nomination counts over grades. Grade-to-grade classroom changes and variations in classmates were addressed by superimposing a classroom cross-classification (Goldstein, 2003; Hox, 2010; Raudenbush & Bryk, 2002; Raudenbush, et al., 2011; Snijders & Bosker, 2012) structure on the longitudinal trends within individuals. This allowed effects of variations among classrooms in patterns of peer nominations to be statistically controlled. It also allowed for the changing effects of classroom environment on nominations of each child to be evaluated, even though teachers, classrooms, and specific classmates changed from one year (grade) to the next (Spangler Avant, et al., 2011). Finally, the approach extended all of the well-known advantages of standard multilevel longitudinal modeling to the analysis of peer nomination data collected repeatedly over time, such as the ability to characterize (group) average patterns of change, capture personal trajectories of change for each sample member, incorporate both time-varying and fixed covariates, and accommodate missing data and varying numbers of observations per child (Hox, 2010; Raudenbush & Bryk, 2002; Singer & Willett, 2003; Snijders & Bosker, 2012). To the best our knowledge, this was the first published application of a cross-classified multilevel longitudinal Poisson model to peer report data, and it opens new avenues for directly addressing more sophisticated questions about the influences of individual, developmental, and contextual factors on children's peer nominations over time.

Heterotypic Continuity

Heterotypic continuity refers to congruencies or predictabilities in patterns of developmental outcomes over time that are found despite differing behavioral manifestations, which are rooted in a child's increasingly sophisticated and refined biological, cognitive, and social capacities and behavioral repertoires (Caspi, 1998). Consequently, the same underlying behavioral tendency or relation with peers may be manifested differently as children develop. Likewise, the social expectations of classmate judges are subject to similar developmental processes, leading to increasingly refined, yet developmentally appropriate expectations of their classmates' behavior. For example, as summarized in Williams and Gilmour (1994, p. 1004), younger children employ very general criteria in deciding which peers they like or dislike, but as they age, their social information processing skills become more sophisticated and their judgments more nuanced. Thus, although peer ratings and nominations elicited from young children are likely subject to strong developmental influences over time, the implicitly age-normed behavioral expectations of classmates, as judges, likely exerts a stabilizing influence on peer report data collected over time. To the degree that behavior of a highly nominated classmate deviates from the social expectations of his or her classmates, even as both the child and classmates are growing and developing over time, he or she will continue to be highly nominated. Because the same item content can often be maintained in peer ratings and nominations even when they are collected over relatively long time intervals, it is tempting to assume that the construct measured was invariant over time. However the same items can take on different meaning for children as they develop. For example, as described above, children's criteria for who they consider a friend becomes more sophisticated with age. Consequently, when interpreting the results of repeated peer reports over time, the implicit age-norming and heterotypic continuity of the behaviors under consideration must always be kept in mind.

INTERPRETING PEER REPORT DATA

Peer report data derives its value from direct assessment of the perceptions of participants with insiders' perspectives on peer relations and peer behavior, as well as access to multiple opportunities to observe and interact with the child across a variety of social situations. Because peer reports are collected from multiple respondents (multiple classmates) they will tend to have stronger psychometric properties than measures collected from a single respondent. Nevertheless, care must be taken when interpreting peer report data.

Normative Change and Individual Differences

One of the central objectives of longitudinal research is explicitly characterizing and analyzing both normative change, as well as inter-individual heterogeneity in growth patterns (Baltes and Nesselroade, 1979). Multilevel linear and nonlinear models (Hox, 2010; Raudenbush & Bryk, 2002;

Singer & Willett, 2003; Snijders & Bosker, 2012) have become standard tools for directly addressing both objectives, and spawned a new generation of questions about continuity and change that cannot be addressed with other methods. The techniques facilitate examination of the shapes of average or normative developmental trajectories, main effect and interactive predictors of these average trajectories, as well as the potentially time-structured influence of some predictors. In addition to the capacity to examine normative patterns of growth and change, multilevel longitudinal modeling also provides estimates of individual growth and change, and how much and in what specific ways it deviates in shape or pattern from normative developmental trajectories (Singer & Willett, 2003; Willett, 1997).

The opportunity to address nuanced questions about both normative and individual growth and change, however, comes at a price; the statistical and measurement demands of longitudinal modeling may contradict key developmental phenomena. From a statistical point of view, it would be ideal if the exact same measure could be used at all assessment points; however, from a developmental perspective, measures need to be age-appropriate and contextually appropriate for the participants at each assessment. Even if the same measure is employed at all time points, because children's capacities to process and understand cognitive and social information grow and become more nuanced over time, is it valid to treat children's *interpretation* of the same measure as consistent over time (Brooks-Gunn, Rock, & Warren, 1989; Dixon, 2005; Singer & Willett, 2003)? Moreover, if measures are collected from intact social groups, how do researchers insure that members of all groups are interpreting and responding to items consistently, insuring comparability of scores across the groups?

Peer report data, in general, and peer nomination data, in particular, are likely to satisfy both statistical and developmental demands on validity. From a statistical and measurement perspective, peer nomination rates are, by definition, comparable across assessment occasions—they are the numbers of nominations received from peers expressed as a proportion of opportunities to receive nominations. In addition, because the information can be elicited from the same question over time, it seems to satisfy all nominal requirements for comparability over time and assessments. More importantly from a developmental point of view, we have argued that the judgments of age-mate (or grade-mate) peers inherently calibrates the growing social and cognitive behavioral repertoires of the children who are rated to the age- or grade-specific social and behavioral expectations of their peers. In this sense, a rated child's behavior and status within a social group is inherently calibrated to the social expectations for behavior within the group, including contextual, cultural, and other collective social considerations. By using multilevel Poisson and cross-classified longitudinal Poisson analysis methods we can recognize essential data characteristics, while still appropriately accounting for heterogeneity among classrooms in their criteria and use of peer nominations (e.g., a class with a relatively elevated proportion of aggressive children). In the same way that linear multilevel models allow for the characterization of both normative (average) patterns of growth and development, as well as individual variations; multilevel Poisson and multilevel cross-classified longitudinal Poisson analysis methods do the same.

Although extant analytic tools can appropriately accommodate variations among classrooms in peer nomination patterns and associated classroom behavioral norms and expectations, much less attention has focused on group-level (classroom-level) social processes that lead to the establishment of behavioral norms, and the consequences for children who violate them. Better-suited to addressing such questions is network analysis, another conceptual and statistical approach to the analysis of peer report data (i.e., friendship nominations and reports on which peers interact with one another). Although detailed description of this family of approaches is beyond the scope of the current chapter, we contrast the strengths of this approach with those we have presented above. Whereas the techniques we have presented above emphasize the characterization of individual children's behavioral characteristics and affiliation patterns in reference to their classroom and grade cohort, network analysis focuses on the composition and structure of social groups, the hierarchical relations among social groups, the position of individuals within the group, and individual-group similarities and differences and their patterns of change over time. The choice of analytic technique for peer report data depends upon the nature of the research question, as the same data can often be analyzed from either perspective.

Severity Versus Reputation

Peer nomination scores are often interpreted as indicative of severity. For instance, if the mean peer exclusion score of child A is significantly more than child B, the statement is often made that child A is more severely excluded than child B. However, peer nominations are technically assessments of reputation rather than severity (Perry, 1995). That is, is it technically more correct to say that child A has a stronger reputation among peers for being excluded, rather than that they are more severely excluded. However, in practice, it can be cumbersome to use the more technically correct language. Although researchers may employ shorter severity-oriented language to achieve cleaner prose, they should nonetheless understand that they are measuring reputation when they employ peer methodology. This is important to recognize because there are instances in which peer reputation may differ from other objective measurements. For instance, when peer exclusion and victimization are measured via peer report, anxious solitary children appear to be similarly elevated on both indices of peer mistreatment. However, when rates of peer exclusion and victimization of anxious solitary children are observed at recess, observational data reveal that peer exclusion occurs in a much greater proportion of intervals than peer victimization (Gazelle, 2008). Thus, peer report data appears sensitive to relative differences among children in extent of reputation for peer treatment, but insensitive to relative differences in the frequency with which children encounter specific forms of peer treatment. When peer reports are correctly framed as measures of reputation, insensitivity to the frequency with which a specific form of peer treatment occurs is not surprising. Ultimately, peer reports are highly useful assessments when employed to assess reputation, but their accuracy depends upon the appropriateness of data interpretation.

Group Versus Dyad

Another common error in interpreting peer report data is to infer dyadic-level phenomena from group-level phenomena, or vice versa. For instance, elevated peer rejection (a group-level phenomenon) does not necessarily indicate that a child has no reciprocated friendships (a dyadic phenomenon) (Howes, Rubin, Ross, & French, 1988). For instance, research indicates that rejected children who have friends demonstrate better adjustment over time (Howes, et al., 1988). Such research into peer relations processes is made possible by conceptually accurate distinctions among group- and dyadic-level constructs.

ETHICS

Observational Studies

Schools and parents sometimes raise concerns about the usage of peer report methodology. The most common concern is that asking children about who they don't like to play with or who displays negative behaviors might cause them to contemplate issues they would not otherwise contemplate. Consequently, the concern is that peers might treat children identified by such nominations poorly, although they might not otherwise do so. However, there is a variety of evidence to diminish these concerns. First, observation of children engaged in answering peer report questions reveals that they answer both positive and negative questions about classmates rapidly, suggesting that these are issues that they have already thought about and are salient to them in their everyday lives. Indeed, when the first author's three-year-old looks at pictures of his classmates he readily points out one child who is "naughty" and states that he does not like this child (without being asked about who he likes or dislikes), in addition to many children he likes. Second, and most importantly, observational research with young children reveals no difference in children's play behavior and treatment of peers before versus after participating in peer report interviews (Hayvren & Hymel, 1984). Although research with older children has indicated that some children report discussing their responses with peers despite being asked not to, these conversations occurred without the knowledge of target children (as do many such conversations among friends). Consequently, researchers have concluded that peer report methods do not result in harm or represent a greater risk than encountered in children's everyday lives (Iverson, Barton, & Iverson, 1997; Iverson & Iverson, 1996). Therefore, there is no evidence that participating in peer reports introduces children to new ideas about their peers or influences their treatment of peers.

Nonetheless, it is common practice for researchers to employ several methods to diminish the potential risk that participating in peer reports could influence treatment of classmates. First, children are always told that their responses are private and that they should not talk about them with other children so that no one's feelings get hurt (but that it's ok to discuss them with their parents). Similarly, older children participating in group-administered interviews are given sheets of paper to help keep their questions out of view of peers. Second, because peer report interviews are conducted with young children individually, there is no possibility that children would react to questions publicly or discuss their responses with one another during the interview. Third, peer report interviews are not administered immediately before recess so that it is not the most immediate issue on children's minds when they are free to interact with one another in an unstructured manner (Bell-Dolan & Wessler, 1994).

Cultural Considerations

Peer report methodology is widely used in North America, Europe, and Australia. In these areas of the world informed permission to conduct research is sought first from schools or child care centers, and then written informed consent is sought from parents. In addition, children must assent or agree to cooperate with peer reports and other research. Written assent is often sought with children five years and older. This usually involves the researcher reading aloud the description of the research task as printed on the assent form in brief, simple language, and asking the child to write his or her name if he or she would like to take part. With younger children, researchers should read a script with the description of the task and record children's verbal wishes to participate or not as assent or the lack thereof.

Peer report methodology has also been employed in many other countries around the world. Schools in China and Russia act "*in loco parentis,*" meaning that they have legal responsibility for the children under their care while the child is at school, and thus the ability to directly consent to the child's participation in research. Consequently, some peer relations researchers have reported that they are not allowed to obtain written parental permission in these cultures (Hart et al., 2000). However, other researchers have obtained written parental permission in China (Chen, Wang, & Cao, 2011). If parents' written informed consent cannot be sought, researchers ask schools to arrange a presentation for parents and explain confidentiality and children's right to refuse or discontinue participation in this context to insure that parents are informed about the research and have an avenue to ask questions or raise concerns. There is also at least one country that has chosen not to participate in research involving peer report methodology (i.e., Japan). It is always important that researchers are informed about local norms and ethics approval procedures and are respectful of these practices.

CONCLUSION

Peer report data provides a unique "inside view" of children's peer relations and social behavior. Furthermore, their multi-informant nature yields good psychometric properties for many constructs in young children from the age of 3 years. Obtaining good psychometrics with peer reports in children ages 3 to 7 years requires individual administration of peer report questions and the use of photographs of peers. Using such methods, reliable peer report information can be obtained with nominations, ratings, or paired comparisons. The choice of administration strategy involves a tradeoff between length of administration time (e.g., high for paired comparisons in particular and ratings are also more lengthy than nominations) and the reliability and stability of data (most studies indicate higher reliability and stability for ratings than nominations).

Contemporary peer relations research tends to focus on peer relations processes rather than status groups and to make fine-grained distinctions between different forms of child behavior and peer treatment. Also, increasing sophistication in the analysis of data in the social sciences is slowly spurring changes in accepted practices for analyzing peer relations data. In the future, we expect to see increasing recognition that techniques which correctly treat peer nomination data as count data (using Poisson models) are advantageous as they may yield increased power. We expect such developments to contribute to the continued flourishing of peer relations research well into the future.

NOTE

1. One anonymous reviewer of this chapter suggested the innovative idea that gamma or Weibull distributions could be productively employed to directly model proportion scores. Although we were unable locate any published application of this method to sociometric nomination data, we agree that it represents a potentially fruitful avenue of exploration.

REFERENCES

Achenbach, T. M., McConaughy, S. H., & Howell, C. T. (1987). Child/adolescent behavioral and emotional problems: Implications of cross-informant correlations for situational specificity. *Psychological Bulletin, 101*(2), 213–232.

Asher, S. R., & Dodge, K. A. (1986). Identifying children who are rejected by their peers. *Developmental Psychology, 22*, 442–449.

Asher, S. R., Singleton, L. C., Tinsley, B. R., & Hymel, S. (1979). A reliable sociometric measure for preschool children. *Developmental Psychology, 15*(4), 443–444.

Atkinson, A. C. (1985). *Plots, transformations, and regression: An introduction to graphical methods of diagnostic regression analysis.* New York, NY: Oxford University Press.

Baltes, P. B., & Nesselroade, J. R. (1979). History and rationale of longitudinal research. In J. R. Nesselroade & P. B. Baltes (Eds.), *Longitudinal research in the study of behavior and development* (pp. 1–39). New York, NY: Academic Press.

Bell-Dolan, D. J., & Wessler, A. E. (1994). Ethical administration of sociometric measures: Procedures in use and suggestions for improvement. *Professional Psychology: Research and Practice, 25*(1), 23–32.

Brooks-Gunn, J., Rock, D., & Warren, M. P. (1989). Comparability of constructs across the adolescent years. *Developmental Psychology, 25*(1), 51–60.

Bukowski, W. M., Sippola, L., Hoza, B., & Newcomb, A. F. (2000). Pages from a sociometric notebook: An analysis of nomination and rating scale measures of acceptance, rejection, and social preference. *New Directions for Child & Adolescent Development, 2000*(88), 11–26.

Cameron, A. C., & Trivedi, P. K. (1998). *Regression analysis of count data.* New York, NY: Cambridge University Press.

Caspi, A. 1998. Personality development across the life course. In W. Damon (Series Ed.) & N. Eiesenberg (Vol. Ed.), Handbook of child psychology: Vol. 3. Social, emotional, and personality development (5th ed, pp. 311–388). New York, NY: Wiley.

Chatterjee, S., & Hadi, A. S. (2006). *Regression analysis by example* (4th ed.). Hoboken, N.J.: Wiley-Interscience.

Chen, X., Wang, L., & Cao, R. (2011). Shyness-sensitivity and unsociability in rural Chinese children: Relations with social, school, and psychological adjustment. *Child Development, 82*(5), 1531–1543.

Cillessen, A. H. N., Bukowski, W. M., & Haselager, G. J. T. (2000). Stability of sociometric categories. In A. H. N. Cillesen & W. M. Bukowski (Eds.), *New directions for child & adolescent development* (Vol. 2000, pp. 75–93). New York, NY: John Wiley & Sons, Inc.

Cohen, A. S., & Van Tassel, E. (1978). A comparison of partial and complete paired comparisons in sociometric measurement of preschool groups. *Applied Psychological Measurement, 2*(1), 31–40.

Cohen, J. (1977). *Statistical power analysis for the behavioral sciences.* New York, NY: Academic Press.

Cohen, J., Cohen, P., West, S. G., & Aiken, L. S. (2003). *Applied multiple regression/correlation analysis for the behavioral sciences* (3rd ed.). Mahwah, N.J.: Erlbaum Associates.

Coie, J. D., & Dodge, K. A. (1983). Continuities and changes in children's social status: A five-year longitudinal study. *Merrill-Palmer Quarterly, 29,* 261–282.

Coie, J. D., Dodge, K. A., & Coppotelli, H. (1982). Dimensions and types of social status: A cross-age perspective. *Developmental Psychology, 18*(4), 557–570.

Coie, J. D., Dodge, K. A., & Kupersmidt, J. B. (1990). Peer group behavior and social status. In S. R. Asher & J. D. Coie (Eds.), *Peer rejection in childhood. Cambridge studies in social and emotional development.* (pp. 17–59). New York, NY: Cambridge.

Connolly, J. A. (1983). A review of sociometric procedures in the assessment of social competencies in children. *Applied Research in Mental Retardation, 4*(4), 315–327.

Coplan, R. J., & Armer, M. (2007). A 'multitude' of solitude: A closer look at social withdrawal and nonsocial play in early childhood. *Child Development Perspectives, 1*(1), 26–32.

Coxe, S., West, S. G., & Aiken, L. S. (2009). The analysis of count data: A gentle introduction to Poisson regression and its alternatives. *Journal of Personality Assessment, 91*(2), 121–136.

Crick, N. R., & Grotpeter, J. K. (1995). Relational aggression, gender, and social-psychological adjustment. *Child Development, 66*(3), 710–722.

Crozier, W. R., & Burnham, M. (1990). Age-related differences in children's understanding of shyness. *British Journal of Developmental Psychology, 8*(2), 179–185.

Diamond, K., Furgy, W. L., & Blass, S. (1993). Attitudes of preschool children toward their peers with disabilities: A year-long investigation in integrated classrooms. *Journal of Genetic Psychology, 154,* 215–221.

Dixon, J. A. (2005). Strong tests of developmental ordering hypotheses: Integrating evidence from the second moment. *Child Development, 76*(1), 1–23.

Dobson, A. J., & Barnett, A. G. (2008). *An introduction to generalized linear models* (3rd ed.). Boca Raton: CRC Press.

Draper, N. R., & Smith, H. (1998). *Applied regression analysis* (3rd ed.). New York, NY: Wiley.

Engle, J. M., McElwain, N. L., & Lasky, N. (2011). Presence and quality of kindergarten children's friendships: Concurrent and longitudinal associations with child adjustment in the early school years. *Infant and Child Development, 20*(4), 365–386.

Epkins, C. C. (1995). Peer ratings of internalizing and externalizing problems in inpatient and elementary school. *Journal of Emotional & Behavioral Disorders, 3*(4), 203.

Faldowski, R. A., Gazelle, H., & Spangler Avant, T. (2012). *Multilevel Poisson models for children's longitudinal sociometric rating data.* Paper presented at the Society for Research in Child Development 2012 Themed Meeting: Developmental Methodology, Tampa, Florida.

Foster, S. L., Bell-Dolan, D., & Berler, E. S. (1986). Methodological issues in the use of sociometrics for selecting children for social skills research and training. *Advances in Behavioral Assessment of Children & Families, 2*, 227–248.

Gardner, W., Mulvey, E. P., & Shaw, E. C. (1995). Regression analyses of counts and rates: Poisson, overdispersed Poisson, and negative binomial models. *Psychological Bulletin, 118*(3), 392–404.

Gazelle, H. (2008). Behavioral profiles of anxious solitary children and heterogeneity in peer relations. *Developmental Psychology, 44*(6), 1604–1624.

Gazelle, H., & Spangler, T. (2007). Early childhood anxious solitude and subsequent peer relationships: Maternal and cognitive moderators. *Journal of Applied Developmental Psychology, 28*(5–6), 515–535.

Goldstein, H. (2003). *Multilevel statistical models* (3rd ed.). New York, NY: Oxford University Press.

Hart, C. H., Yang, C., Nelson, L. J., Robinson, C. C., Olsen, J. A., Nelson, D. A., et al. (2000). Peer acceptance in early childhood and subtypes of socially withdrawn behavior in China, Russia and the United States. *International Journal of Behavioral Development, 24*(1), 73–81.

Hartup, W. W., & Abecassis, M. (2004). Friends and enemies. In P. K. Smith & C. H. Hart (Eds.), *Blackwell handbook of childhood social development* (pp. 285–306). M A Malden: Blackwell.

Hays, W. L. (1994). *Statistics* (5th ed.). Fort Worth: Harcourt College Publishers.

Hayvren, M., & Hymel, S. (1984). Ethical issues in sociometric testing: Impact of sociometric measures on interaction behavior. *Developmental Psychology, 20*(5), 844–849.

Hilbe, J. M. (2007). *Negative binomial regression.* New York, NY: Cambridge University Press.

Hops, H., & Lewin, L. (1984). Peer sociometric forms. In T. H. Ollendick & M. Herson (Eds.), *Child behavioral assessment* (pp. 124–147). New York, NY: Pergamon Press.

Howes, C., Rubin, K. H., Ross, H. S., & French, D. C. (1988). Peer interaction of young children. *Monographs of the Society for Research in Child Development, 53*(1), 1–92.

Hox, J. J. (2010). *Multilevel analysis: Techniques and applications* (2nd ed.): NY : Routledge.

Hymel, S. (1983). Preschool children's peer relations: Issues in sociometric assessment. *Merrill-Palmer Quarterly, 29*(3), 24.

Iverson, A. M., Barton, E. A., & Iverson, G. L. (1997). Analysis of risk to children participating in a sociometric task. *Developmental Psychology, 33*(1), 104–112.

Iverson, A. M., & Iverson, G. L. (1996). Children's long-term reactions to participating in sociometric assessment. *Psychology in the Schools, 33*(2), 103–112.

Jiang, X. L., & Cillessen, A. H. N. (2005). Stability of continuous measures of sociometric status: A meta-analysis. *Developmental Review, 25*(1), 1–25.

Kane, J. S., & Lawler, E. E. (1978). Methods of peer assessment. *Psychological Bulletin, 85*(3), 555–586.

Leflot, G., van Lier, P. A. C., Verschueren, K., Onghena, P., & Colpin, H. (2011). Transactional associations among teacher support, peer social preference, and child externalizing behavior: A four-wave longitudinal study. *Journal of Clinical Child and Adolescent Psychology, 40*(1), 87–99.

Long, J. S. (1997). *Regression models for categorical and limited dependent variables.* Thousand Oaks: Sage Publications.

Maassen, G. H., Steenbeek, H., & Van Geert, P. (2004). Stability of three methods for two-dimensional sociometric status determination based on the procedure of Asher, Singleton, Tinsley, and Hymel. *Social Behavior & Personality: An International Journal, 32*(6), 535–550.

Masten, A. S., Morison, P., & Pellegrini, D. S. (1985). A revised class play method of peer assessment. *Developmental Psychology, 21*(3), 523–533.

McCandless, B. R., & Marshall, H. R. (1957). A picture sociometric technique for preschool children and its relation to teacher judgments of friendship. *Child Development, 28*(2), 139–147.

McConnell, S. R., & Odom, S. L. (1986). Sociometrics: Peer-referenced measures and the assessment of social competence. In P. Strain, M. J. Guralnick, & H. M. Walker (Eds.), *Children's social behavior: Development, assessment, and modification* (pp. 215–284). New York, NY: Academic Press.

McCullagh, P., & Nelder, J. A. (1989). *Generalized linear models* (2nd ed.): New York, NY: Chapman and Hall.

Moreno, J. L. (1934). *Who shall survive? A new approach to the problem of human interelations.* Washington, D.C.: Nervous and Mental Disease Publishing Co.

Muthén, L. K., & Muthén, B. O. (1998/2010). *Mplus User's Guide* (6th ed.). Los Angeles, CA: Muthén & Muthén.

Nelson, D. A., Robinson, C. C., & Hart, C. H. (2005). Relational and physical aggression of preschool-age children: Peer status linkages across informants. *Early Education and Development, 16*(2), 115–140.

Nelson, D. A., Robinson, C. C., Hart, C. H., Albano, A. D., & Marshall, S. J. (2010). Italian preschoolers' peer-status linkages with sociability and subtypes of aggression and victimization. *Social Development, 19*(4), 698–720.

Newcomb, A. F., & Bukowski, W. M. (1984). Longitudinal study of the utility of social preference and social impact sociometric classification themes. *Child Development, 55*(4), 1434.

Olson, S. L., & Lifgren, K. (1988). Concurrent and longitudinal correlates of preschool peer sociometrics: Comparing rating scale and nomination measures. *Journal of Applied Developmental Psychology, 9*, 409–420.

Parker, J. G., & Asher, S. R. (1993). Friendship and friendship quality in middle childhood: Links with peer group acceptance and feelings of loneliness and social dissatisfaction. *Developmental Psychology, 29*(4), 611–621.

Pekarik, E. G., Prinz, R. J., Liebert, D. E., Weintraub, S., & Neale, J. M. (1976). The Pupil Evaluation Inventory. A sociometric technique for assessing children's social behavior. *Journal Of Abnormal Child Psychology, 4*(1), 83–97.

Perry, D. G. (1995). *Uses and abuses of the peer rejection construct.* Florida Atlantic University. Boca Raton, FL.

Philips, B. M., Driscoll, C. J., & Hooe, E. S. (2002). Positive and negative affectivity in children: A multitrait–multimethod investigation. *Journal of Clinical Child and Adolescent Psychology, 31,* 465–479.

Pronin, E., Lin, D. Y., & Ross, L. (2002). The bias blind spot: Perceptions of bias in self versus others. *Personality and Social Psychology Bulletin, 28*(3), 369–381.

Ramsey, P. G. (1995). Changing social dynamics in early childhood classrooms. *Child Development, 66*(3), 764–773.

Rasbash, J., Charlton, C., Browne, W. J., Healy, M., & Cameron, B. (2009). *MLwiN Version 2.1.* Bristol, UK: Centre for Multilevel Modelling, University of Bristol.

Raudenbush, S. W., & Bryk, A. S. (2002). *Hierarchical linear models: Applications and data analysis methods* (2nd ed.) Thousand Oaks, CA: Sage Publications.

Raudenbush, S. W., Bryk, A. S., Cheong, Y. F., Congdon, R. T., & du Toit, M. (2011). *HLM 7: Hierarchical linear and nonlinear modeling.* Lincolnwood, Ill.: Scientific Software Int. Inc.

SAS Institute. (2011). *SAS/STAT® 9.3 User's Guide.* Cary, NC: SAS Institute Inc.

Shell, M. J., & Gazelle, H. (2014). *Observed naturalistic peer interaction sequences in anxious solitary children: Evaluating universal vulnerability, sensitivity to threat, and reputational bias mechanisms.* (Unpublished Manuscript)

Singer, J. D., & Willett, J. B. (2003). *Applied longitudinal data analysis: Modeling change and event occurrence.* New York, NY: Oxford University Press.

Snijders, T. A. B., & Bosker, R. J. (2012). *Multilevel analysis: An introduction to basic and advanced multilevel modeling* (2nd ed.). Los Angeles, CA: Sage.

Spangler Avant, T., Gazelle, H., & Faldowski, R. (2011). Classroom emotional climate as a moderator of anxious solitary children's longitudinal risk for peer exclusion: A child X environment model. *Developmental Psychology, 47*(6), 1711–1727.

Spangler, T., & Gazelle, H. (2009). Anxious solitude, unsociability, and peer exclusion in middle childhood: A multitrait-multimethod matrix. *Social Development, 18*(4), 833–856.

Szewczyk-Sokolowski, M., Bost, K., & Wainwright, A. (2005). Attachment, temperament, and preschool children's peer acceptance. *Social Development, 14*(3), 379–397.

Terry, R. (2000). Recent Advances in Measurement Theory and the Use of Sociometric Techniques. In A. H. N. Cillessen & W. M. Bukowski (Eds.), *Recent advances in the measurement of acceptance and rejection in the peer system: New Directions for Child & Adolescent Development* (Vol. 88, pp. 27–53). New York, NY: John Wiley & Sons, Inc.

Terry, R., & Coie, J. D. (1991). A comparison of methods for defining sociometric status among children. *Developmental Psychology, 27*(5), 867–880.

Vaughn, B. E., Colvin, T. N., Azria, M. R., Caya, L., & Krzysik, L. (2001). Dyadic analyses of friendship in a sample of preschool-age children sttending head start: Correspondence between measures and implications for social competence. *Child Development, 72*(3), 862–878.

Vaughn, B. E., & Mize, J. (1991). *A comparison of two methods for estimating sociometric status in preschool-age children.* Paper presented at the biennial meeting of the Society for Research in Child Development, Seattle WA.

Vaughn, B. E., Shin, N., Kim, M., Coppola, G., Krzysik, L., Santos, A. J., et al. (2009). Hierarchical models of social competence in preschool children: A multisite, multinational study. *Child Development, 80*(6), 1775–1796.

Veldman, D. J., & Sheffield, J. R. (1979). The scaling of sociometric nominations. *Educational and Psychological Measurement, 39*(1), 99–106.

Wasik, B. H. (1987). Sociometric measures and peer descriptors of kindergarten children: A study of reliability and validity. *Journal of Clinical Child Psychology, 16*(3), 218–224.

Willett, J. B. (1997). Measuring change: What individual growth modeling buys you. In E. Amsel & K. A. Renninger (Eds.), *Change and development: Issues of theory, method, and application* (pp. 213–243). Mahwah, NJ: L. Erlbaum.

Williams, B. T. R., & Gilmour, J. D. (1994). Annotation: Sociometry and peer relationships. [Article]. *Journal of Child Psychology & Psychiatry & Allied Disciplines, 35*(6), 997–1013.

Wu, X., Hart, C. H., Draper, T. W., & Olsen, J. A. (2001). Peer and teacher sociometrics for preschool children: Cross-informant concordance, temporal stability, and reliability. *Merrill-Palmer Quarterly, 47*(3), 416–443.

Younger, A. J., & Daniels, T. M. (1992). Children's reasons for nominating their peers as withdrawn: Passive withdrawal versus active isolation. *Developmental Psychology, 28*(5), 955–960.

Younger, A. J., Schwartzman, A. E., & Ledingham, J. E. (1985). Age-related changes in children's perceptions of aggression and withdrawal in their peers. *Developmental Psychology, 21*(1), 70–75.

Younger, A. J., Schwartzman, A. E., & Ledingham, J. E. (1986). Age-related differences in children's perceptions of social deviance: Changes in behavior or in perspective? *Developmental Psychology, 22*(4), 531–542.

CHAPTER 3

SOCIOMETRIC MEASURES FOR PEER RELATIONS RESEARCH WITH YOUNG CHILDREN

Rosanne Burton Smith

The terms sociometry and sociometric connote "companion measure" from the Latin *socius* meaning companion, and *metrum* meaning measure. Sociometric measures are methods for assessing social attractions and repulsions within a group context. They provide relational data reflecting the connections between different group members. These measures contrast with attribute data—assessments of an individual's attitudes, opinions, and behaviors. Despite this distinctiveness, similarity exists in the techniques employed to collect social relational data and attribute data, including interviewing, questionnaires, and rating scales. Individuals making sociometric evaluations are "expert" evaluators, basing interpersonal judgments on their own experiences and feelings; and giving global measures of interpersonal attraction and repulsion (Lyndzey & Byrne, 1968). However, in sociometric studies researchers generally do not examine the reasons for, and the dynamics leading to, an individual's evaluation of another person.

Two types of sociometric measure are employed in research—quantitative measures show the *degree* of acceptance and rejection of individuals within groups, while qualitative measures explore the *patterns* of attraction and repulsion between individuals within groups. During the first half of the twentieth century sociometric research was largely qualitative with adults as the primary focus. Since the 1960s however, research interest in the development of children's peer relationships has seen the burgeoning of quantitative sociometric measurement.

SOCIOMETRIC INVESTIGATION OF YOUNG CHILDREN'S PEER RELATIONSHIPS

Peer relationships initially forged during early childhood are vital to children's later development (Ladd, 2006; Ladd & Troop-Gordon, 2003). According to Rubin, Bukowski and Parker (2006) children learn unique and vital social skills from egalitarian peer relationships that are not available from the family context, because it is based on unequal power and nurturance (Gleason, 2002). From the preschool years onwards peers uniquely teach children the principle of give-and-take and how to resolve conflicts, as well as understanding the mental states of other people (Ladd, 2005; Gifford-Smith & Brownell, 2003). Peer relations are therefore recognized as a significant socializing agent, essential for normal social-emotional development during early childhood and beyond. For this reason peer relations became an important focus for research during the 1980s and continue to be so in the twenty-first century.

Researchers commonly employ observations, questionnaires, rating scales, and sociometric assessments to study children's peer relationships. Informants might be parents, teachers, trained adult observers or children's peers. Each of these data sources is valuable, because they vary in accessibility to information, cognitive bias and relationship to the target child. The information from adults and from children's peers differs significantly along these dimensions. Adult informants' *accessibility* to information about children is "limited in time type and context" (Newcomb, Bukowski & Pattee, 1993, p. 103). Incidents occurring out of adult view can be critical for peer functioning, so peer-based information provides investigators with unique insights into children's peer relations. Peers' understanding of group norms and relationships may be more extensive than parents' or teachers' knowledge (Rubin & Hymel, 1985; Hymel, Closson, Caravita & Vaillancourt, 2011). *Cognitive bias* is evident in the differing social norms of adults and children—children are concerned about facilitating interaction; adults with social regulation. These biases as well as variations in age-related cognitive development affect assessments by child and adult informants.

Moreover, adult information is based on an unequal relationship of varying intimacy with children, depending on whether a parent, a teacher or a stranger is involved in assessment. Children's peers and adults are each susceptible to reputational bias—expectation effects from prior knowledge of the child subject. In particular, peers look for confirmatory evidence of their expectations (Newcomb et al., 1993).

Because it is a *peer-based assessment*, sociometric techniques provide data relevant to a group of individuals who largely determine children's group integration and adjustment. Peer assessment is a cumulative, group-based response to an individual. Multiple peer observers provide a wide perspective, reflecting the opinions of a range of individuals with whom a target child has different personal relationships. In contrast, observations, questionnaires, and rating scales using adults as informants, elicit an individual's response to a target child—for example, a teacher's ratings of a child's behavior.

Using sociometric approaches, researchers can effectively investigate the two distinctive aspects of children's peer relationships—friendship and peer group status. *Peer group status* refers to individual differences in children's standing within an established group such as a day care cluster. Sociometric techniques aggregate the evaluations pertaining to any one individual by all other members of the group, giving each individual a relative social standing within the group. Therefore peer group status measures are metrics associated *with* the individual, and consequently lend themselves to correlation with attribute data, for example ratings of the individual's behavior. Sociometric measures for children have evolved mainly to investigate peer group status, and to a lesser extent, friendship formation. From the 1980s onwards, sociometric measurement has been dedicated to assessing the peer group status of children in classrooms and early learning situations with a view to determining the antecedents and correlates of peer group acceptance and rejection (e.g., Coie & Kuperschmidt, 1983; Dodge, Coie, Pettit, & Price, 1990; Ladd, 2005). Thus sociometric assessment is central to the development and testing of several important theories of peer rejection (e.g, Dodge et al., 2003). During the first decade of the twenty-first century sociometric assessment refocused on assessment of *popularity* and its effects on older school-aged children and adolescents (e.g., Cillessen & Rose, 2005; Cillessen & Marks, 2011; Hymel, Closson, Caravita & Vaillancourt, 2011). However, this line of research has limited relevance to research with young children in the educational context, where *peer acceptance* and interpersonal adjustment continue to be an important issue.

In contrast to peer group status, friendship carries no implications of rank or relative position. It is egalitarian and voluntary—a mutual, dyadic relationship that relies heavily on reciprocation for maintenance. Friendships can be reliably distinguished from general peer group relationships by observation of children's behavior toward each other during the preschool years. Young friends spend more time playing together, and their interactions are typified by greater emotional expressiveness—children who are friends tend to look at each other, talk and laugh together more than they do with acquaintances or nonfriends. They also show greater reciprocity and interdependence (Vaughn, Colvin, Azria, Caya, & Krzysik, 2001). Increasingly from early childhood onwards, friendships are based on similarity, including characteristics such as gender, age and physical appearance as well as humour and play style (Gest, Graham-Bermann, & Hartup, 2001).

Developmental theorists such as Sullivan (1953) recognized the important role of friendships, and the distinctiveness of friendships from general peer relationships and contexts. Bronfrenbrenner (1979) observed that peer relationships occur at different levels and in different spheres of experience; for example, general peer group relationships provide a wider context for the relationships between friends. In 1985 Furman and Robbins developed a model of differential social provisions where friendship provides affection, intimacy and reliable alliance; while general peer relations and peer group status provide a sense of inclusion and identity (Newman & Newman, 2001). Thus it is now widely acknowledged that general acceptance by the peer group is important for psychosocial development, but friendship makes a distinctive contribution to children's adjustment and wellbeing. High status in the peer group is not predictive of positive friendship formation and vice versa (Parker & Asher, 1993; Ladd, Kochenderfer, & Coleman, 1997; Brendgen, Little, & Krappmann, 2000).

Friendships can be identified more accurately through sociometric techniques than by other methods, such as observations or ratings by adults (Ladd & Ettekal, 2009). In research studies from early childhood onwards, investigators have therefore relied heavily upon children's self-reports in the form of sociometric assessments where children name each other as friends or best friends. So, investigators prefer to use sociometric techniques to identify and investigate childhood friendships, since these techniques have greater ecological validity.

Distinctive sociometric approaches and methodologies have evolved over the past 80 years. Their diversity derives from innovation and opportunity in response to research challenges, as well as from researchers' dissatisfaction with the limitations of earlier methods. Sociometric approaches for investigating friendship and peer status are described and evaluated in the following sections. Each approach and how to conduct it is outlined in general terms. Sociometric measurement does not exclusively apply to young children but can be used across the developmental spectrum from early childhood to adulthood. However, specific reference is made to the applicability of each approach to research with young children, as well as any necessary modifications to make the technique suitable for young respondents.

SOCIOMETRIC NOMINATION

Sociometric nomination is the earliest of the sociometric approaches, first developed by Jacob Moreno in the 1930s. Nominations are a simple and highly flexible technique. The investigator develops stimuli called sociometric questions, such as "Who are your friends?" and "Who do you like to play with?" The individual responses to these questions consist of several names, usually from a prescribed group such as a kindergarten class, which is known as a reference group.

Researchers can treat sociometric nomination data *qualitatively*, to uncover the structure of children's social networks using *sociograms*. These are diagrams that visually illustrate social networks. The investigator examines children's choices of individuals from their reference group; constructing a social map that depicts individuals as nodes, for example females as triangles and males as circles. The researcher uses arrows to illustrate the relationship between the named individuals, the direction of the arrow indicating whom has chosen whom as a friend. For example, if Caitlin has chosen Ruby, then the arrow would originate at the triangle representing Caitlin and would point toward Ruby's triangle. Double ended arrows show a reciprocated choice, for example if Ruby chose Caitlin as well. Constructing sociograms for large groups can be arduous and complicated, and they are difficult to interpret. Investigators can present children's sociometric nominations more precisely using s*ociomatrices*. These consist of a grid where children's names are listed across the top as *givers* of nominations and down the side as *receivers* of nominations. It is then a simple matter to use the grid to ascertain who has chosen whom as a friend. *Social network analysis* has evolved from sociomatrices. Here investigators can use probabilistic statistics to give estimates of relationship strength between child dyads and within children's groups.

Methods for Collecting Sociometric Nomination Data

The nomination approach is frequently the approach of choice for early childhood researchers because of its simplicity, rapid administration, ease of understanding, straightforward responses and face validity (Parker, Rubin, Price, & de Rosier, 1995). Sociometric questions are the social equivalent of Piaget's clinical interview, routinely used to uncover young children's understanding of the physical world. Like Piaget's questions concerning the conservations, sociometric nomination questions are open-ended, and require straightforward answers that are taken at face value.

Sociometric nomination is a flexible technique. Researchers can readily modify nominations to suit different purposes in educational research with young children by simply manipulating the sociometric question. For example, researchers can obtain general affiliation data through open-ended questions such as "Who do you play with?" They can collect data on specific relationships by using questions that limit the number of choices, define the social situation, and the type of person to be named (e.g., "Which girls in your play group do you sit with for play lunch?"). Despite their endless variety, sociometric questions fall into three main types. Questions like "Who is your best friend?" access close friendship ties, while "Which children do you prefer to play with?" yields less intimate affiliations based on leisure activities. By asking children about their workmate preferences, investigators can access social relationships of early elementary school children in more formal contexts such as classrooms.

Some research involves investigators collecting both *positive* and *negative* peer nominations. There is a wide variety of methods for collecting these data. Positive nomination can be a simple oral task where investigators ask individuals to name the children in a reference group who are their friends, playmates or workmates. Researchers obtain negative nominations by asking school children to identify least preferred playmates or workmates; and for preschoolers, the children they would rather *not* have as friends or playmates.

Investigators can also design more elaborate nomination methods. They can provide a definition of what is meant by "friend," or they can use class seating plans and imagined scenarios as a context for making sociometric choices. For example, an investigator might say "Let's imaging you're in the playground playing tag (or the child's chosen play activity). Who would you choose to play with you?" If the reference group is large, researchers can present rosters of names as a memory aid for children. The child then circles the names of all the children they prefer to play with as well as those they do not wish to play with (Foster & Crain 2002). Sometimes investigators collect *unlimited nominations*, leaving it up to individual children to identify as many playmates or friends as they wish. Alternately, researchers can collect *limited-choice nominations* where investigators stipulate a standard number of nominations per child, usually between three and five choices.

Nominations can be collected by individual interviews, or alternately in group-based procedures. These involve giving child respondents a proforma where they write down their choices according to the sociometric questions written on the proforma. The investigator guides the group while it fills in the proforma, reading out the questions and helping individual children. However, group administration is only suited to older school-aged children who have reasonable levels of literacy. Group-based procedures present task demands that are too difficult for preschoolers, including reading and writing down the names of their peers, so data are usually collected individually and orally. Young children often find it hard to recall all the members of their preschool class or day care centre group. To overcome this challenge, investigators can use nonverbal nomination methods with preschool children, by presenting photographs of all group members to each child who simply indicates their choices by pointing (e.g., McCandless & Marshall, 1957; Moore & Updegraff, 1964; Singleton & Asher, 1977; Asher, Singleton, Tinsley & Hymel, 1979; Poteat, Ironsmith & Bullock, 1986). This technique is also useful for young elementary students in the early years of formal schooling when their literacy skills might be inadequate for reading rosters of names. Alternately, investigators can read out the names from rosters.

Analyzing and Interpreting Sociometric Nomination Data as Measures of Friendship and Peer Group Status

Investigators can use sociometric nomination to measure both friendship and peer group status. To identify friendships, researchers should apply Bukowski and Hoza's (1989) friendship criteria—the unit is the dyad, and the judgment bilateral and specific in nature. In other words investigators need to look for *reciprocated* nominations on sociomatrices. Friendship involves mutual liking, so strong evidence of reciprocal choices is needed. However, if a child names another as a friend but her nomination is not reciprocated by the other child, then there is weak evidence for friendship. Researchers generally do not regard such one-sided relationships true friendships during childhood. In practice, unilateral friendship nominations show little correspondence to observed friendship behaviors (Hops & Lewin, 1984). Researchers investigating children's friendships usually elicit only positive nominations such as "Who is your best friend?" Negative nominations such as "Who would you *not* have as a friend" are unnecessary and are generally avoided.

For investigating peer group status, investigators sum the nominations for each child from all evaluators in the reference group. This procedure fulfils Bukowski and Hoza's (1989) criteria for measuring peer group status—the unit is the group, and the judgment is unilateral and general in nature. The column totals on a sociomatrix therefore provide a measure of peer group status for individual children. The quantification of sociometric nominations then allows researchers to statistically evaluate individual differences in peer group status.

When researchers explore peer group status, they need to collect negative nominations as well as positive ones. Just because a child is *not* positively nominated as a friend or a playmate does not necessarily mean that she is rejected by her peers, so negative nominations are essential to complete the picture. Positive and negative nominations represent respectively peer acceptance and rejection. These are now widely recognized by theorists as *separate* aspects of children's peer group status; not simply the poles of a single continuum anchored by the extremes of full acceptance and full rejection. In other words children vary *independently* on each dimension of peer group status. For example a child might be low on peer acceptance and also low on peer rejection. Goldman, Corsini, and de Urioste (1980) and Olson and Lifgren (1988) found that correlations between positive and negative nominations were low and often nonsignificant, indicating that the two measures are "distinct indices of social status" (Hymel & Rubin, 1985, p. 254). Furthermore Newcomb et al. (1993) found discrete sets of behavioral correlates for nomination-based peer acceptance and rejection. Taken together, positive and negative nominations represent conceptually distinctive aspects of children's peer group status, with negative nominations providing vital evidence for identifying children with peer relations difficulties.

If researchers use *raw* nominations (i.e., simple sums of nominations) to ascertain children's peer group status, individual status scores vary according to the number of nominators in the reference group. Peer group status measures are therefore not comparable between different-sized groups. For example, the peer group status of a boy in a group of 30 children cannot be validly compared to that of a girl in a group numbering 15 members. The boy is likely to receive more positive nominations than the girl, simply because his group of potential nominators that is twice as large as hers. To be meaningful, raw nominations from different sized reference groups need to be standardized. This is usually achieved by dividing the total nominations the individual child receives by the number of potential nominators (i.e., excluding the target child), yielding a *proportional* status score.

PAIRED COMPARISONS

Paired comparisons are one of the earliest approaches to sociometric assessment, developed soon after Moreno's nomination technique (Koch, 1933). Paired comparisons are an oral technique suitable for young children. The investigator reads out the names of every possible pairing of members in a reference group such as a preschool class, excluding the respondent child. The respondent child then names their preference in each pair. Depending on the size of the reference group, this procedure might involve many choices. For example, a child choosing within a group of just four playmates would make forced choices involving six possible paired comparisons. But in a class of 25 a child would need to make approximately 300 forced choices to complete a full paired comparison procedure (Hops &

Lewin, 1984). So, paired comparisons are an exhaustive technique allowing the evaluation of all group members in relation to all others in the group.

Collecting, Analyzing and Interpreting Paired Comparison Data as Measures of Peer Group Status

The paired comparisons approach does not lend itself easily to measuring friendship—identifying clearly the reciprocation of choice necessary for recognizing friendships is difficult using this technique, due to its forced-choice format. Paired comparisons are therefore employed almost exclusively to measure peer group status. The researcher counts the number of times each group member is chosen using the responses of all other group members. This is then used as an indicator of individual peer group status.

Paired comparisons are an alternative to positive nominations, providing a more exhaustive evaluation of peer preferences than limited-choice nominations do. In limited-choice nominations, responses do not reflect full or equal consideration of all group members. Only the most salient group members are selected, for example in a three-choice nomination task. So, the majority of children—unnominated and minimally nominated individuals—are not actively compared with more salient group members and are therefore not differentiated in terms of peer preference (Cohen & Van Tassel, 1978). On the other hand, paired comparisons provide an exhaustive set of peer preferences from each group member, making it one of the most discriminating sociometric approaches (Kane & Lawler, 1978).

There are distinct measurement advantages for paired comparisons over nominations. However, the arduousness of the procedure for both researcher and respondent is a major drawback (Bullock, Poteat, & Ironsmith, 1988). For example, Koch's (1944) school-aged participants made up to 740 separate preference judgments, taking up to 1.5 hours per child. Lippit (1941) reported that her preschool procedure took up to 12 hours per child. For modern investigators such protracted data collection is a major practical and ethical barrier to research, especially with young children. The original procedure used by Koch and Lippit was entirely oral, but the use of photographs of each group member can greatly accelerate the administration of paired comparisons, with children only needing to point to their preferred peer. For example, Cohen and Van Tassel's (1978) procedure was completed in 30 to 40 minutes on average. Vaughn and Waters (1981) reported that the picture method took up to 45 minutes per preschool child. This is a significant improvement on the time taken for the oral technique, but paired comparisons are still unwieldy compared to limited-choice nominations. These usually take only a few minutes per child, and are generally completed in a single session. Cohen and Van Tassel found that picture-based paired comparisons took ten times longer to accomplish than a four-choice nomination task and took several sessions per child to accomplish. As well, investigators have to administer paired comparisons individually, whereas they can collect nominations using group-based procedures. So nominations yield maximal data in minimal time.

Researchers can however modify the paired comparison technique, preserving many of the measurement advantages while minimizing administration time. Instead of a full set of paired comparisons, the researcher generates a *subset* of stimulus items such as pairs of photographs, representing a random sampling of the total range of choices (e.g., Hops & Lewin, 1984). In line with this, Cohen and Van Tassel (1978) created five different subsets of stimulus pairs to measure peer group status in four-year-old children. These authors found that the reliability of a single subset was highly similar to that of a full paired comparison procedure, and the single subset took a fraction of the time to administer.

Paired comparisons are more discriminating than nominations, and produce more reliable estimates of individual peer group status, especially for young children. However, paired comparisons yield only positive sociometric data, and unlike negative nominations, they cannot access the rejection dimension essential for comprehensive investigations of peer group status. In terms of analysis, paired comparisons yield data that limit the application of parametric statistics. Paired comparisons are ordinal data, so they do not providing direct information about the intervals between rankings of group members, or any overall value in terms of average rankings (Kane & Lawler, 1978). Paired comparisons were originally developed for use with young children, but they present so many conceptual, practical, and statistical limitations, researchers should be wary of using them in peer relations research.

SOCIOMETRIC RATINGS

Sociometric rating scales, sometimes called roster-and-rating techniques, evolved later than either nominations or paired comparisons (e.g., Bonney, 1954), with development continuing through the 1960s, 1970s, and 1980s. Sociometric rating scales consist of a roster of group members with a numerical scale next to each member's name. Scale points usually range from 1 to 5, and refer to a specific criterion for making evaluations, for example, "How much do you like to play with this child?" Respondents indicate one point on the scale to show how much they like to play with each individual on the roster. The higher the numerical value, the more the respondent would like to play with the subject of the evaluation. Investigators then sum the evaluations given to each target child by the whole reference group.

This type of scale yields a single score for each target child, with higher ratings corresponding to greater peer acceptance. Alternately, the numerical points on a sociometric rating scale are linked to descriptors that represent the measurement criterion. For example, Bruininks, Rynders and Gross' (1974) rating scale for elementary school children uses three scale points corresponding to the descriptors "Friend," "All right," and "Wouldn't like." These types of rating scale also produce a score by the method described above, but the ratings reflect a continuum anchored by extreme peer acceptance on one end and extreme peer rejection on the other.

Collecting, Analyzing and Interpreting Sociometric Rating Data as Measures of Friendship and Peer Group Status

Sociometric ratings are problematic for assessing friendships during early and later childhood. Ratings are unilateral evaluations, and do not easily fulfill the accepted criterion of bilateral regard for the identification of friendships. So, researchers may find sociometric ratings problematic in measuring friendship. Nonetheless, Berndt and his colleagues employed ratings instead of limited-choice nominations as a friendship measure (e.g., Berndt, Hawkins, & Hoyle, 1986; Berndt & Hoyle, 1985; Berndt & Perry, 1986). Berndt (1984) assumed that high *unilateral* ratings of likeability given by one child to another validly identify friendship. One-sided sociometric ratings however, fail to demonstrate the reciprocity essential for true friendships (Bukowski & Hoza, 1989). For example, the child who is the subject of the high rating might not give the evaluator a high rating in return. Therefore researchers using sociometric ratings to identify friendships should insist on *reciprocated* high ratings to stringently fulfill Bukowski and Hoza's friendship criteria (Jones, 1984). Researchers can use sociometric ratings in friendship studies to compensate for the under-reporting of reciprocity that occurs with limited-choice nominations. Ratings involve all children evaluating all other children in the group, so it is more likely that reciprocity will be identified. Despite the measurement advantages offered by sociometric ratings, most contemporary researchers continue to regard limited-choice reciprocated positive nominations as the gold standard for friendship identification.

Sociometric ratings measure peer group status more easily than friendship. The investigator determines peer group status by simply summing the ratings received by an individual from all group members, and then averaging them according to the number of evaluators in the reference group ($n-1$). The mean rating from rating scales automatically corrects for group size and allows for easy individual comparisons across different sized groups.

Researchers need to interpret children's responses to sociometric rating scales with care, and especially the responses of young children (Asher & Taylor, 1982). Even older school-age children require training with ratings in order to accurately relate numerical scale points to the evaluation criteria (e.g., Asher et al., 1979). Young children's understanding of rating scales and how to interpret them cannot therefore be assumed, and this validity issue presents a major barrier to their use in early education research. Drawings, pictures and facial icons ("smileys") can facilitate understanding of rating scales for preschoolers and younger elementary school children. For example, Bruininks et al. (1974) provided simple line drawings to help younger children interpret the scale point descriptors. Two stick figures playing ball represented "Friend." "All right" was explained by two figures working side by side at a blackboard. "Wouldn't like" was illustrated by two figures with their backs to each other. Singleton and Asher (1977) used progressively changing facial icons ranging from a full smile to a full frown to represent five numerical points on their sociometric rating scale. Asher et al. (1979) employed a similar approach in a three-point scale for preschool children using a play criterion. Respondents placed photographs of their classmates into one of three boxes displaying a happy, neutral, or sad face, according to which face best indicated their preference for the photographed child as a playmate. Investigators developing sociometric rating scales intended for young children should carefully pilot them and should include mnemonics such as "smileys" to facilitate respondents' understanding of scale points.

Despite their inherent problems for young children, ratings might yield superior measures of peer group status compared to nominations. This is because sociometric rating scales involve multiple judgments. Psychometricians regard measures that include judgments of all group members by all group members as superior representation of a sample's responses. However, some authors assume that in unlimited nominations, the children the respondent fails to nominate as friends can be relegated to a category of nonfriend. If the judgments of all children in a group are canvassed in this way, it yields an exhaustive summary of dichotomous friend/nonfriend judgments by all group members about all group members. Nonetheless, rating scales provide purely *overt* information in the form of graded appraisals of all group members. This contrasts with the *covert* information assumed from unlimited nominations (Kane & Lawler, 1978). In this way sociometric ratings avoid the interpretive difficulties that are associated with sociometric nominations, and are more transparent. Response biases however affect sociometric ratings. They include halo effects, similarity–contrast, leniency–severity and central tendency effects, especially when administered to young children.

Researchers analyzing sociometric rating scale data need to understand the scaling properties of their ratings. Sociometric ratings obtained from simple Likert-type scales such as the ones described above are more closely related to conventional psychometric measures (interval scales) than are nominations (nominal scales) or paired comparisons (ordinal scales). The nomination approach yields categorical data (e.g., friend/nonfriend) which can be simply tallied. Consequently, the summed frequency data used for analysis in many studies might not conform well to the normal distributions that are assumed to underpin parametric statistical analyses. By contrast, sociometric ratings are like mainstream psychometric measures and yield greater range and variability that conform better to the normal distributions required for parametric statistical analyses. So, researchers can validly use sociometric ratings alongside psychometric measures such as ratings of children's behaviors, and can analyze them simultaneously using parametric statistics. On the other hand, nomination-based data are more limited, and strictly speaking require nonparametric statistical analysis. This aspect could limit correlation research where their use in tandem with conventional psychometric ratings might be questionable.

GROUP PREFERENCE RECORDS

Group preference records evolved in the 1930s, at about the same time as paired comparisons (e.g., Newstetter, Feldstein & Newcomb, 1938; Zeleny, 1940, 1960). They represent a distinctive sociometric assessment approach, combining measurement features from sociometric rating scales and nominations. Investigators present a printed roster of all group members—similar to that of a sociometric rating scale—to each member of the reference group. Each member responds categorically in a similar way to sociometric nominations, but classifies all group members in terms of like, dislike and neutral using a forced-choice format. Investigators can administer group preference records to a reference group using group-based methods in much the same way as a rating scale is administered. This method is suitable for older elementary school children who have no difficulty in reading the roster of names and reliably circling just one of the response alternatives for each group member named. However, for young children who have limited attention, literacy skills and understanding of formal test requirements, it is preferable to administer group preference records individually using an interview format. In this way researchers can read out the names of each child on the roster and can ensure the child selects a single response option when evaluating each group member, for example by pointing to an icon representing that option.

Researchers can easily adapt existing rating scales to make a group preference record. For example, Gottlieb and Colleagues modified Bruininks et al. (1974) *Peer Acceptance Scale* for use as a group preference record (e.g., Goodman, Gottlieb, & Harrison, 1972; Gottlieb & Budoff, 1973). Instead of assigning numerical values to the scale points, they used the scale points "Friend," "All right," and "Wouldn't like" as separate response categories. In such adaptation researchers should simply sum the *numbers* of different evaluations—treating individual results as categorical rather than interval data. Alternately, researchers might prefer to use purpose-made group preference records such as the *How I Feel toward Others* instrument, or HIFTO (Agard, Veldman, Kaufman & Semmel, 1978a). The HIFTO is a group preference record developed specifically for a large-scale evaluation project on educational mainstreaming (see Kaufman et al., 1985 for details). Consequently the HIFTO was designed so that it could be understood by school-aged children with intellectual and learning disabilities, with features that also make it useful for sociometrically assessing young children. The instrument includes three sociometric response categories, represented by facial icons—a smile (acceptance), a frown (rejection), and a straight mouth (neutral). The HIFTO has a fourth category "don't know," represented by a question mark. This alternative to the preference categories allows researchers to identify whether a child is not well known to the group (i.e., receives a large number of "don't know" evaluations). Sociometric nominations do not include "don't know" as a possible response. However, with group preference records researchers can use the "don't know" option to ascertain how familiar individual children are to the rest of the reference group.

Collecting, Analyzing and Interpreting Group Preference Record Data as Measures of Friendship and Peer Group Status

Group preference records are designed primarily for assessing individual differences in peer group status (e.g., Kaufman, Agard & Semmel, 1985). However, researchers can also readily measure friendship using reciprocated positive evaluations from group preference records. For example, HIFTO uses a friendship criterion for children to evaluate their peers. The smiling facial icon represents a positive evaluation—"children you regard as friends" (Agard et al., 1978a). Therefore *reciprocated* smiles—those given and received mutually by two group members—would fulfill Bukowski and Hoza's (1989) criteria for friendship measures and would validly indicate the presence of a friendship in the same way as reciprocated friendship nominations.

Identifying friendships using group preference records offers researchers distinct advantages over limited-choice nominations. Group preference records are roster based and so all group members can evaluate all group members. The identification of friends using reciprocated HIFTO smiles for example, is a more reliable method than limited-choice nominations.

This is because group preference records exhaustively canvass peer evaluations in contrast to the partial coverage given by limited-choice nominations. It is therefore more likely that researchers using group preference records will identify *all* friendships in a reference group, rather than the subset available from limited-choice nominations.

To determine the peer group status of an individual from a group preference record, investigators sum the evaluations of an individual by all group members within category, for example separately summing all the smile and frown evaluations for a child assessed with HIFTO. This process yields distinctive acceptance and rejection scores as in nominations. However investigators need to express these raw totals as a proportion of the number of evaluators $(n-1)$ in the same way as nominations are standardized according to group size. These scores are then used to assess individual differences in peer group status. Researchers can use the neutral option offered by peer preference records to ascertain a middle ground position in peer group status, lying somewhere between acceptance and rejection. For example, investigators can use the HIFTO neutral category as a measure of peer toleration (Morrison, 1981a) or indifference (Agard et al., 1978a). So, group preference records provide an additional level of peer group status unavailable from either nominations or ratings. This feature expands traditional conceptualizations of peer group status—a dichotomous construct in sociometric nominations, and a unidimensional variable in sociometric ratings and paired comparisons (Hymel et al., 2011).

Researchers should consider the measurement features and limitations of different sociometric approaches when selecting suitable research instruments. This is also important when they analyze and interpret the data from different approaches. Group preference records offer distinctive measurement features: They combine the advantages of sociometric ratings and nominations in one instrument and at the same time solve the measurement problems of both nominations and ratings. Group preference records allow multiple evaluations, and these contribute to higher reliability in peer group status measures compared to nominations. Sociometric ratings also have higher reliability than nominations, but this feature is achieved at the expense of losing the crucial distinctiveness of the acceptance and rejection dimensions of peer group status. Ratings yield a single score which reflects only peer acceptance; or alternately, both acceptance and rejection simultaneously, as the anchor points of a unidimensional continuum. The forced-choice categorical responses from group preference records are exhaustive and transparent appraisals, solving the problem of covert, imprecise, and incomplete categorization in limited-choice nominations. Moreover, the additional response categories found in group preference records provide a range of dimension-based measures that are more useful for the assessment of individual differences in peer group status. These are limited to acceptance and rejection in nominations. Group preference records acknowledge that children might not know some group members sufficiently to evaluate them interpersonally; and that children might also be indifferent to or simply tolerate some peers, rather than just accepting or rejecting them outright as is the case with nominations.

Sociometric assessment of young children presents a number of methodological challenges to investigators. Sociometric ratings in particular remain problematic for this population. As previously outlined, young children experience difficulties understanding equal intervals and associated numerics and what this means in terms of evaluating peers. Researchers have tried to make sociometric ratings understandable and hopefully valid for use with young children, such as explaining numerical intervals using descriptors or graphics (e.g., Bruininks et al., 1974; Asher et al., 1979). Nonetheless, in view of young children's conceptual limitations, researchers should not confidently treat their responses to rating scales as equal interval data. Investigators can easily overcome the measurement issues in sociometric ratings by adapting them for use with young children by using the numerical points as more straightforward categorical responses alternatives—to make a group preference record.

Group preference records provide researchers with a highly useful a middle-ground alternative to acceptance and rejection that Morrison (1981a, 1981b) and others call a "toleration" measure. This alternative response more sensitively indicates the peer group status of children who may be neither greatly liked nor disliked. This feature is important for sociometrically assessing young children. Peer relationships in the early developmental period do not conform to the strong and enduring likes and dislikes typical of middle and late childhood, but are more fluid and diverse (Coplan & Arbeua, 2009). Dichotomous assessment methods such as nominations conform more closely to the pattern of peer affiliations later in childhood; whereas group preference records with their additional categories capture more accurately the friendship and peer preference patterns of young children.

Group preference records are highly flexible in terms of the ways that responses can be treated, an important feature for researchers investigating peer relations in young children. Researchers can modify the basic measures of the instrument so that subsequent analysis and interpretation is more accurate and reflects the characteristics of the sample. For example, Morrison (1981a, 1981b) separately summed HIFTO acceptance, indifference and rejection evaluations for each class member. Morrison then multiplied each sum by a weighting that mirrored the relative levels of *group* responding in each response category. So, Morrison modified each measure to reflect group response patterns, increasing their ecological validity. This feature is useful when researchers are assessing young children's peer group status, since data treatment like Morrison's takes into consideration the more diverse and less polarized preferences in the group, a pattern that tends to differ from that of older school-aged children (Coplan & Arbeau, 2009; Ladd, Herald, & Andrews, 2006). With recognized age-related differences in friendship formation and patterns of peer preferences, it is important that peer group status data reflect these developmental distinctions.

Researchers can profit from another flexible feature of group preference records. Unlike other sociometric assessment approaches, they can provide a measure of the individual's attitudes *towards* their peers, derived from the summed evaluations they assign *to* other group members. This provides a valuable addition to children's individual peer group status which is derived from evaluations they receive *from* other group members. So, a researcher can readily examine the balance of positive versus negative feeling a child has towards their reference group. For example, the proportion of HIFTO smiles they allocate to group members can be compared with the proportion of HIFTO frowns they allocate. In aggregated form, these measures provide an indication of *group feeling*. Summed smiles provide a measure of group cohesiveness while summed frowns indicate the level of group-based negativity. Summed neutrals indicate the degree of group indifference to members, while summed question marks show acquaintanceship levels in the group. Researchers can compare the proportions of these evaluations to the *possible* or ideal number of evaluations in these categories. This can provide important information on classroom climate (Agard et al., 1978b). These group measures might prove useful in developmental studies examining age-related changes in group cohesiveness from the preschool to the middle school years.

Group-based data from group preference records can also be used normatively. Estimates of negativity expressed by any individual child could be compared to the general level of negativity within the group. For example, if a child allocates significantly higher numbers of frowns to the group than the group norm, this could provide important information for identification of risk. Early identification of such patterns allows for intervention during the preschool years before reputational mechanisms have a chance to work and children's peer group status becomes entrenched (Coie, Dodge, Terry, & Wright, 1991; Masten & Coatsworth, 1998; Buhs, Ladd, & Herald, 2006). Group measures such as cohesiveness are not readily available from either sociometric ratings or nominations. Limited-choice nominations only partially canvass group-based evaluations, making group measures such as cohesiveness meaningless. With nominations it is not possible to evaluate comparative proportions of the multiple evaluation categories available from group preference records. Sociometric ratings yield a single preference score, so comparisons between negative and positive evaluations given by an individual are unavailable.

Group preference records provide definite advantages for measuring peer group status and friendship in young children. Despite a long history of established use, this approach is not as popular in sociometric research as nominations and ratings. Researchers in child disability have actively favored group preference records over other methods, recognizing their measurement advantages for special child populations (e.g., Morrison, 1981a, 1981b, Morrison, Forness, & MacMillan, 1983; Ballard et al., 1977; Gottlieb, Semmel, & Veldman, 1978; Goodman et al., 1972; Gottlieb & Budoff, 1973; Kaufman et al.1985). These advantages equally apply to young elementary and preschool children.

ESTIMATING THE VALIDITY OF SOCIOMETRIC MEASURES

Validity refers to the meaning of psychometric instruments and their scores, and consists of the evidence for the inferences that are made from the results of applying them. Researchers consider validity essential for measures of psychological traits (Kaplan & Sacuzzo, 2009). Some sociometric researchers however, argue that their data are distinctive from psychometric data, representing the individual's reaction to a stimulus person, and not a generalized trait (Lyndzey & Byrne, 1968). Early sociometric investigators therefore did not rigorously apply psychometric validation to their methods.

Researchers formally validate their measures based on the degree of inference involved. Certain types of data such as observation data may not require formal validation, for example, the frequency of verbal exchanges between children in studies of preschooler's interactions. Some sociometricians maintain that their data are low-inference measures similar to observations—for example, a friend is whomever a child nominates as friend. So, they argue the meaning of sociometric data depends on the individual who develops the sociometric measure, similar to the operational definitions of behaviors in observation studies. However, even these lowest inference data are subjected to validation through interrater agreement indices, which can reveal ambiguities and inadequacies in behavioral definitions.

Contemporary researchers now recognize the level of inference even in the most straightforward sociometric data is too great for reliance on face validity alone. For example, developmental factors affect the interpretation of a common sociometric question "Who is your best friend." The question has different meanings for young children compared with older ones. Recent research has indicated that children's conceptions of friendship change dramatically from the preschool years to adolescence depending largely on their cognitive development (Hartup & Abecassis, 2004). For preschoolers then, qualifying the word "friend" with the idea of a "best friend" exacerbates the problem of interpretation. Young children might apply different interpretations depending on age-related social norms and the unique structure of their social circle. "Best friend" evaluations depend to some extent on stability in relationships and enduring connections between children. These aspects of peer relationships are still embryonic in early childhood, compared to middle and late childhood where the term "best friend" might be more validly applied. Rating scales too suffer from interpretive difficulties when used with young children. They employ age-dependent criteria which individuals must decode correctly in order to make valid judgments. Researchers now recognise sociometric stimuli more closely resemble the items on personality or attitude questionnaires, and therefore require formal validation.

In the process of validation a there is a logical sequence of events. Philosophical definition comes first, comprehensively providing the characteristics of phenomena, but also allowing for individual and environmental differences vital in applying theories to improve personal functioning. Theoretical modelling of the processes follows definition, outlining underlying psychological and social phenomena which should lead naturally to methodologies for measurement. Measurement then provides the means for testing and confirming, or alternately, revising and refining theoretical models of behavior.

This ideal sequence has not been followed in sociometric measurement validation. Researchers have tailored sociometric techniques to suit their individual measurement requirements. The current diversity of sociometric approaches and instruments is therefore result of fashion, innovation, personal bias and opportunity; involving pragmatism and empiricism rather than a sound theoretical basis. This problem began during the infancy of sociometry in the early part of the 20th century. Moreno and his disciples were concerned mainly with individual social adjustment, and not with the development of theory relating to friendship and peer group status (Hallinan, 1981). The term "sociometry" coined by Moreno betrays an early bias towards measurement as an end in itself. Early sociometricians therefore put the measurement cart squarely before the theoretical horse, and consequently forgot the definitional harness in their headlong rush towards results. An explosion of validity studies during the 1980s and 1990s was a belated attempt to make sense of the plethora of measures that had emerged over earlier decades, with later researchers doing a great deal of theoretical backtracking in order to validate the methods pioneered in the 1930s and 1940s.

Researchers who develop their own sociometric instruments need to provide independent evidence of validity. However, experimenters generally prefer to use or adapt existing sociometric instruments, and therefore avoid the rather arduous process of instrument validation prior to experimentation. Here investigators must rely on the validity evidence provided by other authors for the different approaches to sociometric assessment and the numerous variants within these approaches. The outcomes of research studies rest largely on the validity of the measures that are collected, so investigators cannot use existing instruments with impunity, assuming that they have adequate validity. Understanding and critically evaluating validity evidence in the literature can guide investigators in selecting sociometric approaches and methods that will yield meaningful data for research projects. The following sections therefore present the validity evidence and validity issues that have been uncovered during the past four decades of investigation. This information acts as a guide to method and instrument selection for investigators, and also provides methodological ideas by which developers can validate their own sociometric instruments.

Validity evidence for sociometric assessment and the methods by which it can be derived are presented as sections addressing the accepted models from the psychometric tradition—content-, criterion-, and construct-related validity evidence (Kaplan & Saccuzzo, 2009). Where possible validity evidence is provided from studies of young children, since validity estimates can vary according to subject age. Nonetheless, the validity of sociometric instruments cannot be established using the limited data from a subset of the population. It is therefore important to gather validity evidence from studies that target individuals from the relevant age groups for whom the instrument is intended. In the case of sociometric approaches and methods, this includes a wide developmental period between early childhood and adulthood. However, much of the validity evidence in the literature relates to the periods of childhood and early adolescence, the key periods of research into friendship and peer group status.

Validating Sociometric Instruments Using Construct-Related Validity Evidence

Construct-related validity refers to the relationship between the instrument and the constructs it measures; vital for tests which represent theoretical dimensions, including friendship and peer group status. So, researchers undertaking construct-related validation of sociometric instruments test whether instruments actually measure the friendship and peer group status phenomena that they purport to measure. This involves investigators accumulating evidence from a wide variety of sources, often concurrent with instrument development. This evidence might be statistical evidence—for example, the variables that are associated with the instrument's measures. Evidence might also take the form of logical deductions and observations related to the theory underlying the dimension being measured (Kaplan & Saccuzzo, 2009).

Evaluating the Equivalence of Sociometric Measures and Its Influence on Construct-Related Validity

The fundamental nature of both friendship and peer group status lie at the heart of construct-related validation of sociometric measures. Several different sociometric approaches including a large range of diverse instruments now exists, all purporting to measure friendship or peer group status or both. Alternative sociometric approaches differ fundamentally however, and yield measures that may mean very different things. Researchers therefore need to cautiously interpret the data from diverse sociometric approaches, taking into consideration the procedural conditions under which they were collected (Hops & Lewin, 1984). For example, measures of peer group status obtained from a group preference record might not be functionally equivalent to those collected using restricted-choice nominations.

There are many individual exemplars of each sociometric approach. These instruments often share a common rationale, but design features can vary from instrument to instrument, raising issues of construct-related validity. Therefore researchers validating sociometric instruments need to answer questions such as these—Does a three-point rating scale such as Bruininks et al.' (1974) *Peer Acceptance Scale* yield measures of peer group status equivalent to a six-point scale such as Rucker et al.'s (1969) *Ohio Acceptance Scale*? How do the different descriptors and criteria used with rating scales affect the measurement of peer group status? Do limited choice nominations measure friendship as exhaustively or as legitimately as unlimited-choice nominations? How do workmate nominations relate to playmate nominations in the measurement of peer acceptance and rejection? These questions should also be set in a developmental context, with children's age also affecting the meaning of measures derived from diverse techniques— for example, do three- and five-point rating scales impact differentially on the responses of preschool children as opposed to late elementary-school children?

Since the 1990s the focus in sociometric research has largely veered away from validity issues, with few contemporary studies tackling the *meaning* of data from different sociometric approaches and their diverse range of instruments. So despite much previous investigation, the relationship between individual sociometric techniques is still far from clear and requires ongoing investigation. This poses a problem for researchers using existing instruments for their research projects, and needing to establish the construct-related validity of their data. One solution to this problem is for researchers to use a multi-method approach, collecting data using several different sociometric approaches. For example researchers could use a group preference record as well as ratings and nominations. Correlating the results of these different methods would give researchers an indication of the degree of overlap in their data and therefore its validity. Differential correlations with outcome data such as children's behaviors would also add construct-related validity evidence to guide researchers in the interpretation of their results. The multimethod approach also raises the possibility of developing indices that *combine* the measures from different sociometric approaches such as nominations and rating scales. These indices might more effectively represent children's friendships and peer group status than single measures do. The results of multimethod studies might therefore enhance the development of theories relating to children's friendship and peer acceptance (Parker et al., 1995; Bukowski & Hoza, 1989; Dodge, Lansford, Burks, Bates, Pettit, Fontaine, & Price, 2003).

The Influence of Group Characteristics on the Construct-Related Validity of Sociometric Data

Groups are fundamental to the meaning of sociometric data, and therefore to construct-related validity. For example, the particular reference group in a study gives relevance to individuals' peer group status and to any individual differences that are detected. Researchers presenting construct-related validity evidence for new sociometric instruments—or when examining the validity of existing instruments—should carefully evaluate how child subjects are sampled. In other words, are legitimate reference groups in fact identified? In this regard, Evans (1966) provides some useful guidelines for researchers. Groups can be broadly defined as two or more people having a common purpose, a definite role, status relationships, rules, and are set apart from nonmembers. Researchers can apply these criteria to test the legitimacy of the groups involved in sociometric research. For example, they can successfully differentiate a kindergarten class from a random collection of children attending a pantomime.

Researchers should also consider the characteristics of the group under study. Groups are differentiated from each other by their purpose, size, duration and composition, and these factors constitute an interpretive backdrop to the data yielded by sociometric measures. *Temporal factors* involving the history and duration of the reference group are highly relevant to the construct-related validity of sociometric data. Groups are not static social phenomena, but instead change in their composition over time. According to Evans (1966) groups develop from simple "togetherness" situations with roles, status and objectives becoming more clearly defined as time goes on. Therefore, early in its evolution a reference group can differ from one at the midpoint of its existence, or at the end of its life. This is particularly pertinent to reference groups such as school classes and early learning groups, which typically have a life of one school year. Recent research has revealed that preschoolers' friendships may be carried over from one school year to the next, but this is modified by the degree of overlap in group membership (Ladd, Herald, &

Andrews, 2006). Researchers should therefore consider the familiarity of the individual group members from previous years, as well as the proportion of new members.

As a context to their data analysis, results and conclusions; investigators need to adequately *describe* the characteristics of the reference groups involved in their research, including the stability of group membership during the life of the group (e.g., a school year), how many members enter and exit the group as well as the point in the evolution of the group's life that the investigator intervened. For example a sociometric study at the beginning of a school year can yield very different results from one at year's end, and can in turn profoundly affect the interpretation of individual sociometric data. Researchers should not lose sight of the fact that sociometric studies capture unique temporal snapshots of a group that is constantly evolving in terms of its membership and its relational dynamics. Despite this reality, many researchers tend to be present the results of sociometric studies as absolutes or generalities regarding peer relationships.

Investigators concerned with construct-related validity need to ask pertinent questions relating to the *purpose* the reference group (e.g., "Does the group reflect a relevant social context for the dimension I am investigating?"). For example, a study of young children's friendships would be more validly carried out in an early learning situation where preschoolers have the opportunity to freely socialize and make friends, than in a pediatric hospital ward. The *nature* of the reference group is also highly relevant to the interpretation of sociometric data, including whether it is voluntary or involuntary. Voluntary groups exist as a consequence of the common interests and objectives of their members, while nonvoluntary groups are a result of legislative or administrative requirements. From early childhood onwards children are organized on a nonvoluntary basis into preschool classes and then elementary school grades. These nonvoluntary groupings have become the common currency of children's sociometric studies. By contrast, fewer studies have considered voluntary groups such as neighbourhood friendship bands which form spontaneously. These groups present practical challenges to investigators, whereas educational and day care organizations have accessible administrative units and organizational features that make them easier environments for sociometric studies.

The data from studies of young children's friendships and peer group status might be particularly constrained by nonvoluntary adult-imposed groupings. It is well recognized that early childhood peer relations are largely determined by the socialisation opportunities controlled by parents and other adults such as day care workers and early educators (Rubin, Bukowski, & Parker, 2006). Some authors have criticized the narrowness and artificiality of day care groupings and school classes as the reference groups for sociometric investigation. Assuming they constitute a natural social boundary might not be legitimate. If the validity of sociometric data is indeed restricted by the artificiality of groupings, researchers are equally constrained in generalizing the results of their investigations. As early as 1981 Hallinan argued children's peer relationship findings might therefore relate to formal environments alone, and could be restricted rather than general in nature. Therefore, in reporting their data and making conclusions, researchers need to acknowledge group-related validity issues and consequent threats to the legitimacy of their data.

Despite the caveats described above, there is evidence to suggest that a degree of continuity exists between involuntary educational groups and voluntary groups such as neighbourhood friendship bands. If schools and early learning facilities are located close to where children live, the continuity of social groupings from the formal to the informal environment is likely to be greater. Thus, formal groupings such as elementary school classes can be the starting point for long-term friendships and informal groupings outside school hours. Furthermore, once constituted, artificial groupings become a social construction in which interactions rapidly lead to social structuring, status relations and rules of behaving (Sherif & Sherif, 1956). This adds legitimacy to researchers treating the results of school-based sociometric studies as general findings reflecting universal aspects of children's peer relations. Nonetheless, researchers need to provide relevant validity evidence in this regard. For example in describing their samples, researchers could provide vital information on the degree to which a school is a neighbourhood school. This would involve mapping the participants' residential addresses and proximity to the school.

The *size* of the reference group is an important consideration affecting the validity of data from sociometric investigations. As well as influencing the meaning of the group-based measures obtained, group size dictates the practical constraints of sociometric methodology. Therefore the reference group for sociometric studies must be *realistically* delimited in size (Evans, 1966). Moreno (1934) originally intended sociometry for small groups, but what is meant by "small" is open to interpretation. Some groups constitute so few members that individual measures are not meaningful. Kane and Lawler (1978) suggested a minimum size of 10 for valid group-based measures which also possess a degree of reliability. Early educational settings such as day care facilities and preschools typically contain fewer individuals than the average elementary or high school class, so there may be a problem of inadequate reference group size in early educational studies. Conversely, some groups can be too large for the meaningful interpretation of sociometric data. Sociometric measures of very large heterogeneous groupings usually reflect a diversity of affiliations that are too complex to collect and analyze. For example, a sociometric study with an entire nursery school or a large day care facility as the reference group would result in less meaningful measures than those relating to smaller sub-groupings such as preschool classes.

Researchers should always consider the size of the reference group when calculating indices of peer group status for any individual. This is a fundamental construct validity issue because peer group status is based on the evaluations of individuals by other group members. The meaning of peer group status can therefore vary fundamentally based on whether it is determined using a group of 10 evaluators or 100 evaluators. As previously discussed, *raw* sociometric data yield measures of peer group status that depend on how many evaluations are given to an individual child; and the methods for standardizing sociometric data according to different group sizes have already been described. For example, nominations received by an individual are routinely divided by the number of nominators excluding the target individual (i.e., $n-1$). This ostensibly allows direct comparison of individuals' peer group status across different-sized groups. Bronfenbrenner (1943) however took issue with such simple indices. He argued that the relative peer group status of any individual does not depend simply on the numerical information in their sociometric score, but also on the range and distribution of all other scores within the group. Researchers should therefore standardize peer group status scores using the z score, which considers both the group mean and the standard deviation.

The Influence of Sub-Group Characteristics on the Construct-Related Validity of Sociometric Data

Construct-related validity issues arise from the size and nature of gender- and ethnically-based subgroups within sociometric reference groups. Research has established that children routinely exhibit significant peer preferences based on ethnicity and gender (e.g., Fabes, Martin, & Hanish, 2004; Barbu, 2003; Aboud, Mendelson, & Purdy, 2003; Lee, Howes, Chamberlain, & Brandt, 2007).

Gender bias can significantly affect the validity of limited-choice sociometric nominations, which are mostly used in preference to unlimited nominations for research projects. For example, in a limited-choice nomination task, bias toward same-gender choices automatically restricts opposite-gender choices, and in practice very few opposite-gender positive nominations are detected. Negative nominations tend to be opposite-gender rather than same-gender. These biases are found in the nomination data of both school-aged and preschool children (Bukowski, Gauze, Hoza, & Newcomb, 1993; Fabes et al., 2004; Barbu, 2003). Hayden-Thomson et al. (1987) maintain that gender bias for this type of data is exaggerated compared to roster-based assessments such as group preference records and ratings that use evaluations by all group members. Children are less likely to cross the gender barrier when they have only limited opportunities to designate their friends and playmates. However, they might have unspecified opposite-gender friendships that would normally be detected in an unlimited nomination task. In this way limited-choice nominations probably exaggerate positive same-gender preferences. Restricting choices in negative nominations could also lead to overstated gender effects, with children predominantly nominating opposite-gender peers. This is due to stronger opposite-gender dislikes taking precedence over milder same-gender dislikes. Conversely, negative same-gender choices hidden in a limited-choice task might be revealed in an unlimited negative nomination task.

Sociometric ratings are also affected by gender bias, with consistent findings of significantly more positive same-gender than opposite-gender ratings (e.g., Bonney, 1954; Reese 1962, 1966; Bruininks et al. 1974; St. John & Lewis, 1975; Singleton & Asher, 1977, 1979; Asher & Hymel, 1981; Sagar et al. 1983; Hayden-Thomson, Rubin, & Hymel, 1987; Blanton et al., 1992; Ramsey, 1995; Burton Smith, Davidson, & Ball, 2001). These studies employed a variety of different sociometric rating scales and rating criteria, and canvassed samples from kindergarten to senior high school. However, due to their inclusiveness, sociometric ratings probably elicit less extreme gender-based responding than limited-choice nominations do. Canvassing the opinions of all class members by all other members more accurately reflects gender-based preferences. Nonetheless, these construct-related validity questions remain largely unanswered because of a lack of direct comparative studies of the differential degree of bias in sociometric nominations, ratings and group preference schedules. In group preference schedules several response alternatives for the expression of interpersonal feelings might also reduce the level of gender-based responding.

Developmental effects on gender bias also impact gender biasing in sociometric data, with weaker gender effects during the preschool years than later in middle childhood when gender segregation reaches its peak (Maccoby, 2000). In a comparative study of third to sixth grade children Burton Smith et al. (2001) found complex patterns of differential gender bias according to method, sex of child and age in playmate nominations, ratings of peer acceptance, and responses to a group preference record using a friendship criterion.

Gender bias raises an important construct-related validity issue for researchers—the equivalence of same-gender, opposite-gender, or both-gender peer evaluations and how well they represent the peer group status of individuals. This in turn poses a difficult methodological decision for researchers—which of these types of data is the most valid for specific studies involving peer group status? Same-gender sociometric evaluations for preschool and early elementary studies are sometimes justified by the observation that peer interactions at this age are almost exclusively same-gender (e.g., Walker, 2009). However, negative sociometric evaluations in these age groups are frequently opposite-gender, so including opposite-gender evaluations is important to improve the ecological validity of data (Cillessen & Marks, 2011). Gender bias can potentially account for a significant amount of variance in individuals' peer group status scores—for example, in a group where boys are in the majority, same-gender bias might exaggerate the peer group status of boys within the group, while diminishing that of girls. Researchers should therefore consider the gender composition as well as the size of the reference group in standardizing sociometric data. Standardizing according to within-group gender distributions involves for example, dividing same-gender evaluations for girls by the relevant number of girls in the reference group minus 1. This simultaneously controls for size and gender bias effects in both-gender data, and is essential for the valid representation of children's peer group status (Bukowski, Sippola, Hoza, & Newcomb, 2000).

Studies of other subgroups within reference groups point to additional biasing effects in sociometric data. Ethnic bias involves a preference for peers of the same ethnicity (Aboud et al., 2003; Lee et al., 2007). However, it is not as strong as gender bias (Aydt & Corsaro, 2003; Martin & Fabes, 2001), and varies according to sociometric approach. For example, Singleton and Asher (1977) showed that acceptance ratings exhibited less racial subgroup bias than did restricted nominations. Subgroup-biasing also occurs in measures of friendship and peer group status for children with cognitive disabilities integrated into ordinary schools. Morrison (1981a, 1981b) asserted that friendship nominations of children with learning and intellectual disabilities by mainstream children are rare. So studies involving inclusive settings might require similar corrections for ethnic and disability-based subgroup bias as those correcting for gender bias in sociometric data.

Even with data manipulation correcting for various biases, the comparison of peer group status between individuals from separate reference groups such as different school classes and preschool groups is still problematic. Therefore researchers should not simply interpret the results of sociometric studies according to the size, gender, ethnic and age composition of reference groups. They should also consider the influence of group members' personal characteristics, the factors leading to group cohesiveness, and group function. All groups vary in the range and patterns of their aggregated attractions and repulsions, and so investigators are bound to interpret the peer group status of any individual with this background in mind. Group preference records such as the HIFTO (Agard et al., 1978b) with their measures of classroom climate provide informative *group* indices. Researchers can use these indices to clarify the relative meaning of individual peer group status across groups, taking into consideration the specific patterns of choice within groups. In this way researchers and early educators can avoid interpreting sociometric measures as absolutes or a general consensus regarding an individual. Instead, sociometric measures are an aggregate of attractions and repulsions by a *particular* group, so friendships and peer group status of individual children are valid only in relation to a specific social system and context (Moreno, 1978).

Validating Sociometric Instruments Using Content-Related Validity Evidence

Content-related validity is the extent to which a measure represents the domain it is meant to cover. Developers can measure this type of validity during the construction, selection and revision of test items or stimuli. The evidence for psychometric content-related validity is logical and deductive rather than statistical, and is generally presented in a qualitative form. It addresses these central questions: Is the instrument adequately constructed? Does it have appropriate task requirements and scale properties? Do the items adequately sample and represent the domain the instrument is supposed to access? How will any interpolating variables affect performance? (Kaplan & Saccuzzo, 2009). These questions are vital to examining the adequacy of the stimuli used in sociometric instruments measuring both friendship and peer group status (Lyndzey & Byrne, 1968).

Content-related validity is relevant to sociometric nomination data, in particular. Sociometric nominations are deceptively simple, so researchers are tempted to assume that responses to nomination questions reflect the dimension apparently stipulated by the sociometric question, with face validity prominent in many studies. However, investigators should critically examine nominations for content-related validity (i.e., making sure the substance of the sociometric question adequately matches the construct being measured). In this way they can check whether the *meaning* of children's responses corresponds to the aspect of peer relations they are investigating. For example, researchers should not assume that playmate choices or seating preferences represent a multidimensional construct such as friendship; instead they assess specific aspects of friendship (Hallinan, 1981). Workmate choices might not reflect friendship, but rather scholastic esteem; especially when children repeatedly nominate the brightest pupil in a class.

The Influence of Child Variables on the Content-Related Validity of Sociometric Nomination Data

Like psychometric measures, sociometric measures are influenced by interpolating variables related to child characteristics such as age, which can significantly impact the validity of sociometric responses. Young children are particularly vulnerable to immediacy effects such as who might be present or absent in their group, or who they might currently be playing with or sitting next to (Berndt, 1984). Nominations by preschoolers can therefore reflect environmental and temporal factors to the same extent as they represent friendship or peer group status. Using pictorial or name rosters can help young children to consider all group members when making selections, which in turn reduces the influence of memory and immediacy effects on nomination responses (Foster & Crain, 2002). However, to control for serial position influences such as recency and primacy effects, researchers should use different randomized orders for both pictorial and name rosters.

Nominations are adversely affected by social desirability; evident in *choosing up*, where the most desirable group member is nominated regardless of specific sociometric criteria. For instance, a child might nominate the most popular child in the play group as their friend, despite the fact that they rarely or never play with this child. Choosing up is more likely in young children's responses than in older school-aged children, and has validity implications for nomination-based measurement of friendships in particular. If many children nominate a popular child, she in turn has a limited opportunity to return these nominations. The criterion for friendship is reciprocated nominations (Bukowski & Hoza, 1989). So, choosing up leads to more unreciprocated choices, and therefore the mutual nominations essential for identifying friendships are under-reported (Jones, 1984). For friendship studies researchers need to minimize choosing up. This can be done by using unlimited nominations. There is greater likelihood of discovering friendships through reciprocation and the threat to the validity of responses by social desirability factors is less extreme.

Social desirability is problematic in studies of peer group status based on limited-choice nominations. This is because choosing one peer necessarily restricts the likelihood of another peer being chosen. Children repeatedly nominating prominent or popular children in the group can therefore artificially inflate the peer group status of some members at the expense of others. Un-nominated children might be more valid selections according to the selection criteria. So, social desirability can also seriously affect peer group status measures from limited-choice nomination data. For this reason, studies of peer group status also benefit from the use of unlimited nominations.

The Influence of Scaling Factors on the Content-Related Validity of Sociometric Nomination Data

In considering content-related validity, researchers should recognize that nominations are a *dichotomous scale,* based on absence or presence of nomination. A substantial proportion of any group administered a nomination task routinely receives no nominations, thus remaining undiscriminated.

Much data are therefore lost through the binary evaluation approach of nominations. As previously outlined, each evaluator only provides *overt* preference data for a minority of a reference group, through the few peers that she names as preferred friends or playmates. The actual status of the majority of the group therefore remains *covert*, in a sort of measurement limbo. In other words, investigators do not have any direct evidence that un-nominated children are in fact "nonfriends"—it is purely an assumption. This feature of nominations becomes even more problematic if the number of choices is limited.

Limited-choice nominations involve validity issues relating to response scoring and interpretation (Hallinan, 1981). The limited-choice nominations from reference groups which vary considerably in size can result in *upward bias*—the tendency for a greater proportion of individuals in smaller groups to receive more extreme scores than those in larger groups (Kane & Lawler, 1978). When sociometric data from different sized groups are combined or when intergroup comparisons are made, upward bias becomes problematic, and simple standardization of nominations will not remove its effects. However, upward bias can be controlled by investigators using different numbers of limited-choice nominations in different sized groups.

In scoring nomination responses, researchers sometimes regard the temporal order in which nominations are given as showing preference strength, with initial choices given greater weight than later choices. However, investigators cannot simply assume that a connection exists between the order of elicitation and a child's preferences. If nominations are to be weighted in terms of preference strength, then investigators should make the order of preference clear in their instructions to children. Investigators could ask children who they would choose *first* as a playmate in an imagined playground scenario involving dyadic play. Then they could obtain second and subsequent choices on the basis of the previously nominated child being absent from the group. For example, "Let's pretend Kyeesha is away sick. Who would you choose then?" (Burton Smith, et al., 2001). This procedure yields an unambiguous ordinal ranking of choices in terms of preference.

The Influence of Task Requirements on the Content-Related Validity of Sociometric Nomination Data

Unlimited nominations allow respondents to define for themselves the parameters of questions such as "Who are your friends?" Using unlimited nominations, a child with one or two close friends can express his preferences just as accurately as a child with a large social circle. The criterion "friend" is therefore likely to have an equivalent and hence a more valid meaning across different child respondents. However, researchers rarely collect unlimited nominations in sociometric studies. They analyze sociometric results using parametric statistics which cannot easily quantify unlimited nomination data. So, in the interests of methodological parsimony and easy analysis, most investigators limit children's choices to a maximum of five positive and five negative nominations (e.g., Kafer & Shannon, 1986; Shannon & Kafer 1984; Berndt, 1984; Burton Smith, et al., 2001). Nonetheless, this is done at the expense of validity, since prescribed choices might not match the actual size of children's friendship or playmate circles.

In friendship studies using limited-choice nominations, both the absence and presence of nominations are open to interpretation. Children might make nominations which do not fit the question criteria, simply to fulfill task requirements. For example, children with no friends or only one friend might nominate children who are not their friends just to complete the three or so nominations the investigator requires. This is more likely to happen with young children who want to please adults, more so than older children. Some children might find the limited number of choices fails to adequately represent their large friendship circle. Thus, limited-choice nominations artificially restrict children who would normally make many choices. Children, who would normally nominate *fewer* peers than the specified number, could be induced to make additional and entirely artificial choices. The meaning of the criterion therefore varies between children, depending on whether the number of choices allowed conforms to their personal circle of friends (Evans, 1966).

In a hypothetical example, a researcher administers a three-choice friendship nomination task to a nursery school class. After the nominations for the whole class have been tallied, one boy and one girl remain un-nominated as friends. The task is repeated a short time later, but using unlimited nominations. When the unlimited nominations are tallied, the boy is nominated three times—once as a child's fourth choice and as the sixth choice of two children. The girl however, remains un-nominated by anyone. The boy and girl who failed to be nominated on the first nomination task differ fundamentally from each other. The girl has remained un-nominated even when the investigator has given her reference group free reign to nominate her. She is therefore probably friendless, being overlooked by all her peers. In the limited-choice nomination the boy would also be initially identified as a friendless, but subsequent to the later unlimited nomination procedure he was chosen as a friend by several of his peers. So unless unlimited-choice nominations are used, the true peer group status of some children is uncertain. These children are only overlooked relative to the degree of choice restriction the investigator has imposed. Therefore the unchosen status of some children in groups might be simply an artefact of the limited choices allowed instead of their actual peer group status. The number of choices allowed in a nomination task also raises the question of the *degree* of friendlessness reflected by limited-choice nominations. Is a child who receives no nominations from a five-choice task more friendless than a child who is identified by a three-choice task? Moreover, *social isolates*—children who neither choose others, nor are chosen as friend or playmate—can be validly identified only by unlimited nominations.

Task difficulty is a factor that can affect the interpretation of unlimited and limited-choice nominations. Unlimited nominations are relatively straightforward, even for young children. Children need only interpret the criterion question, and identify the members of their group accordingly. Here the choices appear to be fairly automatic, and could be achieved intuitively, based on personal feelings of attraction and repulsion. A similar, fairly effortless process would also take place when the investigator's choice restrictions match the child's own personal pool of choices. However, if a match is not present, then a limited-choice nomination task imposes a more complex decision-making process, which might test the capabilities of young children.

For some children there are more group members who fulfill the question criterion such as "friend" than the limited number of choices allows. These respondents might be forced to make complex judgments using multiple criteria in order to decide the children they should exclude:

> Now for my last choice. I really like Jenny, but she doesn't play with me as much as Jane. I've been friends with Jenny longer than Jane, but Jane is really nicer to me than Jenny most of the time...

Children whose smaller friendship circles also do not match the number required, face an equally complex decision-making process:

> Well, I've only really got one friend, that's George, but the lady says I've got to name three friends. I suppose I could say James. He used to be my friend in preschool, but then we had a big fight. I wonder if she really means friends right now in first grade, or could I still count James? He's O.K. to me now, but I don't think he's my friend still. If I say that I've only got one friend she might say it's wrong 'cos you really need to have three...

This sort of thinking may well be in train when children hesitate or take a long time responding to limited-choice nomination tasks. It is therefore important for researchers to make it totally clear to young respondents that they can nominate fewer children than the number stipulated (Parker et al., 1995). This strategy can reduce response error for some children, but it still does not address the decision-making problems for children with larger social circles than the stated number of choices. So despite such remedial strategies, the fundamental task-related validity problems affecting limited-choice nominations remain.

The *context* of nomination questions is important for content-related validity of nomination data. For example, in ascertaining the friendships of early elementary school children, the investigator should examine the range of social contexts from classroom to playground as possible frameworks for sociometric questions. Some situations might have greater relevance to peer group status than others, so investigators could select a context based on what is already known about children's interactions in formal and less formal settings. To more validly access the friendship dimension under study, sociometric questions could then be set in an imagined situation such as a playground scene where children are engaged in a dyadic play activity of their own choice (e.g., Burton Smith, et al., 2001).

There are many content-related validity problems associated with limited-choice nominations. However, investigators could solve these problems relatively simply. They could first elicit unlimited nominations from children, thus controlling many of the variables described above that affect the validity of children's responses. If researchers require limited-choice nominations for statistical purposes, then the first three to five choices could be used. For children who nominate fewer children than the number analyzed, the non-responses could be treated statistically as missing data. This would be preferable to the inclusion of invalid nominations that fail to reflect the nomination criteria. This technique has the advantage of removing the biasing elements involved in limited-choice nominations. At the same time it provides an estimate of the size of children's personal friendship networks—generally between five and seven individuals in unlimited nomination tasks (Evans, 1966). Cillessen and Marks (2011) observe that researchers now recognise compelling reasons for using unlimited nominations in place of limited-choice nominations.

Validating Sociometric Instruments Using Criterion-Related Validity Evidence

Criterion-related validity involves the relationship between measures from an instrument and a performance criterion, involving statistical evidence from correlations known as *validity coefficients*. Validity coefficients provide a numerical indication of the extent of relationship between the instrument and its criterion (Kaplan & Saccuzzo, 2009). Concurrent validity indicates a relationship between two measures in real time, while predictive validity assesses this relationship with temporally offset measures. Both these types of validity evidence, usually applied to psychometric assessments, are also relevant to sociometric assessments. However, in the research literature, predictive validity evidence for sociometric instruments involving longitudinal studies is more limited compared to concurrent validity evidence.

Guidelines for Evaluating the Concurrent Validity Evidence for Sociometric Instruments

Concurrent validity studies examine the extent of similarity between different sociometric approaches, yielding evidence for the validation of new or innovative sociometric approaches. Investigators who wish to validate their own sociometric instruments can correlate children's responses on existing instruments with responses on the new instrument using Pearson's *r* statistic. However, researchers who prefer to use existing instruments and approaches can utilize a substantial body of research in the peer relations literature that has addressed the issue of concurrent validity of sociometric measurement, with most studies carried out between the late 1970s and the mid 1990s. These studies are a valuable resource for investigators who wish to ascertain the degree of *overlap* between potential sociometric measures for their research. Here they should examine the validity coefficients yielded by relevant studies.

The overlap in sociometric approaches and instruments can be affected significantly by the degree of similarity in the *criteria* used to elicit children's responses. Researchers can use a large range of different criteria in the questions for sociometric nominations; and in the instructions for completing rating scales, group preference records, and paired comparisons. Rating scales employed in published peer group status research typically utilize play and general friendship criteria, while nominations involve both playmate and best friend questions. In concurrent validity studies, the agreement between rating scale and nomination data is likely to be higher if the nomination question and the rating scale criterion both concern friendship, or both embrace play; than if the rating scale involved friendship and the nomination concerned play. Investigators establishing concurrent validity should therefore hold the *content* of rating scale criteria and nomination questions constant. In this way the amount of overlap in the *methodology* of sociometric measurement can be more clearly examined. The strength of correlation coefficients indicates the degree of intersection for the two methodologies. Nevertheless, simple correlations cannot show *how* different methodologies influence the meaning of children's responses.

When a lack of overlap is demonstrated between two sociometric measures, there could be wide theoretical or conceptual differences between them. For example, when researchers use nominations to represent peer group status, positive and negative nominations exemplify the two separate acceptance and rejection dimensions of peer group status. In contrast, rating scales use a single score from a unidimensional continuum to represent peer group status. Similar sociometric ratings expressed as *mean scores*, can conceal highly different distributions of peer group evaluations—in other words, two identical averaged sociometric ratings could comprise very different score profiles depicting diverse types of children. For example, a mid-range averaged rating of 3 calculated from a scale ranging from 1 to 5 could comprise a combination of extreme scores (5s and 1s), representing a child who is strongly liked and disliked by different group factions. An average rating of 3 could equally result from combining non-extreme mid-range ratings (2s, 3s, and a few 4s), describing a child that the majority of the reference group finds unremarkable (Thompson & Powell, 1951). This example shows the validity problems that arise through a lack of separation of the two dimensions of acceptance and rejection when ratings are used to representing individual differences in peer group status (Morrison, 1981a).

Evaluating Concurrent Validity Evidence: Are Different Sociometric Approaches Distinctive?

During the 1970s and 1980s progressive discovery of dissimilar measurement properties led a number of authors to conclude that sociometric nominations and ratings assess different aspects of peer group status. In an overview of the literature to that date, Asher and Hymel (1981) maintained that ratings give a measure of general group acceptability, whereas nominations indicate how much peers regard a child as a *preferred* playmate, workmate or friend. This conclusion was based on deductions from the results of previous studies. For example, Hymel and Asher (1977) found that a sizable proportion of children receiving no positive nominations in fact received high positive play ratings. Further, in a study of African-American and Anglo-American children in integrated schools, Singleton and Asher (1977, 1979) found a significant degree of acceptance reflected in sociometric ratings, compared to the typical dearth of cross-race nomination as preferred playmate or best friend in previous studies. French and Waas, (1985) and Hymel and Asher (1977) also found that children receiving few or no peer nominations for playmate were rated quite highly on a play rating measure.

Throughout the 1980s authors increasingly endorsed the distinctiveness of ratings and nominations as measures of peer group status, with further evidence to reinforce this stance (e.g., Schofield & Whitley, 1983; Shannon & Kafer, 1984). Asher and Renshaw (1981) found that children with different rating/nomination profiles also differed in their observed behavior, a finding that was repeated later by Olson and Lifgren's (1988) study with preschool children. Children who were low on both acceptability (ratings) and preference as friends (nominations) were less socially skilled than children who were only low on nominations. This observation is further reinforced by Oden and Asher's (1977) finding of differential improvement in nomination- and rating-based measures of peer group status after social skills training. Friend nominations showed lower and nonsignificant improvement compared to play ratings. The play and friend criteria of the two measures were not uniform in this study confounding the results somewhat, but it would appear that ratings are more sensitive to intervention effects than are nominations. The findings of these diverse studies are understandable in the light of the shortcomings of limited-choice nominations. Children who are not high priority in terms of the play or friendship criterion—including children of a minority ethnicity, children who are not socially skilled or academically prominent in the class—have a much reduced chance of being chosen in a limited-choice nomination task. This is particularly so if the criterion refers to friendship. However, in a rating task based on a roster of all group members, low priority children's data *are* included. Therefore the method-based variance in each approach could largely account for differential findings.

Researchers can examine the concurrent validity of different measures of peer group status by applying two or more measures to the same sample of children and then using Pearson' r statistic to analyze the correlations between pairs of instruments or approaches. Using this methodology, researchers have generally found correlation coefficients ranging from .40 to .70, indicating a moderate to strong relationship between ratings and positive nominations (e.g., Vogel, Conger, & Keane, 1985; Vitaro & Boivin, 1989; Schwarzwald, 1991; Asher & Hymel, 1981; Poteat, Ironsmith, & Bullock, 1986; Olson & Lifgren, 1988). Negative nominations and ratings generally correlate more highly than positive nominations and ratings, indicating a stronger relationship between sociometric ratings and negative sociometric nominations.

Moderate-to-strong correlations seem to constitute firm evidence indicating that two measures are similar and that both assess a common sociometric dimension However, researchers need to evaluate even strong correlations cautiously. They should square the coefficient to ascertain the amount of variance that is accounted for by the two measures. Even with coefficients of .70, only about half of the variance is (49%) in the two measures is *common* or shared between the two measures. More than half of the variance (51%) in this case is *not* common variance, meaning that rating scales and nominations are in fact measuring distinctive aspects of children's peer group status. For example, in a study using nomination and rating scale approaches with preschool children, Musun-Miller (1990), found high and significant correlations, but the average overall agreement between approaches corrected for chance agreement, was only 68%. The remaining 32% of variance unaccounted for by the overlap in the approaches represents unique aspects of peer group status accessed by each measure.

Investigators can use factor analysis and multiple regression analysis in establishing the concurrent validity of diverse sociometric methods such as sociometric nomination and ratings. These analytic techniques are based on simple correlations of the scores of the same sample of children on different instruments. However, factor analysis and multiple regression analyses provide much richer validity information than simple correlations, and in turn, offer the most conclusive evidence for the independence or overlap of sociometric nomination and ratings. For example, Gresham (1981) using factor analysis found that nominations and ratings loaded on independent factors which he labelled as *friendship* and *likeability*. French, Waas, and Tarver Behring (1986), using multiple regression analysis of positive and negative nominations and ratings, revealed a greater degree of overlap between ratings and nominations than that found by Gresham who used only positive nomination data. However there was still considerable *unique* variance accounted for by each approach, suggesting that ratings and nominations each measure something different, as well as having something in common. In a later factor analytic study of ratings and nominations Bukowski, Hoza, and Newcomb (1994) concluded that each approach provided a parallel but not identical measure of peer group status.

Concurrent validity studies of paired comparisons and group preference records are rare in the peer relations literature. Cohen and Van Tassel (1978) examined the overlap between a limited-choice nomination technique and a variant of the paired comparison approach with preschool children. Using simple correlations at three different time points during the school year, these authors found there was little or no overlap between the two approaches when they were used to indicate friendship. When nominations and paired comparisons were used as measures of peer group status, most correlations were moderate to large in size, reflecting a similar degree of overlap to that found between ratings and limited-choice nominations.

The findings of concurrent validity studies have implications for the interpretation of peer group status research based on different methods of data collection. Vogel et al. (1985) concluded that generalizing results across different approaches to sociometric measurement is a questionable procedure. The major methodological difference between nomination and rating approaches appears to lie in the relative comprehensiveness of each approach, so any measures derived from them will always be imperfectly correlated. If nominations were unlimited—i.e., they involved a full ranking of the reference group—the measures would be methodologically more similar and therefore statistically more correlated. Cohen and Van Tassel's (1978) study demonstrated clearly that the comprehensiveness factor is significant in explaining the imperfect correlations between sociometric measures based on full and partial rankings of a group. When the correlations from a limited-choice nomination task were corrected for attenuation, the overlap between nomination and paired comparison approaches improved significantly. Cohen and Van Tassel controlled major methodological differences between limited-choice nominations and paired comparisons. Both measures are variants of a basic nomination approach, so Cohen and Van

Tassel concluded that paired comparisons and nominations were assessing similar choice behaviour. Uncontrolled differences in comprehensiveness contributes substantially to the *lack* of overlap observed in these nomination based measures, and by extension to the lack of overlap with rating scales as well.

From the research reviewed above, it is apparent that different sociometric approaches are distinctive measures of children's peer group status and friendship, each accessing unique variance. They are not interchangeable, and should not be regarded as such. In practice then, using *combinations* of approaches is recommended, increasing the accuracy of identifying children, particularly rejected children who have peer relationship problems in the classroom or early education setting.

Evaluating Concurrent Validity Evidence of Sociometric Data Using External Criteria

Researchers can provide evidence of concurrent validity by correlating sociometric measures of peer group status and with external criteria, such as teacher evaluations of children's peer group status. This procedure indicates the degree of commonality or overlap in peer-based and teacher-based evaluations of children's peer group status. For example, Landau, Milich, and Whitten (1984) found both sociometric and teacher-based evaluations of kindergarten boys showed a high degree of intersection for the acceptance dimension of peer group status. However, there was no significant overlap for the rejection dimension. Olson and Bradfield (1991) Foster, Bell-Dolan, and Berler (1986) also found minimal correlation between sociometric and teacher evaluations of young children's peer group status. Additionally, Wu et al. (2001) showed that sociometric measures of preschool children's peer group status and teachers' assessments correlate to some extent, but they also assess unique aspects of children's peer group status. These concurrent validity findings are important for researchers—there is at best only a moderate degree of similarity in peer and teacher evaluations of children's peer group status. This underlines the need for researchers to access peer-based information in assessing children's peer relationships. Children's peers and adults such as parents and teachers have different accessibility to social information about children, as discussed earlier.

Researchers can establish concurrent validity of sociometric data by using external criterion measures in the form of behavioral indices. This approach, sometimes called the *known groups* approach, involves investigators measuring the peer group status of a sample using sociometric methods and also obtaining behavioral criterion measures about the same sample of children. These criterion measures can come from observations, as well as peer, parental and teacher ratings of social behaviors (Hops & Lewin, 1984). Researchers then use statistical techniques such as analyses of variance or t tests to investigate whether there are significant differences in the behaviors of children with different levels of peer group status—for example whether children with high peer acceptance and those with low peer acceptance are significantly different in terms of aggressive behavior. Correlations such as Pearson's r between sociometric and behavioral measures can also indicate behavioral differences in children with different levels of sociometric status—for example, a pattern indicating that high levels of aggression are *positively* correlated with high levels of peer rejection; and low levels of aggression are *negatively* correlated with high levels of peer rejection.

Detecting differences s between individuals' peer group status and their behaviors are a vital evidence for the validity of sociometric data. Researchers can carry out such validity studies themselves and can also benefit from the results of existing studies in the sociometric literature. Many studies examining the relationship between social behaviors and peer group status are not validity studies *per se*, but fortuitously provide concurrent validity data (for a summary see Newcomb et al., 1993). These studies focus on children's behavior toward their peer group. However, researchers seeking concurrently validity evidence for sociometric data should also examine the behavior of the peer group toward children differing in peer status. In other words researchers need more conclusive evidence that children differing in peer group status not only differ in their own behaviour toward others but are also treated differently by the group (Bukowski &Hoza, 1989). This information constitutes a true, group-based criterion for differentiating peer group status, a measure which is also group-determined. In terms of the research literature, only limited evidence exists of differential peer group behavior toward individuals with varying peer group status, for example, the finding that more accepted children receive greater peer group reinforcement than less accepted children (Gottman, Gonzo, & Rasmussen, 1975; Masters & Furman, 1981). Studies investigating visual attention (Vaughn & Waters, 1981), negative acts (Asher & Hymel, 1981) and punishment (Masters & Furman, 1981) have found group-based behavioral evidence for the validity of peer group status measures.

In order to gain a comprehensive picture of concurrent validity based on the overlap between peer group status and social behavior, investigators examining peer group status and friendship in young children need to target correlation evidence for preschool children as well as for school-aged children. Older school age children and preschoolers vary to a significant degree in social development, and this might impact significantly on the correlates of peer group status for younger children. For example, peer rejection is reliably discriminated by negative social behaviors in older children, but in very young children positive social behaviors appear to be better discriminators (Walter & LaFreniere, 2000). Nonetheless, a few studies suggest broad similarity between the correlates of peer group status in older and younger children (e.g., Keane & Calkins, 2004; Wood, Cowan, & Baker, 2002). Behavioral measures suited to older school-aged children might not be relevant to the social repertoires of preschoolers. Researchers should therefore employ measures that are appropriate for very young children, for example Parten's (1932) typology of play behaviors. Parten provides well-recognized and useful categories of play including nonsocial types of play such as solitary, onlooker and parallel play; and social types of play including associative and cooperative play. Previous researchers have found that nonsocial types of play are related to peer rejection in preschoolers (e.g., Gazelle & Ladd, 2003; Hart et al., 2000; Spinrad et al., 2004); while social types of play are directly associated with peer acceptance (e.g., Walker, 2009; Hart et al., 2000; Nelson et al., 2005). These finding provide concurrent validity evidence of a degree of continuity between early childhood and later developmental periods, where cooperative interactions are consistently associated with peer acceptance (Coie, Dodge, & Kupersmidt, 1990).

ESTIMATING THE RELIABILITY OF SOCIOMETRIC DATA

Reliability refers to consistency of data, and without consistency the meaning of research outcomes is compromised. Also, a lack of reliability threatens the replication of findings which is essential in experimentation. Without consistency in what an instrument measures, researchers do not know whether a particular set of results has in fact been replicated. Psychometric theory based on attribute data recognizes different types of reliability and includes test–retest reliability, parallel forms reliability and split-half reliability (Kaplan & Saccuzzo, 2009). All these types of reliability involve correlations using Pearson's *r* statistic. The coefficients that result from reliability studies are called reliability coefficients.

Evaluating the Applicability of Psychometric Reliability to Sociometric Instruments

Because of fundamental differences between sociometric data and attribute data, psychometric reliability cannot be applied in totality to sociometric data—parallel forms and split-half reliability are inappropriate forms of reliability for sociometric instruments. Parallel forms of cognitive and personality tests are sometimes developed from two or more different selections of test items from a common pool of items. Researchers use *parallel forms reliability* to investigate the consistency of measurement between alternate forms of an instrument, by correlating the responses of a sample of respondents on the separate forms of the test. Their structure and response requirements make it impossible to develop parallel forms of sociometric instruments such as nominations. *Split-half reliability* examines the internal consistency of an instrument by dividing its items randomly into halves and correlating respondents' scores on the two sets of items. However internal consistency cannot be validly applied to sociometric instruments because they do not consist of regular test items like the words found in a vocabulary test for example. Instead, sociometric tests such as rating scales and group preference records consist of rosters—the names or pictures of individuals whom the respondent evaluates. These stimuli do not equate to personality or cognitive test items which must demonstrate an equivalent ability to measure the trait the test is assessing, such as intelligence (i.e., the test should show adequate internal consistency).

Researchers using sociometric measures are concerned only with the third type of psychometric reliability—*test–retest reliability* which assesses the temporal stability of data. This involves correlating individuals' responses to the same instrument at different time points using statistics such as Pearson's r. Test–retest reliability is based on the assumption that behaviors relating to enduring traits should be stable over time. Using this type of reliability with sociometric measures is however controversial—some researchers claim the assumption underlying psychometric test stability is not applicable to sociometric instruments. Sociometric instruments differ fundamentally from psychometric tests because sociometric instruments yield *relational* data representing friendship and peer group status. These dimensions are not enduring personal traits, for example measures of a person's intelligence which are derived from *attribute* data (Scott, 1991).

Significant changes in a person's score on an intelligence test over a short period of time might indicate instability in the test due to shortcomings in its design or items. This assumption is based on the recognition of intelligence as a stable personal trait which should not vary substantially over time. However, changes over time in an individual's peer group status score are more difficult to interpret. The change could reflect a weakness in the design of the sociometric instrument used, or it might simply indicate that peer group status itself is inherently unstable. This problem has never been fully resolved, so researchers should interpret stability coefficients for sociometric instruments with caution. For example Wu, Hart, Draper, and Olsen (2001) recommend careful consideration of what is meant by stability and reliability in relation to sociometric assessment. *Stability* is "a temporal characteristic of the phenomenon or behavior being measured across time", for example peer rejection; while *reliability* is "a psychometric property of a measurement instrument" for example sociometric assessment (p. 420). Using these definitions Wu and Colleagues reasoned that it is possible to reliably measure inherently unstable phenomena. It is also possible to obtain spuriously low reliability estimates for an inherently stable characteristic by using an unreliable instrument.

Factors Affecting the Reliability of Young Children's Sociometric Data

The degree of correlation between sociometric measures over time is influenced by several factors—the age of respondents, the method or sociometric approach, the referent situation or criteria, and the time interval between test and retest. Investigators should always interpret the reliability coefficients obtained from test–retest studies with these factors in mind. This section deals with the variables that affect the stability of sociometric measures, reviewing the reliability evidence from the literature, with a special emphasis on the more problematic stability of young children's sociometric responses.

Findings from studies of psychometric instruments such as intelligence tests show the longer the time interval between test and retest, the smaller the reliability coefficient, reflecting lower agreement between the two sets of test results. It is the same for sociometric tests (Hymel et al., 2011). Psychometricians recognise that test–retest reliability coefficients are affected simultaneously by learning effects (respondents remembering and repeating their initial evaluations) and developmental effects (experiences during the intervening period which might change respondents' initial evaluations on a subsequent evaluation). According to Kaplan and Saccuzzo (2009), learning and developmental effects are major impediments to accurately estimating test–retest reliability, since substantial amounts of the variance in an individual's scores from the two testings can be due to these effects. Like psychometricians, sociometric investigators should therefore carefully consider an appropriate test–retest interval to minimize both learning and developmental effects when estimating the reliability of their data.

The estimates temporal stability of sociometric measures obtained from test–retest reliability studies might be even more susceptible to learning and developmental effects than temporal stability estimates from psychometric assessments. For example, if a researcher assessed the temporal stability of responses in three-choice nomination task using a test–retest interval that was too short, respondents would be able to easily remember their three choices on the first testing. Remembering their initial responses to 100 different items on a cognitive test would be much more difficult. So in a simple nomination task, memory factors could account for most of the similarity between the respondents' choices on the first and second administrations of the task. If a researcher chose a test–retest interval that was too long, for example a whole year, most of the differences in respondents' choices between the first and second testing could be due to developmental effects—for example, substantial changes in the makeup of the respondents' peer group in a study straddling two school years. Estimates of the reliability of young children's sociometric responses might be particularly vulnerable to developmental effects because of the highly dynamic nature of children's relationships during the early developmental period (Hay, Payne, & Chadwick, 2004).

Children's age has a significant influence on the temporal stability of sociometric measures. In studies over many years researchers have found young children's peer group status is less stable than that of older children. In an early article Hops and Lewin (1984) reported a number of studies of temporal stability for limited-choice nominations, with coefficients ranging from .30 to .78. In these studies stability of peer group status scores was greater for elementary-aged children than for preschoolers. Later studies have reinforced this general finding (Hymel et al., 2011). Lower temporal stability in young children's peer group status data reflects the greater fluidity observed in peer relations during early childhood. Young children's peer relations are affected by greater emotional lability, which contributes to on-again, off-again associations. However, Wu et al. (2001) point out that there are also consistencies in young children's peer relationships that can equally influence stability coefficients for peer group status. These include preschool children's increasing social competence as well as their frequent aggressive acts, both of which tend to consolidate the reputations of children during the early childhood period. Estimates of stability therefore depend not only on the adequacy of the sociometric instrument but also on the balance of fluid and stable characteristics in the child sample.

In a review of reliability studies, Hymel (1983) set an age limit for the reliable collection of sociometric data, with sociometric tests "not recommended" for children under four. A lack of stability in very young children's sociometric data could be due to validity issues—their failure to adequately understand sociometric tasks. However more recent studies showed favourable stability results from three-year-olds' sociometric data (e.g, Bost, Vaughn, Washington, Cielinski, & Bradbard, 1998; Lemerise, 1997; Wu et al., 2001). So the lower age limits of applying sociometric techniques is still open to question, and depends greatly on the researcher's ability to develop valid techniques that are appropriate for very young children.

Since the 1970s investigators have examined the differential stability of peer group status derived from various sociometric methodologies. Researchers have consistently found roster-based approaches yield better stability coefficients than do nomination-based approaches. For example Hops and Lewin (1984) reported a number of temporal stability studies for limited-choice nominations, with coefficients ranging from .30 to .78.

Sociometric ratings and paired comparisons exhibited more impressive coefficients in the range of .70 to .80. These findings are generally the same for studies with young children (e.g., Cohen & Van-Tassel, 1978; Asher, Singleton, Tinsley, & Hymel, 1979; Kalfus & Berler, 1985; Boivin & Begin, 1986; Olson & Lifgren, 1988; Bullock, Ironsmith, & Poteat 1988), with only a few exceptions (e.g., Denham & McKinley, 1993). The superior stability of roster methods could be due to ratings and paired comparisons sampling a larger number of evaluations than nominations do. Differences in temporal stabilities could also be due to real differences in the stability of the separate constructs each approach measures (Singleton & Asher, 1977, 1979). For example, nominations measure children's popularity as friends and this might be more variable over time than their general group acceptability, which is measured by rating scales. These considerations should guide researchers' choice of sociometric instruments, especially in studies in early education settings where the stability of children's responses is an important issue.

ASSESSING PEER GROUP STATUS USING SOCIOMETRIC CLASSIFICATION

A large proportion of the sociometric literature involving young children consists of studies employing unidimensional measures of individuals' peer group status. In other words, many researchers have used single measures to reflect children's peer group status, for example the total number of rejection nominations children receive (Coie, Dodge, & Kupersmidt, 1990). Unidimensional measures are calculated in several ways—by averaging sociometric ratings; and by separately summing and standardizing negative and positive nominations, and the distinctive evaluations of group preference records. Investigators have correlated unidimensional measures with a wide range of individual child characteristics in order to discover patterns that might clarify the causes of peer rejection and acceptance (Newcomb et al., 1993).

Researchers however, can make further distinctions in peer group status beyond simple measures of peer acceptance and rejection. For example, children who are not nominated at all are distinctive from children who receive many rejection nominations and few or no acceptance nominations. Similarly, children who receive many acceptance nominations and few rejections appear sociometrically different from those who receive high numbers of both acceptances and rejections. Early sociometricians such as Bronfenbrenner (1943, 1944), Lemann and Solomon (1952), Dunnington (1957), and Gronlund (1959) recognized this fact. They outlined a sociometric approach which combined acceptance and rejection measures to distinguish separate *categories* of sociometrically dissimilar children. For example, Gronlund proposed four rather imprecise sociometric categories—sociometric stars (many positive but few or no negative nominations); controversial children (many positive and many negative nominations); rejected children (few or no positive and many negative nominations); and neglected or isolated children (few or no positive and few or no negative nominations). Such categorization of children is known as *sociometric classification*. Sociometric classification can be used successfully in research with young children, as well as older school-aged children. Therefore, in the following section the methods for classifying children of all ages are described.

Understanding and Evaluating Different Classification Schemes

In 1979 Peery formalized the imprecise descriptive classifications proposed by early sociometricians such as Gronlund (1959), by calculating two mathematically exact indices from combinations of acceptance and rejection nominations by preschool children. Peery's *social impact* index is the total number of positive (acceptance) and negative (rejection) nominations received. It refers to the visibility of an individual within a specific group, but does not measure their social desirability—individuals can gain a high score by receiving many nominations regardless of whether they are negative or positive. Peery's *social preference* index is calculated by subtracting negative from positive nominations. It depends on the relative balance of the group's negative and positive regard for an individual, and can be equated to their social desirability in a specific group. For example, disproportionately more rejection than acceptance nominations yields a negative social preference score, reflecting the group's overriding disapproval. Peery calculated these two indices for each individual and then matched them with specific classification criteria to categorize group members. For example, *rejected children* have above average social impact index scores and negative social preference index scores.

Peery (1979) made a breakthrough in measuring children's peer group status by simultaneously employing social preference and social impact as the defining dimensions of a *two-dimensional* system of sociometric classification. Peery conceptualized sociometric categories schematically. Theoretically orthogonal axes delineate four quadrants in two-dimensional space. A diagram of the model in Peery's (1979) article shows axis lines representing the social impact and social preference dimensions intersecting at right angles, at the zero point on the social preference dimension, and at the arithmetic mean on the social impact dimension. By their scores, researchers can place an individual case in a quadrant of the model which defines four approximately equal sociometric groups, *isolated, rejected, popular* and *amiable* children. Peery's scheme however, does not exhaustively classify any sample. Peery as well as Newcomb and Bukowski (1983) found between 7% and 12% of sampled scores fell directly on an axis, thus excluding these individuals from classification. Peery excluded a further 59% of his sample because they were too closely clustered around the model's central point, the intersection of the two dimensions. He regarded these cases as sociometrically non-extreme children, a majority differentiated from extreme cases such as rejected children who were located nearer the model's periphery.

In an amplification of Peery's (1979) scheme, Coie, Dodge and Copotelli (1982) formalized his excluded cases as an additional sociometric category—sociometric *average* children. Coie and Colleagues used exact statistical criteria based on social impact and social preference scores to classify cases, as well as sums of positive ("liked most"—LM) and negative ("liked least"—LL) nominations. For example, the authors define *rejected* individuals by social preference indices less than minus 1; LM scores less than 0 and LL scores greater than zero. These children are typified by high levels of peer rejection and low peer acceptance, indicating they are the least preferred children in a group. Coie and Colleagues' sociometric classification defines five sociometric groups. Only the popular and rejected categories are conceptually similar to Peery's original classifications. *Popular* children are those with high levels of peer acceptance and low levels of peer rejection, indicating they are the most preferred children in a group. Coie and Colleagues' *controversial* category has no parallel in Peery's scheme. It describes children who have high levels of acceptance as well as rejection, and high social impact in a group. Coie and Colleagues' fifth category *neglected* children combines Peery's *amiable* and *isolated* classifications. Observations showed that Peery's *isolated* children often interacted with their peers, and that "isolated" was in fact a misnomer (Berndt, 1984). Coie and Colleagues, therefore, used the term *neglected* to better describe isolated children, who were defined mainly by low social impact. This category describes the sociometrically "invisible" children in a group, whom other children tend to overlook.

In their classification scheme, Coie et al. (1982) corrected problems associated with Peery's use of raw same- and opposite-gender nominations to calculate social preference and social impact indices. Peery controlled for group size and gender effects in his nomination data by using same-sized, gender-balanced laboratory groups as his child samples. However, investigators cannot artificially manipulate group characteristics in naturally occurring groups such as preschool classes. Researchers have found strong bias in nomination data toward same-gender acceptance and opposite-gender rejection during early and later childhood (e.g., Bukowski et al., 1993). Therefore, social impact and preference indices could vary in relation to the size and gender balance of the nominating group, making it difficult to equate peer group status across different groups of children. Coie and Colleagues used same- and opposite-gender nominations in combination to determine scores and indices for their classification scheme. They standardized their data using group-based means and standard deviations, and also standardized social preference and impact scores within group. Their procedure controlled for size differences in reference groups, providing a constant frame of reference across different sized groups, regarded as important since the earliest sociometric studies (Bronfenbrenner, 1944; Dunnington, 1957). Standardization also allows legitimate comparisons between different sociometric classification categories, which are not possible with Peery's classifications. However, Coie and Colleagues did not control for group differences in gender composition.

The criteria of the 1982 Coie Dodge and Coppotelli (CDC) classification scheme fail to classify a substantial proportion of any sample. Individuals either conform to statistical criteria for *average* status or alternately, for one of the four extreme classifications—*popular, rejected, neglected,* and *controversial.* Nevertheless, some scores fall outside the criteria for average status, and yet do not deviate sufficiently from the norm to warrant extreme classification. These *unclassified* children constituted 57.3% of Coie et al.'s (1982) participants. If researchers' primary concern is identifying groups of sociometrically extreme children such as rejectees, a lack of scheme exhaustiveness is not problematic. An unclassified sociometric "buffer" group might in fact help to differentiate sociometrically extreme children from average ones. However, if a research design requires exhaustive classification; substantial numbers of unclassified participants can threaten the ecological validity of the study and might present problems for statistical analysis through missing cases.

In 1983 Newcomb and Bukowski proposed an exhaustive sociometric classification scheme. Like the Peery and CDC Schemes, it is based on social impact and social preference dimensions. However, it employs classification criteria based on the rarity of nominations calculated using Bronfenbrenner's (1943) binomial probability model, as well as group normative statistics. *Rare scores* are those occurring in less than 5% of cases, based on the size of the nominating group and the relative number of rejection, acceptance and total nominations by the group. For example, rejected status is defined by a rare disliked score plus a liked score below the group mean. Popular status is substantiated by a rare liked score and a disliked score below the group mean. According to the authors, the rare score controls for group size effects, avoiding the need to standardize scores as in the CDC Scheme. Standardization results in loss of accuracy in representing actual social networks. Newcomb and Bukowski also addressed the problem of gender bias in their data by using only same-gender nominations. During early and middle childhood, opposite-gender positive nominations are rare; so excluding opposite-gender nominations would probably result in little loss of data. However, negative nominations are more likely to be opposite-gender than same-gender during early to middle childhood (Bukowski et al., 1993; Fabes et al., 2004; Barbu, 2003). Newcomb and Bukowski's method might therefore artificially restrict the nomination data on which classifications are based, and compromise the ecological validity of sociometric categories. Researchers could instead use the method previously recommended in this chapter—standardizing according to within-group gender distributions, which simultaneously controls for size and gender bias effects in both-gender data.

The five sociometric categories of the Newcomb and Bukowski (NB) Scheme are comparable to the categories created by the CDC Scheme. The two schemes are based on a similar model of classification—the major difference is in the *criteria* used to define the sociometric groups. Despite some obvious shortcomings, the two schemes were most frequently used for sociometric classification in the research literature during the 1980s and early 1990s (see Newcomb et al., 1993 for a review of studies). Nonetheless, in the three decades since Newcomb and Colleagues' study, the CDC Scheme has become paramount in the literature, despite the obvious advantage of the NB Scheme in classifying all children in a specified group (Hymel et al., 2011). Researchers have since developed their own variants of the CDC and NB Schemes (e.g., Dodge, Schlundt, Schocken, & Delugach, 1983; Lazarus & Weinstock, 1984; Terry & Coie 1991).

The most popular classification schemes are based on limited-choice nominations. However, researchers have also produced sociometric classifications based fully or partially on sociometric ratings (e.g., Roistacher, 1974; Singleton & Asher, 1977; Ladd 1983; French, 1988, 1990; Asher & Dodge, 1986; Walker, 2009). Ratings-based classification schemes introduce comprehensive roster-based measures to sociometric classification, increasing the ecological validity and reliability of the sociometric categories. As well, ratings often replace the negative nominations in these schemes, which some researchers find ethically questionable. Collecting negative nominations might also present a barrier to obtaining parental consent for children's participation in sociometric studies (Asher & Dodge, 1986).

Using Sociometric Classification in Research

Sociometric classification solves many of the measurement difficulties associated with unidimensional rating and nomination measures of peer group status. Research designs using unidimensional measures often fail to unravel the complex relationships between children's peer group status and their behavior. Authors such as Coie et al. (1982) and Hymel and Rubin (1985) maintain that in correlation studies, sociometric classification strengthens the relationship between measures of peer group status and child variables such as social behaviors. Separate sociometric status categories demonstrate more meaningful relationships with a variety of behavioral measures, successfully clarifying the confounded effects often obtained in studies employing simple ratings and nominations. For example, research using sociometric classification suggests that different behavioral determinants exist for distinctive typologies of children who have negative peer group status—neglected, rejected, and controversial children (Coie et al., 1990; Newcomb et al. 1993). Sociometric classification therefore has greater ecological validity, permitting more powerful research designs for investigating the evolution of peer rejection, especially during early childhood.

Early education facilitators can profitably apply sociometric classification to groups of young children, to easily identify individuals with imerging problematic peer relations. Classification during the preschool years might therefore facilitate crucial early interventions to increase peer acceptance and consequently reduce unfavorable developmental outcomes during the school years.

Selecting Sociometric Classification Schemes for Research With Young Children

Contemporary researchers in early education settings have a large number of different classification schemes from which to choose. Selecting or developing a suitable scheme for classifying young children should be governed principally by the type of base scores used in the scheme, as well as the need to obtain *valid* scores in this population. Sociometric ratings are problematic for preschoolers, so classifications reliant on these measures may not possess the necessary validity. So, with young children, nomination-based schemes might be preferable. Practical considerations are also important, including ease of quantification and classification, and usefulness in terms of the number and type of categories available. The exhaustiveness of the scheme—whether it classifies all or only some group members is an important consideration in the design of studies, and whether children in the average status group are sufficiently differentiated from extreme sociometric classifications such as rejected and neglected children. The presence an unclassified "buffer" group between average and extreme sociometric status can be important if researchers wish to contrast extreme status with average sociometric status. Cases that are too close to cut-off points might confound the effects being investigated. On the other hand, the presence of an uncategorized group can be problematic for the design of some studies. Consequently investigators should closely review their research *aims* before they select a classification scheme.

The question of category size—the proportion of group members assigned to each category in a classification scheme—is an important consideration in selecting a suitable classification scheme for research with young children. The model underlying the classification scheme and the classification criteria are largely responsible for the relative sizes of the sociometric categories. For instance, in separate studies, Newcomb and Bukowski (1983) and Terry and Coie (1991) compared classifications of the same sample of children using the NB and the CDC Schemes. The NB Scheme's exhaustiveness and the CDC Scheme's non-exhaustiveness resulted in sociometric *average* categories from the two schemes that differed in size by over 40%. Apart from the neglected category, extreme CDC categories were twice to three times larger than the corresponding NB categories. This difference reflects the more conservative NB criteria. A statistical cut-off of .05 for rare social preference scores defining the rejected, controversial and popular categories targets approximately 5% of the population. By contrast, Coie and Colleagues' standard cut-off scores—greater than one *SD* from the mean for the extreme groups—target approximately 15% of the population for the extreme categories, including popular, rejected and controversial children. However, for the CDC neglected category, the criteria are more stringent than the NB criteria.

Investigators need to consider the issue of appropriate size for extreme sociometric groups in relation to the aims and design of their research, as well as the intended statistical analysis. For example, the NB Scheme with its more stringent criteria might yield too few children in the rejected category for meaningful statistical analysis; that is, unless very large samples are recruited. With small administrative units in early education, this could pose a practical barrier to using this scheme. The CDC Scheme identifies about three times as many rejected children from the same sized reference group, thus allowing for smaller, more manageable samples. The proportion of rejected children identified by the CDC Scheme is closer to the proportion identified for negative outcomes in the child population (20%). So using the CDC Scheme might also achieve greater ecological validity. Nonetheless, the NB Scheme could be superior in research projects where more stringent classification criteria correspond to the significance levels needed to show meaningful effects (Terry & Coie, 1991). Categories with proportionally more cases such as CDC categories are more stable over time; but being more behaviorally heterogeneous, they show lower criterion-related validity. Researchers need to balance these pluses and minuses in relation to their own research aims, design and analysis approach.

Sample characteristics significantly affect category size, so researchers cannot rely purely on the specific proportions predicted by certain classification models for the percentages they might find in their own studies. For example Peery's (1979) classification of preschool children distributed his sample evenly over the four quadrants of the model, with approximately 25% in the sample in each of his four categories. Newcomb and Bukowski's (1983) classification of 334 Grade 4 and 5 children using Peery's Scheme yielded the expected distribution of about a quarter in each of the popular and rejected categories, but significantly more amiable children and fewer isolated children than expected. However, differences in categorical proportions do not indicate that one classification scheme is superior, nor do they validate a particular scheme. Validity of classification is addressed in the following section.

Examining the Validity of Sociometric Classifications

Establishing the *validity* of a classification scheme is crucial for investigators using classification data in their research, or for clinical purposes like identifying young children in need of educational interventions, such as rejected children. Validity of classification involves the *accuracy* with which children are categorized into different typologies.

Researchers may wish to develop their own classification schemes or might adapt existing schemes to better suit their research aims and data requirements. In these cases researchers need to provide their own validity evidence for the classification categories they develop. They can present construct-related validity for a new classification scheme by classifying the same sample of children using new and already existing schemes, and relating overlap in classification to elements such as scheme structure and criteria. Low concurrence might indicate scheme-related differences that signal improvements in a new scheme, thus contributing to the *discriminate* validity of the new scheme. Scheme overlap on the other hand is evidence of *convergent* validity and depends heavily on factors such as similarity in the base data and the criteria used for classification. The more similar these aspects are the more likely are overlaps in classifications between existing and new schemes. A major determinant of scheme overlap however, is the exhaustiveness and relative size of sociometric categories. For example, Terry and Coie (1991) found that overlap between the CDC and NB Schemes was minimal due to wide differences in these factors. After adjusting the criteria of each scheme to make them more similar in exhaustiveness and category size, the overlap was much greater, but still less than perfect.

For researchers who wish to employ existing classification schemes, scheme overlap affects selection of the most appropriate scheme. This is especially so if investigators want to identify sociometrically extreme individuals who might be children at risk, for example rejected children. In short, evidence of scheme overlap shows sociometric classification schemes are *not* interchangeable. Investigators should therefore carefully consider the strengths and weaknesses of different schemes according to the specific aims of their research. They should thoroughly examine the validity evidence available for the scheme in the research literature. The following sections aim to summarize this evidence as well as highlighting validity issues pertinent to sociometric classification which beginning sociometric researchers should be aware of.

Model-Based Issues and the Validity of Sociometric Classifications

Most sociometric classification schemes are fully or partially based on sociometric nominations (e.g., Peery, 1979; Coie et al., 1982; Newcomb & Bukowski, 1983; Dodge, Schlundt, Schocken, & Delugach, 1983; Lazarus & Weinstock, 1984; Terry & Coie, 1991; Asher & Dodge, 1986; Walker, 2009). Developers of nomination-based classification schemes make an assumption that dimensions such as social impact and social preference used for classifying children are orthogonal—i.e., they are independent of each other. Failure to demonstrate the orthogonality of these dimensions can present a major threat to construct-related validity of the resulting sociometric classifications. For example the raw acceptance and rejection scores Peery (1979) used to calculate social impact and social preference were moderately correlated, with peer rejection measures making a stronger contribution to both social impact and social preference than peer acceptance (Newcomb & Bukowski, 1983). Consequently Peery's social impact and social preference indices were also moderately and significantly correlated, indicating a lack of independence. This contradicts the orthogonal model Peery depicted for his classification scheme, with the social impact and social preference axes at right angles to each other. Newcomb and Bukowski (1983) in fact discovered a *curvilinear* relationship exists between these dimensions.

Peery's (1979) social impact and social preference dimensions are non-orthogonal because the indices used to represent them are combinations of significantly correlated positive and negative nominations. The degree of correlation between different types of nomination data used in sociometric status indices such as a social preference index is crucial. If positive and negative nominations were perfectly independent of each other ($r = 0$), combining the two measures would produce an index that is fully distinctive from the original nominations. However, if a perfect *inverse* relationship existed between the positive and negative nominations ($r = -1.0$), combining them into an index would add no extra information about an individual's sociometric status compared with either of the two original nomination measures. If the positive and negative nominations are significantly and positively correlated, the meaning of a combined index such as social preference becomes ambiguous (Lyndzey & Byrne, 1968).

In their adaptations of Peery's classification scheme, Coie et al. (1982) and Newcomb & Bukowski (1983) used different modifications to correct for the lack of independence of the social impact and social preference dimensions used to classify children. Coie et al. (1982) successfully eliminated the correlation between the social preference and social impact indices by first standardizing nominations. Rejection and acceptance no longer made unequal contributions to social impact and social preference, and the indices themselves showed zero correlation (Newcomb & Bukowski 1983). However, by standardizing nominations, Coie and Colleagues sacrificed the variability in their data—i.e., the range, mean and standard deviation should be different for diverse groups. This is a fundamental assumption of sociometric measurement—sociometric measures are only interpretable in terms of the specific characteristics of a defined social group (Bronfenbrenner, 1944). Therefore, Coie and Colleagues compromised ecological validity by failing to adequately show the true sociometric variability of different naturally-occurring groups in their base data. Newcomb and Bukowski (1983) preserved group-based variability by standardizing their data using statistically rare scores. These were calculated using group-specific statistics, such as means. But Newcomb and Bukowski also combined acceptance and rejection nominations to measure social impact, and this perpetuates the original problem of correlated measures. These problems involving the orthogonality of dimensions used to classify children can also be found in other classification schemes based on the original CDC and NB Schemes.

Developers of nomination-based classification schemes have contradicted classification models in other ways, giving rise to further validity issues. For example, by specifying sociometric categories based on only *one* of the model's *two* dimensions, they have used social impact and social preference unequally (Newcomb & Bukowski, 1983). For example, the CDC Scheme identifies neglected and controversial children by social impact indices and not social preference indices. Popular and rejected children are classified using social preference indices and not social impact indices (Coie et al., 1982). The NB Scheme shows the same inconsistency—for example, sociometrically average children are classified using social impact indices, but popular and rejected children are not. If a single dimension defines a category of peer group status—such as popular and rejected status by social preference; and average and neglected status by social impact—investigators can only validly interpret any research-based differences they find for these categories in terms of that single dimension For example, differences in the aggressive behavior of rejected and popular children can only be related to social preference, because these two categories are defined using only this dimension (Newcomb & Bukowski, 1983). However, if the social impact and social preference dimensions are in fact *not* independent of each other, any research-based differences could also be interpreted in terms of *either* dimension. The imperfections in the use of social impact and social preference indices to classify children are probably responsible for the lack of predictive validity demonstrated in some classifications, particularly neglected and controversial categories.

Measurement-Based Limitations in Classification Schemes

There are serious validity problems relating to the measurement limitations of the base data used in many sociometric classification schemes. The Peery, CDC and NB Schemes and their variants use the total nominations received by an individual as a measure of social impact. In the CDC scheme, extreme social impact indices are vital for identifying both controversial and neglected status, while social impact is important in defining the NB Scheme's neglected and average categories. High social impact indices are not problematic—they designate a child who is socially prominent and tends to be nominated a great deal either positively, negatively or both. In other words, peers are far from indifferent to these children. However, low social impact indices are not so easy to interpret. Peers might never nominate some children because their behavior or personal characteristics give rise to peer indifference. On the other hand the nominating group might not *know* certain children well enough to nominate them. These children could be recent arrivals to the group, or they might live outside the area surrounding the preschool or day care facility. Therefore it is impossible to adequately separate the "don't care about" and "don't know about" factors in low social impact indices. This in turn results in poor content-and construct-related validity for the neglected category in nomination-based sociometric classifications. For example, in a validity study Dydgon and Conger (1990) found little agreement between a direct measure of neglect in first-grade children and the social impact indices from the NB and CDC Schemes.

Classification schemes currently in widespread use are based on limited-choice nominations, which have many inadequacies in relation to reliability and validity, as previously discussed. Shortcomings include the need for complex decision-making if a respondent's friendship circle either exceeds or falls short of the number of choices the investigator specifies. The criteria children use to include or exclude group members have not been widely explored. This would involve children being asked the *reasons* for including some children and excluding others. However, because we do not know the reasons for non-nomination, we also do not know if a *neglected* child is overlooked because of their personal characteristics. Neglected children may in fact be individuals who narrowly miss out on being nominated purely because of the decision-making processes imposed by limited-choice nomination tasks. In a nomination-based classification scheme such as the CDC Scheme, a low social impact score could place an un-nominated child in the neglected category, but not with the same degree of certainty that an unlimited nomination approach would allow. Investigators can therefore only gauge children's social impact relative to the restrictions of the data gathering technique they use. Social preference indices based on limited-choice nominations are subject to the same constraints. So, both of the indices used to classify children artificially restrict the range of children identified and fail to reflect their actual visibility and relative degree of acceptance and rejection in the reference group. Investigators could overcome these difficulties by using unlimited nominations. However, popular schemes such as the CDC and NB Schemes and their variants avoid unlimited nominations because they are unwieldy in calculating the statistics needed for classification.

Investigators such Asher and Dodge (1986) and Walker (2009) have addressed the validity problems associated with classification schemes based on limited-choice nominations by developing classifications based fully or partially on sociometric ratings. These researchers reasoned that the limitations of dichotomous scaling which are carried over into classifications can be overcome by using comprehensive roster-based measures where all group members evaluate all other members. In fact, ratings-based classification schemes such as Asher and Dodge (1986) yield more stable classifications in preschool children than do pure nomination-based classifications (Cillessen, Bukowski, & Haselager, 2000; Maassen, Boxtel, & Goossens, 2005).

Ratings-based schemes generally substitute low peer acceptance ratings for negative nominations. However, ratings pose a fundamental measurement problem that might jeopardize the validity of the sociometric categories they produce. Ratings characterize children's peer group status as a single composite score rather than the separate measures of peer acceptance and rejection found in nominations. Ratings therefore do not reflect the widely recognized *independent* acceptance and rejection dimensions in nomination-based classification models such as the CDC Scheme. Consequently, classification schemes using ratings to define the dimensions of social preference and/or social impact might produce less accurate classifications, even if the classifications are more reliable.

Evaluating Validity Evidence for the Independence of Sociometric Classifications

Classification schemes aim to place children in discrete, independent categories whose members display similar behavior (Terry & Coie, 1991).

So, criterion-related validity evidence for classifications is the extent to which sociometric categories discriminate groups with behaviors that are theoretically linked to differences in peer group status. To investigate the discriminating ability of their sociometric categories researchers first sociometrically classify a sample of children. Then, using measures from peer and teacher evaluations, investigators create behaviorally homogeneous groupings of children from the same sample, for example children showing high levels of aggression. Researchers then cross-classify children, looking at the number of children who fit both the socometric category and the related behavioral category. For example, children with high levels of aggression should mostly fit the rejected sociometric category. The amount of overlap between the behavioral and sociometric classifications is a measure of the sociometric category's validity (i.e., the "accuracy" of sociometric classification is determined). High levels of overlap signal that there is behavioral homogeneity *within* sociometric categories, with children exhibiting similarity in their behavioral profiles. On the other hand, behavioral differences *between* groups indicate the discriminating power of sociometric categories. For example, rejected children should be discriminated by high levels of aggression, and popular children by low aggression.

Researchers can evaluate the concurrent validity of different classification schemes using the homogeneity and discriminability of their sociometric categories. For example, Newcomb and Bukowski (1983) compared their own scheme with the Peery and CDC Schemes using discriminate analysis, and employing behavioral scores from peer evaluations to validate the sociometric classifications from each scheme. The NB scheme was most successful in the overall classification of children. It produced greater numbers of "accurate" classifications of average children, but the classification accuracy of other sociometric types was slightly to significantly poorer. None of the schemes was successful at accurately classifying neglected children and the NB Scheme showed no success in correctly classifying controversial children. Other studies have also found the controversial and neglected categories are the most disputed, with some authors claiming that in behavioral terms, these categories cannot be adequately separated from the average category (French & Waas, 1985; Rubin, Lemare, & Lollis, 1990). Researchers could shed more light on the validity of such classifications by *first* identifying children with extreme characteristics salient to peer group status, and *then* examining the frequency with which they fall into different sociometric groups.

Concurrent validation of sociometric classifications is described above, but predictive validation is also needed as evidence for the accuracy of classification. Researchers can obtain predictive validity evidence using longitudinal designs and a variety of outcome measures over different time intervals. In this way predictive validity estimates for different sociometric categories are available over short-term to long-term temporal periods. As evidence accumulates about the correlation between initial sociometric classifications and children's behaviour or characteristics at later stages in their development, it provides predictive validity evidence for sociometric categories (Hymel, Vaillancourt, McDougall, & Renshaw, 2002). For example, Bukowski and Hoza (1989) demonstrated differences in self-concept between distinct sociometric categories over a one-year period, providing predictive validity evidence using the developmental outcomes of specific types of sociometric status. Such evidence gives researchers and educators confidence that sociometric categories are clinically meaningful, and that sociometric classification can accurately identify children at risk.

ESTABLISHING THE RELIABILITY OF SOCIOMETRIC CLASSIFICATIONS

Validity estimates increase investigators' confidence that sociometric categories are meaningful. Reliability estimates on the other hand indicate how consistent these classifications are over time. Reliability of sociometric classification therefore involves the temporal stability of different sociometric categories.

Researchers developing their own classification schemes need to provide temporal stability evidence for their sociometric categories. This can be achieved by using longitudinal research designs involving comparisons of children's status categories at several different time points, giving an indication of both short- and longer-term stability of sociometric categories. Using an adequate sample of children so that attrition does not deplete numbers too greatly, researchers should examine the *proportion* of children in the sample who are included in the same category at different time points. Non-parametric statistics such as chi squared can be used to statistically test any differences that are found between the numbers of stable classifications and those that change over time. Investigators can also use this method to examine the temporal stability of specific sociometric categories. For example, the temporal stability of the rejected category could be determined by examining the proportion of children classified as rejected at Time 1 who are also classified as rejected at Time 2.

Investigators opting to use existing classification schemes should critically examine the stability evidence achieved by other authors. For example, Newcomb and Bukowski (1984) demonstrated that the classifications for elementary school children produced by several popular classification schemes were unstable over six to18 months. However, for all sociometric categories the NB Scheme had greater short-term temporal stability than either the Peery or the CDC Schemes. Rejected status was more stable than either neglected or controversial status. Asher and Dodge (1986) reported similar short-term stability for the categories produced by their ratings-based classification scheme.

Investigators need to interpret the temporal stability data relating to young children with circumspection. The peer relationships of preschool children and children in the early elementary years are more dynamic, therefore classification of this age group is typified by change. Both ratings- and nominations-based classifications typically show that around half the children change category over periods of six months to one year (e.g., Olson & Brodfeld, 1991; Walker, 2009). Therefore researchers should not necessarily construe that low reliability coefficients indicate inconsistent sociometric instruments and unreliable classification *methods*. Instead, low reliability coefficients might simply be an artefact, reflecting a developmental period where children's peer group status is still emerging, and is thus more fluid than in middle childhood.

USING GROUP PREFERENCE RECORDS FOR SOCIOMETRIC CLASSIFICATION

The previous sections outline the weaknesses of ratings- and nomination-based sociometric classification schemes, as well as their problematic validity and reliability, especially for use with young children. These problems can be traced to the base measures used to derive the social impact and social preference indices needed for classification. Both sociometric nominations and ratings pose conceptual and task-related difficulties for young children, because of this age group's cognitive limitations. These difficulties have already been discussed in detail in earlier sections. This section offers researchers a solution, by using the responses on group preference schedules to classify children. It has already been demonstrated how group preference schedules overcome the challenges and shortcomings of both limited-choice nominations and sociometric ratings for young children. It therefore makes sense for researchers to base classification young children on measures that are more suited to their specific requirements.

In classification schemes founded on limited-choice nominations, the discrepancy between the small number of nominations allowed and the larger pool of possible nominees frequently produces skewed distributions of nominations. In these distributions there is a great deal of information about a few individuals in the group (those who are frequently nominated), and little or no information about the majority (those who are rarely or never nominated). Because of this *lack* of information, investigators must make inferences about a significant proportion of any group, instead of relying on the "certainties" allowed by the *presence* of their information. Many of the validity and reliability problems of nominations-based classification schemes can be traced to these measurement limitations. It would therefore be preferable to measure social preference and social impact, the keys to classification, by using full information about all group members rather than partial information about some. Group preference records offer this opportunity.

Sociometric classification based on group preference records has several advantages over nomination- and ratings-based classification schemes. It is founded on sociometric measures canvassing the opinions of all group members and thus overcomes measurement problems associated with limited-choice nominations and sociometric ratings. This multi-alternative forced-choice approach effectively tests the sociometric limits by asking children to evaluate all other group members using one of several alternatives—for example the HIFTO's choices of *friend* (accepted), *nonfriend* (rejected), *neither friend nor nonfriend* (tolerated) and *not known* (Agard et al., 1978a). The inclusion of *not known* and *tolerated* options increases the validity of children's choices. Toleration responses permit a sociometric "shade of grey" which is an alternative to either rejecting or accepting group members as friends. The *not known* option allows children to evaluate group members who do not seem to fit any of the other descriptors. This option is potentially a more ecologically valid and sensitive indicator of neglected status than the social impact dimension used in nomination-based classification schemes.

Sociometric test developers using group preference records can base classifications *directly* on aggregated individually-generated independent evaluations of all group members. Newcomb and Bukowski (1983) advocate using "independent measures of social preference and social visibility" (p. 865). Nonetheless, their own nomination-based classification scheme and as well as other schemes, rely instead on *indirect* and incomplete information about group members and on nonorthogonal measures of social impact and social preference. From the range of available sociometric assessment methods, only group preference records allow comprehensive and independent measures of these dimensions by virtue of their roster-based forced-choice format. Respondents must evaluate a target child as *not known* if she is not sufficiently familiar to be evaluated using the remaining descriptors. Measuring social impact (i.e., visibility) directly using the *not known* alternative, would therefore mean that social preference and social impact indices are in fact independent of each other. This is because the *not known* alternative is methodologically and conceptually separated from the remaining response alternatives, all of which measure social preference. As well, using the *not known* and *tolerated* alternatives in a forced choice format effectively separates the "don't know" from the "don't care" dimensions which are confounded in the social impact indices of nomination-based classification schemes.

A direct measure of social impact using a *not known* evaluation appears to be a more valid method of ascertaining the problematic sociometric category of *neglected* children. Classification schemes such as the CDC and NB Schemes typify neglected children as those with rare or statistically low social impact indices, computed from the sum of positive and negative nominations received. However, limited-choice nominations do not exhaustively evaluate all group members, adding to the uncertainty of evaluation, and therefore the lower reliability and validity of this category (Newcomb & Bukowski, 1984; French & Waas, 1985; Rubin, Lemare, & Lollis, 1990). On the other hand, a *not known* alternative independently evaluates the social impact (i.e., visibility) of all group members. In other words, if an individual is not well enough known to be evaluated in terms of their social preference (e.g., HIFTO's *friend, nonfriend* or *tolerated*), they are automatically given a *not known* evaluation. Evaluating neglected or low visibility children this way is therefore more likely to reflect social realities rather than the limitations of the measurement technique itself. Validity and reliability estimates for a group preference record-based neglected/low visibility category should be better than estimates found so far for the neglected categories of nomination-based schemes.

Development of the HIFTO Classification Scheme

Burton Smith, Ball, and Davidson (2012) used principal components analysis of data ($n = 906$) from the HIFTO manual (Agard et al., 1978b), to establish the parameters of a classification scheme based on a group preference record. Three orthogonal factors loading highly on each of HIFTO Neutrals (tolerations), Frowns (rejections), and Questions (don't knows) emerged. The developers used toleration and rejection, the two *independent* social preference factors that emerged from the analysis, to form the dimensions of a two-dimensional orthogonal model for the classification scheme. An acceptance vector represented by HIFTO Smiles was drawn at an oblique angle from the model's origin—the intersections of the toleration and rejection axes. This was based on the relative loadings that acceptance showed on each of the toleration and rejection factors, and defined the sections of the model representing the different status categories. The authors therefore established the parameters of the classification model by examining the actual structure of base responses from the HIFTO. This procedure contrasts with the development of the CDC and NB Schemes where the structure and meaning of sociometric categories as well as the orthogonal nature of the dimensions were assumed rather than subjected to prior validation.

Burton Smith et al. (2012) applied the HIFTO Classification Scheme to a set of data ($n = 308$) grade 3 to 6 children. This allowed for evaluation of the suitability of the scheme for early elementary to late elementary aged school children. Nonetheless, the HIFTO Scheme appears to be suitable for even younger children at preschool level, because it is based on data from a group preference record which is highly accessible by this population. However, the scheme still requires formal evaluation for preschoolers.

The HIFTO Classification Scheme departs from the commonplace practice using *a priori* criteria for separating average from extreme sociometric status, for example in the NB Scheme which arbitrarily sets the criteria for "rare" scores at less than 5% of cases. Instead, the developers of the HIFTO Classification Scheme considered the actual *distributions* of sociometric scores from specific samples prior to setting inclusion/exclusion criteria. So, the number of HIFTO question, smile, neutral and frown evaluations received by individuals were first standardized within grade. Two factor scores were then calculated for each subject by multiplying their scores for acceptance, rejection, toleration, and visibility by the relevant factor loadings from the principal components analysis. A computer graphing program produced a scatterplot based on the two-dimensional model described above. A circle of radius 1.5 *SDs* was then drawn from the origin of the model. Cases falling inside the circle and closer to the model's origin were classified as *average* children while the remaining 29% outside the circle were considered to be sociometrically extreme children. Areas encompassing four extreme sociometric classifications were established by precise geometric subdivision of the model, using the five categories of popular, rejected neglected controversial and average children. *Popular* children fall into the sector defined by the toleration axis, and a vector bisecting the angle between the acceptance vector and the toleration axis. *Rejected* children are defined by a line drawn from the origin which excludes children with positive acceptance scores, and another line bisecting the quadrant containing children with both positive toleration and rejection factor scores. Children in the sector between the rejected and popular children are *controversial*, with positive acceptance and rejection factor scores. Cases located in the sector between popular and rejected children constitute *neglected* children, all of whom are regarded with a greater than average degree of indifference by their peers (i.e., HIFTO "don't knows").

Assessing the Validity of the HIFTO Classification Scheme

Burton Smith et al. (2012) classified 109 Grade 3 to 5 children using the HIFTO, CDC and NB Schemes. Despite targeting a proportion of extreme classifications that was similar to the CDC scheme, the proportional distribution of cases between the five sociometric categories was significantly different. When the HIFTO and CDC *average* categories were equalized by making CDC classifications exhaustive, significant differences disappeared. The HIFTO and NB Schemes produced similar sized average groups, but the proportional distribution of extreme categories was significantly different. Overall, the HIFTO Scheme yielded sociometric classification groups most similar in size to the CDC Scheme.

Cross-tabulations and proportional distribution comparisons with existing schemes provide concurrent validity evidence for the HIFTO Classification Scheme. Cross-tabulations of cases classified by the HIFTO, CDC and NB Schemes suggested that the HIFTO Scheme is fairly robust, producing classifications which overlap with those of established schemes, at least to the degree that established schemes overlap with each other. When the factors influencing scheme overlap were controlled, the HIFTO Scheme classified more concordantly with the CDC and NB Schemes than they did between themselves. The HIFTO Scheme's classification of cases was most similar to the NB Scheme, due to the exhaustiveness of both schemes. However, when the CDC and HIFTO schemes were equalized for exhaustiveness, their concordance level was greater.

Evidence of criterion-based validity for the HIFTO Scheme was provided by discriminate analysis. This revealed the HIFTO Scheme to be at least as accurate in classifying children as the NB Scheme, which is the most successful nomination-based scheme in correctly classifying subjects according to their behavioral profiles (Newcomb & Bukowski, 1983). Over 80% of the sample was correctly classified, data which are consistent with the success rate for the NB scheme.

Uses and Limitations of the HIFTO Classification Scheme

Group preference record-based classifications such as the HIFTO offer several advantages over existing classification schemes. The factor structure of the HIFTO was used to establish an orthogonal two-dimensional model for classification. The scheme is therefore able to allocate children to categories which are based on tested structural assumptions. HIFTO classification yields five sociometric categories similar to other widely used classification schemes. However, unlike other schemes it readily provides a comprehensive social map of the reference group as well. The technique precisely locates every group member in two-dimensional space according to their relative scores on social preference measures. This information can be used to advantage in a variety of educational applications. For example, the HIFTO Scheme graphic with names identifying individuals, could be used in kindergarten classes to give educators and psychologists a clear and precise visual indication of the relative social standing of each member of the class. The distance of individual children in any category from the circular line dividing average from extreme peer group status gives immediate visual feedback about their degree of deviation from average status. For example, two children might be located in the sector defining rejected children. One child however is located close to the periphery of the model while the other is much nearer to the centre of the model and therefore to the average group of children. In this way educators could easily identify the child most in need of intervention—the child nearer to the periphery of the diagram.

CONCEPTUAL AND PRACTICAL RESTRICTIONS OF SOCIOMETRIC CLASSIFICATION

The French philosopher Michel Foucault maintained that all classifications are by nature limited as representations of natural orders because they cannot adequately represent the full range of dimensions by which items can be classified (Bukowski & Hoza 1989). Therefore classification per se is problematic, because of what it leaves out and not because of what it includes. The elegance of sophisticated schemes such as those described above can however be seductive. The elaborate dimensions created to accommodate natural phenomena may become self-serving and cease to reflect the real-life actualities they are meant to represent. This can be seen in the lack of validity for the controversial and neglected sociometric categories which continue to be used in research. These categories did not even exist in Peery's (1979) original two-dimensional classification scheme until they were added during later advances in methodology.

Classifying children may not necessarily indicate something meaningful, but instead, the artificiality of the scheme itself. The evidence for the existence of popular and rejected children is fairly firm, but there is a lack of similar evidence for other less distinctive typologies. This raises the possibility of classification schemes synthetically creating artificial statuses. For example, significant numbers of children classified as controversial and neglected by schemes based on limited-choice nominations might well be casualties of imperfect systems for identifying such children. The lack of validity evidence coupled with the lower temporal stability of these categories should prompt investigators to regard them critically from a theoretical, empirical and practical viewpoint. For example, some researchers seriously question the clinical significance of the neglected category (e.g., Hymel & Rubin, 1985). The relative rarity of controversial children is also suspicious—they might simply be misclassified rejected and neglected children

(Newcomb & Bukowski, 1983). Prophetically, in 1984 Berndt wrote that "The last word on classification schemes for use with sociometric data has probably not been written" (p. 37).

ETHICAL CONSIDERATIONS FOR YOUNG CHILDREN'S PARTICIPATION IN SOCIOMETRIC ASSESSMENTS

Researchers recognise that young children are a vulnerable population due to various developmental factors. Investigators collecting sociometric data from this age group therefore need to carefully consider the question of possible harm from collecting this social information. Eliciting negative peer evaluations in particular raises ethical issues. Identification of rejected and controversial children for example, increases the salience of less accepted group members, and possibly provides opportunities for peer-based and adult typecasting and consequent mistreatment.

However, empirical evidence has repeatedly shown an absence of harmful social consequences from sociometric studies with school-age and preschool children (e.g., Ballard, et al., 1977; Asher & Hymel, 1981; Hayvren & Hymel, 1984; Ratiner, Weissberg, & Caplan, 1986; Bell-Dolan, Foster, & Sikora, 1989; Bell-Dolan, Foster, & Tishelman, 1989; Bell-Dolan, Foster, & Christopher, 1992; Jones, Young, & Friman, 2000). Reviewing the evidence, Denham and Burton (2003) maintain that taking part in sociometric investigations where there are negative evaluations, involves no increased risk for young children than everyday experiences in preschool and day care settings. Foster and Crain (2002) claim that the absence of adverse effects might be attributed to pre-emptive measures in the studies reviewed, such as sensitively wording negative sociometric questions, refraining from sociometric evaluations just prior to free play periods; embedding sociometric procedures in other distracter activities and obtaining agreements from children not to disclose their responses; precautions that Denham and Burton strongly stipulate.

Despite evidence to the contrary, concern persists about detrimental effects of identifying children as social rejects, and this can be a significant factor in low consent rates for children's participation in sociometric studies. Sociometric researchers ideally need to collect *full* data sets based on the aggregated attractions and repulsions of an intact reference group. Exclusion of group members as evaluators and targets can profoundly affect sociometric data collection and analysis. Low participation rates are an acknowledged problem, and are a potential hazard to the validity and reliability of findings (Iverson & Cook, 1994). Seventy to 75% of a group should be included in data collection for valid and stable sociometric measures. If researchers collect unlimited nominations, 60% participation may be sufficient (Cillessen, 2009; Hymel, Closson, Caravita, & Vaillancourt, 2011).

Nonparticipation of sociometrically extreme children might have more impact on research results than the exclusion of average children, biasing results and thus the sociometric picture of the group. It is also possible that sociometrically extreme children such as rejectees, are less likely to participate in sociometric research, given the heightened sensitivity of these children and their parents to peer relations issues. It is unrealistic for researchers to expect perfect participation in every reference group, but they should acknowledge nonparticipation as a potential biasing factor in their sociometric data. They should clearly document and present *participation rates* in each sociometric reference group, so that the effects of non-participation on the data collected can be objectively evaluated by others. Prior to seeking consent, researchers should fully inform parents and guardians about the research procedures and reassure them about possible risks. Appropriate parent education can therefore facilitate consent, and increase participation *rates* (Iverson & Cook, 1994; Denham & Burton, 2003).

Informed consent is an essential prerequisite for the collection of all data pertaining to individuals. Data collection in institutions such as schools and day care centers usually involves approvals at a number of levels, with different stakeholders involved—institutional ethics committees, administrators such as school principals, child workers and teachers whose groups are the focus of data collection, and the parents of potential child participants. This multi-level process can erect obstacles to participation. For example, at a school district level, a lack of approval for research can eliminate whole schools from participation. School principals, teachers and day care centre managers can block classes and groups from research participation. Parents may preclude individual children from participating in research. This impacts differentially on the representativeness of the data collected; from the representativeness of schools in a system for instance, to the classes within a school. Participating classes for example might differ fundamentally in class climate than non-participating classes. More serious threats to sociometric data sampling are within the reference group—from a lack of parental or guardian consent and the subsequent elimination of individual children as evaluators and targets for evaluation.

The effect of non-participation in sociometric data collection means that all evaluations that would otherwise have been provided by non-participants is omitted from the database. It is impossible to gauge the effect of this missing information about the remaining members of the group. However, data *pertaining to* nonparticipants is sometimes available, for example through children making spontaneous nominations of nonparticipating group members. These nominations would be excluded from any subsequent data analysis for the sample, but they allow a fortuitous sociometric profile of non-participating children to be drawn for comparison with the larger sample of participants, and therefore an estimate of the effects of missing cases on the overall representativeness of the data. Checking data representativeness is important, particularly when low participation rates occur.

CONCLUSIONS

Sociometric assessment of young children's peer group status and friendships has enjoyed considerable advances over the past 80 years since these aspects of children's peer relations were first investigated. There are now myriad approaches and variants of techniques to evaluate these important dimensions of children's peer relationships. This chapter provides a practical, methodological, and ethical map for the sociometric researcher, hopefully assisting them to cut a clear path through a veritable jungle of possibilities in selecting and developing suitable sociometric tools for pursuing research with young children.

REFERENCES

Aboud, F. E., Mendelson, M. J., & Purdy, K. T. (2003). Cross-race peer relations and friendship quality. *International Journal of Behavioral Development, 27*, 165–173.

Agard, J. A., Veldman, D. J., Kaufman, M. J., & Semmel, M. I. (1978a). *How I feel towards others: An instrument of the prime instrument battery.* Washington, D.C.: US Office of Education, Bureau of Education for the Handicapped.

Agard, J. A., Veldman, D. J., Kaufman, M. J., & Semmel, M. I. (1978b). *How I feel towards others: an instrument of the prime instrument battery. Technical Report.* Washington, DC: US Office of Education, Bureau of Education for the Handicapped.

Asher, S. R., & Dodge, K. A. (1986). Identifying children who are rejected by their peers. *Developmental Psychology, 22*, 444–449.

Asher, S. R., & Hymel, S. (1981). Children's social competence in peer relations: Sociometric and behavioural assessments. In J. D. Wine & M. D. Smye (Eds.), *Social competence* (pp. 125–157). New York, NY: Guilford Press.

Asher, S. R., & Renshaw, P. D. (1981). Children without friends: Social knowledge and social skills training. In S. Asher & J. Gottman (Eds.) *The development of children's friendships* (pp. 273–296). Cambridge, MA: University of Cambridge Press.

Asher, S. R., Singleton, L. C., Tinsley, B. R., & Hymel, S. (1979). A reliable sociometric measure for preschool children. *Developmental Psychology, 15*, 443–444.

Asher, S. R., & Taylor, A. R. (1982). Social outcome of mainstreaming: Sociometric assessment and beyond. In P.S. Strain (Ed.), Social development of exceptional children (pp. 13–30). Rockville, MA: Aspen.

Aydt, H., & Corsaro, W. A. (2003). Differences in children's construction of gender across culture: An interpretive approach. *American Behavioral Scientist 46*, 1306–1325.

Ballard, M., Corman, L., Gottlieb, J., & Kaufman, M. J. (1977). Improving the social status of mainstreamed retarded children. *Journal of Educational Psychology, 69*, 605–611.

Barbu, S. (2003). Stability and flexibility in preschoolers' social networks: A dynamic analysis of socially directed behavior allocation. *Journal of Comparative Psychology, 117*, 429–439.

Bell-Dolan, D. J., Foster, S. L., & Christopher, J. S. (1992). Children's reactions to participating in a peer relations study: An example of cost-effective assessment. *Child Study Journal, 22*, 137–156.

Bell-Dolan, D., Foster, S. L., & Sikora, D. M. (1989). Effects of sociometric testing on children's behavior and loneliness in school. *Developmental Psychology, 25*, 306–311.

Bell-Dolan, D. J., Foster, S. L., & Tishelman, A. C. (1989). An alternative to negative nomination sociometric measures. *Journal of Clinical Child Psychology, 18*, 153–157.

Berndt, T. J., (1984) Sociometric, social-cognitive, and behavioral measures for the study of friendships and popularity. In T. Field, J. L. Roopnarine & M. Segal (Eds), *Friendship in normal and handicapped children*, (pp. 31–52). Norwood, NJ: Ablex.

Berndt, T. J. (2002). Friendship quality and social development. *Current Directions in Psychological Science, 11*, 7–10.

Berndt, T. J., Hawkins, J. A., & Hoyle, S. G. (1986). Changes in friendship during a school year: Effects on children's and adolescents' impressions of friendship and sharing with friends. *Child Development, 57*, 1284–1297.

Berndt, T. J., & Hoyle, S. G. (1985). Stability and change in childhood and adolescent friendships. *Developmental Psychology, 21*, 1007–1015.

Berndt, T. J., & Perry, T. B. (1986). Children's perceptions of friendships as supportive relationships. *Developmental Psychology, 22*, 640–648.

Blanton, P. W., Smith, D. J., Davidson, P. M., & Popper, W. A. (1992). Peer acceptance in middle childhood among rural and urban boys and girls. *Journal of Genetic Psychology, 154*, 237–248.

Boivin, M., & Begin, G. (1986). Temporal reliability and validity of three sociometric status assessments with young children. *Canadian Journal of Behavioural Science, 18*, 167–172.

Bonney, M. E. (1954) Choosing between the sexes on a sociometric measurement. *Journal of Social Psychology, 39*, 99–114.

Bost, K. K., Vaughn, B. E., Washington, W., Cielinski, K., & Bradbard, M. (1998). Social competence, social support and attachment: Demarcation of construct domains, measurement, and paths of influence for preschool children attending Head Start. *Child Development, 69*, 192–218.

Brendgen, M., Little, T. D., & Krappmann, L. (2000). Rejected children and their friends: A shared evaluation of friendship quality. *Merrill-Palmer Quarterly, 46*, 45–70.

Bronfenbrenner, U. (1943). A constant frame of reference for sociometric research. *Sociometry, 6*, 363–396.

Bronfenbrenner, U. (1944). A constant frame of reference for sociometric research. Part II. Experiment and inference. *Sociometry, 7,* 40–75.

Bruininks, R. H., Rynders, J. E., & Gross, J. C. (1974). Social acceptance of mildly retarded pupils in resource rooms and regular classes. *American Journal of Mental Deficiency, 78,* 377–383.

Buhs, E. S., Ladd, G. W., & Herald, S. L. (2006). Peer exclusion and victimization: Processes that mediate the relation between peer group rejection and children's classroom engagement and achievement. *Journal of Educational Psychology, 98,* 1–13.

Bukowski, W., Gauze, C., Hoza, B., & Newcomb, A. (1993). Differences and consistency between same-sex and other-sex peer relationships during early adolescence. *Developmental Psychology, 29,* 255–263.

Bukowski, W. M., & Hoza, B. (1989). Popularity and friendship: Issues in theory, measurement and outcome. In T. Berndt & G. Ladd (Eds.), *Peer relations in child development* (pp. 15–45). New York, NY: Wiley

Bukowski, W. M., Hoza, B., & Newcomb, A. F. (1994). Using rating scale and nomination techniques to measure friendship and popularity. *Journal of Social and Personal Relationships, 11,* 485–488.

Bukowski, W. M., Sippola, L. K., Hoza, B., & Newcomb, A. F. (2000). Pages from a sociometric notebook: An analysis of nomination and rating scale measures of acceptance, rejection and social preference. In A. Cillessen & W. Bukowski (Eds.) *Recent advances in the study and measurement of acceptance and rejection in the peer system.* (Volume no. 88 in the *New Directions for Child Development Series,* pp. 11–26). San Francisco: Jossey Bass.

Bullock, J., Ironsmith, M., & Poteat, G. M. (1988). Sociometric techniques with young children: A review of psychometrics and classification schemes. *School Psychology Review, 17,* 289–303.

Burton Smith, R., Davidson, J. A., Ball, P. J., (2001) Age-related variations and sex differences in gender cleavage during middle childhood, *Personal Relationships, 8,* 153–165.

Burton Smith, R., Ball, P., & Davidson, J. (2012). *Development and validation of a roster-based sociometric classification scheme.* Unpublished report, School of Psychology, University of Tasmania, Australia.

Cillessen, A. H. N. (2009). Sociometric methods. In K. Rubin, W. Bukowski, & B. Laursen, (Eds), *Handbook of peer interactions, relationships and groups* (pp. 82–99). New York, NY: Guilford Press.

Cillessen, A. H. N., Bukowski, W. M., & Haselager, G. J. T. (2000). Stability of sociometric categories. *New Directions for Child and Adolescent Development, 88,* 75–93.

Cillessen, A. H. N., & Marks, P. E. L. (2011). Conceptualizing and measuring popularity. In A. Cillessen, D. Schwartz, & L. Mayeux (Eds.), *Popularity in the peer system* (pp. 25–56). New York, NY: Guilford Press.

Cillessen, A. H. N., & Rose, A. J. (2005). Understanding popularity in the peer system. *Current Directions in Psychological Science, 14,* 102–105.

Cohen, A. S., & Van Tassel, E. A. (1978). A comparison of partial and complete paired comparisons in sociometric measurement of preschool groups. *Applied Psychological Measurement, 2,* 31–40.

Coie, J., Dodge, K., & Coppotelli, H. (1982) Dimensions and types of social status: A cross-age perspective. *Developmental Psychology, 18*, 557–570

Coie, J. D., Dodge, K. A., & Kupersmidt, J. B. (1990). Peer group behavior and peer group social status. In S. R. Asher & J. D. Coie (Eds.), *Peer rejection in childhood* (pp. 17–59). Cambridge, UK: Cambridge University Press.

Coie, J. D., Dodge, K. A., Terry, R., & Wright, V. (1991). The role of aggression in peer relations: an analysis of aggression episodes in boys' play groups. *Child Development 62*, 812–826.

Coie, J. D., & Kuperschmidt, J. B. (1983). A behavioural analysis of emerging social status in boys' groups. *Child Development 54*, 1400–1416.

Coplan, R. J., & Arbeau, K. (2009). Peer interactions and play in early childhood. In K. H. Rubin, W. Bukowski, & B. Laursen (Eds.), *Handbook of peer interactions relationships, and groups* (pp. 143–161). New York, NY: Guilford Press.

Denham S. A., & Burton R. (2003). *Social and emotional prevention and intervention programming for preschoolers.* New York, NY: Kluwer Academic/Plenum Publishers.

Denham, S. A., & McKinley, M. (1993). Sociometric nominations of preschoolers: A psychometric analysis. *Early Education and Development, 4*, 109–122.

Dodge, K. A., Coie, J. D., Pettit, G. S., & Price, J. M. (1990). Peer status and aggression in boys' groups: Developmental and contextual analyses. *Child Development 61*, 1289–1309.

Dodge, K. A., Lansford, J., Burks, V., Bates, J., Pettit, G., & Fontaine, R. (2003). Peer rejection and social information processing factors in the development of aggressive behaviour problems in children. *Child Development, 74*, 374–393.

Dodge, K. A., Schlundt, D. C., Schocken, I., & Delugach, J. D. (1983). Social competence and children's sociometric status: The role of peer-group entry strategies. *The Merrill-Palmer Quarterly, 29*, 309–336.

Dunnington, M. J. (1957). Investigation of areas of disagreement in sociometric measurement of preschool children. *Child Development, 28*, 93–102.

Dygdon, J. A., & Conger, A. J. (1990). A direct nomination method for the identification of neglected members in children's peer groups. *Journal of Abnormal Child Psychology, 18*, 55–74.

Evans, K. M. (1966). *Sociometry and education.* London: Lowe & Brydon Ltd.

Fabes, R. A., Martin, C. L., & Hanish, L. D. (2004). The next 50 years: Considering gender as a context for understanding young children's peer relationships. *Merrill-Palmer Quarterly, 50*, 260–273.

French, D. C. (1988). Heterogeneity of peer-rejected boys: Aggressive and nonaggressive subtypes *Child Development, 59*, 976–985.

French, D. C. (1990). Heterogeneity of peer-rejected girls. *Child Development, 61*, 2028–2031.

French, D. C., & Waas, G. A. (1985). Teachers' ability to identify peer-rejected children: A comparison of sociometrics and teacher ratings. *Journal of School Psychology, 23*, 347–353.

French, D. C., Waas, G. A., & Tarver-Behring, S. A. (1986). Nomination and rating scale sociometrics: Convergent validity and clinical utility. *Behavioral Assessment, 8*, 331–340.

Foster, S. L., Bell-Dolan, D., & Berler, E. S. (1986) Methodological issues in the use of sociometrics for selecting children for social skills research and training. *Advances in Behavioral Assessment of Children and Families, 2,* 227–248.

Foster, S. L., & Crain, M. M. (2002). Social skills and problem-solving training. In F. W. Kaslow & T. Patterson (Eds.) *Comprehensive handbook of psychotherapy Vol 2 Cognitive-behavioral approaches* (pp. 31–50). New York, NY: Wiley.

Gazelle, H., & Ladd, G. W. (2003). Anxious solitude and peer exclusion: A diathesis-stress model of internalising trajectories in childhood. *Child Development, 74,* 257–278.

Gest, S. D., Graham-Bermann, S. A., & Hartup, W. W. (2001).Peer experience: Common and unique features of number of friendshipos, social network, centrality, and sociometric status. *Social Development, 10,* 23–40.

Gifford-Smith, M. A., & Brownell, C. (2003). Childhood peer relationships: Social acceptance, friendships and peer networks. *Journal of School Psychology, 41,* 235–284.

Gleason, T. R. (2002). Social provisions of real and imaginary relationships in early childhood. *Developmental Psychology, 38,* 979–992.

Goldman, J. A., Corsini, D. A., & de Urioste, R. (1980). Implications of positive and negative sociometric status for assessing the social competence of young children. *Journal of Applied Developmental Psychology, 1,* 209–220.

Goodman, H., Gottlieb, J., & Harrison, R. H (1972). Social acceptance of EMRs integrated into a nongraded elementary school. *American Journal of Mental Deficiency, 76,* 412–417.

Gottlieb, J., & Budoff, M. (1973). Social acceptability of retarded children in nongraded schools differing in architecture. *American Journal of Mental Deficiency, 76,* 412–417.

Gottlieb, J., Semmel, M. I., & Veldman, D. J. (1978). Correlates of social status among mainstreamed mentally retarded children. *Journal of Educational Psychology, 70,* 396–405.

Gottman, J., Gonzo, J., & Rasmussen, B. (1975).Social interaction, social competence, and friendship in children. *Child Development, 46,* 709–718.

Gresham, F. M. (1981). Validity of social skills measures for assessing social competence in low-status children: A multivariate investigation. *Developmental Psychology, 17,* 390–398.

Gronlund, N. E. (1959). *Sociometry in the classroom.* New York, NY: Harper.

Hallinan, M. T. (1981). Recent advances in sociometry. In S. Asher & J.Gottman (Eds.) *The development of children's friendships* (pp. 91–115). New York, NY: Cambridge University Press.

Hart, C. H., Yang, C., Nelson, L. J., Robinson, C. C., Olsen, J. A., Nelson, D. A., et al. (2000). Peer acceptance in early childhood and subtypes of socially withdrawn behaviour in China, Russia and the United States. *International Journal of Behavioral Development, 24,* 73–81.

Hartup, W. W., & Abecassis M. (2004). Friends and enemies. In P. K. Smith and C. H. Hart (Eds.), *Blackwell handbook of of childhood social development* (pp. 285–306). Malden MA: Blackwell.

Hay, D., Payne, A., & Chadwick, A. (2004). Peer relations in childhood. *Journal of Child Psychiatry and Psychology and Allied Disciplines, 45,* 84–108.

Hayden-Thomson, L., Rubin, K. & Hymel, S. (1987). Sex preferences in sociometric choices. *Developmental Psychology, 23,* 558–562.

Hayvren, M., & Hymel, S. (1984). Ethical issues in sociometric testing: The impact of sociometric measures on interaction behavior. *Developmental Psychology, 20*, 844–849.

Hops, H., & Lewin, L. (1984). Peer sociometric forms. In T.H. Ollendick & M. Hensen (Eds.), *Child behavioral assessment: Principles and approaches* (pp. 124–147). New York, NY: Pergamon.

Hymel, S. (1983). Preschool children's peer relations: Issues in sociometric assessment. *Merrill-Palmer Quarterly, 29*, 237–260.

Hymel, S., & Asher, S. R. (1977). *Assessment and training of isolated children's social skills*. Paper presented at the biennial meeting of the Society for Research in Child Development (New Orleans, Louisiana, March 17–20, 1977).

Hymel, S., Closson, L. M., Caravita, S. C., & Vaillancourt, T. (2011). Social status among peers: From sociometric attraction, to peer acceptance to perceived popularity. In P. K. Smith & C. H. Hart (Eds.) *The Wiley-Blackwell Handbook of child social development* (pp. 375–392). Malden, MA: Wiley-Blackwell Publishing.

Hymel, S., & Rubin, K. A. (1985). Children with peer relationship and social skills problems: Conceptual, methodological and developmental issues. In G. Whitehouse (Ed.) *Annals of child development* (Vol. 2, pp. 251–297). Greenwich, CT: JAI Press.

Hymel, S., Vaillancourt, T., McDougall, P., & Renshaw, P. (2002). Acceptance and rejection by the peer group. In P.Smith & C Hart. (Eds.) *The Blackwell handbook of childhood social development* (pp. 265–284) London: Blackwell.

Iverson, A. M., & Cook, G. L. (1994). Guardian consent for children's participation in sociometric research. *Psychology in the Schools, 31*, 108–112.

Jones, D. C. (1984). A multidimensional analysis of social organization in samesex groups of young children. *Ethology and Sociobiology, 5*, 193–202.

Jones, K. M., Young, M. M., & Friman, P. C. (2000). Children's long-term reactions to participating in sociometric assessment. *Psychology in the Schools, 33*, 103–112.

Kafer, N. F., & Shannon, K. A. (1986). Identification of rejected and neglected children. *Psychological Reports, 59*, 163–168.

Kalfus, G. R., & Berler, E. S. (1985). Test–retest reliability of sociometric questionnaires across four grade levels. *Journal of Clinical Child Psychology, 14*, 345–347.

Kane, J. S., & Lawler, E. E. (1978). Methods of peer assessment. *Psychological Bulletin, 85*, 555–586.

Kaplan, R. M., & Saccuzzo, D. P. (2009). *Psychological testing: Principles, applications and issues* (7th ed.). Belmont: Thompson Wadsworth.

Kaufman, M., Agard, J. A., & Semmel, M. I. (1985). *Mainstreaming: Learners and their environment*. Cambridge, MA: Brookline Books.

Keane, S. P., & Calkins, S. D. (2004). Predicting kindergarten peer social status from toddler and preschool problem behavior. *Journal of Abnormal Child Psychology, 32*, 409–423.

Koch, H. L. (1933). Popularity among preschool children: Some related factors and a technique for its measurement. *Child Development, 4*, 164–175.

Koch. H. L. (1944) A study of some factors conditioning the social distance between the sexes. *The Journal of Social Psychology, 20*, 79–107.

Ladd, G. W. (1983). Social networks of popular, average, and rejected children in school settings. *Merrill-Palmer Quarterly, 29*, 283–307.

Ladd, G. W. (2005). *Children's peer relations and social competence: A century of progress.* New Haven, CT: Yale University Press.

Ladd, G. W. (2006). Peer rejection, aggressive or withdrawn behavior, and psychological maladjustment from ages 5 to 12: An examination of four predictive models. *Child Development, 77,* 822–846.

Ladd, G. W., & Ettekal, I. (2009).Classroom peer acceptance and rejection and children's psychological and school adjustment. *Interpersonal Acceptance 1,* 1–3.

Ladd, G. W., Herald, S. L., Slutzky, C.B., & Andrews, R. K. (2004). Preventive interventions for peer group rejection. In L. Rapp-Paglicci, C. N., Dulmus, & J. S. Wodarski (Eds.), *Handbook of preventioninterventions for children and adolescents* (pp. 15–48). New York, NY: Wiley.

Ladd, G. W., Kochenderfer, B. J., & Coleman, C. C. (1997). Classroom peer acceptance, friendship, and victimization: Distinct relational systems that contribute uniquely to children's school adjustment? Child development, *68,* 1181–1197.

Ladd, G. W., & Troop-Gordon, W. (2003). The role of chronic peer difficulties in the development of children's psychological adjustment problems. *Child Development, 74,* 1344–1367.

Landau, S., Milich, R., & Whitten, P. (1984) A comparison of teacher and peer assessment of social status. *Journal of Clinical Child Psychology, 13,* 44–49.

Lazarus, P. J., & Weinstock, S. (1984). Use of sociometric peer nominations in classifying socially ignored versus socially rejected children. *School Psychology International, 5,* 139–146.

Lee, L., Howes, C., & Chamberlain, B. (2007). Ethnic heterogeneity of social networks and cross-ethnic friendships of elementary school boys and girls. *Merrill-Palmer Quarterly 53,* 325–346.

Lemann, T. B., & Solomon, R. L. (1952). Group characteristics as revealed in sociometric patterns and personality ratings. *Sociometry Monographs* (p. 27). Boston: Beacon House.

Lemerise, E. A. (1997). Patterns of peer acceptance, social status, and social reputation in mixed-age preschool and primary classrooms. *Merrill-Palmer Quarterly, 43,* 199–218.

Lippit, R. (1941). Popularity among preschool children. *Child Development, 12,* 305–332.

Lyndzey, G., & Byrne, D. (1968). Measurement of social choice and interpersonal attractiveness. In G. Lyndzey & F. Aronsen, (Eds.), *The handbook of social psychology* (2nd ed., Vol. 2., pp. 542–512) Reading, Mass.: Addison-Wesley.

Maassen, G. H., van Boxtel, H. W., & Goossens, F. A.. (2005). Reliability of nominations and two-dimensional rating scale methods for sociometric status determination. *Applied Developmental psychology, 26,* 51 –68.

Maccoby, E. E. (2000). Perspectives on gender development. I*nternational Journal of Behavior Development, 24,* 398–406

McCandless, B. R., & Marshall, H. R. (1957). A picture sociometric technique for pre-school children and its relation to teacher judgments of friendship. *Child Development, 28,* 139–149.

Martin, C. L., & Fabes, R. A. (2001). The stability and consequences of young children's same-sex peer interactions. *Developmental Psychology, 37,* 431–446.

Masten A. S., & Coatsworth, J. D. (1998). The development of competence in favourable and unfavourable environments. *American Psychologist, 53*, 205–220.
Masters, J. C., & Furman, W. (1981). Popularity, individual friendship selection and specific peer interactions among children. *Developmental Psychology, 17*, 344–350.
Moore, S., & Updegraff, R. (1964). Sociometric status of preschool children related to age, sex, nurturance-giving, and dependency. *Child Development, 35*, 519–524.
Moreno, J. L. (1934/1978). *Who shall survive? A new approach to the problems of human interrelations.* Washington, DC: Mental Diseases Publishing Co.
Moreno, J. L. (1978). *Who shall survive? Foundations of sociometry, group psychotherapy and sociodrama.* Beacon, N Y: Beacon House Inc.
Morrison, G. M. (1981a). Sociometric measurement: Methodological consideration of its use with mildly learning handicapped and nonhandicapped children. *Journal of Educational Psychology, 73*, 193–201.
Morrison, G. M. (1981b). Perspectives of social status of learning handicapped and nonhandicapped students. *American Journal of Mental Deficiency, 86*, 243–251.
Morrison, G. M., Forness, S. R., & MacMillan, D. L. (1983). Influences on the sociometric ratings of mildly handicapped children: A path analysis. *Journal of Educational Psychology, 75*, 63–74.
Musun-Miller, L (1990) Sociometrics with preschool children: Agreement between different strategies. *Journal of Applied Developmental Psychology, 11*, 195–207.
Nelson, D. A., Robinson, C. C., & Hart, C. H. (2005). Relational and physical aggression of preschool-age children: Peer status linkages across informants. *Early Education and Development, 16*, 115–139.
Newcomb, A. F., & Bukowski, W. M. (1983). Social impact and social preference as determinants of children's peer group status. *Developmental Psychology, 19*, 856–867.
Newcomb, A.F., & Bukowski, W.M. (1984). A longitudinal study of the utility of social preference and social impact sociometric classification schemes. *Child Development, 55*, 1434–1447.
Newcomb, A. F., Bukowski, W. M., & Pattee, L. (1993). Children's peer relations: a meta-analytic review of popular, rejected, neglected, controversial and average sociometric status. *Psychological Bulletin, 113*, 99–128.
Newman, B. M., & Newman, P. R. (2001). Group identity and alienation: Giving the We its due. *Journal of Youth and Adolescence, 30*, 515–538.
Newstetter, W. I., Feldstein, M. J., & Newcomb, T. M. (1938). *Group adjustment: a study in experimental sociology.* Cleveland, OH: School of Applied Social Sciences, Western Reserve University.
Oden, S., & Asher, S. R. (1977). Coaching children in social skills for friendship making. *Child Development, 48*, 495–506.
Olson, S. L., & Brodfeld, P. L. (1991). Assessment of peer rejection and externalizing behavior problems in preschool boys: A short-term longitudinal study. *Journal of Abnormal Child Psychology, 19*, 493–503.
Olson, S. L., & Lifgren, K. (1988). Concurrent and longitudinal correlates of preschool peer sociometrics: Comparing rating scale and nomination measures. *Journal of Applied Developmental Psychology, 9*, 409–420.

Parker, J. G., & Asher, S. R. (1987). Peer relations and later personal adjustment: Are low-accepted children at risk? *Psychological Bulletin, 102,* 357–389.

Parker, J. G., & Asher, S. R. (1993). Friendship and friendship quality in middle childhood: Links with peer group acceptance and feelings of loneliness and social dissatisfaction. *Developmental Psychology 29,* 611–621.

Parker, J. G., Rubin, K. H., Price, J. M., & deRosier, M. E. (1995). Peer relationships, child development and adjustment: A developmental psychopathology perspective. In D. Chichetti & D. Cohen, (Eds.) *Developmental psychopathology, Vol. 2: Risk, disorder and adaptation,* (pp. 96–161). New York, NY: Wiley.

Parten, M. B. (1932). Social participation among preschool children. *Journal of Abnormal and Social Psychology, 27,* 243–269.

Peery, J. C. (1979). Popular, amiable, isolated and rejected: A reconceptualization of sociometric status in preschool children. *Child Development, 50,* 1231–1234.

Poteat, G, M., Ironsmith, M., & Bullock, J. M. (1986). The classification of preschool children's sociometric status. *Early Childhood Research Quarterly, 1,* 349–360.

Ramsey, P. G. (1995). Changing social dynamics in early childhood classrooms. *Child Development, 66,* 764–773.

Ratiner, C Weissberg, R. & Caplan, N. (1986) *Ethical considerations in sociometric testing: The reaction of preadolescent subjects.* Paper presented at the 94th annual meeting of the American psychological association, Washington, DC.

Reese, H. W. (1962). Sociometric choices of the same and opposite sex in late childhood. *Merrill-Palmer Quarterly, 8,* 173–174.

Reese, H. W. (1966). Attitudes towards the opposite sex in late childhood. *Merrill-Palmer Quarterly, 12,* 157–163.

Roistacher, R. C. (1974). A microeconomic model of sociometric choice. *Sociometry, 37,* 219–238.

Rubin, K. H., Bukowski, W., & Parker, J. (2006). Peer interactions, relationships and groups. In W. Damon & R.Lerner (Eds.) *Handbook of child psychology* (6th edn). New York, NY: Wiley.

Rubin, K. H., LeMare, L. J., & Lollis, S. (1990). Social withdrawal in childhood: Developmental pathways to peer rejection. In S. R. Asher & J. D. Coie (Eds.), *Peer rejection in childhood* (pp. 17–59). Cambridge, England: Cambridge University Press.

Rucker, C. N., Howe, C. E., & Snider, B. (1969). The participation of retarded children in junior high academic and non-academic regular classes. *Exceptional Children, 35,* 617–623.

Sagar, H. A., Schofield, J. W., & Snyder, H. N. (1983). Race and gender barriers: Preadolescent peer behaviour in academic classrooms. *Child Development, 54,* 1032–1040.

Schofield, J. W., & Whitley, B. E. (1983). Peer nomination vs. rating scale measurement of children's peer preferences. *Social Psychology Quarterly, 46,* 242–251.

Schwarzwald, J. (1991). The use of sociometric indices in appraising social relations in the heterogeneous classroom. Special Issue: Facet theory and its applications. *Megamot, 33,* 549–563.

Scott, J. (1991). *Social network analysis: A handbook.* London: SAGE.

Shannon, K. & Kafer, N. F. (1984). Reciprocity, trust, and vulnerability in neglected and rejected children. *The Journal of Psychology, 117,* 65–70.

Sherif, M., & Sherif, C. (1956). *An outline of social psychology.* New York, NY: Harper.

Singleton, L. C., & Asher, S. R. (1977). Peer preferences and social interaction among third grade children in an integrated school district. *Journal of Educational Psychology, 69,* 330–336.

Singleton, L. C., & Asher, S. R. (1979). Racial integration and children's peer preferences: An investigation of developmental and cohort differences. *Child Development, 50,* 936–941.

Spinrad, T. L., Eisenberg, N., Harris, E., Hanish, L., Fabes, R. A., Kupanoff, K., et al. (2004). The relations of children's everyday non-social peer play behavior to their emotionality, regulation and social functioning. *Developmental Psychology, 40,* 67–80.

St. John, N. H., & Lewis, R. G. (1975). Race and the social structure of the elementary classroom. *Sociology of Education, 48,* 346–368.

Sullivan, H. (1953). *The interpersonal theory of psychiatry.* New York, NY: Norton.

Terry, R., & Coie, J. (1991). A comparison of methods for defining sociometric status among children. *Developmental Psychology, 27,* 867–880.

Thompson, G. G., & Powell, M. (1951). An investigation of the rating-scale approach to the measurement of social status. *Educational and Psychological Measurement, 11,* 440–455.

Vaughn, B. E., Colvin, T. N., Azria, M. R., Caya, L., & Krzysik, L. (2001). Dyadic analyses of friendship in a sample of preschool children attending Head Start: Correspondence between measures and implications for social competence. *Child Development, 72,* 862–878.

Vaughn, B., & Waters, E. (1981). Attention structure, sociometric status, and dominance: Interrelations, behavioral correlates and relationships to social competence. *Developmental Psychology, 17,* 275–288.

Vitaro, F., & Boivin, M. (1989). Peer rejection and adaptation problems among children: Measurement and intervention. *Science et Comportement, 19,* 271–294.

Vogel, J., Conger, J. C., & Keane, S. P. (1985). Comparability of peer-assessment measures: A multitrait-multimethod and selection analytic approach. *Journal of Psychopathology and Behavioral Assessment, 7,* 385–396.

Walker, S. (2009). Sociometric stability and the behavioral correlates of peer acceptance in early childhood. *The Journal of Genetic Psychology, 170,* 339–358.

Walter, J. L., & LaFreniere, P. J. (2000). A naturalistic study of affective expression, social competence and sociometric status in preschoolers. *Early Education and Development, 11,* 109–122.

Wood, J. J., Cowan, P. A., & Baker, B. L. (2002). Behavior problems and peer rejection in preschool boys and girls. *The Journal of Genetic Psychology, 163,* 72–88.

Wu, X., Hart, C. H., Draper, T. W., & Olsen, J. A. (2001). Peer and teacher sociometrics for preschool children: Cross-informant concordance, temporal stability and reliability. *Merrill-Palmer Quarterly, 47,* 416–443.

Zeleny, L. D. (1940). Measurement of social status. *American Journal of Sociology, 45,* 576–582.

Zeleny, L. D. (1960). Status: Its measurement and control in education. In J. Moreno, H. Jennings, J, Criswell, L. Katz, R. Blake, J. Mouton, M. Bonney, M. Northway, C. Loomis, R. Taguiri, & J Nehnevojsa (Eds.), *The sociometry reader.* (pp. 261–265) Glencoe, IL: The Free Press.

CHAPTER 4

USING Q METHODOLOGY IN CONDUCTING RESEARCH WITH YOUNG CHILDREN

Aesha John, Diane Montgomery,
and Amy L. Halliburton Tate

INTRODUCTION

Early childhood research is increasingly focused on participatory approaches, involving children and their families in the research process (Clark, 2005; Darbyshire, Schillera, & MacDougall, 2005; Smith, Duncan, & Marshall, 2005). This shift in philosophy has created a need for a methodology that is simple enough to capture children's voices and at the same time sufficiently detailed, complex, and rigorous to reflect the diversity in the early childhood population. Indeed, the current trends in early childhood research provide rich opportunities for the utilization of Q methodology. Throughout the past several decades, researchers in the field of early childhood have been challenged to broaden the scope and nature of their research with young children. This call to expand the early childhood research paradigm is multidimensional in nature, stemming from several key movements, including those with a focus on social justice and children's rights as well as a focus on exploring cultural diversity in child development. This more comprehensive

Handbook of Research Methods in Early Childhood Education, pages 147–173
Copyright © 2015 by Information Age Publishing
All rights of reproduction in any form reserved.

research paradigm reflects an emphasis on capturing both subjective and objective data, particularly through participatory research involving children, and can benefit from Q methodology.

Traditional research in early childhood education is characterized as being objective in nature, primarily utilizing quantitative methods for gathering data (Barker & Weller, 2003; Darbyshire et al., 2005). Whereas quantitative methods employing experimental designs, observations, questionnaires, and assessment tools provide valuable information about children, they do not provide a viable alternative for gathering children's own perspectives. In part, this is because researchers are concerned that young children might lack the ability to comprehend and accurately respond to survey questions (Scott, 2008). Thus, this type of research is rightfully thought of as research *on* children, as opposed to research *with* children (Einarsdóttir, 2007). Otherwise known as participatory research, research *with* children enables scientists to conduct exploratory research in addition to evaluative research.

The paradigm shift towards participatory research finds its origins in social justice and the Children's Rights Movement, as well as the sociological and postmodern perspectives (Einarsdóttir, 2007). The 1989 United Nations Convention on the Rights of Children led to the recognition of children's legal rights to express their views and have a voice in decisions that affect them (MacNaughton, Smith, & Davis, 2007). This notion of children as "social actors" extends to early childhood research because involving children as active participants in the research process honors their rights to offer their own perspectives. Participatory research also emphasizes children as competent, active constructors of their experiences who are considered valuable, reliable informants (Clark, 2005; Darbyshire et al., 2005). As such, qualitative researchers have been effective in utilizing narrative methodologies, ethnography (e.g., Smith et al., 2005), and interviews (e.g., Davis, 2007; Irwin & Johnson, 2005; Nicholas, Picone, & Selkirk, 2011) in gathering children's own perspectives. However, qualitative approaches present issues such as children's limited ability to construct a narrative or participate in lengthy, in-depth procedures (Irwin & Johnson, 2005). This opens the door to research methodologies such as Q methodology that tap children's perspectives, attitudes, and opinions.

In addition to generating research that explores children's perspectives, researchers have been called to generate a stronger understanding of diversity in childhood experiences. Child development is inextricably linked to culture, as development occurs within a cultural context where children construct their understandings through interactions with the environment and important adults. Woodhead (1999) suggested a movement away from "textbook images" of child development and research seeking to uncover normative development. Early childhood researchers are challenged to move toward "more recognition of diverse environments and to reflect on culture in an inclusive way" (Gillen et al., 2007, p. 208). As researchers continue to explore and refine methodologies to better capture diversity in child development, Q methodology holds promise as a useful tool in this quest.

Hence, in this chapter, we describe Q methodology as an alternative to quantitative and qualitative approaches and highlight its relevance to the early childhood research field. The chapter begins with a detailed description of Q methodology. The steps in Q methodology are substantiated with examples from past early childhood research that utilized Q methodology. Next, we review the Q studies in early childhood field; although few past studies have utilized the methodology, the range of study topics demonstrates the potential of Q methodology in responding to a diverse set of questions. The subsequent section outlines the emerging trends in early childhood research and how these trends present opportunities for the use of Q methodology. We conclude with a section detailing issues that are pertinent to Q methodology. Specifically, we describe some variations within Q methodology, possible limitations of Q methodology and the potential place of Q methodology in the research toolkit.

USING Q METHODOLOGY

Q methodology was designed by William Stephenson (1953; 1967) and described in detail in several subsequent books (Brown, 1980; Watts & Stenner, 2012), monographs (McKeown & Thomas, 2013; van Exel & de Graaf, 2005), chapters (Brown, 1986; Brown, Durning, & Selden, 2008; Gallivan, 1994; Smith, 2001; Stenner, Watts, & Worrell, 2007; Wolf, 1997), and encyclopedia entries (Brown, 2008; Brown & Good, 2010; Robbins, 2005). Yet, with all of this information on relevance and strength of the Q methodology, many researchers remain seemingly unaware of the essential differences and strengths of this unique approach to capturing the viewpoint of individuals.

Q methodology has been recommended for conducting research in many disciplines and fields of study. For example, articles have appeared for research in accounting (Massingham, Massingham, & Diment, 2012), environmental science (Webler, Danielson, & Tuler, 2009), feminism (Kitzinger, 1999), human geography (Eden, Donaldson, & Walker, 2005; Robbins & Krueger, 2000), nursing (Akhtar-Danesh, Baumann, & Cordingley, 2008; Kanim, 2000), parenting (John & Halliburton, 2010), psychology (Watts & Stenner, 2005), and social work (Ellingsen, Storksen, & Stephens, 2010). Many researchers describe the technique, method, and methodology in detail as they report findings of studies. This reporting approach has probably been requested by editors or reviewers to build rigor into the methodology. Although the current electronic listserve (qmethod@kent.edu) of researchers using or curious about Q methodology numbers nearly 750, the use of this research strategy has been overshadowed by other research approaches for decades.

Stephenson garnered respect from his colleagues and students (see Brown & Brenner, 1972) for his innovation in factor analytic models and insightful philosophy of the close connection between research and practice. The procedure of the methodology is staged (sequential or stagewise); staged in this instance implies a step-by-step process, as opposed to a mixed method where the researcher may choose various steps at any stage. The procedure includes developing a concourse, sampling the concourse to result in the Q set, directing participants to sort the items, and analyzing and interpreting the data. Data analysis starts with correlating all items in one sort to the items in all sorts, factoring the correlation matrix, developing z-scores for the statements within each factor, and interpreting the resulting arrays or the typology. For this reason, the methodology is not necessarily mixed, yet includes both qualitative strategies (building the concourse and interpreting the results) and quantitative strategies (calculating correlation, factor analysis, z-scores).

Developing the Concourse

The concourse is considered to be the communicability or the possible responses in order to communicate personal meaning regarding the study topic; it represents a comprehensive set of items related to the research topic, and might be in the form of statements, images, photos, objects, or other medium of expression. The concourse is comprised of the limitless number of ways that can be used to express an opinion about the topic. Each item carries the potential to have a personal, self-referent response from someone who can relate to the topic. In other words, the items or statements are not of a factual nature (e.g., I will be in kindergarten, I am 5-years old, or I will eat lunch at school), which tend to draw yes or no responses and do not assist in communicating a 5-year old child's perspective about transitioning to a full-day program. Rather, the items are subjective and have the potential to draw a range of reactions that a 5-year old may have toward transitioning to a full-day program. For example:

- I am scared to be away from my mom for so long.
- I am excited I will get to spend more time with my friends.
- I will feel all grown-up when I get to spend the entire day in school.
- I want to be home when it is time for my nap.

There are several options for collecting the items in a concourse. One approach is the naturalistic method (McKeown & Thomas, 2013), which involves drawing statements (i.e., items for the Q set) from participants' oral or written responses. To construct a concourse using the naturalistic method, researchers often conduct participant interviews to learn more about the various perspectives and nuances regarding conditions and issues within the topic. Analyzing interview data for the concourse is different from qualitative analyses used to search for connectedness, themes, and common patterns. It is different, because in finding statements or ideas for the concourse, the Q methodology researcher must also incorporate minority views. The opinions that represent a full range of possible responses are chosen. Perspectives can be generated in group settings as well. Moseman (2003) utilized nominal group technique (NGT) to create a concourse for a study on early childhood educators' beliefs regarding the ways children's families can contribute to classroom practices. According to this technique, teachers met in groups of five to six to brainstorm. First, all participants silently recorded their responses to a set of questions; next, they shared their responses with the group and a facilitator recorded the responses on a chart; and finally, the groups discussed and reviewed the listed items. In addition, the researcher transcribed the interviews. Moseman combined the NGT statements with statements pertaining to family competence from experts (researchers and scholars) to create a concourse of 300+ items.

To develop a concourse, a number of past Q methodology studies in the field of early childhood education field have utilized publications as a resource. The National Association of Education for Young Children (NAEYC) publications on early childhood education standards and developmentally appropriate practices were utilized to construct concourses for studies on prevalent classroom practices (Bracken & Fischel, 2006), as well as an international study on beliefs about developmentally appropriate practices among parents and professionals in Hungary (Szente, Hoot, & Ernest, 2002). Similarly, Hurley and Horn (2010) used a list of characteristics developed by the Early Childhood Research Institute on Inclusion to develop a concourse for their study on the characteristics of inclusive classroom settings valued by families and professionals. Early childhood education researchers have also utilized empirical literature to develop a concourse. Sawyer and Campbell (2009) utilized empirical studies on best practices in early intervention to develop a concourse for their study on family participation in their children's early intervention services. Likewise, Hurley, Wehby, and Feurer (2010) used social competence intervention studies published during the previous 10 years to develop their concourse for social behavior goals. Berry (2010), on the other hand, utilized student essays to develop a concourse for a study on preservice and early childhood teachers' attitudes toward inclusion, instructional accommodations, and fairness.

Sampling the Concourse

Consistent with the Q methodology philosophy, the sampling process is representative of the phenomenon or topic under study. This is unlike a traditional factor analytic approach in which the focus is on testing traits in a sample drawn from a population of individuals. The researcher uses a structured or unstructured method to get a Q sample of the many possible items from the concourse. Under the structured method, the researcher uses one or more theories relevant to the research topic to construct a Q sample that has both breadth and depth. Using theory as the structure for sampling, the concourse can be categorized through grouping strategies to facilitate the selection of items that may represent all viewpoints, including a minority viewpoint. For example, in a study on teachers' perspectives of the arts in schools (Hull, 2005), the researcher combined Eisner's (1985) theory on the social contexts of society, school and individual, and Bresler's (1995) four arts integration theoretical categories of co-equal, social, emotional, and subservient integration of arts to education, to produce 12 categories (i.e., Eisner's three categories X Bresler's four categories). Next, the Q researchers tried to fit the 350+ statements collected through interviews into one of the 12 categories. For the statement that could not be accommodated within any of the 12 categories, the researcher added a new grouping of the arts integration category to the Bresler theory; the new category that represented a minority view combined into a single category, the "no arts integrated into other content areas" and "the social and emotional arts integration." This example represents a structured sampling approach, wherein the 12 theoretical areas were used to structure a Q set that consisted of statements articulating diverse opinions.

Another example of structured sampling comes from Berry's (2010) study on the attitudes of preservice and early career teachers regarding inclusion, instructional accommodations, and fairness. The items in the 24-item Q set were sampled to represent two attitudinal dimensions (anxious/confident and positive/negative) toward three areas (inclusion, instructional accommodations, and fairness). Two statements represented each of the 12 categories (4 dimensional extremes X 3 topics). For example, the statement "I think inclusion is a great thing, but I don't know if I myself will always know the perfect adjustment to make" was one of the two statements that represented the category "anxious" about one's own ability, but "positive" attitude toward "inclusion." Similarly, the statement, "I don't think I should have to make modifications for students with special needs" represented the category "confidence," "negative attitude," and "accommodations." The items were sampled from student essays. On the other hand, Moseman (2003) sampled items after conducting a thematic analysis of interview transcripts. To ensure diversity, Moseman drew Q items from each theme and sampled items from the concourse through factorial designs. Although it may seem complex, structured sampling combines the best practices of both naturalistic and theoretical structuring strategies to garner the greatest range in opinions related to the topic.

Under the unstructured approach to sample a concourse, two strategies are mainly utilized to gain a broad representation of the concourse. First, consistent with the homogeneity rule, all items that are alike in some respect are clustered together to generate groups. In the next step, the heterogeneity rule is followed to identify from each group a diverse set of items; each item represents a unique idea or response and makes up the final Q set (other terms used to describe the content of the Q instrument include Q sample, Q statements, and Q items), which usually contain 40–60 such items. Fewer items may be used for very young children. The set of statements or items may be balanced for stating some ideas in a more positive light and others in a more negative light. Researchers are cautioned about balance and are encouraged to recognize that too many negatives may prove cumbersome in the final interpretation of meaning.

Researchers can develop a Q set based on existing survey measures as well. Sexton, Snyder, Wadsworth, Jardine, and Ernest (1998) derived a Q set from a widely used rating scale for a study on family-centered practices that are valued by families receiving early intervention services. The rating scale questions were changed to statements and reworded to make them parent-focused instead of professional-focused. For example, "Do you ask parents what they want before telling them what the program does?" was changed to "Professionals ask parents what they want before telling them what the program does."

Preparing a Q Set

Once the Q set items are finalized, the next step is to design the Q set. The Q set is designed with the participants in mind, and a good Q set design can make the sorting procedure a fun and pleasant experience for the participants. Most Q sets consist of Q items printed on strips of paper or index cards and a sorting surface with a desired distribution pattern (see Figure 4.1). However, it

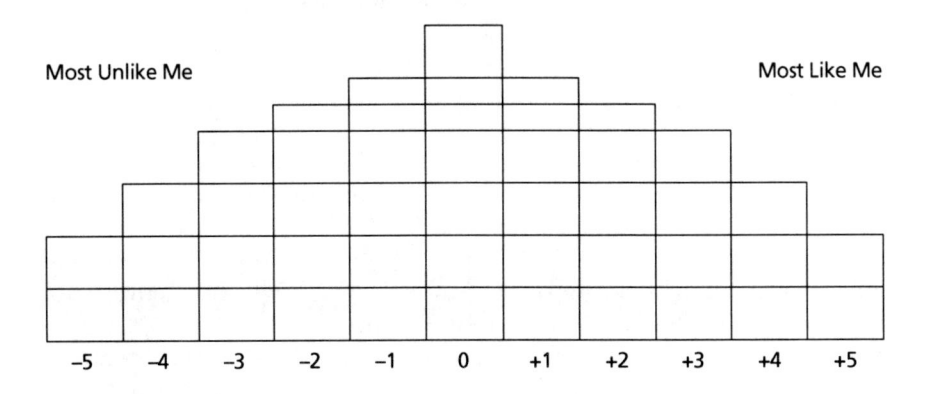

Figure 4.1 Q Sorting Format (Sample for 47 Items)

is possible to have several alternative formats. For example, Q researchers can use magnetic boards and print the Q set on magnetic cards. Magnetic boards and printing paper/cards are available at stores that carry craft and office supplies. With children as participants, it is also a good idea to use pictures for sorting. Figures 4.2 and 4.3 illustrate a preschool child sorting pictures to portray her feelings. Young children may sort toys or objects to communicate preferences or opinions. In a study that aimed to find common types of food choices among three-year olds, children were asked to sort plastic food into a range of bins. Another researcher explored young children's perceptions of art by having them bring in toys, symbols, or objects that were creative art in their opinion and used the unstructured approach (i.e., homogeneity and heterogeneity strategies; see previous section for details) to get a representative sample of objects for a Q set.

Furthermore, there are a number of programs available to conduct the sorting procedure electronically. Programs such as FlashQ (Hackert) and WebQSort (Correa) written by Q researchers can be downloaded for free from the program website. Studies in diverse disciplines have effectively utilized these programs to create participant-friendly online Q sets (e.g., Gruber, 2011). The online Q sets have an advantage in terms of having a wider geographical reach, which ultimately negates the qualities necessary in developing a representative group of people to perform the sort. Although young children may find the electronic format more attractive given their familiarity with and affinity for electronic devices, the face-to-face Q sort sessions often provide valuable information about participants' perspectives. Participants often voice their struggles and confusion as they carry out the sorting; this information can become part of the researchers' field notes and may be used in the post-analysis phase for interpretation of the viewpoints. Of course, it is possible to have an electronic Q set for in-person sorting procedures as well. Thus, it is important for a researcher to keep in mind these pros and cons while making a decision about the Q sorting format.

Selecting the *P* Set

The first decision for the Q researcher in the sorting stage is to purposively construct a *P* set, which consists of individuals who sort the Q set. It is important to find individuals who may hold diverse opinions or attitudes about the study concourse. Past early childhood education Q studies have mostly been conducted with professionals. Depending on the purpose of the study, the *P* sets have been comprised of pre-service teachers (e.g., Berry, 2010), classroom teachers (e.g., Bracken & Fischel, 2006; Szente et al., 2002), and early intervention service providers (e.g., Sawyer & Campbell, 2009). To make the *P* set heterogeneous, Moseman (2003) recruited

Using Q Methodology in Conducting Research With Young Children ■ **155**

Figure 4.2 Using images with young children.

Figure 4.3 Finalizing the sort of images.

primary school teachers from diverse school settings (urban, rural, suburban) who were teaching diverse groups of students (SES, ethnicity) to sort the Q set on developmentally appropriate practices.

To some extent, Q methodology has paved the way for more participatory research in early childhood education, and has enabled researchers to go beyond just service providers' views and seek out the perspectives of family members, who are widely considered to be the key stakeholders in early childhood education. The next step would be to involve young children in research, and rather than collect information *on* children, researchers can carry out research *with* children. Although only one published Q study in early child education research included children in its *P* set (Storksen, Thorsen, Overland, & Brown, 2012), studies in other disciplines demonstrate that the sorting task can be a viable and developmentally appropriate measure for garnering young children's views (De Mol & Buysse, 2008; Sickler et al., 2006).

It is important to note that unlike quantitative research, a large P-sample is not critical to derive findings from a Q study. The viewpoints or factors are considered salient even if they are generated from relatively few Q sorts. One rationale underlying this premise is that the possible ways that items could have been sorted constitute the sample size (N). In other words, the resulting viewpoints based on these sorts emerge despite all other possible combinations. Thus, the viewpoints are considered robust rather than a chance occurrence (John & Halliburton, 2010; Shemmings, 2006).

Furthermore, Q methodology endorses the principles of *atomic uniformity* and *finite diversity* (Brown, 1980), which maintain that although items can be sorted in infinite number of ways (atomic uniformity), the resulting factors can be saturated by relatively few sorts (finite diversity). To uncover robust factors, emphasis is placed on the variability of the *P*-set rather than its size (Smith, 2001). Thus, in early childhood education research, focus should be on gathering perspectives of a diverse set of stakeholders, including children, rather than a large number of participants. Consistent with this premise, some past early childhood education research studies have been carried out with small samples and have included small but diverse *P* sets (e.g., Hurley & Horn, 2010; Sexton et al., 1998). However, some studies have not adhered to this principle and have included *P* sets with more than 50 to 100 sorters (e.g., Berry, 2010; Bracken & Fischel, 2006), which likely contributed to neglecting a minority view and yielding strong one-factor solutions.

The Sorting

The sorters are instructed to sort in two phases with respect to a *condition of instruction*, which is a question the sorters try to address through the sorting process. Most researchers frame a simple condition of instruction such as, "Sort these statements based on your personal viewpoint." However, some researchers provide more elaborate instructions to avoid misinterpretation and ambiguity. For example, Hurley and Horn (2010) framed their condition of instruction as, "Here are the cards that you will sort according to which characteristics of an inclusive early childhood education program you value the most to those you value the least" (p. 340). Overall, it is important to frame a condition of instruction that is clear for the participants to understand and to include definitions for ambiguous terms. On the other hand, sometimes the condition of instruction can simply ask the participant to sort the statements from *most agree* to *most disagree*. Similarly, it is also important to have a corresponding distribution pattern. If the condition of instruction asks the participants to "sort statements based on personal viewpoint," the anchor points would range from *most unlike my viewpoint* to *most like my viewpoint*, whereas if the condition of instruction is "what characteristics do you value?", the anchor points would range from *most not valued* to *most valued*.

Asking a group of people to sort one time is considered an extensive *P* set (McKeown & Thomas, 2013), whereas asking only one person to sort multiple times is an intensive *P* set. For example, an early childhood teacher might sort a set of statements according to the following conditions of instruction in order to discover her perceptions of development:

- What were you like before you started school?
- What is expected of a five-year old?
- What might advanced development for a three-year old look like?
- What did your mother say about you before you started school?
- What was your oldest child like at age five?
- What was your youngest child like at age five?

Intensive studies are often carried out over multiple sessions to ensure against participant fatigue and clear recall of the previous sort. The sorting procedure is conducted in two phases. In the first phase, the sorter is required to read all the statements in the Q set, and put each statement in one of three piles of *most like me, most unlike me,* and a pile in the middle that represents *neutral* or *undecided*. This phase facilitates initial familiarity with the content, while strong positive and negative reactions begin to form in the sorter's mind. In the next phase, the sorter rank orders the statements. This is done through a forced-choice distribution, such that the sorter first places items about which he/she has the strongest opinion in the "most like" and "most unlike" piles; sorters are encouraged to work back and forth until they arrange all the Q set items in a predefined quasi normal distribution pattern (see Figure 4.1). It is important to inform the sorters that they will have a chance to make changes, even after the items are placed in the sorting pattern; knowing that they can rearrange items frees them from worrying about the initial placement.

Group administration is a viable option and has been successfully utilized with teachers of young children, teacher educators, and parents as a means of investigating issues of concern in the field of early childhood. Careful planning before data collection assures that ample data sources are available to aid in the interpretation of findings. If the Q sorts are being carried out in person, the researcher can record relevant participant comments during the sorting process. These comments can later facilitate factor interpretation.

Data Analysis

After data are collected, each of the n sorts is correlated with all other sorts to construct an $n \times n$ correlation matrix. In other words, if the Q set has 40–60 items (statements, pictures, drawings, etc.), all of the item placements are used to calculate the correlation to items in other sorts. The resulting correlation matrix is factor analyzed and rotated as necessary. The unrotated matrix, the results of a varimax rotation, or a hand rotation based on theory or practical considerations may be used to determine the final set of factors. A factor matrix (matrix of factor loadings) of the final set of factors includes the participant sorts that significantly and distinctly define each factor. Figure 4.4 illustrates a factor matrix (X indicates defining sorts) from Weis' (2010) study aimed to explore early childhood educators' perceptions of children's creative leadership characteristics. The three factors in Weis' study were derived from nine early childhood educators' sorts of 47 items in response to three conditions of instructions:

1. What do you believe about your current group of students?
2. What do you believe to be the characteristics of the ideal student?
3. What do you believe to be the characteristics of an adult leader for whom you would like to work?

Next, the defining sorts of each factor (indicated by X in Figure 4.4) are used to calculate a Q item z-score (factor score) for that specific factor. Figure 4.5 illustrates the Q-item z-scores for one out of the three factors from Weis' (2010) study. Finally, the Q item z scores are used to construct the hypothetical ideal sort (also known as factor array). To construct the factor array, the items with the highest z-score are placed in the *most like* column and the items with lowest score are placed in the *most unlike me* column. Figure 4.6 illustrates the factor array for "transformational leadership" factor

QSORT	Transformational	Charismatic	Servant
1 TK02ECEN	0.3045	0.7626X	0.1876
2 TK02ECEF	0.2008	0.2876	0.7690X
3 TK02ECEL	0.0874	0.2523	0.8299X
4 SP03ECEN	0.5950X	0.2474	0.2854
5 SP03ECEF	0.5681	−0.0138	0.5877
6 SP03ECEL	0.3868	0.0012	0.7559X
7 TP01ALTN	0.1764	0.8037X	0.1185
8 TP01ALTF	0.2170	0.4504	0.6969X
9 TP01ALTL	−0.0453	0.4354	0.7212X
10 T122ECEN	0.5002X	0.4284	0.1868
11 T122ECEF	0.5045	0.1823	0.6256
12 T122ECEL	0.1013	0.0081	0.8263X
13 TK01ECEN	0.6530X	0.4074	0.2393
14 TK01ECEF	0.5290X	0.4121	0.4062
15 TK01ECEL	0.2875	0.3272	0.6257X
16 TK23ECEN	0.4629	0.5271X	0.2427
17 TK23ECEF	0.7045X	0.2217	0.3801
18 TK23ECEL	0.5157	0.1713	0.5979
19 TPK1ALTN	0.2155	0.6557X	0.0338
20 TPK1ALTF	0.3738	0.3788	0.6410X
21 TPK1ALTL	0.3387	0.2709	0.7372X
22 TPKK13EN	0.7504X	0.2342	0.0050
23 TPKK13EF	0.8012X	0.2293	0.2685
24 TPKK13EL	0.4148	0.0972	0.7408X
25 T0207ECN	0.6208X	0.2417	0.2768
26 T0207ECF	0.5665	−0.0112	0.6433
27 T0207ECL	0.3174	−0.0844	0.8138X
% expl. Var.	22	14	31

Figure 4.4 Factor matrix from Weis' (2010) study on Early Childhood Teachers' Perceptions of Children's Creative Leadership Characteristics. X indicates a defining sort.

from Weis' study, which was constructed based on z-scores illustrated in Figure 4.5. Note that the statements with the highest factor scores (e.g., Asking questions about puzzling things, wants to know; Energetic, vigorous) in Figure 4.5 are placed in the +5 (*most value*) column in Figure 4.6, and statements with the lowest factor scores (e.g., Disturbing procedures and organization of the group; Quiet, not talkative) are placed in the −5 (*most not value*) column in Figure 4.6.

Typically, the results consist of two to five factor arrays, which are interpreted for meaning. Data sources for interpretation include the factor scores associated with the statements (e.g., Figure 4.5), post-sort interview

FACTOR 1 TRANSFORMATIONAL LEADERSHIP (self, others, groups, organization)

No.	Statement	No.	Z-SCORES
4	4 Asking questions about puzzling things, wants to know	4	2.101
17	17 Energetic, vigorous	17	1.801
36	36 Sense of humor	36	1.499
22	22 Industrious, busy	22	1.435
20	20 Guessing, hypothesizing	20	1.419
42	42 Talkative, verbally fluent	42	1.206
21	21 Independent in thinking	21	1.094
34	34 Self-starting, initiating	34	1.071
27	27 Never bored, always interested	27	1.043
41	41 Stubborn, obstinate	41	−1.046
10	10 Critical of others	10	−1.195
18	18 Fault-finding, objecting, criticizing	18	−1.246
32	32 Reserved, suppressing feelings	32	−1.431
14	14 Domineering, controlling	14	−1.535
19	19 Fearful, apprehensive	19	−1.632
12	12 Disturbing procedures and organization of the group	12	−1.715
30	30 Quiet, not talkative	30	−2.116

Figure 4.5 Q item (statement) Factor Scores (z-scores) for Factor named 'Transformational Leadership' from Weis' (2010) study on Early Childhood Teachers' Perceptions of Children's Creative Leadership Characteristics.

data, demographic information of participants with the defining sorts, and field notes taken while sorting. Utilizing these sources, the researcher develops a holistic description of the factor as well as gives names to the factors or viewpoint that reflect a generalization of their meaning. For example, the three factors that emerged in Weis' (2010) study on early childhood teachers' perceptions of children's creative leadership characteristics were named transformational, charismatic, and servant leadership. In their study exploring daycare children's experiences of divorce, Størksen et al. (2012) named their three factors—well adjusted, mixed feeling, and sadness.

In addition, *consensus items*, which are those statements that achieved similar ratings across all viewpoints, present an opportunity and a practical strategy to build collaboration or community across factors or viewpoints. In contrast, *distinguishing items* indicate the opinions that represent the strongest differences between factors or viewpoints. In summary, the data are analyzed by determining an underlying structure using the position of the statements in the Q sorts to construct a correlation matrix, carrying out factor analysis and rotation, and deriving z-scores for each Q item. The underlying structure is interpreted using multiple sources of quantitative comparisons and qualitative information of the sorters that define the group.

Using Q Methodology in Conducting Research With Young Children ▪ 161

-5	-4	-3	-2	-1	0	1	2	3	4	5
					6 Becoming preoccupied with tasks					
				44 Truthful, even when it hurts	23 Intuitive, insightful	5 Attempting difficult tasks				
			26 Neat and orderly	16 Emotionally aware/sensitive	13 Doing work on time	31 Receptive to ideas of others	35 Self-sufficient			
		25 Obedient, submissive to authority	11 Determined, unflinching	3 Altruistic working for good of others	15 Feeling/expressing emotions strongly	8 Courteous, polite	2 Affectionate, loving	34 Self-starting, initiating		
		18 Fault-finding, objecting, criticizing	1 Adventurous, testing limits	40 Striving for distant goals	28 Persistent, persevering	37 Sincere, earnest	33 Self-confident	27 Never bored, always interested	22 Industrious, busy	
12 Disturbing procedures & organization of the group	14 Domineering, controlling	41 Stubborn, obstinate	7 Conforming, strictly follows rules	46 Willing to accept judgments of authority	29 Popular, well-liked	38 Socially well-adjusted	39 Spirited in disagreements	21 Independent in thinking	20 Guessing, hypothesizing	4 Asking questions about puzzling things, wants to know
30 Quiet, not talkative	19 Fearful, apprehensive	10 Critical of others	24 Liking to work alone	45 Unwilling to accept things on mere say-so	43 Thorough, exhaustive	9 Competitive, trying to win	47 Willing to take risks	42 Talkative, verbally fluent	36 Sense of humor	17 Energetic, vigorous
32 Reserved, suppressing feelings										

Figure 4.6 Factor Array for Factor named 'Transformational Leadership' from Weis' (2010) study on Early Childhood Teachers' Perceptions of Children's Creative Leadership Characteristics.

User-friendly statistical software packages specifically designed for Q sort analysis can be downloaded for free from the Q methodology website (http://qmethod.org/links). Two analytic software packages that have been used in a number of past Q studies include the PQMethod (Schmolck, 2012) and PCQ (Stricklin, 2010) programs. In both programs, once the researcher enters all the participant Q sorts into the program, the program automatically constructs a correlation matrix, conducts a factor analysis, carries out a varimax rotation, computes item z-scores, and generates lists of differentiating and consensus statements.

Reliability

As the Q methodology's focus is on subjectivity, reliability is of little concern to most Q researchers. Some Q researchers, however, have chosen to examine consistency of participant responses through repeated sorts; participants carry out the sorting task more than once, and their repeated sort is compared to the original one to establish reliability or stability of the participant's response. A significant correlation between the two sorts or non-significant *t*-test finding for the difference between the two sorts is used as a reliability indicator. Consistent reliability analysis methods have been employed in past early childhood education Q studies. In Bracken and Fischel's (2006) study, a year after the original sort, 13 out of 66 participants sorted the Q set a second time; their sorts from both time points were significantly correlated and had a non-significant *t*-test finding. In another study, test-reliability was assessed by having 36 practitioners sort the Q set twice within a 15-month interval (Sawyer & Campbell, 2009). Sorts from both time points were significantly correlated, thereby indicating stability or reliability of participant responses.

Validity

As most Q studies focus on subjective topics such as beliefs and perceptions, validity of the instrumentation is of little concern to Q methodologists. To ensure understandability and comprehensibility of the items, some researchers pilot test their Q set with individuals who have a similar background to that of the targeted participants (Bracken & Fischel, 2006). Having the zero, neutral, or middle columns allows for the placement of statements or items that have little meaning or salience to the sorter. However, validity has been addressed in terms of the findings, particularly in the interpretation of the theoretical arrays and the likely bias that researchers might impose on the emergent statement/item arrays.

There are two common techniques used to encourage Q researchers to be reflective, open-minded, and not overly influenced by the theoretical foundation with which they may have started in sampling the concourse. One way to remind the researcher about the temptation of seeing one's own point of view as the correct viewpoint is to perform the sort and add the researcher sort into the analysis. Quickly, the factor matrix provides a comparison of the researcher's view (sort) with the other sorters. Another way of checking the validity of the interpretations of findings is through a post-sort interview. The interview provides the researcher with an opportunity to verify whether the description of the viewpoint accurately reflects participants' beliefs.

Opinion of content and language experts is one way to establish the face validity and content validity of the Q items (Szente et al., 2002); yet, the statements or Q items have no meaning until they are sorted. Moreover, how they might be sorted is unrelated to any apriori categories conceptualized by researchers. To verify their Q study findings, Bracken and Fischel (2006) compared the clusters derived through Q methodology to scores on a standardized measure. Their study assessed existing preschool classroom practices in New York Head Start centers. The two clusters of activities derived through Q sorts, socioemotional and cognitive, were consistent with and significantly correlated to observation ratings of a subsample of classrooms on Early Childhood Evaluation Ratings Scale (ECERS-R; Harms, Clifford, & Cryer, 2005), a standardized classroom observation protocol.

CURRENT APPLICATIONS IN EARLY CHILDHOOD EDUCATION

To shed light on the current status of Q methodology in early childhood research, we review past studies in the field that have utilized Q methodology and conclude with recommendations about early childhood topics that would benefit from the use of Q methodology. Our literature search through the electronic databases PsycInfo and ERIC, using keywords "early childhood" and "Q methodology," yielded a total of 18 publications. Out of those 18, only nine were selected for review as the remaining were either not peer-reviewed or utilized Q methodology procedures that are vastly different from those articulated by Stephenson (1935/1953). Based on their research topic, we grouped the studies in three broad categories: classroom practices, family participation, and inclusion.

Classroom Practices

Szente et al. (2002) carried out a Q methodology study in Hungary to assess teachers' and parents' beliefs about developmentally appropriate practices. Their Q set was based on National Association for the Education of Young Children (NAEYC) guidelines and included 30 items that NAEYC considers developmentally appropriate and 30 items that NAEYC considers developmentally inappropriate. Analysis of the sorts indicated three dominant viewpoints. The first viewpoint emphasized *children's individual development and learning* activities as most developmentally appropriate, the second viewpoint considered *academic practices* (e.g., testing) as most developmentally appropriate, and the third viewpoint regarded *diversity and family involvement* related items as most developmentally appropriate. The researchers carried out postsort interviews and identified subthemes within each viewpoint. These subthemes suggested that each viewpoint included both types of practices: practices that NAEYC considers developmentally appropriate as well as those that it considers inappropriate. These findings illustrate the intracultural diversity of viewpoints among Hungarian parents and teachers, and also indicate that certain practices considered appropriate in the US may not be culturally appropriate in Hungary. Additionally, "belief in developmentally appropriate practices" is not a dichotomous construct (believe or not believe), but rather a diverse construct wherein participants hold viewpoints that endorse a combination of appropriate and inappropriate practices. Standardized questionnaires are likely to miss this diversity of viewpoints.

Rather than teacher beliefs, Bracken and Fischel (2006) used Q methodology to assess existing preschool classroom practices in New York Head Start centers. This study is unique and important because it illustrates that Q methodology is suitable not only for exploring beliefs but also to examine prevalent practices. Sixty-six preschool teachers from nine Head Start centers sorted the items. The results of the Q sort analysis revealed two clusters of activities—Socioemotional and Cognitive—that are characteristic of early childhood classrooms. The participants sorted cognitive or literacy activities as *less characteristic* in preschool classrooms. Moreover, certain activities typically identified as cognitive (e.g., shared book reading, library use) received high scores in the socioemotional cluster.

Finally, Hurley et al. (2010) used Q methodology to evaluate the goals of social skills interventions provided in early childhood education settings. They obtained views of early childhood educators, early childhood special educators, and administrators regarding the social skills that they believed were important for young children to have. This was done to see if the educators' views of children's social competence matched with goals of social competence interventions. Analysis of 36 Q sorts generated three viewpoints with respect to desired social skills in young children. Participants with the first viewpoint believed it was important for interventions to reduce negative behaviors, those with second viewpoint wanted interventions to promote prosocial behaviors, and individuals with the third viewpoint wanted interventions to focus on children's communications skills and good manners.

Family Participation in Early Childhood Education and Intervention

Moseman's (2003) research examined what early childhood educators believed about how children's families can contribute to classroom practices. Three factors were discovered through the analysis of 43 Q sorts. Teachers who identified with the first viewpoint *valued* family competence and believed that parents (a) know their children best, (b) can provide feedback about how classroom practices affect their children, (c) have primary responsibility for their children, and (d) can provide cultural inputs. The study not only helped to identify a viewpoint, but specific behaviors valued by individuals holding the viewpoint. Moreover, within the *valuers* category, the researcher identified high and low valuers based on their factor loadings and interview responses. The second viewpoint was indicative of *categorization*. Teachers with this viewpoint categorized families in terms of their ability/competence, or lack thereof, to provide feedback. They believed that a few select families have the ability to contribute, but that a vast majority may lack sufficient understanding to contribute meaningfully to classroom practices. Individuals with the third viewpoint were labeled *autonomists* because they viewed teachers as independent from families and did not appreciate families' ability/competence to provide feedback. Based on Q sort analysis, qualitative interviews, and NGT, the researcher found that, in general, primary school teachers did not view families as partners in education. Even the *valuers* were selective about the specific areas where families have the competence to contribute.

In another study, researchers used Q methodology to explore beliefs of current practitioners, preservice students, and faculty experts regarding family participation in their children's early intervention services (Sawyer & Campbell, 2009). Sawyer and Campbell developed their 20-item Q set of participation-based and other recommended practices from past literature and empirical studies on early intervention. Their approach to analysis was slightly different than what we describe. Instead of factor analysis, they simply summed the scores for each practice to identify the practices that most frequently received high or low rankings. In their second-level analysis, they separately examined the practitioners' and preservice teachers' rankings. In addition, they used the faculty experts' sort to create a criterion sort, which served as a standard against which practitioners' and preservice teachers' sorts were compared.

In a relatively older, but unique study, Sexton et al. (1998) utilized Q methodology to explore families' views rather than practitioners' views regarding what family-centered practices they value in early intervention services. Based on the sorts of 35 family members, three viewpoints were derived. According to the first viewpoint, optimal family-centered practice consists of professionals communicating in an honest, understandable, and encouraging manner. The second viewpoint indicated that parents in this group viewed early interventions as family-centered when professionals kept them informed and respected family priorities. Parents who constituted the third viewpoint perceived professionals as family-centered, when professionals responded promptly to their requests and made positive comments about their children. Notably, all participants assigned a high priority to professionals meeting families' needs versus just children's needs.

Inclusion

Hurley and Horn (2010) used Q methodology to assess the characteristics of inclusive classroom settings that families and professionals valued most and least. Ten professionals and 10 family members participated in the study and sorted 80 items that were sampled from a list of characteristics developed by the Early Childhood Research Institute on Inclusion. Their analysis generated a single factor, thereby indicating that all participants valued similar characteristics in inclusive settings. Although the study did not generate diverse viewpoints, it did help to identify the characteristics that parents and professionals value in inclusive settings. Typically, one-factor solutions reveal a consensus in the construction of the Q set and may need further research to explore deeper and more personal meanings. Qualitative interviews may assist in highlighting the areas that were untouched in this study.

In a different study, Q methodology was utilized to explore the attitudes of preservice and early career teachers regarding inclusion, instructional accommodations, and fairness (Berry, 2010). Analysis of 60 Q sorts helped to uncover three attitude patterns. The first pattern was labeled *keen but anxious beginners* and was characterized by a positive attitude regarding the three topics but also some anxiety. The second pattern was labeled *positive doers* and was characterized by positive attitude as well as confidence. The third pattern was labeled *resisters* and was characterized by negative attitudes and some amount of anxiety toward inclusion, instructional accommodations and fairness.

EARLY CHILDHOOD RESEARCH TRENDS AND OPPORTUNITIES FOR Q METHODOLOGY

With a focus on participatory research and the charge to explore both subjective and objective data that is culturally relevant comes the need to identify and utilize fresh research methodologies. In short, the challenge for researchers is to generate methods for *scientifically* exploring questions pertaining to human subjectivity; Q methodology provides one avenue for addressing this challenge, and has been conceptualized as a "bridge between human subjectivity and objective quantification" (Sexton et al., 1998, p. 96). Q methodology can be used to capture not only the subjective perspectives of parents, caregivers, teachers, and other important adults in children's lives, but it can be used to capture the subjective perspectives of children as well. In this way, our understanding of children's development would become more thorough, meaningful, and would reflect the perspectives of the participants themselves, be they children or adults.

Q methodology also provides a mechanism for researchers to engage in child-friendly research. Whereas traditional research methods such as questionnaires may be considered "boring" by children (Barker & Weller, 2003), Q sorts are game-like in nature, and are potentially more enjoyable for children. Proponents of child-friendly participatory research suggest the use of multisensory approaches to gathering data, such as photographs, drawings, and diaries (Barker & Weller, 2003; Clark, 2005). Because items in the concourse can include images, photos, objects, and other expressions, Q methodology can accommodate a multisensory approach with children. Figures 4.2 and 4.3 illustrate the use of Q methodology with children as participants (Storksen et al., 2012). Furthermore, Q methodology inherently allows for research to be culturally relevant, as concourses can be developed in native languages and using items that are culturally meaningful.

Clearly, conducting Q research with very young children has its own set of ethical principles to consider. Thorsen and Storksen (2010) established three areas that demand careful consideration. The ethical, methodological and practical advice included some of the following suggestions:

1. Be sensitive to the power and authority researchers have over children.
2. Plan for the sorting of objects that are known to children and with which they are comfortable.
3. Use language, images, time and rapport to provide comfort to the child who is sorting.

CONCLUDING REMARKS

Variations Within Q Methodology

Within Q methodology, there are approaches that are relatively *more popular* than Stephenson's traditional approach to Q methodology. For example, a number of attachment and parenting studies in the past two decades have utilized Q sorting procedures and measures (see van IJzendoorn, Vereijken, Bakermans-Kranenburg, & Riksen-Walraven, 2004 for a review; Pederson, Moran, Sitko, Campbell, Ghesquire, & Acton, 1990) such as the Attachment Q Set (AQS; Waters & Deane, 1985) and Maternal Behavior Q Set (MBQS; Moran, Pederson, & Bento, 1995), which assess attachment and maternal behaviors respectively. Although these measures utilize sorting procedures similar to Stephenson's Q methodology, they differ from Stephenson's approach in two important ways: first, rather than have participants sort Q items based on *subjective beliefs and experiences* (e.g., role of art in learning, transitioning to daycare), the AQS and MBQS require an observer or a parent to sort the Q set items based on *observed behavior* (e.g., child's attachment behaviors toward mother, mother's interaction behavior with child); second, instead of a factor analytic approach, the AQS and MBQS correlate the resulting sorts to a criterion sort (i.e., a hypothetical ideal sort) to derive attachment security and sensitivity scores respectively. These measures are inspired largely by Block's ground-breaking work in applying Q methodology to personality assessment (van IJzendoorn et al., 2004). Block is credited with the development of California Q-Set (CQ-Set), a 100-item personality assessment tool, which has been utilized considerably in both research and clinical settings. Although these approaches have made substantial contributions to field of attachment, parenting, and personality research, they do not necessarily promote participatory research with young children. Hence, our chapter does not detail these approaches but rather just focuses on Stephenson's Q methodology.

Limitations and Future Directions

Past critiques pinpoint two key limitations with respect to Q methodology: The first limitation pertains to the *P* sample (number of participants/sorters), which is both small and purposively (rather than randomly) sampled from the population. Critics argue that this makes Q methodology statistically weak and limits the generalizability of the factors derived from the various Q studies (Robbins, 2005). Some experts also suggest that Q methodology's emphasis on subjectivity perhaps undermines its effectiveness and leads to questionable findings.

The second limitation is the practical difficulty associated with the sorting procedure, which requires sorters to arrange items in a quasinormal distribution. It is possible that such force fitting may cause frustration among participants, but on the other hand a forced distribution format precludes participants' idiosyncratic responses such as extremely high or low ratings for all items or the tendency to rate everything in the middle (Block, 1961). Another practical challenge may be that collecting sorting data with very young children will require more patience, time for sorting, and an individualized setting for sorting. Yet, successful studies reveal the products of young children's thinking. For example, Thorsen and Storksen (2010) conducted a study in which children sorted pictures of various emotions and, peer and adult interactions to determine the ways that children view their family situations. She included children from intact families and children of divorce. Taylor and Delprato (1994) used multiple conditions of instruction with three- and four-year old children. A Q set of pictures was sorted eight times by each child to demonstrate that children can differentiate the expectations that others may have for them.

Q Methodology as Part of the Research Toolkit

Researchers have found Q methodology to be an excellent complement to other methods for better understanding how to address issues in theory, research, and practice. Q was designed to determine areas of similarities and differences, perhaps leading to interventions that can be implemented and explained through ethnography, case studies, or other qualitative methods. According to Brown (1993), Q methodology is simple and elegant and at the same time has a solid scientific foundation. Q methodology employs statistical procedures that are identical to conventional factor analysis such as correlations and principal components analysis (McKeown & Thomas, 2013), and Q sorts rule out the possibility of missing data and unreliable responses (Dennis, 1986). Indeed, Q methodology holds strong promise for research in the field of early childhood.

REFERENCES

Akhtar-Danesh, N., Baumann, A., & Cordingley, L. (2008). Q methodology in nursing research: A promising method for the study of subjectivity. *Western Journal of Nursing Research, 30,* 759–773.

Barker, J., & Weller, S. (2003). "Is it fun?" Developing children centered research methods. *International Journal of Sociology and Social Policy, 23,* 33–58.

Berry, R. W. (2010). Preservice and early career teachers' attitudes toward inclusion, instructional accommodations, and fairness: Three profiles. *Teacher Educator, 45,* 75–95.

Block, J. (1961). *The Q sort method in personality assessment and psychiatric research*. Palo Alto, CA: Consulting Psychologists Press.

Bracken, S., & Fischel, J. E. (2006). Assessment of preschool classroom practices: Application of Q sort methodology. *Early Childhood Research Quarterly, 21*(4), 417–430.

Bresler, L. (1995). The subservient, co-equal, affective and social integration style and their implications for the arts. *Arts Education Policy Review, 96*, 31–37.

Brown, S. R. (1980). *Political subjectivity: Applications of Q methodology in political science*. New Haven, CT: Yale University Press.

Brown, S. R. (1986). Q technique and method: Principles and procedures. In W. D. Berry & M. S. Lewis-Beck (Eds.), *New tools for social scientists: Advances and applications in research methods* (pp. 57–76). Thousand Oaks, CA: Sage.

Brown, S. R. (1993). A primer on Q methodology. *Operant Subjectivity, 16*, 91–138.

Brown, S.R. (2008). Q methodology. In L. M. Given (Ed.), *The SAGE encyclopedia of qualitative research methods* (Vol. 2, pp. 699–702). Thousand Oaks, CA: Sage.

Brown, S. R., & Good, J. M. M. (2010). Q methodology. In N. J. Salkind (Ed.), *Encyclopedia of research design* (Vol. 3, pp. 1149–1155). Thousand Oaks, CA: Sage.

Brown, S. R., & Brenner, D. J. (Eds.) (1972). *Science, psychology, and communication: Essays honoring William Stephenson*. New York, NY: Teachers College Press.

Brown, S. R., Durning, D. W., & Selden, S. C. (2008). Q methodology. In K. Yang & G. R. Miller (Eds.), *Handbook of research methods in public administration* (2nd ed., pp. 721–763). New York, NY: Taylor & Francis.

Clark, A. (2005). Listening to and involving young children: A review of research and practice. *Early Child Development and Care, 175*(6), 489–505.

Darbyshire, P., Schiller, W., & MacDougall, C. (2005). Extending new paradigm childhood research: Meeting the challenges of including younger children. *Early Child Development and Care, 175*(6), 467–472.

Davis, P. (2007). Storytelling as a democratic approach to data collection: Interviewing children about reading. *Educational Research, 49*(2), 169–184.

De Mol, J., & Buysse, A. (2008). The phenomenology of children's influence on parents. *Journal of Family Therapy, 30*(2), 163–193.

Dennis, K. E. (1986). Q methodology: Relevance and application to nursing research. *Advances in Nursing Science, 8*(3), 6–17.

Eden, S., Donaldson, A., & Walker, G. (2005). Structuring subjectivities: Using Q methodology in human geography. *Area, 37*, 413–422.

Einarsdóttir, J. (2007). Research with children: Methodological and ethical challenges. *European Early Childhood Education Research Journal, 15*, 197–211.

Eisner, E. (1985). Aesthetic ways of knowing. In E. Eisner (Ed.). *Learning and teaching the ways of knowing* (pp. 23–36). Chicago: University of Chicago Press.

Ellingsen, I. T., Størksen, I. I., & Stephens, P. P. (2010). Q methodology in social work research. *International Journal of Social Research Methodology: Theory & Practice, 13*, 395–409.

Gallivan, J. (1994). Subjectivity and the psychology of gender: Q as a feminist methodology. In J. Gallivan, S. Crozier & V. Lalande (Eds.), *Women, girls, and achievement* (pp. 29–36). Toronto, Canada: Captus University.

Gillen, J., Cameron, C. A., Tapanya, S., Pinto, G., Hancock, R., Young, S., & Gamannossi, B. A. (2007). 'A day in the life': Advancing a methodology for the cultural study of development and learning in early childhood. *Early Child Development and Care, 177*(2), 207–218.

Gruber, J. S. (2011). Perspectives of effective and sustainable community-based natural resource management: An application of Q methodology to forest projects. *Conservation & Society. 9*, 159–171.

Harms, T., Clifford, R. M., & Cryer, C. (2005). Early Childhood Environment Rating Scale—Revised Edition. New York, NY: Teachers College Press.

Hull, D. F. (2005). *A Q methodological study describing the beliefs of teachers about arts integrated in the curriculum in Oklahoma K-12 schools*. Doctoral Dissertation, Oklahoma State University, Stillwater.

Hurley, J. J., & Horn, E. M. (2010). Family and professional priorities for inclusive early childhood settings. *Journal of Early Intervention, 32*(5), 335–350.

Hurley, J. J., Wehby, J. H., & Feurer, I. D. (2010). The social validity assessment of social competence intervention behavior goals. *Topics In Early Childhood Special Education, 30*(2), 112–124.

Irwin, L. G., & Johnson, J. (2005). Interviewing young children: Explicating our practices and dilemmas. *Qualitative Health Research, 15*(6), 821–831.

John, A., & Halliburton, A. L. (2010). Q methodology to assess child-father attachment. *Early Child Development and Care, 180*(1–2), 71–85.

Kanim, K. (2000). Q methodology: Advantages and the disadvantages of this research method. *Journal of Community Nursing, 15*(4), 8–12.

Kitzinger, C. (1999). Researching subjectivity and diversity: Q methodology in feminist psychology. *Psychology of Women Quarterly, 23*, 267–276.

MacNaughton, G., Smith, K., & Davis, K. (2007). Researching with children: The challenges and possibilities for building child-friendly research. In J. A. Hatch (Ed.), *Early childhood qualitative research* (pp. 167–184). New York, NY: Routledge.

Massingham, P. R., Massingham, R., & Diment, K. (2012). Q methodology: Is it useful for accounting research? *Qualitative Research in Accounting & Management, 9*(1), 66–88.

McKeown, B., & Thomas, D. (2013). *Q methodology*. Thousand Oaks, CA: Sage.

Moran, G., Pederson, D., & Bento, S. (2009). *Maternal Behavior Q-Sort (MBQS)— Overview, Available Materials, and Support*. Available from http://works.bepress.com/gregmoran/48

Moseman, C. (2003). Primary teachers' beliefs about family competence to influence classroom practices. *Early Education and Development, 14*, 125–152.

Nicholas, D. B., Picone, G., & Selkirk, E. K. (2011). The lived experiences of children and adolescents with end-stage renal disease. *Qualitative Health Research, 21*(2), 162–173.

Pederson, D. R., Moran, G., Sitko, C., Campbell, K., Ghesquire, K. and Acton, H. (1990), Maternal Sensitivity and the Security of Infant-Mother Attachment: A Q-Sort Study. *Child Development*, 61: 1974–1983. doi: 10.1111/j.1467-8624.1990.tb03579.x

Robbins, P. (2005). The Q method. In K. Kempf-Leonard (Ed.), *Encyclopedia of social measurement* (Vol. 3, pp. 209–215). San Diego, CA: Elsevier.

Robbins, P., & Krueger, R. (2000). Beyond bias? The promise and limits of Q method in human geography. *Professional Geographer, 52*, 636–648.

Sawyer, L. E., & Campbell, P. H. (2009). Beliefs about participation-based practices in early intervention. *Journal of Early Intervention, 31*(4), 326–343.

Schmolck, P. (2012). PQMethod (Version 2.33) [software]. Available from http://schmolck.userweb.mwn.de/qmethod/downpqwin.htm

Scott, J. (2008). Children as respondents: The challenge for quantitative methods. In P. Chrsitensen & A. James (Eds.) (2nd ed.), *Research with Children: Perspectives and Practices* (87–108). New York, NY: Routledge/Taylor & Francis Group.

Sexton, D., Snyder, P., Wadsworth, D., Jardine, A., & Ernest, J. (1998). Applying Q methodology to investigations of subjective judgments of early intervention effectiveness. *Topics in Early Childhood Special Education, 18*(2), 95–107.

Shemmings, D. (2006). 'Quantifying' qualitative data: An illustrative example of the use of Q methodology in psychosocial research. *Qualitative Research in Psychology, 3*(2), 147–165.

Sickler, J., Fraser, J., Webler, T., Reiss, D., Boyle, P., Lyn, H., Lemcke, K., & Gruber, S. (2006). Social narratives surrounding dolphins: Q method study. *Society & Animals: Journal of Human-Animal Studies, 14*(4), 351–382.

Smith, A., Duncan, J., & Marshall, K. (2005). Children's perspectives on their learning: Exploring methods. *Early Child Development and Care, 175*(6), 473–487.

Smith, N. W. (2001). *Current systems in psychology: History, theory, research, and applications*. Belmont, CA: Wadsworth/Thomson Learning.

Stenner, P., Watts, S., & Worrell, M. (2007). Q methodology. In C. Willig & W. Stainton Rogers (Eds.), *Handbook of qualitative research methods in psychology* (pp. 215–239). London: Sage.

Størksen, I., Thorsen, A. A., Øverland, K., & Brown, S. R. (2012). Experiences of daycare children of divorce. *Early Child Development and Care, 182*, 807–825.

Stephenson, W. (1953). *The study of behavior: Q-technique and its methodology*. Chicago: University of Chicago Press.

Stephenson, W. (1967). *The play theory of mass communication*. Chicago, IL: University of Chicago Press.

Szente, J., Hoot, J., & Ernest, J. (2002). Parent/teacher views of developmentally appropriate practices: A Hungarian perspective. *International Journal of Early Childhood, 34*(1), 24–36.

Taylor, P., & Delprato, D. J. (1994). Q methodology in the study of child phenomenology. *Psychological Record, 44*(2), 171–183.

Thorsen, A. A., & Storksen, I. (2010). Ethical, methodological, and practical reflections when using Q methodology in research with young children. *Operant Subjectivity: The International Journal of Q methodology, 33*, 3–25.

Van Exel, J., & de Graaf, G. (2005). Q methodology: A sneak preview. Retrieved from http://www.qmethodology.net/PDF/Q methodology%20-%20A%20sneak%20preview.pdf

Van IJzendoorn, M. H., Vereijken, C. M. J. L., Bakermans-Kranenburg, M., & Riksen-Walraven, J. (2004). Assessing attachment security with the attachment Q sort: Meta-analytic evidence for the validity of the observer AQS. *Child Development, 75*(4), 1188–1213.

Watts, A., & Stenner, P. (2005). Doing Q methodology: Theory, method and interpretation. *Qualitative Research in Psychology, 2*, 67–91.

Watts, S., & Stenner, P. (2012). *Doing Q methodological research: Theory, method and interpretation.* Thousand Oaks, CA: Sage.

Webler, T., Danielson, S., & Tuler, S. (2009). Using Q method to reveal social perspectives in environmental research. Greenfield, MA: Social and Environmental Research Institute. Retrieved from http://www.seri-us.org/sites/default/files/Qprimer.pdf.

Weis, L. (2010). *Early childhood teachers' perceptions of children's creative leadership characteristics: A Q-study.* Unpublished manuscript, Oklahoma State University, Stillwater, OK.

Wolf, R. M. (1997). Q methodology. In J. P. Keeves (Ed.), *Educational research, methodology, and measurement: An international handbook* (2nd ed., pp. 417–420). London: Elsevier Science.

Woodhead, M. (1999). Reconstructing developmental psychology. *Children and Society, 13*(1), 3–19.

CHAPTER 5

Q-METHODOLOGY AND Q-SORTING AS TOOLS FOR ADDRESSING RESEARCH QUESTIONS IN EDUCATIONAL SETTINGS

Historical Overview and Illustrations Using Three Standardized Q-Sets

Brian E. Vaughn,[1] António J. Santos, and Gabrielle Coppola

Teachers, administrators, education policy makers, and educational researchers face broad assessment challenges in their attempts to create and maintain curricula and learning environments that maximize the opportunities for every child to learn and achieve in schools, from early childhood pre-K programs through graduate and professional training during adulthood. In addition to selecting reliable and valid measures to track students' mastery of and progress through the curriculum materials, a broad range of other assessment issues must be considered. For example, policy makers may desire to increase participation in higher education by historically underserved groups but find that programs designed to accomplish this goal miss their targets and seek to explain why this might be (e.g., Bradley & Miller, 2010); administrators may want to know whether and how teachers' philosophies of instruction interact with delivery of specific aspects of curricula to promote, or impede, student progress (e.g., Lim, 2010; Massetti & Bracken, 2010); or, education researchers may want to identify the behavioral, psychological, and physical foundations of social position(s) in the peer networks found in classrooms or in entire schools to identify potential intervention points to reduce bullying (e.g., Duncan & Owen, 2011).

Readers will recognize that the two domains of education research questions described above have somewhat different goals; namely, a direct focus on child performance within a school setting vs. a focus setting conditions characteristic of different education settings that may interact directly or indirectly with children's abilities and other attributes to affect their academic performance. Most frequently, questions of the first type are evaluated using "objective" assessments that compare a given child to a "standard" of performance in the school setting (e.g., mastery of required curriculum materials and information), where the "standard" may be others in the peer cohort (i.e., how does this child's performance compare to the performance of the peer cohort as a whole) or may be to the child's own prior performance (i.e., has this child's performance improved since the prior assessment). In either case, the assessments used tend to be "objective" (or quantitative) in the sense that all children in the relevant comparison group are evaluated using the same instruments/tests and under similar conditions of testing and the results of assessment can be expressed numerically. Questions focused on setting conditions are often less amenable to standard, objective assessments because these "conditions" will likely differ across settings and these differences will often be idiosyncratic to a given setting. Consequently, different types of assessment will be required and these assessments will likely entail the use of more "subjective" (or qualitative) measures that are not readily standardized across different school settings. Moreover, the results of analyses for these kinds of data may not be expressed numerically (although they may be).

Although both types of question (and the kinds of answers obtained) can provide useful insights into the performance differences characterizing children in academic settings, objective and subjective data are often not treated as being equally meaningful, with more weight being accorded to objective, quantified information than to subjective, qualitative information. The focus of this chapter is to describe a conceptual framework and data collection protocol originally intended to demonstrate that subjective data can be analyzed and interpreted quantitatively. Over time, this framework has evolved into two distinct traditions that can address both objective and subjective questions and can provide numeric analyses and interpretations for both, with each retaining the original data collection protocol. This framework is known in the behavioral, social, and developmental sciences as the Q-method and the procedure common to all Q-methodologies is called Q-sorting. This chapter is intended to provide an historical overview of Q-methodology and illustrate the use of Q-sort approaches to both subjective and objective phenomena relevant to education.

Q-METHODOLOGY: HISTORICAL BACKGROUND

The Q-method has a long (and controversial) history in the behavioral and social sciences, and has recently been incorporated into studies from the education sciences. The conceptual foundation for the Q-method was conceived and first elaborated by William Stephenson (e.g., 1935, 1950, 1953), who was most interested in developing statistically sound means of representing subjective experience at the individual level. Stephenson earned PhD degrees in both physics and psychology and his understanding of physics informed his approach to psychology. He was convinced that subjective experiences were indeterminate in a manner similar to how the behavior of quantum particles was indeterminate, but he also believed that their inherent indeterminacy need not exclude subjective experiences from scientific inquiry. He also described methods for acquiring and analyzing Q-data. Both Stephenson's ideas about individual subjectivity and the methods he proposed for analyzing subjectivity were controversial and his arguments with the statistician Cyril Burt (e.g., 1937, 1938, 1955; Burt & Stephenson, 1939; Stephenson, 1936) concerning the nature of objective and subjective data tended to be resolved in Burt's favor (e.g., Cronbach & Gleser, 1954), within the behavioral sciences.

Whereas Stephenson believed that two very different data matrices were involved when objective (e.g., tests, observations on which n persons were compared; the r-matrix) and subjective (salience of some object/entity or event to the person) experiences (i.e., the Q-matrix) were analyzed; Burt saw a single data matrix in which Q persons were observed over R variables. Whether analysis considered correlations among variables (i.e., the typical analyses of an r-matrix) or among persons (after transposing the data matrix: the Q-matrix), was not especially important to Burt. For him, the data were equivalent. Variations of Burt's view continue to dominate in most sub-disciplines within psychology (with, perhaps, the exception of clinical psychology) but Stephenson's perspective has been adopted in several of the other social sciences (e.g., Brown, 1972, 1980, 1996) and has been quite influential in communication sciences.

Stephenson's approach to data acquisition was also controversial. Because he wished to represent subjective perspectives (i.e., the individual person's point of view or opinion about some domain), he felt it was imperative to construct items that represented the universe of potential opinions or points of view relevant to the given topic or domain. The first task of a Q-methodologist, then, was to survey the range of various points of view on the topic/domain of interest and determine the inherent structure of discourse concerning the domain (e.g., Stephenson, 1978). Items drawn from the universe of potential items such that all major opinions were included became the Q-sample for that domain in a given research study. One interesting implication of this approach is that the universe of potential items for a domain is much larger than the actual Q-sample selected. Therefore, different studies concerning a specific domain could, in principle, use nonoverlapping sets of items in their respective Q-samples, which may be advantageous when the same set of evaluators is asked to evaluate the items on multiple occasions but also raises questions about the comparability of results across rater-groups when different Q-samples are used to elicit points of view.

The task of the participant in a Q-method study is to describe her or his point of view (or opinion) about the domain (e.g., object/entity, event, experience) by rank ordering the items (typically printed on separate cards) in the Q-sample according to the participant's degree of agreement or disagreement with each item. Typically, this is done using a forced distribution of items to categories of agreement/disagreement, which may take quasinormal (see Figure 5.1a) or rectangular (see Figure 5.1b) shapes, depending on how many different perspectives are represented and how many items are included for each perspective. The participant judges each item relative to all other items in the Q-sample in terms of his or her degree of agreement or disagreement with the statement. Items most strongly corresponding to the participant's point of view are placed at one extreme in the distribution and the items most opposite to (i.e., those with which the participant disagrees) the participant's point of view are placed at the other extreme, with the remaining Q-items being placed according to their salience for agreement or disagreement. Items with zero salience (neither similar nor dissimilar to the individual's own point of view/opinion) are placed at the center of the distribution. A common convention is to locate items *uncharacteristic* of the entity being described at the *low* end of the item distribution (e.g., 1, 2, or 3 for a 9-category Q-sort) and to locate the items *characteristic* of the entity at the *high* end (e.g., 7, 8, and 9 for a 9-category Q-sort. The "score" for a given item is the numeric value of the category in which it is placed (i.e., 1, 2, ... 9 for a 9-category Q-sort).

It is frequently recommended that the procedure be implemented in two steps (e.g., Waters & Vaughn, in press). First, items are coarsely divided into

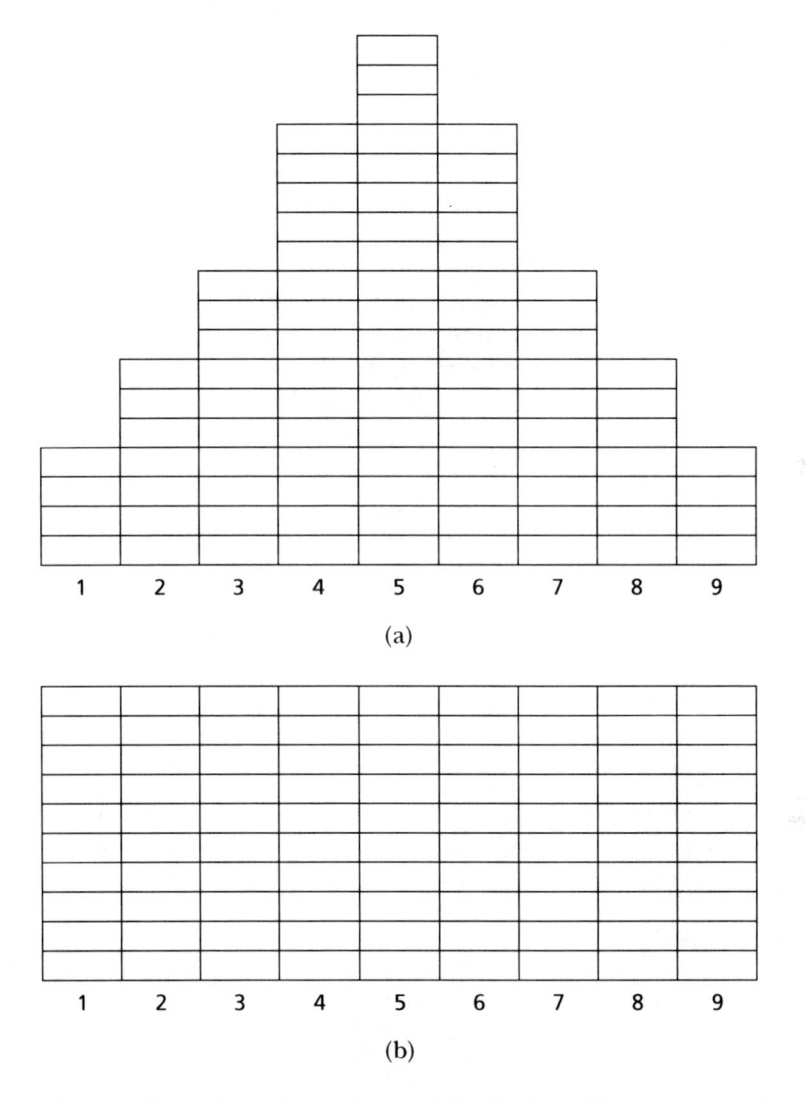

Figure 5.1 (a) Illustration of a quasi-normal distribution of items to categories with a 90-item Q-sort, (b) Illustration of a square distribution of items to categories with a 90-item Q-sort. *Note.* 1 = Most Strongly Disagree/Most Uncharacteristic of Subject; 2 = Strongly Disagree/Very Uncharacteristic of Subject; 3 = Moderate Disagree/Moderately Uncharacteristic of Subject; 4 = Somewhat Disagree/Somewhat Uncharacteristic of Subject; 5 = Neither Disagree nor Agree/Neither Characteristic nor Uncharacteristic of Subject; 6 = Agree Somewhat/Somewhat Characteristic of Subject; 7 = Moderate Agree/Moderately Characteristic of Subject; 8 = Strongly Agree/Very Characteristic of Subject; 9 = Most Strongly Agree/Most Characteristic of Subject.

three categories: those items with which the participant is more or less in agreement; those items with which the participant is more or less in disagreement; and the remaining items. The task is facilitated if these three categories are roughly equal in size. Then each group of items is subdivided according to the required distribution. This sequence is illustrated in Figure 5.2. The process of grouping then comparing items and deciding on the specific location of the items in the fixed scoring distribution is called "Q-sorting."

When a group of participants each sort items from a given Q-sample, it is a common practice to transpose the data matrix so that individual Q-sorts (i.e., contributed by a single individual) are columns in the matrix and Q-items are the rows (i.e., create the Q-matrix) and then to group Q-sorts (i.e., persons) as a function of their item-distributions, using multivariate

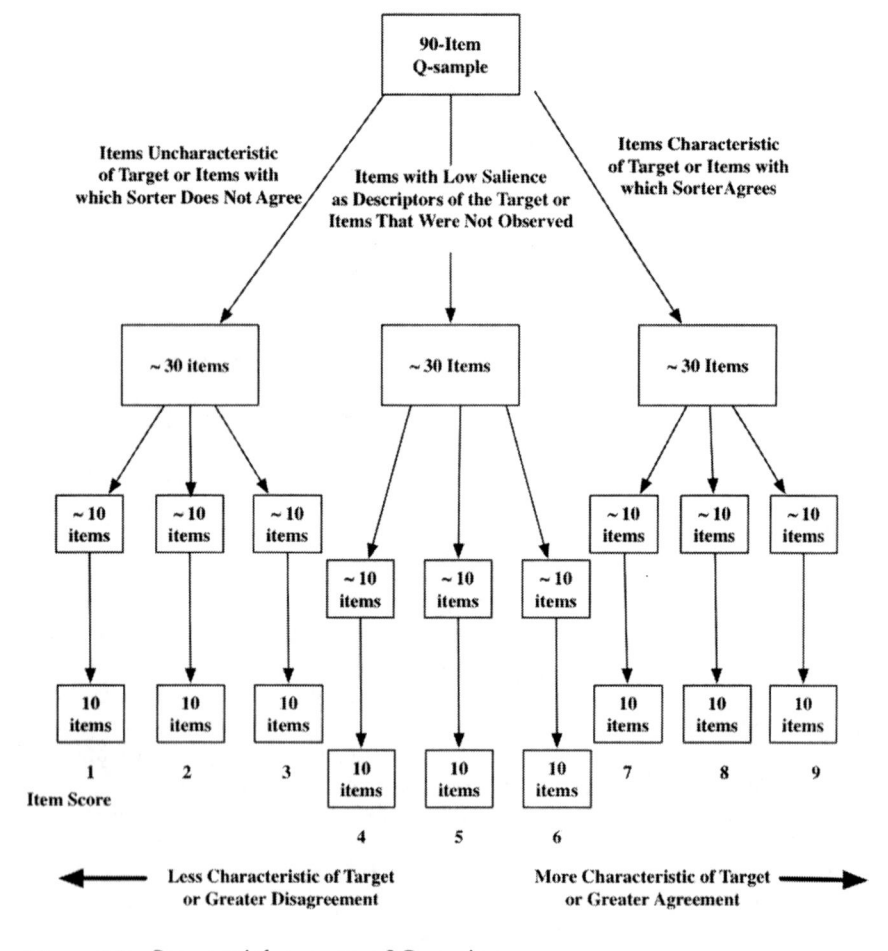

Figure 5.2 Sequential process of Q-sorting.

analyses of one sort or another (e.g., principal components analysis, common factors analysis, or cluster analysis). When the sample of participants truly represents the population of persons holding the full range of opinions/points of view concerning the domain being considered, these analyses will tend to group together those persons sharing a common opinion about that domain as "types" or clusters. Item placements (agreements and disagreements) distinguish a given type from the other types identified in the grouping analysis and allow inferences about the nature of differences in opinions/points of view that distinguish persons of different types. By way of comparison, traditional analyses (i.e., analyses of the r-matrix) group variables together as dimensions along which persons can be ranked or otherwise compared. This person-centered aspect of Q-methodology makes the method very useful for addressing qualitative questions such as those posed in the opening section of this chapter (for specific applications, see Bradley & Miller, 2010; Lim, 2010; Massetti & Bracken, 2010; see also, Webler, Danielson, & Tuler, 2009).

Within the sub-disciplines of clinical and personality psychology, Q-methodology and the Q-sorting procedure (i.e., arranging items into categories based on their salience or importance as descriptors of the object/entity) have been used for over 50 years as tools for assessment, although different research traditions have emphasized (or de-emphasized) the subjective aspects of the methodology. For example, Carl Rogers and associates (e.g., D. S. Cartwright, 1956; R. D. Cartwright, 1957; Rogers & Dymond, 1954) used repeated Q-sort self-descriptions of the "real" and "ideal" self as evidence for therapeutic change (i.e., when the client's real self and ideal self show increased convergence) and they treated the difference between these sorts as an indicator of self-esteem (i.e., smaller discrepancies suggesting higher self-esteem), much in the spirit of Stephenson's original intention for the Q-method as a reflection of the participant's subjective view on him/herself.

Block (e.g., 1961, 2008) also used Q-sort data for assessment in studies of personality and personality development (e.g., J. H. Block & J. Block, 1980) but he was not persuaded by Stephenson's (1953) arguments concerning the differences between matrices of subjective vs. objective data (Block was more inclined to believe that self-descriptions should be considered as objective data). Furthermore, he believed that Rogers' method of quantifying differences between two self-descriptive Q-sorts (as for self-esteem) was not the most efficient way of using Q-data. Over a period of about 20 years, Block (e.g., 1961) and associates devised Q-samples (he preferred the term "Q-sets") as assessment tools for the description of personality in both adults and children, for assessing parental practices, goals, attitudes, and values regarding child-rearing, and as descriptions of specified social environments (e.g., household as a support for children's development).

Many of these Q-sets continue to be used for these purposes by developmental and personality/social psychologists (e.g., Block, Block, & Keyes, 1988; Lanning, 1994; McCrae, Terracciano, Costa, & Ozer, 2006; McNally, Eisenberg, & Harris, 1991; Waters, Garber, Gornal, & Vaughn, 1983; Waters, Noyes, Vaughn, & Ricks, 1985).

Block was also an expert in the psychometric desiderata of scale development, especially the aggregation of item scores as a means of improving scale reliability. He reasoned that trained observers' perceptions of a given object or person (e.g., a research participant) would necessarily reflect subjective impressions of the research participant (or client) based on their unique contacts or interactions with that person. However, when several observers each interacted with the same person, the average of all their descriptions should yield a statistically reliable estimate of the "true" properties of the person. Consequently, when several observers each provide Q-sort descriptions of a research participant (or client/patient in a clinical setting), the average of their Q-sorts of the behavior and personality of the person being described should be more representative of the true qualities of the person than would any single Q-sort description. Because observers (or examiners) would most likely encounter the research participant in somewhat different contexts and with different purposes, and because research participants are likely to behave somewhat differently in different contexts, Q-sort profiles from by different observers should always be imperfectly correlated. Although, these correlation values would be expected to increase when observation settings were similar and occasions of contact with the person overlapped. Nevertheless, the aggregated profile should provide a clearer, more nearly "true" characterization of the person. Thus, the subjective data obtained using Q-methodology can, in some instances, yield objective information about research participants.

DERIVING SCORES FROM Q-SORT DATA

Criterion Sorts

Block (2008; J. H. Block & J. Block, 1980) also pioneered the use of "criterion" Q-sorts as standards for specific dimensional constructs in Q-sort research. When such a criterion for some specific behavioral or personality dimension (e.g., social competence or self-esteem) was established, it became possible to compare a Q-sort description of a specific research participant (or client) with the criterion to estimate the similarity between the individual's Q-sort description and that dimension.

In his own studies of fundamental dimensions of ego functioning, Block (e.g., Block & Block, 1980) invited psychologists with training and research experience using specific personality constructs (i.e., ego-control and ego-resilience) to sort a specially constructed Q-set of items according to a fixed distribution, with the instruction to describe the *hypothetical* person who would be seen at the extreme high end of the distribution of scores for the dimension (e.g., the hypothetical *most* ego-resilient person). Finding that the resulting criterion sorts largely overlapped and yielded aggregate composite scores that are highly reliable, in the statistical sense, the average of these expert Q-sorts became "criterion" for the respective constructs. The reader will recognize that this approach to construct description is similar to computing a traditional Q-factor analysis with only a single common element (i.e., Q-sorts for all experts load on a single factorial dimension). The format of a data matrix for constructing a criterion sort is presented in Table 5.1.

It is important to understand that criterion sorts make use of all items in the Q-set and that when read from the left to right ends of the distribution, the items define the construct from the properties that are the least like (or most negatively salient for) the construct to items that are most descriptive of (or most positively salient for) the construct. Items placed toward the middle of the distribution are of minimal salience for the definition of the construct or dimension. In short, these criterion sorts provide a comprehensive profile of the hypothetical individual at one extreme for the construct being studied.

In Block's approach, the Pearson correlation between Q-sort description(s) of an individual research participant (or client/patient) and

TABLE 5.1 Creating a Criterion Q-Sort

Item #	Criterion Sort #1	Criterion Sort #2	Criterion Sort #3	Criterion Sort #4	Criterion Sort #5	Average Sorts 1–5
Item 1	3	3	4	5	3	3.6
Item 2	7	8	9	8	8	8.0
Item 3	2	2	1	1	1	1.4
Item 4	4	4	3	3	3	3.4
Item 5	6	6	5	6	6	5.8
Item 6	5	4	5	6	5	5.0
Item 7	7	7	6	6	6	6.4
Item 8	1	2	3	1	2	1.8
Item 9	9	9	9	9	8	8.8
...						
Item N	8	8	7	9	7	7.8

Note: After demonstrating substantial cross-sort convergence (correlation) and internal consistency/reliability (Cronbach's alpha), the average score for each item becomes the final criterion value for the item.

the criterion Q-sort for a construct/dimension becomes the individual's "score" for that construct of dimension. This correlation indexes the similarity between the individual and criterion Q-sorts and it can be treated normatively (i.e., can be compared to scores for other research participants/clients). If desired, the r to z transformation can be applied to these correlation values, but this proves unnecessary in practice because the distributions of individual scores for most criterion sorts (in the majority of samples) tend to normality around the sample mean and the relation of r to z is approximately linear within the range of typical criterion scores.

Additional Scoring Options

In addition to criterion scoring for Q-sort data, the data analyst may also compute tests on scores for individual items and/or for scales created from subsets of items in the Q-set. Individual item analyses are useful when the goal of the study is to describe the behavioral or personality context of adaptation in a particular sample or population. Examining the specific Q-items that are correlated with some outcome (e.g., peer acceptance or academic accomplishment in a classroom) helps to characterize the means through which the outcome is achieved and the resources the child is able to bring to bear in achieving those outcomes. It is also informative to discover item contents that are *not* associated with the outcome because this helps limit the range of the outcome dimension (knowing what something is not can be as useful as knowing what that thing is). By the same logic, this procedure can be valuable for comparing groups known to differ on some other critical dimension that may influence adaptive functioning (e.g., groups that differ along dimensions of culture or social positions).

There are, of course, qualifications and limitations associated with analyses at the item level. For example, low frequency and/or multipurpose behaviors (e.g., frowning) may be critical for understanding the outcome being predicted but not achieve a significant association because the activity was not observed (perhaps because a relevant context was not encountered) during the period of observation. There is also an issue concerning the number of expected significant associations (or differences) in the Q-set, especially because many items will have significant associations with other (also correlated with the outcome) items. Combining related items into multi-item scales is one way to avoid the problems with single-item analyses. Scales can be designed on rational (i.e., selected *a priori* from the set of Q-items) and/or on empirical (i.e., selected *post-hoc* because the items are correlates of some outcome variable) bases; in either case, the between item correlations and scale internal consistencies need to be examined to determine the degree of utility that scales will have. Scoring for scales is typically the sum (or average) of items in the scale (after re-scaling items stated negatively).

COMPARING Q-DATA TO TRADITIONAL SCALE DATA

Block (1961) suggested that his approach to the Q-sort method had a range of advantages over traditional rating scale methods of assessing personality and behavior. First, Q-sets are deliberately designed to provide comprehensive characterizations of the phenomena being studied (in the case of Block's California Q- and California Child Q-sets, these phenomena are the behavior, personality, and general adaptive functioning of persons) and this means that many different dimensions relevant to the phenomena under study may be included in a single sort. That is, the universe of content relevant to the phenomena being studied must be surveyed and selected carefully as a part of the process of designing the Q-set. Again, readers will recall that this aspect of Q-sample development was part of Stephenson's overall Q-method. As a result, Q-sorting provides a very economical means of gathering information over a range of relevant dimensions using a limited number of (mostly nonredundant) items (a total of 100 items in the case of the Block California Q-sets). This compares with perhaps 20 to 30 items for a scale intended to measure a single dimension (e.g., "anxiety") using conventional questionnaires or several hundred items in comprehensive temperament or personality assessment instruments such as the Children's Behavior Questionnaire (Rothbart, Ahadi, Hershey, & Fischer, 2001) or the Multidimensional Personality Questionnaire (Tellegen, 1982).

Second, Q-sorting is *ipsative* by design; that is, the sorter evaluates the salience/meaning of each item in the context of the other items rather than frequencies or rates of occurrence *per se* as it is relevant for describing the person. In a way, the Q-sort protocol requires the sorter to rank order the Q-set items as descriptors of the research participant/client. Both Block (1961) and Stephenson (e.g., 1935) argued that the ipsative nature of Q-sorting poses different demands on the Q-sorter than traditional, normative measurement approaches do, because normative measures presume that the rater/observer judges the item in terms of a population of (i.e., is the person being rated now below, at, or above the average expected value compared to the population in the reference group to which the person belongs?). This implies that the rater/observer should know, or at least estimate, the average level and the ranges for the scale or dimension being scored in the reference group. In Q-sorting, the observer need not have knowledge of population norms to provide useful descriptions of the observed person. Finally, Block suggested that the forced choice format of Q-sorting reduces the effects of social desirability response sets (Block, 1965, 1990) that often contaminate data collected using norm-referenced scales.

Waters and Vaughn (in press) noted additional advantages accruing to the Q-sort method. First, it allows (and sometimes requires) the sorter to consider the meaning of behavior within the context in which the behavior is observed. For example, a child's initiation of proximity and contact with the primary caregiver is a key aspect of the secure base phenomenon (e.g., Ainsworth, Blehar, Waters, & Wall, 1978) that is the hallmark of attachment at the end of the first year of life. Waters (1995) included items referencing child-initiated proximity in his *Attachment Q-set* (AQS). However, not every approach by the toddler to the attachment figure that ends in proximity or contact "counts" as an instance of secure base behavior; rather only those approaches interspersed with bouts of exploratory behavior are relevant. So, if a child is being held by the caregiver after having been upset and then gives a signal for release, but after being released the child quickly returns to the caregiver signaling for contact again, the observer would not see this approach as an instance of secure base behavior even though the topography of the approach may be indistinguishable from an approach after a bout of exploration and such an approach would not enter into the placement of items referring to use of the caregiver as a secure base for exploration and haven of safety.

Second, Q-sort procedures separate the description of the phenomena being studied from the scoring of those descriptions. That is, observers can be trained to expert status on the meaning of the items and the standards of observation leading to valid Q-sort descriptions as well as achieve quite high degrees of agreement with other observers without knowing which construct scores will be derived from their Q-sort descriptions of the research participants/clients and without knowing the hypotheses being tested. Indeed, because Q-sets (both *objective* and *subjective*) provide comprehensive descriptions of the phenomena (or points of view) it is frequently possible to define additional constructs using the criterion Q-criterion sort method, which makes testing novel hypotheses feasible using existing data. Thus, even the investigators may not know beforehand all of the hypotheses to be tested from the data generated in a Q-sort study.

A third advantage of Q-sort methods is also due to the fact that a well-constructed Q-set comprehensively describes a given content domain and can give rise to multiple constructs relevant to that domain. When several criterion Q-sorts are created for a given Q-set (e.g., the California Child Q-set (Block & Block, 1980) has been used to generate criterion scores for Ego-control, Ego-resilience, Social Competence, Emotional Regulation, and Self-esteem constructs), all of these constructs can be scored for a given research participant/client from a single Q-sort description. This makes it possible to construct and test alternative hypotheses without obtaining additional data. For example, the Waters AQS (1995) has criterion sorts for both *Attachment Security* and *Dependency* constructs and these tend to show age related changes in their association. At younger ages (i.e., 11 to 18 months of age) these scores tend to have modest positive associations but at older ages they are either uncorrelated or negatively correlated. If an investigator sought to know whether children's tendency to seek proximity and contact with the caregiver at home was a reflection of attachment security or whether this tendency reflected dependency on the parent, assessments of proximity seeking collected independently from the Q-sort observations could be analyzed in relation to both the *Attachment Security* and *Dependency* scores derived from the AQS. Both zero-order correlations and multiple regression analyses would reveal whether the AQS scores were unique, overlapping, or fully redundant predictors of proximity seeking and contact maintenance at home across a range of ages.

An additional advantage of Q-methods is that by virtue of the forced-choice format, observers are motivated to attend closely to the meanings of individual items, which can make descriptions of individual more precise. That is, the Q-sorter is constantly comparing the salience of new items to items already placed in a given category and this helps to keep the content of already-sorted items "in mind" (or, perhaps, in "working memory").

LOGISTICS OF A Q-SORT STUDY: TRAINING, DATA COLLECTION, AND OBSERVER AGREEMENT

As described by Stephenson (e.g., 1953) and Block (e.g., 1961) and discussed above, studies involving Q-methods, whether these are intended to produce subjective or objective data, are multistage efforts. As noted above, the initial step after identifying the topic or domain of phenomena to be studied is to survey the breadth of opinions or constructs that are most relevant to the topic/domain. This may be accomplished by reviewing published and unpublished accounts relevant to the topic/domain or by polling relevant stakeholders (e.g., scholars/researchers, policy makers, members of affected constituencies) from diverse perspectives. This survey leads to the next stage; construction of the Q-sample (or Q-set) items that are designed to reflect the range of viewpoints (or range of constructs) about the topic/domain. At this point, it is wise to pilot test the Q-sample with a relatively small sample of experts and a small sample of individuals who would represent persons most likely to complete the Q-sorts when actual data are gathered to get feedback about the range of coverage for the topic/domain in the Q-sample and clarity of the items themselves. This feedback may lead to revisions of the Q-sample that range from modifying the wording of item statements to adding or deleting items from the Q-sample. These steps would apply to both subjective and objective Q-method studies and they may take considerable time, especially if one goal of the research is to develop a standard set of Q-items for use by many different research teams for a range of purposes (see Vaughn, Deane, & Waters, 1985).

At this point, the step sequences for subjective and objective Q-method studies diverge. Because participants in a subjective Q-sort study are already experts regarding their own opinions and points of view, data collection can begin at this point in the process. However, when Q-sorters are expected to provide objective data about some other person or entity, additional training is required to make certain that all observers share a common understanding the intended meanings of the Q-items *and* the nature of observations that support item placements on the high or low ends of the item-distribution (i.e., salient as a descriptor of the person/entity, either as characteristic or uncharacteristic). Furthermore, decisions regarding the observation interval and behavioral sample required to complete the assessment must be made and this necessarily involves observations in pilot samples. For example, Waters and associates (e.g., Waters & Deane, 1985) determined that a minimum of 2–3 hours for children between 12 and 36 months of age was required to observe a sufficiently diverse set of interactions and contexts (e.g., play, meal/snack, change diaper, integration of childcare with household responsibilities) and yield reliable, valid AQS descriptions. Ideally, multiple observers would spend time over two or more days observing each participating child and parent, although this ideal is often not practical economically. In work with preschool age children, Vaughn and associates have reported that all children in a given classroom (as many as 20 children) can receive reliable and valid Q-sort descriptions when two observers spend 20 hours (each) over a period of at least five observation days in the classroom (e.g., Vaughn, Shin, Kim, Coppola, Krzysik, Santos, et al., 2009).

Observer training is facilitated by clearly written items and with a conservative use of jargon terms. For some items, it will be useful to explicitly define the meaning of low (i.e., uncharacteristic) or middle (i.e., no salience) item placements. For example, Q-item #27 from the AQS (Waters, 1995) refers to whether the child laughs when teased by the mother and the qualifier for low placement states "annoyed when mother teases him or her." An added explanatory note explains that the item should be placed in the middle categories if the mother never teases the child during play or conversations. AQS item #34 refers to the child failing to follow the mother when upset after she leaves the child during a home observation visit, with low placement implying that the child actively goes after her if upset after her leaving, and middle placement meaning that the child is never upset by the mother's leaving during a home observation visit. This kind of careful attention to the phrasing and clarification of the items makes the observer's task easier to accomplish, both at the stage of learning item-meanings and at the stage of actual data collection. Furthermore, having a clear understanding of the items in the Q-set makes it possible for the observer to optimize note-taking and to make relevant queries to the parent for the purpose of gaining information about item-contents that are unlikely to be observed directly (e.g., the AQS, Waters, 1995, includes an item referring to whether or not the child becomes upset when left at home with a babysitter).

At this point, training continues by pairing the novice observer with an experienced, expert observer for the domain being evaluated and having them jointly observe targets from the study population, who may or may not necessarily be actual research participants. During the joint observations, the expert may instruct the novice observer immediately when activities relevant to the Q-set items are occurring, or these instances may be discussed after the observations are completed. After discussing the observations, the pair should jointly work through the Q-sorting process and complete a consensus sort for the target being described. Usually this stage of training is completed in two–four joint observations and assures that the novice has been exposed to the range of observed behaviors and rationales relevant to locating items at different positions in the required item distribution for the Q-sort. After completing this step, the novice observer can be considered "trained" and ready to begin observations for the study sample. After completing observations, each observer follows the three-step procedure illustrated in Figure 5.2 for all observed research participants.

In large-scale studies, in which many observers are describing many different research participants, it may be important to assure that all observers reach a predetermined degree of agreement with the expert observer(s). This is most efficiently accomplished using a standard set of observations based on video records of study participants that have been sorted by the expert observer(s). Video records assure that all observers are tested on the same stimulus set and save the time and expense associated with having the expert(s) complete the observations separately for each novice observer. Not only can observer agreement with the expert be calculated, but also between observer estimates of rater agreement and the reliability of multiple sorts (i.e., the aggregate of all observers) can be obtained easily and efficiently for the training videos. Observer agreement is typically calculated at the full Q-sort level (i.e., bivariate correlation analysis of the Q-matrix) for pair wise comparisons between observers and the reliability of composite Q-sorts (i.e., the average across sorters) can be obtained using Cronbach's alpha coefficient for the same dataset.

When two or more previously trained observers complete Q-sorts on actual study participants, rater agreement and Q-sort reliabilities are estimated in the same manner. The average of independent observers' Q-correlations (after r to z transformation) over the jointly observed cases (a minimum number of 20 cases jointly observed or 20% of the total sample in samples over 100 cases) is their sample-level agreement score. For example, in a study including 100 cases 20 cases would be jointly observed by the same pair of Q-sorters, generating 20 individual Q-correlations. The average of these Q-correlations would be the sample level value of rater agreement. An example of a data matrix for rater agreement/Q-sort reliability is shown in Table 5.2.

When agreement is acceptable for the purposes of the specific research question, the average of multiple sorts can be used to create the final Q-sort description and criterion scores may be computed from this aggregated sort. Alternatively, criterion scores may be derived from the sorts of each observer and the intraclass correlation between these scores is the indicator of agreement. Assuming agreement levels are acceptable for the purposes of the research being conducted, criterion scores may be averaged across observers to derive the scores used to test study hypotheses.

ILLUSTRATIVE EXAMPLES OF Q-METHOD STUDIES WITH RELEVANCE TO EDUCATION QUESTIONS

Thus far, we have described Q-methodology and protocols in a relatively abstract manner so as to suggest potential applications to readers. In this

TABLE 5.2 Q-Matrix for Calculating Observer Agreement When Multiple Observers Observe the Same Sample of Research Participants

Item #	Observer 1, Case 1	Observer 2, Case 1	Observer 1, Case 2	Observer 2, Case 2	...	Observer 1, Case N	Observer 2, Case N
Item 1	3	3	4	5		3	3
Item 2	7	8	9	8		7	6
Item 3	2	1	1	3		3	2
Item 4	4	3	5	6		4	3
Item 5	8	6	2	4		6	4
Item 6	4	4	6	7		5	5
Item 7	4	7	5	4		3	4
Item 8	1	2	8	6		2	3
Item 9	9	9	6	5		6	8
...							
Item N	2	4	3	3		2	3

Note: Observer 1 Q-sort is correlated with Observer 2 Q-sort for each case. The average correlation value (use r to z transformation) over all cases jointly sorted by a specific observer pair is their agreement score.

second major section, we present several illustrative "case studies" using Q-methods to evaluate specific substantive problems similar to those that may be encountered in education settings. The first of these involves construct definition and the generality of such definitions across socio-cultural boundaries. The second case addresses the issue of using two Q-samples to assess a single construct in one study. The third is a demonstration of the utility of Q-data to help "unpack" the dimensional structure of a complex construct. The final example illustrates a means to distinguish between two overlapping but distinct constructs using Q-sort data.

Using Q-Methods to Determine the Generality of Construct Definitions

We have discussed the creation of criterion Q-sort scores above and noted that this task makes use of the Q-method's utility in analyzing unique individual perspectives (i.e., subjective data) in a quantitative manner. When a criterion Q-sort is developed, scientists or other experts with respect to the domain at issue are asked to sort the Q-items so as to describe a person who is at one extreme on the domain. For example, education scientists studying young children's adaptation to the peer group wanted a comprehensive definition of the *Social Competence* construct (e.g., Waters, Garber, Gornal & Vaughn, 1983). They solicited several experts in young children's social behavior and social adaptation to provide descriptions of the hypothetical most socially competent preschool age child using two Q-sets (i.e., California Child Q-set [CCQ], Block & Block, 1980, and Preschool Q-set [PQ], based on a Q-set published by Baumrind, 1967). Finding substantial correlations across the Q-sort descriptions of all informants for Q-sets, Waters and associates averaged the sorts for each Q-item. These criterion Q-sorts became the definition of a highly socially competent preschooler in their subsequent research (e.g., Vaughn & Martino, 1988) and they were found to be correlated with each other as well as with other indicators of social competence (e.g., Vaughn et al., 2009). Waters and Deane (1985) used the same rationale and approach to derive their *Attachment Security* criterion Q-sort for the AQS.

Waters and associates intended that their criterion Q-sorts would serve as behaviorally referenced standard measures for the *Social Competence* and *Attachment Security* constructs and they have become widely adopted by other researchers, especially the AQS *Attachment Security* criterion. However, as these measures reached a broader audience questions were raised concerning potential adjustments to the best definition of attachment security when the construct was assessed in different sociocultural groups. Chen and French (2008) argued that diversities in cultural norms, values and orientations may lead to divergences in the way children's social behavior is interpreted and evaluated, with respect to which behaviors are identified as appropriate in a given social context and, consequently, in how to define the construct of social competence. With reference to attachment security, Harwood (e.g., Harwood, 1992; Harwood, Miller, & Irizarry, 1995) suggested that Latin American cultural values focused mothers' preferences for child behavior differently than in North America and northern Europe and that these preferences would impact what it meant to be securely attached in these cultures. Rothbaum and associates made similar arguments *vis-à-vis* Asian cultures (e.g., Rothbaum, Kakinuma, Nagaoka, & Azuma, 2007; Rothbaum, Morelli, & Rusk, 2010; Rothbaum, Weisz, Pott, Miyaki, & Morelli, 2000). These are clearly fundamental questions for theories of social competence and attachment security insofar as both assume that the core aspects of the domains covered by the theory are features of human nature that should be observable in virtually any human society. The two studies we review here address these questions.

Coppola and Camodeca (2010) conducted a study of preschool children's social competence with an Italian sample and wanted to determine whether cultural differences in collectivistic values (Oyserman, Coon, & Kemmelmeier, 2002) that distinguish Italian from U.S. cultures would influence the definitions of child social competence derived from criterion sorts. They recruited 30 experts from different regions of Italy who represented four distinct academic tracks in the Italian university system including education sciences, developmental psychology, social development, and child clinical psychology and asked them to sort one or the other of the two Q-sets (i.e., CCQ, $N = 16$, or PQ, $N = 14$) to describe the hypothetical most socially competent preschooler.

Q factor analyses for both each of the Q-sorts revealed a single common factor with an eigenvalue greater than 1.0 (i.e., all Q-sorts had their highest loading on the first extracted factor and no other factor accounted for as much as one unit of variance). The common factors accounted for approximately 76% and 72% of the common variance for the CCQ and PQ, respectively. Cronbach's alphas were .98 for the CCQ criterion and .95 for the PQ criterion. This suggests that within Italian academic culture there is a common understanding of what social competence should mean for preschool age children. A subsequent Q factor analysis was computed with the original Waters and associates (1983) *Social Competence* criterion Q-sort included. The result remained clear. Only one factor with an eigenvalue greater than 1.0 emerged in each analysis, with each variable loading strongly on the common factor (i.e., factor loadings ranged from .82–.93 and the loading for the original US criterion Q-sort was .89 for the CCQ analysis; loadings ranged from .82–.93 and the loading for the original US criterion Q-sort was .90 for the analysis of PQ Q-sorts). Out of 172 items for the two Q-sorts, only eight (6 from the CCQ, 2 from the PQ) were placed as much as 1.5 categories apart when the final composite Italian Q-sorts were compared to the US criterion sorts. These results indicate that the definition of *Social Competence* derived from expert sorts of the CCQ and PQ item sets are not meaningfully different from the original U.S. definition and that either of these could be used in Italian samples to obtain valid assessments of child social competence in preschool classrooms.

Posada and associates (e.g., Posada et al., 1995; Posada et al., 2013) have conducted studies examining the cross-cultural generality of the AQS *Attachment Security* criterion Q-sort in response to the kinds of critiques offered by Rothbaum and associates (e.g., Rothbaum et al., 2000). In their initial study, Posada and associates (1995) recruited 104 experts from seven countries (China, Japan, Colombia, Israel, Norway, Germany, and the United States). The experts represented a range of disciplines including early childhood education and developmental psychology. They had a range of expertise regarding the Bowlby/Ainsworth theory of attachment but most had extensive experience observing the behavior of infants and/or young children. Each expert sorted the original version of the AQS (Waters & Deane, 1985) using a common distribution of items to categories to describe optimal secure base behavior for a young child. Based on correlation analyses within each country, Posada and associates created country-level composites for analysis and reported the cross-nation correlations (range of $rs = .78 - .93$) and suggested that the experts held a common understanding of the meaning of attachment security based on secure base behavior across all countries represented. Furthermore, these country-level composite Q-sorts were strongly associated with sorts for the "ideal" child contributed by mothers of children from each culture (range of $rs = .67–.91$). They concluded that most mothers in the countries represented preferred young children who behaved like a child described by experts as securely attached.

In the Posada and associates (2013) study, 75 experts from eight different countries (Canada, Colombia, France, Italy, Japan, Peru, Portugal, and Taiwan,) used the most recent revision of the AQS (Waters, 1995) to test the currently accepted criterion score for *Attachment Security* in terms of its cross-national generality. For the purposes of this chapter, we re-analyzed the resulting data using Q-factor analyses. At the first step, expert sorts from each country were analyzed to determine the number of common factors in the data. In every country represented in the sample, a single common factor accounting for between 65% and 81% of common variance was obtained and no other factor had an eigenvalue greater than 1.0 in any sample. These results indicate that for each country represented there is strong agreement among the experts regarding the Q-sort definition of *Attachment Security*.

In the next step, composites for each country plus the U.S. criterion Q-sort were included in another Q factor analysis. Again a single common factor accounting for over 88% of the variance was obtained (factor loadings range = .91–.98). Thus, using the AQS items to define the meaning of *Attachment Security*, there is a single definition that is applicable across all countries represented in the Posada and associates sample. This is consistent with expectations from attachment theory (e.g., Waters, 1995) and suggests that the cultural critiques of attachment security as being overly influenced by North American and northern European biases about ideal relationships may lack an empirical basis.

As noted above, our goal for describing these studies in some detail is to provide a concrete illustration of how subjective Q-sort data (i.e., how individual experts on a topic define a specific construct when provided with the common language of the Q-set) can be evaluated quantitatively to answer broader questions about the validity of the construct(s) in question. These studies contribute to the understandings of both social competence and attachment security and suggest that the Q-sets and criterion Q-sorts derived from them may be used across a range of sociocultural milieu to yield valuable individual difference information about young children.

Using Multiple Q-Sets to Measure a Single Construct in One Study

When Stephenson first described Q-methods, he assumed that any Q-sample would be a representative set of items from a universe or population of such items and that a different Q-sample might have been drawn randomly from the same item universe that would have been equally representative. This aspect of the Q-method has proven very attractive in studies assuming that objective data can be extracted from subjective observations of persons/entities, in part because current best practices for data analysis emphasize the creation of latent variables for testing many hypotheses. However, it is important to test the assumption that different, partially overlapping Q-samples do, in fact register the same underlying construct(s). Vaughn and associates (2009) demonstrated the utility of using two different Q-sets in their multisample, multinational (i.e., samples from the United States, the Netherlands, and Portugal) study of social competence.

The central premise of the Vaughn and associates (2009) report was that the *Social Competence* construct should be considered a multidimensional construct that would be best modeled as a hierarchical (or second-order) factor in latent variable analyses (i.e., confirmatory factor analysis, CFA). One of the first order dimensions they included as a constituent of *Social Competence* was based on criterion scores for *Social Competence* from CCQ and PQ Q-sorts completed by observers. In each sample, each observer (two per classroom) spent approximately 20 hours in the classroom watching the children and taking notes on their behavior. After completing 20 hours in the classroom, each observer described every participating child using one (or both) of the two Q-sets (i.e., CCQ, PQ) and criterion scores for each child were derived and these served as measured variables in the CFA. This dimension was presumed to represent the social behaviors/skills and personality attributes of a socially competent preschool age child (e.g., Coppola & Camodeca, 2010; Waters et al., 1983).

The CFA was consistent with the hypothesized model in each of the five samples, and the measurement model (i.e., loadings of measured variables on their individual first-order factors) was invariant across all five samples. Focusing explicitly on the first-order factor associated with the Q-sort *Social Competence* criterion scores, in each of the five samples, this factor significantly predicted the CCQ and PQ criterion scores (loadings ranged from .69 to .92, median loading = .765). Furthermore, this first-order factor had strong loadings on the second order factor in all five samples (path coefficients ranged from .74 to .95, median path coefficient = .91). This replicated pattern of findings suggests that the two Q-samples represented by the items from the CCQ and PQ do in fact come from the same item universe and that the composite of the two criterion scores is more reliable and valid indicator of child social competence than either score individually. From the perspective of this chapter, the findings also demonstrate the utility of Q-sort data for gathering normative, objective information about young children.

Using Q-Sort Data to Unpack Meaning for Complex Constructs

The first two examples consider how the criterion scores for Q-sort data can be used to address substantive questions about the generality of construct definitions and the wider utility of the constructs in research. Here we consider how items from Q-sort descriptions can be valuable in determining the breadth of meaning(s) and the possible implications of different measures/constructs. Waters and associates (1983) attempted to determine if a behavioral indicator of social dominance (i.e., attracting attention from peers, Chance, 1967) might be better interpreted as an indicator of social competence in preschool age children. To test this possibility, a team of observers collected data on the frequency with which individual children were targets of their peers' attention while another team independently observed the same children for the purposes of completing Q-sort descriptions using the CCQ and PQ item sets discussed above (total of 172 items) in three classrooms of preschool children ($N = 56$).

Data analyses consisted (in part) of an examination of the Q-item correlations of receiving visual attention, in each classroom and for the combined sample. To be considered a Q-item correlate of visual attention received from peers, Waters and associates (1983) required that the item be significantly associated with visual attention in the combined sample and reach the same level of magnitude in at least two of the three classrooms. Sixty-three of the 172 Q-items (37%) met this criterion. Items with high positive associations (i.e., >.50) included "peer leader," "is admired and sought out by other children," "is self-assertive," and "confident of own ability." Items with high negative associations (i.e., >−.50) included "spectator in social activities," "hesitates to engage," "when in conflict with others tends to give in," and "typically in the role of listener." Waters and associates used hierarchical cluster analysis to group related items (with the caveat that the minimum cluster reliability, Cronbach's alpha, was ≥.80 and the next item added to the cluster reduced cluster reliability). The nine-cluster solution met these criteria (Socially skilled; Engages peers; Active, energetic; Confident vs. anxious; Direct, persistent; Purposive; Open, straightforward; Impetuous vs. reflective; and Feels guilty, with these items being signed negatively). Not surprisingly, the nine cluster scores were themselves significantly correlated (35 of 36 p-values <.01) and all cluster scores were significant correlates of receiving visual attention from peers. Waters and associates (1983) concluded that while many of the correlates of receiving attention from peers were consistent with social dominance, the range of correlates suggested a socially engaged, physically active, and confident child who had positive relationships with peers and who was sought out by peers as a playmate. These features, they argued suggested that social dominance was only a modest aspect of what receiving visual attention implied in the group and concluded that receiving visual attention from peers should be considered an indicator of social competence more broadly.

Defining Boundaries of Related Constructs Using Q-Sort Data

In addition to his enthusiastic support for the Q-sort method to obtain objective behavioral and personality data, Jack Block also championed the use of Q-data for identifying critical distinctions between related constructs (e.g., Block & Kremen, 1996). Throughout his professional career, Block studied adaptive functioning and the complex structures of personality that supported adaptive functioning from childhood to adulthood (e.g., Block, 1961; Block & Block, 1980). He summarized two of these structural aspects as "ego-control" and "ego-resiliency" and he designed and validated a variety of laboratory, observation, and questionnaire measures to describe them (e.g., Block, 1981; Block & Block, 1980). Block & Kremen (1996) focused on the second of these (i.e., ego-resiliency), which they defined thusly: "... the dynamic capacity o an individual to modify a characteristic level of ego-control, in either direction, as a function of the demand characteristics of the environmental context, so as to preserve or enhance system equilibration." Depending on the press of the context, this definition implies the capacity to shift from and to return to the individual's typical level of ego-control when stresses imposed by the environment are no longer present. They also suggested that the notion of "resilience" implies a persoonological quality of the person that applies across time and context; it is not intended as a characterization of a specific encounter with environmental stresses on a single occasion.

Block and Kremen point out that the definition of ego-resiliency implies the exercise of cognitive faculties including control of attention, short-term memory, effortful control, and regulation of action, thought, and affect and that these faculties are often considered as elements of intelligence, broadly construed. This fact, they argued, most likely accounted for published findings demonstrating significant associations between measures of ego-resiliency and IQ (e.g., Funder & Block, 1989; Hart, Hofmann, Edelstein, & Keller, 1997; Robins, John, Caspi, Moffitt, & Strouthamer-Loeber, 1996). These kinds of associations raise potential questions about the implications of individual differences in general intelligence (at least as assessed using standard IQ tests) for the wider meaning of ego-resiliency. That is, should ego-resiliency be considered a subset of what is meant by IQ? To test this question, Block and Kremen "purified" their measures of ego-resiliency (assessed using a 14-item self-report questionnaire) and IQ (assessed using the Wechsler Adult Intelligence Scale, 1981) by controlling the effects of IQ in tests associating ego-resiliency with external variables using partial correlations (and *vice versa*, controlling the effects of ego-resiliency in tests associating IQ with the same set of outcome variables). In their study, outcome variables were the 100 items from Block's *California Adult Q-set* (Block, 1961), based on multiple observations for 95 (49 female) participants in the J. Block and J. H. Block longitudinal study (1980) when they were 23 years of age.

For the young women, 42 of the 100 CAQ items were significantly associated with ego-resiliency when IQ was controlled in the analyses. Ego-resiliency was positive associated with items suggesting social poise, assertiveness, gregariousness, cheerfulness, and as having a sense of meaning in life whereas, negative correlates emphasized issues of self-concern, fearfulness, and rumination. In the sample of young men, 49 CAQ items were significantly correlated with ego-resiliency when IQ was controlled. In addition to the qualities of gregariousness, cheerfulness, and the absence of rumination and fearfulness that characterized the item-correlates for women, ego-resiliency was positively associated with a capacity for commitment, responsibility, ethical behavior, and sympathetic caring in relationships. Negative correlates also included rebelliousness, irritability, fluctuating moods, hostility to others, and feeling cheated in life.

The 24 "pure" IQ CAQ item correlates for women (i.e., ego-resiliency controlled) positively suggested the appearance of high intellectual capacity, valuing intellectual matters, verbal fluency, and a wide range of interests, as well as a tendency to introspection, to complicate simple situations, and a readiness to feel guilt. Negative correlates included assertiveness, interests in the opposite sex, tends to give advice to others, and being protective of those close to him/her. For the male subsample, 31 CAQ item-correlates of IQ were obtained when ego-resiliency was controlled. In addition, to items emphasizing intellective capacity (e.g., values intellectual and cognitive matters; verbal fluency; prides self on being objective, rational), "pure" IQ was positively associated with items suggesting an emphasis on productivity and integrity (e.g., gets things done; is a genuinely dependable and responsible person), as well as a tendency to overcontrol (e.g., fastidious, perfectionistic; tends toward over-control of needs and impulses). Negative "pure" IQ correlates also suggest a mixture of undesirable tendencies (e.g., self-indulgent, self-defeating, unpredictable and changeable with regard to behavior and attitudes, pushes limits, gives up and withdraws from frustration or adversity).

These patterns of results are interesting and useful for understanding both the commonalities and the differences between the constructs of ego-resiliency and IQ. Moreover, they show that objective Q-sort data can serve to identify and illustrate those commonalities and differences, when the Q-set has been designed to represent the range of possible constructs associated with a specific domain (in this case, adaptation to life circumstances).

CONCLUSION

We intended that this chapter should give readers an overview of Q-methodology and the kinds of research questions to which Q-data might be put, so as to suggest that these methods could find applications in education settings. Q-methods have been used in the behavioral, developmental, and clinical sciences to specify operational definitions of abstract constructs, to illuminate distinctions among related constructs, to identify homogeneous subgroups of persons within a larger population, to compare the quality of adaptation to specific contexts for individuals who differ with respect to the salient constructs defined, and to track the development of critical constructs (e.g., social competence, ego-control) over contexts and over time. We have also described the processes that researchers would use in the creation of new Q-samples that might be designed with additional education-relevant questions in mind. We note that these methods are not unknown in the education sciences and that both the Q-method and Q-data are being used now by a few education scientists to address similar kinds of questions in education settings, as indicated by the citation list for the opening paragraphs of the chapter. Hopefully, this chapter will introduce many more researchers to these methods, measures, and analytic approaches. They have proven extraordinarily profitable in our own research efforts and we believe that they can be equally valuable to others.

NOTE

1. Preparation of this chapter was supported in part by NSF grant BCS 0843919. Communication concerning this chapter should be directed to Brian E. Vaughn, Department of Human Development & Family Studies, 203 Spidle Hall, Auburn University, Auburn, AL 36849, email: vaughbe@auburn.edu

REFERENCES

Ainsworth, M. D. S., Blehar, M. C., Waters, E., & Wall, S. (1978). *Patterns of attachment: A psychological study of the strange situation.* Hillsdale, NJ: Erlbaum.

Baumrind, D. (1967). Child care practices anteceding three patterns of preschool behavior. *Genetic Psychology Monographs, 75,* 43–48.

Block, J. (1961). *The Q-sort method in personality assessment and psychiatric research.* Springfield, IL: Charles C. Thomas Publisher.

Block, J. (1965). *The challenge of response sets.* New York, NY: Appleton-Century-Crofts.

Block, J. (1981). Some enduring and consequential structures of personality. In A. I Rabin, J. Aronoff, A. M. Barclay, & R. A. Zucker (Eds.), *Further explorations in personality* (pp. 27–43). New York, NY: Wiley.

Block, J. (1990) More remarks on social desirability. *American Psychologist, 45,* 1076–1077.

Block, J. (2008). *The Q-sort in character appraisal: Encoding subjective impressions of persons quantitatively.* New York: American Psychological Association.

Block, J. H., & Block, J. (1980). The role of ego-control and ego-resiliency in the organization of behaviour. In W. A. Collins (Ed.), *Minnesota symposium on child psychology. Vol. 13. Development of cognition, affect, and social relations* (pp. 39–101). Hillsdale, NJ: Erlbaum.

Block, J., Block, J. H., & Keyes, S. (1988). longitudinally foretelling drug usage m adolescence early childhood personality and environmental precursors. *Child Development, 59,* 336–355.

Block, J., & Kremen, A. M. (1996). IQ and ego resiliency: Conceptual and empirical connections and separateness. *Journal of Personality and Social Psychology, 70*, 349–361.

Bradley, J., & Miller, A. (2010). Widening participation in higher education: Constructions of "going to university." *Educational Psychology in Practice, 26*, 401–413.

Brown, S.R. (1972). A fundamental incommensurability between objectivity and subjectivity. In S. R. Brown & D. J. Brenner (Eds.), Science, psychology, and communication: Essays honoring William Stephenson (pp. 57–94). New York, NY: Teachers College Press.

Brown, S. R. (1980). Political subjectivity: Applications of Q methodology in political science. New Haven, CT: Yale University Press.

Brown, S. R. (1996). Q methodology and qualitative research. *Qualitative Health Research, 6*, 561–567.

Burt, C. (1937). Correlations between persons. *British Journal of Psychology, 28*, 59–96.

Burt, C. (1938). The unit hierarchy and its properties. *Psychometrika, 3*, 151–168.

Burt, C. (1955). [Review of the book *The study of behavior*]. *Occupational Psychology, 29*, 58.

Burt, C., & Stephenson, W. (1939). Alternative views on correlations between persons. *Psychometrika, 4*, 269–281.

Cartwright, D. S. (1956). *A coefficient of consistency over T Q sorts*, Counseling Center Discussion Paper, Vol. II, April, 1956.

Cartwright, R. D. (1957). Effects of psychotherapy on self-consistency. *Journal of Counseling Psychology, 4*, 15–22.

Chance, M. R. A. (1967). *Attention structure as the basis of primate rank orders.* Man NS 2: 4.503–518.

Chen, X., & French, D.(2008). Children's social competence in cultural context. *Annual Review of Psychology 59*, 591–616.

Coppola, G., & Camodeca, M. (2010). *La metodologia Q-Sort. Valutare la competenza sociale nella scuola dell'infanzia* [The Q-Sort methodology. The assessment of social competence in kindergarten]. Roma: Carocci Editore.

Cronbach, L. J., & Gleser, G. C. (1954). [Review of the book *The study of behavior*]. *Psychometrika 19*, 327–330.

Duncan, N., & Owens, L. (2011). Bullying, social power and heteronormativity: Girls' constructions of popularity. *Children and Society, 25*, 306–316.

Funder, D. C., & Block, J. (1989). The role of ego-control, ego-resiliency, and IQ in delay of gratification in adolescence. *Journal of Personality and Social Psychology, 57*, 1041–1050.

Hart, D., Hofmann, V., Edelstein, W., & Keller, M. (1997). The relation of personality types to adolescent behavior and development: A longitudinal study of Icelandic children. *Developmental Psychology, 33*, 195–205.

Harwood, R. L. (1992). The influence of culturally derived values on Anglo and Puerto Rican mothers' perceptions of attachment behavior. *Child Development, 63*, 822–839.

Harwood, R. L., Miller, J. G., & Irizarry, N. L. (1995). Culture and attachment: Perceptions of the child in context. *Culture and human development.* New York: Guilford Press.

Lanning, K. (1994). Dimensionality of observer ratings on the California Adult Q-set. *Journal of Personality and Social Psychology, 67,* 151–160.

Lim, C. (2010). Understanding Sinaporean preschool teachers' beliefs about literacy development: Four different perspectives. *Teaching and Teacher Education, 26,* 215–224.

Massetti, G. M., & Braken, S. S. (2010). Classroom academic and social context: Relationships among emergent literacy, behavioral functioning, and teacher curriculum goals in kindergarten. *Early Child Development and Care, 180,* 359–375.

McCrae. R. R., Terracciano, A., Costa, P. T., & Ozer, D. J. (2006). Person-factors in the California Adult Q-Set: Closing the door on personality trait types? *European Journal of Personality, 20,* 29–44.

McNally, S., Eisenberg, N., & Harris, J. D. (1991). Child-rearing practices and values: A longitudinal study. *Child Development, 62,* 190–198.

Oyserman, D., Coon, H. M., Kemmelmeier, M. (2002). Rethinking individualism and collectivism: Evaluation of theoretical assumptions and meta-analyses. *Psychological Bullettin, 128,* 3–72.

Posada, G., Gao, Y., Fang, W., Posada, R., Tascon, M., Schoelmerich, Sagi, A., Kondo-Ikemura, K., Ylaland, W., & Synnevaag, B. (1995). The secure base phenomenon across cultures: Children's behavior, mothers' preferences, and experts' concepts. In E. Waters, B. Vaughn, G. Posada, & K. Kondo-Ikemura (Eds.), *Caregiving, cultural and cognitive perspectives on secure-base behavior and working models: New growing points of attachment theory and research.* Monographs of the Society for Research in Child Development. Nos. 2–3, pp. 27–48.

Posada, G., Lu, T., Trumbell, J., Kaloustian, G., Trudel, M., Plata, Peña, P. P, . . . Lay, K. L. (In press). Is the secure base phenomenon evident here, there, and anywhere? A cross-cultural study of child behavior and experts' definitions. *Child Development.* DOI: 10.1111/cdev.12084

Robins, R. W., John, O. P., Caspi, A., Moffitt, T., & Strouthamer-Loeber, M. (1996). Resilient, overcontrolled, and undercontrolled boys: Three replicable personality types. *Journal of Personality and Social Psychology, 70,* 157–171.

Rogers, C. R., & Dymond, R. F. (Eds.). (1954). *Psychotherapy and personality change.* Chicago: University of Chicago Press.

Rothbart, M. K., Ahadi, S. A., Hershey, K. L., & Fischer, P. (2001). Investigations of temperament at three to seven years: The Children's Behavior Questionnaire. *Child Development, 72*(5), 1394–408.

Rothbaum, F. Morelli, G., & Rusk, N. (2010). Attachment learning and coping: The interplay of cultural similarities and differences. In M. J. Gelfand, C-Y Chiu, & Y-Y. Hong (Eds.) *Advances in culture and psychology* (Vol. 1., pp. 153–216). New York, NY: Oxford University Press.

Rothbaum, F., Weisz, J., Pott, M., Miyake, K., & Morelli, G. (2000). Attachment and culture: Security in the Unites States and Japan. *American Psychologist, 55,* 1093–1104.

Stephenson, W. (1935). Correlating persons instead of tests. *Character and Personality, 4,* 17–24.

Stephenson, W. (1936). The inverted factor technique. *British Journal of Psychology, 26,* 344–361.

Stephenson, W. (1950). A statistical approach to typology: The study of trait universes. *Journal of Clinical Psychology, 6,* 26–38.
Stephenson, W. (1953). *The study of behavior: Q-technique and its methodology.* Chicago: University of Chicago Press.
Stephenson, W. (1978). Concourse theory of communication. *Communication, 3,* 21–40.
Tellegen, A. (1982). *Brief manual for the Multidimensional Personality Questionnaire.* Unpublished manuscript, University of Minnesota, Minneapolis. (Renamed Multidimensional Personality Questionnaire.)
Vaughn, B. E., Deane, K., & Waters, E. (1985). The impact of out-of-home care on child–mother attachment quality: Another look at some enduring questions. In I. Bretherton & E. Waters (Eds.), *Growing points of attachment theory and research.* (pp. 110–135). Monographs of the Society for Research in Child Development, 50 (Serial No. 209).
Vaughn, B. E., & Martino, D. (1988). Age related Q-sort correlates of visual regard in groups of preschool children. *Developmental Psychology, 24,* 589–594.
Vaughn, B. E., Shin, N., Kim, M., Coppola, G., Krzysik, L., Santos, A. J., Peceguina, I.,... Korth, B. (2009). Hierarchical models of social competence in preschool children: A multi-site, multi-national study. *Child Development, 84,* 1896–1905.
Webler, T., Danielson, S., & Tuler, S. (2009). *Using Q method to reveal social perspectives in environmental research.* Greenfield MA: Social and Environmental Research Institute. Retrieved from: http://www.seri-us.org/sites/default/files/Qprimer.pdf
Waters, E. (1995). The attachment Q-set (version 3.0). In E. Waters, B. Vaughn, G. Posada, & K. Kondo-Ikemura (Eds), *Caregiving, cultural, and cognitive perspectives on secure base behavior and working models: New growing points of attachment research.* Monographs of the Society for Research in Child Development, 60 (Serial No. 244).
Waters, E. & Deane (1985).
Waters, E., Garber, J., Gornal, M., & Vaughn, B.E. (1983). Q-sort correlates of social competence. *Developmental Psychology, 19,* 550–560.
Waters, E., Noyes, D., Vaughn, B. E., & Ricks, M. (1985). Social competence and self-esteem: A Q-sort analysis of conceptual and empirical similarities between related constructs. *Developmental Psychology, 21,* 508–522.
Waters E., & Vaughn, B. E. (in press). Assessing secure base behavior in naturalistic environments: The Attachment Q-set. In E. Waters, B. E., Vaughn, & H. S. Waters (Eds.), *Measuring attachment: A handbook of methods.* New York, NY: Guilford.
Wechsler, D. (1981). *Manual for the Wechsler Adult Intelligence Scale-Revised.* New York, NY: Psychological Corporation.

CHAPTER 6

THE DELPHI PROCESS

Ian P. Sinha and Olivia N. Saracho

INTRODUCTION

For more than six decades, researchers have searched for a way to collect information based on the knowledge and experience of experts in a field which will guide them in making decisions and predictions about the future. Several researchers have used the Delphi process to elicit and refine the combined opinion and expertise of a panel of experts to reach a consensus.

Consensus research methods can be used to examine how effective decisions are made in situations where there is inconsistent or scarce information. They include brainstorming, nominal group technique, and the "Delphi" survey technique, which is a systematic method to acquire the opinions and, preferably a consensus from a panel of experts on a specific issue. The Delphi technique is a method of ascertaining the opinions of a group of experts to reach consensus around areas of uncertainty. The process entails a series of questionnaires that are completed anonymously by a group of participants, each of whose opinion is accounted for when the final consensus is reached.

Since the Delphi technique has been extensively used and modified in many ways, the purpose of this chapter is to provide a definition and history of the Delphi technique as well as discuss (a) consensus development methods, (b) the use of the Delphi as a research technique, (c) steps in designing a Delphi research study, and (d) important methodological considerations for researchers and highlight potential pitfalls. The chapter concludes with recommendations for the reporting of studies that utilize the Delphi technique, such that researchers reading the report will be able to comprehensively understand and critique the methods and results. The chapter deals mainly with the use of the Delphi process for reaching consensus in order to formulate a "list," as this is the manner in which it is most likely to be used; but the methodological recommendations also pertain to studies that use the technique for other purposes. This chapter does not deal with the development and validation of questionnaires, which are covered elsewhere in this book.

DEFINITION

Delphi is a systematic method to build group consensus using a panel of experts that avoids the logistical and other challenges and group dynamic concerns that are related to more conventional collaborative procedures. There are several descriptions and definitions of the Delphi technique. For example, Delbecq, Van de Ven, and Gustafson (1975) define it as "a method for the systematic solicitation and collection of judgments on a particular topic through a set of carefully designed sequential questionnaires interspersed with summarized information and feedback of opinions derived from earlier responses" (p. 10). Fish and Busby (2005) refer to the Delphi technique as a process that is used to negotiate a reality that can be used to improve a specific field, prepare for the future, or modify the future by predicting its situations. All definitions indicate that the Delphi technique is an outstanding method to have continuous and organized communication between groups of competent experts in a precise field to establish an acceptable resolution to a complicated problem (Linstone & Turoff, 1975).

HISTORY

The Delphi technique is named after the ancient Greek town of Delphi. This research method has historical roots with the ancient Greek God of light, purity, the sun and prophecy. According to the myth, after slaying the dragon Python in Delphi, Apollo seized the temple in Delphi that had the well-known oracle,[1] Pythia. Apollo allegedly communicated through this oracle to the ancient Greeks to forecast the future (Fish & Busby, 2005). From this modest mythological initiation, Delphi has progressed into an enduring wide spreading research methodology.

In 1948 the Rand Corporation conducted the first Delphi experiment for military research and defense matters. They used the name "Project Delphi" (Dalkey & Helmer, 1963) in developing a consensus among United States experts concerning Soviet opinions on optimal American industrial targets and the quantity of firepower that was needed for their demolition (Linstone & Turoff, 1975). In 1963, the Delphi technique flourished after the publication of the first article that described it. Between 1950 and 1963, Helmer and Dalkey used the Delphi technique at the Rand Corporation to conduct numerous experiments that were related to defense (Gupta & Clarke, 1996).The Delphi technique had a huge increase in usage throughout the 1960s and 1970s. It broke out onto the scientific setting with Gordon and Helmer-Hirschberg's 1964 study that predicted long-range trends in science and technology. In the present research community, the Delphi technique is frequently used in fields such as education, psychology, sociology, political science, human health, transportation, and the environment (Fish & Busby, 2005). Thus, the Delphi technique has become a widely used research method in a variety of disciplines.

CONSENSUS DEVELOPMENT METHODS

Evidence-based guidelines are found in consensus development methodologies such as open group discussions, nominal group technique, and Delphi technique. A careful consideration of the methodology improves the outcomes of the consensus process and evidence-based guidelines.

Consensus—Why Is It Important, and How Can It Be Reached?

Ideally, guidelines and recommendations in education should be based on evidence derived from rigorously conducted research. If such evidence is lacking, uncertainty may remain about particular questions. Let us consider the development of a curriculum for teaching history to first grade pupils. Some may advocate that young children should learn about recent local history, others that history lessons should start at the beginning of civilization, and an alternative opinion would be that lessons should focus on specific historical events.

Although each of these approaches has merits, a judgment must ultimately be made about which is used. For example, Feinberg, Saracho, and

Spodek (1990a) assumed that the historical tradition of Jewish education is a main source for a Jewish curriculum. In identifying innovative approaches to a sectarian curriculum for early childhood Jewish schools, Feinberg, Saracho, and Spodek (1990b) used the Delphi technique to identify Jewish sectarian content that would be appropriate for young children in Jewish early childhood education religious programs. The Delphi approach enabled them to compare the practitioners' ideas in making Jewish curriculum choices.

The responsibility for making such a judgment could rest either with one individual or a group. The collective recommendations of a group are likely to be more credible, because they are based on a wider range of experiences and knowledge. In research, three main methods can be used to reach consensus: open group discussion, Nominal Group technique, and the Delphi technique. Although this chapter relates to the Delphi technique, the other related methods are briefly discussed below.

Open Group Discussions

The use of group-based techniques to generate ideas and solve problems is customary in many disciplines and for many purposes. Open group discussions can either be structured, in which a facilitator leads the group through discussion points, or unstructured, in which the dialogue is not driven by a facilitator. The overall group opinion can be ascertained either by the facilitator interpreting the group feeling or by way of a vote. The advantages of open group discussion are that a fruitful debate between participants can generate new ideas, resolve differences, or highlight problems that should be addressed.

The main problems with open group discussion relate to group dynamics; because certain types of personalities can inhibit debate, reduce productivity, and compromise the credibility of the pooled opinion. These may include participants that dominate the decision making process, are unwilling to change their position once publicly taken, do not voice disagreement with people more senior than themselves, acquiesce for the sake of reaching consensus, or are reluctant to mention a new idea, because they are afraid of being criticized.

Nominal Group Technique

Nominal Group Technique (NGT) aims to reduce problems of group dynamics by focusing discussion in a very structured fashion. A panel of experts, typically between 10 and 15 members in number, discusses one clearly defined problem at a time, at a face-to-face meeting. Each participant shares their opinion with the group without interruption and then an anonymous vote is taken. There should be a pre-determined definition of what constitutes consensus, disagreement, or uncertainty amongst the group.

Using this technique, specific problems can be discussed in order to generate ideas and share opinions. Each participant's view is heard by the group, and incorporated equally in the vote. This means that the final group decision is less likely to be swayed by a vocal minority or by people of seniority. The disadvantages are that only a small group can be involved and they must all convene at the same place and time. Problems of group dynamics are not completely overcome; because even if the vote is anonymous, the process of stating opinions and sharing ideas is not.

THE USE OF DELPHI AS A RESEARCH TECHNIQUE

The Delphi is a research technique that has been extensively applied to a broad range of problems in a variety of areas. Since the technique was established in the early 1950s at the Rand Corporation, many deviations of the Delphi have emerged to guide researchers to examine their unique problems. Sinha, Smyth, and Williamson (2011) point out that:

- Studies that use the Delphi process for gaining consensus around a core outcome set of variables should be of sufficiently high quality in order for their recommendations to be considered valid.
- Studies that used the Delphi technique vary in their methodology and reporting.
- The quality of studies that use the Delphi process is improved when everybody is involved in the process. For example, in a classroom study young children, teachers, parents, administrators, the community, and anybody who has knowledge of the subject matter should participate in the study.
- Researchers and facilitators should avoid imposing their views on participants to minimize the participants' dropout rate.
- Methodological procedures and decisions should be clearly described for publication purposes.

In the Delphi technique, a panel of participants, each with relevant expertise, anonymously answers a series of questionnaires. After each "round" of questions, the group response is fed back to participants. The result of each round determines the composition of the subsequent questionnaire. Improved global communication enables involvement of geographically distant participants in larger numbers than can be achieved in face-to-face discussion. Partly for this reason, the Delphi technique is an increasingly popular method of reaching consensus. Some examples of its use are shown in Table 6.1.

TABLE 6.1 Possible Uses of the Delphi Technique in Early Childhood Education

Making a "List"

- Topics for inclusion in curricula
- Prioritizing research topics
- Developing a list of suitable school trips
- Agreeing to suitable questions for quizzes or examinations
- Identifying areas of agreement or disagreement
- Highlighting differences between parents' and teachers' views about curricula
- Identifying discrepancies in approaches to teaching

ADVANTAGES OF THE DELPHI APPROACH

The Delphi approach has advantages over less structured methods of reaching consensus, but the fundamental aspects of the Delphi technique can be scrutinized. Some of its advantages are that it uses (a) anonymity, (b) experts in the area of study, and (c) sequential rounds of voting where participants provide feedback in each round.

Anonymity

The Delphi approach is a democratic and structured approach that shields the participants' anonymity. Traditionally, participants in a Delphi study do not interact with each other directly, which helps avoid situations where certain individuals dominate the group. When participants consider their answers in light of the group response, they are not pressured to tailor their opinion to publically agree with individuals who are more senior, vocal, or domineering. Anonymity, however, means that participants are not individually accountable for the quality of their responses.

The Use of "Experts"

It seems implicit that if consensus is to be reached on a particular topic, participants with relevant expertise should be consulted. However, this raises questions about what constitutes "expertise." It is tempting to suggest that experts are those with influential names, who work at prestigious institutions. It is important to remember, however, that others may have experience that is more extensive, recent, or relevant, with regard to the particular topic in hand. Table 6.2 provides examples of experts in different areas that were used in early childhood education studies that used the Delphi approach.

TABLE 6.2 Purposes, Rounds, and Experts in Early Childhood Education Delphi Studies

Study	Purpose	Rounds	Experts
Feinberg, Saracho, & Spodek (1990a)	Identify sectarian curriculum content for Jewish early childhood education programs	2	National Jewish Early Childhood Network members ($n = 154$)
Kim, Lee, Suen, & Lee (2003)	Identify concepts of young children's readiness in Korea	4	Early childhood education experts in Korea ($n = 22$)
Osborne, Collins, Ratcliffe, Millar, & Duschl (2003)	Identify key ideas that are essential in a science curriculum	3	Leading international educational scientists ($n = 22$)
Samarakkody, Fernando, Perera, McClure & De Silva (2010)	Develop and validate a 54 item screening instrument for early identification of behavioral problems for children aged 4-6 years	3	Experts from relevant fields: Pediatrics, Child Psychiatry, Community Medicine and Child Psychology ($n = 15$)
van den Heuvel-Panhuizen & Elia (2012)	Identify characteristics of picturebooks that can be used to support young children's learning of mathematics	4	Experts on children's literature in early childhood mathematics education or on the use of literature in mathematics education ($n = 7$)

Sequential Rounds of Voting That Provide Feedback to Participants

The Delphi approach aims to reach consensus as the process progresses. Results from each round are used to inform the subsequent questionnaire. After each questionnaire, presentation of the overall group opinion (e.g., the number of participants who voted for or against a suggestion) enables participants to consider their opinion in light of what the group thinks and either stick to their original choice or change their mind. Table 6.3 provides examples of the different rounds that were used in Delphi studies in early childhood education.

If an individual's opinions do not match those of the overall group, this feedback can cause problems. Some people may change their answers just to reach consensus with the rest of the group. They may even drop out of the process, if they feel that the final group consensus will not match their own views. The steps in designing and implementing a Delphi study may help avoid these problems.

TABLE 6.3 Differences in Rounds in Early Childhood Education Delphi Studies

Study	Round 1	Round 2	Round 3	Round 4
Feinberg, Saracho, & Spodek (1990a)	Experts identified Jewish sectarian content items to teach young children	Experts prioritized these content items in order of perceived importance		
Kim, Lee, Suen, & Lee (2003)	Experts rated a list of 23 items and open-ended questions on a 3 point scale	Experts ranked order the final 23 items in order of importance	Experts revised their ranking based on all of the second round rankings and provided a written rationale for any discrepancies (e.g., rank of this item should be higher because . . .).	Experts finalized their ranking order based on all of the third round rankings and reasons that the items should be ranked higher or lower.
Osborne, Collins, Ratcliffe, Millar, & Duschl (2003)	Experts provided extensive comments on key ideas that are essential in a science curriculum, which were categorized into 30 themes.	Experts rated the importance of each theme on a 5-point Likert scale, where 18 items had the highest rating.	Experts rated each of the 18 themes, justified their rating, and suggested terminology that would reflect the essence of each science idea.	

(continued)

TABLE 6.3 Differences in Rounds in Early Childhood Education Delphi Studies (continued)

Study	Round 1	Round 2	Round 3	Round 4
Samarakkody, Fernando, Perera, McClure & De Silva (2010)	Experts assessed and commented on a preliminary list of 54 items to be included in a screening instrument. They rated each item on a five point scale as: 1. Most important; 2. Important; 3. Don't know; 4. Unimportant; 5. Should be deleted.	Experts rated the items from the first round that were considered "Most important" or "important" and generated new items.	Experts rated items from the second round that had a positive rating of 80% and suggested modifications to create a 15 item instrument.	
van den Heuvel-Panhuizen & Elia (2012)	Experts described learning-supportive characteristics of picturebooks that can help kindergartners to learn mathematics. Next, they identified which points in a framework could be removed, added to, or reformulated.	Experts responded to the adaptations from the first round. Then they identified which aspects are important when evaluating the learning-supportive characteristics of picturebooks.	Experts used the final revision of the framework to evaluate three picturebooks for a program that would support kindergartners in developing mathematical skills and understanding. Then they evaluated the Delphi method.	Experts met in person, discussed the results of the Delphi method, and rated on a five-point scale the importance of the characteristics included in the revised framework.

STEPS IN DESIGNING A DELPHI PROCESS[2]

Researchers differ in their degree of interpretation and flexibility, but a classic Delphi process is based on a set of standard procedures. Although researchers who use the Delphi technique differ in their methodology and how they report their study, they usually follow a set of similar basic procedures such as how they (a) determine the aims, scope, and length of the project; (b) start the process; (c) select the panel of experts; (d) decide the medium for conducting the study; (e) consider the anonymous process; (6) identify how consensus is reached; (f) resolve what to do if participants do not respond; (g) establish the reliability and validity estimates; and (h) determine how to report a Delphi study. These steps are described in the following section.

Determine the Aims, Scope, and Length of the Project: What Is Needed and What Is Feasible?

The traditional approach to the Delphi technique is to allow participants to determine the issues and questions they wish to answer (hence reducing researcher bias) by way of open questioning in the first round. This differs from the approach in most other research studies, in which the question should be clearly defined a priori. We would recommend that even if participants determine the topics that will be considered during the Delphi process, the researchers should clearly define the scope and aims of the group, particularly in terms of the population to whom the recommendations of the group will pertain (for example do the recommendations relate to one school or is the output expected to be a national recommendation). The participants determine the issues and reach consensus in several rounds. Powell (2003) suggests the following for the first and subsequent rounds.

First Round

The first round is generally unstructured and searches for open responses. Participants have the freedom to expand and strengthen the topic that is being studied. The responses are qualitatively analyzed and used as the basis to create the second and subsequent surveys. In the first round the participants identify issues that will be addressed in later rounds. Open-ended questions augment the richness of the data that are collected. Conversely, alternative methods are used such as semistructured questions in their first round or a prearranged questionnaire.

Succeeding Rounds

The second and following rounds are more precise such as using questionnaires for quantification that have rating or ranking techniques. Since researchers provide the results to the participants from preceding rounds, there seems to be conformity to a consensus of opinion. This is the only contact that occurs among participants. Researchers usually use three rounds but more rounds may be possible depending on time, cost and possible participants' fatigue.

Table 6.2 provides different examples of the purposes, rounds, and experts that were used in early childhood education studies that used the Delphi approach. The scope of the project is determined based on time and resources available to the facilitator; because the development of questionnaires, collation of responses, communication with participants, and analysis of data can be labor intensive. The time required for data analysis after each round will depend on the number of participants, the length of questionnaires, and the type of data collected (for example, open questioning techniques will generate data that take longer to analyze). Table 6.2 shows the number of rounds that were used in early childhood education studies while Table 6.3 shows the experts' tasks for each round.

The tasks included prioritizing, rating, and revising and justifying their rankings. Researchers should plan in advance the number of rounds of questions. They may either specify a set number of rounds or state that the process will continue until a consensus is reached. The former approach prevents the process from "dragging on" but risks premature termination of the project before some issues are resolved. If the latter approach is used, the final consensus may reflect a more considered group opinion; but risks "participant fatigue," which may lead to some individuals dropping out of the study or changing their responses simply to reach consensus.

Whichever approach is used, it is important that the length of a Delphi process is considered in terms of numbers of rounds rather than by length of time—in other words it is not appropriate to say, "We will continue the Delphi process for six months regardless of how many rounds we can fit in during this period."

How Should You Start the Process? Begin by Asking Open-Ended Questions

In studies that use the Delphi process to formulate a list, it is essential that the initial "long list" is not generated by the researchers or facilitators but rather by the participants. For example, rather than asking, "Which of the following topics should be included in the curriculum?" the question in the first round should be, "Which topics do you feel should be included in the curriculum?" Open ended questions can be used to help participants generate their own ideas. Table 6.4 provides examples of open-ended

TABLE 6.4 Suggested Open-Ended Questions

Experts' & Concepts	Open-ended Questions
Children's (ages 3–5) concepts of reading (Saracho, 1984)	1. What do you see in reading? 2. Who reads? 3. Where do people read?
Children's (ages 3–5) perceptions of reading (Saracho, 1986)	1. What does reading mean to you? Their responses from this statement identified and described their perceptions of reading. 2. Where do boys and girls read?
Children's (ages 3–5) attitudes toward reading (Saracho, 1986)	1. How do boys and girls behave when they like reading? 2. How do boys and girls behave when they do not like reading?
Families' contributions to their young children's literacy development (Saracho, 2000)	1. What does your child read with you at home? 2. What does your child read with you when you're away from home? 3. What board games does your family play that have letters, pictures, or numbers? 4. What games do you and your child play that involve letters, pictures, or numbers? 5. What TV programs do you and your child watch together?
Families or teachers' selection of books (Saracho & Spodek, 2010).	1. What types of books do you read to children? 2. What are the names of the books that you read to children?
Teachers' multifaceted roles (Saracho, 1988)	1. What do you do in your classroom? 2. What do you do outside your classroom to prepare to teach? 3. What type of interactions do you have with your classroom children?

questions in a variety of areas (e.g., multifaceted roles of teachers, genres in children's literature, emergent literacy, and family literacy).

Using open-ended questions is an approach that (a) avoids situations where the items for consideration are biased towards the researcher's opinions and (b) is more likely to generate a diverse long list of items. Table 6.3 shows how different researchers initiated the first round. Some participants identified content items (Feinberg, et al., 1990a), key ideas (Osborne, Collins, Ratcliffe, Millar, & Duschl, 2003), or characteristics (van den Heuvel-Panhuizen & Elia, 2012). Other participants evaluated a preliminary list of items and open-ended questions (Kim, Lee, Suen, & Lee, 2003, Samarakkody, Fernando, Perera, McClure & De Silva, 2010).

Typically three rounds of questionnaires are sent to a preselected expert panel, although the decision over the number of rounds is largely pragmatic. Tables 6.2 and 6.3 show that the number of rounds can range from two to four.

Select the Panel: "Shop Floor" or "Ivory Tower"?

The selection of the panel needs to consider the size of the panel and qualifications of experts. Involving senior experts in the field can increase the credibility of the group, but researchers must consider those individuals for whom the recommendations from the Delphi process are being formulated. If the recommendation relates to teachers, for example, their current insight into the problems and solutions of their job will be invaluable. Involving individuals who are working "on the shop floor" will also foster a feeling of ownership, which is invaluable at the point of implementing recommendations or guidelines. A top-heavy, "ivory tower" approach, in which collective wisdom is handed down, is likely to fail if recommendations are unfeasible in practice (such that people *cannot* implement them) or if they foster resentment (such that people *will not* implement them).

Researchers may also wish to consider involving parents in formulating recommendations. This may not always be appropriate, but in some cases (for example determining the suitability of subject matter for a curriculum) parents can provide invaluable insight. Some researchers may even feel confident enough to tailor the Delphi process to involve children. This is appropriate when children are the experts on the topic. For example, when Saracho (1984) examined the children's concepts about reading before formal reading instruction, she used three- to five-year-old children. The experts are those individuals who have the most knowledge about the subject. In addition, they represent the entire population that is being studied.

The number of participants required will vary immensely, according to the topic. Table 6.2 shows how different studies had a different number of experts that ranged from 7 to 154 experts. In general, one way to estimate the required number would be to ask, "Within the constraints of the resources available to me, how many participants would add sufficient credibility to these recommendations such that they would change practice?"

Once the types and number of participants are specified, it is then necessary to identify individuals who should be invited to the panel. Researchers may wish to involve people they know who have an interest in the topic at hand. This may increase response rates and is probably the most convenient method to use but will generate biased results if only people who are known to agree with the researchers are invited. Opening the process to a whole population (e.g., a professional body, all the mathematics teachers in a particular state) is more difficult to arrange, but it diversifies the opinions within a group and is a more rigorous approach to sampling.

Decide the Medium for Conducting the Delphi Process

Advances in communication technology have meant that questionnaires will almost certainly be administered electronically. Reputable cost-free web-based survey providers include Survey Monkey (www.surveymonkey.com) and Survey Gizmo (www.surveygizmo.com). These resources also provide basic analyses of quantitative data. Email surveys may be used, but these are more time consuming for the facilitator, especially if several participants are involved. Simple measures may improve response rates to email questionnaires, such as embedding the questionnaire in the email rather than more laborious methods by which participants must download forms.

The Delphi technique can also be used to reach consensus at a meeting. Although this allows people to reach consensus in a shorter time, problems with group dynamics are likely to surface and these may negate the innate advantages of the Delphi process. If this approach is used, we would strongly recommend that, at the very least, the voting is done anonymously rather than by "show of hands."

Consider How Anonymous the Process Will Be

There are varying degrees of anonymity in a Delphi process. In "totally anonymized" studies, participants do not know who is involved in the group and voting is done anonymously such that nobody knows who provided what response. In "pseudoanonymized" studies, group members know who the other participants are, even if they do not know their responses. Although knowledge that like-minded or influential people are involved may stimulate some people to participate, the main problem with pseudoanonymity is that people may know other group members' opinions and this may bias their responses.

Identify How Consensus Is Reached

This involves methodological decisions for which there is little guidance but is crucial to the final results. Researchers must determine how the process progresses after each round, which will require a definition of "consensus." In most examples such as those listed in Table 6.1, the aim of the Delphi process is to formulate a list of some sort. In such situations, participants are likely to be presented in early rounds with a "long list" of items, for each of which they indicate whether it should be included in the final list (either by voting "yes or no" or by administering a score). Even in early rounds, there are likely to be some items for which the group feeling is already evident (either that the item *should* be included in the final list or that it *should not*). These items could be removed to reduce workload in subsequent questionnaires.

The Delphi process is rather difficult to use with young children but it is to their advantage that with this process, they have more time to think about their answers. In addition, the use of experts and various rounds for consensus may be helpful in a research study. However, for young children the procedures need to be modified for their open-ended questions and responses to a list of items.

- *Open-ended questions.* For open-ended questions, young children's responses are tape recorded and the tape is mailed to the researcher. They can also dictate their responses to an adult who records and mails or e-mails the responses to the researchers. For young children, the number of items (such as 5 to 10 items) should be small.
- *List of items.* In relation to responding to a list of items, the younger the children, the smaller the number of items. In addition, since some children are not able to read, the items for these children should include both pictures and written words. If researchers want children to rank order the items, they need to provide them with a set of cards with words and pictures. Children can then arrange the cards based on their preference. An adult needs to take the cards that have been ranked and either mail them or e-mail their ranking order to the researcher. If a rating scale is used, children whose ages range from three to five years should have a 3-point rating scale (Saracho, 1986). The children's ratings can either be mailed or e-mailed to the researcher. Since the number of items for young children is small, researchers need to increase the number of experts to obtain a higher reliability estimate and power in the quantitative analyses.

Decisions relating to this aspect of methodology are crucial, because they determine the composition of the questionnaire in each round. Advantages and disadvantages of different methodological approaches are listed in Table 6.5.

TABLE 6.5 How a Delphi Process May Progress

Approach	Advantage	Disadvantage
Decision 1: Should Items Be Removed After Each Round?		
Not removing any items— i.e., all items listed in Round 1 are voted for in each subsequent round of the Delphi	Participants can change their mind as the process progresses, even if the group felt strongly about an item in an early round.	Decreased efficiency: Questionnaires include items already felt to be/not be in the final list.
Removing items which are less popular, and/or those which appear to be particularly popular	Increased efficiency: Questionnaires focus on uncertain/controversial issues.	If the group felt strongly about an item in an early round, there is no scope to amend this.
Decision 2: Which Items Should Be Removed From the List, and Which Should Be Carried Forward to the Next Round?		
Threshold for carrying items forward or removing them from the list is an absolute cutoff i) a SCORE (e.g., only items with a median score of > 8/10 are carried forward) ii) a RANKING (e.g., the 10 least popular items are removed from the list)	Easy and convenient	i) The cutoff is arbitrary. ii) Can mask major disagreement (an item can be included/not included in the final list even if a minority feel strongly against this). iii) If ranking is used, low-scoring items can be included in the final list, because they were better than the alternatives.
Threshold for carrying items forward/removing them from the list is a cutoff relative to other items (e.g., Items are carried forward if their mean score is greater than the mean score for all the outcomes combined)	i) The threshold is less arbitrary than an absolute cut-off score or rank. ii) Items which would have attained a predefined cutoff score, but would not have ranked highly ("not popular") are not carried forward.	The "fate" of each item is affected by anomalous results (e.g., if one item attains a falsely high score, the mean score for all items is raised. Other outcomes may then be removed from the list, even though they are actually "popular").
Double-edged threshold: Decision to carry an item forward considers views both for and against its inclusion(e.g., an item is carried forward only if >80% of participants scored it >7/10, and <5% of participants score it <3/10).	Takes into consideration the risk that a single threshold may mask major disagreement—e.g., with a single threshold, an item could be included in the final list if most people felt that it should be, even if the minority feel strongly that it should not.	i) More complicated to analyze. ii) If it is a controversial or uncertain topic, a consensus list may not contain any items!

Note: This is only relevant for Delphi processes aiming to formulate a "list."

Decide What to Do if Participants Do Not Respond

Achieving a poor response rate is a concern for all researchers who utilize questionnaires or other survey techniques. In the Delphi process, *attrition* of participants, as the study progresses, may be even more worrying. This is because participants with opinions that differ from the overall group response or whose feelings on the topic are equivocal are more likely to not respond to questionnaires. If experts with minority views drop out, the degree to which the group agreed with the final recommendations is overestimated and the result is a biased representation of how the group actually felt.

Researchers could either invite all participants who completed the first round to then complete each subsequent questionnaire, regardless of whether they did not respond to one or they could choose to exclude them from the remainder of the study. Researchers may also wish to include "new" participants as the study progresses. The advantages and disadvantages of these approaches are summarized in Table 6.6.

Whichever approach is taken, it is important that the facilitator inspires experts to want to become (and remain) involved. The effectiveness of this "personal" approach can be immense but so can the effort involved. For example, Feinberg and Associates (1990a) gave the participants extra time to respond and after two months those participants who had not responded were telephoned and again encouraged to respond. In addition, researchers can offer to acknowledge participants' names in any publications that arise from the work, ensuring that the aim of the project is presented in such a way that it is shown to be important and planning the study so as to minimize the workload for participants. Attrition can be reduced by explaining the importance of remaining in the study at the outset (for an

TABLE 6.6 Approaches to Nonresponders and Adding New People as the Delphi Process Progresses

Approach	Advantages	Disadvantages
Inviting people who did not respond to a particular round to participate in subsequent rounds	Acknowledges that people may miss one round but would like to remain involved.	Decreased efficiency: Some people who do not respond to one round may not wish to remain involved.
Excluding people who did not respond to a particular round from subsequent rounds	Increased efficiency: If people do not respond to one round, they may not wish to remain involved.	If people do not respond, it may be because they hold a minority or equivocal views, so the final result is biased.
Inviting new participants as the process progresses	Some people may not have known about the Delphi process at the outset, and may wish to get involved later in the process.	If this is not regulated, the final group may look very different from the panel that started the process.

> **BOX 6.1 EXAMPLE TEXT TO EXPLAIN TO PARTICIPANTS THE IMPORTANCE OF NOT DROPPING OUT OF THE DELPHI PROCESS (FROM SINHA ET AL 2011)**
>
> Thank you for agreeing to participate in our study. It is very important that you complete the questionnaires in each round. The reliability of the results could be compromised if people drop out of the study before it is completed, because they feel that the rest of the group does not share their opinions. If people drop out because they feel their opinions are in the minority, the final results will overestimate how much the sample of participants agreed on this topic.

example, see Box 6.1) and by contacting non-responders individually to remind them complete the questionnaires, and ask whether they are not responding because they feel their views are in the minority.

Determine Reliability and Validity in the Delphi Process

In Delphi-based surveys, the number of participants may be small and participants are chosen based on their expertise instead of at random. Among the traditional research methods this is considered to affect the possibility of bias and jeopardizing both reliability and validity. The results from a Delphi study are strengthened when researchers establish acceptable reliability and validity measures.

Reliability

Many researchers assume that the consensus in the Delphi process may be sufficient in determining the study's reliability. Problems emerge when the reliability and accuracy of the Delphi technique are measured. To assess reliability, the internal correlation coefficient (Cronbach's alpha) can be calculated among the rounds. Thus, reliability of the Delphi can be determined by means of the intraclass correlation coefficient. Reliability can be determined by distinguishing between reliability (the proportional consistency of variance among raters) and agreement (which looks at the extent to which raters make essentially the same rating (Tomasik, 2010).

Typically increasing the number of group members will increase the reliability of group judgment. Combining individual judgments is usually better. An increase in the number of judges increases the reliability when the responses are combined. Murphy, Black, Lamping, McKee, Sanderson, Askham, and Marteau (1998) assume that as the number of experts increases, the reliability of a combination of responses increases. Nonetheless, they also state that:

There is very little actual empirical evidence on the effect of the number of participants on the reliability or validity of consensus processes. (p. 37)

According to Sackman (1975), Delphi studies are usually insensitive to the outcomes of reliability measurements and scientific validation. Since the technique is supposed to adjust for lack of conclusive data by drawing on, and sharing, the experts' knowledge and experience, it does not need the same validation criteria as hard science. Murphy et al. (1998) point out that the Delphi method and other consensus development approaches are not considered scientific methods that develop new knowledge. This procedure makes the best use of accessible information using the participants' scientific data or their combined knowledge.

Validity

Validity of the Delphi technique can be determined in a variety of ways.

- Content validity can be examined using the results from the study and comparing them with published related research studies.
- A panel of experts in the area of study can assess the results of the study.
- Construct validity can be determined by comparing the results from the Delphi study with those of other methods (Tomasik, 2010). Perhaps a sample of the population can be used to examine the same research problem with a different research method. Then the results of both research methods for this population can be compared.

Some researchers determine the validity by comparing the results from the study with two or more Delphi studies on the same subject, using Pearson, kappa, or rank-order coefficients. However, this strategy is not very efficient or useful. It is best to use the respondents' numerical ratings when such ratings are normally distributed.

Until definite components (e.g., group composition, number of rounds, consensus criterion, and feedback) of the Delphi method become standardized, researchers can use whichever estimate of reliability and validity is relevant to any study. However, the generalizability is challenged in the results of the study. Participation of representative experts in the study may somewhat help with the interpretation of the results (Tomasik, 2010).

How to Report a Delphi Process

It is crucial that the methods and results of any Delphi process are described thoroughly to maintain transparency and enable the reader to

TABLE 6.7 Recommended Aspects of the Delphi Process That Should Be Reported When the Study Is Disseminated

Size and Composition of the Panel
- Number of participants—the total number invited, and the number who completed the first round
- Types of participants (e.g., teachers, principals, parents)
- Proportion of each type of participant
- How participants were identified/sampled

Methodology of the Delphi Process
- Administration of questionnaires (e. g ., postal, email, internet, in person)
- How items were generated for the first questionnaire: Were these provided by the researchers, or generated by the participants? If these were provided by researchers, they should describe how the list was generated.
- What was asked in each round—where possible, the questions should be made available.
- Information, known to the researchers, which was provided to participants before the first round—this may influence the participant responses.
- How the overall group response was fed back to participants.
- The process after each round by which the questionnaires were refined—e.g., What was the threshold for cutting down from a long-list to a short list, and how was this used to generate the final list?
- Level of anonymity (total or quasianonymity)
- A priori definition of "consensus"
- Were nonresponders invited to subsequent rounds or excluded from the study? Were extra people invited?

Results
- Number of respondents to each round
- Number who completed every round
- Results for each question or item in each round
- Group response for each question/item (final round)
- Distribution of response for each item (final round)
- Clear list of final recommendations

Source: Adapted from Sinha et al, 2011

critique the methods and recommendations. Items that should be reported in all studies using the Delphi technique are listed in Table 6.7.

CONCLUSIONS

The Delphi technique is a series of sequential questionnaires or "rounds" that is combined with organized feedback that is used to reach the most reliable consensus of opinion of a group of experts. This method is valuable for situations where individual judgments are used and combined to concentrate on a need of agreement or incomplete state of knowledge.

Basically, the Delphi is predominantly used for its capacity to structure and organize group communication.

The most important qualities of the Delphi technique are its series of rounds with their immediate feedback, which helps the participants evaluate their own responses. Indicators of well-planned and well-conducted research include the use of three or more rounds, allowing the participants to assess and argue their responses after knowing the other opinions, and the participants' anonymity. Although the Delphi process is conducted in various forms, the basic steps and characteristics that are described here are standards that are found in most studies.

The Delphi process can be an excellent way of reaching consensus, if conducted properly. Methods for using the Delphi technique vary immensely. It is vital that the right participants are selected, the right questions are asked, and attrition bias is minimized. The methods and results should be reported thoroughly, to enable critique and appraisal.

NOTES

1. The word oracle in Greek can mean several related things. It means a God who predicts the future, like Apollo, the wise God who can tell the future.
2. Terminology: In this section the terms "researcher" and "facilitator" may appear to be used interchangeably, but there are differences. "Facilitators" are specifically those people involved in running the Delphi process (such as sending questionnaires, analyzing results after each round, and sharing feedback to participants). "Researchers" are those people involved in planning, designing, or presenting the final recommendations on behalf of the group. The terms are not mutually exclusive.

REFERENCES

Dalkey, N., & Helmer, O. (1963). An experimental application of the Delphi method to the use of experts. *Management Science, 9*(3), 458–467.

Delbecq, A. L., Van de Ven, A. H., & Gustafson D. H. (1975). *Group techniques for program planning: A guide to nominal and Delphi processes.* Glenview, IL: Scott, Foresman and Co.

Feinberg, M., Saracho, O. N., & Spodek, B. (1990a). Early childhood curriculum in Jewish education. *Early Child Development and Care, 61,* 27–33.

Feinberg, M., Saracho, O. N., & Spodek, B. (1990b). Identifying sectarian content for Jewish early childhood educational programs. *International Journal of Early Childhood, 22*(2), 23–38.

Fish, L., & Busby, D. M. (2005). The Delphi method. In Piercy, F. P., & Sprenkle, D. H. (Eds.), *Research methods in family therapy* (2nd ed., pp. 238–253). New York, NY: Guilford Press.

Gupta, U. G., & Clarke, R. E. (1996) Theory and Applications of the Delphi Technique: A Bibliography (1975–1994). *Technological Forecasting and Social Change, 53*, 185–211.

Kim, J., Lee, Y., Suen, H., & Lee, G. S. (2003). A Delphi study of young children's readiness in Korea: Challenges and implications for early childhood schooling. *Educational Research and Evaluation: An International Journal on Theory and Practice, 9*(4), 345–355.

Linstone, H. A., & Turoff, M. (Eds.) (1975). *The Delphi method: Techniques and applications*. Reading, MA: Addison-Wesley.

Murphy, M. K., Black, N. A., Lamping, D, L., McKee, C. M., Sanderson C.F. B., Askham, J., & Marteau, T. (1998). Consensus development methods, and their use in clinical guideline development. *Health Technology Assessment* 1998 2(3).

Osborne, J., Collins, S., Ratcliffe, M., Millar, R., & Duschl, R. (2003). What "Ideas-about-science" Should be taught in school science? A Delphi study of the expert community. *Journal of Research in Science Teaching, 40*(7), 692–720.

Powell, C. (2003). The Delphi technique: Myths and realities. *Journal of Advanced Nursing, 4*(4), 376–382.

Sackman, H. (1975). *Delphi critique*. Lexington, Massachusetts: DC Health.

Samarakkody, D. C., Fernando, D. N., Perera, H., McClure, R. J., & De Silva, H. (2010). The Child Behaviour Assessment Instrument: Development and validation of a measure to screen for externalising child behavioural problems in community setting. *International Journal of Mental Health Systems, 4*(13). Retrieved from http://www.ijmhs.com/content/4/1/13

Saracho, O. N. (1984). Young children's conceptual factors of reading. *Early Child Development and Care, 15*(4), 305–314.

Saracho, O.N. (1986). The development of the preschool reading attitudes scale. *Child Study Journal, 16*(2), 113–124.

Saracho, O.N. (1988). A study of the roles of early childhood teachers. *Early Child Development and Care, 38*, 43–56.

Saracho, O. N. (2000). Assessing the families' perceptions of their young children's acquisition of literacy. *Early Child Development and Care, 161*, 83–91.

Saracho, O. N., & Spodek, B. (2010). Families' selection of children's literature books. *Early Childhood Education Journal, 37*(5), 401–409.

Sinha, I. P., Smyth, R. L., & Williamson, P. R. (2011). Using the Delphi technique to determine which outcomes to measure in clinical trials: Recommendations for the future based on a systematic review of existing studies. *PLoS Medicine, 8*(1), e1000393. Retrieved from http://www.plosmedicine.org/article/info%3Adoi%2F10.1371%2Fjournal.pmed.1000393

Tomasik, T. (2010). Reliability and validity of the Delphi method in guideline development for family physicians. *Quality in Primary Care, 18*(5), 317–326.

van den Heuvel-Panhuizen, M., & Elia, I. (2012). Developing a framework for the evaluation of picturebooks that support kindergartners' learning of mathematics. *Research in Mathematics Education, 14*(1), 17–47.

CHAPTER 7

USING THE CRITICAL INCIDENT TECHNIQUE IN EARLY CHILDHOOD RESEARCH

Beth S. Rous

In 1954, John Flanagan, described a research technique for observing human behaviors and identifying participant perceptions from what he described as "critical incidents" in the participant's life. Flanagan (1954) defined critical incidents as:

> any observable human activity that is sufficiently complete in itself to permit inferences and predictions to be made about the person performing the act. To be critical, an incident must occur in a situation where the purpose or intent of the act seems fairly clear to the observer and where its consequences are sufficiently definite to leave little doubt concerning its effects. (p. 327)

Since this time, the Critical Incident Technique (CIT) has been used as a research method across a variety of fields, including education, psychology, medicine, and business. This chapter will provide an overview of the historical roots of the CIT, procedures to support the use of the CIT as a research method, followed by recommendations related to ensuring the credibility and trustworthiness of findings when using the CIT. To help explicate the potential use of the CIT in early childhood research, a study conducted by the author will be used for illustrative purposes (Rous, 2004; Rous 2001), with additional examples provided from two additional unpublished studies (Calabrò & LaRocco, 2006; Dogaru, Rosenkoetter, & Rous, B., 2009). General information about these studies in presented in Table 7.1.

HISTORICAL PERSPECTIVE

Flanagan (1954), a psychologist, developed the CIT as a result of his work with the U.S. Army Air Core during World War II. As part of this research, Flanagan was interested in the exploring effective pilot performance during combat missions. When first describing the CIT in 1954, Flanagan acknowledged the technique was not new, but built on years of research involving human observation. Much of the development of the CIT research process came out of a series of studies conducted through the American Institute for Research (AIR) and the Aviation Psychology Program which began in

TABLE 7.1 Exemplar CIT Studies in Area of Early Childhood

Study	Sample	Purpose	Methods
Calabro & LaRocca (2006)	14 primary teachers from 9 schools across 7 school districts	Identify strategies teacher use to promote student academic, social, and behavioral development	Individual interviews of 60–90 minutes; teachers asked to reflect on and describe "significant or memorable instructional experiences"
Dogaru, C., Rosenkoetter, S., & Rous, B. (2009)	37 parents of children with disabilities and 28 service providers	Identify effective and ineffective practices related to transition of young children with disabilities	Web-based and paper open-ended questionnaires asked participants to recount a transition experience, describe the outcomes of the experience
Rous, B. (2004) Rous, B (2001)	197 public preschool teachers from one state	Identify leadership behaviors of those who provide instructional supervision in preschool classrooms	Open-ended questionnaire asked teachers to describe a behavior used frequently that positively or negatively influence classroom teaching, an example of the impact, and feelings about the behavior

1947. Additional work on the CIT method was conducted at the University of Pittsburg, extending application to other occupations and areas, including dentistry, business, higher education, and medicine. By 1954, Flanagan was able to present specific steps and procedures for using the CIT research method based on this work.

Since this original publication, the CIT method has evolved through application and use across a number of disciplines. Not surprisingly, the terms used to describe the method have varied and evolved as well (Butterfield, Borgen, Amundson, & Maglio, 2005; Fivars & Fitzpatrick, 2001). For example, when reviewing the limited literature of studies using the CIT in early childhood and education, terms such as the Critical Incident Technique (e.g., Tulley & Chiu, 1998), critical incident approach (e.g., Foster, DeLawyer, & Guevremont, 1986; Gilbert & Priest, 1997); critical incident reporting (e.g., Gettinger & Stoiber, 1998); and critical incident reflections (e.g., Wopereis, Sloep, & Poortman, 2010) all refer to the same general research method outlined by Flanagan.

In 2009, Butterfield, Borgen, Maglio and Amundson proposed the *Enhanced Critical Incident Technique* (ECIT) as a way to better support researchers in applying the steps and processes of the CIT. The ECIT expanded on the original work by Flanagan (1954) by including three new components to the five step process:

1. Nine credibility checks
2. Contextual questions
3. Questions to participants to elicit items that helped or hindered the situation

Today, the CIT continues to be prevalent among research techniques used in some fields, such as social work, criminal justice, psychology and nursing. Its use in the fields of early childhood, early education and education was prevalent from 1960 to 1990 but has since declined. Currently, use of the CIT method in the field of education is much more common in dissertation studies than in published literature.

THE CRITICAL INCIDENT TECHNIQUE RESEARCH PROCESS

The Critical Incident Technique generally falls within the qualitative paradigm of research methods. However, some studies using the CIT have also included quantitative methods as part of the study design. From the onset, Flanagan (1954) described the CIT as a flexible process with an emphasis on collecting information on specific events, activities or behaviors, identified as critical incidents, which can be used to help address practical problems in the field. Within the qualitative paradigm, the overarching benefit of the CIT is that it provides a specific set of steps or procedures to help collect, analyze, and organize a discrete set of behaviors related to the phenomenon of interest. The CIT has been used across disciplines as a means to analyze the effectiveness of job practices, (e.g., Manley-Casimir & Wasserman, 1989; Rous, 2004) scale development (e.g., Smith and Kendall, 1963; Alvarez & Bernardin, 1973) and organizational research (e.g., Symon & Cassell, 1998).

To help the researcher situate the CIT within the traditional qualitative research traditions as presented by Cresswell (1998), Butterfield et al., (2005) proposed five distinctive features of the CIT which will set the frame for the remainder of this chapter.

1. Focus is on critical events, incidents, or factors that help promote or detract from the effective performance of some activity or experience of a specific situation or event;
2. Discipline origin is from industrial and organizational psychology;
3. Data collection is primarily through interview, either in person individually or in groups) or via telephone;
4. Data analysis is conducted by determining the specificity or generality of the categories; and
5. Narrative form is that of categories with operational definitions and self-descriptive titles (p. 434).

A key component in the CIT is the identification of the "critical incident(s)" to be explored. The definition of incident proposed by Flanagan (1954) was: "any observable human activity that is sufficiently complete in itself to permit inferences and predictions to be made about the person performing the act" (p. 327). Further, these incidents should be significant to the participants of the study so they are able to (a) clearly describe a situation, (b) account for the actions and behaviors of those involved in the situation, and (c) reflect on an outcome or response to the situation. The remainder of this section will provide an overview of the five steps described by Flanagan (1954) to implement a study using the CIT within the context of early care and education (see Figure 7.1).

As mentioned previous, a study conducted by Rous (2004) will be used to illustrate steps in the CIT process. However, it should be noted while the study provides examples in keeping with critical dimensions of the CIT, areas for improvement within the study design and implementation will also be addressed. Additionally, since the published study does not contain all methodological details given limited publication space, additional details will be provided as needed.

> 1. Identify the general aims of the activity under study by providing a functional description from which to judge the effectiveness or success of the activity.
> 2. Develop plan for how to gather data or "incidents," including specifications for ensuring consistent data collection processes.
> 3. Collect the data by observation, interview, group interview, questionnaire, written records.
> 4. Analyze the data by identifying a frame of reference, creating categories and identifying general behaviors.
> 5. Interpreting and reporting the findings, with care to review and identify judgments made in both collecting and analyzing the data.

Figure 7.1 Five steps originally employed in CIT (Flanagan, 1954).

Step 1: Identify the General Aims

Like most research methodologies, the identification of the general aims of the study provides the foundation upon which data collection and analysis processes are built. As originally presented by Flanagan (1954), when using the CIT, the basic premise is there are particular problems of interest within a system that need to be addressed. The CIT has also been used to identify areas within a system that could potentially be problematic. Overall, the general idea behind the CIT is to identify the success and/or effectiveness of practices or activities and the behaviors or actions that lead to these practices.

In the area of early care and education, areas of study for which the CIT may be appropriate include the exploration of specific job functions for teachers, aides, assistant teachers, principals and/or other administrators and the understanding of the degree to which these job functions are perceived as effective. Other potential areas of study would include the success or failure of the organizational processes in helping meet the goals of the organization. At the child and family level, the CIT may be appropriate for exploring the service and supports they receive in early care and education systems. Examples of potential areas of study appropriate for the CIT methodology can include, but are not limited to

- teaching strategies and instructional practices;
- identification of competencies for teachers, leaders, and other organizational staff;
- teacher, administrator, and staff performance and job satisfaction;
- administrator roles in instructional supervision within classrooms;
- decision-making, leadership, communication, and change within an organization;

- family experiences with early childhood programs, teachers, and administrators;
- specific child experiences in early childhood programs (e.g., peer to peer interactions, transition into and out of programs, etc.); and
- design and implementation of professional development to support early childhood staff.

In the Rous (2004) study, the overarching focus was to identify supervisor behaviors that influenced preschool teacher's instruction. Specifically, the aim was to identify behaviors that positively and negatively impacted teachers' instructional practices and teachers' feelings about the use of these supervisor behaviors. The basic assumption was there were a set of behaviors used by instructional supervisors that could be elicited and described by the teachers they supervised.

Step 2: Identify Events to Be Collected

The second step in the process, determining the incidents or events to be collected, is one of the most critical steps as it will determine the degree to which the aims of the study are met (Flanagan, 1954). The identification of events requires the researcher to focus on observable and/or measurable behaviors. While the initial goal of the CIT as outlined by Flanagan (1954) was a focus on overt behaviors, over time the CIT has been used to study both "psychological concepts or factual events" as well (Butterfield, 2005; p. 480). These events can be defined as remarkable and/or extreme events that can be easily recalled by participants in the study. As described by Chell (2006), the CIT approach "captures the thought processes, the frame of reference and the feelings about an incident or set of incidents" (p. 47). The purpose is to have the participant clearly describe an event that helps support or undermine their effective performance or their individual experiences within a defined situation. Since the events are at the heart of the study, the researcher must ensure data are collected from those participants in the best position to both recall the events in question and to make judgments on the critical nature of the events to be reported.

In the Rous (2004) study of preschool instructional supervisor behaviors, public school preschool teachers were asked to "describe a behavior their instructional supervisor used frequently that positively or negatively influenced their classroom teaching" (p. 272). Based on responses provided, participants were then asked to provide an example of the impact of this behavior on their instructional practices and their feelings about the behavior. Key to the gathering of the information from participants was the direction to provide real-life examples of the impact based on their experiences. From this example, three key features of critical incidents as described by Flanagan (1954) were met:

1. A description of a particular situation (i.e., the instructional supervisor's behavior)
2. An account of the behavior from a key play (i.e., the teacher receiving instructional supervision from an administrator)
3. A reflection of the outcome or response to the situation (i.e., teacher feelings about the supervisor behavior)

Step 3: Collection of Data

In keeping with traditional qualitative methodology, CIT research typically takes place in natural settings with the researcher serving as the key instrument (Creswell, 2007). When outlining the CIT in his original work, Flanagan (1954) indicated a preference for observations to gather incidents, but acknowledged multiple methods, specifically the use of questionnaires and interviews (individual or group) and record forms. The CIT could also be used in combination with other methods as part of a larger study (Gremler, 2004). For example, a part of the development of a survey instrument might include the use of the CIT to gather participant stories to facilitate the identification of relevant survey items and/or questions.

Depending on the field of study, different data collection methods are more prevalent. For example, Butterfield et al. (2009) indicated in-person interviews are a preferred method in counseling psychology while Gremler (2004) reported interviews as the most frequent method as well in service research. Interviews and written data collection are reported most often in nursing research employing the CIT (Bradbury-Jones & Tranter, 2008).

When considering the data collection method to be used, several aspects should be considered. Direct participant *observation* as originally described by Flanagan (1954) may be appropriate when the investigator is interested in behaviors that are explicit in nature. Observations can be conducted by the researcher or trained observers who work in the organization under study. As indicated by Flanagan (1954) *record forms* are often used during the observation to ensure accuracy of data collected. When conducting observations, the steps outlined by Creswell (2007; p 134) can be helpful, specifically related to the design of an observational protocol to support the recording process. This recording form should take into consideration the specific defining characteristics of the CIT including the situation, the action and outcome. While observations were often used in early CIT research, the approach is much less common with research conducted in the last 20 years, potentially due to the cost associated with observational studies. However in the area of early childhood, observations are often used to help measure the quality of the environment in which children spend time, as well as the interactions between adults and children. Using the CIT as a component of these studies provides a unique opportunity for early childhood researchers.

Interviews can be conducted for each individual or with an entire group of participants. Due to the nature of the CIT, open-ended, semistructured interview protocols are typically most appropriate. As compared to the use of questionnaires or direct observation, the interview is advantageous in that it allows the researcher the option to probe for additional detail on the basis of both nonverbal cues and on interview responses. This option is especially valuable when participants recount the impacts or effects of the behavior under exploration. As with observations, the use of a formal interview protocol can help ensure the critical dimensions are covered: situation, action, and outcome. Other critical decisions with the use of interviews include the length of the interviews and/or number of interviews to be conducted to fully explore the phenomenon under study and to ensure the researcher is able to gather a consistent level of detail from all participants. Butterfield et al., (2009) provides a detailed example of considerations when using interviews as part of a study using the CIT.

Questionnaires and/or surveys may be especially helpful during studies of behaviors that are more difficult to observe and/or involve activities such as decision-making. To implement the CIT with questionnaires, the researcher must make critical decisions about the degree of structure to be provided to participants. Open-ended questions can allow for full descriptions of the behaviors under study, while close-ended items help to identify participant demographics and contextualize information, which is critical for situating the study and interpreting the findings. As with most questionnaires, researchers should field-test or pilot the questionnaire in advance to ensure the instrument will elicit the type and level of information needed to address the general aims of the study. As compared to direct observation of participants, the use of questionnaires for studies using the CIT is relatively economical and can support data collection from a large group of participants. Limitations of this approach to data collection include both the time needed for respondents to fully describe the situation, behaviors and outcomes and the degree to which they can fully explicate these responses in writing, which can result in limited data available for analysis.

In the Rous (2004) study, a questionnaire was designed to elicit stories from participants about their experiences related to instructional supervisor behavior. The design of the questionnaire was replicated from another study using the CIT to investigate instructional supervisor behavior with teachers in public school settings (Blasé & Blasé, 1999). However, given the population of interest in the Rous (2004) study, additional questions were added to the questionnaire to gather information about the context for instructional supervision at the preschool level from which findings could be interpreted (i.e., demographic information about participants; the title of the person providing instructional supervision, as well as demographic information about the supervisor; the participants understanding of Developmentally Appropriate Practices). The questionnaire was dissemination to all teachers in the state via first class postal service, with repeated contacts to help increase the return rate.

Due to the multiple data collection methods available, using the CIT requires researchers to have a clear understanding of appropriate practices related to the method chosen. While detailed descriptions of each method (i.e., interview, questionnaire, and observation) and appropriate analysis techniques are not feasible in this chapter, additional information on these methods is available throughout this handbook. Regardless of the data collection method used in the study, the researcher must attend to procedures designed to help ensure participants provide specific information in their reports. To support this process, the American Institute of Research (1998) proposed five guiding questions to help elicit critical incidents:

- What preceded and contributed to the incident?
- What did the person or people do or not do that had an effect?
- What was the outcome or result?
- What made this action effective or ineffective?
- What could have made the action more effective?

Without detailed descriptions of the situation, actions and outcomes, it is impossible to obtain accurate and reliable data needed to meet the basic requirements of the CIT methodology. At a minimum, procedures must ensure the researcher can understand each participant's perspective on the reported event and identify the implications of that perspective on the system or organization. To this end, piloting and/or field testing observational or interview protocols and/or questionnaires is necessary to determine the level of direction and guidance needed to ensure detailed information is provided by participants.

Plans for data collection must take into consideration the sample size needed to address the study aims. When determining the sample size within CIT, the number of participants is less important than the number of incidents gathered (Flanagan, 1954). There is no hard and fast rule on the number of incidents required for a study as the number will be dependent on the complexity of the research questions within the study and the quality of the data provided by participants. However, researchers can consider the recommendations from Flanagan (1954) that suggests if only two to three behaviors per 100 critical incidents are identified, coverage is achieved. At the onset of the study, the researcher should identify a target range for the number of incidents to collect (e.g., 50 to 100) that can serve as a guide during the data collection process. Once analysis begins, exhaustiveness can be used as a measure of the appropriate number of incidents.

Step 4: Analysis of Data

The CIT process assists the researcher in focusing on participant perspectives of an event of interest. In a synthesis of studies using the CIT in service research, Gremler (2004) identified two primary data analysis approaches which are equally appropriate to studies conducted in the area of early care and education. The first is interpretive, seeking to understand the experiences of the participant. Second, is the use of content analysis methods (Kassarjian, 1977) which includes reporting events that have taken place. CIT data can be reported both qualitatively, using codes and categories that emerge from the data, as well as quantitatively, by reporting the type and number of incidents as part of the findings. For example, in addition to identified response categories Calabrò & LaRocco (2006) provided data on the number of participants who reported strategies within each category as part of their analysis process, which is consistent with the participation rate calculations reported by Butterfield et al. (2005) and Butterfield et al. (2009). Both Dogaru et al. (2009) and Rous (2004) presented the number of text codes across the identified categories.

Consistent with other qualitative approaches in research, an inductive approach to data analysis is typically used within studies employing the CIT, meaning categories emerge from the data through an iterative process (Creswell, 2007). However, to ensure fidelity within the CIT process, there are three steps recommended by Flanagan (1954) and supported through Butterfield et al. (2005). These include:

1. Identifying the frame of reference based on the purpose of the study.
2. Using an inductive approach to identify categories.
3. Deciding on the specificity or generality needed when reporting the data.

Through the analytic process, the researcher identifies categories based on the issues and behaviors identified by participants, which are then defined and self-titled as part of the analysis process.

In keeping with contemporary methods of data analysis within the qualitative paradigm, criteria of rigor should be equally applied to ensure the trustworthiness of the data and findings. Several steps can facilitate the analysis data gathered through the CIT method. First, as mentioned previously, the number of incidents recorded is more important than the number of participants within the study (Flanagan, 1954). Often during a CIT study, participants may identify numerous incidents, particularly during individual interviews when they become comfortable telling their "story" to the researcher or interviewer. Therefore, the inductive analysis approach based on written transcripts and/or narrative data allows the researcher to determine emerging categories, define and self-title those categories which can be explored across incidents until saturation has been reached.

Second, context is an important factor in studies using the CIT process (Flanagan, 1954; Butterfield et al., 2005). This is particularly important in understanding the events participants choose to describe and in detailing the decisions they make during the event. Keeping in mind the general purpose of the CIT method, which is to identify practices or activities and the behaviors or actions that lead to the practices, the researcher must analyze the circumstances surrounding events, both before and after. Situational analysis of events can help the researcher identify the degree to which participants are likely to make the same decisions given similar circumstances. In this way, effective and ineffective practices can be linked with specific behaviors based on the decisions of the participants at the time of the event.

Third, organization of the data is critical given the potential complexity of the events and contextual information provided by participants. There are multiple data analysis strategies that have been used in CIT studies to help organize data. For example, Rous (2004) used a code-and-retrieve analysis process (Richards & Richards, 1994) to assist with complex coding to support the identification of categories. This process involves identifying relevant experiences which are assigned a short code, collecting examples of the experience across all respondents, and determining commonalties, differences, and patterns among experiences. Dogaru et al., (2009) used a more generalized inductive approach of narrative analysis (Thomas, 2006) to identify codes and categories. The use of categories of codes (Bogdan & Bilken, 1992) to sort events *a priori* is another analysis option. Examples of those particularly salient for studies using CIT include categories related to processes, context, and activity/strategies. Both Calabrò & LaRocco (2006) and Dogaru et al., (2009) used a conceptual framework to help identify themes and or categories into which data text segments were organized. Within all of these approaches, analysis of CIT data can also be conducted using the interview or survey questions as a sorting scheme for initial analysis, followed by cross question analysis.

In the Rous (2004) study, three stages were completed as part of the initial analysis process. First, verbatim transcriptions of responses were made. Second, each of the six questions were treated as a separate response (i.e., question one and four responses related to describing the behavior (positive and negative); questions two and five related to real-life examples; and question three and six related to feelings about the behavior). In this study, participants commonly provided multiple behaviors across the questions. For example:

1. Please describe a behavior your instructional supervisor uses frequently that positively influences your classroom teaching?

   Considers me a part of school, gave me a new playground [sic]. Support, understanding what we do. Positive evaluations. Praise/encouragement/ rewards. Suggestions to improve instruction, P.D. for my needs...

2. Please provide a real-life example of the effect (impact) that the behavior has on your instructional practices in the classroom.

   During screening done in classroom [she] provides title aides to help. Received a new autistic child who was very difficult with behaviors, principal came [and] stayed to help me most of week. [She] immediately called appropriate people for support for me and had additional special education aide one week. During observation in classroom, [she] provided feedback on developmental approach, suggestions for higher level questioning skills, which I implemented

3. What feelings do you have about the instructional supervisor's behavior you described?

   I like her help/support. [It] makes my job easier [and] she makes me feel that I have a positive impact on students.

Third, responses to each question were analyzed as a text unit from which multiple behaviors could be identified. This resulted in the identification of 1,485 behaviors across 888 text units. Codes were attached to each behavior and defined, followed by the identification of categories, which were additionally defined. Examples of a code and category definitions are included in Figure 7.2.

Within this study, the three steps recommended by Flanagan (1954) were met in the following ways. First, the frame of reference for the analysis was to be able to use the results to understand both who provides instructional support to preschool teachers housed in public school settings and support those supervisors in providing information on practices that both facilitated and inhibited the instruction in preschool classrooms. Second, an inductive approach was used to identify the codes and categories of behaviors. Finally, in this study, multiple behaviors were presented in participant's written responses, thus the approach was to identify more specific behaviors that both facilitated and inhibited the teachers' instruction.

In addition to manual coding of data, there are a number of software programs and analytic tools which can be particularly helpful with complex

> **Professional Development**
> *Activities involving ongoing dialogue between the instructional supervisor and the teacher which resulted in professional growth. Formal behaviors were those in which the instructional leader had direct interaction with the teacher. Informal behaviors were those that included specific traits of the supervisor such as organizational skills and attitudes.*
>
> | | |
> |---|---|
> | Feedback | Provides specific feedback about teaching strategies, classroom organization, etc., feedback related to review of lesson plans, Conducts teacher evaluations with feedback |
> | Suggestions | Provides suggestions and ideas about how to provide classroom instruction, including specific strategies for working with children, models instructional practices and/or presents a positive role model for staff and children, Presents a calm style/demeanor in classroom or during crisis situations |
> | Interaction | Provides or supports meetings and/or interaction with other teachers or staff |
> | Training | Supports training, workshops, conferences or other professional development activities |
> | Autonomy | Allows flexibility or autonomy on the part of teachers; staff participate in decision making related to classroom practices |

Figure 7.2 Sample of operational definitions of categories and codes for positive/facilitative behaviors identified.

narrative data gathered through CIT methods. These include both open source software packages (e.g., Compendium, CAT—Coding Analysis Toolkit) and for purchase (e.g., QRS NVivo, Atlas.ti). Rous (2004) reported using QRS NUD*IST (now NVivo) to support analysis. Dogaru et al., (2009) used both Microsoft Excel® and MAXQDA 2007© to support text analysis.

Regardless of the data analysis approach chosen, researchers using the CIT should clearly define the codes and categories identified. Within the CIT process, one distinguishing feature is the operationalization of the categories. This process will support the trustworthiness and credibility of the findings. As an example, the operationalized categories identified through the analysis process presented by Rous (2004; see Figure 7.2) was also used to support independent judgment procedures as a credibility check for the study.

Step 5: Report the Findings

As with all research, the interpretation and report of the findings should match the intended audience. In this chapter, the focus will be on reporting findings that promote the replication of the study. This is especially important given the limited number of studies in the field of early childhood that use the CIT process. Because the CIT relies on participants to provide information about critical events as they tell their story, researchers must take great care to ensure narrative data presented in the findings and discussion sections do not identify individual participants. At times, this may result in the selection of narrative data that may be less illustrative than other excerpts.

In 2009, Rosenkoetter, Schroeder, Rous, Hains, Shaw, & McCormick conducted a review of the literature related to the transition of young children. As part of this review, they found many studies lacked the methodological detail needed to either replicate or generalize findings. This is consistent with findings by Gremler (2004) as it relates to studies using CIT methods. Based on these observations, researchers should include detailed procedural processes when they report the findings from their studies. One approach is to carefully follow the first four steps provided by Flanagan (1954). To start, a clear explanation of the problem or issue to be addressed through the study and how the CIT method helped examine the issue should be presented. The critical incident or event should be operationalized for the reader as this will serve as the unit of analysis for the study. The operationalization should include any criteria used to include or exclude data (incidents) from the analysis process. Providing copies or detailed descriptions of the interview/observational protocols and/or questionnaires can help other researchers determine the extent to which participants had ample opportunity to provide the detail needed for inclusion of the incident in the analysis process.

While it is important to describe the sample for the study, the number of critical incidents reported across participants in equally important, especially if the study design can elicit multiple incidents from participants. Within the analysis phase, researchers should clearly illustrate the processes used to develop the categories, including definitions. Finally, steps taken to address both the credibility and trustworthiness of the data analysis should be presented. Additional information on methods that can be used in studies using the CIT in presented in the following section.

Based on his research synthesis, Gremler (2004) provided recommendations related to reporting findings, two of which are particularly salient for researchers in the field of early care and education. First is the consideration of studies using the CIT that include dyadic perspectives across an incident. Dogaru et al., (2009) collected transition stories from multiple perspectives, both parents of young children as well as providers of their care (early intervention specialists, teachers, administrators); however, they did not use a matched parent—professional sample who reported on the same incident.

Second, Gremler (2004) recommended more emphasis on the "physical environment" in which the incident occurred. His premise is that the environment can influence the interactions under study. In the area of early care and education, both the organizational and classroom environments can play a critical role in the types of services and instructional supports provided to young children, so should be considered in studies using the CIT. In the Rous (2004) example, which included a questionnaire disseminated to 435 teachers, information about the environment in which instruction occurred was gathered through several demographic questions that included the school setting and teacher understanding of developmentally appropriate practices. A limitation in this study however, was the lack of data elicited about the specific classroom settings (e.g., location, size) in which the instruction took place.

THE RELIABILITY AND VALIDITY OF THE CIT METHOD AND FINDINGS

Another key consideration is the reliability and validity of the CIT method and findings. There have been a number of researchers who have examined the CIT method and determined the soundness of the approach when implemented using the five steps presented by Flanagan (1954). In 2005, Butterfield et al. published a review of 50 years of research using the CIT in the area of counseling psychology. As part of this review, they identified two studies on the reliability and validity of the CIT method that are commonly cited. A general overview of these studies and their findings are presented in Table 7.2.

With evidence to support the CIT process as a valid and reliable study approach, the emphasis for the researcher is on ensuring the study produces results that have both internal validity (credibility, believability, plausibility of findings and results) and are trustworthy (credible, transferable, dependable, and confirmable). One important consideration in this process is the degree to which the researcher can elicit enough detailed stories (incidents) from participants that elucidate the problem to be addressed. This in turn increases the overall validity and trustworthiness of the findings. Based on a decade of studies using the CIT at the University of British Columbia, Department of Educational and Counseling Psychology and Special Education, Butterfield et al. (2005) presented nine emerging credibility checks for researchers. These are combined with additional methods found in CIT studies reviewed for this chapter to present a list of validity and credibility checks to be considered by those using the CIT method.

Independent extraction involves an independent review of data by another researcher familiar with the CIT method. Butterfield et al., (2005) reported

TABLE 7.2 Commonly Cited Studies of Reliability and Validity of CIT as a Research Method

Study	Method	Findings
Andersson, B. E., & Nilsson, S. G. (1964). Studies in the reliability and validity of the Critical incident technique. *Journal of Applied Psychology, 48*, 398-403.	Interviews and Questionnaires with grocery store managers; 1800 incidents collected; statistical analysis of reliability within and across data collection methods; agreement on category placement; content validity of categories with literature; validity of the subcategories.	Information collected using CIT method is both reliable and valid.
Ronan, W. W., & Latham, G. P. (1974). The reliability and validity of the critical incident technique: A closer look. *Studies in Personnel Psychology, 6*(1), 53-64.	Job performance of businessmen in pulpwood production; reliability of the categorization using inter-judge, test-retest and intra-observer; content validity; construct validity, relevance; concurrent validity	Satisfactory reliability and validity results.

a common acceptable percentage of a randomly selected sample of 25% of the total number of incidents (i.e., transcripts, etc.) gathered. This second researcher extracts the "critical" incidents based on the criterion set by the researcher. Incidents are then compared and level of agreement is calculated (i.e., agreements divided by agreements plus disagreements). Once calculated, discrepancies are discussed and differences resolved, with the expectation of 100% agreement across researchers.

Independent judge refers to the agreement of the original coder and an independent judge on the placement of extracted incidents into specific existing categories. This is sometime also referred to as inter-coder reliability. This method is similar to independent extraction in that a random selection of incidents (e.g., narrative responses, transcripts, etc.) are pulled for analysis and simple agreement calculations are used with a higher percent agreement corresponding with a higher level of credibility. The researcher should set an acceptable level of agreement (e.g., 80%) and as with the independent extraction, discussions between researcher and independent judge can be used to refine categories and definitions, followed by another round of randomly coded incidents until acceptable percentages are reached.

Participant cross-checking allows the researcher to check with a participant to confirm their "incidents" are correctly placed into categories identified. A similar method employed by Calabrò & LaRocco (2006) was *member checking* (Lincoln & Guba, 1985) to confirm participant meaning as part of the interview process through the use of probes, restating participant information to confirm its accuracy. Cross checking can be conducted in a number of ways including confirmation as part of a follow-up interview or survey, as well as providing a list of categories derived from the participants "incidents" for review and verification. Key questions for participants would address

1. the accuracy of the reported incident and/or categories derived,
2. missing information,
3. needed revisions, and
4. additional information needed.

Procedural reliability can also be used when interviews and/or observations are used to as the primary data collection method. Butterfield et al., (2009) referred to this as interview fidelity. This process involves ensuring protocols and data collection methods are followed. For interviews, this can involve checks on a randomly selected number of interview tapes. For observations, it can involve a second observer. The process includes development of a checklist from which the third party determines if questions and/or procedures were presented and followed as outlined. Items included on the checklist are dependent on the degree of structure within the interview or observation. For example, with a structure interview, items of import might include informed consent, the degree to which the questions were presented appropriately and in the right order, the degree to which the interviewer probed appropriate and/or refrained from leading questions, etc.

Flanagan (1954) presented the concept of *exhaustiveness* of the data as one method for determining when incident categorization is complete. This concept is similar to data saturation (Morse, 1995) or redundancy (Lincoln and Guba, 1985). The use of test or holdout samples (holding up to one half of incidents) is also as a validation method that can be used once categories had been developed from a portion of the data (Butterfield et al., 2005; Butterfield et al., 2009; Gremler, 2004).

Expert review involves the use of experts to validate the categories identified through the analysis. This step in the process is completed after the final categories have been identified and defined. Using two or more experts who have content knowledge based on the area of study, the categories are presented along with guiding questions related to the whether the categories make sense, are useful or surprising, and if there are categories that may be missing. From this point, the researcher determines if the results from the expert review responses warrant additional data analysis or confirm the findings.

Theoretical validity (Maxwell, 1992) can also be used to support findings, linking them with existing empirical research. The first step in the process is to document whether the assumptions underlying the study are supported by the research literature. The second step is to determine the degree to which the categories that emerge from the study are supported through the literature. In some cases, existing literature to be used to develop a theoretical or conceptual framework that can be used *a priori* can help validate findings, especially when used concurrently with other methods as presented in this chapter. Examples of this process can be found in the Calabrò and LaRocco, 2006 and Dogaru et al., 2009 studies.

Finally, *participation rates* involves calculating the number of participants for whom a recalled incident falls within a specific category identified by the participant. This requires the researcher to carefully document, by participant, each incident by category identified. For example, in the Rous (2004) study, participant was assigned a code and each text unit was the assigned to a participant. By using a software package (QRS NUD*IST; now NVivo) to support data analysis, each code was linked to a category, thus calculations could be conducted on the number of participants whose incidents fell under each category identified. This allowed reporting of the final categories and findings in order from the highest to the lowest participation rates.

MAKING THE CASE FOR THE CIT IN EARLY CHILDHOOD

The Critical Incident Technique is a research method that currently appears to be under-utilized in the area of early care and education. There are a number of benefits to the use of the CIT in our field. First, the CIT method allows participants to choose the events they recount based on their perceptions of what is relevant to the researcher. The "story-telling" nature of CIT research reflects an important component of early childhood development and instructional strategies, which might serve as an additional incentive for participation in the study.

Second, the CIT is particularly useful when exploring phenomenon for which we have little information or understanding. Most recently within the field of early childhood, there has been an emphasis on improving the quality of early care and education environments, as well as integrating services and systems. Given the paucity of research in these areas, the CIT offers the opportunity to explore these areas to support the generation of new constructs, concepts, and theories.

Third, the overall purpose of the CIT is to identify effective (and ineffective) practices related to a real-life set of issues or problems faced in an organization. This fits well into the current drive in the field of education to identify evidence based practices at both the organizational and classroom levels. In fact, one definition of evidence based practice includes those practices identified by those who have experience in the field. Buysse, Wesley, Snyder, & Winton (2006) state that "Evidence-based practice is a decision-making process that integrates the best available research evidence with family and professional wisdom and values" (p. 12). Using data gathered through studies using the CIT can support changes in organizational policies and practices to improve the effectiveness of services provided.

The CIT method is not without its limitations. As presented in the section on reliability and validity, researchers must identify and include multiple methods to ensure the credibility of findings. Of particular concern in the CIT process is the role of research bias throughout the process. During step five of the CIT as presented by Flanagan (1954), a critical component is the need of proper interpretation of the data and the need to ascertain if bias was introduced at any stage in the proceeding fours steps of the process. Finally, the CIT was presented by Flanagan (1954) as a flexible process that can be modified to fit the topic of study. While this flexibility can be seen as a strength of the model, it requires due diligence on the part of the researcher to ensure the methods used across the five steps are well planned and documented.

REFERENCES

American Institutes for Research (AIR). (1998, April). The critical incident technique. *AIR Web Page*. [On-line]. Retrieved July 2006 from www.air.org/airweb/about/critical.html.

Alvarez, K. M., & Bernardin, H. J. (1973). *Behaviorally based rating scales for patrolmen: A step-by-step description of their development* [Abstract]. (Grant No. 371-86-10-A1). Washington, DC: Law Enforcement Assistance Administration.

Andersson, B. E., & Nilsson, S. G. (1964). Studies in the reliability and validity of the Critical incident technique. *Journal of Applied Psychology, 48,* 398–403.

Blasé, J., & Blasé, J. (1999). Principals' instructional leadership and teacher development: Teachers' perspectives. *Educational Administration Quarterly. 35*(3), 349–379.

Bogdan, R. C., & Biklen, S. K. (1992). Qualitative research for education: An introduction to theory and methods (2nd ed.). Boston, MA: Allyn & Bacon.

Butterfield, L. D., Borgen, W. A., Amundson, N. E., & Maglio, A.-S. T. (2005). Fifty years of the critical incident technique: 1954–2004 and beyond. *Qualitative Research, 5*(4), 475–497.

Butterfield, L. D., Borgen, W. A., Maglio, A.S. T., & Amundson, N. E. (2009). Using the enhance critical incident technique in counsellingn psychology research. *Canadian Journal of Counselling, 43*(4), 265–282.

Buysse, V., Wesley, P. W., Snyder, P., & Winton, P. (2006). Evidence-based practice: What does it really mean for the early childhood field? *Young Exceptional Children, 9*(4), 2–11.

Bradbury-Jones, C., & Tranter, S. (2008). Inconsistent use of the critical incident technique in nursing research. *Journal of Advanced Nursing, 64*(4), 399–407.

Calabrò, M. R., & LaRocco, D. J. (2006). *A qualitative investigation of primary teachers' intentional strategies for promoting development in early childhood.* Paper presented at the Annual Meeting of the Northeast Educational Research Association (37th, Kerhonkson, NY, Oct 18–20, 2006). 22 pp.

Chell, E. (2006). Critical incident technique. In C. Cassell & G. Symon (Eds.), *Essential guide to qualitative methods in organizational research,* (pp. 45–60). London: Sage.

Creswell, J. W. (2007). *Qualitative inquiry and research design: Choosing among five traditions* (2nd ed.). Thousand Oaks, CA: Sage.

Dogaru, C., Rosenkoetter, S., & Rous, B. (2009). *A critical incident study of the transition expereince of young children with disabilities. Recounts by parents and professionals.* Technical Report #6. Lexington University of Kentucky, Human Development Institute, National Early Childhood Transition Center. Available at http://www.hdi.uky.edu/SF/NECTC/Publications/papers.aspx

Fivars, G., & Fitzpatrick, R. (2001). *The critical incident technique bibliography* [Electronic Copy]. Retrieved from http://www.apa.org/pubs/databases/psycinfo/cit-intro.pdf

Flanagan, J. C. (1954). The critical incident technique. *Psychological Bulletin, 51*(4), 327–358.

Foster, S. L., DeLawyer, D. D., & Guevremont, D. C. (1986). A critical incidents analysis of liked and disliked peer behaviors and their situational parameters in childhood and adolescence. *Behavioral Assessment, 8,* 115–133.

Gettinger, M., & Stoiber, K. C. (1998). Critical incident reporting: a procedure for monitoring children's performance and maximizing progress in inclusive settings. [Feature Article]. *Early Childhood Education Journal, 26*(1), 39–46.

Gilbert, J., & Priest, M. (1997). Models and discourse: A primary school science class visit to a museum. *Science Education, 81*(6), 749–762.

Gremler D. D. (2004). The critical incident technique in service research. *Journal of Service Research (7)*1, 65–89.

Kassarjian, H. H. (1977, June). Content analysis in consumer research. *Journal of Consumer Research, 4,* 8–18.

Lincoln, Y. S., & Guba, E. G. (1985). *Naturalistic enquiry.* Newbury Park, CA: Sage.

Manley-Casimir, M., & Wassermann, S. (1989). The teacher as decision-maker: Connecting self with the practice of teaching [Abstract]. *Childhood Education, 65*(5), 288–293. (PS516905).

Maxwell, J. A. (1992). Understanding and validity in qualitative research. In A. M. Huberman & M. B. Miles (Eds.), *The qualitative researcher's companion,* (pp. 37–64). Thousand Oaks, CA: Sage Publications.

Morse, J. M. (1995). The significance of redundancy. *Qualitative Health Research, 8,* 443–445.

Richards T. J., & Richards, L. (1994). Using computers in qualitative research. In N. K. Denzin & Y. S. Lincoln (Eds), *Handbook of qualitative research* (pp. 445–462). Thousand Oaks, CA: Sage Publications.

Ronan, W. W., & Latham, G. P. (1974). The reliability and validity of the critical incident technique: A closer look. *Studies in Personnel Psychology, 6*(1), 53–64.

Rosenkoetter, S., Schroeder, C., Rous, B., Hains, A., Shaw, J., & McCormick, K. (2009). A review of research in early childhood transition: Child and family studies (Technical Report #5). Lexington, KY: University of Kentucky, Human

Development Institute, National Early Childhood Transition Center. Available at http://www.hdi.uky.edu/NECTC/Home.aspx

Rous, B. (2004). Teacher perspectives of instructional supervision and behaviors that support preschool instruction. *Journal of Early Intervention 26*(4), 266–283.

Rous, B. (2001). *Instructional leadership in Kentucky public preschool programs: Teacher perceptions of leader instructional influence.* Retrieved from ProQuest Dissertations and Theses database. (UMI No. 3032617).

Smith P., & Kendall, L. (1963). Retranslation of expectations: An approach to the construction of unambiguous anchors for rating scales. *Journal of Applied Psychology 47*, 149–155.

Symon, G., & Cassell, C. (Eds.). (1998). *Qualitative methods and analysis in organizational research: A practical guide.* London, England UK: Sage Publications Ltd.

Thomas, D. R. (2006). A general inductive approach for analyzing qualitative evaluation data. *American Journal of Evaluation, 27*(2), 237–246.

Tulley, M., & Chiu, L. H. (1998). Children's perceptions of the effectiveness of classroom discipline techniques. *Journal of Instructional Psychology, 25*(3), 189–197.

Wopereis, I. G. J. H., Sloep, P. B., & Poortman, S. H. (2010). Weblogs as instruments for reflection on action in teacher education. *Interactive Learning Environments, 18*(3), 245–261.

CHAPTER 8

UTILITY OF IMPLEMENTATION AND INTERVENTION PERFORMANCE CHECKLISTS FOR CONDUCTING RESEARCH IN EARLY CHILDHOOD EDUCATION

Carl J. Dunst, Carol M. Trivette, and Melinda Raab

INTRODUCTION

This chapter includes a description of the development and utility of performance checklists for assessing and measuring adherence to different kinds of practices as part of conducting research with young children. Checklists can take on different formats (yes/no, Likert scales, etc.) and can be used to assess adoption and use of practices constituting the focus of investigation. An implementation sciences framework is used to distinguish between two types of early childhood practices, describe the differences between the two types of practices, describe how the two practices are related, and illustrate how checklists can be used to measure adherence to the key characteristics of both types of practices. The two types of practices are ones used by early childhood teachers to promote and enhance child learning and development (e.g., Bennett-Armistead, Duke, & Moses, 2005; National Association for the Education of Young Children, 2005; Sandall, Hemmeter, Smith, & McLean, 2005) and ones used by professional development staff to promote early childhood teachers' use of research-based or recommended early childhood practices (e.g., Neuman & Kamil, 2010; Skiffington, Washburn, & Elliott, 2011; Snyder et al., 2012).

The content of the chapter is based on research our colleagues and ourselves have conducted (e.g., Dunst & Raab, 2010; Dunst, Trivette, & Deal, 2011; Trivette, Dunst, & Hamby, 2010; Trivette, Raab, & Dunst, 2012b) as well as research conducted by others investigating the usefulness of checklists for discerning the extent to which evidence-based or recommended practices are used in the manner intended by practitioners in early childhood programs (e.g., National Association for the Education of Young Children, 2005; Sandall et al., 2005) as well as by practitioners in other fields (e.g., Alkon, To, Wolff, Mackie, & Bernzweig, 2008; Lattimore, Stephens, Favell, & Risley, 1984; Lockyer et al., 2006; Shen, Hao, Tam, & Yao, 2007). Our own research has included, but has not been limited to, the investigation of early childhood classroom practices (Dunst, McWilliam, & Holbert, 1986; Trivette & Raab, 2011); early intervention practices (Dunst, 2004; 2011); infant, toddler, and preschool early literacy and language intervention practices (Dunst, Jones, Johnson, Raab, & Hamby, 2011); everyday naturally occurring learning opportunity practices (Dunst et al., 2001; Dunst, Bruder, Trivette, & Hamby, 2006); interest-based child learning practices (Dunst & Raab, 2011; Swanson, Raab, Roper, & Dunst, 2006); parent capacity-building intervention practices (Dunst & Trivette, 2011a; Swanson, Raab, & Dunst, 2011); capacity-building practitioner help-giving practices (Dempsey & Dunst, 2004; Trivette & Dunst, 2007); and family-centered help-giving practices (e.g., Dunst & Trivette, 2010; Trivette & Dunst, 2007). This research and practice has led to the development of many different kinds of performance checklists for measuring practitioner and parent use of the above practices as well as other kinds of early childhood, parenting, and family support practices (e.g., Dunst, Raab, Trivette, & Swanson, 2010; Dunst, Trivette, Raab, & Masiello, 2008; Raab & Dunst, 2006; Roper & Dunst, 2006; Trivette & Dunst, 2004; Wilson & Dunst, 2004).

IMPLEMENTATION SCIENCES FRAMEWORK

Implementation science and implementation research focuses on the adoption and use of evidence-based intervention practices and the methods and procedures best suited for promoting practitioner use of the practices

(Eccles & Mittman, 2006). According to Kelly and Perkins (2012), implementation science is concerned with an understanding of the processes, procedures, and conditions that promote or impede the transfer, adoption, and use of evidence-based intervention practices in the context of typical, everyday settings (e.g., early childhood classrooms). Eccles et al. (2009) describe implementation research as the "scientific study of methods to promote the systematic uptake of clinical [intervention] research findings and other evidence-based practices into routine practice" (p. 18). The term *evidence-based practices* is used in this chapter to mean practices that have been scientifically investigated with a focus on the identification of the key characteristics of the practices that are empirically related to hypothesized outcomes where the relationships between the characteristics and consequences of the practices have been replicated under a variety of differing conditions (Dunst & Trivette, 2009b; Dunst, Trivette, & Cutspec, 2007).

Implementation and Intervention Practices

An implementation science framework includes an important distinction between implementation practices and intervention practices. Fixen, Naoom, Blasé, Friedman, and Wallace (2005) in their review and analysis of the state of implementation science research, differentiated between these two types of evidence-based practices and the outcomes of the practices. Implementation practices refer to the methods, procedures or activities used to promote adoption and use of intervention practices, and intervention practices refer to the methods, procedures or activities used to promote changes in an individual's or group's behavior or development. Accordingly, implementation practices are defined as the methods and procedures used by implementation agents (coaches, supervisors, instructors, trainers, etc.) to promote practitioners' adoption and use of evidence-based intervention practices, whereas intervention practices are defined as the methods and strategies used by intervention agents (early childhood teachers, early interventionists, parent educators, etc.) to affect changes or produce desired outcomes in a targeted population or group of recipients (e.g., preschool children). For example, Snell et al. (2013), in a review of 69 professional development studies to promote preschool teachers' use of different kinds of classroom practices, found that a number of implementation practices (e.g., instructor modeling, demonstration and feedback) were effective in changing preschool teachers' practices. In a similar manner, McCabe and Altamura (2011) reviewed and analyzed preschool classroom intervention practices that were effective for enhancing young children's social and emotional competence.

From an applied perspective of implementation science and research, it is of practical value to have as clear an understanding as possible of the active ingredients (Clark, 2009) or key characteristics (Dunst & Trivette, 2009b) of both evidence-based implementation practices and evidence-based intervention practices. Any implementation practice or intervention practice can be conceptualized and operationalized as "made up" of different features and elements (e.g., the different activities in an early childhood curriculum) where certain characteristics or combination of characteristics of the practices are found to be more important than others as determinants of the use of either implementation practices or intervention practices. For example, as part of a line of meta-analytic research on the key characteristics of adult learning methods (an implementation practice), we were able to identify the particular practices that best explained optimal learner outcomes (Dunst & Trivette, 2012b; Dunst, Trivette, & Hamby, 2010). The findings in turn were used to develop an evidence-based approach to professional development (Dunst & Trivette, 2009a). Similarly, a meta-analytic line of research on the key characteristics of adult–child interactions found to be associated with optimal child outcomes (Dunst & Kassow, 2008; Trivette, 2007) resulted in the identification of the particular interactive behavior that best explained child outcomes. The findings in turn were used to develop an evidence-based approach to responsive teaching (Raab & Dunst, 2009). These particular implementation and intervention practices are used in this chapter to illustrate the development of performance checklists for assessing adherence to the practices.

Implementation and Intervention Fidelity

An implementation sciences framework can be taken one step further for both understanding its applicability and establishing the foundation for developing implementation and intervention practices checklists. Neither implementation nor intervention practices, no matter their evidence base, are likely to have intended effects if they are not used in a manner that includes the key characteristics of the practices. Using either or both implementation and intervention practices in the manner found effective from research findings is what is meant by the fidelity of use of a practice (Carroll et al., 2007; Gearing et al., 2011). Accordingly, implementation fidelity refers to the degree to which coaching, in-service training, instruction, or any other kind of evidence-based professional development practice is implemented as intended and has the effect of promoting the adoption and use of evidence-based intervention practices (Trivette & Dunst, 2011). In turn, intervention fidelity refers to the degree to which evidence-based intervention practices are used as intended by early childhood practitioners or other intervention agents and have expected or intended benefits (Dunst, Trivette, McInerney et al., 2008).

Most models and approaches to fidelity make a distinction between the *quantity* and *quality* of the adoption and use of a practice (see Dunst et al., 2008). Quantity refers to *how much* a practice was used, and quality refers to *how well* a practice was used (Dane & Schneider, 1998). The difference between the quantity and quality of fidelity is best understood by recognizing the fact that either or both implementation and intervention practices need to be delivered in amounts and in ways that include the key elements of the practices if they are likely to have intended effects (Gearing et al., 2011; Warren, Fey, & Yoder, 2007). As described in a later section of the chapter, checklists are one way of determining the extent to which implementation and intervention practices are used with fidelity.

Relationships Between Implementation and Intervention Practices

Figure 8.1 shows the relationships between evidence-based implementation practices and evidence-based intervention practices and how the adoption and use of implementation and intervention practices with fidelity would in turn be expected to have hypothesized benefits and outcomes. The relationships depicted in the framework lead to a number of

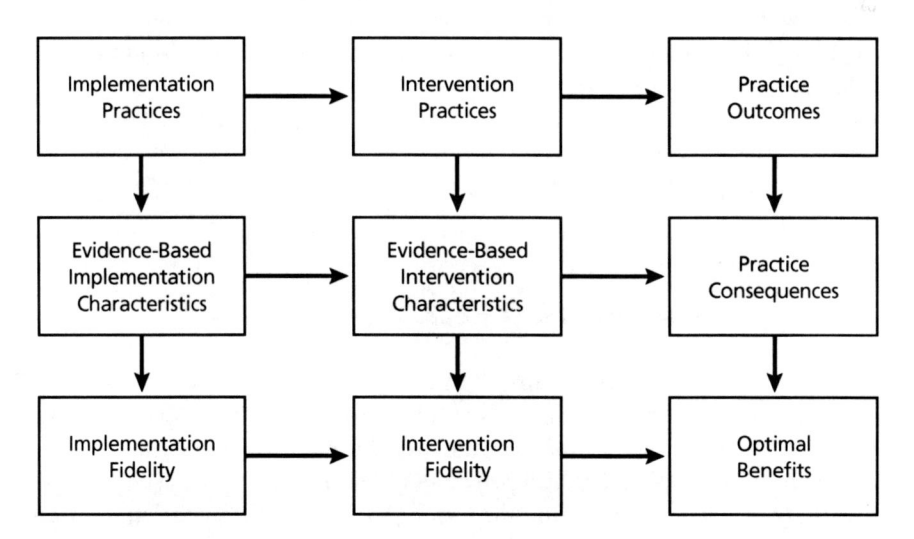

Figure 8.1 Framework for showing the relationships between the fidelity of evidence-based implementation practices, evidence-based intervention practices, and the outcomes and consequences of the practices.

hypotheses where checklists could be used to measure the fidelity of both implementation and intervention practices (Dunst, 2012; Dunst & Trivette, 2012a) and in turn be used to evaluate the extent to which variations in implementation and intervention fidelity are related to variations in early childhood education outcomes (Dunst, 2012). The main hypotheses that could be tested using checklists to measure fidelity include the following:

- *Variations in implementation fidelity should be related to variations in intervention fidelity.* Tests of the hypothesis would include evaluation of the relative importance of the quantity and quality of implementation fidelity, and the interactions between the types and elements of fidelity.
- *Variations in intervention fidelity should be related to variations in practice outcomes.* Tests of the hypothesis would include evaluation of the relative importance of the quantity and quality of intervention fidelity, and the interactions between the types and elements of fidelity.
- *Variations in intervention fidelity should mediate the relationship between implementation fidelity and practice outcomes.* Tests of the hypothesis would include evaluation (to the extent possible) of the complex relationships between the quantity and quality of implementation and intervention fidelity and the outcomes of the evidence-based practices.

Later in the chapter, we illustrate how variations in the implementation fidelity of an evidence-based approach to professional development are related to variations in early childhood practitioners' use of a naturalistic teaching practice with young children in preschool classrooms. The examples that are used show why it is important to differentiate between the two types of practices as well as highlight the manner in which the practices are empirically related.

PERFORMANCE CHECKLIST INDICATORS

The term *checklist* is used in this chapter to refer to a list of indicators or criteria informed by research findings that, taken together, represent the key characteristics of the practice the checklist indicators are intended to measure (Stufflebeam, 2000). A *performance checklist* refers to a list of indicators that are used to determine the extent to which an implementation or intervention agent's performance mirrors the characteristics of a practice that has evidence-based key features and elements (Roper & Dunst, 2006; Stufflebeam, 2000; Westgaard, 2001).

One of the most useful frameworks for developing checklist indicators for either research or practice is described by Babbie (2009) in his book *The Practice of Social Research*. The framework differentiates between conceptualization, operationalization, and measurement, and explicitly considers the manner in which the three elements are related. Figure 8.2 shows an adaptation of the Babbie (2009) framework depicting the progression from conceptualization to measurement of the fidelity of a practice constituting the focus of investigation. The framework has proven especially useful in our own research for developing implementation and intervention practice checklists and for ascertaining the fidelity of either or both types of practices.

Conceptualization

Conceptualization refers to the process of identifying as precisely as possible what one means by a concept, construct, or practice. As stated by Babbie (2009), "conceptualization produces a specific, agreed-upon meaning of a concept for the purpose of research" (p. 122).

For example, suppose we want a better understanding of the meaning of teacher responsiveness in the context of early childhood practitioners interacting with young children in early childhood classrooms. The first

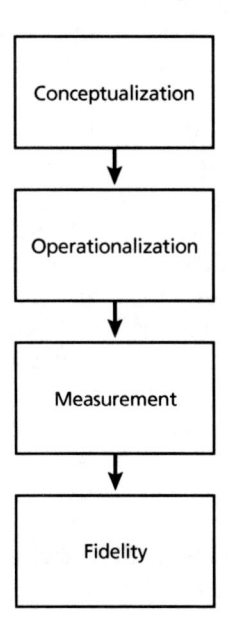

Figure 8.2 Process for developing evidence-based checklist items for assessing adherence to the practice indicators.

step in doing so would be to develop a working definition of the construct in order to be able to develop indicators that can be used to determine if a teacher is or is not responsive to young children's behavior in a classroom setting. We might, for example, define teacher responsiveness as those emotional and sensitive behavior that engage and sustain child participation in learning activities where a teacher's responses to a child's behavior are used to reinforce child production of social and nonsocial competence (e.g., Bakermans-Kranenburg, van IJzendoom, & Juffer, 2008; Dunst & Kassow, 2007; Nievar & Becker, 2008). As noted by Babbie (2009), conceptualization gives meaning to a concept (or practice) and provides a foundation for specifying the indicators of a concept or practice.

Operationalization

The process of developing the indicators of a construct or practice is what we mean by operationalization. Indicators are the items on a checklist that are used to measure the presence (use) or absence (nonuse) of a practice that is the focus of investigation. So, for example, we might use teacher positive affect, warmth, following a child's lead, sensitivity to child initiations, adult–child turn-taking, and shared teacher–child interests as indicators of teacher responsiveness.

A construct or practice can be either unidimensional or multidimensional, and therefore, the operationalization of a construct or practice can include either a single set of indicators or two or more subsets of indicators. In our research investigating the key characteristics of interest-based child learning, for example, we have been able to identify a unidimensional set of indicators that taken together, operationally define what we mean by interest-based child learning opportunities (Dunst et al., 2001). The indicators include such things as the use of personal child interests as the basis for selecting child learning activities, sustained child engagement in the activities, opportunities to practice existing skills and learn new behavior, child exploration of the range of consequences of different actions, and opportunities to develop a sense of mastery. In contrast, as part of a line of research on family-centered help-giving practices, we have consistently found two subsets of practices (relational help-giving and participatory help-giving) with each subset having their own unique indicators (Dunst, Trivette, & Hamby, 1996; Trivette & Dunst, 2007). Relational indicators include such things as active and reflective listening, treating families with dignity and respect, and sharing information in a complete and unbiased manner. Participatory indicators include such things as informed family decision-making, active family engagement in obtaining desired resources, and the use of capacity-building help-giving methods and strategies to strengthen family competence. The indicators for both interest-based child learning and family-centered helpgiving have been used to develop performance checklists for both types of practices (e.g., Dunst, Herter, & Shields, 2000; Wilson & Dunst, 2004).

Measurement

Once the indicators of a construct or practice have been developed, the next step is to decide how to measure the use or nonuse of the indicators by either implementation or intervention agents. The nature of the construct or practice typically dictates which kind of measurement procedure is used for assessing adherence (i.e., fidelity). This can range from observational counts of the use or nonuse of checklist indicators, time sampling, dichotomous scoring (e.g., yes or no), Likert scaling, or any other method that makes sense for the construct or practice being investigated.

Checklists in general, and performance checklists in particular, constitute one way of going from conceptualization to operationalization to measurement as part of research in early childhood education or other fields of research. We have found performance checklists of particular value in our research and practice as a way of measuring the use of the key characteristics of both evidence-based implementation and intervention practices, and for establishing the fidelity of use of either or both of the practices. The Appendix includes a list of the sources of the checklists we have developed as well as references to other sources of information on different types of performance checklists. We now describe the process of developing checklists for both implementation and intervention practices.

DEVELOPMENT OF EVIDENCE-BASED PERFORMANCE CHECKLISTS

The process that we have used to develop performance checklists is to start with a research synthesis or meta-analysis of a targeted practice to identify the evidence-based characteristics of the practice which in turn are used to develop checklist indicators. The approach that we use for examining studies of a targeted practice is called a *practice-based research synthesis* (Dunst, Trivette, et al., 2007). This type of research synthesis or meta-analysis explicitly focuses on identifying, unpacking, and disentangling the active ingredients or key features of a practice that matter most in explaining study outcomes (Dunst & Trivette, 2009b, 2012a; Lipsey, 1993) where the evidence-based characteristics that are identified are used to develop performance checklist indicators. This process is illustrated next for both an implementation and an intervention practice.

Example of an Implementation Practice Checklist

Professional development in early intervention and early childhood programs has constituted the focus of our research and practice for a number of years (e.g., Dunst & Raab, 2010; Dunst, Trivette, & Deal, 2011; Trivette & Dunst, 2000). One of the major activities in this line of research was a meta-analysis of four adult learning methods (Dunst, Trivette et al., 2010) and the investigation of the conditions under which the learning methods had optimal learner benefits and outcomes (Dunst & Trivette, 2011b, 2012b). The adult learning methods constituting the focus of investigation were accelerated learning (Meier, 2000), coaching (Hargreaves & Dawe, 1990), guided design (Wales & Stager, 1972), and just-in-time training (Beckett, 2000). These particular adult learning methods were selected because they have been subjected to experimental evaluations and the implementation practices have been used with early intervention practitioners and early childhood teachers (Bowman & McCormick, 2000; Cain, Rudd, & Saxon, 2007).

Findings reported in *How People Learn* (Bransford et al., 2000), a literature review of the science of learning, were used to develop operational definitions of six adult learning practices where the adult learning methods in each study were coded in terms of the practices used to present new information or knowledge to learners, engage the learners in the use of the information or knowledge, and the methods to promote learner deep understanding of the knowledge or practice.

Presentation included the methods and procedures used by coaches, instructors, or trainers to

1. introduce new knowledge, material, or practices to learners; and
2. illustrate or demonstrate the use of the knowledge, material or practices for the learners.

Application included the methods and procedures to engage learners in

1. the use of the knowledge, material, or practices; and
2. evaluation of the outcomes or consequences of application

Deep understanding included the methods and procedures for engaging learners

1. in reflection on their totality of learning experiences and
2. self-assessment of mastery of newly acquired learner knowledge or skills.

More than 30 different adult learning methods were used to present new knowledge and practices, have learners apply new knowledge and skills, and promote learner deep understanding of the knowledge or practice. The particular practices found most effective in promoting adult learner knowledge and skills are shown in Table 8.1. Findings showed that the more actively involved learners were in mastering new knowledge or practice and the more instructors or trainers supported and facilitated the learning process, the better the learner outcomes. The findings also demonstrated that how instructors engaged learners, provided guidance, orchestrated learner self-evaluation and reflection, and encouraged and supported deeper learner understanding, the more effective were the learner outcomes. The only practice found effective in terms of learner assessment of his or her mastery of the material or practice constituting the focus of investigation was the use of standards-based performance checklists.

TABLE 8.1 Cohen's *d* Effect Sizes for the Most Effective Adult Learning Method Practices

Characteristics/Practices	Number Studies	Effect Sizes	Mean Effect Size	95% Confidence Interval	Z
Introduction					
Out of class learner activities/self instruction instruction	9	11	.64	.52–.77	10.43**
Classroom/workshop presentations	21	31	.63	.53–.72	13.14**
Preclass learner exercises	5	5	.54	.38–.71	6.44**
Illustration/Demonstration					
Role playing/simulations	14	21	.55	.42–.68	8.20**
Learner informed input	4	4	.53	.34–.72	5.41**
Practicing					
Real life application	9	13	.94	.79–1.09	12.15**
Real life application + role playing	5	7	.86	.61–1.03	6.75**
Problem solving tasks	13	19	.49	.39–.58	10.10**
Evaluation					
Assess strengths/weaknesses	7	9	.94	.65–1.22	6.49**
Review experience/make changes	16	24	.47	.38–.56	10.19**
Reflections					
Performance improvement reviews	4	6	1.27	.89–1.65	6.56*
Journaling/behavior suggestion	5	5	.82	.52–1.12	5.33**
Mastery					
Standards-based self assessment	8	11	.86	.72–.99	12.47**

Note: Z is a measure of the strength of the relationships among measures. *$p<0.01$. **$p<0.0001$

The findings from the meta-analysis were used to develop an approach to professional development called a *Participatory Adult Learning Strategy* (PALS; Dunst & Trivette, 2009a) which has been the foundation for developing PALS checklists for providing professional development to early childhood practitioners to promote their adoption and use of different kinds of evidence-based early childhood practices. Exhibit A shows examples of PALS checklist indicators that have been used for evaluating the

Exhibit A
Examples of PALS Checklist Indicators

Trainer/Coach _____ Practice _____			
Did the trainer or coach use the following practices as part of promoting practitioner understanding and use of the targeted early childhood practice?		Yes	No
Presentation — Introduction	1. Solicited practitioner identification or description of what he/she expected to learn from the training		
Presentation — Introduction	2. Provided a detailed description or explanation of the practice		
Presentation — Illustration	3. Used practitioner knowledge or experience with the practice or similar practices to provide example(s) of the practice		
Presentation — Illustration	4. Demonstrated the use of the practice either *in vivo* or through role playing		
Application — Practicing	5. Engaged the practitioner in the use of the practice either *in vivo* or through role playing		
Application — Practicing	6. Provided the practitioner trainer-guided practice using the practice		
Application — Evaluation	7. Engaged the practitioner in evaluation of his/her experience using the practice		
Application — Evaluation	8. Provided the practitioner feedback based on trainer observation of practitioner use of the practice		
Deep Understanding — Reflection	9. Engaged the practitioner in self-assessment of his/her understanding of both the use and consequences of the practice		
Deep Understanding — Reflection	10. Had the practitioner assess his/her performance to identify next steps in the learning process		
Deep Understanding — Mastery	11. Had the practitioner use a checklist or set of performance standards to assess his/her overall understanding and mastery of the practice		
Deep Understanding — Mastery	12. Provided the practitioner opportunities to use the practice in different settings and with different children		

extent to which a trainer or coach engages early childhood practitioners in learning to use responsive teaching as an instructional practice with preschoolers. The targets of appraisal of the indicators are the trainer's or coach's use of practices consistent with the findings from the meta-analysis of the adult learning methods (Dunst, Trivette et al., 2010). The exhibit includes side headings for illustrating which items are indicators for which PALS practices (Dunst & Trivette, 2009a). Measure of adherence to practice indicators could be ascertained by observations, behavior ratings, Likert scaling, or another method that evaluates either or both the quantity and quality of the trainer or coach practices.

Example of an Intervention Practice Checklist

One early childhood instructional method that has been the focus of our research and practice is responsive parenting (Landry, Smith, & Swank, 2006) and responsive teaching (May, 2010). The research foundations for the instructional practice have been research studies of different naturalistic teaching methods (Dunst, Raab, & Trivette, 2011; Kaiser & Trent, 2007; Kassow & Dunst, 2007; Trivette, 2007) and meta-analyses of adult–child interaction research studies (e.g., DeWolf & van Ijzendoorn, 1997; Dunst & Kassow, 2008; Nievar & Becker, 2008; Roberts & Kaiser, 2011). The focus of our analyses of these two lines of integrative research has been the identification of the key characteristics of responsive teaching (and parenting) associated with optimal child benefits.

The adult behavioral characteristics consistently found related to positive child behavioral and developmental outcomes include positive affect and warmth, following a child's lead and interests, interpreting a child's behavior as an intent to communicate or interact, engaging in joint attention with a child, responding contingently to a child's behavior, and providing support and encouragement to engage in new and different behavior.

Findings from the various research syntheses and meta-analyses were used to develop an evidence-based instructional practice called the *Magic Seven Steps to Responsive Teaching* (Raab & Dunst, 2009). The key characteristics of this evidence-based instructional practice have been used to develop a number of different responsive teaching performance checklists. Examples of checklist indicators for this instructional practice are shown in Exhibit B. The indicators, taken together, constitute a child-centered approach to instruction which emphasizes teacher or parent sensitivity and responsiveness to a child's interactional behavior, adult support and encouragement, and efforts to promote expansions and elaborations in child competence. Adherence to the indicators could be measured through

Exhibit B
Examples of Responsive Teaching Checklist Indicators

Teacher/Practitioner _____ Setting _____		
Did the teacher or early childhood practitioner use the following practices as part of his or her interactions with the children in his/her classroom?	Yes	No
Setting the Stage — 1. Engaged the child in interest-based learning activities		
2. Paid attention to and noticed when and how the child attempted to interact with people and objects		
3. Provided the child ample time to initiate interactions with people, objects, or other materials		
Responsiveness — 4. Responded promptly and positively to the child's behavior in ways that matched the amount, pace, and intent of the child's behavior		
5. Responded to the child's behavior with comments, joint interaction, and gestures to support and encourage child engagement in the activity		
6. Responded to the child in ways that encouraged him or her to use his or her behavior in new and different ways		
Elaboration — 7. Used a variety of materials or arranged the environment in ways to encourage the child to use his or her behavior in new and different ways		
8. Provided the child frequent opportunities to practice newly learned abilities as part of learning activities		
9. Encouraged the child to elaborate or expand on his or her behavior in ways that were increasingly more complex		

observations, behavior ratings, Likert scaling, or another method for assessing fidelity of use of the instructional practice.

Measuring the Fidelity of Implementation and Intervention Practices

The manner in which implementation and intervention checklists have been used to assess fidelity, where variations in coaching fidelity are related to variations in early childhood classroom practices, is illustrated from a study in which PALS was used as the implementation practice (Dunst & Trivette, 2009a) and responsive teaching was used as the intervention practice (Raab & Dunst, 2009). The study was conducted in 18 Head Start classrooms, all but one of which included one teacher and one teacher assistant (Trivette, Raab, & Dunst, 2012a).

Professional Development

PALS was used to conduct training to promote both teacher and teacher assistant adoption and use of responsive teaching (as well as other classroom practices) (see Trivette et al., 2012a). Training was conducted on-site in the Head Start classrooms and primarily in the teachers' classrooms. The coach met with each teacher and teacher assistant once a week for four months where the coach used PALS practices to promote teacher and teacher assistant understanding and use of responsive teaching practices. The coach spent, on average, 60 minutes with a teacher and teacher assistant during each on-site visit. In the largest majority of coaching sessions (94%), the coach worked with both the teacher and teacher assistant at the same time.

Exhibit C includes examples of the checklist indicators that were used to assess coach adherence to the PALS approach to training and the Likert scale for measuring the degree of coach adherence to the PALS indicators. (The actual checklist included 20 indicators.) Fidelity was considered established if the coach received ratings of 4 or 5 on 85% of the indicators by both the teachers and teacher assistants. Figure 8.3 shows the percent of indicators that were rated in this manner. Fidelity was achieved in 14 of the 17 classrooms as evidenced by the percent of indicators meeting the a priori established criterion and by the fact that the criterion was met for both the teachers and teacher assistants in the 14 classrooms.

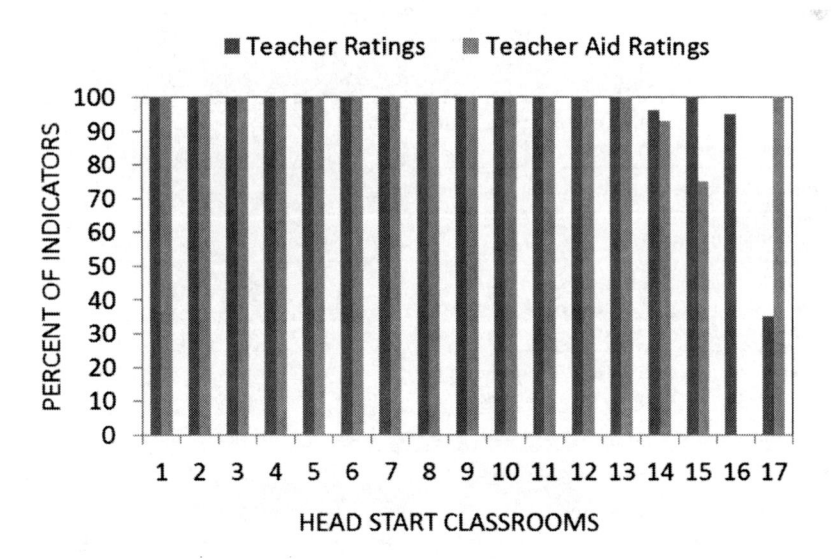

Figure 8.3 Percent of professional development (implementation practice) indicators meeting the criterion of coach fidelity in the Head Start classrooms.

Exhibit C

Examples of the PALS Head Start Coaching Checklist Indicators

Trainer/Coach _____ Program Name _____	Teacher/Teacher Assistant _____ Classroom _____				
Indicate how true each statement is about the training you received from the Head Start Coach.	Not At All True	A Little True	Somewhat True	Mostly True	Very Much True
It was helpful to have the coach provide examples/illustrations of the important features of the responsive teaching practices	1	2	3	4	5
I had different types of opportunities to learn how to use the responsive teaching practices	1	2	3	4	5
The coach provided me enough time to understand how to implement the responsive teaching practices	1	2	3	4	5
The experiences I had while learning to implement the responsive teaching practices kept me highly engaged	1	2	3	4	5
The coach provided me enough opportunities to use the responsive teaching practices in my classroom	1	2	3	4	5
The coach was enthusiastic about ways I could gain a better understanding of the responsive teaching practices	1	2	3	4	5
The coach provided frequent opportunities for me to use the responsive teaching practices	1	2	3	4	5
My discussions with the coach helped me identify ways I could gain a greater understanding of the responsive teaching practices	1	2	3	4	5
The coach illustrated the key characteristics of the responsive teaching practices in various ways	1	2	3	4	5
When I used the responsive teaching practices in my classroom, the coach provided me just enough assistance to be successful	1	2	3	4	5
My discussions with the coach about my use of the responsive teaching practices helped me reflect on what I did and how it worked	1	2	3	4	5
My conversations with the coach helped me identify next steps in improving my use of the responsive teaching practices	1	2	3	4	5

Responsive Teaching

The teachers' and teacher assistants' use of responsive teaching was assessed on three occasions, prior to the beginning of the PALS training on the

Utility of Implementaion and Interventon Performance Checklists ▪ **263**

Exhibit D

Examples of the Head Start Responsive Teaching Checklist Indicators

Teacher/Assistant _____ Observer _____ Program Name _____ Classroom _____				
Indicate the extent to which the teacher or teacher Assistant used the following practices as part of his or her interactions with the children in the classroom.	Not At All Used	Used A Little	Used Some-of-the-Time	Routinely Used
Let the children take the lead and make choices in interactions with objects and people	1	2	3	4
Paid attention to and focus on what captures and maintains the children's attention	1	2	3	4
Interpreted the children's behavior as intents to interact with objects and people	1	2	3	4
Responded promptly and positively to the children's behavior to help the children learn how using their behavior can make interesting things happen	1	2	3	4
Responded to children's initiations in ways that help them maintain engagement with objects and people (e.g., make comments, provide acknowledgement, use gestures, etc.)	1	2	3	4
Joined in the children's play and engaged in turn taking with the children	1	2	3	4
Provided the children the least assistance necessary to help them use new behavior and explore their capabilities	1	2	3	4
Provided the children multiple opportunities throughout the day to produce and practice new behavior	1	2	3	4

instructional practice, two months later, and four months after training was initiated. The observations and ratings of use of responsive teaching were made by an independent observer in the Head Start classrooms who was unaware of the teachers' and teacher assistants' judgment of coaching fidelity. Examples of the checklist indicators for measuring teacher and teacher assistant use of the responsive teaching practices are shown in Exhibit D. A 4-point Likert scale was used to assess fidelity of use of the practices. Fidelity was considered achieved if the classroom staff were rated as using the practice indicators some-of-the-time or routinely on 85% of the items.

Figure 8.4 shows the average percent of indicators rated either a 3 or 4 at each measurement occasion and the 95% confidence intervals for the averages. Staff training on responsive teaching was conducted between the Times 2 and 3 observations. As would be expected, the adherence ratings were below the criterion prior to training but reached 81% and 82%, respectively, at the times after training was initiated. The reason the average percents did not reach the a priori criterion can be discerned from

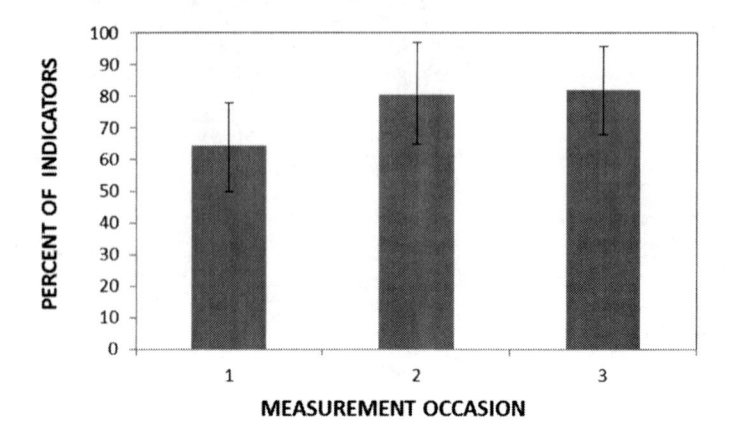

Figure 8.4 Percent of responsive teaching (intervention practices) indicators and the 95% confidence intervals for the indicators meeting the criterion of teacher and teacher assistant fidelity.

the 95% confidence intervals which are metrics for the range of individual classroom staff scores around the averages. As can be seen by examination of the confidence intervals, the criterion was reached in some of the classrooms at all three measurement occasions and not reached in other classrooms the two other times fidelity was assessed. Inspection of the raw data showed that fidelity was achieved in seven classrooms at Time 1 and in 13 classrooms at both Times 2 and 3. In the five classrooms where fidelity was not reached, the percents at the different measurement occasions were zero or near zero suppressing the averages for all classrooms combined.

Relationship Between Implementation and Intervention Fidelity

The manner in which variations in implementation fidelity were related to variations in intervention fidelity was assessed using the PALS fidelity checklist indicators as a predictor measure and the responsive teaching fidelity checklist indicators as the outcome measure. The sum of the ratings on the 20 PALS coaching practice indicators was used as the measure of implementation fidelity, and the sum of the ratings of the eight responsive teaching practice indicators was used as the measure of intervention fidelity.

The means, standard deviations, and ranges for the implementation and intervention measures are shown in Table 8.2. The mean implementation ratings for the teachers and teacher assistants were nearly identical, but for both of the staff, the fidelity ratings varied by 35 to 40 points. The mean ratings of the teachers and teacher assistants' use of the instructional practice

TABLE 8.2 Means, Standard Deviations and Ranges for the PALS Coaching (Implementation) and Responsive Teaching (Intervention) Scores in the Head Start Classrooms

	Measures				
Type of Practice	Number of Scale Items	Number of Classrooms	Mean	Standard Deviation	Range
Implementation Practice					
Teacher Ratings	20	18	93.00	9.59	66–100
Teacher Assistant Ratings	20	17	92.53	11.15	59–100
Intervention Practice					
Time 2	8	18	25.39	5.84	12–32
Time 3	8	18	25.89	5.12	14–32

increased somewhat between the two measurement occasions, but there was considerable variability in the ratings of the staff's use of responsive teaching. The findings for both the implementation and intervention practices measures reflect the reality of applied research studies; no matter how much one attempts to establish fidelity in the early childhood setting constituting the focus of investigation, that standard is rarely met. The variability in the fidelity scores, however, permits tests of the relationship between implementation and intervention fidelity as illustrated next.

We first examined the relationship between implementation and intervention fidelity by computing the correlations between the PALS and responsive teaching measures to determine the degree of covariation between the two types of practices. The correlations between implementation fidelity and responsive teaching fidelity were $r = 0.59$, $p = 0.010$ at Time 2, and $r = 0.48$, $p = 0.043$ at Time 3. As predicted, based on Hypothesis 1 described earlier (p. 252), variations in implementation fidelity were related to variations in intervention fidelity.

Further analysis of the data were performed for illustrative purposes by categorizing the classrooms into low, medium, and high fidelity groups using a tripartite split of the implementation fidelity scores. The average implementation fidelity scores for the three groups were 82, 96, and 100, respectively. We therefore expected to find the largest differences in the classroom staff's responsive teaching scores between the low fidelity and both the medium and high fidelity groups, and the smallest differences between the medium and high fidelity groups based on size of the differences in the average implementation fidelity scores.

The focus of analysis was the differences in the responsive teaching practices for the three groups at Times 2 and 3 which were observed after training was initiated on the intervention practice. Cohen's d effect sizes for the

TABLE 8.3 Means, Standard Deviations, and Cohen's *d* Effect Sizes for the Between Implementation Fidelity Group Contrasts

Intervention Practice	Time	Implementation Fidelity						Between Group Cohen's *d*		
		Low (L)		Medium (M)		High (H)				
		Mean	SD	Mean	SD	Mean	SD	*L* vs. *M*	*L* vs. *H*	*M* vs. *H*
Responsive Teaching	2	21.50	7.18	26.67	4.63	28.00	3.85	0.88	1.18	0.31
Responsive Teaching	3	23.17	6.43	28.83	4.17	27.67	4.08	1.07	0.85	0.28

above three contrasts were used to evaluate whether the pattern of results were consistent with expectations. The results are shown in Table 8.3 where the sizes of effect for the three between group contrasts show the manner in which variations in implementation fidelity were related to variations in intervention fidelity. The four effect sizes for the low versus medium and low versus high fidelity group contrasts were all large to very large, whereas the sizes of effect for the medium vs. high fidelity group contrasts were both small (Lipsey & Wilson, 2001).

Although we recognize the fact that the two sets of analyses (correlations and effect sizes) are rather simplistic and the sample sizes in the analyses were quite small, we believe that the data and findings demonstrate that it is possible to investigate the relationship between implementation fidelity and intervention fidelity. In terms of the purposes of this chapter, the analyses illustrate how performance checklists can be used to investigate those relationships.

DISCUSSION

The approach to developing performance checklists, and using the checklists to assess the fidelity of either or both implementation practices and intervention practices, is but one way of measuring adoption and adherence to early childhood or other kinds of practices. Both the implementation sciences framework (Kelly & Perkins, 2012; Tansella & Thornicroft, 2009) and the framework for developing evidence-based performance checklist indicators (Babbie, 2009), taken together, provide researchers guidance for developing and using performance checklists for investigating a wide range of early childhood practices and the methods and procedures for promoting adoption of the practices.

Findings from our research have consistently indicated that variation in adherence to implementation practice indicators is related to variation in adherence to early childhood intervention practices (e.g., Dunst & Raab,

2010; Dunst, Trivette, & Deal, 2011; Trivette, Dunst, Hamby, & Pace, 2007; Trivette et al., 2012a), and that variation in adherence to early childhood intervention practice indicators is related to variation in changes or improvements in children's behavior and development (Dunst, Pace, & Hamby, 2007; Dunst & Raab, 2007; Trivette et al., 2007; Trivette et al., 2012b). Meta-analyses of both implementation practices research (Dunst, Trivette, Meter, & Hamby, 2011) and intervention practices research (e.g., Dunst & Kassow, 2008; Trivette, Dunst, & Gorman, 2010) has proven illuminating in terms of identifying the particular practices that matter most in terms of explaining study outcomes. These practices, in turn, have been used to develop evidence-based performance checklist indicators (Raab & Dunst, 2006; Raab, Dunst, & Trivette, 2010). These performance checklists have been used in both research and practice for promoting early childhood practitioners' as well as parents' adoption and use of the evidence-based practices that have constituted the focus of our research investigating the conditions under which both implementation and intervention fidelity can be achieved.

We conclude by reiterating what we consider some of the most important considerations in developing performance checklists. Checklists for practices the indicators are intended to measure are more likely to be useful if the process depicted in Figure 8.2 is used to systematically develop checklist indicators. The interested reader is referred to Babbie (2009) for additional guidelines for developing checklist indicators. The reader is also referred to Stufflebeam (2000) for a detailed checklist for how to develop operationally defined checklist indicators (see also Westgaard, 2001).

A second important consideration is to use, to the extent possible, findings from meta-analyses or research syntheses investigating the active ingredients or key characteristics of a practice of interest to be sure checklist indicators are evidence-based or at least research-informed. This ensures or at least increases the probability that the most important features and elements of a practice are the focus of either research or practice.

Finally, we cannot emphasize enough the importance of the difference between implementation practices and intervention practices and why one should consider both as part of investigating the adoption and use of evidence-based early childhood practices. No intervention practice, no matter its evidence base, is likely to be adopted and routinely used, if the implementation methods and strategies used to promote adoption of intervention practices are not themselves evidence-based and used with fidelity in order to promote early childhood practitioners' routine use of an evidence-based early childhood practice (Fixsen et al., 2005). It is for this reason that we have advocated for the development and use of both implementation and intervention practices checklists as part of early childhood research.

ACKNOWLEDGEMENT

The content of this chapter is based, in part, on research findings from the Professional Development Strategies for Promoting Head Start Teacher Effectiveness Project funded by the U.S. Department of Health and Human Services, Administration for Children and Families, Office of Planning, Research and Evaluation (# 90YR0012). The opinions expressed, however, are those of the authors and do not necessarily reflect the official position of the funder.

REFERENCES

Alkon, A., To, K., Wolff, M., Mackie, J. F., & Bernzweig, J. (2008). Assessing health and safety in early care and education programs: Development of the CCHP Health and Safety Checklist. *Journal of Pediatric Health Care, 22,* 368–377.

Babbie, E. R. (2009). *The practice of social research* (12th ed.). Belmont, CA: Wadsworth.

Bakermans-Kranenburg, M., van IJzendoom, M., & Juffer, F. (2008). Less is more: Meta-analytic arguments for the use of sensitivity-focused interventions. In F. Juffer, M. Bakermans-Kranenburg, & M. van IJzendoom (Eds.), *Promoting positive parenting: An attachment-based intervention* (pp. 59–74). New York, NY: Taylor and Francis.

Beckett, D. (2000). Just-in-time training as anticipative action and as inferential understanding. In C. Symes (Ed.), *Proceedings [of the] International Conference on Working Knowledge: Productive learning at work* (pp. 15–20). Sydney, Australia: University of Technology, Research Centre for Vocational Education and Training. Retrieved from ERIC database. (ED451388).

Bennett-Armistead, V. S., Duke, N. K., & Moses, A. M. (2005). *Literacy and the youngest learner: Best practices for educators of children from birth to 5.* New York, NY: Scholastic.

Bowman, C. L., & McCormick, S. M. (2000). Comparison of peer coaching versus traditional supervision effects. *Journal of Educational Research, 93,* 256–261.

Bransford, J. D., Brown, A. L., Cocking, R. R., Donovan, M. S., Bransford, J. D., & Pellegrino, J. W. (Eds.). (2000). *How people learn: Brain, mind, experience, and school.* Washington, DC: National Academy Press.

Cain, D. W., Rudd, L. C., & Saxon, T. F. (2007). Effects of professional development training on joint attention engagement in low-quality childcare centers. *Early Child Development and Care, 177,* 159–185.

Carroll, C., Patterson, M., Wood, S., Booth, A., Rick, J., & Balain, S. (2007). A conceptual framework for implementation fidelity. *Implementation Science, 2,* 40.

Clark, R. E. (2009). Translating research into new instructional technologies for higher education: The active ingredient process. *Journal of Computing in Higher Education, 21,* 4–18.

Dane, A. V., & Schneider, B. H. (1998). Program integrity in primary and early secondary prevention: Are implementation effects out of control? *Clinical Psychology Review, 18,* 23–45.

Dempsey, I., & Dunst, C. J. (2004). Helpgiving styles and parent empowerment in families with a young child with a disability. *Journal of Intellectual and Developmental Disability, 29,* 40–51.

DeWolf, M. S., & van Ijzendoorn, M. H. (1997). Sensitivity and attachment: A meta-analysis on parental antecedents of infant attachment. *Journal of Marriage and the Family, 68,* 571–591.

Dunst, C. J. (2004). An integrated framework for practicing early childhood intervention and family support. *Perspectives in Education, 22*(2), 1–16.

Dunst, C. J. (2011). Advances in theory, assessment, and intervention with infants and toddlers with disabilities. In J. M. Kauffman & D. P. Hallahan (Eds.), *Handbook of special education* (pp. 687–702). New York, NY: Routledge.

Dunst, C. J. (2012, February). *Framework for conceptualizing the relationship between evidence-based implementation and intervention practices.* Presentation made at the Conference on Research Innovations in Early Intervention, San Diego, CA. Available at http://utilization.info/presentations.php.

Dunst, C. J., Bruder, M. B., Trivette, C. M., Hamby, D., Raab, M., & McLean, M. (2001). Characteristics and consequences of everyday natural learning opportunities. *Topics in Early Childhood Special Education, 21,* 68–92.

Dunst, C. J., Bruder, M. B., Trivette, C. M., & Hamby, D. W. (2006). Everyday activity settings, natural learning environments, and early intervention practices. *Journal of Policy and Practice in Intellectual Disabilities, 3,* 3–10.

Dunst, C. J., Herter, S., & Shields, H. (2000). Interest-based natural learning opportunities. In S. Sandall & M. Ostrosky (Eds.), *Natural environments and inclusion* (Young Exceptional Children Monograph Series No. 2) (pp. 37–48). Longmont, CO: Sopris West.

Dunst, C. J., Jones, T., Johnson, M., Raab, M., & Hamby, D. W. (2011). Role of children's interests in early literacy and language development. *CELLreviews, 4*(5), 1–18. Available at http://www.earlyliteracylearning.org/cellreviews/cellreviews_v4_n5.pdf.

Dunst, C. J., & Kassow, D. Z. (2007). *Characteristics of interventions promoting parental sensitivity to child behavior* (Winterberry Research Syntheses Vol. 1, No. 13). Asheville, NC: Winterberry Press.

Dunst, C. J., & Kassow, D. Z. (2008). Caregiver sensitivity, contingent social responsiveness, and secure infant attachment. *Journal of Early and Intensive Behavior Intervention, 5,* 40–56.

Dunst, C. J., McWilliam, R. A., & Holbert, K. (1986). Assessment of preschool classroom environments. *Diagnostique, 11,* 212–232.

Dunst, C. J., Pace, J., & Hamby, D. W. (2007). *Evaluation of the Games for Growing tool kit for promoting early contingency learning* (Winterberry Research Perspectives Vol. 1, No. 6). Asheville, NC: Winterberry Press.

Dunst, C. J., & Raab, M. (2007). *Evaluation of an evidence-based practice guide for increasing preschoolers prosocial peer interactions* (Winterberry Research Perspectives Vol. 1, No. 5). Asheville, NC: Winterberry Press.

Dunst, C. J., & Raab, M. (2010). Practitioners' self-evaluations of contrasting types of professional development. *Journal of Early Intervention, 32,* 239–254.

Dunst, C. J., & Raab, M. (2011). Interest-based child participation in everyday learning activities. In N. M. Seel (Ed.), *Encyclopedia of the sciences of learning.* (pp. 1621–1623). New York, NY: Springer.

Dunst, C. J., Raab, M., & Trivette, C. M. (2011). Characteristics of naturalistic language intervention strategies. *Journal of Speech-Language Pathology and Applied Behavior Analysis, 5*(3–4), 3–16.

Dunst, C. J., Raab, M., Trivette, C. M., & Swanson, J. (2010). Community-based everyday child learning opportunities. In R. A. McWilliam (Ed.), *Working with families of young children with special needs* (pp. 60–92). New York, NY: Guilford Press.

Dunst, C. J., & Trivette, C. M. (2009a). Let's be PALS: An evidence-based approach to professional development. *Infants and Young Children, 22*(3), 164–175.

Dunst, C. J., & Trivette, C. M. (2009b). Using research evidence to inform and evaluate early childhood intervention practices. *Topics in Early Childhood Special Education, 29,* 40–52.

Dunst, C. J., & Trivette, C. M. (2010). Family-centered helpgiving practices, parent-professional partnerships, and parent, family and child outcomes. In S. L. Christenson & A. L. Reschley (Eds.), *Handbook of school-family partnerships* (pp. 362–379). New York, NY: Routledge.

Dunst, C. J., & Trivette, C. M. (2011a, May). *Characteristics and consequences of family capacity-building practices.* Presentation made at the 3rd conference of the International Society on Early Intervention, New York, NY. Available at http://utilization.info/presentations.php.

Dunst, C. J., & Trivette, C. M. (2011b). Disaggregating adult learning practices to identify what works best in explaining learner outcomes. In C. Prachalias (Ed.), *Proceedings of the Seventh International Conference on Education* (Vol. 1) (pp. 55–61). Athens, Greece: National and Kapodistrian University of Athens.

Dunst, C. J., & Trivette, C. M. (2012a). Meta-analysis of implementation practice research. In B. Kelly & D. F. Perkins (Eds.), *Handbook of implementation science for psychology in education* (pp. 68–91). New York, NY: Cambridge University Press.

Dunst, C. J., & Trivette, C. M. (2012b). Moderators of the effectiveness of adult learning method practices. *Journal of Social Sciences, 8,* 143–148.

Dunst, C. J., Trivette, C. M., & Cutspec, P. A. (2007). *Toward an operational definition of evidence-based practices* (Winterberry Research Perspectives Vol. 1, No. 1). Asheville, NC: Winterberry Press.

Dunst, C. J., Trivette, C. M., & Deal, A. G. (2011). Effects of in-service training on early intervention practitioners' use of family systems intervention practices in the USA. *Professional Development in Education, 37,* 181–196.

Dunst, C. J., Trivette, C. M., & Hamby, D. W. (1996). Measuring the helpgiving practices of human services program practitioners. *Human Relations, 49,* 815–835.

Dunst, C. J., Trivette, C. M., & Hamby, D. W. (2010). Meta-analysis of the effectiveness of four adult learning methods and strategies. *International Journal of Continuing Education and Lifelong Learning, 3*(1), 91–112.

Dunst, C. J., Trivette, C. M., McInerney, M., Holland-Coviello, R., Masiello, T., Helsel, F., & Robyak, A. (2008). Measuring training and practice fidelity in capacity-building scaling-up initiatives. *CELLpapers, 3*(1), 1–11. Available at http://www.earlyliteracylearning.org/cellpapers/cellpapers_v3_n1.pdf.

Dunst, C. J., Trivette, C. M., Meter, D., & Hamby, D. W. (2011). Influences of contrasting types of training on practitioners' and parents' use of assistive technology and adaptations with infants, toddlers and preschoolers with disabilities. *Practical Evaluation Reports, 3*(1), 1–35. Available at http://practical-evaluation.org/reports/CPE_Report_Vol3No1.pdf.

Dunst, C. J., Trivette, C. M., Raab, M., & Masiello, T. L. (2008). Caregiver-mediated everyday language learning practices: II. Implementation methods and procedures. *Practically Speaking, 1*(2), 1–12.

Eccles, M. P., Armstrong, D., Baker, R., Cleary, K., Davies, H., Davies, S., Glasziou, P., ... Sibbald, B. (2009). An implementation research agenda. *Implementation Science, 4*(1), 18–25.

Eccles, M. P., & Mittman, B. S. (2006). Welcome to Implementation Science. *Implementation Science, 1*(1), 1–3.

Fixsen, D. L., Naoom, S. F., Blase, K. A., Friedman, R. M., & Wallace, F. (2005). *Implementation research: A synthesis of the literature.* Tampa, FL: University of South Florida. Retrieved from http://www.fpg.unc.edu/~nirn/resources/publications/Monograph/pdf/Monograph_full.pdf.

Gearing, R. E., El-Bassel, N., Ghesquiere, A., Baldwin, S., Gillies, J., & Ngeow, E. (2011). Major ingredients of fidelity: A review and scientific guide to improving quality of intervention research implementation. *Clinical Psychology Review, 31,* 79–88.

Hargreaves, A., & Dawe, R. (1990). Paths of professional development: Contrived collegiality, collaborative culture, and the case of peer coaching. *Teaching and Teacher Education, 6,* 227–241.

Kaiser, A. P., & Trent, J. A. (2007). Communication intervention for young children with disabilities: Naturalistic approaches to promoting development. In S. L. Odom, R. H. Horner, M. E. Snell, & J. Blacher (Eds.), *Handbook of developmental disabilities* (pp. 224–245). New York, NY: Guilford Press.

Kassow, D. Z., & Dunst, C. J. (2007). *Relationship between parental contingent-responsiveness and attachment outcomes* (Winterberry Research Syntheses Vol. 1, No. 1). Asheville, NC: Winterberry Press.

Kelly, B., & Perkins, D. F. (Eds.). (2012). *Handbook of implementation science for psychology in education.* New York, NY: Cambridge University Press.

Landry, S. H., Smith, K. E., & Swank, P. R. (2006). Responsive parenting: Establishing early foundations for social, communication, and independent problem-solving skills. *Developmental Psychology, 42,* 627–642.

Lattimore, J., Stephens, T. E., Favell, J. E., & Risley, T. R. (1984). Increasing direct care staff compliance to individualized physical therapy body positioning prescriptions: Prescriptive checklists. *Mental Retardation, 22,* 79–84.

Lipsey, M. W. (1993). Theory as method: Small theories of treatments. *New Directions for Program Evaluation, 57,* 5–38.

Lipsey, M. W., & Wilson, D. B. (2001). *Practical meta-analysis* (Applied Social Research Methods Series Vol. 49). Thousand Oaks, CA: Sage.

Lockyer, J., Singhal, N., Fidler, H., Weiner, G., Aziz, K., & Curran, V. (2006). The development and testing of a performance checklist to assess neonatal resuscitation megacode skill. *Pediatrics, 118,* e1739–e1744.

May, P. (2010). *Child development in practice: Responsive teaching and learning from birth to five.* New York, NY: Routledge.

McCabe, P. C., & Altamura, M. (2011). Empirically valid strategies to improve social and emotional competence of preschool children. *Psychology in Schools, 48*(5), 513–540.

Meier, D. (2000). *The accelerated learning handbook: A creative guide to designing and delivering faster, more effective training programs.* New York, NY: McGraw Hill.

National Association for the Education of Young Children. (2005). *NAEYC early childhood program standards and accreditation criteria: The mark of quality in early childhood.* Washington, DC: Author.

Neuman, S. B., & Kamil, M. L. (2010). *Preparing teachers for the early childhood classroom: Proven models and key principles.* Baltimore, MD: Brookes.

Nievar, M. A., & Becker, B. J. (2008). Sensitivity as a privileged predictor of attachment: A second perspective on De Wolff and van IJzendoorn's meta-analysis. *Social Development, 17,* 102–114.

Raab, M., & Dunst, C. J. (2006). Checklists for promoting parent–mediated everyday child learning opportunities. *CASEtools, 2*(1), 1–9. Available at http://www.fippcase.org/casetools/casetools_vol2_no1.pdf.

Raab, M., & Dunst, C. J. (2009). *Magic seven steps to responsive teaching: Revised and updated* (Winterberry Practice Guides). Asheville, NC: Winterberry Press.

Raab, M., Dunst, C. J., & Trivette, C. M. (2010). Adult learning process for promoting caregiver adoption of everyday child language learning practices: Revised and updated. *Practically Speaking, 2*(1), 1–8.

Roberts, M. Y., & Kaiser, A. P. (2011). The effectiveness of parent-implemented language interventions: A meta-analysis. *American Journal of Speech-Language Pathology, 20,* 180–199.

Roper, N., & Dunst, C. J. (2006). Early childhood intervention competency checklists. *CASEtools, 2*(7), 1–14.

Sandall, S., Hemmeter, M. L., Smith, B. J., & McLean, M. E. (2005). *DEC recommended practices: A comprehensive guide for practical application in early intervention/early childhood special education.* Longmont, CA: Sopris West.

Shen, L.-Y., Hao, J. L., Tam, V. W. Y., & Yao, H. (2007). A checklist for assessing sustainability performance of construction projects. *Journal of Civil Engineering and Management, 13,* 273–281.

Skiffington, S., Washburn, S., & Elliott, K. (2011). Instructional coaching: Helping preschool teachers reach their full potential. *Young Children, 66*(3), 12–19. Retrieved from http://www.naeyc.org/yc/

Snell, M. E., Forston, L. D., Stanton-Chapman, T. L., & Walker, V. L. (2013). A review of 20 years of research on professional development interventions for preschool teachers and staff. *Early Child Development and Care, 183*(7), 857–873.

Snyder, P., Hemmeter, M. L., Meeker, K. A., Kinder, K., Pasia, C., & McLaughlin, T. (2012). Characterizing key features of the early childhood professional development literature. *Infants and Young Children, 25*(3), 188–212.

Stufflebeam, D. L. (2000, July). *Guidelines for developing evaluation checklists: The Checklists Development Checklist (CDC).* Kalamazoo: Western Michigan University, Evaluation Center. Retrieved from http://www.wmich.edu/evalctr/checklists/

Swanson, J., Raab, M., & Dunst, C. J. (2011). Strengthening family capacity to provide young children everyday natural learning opportunities. *Journal of Early Childhood Research, 9,* 66–80.

Swanson, J., Raab, M., Roper, N., & Dunst, C. J. (2006). Promoting young children's participation in interest-based everyday learning activities. *CASEtools, 2*(5), 1–22.

Tansella, M., & Thornicroft, G. (2009). Implementation science: Understanding the translation of evidence into practice. *British Journal of Psychiatry, 195*, 283–285.

Trivette, C. M. (2007). *Influence of caregiver responsiveness on the development of young children with or at risk for developmental disabilities* (Winterberry Research Syntheses Vol. 1, No. 12). Asheville, NC: Winterberry Press.

Trivette, C. M., & Dunst, C. J. (2000). *Effectiveness of onsite, intensive training on practitioners' adoption of family systems intervention practices.* Unpublished final report, Orelena Hawks Puckett Institute, Asheville, NC.

Trivette, C. M., & Dunst, C. J. (2004). Evaluating family-based practices: Parenting Experiences Scale. *Young Exceptional Children, 7*(3), 12–19.

Trivette, C. M., & Dunst, C. J. (2007). *Capacity-building family-centered helpgiving practices* (Winterberry Research Reports Vol. 1, No. 1). Asheville, NC: Winterberry Press.

Trivette, C. M., & Dunst, C. J. (2011, August). *Implementation with fidelity: How to get changes in early childhood classroom practices.* Paper presented at the Global Implementation Conference, Washington, DC.

Trivette, C. M., Dunst, C. J., & Gorman, E. (2010). Effects of parent-mediated joint book reading on the early language development of toddlers and preschoolers. *CELLreviews, 3*(2), 1–15.

Trivette, C. M., Dunst, C. J., & Hamby, D. W. (2010). Influences of family-systems intervention practices on parent-child interactions and child development. *Topics in Early Childhood Special Education, 30*, 3–19.

Trivette, C. M., Dunst, C. J., Hamby, D. W., & Pace, J. (2007). *Evaluation of the Tune In and Respond tool kit for promoting child cognitive and social-emotional development* (Winterberry Research Perspectives Vol. 1, No. 7). Asheville, NC: Winterberry Press.

Trivette, C. M., & Raab, M. (2011, April). Relationship between teacher characteristics, professional development procedures, and teachers' adoption of classroom practices. In W. DeCourcey & L. Hoard (Chairs), *Coaching/mentoring: For whom and under what conditions.* Symposium conducted at the biennial meeting of the Society for Research in Child Development, Montreal, Canada.

Trivette, C. M., Raab, M., & Dunst, C. J. (2012a). An evidence-based approach to professional development in Head Start classrooms. *NHSA Dialog, 15*, 41–58.

Trivette, C. M., Raab, M., & Dunst, C. J. (2012b). Steps to successful professional development in Head Start. *NHSA Dialog, 15*, 127–134.

Wales, C. E., & Stager, R. A. (1972). The design of an educational system. *Engineering Education, 62*, 456–459, 488.

Warren, S. F., Fey, M. E., & Yoder, P. J. (2007). Differential treatment intensity research: A missing link to creating optimally effective communication interventions. *Mental Retardation and Developmental Disabilities, 13*, 70–77.

Westgaard, O. (2001). *Performance checklists.* Retrieved from http://eppic.biz/2011/09/03/from-my-archives-performance-checklists-by-odin-westgaard/

Wilson, L. L., & Dunst, C. J. (2004). Checking out family-centered helpgiving practices. In E. Horn, M. M. Ostrosky, & H. Jones (Eds.), *Family-Based Practices* (Young Exceptional Children Monograph Series No. 5) (pp. 13–26). Longmont, CO: Sopris West.

APPENDIX

Sources of Information on Performance Checklists

Alkon, A., To, K., Wolff, M., Mackie, J. F., & Bernzweig, J. (2008). Assessing health and safety in early care and education programs: Development of the CCHP Health and Safety Checklist. *Journal of Pediatric Health Care, 22,* 368–377. doi:10.1016/j.pedhc.2007.11.002

Baker, C., Medves, J., Luctkar-Flude, M., Hopkins-Rosseel, D., Pulling, C., & Kelly-Turner, C. (2012). Evaluation of a simulation-based interprofessional educational module on adult suctioning using action research. *Journal of Research in Interprofessional Practice and Education, 2,* 152–167. Retrieved from http://www.jripe.org/index.php/journal/index

Basile, C. G. (2000). Environmental education as a catalyst for transfer of learning in young children. *Journal of Environmental Education, 32,* 21–27. doi:10.1080/00958960009598668

Browder, D. M., Trela, K., & Jimenez, B. (2007). Training teachers to follow a task analysis to engage middle school students with moderate and severe developmental disabilities in grade-appropriate literature. *Focus on Autism and Other Developmental Disabilities, 22,* 206–219. doi:10.1177/10883576070220040301

Dunst, C. J., Trivette, C. M., Meter, D., & Hamby, D. W. (2011). Influences of contrasting types of training on practitioners' and parents' use of assistive technology and adaptations with infants, toddlers and preschoolers with disabilities. *Practical Evaluation Reports, 3*(1), 1–35. Available at http://practical-evaluation.org/reports/CPE_Report_Vol3No1.pdf

Gallagher, C., Rabinowitz, S., & Yeagley, P. (2001). *Key considerations when measuring teacher effectiveness: A framework for validating teachers' professional practices (AACC Report).* San Francisco and Los Angeles, CA: Assessment and Accountability Comprehensive Center.

Hall, L. J., Grundon, G. S., Pope, C., & Romero, A. (2009). Training paraprofessionals to use behavioral strategies when educating learners with autism spectrum disorders across environments. *Behavioral Interventions, 25,* 37–51. doi:10.1002/bin.294

Herbert-Jackson, E., O'Brien, M., Porterfield, J., & Risley, T. R. (1977). *The infant center: A complete guide to organizing and managing infant day care.* Baltimore: University Park Press.

Hundert, J., & Hopkins, B. (1992). Training supervisors in a collaborative team approach to promote peer interaction of children with disabilities in integrated preschools. *Journal of Applied Behavior Analysis, 25,* 385–400. doi:10.1901/jaba.1992.25-385

Kaczorowski, J., Levitt, C., Hammond, M., Outerbridge, E., Grad, R., Rothman, A., & Graves, L. (1998). Retention of neonatal resuscitation skills and knowledge: A randomized controlled trial. *Family Medicine, 30,* 705–711. Retrieved from http://www.stfm.org/fmhub/

Kunz, G. G. R., Lutzker, J. R., Cuvo, A. J., Eddleman, J., Lutzker, S. Z., Megson, D., & Gulley, B. (1982). Evaluating strategies to improve careprovider performance on health and developmental tasks in an infant care facility. *Journal of Applied Behavior Analysis, 15,* 521–531.

Lattimore, J., Stephens, T. E., Favell, J. E., & Risley, T. R. (1984). Increasing direct care staff compliance to individualized physical therapy body positioning prescriptions: Prescriptive checklists. *Mental Retardation, 22,* 79–84.

Lockyer, J., Singhal, N., Fidler, H., Weiner, G., Aziz, K., & Curran, V. (2006). The development and testing of a performance checklist to assess neonatal resuscitation megacode skill. *Pediatrics, 118,* e1739–e1744. doi:10.1542/peds.2006-0537

Marshall, N. (1983). Using story grammar to assess reading comprehension. *Reading Teacher, 36,* 616–620. Retrieved from http://www.reading.org/General/Publications/Journals/RT.aspx

McSwain, C., Mahan, J. M., & Herrin, T. J. (1979). The use of a criterion performance checklist to improve efficiency and effectiveness in a CPR self-teaching program. *Journal of Medical Education, 54,* 736–738. doi:10.1097/00001888-197909000-00010

McWilliam, R. A. (Ed.). (2010). *Working with families of young children with special needs* (What works for special-needs learners). New York: Guilford Press.

Morgan, P. J., Cleave-Hogg, D., DeSousa, S., & Tarshis, J. (2004). High-fidelity patient simulation: Validation of performance checklists. *British Journal of Anaesthesia, 92,* 388–392. doi:10.1093/bja/ach081

Morgan, P. J., Lam-McCulloch, J., Herold-McIlroy, J., & Tarshis, J. (2007). Simulation performance checklist generation using the Delphi technique. *Canadian Journal of Anesthesia, 54,* 992-997. doi:10.1007/BF03016633

Mott, D. W. (2006). Checklists for measuring adherence to resource-based intervention practices. *CASEtools, 2*(3), 1–8. Available at http://www.fippcase.org/casetools/casetools_vol2_no3.pdf

O'Brien, M., Porterfield, J., Herbert-Jackson, E., & Risley, T. R. (1979). *The toddler center: A practical guide to day care for one- and two-year olds.* Baltimore: University Park Press.

Paul, C. L., Redman, S., & Sanson-Fisher, R. W. (1997). The development of a checklist of content and design characteristics in printed health education materials. *Health Promotion Journal of Australia, 7,* 153–159.

Plavnick, J. B., Ferreri, S. J., & Maupin, A. N. (2010). The effects of self-monitoring on the procedural integrity of a behavioral intervention for young children with developmental disabilities. *Journal of Applied Behavior Analysis, 43,* 315–320. doi:10.1901/jaba.2010.43-315

Raab, M., & Dunst, C. J. (2006). Checklists for promoting parent-mediated everyday child learning opportunities. *CASEtools, 2*(1), 1–9. Available at http://www.fippcase.org/casetools/casetools_vol2_no1.pdf

Raab, M., Dunst, C. J., & Trivette, C. M. (2010). Adult learning process for promoting caregiver adoption of everyday child language learning practices: Revised and updated. *Practically Speaking, 2*(1), 1–8.

Reinke, W. M., Lewis-Palmer, T., & Merrell, K. (2008). The Classroom Check-up: A classwide teacher consultation model for increasing praise and decreasing disruptive behavior. *School Psychology Review, 37,* 315–332. Retrieved from http://www.nasponline.org/publications/spr

Roper, N., & Dunst, C. J. (2006). Early childhood intervention competency checklists. *CASEtools, 2*(7), 1–14.

Sawyer, T., Sierocka-Castaneda, A., Chan, D. H., Berg, B., Lustik, M., & Thompson, M. (2011). Deliberate practice using simulation improves neonatal resuscitation performance. *Simulation in Healthcare, 6*, 327–336. doi:10.1097/SIH.0b013e31822b1307

Schectman, J. M., Schorling, J. B., Nadkarni, M. M., Lyman, J. A., Siadaty, M. S., & Voss, J. D. (2004). The effect of physician feedback and an action checklist on diabetes care measures. *American Journal of Medical Quality, 19*, 207–213.

Shen, L.-Y., Hao, J. L., Tam, V. W. Y., & Yao, H. (2007). A checklist for assessing sustainability performance of construction projects. *Journal of Civil Engineering and Management, 13*, 273–281. doi:10.1080/13923730.2007.9636447

Stufflebeam, D. L. (2000, July). *Guidelines for developing evaluation checklists: The Checklists Development Checklist (CDC)*. Kalamazoo, MI: Western Michigan University, Evaluation Center. Retrieved from http://www.wmich.edu/evalctr/checklists/

U.S. Department of Health and Human Services, Administration for Children and Families. (2000). A checklist for early childhood curriculum. *Head Start Bulletin, 67*, 1–3.

Vandergrift, L. (1999). Facilitating second language listening comprehension: Acquiring successful strategies. *ELT Journal, 53*, 168–176. doi:10.1093/elt/53.3.168

Westgaard, O. (2001). *Performance checklists*. Retrieved from http://eppic.biz/2011/09/03/from-my-archives-performance-checklists-by-odin-westgaard/

Wright, M. C., Phillips-Bute, B. G., Petrusa, E. R., Griffin, K. L., Hobbs, G. W., & Taekman, J. M. (2009). Assessing teamwork in medical education and practice: Relating behavioural teamwork ratings and clinical performance. *Medical Teacher, 31*, 30–38. doi:10.1080/01421590802070853

CHAPTER 9

ETHICAL, NARRATIVE, AND PROJECTIVE PROCESSES IN RESEARCH INTERVIEWS WITH YOUNG CHILDREN

Helen L. Cameron

INTRODUCTION

This chapter focuses on individual research interviews with young children between the ages of three and eight. It addresses the practical, ethical and challenging aspects of research when the levels of ability in self-expression in the child limited by their age. The author has a wide background of qualitative research with children and adults and accepts that no chapter can explain everything about interviewing children. The range of references provided however, will enable keen researchers to read further on the range of issues explored in this chapter.

Interviewing young children for research is an enjoyable and worthwhile activity. Several authors express enthusiasm for involving the young child in research. Irwin and Johnson (2005) for example, suggest that children as young as four years "can provide important insights into their daily lives and health experiences" (p. 822). Certainly research with children is now

Handbook of Research Methods in Early Childhood Education, pages 277–321
Copyright © 2015 by Information Age Publishing
All rights of reproduction in any form reserved.

seen as providing valuable insights into all aspects of their lives. Children are seen as active participants and given roles that make them pivotal in the direction and focus of the research. There is a large range of studies reported in the literature where children have been invited to participate actively in the research in ways that recognize their competence and free will. (Danby, Ewing, & Thorpe, 2011; Einarsdottir, Dockett, & Perry, 2009).

The free will of children in research projects has been protected in terms of their human rights in the *United Nations Convention on the Rights of the Child* (UNCRC: United Nations (1989) which gave momentum to an "emancipatory rights-based approach to the study of children." This is also a publication that is seen as enshrining the child's "freedom of expression" on all matters that affect them in research (Gray & Winter, 2011, p. 310).

As a result of children being increasingly involved actively in research, approaches and the processes used in research have shifted. Children, once seen as unreliable and incomplete objects to be studied, are now viewed as social agents or "experts" on their own lives (De Jong & Berg, 2008). Shifts in the dominant views of children have also brought methodological changes in research, including adaptation of more traditional methods such as observation, interviews and questionnaires and the development of multi-method approaches involving art, camera work and other activity based on projective approaches (Fargas-Malet, McSherry, Larkin, & Robinson, 2010).

In their book, Clark and Moss (2011) describe their mosaic approach as a multimethod one, involving two main stages. The first stage is focused on "gathering documentation through 'observation' by researchers, teachers and parents and 'child conferencing'" (Clark & Moss, 2011, pp. 15–18). This is described as a form of reflective interviewing involving a range of other participatory activities. The second stage is about "piecing together information for dialogue, reflection and interpretation" (Clark & Moss, 2011, p. 38). This approach conflates several separate steps in the analysis of data, as is described later on in the chapter.

Despite children's greater involvement in research, there a need for more clarity in term of practical challenges inherent in conducting interviews with children (Irwin & Johnson, 2005). Others call for further "robust, critically reflective and practically useful scholarship of research with young children," one that moves "beyond the sanitized, linear account of the mythical problem-free study" (Darbyshire, Schiller, & McDougal, 2005, p. 469). For instance, blocks to their participation can still occur. Many researchers encounter difficulty in gaining access to children. Gatekeepers, parents or other guardians may present objections to their child being involved in a study. Gatekeepers who block children from being involved in research, "marginalize children and reinforce discourses that construct children as being unable to decide for themselves whether or not they will participate" (Campbell, 2008, pp. 41, 42).

The skilled researcher then, requires the ability to facilitate communication not only with young children but also with their parents and other gatekeepers. When researchers are interested in a child's perspective, any interview process needs to be conducted with all due care and with consideration of the age, comfort and safety of the young subject. Researchers should not impose their own agenda and instead should offer opportunities for the young child to give their viewpoints and opinions, even if these may not exactly always match the purpose of the research.

In this regard, narrative approaches are seen as central in research with children. These allow the incorporation of a flexible mosaic of noninvasive and supportive techniques for conducting interviews and for analyzing data from these. Narrative research offers "no overall rules about suitable materials or modes of investigation, or the best level at which to study stories" (Squire, Andrews, & Tamboukou, 2008, p. 1). Any research processes employed however, needs to be "relevant, meaningful and important" (Dockett & Perry, 2007, p. 518) and to avoid any activity that risks trivializing a child's involvement. Empathic, narrative approaches are least likely to do so, as the child's story is seen as centrally important.

So despite views that children are able to actively contribute in research projects, all researchers, including those who may also be teachers, psychologists, social workers or counselors, need to be aware of continuing challenges to their involvement and of ethical principles in negotiating these. Research with young children requires high levels of ethical mindfulness and the next section focuses on a range of matters relevant to ethical research.

ETHICAL MANAGEMENT OF THE YOUNG CHILD IN RESEARCH

Ethical management of the researcher's relationship with the child rests on a range of complex issues. These include general ethical mindfulness, the troubled area of confidentiality, negotiating consent and assent and mandated reporting in research with young children between three and eight years.

Ethical Mindfulness in Research With Children

Conducting research with young children can present ethical and practical dilemmas for many researchers, calling for ethical mindfulness and a working knowledge about professional and legal aspects of relationships with young research subjects. As Warin (2011) expresses it, in discussing her research with children, "Ethics in practice is a set of day-to-day practical negotiations and compromises. It stresses the dilemma-laden nature of research and the unanticipated" (p. 807). There is also inevitable ambiguity between a researcher's aim to study private features of children's lives, thus risking objectifying them as being somewhat exotic and on the other hand, accepting children's ideas and feelings and actively involving them in the research. Brostrøm (2006) poses the following important question "If we truly respect children and childhood, when and to what extent is it in the children's best interest for them, knowingly or unknowingly, to help adults uncover details of their everyday life and secret spaces?" (p. 241) As Huber and Clandinin (2002) also state it is important "to attend to the aftermath for children's lives as their first concern" (pp. 800–801). Ethical researchers are mindful of any impact they have on children involved in their research. Flewitt (2005) in describing her study with preschool children accepts that "Ethical issues arise in all aspects of research and are particularly salient when studying vulnerable members of society" (p. 21). This is especially the case for young children as they face the challenges involved in starting school.

Negotiating with the parents or other guardians of children can present ethical dilemmas. Parents might feel obliged to agree to their child being involved in the study, fearing that "refusing to take part could damage either their relationship with the staff or the services their child receives" (Flewitt, 2005, p. 554). Ethical mindfulness then, encompasses children, parents and other carers.

Research by "insiders"—teachers for instance or other professional workers who already have a relationship with the children—may pose additional ethical challenges, as discussed by Kim (2012) and Einarsdottir (2007). Where existing power based relationships add coercive elements to the research process there can be dilemmas "that insiders could face concerning research ethics, power relations and interview reciprocity," (Kim, 2012, p. 274). Heightened levels of reflexive and ethical mindfulness are required to protect the "insider" researcher, the children and their carers in these circumstances.

Reflexivity is a central motif in ethical mindfulness in research and is demonstrated through the researcher's willingness to "emerge from behind the secure barrier of anonymity and own up to their involvement" (Etherington, 2007, p. 611). Ethical researchers are well advised to keep a reflective research journal where they record experiences, thoughts and feelings about their work with children in their research. Material from a reflective research journal, based on observations of the child and notes on research activities and related issues, may usefully form part of the data in the analysis phase.

This journal process assists the researcher to maintain a thoughtful, aware and reflexive approach to the research. Small entries can be added during the work day, for example during or after involvement in research with children. It may also serve as a summary activity at the end of a work day. The journal supports the development of trustworthiness and rigor and if these form part of the data for analysis, the entries need to be both thoughtful and clear. Computer based journals, using lap tops work well for many researchers.

Ortlipp (2008) suggests other benefits in keeping and using reflective research journals which "went beyond achieving methodological rigor and paradigmatic consistency" (p. 704). Critical self-reflection has positive effects on the research process and Ortlipp (2008) found beneficial changes were made to "the research design, methods used, and approaches" (p. 704).

Research interviews assist children to describe their world to the researcher and when conducted ethically, they demonstrate respect for the child's contribution to the research. Ethical mindfulness in research requires a considered approach, entailing self-awareness on a number of levels. As Nutbrown (2010) comments on her own research with children, "We have to be clear about our values, the importance we give to children's actions and views, how we value their perceptions, and how useful their view of the world is. This calls for self-reflexivity, for integrity, and for honesty" (p. 11). To maintain ethical research practices, in addition it is important to have a high appreciation of the importance of confidentiality and informed consent/assent issues. This will ensure the research interview commences and proceeds well, from perspectives of young children, their parents, teachers, other gate keepers, researchers and in reference to any guidelines.

Confidentiality

The regulation of social research is rapidly evolving in response to a variety of institutional, legal, political and moral influences. Consequently all researchers involved in research with children are advised to keep themselves updated on current requirements and ethical rulings. Some of these parameters are defined by their own institutions or are set out by local organizations, as well as by state and/or federal organizations with purview over research activities (Wiles, Heath, Crow, & Charles, 2005). This also involves balancing a range of competing interests, including the aims of the research, the interests and rights of the children and those of any gatekeepers. Some guidelines concern confidentiality in child focused interviews for research and for other purposes.

The issue of confidentiality is important and complex in research settings where young children are involved (Ivey & Ivey, 2008). Young children deserve to know what can remain confidential and what may need to be reported to others. This can be expressed as the difference between what can remain "just between you and me" and what may need to be told to others "to stop someone from getting hurt" (Thompson & Randolph, 2000, p. 35). This requires fine judgment however, and some young children may not have the capacity to understand what this means. It then becomes essential to assist younger children to understand how confidentiality will work in terms of the research project.

Many young children lack experience of being given the right to receive confidentiality. They see and hear teachers, parents and other adults talking about them often in public venues as though their lives are public property. Older children, around eight or nine, can probably comprehend confidentiality but younger children around five or six are less likely to understand these issues. Hurley and Underwood (2002) add that "if the majority of younger children do not believe confidentiality will be held for them, then the validity of their responses is in jeopardy" (p. 140). Cameron (2008) mentions a possible "clash of expectations about confidentiality" (p. 151) when what has been revealed may need to be reported to others. It is better to warn in advance about the researcher's obligation to share particular matters with others, if children have the capacity to understand about any limits imposed on the extent of confidentiality, especially if protection issues arise.

It is important that in a research interview the child feels safe to share. This is tricky when they also deserve to know that if they share information is about risks to themselves or others, confidentiality cannot be assured (Neill, 2005). Williams and Goodenough (2005) state that the basis of any informed consent or assent is the need to understand "how far they will be afforded anonymity and confidentiality" (p. 404). Munro and Parton (2007) agree that "confidentiality is of crucial importance for many children" (pp. 15, 16) and if this is damaged they may hesitate to share anything of importance with the researcher.

It needs to be stressed here that the extent to which young children understand the researcher's ability to provide complete confidentiality is not the only issue. Rather what is important too is that the researcher does not make blanket assurances to the child about things being "just between us" in encouraging disclosure which then requires the researcher to consider telling someone else. In telling others what the child has said, the researcher risks the child feeling betrayed if information has to another person, even if this is for the child's protection (Geldard & Geldard, 2002). So confidentiality is always, to some extent, conditional and should not be described otherwise.

The possibility of a clash with confidentiality is accentuated in the light of the fact that in some legislative arenas, researchers may be required to report to others their suspicion that a child could be in danger of being harmed. This may present additional dilemmas for ethical researchers who fear breaking a confidentiality agreement and betraying the trust of the child. Nonetheless, researchers need to be prepared to deal with these issues in working with young children. Williamson and Goodenough (2005) note that although child protection issues may not arise, it is recognized good practice to prepare for this when planning any research involving children. For this reason, although it is not intended to be a central focus, this chapter now includes a brief discussion of mandated reporting in reference research with children.

Mandated Reporting Obligations in Research

Researchers should acquaint themselves with legislative or other rulings in reference to their obligation to report suspected abuse of any children they interview. There is considerable variety in legislative rulings on mandated reporting and consequently it needs to be noted that, depending on their location, researchers may or may not come under any legal guidelines. There is still considerable diversity in rulings despite some limited progress toward uniformity of approach. Munro and Parton (2007) focus on the progress in England towards introducing a uniform mandatory reporting system and note that in many countries "the introduction of a mandatory reporting system provided a central pillar in the emergence of new policies and practices in response to concerns about child abuse from the early 1960s onwards" (p. 5). There is a lack of agreement within and between nations and states about how these guidelines should be applied, as noted by Wallace and Bunting (2007).

Internationally, few countries appear to have mandatory reporting laws covering child abuse. The United States, Australia, and Canada are the main countries that pursue this as an approach, although a range of other countries including Argentina, Sweden, Denmark, Finland, Israel, Kyrgyzstan, the Republic of Korea, Rwanda, Spain, and Sri Lanka have been identified as adopting some form of mandatory reporting legislation. Nonetheless, voluntary reporting systems are considered to be much more common (Wallace & Bunting, 2007, p. 4).

Mathews and Kenny (2008) agree adding that although mandatory child abuse reporting laws have been developed in particular detail in the United States, Canada, and Australia, "the terms of these laws differ in significant ways, both within and between these nations" (p. 50) mainly in reference to who is required to report. It is still unresolved both in terms of who is mandated to report and also in term of what happens when a report is made. Munro and Parton (2007) note that "while there is a mandatory requirement to report... there is not an equivalent legal duty to offer any service for those so identified" (p. 17). The whole area of mandatory reporting can be undermined by concerns for confidentiality; poor resourcing and questionable follow up if a report is made.

Even with best intentions of the researcher and the child's full understanding of the purpose and scope of the research, unintended matters may still arise related to physical, mental or sexual harm of the child. If this occurs then, careful and thoughtful attention to correct process is essential. Researchers need to resolve which legislative rulings have impact on their practice in reference to mandated reporting. The child must be sensitively informed that the researcher feels a need to tell someone about the harm the have talked about. Before this the researcher should carefully check they have not misinterpreted the child's story in any way (Saywitz, Lyon, & Goodman, 2011). Ethically mindful consideration of who to inform of the suspected abuse is important. Concern for the confidentially between researcher and child may cause researchers to hesitate about whether to let someone know about what may only be a suspicion. Discussion with a mentor or other person trusted by the researcher then may assist in making the decision to take the matter further.

The regulation of social research is rapidly evolving, in response to a variety of institutional, legal, political and moral influences. The terms consent and assent are generally used to differentiate levels of legal competency of young people in research. Gaining consent and assent in researching children's experiences remains a highly contested process, one that is "unable to account for the messy, compromised position of research participants, especially children in schools" (Gallagher Haywood, Jones, & Milne, 2010, p. 470). Negotiating the process often comes down to the individual researcher's sense of ethical mindfulness about this matter. Neill (2005) notes too that "research data gathered through any form of coercion would be of questionable validity, as there would be no way of establishing whether the child had actually shared their own views and experiences" (p. 49). Any coercion is also unethical and suggests the absence of effective processes relating to consent and assent. In most qualitative research, where the intention is to allow the child to freely explore certain issues, even young children can exercise considerable control in assenting to the research and possess self-decision about what to share.

Informed Consent

Informed consent is where the parent or guardian gives permission for a child to be involved in research. Consent to participate in research is also related to the varying benchmarks about "age of consent" that exist across states, territories and countries, although this is usually 16 years. So, informed consent in research with young children in the age range of three to eight, almost always involves an adult gate-keeper who is in a position to provide permission or consent for a child to participate. This is the general definition of informed consent in this chapter.

Ivey and Ivey (2008) suggest it is usually necessary to gain consent or "written parental permission" (p. 81) from the legal caregiver when a young child is to be interviewed. Wilson and Powell (2001) note that "Legal consent is a complex issue" (p. 28), and agree that "local and procedural guidelines should always be consulted" thus respecting different procedures of the agency, state and/or country in which the research is conducted. This is especially important if aspects of the information gained from research with children, will form part of any publication.

Where informed consent in medical research has a long history, social research has lagged behind in this regard. Neill (2005) states that if the current law on consent to medical treatment for children were applied to consent to participate in social research, a "child's refusal to participate could be overridden by anyone with parental responsibility" (p. 49). However she goes on to suggest that in social research it would not be usual to allow parents to dictate their child's participation.

There are problems too when a project is long, extends over a year or so and consent is only asked for at its beginning. In such cases, a problem can arise when parents misplace or misunderstand the information that researchers provide them and "quite often they forget that they have consented to a research project at all" (Williams, 2005, p. 52).

Active and Passive Consent

In research matters there is also the difference between *active* and *passive* consent. If parents are given a form to provide their consent but elect not to return it, this is considered by some to be *passive* consent as the parents were given the chance to agree. If parents sign and return a form giving permission for their child to be interviewed, this is termed *active* consent. Berg (2001) is critical of the differentiation between these two forms of consent and sees it as interference if various jurisdictions demand active consent before research can proceed. Generally, it is preferable if parents or other gatekeepers *can* provide active consent. For guidance, examples of an Informed Consent Information Letter and Consent Form are included as Appendix 1 to this chapter, but customization is necessary in many instances to make it appropriate for particular research purposes. Note this form also seeks consent to record the interview and other activities. As these recordings will usually comprise essential aspects of the data, this aspect of consent may be essential for the success of the research.

Consent by a parent or guardian however, does not necessarily ensure the child's agree to be involved in the research nor that the child is seeking involvement from an informed base. In some settings collaborative negotiation, involving parents, children and others with a duty of care, may lead to a more satisfactory level of informed agreement involving the young child as well as any gatekeepers. This process may also lead to the establishment of the child's informed assent.

Informed Assent

Informed assent is the term used by many to indicate a process where a young child gives their own agreement to be involved in a research project. There is considerable literature about children and their ability to give informed assent in research, for instance see Cocks (2006), Conroy and Harcourt (2009), Spriggs (2010), and Harcourt (2011). A sociological view portrays children "as already competent participants in their everyday worlds and capable of participation in or withdrawal from research" (Farrell, 2005, p. 6) which suggests the child has decision making capacity in all research framed interactions involving them.

The term "assent" gives recognition of the child's decisional power that lies between having no legal capacity to consent to be involved in research and full decisional authority. Negotiating the child's assent for being a participant in the research may often also involve seeking agreement to record the proceedings, even if this may have limited legal standing. The analysis process in research may depend on accurate data being recorded so if necessary this means seeking a parent's consent as well as the child's assent to ensure this. Please refer to the example Assent Information Sheet and Assent Form in Appendix 2 but note these may need to be customized for particular use in research.

Alderson and Morrow (2004) comment that assent can have a "spurious quasilegal status" (p. 97) based on a partly informed decision by the child to participate in the research. They also suggest that assent may disguise a child's refusal because it can mean "at least not refusing" (Alderson & Morrow, 2004, p. 97), although this would constitute unethical practice by a researcher. Alderson (2005) recommends that "this uncertainty in social research, about when it is reasonable to rely on children's consent alone, needs to be sorted out" because of its complexity which can be beyond many researchers' (p. 34) capacity to sort out themselves, This is not supported by those advocating informed assent. Views of the "agentic child" have grown in strength among researchers (Cocks, 2006, p. 254). Others point out that giving assent does not necessarily protect the child from harm and nor should it in any way override the rights of the child to opt out of the research at any later stage (Miller & Nelson, 2006).

Research has demonstrated that it is difficult to define an age at which children can grasp the concepts involved in assent and Bray (2007) adds that "the often quoted age of seven years as the threshold for the capacity to assent has no regulatory status" (p. 449) as it is based on spurious rulings about developmental milestones and has little validity. She suggests that age is not the only consideration as a child's maturity is not age dependent.

The child's ability to assent to take part in research is a complex. For example, with a very young child this assent may extend only into the immediate future and the child may not remember they have agreed nor understand the importance of their assent. Conroy and Harcourt (2009) add to this point by asking "do we thus assume that the assent of a preschool child will stand forever?" (p. 163). It is suggested that in working with children it is important to "establish an informed assent process whereby children have the opportunity to build understanding about their participation in the research process, before they agree to participate" (Conroy & Harcourt, 2009, p. 163). Harcourt, (2011 extends this understanding by suggesting a multi-layered process in the following account that provides an exemplar for gaining children's assent:

> The children... decided that they could write "OK" as their agreement mark/signature. They also decided that they would need to write "OK" (using a different color) each time they agreed to work with the adults.... With this type of ownership over agreement, the researcher was reasonably confident that the children had understood the informing process and were genuinely interested in participating. (Harcourt, 2011, p. 336)

Warin (2011) agrees with Harcourt that part of ongoing ethical mindfulness in matters of informed assent is about being able to consider a child's assent to be part of a "continuing process within the researcher–participant relationship rather than a one-off event" (p. 812). Informed assent for research with young children thus needs to remain a living contractual arrangement, negotiated before and revisited at times during and after the research. As Cocks (2006) remarks, "flowing through each of the core issues of the ethical framework, particularly through the application of 'assent', is the reflexivity of the researcher" (p. 261), again suggesting the value of ethical mindfulness and the reflective research journal.

In summary, it remains of value to seek both informed consent and assent and to affirm this from time to time, as suggested by Harcourt (2011). Ethical researchers need to consider all the issues and processes relating to confidentiality. mandated reporting and consent and assent before, during and following research with young children. A good understanding of these complex issues in research with young children provides part of the contextual framing of the young child's capacity to engage in a research interview.

The success of the research interview also rests firmly on the strength of the researcher's skills and abilities in managing the process of preparing for the interaction and in conducting it. The chapter now describes these, presuming ongoing awareness of the ethical issues explored in the preceding section.

PRACTICAL PREPARATION FOR THE CHILD-FOCUSED NARRATIVE INTERVIEW

A sound appreciation of what is required to encourage the child's narrative is important including the need for a period of observation and free play where the child's language can be assessed. A range of materials and media are required to meet this variation in language and comprehension of the young child. This will assist researchers to approach an interview with sensitivity. In children between in the lower end of the age range of three and eight years, problems in syntax and grammar in language may cause misunderstandings between the child and the researcher. The researcher who is "equipped with knowledge of developmental trends" (Saywitz, 2002, p. 7) and takes time to observe the young child, is much more likely to use approaches and activities, that match the child's level of functioning. In research interviews with any child however there are some very practical matters that will allow researchers to begin an interaction in a positive and well organized manner.

In practical terms, before commencing any child focused interaction it is essential to consider general aspects of the research and to organize the physical location, including the furniture and other facilities. Secondly, prior to beginning the interview, a loose structure of questions and activities should be designed, one that provides a guide to the researcher without blocking the child from expressing their views and interests. Thirdly, processes related to rapport, sharing the purpose of the interview, and establishing some "ground rules" need to be considered.

General Preparation

In all individual interviews with young children, it is important that researchers organize themselves well before encountering the young person. If the researcher is to establish "open interaction, and co-operation between the researcher and children," it is important to leave sufficient time get acquainted in order to "win their trust" (Kyronlampi-Kylmanen, & Maatta, 2011, p. 87). Aspects of this thoughtful approach to an interview are especially pertinent for working with very young children where it is important that the interview is child focused and age appropriate. If the child is very young, for instance between 3 and 5 years of age, verbal ability may be very limited and parents may wish to be present. This may sometimes posing additional challenges in settling the child and conducting the interview. Saywitz et al. (2011) note that "it should not be assumed that a parent's presence will decrease stress" (p. 341) in the young subject and that it may be useful to consider asking a parent to sit behind the child, out of their direct view. In all research interviews with children aged between three and eight, careful planning and background organization is essential in preparing for interactions with these young people.

The Physical Setting

Preparing the room in advance in which the research interview is to take place is always important and is particularly relevant when the person to be talked with is a child. Wilson and Powell (2001) refer to the size difference between young children and adult interviewers and stress that the furniture should minimize this. This means asking children to sit in child proportioned chairs which are the right size for them. The dilemma is this may mean the adult researcher has to sit uncomfortably in a child sized chair unless some compromise can be reached. It becomes essential then to obtain furniture that enables both researcher and child to sit on an equal level. At times this may mean both sitting on the floor or on cushions if this is feasible. As well, it is advisable to avoid sitting behind a desk as this may remind children of authority figures in their life and discourage their trust and free narrative.

Irwin and Johnson (2005) suggest that often neither the researcher nor the child will sit down, as it is often preferable "to tailor the interview space to the expressional style of the child" (p. 826), and to think beyond the spaces often associated with conventional interviews. "Some children might best be interviewed as they walk, play, or are enjoying outdoor spaces, in what we refer to as kinetic conversations" (Irwin & Johnson, 2005, p. 826). They also mention that "kinetic conversations can be technically challenging," but suggest it is worth it as it yields more complete and "more naturalistic expressions of children's experiences for some children" (Irwin & Johnson, 2005, p. 826). This would suggest the value of a digital recorder that can move with the researcher.

Other objects in the room, such as photographs, toys and books, need to be analyzed for their impression on the child. Saywitz, Lyon, and Goodman (2011) suggest there is general acceptance of "an age-appropriate, private, child-friendly setting with minimal distraction" (p. 341) when interviewing young children. Likewise, Thompson and Rudolph (2000) warn against having unnecessary clutter and things that are visually or audibly distracting (brightly colored toys that make noises, a loudly ticking clock and so on) especially for young children who are restless or have difficulty concentrating, as do very young children. Wilson and Powell (2001) also suggest the considered use of dolls or other toys and note their distracting nature in some situations. They recommend carefully matching these to the purposes of the interview and the child's age.

The interview room should not be sterile however and Thompson and Rudolph (2000) suggest having a soft, comfortable floor covering, pillows and soft toys around, especially for younger children. Even live pets such as a gentle, friendly dog, cat or rabbit can help ease tension at the beginning of the interview but only if it can be established in advance that the child is not allergic to and has no phobias about these pet animals.

A Loose Interview Structure

Focusing the child on some particular issues is often necessary in research. Advance preparation of areas of focus is especially important to attain research goals. In such a case, it is advised to have a list of prompts related to points of focus to act as possible lines of enquiry. Prompts must be carefully expressed as encouraging enquiries and in very plain language—the simpler the better for the younger child. De Jong and Berg (2008) advise the use of what they term "everyday language" and the avoidance of "large words that seem to talk down to the child" (p. 182). However because it is never known just what the child will say or focus on, any list of prompts need to be limited to basic structures to act as a loose guide for the researcher. Wilson and Powell (2001) caution about seeing these as being asked directly of the child and agree these should be seen as a guide, to assist the researcher to estimate the progress over intended issues.

For a variety of reasons, the interview will usually be recorded for which the child's assent and the parent's consent needs to be sought, as discussed previously. See Appendix 1 and 2 for examples of forms for these purposes. Whatever the intended focus of the research, careful planning of the first research interview will best ensure that it and any following encounters with the child, proceed smoothly.

To get the research interview underway, some other processes need attention including establishing rapport, gaining a sense of shared purpose, discussing ground rules to help the young client know a little about what to expect and managing the consent process. In all research involving children it is helpful to spend time establishing some shared basis for the work together. This may provide assurance to the young person about the intentions of the researcher and guidance about what is expected of them. The establishment of rapport may take time but this is an essential basis for an effective research interview, so should not be viewed by researchers as a two minute job before getting down to the real business.

Establishing Rapport

Establishing rapport with young children is not always able to be achieved in the first encounter and it has been accentuated that "particularly in our current social context... children are encouraged to be wary of unknown adults" (Irwin & Johnson, 2005, p. 823). Adults understand that getting to know one another is a usual part of the social process and is a common aspect of many professional or research encounters, whereas many young children have very limited understanding of this. Saywitz et al. (2011) say that although it is commonly mentioned that "interviewers need to spend time establishing rapport"... "there is little scientific data available on the methods" (p. 343) for doing so. Saywitz et al. (2011, p. 344) do suggest however that "Time spent on narrative practice," for example showing support for the child's full explanations "may serve the goal of furthering rapport" (p. 344). In other words, empathic responding to affirm the child's view of things right from the start has rapport building qualities as it shows respect for the child's ideas.

Danby et al. (2011) discuss the importance of "planning for the interview and building familiar contexts where both the children and the interviewer feel comfortable" (p. 81) as well as building rapport with children. Punch (2002) suggests that a reason why child research is challenging is because adults often fear they come across as "patronizing" (p. 328), or will behave awkwardly and fail to make a connection with the child. All researchers need to see it as a priority to attempt to establish an initial working relationship to build rapport with the child and when required, with the parent also. This suggests some initial process of gentle conversation although Wilson and Powell (2001) caution that the researcher should not expect to become best friends with the child. Saywitz et al. (2011) suggest that the rapport building time can be also used as a form of conversation training, to demonstrate to the young child that he or she will be listened to carefully. The child needs assurance that they can talk about anything to start with in as much detail as they like and in their own words.

Sharing the Purpose of the Interview

It is often the case that young children have limited understanding about the reasons for their involvement in the research process, even after providing informed assent. When there are special constraints, such as a child's very young age, it is important to consider how to describe the research purpose so as to provide the best understanding for the child. Sometimes this will focus on explaining aspects of the process to a very young child as in, "We are going to look at these pictures together and talk about them." The language capacity for children can be hard to judge until further discussion takes place with them and age is not the best predictor of verbal ability. Sharry (2004) agrees and points out that a six year old may have "speech and language difficulties" whereas a younger preschool child may have excellent communication skills and be "able to engage in imaginative reflective exercises and to ask challenging questions" (p. 58). This underlines the need for an initial period where some assessment of the child's verbal capacity can be made.

Most young children lack experience in being interviewed and Thompson and Randolph (2000) also note that sometimes "parents and teachers may have given [children] misinformation that could result in mistrust" (pp. 32–35) of the person conducting the interview. Thompson and Randolph (2000, pp. 33, 34) advocate a range processes to gently overcome the child's fear about the process including explaining the research purpose in child accessible language. Just what is said will vary according to the age of the child but it should be accepted that spending time developing rapport is a good investment. This allows the researcher to gain an understanding of the young person, to better match communication style to the particular child (Sharry, 2004, p. 58).

Establishing Some Ground Rules

Usually the researcher is a stranger and most young children lack any understanding of what to expect or how to behave in the interview setting. A child who feels anxious and unsure of what to expect or how things will happen is unlikely to provide their best account of the issues under discussion. The younger the child, the less background understanding she or he will have as a guide to the purpose, process and rules of the encounter. Early on it is important to discuss how long the interview will take. In general, shorter interviews will suit younger children and breaks may help a restless or very young child to come back for some more conversation. As described by Irwin and Johnson, (2005), it may be preferable to abandon sitting down at times and to conduct the interaction walking around the room or even outside, depending on the weather. These possible arrangements need to be considered in advance and mentioned to the child and/or parent at the beginning of the interview.

Ground rules include guidance about a range of processes that many adults take for granted. This may include simple things like what to call the research interviewer and much more complex things like how to talk about issues. Wilson and Powell (2001) refer to several helpful ground rules that can be established early in the interview to guide the child. They suggest it is useful to offer the child some ideas about how to deal with the interviewer, such as "If I misunderstand something please tell me"; "If you don't understand something please tell me," or "It is OK to say 'I don't know' or 'I don't remember' to questions I ask" (Wilson & Powell, 2001, p. 35). Other ground rules refer to suggesting to the child that it is fine if they cannot remember something, that the child can use any words they wish to explain things and that the researcher will not get upset at anything the child says. As well there may be additional things that the interviewer wishes to impress upon the child, such as to "only talk about things that have really happened" (Wilson & Powell, 2001, pp. 34, 35) and if they cannot remember something, not to guess or make things up (Wilson & Powell, 2001).

The interviewer needs to be mindful that explaining these ground rules provides no guarantee that children will follow them during the interview. For instance, younger children, particularly those under the age of six, are more likely to accept fictional accounts as true and to give an answer (perhaps even a made-up one) especially if they do not understand a question, despite the researcher's or practitioner's overt encouragement to say "I don't know" and the existence of good rapport (Wilson & Powell, 2001, p. 34; Saywitz et al., 2011, p. 339).

The overriding concern during the research interview remains the facilitation of the child's free expression. This is seen as best achieved through the use of narrative approaches and the use of other processes that are child focused and age appropriate and which maximize the child's comfort as well as the value of the information elicited. Appreciating the young child's narrative is viewed as a key feature of effective research with young children. Projective activities discussed later in this chapter, need to be used with care, particularly if these produce thoughts and feelings which require some interpretation of the young person's meaning. These features of effective and ethical practice in research with young children are emphasized by Morison et al. (2000) who also acknowledge the importance of age appropriate practices.

EMPATHIC PROCESSES IN ENCOURAGING THE YOUNG CHILD'S FREE NARRATIVE

At its simplest level, the beginning of the interview process and building rapport, as mentioned previously, can be assisted through a period of free talk and activity before focusing on research questions, as this helps the child to settle in. This period of free narrative and play also provides the researcher with some valuable insight into the child's communication style and speech patterns. This initial informal conversation supports the building of a supportive and empathic researcher style.

The Value of Empathic Reflections

Once the research focused conversation begins, many authors, who discuss working with children, emphasize the essential value of empathic reflective responses in helping the child to tell her story. Depending on the age of the child, empathic responses assist in eliciting a more complete story. As Kyronlampi-Kylmanen and Maatta (2011) note however, "it is difficult for an adult to keep track of a child's story"... as "the children's vividness and talkativeness also confused the interviewer" (p. 89). They add that a confused researcher did not seem to concern the children.

Ivey and Ivey (2008), De Jong and Berg (2008), Egan (2007), Wilson and Powell (2001), and Thompson and Rudolph (2000) suggest that the child's free narrative is supported by the researcher using reflections to show empathy and understanding. This is not to suggest that questions and prompts are never used but that there needs to be a balance of responses so any research interview with a young child does not deteriorate into an interrogation. A child focused approach means listening to the child's story and using short empathic reflections to encourage free narrative wherever possible. It also means keeping an open mind, "despite any background information you have" (Wilson & Powell, 2001, p. 44).

Being heard and understood is important to children. Because many young children lack conversational initiative, some invitations to talk in beginning a discussion are often needed. Expressing thoughts out loud by the researcher as in "Let's see—I wonder if you can tell me about your school friends" and if the child then says "Jenny and Fiona are my best friends—we play after school" then a reflective response could be something like *"Two* best friends—and it sounds like you play together often." If the child then continues with this theme, there is material to form the basis of another reflection.

If the conversation falters, as may happen with young children, an open prompt like "What sort of games do you play?" may help to keep the conversational on track. Reflecting the child's feelings in plain language is also important, such as "I think that seems to make you happy" or about something else "I wonder if that might feel a bit scary." Reflective skills, when established in the behavioral repertoire of the ethical researcher, provide a solid basis for establishing rapport, getting the interview underway and encouraging the child to begin tell her story. Empathic, narrative processes have a central place in child focused research. "In the last two decades, narrative has acquired an increasingly high profile in social research" (Squire et al, 2008, p. 1).

Narrative Approaches in Research Interviews

Narrative approaches in managing research interviews help to build the relationship between researcher and the young child and as stated by Huber, Murphy, and Clandinin (2011) "relationships live at the heart of narrative inquiry" (p. 13). This emphasizes the central importance of establishing rapport and trust with the young child from the beginning. "Narrative is a popular portmanteau term in contemporary western social research" according to Squire et al. (2008, p. 2) a research approach that is also flexible and child focused. Etherington (2007) cautions here however that a "researcher can usually provide information about the purposes and practices of research in advance but may not be able to provide information about processes that have yet to unfold, in particular when using heuristic or narrative inquiry" (p. 601).

Using a narrative inquiry methodology is about adopting a particular "view of experience as phenomenon under study" (Connelly & Clandinin, 2006, p. 375). Story, in narrative approaches, is a "portal through which a person enters the world and by which their experience of the world is interpreted and made personally meaningful" and this is "first and foremost a way of thinking about experience" (Clandinin & Huber, 2010, p. 2). Squire et al. (2008) suggest that "unlike other qualitative research perspectives, narrative research offers no overall rules about suitable materials or modes of investigation, or the best level at which to study stories" (p. 1). Despite this, many researchers still favor a narrative approach as it enables a view containing layers of meaning and allows the researcher "to bring them into useful dialogue with each other, and to understand more about individual and social change" (Squire et al., 2008, p. 1).

Griffin (2003) mentions the suitability of narrative approaches "for work with children" and notes that "narrative approaches often incorporate behavioural elements, as well as aspects of other therapeutic models" and "shares with CBT a preference for conscious cognitive strategies" (p. 34). Narrative inquiry does suggest a particular use of language where the researcher will encourage "storying" in an externalized form where the child is separated from any problems they may describe (Geldard & Geldard, 2004, p. 40). Externalization is the basis of narratives build up through the research conversation. Hayward (2003) champions the application of holistic approaches in narrative inquiry.

Riessman (2008) offers three key points to guide researchers who use narrative approaches. First, she suggests it is important to think about how the idea of the narrative is to be employed in the research, second she emphasizes the importance of appreciating language and form in the investigation, which she refers to as "the building blocks of narrative" (p. 153). Third, she refers to the importance of the context in interpretive processes, and notes how "different physical spaces can open up (or close down) discursive spaces" (p. 154). She adds that "no story speaks for itself but instead requires interrogation and contextualization" (p. 155). Central to narrative research is the idea that speakers retain "control over how their experiences are represented" (p. 154).

Mulvaney sees that the child's ability to sustain a narrative about their life experiences is dependent on language and sustained memory both of which begin in early infancy—with some rudimentary "scripts" which in narrative approaches are described as "linguistic structures" within which "language is fundamental to the construction of individual narratives," and in the "representation of memory" (Mulvaney, 2011, p. 1154).

Scripts have also been defined as cognitive frameworks for events, which are memories about what usually or typically occurs in a child's life (Santrock, 2005). "The process of narrative construction initially emerges as a social construction through which children recall important details and impart meaning on narratives by discussing it with social partners" (Mulvaney, 2011, p. 1154). As an example, Tang (2006) suggests "a script about going to the supermarket will likely include taking a shopping cart, selecting merchandises, putting the purchases in the shopping cart, and paying at the checkout counter" (p. 139) with accompanying feelings and thoughts.

The Development of a Child's Narrative Ability

It is only when children begin to use symbols within their thought processes that that are able to build personal narratives. Mulvaney (2011) notes that the "ages from two to four years represent a period of developmental change that results in the capability to produce logically and sequentially organised scenes that can be recalled independently" (p. 1154), citing commentators such as Miller and Sperry, (1988) and Nelson and Fivush, (2004) on this early development. Narrative construction becomes more complex by the age of four, as the preschool years provide opportunities for crucial scripts to develop, ones representing relationships, social behavior and gender roles. "Children develop and learn the skills of storytelling most often in parent–child interactions" (Irwin & Johnson, 2005, p. 827) which Mulvaney (2011) describes as being "conceptualised as a process of narrative construction" (p. 1157). These ideas and concepts will go on developing even if, to some extent, they remain influenced over ensuing years by the initial scripts formed during earlier years (Mulvaney, 2011, p. 1155).

The period of early childhood, between the ages of three and eight however, is also a time when early influences on script formation gradually lessen to the point where the child has more independence in script construction. Children begin to rely "less on adults to aid them in their construction" (Mulvaney, 2011, p. 1155). He cautions however that development is strongly impacted by social and cultural influence (Mulvaney, 2011). This underlines the importance of taking time to assess the young child's capacity to describe events in their life. It is essential to neither overestimate nor underestimate their independence of thought as well as their linguistic capacity. The young child also needs supportive encouragement to tell their story in their own language and at their own pace.

As Squires et al. (2008) note… "we are part of the data we collect; our presence is imprinted upon all that we do" (p. 17). Huber and Clandinin (2002) describe the heavy burden they feel in being the responsible adults hearing the children's stories. They add that they began to see "that we needed to be guided by relationships, by the shared narrative unities of our lives" with those of the children. "Engaging with one another narratively shifts us from questions of responsibility understood in terms of rights and regulations to thinking about living and life, both in and outside classrooms and on and off school landscapes" (Huber & Clandinin, 2002, p. 797).

A child-centered process, necessary to facilitate a child's free narrative, features low-key processes and a gentle approach that demonstrates understanding. Excessive use of direct questioning is to be avoided if the researcher is hoping to encourage the child's trust. It needs to be realized also that many young children do not relate their stories sequentially and so a patient, reflective approach is required to gradually build up a full picture of the child's world. Empathic listening can have a profoundly positive effect and skills supporting the child's free narrative are both nonverbal and verbal.

Nonverbal Presence of the Interviewer

Awareness of nonverbal attentiveness is important in that nonverbal behaviors convey messages from the researcher to the child—both as intentional process and at times as an accidental conveyance of meaning. A sensitive researcher will also be alert for nonverbal messages from the child—that she is restless, anxious or tired for example—thus allowing an appropriate response. The researcher intent of completing an interview, can easily neglect to notice what is happening to the child who may be too polite to say anything about what they are feeling. Kyronlampi-Kylmanen and Maatta (2011) note that "whether they think of pleasing the researcher depends partly on power sharing and how the children see the researcher" (p. 91). Keeping the child's needs foremost is part of a researcher's obligation in working with young people, as many lack confidence in their right to ask for consideration.

As the child speaks, the attentive researcher maintains gentle but consistent eye gaze and as a sign of respect keeps distracting movements or other signs of inattention to a minimum. Wilson and Powell (2001) stress the special sensitivity of young children to apparent non-attention such as when the interviewer's gaze wanders out the window and note that children often stop talking when they see the researcher's attention lapse momentarily.

Ivey and Ivey (2008) refer to the nonverbal realm as comprising "visual/eye contact," "vocal qualities," "verbal tracking," and "attentive and authentic body language" (pp. 48–52). They also mention "the value of nonattention"—of use sometimes if the child's focus goes way off track—and the "usefulness of silence" to leave plenty of space for the child to talk. The vocal qualities referred to by Ivey and Ivey (2008) encompass vocal tone, speech rate and verbal tracking—all related to staying focused on the child in an attentive, gentle and flexible manner. Egan (2007) uses the acronym SOLER to refer to the qualities of the attending position recommended for interviewers. The S refers to *squaring off*, the O to using an *open posture*, the L to *leaning* forward slightly, the E for *eye contact*, and the R for a *relaxed* or natural use of the preceding behaviors.

Nonverbal or sub-vocal processes, used appropriately, convey messages that the researcher is staying with the child and wants to hear her story. There is every reason to believe that young children are highly sensitive to these subtle nonverbal and verbal cues. "A nonverbal expression, such as a look and smile, is an important way to support a child in an interview situation" (Kyronlampi-Kylmanen & Maatta, 2011, p. 90). It is important that the researcher is skilled in both non-verbal and verbal communication.

Occasional Subvocal encouragers

Gentle encouragers such as "Mmm," "Oh," or "OK" and head nods help to keep the conversation rolling. Small sounds and head movements encourage the child's free narrative and are usefully applied, especially when the researcher wishes to hear more of the child's story without interrupting. Note that none of these *nods* or *sounds* replaces good reflective responding in demonstrating understanding of the young child's story. The researcher needs to monitor these subvocal behaviors, as constant nodding or repeating a sound can be distracting to the child.

In addition, it is important to restrict the use of single word exclamations such as "Great!" "Wonderful!" "Wow!" "Terrific!" "Cool!" Use of informal terms such as these or similar, does not encourage trust and paradoxically, may discourage the child from telling the whole story which may include some "noncool" parts (Cameron, 2005, p. 603).

Use of "Door Openers"

Door openers are initial prompts and nonverbal behaviors that offer encouragement to begin to speak about an issue (Cameron, 2008). Likewise, occasional open prompts are useful like "What happened next?" as suggested by Wilson and Powell (2001, p. 51) and Ivey and Ivey (2008, pp. 60–62). These act as invitations to begin the story. These are also signaled through encouraging eye gaze and other warm, friendly aspects of style as well as through verbal prompts that ask the child for free information about an issue (Geldard & Geldard, 2002). For example, a prompt like "Tell me some more about that" is open and invites the child to respond however she wishes (p. 100).

Appropriate Attentive Silence

Getting the child's narrative started needs a patient approach and tolerance of silence. According to Wilson and Powell (2002) it requires "the ability to... hold one's tongue" (p. 51). Interviewers often need to sit in silence with a child and to resist the need to fill conversational spaces, particularly by asking questions. The child may be thinking, for example, but the researcher feels pressured to maintain the dialogue. Keeping quiet is challenging, as many people have "low tolerance for conversational silence" (Cameron, 2008, p. 17). Note that this is an active form of silence. It means that whilst remaining silent, the researcher observes the child, maintains gentle eye contact and keeps their own distracting body movements under control. As can be seen, a picture of the researcher as an intentional and deliberate communicator is emerging here.

Helping Conversation to Begin Gently

The major task for the researcher at the beginning of the interview is about finding ways to connect with the child and to establish a context where the child feels safe to tell their story. Most children feel anxious and a bit confused when they encounter the researcher for the first time, especially if they are a stranger. This contrasts with most adults who approach a research interview with some sense of what to expect from the process, have their own agenda and often know what they want to talk about. As noted by Thompson and Randolph (2000) and De Jong and Berg (2008) however, children may be in a kind of *involuntary* role—often having been encouraged to take part by a parent, teacher or other person in some sort of authority over them. Therefore, it is important to begin the research interview by seeking ways of helping the child to begin to see some value in being with the researcher, to find the relevance for them and in helping them to relax.

The application of activities like free form drawing, playing with clay or similar low-key activities may help to relax the child. The beginning the conversation can occur as they play, by encouraging the child to talk about things they already know and see as relatively unthreatening. This includes their name, when their birthday occurs, their favorite subject/activity at school; their teacher's and best friends' names, siblings or pets and so on. Focus on these issues may reduce the child's concerns about being able to know the so-called "right answers" to things—a common type of performance anxiety for children beginning any interview process. The researcher may also take the opportunity to provide some brief description of the research project. As the child begins to relax a little, if the researcher uses noninvasive responses, the child may feel confident to talk about other things they may not readily "know" and which are more related to the purpose of the research.

Many believe managing an interview with a young child is just about asking the right questions, as is suggested by Wilson and Powell (2001, p. 41). They also note that many interviewers feel panic that they might not be able to think of the "right," or *any* questions to ask. Performance anxiety affects the researcher too! But using too many questions will not comfort an anxious researcher nor help the child feel listened to. Some questions mislead the child into answering wrongly. For instance, closed questions requiring a yes/no answer produce many response errors according to Tang (2006, p. 138), who also refers to the superiority of what she terms "wh" questions—who, what, where, when questions. She says that "wh" questions are "superior to yes/no questions in reducing errors." They also help children to be willing to say "I don't know" when answering some questions, "seldom elicited by yes/no questions" (Tang 2006, p. 138). This clearly suggests avoiding closed question and instead to use open forms of enquiries and invitations. Ivey and Ivey (2008, p. 70) caution against using too many questions, *both* closed and open ones. Young children may even experience difficulty with the scope of some open probes, especially "why" questions. This then points to the value of using a broad platform of reflective responses in preference to asking many questions in conducting research interviews with young children.

Epstein, Stevens, McKeever, and Baruchel (2006) caution however, that "although there is a trend toward using interviews with children" to solicit their thoughts, feelings and ideas, these traditional interviews can be limited in their suitability. Talk then is not everything in child based research interviews.

USING PROJECTIVE ACTIVITIES IN RESEARCH INTERVIEWS

Projective techniques are activities involving a range of media, especially useful when the required information is difficult to obtain by direct methods during interviewing. This may be because the child has limited verbal capacity or willingness to talk directly to the researcher or the matter being studied. The media used in projective activities during an interview, can involve paints, pencils, clay, camera, dolls, and internet technology. The idea is not to make these activities separate from the interview, but rather to integrate them as far as possible, so they become part of the process

Many projective activities have been adapted from play therapy which has wide and long-standing application in child counseling and therapy fields, especially with young clients with blocks to their expression. Seminal perspectives are provided by Machover (1935), Amster (1943), Axline (1989) and Hulse (1951) who are early advocates of drawing, drama and other projective techniques in exploring the world of the child. In the 1940s Virginia Axline began to develop nondirective play therapy based on some principles related to Carl Rogers' therapy and based on a "firm belief in a child's capacity for positive growth and change" (Webb 2007, p. 46). From Axline and these other pioneers has come a range of now quite mainstream practices involving projective activities as adjuncts to the usual processes of conversation in conducting interviews with children.

The basic principle of any technique that is projective is that it acts to release the child from or supplements the usual discussion based processes and invites their involvement in an expressive and imaginative activity. Note this does not rule out further ongoing talk. Because of inherent difficulties in analyzing data gathered through these range of qualitative processes involving interviews and other activities, researchers are well advised to record proceedings as best they can, using audio and video techniques. Of course, this recording needs to be included in any consent or assent process.

The value of a projective technique in research interviews with young children is that the child is able to "project" what he or she thinks about others or him or herself onto the image, sometimes separating emotional reactions from the image. This is thought to be more accurate than asking the child directly to describe his or her views or feelings and is quite useful when conducting research with younger children, especially those within the range of three to five years (Ivey, 2012).

The stress on verbal research processes in child based research may suggest more active play or projective methods have only a minor role in social research although they have been part of child therapy for some considerable time. Research has remained primarily word-based and projective methods "in particular their capacity to reveal 'the truth' has been questioned" (Harper, 2002, p. 17). Qualitative researchers however, reject the idea of searching for "the truth" and instead place emphasis of the child's narrative about their life. Processes other than talk in qualitative research can encourage children to share their life experiences, through activities than can be fun and relaxing.

Clark (2005, p. 494) describes "a range of techniques for listening to young children which shift the balance away from the written or spoken word to visual or multisensory approaches." Punch (2002, p. 329) cautions however that a "reflexive and critical approach is needed in order to recognize their disadvantages and limits, as well as the reasons" for applying projective techniques. She suggests questioning whether they are used only because they are fun, or "because they also generate useful and relevant data." This suggests the need for an ongoing ethical and reflective approach.

Many of these imaginative (and imagination based) activities have application in conducting research interviews with children. Of course, it is advisable for researchers to have a range of resources on hand including appropriate books and pictures, a supply of paper, paste, drawing and painting implements, different play figures such as dolls or puppets and online facilities. Some of these may be of use initially in a free-form manner to put the child at ease. Later, as the interview unfolds, they can be applied to provide a means of encouraging the child in directed narratives, related to the research goals.

Children's Drawing, Painting, and Photography in Narrative Interviews

Many children find it comforting to have a painting or drawing to do as they chat with the researcher and the accompanying narrative in particular, may provide valuable insight into her or his life. There are several benefits of using art in the interview. It can provide access to "unconscious, tangible symbols of the child's emotions" and better self-awareness through non-threatening forms of expression which are "open to self–interpretation" often described as a kind of "window to the unconscious" (Henderson,

2000, pp. 377, 388). Art based materials are also easily combined with other projective activities such as the use of cameras

The use of drawing as meaning-making is about the child making the drawing and talking about it as they do so or after they complete it. Wright (2007) notes the complexity of children's drawings as a non-verbal activity explicated with verbal signs as children talk about their product. The researcher will need to take photographs of children's drawings and paintings so there is a record for further analysis and to record the child's commentary. Combined with a sensitively managed interview, drawing can supplement and expand the meaning of the child's expression.

Practical considerations surround the use these art-based techniques in an interview. The researcher needs to be willing to supply sufficient choice of media to suit the individual child. Some children will enjoy working with paint, crayons or cameras whereas others may prefer a simple pencil. Colored paper shapes, for pasting on to sheets of paper, glitter or leaves and other things from nature may help a child who feels unable to draw or paint, to build up a picture. Allowing free choice of materials means the researcher needs to maintain a full range of supplies. As well, some art techniques—like painting—may not be suited to all interview settings. For examples, painting with very young children can be rather messy. The researcher may need to supply protective smocks or aprons and ask permission for the child to join in the activity from teachers or parents. The use of these techniques and materials also need to be feasible within the time frame allowed for the research interview.

To get the child started, the researcher might suggest something like "How about drawing or painting a picture of how you feel at school—what would this look like?" or "How would your family look if you used these cut outs?" The researcher may need to help the child to begin the drawing or painting and it is important that some talk surrounds and follows the creative process, for example asking the child to comment on her picture.

Dockett and Perry (2007) were interested in children's first year at school as displayed in a drawing and the child's reflections on this. They described how they took copies of the drawing with color cameras and they stress how important is "not asking children for the drawing is that we regard it as unreasonable to expect children to spend considerable time and energy creating a drawing, only to have it taken away" (Dockett & Perry, 2007, p. 515). Photographing children's art is also essential to gathering data for further analysis.

The child's description of their art work is an essential part of the process. Of course, in applying any of the projective activities described in this section, the child's commentary needs to be recorded as are their actions and products, as these will all comprise essential aspects of the data for analysis later on.

Modeling with play dough or plasticine can also provide a useful medium for young children many of whom will enjoy modeling material for its tactile qualities and its soothing effects. Play dough can be cheaply made from flour paste and plasticine is relatively economical as it can be re-used. Clay-like materials may provide more flexibility of use than painting or drawing, as what has been modeled can be easily rolled up and remodeled. Some children do not find modeling with clay helps them to express their thoughts, as may also be the case for painting, drawing or photography. Einarsdottir, Docket, and Perry (2009) agree, and report that although "many of the children involved in these studies seemed eager to draw" in each of their studies some children said they "couldn't draw or avoided the drawing activity" (p. 228). This merely underlines the idiosyncratic nature of children, indicating that the researcher may need to be flexible, to think ahead and not see the success of the research project resting entirely on the use of particular materials or techniques.

Photography is seen as "an expanding method in research with children" (Einarsdottir, 2006, p. 527). She notes that by giving the children cameras (some supervised and some unsupervised) they took pictures, photographing whatever they wished. The children thus became the experts on these pictures when they described them to the researcher. This process was also found to be "beneficial when working with young children or children with poor written or verbal language" (Einarsdottir, 2006, p. 527).

Clark (2005) describes a flexible child focused process where creative maps are used by the young children as they take adults—such as the researcher or others–on a guided tour around their school. This map creation involves "children taking photographs, making drawings and audio recordings which are then incorporated into these maps by the children" (Clark, 2005, p. 496). This activity is a means of empowering young children in the research process as well assisting them to express their feelings and views. There is a wide range of other media and processes, some of which may be creatively applied to supplement research interviews with young children.

Using Puppets and Dolls

The use of puppets and dolls can assist in setting up "pretend" activities and may support a dramatic role play of people and incidents in the child's life. Axline (1989) originally suggested wide uses for puppets with suitable children. Henderson (2000) refers to a list of considerations in selecting these puppets for use in working with children. These include ease of manipulation so that any puppets fit both children's and adult's hands and that figures and dolls are able to be easily cleaned.

Dolls used as part of a dramatic projective activity in research are most suitable for working with children who have reasonable verbal skills. A tea-party with dolls may demonstrate who the child might invite from their class, initiating conversations about friends. A dinner-table set, using a make believe family of dolls, may assist in exploring family dynamics. Likewise, a mock-up of a school class room or other scenarios may enable the acting out or description of the relationships between the child and other people in their life.

Wilson and Powell (2001) caution against the use of dolls with very young children except for the purposes of free play; they make the point that "A five-year-old girl who plays with a Barbie doll will rarely think that the doll represents her—she is more likely to pretend she is Barbie" (p. 31). Their field of application is primarily with children who may have been abused, so they suggest that children should be around six or seven before they are seen as capable of understanding the idea that a doll is a symbolic representation of the child or another person in their life (Wilson & Powell, 2001, p. 31). Jesuvadian and Wright (2011) disagree as they are talking more broadly about research with a range of children. They are enthusiastic about the use of Persona dolls in research with quite young children and suggest them as a useful medium to introduce cultural and disability issues in research, as does Clark (2005).

Persona dolls were created first by Kay Tau in California for use in her pre-school, according to Etienne, Verkest, Kerem and Meciar (2008). As Irish (2009) describes them, "Persona Dolls are large boy or girl rag dolls, carefully dressed like regular preschool children" and that these are child sized and can have a range of skin color and dress to match the ethnic diversity of a community in which the research takes place. Etienne et al. (2008) describe the modern use of dolls in research as functioning in the same way as puppets, "but without any strings" (p. 9). Jesuvadian and Wright (2011) describe how using Persona dolls in research with young children (ages 4–6) "can capture and foreground the child's voice in order to understand his/her world views in a setting that is both safe and conducive to engagement" (p. 277).

Persona Dolls provide a non-threatening approach to encouraging children to talk about inclusion, identity and diversity issues that impact on their lives and that of their families. Jesuvadian and Wright (2011) used these dolls "to raise authentic voices of the children by engaging both their hearts and minds. The resulting data was rich and opened a portal into the very heart of a child's world" (p. 284).

Generally, to use dolls, the researcher needs to acquire a sufficient number and range of "characters" or "personas" so the child can choose freely from the range offered to represent different people that are part of their story or narrative. Children are then invited to introduce the characters to the researcher and to describe or act out a story. The activity and the child's commentary all need to be recorded in photographs and on audio for analysis.

Internet Technology as Projective Research Tools

Finally in this discussion of projective techniques, computers and the internet deserve attention as these provide a set of resources that can be used in a number of ways in research interviews with young children. Technological development and children's increased familiarity with the internet means this is now a central part of many children's lives. Nilsson and Folkestad (2005) describe that in "a study by Nilsson (1992) it was found that young children, aged three to six, had their own tape recorders, thus being able to play recorded music on their own." Many children today have their own IPods, MP3 players and computers through which they explore music and games and many develop considerable expertise in working with these devices.

Cohen (2011) describes the learning advantages of online tools for children which he suggests can be applied from the age of two years and it is not hard to see how these can be applied to support research with young children as another form of projective activity in interviews. Cohen (2011) suggests how an online tool "allows younger children (two years old and older) to access and play productively with a sophisticated media technology platform" (p. 1). He suggests further research is needed into how young children (ages two-to-eight) approach touch screen devices. He states it is important to understand "how children master the challenges of age appropriate applications (Apps)" (Cohen, 2011, p. 4) and to examine how these can be applied in a research project with young children.

Nilsson and Folkestad (2005) say that in their study children demonstrated creative ability in "music making in many different ways" and note that "even very young children gain musical knowledge and competence by taking part in the media world at home, in school, or during their leisure time" (p. 35). Children may have media competence at a level beyond that of the adults around them.

Punch (2002) concludes "A combination of techniques can enable the data-generation process to be fun and interesting for the participants" (p. 336). Cohen (2011), however, points out that children's "prior experience impacts both the activity and the content that they find appealing." He adds that "transfer of learning from computer games, cell phones and other media is critical to iPad and App learning" (p. 8) which may have implications in research settings where children lack this background of familiarity. Of course it is clear that these technical applications need to be age and experience appropriate if they are to be used as an effective research technique Social disadvantage may limit some children's access to any of these devices and this will impact on the value of using these devices in interviews with some children.

In general then, with appropriate consideration for the child's age and capabilities, there is value in allowing children to show, draw, act out, photograph, record and play as this lessens reliance on the child's ability to use verbal language during the research interview. These activities aid memory retrieval to some extent during interviews, as "young children tend to be reliant on external (or contextual) retrieval cues when recalling past events" (Pipe et al., 2002, p. 162) and often need other encouragement to explain and describe things.

Projective activities incorporated into the research interview, such as those using dolls, art or touch screen processes, can be usefully combined in research to produce interesting data from involved children. Attention needs to be paid to the accurate recording of the children's words in describing their art or other products and in photographing and making video or DVD recording of activities and the products. Of course, this entire data gathering process needs to done with the consent and assent of parents and children.

Concluding the Interview

All interviews, including those using projective activities, need to be concluded carefully; with thanks to the child and through offering them the chance to ask any questions or comment on how it all went. The researcher may wish to comment on whether further interviews will take place or if this is the only or final one. What will happen to the data–their recorded words, photographs of their art or other products—should be explained again if needed. Some mention again of assent may be appropriate at this point.

Sometimes it may be appropriate to offer a reward for being involved. The researcher could ask the child to select a reward from an appropriate range of small items organized in advance. This could include pens or pencils, erasers, small toys, colourful small sticky note blocks, small wring pads, small tissue packs or other similar items that the child can easily take with them. It is not recommended to offer sweets, for obvious reasons.

At this point the chapter moves on to discuss how the qualitative research data is viewed, focused, organized, categorized and interpreted in the analysis stage. The integrity of the data can be reasonably assured when ethical mindfulness is maintained and when there is compatibility between the research approaches and the research strategies during data gathering process in the interviews.

VALIDITY AND RELIABILITY AND ANALYZING DATA FROM INTERVIEWS AND PROJECTIVE PROCESSES

Using qualitative processes such as narrative interviews also employing projective activities requires ethical rigor in organizing and selecting results and in analyzing these. This is partly due to the need in qualitative research for interpretation of the child's responses, actions and products such as art work. As well, rigor needs to be established in terms of an explanation of the analytical lens through which the data are examined (Bond, Ramsey, & Boddy, 2011, p. 10). An ethically managed qualitative analysis can help the researcher to make sense of and "understand a situation that would otherwise be enigmatic or confusing" (Eisner, 1991, p. 58). In qualitative research, reliability and validity are contested processes as they derive from quantitative and positivist research paradigms. More applicable researcher qualities involve "trustworthiness, quality, and rigor" (Golafshani, 2003, p. 602) Nonetheless, some discussion of reliability and validity is required in this chapter.

Reliability Issues

Reliability in quantitative research refers to the extent to which results are consistent over time and that results of a study can be reproduced using a similar methodology. This is a questionable process in qualitative research as knowledge is seen by those using qualitative processes to be socially constructed and changing over time and under different circumstances. Since interviews and projective processes techniques are characterized by a high degree of openness, this means there are no "right" answers or responses and as the interview is a "one off" event, the research processes are often difficult if not impossible to replicate.

Some projective instruments have been standardized in that they have been tested with a "sufficient number of administrations and with a statistically sufficient number of participants to demonstrate that the results are reliable" (Ivey, 2012, p. 180). But the ways in which these are integrated into the research interview can be idiosyncratic and are unable to be replicated. So applying qualities related to reliability—the consistency issue and reproduction of results—is inappropriate.

The concept of reliability is often viewed as not fitting into qualitative research, especially when this involves narrative interviews. In addition to the interview processes, the use of multiple methods, such as empathic interviews, observation of projective activities and recording these will lead to more diverse results, making concepts of both reliability and validly inapplicable (Golafshani, 2003, p. 604).

Validity Issues

Validity refers to the extent that means of measurement are accurate and whether they are actually measuring what they are intended to measure. These concepts, also belonging to a more positivist paradigm, may not apply to the qualitative research. "Unlike quantitative researchers who seek causal determination, prediction, and generalization of findings, qualitative researchers seek instead illumination, understanding, and extrapolation" (Hoepfl, 1997). This renders ideas of intention and "accuracy" redundant. Rather than seeking ways to reframe a quantitative term like validity however, more appropriate researcher characteristics informing qualitative research intentions are quality, rigor and trustworthiness as discussed by Golafshani (2003, p. 602).

Analyzing Qualitative Data From Narrative Interviews and Projective Research Processes

In order to provide some stable basis of data it is essential that audio or video recording of interactions and other activities occurs, with the appropriate assent or consent procedures. Qualitative data from narrative interviews, including those involving projective activities, will consist of audio recordings of the child's words, photographs of art work or other products, video or DVD recording of the child's actions and the researcher's written observations. Data from these all need to be subjected to analysis and interpretation to make meaning from these. The reflective research journal, made by the researcher during the data gathering process and added to soon after it, can form a valuable part of the data.

Taylor-Powell and Renner (2003) recommend a series of steps for analyzing narrative data. They suggest the process is a fluid one and moving back and forth between steps is more likely than a lock/step forward progress through these. Review of all the recorded data provides the basis for the first step in analysis, as this is about getting to know the data. This familiarization involves sitting down with all the material, in its varied forms and spending time looking, listening and thinking about it. Photographs of children's art work or other products, if relevant to the data, needs to be spread out so they can be viewed in relation to each other.

The second process is about considering how to focus the data for analysis. Interviews with or without projective activities, will usually include some material that is not useful to include, so it is possible that only some data will be selected for particular attention. The process in this second step includes selecting children's verbal responses to particular questions and commentary made during the projective activities. Focusing here may also involve deciding what to select for inclusion from the child's recorded actions, photographs of their drawings, paintings made in the interview. Again the researcher's recorded observations and reflections can be included for review in this focusing step.

The third process is some form of categorization of this selected data. This involves identifying themes or patterns of children's speech or behavior/actions and organizing these into meaningful categories. Narrative inquiry defines five approaches for categorizing told stories and these clearly derive from qualitative theory frames. These include a psychosocial developmental approach; an identity approach with a focus on how people construct themselves within different contexts; a sociological approach with a focus on specific aspects of people's lives; a narrative ethnographic approach and an auto-ethnographic approach. Narrative inquirers attend to both "personal conditions and, simultaneously, to social conditions" (Clandinin & Huber, in press) and in categorizing children's words, activities and products this becomes very complex, as children's lives are often fluid.

The fourth step is about looking for patterns, themes and connections between these categories. It is also about deciding how important each of these seems to be. This might also involve counting how often a theme comes up in the data. This is not about statistics but rather the focus is on gaining a rough estimate about which themes occur most frequently. Analyzing drawings and paintings may involve a more hands-on process, with images spread out and compared for common or diverse features and how these relate to the particular child's commentary about these and the research questions. A marriage between the child's product and their words however, needs to take place to enable a complete analysis.

The final step is that of interpreting and bringing all the themes and connections together into a meaningful pattern that supports an explanation of the findings (Taylor-Powell & Renner, 2003). Approaches to analyzing the data produced from qualitative processes usually do include interpretive approaches (Catterall & Ibbottson, 2000). Interpretive forms of analysis assist in making sense of data from projective activities and interviews, even with their inherent challenges.

When data is primarily text—as in spoken or written words—content analysis can be employed as "a systematic, replicable technique for compressing many words of text into fewer content categories based on explicit rules of coding" (Stemler, 2001). There are several software packages which facilitate content analysis of interview responses, some of which are free to download (qualitative analysis software applications are able to be downloaded from http://www.pressure.to/qda/). N6 and NVivo are provided on many university servers to networked PCs or may be available as a CD-ROM for home installation (Hannan 2007).

Content analysis may have limited applicability when data is pictorial as when produced through photographing or recording the child's drawing or their doll play for instance on a video or DVD.

An inductive thematic analysis also complements qualitative analysis as it has a theory based in the belief that experience and data is built through interactions with others rather than from adopting pre-existing structures and applying them to the situation. At times a web-like illustration, as in thematic network analysis, may be used to enrich the data analysis process.

Catterall and Ibbottson (2000) note that "researchers find considerable consistency in responses generated by projective techniques" (p. 251) but that interpreting these and other responses from interviews can be difficult.

Negotiating Interpretive Analysis

Interpretation is an essential process in qualitative analysis of data. As described, the final step in analyzing data is that of making sense of the connections and meaning from the children's words and products. It has been acknowledged for some decades researchers interpret data in significantly different manners and for some this calls into question the reliability and validity of research techniques (MacFarlane & Tuddenham, 1951). Interpretation of data needs to inevitably include the psychological motivations and views of the respondent child and the some extent, the researcher.

A major ethical issue concerns the care with which researchers interpret the child's thoughts and memories flowing from imaginative and creative projective activities. As Baker-Ward and Ornstein (2002) note, it is important to be cautious about interpreting the child's representations, especially if these rely on memories about past events. Dockett and Perry (2007) challenge adult led talk about drawings for instance, stressing the importance of "ensuring that the interpretation belongs with the child, rather than the researcher." They add that the focus needs to be on the "message of the drawing, rather than the skill in drawing."

Narrative interviews incorporating projective activities, used sensitively and applied with age appropriateness to the individual child, can provide a rich source of additional information. Interpreting the meaning of children's expressions requires care. Clark (2005) also expresses concern about making general conclusions about what has been revealed especially if these are based on a small number of studies undertaken or on limited numbers of children. This is more about generalizing than interpreting the meaning of words or drawings.

It is important that in forming an interpretive analysis, researchers do not build adult meaning from what children say nor draw firm conclusions from what a child paints, enacts or constructs in any medium. Pipe et al. (2002) note that "interpreting what children do (or draw) is considerably more risky than listening to what they say" (p. 170). It is still possible to misinterpret what the child says, especially with very young children who may experience difficulty in clearly explaining their ideas or who present material non-sequentially.

Ethical mindfulness in child based research may lead to an increasing challenge of concepts of tacit knowledge. It may also energize stronger demands for ethical standards to be brought to bear in exploring qualitative and projective activities in child based research. Narrative and projective research processes applied in child based research offer rich opportunities for new discovery and increasing dialogue. Cautions underline the need for ethical mindfulness in analysis and well as quality, rigor and trustworthiness in conducting research with children and in analyzing data.

In this section then, it is contended that neither reliability nor validity can be usefully applied to data drawn from narrative interviews and projective activities used conducted ethically with young children. Consequently, researchers need to seek quality by faithfully recording verbal and nonverbal outcomes and applying appropriate analysis of these with rigor and trustworthiness.

Ethical researchers also need to strive to create research providing "safe, respectful, meaningful environments for children to offer their thoughts without fear of... being misunderstood by adults" (Schiller & Einarsdottir, 2009, p. 128). Working collaboratively with other researchers can also assist in understanding how meaning can be extracted, analyzed, categorized and interpreted from data in forms that honor the child's interests and intentions.

RECOMMENDATIONS AND SUMMARY

Further research with young children, employing the range of processes discussed in this chapter, may bring to light new applications. The author recommends that researchers employ processes and ways to increase rigor within their research with children. Further development of research practices related to research design and analysis used to evaluate results from research with young children will contribute significantly to the experiences of future research.

Researchers should remain aware of the gap between a child's expression and the meaning adults construct from this and to be especially cautious about making assumptions especially those based on researcher's views or in overzealously seeking the research goals. Dockett and Perry

(2007) mention the need for balance between research that recognizes the unique contribution of children's voices in research but which also does not define conclusions that in any way misrepresent their views. This is not to deny the young child's ability to provide an accurate account of their experiences, but rather it stresses the gulf that separates adults and young children in terms of shared language and meaning. The best information is gained when a child feels appreciated, understood and in control of the direction of their disclosure and where researchers practice their art with rigor and trustworthiness It is recommended that researchers hold these ideals firmly in their minds in conducting ethical interviews and applying qualitative analysis of data emerging form child focused research.

Young children are a challenging proposition for the researcher and gaining an accurate understanding of the child's story is an ethical art in itself. Irwin and Johnson (2005) conclude their paper by saying, "researchers who embark on work with young children need to forge a new understanding of the standards for quality in qualitative research with children" (p. 829). These standards are exacting and require a high level of ethical mindfulness from researchers.

In conclusion then, a range of factors impact on the clarity and veracity of information gained from interviewing the young child for research purposes. This chapter has provided an analysis of key skills and processes required to conduct quality research in child focused interviews, with ethical principles described as a foundation. The facilitation of the child's free narrative remains a central motif in managing the child focused interview. The use of gentle beginning processes and empathic responses are emphasized as features of ethical effectiveness in the interview. A range of media and other processes involved in the use of projective activates have been described along with cautions about interpretation of meaning in the analysis of these.

Young children's minds and bodies are in a state of constant growth and memories of experiences may lay beyond the child's reach. Encouraging the narrative and valuing it as an honest approximation of the young child's memory of experience is a matter of gentle cooperation between the child and the ethically motivated researcher. Ethical mindfulness in research with children provides a platform of guidance. Although these principles suggest moving with care, they need not preclude taking pleasure in the research journey and in the company of young children. They are a joy.

APPENDIX 1

Informed Consent

Information Letter and Consent Form

Date: _____

Dear Parent or Guardian,

    We are conducting a research study entitled "_____" with _____ grade students at _____ School/other setting. We are interested in examining _____. With the permission of _____, we are requesting that you allow your _____ to participate.

    Participants in the study will be asked to _____.
Participants will also complete a brief interview about _____.
The total time to participate in the study will be approximately _____ minutes. Students who participate will complete the study during _____.
(There will be no loss of academic class time.)

There are _____ foreseeable risks to participating in the study.

We may need to record some things your child says and does during the study. This will be done using still cameras, video, DVD or on a voice recorder. We assure you your child will not be identified on any recordings and these will be destroyed after the study is complete.

    No names will be used on any research forms so all responses will be anonymous. No one outside the research team will have access to any of the information collected. Information will be kept at _____
in a locked file cabinet, accessible only to the researchers.

    Participation in the study is entirely voluntary and there will be no penalty for not participating. As well, all students for whom we have parental consent will be asked if they wish to participate and only those who assent will be involved. Moreover, participants will be free to stop taking part in the study at any time.

    Should you have any questions about the study or, if you would like to learn more about your child's rights as a research participant please contact _____ at _____.

    Please give your permission **by signing the enclosed consent form**, adding your child's name and posting it in the stamped, return addressed envelope or by returning it by hand to _____ Please keep this letter for your records.

Sincerely (signature) _____

_____ (Researcher's Name)

_____ (Company, School or University

Consent to Participate

I have read the attached informed and consent letter and agree to have my child participate in the study entitled "_____."

Child's Name

_____

Parent's or Guardian's Name (please print)

_____

Parent's or Guardian's Signature   Date

_____

APPENDIX 2

Subject's Initials _____

ASSENT INFORMATION FORM FOR CHILD (AGES 3–8)

Either give to child to read or read it to them

You are being invited to take part in a research study. We are doing this to learn more about _____. If you agree to be in this study, you will meet with someone who will ask you questions about _____.

You will also be asked to _____.

We will keep everything you tell us private. But if you tell us that you have feelings of hurting yourself or someone else, we will have to tell someone about that. If you tell us someone hurt you, we would have to tell someone about that too, but not the person who hurt you.

For this research study, we will need to record some things you make or do on a camera, a video recorder or DVD or that you say on a voice recorder but we promise you will not be identified on these recordings and they will be destroyed after the study finishes.

If you have any questions, you can ask (*researcher, teacher or* _____, who is conducting this study.

You do not have to be in the study if you do not want to and you can stop at any time.

Child's Assent: I have been told about the study and know why it is being done and what I will be asked to do. I also know that I do not have to do it if I do not want to. If I have questions, I can ask *(name)* _____
or _____. I can stop at any time.

My parents/guardians know that I am being asked to be in this study.

PLEASE SIGN OR TICK THE NEXT PAGE IF YOU AGREE TO BE PART OF THIS STUDY.

You can keep this form, whether you agree to be involved or not.

Informed Assent Form

Study title: _____

Please tick one of these to participate in this study

☐ Yes—I agree to take part

☐ No—I do not agree to take part

Child's Name: _____

YOU CAN ALSO SIGN BELOW HERE

_____   _____
Child's Signature   Date

REFERENCES

Alderson, P. (2005). Designing ethical research with children. In A. Farrell (Ed.), *Ethical research with children* (pp. 25–36). Maidenhead: Open University Press.

Alderson, P., & Morrow, V. (2004). *Ethics, social research and consulting with children and young people,* Ilford: Barnardo's.

Amster, F. (1943). Differential uses of play treatment of young children. *American Journal of Orthopsychiatry, 13,* 62–68.

Axline, V. (1989). *Play therapy,* New York, NY: Ballantine Books. (original publication 1947)

Baker-Ward, L., & Ornstein, P. (2002). Cognitive underpinnings of children's testimony. In H. Westcott, G. Davies, & R. Bull (Eds.) *Children's testimony: A handbook of psychological research and forensic practice* (pp. 21–35). Chichester: John Wiley & Sons.

Berg, B. (2001). *Qualitative research methods for the social sciences.* Boston, MA: Allyn and Bacon.

Bond, D., Ramsey, E., & Boddy, C. R. (2011). Projective Techniques: Are they a Victim of Clashing Paradigms? C., MPRA Paper No. 33331. Retrieved from http://mpra.ub.uni-muenchen.de/33331/

Brostrøm, S. (2006). Children's perspectives on their childhood experiences. In J. Einarsdottir & J. Wagner (Eds.), *Nordic childhoods and early education: Philosophy, research, policy and practice, in Denmark, Finland, Iceland, Norway, and Sweden,* (pp. 223–256). Greenwich CT: Information Age.

Bray, L. (2007). Developing an activity to aid informed assent when interviewing children and young people. *Journal of Research in Nursing. 12*(5), 447–457.

Campbell, A. (2008). For their own good: Recruiting children for research. *Childhood, 15*(1) 30–49.

Cameron, H., (2008). *The counseling interview: A guide for the helping professions.* New York, NY: Palgrave MacMillan.

Cameron, H., (2005). Asking the hard questions: A guide to ethical practices in interviewing young children. *Early Child Development and Care, 175*(6), 597–610.

Catterall, M., & Ibbottson, P. (2000) Using Projective techniques in education. *Research, British Educational Research Journal, 26*(2) 245—256.

Clandinin, D. J., & Huber, J. (2010). Narrative Inquiry. In B., McGaw, E., Baker, & P. , Peterson (Eds.), *International Encyclopedia of Education* (3rd Ed.). New York, NY: Elsevier.

Clark, A., & Moss, P. (2011). *Listening to young children: the Mosaic approach,* London: National Children's Bureau for the Joseph Rowntree Foundation.

Clark, A. (2005). Listening to and involving young children: A review of research and practice. *Early Child Development and Care, 175*(6), 489–505,

Cocks, A. (2006). The ethical maze: Finding an inclusive path towards gaining children's agreement to research participation. *Childhood, 13*(2), 247–266.

Cohen, M. (2011). *Young children, Apps & iPad.* Michael Cohen Group LLC, Department of Education Ready to Learn Program, New York.

Connelly, F. M., & Clandinin, D. J. (2006). Narrative inquiry. In J. L. Green, G. Camilli, & P. Elmore (Eds.), *Handbook of complementary methods in education research* (3rd ed., pp. 477–487). Mahwah, NJ: Erlbaum.

Conroy, H., & Harcourt, D. (2009). Informed agreement to participate: Beginning the partnership with children in research. *Early Child Development and Care, 179*(2), 157–165.

Danby, S., Ewing, L., & Thorpe, K. (2011). The novice researcher: Interviewing young children. *Qualitative Inquiry, 17*(1), 74–84.

Darbyshire, P., Schiller, W., & MacDougall, C. (2005). Extending new paradigm childhood research: meeting the challenges of including younger children. *Early Child Development and Care, 175*(6) 467–472.

De Jong, P., & Berg, I., K. (2008). *Interviewing for solutions.* Belmont, CA: Thomson/Brooks/Cole.

Dockett, S., & Perry, B. (2007). Trusting children's accounts in research. *Journal of Early Childhood Research, 5*(1), 47–63.

Egan, G. (2007). *The skilled helper: A problem-management approach to helping* (6th ed.). Belmont, CA: Thomson/Brooks/Cole.

Einarsdottir, J. (2006). Playschool in pictures: Children's photographs as a research method. *Early Child Development and Care, 175*(6), 523–541.

Einarsdottir, J. (2007). Research with children: Methodological and ethical challenges. *European Early Childhood Education Research Journal, 15*(2), 197–211.

Einarsdottir, J., Dockett, S., & Perry, B. (2009). Making meaning: Children's perspectives expressed through drawings. *Early Child Development and Care, 179*(2), 217–232.

Eisner, E. W., (1991). *The enlightened eye: Qualitative inquiry and the enhancement of educational practice.* New York, NY: Macmillan.

Epstein, I., Stevens, B., McKeever, P., & Baruchel, S. (2006). Photo elicitation interview (PEI): Using photos to elicit children's perspectives. *International Journal of Qualitative Methods, 5*(3), 1–9.

Etherington, K. (2007). Ethical research in reflexive relationships. *Qualitative Inquiry, 13*(5), 598–616.

Etienne, R., Verkest, H., Kerem, E., & Meciar, M. (2008). *Developing practice-based research with persona dolls for social and emotional development in early childhood.* Institute for Policy Studies in Education, London Metropolitan University: London, UK. Retrieved from http://www.londonmet.ac.uk/fms/MRSite/Research/cice/pubs/practice/practice-03.pdf

Fargas-Malet, M., McSherry, D., Larkin, E., & Robinson, C. (2010). Research with children: methodological issues and innovative techniques. *Journal of Early Childhood Research, 8*(2), 175–192.

Farrell, A. (2005). Ethics and research with children. In A. Farrell (Ed.) *Ethical research with children,* (pp. 1–14). Maidenhead, Berkshire: Open University Press.

Flewitt, R. (2005). Conducting research with young children: Some ethical considerations. *Early Child Development and Care, 175*(6), 553–565.

Gallagher, M., Haywood, S., Jones, M., & Milne, S. (2010). Negotiating informed consent with children in school-based research: A critical review. *Children and Society, 24,* 471–482.

Geldard, K., & Geldard, D. (2002). *Counselling children: A practical introduction.* London: Sage Publications.

Golafshani N. (2003) Understanding reliability and validity in qualitative research. *The Qualitative Report, 8*(4) 597–607.

Gray, C., & Winter E. (2011): Hearing voices: Participatory research with preschool children with and without disabilities. *European Early Childhood Education Research Journal, 19*(3), 309–320.

Griffin, M. (2003). Narrative behavior therapy: Integration in practice. *Australian and New Zealand Journal of Family Therapy, 24*(1), 33–37.

Hannan A., (2007) *Interviews in Education Research*, Faculty of Education, University of Plymouth. Retrieved from http://www.edu.plymouth.ac.uk/resined/interviews/inthome.htm

Harcourt, D. (2011). An encounter with children: Seeking meaning and understanding about childhood. *European Early Childhood Education Research Journal, 19*(3), 331–343.

Hayward, M. (2003). Critiques of narrative therapy: A personal response. *New Zealand Journal of Family Therapy, 24*(4), 183–189.

Harper, D. (2002). Talking about pictures: A case for photo elicitation. *Visual Studies, 17*, 13–26.

Henderson, D., (2000). Play therapy. In C., Thompson & L., Rudolph (Eds.) *Counseling children* (pp. 373–399). Belmont, CA: Wadsworth Brooks/Cole.

Hoepfl, M. C. (1997). Choosing qualitative research: A primer for technology education researchers. *Journal of Technology Education, 9*(1), 47–63.

Huber, J., & Clandinin, D. (2002). Ethical dilemmas in relational narrative inquiry with children, *Qualitative Inquiry, 8*(6), 785–80.

Huber, J., Murphy, S., & Clandinin, D. (2011). Narrative inquiry as relational multiperspectival inquiry. In J., Huber, S. Murphy & D., Clandinin (Eds.), *Places of curriculum making: Narrative inquiry into children's lives in motion* (pp. 11–26). Emerald Social Sciences Book Series UK: Bingley.

Hulse, W. (1951). The emotionally disturbed child draws his family. *Quarterly Journal of Child Behavior, 3*, 152–174

Hurley, J., & Underwood, M. (2002). Children's understanding of their research rights before and after debriefing: Informed assent, confidentiality, and stopping participation. *Child Development, 73*(1), 132–143.

Irish, N., (2009). *Evaluating the effectiveness of an ububele-persona doll: emotional literacy programme for preschoolers from Alexandra Township*, Retrieved from http://wiredspace.wits.ac.za/bitstream/handle/10539/7022/9811711P-Full-Research-report.pdf?sequence=1

Irwin, L., & Johnson, J. (2005). Interviewing young children: Explicating our practices and dilemmas. *Qualitative Health Research, 15*(6) 821–831.

falseIvey, J. (2012). Demystifying Research: Projective Research Techniques *Pediatric Nursing 38*(3.), 153–182.

Ivey, A., & Ivey M. (2008). *Essentials of intentional interviewing: Counseling in a multicultural world*. Belmont CA: Thomson Brooks/Cole.

Jesuvadian, M., & Wright, S. (2011). Doll tales: Foregrounding children's voices in research. *Early Child Development and Care, 181*(3), 277–285.

Kim, H. (2012). Research with children: Challenges and dilemmas as an insider researcher. *Early Child Development and Care, 182*(2), 263–276.

Kyronlampi-Kylmanen, T., & Maatta, K. (2011). Using children as research subjects: How to interview a child aged 5 to 7 years. *Educational Research and Reviews. 6*(1) 87–93.

MacFarlane, J., & Tuddenham R. (1951). Problems in the validation of projective techniques. In H. Anderson and G. Anderson (Eds.). *An introduction to projective techniques* (pp. 26–54). Englewood Cliffs, NJ: Prentice-Hall.

Machover, K. (1935). Human figure drawings of children, *Journal of projective techniques, 17*, 85–91.

Mathews, B., & Kenny, M. (2008). Mandatory reporting legislation in the United States, Canada, and Australia: A cross-jurisdictional review of key features, differences, and issues. *Child Maltreatment, 13*(1), 50–63.

Miller, V., & Nelson, R. (2006). A developmental approach to child assent for non-therapeutic research. *Journal of Pediatrics, 149*(1), supplement, 25–30.

Morison, M., Moir, J., & Kwansa, T. (2000). Interviewing children for the purposes of research in primary care. *Primary Health Care Research and Development, 1*, 113–130.

Mulvaney, M. (2011). Narrative processes across childhood. *Early Child Development and Care, 181*(9), 1153–1161.

Munro, E., & Parton, N. (2007). How far is England in the process of introducing a mandatory reporting system? *Child Abuse Review, 16*(1), 5–16.

Neill, S. (2005). Research with children: A critical review of the guidelines. *Journal of Child Health Care, 9*(1), 46–58.

Nilsson, B., & Folkestad, G. (2005). Children's practice of computer-based composition. *Music Education Research, 7*(1), 21–37.

Nutbrown, C. (2010). Naked by the pool? Blurring the image? Ethical issues in the portrayal of young children in arts-based educational research. *Qualitative Inquiry, 17*(1), 3–14.

Ortlipp, M. (2008). Keeping and using reflective journals in the qualitative research process. *The Qualitative Report, 13*(4), 695–705.

Pipe, M., Salmon, K., & Priestley, G. (2002). Enhancing children's accounts: How useful are non-verbal techniques? In H., Westcott, G., Davies & R., Bull (Eds.), *Children's testimony: A handbook of psychological research and forensic practice*, (161–174). Chichester: John Wiley & Sons.

Punch, A. (2002). Research with children: the same or different from research with adults? *Childhood, 9*(3), 321–341.

Riessman, C., (2008). Concluding Comments, In M.Andrews, C. Squire & M. Tamboukou (Eds.) *Doing Narrative Research* (pp. 152–155). Sage books. doi 10.4135/9780857024992, Retrieved on 13/03/12 at http://srmo.sagepub.com.ezlibproxy.unisa.edu.au/view/doing-narrative-research/d2.xml

Santrock, J., (2005). *Children* (8th Ed.). Boston, MA: McGraw-Hill.

Sartori, R., (2010). Face validity in personality tests: psychometric instruments and projective techniques in comparison, *Quality and Quantity, 44*(4), 749–759. Doi 10.1007/s11135-009-9224-0

Saywitz, K., Lyon, T., & Goodman, G. (2011). Interviewing children. In J. E. B. Myers (Ed.), *The APSAC handbook on child maltreatment* (3rd ed., pp. 337–360). Thousand Oaks, CA: SAGE.

Saywitz, K. (2002). Developmental underpinnings of children's testimony. In H. Westcott, G. Davies & R. Bull (Eds.), *Children's testimony: A handbook of psychological research and forensic practice* (pp. 3–19). New York, NY: John Wiley & Sons.

Schiller, W., & Einarsdottir, J. (2009). Special issue: Listening to young children's voices in research—changing perspectives/changing relationships. *Early Child Development and Care, 179*(2), 125–130.

Sharry, J. (2004). *Counselling children, adolescents and families.* Thousand Oaks, CA: SAGE.

Spriggs, M. (2010). *Understanding consent in research involving children: The ethical Issues, A handbook for human research, ethics committees and researchers.* Retrieved from http://www.mcri.edu.au/projects/ConsentInResearch/

Squire, C., Andrews, A., & Tamboukou, M. (2008). What is narrative research? In M.Andrews, C. Squire, & M. Tamboukou (Eds.), *Doing narrative research* (pp. 1–21). Thousand Oaks, CA: SAGE.

Stemler, S. (2001). An overview of content analysis. *Practical Assessment, Research and Evaluation, 7*(17). Retrieved from http://PAREonline.net/getvn.asp?v=7&n=17

Tang, C. (2006). Developmentally sensitive forensic interviewing of preschool children; Some guidelines drawn from basic psychological research. *Criminal Justice Review, 31*(2), 132–145.

Taylor-Powell, E., & Renner, M. (2003). Analyzing qualitative data, *Program Development and Evaluation,* University of Wisconsin. UW-Extension Program Development and Evaluation. Retrieved from www.uwex.edu/ces/pdande

Thompson, C., & Rudolph, L. (2000). *Counseling children.* Belmont, CA: Wadsworth Brooks/Cole.

Wallace, I., & Bunting, L. (2007). *An examination of local, national and international arrangements for the mandatory reporting of child abuse: the implications for Northern Ireland,* NI Policy and Research Unit, Northern Ireland, Retrieved from http://www.nspcc.org.uk/Inform/publications/downloads/mandatoryreportingNI_wdf51133.pdf

Warin, J. (2011). Ethical mindfulness and reflexivity: Managing a research relationship with children and young people in a 14-year qualitative longitudinal research (QLR) study. *Qualitative Inquiry, 17*(9), 805–814.

Webb, N. (2007). Crisis intervention play therapy with children. In N., Webb (Ed.), *Play therapy with children in crisis: Individual group and family Treatment.* (pp. 45–70, 3rd ed.). New York, NY: The Guilford Press.

Wiles, R., Heath, S., Crow, G., & Charles, V. (2005). *Informed consent in social research: A literature review,* ESRC National Centre for Research Methods, NCRM Methods Review Papers, University of Southampton, Retrieved from http://eprints.ncrm.ac.uk/85/1/MethodsReviewPaperNCRM-001.pdf.

Williams, G. (2005). Bioethics and large-scale biobanking: Individualistic ethics and collective projects. *Genomics, Society and Policy, 1,* 50–66.

Williamson, E., & Goodenough, T. (2005). Conducting research with children: The limits of confidentiality and child protection protocols. *Children and Society, 19,* 397–409.

Wilson, C., & Powell, M. (2001). *A guide to interviewing children: Essential skills for counsellors, police, lawyers and social workers.* Sydney: Allen and Unwin.

Wright, S. (2007). Young children's meaning-making through drawing and 'telling': Analogies to filmic textual features. *Australian Journal of Early Childhood, 32*(4), 37–48.

CHAPTER 10

STORY COMPLETION PLAY NARRATIVE METHODS FOR PRESCHOOL CHILDREN

Shira Yuval-Adler and David Oppenheim

Most research involving the socio-emotional development of young children and their adjustment relies on adult reports or observations, and much less research relies on children's perspectives—how they understand and organize their experience. The story completion play narrative methods described in this chapter address this gap. In these methods the interviewer begins a story using dolls and props and invites the child to complete the story in action and words. The stories touch on a range of emotional issues embedded in family relationships, and are presented in a dramatic fashion designed to draw the child into a particular emotional issue, problem, or conflict. These methods provide the researcher with a standardized approach to elicit children's play narratives and learn about children's "internal world." Researchers interested in the socio-emotional development of young, preschool age children in both low and high risk ecologies are likely to find the methods described in this chapter as important additions to their research methods tool box.

Because methods using doll play have a long history in psychology, we begin by setting the current research in its historical context. Next we describe the MacArthur Story Stem Battery (Bretherton, Oppenheim, Buchsbaum, Emde, & the MacArthur Narrative Group, 1990a) and the Attachment Story Completion Task (Bretherton, Ridgeway, & Cassidy, 1990b), the two methods that have garnered the most research in the field, and we also present the Manchester Child Attachment Story Task (Green, Stanley, Smith, & Goldwyn, 2000), a third story completion approach which has also generated much research. We move after that to reviewing the research using the story completion methods and we organize this review according to six domains of child, parent, and family functioning. We conclude with guidelines for researchers and a methodological and theoretical discussion.

THE HISTORY OF DOLL PLAY RESEARCH

Interest in young children's doll play as an avenue into their inner world has a long history in psychology. The early steps were made by child clinicians: Anna Freud (1928) attributed the first therapeutic use of doll play to Melanie Klein who employed it as a procedure for the diagnosis and treatment of disturbed children. Other psychoanalytic writers, such as Waelder (1933), Winnicott (1958), and Erikson (1950) also focused on play as a way to learn about the conflicts and emotional experiences of young children. Clinicians from others schools of thought (e.g., Axline, 1947) were also impressed by the way young children's doll play reveals the sources of their fears and anxieties, and also how such play could be used as a therapeutic method for young troubled children.

Spurred by the clinical use of doll play and intrigued by how such play can help assess young children's motivations, perceptions of the family environment, and personality, researchers during the 1930s, 1940s, and 1950s began investigating doll play systematically. In such studies young children were observed in more or less standardized settings which included dolls and play materials. One of the prominent researchers in this field, Robert Sears, has written compellingly about the experience of observing a young child's doll play (Sears, 1947). He described how the child initially makes a few tentative steps, touching and manipulating the dolls, arranging the doll furniture, and creating a setting for the play. He then proceeds to describe how the child gets increasingly more involved in the play, more intent on the dolls, and less reactive to the observer. The child begins to develop play themes and enact them with the dolls and the props, and Sears describes his experience observing the child (p. 190): "Then the observer has a feeling the blinds have gone up, and he is seeing the inner person of the child. It is as if the child were making him see this family world as the child himself sees it—or, perhaps, as he would like to see it." Alongside with his excitement, emotional engagement with children's doll play and the importance he attributes to it, Sears is quick to caution the reader of the ambiguous nature of the play. He adds that such play can be "dangerously fertile ground to the projection of our own interpretative predilections" (p. 191). Thus in the writing of this early pioneer we already see the tension between the great potential of doll play for understanding the emotional development and inner worlds of young children alongside the complexities inherent in this research. In fact, the remainder of Sears' (1947) paper involves a list of methodological issues to be considered when conducting doll play research. Against the backdrop of this history this chapter will maintain the dual focus both on how doll play reflects children's emotional development and the methodological issues involved in this line of research.

A 1962 *Psychological Bulletin* paper by Levin and Wardwell summarized several decades of research on children's doll play, including that conducted by Sears. The authors carefully described the range of methods, equipment, and procedures used, and the findings around issues such as aggression, doll choice, stereotypes and prejudice in young children. While considerable research has been conducted, Levin and Wardwell's overview of the field was sobering. The authors write that "an overall body of sensible, interrelated findings is not apparent" and that "there are almost as many islands of findings as there are researchers" (Levin & Wardwell, 1962, p. 50). While the review has a somewhat pessimistic tone, the authors point to desired future research directions. One of their main recommendations appears, in hindsight, to forecast the story completion techniques that are the focus of this chapter. Levin and Wardwell (1962) recommend that play elicitation should be more structured and clear in order to facilitate interpretation. As an example they describe Lynn and Lynn's (1959) "Structured Doll Play Test" in which children are presented with 10 situations that involve a predetermined arrangement of dolls and furniture and are presented with various choices (e.g., placing the child in a bed or a crib) or asked to complete a scenario (e.g., the child doll is injured). This procedure can be seen as a very early precursor of the story completion approaches described in this chapter, although, as we will see, the theoretical underpinnings and the guiding questions have changed considerably, as has our knowledge of early social, emotional, and cognitive development.

The changing *Zeitgeist* regarding doll play research is also reflected in the terminology chosen to describe these methods. Clinicians have often referred to methods that elicit doll play as "projective doll play" techniques based on the assumption that children identify with the child doll, see the other dolls as portraying their family members, and project onto their play unconscious wishes, fears, and motivations in relation to their actual families and life circumstances. During the era between the

1930s to the 1960s researchers referred to these methods as "doll play" research. Since the late 1980s there has been a resurgence of interest in the research use of doll play and new techniques have been developed. We will refer to these techniques as *story-completion techniques* because all share the central feature in which the examiner presents, using dolls and props, a play enactment of a beginning of a story and the child is asked to complete the story using narration and play. We will refer to children's productions as play narratives to emphasize the enacted, playful, and narrative quality of these methods.

STORY COMPLETION METHODS

The majority of studies using doll play methodologies since the late 1980s employed story completion tasks, in which children enact play narratives in response to story beginnings (referred to sometimes as *stems*). Each story-stem presents the child with an emotionally evocative and often conflictual relationship-oriented story beginning and invites the child to "take over" at the high point of the story, develop a narrative and provide a resolution. Story stems appear to act as a catalyst that requires the child to complete a story that can reveal the child's subjective attitudes, feelings and emotions (Robinson, Herot, Haynes, & Mantz–Simmons, 2000). In addition, completing a story rests on the child's ability to organize his feelings into coherent stories, to regulate his emotions, and draw on his scripted inner representation of his world, his unique individual experience as well as his cultural and ethnic background.

Within the context of the renewed interest in story completion tasks several assessments have been developed of which two have been most commonly used: the Attachment Story Completion Task (ASCT; Bretherton et al., 1990b) and the MacArthur Story Stem Battery (MSSB; Bretherton et al., 1990a). The ASCT includes five story stems, each focusing on a specific attachment probe (mishap, fear, pain, separation, and reunion) thought to arouse the child's attachment system. The MSSB includes a battery of 15 story stems (some of which are common to the ASCT), dealing with family relations (e.g., parent–child attachment, marital and peer conflicts, family triad), moral rules (prohibitions and transgressions), moral emotions (guilt, shame or empathy) and competence. Several of the ASCT stems were incorporated into the MSSB, and thus the tasks are partially overlapping. The differences between the tasks are in the specific story-stems they include and their theoretical focus: the ASCT was designed to assess attachment representations while the MSSB was designed to assess, more broadly, children's emotion narratives in response to a wide set of emotion and conflict themes (see Table 10.1).

Story Completion Play Narrative Methods for Preschool Children ▪ 327

TABLE 10.1 Summary of the MSSB and ASCT Story Stems

Story-Stem	Brief Description	Issues	Story-Stem Method
Birthday Story	Mother invites the whole family to celebrate a birthday for the older brother.	Introduction, modeling of narration with family figures; "Warm-up" story stem	ASCT; MSSB
Spilled Juice	One of the children accidentally spills the pitcher of juice at the dinner table.	Parent as attachment and authority figure in response to transgression	ASCT; MSSB
Lost Dog	Part I: When going outside to play, a child discovers the family dog is gone. Part II: The dog returns.	Concern for/sadness about a lost animal Joyful, angry, or avoidant reunion response	MSSB
Mom's Headache	The mother has a headache, turns off the TV, and asks the child to be quiet. A friend comes over and asks to watch an exciting TV show.	Empathy with mother's headache/compliance with mother's request vs. compliance with friend request, selfish pleasure; resistance to temptation	MSSB
Gift for Mom or Dad	The child drew a beautiful drawing at preschool and shows it to his parents. The interviewer asks whether the child will give the picture to mom or dad.	Does the child favor the same sex or opposite sex parent? How does child deal with triadic dilemma?	MSSB
Three's a Crowd	A child is playing with his or her friend. The child's sibling wants to play too, but the friend says: "If you let your little brother play, I won't be your friend anymore."	Loyalty to friend versus loyalty to sibling; conflict resolution by children or parental intervention	MSSB
Hot Gravy	A child is warned by the mother not to touch the pot of gravy on the stove, but becomes impatient, touches the pot, and gets burned.	Noncompliance with maternal request and parent as authority/attachment figure	MSSB
The Lost Keys	The mother accuses the father of having lost her keys; an argument ensues.	Child response to parental conflict	MSSB
Stealing Candy	A child asks the mother for candy at the store, but she refuses. The child takes a candybar while the mother is not looking and is discovered by the cashier.	Getting caught during a transgression, owning up to a misdeed	MSSB

(continued)

TABLE 10.1 Summary of the MSSB and ASCT Story Stems (continued)

Story-Stem	Brief Description	Issues	Story-Stem Method
Departure	The parents go on an overnight trip while the grandmother babysits.	Separation from parents	ASCT; MSSB
Reunion	The parents return from their trip.	Reunion quality	ASCT; MSSB
The Bathroom Shelf	Part I: The mother announces that she has to leave and warns the children not to touch anything on the bathroom shelf. While the mother is gone, one of the children cuts his finger and asks for a Band-Aid. Part II: The mother returns.	Compliance with maternal request versus empathy with sibling	MSSB
Climbing a Rock at the Park	Version 1: At the park, the child tells the parents that he will climb to the top of a very high rock. The mother warns the child to be careful.	Child mastery/pride Parental response to accident Parents as attachment figures	MSSB; ASCT
Hurt Knee	Version 2: At the park, the child tells the parents that he will climb to the top of a very high rock. After climbing the rock, the child falls and hurts his knee.		
Exclusion	Mother and father are sitting on the family couch, talking. They tell the child they would like to spend some time alone and ask the child to play in his room. After the child leaves (if necessary with assistance from the interviewer), the parents kiss.	Child's response to being excluded from the parental dyad (compliance with parental request); child's reaction to parental intimacy	MSSB
The Cookie Jar	One of the siblings takes a cookie from the jar in the kitchen and is reminded by the other sibling that the parents said not to take cookies. The first sibling then asks, "Please don't tell mom or dad about it." At this point, the parents enter.	Honesty or compliance with rule versus loyalty and/or empathy to sibling	MSSB
Monster in the Bedroom	The child wakes up during the night and thinks there is a monster in his room.	Child coping with fears Parents as attachment figures	ASCT; MSSB
Family Fun	The whole family discusses their plans for their day off.	Concluding story; designed to allow a positive, relaxed ending to the story task	MSSB

In both the MSSB and the ASCT each story stem begins with a description of a scenario enacted by the interviewer using a standard doll family consisting of a mother, father, and two siblings of the same sex as the subject child, together with other figures required by specific stems (e.g., child's friend). The interviewer leaves the unfolding drama at the cusp of a dilemma or problem accentuated using dramatic affective displays that often include moderately strong negative emotions, and asks the child to "Show me and tell me what happens next." In order to scaffold the child's response, in addition to nondirective comments such as "Does anything else happen in the story?" each stem has a specific set of follow-up probes. For example, in the "Mother's Headache" stem (see Table 10.1), the subject is faced with the conflict between the desire to watch a favorite television program and the prohibition to turn the television set on because the mother does not feel well. If the subject leads the story by adopting one side of the dilemma (e.g., by turning on the TV without an explanation), the interviewer probes (once) by presenting the other side: "But what about mom's headache?" Alternatively, if the child adopts the other side of the dilemma (e.g., by refusing the friend's request to turned on the TV), the interviewer enacts the friend character imploring "Oh come on! I know you'll really like it."

Children are encouraged to enact the story completion using both words and play action. Interviewers are carefully trained to facilitate the child's development of narratives and to refrain from promoting a question and answer style. The careful attention to a warm-up period before the battery is administered, the pacing and presentation of the stories in a way that is sensitive to the child's emotional state, and the playful "feel" of the story-stem delivery, are all intended to get the child into a play-narrative "mode." All of this goes hand in hand with standard administration which includes careful control of the exact wording of the scripts, the conditions under which the follow-up probes are used and their exact wording, the specific dolls and props that are used, their arrangement on the table, and a standardized order of the stems (Oppenheim, 2006; for more details about the administration of the MSSB—see Bretherton and Oppenheim, 2003; for more details about the administration of the ASCT—see Bretherton et al., 1990b).

Following the development of the ASCT and the MSSB, and consistent with the recommendation of Bretherton and Oppenheim (2003) that researchers develop additional story stems according to their research questions, several variations of the story-completion method have been developed, including assessments with additional and/or different story stems (e.g., Shields, Ryan, & Cicchetti, 2001; Shamir, Du Rocher-Schudlich, & Cummings, 2001), figures (e.g., animal dolls instead of human dolls; Hodges, Steele, Hillman, & Henderson, 2003a), degree of emotional engagement of the method of story delivery (Green et al., 2000), administration media (e.g., computerized task; Minnis et al., 2006) and for various ages of participants (e.g., school-age children; Granot & Mayseless, 2001). Although these measures vary in some of the features of the method, they share a common core: children are presented with a set of structured story stems, typically facilitated with dolls representing the self and others, in order to elicit play narrative completions.

A particularly noteworthy variation of the story-completion method which has received considerable empirical support is the Manchester Child Attachment Story Task (MCAST; Green et al., 2000). Like the ASCT, this method was designed to examine the internal representation of attachment relationships in young school-age children using six story stems designed to elicit attachment-related play. Unlike the MSSB and the ASCT, however, the MCAST emphasizes children's identification with the doll figures by asking them to choose a doll that represents them and a doll that represent the child's caregiver. Also different from the MSSB and ASCT, this method includes several structured probes, which are asked at the end of each story, and involve "stepping outside" the narrative frame with questions such as what the dolls are feeling and what they would like to do.

Several guiding points regarding the use of story completion methods are important to mention:

1. Close attention should be paid to the roles of the interviewer during the story completion tasks. The interviewer must support the engagement of the child with the stories adopting a patient, attentive and even curious stance. Additionally, the interviewer must support the regulation and psychological safety of the child. This is particularly relevant when dealing with high risk children with whom the stems can trigger overwhelming memories of traumatic life experiences.
2. Because the story-stems evoke emotions in the children, researchers are encouraged to sequence the stories carefully so as to promote engagement in the task without overwhelming the child.
3. While careful following of the instructions regarding story administration is important, ultimately the usefulness of the battery is not based on literal adherence to story administration guidelines but rather on following the battery's spirit of facilitating play-narrative enactments.
4. It is possible to draw from the battery a subset of stories according to the theoretical focus on the study.

CODING STORY COMPLETIONS

Several approaches to coding children's story completions have been developed, and in this section we will describe them briefly while emphasizing their commonalities. More specific details about the codes used by researchers will be described in the subsequent part of this chapter in which we describe specific studies. In general, approaches to coding children's story completions have emphasized three dimensions, reflecting three levels of analysis:

1. The organization of the narrative, including its coherence.
2. The content of the narrative, or more specifically the predominant emotional themes or representations characteristic of the narrative.
3. Children's behavior during the narrative task and their interactions with the interviewer (Oppenheim, 2006; Page, 2001).

The first dimension of *organization* of the narrative has typically focused on the coherence of the stories. This dimension addresses the degree to which the child responds to the story stem with a logical sequence of events, the degree to which the child addresses and resolves the conflict or dilemma presented in the stem, as well as the degree of elaboration in the child's response. Coherence has typically been assessed using a scale that is applied to each story completion separately, following which mean scores are formed based on all story completions or on groups of stories that are selected based on common themes (e.g., stories that introduce attachment themes or discipline themes; Sher-Censor and Oppenheim, 2004). A slightly different approach designed to be particularly sensitive to incoherence due to its putative role as a marker of emotion dysregulation has been to dichotomize the scale into a coherent/incoherent split and count the number of incoherent story completions the child has produced (see Olds et al., 2004).

The second dimension involves *dominant emotional themes or representations*. These have been coded using various approaches such as identifying specific content themes (e.g., empathy/helping, aggression, Robinson & Mantz-Simmons, 2003; prosocial, limit setting, Steele et al., 2003b) and forming overall scores based on the number of such themes within and across story completions. An additional approach involved assessing representations of parental figures or child figures in the story completions with particular emphasis on the emotional tone and relational quality of the representation (e.g., positive, negative, controlling, disciplining; see Oppenheim, Emde, & Warren, 1997a; Toth, Cicchetti, Macfie, & Emde, 1997). Page (2001) emphasized that the positive and negative forms of these themes should be considered as two distinct components and not two poles of one dimension, since, in many cases (e.g., Oppenheim et al., 1997a), they appear to be orthogonal. Finally, the third dimension of *child's behavior during the narrative tasks* refers to codes such as children's responsiveness to, involvement of, or controlling of the interviewer (Robinson,

Mantz-Simmons, Macfie, Kelsay, Holmberg, & the MacArthur Narrative Working Group, 2007).

The three dimensions of organization, affective themes and child's behavior are represented in the main coding system that has been developed for the MSSB (Robinson & Mantz-Simmons, 2003; Robinson et al., 2007). Other coding systems of the MSSB or other story-completion approaches also rely on these dimensions in coding children's responses, although the dimensions are not necessarily coded separately. For example, in the ASCT Bretherton et al. (1990b) consider stories as secure when the presentation is fluent and coherent and story resolutions are benign, and consider stories as insecure when the child avoids the story issue and provides incoherent or odd responses. An additional global approach to coding story completions focuses on dimensions related to attachment security (e.g., security, deactivation, hyperactivation and disorganization) and uses a 65 item Q-sort (Miljkovitch, Pierrehumbert, Bretherton, & Halfon, 2004) that can be applied both to ASCT and MSSB narratives.

Several guiding points regarding coding children's story completions are important to mention:

1. Many studies, particularly those using the Robinson and Mantz-Simmons (2003; Robinson et al., 2007) coding system, code children's narratives from video tapes. However, there is also a considerable body of research that uses transcripts rather than- or in addition to video tapes for coding children's narratives. Each approach has its advantages: Video tapes are particularly useful for the assessment of nonverbal behavior as well as children's reactions towards the task and the experimenter. Transcripts, on the other hand, are particularly useful for assessing verbal expressions. Also, by removing visual information, transcripts facilitate focusing on the narrative (rather than, for example, on the child's behavior) and increase accuracy in coding.
2. Since there are several approaches to coding story stems, the choice of the coding method should be governed by the specific aims of each study (Bretherton & Oppenheim, 2003). The age of the child is also a factor to consider because many of codes (e.g., coherence) are clearly a function, in part, of children's development. Finally, the size of the sample is also relevant for the choice of codes. Considering statistical power, global, categorical codes that classify children into groups (e.g., secure vs. insecure attachment) may be more appropriate for larger samples whereas continuous codes may be appropriate for both larger and smaller samples.

EMPIRICAL RESEARCH USING THE STORY COMPLETION TASKS: A REVIEW

In this section we summarize empirical evidence regarding the associations between story completion tasks and six domains of child and family functioning. These are: children's attachment, parents' attachment, parenting, children's social-emotional development, measures of the child's family environment, and children's clinical diagnoses. In our review of each domain we will introduce the rationale for why story completions should be associated with the domain, review selected studies, and discuss the studies' implications and limitations. Because there are numerous studies within each domain, we also provide a comprehensive list of all the studies pertaining to each of the domains in tables, one for each domain. We highlight in each section studies that were pioneering, examined a unique population, or had a particularly rigorous design. It is worth noting that a few studies appear in several tables because they include measures that belong to more than one domain.

Story Completion Tasks and Attachment

One of the main incentives behind the development of story completion tasks came from attachment theory, and therefore the first body of research we review involves the associations between story completions and observational assessments of children's attachment to their parents. According to attachment theory (Bowlby, 1982) children form representations or Internal Working Models (IWMs) of their attachment figures' availability and responsiveness in particular contexts, and these representations are thought to influence children's self-perceptions as being worthy of care, love, and acceptance (Bretherton & Munholland, 2008). In addition, IWMs consist of rules that guide children's processing of attachment-related information and their regulation of affect and behavior (Bowlby, 1982; Bretherton, 1985). Children's completion of story stems that touch on attachment themes, such as separation, are thought to be influenced by their IWMs of attachment, both in the themes children narrate (e.g., the maternal character attending to the child's needs) and also in the organization of the child's narration (e.g., the coherence of the narrative). Specifically, secure children are expected to develop flexible, open, and free access to their thoughts, feelings and memories and therefore to produce emotionally coherent story-completions, whereas insecure children's access to attachment related thoughts, feelings and memories might be limited, distorted, or biased. This is thought to limit their ability to produce emotionally coherent story completions (Oppenheim & Waters, 1995).

Findings from attachment studies using story completion tasks have provided support for these hypotheses. Generally speaking, children's attachment as assessed in infancy or later has been found to be related to their narrative productions (see Table 10.2 for a list of studies). For example, in a pioneering study, Bretherton and her colleagues (Bretherton et al., 1990b) reported that attachment security assessed at 37 months using the ASCT was predicted by attachment as assessed at 18 months using the Strange Situation Procedure (SSP; Ainsworth et al., 1978), the gold standard for assessing infant attachment security. Specifically, children who had secure attachments to their mothers as infants narrated at 37 months fluent and coherent stories, displayed coping behaviors of the child and parent figures, and provided positive endings to the stories. In contrast, children who had insecure attachments to their mothers as infants provided as toddlers incoherent or odd responses to the stems, and/or showed avoidance of the story issue.

Support for the association between children's attachment and their subsequent narratives was also provided by Sher-Censor and Oppenheim (2004), who distinguished between the coherence and the content of the narratives (the "how and "what" of the narrative). They used the MSSB (and not the ASCT) and could therefore examine separately story stems that were attachment related (e.g., separation) and stories that touched on emotional issues not directly related to attachment (e.g., conflict around maternal prohibition). The coherence of preschoolers' MSSB narratives and, to a certain extent, the content of their narratives, were linked to child-mother attachment assessed 3.5 years earlier in the SSP. Children who, as infants, had secure attachments to their mothers narrated stories that were more coherent when compared to children who had ambivalent or disorganized attachments in infancy. In addition, children who had disorganized attachments to their mothers as infants described in their attachment stories less competent children (i.e., describing the child protagonist as ignoring the problem, being aggressive, helpless, and failing to resolve the issue raised in the stems) than children who had secure attachments in infancy. Similar findings were reported by researchers who used the Attachment Q-Sort (AQS; Waters & Deane, 1985), another well-accepted measure of early attachment which is based on home observations (e.g., Bretherton et al., 1990b; Smeekens, Riksen-Walraven, & van Bakel, 2009; Wong et al., 2011).

Concurrent and longitudinal links between children's responses to story completion tasks and attachment security were also found in several studies of older children (e.g., Solomon, George, & De Jong, 1995; Moss, Bureau, Béliveau, Zdebik, & Lépine, 2009). To assess attachment these studies used either a Separation-Reunion procedure (Main & Cassidy, 1988) analogous to the SSP or a self-report Attachment Questionnaire (Kerns, Klepac, & Cole, 1996; Kerns, Aspelmeier, Gentzler, & Grabill, 2001). For example, Solomon et al. (1995)

TABLE 10.2 Studies of Children's Story Completion Tasks and Attachment

Study	Sample	Story Stem Method	Main Findings
Bretherton et al., 1990b	n=29; low risk sample; longitudinal study; children's ages: 18, 25, and 37 months.	ASCT	Attachment security assessed by the ASCT at 37 months was significantly correlated with the SSP at 18 months, with maternal attachment Q-Sort at 25 & 37 months and with the Separation-Reunion procedure at 37 months.
Bureau & Moss, 2010	n=104; low risk sample; longitudinal study; children's ages: 6 and 8 years old.	Part of the ASCT	Concordance between age 6 attachment behaviors (Separation-Reunion procedure) and age 8 doll play attachment representations.
Dubois-Comtois, Cyr, & Moss, 2011	n=83; low risk sample; longitudinal study; children's ages: 5.5 and 8.5 years old.	Modified ASCT (Granot & Mayseless, 2001)	Correspondence between attachment behaviors (Separation-Reunion procedure) and representations for secure-confident, ambivalent-preoccupied, and disorganized-frightened groups.
Gloger-Tippelt, et al., 2002	n=28; low risk sample; longitudinal study; children's ages: 12 months (SSP) and 6 years old (ASCT).	ASCT	An association was found between the Strange Situation classification at the age of 1 and attachment classification in the ASCT at the age of 6 (relying on the twofold distinction: secure vs. insecure).
Granot & Mayseless, 2001	n=113; low risk sample; children's ages: 9.5–11.5 years old.	modified ASCT	An association was found between story completion security categories and self report measure of attachment security (Kerns, Klepac, & Cole, 1996).
Kerns, Brumariu, & Seibert, 2011	n=87; low risk sample; ages: 10–12 years old.	modified ASCT (Granot & Mayseless, 2001)	An association was found between the story completion task and an attachment questionnaire (the Security Scale–Kerns, Aspelmeier, Gentzler, & Grabill, 2001).
Moss, et al., 2009	n=104; low risk sample; longitudinal study; children's ages: 6 and 8 years old.	MSSB	An association was found between the coherence and the dominant emotional themes of children's narratives and their attachment behaviors, assessed 2 years earlier (using the Separation-Reunion Procedure).

(continued)

TABLE 10.2 Studies of Children's Story Completion Tasks and Attachment (continued)

Study	Sample	Story Stem Method	Main Findings
Oppenheim, 1997	n=35; low risk sample; children's age: 35-58 months.	Attachment Doll-Play Interview	An Association was found between children's responses to the Attachment Doll-Play Interview and children's attachment behaviors during separations and reunions in a preschool setting. However, no associations were found with the attachment Q-Sort security ratings.
Sher-Censor & Oppenheim, 2004	n=113; low risk sample; longitudinal study; children's ages: 12 months (SSP) and 4.5 years old (MSSB)	MSSB	The coherence of preschoolers' MSSB narratives and, to a certain extent, the content of their narratives, were found to be linked to child-mother attachment assessed 3.5 years earlier in the SSP.
Smeekens, et al., 2009	n=111; low risk sample; longitudinal study; children's ages: 15 months (Short SSP, AQS) and 5 years old (ASCT).	ASCT	Both AQS security and Shortened SSP security were found to significantly and independently contribute to the prediction of the security of the children's attachment representation at 5 years.
Solomon, et al., 1995	n=69; low risk sample; age: 6 years old.	ASCT	Correspondence was found between the Separation-Reunion procedure and the ASCT, while using a four-category (A-B-C-D) classification system in evaluating children's attachment security.
Wong, et al., 2011	n=121; low risk sample; longitudinal study; ages: 2.5 (AQS) and 4 years old (ASCT).	ASCT	The coherence and security of ASCT stories were predicted by children's organization of their secure base behaviors assessed 1.5 years earlier (AQS).

found correspondence between attachments assessed using the Separation-Reunion procedure and the ASCT of 6 year old children. Children with a secure child-parent attachment told confident stories with resolution of negative events (e.g., caregiver dolls rescuing the child dolls and child dolls showing competent behavior and pleasure with reunion). Children with an insecure, disorganized attachment told "frightened" stories with uncontrolled, unresolved danger themes. Children with an insecure, ambivalent attachment told "busy" stories with much digression and attention to irrelevant detail.

Several methodological issues regarding this body of work are worth noting:

1. While four of the studies regarding the associations between attachment and story completion tasks were longitudinal (Bretherton et al., 1990b; Gloger-Tippelt et al., 2002; Sher-Censor & Oppenheim, 2004; Smeekens et al., 2009), many other studies examined *concurrent* links between attachment and narratives. Concurrent links, although important, are less persuasive for supporting the argument that children's attachment histories are reflected in their story completions. Additionally, the Separation-Reunion procedure (Main & Cassidy, 1988) and even more so the Attachment Questionnaire (Kerns et al., 1996, 2001) have received less support as measures of attachment when compared with the SSP (Ainsworth et al., 1978) or the AQS (Waters & Deane, 1985).
2. Most, if not all of these studies, involved nonclinical, low risk samples, and it is important to extend the findings to high risk populations.
3. The studies in this section aimed to assess children's IWMs of attachment through their story completions. Such models are thought to be specific to the child's attachment to each of his or her caregivers, so that children should have a separate model for each attachment relationship. It is unclear which of these models is tapped by the story-completion task, however. Does that depend on parental doll presented in the stem (i.e., mother or father)? Or do children have generalized working models, as is the case with adults? One way to help resolve this issue is to set up parallel pairs of stories in which fathers or mothers are alternately included.

Story Completion Tasks and Parents' Attachment Organization

One of the most robust findings stemming from several decades of attachment studies involves the intergenerational transmission of attachment patterns. Researchers have consistently shown that the security of infants' attachment relationship with their mothers can be predicted from the mothers' (and in some cases the fathers') representations of attachment as assessed using the Adult Attachment Interview (AAI; George et al., 1985; Hesse, 2008; Main & Goldwyn, 1985). Parents with secure representations have been found to foster secure attachments in their children, whereas parents with insecure representations (Dismissing, Preoccupied, or Unresolved) have been found to foster insecure attachments in their children. Attachment researchers explain this link by arguing that the flexibility, coherence, and well regulated state of mind that characterizes the representations of secure parents apply not only to their thinking about their past attachments (as measured in the AAI) but also to their thinking and perception of their children's emotional signals and their responses to them. Secure parents are therefore expected to respond sensitively to their children and foster their secure attachments to them.

In the last decade, researchers have begun to address the intergenerational transmission of attachment patterns beyond infancy using story completion approaches, and revealed significant similarities between mothers' representations of attachment relationships, as reflected in their AAIs, and children's representation of attachment relationships, as reflected in their responses to story completion tasks (for extensive references see Table 10.3). Several studies are particularly noteworthy.

Correspondence between maternal AAI classifications and six-year-olds' attachment representations (each classified dichotomously as secure or insecure) was found in a study conducted by Gloger-Tippelt et al. (2002). Mothers who were secure had children who were more likely to be open to the affect induced by the story stems, address feelings of pain, fear, or separation anxiety frankly, and express confidence that competent adults will help, comfort, and protect them. Mothers who were classified as insecure on the AAI had children who denied pain and fear, attempted to gloss over painful and distressing experiences, or presented frightening, bizarre story endings. Thus, the openness and flexibility characteristic of secure mothers as well as the dismissing or preoccupied stance characteristic of insecure mothers were reflected in analogous ways in children's story completions.

In another study linking the AAI to children's narratives, Miljkovitch et al. (2004) used mothers' and fathers' AAI classifications to predict three-year-olds' responses to the ASCT. These researchers assessed four attachment dimensions in the ASCT using a Q-sort procedure: security, deactivation, hyperactivation and disorganization. Mothers' (but not fathers') AAIs were meaningfully related to these dimensions. Mothers and children used similar representational attachment strategies, and this held not only with respect to overall security vs. insecurity dimension but also with respect to the specific insecure strategy adopted by the parent and child (i.e., deactivation and hyperactivation). In addition, these results document that a

Story Completion Play Narrative Methods for Preschool Children • 339

TABLE 10.3 Studies of Children's Story Completion Tasks and Parents' Attachment Organization

Study	Sample	Story Stem Method	Main Findings
Bernier & Miljkovitch, 2009	n=28; full-custodial divorced fathers / married fathers and their children; children's ages: 4-6 years old	ASCT	Paternal preoccupation with past attachment experiences was associated with child hyperactivation in the full-custodial group. No intergenerational transmission of attachment was found with married fathers.
Gloger-Tippelt et al., 2002	n=28; low risk sample; longitudinal study; ages: 5 (AAI), 6 years (ASCT).	ASCT	Correspondence was found between maternal AAI classifications and children's attachment representations (secure vs. insecure).
Goldwyn, Stanley, Smith, & Green, 2000	n=34; low risk sample; ages: 5-7 years old.	MCAST	Concordance was found between unresolved status of maternal AAI and children's disorganized attachment representation.
Howes et al., 2011	n=88; longitudinal sample of Mexican immigrant mothers and their children; ages: 14 (AAI) and 54 months (MSSB)	MSSB	Early maternal security AAI scores were associated with preschool story stem scores (security, coherence, emotional integration and deactivation).
Miljkovitch et al., 2004	n=31; low risk sample of fathers, mothers and children; ages: 3 years old.	ASCT	Associations were found between maternal AAI classifications and child ASCT Q-scores (security, deactivation, hyperactivation and disorganization). No father-child associations were found.
Steele et al., 2003a	n=61; high risk sample of adopted and previously maltreated children and their adopting mothers; ages: 4-8 years old.	Little Pig (Hodges et al., 2003a)	Significant associations were found between maternal state of mind regarding attachment (secure vs. insecure) and their adopted children's story completions.
Steele et al., 2003b	n=86; low risk sample; longitudinal study; ages: prenatal and 5 years.	MSSB	Maternal AAI, collected during pregnancy, identified as coherent and secure, predict a central organizing feature of children's narratives (the extent to which children resolved social and emotional dilemmas by referencing an authoritative parent).

representational assessment of the four attachment dimensions can already be of value with children as young as three years of age. They are also relevant for the question raised earlier whether children's narratives are reflection of a specific or general working model of attachment: The results of this study seem to suggest that the story stems assessed a specific model, that involving the mother.

Particularly noteworthy due to its longitudinal design is the study conducted by Steele and her colleagues (Steele et al., 2003b). The researchers found that secure maternal AAIs collected during pregnancy predicted the extent to which children resolved the MSSB dilemmas by referencing an authoritative parent. When maternal interviews were insecure, either dismissing or preoccupied regarding attachment, children were less likely to depict mothers as possessing authoritative characteristics, long recognized as an attribute of effective parenting. Steele and her colleagues also examined the intergenerational transmission of representations of attachment in a sample of adopted and previously maltreated children (Steele, Hodges, Kaniuk, Hillman, & Henderson, 2003a). They found that mothers whose AAIs were judged insecure were likely to have adopted children who, three months after placement, provided story completions with higher levels of aggression, as compared to the stories provided by children adopted by mothers with secure AAIs. Children whose adoptive mothers provided AAIs indicative of unresolved (as opposed to resolved) mourning regarding past loss or trauma provided story completions with higher scores for emotional themes such as: "parent appearing child-like," "adult aggression" and lower scores for emotional themes such as "realistic mastery of the child" and "asking sibling or peer helps." These findings suggest that unresolved mourning in a parent may exacerbate the worries of a recently adopted child and may reflect children's difficulty to use an organized strategy to deal with the conflict depicted in the stems.

In sum, the results of cross generational studies offer additional evidence for the validity of the story completion tasks as a measure of attachment. Additional research is needed to examine the mechanisms underlying this cross generational effect, however. Like many parenting studies it is not possible to separate similarities due to shared genetics from those that are the result of the emotional communication between the parent and child. Insight into this issue and to the important role of parental state of mind in relation to attachment in shaping children's representations could be gleaned from intervention studies which focus on promoting parents' resolved/secure state of mind (e.g., the Circle of Security intervention—Hoffman, Marvin, Cooper, & Powell, 2006).

Story Completion Tasks and Parenting

In studying children's story-stem narratives, some researchers and clinicians have hypothesized that children's story completions reflect their perceptions of the parenting they have experienced and their relationships with their parents (e.g., Emde, 2003; Oppenheim et al., 1997a; Robinson, et al., 2000). Therefore, it is expected that links would be found between children's depictions of parents in their story completions and independent assessments of the parenting they receive. As can be seen in Table 10.4, children's responses to story completion tasks have indeed been linked with several aspects of parenting, including sensitivity, warm and engaged parenting and empathy.

Particularly noteworthy are the findings of Toth, Maughan, Manly, Spagnola, and Cicchetti (2002) that, in a study of maltreated children, compared a relationship-based intervention with a psycho-educational intervention using a randomized clinical trial design. Toth et al. (2002) showed a decline in negative portrayals of mothers and children and an increase in positive mother–child expectations in MSSB child narratives—but only in the group receiving the relationship-oriented intervention. These findings suggest a specific link between the emotional qualities of the mother–child relationship, which presumably improved in the relationship-oriented intervention, and children's MSSB narratives, and support the notion that portrayals of parents in children's story completions reflect the parenting they experience.

Focusing on one dimension of parenting thought to be particularly important for children's healthy emotional development, maternal sensitivity, Goodman, Berlin, and Brooks-Gunn (1998) found that the sensitivity of African-American, low-income teenage mothers to their preschool children's cues during a play session was associated with children's ASCT narratives, particularly in terms of the security they reflected. Similarly, but in the context of a low-risk sample, Laible, Carlo, Torquati, and Ontai (2004), found that warm parenting (as reported by the parents) was associated with preschool age children's representations of prosocial themes in the ASCT stories, whereas harsh parenting predicted the use of aggressive themes.

An additional related body of research focused on the joint construction of stories by children and their parents, referred to as narrative coconstructions (Oppenheim & Koren-Karie, 2009). Such coconstructions are thought to have great significance for the child's emotional development in general, and their capacity to narrate openly and coherently about emotional themes such as in story completion tasks, more specifically (Bowlby, 1988; Bretherton, 1990; Waters & Cummings, 2000). During coconstruction dialogues the parent not only supports the child's acquisition of narrative skills, but also provides the emotional security needed to develop narratives

TABLE 10.4 Studies of Children's Story Completion Tasks and Parenting

Study	Sample	Story Stem Method	Main Findings
4a Story Completion Tasks and Parenting Style			
Goodman et al., 1998	$n = 93$; African-American, low-income teenage mothers and their children; ages: 3-5 years old.	ASCT	Mothers' sensitivity to their children's cues during play sessions predicted children's level of attachment security, as reflected in their ASCT narratives.
Kerns et al., 2011	$n = 87$; low risk sample; age: 10-12 years old	Modified ASCT (Granot & Mayseless, 2001)	Secure attachment representations (as assessed with the story completion task) were linked with warm and engaged parenting in middle childhood.
Laible et al., 2004	$n = 74$; low risk sample; ages: 6 years old.	ASCT	Warm parenting predicted child's representation of prosocial themes, whereas harsh parenting predicted the child's use of aggressive themes.
Robinson & Eltz, 2004	$n = 193$; African-American, low-income mothers and their children; longitudinal study; ages: 2 and 6 years old.	MSSB	Associations were found between maternal characteristics (e.g., lack of empathy) and child's MSSB narratives (e.g., child emotional themes).
Sher-Censor, Grey, & Yates, 2013	$n = 195$; ethnically diverse sample; ages: 45-54 months of age	MSSB	Mothers' narrative coherence, but not their narrative affective content, was related to preschoolers' narrative coherence and positive portrayal of the relationship.
Splaun, Steele, Steele, Reiner, & Murphy, 2010	$n = 92$; mother-child dyads where the children are at high-risk for psychopathology due to exposure to potentially abusive or neglectful circumstances; ages: 4-8 years old.	ASCT	Mothers who expressed high levels of joy, competence, confidence, and low anger in the Parent Development Interview had children who were able to address negative themes and feelings in their ASCT stories and resolve the central story dilemma.
Toth et al., 2002	$n = 122$; maltreated/nonmaltreated children; intervention study with 4 groups; Ages: 4, 5 years old.	MSSB+ASCT	Significant decline in negative portrayals of mothers and children and an increase in positive mother–child expectations in MSSB child narratives were found—but only in the group receiving the relationship oriented intervention (Psychotherapy).

(continued)

TABLE 10.4 Studies of Children's Story Completion Tasks and Parenting (continued)

Study	Sample	Story Stem Method	Main Findings
4b Story Completion Tasks and Parental Co-Construction			
Dubois-Comtois et al., 2011	$n = 83$; low risk sample; longitudinal study; ages: 5.5 and 8.5 years old	Modified ASCT (Granot & Mayseless, 2001)	Longitudinal links were found between the affective quality of mother–child conversations in early childhood and later attachment representations.
Laible, 2006	$n = 51$; low risk sample, children's ages: 3–5 years old.	MSSB	The quality of mother–child discourse was related to children's representations of relationships. In addition, the quality of the attachment relationship moderated the influence of maternal positive expressiveness on children's representations.
Laible, 2011	$n = 50$; low risk sample; age: 4 years old.	MSSB	The quality of mother–child discourse during reminiscing about children's negative events was related to children's representations of relationships.
Laible & Thompson, 2002	$n = 63$; low risk sample; longitudinal study; ages: 30 and 36 months old	shortened version of the MSSB	Mothers' ability to resolve conflicts (30 months) was associated with coherence and prosocial themes in children's narratives (36 months).
Oppenheim et al., 1996	$n = 51$; low risk sample; age: 3.5 years old.	MSSB	Maternal and paternal co-constructions were linked with coherence, prosocial themes, and discipline themes in children's MSSB narratives.
Oppenheim, Nir, Emde, & Warren, 1997b	$n = 51$; low risk sample; longitudinal study; children's ages: 4.5 and 5.5 years old. Same sample as Oppenheim et al., 1996.	MSSB	An association was found between children's co-constructed narratives with their mothers and their ability to construct emotionally well-organized and regulated narratives independently (at ages 4.5 and 5.5).

around challenging, complex, and affectively charged themes. This sense of security facilitates the child's exploration of her internal world knowing that the parent is a reliable and sensitive partner and guide (Bretherton, 1990). Parents support such exploration by following their children's lead, encouraging them to talk about a wide range of emotional topics, helping them organize their experiences into an emotionally coherent and meaningful narrative, and stressing the child's strengths as well as the adults' protection of the child (Etzion-Carasso & Oppenheim, 2000; Koren-Karie, Oppenheim, Haimovich, & Etzion-Carasso, 2003; Oppenheim, 2006).

Empirical support for the significance of mother–child dialogues and narrative coconstructions to children's independent narratives comes from several studies (see Table 10.4b). For example, Oppenheim, Emde, and Wamboldt (1996) linked maternal and paternal coconstructions with coherence, prosocial themes, and discipline themes in 3.5-year-olds' MSSB narratives; children who had parents who were more sensitive in guiding them in the coconstruction task, and who were part of a dyad characterized by relatively high levels of shared affect, constructed MSSB narratives that were more emotionally coherent. These results suggest that children's construction of narratives about emotion and conflict themes is based on their co-constructive transactions with their parents. Along similar lines, Laible (2006, 2011) observed mothers and children reminiscing about children's past emotional and moral behavior, and found that mothers who were highly elaborative, who discussed emotions frequently with their children, and expressed high levels of positive affect during reminiscing, had children with prosocial representations of relationships and with advanced levels of emotional understanding.

In sum, studies of parenting style and narrative co-constructions have shown that parents' behavior when interacting with their children (e.g., their sensitivity, warmth, empathy and structuring) represent an important arena in which children develop their emotion narrative skills. Several limitations of this group of studies are worth noting, however.

1. Most of the studies regarding story completion tasks and parenting styles examined concurrent links, while little if any research regarding the associations between early parenting styles and later narratives has been done. Because studies with concurrent assessments of both parental behavior and child narration leave the issue of the direction of effects open (i.e., whether parenting shapes children's narratives or whether children who are better adjusted produce more positive narratives and are easier to parent), additional longitudinal studies are needed.
2. Most studies regarding the association between children's story completions and general parenting attitudes or practices are based

on parental self-reports regarding their parenting style. Self report measures are more prone to bias and are considered as less reliable compared to observational measures. Thus, there is need for additional studies in which parenting would be assessed objectively from observations.

Story Completion Tasks and Children's Social-Emotional Development

Many investigators using story completion tasks have asked whether it is possible to link this procedure with measures that reflect children's socioemotional adaptation, "outside" the world of narrative (e.g., Oppenheim, 2003; Page & Bretherton, 2001; Verschueren & Marcoen, 1999). One reason for this pursuit was to evaluate whether story completion tasks can be used as self-report measures of the emotional well being of young children with whom traditional self report measures have not been found useful. A related incentive involved providing a "voice" for young children, rather than relying only on adults to report about children's emotional lives. A final incentive involved generating hypotheses involving the causal role of children's internal representations and emotional processes in their behavioral and emotional functioning and mental health (Bretherton & Munholland, 1999; Main, Kaplan, & Cassidy, 1985; Oppenheim, 2003; Robinson, 2007). A growing body of research has provided supportive evidence for the link between children's narratives and their socioemotional functioning, including their general adaptation, behavior problems, symptoms and social competence, in both low and high risk populations (see Table 10.5 for a list of studies). Here are some of the main findings.

In a longitudinal study of children aged three, four, and five years, Warren, Oppenheim, and Emde (1996) found associations between the emotional themes in children's narratives and externalizing behavior problems. Children who displayed more distress during play and who portrayed more destructive themes in their MSSB narratives at four and five years of age were rated by their teachers and parents as having more externalizing behavioral problems. Using the same sample, Oppenheim et al. (1997a) found that children who represented mothers in their play narratives as more positive, more disciplinary, and less negative had fewer behavior problems as reported by their mothers, both at age four and five. In addition, the longitudinal analyses showed cross-lag associations between representations of mothers and children's behavior problems (i.e., representations of mothers at four predicting behavior problems at five, and behavior problems at four predicting representations of mothers at five), suggesting that the representation variables capture enduring and relatively stable features of children's

TABLE 10.5 Studies of Children's Story Completion Tasks and Their Social Emotional Development

Study	Sample	Story Stem Method	Main Findings
Bascoe, Davies, Sturge-Apple, & Cummings, 2009	n = 210; low risk sample; longitudinal study; children's age: 7 years old.	Revised MSSB (MSSB-R)	Children's insecure representations of the interparental relationship were indirectly related to their academic functioning through association with their negative information processing of stressful peer events.
Brumariu & Kerns, 2010	n = 87; low risk sample; children's ages: 10-12 years old.	Modified ASCT (Granot & Mayseless, 2001)	An association was found between attachment patterns (using the story completion task) and different types of anxiety symptoms.
Davies, Woitach, Winter, & Cummings, 2008	n = 216; low risk sample; longitudinal study; age: 6 years old.	Revised MSSB (MSSB-R)	Children's insecure representations of interparental relationships predicted parent reports of children's attention difficulties 1 year later. Attention difficulties accounted for an average of 34% of the association between insecure internal representations and school problems.
Futh et al., 2008	n = 113; ethnically diverse sample of children from a high psychosocial risk; children's mean age: 66 months.	MCAST	Attachment narrative scales (security, coherence, and disorganization) were associated with multiple indices of children's behavioral and emotional adjustment, prosocial behavior and competence.
Granot & Mayseless, 2001	n = 113; low risk sample; children's ages: 9.5-11.5 years old.	Modified ASCT	Attachment security was associated with indices of children's adjustment to school.
Hubbs-Tait et al., 1996	n = 27; children of adolescent mothers; longitudinal study; age: 44 months old	ASCT	Disorganized and insecure ASCT responses predicted children's externalizing behavior problems and discriminated children in the clinical from those in the normal range for externalizing problems.
Kerns, Abraham, Schlegelmilch, & Morgan, 2007	n = 52; low risk sample; ages: 9-11 years old	Modified ASCT (Granot & Mayseless, 2001)	Attachment security was associated with mood and emotion regulation in the classroom.
Miljkovitch, Pierrehumbert, & Halfon, 2007	n = 71; low risk sample; age: 3 years old.	ASCT	Representations of supportive caregiving negatively predicted mother-reported internalizing problems, whereas positive resolution and attachment strategies did not.

(continued)

TABLE 10.5 Studies of Children's Story Completion Tasks and Their Social Emotional Development (continued)

Study	Sample	Story Stem Method	Main Findings
Moss et al., 2009	$n = 104$; low risk sample; longitudinal study; children's ages: 6 and 8 years old.	MSSB	Children's narrative conflict themes predicted both level of externalizing and total behavior problems, even after controlling for variance explained by gender and disorganized attachment behavior.
Oppenheim, 1997	$n = 35$; low risk sample; children's mean age: 44 months	Attachment Doll-Play Interview	Associations were found between children's responses to the Attachment Doll-Play Interview and children's self-esteem and age-appropriate attention-seeking strategies (teacher's reports).
Oppenheim et al., 1997a	$n = 51$; low risk sample; longitudinal study; ages: 4.5 and 5.5 years old; Same sample as Warren et al., 1996.	MSSB	An association was found between children's representations of mothers in their play narratives and children's behavior problems. In addition, Longitudinal analyses showed cross-lag associations between representations of mothers and children's behavior problems (i.e., representations of mothers at 4 predicting behavior problems at 5).
Page et al., 2011	$n = 46$; children from high-risk backgrounds and demographically matched group; children's mean age: 6:10 years.	MSSB and ASCT	Children's narratives were associated with measures of children's psycho-social adaptation and risk and also differentiated socially competent children from those with psycho-social risks of externalizing behavior problems and social isolation (mother-reports), and peer's vulnerability and internalizing problems (teacher-reports).
Page & Bretherton, 2001	$n = 66$; post-divorce families; children's mean ages: 4.5 years old.	ASCT (adapted for post-divorce families)	Children's enactments of child–mother attachment behavior were the best predictor of children's social competence. Portrayals of the mother figure were related to teachers' assessments of low-conflict in the relationship with the child.
Shields et al., 2001	$n = 121$; maltreated and non-maltreatment children; ages: 8–12 years old.	Rochester Parenting Stories	Maladaptive representations were associated with emotion dysregulation, aggression, and peer rejection, whereas positive/coherent representations were associated with prosocial behavior and peer preference.
Solomon et al., 1995	$n = 69$; low risk sample; age: 6 years old.	ASCT	Frightening themes in children's ASCT responses were associated with children's aggressive behavior towards peers.

(continued)

TABLE 10.5 Studies of Children's Story Completion Tasks and Their Social Emotional Development (continued)

Study	Sample	Story Stem Method	Main Findings
Stacks, 2007	$n = 53$; low risk sample; children's ages: 44-68 months old.	ASCT	Story content was associated with externalizing behavior only for children classified as ambivalent.
Stadelmann, Perren, Groeben, & von Klitzing, 2010	$n = 187$; clinical and community sample; longitudinal study; ages: 5, 6 years old;	MSSB	Children's negative parental representations were associated with children's behavior and emotional problems. Children's whose parents were separated and who showed negative parental representations, had a significant greater increase in conduct problems than other children.
Stadelmann et al., 2007	$n = 153$; longitudinal study; low risk sample; children's ages: 5, 6 years old.	MSSB	Children's parental representations were associated with children's symptoms/strengths at age 5 and 6. Children's representations were the only predictor of changes in symptoms/strengths between 5 and 6.
Verschueren & Marcoen, 1999	$n = 80$; low risk sample; children's age: 5 years old	ASCT	Children's secure attachment representations were negatively correlated with anxious/withdrawn behavior problems.
Verschueren, Marcoen, & Schoefs, 1996	$n = 50$; low risk sample; children's age: 5 years old	ASCT	An association was found between the security of the child-mother attachment representation and the positiveness of the self.
von Klitzing & Bürgin, 2005	$n = 38$; low risk sample; longitudinal study; ages: 4 years old.	MSSB	Children's narratives characteristics (e.g., coherence) were negatively associated with the number of children's behavioral problems.
von Klitzing et al., 2000	$n = 652$ twins; low risk sample; longitudinal study; children's ages: 5 and 7 years old.	MSSB	Aggressive themes in children's MSSB narratives were significantly correlated with behavior problems. In addition, children who told repeated aggressive/incoherent narratives had more behavior problems than those who did not show this narrative pattern.

(continued)

TABLE 10.5 Studies of Children's Story Completion Tasks and Their Social Emotional Development (continued)

Study	Sample	Story Stem Method	Main Findings
von Klitzing, Stadelmann, & Perren, 2007	$n = 187$; clinical and community sample; children's age: 5 years old.	MSSB	Pro-social and disciplinary themes, as well as coherence and quality of narration were associated with children's social competence (the associations were prominent in the clinical children).
Warren et al., 2000	$n = 35$; low risk sample; longitudinal study; children's ages: 5 and 6 years old.	MSSB	Negative expectations in the narratives of 5-year-olds predicted internalizing and anxiety symptoms at 6 years of age.
Warren et al., 1996	$n = 51$; low risk sample; longitudinal study; children's ages: 3,4,5 years old	MSSB	The emotional narrative themes of 4 and 5 years old were associated with externalizing behavior problems.
Woolgar, Steele, Steele, Yabsley, & Fonagy, 2001	$n = 86$; low risk sample; age: 5 years old.	MSSB	Children's MSSB themes were related to their awareness of moral emotions and to ratings of externalizing and internalizing problems.
Zahn-Waxler et al., 1994	$n = 89$; children at low, moderate and high risk for externalizing disorders; ages: 4–5 years old.	Narratives involving interpersonal conflict/distress	Risk for externalizing disorder was associated with children's narratives (e.g., children with oppositional and antisocial behavior enacted more aggression in their stories)

socioemotional development. Similar results were also obtained from the MacArthur Longitudinal Twin study (Emde et al., 1992), which included an unusually large, nonclinical sample (n = 652 twins) in two time points (five and seven years old). Narratives were defined as aggressive/incoherent when at least 25% of narratives were aggressive and clearly incoherent or at least 50% of narratives were aggressive and somewhat incoherent, and children who created such narratives had more behavior problems than those who did not (von Klitzing, Kelsay, Emde, Robinson, & Schmitz, 2000).

Studying psychopathology symptoms in children, Warren, Emde, and Sroufe (2000) examined whether certain internal representations could predict later symptoms of internalizing and anxiety disorders. They discovered that negative expectations of self and others in the narratives of five-year-olds predicted mother, father, and teacher reports of internalizing and anxiety symptoms and mother reports of separation anxiety, overanxious, and social phobia/avoidant disorder symptoms in the children at six years of age. It is worth noting that children's negative expectations predicted later anxiety in these analyses better than parental anxiety and child temperament. Additional support for the association between children's narratives and their symptoms and, conversely, strengths was provided by Stadelmann, Perren, Wyl, and von-Klitzing (2007). They showed that children's MSSB parental representations at age five were associated with their symptoms and strengths, one year later. Additionally, negative parental representations at age five predicted an increase in conduct problems, whereas positive parental representations at age five predicted an increase in prosocial behavior.

Other studies have focused on the associations between children's narrative responses and their social competence. For example, Page and Bretherton (2001) examined attachment representations of children from post-divorce families in relation to teachers' or child-care providers' perceptions of their social competence. They found that children's enactments of child–mother attachment behavior in their ASCT were the best predictor of their social competence. In addition, portrayals of the mother figure as protective, comforting and supportive of the child figure were related to teachers' assessments of low conflict in the relationship with the child, but unexpectedly were not associated with peer relations.

The associations between children's narrative responses and their socioemotional functioning were also examined in high-risk populations. For example, Shields et al. (2001) compared narratives of maltreated and nonmaltreatment children and found that maladaptive representations were associated with emotion dysregulation, aggression, and peer rejection, whereas positive/coherent representations were related to pro-social behavior and peer preference. It appears that the emotional quality of children's representations of caregivers and the coherence of these representations serve an important regulatory function in the peer relationships of at-risk children. More recently, the clinical correlates of the MCAST narratives (the Manchester Child Attachment Story Task; Green et al., 2000) were examined in an ethnically diverse sample of high risk school-age children. Attachment narrative scales indexing security, coherence, and disorganization were associated with multiple indices of children's behavioral and emotional adjustment, prosocial behavior and competence. These associations held across ethnic groups and were independent of psychosocial risk (Futh, O'Connor, Matias, Green, & Scott, 2008).

In sum, there is a growing body of research supporting the associations between children's story completions and their social-emotional adaptation, including their general adaptation, behavior problems, symptoms, and social competence. These studies provide additional support for the use of story completion tasks as a measure of the young child's social-emotional experience. Nevertheless, there are few limitations which are important to note.

1. The assessment of symptoms and strengths of the child in some of the studies are based on one reporter (e.g., teacher / mother report), without corroboration from additional reporters and contexts.
2. Most studies in this domain use behavior checklists to assess children's symptoms and report on associations between the story completions and the number of behavior problems the child exhibits. However, it is not clear that variability in behavior problems under the clinical cut-off, as is typical of most low risk samples, and variability that crosses the clinical cut-off have the same meaning. The variability within the normal range may be an indication of individual differences (e.g., temperament based) that are not markers of psychopathology.

Story Completion Tasks and Measures Reflecting the Child's Family Environment

So far we have reviewed studies linking the emotional qualities of parent–child relationships and children's story-stem narratives. However, as many theories of children's socioemotional development emphasize, the broader family ecology may have a unique contribution to children's development beyond that of the dyadic parent–child relationships (McHale, 2007; Minuchin, 1985). In line with this approach, a group of studies focused on children's story-stems in relation to measures reflecting the emotional climate in the family or various family constellations (see Table 10.6a.). Here are some of the main findings.

TABLE 10.6 Studies of Children's Story Completion Tasks and Measures Reflecting the Child's Family Environment

Study	Sample	Story Stem Method	Main Findings
6a Family Climate			
Bretherton & Page, 2004	$n = 71$; children of separated/divorced families; ages: 54–60 months.	ASCT +MSSB	Children's story themes were predicted from maternal representations, maternal depressive symptoms and perception of the child's father. Gender differences were found in children's enactments of divorce-related and child-empathy themes.
Davies, Sturge-Apple, Winter, Cummings, & Farrell, 2006	$n = 223$; low risk sample; longitudinal study; age: 6 years old.	revised MSSB (MSSB-R)	Interparental withdrawal and hostility was concurrently associated with children's negative internal representations of interparental conflict.
Du Rocher-Schudlich, Shamir, & Cummings, 2004	$n = 47$; low risk sample; children's ages: 5–8.	Family Stories Task (FAST)	Several associations were found between children's negative representations and parents' conflict strategies. In addition, children's representations of parent–child relations served as a mediator between marital conflict and children's notions about conflict behavior towards peers.
Dubois-Comtois & Moss, 2008	$n = 49$ families; low risk sample; longitudinal study; ages: 5.5, 8.5 years.	modified ASCT (Granot & Mayseless, 2001)	Contemporaneous family interactions (age=8.5) predicted children's attachment representations, after controlling variance explained by prior mother–child interactions (age=5.5).
Gloger-Tipplet & Konig, 2007	$n = 101$; children of single mothers (from divorced families) and two parent families; children's ages: 6 years old.	ASCT	Children of single mothers demonstrated fewer secure and more insecure attachment representations compared to children from two parent families. Significant gender effects emerged in children of single mothers.

(continued)

TABLE 10.6 Studies of Children's Story Completion Tasks and Measures Reflecting the Child's Family Environment (continued)

Study	Sample	Story Stem Method	Main Findings
McHale, Neugebauer, Radin Asch, & Schwartz, 1999	$n = 49$; low risk sample; longitudinal study; children's age: 4.5 years old.	Family Doll Placement Technique	Depictions of affection and aggression among family figures were relatively commonplace, related to mothers' reports of family climate, and stable across a 1-month period.
Shamir et al., 2001	$n = 47$; low risk sample; ages: 5-8 years old.	Family Stories Task (FAST)	Parental marital conflict strategies were related to children's representations of family relationships. Moreover, parents' self-reported parenting styles added to the understanding of children's representations.
Schermerhorn, Cummings, & Davies, 2005	$n = 115$; low risk sample; longitudinal study; age: 6 years old.	Revised MSSB (MSSB-R)	Destructive marital conflict predicted more negative child emotional reactivity in MSSB narratives, which predicted greater child perceived agency (also in the MSSB). By contrast, children's perceived agency at Time 1 was negatively related to marital conflict at Time 2.
Stadelmann et al., 2010	$n = 187$; clinical and community sample; longitudinal study; ages: 5, 6 years old;	MSSB	Negative parental representations were associated with children's behavioral/emotional problems. In addition, children of separated parents, who had negative parental representations, had a significantly higher increase in conduct problems between the ages of 5 and 6 than all other children.
von Klitzing & Bürgin, 2005	$n = 38$; low risk sample; longitudinal study; ages: prenatally (triadic capacity) and 4 years old (MSSB).	MSSB	Positive associations were found between parental triadic capacities and the coherence/number of positive themes in children's narratives.

(continued)

TABLE 10.6 Studies of Children's Story Completion Tasks and Measures Reflecting the Child's Family Environment (continued)

Study	Sample	Story Stem Method	Main Findings
Yoo, Adamsons, Robinson, & Sabatelli, 2013	$n = 421$; low risk sample—families of twins; longitudinal study; ages: 14, 36 months (paternal distress) and 5 years (paternal distress and MSSB).	MSSB	Children's narratives of family conflict were more common when fathers reported greater distress, but their narratives of family harmony were not significantly affected.
6b Child Maltreatment			
Buchsbaum et al., 1992	$n = 100$; maltreated/nonmaltreated children; ages: 4–5 years old.	MSSB + additional stems	Maltreated children's narratives showed more negative themes (e.g., aggression, neglect behaviors) than did those of the controls.
Clyman, 2003	$n = 83$; maltreated/nonmaltreated children; age: 5 years old; same sample as Buchsbaum et al., 1992.	MSSB + additional stems	Maltreated children showed less prosocial behavior, more disobedience, more sexual behavior, and fewer characters in distress than did the nonmaltreated children.
Macfie, Toth, Rogosch, Robinson, Emde, & Cicchetti, 1999	$n = 107$; maltreated/nonmaltreated children; age: 5 years old; same sample as Toth et al., 1997.	MSSB	Maltreated children depicted fewer parental and child doll responses and more child participant responses to relieve distress, than nonmaltreated children. Role reversal was associated with physical abuse.
Macfie, Cicchetti, & Toth, 2001	$n = 78$; maltreated/nonmaltreated children; longitudinal study; ages: 4 and 5 years old.	ASCT	Maltreated children demonstrated more dissociation than did nonmaltreated children. Over a 1 year period, dissociation increased for maltreated children but did not do so for nonmaltreated children.
Shields et al., 2001	$n = 121$; maltreated/nonmaltreatment children; ages: 8–12 years old.	Rochester Parenting Stories	Maltreated children's representations were more negative/constricted and less positive/coherent than those of nonmaltreated children.

(continued)

TABLE 10.6 Studies of Children's Story Completion Tasks and Measures Reflecting the Child's Family Environment (continued)

Study	Sample	Story Stem Method	Main Findings
Stronach et al., 2011	n = 123; maltreated/nonmaltreated children; age: 4 years old.	MSSB	Maltreatment was associated with less positive global representations of the mother–child relationship relative to the nonmaltreated group.
Toth et al., 1997	n = 107; maltreated/nonmaltreated children; age: 5 years old	MSSB	The narratives of the maltreated children contained more negative representations and the children were more controlling and nonresponsive to the interviewer, compared to the nonmaltreated group.
Toth, Cicchetti, MacFie, Maughan, & Vanmeenen, 2000a	n = 93; maltreated/nonmaltreated children; longitudinal study; ages: 4 and 5 years old.	ASCT	Maltreated children depicted more negative representations (including both a negative and a grandiose self). Over time there was a marginal interaction between maltreatment and children's representations.
Toth, Cicchetti, MacFie, Rogosch, Maughan, 2000b	n = 65; maltreated/non-maltreated children; ages: 4–5 years old.	MSSB	The narratives of maltreated children contained more conflictual and fewer moral-affiliative themes.
Venet, Bureau, Gosselin, Capuano, 2007	n = 74; neglected children and control group; ages: 4–5 years old.	ASCT	A significant difference in attachment representation classifications was found between the neglected group and the control group, even after controlling for socio-economic status and maternal stress.

(continued)

TABLE 10.6   Studies of Children's Story Completion Tasks and Measures Reflecting the Child's Family Environment (continued)

Study	Sample	Story Stem Method	Main Findings
Waldinger, Toth, & Gerber, 2001	$n = 71$; maltreated/nonmaltreated children; ages: 4–5 years; subset of a sample studied by Toth et al., 1997.	MSSB	Significant differences were found among the physically abused, sexually abused, neglected and comparison group with respect to the predominance of specific relationship themes in their stories (e.g., representation of self and other, wishes to be close to other).
6c Parental Psychopathology and Trauma			
Cummings, Schermerhorn, Keller, & Davies 2008	$n = 212$; low risk sample; longitudinal study; children's age: 6 years old (at time 1).	MSSB	Children's interparental and attachment representations were found to be an explanatory variable for the effects of parental depressive symptoms on child externalizing symptoms. In addition, maternal depressive symptoms predicted changes in children's representations of marital and attachment relationships over time.
Macfie & Swan, 2009	$n = 60$; children whose mothers have Borderline Personality Disorder (BPD) and normative comparisons. Ages: 4–7 years old.	ASCT + MSSB	In contrast to comparisons, children whose mothers had BPD told stories with poorer emotion regulation and more negative/bizarre themes. In the sample as a whole, associations were found between maladaptive narrative representations and maternal self reports.

(continued)

TABLE 10.6 Studies of Children's Story Completion Tasks and Measures Reflecting the Child's Family Environment (continued)

Study	Sample	Story Stem Method	Main Findings
Murray, Woolgar, Briers, Hipwell, 1999	$n = 95$; children of depressed and nondepressed mothers; children's age: 5 years old	Dolls' House Play	Children's social representations showed systematic relationships with family adversity (maternal depression and parental conflict) in interaction with the child's gender. Children's play was also associated with several aspects of their wider experience (e.g., mother–child interactions, emotional adjustment).
Oppenheim et al., 1997a	$n = 51$; low risk sample; longitudinal study; ages: 4.5, 5.5 years old; same sample as Warren et al., 1996.	MSSB	Children's representations of mothers in their play narratives were associated with mothers' report of psychological distress. Similar findings, with the focus on the emotional resolution of MSSB narratives, were reported by Oppenheim (2003).
Robinson, 2011	$n = 735$; mothers receiving prenatal services; longitudinal study; ages: prenatal (obstetrical health behaviors), 2, 4 (child empathy) and 6 years old (MSSB).	MSSB	As 6 years old, Children of substance using mothers had dramatically lower levels of prosocial representations of family relationships and higher levels of disrupted and dysregulated representations of family relationships. Their ability to tell a coherent story of positive family life was dramatically affected by their mother's prenatal behaviors and attitudes.
Schechter et al., 2007	$n = 25$; referred sample of traumatized mothers and their children; ages: 4–7 years old.	MSSB	Traumatized mothers experience and symptoms prior to their child's turning 4 years old adversely affected their child's mental representations from ages 4–7 years.

(continued)

TABLE 10.6 Studies of Children's Story Completion Tasks and Measures Reflecting the Child's Family Environment (continued)

Study	Sample	Story Stem Method	Main Findings
Toth et al., 2009	$n = 99$; mothers with a history of major depressive disorder/ no history of mental disorder and their toddlers; longitudinal study; ages: 20, 36, & 48 months old.	MSSB	Early-occurring maternal depression had a negative impact on children's negative and positive representations of parents. Attachment security mediated the relation between depressive symptoms and negative representations.
Woolgar & Murray, 2010	$n = 94$; children of depressed and nondepressed mothers; age: 5 years old; same sample as Murray et al., 1999	Dolls' House Play	Representations of fathers were unrelated to maternal mood, but were associated with parental conflict. Representations of child care for the father predicted poor child adjustment, but only in children exposed to maternal postnatal depression.
6d Domestic Violence			
Grych, Wachsmuth-Schlaefer, & Klockow, 2002	$n = 46$; children of battered woman and comparison group; ages: 3.5 to 7 years.	MSSB	Differences were found between children who were exposed to violence and comparison group with respect to several indices of MSSB narratives. Interparental aggression uniquely predicted representations of conflict escalation and avoidance after accounting for parent–child aggression, and the two types of aggression had additive effects in predicting positive maternal representations.
Minze, McDonald, Rosentraub, & Jouriles, 2010	$n = 57$; community sample; ages: 4–5 years.	MSSB	Intimate partner violence (IPV) was negatively associated with narrative coherence.

(continued)

Story Completion Play Narrative Methods for Preschool Children ▪ 359

TABLE 10.6 Studies of Children's Story Completion Tasks and Measures Reflecting the Child's Family Environment (continued)

Study	Sample	Story Stem Method	Main Findings
Stover, Horn, & Lieberman, 2006	n = 40; children from families with histories of domestic violence; children's ages: 27–71 months old.	MSSB	Boys, especially those who did not visit regularly with their fathers, had more negative representations of their mothers, than girls. Girls represented their parents more positively than boys, regardless of other family circumstances. Severity of violence did not predict negative parental representations in the sample.
6e Incarcerated Mothers			
Poehlmann, 2005	n = 54; children whose mothers were currently incarcerated; ages: 2.5–7.5 years.	ASCT	Most children were classified as having insecure relationships with mothers and caregivers. Secure relationships were more likely when children lived in a stable caregiving situation, when children reacted to separation from the mother with sadness rather than anger, and when children were older.
6f Adopted and Institutionalized Children			
Hodges, Steele, Hillman, Henderson, & Kaniuk, 2003b; 2005	n = 61; infancy / late adopted children; longitudinal study; mean age at first assessment: 5–6 years old.	Little Pig Stems (Hodges et al., 2003a)	The children in the late adopted group presented more indicators of avoidance and disorganization, more negative representations of adults and children, and a greater presence of aggression in their narratives, in compare to the infancy adopted group.
Hodges, Steele, Kaniuk, Hillman, & Asquith, 2009	n = 100; infancy / late adopted children (previously maltreated children); longitudinal study; mean age at first assessment: 5–6 years old.	Little Pig Stems (Hodges et al., 2003a)	Two years after placement, the late adopted children showed a significant increase in "security" construct and in their positive emotional themes. However, mean scores on the "insecurity" and "disorganization" constructs did not decrease significantly and major differences remained between them and the comparison group.

(continued)

TABLE 10.6 Studies of Children's Story Completion Tasks and Measures Reflecting the Child's Family Environment (continued)

Study	Sample	Story Stem Method	Main Findings
Katsurada, 2007	n = 32; institutionalized Japanese children and comparison group; ages: 4–6 years old.	ASCT	No secure attachment was found in the institutionalized children, and disorganized attachment was more prevalent in the institutionalized children versus the comparison group.
Minnis et al., 2006	n = 84; children in foster care and school controls; ages: 4–9 years old.	Computerized-MSSB (CMSSB)	Children in foster care showed significantly poorer coherence of narrative, less intentionality and greater avoidance on the CMSSB compared to a school comparison group.
Román & Palacio, 2012	n = 148; internationally adopted children/control group—children living with their birth families with no experience of maltreatment/children who were living in institutions; ages: 4–8 years old;	Little Pig (Hodges et al., 2003a) + part of the MSSB	The mental representations of attachment of the internationally adopted children, at an average of three years following their adoption, were more negative (as reflected in higher scores for insecurity, avoidance and disorganization in children's narratives) than those of the control group, but similar to those of the institutionalized children.
Vorria et al., 2006	n = 100; adopted children (previously reared in institution)/children reared in their own two-parent families; longitudinal study; ages: 1, 4 years old.	ASCT	At four years adopted children had a lower score than the comparison children for story resolution, narrative coherence, prosocial themes and a higher score on avoidance, while differences in atypical and negative themes were not significant.

The influence of mother–child and family interactions on the development of child attachment representations in middle childhood were examined by Dubois, Comtois, and Moss (2008). Mother–child interactions were observed during a snack time in a lab setting (Moss, Rousseau, Parent, St-Laurent, & Saintonge, 1998) when children were five to six years old. Three years later, children's attachment representations were assessed using a doll play narrative procedure in the lab setting. Within six months of the second lab visit, family interactions were filmed during mealtime. Results showed clear differences between attachment groups (as assessed using doll play) on quality of mother–child and family interaction with the secure group showing highest and the disorganized group showing lowest quality interactions. In addition, whole family observations were better predictors of children's story completions than mother-child observations (although a significant limitation was that the family observations were conducted 6 months *after* the story completions were assessed).

Additional support for the importance of considering family relationships came from a study by von Klitzing and Bürgin (2005) who examined the associations between parental capacities for triadic (mother–father–child) relationships assessed prenatally, and the story completions of their offspring at preschool age. Thirty-eight couples were interviewed during their first pregnancy to assess their "triadic capacity," that is, their ability to anticipate their family relationships without excluding either themselves or their partners from the relationship with the infant. Four years later, children's MSSB story stems were assessed. Results showed that couples' "triadic capacity" was associated with more coherent and positive MSSB narratives at preschool, emphasizing the significance of couples' capacity to envision themselves as a triad even before the baby is born for the child's development.

Other family studies examined the links between the marital relationship and children's narratives. For example, Davies, Sturge-Apple, Winter, Cummings, and Farrell (2006) sought to identify developmental change and stability of child reaction patterns to interparental conflict in the context of family relations. Studying a large sample (n = 223) of 6-year-old children and their parents, followed over the course of one year, they found that interparental withdrawal and hostility each uniquely predicted child distress reactions to conflict (as reflected in their MSSB narratives) even after statistically controlling for parental warmth. A related group of studies highlighted risk factors in the family environment and their reflections in children's story completions. In Tables 10.6b–10.6f, we summarized studies that pertain to the following risk area in children's family environment: child maltreatment, parental psychopathology and trauma, domestic violence, maternal incarceration, and foster care or institutionalization. We review next findings regarding two of the risk domains which have received most attention: child maltreatment and parental psychopathology.

Child Maltreatment

When comparing the narratives of maltreated children to the narratives of nonmaltreated children matched for age, gender, race, and receptive language ability, Buchsbaum, Toth, Clyman, Cicchetti, and Emde, (1992) found that maltreated children's narratives showed more themes involving inappropriate aggression, punitiveness, abusive language, neglect, and sexualized behaviors than did those of the controls. In the narratives of the maltreated children, the child doll received less help from the other dolls. Moreover, maltreated children included more statements about the protagonist doll as bad. Additional findings from this sample were reported by Clyman (2003) who found that maltreated children showed less prosocial behavior, more disobedience, more sexual behavior, and fewer characters in distress than did the nonmaltreated children. These findings suggest that maltreated children may display signs of their abuse, as well as possible consequences of the abuse (more disobedience), in their narratives.

Parental Psychopathology

Several studies have examined the associations between children's narratives and parental psychopathology. For example, Toth, Rogosch, Sturge-Apple, and Cicchetti (2009) examined the relations between maternal depression and children's representations of parents and self. Participants included toddlers and their mothers with a history of major depressive disorder or no history of mental disorder. Depressive symptoms were assessed at three time points (20, 36, and 48 months), while representations of parents and self, using the MSSB, were assessed when the children were 36 and 48 months old. Results showed that higher levels of maternal depressive symptoms at Time 1 (20 months) predicted increases in children's negative representations of parents and decreases in positive representations of parents from Time 2 (36 months) to Time 3 (48 months), suggesting a negative impact of early-occurring maternal depression on children's negative and positive representations.

In another study linking parental psychopathology to children's narratives, Schechter et al., (2007) investigated the impact of maternal exposure to family violence, maltreatment, and related posttraumatic stress disorder (PTSD) on young children's mental representations of self and caregivers. Mothers' experience of domestic violence and severity of violence-related PTSD symptoms predicted more dysregulated aggression, attentional bias to danger and distress, as well as more avoidance of and withdrawal from conflicts presented in the children's story stems. Less narrative coherence was also noted. Also studying the link between maternal psychopathology and child narratives, Macfie and Swan (2009) studied mothers with Borderline Personality Disorder (BPD) and their children. In contrast to comparison children and controlling for major depressive disorder, children whose mothers had BPD told stories with the following: (a) more parent–child role reversal, more fear of abandonment, and more negative mother–child and father–child relationship expectations; (b) more incongruent and shameful representations of the self; and (c) more confusion of fantasy and reality. Additionally, associations were found between maternal borderline features and maladaptive narrative composites.

In sum, studies linking children's narratives with measures reflecting the child's family environment suggest that children's responses to story completion tasks reflect their current and past family environment. However, only few of the studies deal with the mechanisms underlying children's narratives, which leaves open the question as to how characteristics of children's family environment, including risk and protective factors, affect children's narratives. This and additional limitations will be revisited in the general discussion.

Story Completion Tasks Among Children With Clinical Diagnoses

As mentioned earlier, research on preschool disorders and diagnoses is almost entirely based on caregiver report or observations. The sole reliance on adult informants is limited because it gives no place to the perspective of the preschool-age child him- or herself (Belden, Sullivan, & Luby, 2007). Following the development of the story completion techniques researchers and clinicians began to ask whether they can be used as self-report measures for young children, and the last decade has seen a growing body of research supporting this direction (see Table 10.7).

For example, Green, Stanley, and Peters, (2007) examined the narratives of a clinical sample with externalizing disorder and found high levels of represented attachment disorganization in the MCAST narratives of the clinical sample compared to population norms. Additionally, ADHD diagnosis was associated with higher levels of attachment disorganization in children's narratives. Other studies have focused on children with mood disturbances. For example, Belden et al. (2007) studied a large sample (n = 279) that included preschoolers with depressive and disruptive disorder and healthy controls. The researchers found that preschoolers' depression severity was associated with their representations of their mothers' caregiving behaviors as assessed by the MSSB. In particular, preschoolers with higher depression severity scores represented their mothers as more negative and more often as showing disciplinary behaviors. This finding

TABLE 10.7 Studies of Children's Story Completion Tasks and Clinical Diagnosis

Study	Sample	Story Stem Method	Main Findings
Belden et al., 2007	n = 279; The sample included healthy, depressed, and disruptive disordered preschoolers; longitudinal study; ages: 3–5 years old.	MSSB	Higher depression severity was associated with preschoolers' greater use of negative and disciplinarian maternal representations. Maternal representations were associated with mothers' later supportive/nonsupportive behaviors and affect.
Beresford, Robinson, Holmberg, & Ross, 2007	n = 32; children with mood disturbances / typically developing children; ages: 3.5–6 years old.	MSSB	Comparison of the referred and typically developing children showed that specific story contexts varied in eliciting responses reflecting disorganization and thought disturbance from the referred children.
Green et al., 2007	n = 61; children with externalizing disorder; ages: 4–9 years old;	MCAST	Disorganized attachment representations showed a high prevalence and independent associations with attention deficit symptomatology and maternal Express Emotion.
Hill, Fonagy, Lancaster, & Broyden, 2007	n = 66; referred boys for disruptive behavior problems / nonreferred boys; age: 5–8 years old	MSSB + newly created stems	Referred boys had elevated aggression and lower intentionality scores across all stems compared to nonreferred boys. However, there was a story type by group interaction: referred boys had substantially lowered intentionality in response to the distress stems, but not the conflict stems.
Hutchison, Beresford, Robinson, & Ross, 2010	n = 31; children with mood dysregulation / typically developing children; ages: 3.5–6 years-old.	MSSB	Significant differences were found among children with mood dysregulation and a comparison group with respect to unusual use of story props.

(continued)

TABLE 10.7 Studies of Children's Story Completion Tasks and Clinical Diagnosis (continued)

Study	Sample	Story Stem Method	Main Findings
Luby et al., 2009	n = 305; depressed, anxious, disruptive disordered preschoolers, as well as healthy children; ages: 3–6 years old.	MSSB	Based on preschoolers' emotion themes during the MSSB task, depression severity was related to preschoolers' expressions of shame.
Wai-Wan & Green, 2010	n = 77; children with externalizing disorder; ages: 4–11 years old.	MCAST	Specific atypical themes were associated with the extent of child psychopathology and were modified by exposure to maternal depressed mood.
Children With a Physical Diagnosis			
Murry et al., 2010	n = 170; Children with cleft lip and controls; longitudinal study; ages: infancy and 7 years old.	Doll play task	Child representations revealed difficulties among children with cleft lip in social relationships.
Spagnola & Fiese, 2010	n = 53; low income preschoolers with asthma; ages: 3-5 years old.	Family Narrative story stem (Fiese & Sameroff, 1999)	Children's family narratives predicted children's behavior problems, while narrative about family response to asthma symptoms did not.

suggests that depressive symptoms may have an impact on the development of young children's experience and expectations of their primary relationships. In addition, the results show that the MSSB narrative technique may be useful for identifying and characterizing negative internal experiences that differentiate preschoolers with high levels of depressive symptomatology from those who are nondepressed.

In sum, there is a growing body of research linking clinic-referred children's narratives to their identified disorders, suggesting that story completion approaches could be a valuable addition to the tools available for the child clinician (Emde, 2007; Murray, 2007; Robinson, 2007). A number of limitations are worth noting, however.

1. Similar narrative responses seem to be associated with a number of different clinical problems. For example, portraying the parent dolls negatively could be associated with troubled parent–child relationships, behavior problems and/or depression. Thus, it seems important for future research to include measures of multiple differentiated aspects of the narrative to clarify what type of narrative responses are associated with which specific clinical outcome.
2. Additional research is needed to validate the story completion tasks against disorders that have not been yet examined and to refine procedures for clinical use.

CONCLUSIONS AND FUTURE DIRECTIONS

Since the renewed interest in doll play methods more than two decades ago, story completion tasks have been extensively studied. Close to one hundred studies on several thousands of subjects living in wide range of circumstances, socioeconomic contexts, and countries have been conducted. The populations studied were diverse, including high and low risk samples, children of divorced parents, children with clinical diagnoses, adopted children, children growing with parents who are mentally ill, children of incarcerated mothers and more. A rich and relatively consistent body of knowledge has emerged, providing the basis for future studies and theory development.

The studies reviewed in this chapter have linked children's story completions to six domains pertaining to child, parent, and family functioning and taken together have shown a wide network of associations around story completion methods. In general, the emotional coherence of children's narrative responses—that is, their ability to address the core emotional theme presented in the story-stem while developing a coherent narrative that includes positive representations and leads to a constructive resolution—was found to be associated with more optimal socioemotional functioning of the child and an environment characterized by a favorable emotional climate.

To account for these findings researchers have used a range of different, albeit related concepts. Children's story completions have been described as representing their perceptions of themselves and others, their representations or Internal Working Models of relationships, their efforts to organize or make sense of their emotional experiences, ways of understanding the world and resolving conflicts, or capacity to produce a coherent narrative response to an emotionally charged story stem. In other words, the story-stem approach does not represent a single measure designed to assess a single construct, but rather a standardized method to elicit young children's narratives around emotional themes which can be used for different purposes depending on the research question at hand. As the breadth of research reviewed in this chapter attests, the richness of children's responses to the story stems has been mined by investigators to examine a wide variety of issues related to children's social emotional development and adjustment.

Beyond their value for studying children's "inner world," the developmental researcher interested in young children's socio-emotional development may find story completion methods useful for the following practical reasons:

1. Detailed manuals are available for the administration of the stems, including specific wording, follow-up probes, and the use and placement of dolls and props.
2. Detailed manuals are available for coding children's stories (although it is important to keep in mind that obtaining inter-rater reliability may require considerable training).
3. Story-stem methods can be used with children as young as three-years-old, although more reliable results are likely to be obtained with older preschoolers. This is particularly true in the case of high-risk children.
4. Researchers have the flexibility to choose sub-sets of stories according to the research question at hand and/or develop additional stems. While this strategy diminishes to some extent the comparability between studies, it increases the scope of research questions that can be addressed using the story-completion method.
5. The story-stem methods are relatively easy and quick to administer, portable, enjoyable for children, and culturally flexible. However, it is important for interviewers to have clinical sensitivity in order to administer the procedures appropriately.

6. Story-completion methods help obtain rich data directly from young children beyond adult reports about the child or direct observations.
7. Story-completion methods can be useful not only for the child researcher but also for the child clinician, who can use the extensive research on these methods to support the interpretations of children's play enactments.
8. Story completion methods have good psychometric properties as evidenced by high inter-rater reliability and extensive support for validity.

Methodological Issues and Directions for Future Research

We close this chapter by discussing several theoretical and methodological issues regarding story completion research, and we begin with the issue of direction of effects. As mentioned above, rather consistent associations have been found between children's story completions and various aspects of their development and environment. However, because most of the studies reviewed in this chapter were correlational, the direction of effects between these correlates and children's story-stem narratives is not clear. Are children's story stems outcomes of the various correlates? This seems to be the idea behind many of the studies reviewed in this chapter. For example, researchers set out to examine whether parenting shapes children's story completions. However, the opposite direction of effect can often not be ruled out. To continue with the same example—it is also possible that some intrinsic child characteristic (e.g., self-regulation) elicits more positive parenting and is also reflected in the child's story stem narratives. Additionally, the "third variable" explanation is also often hard to rule out. Namely, that a variable other than parental or child characteristics (e.g., the quality of the marital relationship), impacts both the parental measure and the child measure and accounts for the association between them.

Some of the studies reviewed in this chapter tried to address this issue and to disambiguate the direction of effects. For example, a subset of the studies linking attachment to children's narratives used a longitudinal design: attachment was measured early and children's story stems were measured later. Such a design is certainly much stronger and supports the conclusion that attachment plays a causal role in shaping children's narratives. However, it cannot rule out a "third variable" explanation. Other studies used statistical control to deal with the third variable problem. For example, in their study of maltreated children, Venet, Bureau, Gosselin, and Capuano (2007) found a significant difference in attachment representation classifications between the neglected group and the control group, even after controlling for socio-economic status and maternal stress.

Experimental designs are, of course, the strongest in terms of establishing causal links. For example, the Toth et al. (2002) study showed that among maltreated children, only those that received an intervention designed to improve the emotional quality of the parent child relationship showed improvements in their story stem narratives. Such a finding, supported by the methodological strength of a randomized clinical trial, is of great importance in establishing direction of effects, and more studies using such designs are clearly needed.

A closely related issue involves the mechanisms linking the putative causal factor (e.g., parental psychopathology, family risk factors) to children's story stem narratives. For example, why is it that the narratives of children from maltreating families include more negative themes and less positive and coherent representations when compared with a control group (e.g., Buchsbaum et al., 1992; Clyman, 2003; Macfie et al., 1999; Shields et al., 2001)? What are the pathways that link the two measures? It is possible that maltreatment leads to emotion dysregulation, particularly around fear or anger themes, and that such dysregulation impacts the story completions children develop. It is also possible that maltreatment is associated with parent–child communication patterns that are mis-attuned and insensitive, if not outright hostile and/or withdrawn, so that maltreated children experience much less opportunities to learn how to construct emotionally coherent narratives. Obviously, the two explanations are not mutually exclusive, and additional mechanisms can also be envisioned. Thus, more research on the mechanisms contributing to variability in children's story completions is needed.

One mechanism that has received attention involves the contribution of parent–child emotion dialogues to children's story completions. Studies of parent–child dialogues have shown that mothers who sensitively guide their dialogues with their children regarding past emotional experiences, have children who are more capable to develop coherent emotion narratives independently (Oppenheim & Koren-Karie, 2009). The studies assessing such dialogues advanced our understanding of the mechanisms that may link general characteristics of the child's environment (e.g., maltreatment, parental mental illness) to children's story-stems. However, none of the studies examined the general characteristics of the children's environment *together with* the mechanisms that may link such characteristics to children's narratives. Also rare are studies that try to tease apart the various different mechanisms that may shape children's narratives and examine their relative contributions. In methodological language, more integrative multivariate studies are needed in order to investigate the various pathways that may contribute to variability in children's story stems.

The emotional and cognitive processes tapped by story completion methods can be not only outcomes of earlier or concurrent influences but also processes that play an important role in shaping children's future development. In other words these processes can serve as "filters" or schemata through which the child experiences the world. Through mechanisms of self-fulfilling prophecies, such filters can forecast children's developmental outcomes. For example, Du Rocher-Schudlich, Shamir, and Cummings (2004) showed that children's internal representations of parent–child relations as assessed using story completions served as a mediator between marital conflict and children's notions about conflict behavior towards peers. An additional, impressive example is the Stadelman, Perren, Groeben, and von Klitzing (2010) study that showed that, after controlling for gender and early (age five) symptoms, children of separated parents who showed negative parental representations had a greater increase in conduct problems between the ages of five and six years than all other children. Thus, children's representations of parent–child relationships moderated the impact of parental separation on the development of conduct problems. In conclusion, story stem approaches can reveal more than how the child is passively impacted by his or her experiences. Rather, acting as mediating or moderating variables they can uncover internal mechanisms that may predict developmental outcomes. More studies to support this conjecture are needed.

In conclusion, the past two decades have witnessed a significant resurgence of interest in children's doll play as assessed using story completion approaches. Unlike the somewhat pessimistic conclusions of Levin and Wardwell's (1962) review of doll play research from the era between 1930 and 1960, we feel that a relatively coherent body of findings has emerged. This may be due to the different theoretical questions that guide current research, the availability of video recording that made coding more accurate, and the methodological advances in research design. Most importantly, perhaps, is that in contrast with earlier research which provided very little structure to children's doll play, the story-stem approach guides children into specific areas of interest to the researcher and uses probes to clarify children's responses. As mentioned earlier, the added structure is very much in line with the recommendations provided by Levin and Wardwell (1962), although these recommendations were probably not the reason why the semi-structured story completion approach was espoused (see Bretherton & Oppenheim, 2003, for an account of the background for the development of story completion approaches).

Researchers who are considering using story stem approaches now have a much more solid base than those who began using this method some 20 years ago. There is much more technical knowledge available regarding how to best use story completion approaches, and there are many findings on which researchers can base future studies. Additionally, there are many open research questions, only a few of which we discussed above. Thus, researchers can share the excitement observing young children's doll play, so vividly described by Sears (1947), as they design studies to better understand preschool children's emotional development.

REFERENCES

Ainsworth, M. D. S., Blehar, M. C., Waters, E., & Wall, S. (1978). *Patterns of attachment: A psychological study of the Strange Situation.* Hillsdale, NJ: Erlbaum.

Axline, V. M. (1947). *Play therapy.* New York, NY: Ballantine Books.

Bascoe, S. M., Davies, P. T., Sturge-Apple, M. L., & Cummings, E. M. (2009). Children's representations of family relationships, peer information processing, and school adjustment developmental psychology. *American Psychological Association, 45*(6), 1740–1751.

Belden, A. C., Sullivan, J. P., & Luby, J. L. (2007). Depressed and healthy preschoolers' internal representations of their mothers' caregiving: Associations with observed caregiving behaviors one year later. *Attachment and Human Development, 9*(3), 239–254.

Beresford, C., Robinson, J. L., Holmberg, J., & Ross, R. G. (2007). Story stem responses of preschoolers with mood disturbances. *Attachment and Human Development, 9*(3), 255–270.

Bernier, A., & Miljkovitch, R. (2009). Intergenerational transmission of attachment in father–child dyads: The case of single parenthood. *The Journal of Genetic Psychology, 170*(1), 31–51.

Bowlby, J. (1982). *Attachment and loss, Vol. 1: Attachment* (2nd ed.). New York, NY: Basic Books.

Bowlby, J. (1988). *A secure base: Parent–child attachment and healthy human development.* New York, NY: Basic Books.

Bretherton, I. (1985). Attachment theory: Retrospect and prospect. *Monographs of the Society for Research in Child Development, 50* (1–2, serial no. 209), 3–35.

Bretherton, I. (1990). Open communication and internal working models: their role in the development of attachment relationships. In R. A. Thompson (Ed.), *Nebraska symposium on motivation: Socioemotional development* (pp. 59–113). Lincoln: University of Nebraska Press.

Bretherton, I., & Munholland, K. A. (1999). Internal working models in attachment: A construct revisited. In J. Cassidy & P. Shaver (Eds.), *Handbook of attachment theory* (pp. 89–111). New York, NY: Guilford.

Bretherton, I., & Munholland, K. A. (2008). Internal working models in attachment relationships. In J. Cassidy & P. R. Shaver (Eds.), *Handbook of attachment: Theory, research, and clinical application* (2nd ed., pp. 102–127). New York, NY: Guilford Press.

Bretherton, I., & Oppenheim, D. (2003). The MacArthur Story Stem Battery: development, administration, reliability, validity, and reflections about meaning. In R. Emde, D. P. Wolf, & D. Oppenheim (Eds.), *Revealing the inner worlds of young children: The MacArthur Story Stem Battery and parent–child narratives* (pp. 55–80). New York, NY: Oxford University Press.

Bretherton, I., Oppenheim, D., Buchsbaum, H., Emde, R. N., & the MacArthur Narrative Group (1990a). *MacArthur Story-Stem Battery.* Unpublished manual.

Bretherton, I., & Page, T. F. (2004). Shared or conflicting working models? Relationships in postdivorce families as seen through the eyes of mothers and their preschool children. *Development and Psychopathology, 16,* 551–575.

Bretherton, I., Ridgeway, D., & Cassidy, J. (1990b). Assessing internal working models of attachment relationship: An attachment story completion task for 3-year-olds. In M. T. Greenberg, D. Cicchetti, & E. M. Cummings (Eds.), *Attachment in the preschool years: Theory, research, and intervention* (pp. 273–308). Chicago: University of Chicago Press.

Brumariu, L. E. & Kerns, K. A. (2010). Mother–child attachment patterns and different types of anxiety symptoms: is there specificity of relations? *Child Psychiatry & Human Development, 41,* 663–674.

Buchsbaum, H. K., Toth, S. L., Clyman, R. B., Cicchetti, D., & Emde, R. N. (1992). The use of a narrative story stem technique with maltreated children: Implications for theory and practice. *Development and Psychopathology, 4,* 489–493.

Bureau, J. F., & Moss, E. (2010). Behavioural precursors of attachment representations in middle childhood and links with child social adaptation. *British Journal of Developmental Psychology, 28,* 657–677.

Clyman, R. B. (2003). Portrayals in maltreated children's play narratives: representations or emotion regulation? In R. N. Emde, D. P. Wolf, & D. Oppenheim (Eds.), *Revealing the inner worlds of young children: The MacArthur Story Stem Battery and parent–child narratives* (pp. 201–221). New York, NY: Oxford University Press.

Cummings, E. M., Schermerhorn, A. C., Keller, P. S., & Davies, P. T. (2008). Parental depressive symptoms, children's representations of family relationships, and child adjustment. *Social Development, 17,* 278–305.

Davies, P. T., Sturge-Apple, M. L., Winter, M. A., Cummings, M. E., & Farrell, D. (2006). Child adaptational development in contexts of interparental conflict over time. *Child Development, 77,* 218–233.

Davies, P. T., Woitach, M. J., Winter, M. A., & Cummings, E. (2008). Children's insecure representations of the interparental relationship and their school adjustment: The mediating role of attention difficulties. *Child Development, 79*(5), 1570–1582.

Du Rocher Schudlich, T. D., Shamir, H., & Cummings, E. M. (2004). Marital conflict, children's representations of family relationships, and children's dispositions towards peer conflict strategies. *Social Development, 13,* 171–192.

Dubois-Comtois, K., Cyr, C., & Moss, E. (2011). Attachment behavior and mother–child conversations as predictors of attachment representations in middle childhood: A longitudinal study. *Attachment & Human Development, 13*(4), 335–357.

Dubois-Comtois, K., & Moss, H. (2008). Beyond the dyad: Do family interactions influence children's attachment representations in middle childhood? *Attachment & Human Development, 10*(4), 415–431.

Emde, R. N. (2003). Early narratives: A window to the child's inner world. In R. Emde, D. P. Wolf, & D. Oppenheim (Eds.), *Revealing the inner worlds of young children: The MacArthur Story Stem Battery and parent–child narratives* (pp. 3–26). New York, NY: Oxford University Press.

Emde, R.N. (2007). Engaging imagination and the future: Frontiers for clinical work. *Attachment & Human Development, 9*(3), 295–302.

Emde, R. N., Plomin, R., Robinson, J., Corley, R., DeFries, J., Fulker, D. W., Reznick, J. S., Campos, J., Kagan, J., & Zahn-Waxler, C. (1992). Temperament, emotion, and cognition at fourteen months: The MacArthur longitudinal twin study. *Child Development, 63*(6), 143–1455.

Erikson, E. H. (1950). *Childhood and society.* New York, NY: Norton.

Etzion-Carasso, A., & Oppenheim, D. (2000). Open mother–preschooler communication: Relations with early secure attachment. *Attachment & Human Development, 2*, 347–370.

Fiese, B. H., & Sameroff, A. J. (1999). The family narrative consortium: A multidimensional approach to narratives. *Monographs of the Society for Research in Child Development, 64*(2, Serial No. 257), 1–34.

Freud, A. (1928). Introduction to the technic of child analysis. *Nervous and Mental Disease Monograph series, 48.*

Futh, A., O'Connor, T. G., Matias, C., Green, J., & Scott, S. (2008). Attachment narratives and behavioral and emotional symptoms in an ethnically diverse, at-risk sample. *American Academy of Child and Adolescent Psychiatry, 47*(6), 709–718.

George, C., Kaplan, N., & Main, M. (1985). *An adult attachment interview: Interview protocol.* Unpublished manuscript, University of California, Berkeley, Department of Psychology.

Gloger-Tippelt, G., Gomille, B., Koenig, L., & Vetter, J. (2002). Attachment representations in 6-year-olds: Related longitudinally to the quality of attachment in infancy and mothers' attachment representations. *Attachment & Human Development, 4*(3), 318–339.

Gloger-Tippelt, G., & Koenig, L. (2007). Attachment representations in 6-year-old children from one and two parent families in Germany. *School Psychology International, 28*, 313–330.

Goldwyn, R., Stanley, C., Smith, V., & Green, J. (2000). The Manchester child attachment story task: Relationship with parental AAI, AST and child behaviour. *Attachment & Human Development, 2*(1), 71–84.

Goodman, G., Aber, J. L., Berlin, L., & Brooks-Gunn, J. (1998). The relations between maternal behaviors and urban preschool children's internal working models of attachment security. *Infant Mental Health Journal, 19*(4), 378–393.

Granot, D., & Mayseless, O. (2001). Attachment security and adjustment to school in middle childhood. *International Journal of Behavioural Development, 25*(6), 530–541.

Green, J., Stanley, C., & Peters, S. (2007). Disorganized attachment and atypical parenting in young school age children with externalizing disorder. *Attachment & Human Development, 9*(3), 207–222.

Green, J., Stanley, C., Smith, V., & Goldwyn, R. (2000). A new method of evaluating attachment representations in young school-age children: The Manchester child attachment story task. *Attachment & Human Development, 2*(1), 48–70.

Grych, J. H., Wachsmuth-Schlaefer, T., & Klockow, L. L. (2002). Interparental aggression and young children's representations of family relationships. *Journal of Family Psychology, 16*(3), 259–272.

Hesse, E. (2008).The Adult Attachment Interview: Protocol, method of analysis, and empirical studies. In J. Cassidy & P. R. Shaver (Eds.), *Handbook of attachment: Theory, research, and clinical applications* (2nd ed., pp. 552–598). New York, NY: Guilford Press.

Hill, J., Fonagy, P., Lancaster, G., & Broyden, N. (2007). Aggression and intentionality in narrative responses to conflict and distress story stems: An investigation of boys with disruptive behaviour problems. *Attachment & Human Development, 9*(3), 223–237.

Hodges, J., Steele, M., Hillman, S., & Henderson, K. (2003a). Mental representations and defenses in severely maltreated children: A Story Stem Battery and Rating System for clinical assessment and research applications. In R. N. Emde, D. P. Wolf & D. Oppenheim (Eds.), *Revealing the inner worlds of young children: The MacArthur Story Stem Battery and parent–child narratives* (pp. 240–267). New York, NY: Oxford University Press.

Hodges, J., Steele, M., Hillman, S., Henderson, K., & Kaniuk, J. (2003b). Changes in attachment representations over the first year of adoptive placement: Narratives of maltreated children. *Clinical Child Psychology and Psychiatry, 8*(3), 351–368.

Hodges, J., Steele, M., Hillman, S., Henderson, K., & Kaniuk, J. (2005). Change and continuity in mental representations of attachment after adoption. In D. M. Brodzinsky & J. Palacios (Eds.), *Psychological issues in adoption: Research and practice* (pp. 93–116). Westport, CT: Praeger.

Hodges, J., Steele, M., Kaniuk, J., Hillman, S., & Asquith, K. (2009). Narratives in assessment and research on the developments in maltreated children. In N. Midgley, J. Anderson, E. Grainger, T. Nesic-Vuckovic, & C. Urwin (Eds.), *Child psychotherapy and research: New approaches, emerging findings* (pp. 200–213). New York, NY: Routledge.

Hoffman, K. T., Marvin, R. S., Cooper, G., & Powell, B. (2006). Changing toddlers' and preschoolers' attachment classifications: The circle of security intervention. *Journal of Consulting and Clinical Psychology, 74*(6), 1017–1026.

Howes, C., Vu, J.A., & Hamilton, C. (2011). Mother-child attachment representation and relationships over time in Mexican-heritage families. *Journal of research in childhood Education, 25*, 228–247.

Hubbs-Tait, L., Hughes, K. P., McDonald Culp, A., Osofsky, J. D., Hann, D. M., Eberhart Wright, A., & Ware, L. M. (1996). Children of adolescent mothers: Attachment representation, maternal depression, and later behavior problems. *American Journal of Orthopsychiatry, 66*, 416–426.

Hutchison, A. K., Beresford, C., Robinson, J., & Ross, R. G. (2010). Assessing disordered thoughts in preschoolers with dysregulated mood. *Child Psychiatry & Human Development, 41*, 479–489.

Katsurada, E. (2007). Attachment representation of institutionalized children in Japan. *School Psychology International, 28*(3), 331–345.

Kerns, K. A., Abraham, A. A., Schlegelmilch, A., & Morgan, T. (2007). Mother-child attachment in later middle childhood: Assessment approaches and associations with mood and emotion regulation. *Attachment & Human Development, 9*, 33–53.

Kerns, K. A., Aspelmeier, J. E., Gentzler, A. L., & Grabill, C. (2001). Parent–child attachment and monitoring in middle childhood. *Journal of Family Psychology, 15*, 69–81.

Kerns, K .A., Brumariu, L. E., & Seibert, A. (2011). Multi-method assessment of mother–child attachment: Links to parenting and child depressive symptoms in middle childhood. *Attachment & Human Development, 13*(4), 315–333.

Kerns, K. A., Klepac, L., & Cole, A. K. (1996). Peer relationships and pre-adolescents' perceptions of security in the child–mother relationship. *Developmental Psychology, 32*, 457–466.

Koren-Karie, N., Oppenheim, D., Haimovich, Z., & Etzion-Carasso, A. (2003). Dialogues of seven-year-olds with their mothers about emotional events: Development of a typology. In R. N. Emde, D. Wolf, & D. Oppenhiem (Eds.), *Revealing the inner worlds of young children: The MacArthur Story Stem Battery and parent–child narratives* (pp. 355–387). New York, NY: Oxford University Press.

Laible, D. (2006). Maternal emotional expressiveness and attachment security: Links to representations of relationships and social behavior. *Merrill-Palmer Quarterly, 54*, 645–670.

Laible, D. (2011). Does it matter if preschool children and mothers discuss positive vs. negative events during reminiscing? Links with mother-reported attachment, family emotional climate, and socioemotional development. *Social Development, 20*(2), 394–411.

Laible, D., Carlo, G., Torquati, J., & Ontai, L. (2004). Children's perceptions of family relationships as assessed in a doll story completion task: Links to parenting, social competence, and externalizing behavior. *Social Development, 13*(4), 551–569.

Laible, D., & Thompson, R. (2002). Early parent–child conflict: Lessons in emotion, morality, and relationships. *Child Development, 73*, 1187–1203.

Levin, H., & Wardwell, E. (1962). The research uses of doll-play. *Psychological Bulletin, 59*, 27–56.

Luby, J., Beiden, A., Sullivan, J., Hayen, R., McCadney, A., & Spitznagel, E. (2009). Shame and guilt in preschool depression: evidence for elevations in self-conscious emotions in depression as early as age 3. *Journal of Child of Psychology and Psychiatry, 50*, 1156–1166.

Lynn, D. B., & Lynn, R. (1959). The Structured Doll Play Test as a projective technique for use with children. *Journal of Projective Techniques, 23*, 335–344.

Macfie, J., Cicchetti, D., & Toth, S. L. (2001). The development of dissociation in maltreated preschool-aged children. *Development and Psychopathology, 13*, 233–254.

Macfie, J., & Swan, S. A. (2009). Representations of the caregiver-child relationships and of the self, and emotion regulation in the narratives of young children whose mothers have borderline personality disorder. *Development and Psychopathology, 21*, 993–1011.

Macfie, J., Toth, S. L., Rogosch, F. A., Robinson, J., Emde, R. N., & Cicchetti, D. (1999). Effect of maltreatment on preschoolers' narrative representations of

responses to relieve distress and of role reversal. *Developmental Psychology, 35,* 461–465.
Main, M., & Cassidy, J. (1988). Categories of response to reunion with the parent at age six: Predictable from infant attachment classifications and stable over a 1-month period. *Developmental Psychology, 24,* 415–526.
Main, M., & Goldwyn, R. (1985). *Adult attachment classification system.* Unpublished manuscript, University of California, Berkeley.
Main, M., Kaplan, N., & Cassidy, J. (1985). Security in infancy, childhood, and adulthood: A move to the level of representation. *Monograph of the Society for Research in Child Development, 50*(1–2), 66–104.
McHale, J. P. (2007). When infants grow up in multiperson relatioonship system. *Infant Mental Health Journal, 28,* 370–392.
McHale, J. P., Neugebauer, A., Radin Asch, A., & Schwartz, A. (1999). Preschoolers' characterizations of multiple family relationships during family doll play. *Journal of Clinical Child Psychology, 28,* 256–268.
Miljkovitch, R., Pierrehumbert, B., Bretherton, I., & Halfon, O. (2004). Associations between parental and child attachment representations. *Attachment & Human Development, 6,* 305–325.
Miljkovitch, R., Pierrehumbert, B., & Halfon, O. (2007). Three-year-olds' play narratives and their associations with internalizing problems. *Clinical Psychology and Psychotherapy, 14,* 249–257.
Minnis, H., Millward, R., Sinclair, C., Kennedy, E., Greig, A., Towlson, K., Read W, & Hill, J. (2006). The Computerized MacArthur Story Stem Battery—A pilot study of a novel medium for assessing children's representations of relationships. *International Journal of Methods in Psychiatric Research, 15*(4), 207–214.
Minuchin P. (1985). Families and individual development: provocations from the field of family therapy. *Child Development, 56,* 289–302.
Minze, L., McDonald, R., Rosentraub, E., & Jouriles, E. (2010). Making sense of family conflict: Intimate partner violence and preschoolers' externalizing problems. *Journal of Family Psychology, 24*(1), 5–11.
Moss, E., Bureau, J. F., Béliveau, M. J., Zdebik, M., & Lépine, S. (2009). Links between children's attachment behavior at early school-age, their attachment-related representations, and behavior problems in middle childhood. *International Journal of Behavioral Development, 33*(2), 155–166.
Moss, E., Rousseau, D., Parent, S., St-Laurent, D., & Saintonge, J. (1998). Correlates of attachment at school-age: Maternal-reported stress, mother–child interaction and behavior problems. *Child Development, 69,* 1390–1405.
Murray, L. (2007). Future directions for doll play narrative research: A commentary. *Attachment & Human Development, 9*(3), 287–293.
Murry, L., Arteche, A., Bingley, C., Hentges, F., Bishop, D. V. M., Dalton, L., Goodacre, T., Hill, J., & the Cleft Lip and Palate Study team (2010). The effect of cleft lip on socio-emotional functioning in school-aged children. *Journal of Child Psychology and Psychiatry, 51*(1), pp 94–103.
Murray, L., Woolgar, M., Briers, S., & Hipwell, A. (1999). Children's social representations in dolls' house play and theory of mind tasks, and their relation to family adversity and child disturbance. *Social Development, 8,* 179–200.

Olds, D. L., Kitzman, H., Cole, R., Robinson, J., Sidora, K., Luckey, D. W., Henderson, C. R., Hanks C, Bondy J., & Holmberg, J. (2004). Effects of nurse home-visiting on maternal life course and child development: Age 6 follow-up results of a randomized trial. *Pediatrics, 114*, 1550–1559.

Oppenheim, D. (1997). The attachment doll play interview for preschoolers. *International Journal of Behavioral Development, 20*, 681—697.

Oppenheim, D. (2003). Children's Emotional Resolution of MSSB Narratives: Relations with child behavior problems and parental psychological distress. In R. Emde, D. P. Wolf, & D. Oppenheim (Eds.), *Revealing the inner worlds of young children: The MacArthur Story Stem Battery and parent–child narratives* (pp. 147–162). New York, NY: Oxford University Press.

Oppenheim, D. (2006). Child, parent, and parent–child emotion narratives: Implications for developmental psychopathology. *Development and Psychopathology, 18*, 771–790.

Oppenheim, D., Emde, R. N., & Wamboldt, F. S. (1996). Associations between 3-year-olds' narrative co-constructions with mothers and fathers and their story completions about affective themes. *Early Development and Parenting, 5*(3), 149–160.

Oppenheim, D., Emde, R. N., & Warren, S. (1997a). Children's narrative representations of mothers: Their development and associations with child and mother adaptation. *Child Development, 68*, 127–138.

Oppenheim, D., Goldsmith, D., & Koren-Karie, N. (2004). Maternal Insightfulness and preschoolers' emotion and behavior problems: Reciprocal influences in a therapeutic preschool program. *Infant Mental Health Journal, 25*, 352–367.

Oppenheim, D., & Koren-Karie, N. (2009). Mother-Child emotion dialogues: A window into the psychological secure base. In J. A. Quas, & R. Fivush (Eds.), *Emotion and memory in development: Biological, cognitive, and social considerations* (pp. 142–165). Oxford: University Press.

Oppenheim, D., Nir, A., Warren, S., & Emde, R. (1997b). Emotion regulation in mother-child narrative co-construction: Associations with children's narratives and adaptation. *Developmental Psychology, 33*(2), 284–294.

Oppenheim, D., & Waters, H. S. (1995). Narrative processes and attachment representations: Issues of development and assessment. *Monographs of the Society for Research in Child Development, 60* (2–3, Serial No. 244), 197–215.

Page, T. (2001). The social meaning of children's narratives: A review of the Attachment based Narrative Story Stem technique. *Child and Adolescent Social Work Journal, 18*(3), 171–187.

Page, T., Boris, N. W., Heller, S., Robinson, L., Hawkins, S., & Norwood, R. (2011). Narrative story stems with high risk six year-olds: Differential associations with mother- and teacher reported psycho-social adjustment. *Attachment & Human Development, 13*(4), 359–380.

Page, T., & Bretherton, I. (2001). Mother– and father–child attachment themes in the story completions of preschoolers from post-divorce families: Do they predict relationships with peers and teachers? *Attachment & Human Development, 3*, 1–29.

Poehlmann, J. (2005). Representations of attachment relationships in children of incarcerated mothers. *Child Development, 76*, 679–696.

Robinson, J. (2007). Story stem narratives with young children: Moving to clinical research and practice. *Attachment & Human Development, 9*(3), 179–185.

Robinson, J. (2011, April). *Maternal prenatal substance use: Long term associations with empathy and behavior problems at age 6 years.* Poster presented at the biennial meeting of the Society for Research in Child Development, Montreal, Quebec, Canada.

Robinson, J., Herot, C., Haynes, P., & Mantz-Simmons, L. (2000). Children's story stem responses: A measure of program impact on developmental risks associated with dysfunctional parenting. *Child Abuse and Neglect, 24*, 99–110.

Robinson, J., & Mantz-Simmons, L. (2003). The Mac-Arthur Narrative coding system: One approach to highlighting affective meaning making in the MacArthur Story Stem Battery. In R. N. Emde, D. P. Wolf, & D. Oppenheim (Eds.), *Revealing the inner worlds of young children: The MacArthur Story Stem Battery and parent–child narratives* (pp. 81–91). New York, NY: Oxford University Press.

Robinson, J., Mantz-Simmons, L., MacFie, J., Kelsay, K., Holmberg, J., & the MacArthur Narrative Working Group. (2007). *MacArthur Narrative Coding Manual.* Unpublished manuscript.

Román, M., & Palacio, J. (2012). Attachment representations in internationally adopted children. *Attachment and Human Development, 14*(6), 585–600.

Schechter, D. S., Zygmunt, A., Coates S. W., Davies, M., Trabka, K. A., McCaw, J., . . . Robinson, J. L. (2007). Caregiver traumatization adversely impacts young children's mental representations on the MacArthur Story Stem Battery. *Attachment & Human Development, 9(3)*, 187–206.

Schermerhorn, A. C., Cummings, E. M., & Davies, P. (2005) Children's perceived agency in the context of marital conflict: Relations with marital conflict over time. *Merrill-Palmer Quarterly, 51*(2), 121–144.

Sears, R. R. (1947). Influence of methodological factors on doll play performance. *Child Development, 18*, 190–197.

Shamir, H., Du Rocher-Schudlich, T., & Cummings, E. M. (2001). Marital conflict, parenting styles, and children's representations of family relationships. *Parenting, 1*(1), 123–151.

Sher-Censor, E., Grey, I., & Yates, T. M. (2013). The intergenerational congruence of mothers' and preschoolers' narrative affective content and narrative coherence. *International Journal of Behavioral Development, 37*(4), 340–348.

Sher-Censor, E., & Oppenheim, D. (2004). Coherence and representations in preschoolers' narratives: Associations with attachment in infancy. In M. W. Pratt & B. H. Fiese (Eds.), *Family stories and the life course* (pp. 77–108). Mahwah, NJ: Erlbaum.

Shields, A., Ryan, R. M., & Cicchetti, D. (2001). Narrative representations of caregivers and emotion dysregulation as predictors of maltreated children's rejection by peers. *Developmental Psychology, 37*, 321–337.

Smeekens, S., Riksen-Walraven, J. M., & van Bakel, H. J. A. (2009). The predictive value of different infant attachment measures for socioemotional development at age 5 years. *Infant Mental Health Journal, 30*, 366–383.

Solomon, J., George, C., & De Jong, A. (1995). Children classified as controlling at age six: Evidence of disorganized representational strategies and aggression at home and at school. *Development and Psychopathology, 7*, 447–463.

Spagnola, M., & Fiese, B. H. (2010). Preschoolers with asthma: Narratives of family functioning predict behavior problems. *Family Process, 49,* 74–91.

Splaun, A. K., Steele, M., Steele, H., Reiner, I., & Murphy, A. (2010). The congruence of mothers' and their children's representations of their relationship. *The New School Psychology Bulletin, 7*(1), 51–61.

Stacks, A. M. (2007). Behavior narratives and its relation to attachment classification and externalizing defensive dysregulation in preschool children's attachment story. *School Psychology International, 28,* 294–312.

Stadelmann, S., Perren, S., Groeben, M., & von Klitzing, K. (2010). Parental separation and children's behavioral/emotional problems: The impact of parental representations and family conflict. *Family process, 49,* 92–108.

Stadelmann, S., Perren, S., Von Wyl, A., & Von Klitzing, K. (2007). Associations between family relationships and symptoms/strengths at kindergarten age: What is the role of children's parental representations? *Journal of Child Psychology and Psychiatry, 48,* 996–1004.

Steele, M., Hodges, J., Kaniuk, J., Hillman, S., & Henderson, K. (2003a). Attachment representations and adoption: Associations between maternal states of mind and emotion narratives in previously maltreated children. *Journal of Child Psychotherapy, 29,* 187–205.

Steele, M., Steele, H., Woolgar, M., Yabsley, S., Fonagy, P., Johnson, D., & Croft, C. (2003b). An attachment perspective on children's emotion narratives: Links across generations. In R. N. Emde, D. P. Wolf, D. Oppenheim, & D. Wolf (Eds.), *Revealing the inner worlds of young children: The MacArthur Story Stem Battery and parent–child narratives* (pp. 163–181). New York, NY: Oxford University Press.

Stover, C. S., Van Horn, P., & Lieberman, A. F. (2006). Parental representations in the play of preschool aged witnesses of marital violence. *Journal of Family Violence, 21*(6), 417–424.

Stronach, E. P., Toth, S. L., Rogosch, F., Oshri, A., Manly, J. D., & Cicchetti, D. (2011). Child maltreatment, attachment security, and internal representations of mother and mother–child relationships. *Child Maltreatment, 16,* 137–145.

Toth, S. L., Cicchetti, D., Macfie, J., & Emde, R. N. (1997). Representations of self and other in the narratives of neglected, physically abused, and sexually abused preschoolers. *Development and Psychopathology, 9,* 781–796.

Toth, S. L., Cicchetti, D., Macfie, J., Maughan, A., & Vanmeenen, K. (2000a). Narrative representations of caregivers and self in maltreated pre-schoolers. *Attachment & Human Development, 2,* 271–305.

Toth, S. L., Cicchetti, D., Macfie, J., Rogosch, F. A., & Maughan, A. (2000b). Narrative representations of moral-affiliative and conflictual themes and behavioral problems in maltreated preschoolers. *Journal of Clinical Child Psychology, 29,* 307–318.

Toth, S. L., Maughan, A., Manly, J. T., Spagnola, M., & Cicchetti, D. (2002). The relative efficacy of two interventions in altering maltreated preschool children's representational models: Implications for attachment theory. *Development and Psychopathology, 14,* 877–908.

Toth, S., Rogosch, F., Sturge-Apple, M., & Cicchetti, D. (2009). Maternal depression, children's attachment security, and representational development: An organizational perspective. *Child Development, 80,* 192–208.

Venet, M., Bureau, J. F., Gosselin, C., & Capuano, F. (2007). Attachment representations in a sample of neglected preschool-age children. *School Psychology International, 28*(3), 264–293.

Verschueren, K., & Marcoen, A. (1999). Representation of self and social emotional competence in kindergartners: Differential and combined effects of attachment to mother and to father. *Child Development, 70,* 183–201.

Verschueren, K., Marcoen, A., & Schoefs, V. (1996). The internal working model of self, attachment, and competence in five-year-olds. *Child Development, 67,* 2493–2511.

von Klitzing, K., & Bürgin, D. (2005). Parental capacities for triadic relationships during pregnancy: Early predictors of children's behavioral and representational functioning at preschool age. *Infant Mental Health Journal, 26*(1), 19–39.

von Klitzing, K., Kelsay, K., Emde, R. N., Robinson, J., & Schmitz, S. (2000). Gender-specific characteristics of 5-year-olds' play narratives and associations with behavior ratings. *Journal of the American Academy of Child and Adolescent Psychiatry, 39,* 1017–1023.

von Klitzing, K., Stadelmann, S., & Perren, S. (2007). Story stem narratives of clinical and normal kindergarten children: Are content and performance associated with children's social competence? *Attachment and Human Development, 9*(3), 271–286.Vorria, P., Papaligoura, Z., Sarafidou, J., Kopakaki, M., Dunn, J., van IJzendoorn, M. H., & Kontopoulou, A. (2006). The development of adopted children after institutional care: A follow-up study. *Journal of Child Psychology and Psychiatry, 47*(12), 1246–1253.

Waelder, R. (1933). The psychoanalytic theory of play. *Psychoanalytic Quarterly, 2,* 208–224.

Waters, E., & Cummings, E. M. (2000). A secure base from which to explore relationships. *Child Development, 71,* 164–172.

Waters, E., & Deane, K. (1985). Defining and assessing individual difference in attachment relations: Q-methodology and the organization of behavior in infancy and early childhood. *Monographs of the Society for Research in Child Development, 50*(1–2, Serial No. 209), 41–65.

Wai-Wan, M., & Green, J. (2010). Negative and atypical story content themes depicted by children with behavior problems. *Journal of Child Psychology and Psychiatry, 51*(10), 1125–1131.

Waldinger, R. J., Toth, S. L., & Gerber, A. (2001). Maltreatment and internal representations of relationships: Core relationship themes in the narratives of abused and neglected preschoolers. *Social Development, 10*(10), 41–58.

Warren, S. L. (2003). Narratives in risk and clinical populations. In R. Emde, D. P. Wolf, & D. Oppenheim (Eds.), *Revealing the inner worlds of young children: The MacArthur Story Stem Battery and parent–child narratives* (pp. 222–239). New York, NY: Oxford University Press.

Warren, S. L., Emde, R. N., & Sroufe, L. A. (2000). Internal representations: Predicting anxiety from children's play narratives. *Journal of the American Academy of Child and Adolescent Psychiatry, 39,* 100–107.

Warren, S. L., Oppenheim, D., & Emde, R. N. (1996). Can emotions and themes in children's play predict behavior problems? *Journal of the American Academy of Child and Adolescent Psychiatry, 34*, 1331–1337.

Winnicott, D. W. (1958). *Collected papers: Through paediatrics to psycho-analysis.* New York, NY: Basic Books.

Wong, M., Bost, K. K., Shin, N., Veríssomo, M., Maia, J., Monteiro, L., ... Vaughn, B. E. (2011). Preschool children's mental representations of attachment: antecedents in their secure base behaviors and maternal attachment scripts. *Attachment & Human Development, 13*(5), 489–502.

Woolgar, M., & Murray, L. (2010). The representation of fathers by children of depressed mothers: Refining the meaning of parentification in high-risk samples. *Journal of Child Psychology and Psychiatry, 51*(5), 621–629.

Woolgar, M., Steele, H., Steele, M., Yabsley, S., & Fonagy, P. (2001). Children's play narrative responses to hypothetical dilemmas and their awareness of moral emotions. *British Journal of Developmental Psychology, 19*, 115–128.

Yoo, Y. S., Adamsons, K. L., Robinson, J. L., & Sabatelli, R. M. (2013). Longitudinal influence of paternal distress on children's representations of fathers, family cohesion, and family conflict. *Journal of Child and Family Studies*, 1-17. doi: 10.1007/s10826-013-9870-7

Zahn-Waxler, C., Cole, P. M., Richardson, D. T., Friedman, R. J., Michel, M. K., & Belouad, F. (1994). Social problem solving in disruptive preschool children: Reactions to hypothetical situations of conflict and distress. *Merrill Palmer Quarterly, 40*, 98–119.

CHAPTER 11

USING MIXED METHODS IN RESEARCH WITH YOUNG CHILDREN ACROSS CULTURES AND CONTEXTS

Linda Liebenberg and Michael Ungar

INTRODUCTION

The past two decades have seen an ever increasing discourse arguing for a more decentered understanding of children that incorporates multiple perspectives, greater focus on the views and experiences of children themselves, and greater inclusion of cultural and contextual variation in the groups we study (Grover, 2004; Hill, 2006; James & Prout, 1990; Luthar, 1999; Ungar, 2011). Researchers and practitioners are more aware than ever that what is experienced as a risk or is traumatic in one environment may be experienced quite differently in another (Tedeschi & Calhoun, 1996; Wong & Wong, 2006). Likewise, how resources build individual and collective capacity is very different depending on the context in which they function (Johnson-Powell & Yamamoto, 1997; Ungar, Brown, Liebenberg, Othman, Kwong, Armstrong, & Gilgun, 2007). Without research designs that allow for multiple perspectives of healthy development, risks and resources, our findings will remain culturally biased, reflecting the dominant theories of child development that have been built from the experiences of a small percentage of the world's children (Grover, 2004; Christensen, 2004). It is becoming increasingly apparent that we need to more accurately document person-environment interactions, negotiate with marginalized populations what their experiences mean to them (is their behavior adaptive or maladaptive?), and develop interventions that are effective locally (Masten & Powell, 2003; Liebenberg & Ungar, 2009; Ungar, 2011). Nicotera (2008), for example, discusses critically the need for better understanding of the processes at play in the lives of children with regards to the impact of neighborhoods. She points to the continuing practice of using census or administrative data in studies of children and neighborhoods that are unable to account for context specific processes that are not measured through surveys. Similarly, Jones and Sumner (2009) critique the emphasis placed on epidemiological data in child development studies, arguing that such an approach fails to account for the complexity of children's experiences with regards to both risk and well-being. Simultaneously though, we are reminded of the need for large scale quantitative studies that can situate children's experiences within larger socio-economic and political realities (Bradford Brown, Larson, & Saraswathi, 2002; Hood, Kelley, & Mayall, 1996). It is for these reasons that while critiquing the pervasive use of epidemiological and census-type data, authors such as Nicotera (2008) and Jones and Sumner (2009) advocate the use of mixed methods in research with children.

Much of our own work explores the use of available qualitative and quantitative research tools and methods in ways that best access the experiences of culturally marginalized children and youth, while simultaneously achieving rigorous, valid and reliable data sets (Liebenberg, 2009; Liebenberg, Ungar, & Theron, in press; Ungar & Liebenberg, 2005; 2011). As resilience researchers we are constantly challenged to find ways of understanding how young people facing persistent risks in their lives navigate through these obstacles and make use of the resources that facilitate their well-being (Ungar, 2005; 2011). Our focus requires an exploration of the experiences of young people themselves, while at the same time understanding the relational and cultural contexts in which they find themselves. Lack of homogeneity amongst children as a group compounds the complexity of this task. The multiple factors impacting the experiences of children, including but not limited to culture, internal family dynamics, and socioeconomic positioning of the family, need to be accounted for in child development research. Given this complexity, understanding the nuances in the similarities and differences across contexts and cultures is an imperative of our work as researchers and informs our approach to research design.

As part of our efforts to address these concerns, we have made extensive use of mixed methods. Indeed, the call for greater attention to the nuanced experiences of marginalized populations appears consistently accompanied by the promotion of a mixed methods design (Mason, 2006; Onwuegbuzie & Leech, 2005). Drawing on Tashakkori and Creswell's (2007) definition of mixed methods research, as well as Merten's (2003) transformative-emancipatory approach, we have woven together iterative stages of qualitative and quantitative data gathering that support the exploration of emic (heterogeneous, indigenous) and etic (homogeneous) understandings of risk and resilience (Tweed & DeLongis, 2006). By doing this, we have been successful in uncovering unnamed processes and better understanding those processes previously identified and named.

Numerous authors have highlighted the value of using a mixed methods approach in research. These benefits include: drawing on the strengths of both qualitative and quantitative methods, each approach compensating for the limitations of the other (Creswell, Plano Clark, Gutmann, & Hanson, 2003); strengthening reliability, validity and generalizability of data through increased trustworthiness and authenticity of research process (Barton, 2005); and more holistic and stronger results stemming from research (Johnson & Onwuegbuzie, 2004) that integrate perspectives of a phenomenon at varying conceptual levels (Todd, Nerlich, & McKeown, 2004). Jones and Sumner (2009) explain, however, that while existing labels attached to mixed methods "might suggest that mixed methods simply entails taking a quantitative method and adding a qualitative method, giving equal weight to each.... there are numerous possible combinations, each with assumptions regarding the respective roles, relative importance and desired sequencing of qualitative and quantitative approaches" (p. 35). Their comment highlights the careful consideration that should be given to the ways in which methods available to researchers are integrated—and the missed opportunities when we default to research designs that ignore both emic and etic perspectives.

This chapter reviews the case for iterative mixed methods design in research with children, describing the process used by researchers at the Resilience Research Centre during the development of the Child and Youth Resilience Measure (CYRM-28). We then explore in detail a second key feature of the approach we have used: the integration of multiple perspectives during all stages of the research project, with specific focus on the integration of children's own understandings of resilience. We use primarily examples from a study that used both the CYRM-28 and qualitative methods, the International Resilience Project (IRP), to illustrate our argument. We will also weave in examples from other research where necessary to expand on the options available to researchers, commenting on their adaptation for use with younger children, specifically those aged four to eight years old. Only those aspects of the IRP that relate to the current discussion are included. More detailed information of the study can be found elsewhere (Ungar & Liebenberg, 2005, 2011).

HOW AND WHEN TO USE AN ITERATIVE MIXED METHODS APPROACH

Many researchers in the field of child and youth resilience and health outcomes have promoted the use of "multiple" methods as means of ensuring veracity of findings (Glantz & Sloboda, 1999; Luthar, 1999) though the qualitative and quantitative portions of the research tend to stand apart from each other. Less attention has been given to the use of mixed methods in an iterative manner to inform research design as studies progress. An iterative approach to mixed methods means that each stage of the research can inform the next.

Initial research phases, for example, can include a review of existing quantitative data bases (such as epidemiological, census or administrative data) to appraise the prevalence of an issue within and across population groups. Simultaneously, qualitative integration of local perspectives on the problem under study elucidates indigenous concerns and understandings regarding the issue. Collectively, this information underscores the need for the research to occur on micro and macro levels simultaneously, as well as highlights local relevance of the issue, furthering contextualization. Such an approach means that consecutive research phases are well established, an authentic account of the participants' experiences is established, and trustworthiness of the resulting findings is improved (Lincoln & Guba, 1985). Building on this understanding of mixed methods approaches and the ensuing benefits, we have argued elsewhere that the use of mixed methods can help address concerns related to the internal validity and generalizability of the resilience construct (Ungar & Liebenberg, 2011).

Use of a mixed methods approach also establishes the opportunity to better inform research design and field relations by obtaining local input on approaches used in the research. While community input can be obtained by establishing local advisory committees (Ungar & Liebenberg, 2005), integration of qualitative approaches in meetings with such committees can help members engage more critically with the concern or question at hand. Certainly, when working with marginalized populations including young children, the use of more creative elicitation techniques, using images or cultural artifacts for example, can be especially beneficial.

Several authors have discussed the importance of obtaining the input of children in the design of research as well (see for example Boyden & Ennew, 1997; Punch, 2002; Scott, 2000). Barker and Weller (2003) have shown that many children experience conventional approaches to research

Using Mixed Methods in Research With Young Children ■ **387**

as intimidating or boring, failing to understand the relevance of the study. They say in particular that "researchers need to be aware that what adults perceive as children friendly and empowering for children may be seen by participants as adult centered and an imposition" (p. 36). A multi-method approach that integrates children's comments on prospective design and content contributes to better buy-in from a greater number of participants.

The model we are proposing here reflects a triangulated design, the purpose of which is to "obtain different but complementary data on the same topic" (Morse, 1991, p. 122) with a view to validating results through a process of comparing and contrasting across actors and data types (Creswell & Plano Clark, 2007). More specifically, an adaptation of the multilevel model is presented (see Figure 11.1). As Creswell and Plano Clark (2007) explain, qualitative and quantitative methods "are used to address different levels

Contextualisation phase

Micro/Local

Exploring
- *Qualitative* -
Identify issues of relevance to local context

⟵⟶

Macro/Global

Explaining
- *Quantitative* -
Explore the prevalence of an issue

Design phase

LAC consultation
*Confirm focus
* Confirm research design
* Identify sample
*Pilot instruments
* Confirm ethical approaches

Research phase

Explaining
- *Qualitative* -
Uncovering processes associated with research focus

Exploring
- *Quantitative* -
Establishing prevalence and patterns of research focus within population

Interpretation and dissemination phase

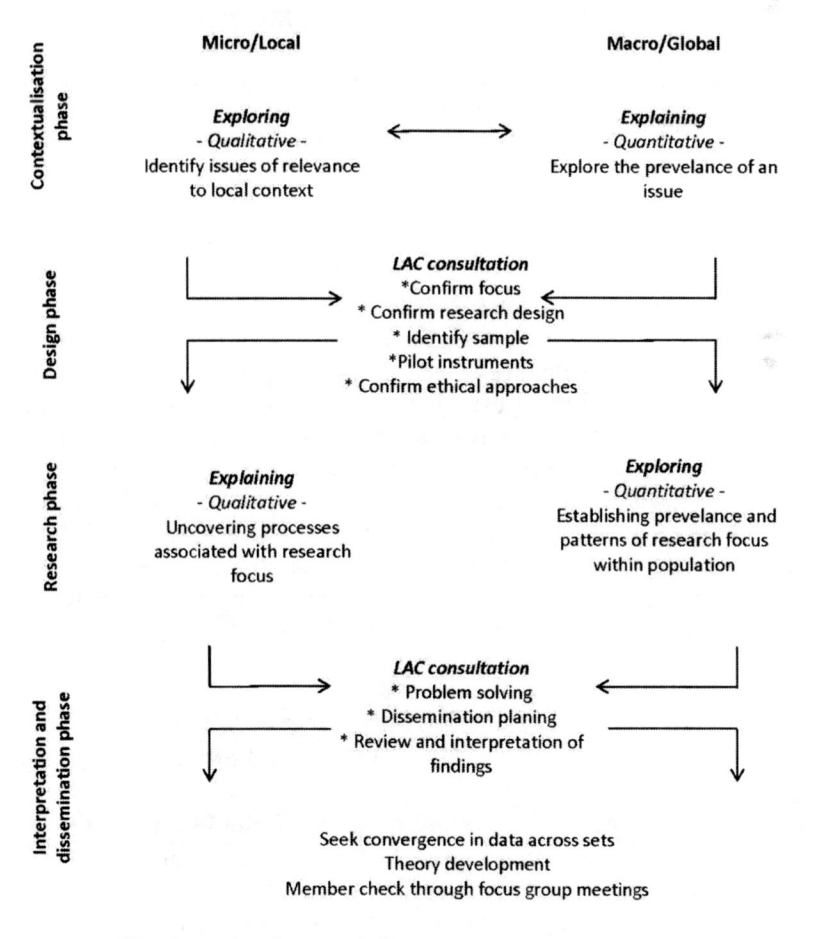

LAC consultation
* Problem solving
* Dissemination planing
* Review and interpretation of findings

Seek convergence in data across sets
Theory development
Member check through focus group meetings

Figure 11.1 The Iterative Research Process.

within a system [and] findings from each level are merged together into one overall interpretation" (p. 65). We propose an adaptation of this approach into one that includes repeated research phases that inform each other iteratively, depending on whether the research team is explaining or exploring the research question. In instances where researchers are exploring a topic or population, qualitative approaches precede the use of quantitative approaches. In this way researchers are able to explore and determine key issues and concerns at a local level that are then integrated into a quantitative phase. Here, themes emerging from the qualitative stage inform review of national and international data bases establishing the prevalence and importance of issues emerging at a local level within a broader context. Once mixed methods approaches have been used to contextualize the research focus and establish the remainder of the research approaches, the process of exploring the research theme in greater depth may integrate a quantitative approach followed by a qualitative approach. This procedure allows research teams to gain an understanding of the prevalence of various issues to a population of youth, as well as patterns surrounding the issue, and then to understand and explain the dynamics of these findings. Alternatively, a process that begins with qualitative investigation of the research focus followed by quantitative approaches allows researchers to possibly identify previously unknown or unconsidered aspects of the research question and then determine the extent to which these aspects can be generalized to a broader or alternative population.

The decisions surrounding the finer details of an iterative research process should be driven by the research question and context. Context includes capacities and expertise of the research team; funding and its implications for staff and analysis resources (such as training and software); the timing and time availability for both data gathering (sequencing); and, analysis of the data (including how findings within the research process will be used to inform subsequent steps). Once strengths and limitations have been identified in relation to the research question, adjustments can be made in relation to how much weight is accorded to each approach (i.e., qualitative and quantitative).

AN ITERATIVE MIXED METHODS EXAMPLE: THE INTERNATIONAL RESILIENCE PROJECT

The following is an account of the International Resilience Project (IRP): a research program aimed at exploring both etic and emic conceptualizations of resilience (Ungar & Liebenberg, 2005). Given the lack of focus on children living outside minority world countries (also referred to as the "West" or "Developed World," where a numerically small group of people extoll a dominant ideology) in the study of resilience preceding the IRP, the goal of the study was to introduce a more cross-cultural understanding of resilience, one that would hold greater relevance to children's experiences in majority world countries (traditionally referred to as the "Third World" or the "Developing World," reflecting conditions experienced by the majority of the world's population). A second goal of the project was to develop a culturally sensitive measure of resilience. Given the study's two goals, a research design had to be used that would account for divergence across research sites and allow for insight into a dynamic construct (Barton, 2005). Simultaneously, the research team's use of an ecological model (Masten, 2001; Rutter, 1987) necessitated integration of at least micro and mezzo level influences on resilience. An iterative mixed methods design seemed best suited to address these considerations.

Mertens (2003) in particular highlights the value of mixed methods approaches in integrating multiple perspectives in research aligning it well with understanding micro and mezzo processes with a view to research that can impact or transform the status quo. Similarly, authors such as Onwuegbuzie, Bustamante, and Nelson (2010) have argued the value of mixed methods approaches for instrument design, particularly when concerns regarding validity across cultures are present.

Recognizing the need for a multiplicity of perspectives the first goal of the IRP was to include numerous research sites with as much heterogeneity between them as possible. As a result, 14 sites in 11 countries on five continents were included in the study. The commonality between all sites was that children included in the study be facing at least three persistent risks to their psychological well-being (e.g., poverty, exposure to violence, the mental illness of a parent).

Inclusion of varied research sites was however insufficient in terms of introducing multiple perspectives. Diversity of perspective and experience had to also filter down into each site in terms of people participating in the study. Because of this, both children and adults were included in the research at each site. Equal numbers of boys and girls were invited to participate. Purposeful selection was used to include young people facing many risks, but considered by their community to be doing well, and an equal number of children considered by their community to not be doing well. This design ensured understanding of those factors that were similar for children within a particular site (i.e., risk), as well as those factors that were divergent (i.e., availability of resources relevant to resilience processes), providing better perspectives on the impact of personal and contextual factors on outcomes for children. Children's perspectives were included through the use of qualitative and quantitative approaches to the research (outlined in greater detail below).

With regards to adults on the advisory committees, variety was also sought in terms of who was invited to participate. The common criterion was that people invited should be seen as having something important to say about the way children grow up in the local community and the risks they face. In this way, adults invited into the study included parents and professionals working with children (such as teachers, social workers, mental health practitioners, and so forth). Adults who themselves were seen as having grown up well in spite of facing significant challenges were also invited to participate in the study. Adults' perspectives were also included in the study through the use of focus group interviews.

Research at each site was led by a local research team and a Local Advisory Committee (LAC). LACs consisted of approximately six people who had something important to say about children in the community where the research was occurring, but who were not participating in the core research itself. Again, these individuals included caregivers, parents, professionals working with children such as teachers, librarians, or program staff, and children themselves.

During the first phase of the study, local research teams at each site gathered information on risks and positive factors through two approaches. First a scan was done of all existing academic and grey literature, together with available local and national statistics. This information was used to develop an understanding of the prevalence of risks and healthy outcomes within the local and national context. This understanding was expanded on through qualitative focus group interviews held with adults regarding the risks children face as well as what healthy outcomes look like within the immediate research site.

The second phase involved inviting children and adults to participate in further focus groups, separately. The many ways in which children thrive when faced with adversity locally were explored. Following the focus group interviews, local research teams analyzed the data to extrapolate themes which were then converted into potential questions for inclusion in a quantitative measure of resilience. Resulting questions were then grouped, again by the local research teams, according to an agreed upon ecological model consisting of individual, relational, contextual, and cultural components of resilience. Following the generation and grouping of questions, LACs reviewed the information and provided recommendations for further refinements in language or addition of new questions. Once local agreement had been reached regarding questions and how they were worded and grouped, questions from all 14 sites were integrated into a single pool of questions. The original grouping of questions by ecological theme was retained, ensuring that the understanding of each question by the local research team was incorporated into the larger group of questions. Questions with similar themes that were common across all sites were then retained for use in a uniform measure of resilience. An instrument which originally consisted of 58 items was returned to each site's LAC for review and comment (for more information on this process see Ungar & Liebenberg, 2005; 2011). The final version of the measure, the Child and Youth Resilience Measure with 28 questions, was the result of this design process (Liebenberg & Ungar, 2011).

Once agreement had been reached on the content of the longer measure it was translated at each site. Even in instances where the local language was English, teams scrutinized the phrasing of each item so as to ensure relevance within the local context. Also, local research teams worked together with LACs to translate items in ways that retained the intended meaning or content of each question, rather than translating the literal meaning of words. Following translation, the measure was piloted with children in the community to obtain their feedback on the questionnaire: Were questions relevant? Were they phrased in a manner that made sense to children? What were the children's opinions on the format of the questionnaire as a whole and the format of the likert-type response options? Should these be numbers or actual words? Was the visual presentation of the response options appealing to children? What revisions would children suggest making to the measure?

At each site, groups of children were then invited to participate in the core data gathering of the study. First, at least 60 children were invited to complete the newly developed quantitative measure. As previously mentioned, purposive sampling was used, and children were ordinarily identified and referred by the LAC. From this large group, a subsample of children was invited to participate in further qualitative data gathering. Again, these children were identified by the LAC who used the same "global" criteria as the group of children in the larger quantitative study (equal numbers of boys and girls, all facing significant risks, some considered to be doing well, and some not). Qualitative interviews explored local definitions and perceptions of risk and health (using a holistic understanding of health); children's understanding of local challenges; strategies and resources children used to manage these challenges; and stories of successful navigation through risk.

The manner in which qualitative data were gathered was site-specific. Local researchers reviewed all available methods, and in collaboration with the LAC, selected those methods that were most culturally and contextually relevant to children locally. Methods selected included standard individual interviews and focus group interviews; group interviews integrating cultural artifacts (such as talking sticks in sharing circles); and visual methods (drawings, collages, photographs, or video). Simultaneously, additional adults were invited to participate in a further qualitative phase of the study, also making use of methods that made most sense locally and focused on the same topics.

Qualitative and quantitative data gathered during this phase of the study was then analyzed simultaneously using modes of analysis that would best highlight local or indigenous experiences, processes and understandings of resilience. Qualitative data was analyzed using a constructionist framework (Charmaz, 2006; Clarke, 2005) and grounded theory analysis (Glasser & Strauss, 1967; Strauss & Corbin, 1990), allowing theory to emerge from the lived experiences of participants themselves. Principal components analysis was used to analyze the quantitative data (DeVellis, 2003; Noar, 2003). As with the qualitative data analysis, this approach to the quantitative data analysis facilitated youth interpretations of individual items to inform the latent structures of the measure, and in doing so, the underlying structure of resilience processes as they are experienced across cultures and contexts.

While many authors use content analysis in their analysis of qualitative data allowing for integration of this data into quantitative analysis (see for example Nicotera, 2008), we chose a process that would allow findings from each data set to either challenge or confirm what was being found in the other data. Rather than integrating quantitative and qualitative data into a single analysis, we compared results from a separate analysis of each. Similarly, we compared findings emerging from the qualitative data of youth, with the findings emerging from the qualitative data of adults. This process proved useful not only in reaffirming emerging findings, but findings from the qualitative data analysis helped make sense of the complexity in factor structures emerging in the quantitative data (see Ungar & Liebenberg, 2011 for further discussion). Findings were then returned to LACs for comment. Only once consensus was reached on findings, were results published. Focus groups were audio-taped ensuring that community comment on the data was retained.

CONTEXTUAL RELEVANCE I: INCLUDING MULTIPLE PERSPECTIVES ON DESIGN AND DATA GATHERING

Meaningful research begins in the design phase of a study. While researchers bring expertise to this process, what they often lack is contextual expertise: what are the day-to-day realities of a particular child population and what do they experience in their particular context or community? Who knows a child best in high-risk contexts can vary greatly. While it may appear most sensible and appropriate, for example, to ask parents of children to complete a questionnaire on their child's play activities, the reality may be that in a particular community, extended family members, or preschool teachers may be a more meaningful source for this information. Similarly, while questionnaires may seem to be an efficient means of gathering data quickly and from a large sample of caregivers, when conducting research in previously un-researched communities, our choice of data collection tool could reinforce cultural and contextual biases of the researchers by reflecting only what community outsiders believe are the important variables to study (like children's play rather than children's work) (Smith, 1999; Liborio & Ungar, 2010). In such instances, qualitative observation may be much better suited to initial phases of research (Karlsson, 2001; Liebenberg, 2009; Young & Barrett, 2001). Even then, however, appropriateness of the chosen approach and research focus should be confirmed as appropriate by members of the community.

The best means of ensuring the appropriateness of the research focus and ensuing design is to engage key informants in the planning of research projects. Inviting relevant adults as well as children themselves into the process will ensure that research is not only much more appropriate to the context, but that it is relevant to the population in question. It is our experience that Local Advisory Committees (LACs) can be extremely valuable in this regard. As mentioned previously, LACs are made up of a small group of individuals, who have something important to say about children in the community where research is taking place, but who are not actively participating in the research study as research participants. LACs should consist of a variety of people who can bring differing perspectives to the research. In the example of the IRP, members were caregivers, parents, people who work with children such as teachers, librarians, or program staff, and children themselves. The key is to ensure mixed perspectives. When working with younger groups of children, it is advisable to run separate focus groups with children, obtaining their input on pre-established research plans rather than asking for their input from the outset. The latter process could place an unnecessary burden on child advisors, asking for their input despite their lack of research knowledge. Ensuring inclusion of all perspectives can be a balancing act, and researchers should be cautious about letting adults speak for children, rather than integrating the information adults provide with the perspectives of children (Greene & Hill, 2005).

Community input through the use of LACs can also increase relevance of the research, ensuring that key issues related to the research questions are focused on. LACs can identify key areas related to the research questions that are perhaps being overlooked and make suggestions about how to include these in the study. LACs can also direct sample selection, ensuring that those members of the community—children or adults—are invited to participate. LACs also comment on questions included in questionnaires and/or interview guides, seeing if items are worded appropriately and if any should be changed or omitted from the instrument in order to fit with the worldviews of people locally. Translation problems and how best to deal with these can also be discussed by LACs; LACs can also provide important feedback regarding the ethics of a research project, too. While it is essential to obtain institutional ethics approval from the research team's own institution, as well as any other required departmental approvals, LACs can ordinarily make important contributions regarding contextual safety and local ethics issues. For example, is it reasonable to expect parental consent in a study? If not, how should this situation be dealt with: whose consent should be obtained and how? Similarly, if participants disclose harm, should this be reported and to whom? Finally, LACs can provide important commentary on findings and ensure that interpretations of the data are contextualised locally as well as advise researchers on how best to disseminate these findings to ensure community uptake. In this last role as knowledge mobilizers, LACs broker broader community participation in the research.

Regular meetings with LACs will allow for community input on issues as they arise in the research. LACs are instrumental in contextualising a study when they help answer the following questions:

- Who should we study?
- What should we ask them?
- What should we look at to learn about the phenomenon in question (for example resilience)?
- What are the biggest challenges children in this community face?
- What are some of the common things that help children cope with the challenges they face?
- What do people in this community think helps children cope with challenges?
- How do we get participants interested in the project?
- Where, when and how should we go about collecting information from people (children and adults) in the community?

Audio recordings of meetings with LACs can be useful later when writing up the study and its findings.

CONTEXTUAL RELEVANCE II: INCORPORATING THE PERSPECTIVES AND VOICE OF CHILDREN IN THE RESEARCH PROCESS

The capacity of young children to participate in and indeed comment on the design of research is often underestimated. For this reason, children are often excluded, and their perceptions and experiences are retold by, and reframed through, the perceptions of the adults around them (Greene & Hill, 2005; Greig, Taylor, & MacKay, 2007; Punch, 2002). Increasing use of creative research techniques such as image-based methods is producing a range of research experiences that testify to the capacity of children as research participants (see for example Cavin, 1994; Clark, 1999; Young & Barrett, 2001). More importantly, these studies highlight the profound ways in which children are able to contribute to our adult perceptions of their experiences, and the important ways these perspectives differ (Dallape, 1996; Karlsson, 2001; Prout, 2001).

More important, perhaps, are those studies that have involved young children as coresearchers which confirm their capacity not only to participate in research, but also to inform research focus and processes. Burke (2008), for example, engaged seven-to-eleven-year-olds as researchers of spaces and places in communities available for play using photo-elicitation methods. While her experience of the core research process mirrors that of other researchers such as Karlsson (2001) and Young and Barrett (2001), it is her experience with participants as coresearchers that is particularly noteworthy. She explains how conversations between herself as adult researcher and the children as co-researchers during initial stages allowed for the establishment of "a collective understanding of the intention of the activity... and... notions of rights, responsibilities and the relationship between research and change" (p. 27). Similarly, Johnson (2008) effectively recruited children as coresearchers in her ethnographic study of school spaces by providing workshops about designing and conducting research for potential participants before the actual study. Through the use of photographs, books and the children's own drawings, she was able to educate children about her intended research and the related methods as well as obtain their input on the research question. Perhaps most valuable is Turtle, McElearney, and Scott's (2010) documentation of how they involved children as consultants to a research program, where children provided feedback on the instruments and procedures used in the study. In that project, children commented on the format and content validity of a proposed questionnaire, devised guidelines for participant safety in a photo elicitation component of the study, and identified and then helped explore key outcomes for the research.

Collectively, the work of these and other researchers demonstrates that young children are capable of active participation in various stages of research programs, including design and data analysis. Drawing on these experiences, and many others like them, researchers can creatively integrate children into pilot projects where relevance and appropriateness of research focus and design can be explored prior to the actual studies themselves. Children can also be included in the review of the findings during and following fieldwork.

Greig, Taylor, and MacKay (2007), in particular, point to the value of qualitative approaches in piloting processes with children and suggest integrating methods that allow the researcher to enter the world of the child, methods with which children will be familiar, such as play with puppets, sand and drawing. Their suggestion echoes that of Freire's (1973) who valued curiosity, action and reflection during pedagogical interventions. These suggestions relate to the more fundamental consideration of ensuring children as participants understand why the research is taking place—its relevance; and that what adults ask of them as participants is manageable given children's own capacities. Greig and colleagues also emphasize the importance of children feeling comfortable with the research process—be it design, consultation or data gathering—and suggest giving participants the opportunity to adjust to the research setting, research tools and fieldworkers (see also Barker & Weller, 2003; Punch, 2002).

Researchers can use these more creative approaches in group work with child advisory committees (CACs) (Coad & Evans, 2008) to explore meaningful ways of explaining the focus and purpose of the research to the sample of children who will be involved in the study as well as identifying meaningful ways of explaining research rights and ensuring participant assent or consent. Researchers can also use these approaches to ensure that data collection methods make sense to children locally, and that these approaches are appealing. CACs can further ensure that questions are worded so as to be understood by participants and that in the case of quantitative data, response options can be understood by children, reducing response bias. In this regard, Greig, Taylor, and MacKay (2007) cite innovative work by MacKay (2006) for getting children aged five to answer Likert-type questions using jam jars to effectively manage social desirability in responses. Similarly, Evans et al. (2007) used innovative game formats to develop reliable and valid measures of environmental attitudes and behaviors of first and second grade students. Finally, through the use of pictures, stories, puppet shows and so forth, findings emerging from data can be relayed to children for comment and member checking as the research progresses.

RELIABILITY AND VALIDITY IN ITERATIVE MIXED METHODS PROCESSES

Reliability and validity of a research study based on a mixed methods approach that integrates multiple perspectives is increased due to greater rigor in both design and process. Richardson and St. Pierre (2005) explain that use of mixed methods results in related yet distinct collections of data that when analyzed provides an opportunity for "crystalisation" rather than triangulation of findings. Data gathered by multiple means will access varying dimensions of the phenomenon in question. Integration of multiple perspectives that are then confirmed in the analysis improves validity of findings and conclusions. As findings emerge from the analysis of one data set, will serve to confirm or challenge findings emerging from an alternative data set, resulting in a rich and complex understanding of the phenomena.

Furthermore, a contextualization phase integrating review of existing quantitative data and localized qualitative voice ensures that appropriate and relevant issues are focused on in the research. Qualitative contextualization processes also ensure that research is conducted in ways that are appropriate to the local context. Data quality is therefore improved because existing constructs and instruments that may not have local relevance are not simply imported, but rather challenged. Finally, embedding opportunities for commentary by participants and the wider community in the research process ensures that multiple perspectives are captured and directly inform both findings and emerging theories. Collectively these improvements in design, data gathering and analysis heighten reliability and validity of research.

CONCLUSION

In this chapter we have described the use of an iterative mixed methods approach when conducting research with children. The argument for the use of mixed methods is driven by the call for a decentered understanding of children that incorporates greater focus on the experiences and perspectives of children themselves. Such an approach is particularly relevant given the heterogeneity of "childhood" and the need to understand the diversity and similarities that exist across cultures and contexts. In this way, iterative mixed methods are particularly well suited for use in studies that focus on cross-cultural issues. The proposed approach is demonstrated in an example of the International Resilience Project, a study of resilience across 14 sites. The discussion of the use of mixed methods is expanded to include consideration of community voice and the voice of children themselves. Community and participant direction of research approaches and processes ensures that dominant theories and conventional research approaches are not simply imported into communities and used in ways that further the marginalization of groups (Denzin & Lincoln, 1998; Smith, 1999). Strategies for achieving this are reviewed. The chapter concludes with an explanation of how an iterative mixed methods approach that integrates community comment on the research process increases reliability and validity of the findings.

While the use of mixed methods research with children that emphasize participation and contextualization deserves greater attention from researchers, this approach certainly has the potential to contribute to a better understanding of the diversity and complexity of their experiences.

In particular, as shown with the IRP, when mixed methods are used in an iterative approach that ensures the approaches used are of relevance to children, the quality of data and subsequent findings are enhanced. Including youth perspectives in data analysis, through the use of member checks, further ensures validity of findings. Key to this process is that the use of mixed methods allows for innovative integration of children into studies as co-researchers, or at the very least as collaborators of the research process. As Turtle, McElearney, and Scott (2010) conclude, "participative research [with children] develops awareness in the research sector of children and young people's perspectives and issues of concern to them, and yields more valid data and research process than might otherwise be the case" (p. 79).

Punch (2002), however, cautions against over simplifying the capacity of children as researchers, encouraging those leading studies to give careful consideration to how children are included. The use of LACs and CACs is particularly important in this regard; integrating children into LACs or CACs, obtaining their perspectives on issues of design in ways that make sense to children, is at least a starting point for effective integration. When done appropriately, and with regard to children's capacities developmentally, the results of the research will be arguably more valid and reliable.

REFERENCES

Barker, J., & Weller, S. (2003). "Isn't it fun" Developing children centred research methods. *The International Journal of Sociology and Social Policy, 23*(1), 33–58.

Barton, W. H. (2005). Methodological challenges in the study of resilience. In M. Ungar (Ed.), *Handbook for working with children and youth pathways to resilience across cultures and contexts* (pp. 135–147). Thousand Oaks, CA: Sage.

Boyden, J., & Ennew, J. (Eds.). (1997). *Children in focus: A manual for experiential learning in participatory research with children*. Stockholm: Radda Barnen.

Bradford Brown, B., Larson, R. W., & Saraswathi, T. S. (Eds.). (2002). *The world's youth: Adolescence in eight regions of the globe*. Cambridge: Cambridge University Press.

Burke, C. (2008). "Play in focus" Children's visual voice in participative research. In P. Thomson (Ed.), *Doing visual research with children and young people* (pp. 23–36). New York, NY: Routledge.

Cavin, E. (1994). In search of the viewfinder: A study of a child's perspective. *Visual sociology, 9*(1), 27–41.

Charmaz, K. (2006). *Constructing grounded theory: A practical guide through qualitative analysis*. Thousand Oaks, CA: Sage.

Christensen, P. H. (2004). Children's participation in ethnographic research: Issues of power and representation. *Children and Society, 18*, 165–176.

Clark, C. D. (1999). The autodriven interview: A photographic viewfinder into children's experiences. *Visual Sociology, 14,* 39–50.
Clarke, A. E. (2005). *Situational analysis: Grounded theory after the postmodern turn.* Thousand Oaks, CA: Sage.
Coad, J., & Evans, R. (2008). Reflections on practical approaches to involving children and young people in the data analysis process. *Children and Society, 22,* 41–52.
Creswell, J. W., Plano Clark, V. L., Gutmann, M. L., & Hanson, W. E. (2003). Advanced mixed methods research designs. In A. Tashakkori & C. Teddlie, C. (Eds.), *Handbook of mixed methods in social and behavioral research* (pp. 209–240). Thousand Oaks, CA: Sage.
Creswell, J. W., & Plano Clark, V. L. (2007). *Designing and conducting mixed methods research.* Thousand Oaks, CA: Sage.
Dallape, F. (1996). Urban children: A challenge and an opportunity. *Childhood, 3,* 283–294.
DeVellis, R. F. (2003). *Scale development: Theory and applications* (2nd ed.). Thousand Oaks, CA: Sage.
Denzin, N. K., & Lincoln, Y. S. (1998). Introduction: Entering the Field of Qualitative Research. In N. K. Denzin & Y. S. Lincoln (Eds.), *Collecting and Interpreting Qualitative Materials* (pp. 1–34). London: Sage.
Evans, G. W., Brauchle, G., Haq, A., Stecker, R., Wong, K., & Shapiro, E. (2007). Young children's environmental attitudes and behaviours. *Environment and behaviour, 39*(5), 635–659.
Freire, P. (1973). *Pedagogy of the oppressed.* New York, NY: Seabury Press.
Glantz, M. D., & Sloboda, Z. (1999). Analysis and reconceptualization of resilience. In M. D. Glantz & J. L. Johnson (Eds.), *Resilience and development: Positive life adaptations* (pp. 109–126). New York: Kluwer Academic/Plenum.
Glasser, B., & A. Strauss. 1967. *The discovery of grounded theory: Strategies for qualitative research.* Chicago Illinois: Aldine.
Greene, S., & Hill, M. (2005). Researching children's experience: Methods and methodological issues. In S. Greene & D. Hogan (Eds.), *Researching children's experience: Methods and approaches* (pp. 1–21). London: Sage.
Greig, A., Taylor, J., & MacKay, T. (2007). *Doing research with children* (2nd ed.). London: Sage.
Grover, S. (2004). Why won't they listen to us? On giving power and voice to children participating in research. *Childhood, 11*(1), 81–93.
Hill, M. (2006). Children's voices on ways of having a voice: Children's and young people's perspectives on methods used in research and consultation. *Childhood, 13*(1), 69–89.
Hood, S., Kelley, P., & Mayall, B. (1996). Children as research subjects: A risky enterprise. *Children and society, 10,* 117–128.
James, A., & Prout, A. (Eds.). (1990). *Constructing and reconstructing childhood: Contemporary issues in the sociological study of childhood.* Basingstoke: Falmer Press.
Johnson, K. (2008). Teaching children to use visual research methods. In P. Thomson (Ed.), *Doing visual research with children and young people* (pp. 77–94). New York, NY: Routledge.

Johnson, R. B., & Onwuegbuzie, A. J. (2004). Mixed methods research: A research paradigm whose time has come. *Educational researcher, 33*(7), 14–26.

Johnson-Powell, G., & Yamamoto, J. (Eds.). (1997). *Transcultural child development: Psychological assessment and treatment.* New York, NY: John Wiley & Sons.

Jones, N., & Sumner, A. (2009). Does mixed methods research matter to understanding childhood well-being? *Social Indices Research, 90,* 33–50.

Karlsson, J. (2001). Doing visual research with school learners in South Africa. *Visual Sociology, 16*(2), 23–37.

Liborio, R., & Ungar, M. (2010). Children's labour and work as a risky pathway to resilience: Children's growth in contexts of poor resources. *Psicologia Reflexao e Critica, 23*(2), 232–242.

Liebenberg, L. (2009). The visual image as discussion point: Increasing validity in boundary crossing research. *Qualitative Research, 9*(4), 441–467.

Liebenberg, L., Ungar, M., and Theron, L. (in press/available online first). Using video observation and photo elicitation interviews to understand obscured processes in the lives of resilient youth. *Childhood.* DOI: 10.1177/0907568213496652

Liebenberg, L., & Ungar, M. (2009). Introduction: The challenges of researching resilience (pp. 3–25). In L. Liebenberg & M. Ungar (Eds.), *Researching youth resilience.* Toronto: University of Toronto Press.

Lincoln, Y., & Guba, E. (1985). *Naturalistic inquiry.* Thousand Oaks, CA: Sage.

Luthar, S. S. (1999). *Poverty and children's adjustment.* Thousand Oaks, CA: Sage.

Mason, J. (2006). Mixing methods in a qualitatively driven way. *Qualitative research, 6*(1), 9–25.

Masten, A. S. (2001). Ordinary magic: Resilience processes in development. *American Psychologist, 56,* 227–238.

Masten, A. S., & Powell, J. L. (2003). A resilience framework for research, policy, and practice. In S. S. Luthar (Ed.), *Resilience and vulnerability: Adaptation in the context of childhood adversities* (pp. 1–28). New York, NY: Cambridge University Press.

Mertens, D. M. (2003). Mixed methods and the politics of human research: The transformative emancipatory perspective. In A Tashakkori & C. Teddlie (Eds.), *Handbook of mixed methods in social and behavioral research* (pp. 135–164). Thousand Oaks, CA: Sage.

Morse, J. M. (1991). Approaches to qualitative-quantitative methodological triangulation. *Nursing research* (40), 120–123.

Nicotera, N. (2008). Children speak about neighborhoods: Using mixed methods to measure the construct neighborhood. *Journal of community psychology, 36*(3), 333–351.

Noar, S. M. (2003). The role of structural equation modeling in scale development. *Structural Equation Modeling, 10,* 622–647.

Onwuegbuzie, A. J., Bustamante, R. M., & Nelson, J. A. (2010). Mixed research as a tool for developing quantitative instruments. *Journal of Mixed Methods Research, 4*(1), 56–78.

Onwuegbuzie, A. J., & Leech, N. J. (2005). On becoming a pragmatic researcher: The importance of combing quantitative and qualitative methodologies. *International Journal of Social Research Methodology, 8,* 375–387.

Prout, A. (2001). Representing children: Reflections on the 5–16 program. *Children and Society,* 15, 193–201.
Punch, S. (2002). Research with children: The same or different from research with adults. *Childhood,* 9(3), 321–341.
Richardson, L., & St. Pierre, E. A. (2005). Writing: A method of inquiry. In N. K. Denzin & Y. S. Lincoln (Eds.), *The Sage Handbook of Qualitative Research* (3rd ed., pp. 959–978). Thousand Oaks, CA: Sage.
Rutter, M. (1987). Psychosocial resilience and protective mechanisms. *American Journal of Orthopsychiatry,* 57, 316–331.
Scott, J. (2000). Children as respondents: The challenge for quantitative research. In P. Christensen & A. James (Eds.), *Research with children: Perspectives and practices* (pp. 98–135). London: Falmer Press.
Smith, L. T. (1999). *Decolonising methodologies: Research and indigenous peoples.* London: Zed Books.
Strauss, A., & Corbin, J. (1990). *Basics of qualitative research: Grounded theory procedures and techniques.* Newbury Park, California: Sage.
Tashakkori, A., & Creswell, J. W. (2007). Editorial: The new era of mixed methods. *Journal of Mixed Methods Research,* 1(1), 3–7.
Tedeschi, R. G., & Calhoun, L. G. (1996). The Posttraumatic Growth Inventory: Measuring the positive legacy of trauma. *Journal of Traumatic Stress,* 9, 455–471.
Todd, Z., Nerlich, B., & McKeown, S. (2004). Introduction. In Z. Todd, B. Nerlich, S. McKeown & D. D. Clarke (Eds.), *Mixing methods in psychology: The integration of qualitative and quantitative methods in theory and practice* (pp. 3–16). New York, NY: Psychology Press, Taylor and Francis Group.
Turtle, K., McElearney, A., & Scott, J. (2010). Involving children in the design and development of research instruments and data collection procedures: A case study in primary schools in Northern Ireland. *Child care in practice,* 16(1), 57–82.
Tweed, R. G., & DeLongis, A. (2006). Problems and strategies when using rating scales in cross–cultural coping research. In P. T. P. Wong & L. C. J. Wong (Eds.), *Handbook of multicultural perspectives on stress and coping* (pp. 203–221). New York, NY: Springer.
Ungar, M. (2005). Pathways to resilience among children in child welfare, corrections, mental health and educational settings: Navigation and negotiation. *Child and Youth Care Forum* 34(6), 423–444.
Ungar, M. (2008). Resilience across cultures. *British Journal of Social Work,* 38, 218–235.
Ungar, M. (2011). The social ecology of resilience: Addressing contextual and cultural ambiguity of a nascent construct. *American Journal of Orthopsychiatry,* 81, 1–17.
Ungar, M., Brown, M., Liebenberg, L., Othman, R., Kwong, W. M., Armstrong, M., & Gilgun, J. (2007). Unique pathways to resilience across cultures. *Adolescence,* 42(166), 287–310.
Ungar, M., & Liebenberg, L., (2011). Assessing resilience across cultures using mixed-methods: Construction of the child and youth resilience measure-28. *Journal of Mixed-Methods Research,* 5(2), 126–149.
Ungar, M., & Liebenberg, L. (2005). Resilience across cultures: The mixed methods approach of the International Resilience Project. In M. Ungar (Ed.),

Handbook for working with children and youth pathways to resilience across cultures and contexts (pp. 211–226). Thousand Oaks, CA: Sage.

Wong, P. T. P., & Wong, L. C. J. (Eds.). (2006). *Handbook of multicultural perspectives on stress and coping.* New York: Springer.

Young, L., & Barrett, H. (2001). Adapting visual methods: action research with Kampala street children. *Area, 33*(2), 141–152.

PART II

QUALITATIVE RESEARCH METHODOLOGIES

CHAPTER 12

GROUNDED THEORY

Robert Thornberg, Lisa M. Perhamus,
and Kathy Charmaz

Early childhood education is an area of practice and research that involves many complex processes such as human interaction, teaching and learning, child development and socialization, peer influences and group dynamics, classroom management and instruction, and curriculum development and program evaluation. In the early childhood classroom, children and teachers are constantly negotiating and forming meanings about each other and the world through play and inquiry based projects. A child-centered early childhood classroom is about fostering curiosity, encouraging exploration, embracing discovery and, of critical importance, honoring process over product. Experienced teachers understand the importance of balancing structure and freedom. Indeed, experienced teachers know that children's sense of freedom to explore their world flourishes best when the structure of their learning environment provides them with the safety and consistency to let their curiosity lead the way. The structure of an early childhood environment provides a net, so to speak, that metaphorically holds children safely and frees them to really dive in to learn about the world around them.

Grounded theory is a bit like this net. The tools of grounded theory provide the researcher a structured approach to sorting through data that, in turn, frees the researcher to fully dive into the data, explore the happenings in the data and discover the analytic stories the data tell. Like early childhood education itself, grounded theory is an approach to data analysis that honors process over product (committed to the process of doing research rather than being preoccupied with producing a particular result) and that works in that exciting tension area between structure and freedom, routine and playfulness, consistency and surprise. In this chapter, we present an overview of grounded theory and how researchers can use it in their own work. Consistent with grounded theory's commitment to collecting and analyzing data prior to conducting the literature review, this chapter discusses the processes of grounded theory first and concludes with a literature review of early childhood education research's uses of grounded theory. We will present various grounded theory methods, the logic of specific grounded theory strategies, provide examples that illustrate these methods and strategies, and discuss the ways in which the field of early childhood education can continue to enrich its research with the methods of grounded theory. Keeping the net metaphor in mind might be helpful. Consistently using the methods and strategies that we discuss in this chapter will provide readers with a structure that will guide their research process and keep them "on track" for conducting rigorous research, and this structure (and the security it can offer them through the research process) will free them to fully explore their data. Like young children who playfully roll around on the floor, researchers can roll around in their data, trusting through the grounded theory process that when they stand up, they will have findings to share.

Before we begin, we must ask, what is grounded theory? Grounded theory is a systematic general method for analyzing qualitative data and constructing theories from the studied data through successive levels of analysis (Charmaz, 2006; Corbin & Strauss, 2008; Glaser & Strauss, 1967). Many scholars have almost equated the term, grounded theory, with inductive qualitative research (e.g., Cohen, Manion & Morrison, 2007; Johnson & Christensen, 2008; Silverman, 2005). Induction in grounded theory means that "you start with individual cases, incidents or experiences and develop progressively more abstract conceptual categories to synthesize, to explain and to understand your data and to identify patterned relationships within it" (Charmaz, 1995, p. 28).

Grounded theory begins with open-ended inductive inquiry but its distinctive characteristics also include comparative, interactive, and iterative methods. Barney G. Glaser and Anselm L. Strauss (1967), the originators of grounded theory, imbued the method with strategies to examine, analyze, and conceptualize individual and collective actions and processes. The term, grounded theory, usually means the method with its strategies but also refers to the product of this research process, the generated theory on the studied phenomenon. A theory states relationships between abstract concepts and may aim for either explanation or understanding. From its beginnings, Glaser and Strauss (1967) intended researchers to use grounded theory to construct fresh theories of the studied data. Nonetheless, grounded theory strategies help diverse researchers to clarify and specify their ideas, although they may not aim to construct theory. Since 1967, grounded theory has been further developed in different versions. The classic or Glaserian version has emphasized an unbiased researcher position, the rejection of epistemology and preconception, and the emergence of concepts and theory by using grounded theory methods (e.g., Glaser, 1978, 1998, 2005). The Straussian version has a more technical procedure, using a particular coding paradigm to sort data and codes into a matrix of causal, intervening and contextual conditions as well as actions/interactions and consequences (Corbin & Strauss, 2008; Strauss & Corbin, 1990, 1998). The constructivist version is rooted in pragmatism and relativist epistemology, takes a middle ground between the realist and postmodernist positions. It assumes that neither data nor theories are discovered, but constructed by the researchers as a result of their interactions with the field and its participants. Data are therefore seen as co-constructed and always colored by the researchers' perspectives (e.g., Charmaz, 1995, 2000, 2006).

COLLECTING DATA AND THEORETICAL SAMPLING

Grounded theory is not limited to any particular method for gathering data but uses data collection methods that best fit the actual research problem and the ongoing analysis of the data. It specifies strategies and methods of *analysis*, not data collection methods, and remains open to a range of methods of data collection, such as qualitative interviews, field observations, informal conversations, focus groups, documents, questionnaires and diaries. Furthermore, grounded theorists gather and analyze data simultaneously throughout the whole research project (Charmaz, 2006; Corbin & Strauss, 2008; Glaser, 1979; 1998; Glaser and Strauss, 1967). Codes and concepts are constructed and developed from data during analysis, which in turn guides further collection of data. When grounded theorists have defined tentative theoretical categories, they engage in *theoretical sampling*, which involves seeking data to enable them to fill out the analytic properties of their defined categories. With this analytic emphasis, theoretical sampling helps researchers to develop robust theoretical categories. Theoretical sampling thus occurs later in the analytic process and also helps researchers to define variation in the category(ies) and relationships between categories. For example, in an early childhood education study about health and school, Perhamus' (2009) data analysis revealed the category of "feeling at risk." Theoretical sampling, further examination of the data from which each of the categories had emerged, illustrated that the "feeling at risk" category included "properties" of what study participants experienced as risk, which included fears around issues of death and dying, limited quality of life, loss of family traditions, an inability to stop generational problems such as substance abuse and mistrust that the school would teach health in ways that honored each family's cultural heritage. Through theoretical sampling, Perhamus was able to identify a deeper level of categories and allowed her to explore the relationships between these categories.

Because theoretical sampling emerges from the analytic process and is conceptually driven, it differs considerably from initial sampling, although the differences are often unrecognized. Initial sampling may start by taking demographic variables into account. Hence in an interview project on kindergarten teachers' teaching styles, researchers may decide to reproduce the percentages of female and male teachers in their initial sample. But after they construct abstract categories from their interview data, then they sample to develop these categories. According to Glaser and Strauss's (1967) original definition of theoretical sampling, the researcher "decides what data to collect next and where to find them, in order to develop his theory as it emerges" (p. 45). Hence, as Corbin and Strauss (2008) put it, "the researcher is like a detective. He or she follows the leads of the concepts, never quite certain where they will lead, but always open to what might be uncovered" (p. 144).

Researchers start with a method or a set of methods of data collection that first fit the initial research problem. If, for example, a single researcher or a team of researchers aim to examine peer conflicts among kindergarten children, they might start with identifying, gaining access to and doing field observations in one or more kindergarten class in order to openly explore what happens when peer conflicts occur. However, questions, clues and preliminary insights might soon emerge that lead the researchers to be more focused on particular events, situations or processes in their field observations, to initiate informal conversations with children, or to ask children to make drawings on certain events and conduct qualitative interviews based on these drawings. Hence, the analysis of data evokes new questions, insights, hunches, "Aha!" experiences or hypotheses, which might lead researchers to change or add a new data collection method. Once grounded theorists begin to construct tentative categories, they focus on obtaining data to illuminate the categories, fill out their properties, and define their implications. This iterative process keeps the researchers focused on checking and refining their constructed codes and categories, and, at the same time, helps to keep the researchers from becoming overwhelmed and unfocused in data collection and analysis. Theoretical sampling continues until the study reaches *theoretical saturation*, which is "the point in the research when all the concepts are well defined and explained" (Corbin & Strauss,

2008, p. 145). The constructed grounded theory and its categories are saturated when "gathering fresh data no longer sparks new theoretical insights, nor reveals new properties of your core theoretical categories" (Charmaz, 2006, p. 113). Nevertheless, judging theoretical saturation is always tricky and the grounded theorist has to be constantly open to what is going on in the field, actively interact with and reflect upon the data and the generated concepts, and use grounded theory guidelines wisely.

CODING

Because data gathering and analysis go hand in hand in grounded theory, the researcher begins *coding* as the first data start to emerge in the study. According to Charmaz (2006), coding refers to "naming segments of data with a label that simultaneously categorizes, summarizes, and accounts for each piece of data" (p. 43). Pidgeon and Henwood (1996) describe it as "the tentative development and labelling of concepts in the text that the researcher considers to be of potential relevance to the problem being studied" (p. 92). Instead of applying preconceived categories and concepts from the pre-existing literature (and hence only see what other scholars already have seen), researchers create their codes by defining what they see in the data. By scrutinizing data and constantly comparing data with data, codes with data, and codes with codes, the researcher follows the data and remains open to what the data may be indicating rather than forcing the data to fit a preconceived analytic framework. "Coding gets the analyst off the empirical level by fracturing the data, then conceptually grouping it into codes that then become the theory which explains what is happening in the data" (Glaser, 1978, p. 55). A critical component in this process is to interact with and ask analytical questions of the data. Some variation is evident in ways of coding between different versions of grounded theory (Charmaz, 2006; Clarke, 2005; Corbin & Strauss, 2008; Glaser, 1998). A constructivist position of grounded theory (Charmaz, 2000, 2003, 2006) argues that coding consists of at least two phases: initial coding and focused coding. Nevertheless, coding is not a linear process. The researchers move flexibly back and forth between the different phases of coding to be sensitive to their own data and analysis, although they do more initial coding at the beginning than at the end of the study.

Initial Coding

Initial coding (also known as open coding) is the first phase of coding. While the researchers move carefully but quickly through the data, they compare data with data, stay close to the data and remain open to examining what they interpret is going on in the data. During the initial or open phase of coding, Glaser (1978, p. 57; 1998, p. 140) states that the researchers ask:

- What is actually happening in the data?
- What are these data a study of?
- What category does this incident, statement, or segment of data indicate?
- What is the participant's main concern?

In addition, Charmaz (2006) adds the following questions as a help to search for and identify what is happening in the data and to scrutinize the data critically and analytically:

- What do the data suggest? Pronounce?
- From whose point of view?
- What do actions and statements in the data take for granted?
- What process(es) is at issue here? How can I define it?
- How does this process develop?
- Under which conditions does this process develop?
- How does the research participant(s) think, feel and act while involved in this process?
- When, why, and how does the process change?
- What are the consequences of the process?

Coding and its analytical questioning help researchers to probe, identify details and become acquainted with the data, see the familiar in a new light, avoid forcing data into preconceptions, think outside the box, gain distance from their own and their participants' taken-for-granted assumptions, think abstractly about the data, and develop provisional codes, ideas and answers to investigate further (Charmaz, 2003; Corbin & Strauss, 2008; Glaser, 1978, 1998). Initial coding is performed by reading and analyzing the data word by word and line by line, and then defines actions or events within the data. During this careful reading, the researchers construct initial codes that represent or refer to the meaning they interpretatively see in a single word, a couple of words, a sentence, or a couple a sentences. The labels they construct might be a single word or a couple of words. Charmaz (2006) advises researchers to remain open, stay close to the data, and keep the codes simple, short, while preserving actions, and moving quickly through the data when doing initial coding. With reference to Glaser (1978), she highlights that coding with gerunds (noun forms of verbs) helps the researchers to detect and remain focused on process and action. "Action codes show what is happening and what people are doing. These codes move us away from topics, and if they address structure, they reveal how it is constructed through action" (Charmaz & Belgrave, 2012, pp. 356–357). Using verbs to label the code forces the researcher to stay focused on the action in the data and the *process* aspect of situations. Grounded theory helps the researcher identify what is happening in the data and focuses the researcher's eye on how meaning is being constructed. Examples of such codes might be "avoiding others," "student grouping," and "becoming sad." It is crucial to make sure that the codes fit the data rather than forcing the data to fit them. In the example in Table 12.1, Perhamus conducts line-by-line initial coding of an interview from a study about the culturally varied health needs of students and families in an inner-city elementary school (2009). The study aimed to capture how young children experience and make sense of health messages from their families and school. The excerpts are taken from interviews with a five-year-old boy who was still quite young in his language development. Because young children's primary means of communication is physical, Perhamus (2009, 2010b) took the position that her data required moving

TABLE 12.1 Initial Coding

Transcript Data	Initial/Open Coding
Interviewer: Hm. What ideas do you have?	
Anthony: Lots.	Being evasive
I: Can you tell me some of them?	
A: You'll have to see (Interview, January 2008).	Building something (playing) instead of talking
	Showing me with his body
Anthony: So this is the cage.	
Interviewer: How do you think they feel in that cage?	Explaining to me
A: A little sad.	
I: What makes them feel so sad?	Feeling sad
A: Because they can't get out. The cage is here next year... Their bed is right here. But they cannot get out there. This is the emergency exit (Interview, January 2008).	Being trapped
	Identifying a way out/emergency
Anthony: This is for no one can come in and this is the privacy (he has blocked off one area)...And I have my own privacy sometimes.	exit
Interviewer: How does it feel to have your own privacy?	Explaining to me
	Creating privacy
A: (He lies down, stretches out his body as if he is relaxed and smiles as he breathes in deeply). *Ah!* (Interview, January 2008).	Showing me with his body

beyond spoken words. She designed a methodological tool for collecting data with young children, a semi-structured game called "Tell Me About It" (as an alternative to the researcher interview), and she considered all of the child's actions as valuable data. Body movements, gestures, phonetic utterances and play choices are common forms of communication for young children and, thus, were all documented as part of the interview record, transcribed and coded.

Note that the codes are kept close to the data and how Perhamus uses gerunds and, therefore, gains a strong sense of action, process, and sequence. Researchers who conduct grounded theory always treat their constructed codes as provisional and open for revision, elaboration, and refinement when being compared with new data and other codes in order to improve their fit with data. Researchers remain as open-minded and sensitive to the data as possible.

While coding, researchers use the *constant comparative method*, which means that they compare newly collected data with previously collected data, data with code, and code with code, to find similarities and differences (Glaser and Strauss, 1967). Initial coding and constant comparative practices result in sorting and clustering of initial codes, and revisions of codes and constructions of new, more elaborated codes by merging or integrating initial codes which are very similar to each other.

Focused Coding

The transition from initial coding to *focused coding* occurs when the researcher (a) "discovers" those initial codes that reappear most frequently or make the most analytical sense of what is going on in the data, and (b) begins to use these codes to sift through and sort large amounts of data (Charmaz, 2000, 2003, 2006). Glaser (1978, 1998, 2005) states that the initial or open coding ends when the grounded theorist has identified a core category, which is the most significant and frequent code that is also related to as many other codes as possible. The core category becomes a guide for further data collection and coding. Glaser (1978, 1998) labels this phase, in which subsequent data collection and coding are delimited to the core category, as selective coding. Thornberg and Charmaz (2012) have argued that the constructivist position of grounded theory (Charmaz, 2006), which uses focused codes rather than a single core category, offers a more sensitive and flexible approach in its guidelines for coding and further data collection. A focused coding approach identifies codes that index key meanings, actions and processes in the data and across the data. As opposed to core categories, focused codes allow the researcher to be open to the possibility of more than just one significant or frequent initial code

Grounded Theory ▪ **413**

in order to conduct further data gathering and coding. During the focused coding, the researcher still remains sensitive and open to determining the adequacy of those codes, to modifying them and to being surprised by the data (note that constructivist grounded theory does not reject the possibility of coming up with one core category, but is not confined to that possibility). Focused codes are more directed, selective, abstract, and conceptual than the initial codes. They help the grounded theorist to begin to synthesize and explain larger segments of data. Focused codes cut across multiple data and therefore represent recurrent themes or processes. The excerpt in Table 12.2 below comes from an interview with a 5-year-old girl. The table illustrates how Perhamus conducted focused coding on both her interview data and memo writing that she did during transcription to help cue herself to possible emerging patterns in the data.

As can be seen in Table 12.2, the focused codes capture and synthesize the main themes in the statements. In addition, the excerpt illustrates how collecting data from young children can be challenging for the adult researcher who, even with the highest commitment to conducting child-oriented research, still must acknowledge that s/he approaches the research situation with an adult frame. There may be times during the data collection process, perhaps even during initial coding, that appear to be almost nonsensical to the researcher because children's and adult's meaning-making can be so different. It is important for the researcher to remain active in interviews and to remain alert for interesting leads (Charmaz & Belgrave, 2012) even when it seems that the data collection process is not yielding fruitful results. All data is meaningful. Often times it is not until later in the coding and analysis process that we have that "Aha!" moment, excitedly understand the data differently and actually "discover" meaningful content in the data.

The excerpt in Table 12.2 also illustrates how cultural differences are part of the researcher/research participant relationship and how culturally shaped meaning-making processes are an important part of the data. Grounded theory's analytic coding tools offer a way for researchers to identify and sort through the more subjective dimensions of research, such as tensions between child and adult orientations to time and space and cultural differences between research participant and researcher. In this excerpt, Perhamus records and codes an interview that emerged through playing "Tell Me about It." Perhamus is a white, Western, adult woman, and Ariel is a black, Puerto Rican five year old child. Ariel also continues to struggle with the ramifications of being born addicted to crack cocaine due to her biological mother's drug use. Perhamus does not know at the time of data collection whether Ariel's "jumpy" play and interaction is due to Ariel's development delays, chronological age, culturally shaped meaning-making and communication, individual personality or Perhamus' own cultured interpretation of Ariel's actions—such analysis comes later in the grounded

TABLE 12.2 Focused Coding

Transcript Data & Memo-Writing	Focused Coding
Ariel: But how do we make a square.	Orienting action
Interviewer: Hm.	Connecting moment
A: Um.	
I: Let's use your ideas.	
A: Oh!!! (another dramatic, loud, gasping for air exclaim) We could just do this. Mush it together.	
I: OK	
A: Like this (she mushes playdough), and then, we can make a square.	
I: How does a house keep them safe?	
A: Um, by making a bed and some playdough houses and window. Aahh (gasping sound likes she's suddenly frightened). A street.	Sensory communication
I: They need a street?	
A: Guess what?	Shifting narrative
I: What?	Connecting moment
A: On our vacation,	
I: Yeah.	
A: me, Mommy and Grandma are going to Sesame Street.	
I: You are?!	
A: Uh, yeah. And they're gonna, and we're gonna eat cookies with Cookie Monster.	
I: Oh, that's so cool.	
A: And Elmo's favorite fruit is banana.	
I: Wow.	
A: I don't know if they're going to talk or not.	
I: So you're going to follow that Sesame Street to all of those good things.	
A: Oh, darn.	
I: I wonder if Big Bird has a house that keeps him safe (note: trying to bring us back to the game card).	
A: I have no idea. Oh!! (another dramatic gasp). A nest!	
I: A big nest, you're right.	
A: Cause we saw at the, what the heck. Oh, I have something. Let me do this. And it could just open like that (she has mushed the playdough together)...so, so, so-so-so-so, so we could put this here. And this	Shifting narrative Physical communication
(*Memo:* Throughout the interview she is rather non-specific. A lot of saying "this" without further explanation of	

(continued)

TABLE 12.2 Focused Coding (continued)

Transcript Data & Memo-Writing	Focused Coding
what "this" is and I find my efforts to clarify are rather ineffective. I experience the interview as light and fun, she is playful and engaged, but it is also rather jumpy—moving quickly from one thing to another within the same project of a moment, and it is sometimes hard to follow. At least from my adult perspective, even though I always try to enter the child's world, it seems that she does not have one thing in mind that she follows through over a few minutes (like some of the children who build something). It seems more like each moment is "open" to her and she sort of looks around for what to fill it with. It's like she moves spontaneously through space and time, without an overtly apparent plan. At the same time, during the first visit and now, she often returns to her original idea through her "spontaneous" movements/actions/words/choices. It is a little hard for me to follow her rhythm—when she is being spontaneous with apparently disconnected actions and when she is adding on to an idea she has.)	Physical communication Adult/child orientation tension Present orientation

...

A: Blue playdough come out! Oh, great.	
I: And whenever you feel like we're done building something to keep these girls safe, we'll roll the die again and pick a different card.	
A: (banging the playdough container) Great.	
I: I think you have to talk to it again.	
A: OK. (yelling) Blue playdough	
I: (we're both talking to the container) Excuse me, blue playdough, please come out to play. Hello? That's not going to work. (I stick my finger in the container to loosen the playdough's suction to the sides) Now maybe it will come out.	Connecting moment
A: (big slam of the container) Aeyh! (yell) ... Ah ah schja! (acting shocked) (Note: I am spelling her dramatic exclamations phonetically) Oh, my... Now we need, now we, um, now we need the white.	Sensory communication
I: I wonder if the white will come out.	
(*Memo:* I just had the realization that with children, calibrating how much I respond and interact and how much I stay silent is much different from adults. With adults, I have had to work at staying quiet more, doing less talking, letting there be silence and finding that the silence eventually gives way to them taking their story a bit further. With children, the tangible interaction is more	Adult/child orientation tension

(continued)

TABLE 12.2 Focused Coding (continued)	
Transcript Data & Memo-Writing	**Focused Coding**
important—their "stories" emerge from the interaction (even if they are not directly responding to me). I would say this is true for adult interviews also, but I would define interaction differently for the two groups, children and adults. As I transcribe, I see that I responded a lot, even with little silly remarks, with Ariel—perhaps even a bit more than with some others. I think I am responding to her—sort of trying to engage with her through her rhythm.)	

theory research process. However, it all gets documented and coded so that such analysis can emerge truly grounded in the data. For researchers collecting data with young children like the girl Ariel, it is important to simply collect, even in situations in which we feel that we do not seem to get "meaningful data"—we see the patterns later.

In the next step of making sense of the data, grounded theorists examine and decide which codes best capture what they see happening in the data, and raise the focused codes to tentative conceptual *categories* by giving them conceptual definitions and by beginning to assess the relationships between them (Charmaz, 2003, 2006). Researchers use the constant comparative method in order to generate and refine categories (Charmaz, 2003; Thornberg & Charmaz, 2012):

- Comparing and grouping codes, and comparing codes with emerging categories
- Comparing different incidents (e.g., social situations, actions, social processes, or interaction patterns)
- Comparing data from the same or similar phenomenon, action, or process in different situations and contexts
- Comparing different people (their beliefs, situations, actions, accounts, or experiences)
- Comparing data from the same individuals at different points in time
- Comparing specific data with the criteria for the category
- Comparing categories in the analysis with other categories.

Theoretical Coding

According to Glaser's (1978, 1998, 2005) version of grounded theory, *theoretical coding* is a sophisticated level of coding that researchers conduct in the later stages of GT analysis, At this point, they analyze how categories and codes generated from data might relate to each other as hypotheses to be integrated into a theory. In theoretical coding, this is achieved by inspecting, choosing and using *theoretical codes* as analytical tools for examining, organizing and conceptualizing how the categories and codes generated from data may relate to each other. Even within a constructivist position of grounded theory, researchers might take advantage of theoretical coding (Charmaz, 2006; Thornberg & Charmaz, 2011, 2014; Thornberg, 2012a, 2012b).

What is theoretical coding and what are theoretical codes? Glaser (1978) uses the term *substantive codes* to refer to the codes that have "emerged" and developed from the data through the constant comparative method and engaging in the earlier phases of coding (which in our constructivist grounded theory terminology would be initial codes and focused codes). In contrast to these empirical substantive codes, theoretical codes are ideas and perspectives that researchers import to the research process as analytical tools and lenses from outside, from a body of background knowledge of a range of theories. Theoretical codes refer to "underlying logics that could be found in pre-existing theories" (Thornberg, 2012a, p. 89), and they "give integrative scope, broad pictures and a new perspective" (Glaser, 1978, p. 72). Theoretical codes "specify possible relationships between categories you have developed in your focused coding... [and] may help you tell an analytic story that has coherence" (Charmaz, 2006, p. 63).

Glaser (1998, 2005) encourages students and researchers to study numerous theories across different disciplines in order to identify, figure out, and learn numerous theoretical codes embedded in these theories and how the theoretical codes are used. According to Glaser (2005), the more theoretical codes the researchers learn, the more they have "the variability of seeing them emerge and fitting them to the theory" (p. 11). Expanding the repertoire of theoretical codes and how they could be used enhances researchers' *theoretical sensitivity*, in other words, their ability to "discover" relationships between their categories that lead them to develop a grounded theory. In order to facilitate students and researchers to get started with theoretical coding, Glaser has elaborated a list of theoretical codes organized in a typology of *coding families* (Glaser, 1978, pp. 72-82; Glaser, 1998, pp. 170–175; Glaser, 2005, 21–30). Examples of coding families presented by Glaser are:

- *The "six C's":* Causes, contexts, contingencies, consequences, covariances and conditions
- *Process family:* Phases, stages, progressions, passages, transitions, careers, trajectories, sequencings, cycling, etc.
- *Degree family:* Limit, range, grades, continuum, level, etc.

- *Dimension family:* Dimensions, sector, segment, part, aspect, section, etc.
- *Type family:* Type, kinds, styles, classes, genre, etc.
- *Strategy family:* Strategies, tactics, manipulation, maneuverings, dealing with, handling, techniques, goals, arrangements, dominating, positioning, etc.
- *Identity-self family:* Self-image, self-concept, self-worth, self-evaluation, identity, transformations of self, etc.
- *Basic Family:* Basic social process, basic social psychological process, basic social structural process, basic psychological process, etc.
- *Cutting point family:* Boundary, cutting point, turning point, breaking points, point of no return, etc.
- *Cultural family:* Social norms, social values, social beliefs, etc.
- *Consensus family:* Agreements, contracts, definitions of situation, conformity, nonconformity, homogeneity, heterogeneity, conflict, etc.
- *Paired opposite family:* ingroup–outgroup, in–out, manifest–latent, explicit–implicit, overt–covert, informal–formal, etc.

Glaser presents many more coding families and his list of them is by no means exhaustive. Also note the considerable overlapping between coding families (e.g., the cutting point family could be seen as a set of members of the degree family, and overlapping between cultural family and consensus family is obvious). Moreover, Charmaz (2006) highlights that whereas several coding families are absent from Glaser's list, other coding families appear rather arbitrary and vague. As Thornberg and Charmaz (2012) recently argue, instead of being hypnotized by Glaser's list of coding families, researchers should investigate all kinds of pre-existing theories they encounter in different research disciplines or domains in order to figure out for themselves their embedded theoretical codes and how these codes are used in the theories.

In her study on how young children navigate culturally shaped meanings of health and wellness, Perhamus (2009) could see different possibilities for relating and organizing the categories she had constructed to reflect her data and the content of her categories. Children actively constructed their subject positions in social relationships, including the researcher/participant relationship, and through their social interactions children moved fluidly between their various subject positions ("student," "daughter/son," "friend," "research participant," etc.). A main category generated from her analysis was situating processes, which refer to how children positioned themselves in the research interaction. She then filled in the depth of this category by identifying that the children demonstrated two kinds of action during situating processes: orienting action (how the children were positioning themselves in relationship to the adult researcher) and present action (the action of a child's talk and play on its own terms). "Situating processes" described a particular yet overarching social process while "orienting action" and "present action" indexed specific kinds of actions in the social process. More than being two distinct kinds of actions, her data demonstrated that orienting action and present action were two layers of one action, a data-grounded analysis that became an important aspect of the theory-building afforded by the research. Hence, we can see some of Glaser's coding families embedded in Perhamus' conceptualization: For example, Basic Family (situating processes), Strategy Family and Identity-Self Family (positioning self in interaction; orienting action, present action), Dimension Family (two layers of one action), and Type Family (various subject positions). In Perhamus' (2009, 2010a) research, the data-grounded analysis of present and orienting action became an important aspect of her theory-building work on the contemporary sociology of childhood. Analyzing the theoretical embeddedness of one's codes and categories affords grounded theorists a rich and rigorous way to "enter" the data at a deeper level and to more fully explore the analytic stories found in the data.

Theoretical codes offer a way to see multiple angles and possibilities in one's data and should, therefore, be used carefully by rigorously comparing the theoretical codes with data, codes, categories, and memos in order to figure out which theoretical codes best describe or explain the constructed categories and how they might relate to each other and integrated into a grounded theory. Glaser (1978) claims that theoretical codes must not be forced into the analysis but have to earn their way in by constant comparisons. In addition, from a constructivist position of grounded theory, we argue that codes and categories developed from initial and focused coding can be related to each other and organized in many different ways depending on the researchers' knowledge and meaning-makings of theoretical codes as well as on their preferences and perspectives as researchers. A grounded theory does not already exist out there in reality to be found. Constructivist grounded theory is always an interpretation, one among many possibilities of understanding reality. However, because the interpretation is completely grounded in the data and entirely constructed by the researchers through rigorous and emergent processes of coding, category-building, memo-writing, and sorting, the grounded theory interpretation rests solidly on empirical evidence.

MEMO WRITING AND SORTING

As a result of the iterative process of data collection, coding and analyzing, researchers will now and then come up with questions, ideas and insightful thoughts. Even though researchers think their ideas are really brilliant and therefore easy to remember, they must not trust their brain as a memory store for their ideas. As soon as they begin coding and analyzing, they also have to write down their analytical, conceptual or theoretical notes as *memos* in order to remember them. Memos could be defined as "the theorizing write-up of ideas about codes and their relationships as they strike the analyst while coding" (Glaser, 1978, p. 83) "the narrated records of a theorist's analytical conversations with him/herself about the research data" (Lempert, 2007, p. 247), and the "documentation of the researcher's thinking process and theorizing from data" (Thornberg, 2012b, p. 254). By *memo writing*, the researcher steps back and ask, "What is going on here?" and "How can I make sense of this?"

Writing successive memos throughout the research process helps researchers to clarify thinking on certain topics or aspects in their study, and to reflect upon, gain an analytical distance to and examine their codes and categories as well as possible relationships between them. Memo writing is about putting things down on paper and thus makes codes, categories, thoughts, reflections, and ideas manageable while also stimulating further theorizing. Memo writing is a prerequisite for theoretical sampling. By memo writing, researchers learn what data they have to collect next in order to answer their questions, elaborate their ideas, make incomplete categories more complete, or examine further their hypothetical associations between categories. According to Lempert (2007, p. 249), memos do the following things:

- Provide a means for the researchers to engage in and record intellectual conversations with themselves about the data
- Clarify processes by explaining and defining properties and characteristics
- Allow researchers to gain the analytic distance that enables movement away from description and into conceptualization
- Record research and analytical progress, as well as thoughts and feelings, about data and directions for further collection and/or analysis
- Distinguish between major and minor codes and categories
- Maintain a "storehouse of analytical ideas" (Strauss & Corbin, 1998, p. 220) available for sorting, ordering, re-ordering, and retrieval
- Do what people in research situation probably cannot to, that is, identify patterns and their properties for both general and specific situations (Strauss & Corbin, 1998)
- Facilitate the generation of theory

As with codes and categories, the researcher treats each memo as partial, provisional and modifiable. Whereas some memos will be revised and elaborated, others will be rejected during the path of the study. The *early memos* at the beginning of the study are often shorter, less conceptualized, and filled with analytical questions and hunches. According to Charmaz (2006), early memos are used to explore and fill out the constructed codes, and to direct and focus further data gathering. Exhibit 12.1 illustrates an early memo from Thornberg's (2008b) study on schoolchildren's meaning-makings of school rules.

As can be seen in Exhibit 12.1, Thornberg took an active, open, and critical stance by constructing analytic questions about the school rules as he encountered them in his ethnographic fieldwork and informal conversation with students and teachers. All questions in the memo above could be linked to the basic question in initial coding, "What is happening or actually going on here?" The memo ends with a short list of what to do

---

EXHIBIT 12.1

EARLY MEMO EXAMPLE

How do students perceive all these school rules?

The students are exposed to and expected to accept and comply with a huge amount of rules in school. Some of the rules are printed in posters on walls in classrooms and corridors. Much more of them are quoted or made explicit by teachers or students in their everyday conversations. They are often quoted to correct behavior. Some of the rules are also explained and justified by teachers in their interactions with students. Field notes, audio-recordings and informal conversations with students indicate that many students have a lot of thoughts and opinions about school rules. They seem to like some of the rules, but dislike or question others. Why?

- How can I get an overview of all these school rules embedded in students' school life?
- How can I categorize school rules based on similarities and differences considering their content and how teachers talk about and justify them in their conversations with students and in their informal conversations with me?
- How do the children make meaning of the school rules, and how do their meanings vary across different school rules?

What I need to do:

- Make a list of all school rules that teachers and students are talking about or can be find on posters. Coding, sorting, and categorizing them (this will be my first step).
- Conduct more informal conversations with students and qualitative interviews or focus groups with students about their thoughts, feelings, and concerns about different school rules (this will be my second step).

next in order to guide further data collection and coding, and hence, illustrates how theoretical sampling can take place in and be built upon memo writing. Later in the research process, memos become more elaborate and conceptual. Charmaz (2006) terms these as *advanced memos*, since the researchers focusing on (a) tracing and categorizing data subsumed by their topic, (b) describing how their category emerges and changes, (c) identifying the beliefs and assumptions that support it, (d) telling what the topics looks and feels like from various vantage points, (e) placing it within an argument, and (f) making comparisons (e.g., comparing different people or different situations; comparing categories in the data with other categories; comparing sub-categories with general categories for fit or with each other, or making comparisons with existing literature).

In Exhibit 12.2, Thornberg (2008b) has come further in his data collection, coding and analysis. He has now identified a pattern in the schoolchildren's meaning-making of school rules. Note that the memo begins with a title, "How students make meaning of school rules." Meaning-making of school rules is actually the main category in the memo, and could be understood as a basic social reasoning process, which in turn is related to the constructed category system of school rules. Meaning-making of school rules consists of four sub categories (relational explanations, structuring explanations, protecting explanations, and meaning-making difficulties) which correspond to the four main categories of school rules (relational rules, structuring rules, protecting rules, and etiquette rules). Making meaning in terms of perceiving a reasonable explanation behind the rule is also linked to how to value the rule.

EXHIBIT 12.2

ADVANCED MEMO EXAMPLE

How students make meaning of school rules

In school, there exists a set of school and classroom rules in order to coordinate, regulate and organize the individuals and their activities in school, to establish and maintain an environment conducive to learning in classroom and to create order and safety in school (e.g., McGinnis, Frederick & Edwards, 1995; Malone & Tietjens, 2000). According to the new sociology of childhood (e.g., Corsaro, 1997; Prout & James, 1997) and the socio-cognitive domain theory (Nucci, 2001; Neff & Helwig, 2002; Turiel, 1983, 1998), children are not just passive receivers in their socialization process, but interpret their experiences and reflect on them. Some social norms or rules will be accepted while others will be questioned or doubted, or even rejected by them. A core process in the findings is *meaning-making of school rules* which refers to the way students justify and explain the points or reasons behind rules.

The categories of school rules

According to my ethnographic fieldwork, the students are exposed to a muddle of different school rules embedded in the everyday school life. In the analysis of the rules (see the draft, "A categorization of school rules") four main categories of school rules that seem to be relevant in students' meaning-making emerged: (a) *relational rules*, i.e., rules about how to act and not to act towards other people (e.g., don't hit, kick or tease others), (b) *structuring rules*, i.e., rules aimed at structuring and maintaining the activities that take place in the school or at structuring and maintaining the physical milieus where the activities take place (e.g., be quiet in the classroom), (c) *protecting rules*, i.e., rules about safety and health (e.g., don't run in corridors), and (d) *etiquette rules*, i.e., rules which manifest customs or traditions (e.g., don't wear your cap in classroom). In accordance with the prototype model of categorization (cf., Dey, 1999), these rule categories overlap in some degree (e.g., the banning of swearing is an etiquette rule in regard to swearing when, for example, talking about a movie or telling a story, but a relational rule in regard to swearing at others), which in turn reflects the multifarious complexity of the school rules and school life.

Students' meaning-making of school rules

According to the analysis of group interviews and informal conversations with students, they think that many school rules are good and important in order to make school a pleasant place to be in. However, how students make meaning of rules varies across the rule categories. Relational rules are explained and justified by the students in terms of relational explanations (transgressions have negative consequences in terms of harming others; following the rule has positive consequences in terms of well-being of others).

> *Jonathan:* You are not allowed to hit anyone.
> *Interviewer:* You aren't? How come?
> *Jonathan:* Because the other person can get hurt.
> *Alex:* Yes, and becomes upset.
> (From group interview 2A:7; three boys in second grade)

As in the excerpt, the students primarily and most frequently explain these rules with reasons about preventing students from harming or hurting other students, or from making students upset, unhappy, frightened, or feeling left out.

Structuring rules are most often explained and justified in terms of structuring explanations (transgressions result in interrupting or destroying ongoing activities or interrupting or hindering those who are participating in the activities).

> *Interviewer:* You have to raise your hand? How come?

> *Rasmus:* Otherwise, everyone might speak at the same time, and then you can't hear who is who, who is speaking.
> *Jesper:* You can't hear. You can't here the person who is speaking
> (From group interview KB:3; three boys in kindergarten class)

Protecting rules are usually explained and justified in terms of protecting explanations (preventing accidental injury and ill health; promoting health). They often reason that transgressions of these rules result in ill health or risks of accidents where the transgressor and/or others unintentionally get hurt.

> *Interviewer:* How come it's not allowed to cycle in the playground?
> *Amanda:* Playground? You have no control. People may come up behind you or something, and from the side, and then maybe you can run into them.
> (From group interview 5A:4; two girls in fifth grade)

While the children make sense of relational rules, structuring rules and protecting rules, it appears to be more difficult for them to explain and justify, and hence make sense of, etiquette rules. They usually do not know the point of these rules. The often tell me that "it's just a rule" or just something the teachers have thought up. Hence, etiquette rules usually result in meaning-making difficulties. In addition, many students think these rules are arbitrary. They argue that transgressions of them do not have any negative effects. "The thing about caps that actually don't disturb anyone and you don't start fighting because of them or anything. Why can't you wear them? I really wonder" (second-grade girl, from group interview 2B:6).

The relation of meaning-making and valuing

The meanings students make of school rules appear to affect how they value them. The relational rules are valued as the most important rules. They exist to prevent students from harming each other. A transgression of a relational rule is judged to be wrong even if they imagine a situation in which their teachers have cancelled the actual rule. The consequence would be harming others whether the rule exists or not.

Many students also value some of the protecting rules as the most important rules, and refer to their function of preventing students from getting hurt by accidents. However, if students judge that there is actually no risk of accidents or ill-health, then they seem to think that it would be okay to do the forbidden act (e.g., "I don't crash into other people. I look where I'm going"). How students value protecting rules depends on how they perceive risk and skills. If they perceive that the forbidden act would result in ill-health or may lead to accidental injury, then they judge this act to be wrong independent of the rule exists or not. However, those who think it is okay to run in corridors,

Grounded Theory • 425

> to cycle or skate-role in the playground, and so forth, often argue that the risk of accidents or ill-health is very low or non-existent.
>
> Moreover, a lot of students also claim that structuring rules are important, since they prevent the activities in school from being interrupted or spoiled. Many students judge transgressions of structuring rules to be wrong even if these rules would be removed. Nevertheless, some students value structuring rules as not so important. The variation here was dependent on how students value the activities (deskwork in the classroom, circle-time or such like) that structuring rules support and uphold as well as other activities that would be in conflict with them (e.g., "Math is boring. Just sitting and working is boring. Dreadfully boring. Talking is much more fun"; a boy from group interview 5B:8; three boys in fifth grade).
>
> In contrast to these three rule categories, etiquette rules are normally valued as least important or unnecessary, which could, at least in part, be explained by students' problems in making meaning of these rules. Students often express criticism and negative attitudes towards etiquette rules in their conversations with me, but most of them, particularly the younger ones, do not openly tell their teachers about their criticism.
>
> ### Some conclusions
> How students make meanings of rules seems to (a) be related to rule category, and (b) affect how they value rules. If teachers want students to accept a rule it appears to be important that students (a) can make sense of the rule (i.e., perceive or recognize the reasons behind the rule), and (b) believe in the rule explanations (i.e., that the reason behind the rule is perceived as reasonable and trustworthy).

During focused coding, grounded theorists use memos to raise focused codes into tentative conceptual categories. They start a memo with a title, which is usually the tentative name of the category. Then they try to write down a working definition of the category and explore its properties. Excerpts from data are used.

Another memo-writing strategy is to write the memos during the interview transcription process and to treat the memo as part of the interview record (Perhamus, 2009, 2010b). This type of memo-writing, which Perhamus terms *transcriptive memo-writing*, incorporates ideas of constructivism, researcher subjectivity, multiplicity and fluidity of meaning, and the importance of viewing a research situation through several contextual lenses. A simple strategy, it is the timing of this writing that is the key. Though additional memo-writing occurs later, as the data analysis develops, this strategy uses transcriptive memos as the initial memo-writing. Transcriptive memos are not titled or re-worked through data analysis. The analytic refinement occurs during write-up but leaves the memo itself in tact as it was first written during transcription. Transcriptive memo-writing encourages the researcher to "re-experience" interview moments during the transcription process. Being "in" the interview once again, the researcher not only recalls the interview in more detail, s/he is "there" again. Sensory memory is activated. The researcher can smell and hear the interview setting again. If a participant cried during part of the interview, hearing those tears again can stir emotion in the researcher that s/he might have felt while doing the interview. Or, if the boundaries of being in the researcher role restricted the researcher's freedom to actually feel the emotion in that researcher/participant social interaction—that human moment—there is freedom during the transcription process to feel that which one originally kinesthetically contained.

Transcriptive memo-writing is a strategy for tapping into these sensory-activated moments and is a textual space for recording the researcher's kinesthetic experiences and analysis of these experiences. In this way, transcriptive memo-writing deepens the analytic reflection of data. The researcher's re-experience of the interview, now recorded in the transcript itself, becomes part of the ethnographic record. As part of the ethnographic record, the researcher's "re-experience of the interview" is textually visible, kinesthetically accessible material for self-reflexive analysis of how her/his subjectivity became part of the interview. Table 12.2 provides two examples of transcriptive memos.

As the research process develops, memos become increasingly comprehensive and conceptualized. During the theoretical coding, researchers more intensely compare, sort, and integrate their memos. Analytical stories that have coherence begin to emerge in memos. Through *memo sorting*, grounded theorists investigate patterns across memos by comparing categories, relationships between categories, and theoretical codes. The aim of memo sorting is to explore, create and refine theoretical relationships, and integrating categories into a grounded theory. Memo writing and memo sorting are crucial in order to construct a grounded theory and to write drafts of papers.

THE DISPUTED LITERATURE REVIEW

Grounded theory is usually described as an inductive research approach in which the researcher constructs a theory from the data. According to the original grounded theory (Glaser & Strauss, 1967) and the Glaserian grounded theory (e.g., Glaser, 1978, 1998, 2005), researchers have to be unbiased and, moreover, a *tabula rasa*, untouched by earlier theory and research about the topic. Therefore Glaser and Strauss advocated delaying the literature review in the substantive area of the study until the analysis is nearly complete. Glaser (1978, 1998) argued that his strategy would keep researchers as free and open as possible to discovery, and avoid "contamination," i.e., to avoid forcing data into pre-existing concepts that might distort or do not fit the data.

However, based on her many conversations with Strauss, Charmaz (2006) states that for Strauss, the argument in the book *Discovery of Grounded Theory* (Glaser & Strauss, 1967) was rhetorical. Strauss and Corbin (1990) clarify their position by stating, "We all bring to the inquiry a considerable background in professional and disciplinary literature" (p. 48). The very idea of a researcher who gathers and analyses data "theory-free," without any prior theoretical knowledge and preconceptions has been strongly challenged by scientist philosophers (e.g., Chalmers, 1999; Hanson, 1965; Thayer-Bacon, 2003) and later grounded theorists (Bryant, 2009; Charmaz, 2006; Clarke, 2005; Dey, 1999; Dunne, 2011; Kelle, 1995, 2007; Lempert, 2007; Schreiber, 2001). In contrast to Glaser's position, Strauss and Corbin (1990, 1998) argue that researchers can use the literature more actively in grounded theory as long as they do not allow it to block creativity and obstruct discovery. According to them, familiarity with relevant literature can enhance sensitivity to subtle nuances in data, provide a source of concepts for making comparisons to data, stimulate questions during the analysis process (e.g., when there is a discrepancy between a researcher's data and the findings reported in the literature), and suggest areas for theoretical sampling. From the constructivist position of grounded theory, we argue that what researchers see or define in the data also relies in part upon the perspectives that they bring to it. "Rather than seeing your perspectives as truth, try to see them as representing one view among others" (Charmaz, 1995, p. 38), which indeed is a way of remaining open-minded. As Dey (1999) puts it, "There is a difference between an open mind and an empty head" (p. 251).

Dunne (2011) argues that the dictum of not reading literature early in the research process as a solution to the fear of contamination and forcing is an extreme position that underestimates researchers' ability to reflect upon the links between extant theories and their data collection and analysis. Instead of running the risk of reinventing the wheel, missing well-known aspects and coming up with trivial products or repeating others' mistakes, the researchers should take advantage of the pre-existing body of related literature to enhance their theoretical sensitivity and to deepen their theoretical insights (Thornberg, 2012b). A constructivist grounded theorist neither dismisses the literature nor applies it mechanically to data but, rather, uses it as a possible source of inspiration, ideas, "Aha!" experiences, creative associations, critical reflections and multiple lenses (Thornberg, 2012b; Thornberg & Charmaz, 2012). Instead of pure induction, we recognize the powerful interplay between induction, in which researchers are never a *tabula rasa*, and abduction, in which pre-existing theories and concepts are treated as provisional, disputable and modifiable conceptual proposals or hypotheses. Abduction is a selective and creative process that involves careful investigating each possible hypothesis to see which one explains a particular segment or set of data better than any other hypothesis (Douven, 2011; Pierce, 1958).

Thornberg conducted a research project to investigate values education in everyday school life. He was informed by a broad plurality of theories and concepts in moral development, normative ethics, values education, social psychology, micro sociology, and educational ethnography. During the research process, Thornberg consulted this pre-existing knowledge base in a theoretically agnostic manner (i.e., took a critical stance toward all extant theories and concepts, and treated them as provisional, disputable, and modifiable conceptual proposals; see Charmaz, 2006; Henwood & Pidgeon, 2003; Thornberg, 2012b) while he constantly compared data with data, data with codes, codes with codes, and so forth. Quite early in his fieldwork he found that the teachers' main concern in values education was to attempt to influence or teach students to be nice and kind to each other and to behave well in the classroom and other school areas. Hence, their everyday practice of values education mainly concerned trying to get students to understand and follow rules in school. Through theoretical sampling the literature on school rules (Thornberg, 2012b), Thornberg investigated what others had written about school rules and found no empirical research in which the content of school rules actually had been explored and analyzed in terms of developing a comprehensive and analytical overview of school rules (e.g., a well-developed typology or classification system). Hence, his ongoing literature review indicated this neglect and therefore justified taking an urgent empirical path to make new contributions. It was also a natural path to take based on theoretical sampling within his research project since teaching students to understand and follow rules in school appeared to be the teachers' main concern in values education. Therefore, he advanced the research process by systematically analyzing the huge amount of school rules embedded in everyday school life in order to develop a useful schema for classification. This grounded category system of school rules was later published (Thornberg, 2008a) and demonstrates how the rigor and depth afforded by grounded theory research can contribute to bodies of knowledge, fields of research and professional practices.

Informed by micro-sociological theories such as symbolic interactionism, ethnomethodology, and social constructionism as well as ethnographic and other qualitative research on norms and moral life of schools, Thornberg continued the analysis by comparing data, substantive codes and memos with theoretical codes and extant concepts such as "informal norms," "social order," "hidden curriculum," "social construction," "negotiation," "moral practice," "shared meaning," and "resistance." His analytical work resulted in a grounded theory of the latent morality of the good student embedded in school rules and teachers' everyday rule work (Thornberg, 2009), and a grounded theory of rule inconsistencies in school (Thornberg, 2007). Moreover, in addition to and as a consequence of the teachers' main concern, Thornberg was interested in the students' main concern(s) regarding school rules and teachers' rule work, and how they make meaning of these things. His data collection and analysis guided him to compare his data and codes with a particular theory of moral development—the social-cognitive domain theory. In one of his memos, Thornberg wrote:

> When I examine if there are general patterns of meaning-making of rules among students, I have to compare [my data, codes, categories and theoretical ideas] with socio-cognitive domain theory (Turiel, Nucci etc.): research indicates that children differentiate between morality and social conventions, judge moral transgressions as more wrong than conventional transgressions, and reasoning in different ways due to social knowledge constructed and organized in different domains (moral domain, conventional domain, and personal domain). Instead of testing or verifying the domain theory, I should explore and compare the students' criteria for judging rules as important or good vs. non-important or bad, as well as their meaning-makings of school rules in relation to my category system of school rules and make comparison within and between the rule categories. The outcome can then be compared with the socio-cognitive domain theory.

As the excerpt from his memo shows, even though Thornberg was informed by socio-cognitive domain theory, he did not use that theory in a deduced way to mechanically apply it on data. He conducted an abductive reasoning. Instead of forcing, he decided to systematically investigate how students value and make meaning of school rules, and then compared their meaning-makings in relation to the different rule categories that he had developed earlier. Thus, Thornberg remained theoretically agnostic as well as grounded in data by constant comparison, coding, theoretical sampling, and memo-writing. The analysis resulted in a grounded theory of students' meaning-making of school rules (Thornberg, 2008b). According to Strauss and Corbin (1998), the grounded theory approach can, in addition to developing a grounded theory, also be used to "elaborate and extend existing theories" (p. 12). By comparing his grounded theory with the socio-cognitive domain theory, Thornberg actually challenged and elaborated the socio-cognitive domain theory (Thornberg, 2008b). This grounded theory has recently been tested and supported in an experimental quantitative study (Thornberg, 2010b), in accordance with a pragmatic epistemology (Biesta, 2010; Morgan, 2007) and a mixed methods exploratory sequential design (Creswell & Plano Clark, 2011). See Thornberg (2012b) for a further discussion on how to take advantage of knowing and using the literature in an open-minded and data-sensitive way without forcing it on the data and the analysis, such as theoretical agnosticism, theoretical pluralism, theoretical sampling of literature, and theoretical playfulness.

GROUNDED THEORY RESEARCH IN THE FIELD OF EARLY CHILDHOOD EDUCATION

Contemporary research in the field of early childhood education (ECE) illustrates the wide-ranging contributions grounded theory studies can make to the field of early childhood educational research and practice. Recent foci of ECE grounded theory research has included program assessment issues (MacDonald, 2007); early literacy practices (Perry, Kay, & Brown, 2008; Williams & Lundstrom, 2007); classroom interactions (Bose & Hinojosa, 2008; Gillanders, 2007); instructional issues for general and inclusive classrooms (Burgess, et al, 2010; DeVore & Russell, 2007; Eckoff, 2009; Gilbert, 2009; Shearn, 2006); teachers' work with and children's reasoning about rules (Thornberg, 2007, 2008b, 2009); children's conceptual learning (Rosemberg & Silva, 2009); bystander behavior (Thornberg, 2010a); identity construction (Fluckiger, 2010); teacher beliefs and practices around teaching and learning (Blay & Ireson, 2009; Boyer, 2010; Edwards, 2005; Filipenko, 2004; Lin, Gorrell & Silvern, 2001; Lynch, 2009; Robson & Fumoto, 2009); transition from preschool to kindergarten and parent choice (Deyer & Barta, 2001; Dockett & Perry, 2004; Malsch, Green & Kothari, 2011; Noble, 2007); family dynamics (Maul & Singer, 2009); and policy and curriculum analysis (Roehrig, et al, 2008; Sofou & Tsafos, 2010). The scope of this research attests to the diversity of grounded theory's application and its continued relevance across fields of research. A review of the literature reveals that the main tenets of grounded theory (coding, constant comparison, categorizing, theoretical sampling, memo-writing and theory-building), while employed with some variation according to the researcher, guide the researcher through a process of data analysis that is grounded in "what is happening in the data."

Recent international attention to the importance of education in the early years has yielded several meaningful grounded theory studies that may be helpful to early childhood researchers, educators and policy makers. Fluckiger (2010) researched how 5 year old children actively constructed their cultural identities across the contexts of home, pre-school and the first year of elementary school in Australia and termed the process by which children do this as "world-building" (2010). Following the work of Greckhamer and Koro-Ljumgberg (2005) and Charmaz (2002), Fluckiger worked with emergent themes to identify social processes in the data and to eventually integrate "categories into a theoretical framework that specifies causes, conditions and consequences of the processes studied" (2010, p. 102). Sorting data through levels of coding, category building and conceptually mapping the relationships between them, Malsch, Green and Kothari (2011) developed a conceptual model through their research that illustrates parental perception of their involvement with their children's transition from Head Start to kindergarten in the United States. Using the constant comparative method and discovering categories and themes of their in-depth interview data, Sofou and Tsafos (2010) were able to identify how teachers in Greece made sense of a new national curriculum, both in theory and in practice. Like Thornberg's (2012b) work in Sweden that carefully sorts through the relevant literature and pertinent theoretical perspectives, the work of Rosemberg and Silva (2009) embraces cognitive and linguistic perspectives in its grounded theory research on how kindergarten teachers in Argentina develop strategies to aid in children's conceptual development. Studying Taiwanese pre-service teachers' beliefs about early childhood teaching and learning, Lin, Gorrell, and Silvern (2001) did initial coding, traced emerging themes and their dimensions and derived 6 categories to develop a model that illustrates the relationship between teacher belief and practice. Research by Roehrig, et al. (2008) on ECE teacher use of assessment data to improve instruction robustly details their grounded theory process of open coding, developing categories, tracing relationships between categories through the constant comparative method, using axial coding and identifying when they had reached the point of theoretical saturation. Their research produced a theoretical model that depicts teacher's experiences of the supports and barriers to using assessment data and offers ECE policy makers (e.g., regarding funding for Reading First Programs) important information about how to most successfully implement literacy programs and mandates.

While this summary of recent ECE grounded theory research is brief and by no means comprehensive of all of the important research happening in the field of ECE research, it does provide students, researchers and scholars who are interested in conducting grounded theory analysis some examples of how various researchers have used grounded theory. Perhaps most importantly, recognizing that the constructivist approach to employing grounded theory is both structured (in its rigorous insistence on constantly comparing data to data, code to code, code to data, memo to memo, etc.) and flexible (in its acknowledgement of the subjectivity in the research process) supports empirically grounded, novel research.

QUALITY IN GROUNDED THEORY RESEARCH

Finally, to sort through the vast literature that details ECE grounded theory research, one must be able to judge the quality of a grounded theory study. In their initial statement of grounded theory Glaser and Strauss (1967) argued that qualitative research must be judged from its own canon and not have the canon of quantitative inquiry imposed on it. Like Corbin and Strauss (2008), we are not comfortable using the terms "validity" and "reliability" when discussing quality in qualitative research, since these terms are rooted in and based on the logic and art of measurement and other aspects of quantitative research (e.g., reliability refers to the consistency or stability of measuring phenomena, which is evaluated by statistical methods such as Cronbach's alpha). We use the broad concept of quality to refer to credibility and usefulness of research and research findings. The concept of quality is more suitable for qualitative studies. In this regard, Glaser's (1998) presents workability, relevance, fit, and modifiability as his four criteria of product proof because he argues that the proof is in the outcome. "Does the theory *work* to explain relevant behavior in the substantive area of the research? Does it have *relevance* to the people in the substantive field? Does the theory fit the substantive area? Is it readily *modifiable* as new data emerge?" (p. 17).

In addition, Corbin (Corbin & Strauss, 2008, pp. 305–307) later presented a set of criteria for GT studies, in which there are some overlaps with Glaser's criteria:

1. Do the findings *fit* the experiences of the readers and the participants as well?
2. How *applicable/useful* are the findings for policy and practice?
3. Are the findings organized around *concepts* rather than a mass of uninterpreted data?
4. Is the *context* described so that the reader can more fully understand the findings and its concepts?
5. Do the findings "make sense" by presenting a *logical* flow of ideas or are there gaps or missing links in the logic?
6. Are there *depth* in the findings, i.e., descriptive details that add richness and variation in addition to the presentation of concepts and links between concepts?
7. Has *variation* been built into the findings to demonstrate the complexity of human life?
8. Are there *creative* aspects in the findings, i.e., do the findings say something new, put old ideas together in new ways, or lead to new understandings?

9. Does the researcher demonstrate *sensitivity* to the participants and to the data?
10. Have the *memos* grown in depth and degree of abstraction as the research moves along? For Charmaz (2006), criteria for grounded theory studies are presented in Box 12.1.

BOX 12.1   Charmaz' Criteria for Grounded Theory Studies

Credibility
- Has your research achieved intimate familiarity with the setting or topic?
- Are the data sufficient to merit your claims? Consider the range, number, and depth of observations contained in the data.
- Have you made systematic comparisons between observations and between categories?
- Do the categories cover a wide range of empirical observations?
- Are there strong logical links between the gathered data and your argument and analysis?
- Has your research provided enough evidence for your claims to allow the reader to form an independent assessment–and *agree* with your claims?

Originality
- Are your categories fresh? Do they offer new insights?
- Does your analysis provide a new conceptual rendering of the data?
- What is the social and theoretical significance of this work?
- How does your grounded theory challenge, extend, or refine current ideas, concepts, and practices?

Resonance
- Do the categories portray the fullness of the studied experience?
- Have you revealed both liminal and unstable taken-for-granted meanings?
- Have you drawn links between larger collectivities or institutions and individual lives, when the data so indicate?
- Does your grounded theory make sense to your participants or people who share their circumstances? Does your analysis offer them deeper insights about their lives and worlds?

Usefulness
- Does your analysis offer interpretations that people can use in their everyday worlds?
- Do your analytic categories suggest any generic processes?
- If so, have you examined these generic processes for tacit implications?
- Can the analysis spark further research in other substantive areas?
- How does your work contribute to knowledge? How does it contribute to making a better world?

(*Source:* Charmaz, 2006, pp. 182–183)

What each of these "quality checks" has in common is a sense of openness and sensitivity through the research process as well as an ability to theorize from the data while maintaining the integrity of staying close to the data. It is important to understand all of the aspects that constitute solid grounded theory research because it will strengthen the researchers' own research skills. Understanding what makes a strong grounded theory study helps researchers to evaluate studies that claim to use grounded theory, aiding their decisions about which research to incorporate, and enriching their own capacity to conduct grounded theory research.

Becoming familiar with the tools of grounded theory takes practice. Developing rich, nuanced analysis through grounded theory takes even more practice! Researchers have to allow themselves to be confused; it shows openness to new insights. To be lost in their data means that they are following their data. They have to pay attention to the tensions and silences of their data; it allows them to hear the analytic stories in their data. They have to notice the patterns that emerge through their data; it indicates where to go next. Immersing themselves in the data in this way is another kind of "check"—an internal check of sorts that pushes them to stay focused on the process of doing research and to be less preoccupied with what the research process will produce. Grounded theory's rigor, across each of the criteria check areas, lies in its attention to process. It is how researchers use grounded theory methods and strategies through the process of data analysis and continued data collection that gives the research findings depth, credibility, relevance and usefulness.

Finally, grounded theory findings will reflect resonance and originality if researchers have systematically used grounded theory methods and strategies with diligence, integrity and a willingness to remain open to new ways of seeing. Remember our safety net metaphor? Methodical employment of grounded theory tools keeps the research safety net strong and frees the researchers to explore their data, investigate hunches and seek deeper insights. Like the young child who enters the early childhood classroom, the researcher enters the research setting(s) and, later, "enters" the data. A researcher might be like the energetic child who runs into the classroom on that first day, excited to explore the environment; perhaps being more like the timid child who enters cautiously, unsure of what may unfold in this environment; or maybe like the child whose uncertainty about what school will be like keeps her/his feet planted at the door, waiting for the teacher to come gently take her/his hand.

Through its various processes and stages, grounded theory supports researchers and challenges them to dig deep into what the excitement, timidity, and need for guidance can afford them in the research process. It is great to start the research with enthusiasm and to have that excitement reignited through stages of coding, category building and memo-writing. It makes sense to feel timid about developing memos further, refining their titles and making preliminary theoretical connections about the patterns seen in the data. And researchers are not alone in having self-doubt as they reach the point of finalizing their analysis and in wishing for that guiding hand to reassure them that they findings are solid, interesting and useful. Remember that the data is the environment of the researchers and that the methods and strategies of grounded theory are that outstretched hand, ready to hold the researchers steady and guide them through the process of sorting through their data. The researchers have to trust the structure of grounded theory to allow them the freedom to enter their data from multiple angles.

REFERENCES

Biesta, G. (2010). Pragmatism and the philosophical foundations of mixed methods research. In A. Tashakkori, & C. Teddlie (Eds.), *SAGE handbook of mixed methods in social & behavioral research* (pp. 95–117). Thousand Oaks, CA: Sage.

Blay, J., & Ireson, J. (2009). Pedagogical beliefs, activity choice and structure, and adult-child interaction in nursery classrooms. *Teaching and Teacher Education, 25,* 1105–1116.

Bose, P., & Hinojosa, J. (2008). Reported experiences from occupational therapists interacting with teachers in inclusive early childhood classrooms. *American Journal of Occupational Therapy, 62,* 289–297.

Boyer, W. (2010). Empathy development in teacher candidates. *Early Childhood Education Journal, 38,* 313–321.

Bryant, A. (2009). Grounded theory and pragmatism: The curious case of Anselm Strauss. *Forum: Qualitative Social Research, 10* (3), Art. 2, http://nbn-resolving-de/urn:nbn:de:0114-fqs090325

Burgess, J., Robertson, G., & Patterson, C. (2010). Curriculum implementation: Decisions of early childhood teachers. *Australian Journal of Early Childhood, 35*(3), 51–59.

Chalmers, A. F. (1999). *What is this thing called science?* (3rd ed.). New York, NY: Open University Press.

Charmaz, K. (1995). Grounded theory. In J. A. Smith, R. Harré, & L. van Langenhove (Eds.), *Rethinking methods in psychology* (pp. 27–49). London: Sage.

Charmaz, K. (2000). Grounded theory: Objectivist and constructivist methods. In N. K. Denzin, & Y. S. Lincoln (Eds.), *Handbook of qualitative research* (2nd ed., pp. 509–535). Thousand Oaks, CA: Sage.

Charmaz, K. (2002). Qualitative interviewing and grounded theory analysis. In J. F. Gubrium, & J. A. Holstein (Eds.), *Handbook of interview research: Context and method* (pp. 675–694). Thousand Oaks, CA: Sage.

Charmaz, K. (2003). Grounded theory. In J. A. Smith (Ed.), *Qualitative psychology: A practical guide to research methods* (pp. 81–110). London: Sage.

Charmaz, K. (2006). *Constructing grounded theory.* London: Sage.

Charmaz, K., & Belgrave, L. L. (2012). Qualitative interviewing and grounded theory analysis. In J. F. Gubrium, J. A. Holstein, A. B. Marvasti, & K. D. McKinney (Eds.), *The SAGE handbook of interview research* (2nd ed., pp. 347–365). Thousand Oaks, CA: Sage.

Clarke, A. E. (2005). *Situational analysis: Grounded theory after the postmodern turn.* Thousand Oaks, CA: Sage.

Cohen, L., Manion, L., & Morrison, K. (2007). *Research methods in education* (6th ed.). New York, NY: Routledge.

Corbin, J., & Strauss, A. (2008). *Basics of qualitative research: Techniques and procedures for developing grounded theory* (3rd ed.). Thousand Oaks, CA: Sage.

Creswell, J. W., & Plano Clark, V. L. (2011). *Designing and conducting mixed methods research* (2nd ed.). Thousand Oaks, CA: Sage.

DeVore, S. & Russell, K. (2007). Early childhood education and care for children with disabilities: Facilitating inclusive practice. *Early Childhood Education Journal, 35,* 189–198.

Dey, I. (1999). *Grounding grounded theory.* San Diego: Academic Press.

Dockett, S. & Perry, B. (2004). Starting school: Perspectives of Australian children, parents and educators. *Journal of Early Childhood Research, 2,* 171–189.

Douven, I. (2011). Pierce on abduction. In E. N. Zalta (Principal Ed.), *Stanford encyclopedia of philosophy.* Retrieved from http://plato.stanford.edu/entries/abduction/pierce

Dunne, C. (2011). The place of literature review in grounded theory research. *International Journal of Social Research Methodology, 14,* 111–124.

Edwards, S. (2005, March). Children's learning and developmental potential: Examining the theoretical informants of early childhood curricula from the educator's perspective. *Early Years, 25*(1), 67–80.

Filipenko, M. (2004). Constructing knowledge about and with informational texts: Implications for teacher-librarians working with young children. *School Libraries Worldwide, 10,* 21–36.

Fluckiger, B. (2010). Culture-switching in different worlds: Young children's transition experiences. *Australasian Journal of Early Childhood, 35,* 101–108.

Gilbert, A. (2009). Utilizing science philosophy statements to facilitate K-3 teacher candidate's development of inquiry-based science practice. *Early Childhood Education Journal, 36,* 431–438.

Gillanders, C. (2007). An English-speaking prekindergarten teacher for young Latino children: Implications of the teacher-child relationship on second language learning. *Early Childhood Education Journal, 35,* 47–54.

Glaser, B. G. (1978). *Theoretical sensitivity.* Mill Valley, CA: Sociology Press.

Glaser, B. G. (1998). *Doing grounded theory: Issues and discussions.* Mill Valley, CA: Sociology Press.

Glaser, B. G. (2005). *The grounded theory perspective III: Theoretical coding.* Mill Valley, CA: Sociology Press.

Glaser, B. G., & Strauss, A. L. (1967). *The discovery of grounded theory.* Chicago: Aldine.

Greckhamer, T., & Koro-Ljungber M. (2005). The erosion of a method: Examples from grounded theory. *International Journal of Qualitative Studies in Education, 18,* 729–750.

Hanson, N. R. (1965). *Patterns of discovery: An inquiry into the conceptual foundations of science.* Cambridge: Cambridge University Press.

Henwood, K., & Pidgeon, N. (2003). Grounded theory in psychological research. In P. M. Camic, J. E. Rhodes, & L. Yardley (Eds.), *Qualitative research in psychology: Expanding perspectives in methodology and design* (pp. 131–155). Washington, DC: American Psychological Association.

Johnson, B., & Christensen, L. (2008). *Educational research: Quantitative, qualitative, and mixed approaches* (3rd ed.). Thousand Oaks, CA: Sage.

Kelle, U. (1995). Theories as heuristic tools in qualitative research. In I. Maso, P. A. Atkinson, S. Delamont, & J. C. Verhoeven (Eds.), *Openness in research: The tension between self and other* (pp. 33–50). Assen: van Gorcum.

Kelle, U. (2007). The development of categories: Different approaches in grounded theory. In A. Bryant & K. Charmaz (Eds.), *The SAGE handbook of grounded theory* (pp. 191–213). Thousand Oaks, CA: Sage.

Lempert, L. B. (2007). Asking questions of the data: Memo writing in the grounded theory tradition. In A. Bryant, & K. Charmaz (Eds.), *The SAGE handbook of grounded theory* (pp. 245–264). Thousand Oaks, CA: Sage.

Lin, H. L., Gorrell, J., & Silvern, S. (2001). Taiwan's early childhood preservice teachers' professional beliefs. *Journal of Research in Childhood Education, 15,* 242–255.

Lynch, J. (2009). Preschool teachers' beliefs about children's print literacy development. *Early Years, 29,* 191–203.

MacDonald, M. (2007). Toward formative assessment: The use of pedagogical documentation in early elementary classrooms. *Early Childhood Research Quarterly, 22,* 232–242.

Malsch, A. M., Green, B. L., & Kothari, B. K. (2011). Understanding parents' perspectives on the transition to kindergarten: What early childhood settings and schools can do for at-risk-families. *Best Practices in Mental Health, 7,* 47–66.

Maul, C., & Singer, G. (2009). "Just good different things": Specific accommodations families make to positively adapt to their children with developmental disabilities. *Topics in Early Childhood Special Education, 29,* 155–170.

Morgan, D. L. (2007). Paradigms lost and pragmatism regained: Methodological implications of combining qualitative and quantitative methods. *Journal of Mixed Methods Research, 1,* 48–76.

Perhamus, L. (2009). In the name of health and wellness: An analysis of how young children, their families and school navigate the moralizing dynamics of health promotion. University of Rochester). *ProQuest Dissertations and Theses,* http://search.proquest.com/docview/304989251?accountid=13567

Perhamus, L. (2010a). "But your body would rather have this...": Conceptualizing health through kinesthetic experience. *The International Journal of Qualitative Studies in Education, 23,* 843–866.

Perhamus, L. (2010b). Entering the experiential world of children's meaning-making: Methodological considerations for developing child-centered research. Paper presented at the May, 2010 American Educational Research Association Annual Meeting. Denver, Colorado.

Perry, N., Kay, S. M., & Brown, A. (2008). Continuity and change in home literacy practices of Hispanic families with preschool children. *Early Child Development and Care, 178,* 99–113.

Pidgeon, N., & Henwood, K. (1996). Grounded theory: Practical implementation. In J. T. E. Richardson (Ed.), *Handbook of qualitative research methods for psychology and the social sciences* (pp. 86–101). Leicester: The British Psychological Society.

Pierce, C. S. (1958). *Collected papers of Charles Sanders Pierce. Vol. VII: Science and philosophy.* Cambridge: Harvard University Press [Edited by A. W. Burks].

Robson, S., & Fumoto, H. (2009). Practitioners' experiences of personal ownership and autonomy in their support for young children's thinking. *Contemporary Issues in Early Childhood, 10,* 43–54.

Roehrig, A., Duggar, S. W., Moats, L., Glover, M., & Mincey, B. (2008). When teachers work to use progress monitoring data to inform literacy instruction: Identifying potential supports and challenges. *Remedial and Special Education, 29,* 364–382.

Rosemberg, C. R., & Silva, M. L. (2009). Teacher-children interaction and concept development in kindergarten. *Discourse Processes, 46,* 572–591.

Shearn, P. (2006). Teaching practice in safety education: Qualitative evidence. *Research Papers in Education, 21,* 335–359.

Silverman, D. (2005). *Doing qualitative research* (2nd ed.). London: Sage.

Sofou, E., & Tsafos, V. (2010). Preschool teachers' understandings of the national preschool curriculum in Greece. *Early Childhood Education Journal, 37,* 411–420.

Schreiber, R. S. (2001). The "how to" of grounded theory: Avoiding the pitfalls. In R. S. Schreiber & P. N. Stern (Eds.), *Using grounded theory in nursing* (pp. 55–83). New York, NY: Springer Publishing Company.

Strauss, A., & Corbin, J. (1990). *Basics of qualitative research.* Newbury Park: Sage.

Strauss, A., & Corbin, J. (1998) *Basics of qualitative research* (2nd ed.). Thousand Oaks, CA: Sage.

Thayer-Bacon, B. J. (2003). Pragmatism and feminism as qualified relativism. *Studies in Philosophy and Education, 22,* 417–438.

Thornberg, R. (2007). Inconsistencies in everyday patterns of school rules. *Ethnography and Education, 2*(3), 401–416.

Thornberg, R. (2008a). A categorisation of school rules. *Educational Studies, 34*(1), 25–33.

Thornberg, R. (2008b). School children's reasoning about school rules. *Research Papers in Education, 23*(1), 37–52.

Thornberg, R. (2009). The moral construction of the good pupil embedded in school rules. *Education, Citizenship and Social Justice, 4,* 245–261.

Thornberg, R. (2010a). A student in distress: Moral frames and bystander behavior in school. *The Elementary School Journal, 110,* 585–608.

Thornberg, R. (2010b). A study of children's conceptions of school rules by investigating their judgments of transgressions in the absence of rules. *Educational Psychology, 30,* 583–603.

Thornberg, R. (2012a). Grounded theory. In J. Arthur, M. Waring, R. Coe, & L. V. Hedges (Eds.), *Research methods & methodologies in education* (pp. 85–93). Thousand Oaks, CA: Sage.

Thornberg, R. (2012b). Informed grounded theory. *Scandinavian Journal of Educational Research, 56,* 243–259.

Thornberg, R., & Charmaz, K. (2012). Grounded theory. In S. D. Lapan, M. T. Quartaroli, & F. J. Reimer (Eds.), *Qualitative research: An introduction to methods and designs* (pp. 41–67). San Francisco, CA: John Wiley/Jossey-Bass.

Thornberg, R., & Charmaz, K. (2014). Grounded theory and theoretical coding. In *SAGE Handbook of qualitative analysis* (pp. 153–169). Thousand Oaks, CA: Sage.

Williams, C., & Lundstrom, R. (2007). Strategy instruction during word study and interactive writing activities. *The Reading Teacher, 61,* 204–212.

CHAPTER 13

CONDUCTING EARLY CHILDHOOD QUALITATIVE RESEARCH IN THE TWENTY-FIRST CENTURY

J. Amos Hatch and Chonika Coleman-King

The aim of this chapter is to give readers an overview of early childhood qualitative research as it is evolving at the present time. We believe that qualitative approaches to systematic inquiry provide information and insights that bring knowledge and understanding to the important work of early childhood educators at all levels that are unavailable from other sources. The unique ability of qualitative inquiry to explore the lived realities of young children and the adults who work with them makes it an invaluable research tool. As much as at any time in the past, the field of early childhood education needs well designed, rigorously done, qualitative studies that reveal for inspection what is going on in all types of settings that include young children and those who educate and care for them. Early childhood qualitative research is well positioned to provide data-based findings that can shape early childhood theory, research, policy and practice in the twenty-first century.

In this chapter, we divide our discussion into topics that we think are important to understanding contemporary early childhood qualitative research: Characteristics of Early Childhood Qualitative Research; Key Considerations for Conducting Early Childhood Qualitative Research; Types of Early Childhood Qualitative Research; and Issues in Conducting Early Childhood Qualitative Research. While all of the topics covered have broader implications for qualitative research in general, we have tried to provide examples and explanations that link directly to the concerns and interests of early childhood researchers.

CHARACTERISTICS OF EARLY CHILDHOOD QUALITATIVE RESEARCH

In this chapter, we adopt the standard of the early childhood education community and consider early childhood to be birth through age eight (Copple & Bredekamp, 2009). We take early childhood qualitative research to be inquiry of the type described below that focuses on individuals (children and adults), practices, policies and institutions involved in the care and education of children birth to age eight. For a definition of qualitative research, we start with Shank's (2006) assertion that it is "systematic empirical inquiry into meaning" (p. 5). By *systematic*, Shank means that the research is carefully planned and ordered, not random or haphazard in design. By *empirical*, he means that this type of inquiry depends on the collection of data that are grounded in the world of experience. The phrase *inquiry into meaning* denotes qualitative researchers' desire to understand how others make sense of their experience. In Denzin and Lincoln's (2008) words, "qualitative researchers study things in their natural settings, attempting to make sense of, or interpret, phenomena in terms of the meanings people bring to them" (p. 4).

Building on this definition, we see several characteristics that distinguish qualitative research from other forms of inquiry. The elements described are adapted from a chapter on early childhood qualitative research published in the *Handbook of Research on the Education of Young Children* (Spodek & Saracho, 2006). In preparing this section, we started with characteristics described in the *Handbook* chapter (Hatch & Barclay-McLaughlin, 2006) and compared these to defining elements found in three recent textbooks focused on qualitative research methods (Creswell, 2007; McMillan & Schumacher, 2010; Merriam, 2009). The list below is organized with the most frequently cited characteristics across the four sources coming first. We recognize that not every qualitative study will have all of these components, but the list provides a reference point for discriminating qualitative work from other forms of research.

Natural Settings

All four of the sources cited above noted that a hallmark of qualitative studies is that they are undertaken in natural settings; as is noted in the definition above, context matters in qualitative research. Capturing the enactment of social phenomena in the natural contexts in which they occur is an essential attribute of qualitative inquiry. Rather than creating contrived environments in which "extraneous variables" can be controlled, qualitative researchers seek to capture and make sense of the complex contexts in which real-world social activity takes place. The classic example of using controlled environments to study early childhood social phenomena is "strange situation" research, in which babies, their mothers, and other adults experience a standardized series of separation and reunion episodes in a laboratory setting (Ainsworth, Blehar, Waters, & Wall, 1978). Babies' levels of attachment are determined based on quantitative data in the form of frequency counts of predetermined behaviors observed in the babies during these episodes. In contrast, qualitative data collection happens "at the site where participants experience the issue or problem under study" (Creswell, 2007, p. 37). So qualitative researchers interested in relationships between adults and infants would not set up contrived situations in laboratories, preferring to study interactions between babies and their caregivers in natural surroundings such as maternity wards, homes, and child care settings (see Hatch, 1995a).

Researcher as Data Collection Instrument

All four sources also identified as critical the role of the qualitative researcher as one who collects data directly. Qualitative data are almost always comprised of field notes from participant observation, interview transcriptions, and/or artifacts (e.g., documents, photographs, children's work) that represent the context under examination. These data are empirical representations of the lived experiences of complex human beings who are negotiating complex social situations. Qualitative researchers want to collect these data directly. They resist relying on instruments designed by others (e.g., checklists or questionnaires) because using such tools means, "the researchers are not then as "close" to the data as they need to be for a full understanding" (McMillan & Schumacher, 2010, p. 323).

Flexible Design

All four sources listed flexible or emergent design as an important characteristic of qualitative research. As Hatch and McLaughlin (2006) argue, "Because the act of doing qualitative research often leads researchers in directions they did not anticipate as studies are planned, research questions, methods, and analysis procedures are often altered as studies are implemented" (p. 498). While it is vital to have a solid research design in place prior to beginning a qualitative project, it is important to realize that there is an emergent quality to this kind of inquiry. It is not unusual for researchers to make changes in their studies in response to what they find out as they begin collecting and processing their qualitative data. This way of conceptualizing research is different from more traditional approaches that emphasize data collection according to a predetermined protocol designed to test a predetermined hypothesis.

Inductive Data Processing

In qualitative studies, "researchers gather data to build concepts, hypotheses, or theories rather than deductively testing hypotheses as in [quantitative] research" (Merriam, 2009, p. 15). The inductive nature of qualitative research was noted as an important characteristic in three of the sources examined. In contrast to quantitative research, the logic of qualitative work flows from specific to general. Qualitative researchers collect specific examples of the phenomena under study and then use inductive analysis processes to uncover patterns, generalization, themes or theories in the data. This approach requires rigorous data analysis procedures that provide ways for qualitative researchers to process large amounts of information and inductively generate findings that are solidly represented in the specifics of the data collected.

Participant Perspectives

Three sources also noted that a prominent feature of qualitative studies is their focus on capturing the understandings that participants use to make sense of their experiences in particular contexts. Observing and interviewing study participants and collecting artifacts generated by them produce data that provide insights into "the insider perspectives of actors in specific social settings" (Hatch & McLaughlin, 2006, p. 15). Participant perspectives on the social phenomena being studied are the researcher's gateway into understanding how social contexts such as early childhood settings work. Qualitative researchers depend on capturing the perspectives of individual participants in enough depth to adequately represent those perspectives in their research reports.

Complexity

The complex nature of qualitative research projects was also noted by three of the sources studied in the preparation of this section. In the words of McMillan and Schumacher (2010),

> Central to qualitative research is the belief that the world is complex and that there are few simple explanations for human behavior. It follows, then, that the methods that investigate behavior, as well as the explanations, need to be sufficiently complex to capture the true meaning of what has occurred (p. 324).

Qualitative approaches do not attempt to reduce or "control" the complexity inherent in the real world, as quantitative researchers believe their statistically driven approaches do. Rather, qualitative researchers engage the complexity of the world by utilizing complex data collection and analysis techniques to generate complex research reports.

Extended First-Hand Engagement

Even though the final two characteristics we will describe were found in only two of the sources cited above, we believe they are vital to distinguishing qualitative research from other forms of systematic inquiry. Extended first-hand engagement with the field and with the data generated in the field makes qualitative work different from most quantitative approaches we know about. In order to capture the complexity inherent in social contexts, qualitative researchers expect to spend "long periods of direct engagement" (Hatch & McLaughlin, 2006, p. 498) in those contexts. Further, extended direct engagement with data generated in the field is required in order for researchers to make sense of what has been captured in their qualitative data. This is in sharp contrast to most quantitative procedures for collecting and analyzing data.

Meaning

As Merriam (2009) explains, "qualitative researchers are interested in how people interpret their experiences, how they construct their worlds, what meaning they attribute to their experiences" (p. 14). Capturing the meanings that research participants use to navigate their social existence is a primary focus of qualitative research projects. Rather than trying to predict future outcomes based on statistically significant quantitative relationships among variables, qualitative researchers are interested in understanding the meanings human beings bring to their experiences in social contexts. In early childhood, qualitative scholars believe that understanding the meanings that young children, their teachers and others involved make of their experiences in early childhood settings is as valuable for improving the field as quantitative studies of variables in relation to other variables.

KEY CONSIDERATIONS FOR CONDUCTING EARLY CHILDHOOD QUALITATIVE RESEARCH

Having identified defining characteristics of qualitative inquiry, in this section, we describe six elements directly related to the design and implementation of high-quality qualitative studies in early childhood contexts: Theory, Research Questions, Research Contexts and Participants, Data Collection, Data Analysis, and Findings. As each is discussed, specific guidance for applying these elements to the conduct of early childhood qualitative research is offered.

Theory

What is the place of theory in early childhood qualitative research? For research of any ilk to be considered legitimate, it must be theoretically grounded. In order for research methods of any type to be respected as viable means for gathering information about the world, they much be supported by a strong theoretical foundation. For the findings of any kind of research enterprise to be taken seriously, they must be connected to the relevant theories of the field. A well-developed theoretical framework is central to conducting and understanding all systematic empirical inquiry, including early childhood qualitative research.

A theoretical foundation for qualitative researchers has been defined as, "the system of concepts, assumptions, expectations, beliefs, and theories that supports and informs your research" (Maxwell, 2005, p. 33). Without a theoretical foundation, it is hard to imagine how any researcher would know where to begin to conceptualize, design, carry out, or interpret a study. Hatch (2002) makes a distinction between two kinds of theory related to qualitative research: methodological and substantive. We believe both are essential in the development and execution of early childhood qualitative studies.

When researchers articulate their methodological theories, they are revealing the scaffolding on which they base their decisions about what kinds of questions they will ask, what kinds of data they will gather, what kinds of analysis they will do, and what forms their findings will take. As will be described later in this chapter, there are many methodological approaches within the qualitative research domain. Each methodology has its own theoretical foundations, and it is vital for early childhood qualitative researchers to explore their own assumptions about how the world is or is not ordered (ontology), how knowledge about the world can be gained (epistemology), and what tools are appropriate given these metaphysical assumptions (methodology) (see Denzin & Lincoln, 1994; Hatch, 2002). Different qualitative methods are rooted in different sets of assumptions that define different research paradigms. We see no reason why any of the methods described later in this chapter would be excluded as possibilities for a study of early childhood phenomena; but we caution that an understanding and explication of methodological theory is vital to establishing a firm foundation for any early childhood qualitative study.

Substantive theories provide frameworks that allow researchers to locate, explain, and interpret the substance of their investigations. These are the conceptual frameworks that allow researchers to connect their work to the organized bodies of knowledge that make up the substantive dimensions of their fields of study. Without establishing some direct relationship to the extant substantive theories in the field, it will be hard for researchers to make any claims about the quality, salience, or importance of their findings. Some studies may verify elements of existing theories, others may modify accepted theoretical postulates, and some may debunk existing theories; but, all need to make connections to some kind of theoretical base in order to enter into the scholarly conversations of the field. Examples of substantive theories that have had a powerful influence in early childhood practice and research include constructivism, sociocultural theory, behaviorism, maturationism, psychoanalytic theory, and ecological theory. Many other important substantive theories (some of which critique what they consider to be the hegemonic influence of those listed) provide legitimate platforms for examining social phenomena in early childhood settings. The point here is that high quality early childhood qualitative studies are firmly supported by well-developed methodological and substantive theoretical bases.

Research Questions

What kinds of research questions do early childhood researchers ask? We consider the articulation of research questions to be one of the most important acts a researcher undertakes. Everything that follows in the design and implementation of a research project should be focused on answering the research questions of the study. While research questions sometimes change as qualitative studies unfold, a set of questions needs to be in place from the outset of the study. An absence of solid research questions can lead to bad decisions about where and how to collect data, how to process data once in hand, and how to make sense of what is discovered in the data.

Qualitative research questions are based on the opposite logic of the questions quantitative researchers ask. Qualitative researchers are not interested in testing null hypotheses or looking at relationships between dependent and independent variables. Qualitative research questions should be "open-ended, evolving, and nondirectional; restate the purpose of the study in more specific terms; start with words such as 'what' or 'how' rather than 'why'; and [be] few in number" (Creswell, 2007, p. 107). They give focus to the study without limiting what the researcher can discover once he or she is in the field. They identify a piece of territory that the researcher plans to explore without predetermining what precise elements will have an impact on the phenomenon under investigation. Their aim is most often to describe, explore, and/or explain phenomena that are little understood, or in certain kinds of studies, to engage in social action or raise consciousness about issues of inequality or injustice (see Marshall & Rossman, 2006).

Qualitative research questions typically include one broad "central" or "overarching" question followed by a small number of more focused, but still open-ended, subquestions (see Creswell, 2007; Hatch, 2002). A broad central question should capture the overall intent of the study, while limiting the study's breadth by defining the boundaries of the inquiry. Subquestions then carve out particular elements within the broader question that sharpen the focus of the study. For example, in a study of integrated (i.e., inclusive) early education programs in Hong Kong (Cheuk & Hatch, 2007), the overarching research question was: "What are teachers' perspectives on the provision of early childhood education for children with disabilities in integrated kindergarten contexts in Hong Kong?" Two subquestions for this study were: "How do early childhood teachers describe their experience with integration?" and "According to the teachers, what does instruction look like in integrated kindergarten programs?" (p. 419). The central question established that the study explored a particular group's (teachers) perspectives on a particular topic (inclusive programs for young children with disabilities) in a particular context (integrated kindergarten programs in Hong Kong). The subquestions highlighted specific elements among many subareas that could have been explored within the broad overarching question. It is worth noting that because of the focus of the study, all of the research questions stipulate that it is only the teachers' perspectives that are being examined.

Research questions are the lynchpin for all research projects, and early childhood qualitative studies are no exception. Qualitative research questions should grow out of the researcher's methodological and substantive theories. It makes no sense to ask research questions that are not answerable given the methodological assumptions of the researcher or are disconnected from the substantive theory of the field. Once established, solid research questions should lead early childhood qualitative researchers' decision making about the rest of the research process, including decisions about where and with whom the study should be conducted.

Research Contexts and Participants

How are research contexts and study participants selected for early childhood qualitative research projects? For starters, proximity, convenience, or familiarity should not be at the top of a list of reasons for choosing research settings or participants. We are surprised at the number of "backyard" studies we see in early childhood qualitative research, that is, studies done in the researchers' own classrooms or with their own colleagues. While many action research projects are designed so that practitioners can systematically study their own practices (see Rust, 2007), most other qualitative studies are better undertaken in contexts that are unfamiliar to researchers and with participants who are not otherwise affiliated with those completing the studies. As Berger and Kellner (1981) wrote more than 30 years ago, "It may be true that familiarity breeds contempt; more relevantly for the interpreting social scientist, familiarity breeds inattention" (p. 34). It is difficult at best to see with new eyes that which researchers are used to seeing every day; and it is especially difficult to explore the taken for granted assumptions that "insiders" use to make sense of their surroundings when researchers themselves have insider status. Except for carefully designed action research projects, in which practitioners systematically document their practice in order to improve it, we recommend that criteria for selecting contexts and participants like those outlined below be applied in most early childhood qualitative studies.

The central consideration for selecting contexts and participants for an early childhood qualitative study should be the likelihood that data will be available to answer the research questions adopted by the researcher. Whatever early childhood phenomena are under investigation, they are manifested in particular contexts by particular individuals. In an optimum research context, the social phenomenon of interest will be an important facet of the daily experience of those operating in that context. Further, qualitative researchers need to keep in mind that "objects and events have equivocal and undetermined meanings without a discernable context"

(Holstein & Gubrium, 2008, p. 178), so the selection of contexts and participants is vital to the planning (and reporting) of qualitative studies. If, for example, the researcher is interested in studying kindergarten children's experience with socio-dramatic play, a primary consideration will be finding contexts in which such play is likely to be observed. Further, it will be important to recognize and take account of the impact of the contexts selected on the expressions of socio-dramatic play observed.

Most research methods books offer guidance for sample selection in qualitative studies, providing lists of strategies and describing attributes of each (e.g., Miles & Huberman, 1994; Patton, 2002). These descriptions can be useful for thinking about and naming strategies for selecting research contexts and participants, but the essential point is that the phenomenon of interest has to be present in the context and researchers have to have access to data that will make it possible to answer their research questions. Such an approach has been called "purposeful sampling" (Cresswell, 2007; Merriam, 2009), and we recommend it as a solid starting place for making decisions about contexts and participants.

Novice early childhood qualitative researchers often wonder about how many research participants are needed for their studies. Unlike most quantitative studies in which large numbers are thought to be essential, "qualitative researchers argue that no direct relationship exists between the number of participants and the quality of the study" (Hatch, 2002, p. 48). Different kinds of qualitative studies and different kinds of research questions lead to different answers to the "how many" question. In qualitative work, it is possible to focus on a particular context or a small number of participants and generate important work that reveals the intricacies of how those contexts work and how individuals operate; but if the focus is tight and the number small, then the depth of the data must be significant. On the other hand, it is possible to design studies that focus on the perspectives of large groups of individuals who work in many contexts. In the later kinds of studies, the data set will be broader but lack the depth of a more tightly focused study. For example, one researcher might spend an extended period of time observing the peer interactions of a target group of six kindergarten children; while another might interview 50 kindergarten teachers about the place of peer interactions in their classrooms. Both could generate rich data sets from which important insights into the phenomena in question could be obtained.

Data Collection

How are data collected in early childhood qualitative studies? Qualitative researchers want to understand the phenomena they are studying from the perspectives of the participants in their studies. In order to reveal those perspectives, three kinds of qualitative data are most commonly utilized: observations, interviews and artifacts (Hatch, 2002). The kinds of studies being implemented and the kinds of research questions being asked will determine which kind or kinds of data will be most useful. Each of these broad categories of data collection is described below, and specific strategies within each category are discussed. In addition, several specialized data collection strategies that have been useful in qualitative studies designed specifically to elicit the perspectives of young children are described.

Participant observation has a long history in the social sciences, having its roots in ethnographies conducted by early anthropologists who spent extended periods of time living among distant groups and mapping the knowledge that group members used to make sense of their cultures (e.g., Malinowski, 1922; Mead, 1928). Participant observers seek to make a careful record of what those they are studying say and do in the naturally occurring contexts in which they operate. They make field-notes as they observe, writing down (or typing) as much detail as possible while they are in the research context, then filling in their notes soon after leaving the scene. In early childhood studies, observations may take place in classrooms, playgrounds, meeting rooms, homes, or any other contexts in which phenomena of interest might be enacted. Whatever the context, making a careful descriptive record of the events and conversations observed is the goal of participant observation, and the skills associated with watching carefully, listening closely, and recording accurately are essential to the collection of useful qualitative data.

Different levels of participation are appropriate for different studies and contexts. Many early anthropologists tried to act as full participants in the cultures they were studying; believing that the best way to understand insider perspectives was to try to negotiate cultural norms and expectations as an active participant. Other researchers occupy less participatory roles as they collect observation data. Spradley (1980) identified passive, moderate, and active levels of participation for qualitative researchers. Levels of participation have an impact on how the researcher will be perceived within the contexts of the study, what kinds of data will be collected, and how well the researcher will be able to make a record of that data (Hatch, 2002). In early childhood studies, decisions about levels of involvement with participants (especially when the participants are young children) are very important. While adult researchers have tried to take on the role of children as they collected participant observation data, most put more emphasis on observation and less on participation, often acting as a "fly on the wall" and trying to be as unobtrusive as possible in the research scene. In his microethnographic study of young children's peer culture, Corsaro (1985) became "Big Bill" to the three- and four-year-olds in his study, collecting participation data while enacting the role of a preschooler. Other early childhood researchers have critiqued attempts by adult researchers to enter research scenes as child participants because of the impact of power, size and gender differences involved and because such efforts wrongly assume that adults and children occupy completely separate social spheres, thus constructing young children as "little aliens to the dominant [adult] culture, the exotic objects of some other culture" (Alldred, 1998, p. 152).

Observation data can also be collected electronically. Digital video and sound recording technology can be used to capture primary or supplemental data in qualitative studies. Applying digital video technology directly to early childhood studies, Walsh et al. (2007) describe several advantages of this data collection strategy: (a) video captures details that are often missed in direct observation; (b) video can be slowed down, paused, and reviewed as many times as necessary to comprehend complex events and conversations; (c) video data can be revisited in various ways at various times for various purposes; and (d) digital video data are in a format that lends itself to a variety of data analysis approaches, especially those supported with contemporary computer programs. It should be noted that the use of video data brings with it special ethical responsibilities. Almost all universities require researchers to have human subjects' approval before conducting research that involves children, and that approval is often conditional on protecting the identities of participants. Researchers using video technologies (especially with young children) must take extra care as they gather, process, and present their data. Our view is that digitally recorded observations need to be converted into text as part of the research process, and raw data that include images of children should not be shared without the explicit knowledge and consent of participants.

Interviewing provides the qualitative researcher with ways of capturing participant perspectives that are unavailable via observation or any other data collection strategy. Effective interviews encourage informants to reveal the meaning structures they use to think about and act in their social worlds. In Patton's (2002) words, interviews tell researchers what is "in and on someone else's mind" (p. 341). Qualitative interviewers ask open-ended questions and invite informants into a conversation that reveals the participants' taken-for-granted assumptions about how they perceive their worlds.

Hatch (2002) described three basic types of qualitative interviews: informal, formal, and standardized. *Informal interviews* are usually incorporated into studies that include observation, so the researcher is present in the research scene and takes advantage of opportunities to ask questions of participants as they come up. Informal interviews most often happen spontaneously and, by definition, do not include sitting down with a predetermined set of questions. Researchers must be sure participants know that all of their conversations with researchers are data (i.e., they are "on the record"), even though these spontaneous interactions may not seem like interviews; and researchers should make written records of informal interviews as soon as possible after the conversations occur.

Formal interviews are "planned events that take place away from the research scene for the explicit purpose of gathering information from an informant" (Hatch, 2002, p. 94). Formal interviews (also call structured, semi-structured, or in-depth interviews) are often used to supplement participant observation studies, but they are used as the principal or only data collection strategy in some kinds of qualitative work. Researchers frequently bring lists of guiding questions to formal interviews, but these are meant to help the researcher remember to cover certain territory based on research purposes. Questions are open-ended, and effective interviewers listen carefully for opportunities to encourage informants to explain, give examples of, and reflect on statements the participants have made.

Standardized interviews are made up of open-ended questions, but the questions are asked in the same way and in the same order to each informant. In some ways, standardized interviews are more like open-ended questionnaires than informal and formal qualitative interviews, except that the interviewer (rather than the informant) records the responses. These kinds of interviews do not work for all kinds of qualitative studies, but they are efficient ways to collect data related to participant perspectives that can be easily compared across a large number of informants (Hatch, 2002).

Focus group interviews are a qualitative interview strategy in which researchers interview groups of participants, rather than having one-on-one conversations. Because individuals think, behave, and talk differently in groups than they do when interacting one-on-one with an interviewer, focus group interviews are designed differently and generate different kinds of data than traditional research interviews. In their description of designing and implementing focus group studies in early childhood settings, Ryan and Lobman (2007) note that "the data gathered from a focus group interview are framed not only by individual experience but also by the social nature and dynamics of the group" (p. 63). Focus groups make it possible to gather information on a particular topic from a particular group in a relatively efficient manner.

In early childhood qualitative studies, when young children are the informants whose perspectives researchers are trying to capture, interviewing them individually or in focus groups becomes especially complex. As Graue and Walsh (1998) point out, "The typical sit-down research interview is difficult to conduct with children. The younger the children are, the more difficult it is" (p. 113). Children's lack of familiarity with researcher-informant role expectations in interview contexts, their expectation that adults ask questions for which there is one right answer, and the built in differences in power and experience make it difficult to get children share what is really on their minds (Hatch, 1990). Young children "know more than they know they know" (Graue & Walsh, 1998, p. 113), but getting them to share what they know is tricky at best. Graue and Walsh (1998) share some general strategies for conducting interviews with young children, including interviewing them in pairs or small groups, using props to stimulate conversation, asking hypothetical questions and third-person questions, keeping interviews short and conversational, and timing interviews so that children are not pulled from more interesting activities in the classroom. Others have identified specific approaches to enhancing the chances of successfully gathering young children's perspectives through interviews, including the use of children's drawings (Einarsdottir, Dockett, & Perry, 2009); photographs taken by children (Clark & Moss, 2001); photographs shown to children (Stephenson, 2009); props such as toys, dolls and puppets (Brooker, 2001); and questionnaires that have been adapted for young children (Einarsdottir, 2007).

Unobtrusive data collection is any form of data gathering that takes place without having an effect on the phenomenon being examined. Unobtrusive data are nonreactive, that is, they are not processed through the perceptions, interpretations and biases of research participants. Hatch (2002) identified several types of unobtrusive data that are often collected in qualitative studies. Below, we describe some of those types of unobtrusive data and provide examples that might be collected in an early childhood qualitative study.

Artifacts are material objects that participants use as part of their everyday activities (e.g., researchers may examine the collection of math materials that a teacher uses as part of instruction in a first grade classroom). *Traces* are the unintended residue of human activity that provides evidence of how people operate in certain settings (e.g., researchers may study wear patterns on classroom carpeting to help inform their understandings of classroom activity in a kindergarten). Documents are official communication tools that all institutions use to manage their activities (e.g., researchers may collect minutes from school board meetings to document decision making related to the creation of a public preschool program). *Personal communications* are unofficial written expressions that participants create in order to share information with others or to make notes or record reflections for themselves (e.g., researchers may ask for access to the personal diaries of primary teachers who have decided to leave the profession after only a few years of teaching). *Records* are special kinds of documents with which institutions keep track of various facets of their enterprise (e.g., researchers may study the cumulative report cards of third graders identified for special education services). *Photographs* that were taken for purposes other than those of the research qualify as potentially valuable sources of information (e.g., researchers my collect photographs of annual "graduation" ceremonies from local Head Start centers).

The ubiquitous use of the Internet and the explosion of social media outlets, smart phones and computer applications have generated several new forms of unobtrusive data (e.g., emails, listserve postings, text messages, blogs, videos, and social media text and image postings). New computer-based technologies have also made access to electronic versions of many of the unobtrusive data described above possible. While there are serious ethical, legal, and methodological issues associated with the use of online information (see Merriam, 2009), these sources offer a potentially valuable source of unobtrusive data. As noted above, context is vital to understanding the meanings individuals make of their social circumstances. Online data are different in form and substance from more traditional data, and the contexts within which they are created and interpreted are different as well. Given that notions of context, relationships, communication, and identity are being redefined in cyberspace, special care should be taken when gathering, analyzing and reporting data collected from the Internet (see Hewson, Yule, Laurent, & Vogel, 2003). Along with the massive potential to gain access to unobtrusive data that were unknown a few years ago, early childhood researchers need to be aware of the limitations in making sense of such data in traditional ways.

Specialized data collection strategies have been developed specifically for eliciting the perspectives of young children, some of which were noted above in the section on interviewing young children. A prominent example of a specialized set of data collection strategies for listening to the voices and gathering the perspectives of young children is the "mosaic approach" (Clark, 2007; Clark & Moss, 2001). Developed in England and strongly influenced by Rinaldi's (2001) "pedagogy of listening" concept, the mosaic approach combines traditional data collecting strategies with participatory tools that children can use to be actively engaged in the research process. Some of the tools utilized by children include using cameras, leading tours, making books, and creating maps. Data from these tools are combined with data researchers collect to form a "mosaic" that children and adults jointly discuss, interpret and apply (Clark, 2007).

Other researchers interested in gathering young children's perspectives through engaging children as active participants in the research process have recommended the use of several additional specialized strategies. These include creating opportunities for verbal, graphic and expressive responding on the part of children (Schiller & Einarsdottir, 2009). Examples of ways to elicit verbal responses include having informal conversations, discussing books, playing games, and showing children photographs, artifacts, videos, and props (Dockett, Einarsdottir, & Perry, 2009; Einarsdottir, 2007). Graphic response options include encouraging children to make drawings, maps, diagrams, and journal entries (Darbyshire, MacDougall, & Schiller, 2005; Dockett, Einarsdottir, & Perry, 2009; Einarsdottir, 2007). Examples of expressive data generating tools researchers have utilized to engage young children include having them take photographs with digital and disposable cameras, make audio and video recordings, and generate narratives of their experience (Einarsdottir, 2007; Schiller & Einarsdottir, 2009). Dockett et al. (2009) point out the importance of using a wide range of strategies in studies of children's perspectives so that children will have a choice in how they participate and the voices of children with a wide range of competencies will be included.

Data Analysis

How are data analyzed by qualitative researchers studying early childhood settings? In order for research findings to be taken seriously, a clear description of rigorous, systematic data analysis is essential. In our preparation of this chapter and in our experience as editors, reviewers, and readers of qualitative research reports, we have noticed that such descriptions are often lacking. While this may be due in part to space limitations in journal articles and the complexity of describing analytic processes, we are concerned that data analysis methods utilized in some qualitative work may be less well developed than they should be. In the sections below, we offer an overview of qualitative data analysis processes, an example of the data analysis phases utilized in one early childhood study, and a brief discussion of electronic programs that support qualitative data analysis.

We agree with Merriam's (2009) general description of the data analysis enterprise:

> Data analysis is the process of making sense out of the data. And making sense out of the data involves consolidating, reducing, and interpreting what people have said and what the researcher has seen and read—it is the process of making meaning. Data analysis is a complex process that involves moving back and forth between concrete bits of data and abstract concepts, between inductive and deductive reasoning, between description and interpretation. (pp. 175–176)

Good qualitative studies generate voluminous data sets, and making sense of these data sets requires careful and systematic processing. Because much qualitative data will be in the form of text or electronic images, computer programs that automatically organize files can be especially helpful.

A necessary first step in any qualitative analysis is to develop ways to manage the sheer volume of data. Observational field-notes should be carefully labeled as they are stored, including setting up files that note exactly when

Conducting Early Childhood Qualitative Research in the Twenty-First Century ■ 457

and where the observations took place. Interview data should be similarly tagged so that file labels quickly identify (at the least) who was interviewed and when. Unobtrusive data in whatever form should be labeled as well so that it is clear what the data are and where and why they were collected. Qualitative data analysis involves looking for patterns, categories, and themes across data segments, so keeping track of the data segments from which original data elements came is critical. Setting up a consistent data management system from the outset will make this kind of tracking possible. It should go without saying that all data files must be backed up in multiple places in case of computer problems. Nothing is more devastating to a research project than the loss of data.

The general process of making meaning of mountains of data starts with some kind of initial coding strategy. Most coding approaches are inductive in nature and require the researcher to examine individual pieces of data that have relevance to the study and to assign some kind of code that represents the meaning the researcher interprets in those data pieces. Open coding as described in grounded theory approaches (e.g., Corbin & Strauss, 2008) is the archetype of this kind of early analysis step. There are several approaches to this initial coding process (some of which are described below), but the general goal is to begin to parse the data by identifying what segments of information may be important to the study and applying a symbolic code based on an initial interpretation about what those segments might mean. Again, it is critical that researchers have some kind of system for keeping track of the many codes that will be generated. It is also important to remember that the complete data set should be coded, rather than stopping once apparently powerful or interesting codes are identified.

The next general data analysis process involves taking a look across codes for potential connections and relationships. This step involves looking for patterns across the codes discovered in the initial analytic pass. Such patterns are at this point tentative and the thinking involved is still inductive. The researcher is looking across all of the codes generated in the first round to see what codes might go together and how they might be related. As potential patterns and relationships are pulled out, researchers write memos to themselves or use other means of keeping track of this emergent process. The final product of this stage is a summary of salient patterns found in the data, usually in the form of taxonomies, outlines or graphic representations.

A third general step is often deductive in nature. The researcher completes a careful search of the entire data set to look for evidence that supports or does not support the hypothetical categories of meaning generated so far. During this process, some categories are confirmed, some are discarded, and some are modified based on what the data have to say. The outcome of this third general step will be generalizations, patterns, categories, or themes that are supported in the data. It is important for researchers to make a record during these analytic processes of where data bits that support particular findings are located in the data and to watch for especially powerful data excerpts so that these can be used as examples when the final products of the data analysis are written up.

The steps described represent our overview of the general processes of data analysis across many specific types. Almost all data analysis models include these general steps, but each model will have its own way of dealing with each step, often including many substeps to guide the researcher more deeply into the data. While every qualitative study is unique and researchers most often develop data analysis strategies based on their individual studies, several data analysis models are described in the qualitative research literature. Examples of widely used data analysis models include those presented by Glaser and Strauss (1967), Hatch (2002), Miles and Huberman (1994), and Spradley (1980).

By way of an example specific to early childhood qualitative research, we next summarize the data analysis steps utilized in a dissertation study of a first year teacher's implementation of a critical literacy curriculum in an urban first grade classroom (Meller, 2008). For this study, the researcher modified Hatch's (2002) "typological" and "inductive" models and completed her data analysis utilizing the phases described below:

- Phase one consisted of rereading the data, scanning it for completeness and reacquainting the researcher with the data set.
- Phase two began with identifying the typologies to be used to parse the data.
- Phase three consisted of reading the data and highlighting entries related to the selected typologies.
- During phase four, the main ideas of each typology were recorded on summary sheets.
- Phase five consisted of inductively coding the main ideas on the summary sheets.
- During phase six, the raw data were highlighted according the codes developed in phase five.
- Phase seven consisted of creating a conceptual outline that summarized themes and subthemes identified to this point.
- In phase eight, excerpts that supported the themes and subthemes were identified and pasted into the conceptual outline.
- Phase nine consisted of writing generalizations that captured the findings to this point.
- Phase ten included writing interpretations that facilitated reporting the generalizations as a narrative (Meller, 2008).

Several computer programs have been developed to support the complex processes involved in qualitative data analysis. It is our view that such programs can be helpful for managing and organizing the large amounts of data most qualitative studies generate, but that these programs cannot do the "mindwork" (Wolcott, 1995, p. 155) required to discover the meaning in data. No computer programs have been developed to date that can simulate the reasoning and interpretive faculties required to make sense of the social phenomena captured in a well-developed qualitative data set. As Bogdan and Biklen (2007) summarize, "the computer program only helps as an organizing or categorizing tool, and does not do the analysis for the researcher" (p. 187).

Keeping their limitations in mind, there are, nonetheless, several programs that are used to support qualitative work. Software programs specifically designed for managing and analyzing digital video-data (i.e., *Transana, Transtool, The Observer,* and *Gamebreaker*), along with their applications to early childhood studies, are described by Walsh et al. (2007). These scholars note that the programs described can accomplish several tasks associated with data processing and analysis, including creating transcripts of videos, linking places in the transcripts to frames in the video, defining and marking codes, creating chronological records, and producing individual movies and presentations. Several other computer programs designed for working with more traditional qualitative data (*Atlas.ti, QSR NVivo, HyperRESEARCH,* and *MAXqda*) are described by Creswell (2007). It should be remembered that these programs are updated frequently and brand new programs are developed continuously.

TYPES OF QUALITATIVE METHODS USED IN EARLY CHILDHOOD RESEARCH

Qualitative research makes an important contribution to the dynamic body of scholarly work that exists in the early childhood field. Qualitative studies allow for deeper understanding of early childhood phenomena that carry multiple meanings and socially constructed interpretations of the world (Merriam, 2002). As such, qualitative research methods provide frameworks for examining the experiences of young children and the adults who work with them in their natural setting and provide inquiry tools that uncover the ways in which individuals make meaning of their experiences. Qualitative studies in early childhood education make it possible to gather information about the perspectives and experiences of adults who live and work with children and provide useful insight into the experiences and perspectives of children themselves (Darbyshire, MacDougall, & Schiller, 2005).

Depending on the phenomenon being studied, researchers must determine which methods will yield data that most adequately answer the questions being posed as well as assess the feasibility of utilizing particular methods. Because qualitative research often requires a great deal of direct contact between the researcher and research participants, the ability to choose a particular method can be constrained by a researcher's ability to commit to the time requirement necessary to engage in some types of qualitative inquiry.

Our goal in the preparation of this section was to survey the early childhood qualitative research reported over the past several years to determine which qualitative methods were being used. We also wanted to provide readers with examples of the kinds of studies we found. To accomplish these aims, we used a variety of search engines to scan the literature in search of methodologically sound examples of qualitative studies published within the last ten years. As we began our search, we focused on the following methodological frameworks: ethnography, microethnography, ethnomethodology, participant observation, interview studies, focus groups, artifact analysis, grounded theory, naturalistic inquiry, narrative, phenomenology, case studies, and action research.

It became evident that certain types of qualitative inquiry were published more frequently in the field of early childhood, while other methods in our initial list were not found. Our search revealed that early childhood qualitative studies published across a wide array of journals were dominated by case studies, interviews, and focus groups, that is, they were the most frequently used methods among the studies examined. Second to case studies, interviews, and focus groups were studies that used methods such as ethnography, microethnography, and ethnomethodology; and studies that relied on grounded theory and action research appeared to a lesser extent in the published literature examined. We also noted that methods such as participant observation were often combined with other ethnographic methods rather than being used independently.[1]

Below, are examples of studies in early childhood that utilized the qualitative methods discovered in our search. The methods included are organized according to the frequency with which they appeared in journals, with the most frequently cited methods appearing first. In the subsections to follow, we give a brief overview of each type of research, and then describe a recent study that stands as an example of the application of that method in early childhood contexts.

Case Studies

Case studies allow for the in-depth examination of a particular phenomenon or social unit that occurs within a bounded system, such as a particular program, group, context, or event (Merriam, 2002). Generally, the purpose of a qualitative case study is to unearth processes or insider interpretations regarding a specific phenomenon or entity. In this kind of work, the unit of analysis is considered to be "the case" (Merriam, 2002). Case studies allow for the examination of issues too complex for experimental designs and are generally used when someone wants to understand how contextual conditions might be pertinent to a particular phenomenon (Yin, 2002). Although the use of case study methods should not be restricted to exploratory research, they can be useful in providing information that informs the direction of future qualitative and quantitative studies.

In an example of a qualitative case study, McRae and Ellis (2012) examined a group of White first-graders' perceptions of diversity in their school environment. This study is classified as a case study, in part, because the first grade classroom and larger school community served as a bounded system in which researchers studied a particular phenomenon—the perceptions of diversity among a set group of students. McRae and Ellis justified the use of case study as a suitable methodology stating that the case study format provided for an evaluative analysis that allowed them to describe, explain, and interpret their data.

Data collection included observations of the first-graders in the school, as well as an analysis of photographs students took of their perceived representations of diversity. The images were later coded and themes were developed. Many of these themes reflected tensions in the ways that diversity was addressed and the presence of messages that counter an inclusive perspective. For the first graders, diversity was commonly represented by the following themes: "(a) difference from self as diversity, (b) representation of iconic diversity, and (c) symbolism of embracing or shunning others" (McRae & Ellis, 2002, p. 18). The images demonstrated that the children were aware of differences in speech, mobility, academic ability, gender, emotion, behavior, and culture, among other categories of difference. The study calls for educators to actively engage young children around their understandings of diversity so that they are not left with distorted and hurtful preconceptions.

Interviews

Interviews are commonly used qualitative data collection procedures. Interviews are often used as a primary source of data collection, and in other instances, interviews support other qualitative data by providing means for triangulating data (i.e., comparing interviews to data from other sources). In studies that utilize interviews as a primary source of data collection, an interview protocol is created using open-ended questions. However, interviews are rarely restricted to questions stated on the interview protocol. As an interview progresses, additional questions may arise based on prior responses to questions or the interviewer may feel the need to ask follow-up questions in an effort to gain additional insight (Hatch, 2002; Seidman, 2005)).

In an effort to better understand the ways in which childcare providers offer work–family support to low-income families, Bromer and Henly (2009) interviewed various types of childcare providers such as family and neighbor providers, licensed family child care centers, and center-based teachers. Two interviews were conducted with each provider. The first interview was a telephone interview to collect demographic information regarding the number of children served, hours worked, and relationship to children in care. The second interview was an in-depth semi-structured interview that lasted one hour on average. Childcare providers were asked to share how they entered the field, the relationships they have with children and families, and what kinds of support the provider offers to families. The interviewers generally asked a lead question followed by several probing questions depending on the participant's response.

In reporting the results of the study, Bromer and Henly (2009) relied heavily on quotes from interviews to support their analysis. This is an important characteristic of studies that utilize interviews as a preferred method of data collection. Multiple salient understandings were discovered through this inquiry. Findings indicated that childcare providers offered substantial logistical and economic help to parents. Family and friends tended to offer the most generous support by making flexible payment arrangements and defraying the cost of care. Licensed family childcare arrangements also offered support, but were constrained by professional guidelines and policies. This study gives insight into the effects of childcare on parents and how support for parents can vary depending on the models of care.

Focus Groups

The group dynamic is central to focus group interviews as each participant draws from and responds to the perspectives of others. It is through the interaction of the group that essential data are drawn. These data help reveal information that might not have been garnered from a one-on-one interview (Morgan, 1997). In focus groups, the researcher plays the role of a moderator rather than consistently posing specific questions throughout. This allows the group to take its own direction within the confines of the focal topic. Focus groups bring together a set of individuals with something in common or to discuss a common issue. Focus groups can serve as a tool for enabling children to share their perceptions of the world through their own lens rather than being mediated by adults' interpretations of their experiences (Darbyshire, et al. 2005). Young children are used to working in group settings and may be more comfortable interacting with their peers than in one-on-one interviews with an adult researcher.

The focus group interview was the primary research method used by Lara-Cinisomo et al. (2009) in a study of early childhood educators' perspectives on key preschool class experiences. The aim of the study was to reveal how early childhood educators from public centers, private centers, and family childcare programs understood the needs of children as they prepared to enter kindergarten. According to the authors, "Focus groups were deemed the most appropriate method of data collection because they allow informants to openly discuss their beliefs without feeling targeted, which can occur in a one-on-one interview" (Lara-Cinisomo et al., 2009, p. 9). The focus group format also allowed the participants to steer the direction of the conversation and highlight issues they found most salient within the broader topic.

Key findings in this study indicated that the caregivers felt the following areas were of key importance: teacher–child interactions, learning environments, and learning opportunities. However, variation was evident in the ways in which private centers, public centers, and family-based caregivers thought about each area. The study generated insight into the types of care children might receive in different types of settings as they prepare to enter kindergarten.

Ethnography

For some, the term ethnography is synonymous with qualitative research. We do not share that perspective. For us, ethnography is a particular type of qualitative work. Ethnography encompasses the opportunity to overtly or covertly observe and document the occurrences of people's daily lives over an extended period of time. This might include, "...watching what happens, listening to what is said, asking questions, collecting whatever data are available to [shed] light on the issues that are the focus of the research" (Hamersley & Atkinson, 1995, p. 1). The purpose of ethnographic observations often includes the desire to understand a cultural group and how individuals make sense of the world within a particular cultural orientation. As a result, ethnographers may also use formal and informal interviews, participation in daily activities, and the collection of artifacts to make sense of their observations and triangulate data (Hatch, 2002).

The documentation of ethnographic observations occurs through the process of writing field notes that record what happens during the observation and filling them in immediately after the observation has occurred. Field notes and other sources of data are used together to generate findings, which are reported through the use of vignettes, quotes, and rich descriptions of events. Buchbinder et al. (2006) provide a review of ethnographic research projects completed in child care contexts around the globe, arguing that ethnographic research models make possible not only the study of locations where child development happens, but also the examination of such places as sources of "enculturation and social reproduction" (p. 59).

In an exemplary early childhood ethnographic study, Long et al. (2007) explored children's play in multilingual and multicultural contexts. Each of the participants was from a nondominant culture. The ethnographers observed a Bangledeshi British child and her sister who lived in London, a Puerto Rican child in the Midwest United States, and an American child who lived in Iceland. The researchers sought to understand how these children scaffold their learning outside of school with a focus on what they know rather than a deficit perspective that generally highlights what children from non-dominant cultures do not know. Multilingual and multicultural characteristics of the participants studied helped researchers to learn how these children "drew on multiple worlds to create new contexts for teaching and learning through play" (p. 243). The researchers found that the children learned a variety of academic concepts, including language, literacy, and mathematics by "playing" school and mimicking experiences in religious institutions. It was also through play that the children took risks with cultural roles and routines. The researchers highlighted the value of play as a site where children can take control of their own learning.

Microethnography

Micoethnographies, generally taken up by sociolinguists, focus on the minute details of face-to-face interactions within a given context (Hatch, 2002). These interactions are typically captured on video and later analyzed. Discourse analysis procedures provide tools for understanding the complex dynamics of conversations, as well as how individuals come to understand and integrate divergent views regarding a particular issue or topic (Wetherell, Taylor, & Yates, 2001).

Given the current educational climate in which accountability measures strongly influence curricula in early childhood settings, Wohlwend (2007) sought to understand how early childhood teachers engage in discourse around play, which has been eliminated from many public school classrooms. This research attempted to capture the tensions inherent in teachers both wanting to protect play practices and comply with institutional expectations and revealed how this tension manifested in the language and discourse of early childhood teachers.

Wohlwend (2007) employed a microethnographic analysis of conversations that occurred during one discussion between two kindergarten and three first-grade teachers. During the discussion session, the teachers were asked to view video clips, record their impressions of the learning center activities on the tape, and categorize the learning center activities as either work or play. The tape was stopped periodically to allow opportunities for the teachers to discuss their ideas.

It was through this discussion that the microethnographic methods enabled Wohlwend (2007) to make sense of how teachers understood and enacted the phrase, "Play is a child's work." The phrase legitimated a variety of teaching practices and through discussion teachers were able to resolve and affirm conflicting perspectives. As part of the research process, teachers hybridized the terms *play* and *work* to call it "plurk." This hybridization helped them to reconcile two dissonant discourses and encouraged the improvisation of a new understanding of their teaching as well as potential opportunities to transform their work. The study revealed not only for the researcher, but also for the teachers that there is power in the discourses used, and teachers have agency in the face of accountability pressures to reconcile divergent models of teaching.

Ethnomethodology

Ethnomethodologists use in-depth discourse analysis from observations and interviews to understand the strategies individuals use to engage in common daily tasks. Ethnomethodologists explore participants' understanding of what is going on in the present moment as they reflect upon and explain what the participants perceive to be happening (Davidson, 2011). According to Davidson (2011), the ethnomethodological "approach results in descriptions of the ways members of society bring about an orderly world as a local and everyday (or mundane) accomplishment" (p. 26). Fine-grained linguistic analyses are used in conjunction with ethnomethodology to examine the types of responses that arise through dialogue as individuals engage in everyday tasks.

Davidson (2011) used ethnomethodology to understand how digital literacy practices are acquired in context and how interactions with adults contribute to children's acquisition and use of such practices. Data collection included the use of video recordings of young children using computers at home. Although four children participated in the study, Davidson's analysis focused on one family's interactions as their son conducted a Google search for information regarding a green basilisk lizard. Through specific documentation and analysis of interactions and discussion, Davidson found that the ordinary task of conducting a Google search was mediated by this young child's interactions with his family and demonstrated how this child made sense of print and images to learn about the world using digital technology.

Grounded Theory

Grounded theory methodology is used when the primary purpose of the work is to develop a substantive theory that deals with real-world situations in a localized context (Glaser & Strauss, 1967). Grounded theory requires in-depth comparison of data to confirm patterns grounded in the data that lead to the development of a particular theoretical framework. Strauss and Corbin (1998) describe elaborate coding processes to be applied in several stages, including (a) a microscopic examination of the data; (b) open coding that breaks data down into discrete parts; (c) axial coding to discover related categories; (d) selective coding to integrate existing categories; (e) coding for process to expose the dynamics of the emerging theory; and (f) creation of a conditional/consequential matrix to explore relationships between the contexts of the study and beyond (pp. 57–181). Grounded theory applied in this complex way offers insight into how we might understand a particular phenomenon and the relationships among various categories and characteristics.

MacDonald (2007) utilized grounded theory in a study designed to investigate the use of a Reggio Emilia style of pedagogical documentation in five kindergarten classrooms. MacDonald interviewed parents and classroom teachers about the use of the techniques and later analyzed the transcriptions of interviews using grounded theory to determine themes and patterns. The study was designed in response to the need of teachers and parents to adequately address children's literacy development.

The Reggio Emilia style of documentation proved useful to parents and teachers as it enabled them to learn more about "the children's strengths, interests, and curiosities beyond what is traditionally assessed" (p. 241). This method was also deemed to be a possible alternative to traditional standardized tests because it was able to capture the nuances in teaching and learning. The possibility for this style of documentation to augment traditional assessment by offering evidence to support or refute assessment data was also noted, as were challenges to implementing such an approach in U.S. schools.

Action Research

While there are several types, action research essentially provides an opportunity for those who are typically considered research subjects to play a central role in conducting research that has a practical outcome related to the lives or work of the participants (Stringer, 1999). The investigators in an action research project ask questions relative to a process, event, or setting in which they are active participants during the data collection process. Action research is also thought of as practitioner research and often taken up by teachers, social workers, and healthcare professionals (Stringer, 1999). The context specific challenges of these professions lead individuals to pursue their own inquiry by exploring the outcome of an intervention or the steps towards addressing a particular issue. Action research can be a continuous process of inquiry as it serves to build professional expertise or meet particular contextualized goals.

After noticing the way in which preschool children segregated themselves on the basis of gender stereotypes, Daitsman (2011) decided to conduct an 18-month action research project to find out more about the gender constructions of children ages two to seven. The researcher engaged the children in story dictation and dramatization by first writing out the dictated stories of the children and then having the entire class participate in a dramatization of each child's story. Both the dictations and dramatizations were audio and video recorded. The researcher kept a journal with reflections regarding his work with the children and also watched the videos with the children to get their reactions about potentially gendered dramatizations.

Findings from the study demonstrate that the more experience children had with story dictation, the more likely they were to tell stories focused around gender stereotypes. While the children most often told stories related to their gender, they also told gender-neutral stories almost 30 percent of the time. Additionally, children's gendered stories were often informed by the types of stories the teachers read to the students that day in school. The researcher also found that engaging the children in discussion about their gender assumptions led to more flexibility on the part of the students and more acceptance of the opposite gender.

ISSUES IN CONDUCTING EARLY CHILDHOOD QUALITATIVE RESEARCH IN THE TWENTY-FIRST CENTURY

In this section, we address four salient issues related to doing early childhood qualitative studies. As is evident from the foregoing discussions, many kinds of qualitative research are being done in contemporary early childhood settings, and each kind of study has its own issues. In addition, because qualitative studies are unique, each study generates issues that are particular to the special dimensions of the work at hand. Still, some issues reach across qualitative research paradigms and specific studies. Four prominent examples of such issues are taken up below.

Protecting Children's Rights Versus Listening to Children's Voices

Studies involving young children that are undertaken from any research perspective present complex ethical issues. Because children are legally ineligible to give "informed consent" in virtually all jurisdictions, adult parents or guardians are charged with the legal responsibility of agreeing to their child's participation in a research project. While "assent" is usually asked of the child, issues of power and understanding often make obtaining the child's informed agreement suspect at the least (Conroy & Harcourt, 2009). Informed consent is only one ethical issue that is magnified when participants are young children. Questions of unequal power relations, concerns about who benefits from research processes and outcomes, and issues related to relationships between researchers and participants before, during, and after research projects are all more sensitive when young children are involved (see Hatch, 1995b).

Over the past 20 years, many qualitative researchers have shifted from doing research *on* children to doing research *with* children. Contemporary qualitative researchers who seek to give voice to children's perspectives have adopted a postmodern stance that positions children as social actors in their own right, that is, competent members of society who have their own legitimate points of view (Mayall, 2002). In the words of Einarsdottir (2007), research that gives voice to children is "built on the conviction that children, just like adults, hold their own views and perspectives, have the right to be heard, and are able to speak for themselves if the right methods are used" (p. 199). This stance acknowledges children's fundamental right to participate in the decisions that impact their lives and express their own opinions, as codified in the *Convention on the Rights of the Child* (1989) drawn up by the United Nations.

The ethics related to studies in which children's active participation is part of the research process from start to finish are even more complex than in research that positions children as static objects to be examined by adult experts. When the claim is made that researchers are listening to the voices of children, special care must be taken to ensure that children's right to participate does not overshadow their right to be protected (Schiller & Einarsdottir, 2009). Moss, Clark, and Kjorholt (2005) point out several potential risks associated with projects designed to "listen" to children's voices, including: the process of listening may become a way to support existing power relations between adults and children; listening can become a means to govern the child more effectively; listening and participation may become a means by which the child is created as a particular kind of subject; and listening can distort the authenticity of the child's voice.

Given these and other risks, researchers who study early childhood contexts, especially those who want to partner with young children in research endeavors, need to take seriously their ethical obligation to protect young children from any negative consequences associated with participation in their studies. Gaining genuine informed agreement is a necessary first step. Conroy and Harcourt (2009) point out that early childhood qualitative researchers need to spend more time on the process of informing children about their participation in a research project, rather than focusing on gaining the documentation of that assent. Further, these researchers and others (e.g., Dockett, Einarsdottir, & Perry, 2009) recommend that children's agreement to participate should not happen only at the outset of the study, but should be revisited as the study unfolds. Children must have opportunities to withdraw from a study at any time and be reminded of the option to do so. In sum, early childhood qualitative researchers have a moral obligation to protect children's rights by constantly asking how the best interests of their young participants are being served as studies are designed, implemented, and written up. An elemental questions for all early childhood researchers should be: "Can we justify this intrusion into the private lives of children?" (Dockett, Einarsdottir, & Perry, 2009, p. 293).

Reliability, Validity, and Generalizability Versus Trustworthiness

Kuhn (1970) made the case that scientists cannot put forth arguments that are logically compelling to those operating within paradigms that are different from their own. He pointed out that different research paradigms operate on different ontological, epistemological and methodological assumptions—indeed, having a unique set of assumptions about how the world is (or is not) ordered, what can be known, and how we can generate knowledge about the world is what defines a paradigm. Arguments for reliability, validity and generalizability are firmly rooted in assumptions of the positivist paradigm. Positivist researchers assume the existence of an objective universe that has order independent of human perspectives. They believe that reality exists and is driven by universal principles that can be discovered using quantitative measures. For positivists, knowledge is made up of facts that have been scientifically verified and theories and laws based on those facts (Hatch, 2002). Qualitative researchers who operate within paradigms that reject positivist assumptions (see Guba & Lincoln, 1994; Hatch, 2002) set an impossible task for themselves when they try to argue that their studies meet criteria for assessing the quality of quantitative studies. That does not mean that qualitative researchers are left without the responsibility of systematically demonstrating the warrant of their approaches and the quality of their work; it only means that it makes no logical sense to apply the positivist constructs of reliability, validity and generalizability to the assessment of qualitative studies.

Lincoln and Guba (1985) proposed criteria associated with trustworthiness as an alternative for assessing the rigor of qualitative studies, and their model continues to be the standard for giving legitimacy to qualitative research. Lincoln and Guba (1985) identified four interconnected elements that make up trustworthiness: credibility, transferability, dependability, and confirmability. Credibility means demonstrating the "truth value" of the inquiry by showing that multiple representations of reality have been provided and that the reconstructions of the researcher are credible to the participants who supplied the original data. Lincoln and Guba (1985) propose several research techniques to establish credibility: *prolonged engagement* (spending sufficient time in the field); *persistent observation* (examining important elements in depth); *triangulation* (applying different data sources, methods, investigators, and theories); *peer debriefing* (sharing research processes and findings with peers); *negative case analysis* (looking for different or disconfirming explanations); *referential adequacy* (archiving data for later comparison); and *member checks* (attaining feedback from those being studied).

Addressing transferability means providing enough information to potential users of research findings that they can assess the applicability of the study to their own situations. Lincoln and Guba (1985) propose the use of *thick description* as a way to address transferability concerns. Thick descriptions include enough contextual detail that readers can make their own judgments about how well the research findings apply to their own settings.

Lincoln and Guba (1985) address the criteria of dependability and confirmability by suggesting the use of an *inquiry audit*, including an *audit trail.* An inquiry audit can bolster a study's dependability and confirmability by providing a careful analysis of records generated at all stages of the inquiry. Lincoln and Guba (1985) conclude their description of research techniques that bolster trustworthiness by presenting reflexive journal writing as a strategy that reaches across all of the criteria for enhancing trustworthiness. A reflexive journal should include a daily record of the nuts and bolts implementation of the study, a personal diary recording the researcher's reflections, and a methodological log detailing the decision processes of the study's implementation.

Over the years, early childhood qualitative researchers have been challenged by their quantitative colleagues with such questions as: "How do know that your data represent what is really happening?"; "How do you know that you are recording and interpreting data objectively?; or "How can your findings be generalized?" Our view is that these are legitimate questions for one quantitative researcher to ask another, but that qualitative researchers have to step outside the metaphysical assumptions at the core of their paradigms to try to respond to such challenges. Qualitative researchers' ways of conceptualizing the research process are fundamentally different from those of their quantitative colleagues. As Kuhn (1970) pointed out, scientists from competing paradigms effectively talk past one another when their metaphysical assumptions are not aligned. Therefore, early childhood qualitative researchers should avoid the trap of justifying their work in terms of meeting criteria determined by positivist research assumptions. Instead, they should apply constructs such as trustworthiness to establish the legitimacy of their work.

Scientifically Based Research Versus Qualitative Studies

Qualitative research in the United States, including qualitative studies done in early childhood settings, has been under attack over the past decade. Rooted in the work of the National Reading Panel (2000), "No Child Left Behind" legislation (see Giangreco & Taylor, 2002), and the National Research Council (2002) report entitled, "Scientific Research in Education," a concentrated effort was undertaken to define legitimate methods for educational researchers. Criteria for what has been labeled "scientifically based" research have been identified, and governmental funding for research and for materials that are used in education programs has been restricted to projects and materials that meet the scientifically based criteria. The criteria are based on positivist research assumptions, for which research protocols in medical research and experimental psychology are held up as exemplars. In effect, certain types of research (i.e., quantitative studies with large sample sizes and double-blind research procedures) have been officially sanctioned as the only kinds of legitimate research, while research approaches such as qualitative studies have been relegated to less than normal status (Erickson, 2005; Hatch, 2007a).

In the United States, this systematic devaluation of alternative forms of knowledge production has had a powerful impact on public and private research funding, doctoral level research preparation programs, and publication patterns in top-tier journals. The impact of applying the scientifically based standard is a genuine issue for scholars interested in doing qualitative studies in early childhood settings (Hatch, 2007a). As a result of the adoption of scientifically based criteria in early childhood, qualitative researchers have more difficulty finding external funding for their projects, doctoral students have more difficulty building support for their qualitative dissertations, and scholars have more difficulty publishing qualitative research reports.

We analyzed the research reports published over the past ten years in *Early Childhood Research Quarterly* (*ECRQ*), the journal that is ranked highest among early childhood journals by Journal Citation Reports (ISI Web of Knowledge, nd). Based on the authors' descriptions, we classified the 315 research articles published in *ECRQ* from the 2002 through 2011 volumes as quantitative, qualitative, or mixed methods. We did not include editorials, book reviews, or theoretical, practical, or policy-related essays in our count. We found that only 13 qualitative research reports (4.1%) and nine mixed methods reports (2.9%) were published in *ECRQ* over the ten-year period. Of particular note, over the most recent three years, of 112 research articles published in *ECRQ*, only two were identified as qualitative studies and two as mixed methods (1.8% each). We offer this crude analysis only to illuminate the current difficulties in publishing qualitative research in top-tier journals, and we take that to be directly related to the reification of the scientifically based standard in early childhood educational research.

Methodological Rigor Versus Weak Data and Shallow Analyses

While issues over narrow definitions of reliability, validity and generalizability and scientifically based research emanate from outside sources, we see the widespread lack of rigor in early childhood qualitative research as an issue that is internal to the early childhood qualitative research community. As mentioned above, when we searched the literature in preparing this chapter, we studied scores of early childhood research reports. One of our impressions is that too many of these published reports were based on what appeared to be thin data sets and shallow data analyses. We recognize that publishing article-length research reports is problematic for qualitative researchers because the strict page limits of research journals often keep descriptions of data collection and analysis procedures to a few paragraphs. However, the patterns we observed on our analyses make us concerned about the rigor with which many early childhood research projects are undertaken.

As noted above, there appears to be less and less space available to qualitative scholars in top-tier early childhood research journals. This means that the work needs to be especially well done and the criteria for qualitative rigor carefully applied. In addition, descriptions of how data are gathered and how analyses are undertaken need to be much more detailed than we observed in many of the articles we examined. It is hard to presume that data are adequate to support the generalizations of a qualitative study when data collection methods are not spelled out. And, it is hard to trust the efficacy of qualitative findings when the description of data analysis processes in limited to phrases like "an inductive analysis was completed" or "grounded theory guided the analysis."

We offer the following questions developed by Hatch (2007b, pp. 224–242) as tools for assessing the quality of early childhood qualitative studies. We hope they will offer a guide for novice researchers who are learning to do qualitative work and for anyone who needs criteria by which to assess the quality of the research reports they are reading. The questions are:

- Has the researcher located himself or herself in relation to particular qualitative paradigms?
- Has the researcher selected appropriate qualitative research approaches, given his or her paradigm choices?
- Has the researcher described his or her methodological and substantive theory bases?
- Has the researcher articulated a set of research questions that make sense given his or her methodological and substantive theories?
- Has the researcher described the research context and provided a rationale for why the context was selected?
- Has the researcher described research participants, explained criteria for selecting them, and justified their level of involvement?
- Has the researcher described all of the data collected as part of the study, making it clear how, when, and why the data were collected?
- Has the researcher explained and justified data analysis procedures used in the study, making it clear how and when data were analyzed?
- Has the researcher written his or her report using a narrative form that communicates findings clearly?
- Has the researcher presented findings that flow logically from his or her paradigmatic assumptions, methodological orientation, research questions, data, and analysis?

SUMMARY

In this chapter, we described the characteristics of early childhood qualitative research, discussed key elements necessary for the conduct of an early childhood qualitative research project, provided descriptions and examples of kinds of early childhood qualitative studies published over the past ten years, and identified key issues that face early childhood qualitative researchers in the second decade of the twenty-first century. In spite of the issues mentioned in the last section, we are hopeful that early childhood qualitative research will continue to grow and develop. Qualitative studies offer special insights into the lived realities of young children, their families, and the adults who work with and on behalf of them. They provide conceptual richness and contextualized understandings that are unavailable in research based on statistical analyses of carefully controlled variables. In an era where finding "what works" seems to be the watchword for traditional educational researchers, we recommend qualitative studies as tools for finding out how things really work for real people in real settings.

NOTE

1. The present *Handbook* includes separate chapters about these methods, including case studies, interviews, checklists, microethnography, grounded theory, observations, etc.

REFERENCES

Alldred, P. (1998). Ethnography and discourse analysis: Dilemmas in representing the voices of children. In J. Ribbens & R. Edwards (Eds.), *Feminist dilemmas in qualitative research: Public knowledge and private lives* (pp. 147–170). London: Sage.

Berger, P. L., & Kellner, H. (1981). *Sociology reinterpreted: An essay on method and vocation.* Garden City, NY: Anchor Books.

Bogdan, R. C., & Biklen, S. K. (2007). *Qualitative research for education: An introduction to theory and methods, 5th Edition.* Boston: Pearson.

Bromer, J., & Henly, J. (2009). The work-family support roles of child care providers across settings. *Early Childhood Research Quarterly, 24,* 271–288.

Brooker, L. (2001). Interviewing children. In M. G. Naughton, S. Rolfe, & I. Siraj-Blanchford (Eds.), *Doing early childhood research: International perspectives on theory and practice* (pp. 162–179). Buckingham, UK: Open University Press.

Buchbinder, M., Longhofer, J., Barrett, T., Lawson, P., & Floersch, J. (2006). Ethnographic approaches to child care research: A review of the literature. *Journal of Early Childhood Research, 4*(1), 45–63.

Cheuk, J., & Hatch, J. A. (2007). Teachers' perceptions of integrated kindergarten programs in Hong Kong. *Early Child Development and Care, 117,* 417–432.

Clark, A. (2007). A hundred ways of listening: Gathering children's perspectives in their early childhood environment. *Young Children, 62*(3), 76–81.

Clark, A., & Moss, P. (2001). *Listening to young children: The Mosaic approach.* London: National Children's Bureau.

Conroy, H., & Harcourt, D. (2009). Informed agreement to participate: Beginning the partnership with children in research. *Early Child Development and Care, 179*(2), 157–165.

Copple, C., & Bredekamp, S. (Eds.). (2009). *Developmentally appropriate practice in early childhood programs, 3rd edition.* Washington DC: National Association for the Education of Young Children.

Corbin, J., & Strauss, A. (2008). *Basics of qualitative research, 3rd Edition.* Thousand Oaks, CA: Sage.
Corsaro, W. A. (1985). *Friendship and peer culture in the early years.* Norwood, NJ: Ablex.
Creswell, J. W. (2007). *Qualitative inquiry and research design: Choosing among five approaches, 2nd Edition.* Thousand Oaks, CA: Sage.
Daitsman, J. (2011). Exploring gender identity in early childhood through story dictation and dramatization. *Voices of Practitioners, 6*(1), 1–12.
Darbyshire, P., MacDougall, C., & Schiller, W. (2005). Multiple methods in qualitative research with children: More insight or just more? *Qualitative Research, 5*(4), 417–436.
Davidson, C. (2011). Seeking the green basilisk lizard: Acquiring digital literacy practices in the home. *Journal of Early Childhood Literacy, 12*(1), 24–45.
Denzin, N. K., & Lincoln, Y. S. (1994). Introduction: Entering the field of qualitative research. In N. K. Denzin & Y. S. Lincoln (Eds.), *Handbook of qualitative research* (pp. 1–18). Thousand Oaks, CA: Sage.
Denzin, N. K., & Lincoln, Y. S. (2008). Introduction: The discipline and practice of qualitative research. In N. K. Denzin & Y. S. Lincoln (Eds.), *Strategies of qualitative inquiry, 3rd Edition* (pp. 1–44). Thousand Oaks, CA: Sage.
Dockett, S., Einarsdottir, J., & Perry, B. (2009). Researching with children: Ethical tensions. *Journal of Early Childhood Research, 7*(3), 283–298.
Einarsdottir, J. (2007). Research with children: Methodological and ethical challenges. *European Early Childhood Education Research Journal, 15*(2), 197–211.
Einarsdottir, J., Dockett, S., & Perry, B. (2009). Making meaning: Children's perspectives expressed through drawings. *Early Child Development and Care, 179*(2), 217–232.
Erickson, F. (2005). Arts, humanities, and sciences in educational research and social engineering in federal education policy. *Teachers College Record, 107,* 4–9.
Giangreco, M. F., & Taylor, S. J. (2002). Scientifically based research and qualitative inquiry. *Research and Practice for Persons with Severe Disabilities, 28,* 133–137.
Glaser, B. G., & Strauss, A. L. (1967). *The discovery of grounded theory: Strategies for qualitative research.* Mill Valley, CA: Sociology Press.
Graue, M. E., & Walsh, D. J. (1998). *Studying children in context: Theories, methods, and ethics.* Thousand Oaks, CA: Sage.
Guba, E. G., & Lincoln, Y. S. (1994). Competing paradigms in qualitative research. In N. K. Denzin & Y. S. Lincoln (Eds.), *Handbook of qualitative research* (pp. 105–117). Thousand Oaks, CA: Sage.
Hamersley, M., & Atkinson, P. (1995). *Ethnography: Principles in practice, 2nd Edition.* New York, NY: Routledge.
Hatch, J.A. (1990). Young children as informants in classroom studies. *Early Childhood Research Quarterly, 5,* 251–264.
Hatch, J. A. (1995a). Studying childhood as a cultural invention. In J. A. Hatch (Ed.), *Qualitative research in early childhood settings* (pp. 118–133). Westport, CT: Praeger.
Hatch, J. A. (1995b). Ethical conflicts in classroom research: Examples from a study of peer stigmatization in kindergarten. In J. A. Hatch (Ed.), *Qualitative research in early childhood settings* (pp. 213–223). Westport, CT: Praeger.

Hatch, J. A. (2002). *Doing qualitative research in education settings.* Albany: State University of New York Press.

Hatch, J. A. (2007a). Back to modernity? Early childhood qualitative research in the 21st century. In J. A. Hatch (Ed.), *Early childhood qualitative research* (pp. 7–22). New York: Routledge.

Hatch, J. A. (2007b). Assessing the quality of early childhood qualitative research. In J. A. Hatch (Ed.), *Early childhood qualitative research* (pp. 223–244). New York: Routledge.

Hatch, J. A., & Barclay-McLaughlin, G. (2006). Qualitative research: Paradigms and possibilities. In B. Spodek & O. Saracho (Eds.), *Handbook of research on the education of young children, 2nd Edition* (pp. 497–514). Mahwah, NJ: Lawrence Erlbaum.

Hewson, C., Yule, P., Laurent, D., & Vogel, C. (2003). *Internet research methods: A practical guide for the behavioral and social sciences.* London: Sage.

Holstein, J. A., & Gubrium, J. F. (2008). Interpretive practice and social action. In N. K. Denzin & Y. S. Lincoln (Eds.), *Strategies of qualitative inquiry, 3rd Edition* (pp. 173–202). Thousand Oaks, CA: Sage.

ISI Web of Knowledge. (nd). *Journal citation reports.* Retrieved from http://admin-apps.webofknowledge.com.

Kuhn, T. S. (1970). *The structure of scientific revolutions.* Chicago: University of Chicago Press.

Lara-Cinisomo, S., Fuligni, A. S., Daugherty, L., Howes, C., & Karoly, L. A. (2009). A qualitative study of early childhood educators' beliefs about key preschool classroom experiences. *RAND Working Paper* No. WR- 656. Retrieved from http://dx.doi.org/10.2139/ssrn.1333307

Lincoln, Y. S., & Guba, E. G. (1985). *Naturalistic inquiry.* Beverly Hills, CA: Sage.

Long, S., Volk, D., & Gregory, E. (2007). Intentionality and expertise: Learning from observations of children at play in multilingual, multicultural contexts. *Anthropology & Education Quarterly, 38*(3), 239–259.

MacDonald, M. (2007). Toward formative assessment: The use of pedagogical documentation in early elementary classrooms. *Early Childhood Research Quarterly, 22,* 232–242.

Malinowski, B. (1922). *Argonauts of the Western Pacific.* London: Routledge.

Marshall, C., & Rossman, G. (2006). *Designing qualitative research, 4th Edition.* Thousand Oaks, CA: Sage.

Maxwell, J. A. (2005). *Qualitative research design: An interactive approach, 2nd Edition.* Thousand Oaks, CA: Sage.

Mayall, B. (2002). *Towards a sociology of childhood.* Maidenhead, UK: Open University Press.

McMillan, J. H., & Schumacher, S. (2010). *Research in education: Evidence-based inquiry, 7th Edition.* Upper Saddle River, NJ: Pearson.

McRae, A., & Ellis, J. B. (2012). Early childhood perceptions of diversity: A case of addressing multicultural education in the classroom. *Journal of Teaching and Learning, 8*(1), 13–26.

Mead, M. (1928). *Coming of age in Samoa.* New York: William Morrow & Company.

Meller, W. B. (2008). *A critical literacy case study: The journey from pre-service exploration to in-service implementation.* Unpublished Doctoral Dissertation. Knoxville: University of Tennessee.

Merriam, S. (2002). Introduction to qualitative research. In S. Merriam (Ed.), *Qualitative research in practice: Examples for discussion and analysis* (pp. 3–17). San Francisco, CA: Jossey-Bass.

Merriam, S. B. (2009). *Qualitative research: A guide to design and implementation.* San Francisco, CA: Jossey-Bass.

Miles, M. B., & Huberman, A. M. (1994). *Qualitative data analysis: A sourcebook of new methods, 2nd Edition.* Thousand Oaks, CA: Sage.

Morgan, D. L. (1997). *Focus groups as qualitative research, 2nd Edition.* Thousand Oaks, CA: Sage.

Moss, P., Clark, A., & Kjorholt, A. T. (2005). Introduction. In A. Clark, A. T. Kjorholt, & P. Moss (Eds.), *Beyond listening: Children's perspectives on early childhood services* (pp. 1–16). Bristol, UK: Polity Press.

National Reading Panel. (2000). *Report from the National Reading Panel.* Washington, DC: National Institute for Child Health and Human Development.

National Research Council. (2002). *Scientific research in education.* Washington, DC: National Academy Press.

Patton, M. Q. (2002). *Qualitative research and evaluation methods, 3rd Edition.* Thousand Oaks, CA: Sage.

Rinaldi, C. (2001). A pedagogy of listening. *Children in Europe, 1*(1), 2–5.

Rust, F. O. (2007). Action research in early childhood contexts. In J. A. Hatch (Ed.), *Early childhood qualitative research* (pp. 95–108). New York: Routledge.

Ryan, S., and Lobman, C. (2007). The potential of focus groups to inform early childhood policy and practice. In J. A. Hatch (Ed.), *Early childhood qualitative research* (pp. 63–74). New York: Routledge.

Schiller, W., & Einarsdottir, J. (2009). Listening to young children's voices in research: Changing perspectives/changing relationships. *Early Child Development and Care, 179*(2), 125–130.

Seidman, I. (2005). *Interviewing as qualitative research: A guide for researchers in education and the social sciences.* New York: Teachers College Press.

Shank, G. D. (2006). *Qualitative research: A personal skills approach, 2nd Edition.* Upper Saddle River, NJ: Pearson.

Spodek, B., & Saracho, O. N. (Eds.). (2006). *Handbook of research on the education of young children.* Mahwah, NJ: Lawrence Erlbaum.

Spradley, J. P. (1980). *Participant observation.* New York: Holt, Rinehart & Winston.

Stephenson, A. (2009). Horses in the sandpit: Photography, prolonged involvement and 'stepping back' as strategies for listening to children's voices. *Early Child Development and Care, 179*(2), 131–141.

Strauss, A., & Corbin, J. (1998). *Basics of qualitative research: Techniques and procedures for developing grounded theory.* Thousand Oaks, CA: Sage.

Stringer, E. (1999). *Action research, 2nd Edition.* Thousand Oaks, CA; Sage.

United Nations (1989). *Convention on the Rights of the Child.* Retrieved from http://www.ohchr.org/en/professionalinterest/pages/crc.aspx, http://untreaty.un.org/cod/avl/ha/crc/crc.html, and http://www.unhchr.ch/htm/menu3/b/k2crc.htm (this link did not work)

Walsh, D. J., Nesrin, B, Lee, T. B., Chung, Y-H, & Chung, K. (2007). Using digital video in field-based research with children. In J. A. Hatch (Ed.), *Early childhood qualitative research* (pp. 43–62). New York: Routledge.

Wetherell, M., Taylor, S., & Yates, S. J. (Eds.). (2001). *Discourse as data: A guide for analysis.* Thousand Oaks, CA: Sage.

Wohlwend, K. (2007). More than a child's work: Framing teacher discourse about play. *UCLA Journal of Education and Information Studies, 3*(1), 1–25.

Wolcott, H. F. (1995). *The art of fieldwork.* Walnut Creek, CA: AltaMira.

Yin, R. (2002). *Case study research: Design and methods, 3rd Edition.* Thousand Oaks, CA: Sage.

CHAPTER 14

INNOVATIVE QUALITATIVE RESEARCH METHODS WITH CHILDREN AGED 4–7 YEARS

Karen Winter

There is a growing body of research that spans many disciplines including education, health, social work, sociology, psychology, planning and the environment and that uses innovative qualitative methods to support and facilitate the involvement of young children, aged seven years and under, in the research process. The field of early childhood education has made a major contribution in this area with research that details the experiences and perspectives of very young children regarding the design and delivery of preschool provision (Clark, McQuail, & Moss, 2003; Einarsdottir, 2005; Pascal & Bertram, 2009, 2011; Gray & Winter, 2011; Clark & Moss, 2011), their transition into and experiences of primary schooling (Dockett & Perry, 2005; 2005a) and the interaction of gender, race and class in young children's social relationships with peers and staff in primary school settings (Connolly, 2004; 2008).

In other related disciplines, such as health for example, important insights have been gained from research that has used innovative qualitative methods regarding young children's experiences of chronic illness (Christie et al., 2011), experiences of pain (Kortesluoma, Hentinen, & Nikkonen, 2003), and their perceptions regarding their care/support needs when suffering from serious illnesses (Horstman, Aldiss, Richardson, & Gibson, 2008). Furthermore in the field of social care, research has made a major contribution to our understanding of young children's experiences of their daily lives within their local communities (Dockett, Perry, & Kearney, 2012); their families (Nixon & Halpenny, 2010), while living in the state care system (Winter, 2012a) and when facing family adversity such mental illness (Fox, Buchanan-Barrow, & Barrett, 2007).

This chapter explores reasons for the growth in the use of innovative methods, the underlying principles through which the engagement of young children has been achieved, and the different types of method with detailed case examples. For each method some of the main critical issues are identified and discussed in further detail. The latter sections of the chapter focus on contemporary issues regarding the use of innovative methods particularly focusing on some of the common concerns and criticisms regarding the use of innovative qualitative methods pertaining to issues of trustworthiness, reliability, validity and generalizability.

FACTORS LEADING TO THE GROWTH IN THE USE OF INNOVATIVE METHODS

The large body of research involving young children, that is based upon a participatory framework and employs a wide range of innovative qualitative methods, is in stark contrast to the historical dearth of research regarding young children that was apparent up until about 20 years ago. In periodic reviews writers (Clark et al., 2003; Clark, 2005; Corsaro, 2010) have examined the reasons for this growing interest and two themes emerge as having had a critical impact namely changing constructions of childhood and children's rights. These have had the effect of redefining our understanding of childhood and repositioning children as rights bearers, active citizens with varying degrees of social agency as opposed to passive individuals.

In relation to constructions of childhood our views regarding the capacities and competencies of young children to be involved in research have been challenged by the emergence of new ways of thinking about childhood introduced through the sociology of childhood. Sociological frameworks have challenged the "taken for granted" meanings regarding children, that have previously been heavily influenced by a narrow and rigidly applied Piagetian developmental discourse which is associated with age as synonymous with social and cognitive ability, whereas sociological approaches also examine the influence of social and cultural factors on our understandings of childhood and the lives of children (Jenks, 1982; James, Jenks, & Prout, 1998; Corsaro, 2010).

As Jenks (1982) has explained, evidence has shown that "cross-culturally children vary enormously in terms of their degree of responsibility, the expectations held of them, their level of dependency, need for care, life expectation and more generally the nature of their relationship with adults" (p. 205). Prout and James (1997) have reiterated this when they stated that "the immaturity of children is a biological fact of life but the ways in which this immaturity is understood and made meaningful is a fact of culture" (p. 8). Prout and James (1997) outlined a set of key principles underpinning a sociological approach to the study of childhood. These are as follows: first, as already highlighted, childhood is to be understood as a social construction; secondly childhood is a variable of social analysis and can never be separated from other social variables such as class, gender, or ethnicity; thirdly childhood and children's social relationships are worthy of study in their own right; fourthly children are and must be seen as active in the construction and determination of their own social lives, the lives of those around them and the societies in which they live; fifthly qualitative methodologies such as ethnography are useful in that they allow children a more direct voice; and sixthly the emergence of a new paradigm of childhood sociology should engage in and respond to the process of reconstructing childhood in society. One of the hallmarks of this theoretical framework is then that children of all ages are constructed as people, as individuals able to form a view, contribute, influence and to share responsibility in relationships including research processes (Jenks, 1982; James & Prout, 1997; Mayall, 2002; James & James, 2004; Corsaro, 2010).

Concurrent with the development of a new theoretical approach to the study of childhood has been the emergence of legal frameworks that provide the statutory footing to the focus on children in particular the *United Nations Convention on the Rights of the Child* (UNCRC) (United Nations, 1989). Fundamentally what this Convention does is threefold: firstly to establish children as a group requiring separate and special "rights" provisions; and secondly to establish children as citizens who can exercise rights; and thirdly to create a set of standards and principles with which the practices of its signatories (State Parties) should comply and against which legislation, policy and practice should be evaluated. The UNCRC (United Nations, 1989) is underpinned by four fundamental principles: the right to nondiscrimination (Article 2); the best interests' principle (Article 3); the right to life, survival and development (Article 6); as well as the right to express views freely and to have the view taken seriously (Article 12). Commonly the UNCRC is divided into three broad indivisible categories of rights, often labeled the "three P's" and known as rights to provision, protection and participation.

The use of innovative methods in research with young children is often tied in with their participation rights. While the Convention does not mention a participation right *per se* several of the Convention's Articles cover the various elements of what are loosely known as participation rights: the right to information (Article 13), the freedom to express views and to have his or her views taken into account in all matters affecting the child (Articles 12), freedom of information (Article 13), of thought, conscience and religion (Article 14), and of association and peaceful assembly (Article 15). They also include rights to participate as a member of a group (Article 15), in cultural and artistic activities (Article 31), and in due legal process in the judicial system (Article 40).

Children's exercise of their "participation rights" is inextricably linked to the obligation placed on adults to provide information to them, to support their involvement and to permit influence in decision-making. As argued by Lundy (2007), within this framework, the focus on "voice" is not enough because it fails to capture adequately the social context, which gives rise to children's participation. For this reason Lundy (2007) suggests an integrated framework: space, voice, audience and influence. It is the indivisible relationship between all four of these factors that facilitates and supports children to exercise their participation rights.

In relation to younger children there are particular factors peculiar to their age, vulnerability and social status that are acknowledged in the UN-CRC and considered further in a series of *General Comments* published by the United Nations (the purpose of which is to provide detailed advice on the practical meaning of children's rights as defined within the UNCRC). In relation to age *General Comment No. 7 Implementing Child Rights in Early Childhood* (UN, 2005) notes that young children are exposed to age related discrimination where "they have been regarded as undeveloped, lacking even basic capacities for understanding, communicating and making choices. They have been powerless within their families and often voiceless and invisible within society" (p. 6–7, para. 14). Secondly young children are vulnerable, depending on adults to provide the opportunities for them to progressively exercise their rights and these processes rely on adults who have the commitment, knowledge and resources to support children in this regard. Thirdly, young children's "rapid transformations in physical, cognitive, social and emotional functioning draws attention to processes of maturation and the evolving capacities of young children to understand and exercise their rights" and emphasizes the responsibility of adults "to continually adjust the levels of support and guidance they offer a child" (p. 8, para. 17).

As further explained in *General Comment No. 7* (United Nations, 2005) "Evolving capacities should be seen as a positive, enabling process, not as an excuse for authoritarian practices that restrict children's autonomy and self-expression and which have traditionally been justified by pointing to children's relative immaturity and their need for socialization" (p. 8, para. 17). Bearing in mind young children's experience of age related discrimination, their vulnerability, dependency and their evolving capacities, the research that seeks to provide opportunities to children to be involved and to exercise their rights is underpinned by a common set of shared principles that form an overarching ethical framework for the conduct of research relationships and processes. These are outlined in the subsequent section before the chapter then moves on to consider the different types of innovative method, how, when and why they are used and some of the critical issues regarding their use.

ETHICAL PRINCIPLES INFORMING USE OF INNOVATIVE RESEARCH METHODS

Research relationships with young children are the subject of stringent ethical frameworks that aim to strike the balance between protecting children from harm, abuse and exploitation while also supporting them in opportunities to be involved in research (Alderson & Morrow, 2011; Powell, 2011). Complimented by other interconnected frameworks such as that outlined in *UN General Comment No. 12 The Right of the Child to be Heard* (United Nations, 2009), there are a series of practice principles that give effect to those aims as outlined and discussed below.

Transparent and Informative

The aims, purpose, methods of research and the nature, scope and likely impact of young children's involvement in research projects must be clearly and fully outlined in ways that are accessible, diversity friendly and appropriate to the age and ability of the child(ren) concerned (Alderson & Morrow, 2011). On a practical level this involves researchers thinking through the mode of information sharing such as DVD/CD; leaflet; drawings; and information packs either directly to the child or to their main carer who then spends time talking through the information with the child concerned. A combination of both is often necessary. Information should be provided in a format that it can be revisited—commonly research participants (in this case children and/or their carers) wish to be reminded about the research study (Winter, 2011). Attention should be paid to layout, text, colour and the amount of technical information made available. An example of an information leaflet that was designed by Winter (2012a) for a young child's involvement in a research project about their views of being in care can be seen in Appendix One.

Voluntary

Children should not be coerced into being involved in research and/or to remain involved in research projects. In this regard careful attention needs to be given to consent/assent processes. Assent is defined as the act of agreeing to be involved in a research project, relating to children who have no legal right, by virtue of their age, to consent and where their understanding of all issues may not be fully formed. It can also be taken to refer to those children who have not refused to be involved. Consent, on the other hand, indicates an active decision to take part. Alderson & Morrow (2011) prefer the term consent—they question the status of a decision by a child to be involved when it is acknowledged that they may not have full understanding. They also point out that an assent process has the potential to act as a "cover-up" for children who do not really want to take part (p. 103). The consent process should be constructed as "opt-in" rather than "opt-out." An "opt-in" approach means that children have to actively decide to take part in the research project whereas an "opt-out" approach means that children could be included without actively having had the opportunity to decide to be involved. The process of securing consent from children may involve also securing consent from birth parents, carers and/or key professionals. Negotiating access and consent with gatekeepers, who to varying degrees exercise control over access to children, can be costly and time consuming and in practical terms means being clear about the purpose of the research, the terms and conditions of involvement, the risks and the benefits (Butler and Williamson, 1994; Cocks, 2006). Successfully securing consent should not be regarded as a "one-off" tick box exercise but as an ongoing process. In practical terms this means creating spaces throughout each stage of a research project for children to be reminded about the aims and purpose of the study and that they can stop their involvement at any time without fear of negative consequences for them and/or their family (Mason & Hood, 2011). The Appendix contains an example of a consent sheet, also designed by Winter (2012), illustrating some of these points.

Respectful

Being respectful of young children involves researchers engaging with young children as subjects rather than objects of the research (Morrow,

2008; Alderson & Morrow, 2011; Christensen, 2004). This relies on building up respectful relationships with children and sensitively supporting their choices and freedoms during the research process, being flexible and offering opportunities for negotiation, collaboration and the co-construction of meanings and striving to develop a mutual understanding between the researcher and the child participants (Barker & Weller, 2003; Alderson & Morrow, 2011; Christensen, 2004; Dockett & Perry, 2007) about the research and the significance of the child's participation in it. An important part of viewing children as subjects and not objects is respect for their social agency—that is the degree to which they can exert their own strategies to challenge, control, and change certain aspects of the research and to develop their own strategies for including and/or excluding the researcher in the research process (Christensen & James, 2008; Connolly, 2008).

Researchers also need to be respectful of the capacities, choices and preferences of young children. Researchers should avoid making assumptions about what they think are the preferred ways for children to communicate. Hill, Davis, Prout, & Tisdall (2006) indicate that children need to be comfortable with the method being used and for some the method may not be known to them but for other young children they may enjoy using materials unavailable or not allowed at home. On a practical level this means the researcher engaging in a process of ongoing negotiation with the child during the course of the research process rather than imposing methods (p. 79). Hence as Punch (2002) argues "The choice of methods not only depends on the age, competence, experience, preference and social status of the research subjects but also on the cultural environment and the physical setting, as well as the research questions and the competencies of the researcher" (p. 338).

Children should be free to chose and use the available methods in the ways they wish. In my own research I had a finite number of arts based methods in each interview session with a child –the list was not limitless. However within the structured space of the interview encounter children were able to exercise some choice and some autonomy. For example some children made drawings and models. Some did not use the materials at all. Sometimes it was less a case of the methods available than offering time, space, my attention, genuine interest, and respect for the child's value, worth and dignity that encouraged the children to share their views (Christensen, 2004).

In my own research, part of which is reported later in this chapter, I found that there was no perfect method but a huge reliance on researcher confidence, skill, responsiveness, reflexivity, flexibility, and creativity (Christensen, 2004) so that the child and I could negotiate our way through the process, its ups and downs and could deal with what was often "(the) messy and (the) unpredictable" (Darbyshire, MacDougall, & Schiller, 2005,

p. 418). Connected with this, research should also respect children's individuality taking account of differences such as social class, age, gender, disability, religion, ethnicity, or culture (Punch, 2002). According to Christie et al. (2011), these processes should also all take place in a context where "young children's language development, concrete thinking and developmental level, current cognitive level, capacity, knowledge, and opportunities provided by the environment" need to be factored in (p. 6).

Relevant

UN General Comment No. 12 (2009) states that:

> the issues on which children have the right to express their views must be of real relevance to their lives and enable them to draw on their knowledge, skills and abilities. In addition, space needs to be created to enable children to highlight and address the issues they themselves identify as relevant and important. (p. 30, para. 134)

Applied to research processes there is an onus to draw up research agendas that reflect children's own concerns and to involve them, where possible, in the development of research questions, suitable methods and in the analysis and dissemination of findings. This involves researchers being critically reflective regarding the development of research agendas, the underpinning drivers and their own influence on the agenda (Alderson & Morrow, 2011; Powell, 2011).

Child Friendly and Inclusive

To successfully achieve full engagement and to ensure that existing patterns of age related discrimination and marginalisation are not repeated in research processes, research environments and methods need to be adapted to young children's preferences, strengths and abilities recognising that these vary from child to child. On a practical level this can be challenging in that some writers argue that the use of so called child friendly techniques such as drawing and art based methods and the interpretation of the meaning of those artefacts by adults reinforces negative stereotypes of children as unable or unwilling to explain their own work (Backett-Milburn & McKie, 1999; Coates & Coates, 2006; Einarsdottir, Dockett, & Perry, 2009; Christie et al., 2011). These authors have also noted that there has been a concern that the production of drawings and writings often encourages a focus on the finished product as opposed to the social processes, interactions, commentary that accompanies the construction of the picture. Achieving an inclusive and ethical approach, as will be seen later in the chapter, relies on researchers recording the child's narrative that accompanies the drawing or artwork so that it is the child's meaning about the drawing, its content and its significance that is reported in findings.

Safe and Sensitive to Risk

The act of reporting findings or placing into the public domain the perceptions, experiences, feelings and views of young children that may have been hitherto hidden and that might challenge existing norms and/or adult practices/perceptions can create risks for children. For example research that involves collecting data from children around issues such as child labour, domestic violence and abuse, parental substance misuse, experiences of living in state care involves benefits (such as enhancing knowledge with the aim of developing policies and practices that better support children) but these have to be weighed up against the potential harm, risk, and distress caused to children (where their involvement may exacerbate the likelihood of further abuse, put their lives in danger and/or cause undue personal stress, anxiety and distress) (Butler & Williamson, 1994; Johnson, 2011; Winter, 2011).

This does not mean that researchers avoid tackling difficult issues with young children (who themselves may experience their involvement in research as partly therapeutic and cathartic) but that researchers' provide a full appraisal of the risks and benefits and identify what they have put in place to alleviate and manage risk (Alderson & Morrow, 2011; Powell, 2011; Winter, 2011). This includes adhering to protocols regarding the collection and storage of anonymized information only, ensuring that findings contain no identifiable information and also ensuring that where necessary children have access to support services (counselling, confidential help lines, identified professionals who can offer support) (Winter, 2011).

Accountable and Supported By Training

As researchers we are used to being accountable to funders and institutions for the progress and completion of projects. However at the heart of research practice are the young children who have given up their time and invested emotional energy to be involved in the research project. We are accountable to them and we therefore have an obligation to report back to them on: what they said and shared; what significance their involvement has had and will have; how and in what ways the findings will be reported; what has been done or will be done with the findings; when and in what ways they might benefit both in the long and short term from the sharing of those findings (Alderson & Morrow, 2011; Powell, 2011). Additionally there should be discussion about whether in the design of the reports and the broader dissemination of findings this could involve the children themselves without exposing them to risk of harm and/or exploitation. In terms of supporting both adults and children to maximise the benefits of being involved in research together training should be provided for both children and researchers to develop knowledge, skills and improve levels of confidence (Powell, 2011). Having outlined the ethical principles that should underpin research processes that involve the use of qualitative innovative methods with young children the remainder of this chapter outlines definitions and different types of innovative method and provides detailed case examples of their use in practice. This is used as a platform for broader discussions regarding critical issues in the use of innovative methods before finishing with an overview of contemporary concerns and criticisms relating to the current state of knowledge and practice in this area.

DEFINITIONS OF "INNOVATIVE" METHODS

Writers (James, 2007; Gallacher & Gallagher, 2008; Holland, Renold, Ross, & Hillman, 2008: Travers, 2009) have noted that innovative methods have been an inherent part of both professional practice (as part of therapeutic, teaching and learning approaches) as well as a research methodology for a long time. Given the wide use of the term "innovative" it is important to reflect on its meanings. Travers (2009) and Taylor and Coffey (2009) have sought to address definitional issues. Concerned by the varied and nebulous references to the term these writers define an innovative method as: a new method; a pre-existing method used in a new way; and/or the use of methods associated with other disciplines into a new field of enquiry. Taylor and Coffey (2009) also argue that the term innovative should not be used to describe the method alone but should capture its application in practice reflecting a social process—a reciprocal relationship between the idea, the researcher (as the technician of the new idea/approach) and the user (research participant) of the idea (p. 14).

Bearing this in mind, innovative methods with young children could include the development of new methods and/or methods used elsewhere but used for the first time with young children. In general terms innovative methods share several other common characteristics: they tend to be designed with children's preferences and strengths in mind; they aim to elevate into the public domain children's perspectives that have been hitherto hidden by virtue of children's marginalised status and difficulties gaining access to them. They are designed to be inclusive, to facilitate the communication process and empower children in relation to the adult researcher. In this chapter the scope of research reviewed that uses innovative methods with young children aged 7 years and under is drawn from a multi-disciplinary perspective and includes research in health, social care as well as early childhood education. This allows for the full range of innovative methods to be considered and also highlights to researchers the benefit of developing multi-disciplinary perspectives in relation to early childhood research given the interconnected nature of the various research questions, designs and findings.

TYPES OF INNOVATIVE METHODS

This section of the chapter considers the main types of innovative method and provides the following: an overview of the research knowledge that uses the method; practical examples as to how the method is used; and a discussion regarding some of the critical issues to consider when using the method (See Table 14.1).

DRAWING, WRITING AND BOOKS

Drawing has long been used as a therapeutic, diagnostic and research tool (Rollins, 2005). On one level and reflective of an "age and stage" developmental discourse, the use of drawing as a research method is seen as reflecting a natural part of children's developmental progress with children using "drawings" as their own language, an alternative language that enables them, before they acquire complete fluency in verbal language, to express their inner world, feelings and thoughts (Hamama & Ronen, 2009, p. 93).

TABLE 14.1 Types of Innovative Method: General and Specific

General method	Specific examples
Drawing, writing and books	Mapping, spider diagrams, timelines, Venn diagrams, daily activity schedules/daily routine diagrams, circle maps, scrapbooks and storybooks.
Photographic and video methods	Photo elicitation, photo elicitation interviews (PEI's), photo novella, photovoice, digital photography, participatory photo mapping (PPM), stimulated video recall/video stimulated accounts, video diaries/participatory video processes.
Arts based methods	Research initiated role play (PIRP), games, puppets, construction using Lego and construction using shoe-boxes
Interviews and focused groups	Semi-structured and structured

An example of this is in psychological research with young children where a focus has been on young children's ability to make visual representations of the objects in the world around them (Einarsdottir et al., 2009, p. 218).

Further examples, drawn from the field of psychiatry, indicate that clinicians have used drawings as a diagnostic and measurement tool with the aim of assessing children's development and wellbeing (Moschini, 2005; Hamama & Ronen, 2008). Applied in this way the technique is, according to Horstman et al. (2008), "an innovative and developmentally appropriate method to gain access to children's perspectives because children's ability to retrieve information that is encoded about their experiences may be more readily accessed by stimulating their perception senses than by semantic stimulus" (p. 1001).

Moving away from the measurement of children's abilities and well being and focusing on seeking to gain children's perspectives, recent research in the field of early childhood education that uses the method (Dockett & Perry, 2005, 2005a; Clark et al., 2003; Clark & Moss, 2011) is underpinned by a rights based and social competence framework asserting that "all young children have the competence to engage in research as sophisticated thinkers and communicators and that the inclusion of children's views are pivotal if we are to understand their life worlds" (Harcourt & Einasdottir, 2011, p 301). The facilitating effect on children's ability to talk about particular issues if drawing is introduced has been the subject of systematic review and meta analyses (Driessnack, 2005, 2006) with the results (Driessnack, 2006) having indicated that "introducing the opportunity to draw to young children before they are interviewed appears to be a robust strategy with a large overall effect size" (p. 1415). What this indicates is that it is not just the facilitating effect of introducing drawing to young children that is important but that this then has an impact on how well young children engage with any subsequent interview process.

Building on the earlier reviews of literature in this area (Driessnack, 2005, 2006), Driessnack and Furukawa (2012) have undertaken a review of over 200 articles, involving drawing and writing and other arts based research in research with children aged 7–12 years. The review focused on the children's narratives, interpretation and information surrounding the drawing not on drawing skills *per se* and where the drawing acted to support and facilitate the child to explore issues related to the research (Einarsdottir et al., 2009; Driessnack & Furkuwana, 2012). It was found that researchers used drawings in two main ways either impromptu (produced at the directive of the researcher) or spontaneous (created without researcher direction).

Tasks included inviting a child to draw a picture of themselves, of someone else involved in a particular event (for example receiving medical intervention) (Horstman et al., 2008), an event such as starting school (Dockett & Perry, 2005; Einarsdottir et al., 2009), something, for example "my favorite place", (Young and Barrett, 2001), or a feeling such as fear (Driessnack, 2006) or pain (Kortesluoma et al., 2003) and then inviting discussion around what has been drawn in the picture and what narrative the child attaches to the picture. Findings were reported in terms of children's perspectives and experiences.

Specific Types of Drawing/Writing

Beyond research that refers to generic drawing techniques as a method to report on young children's views, experiences and perspectives on various aspects of their lives and experiences there is literature that also reports the use of particular types of drawing and diagram to involve young children in the research process. These include mapping, spider diagrams, time lines, Venn diagrams, daily routine diagrams and circle maps. The research knowledge on these specific types of drawing will briefly be described in turn before considering some of the critical issues that researchers encounter when using this type of method.

Mapping involves researchers inviting children to draw maps of their social and physical environments (Morrow, 2008; Darbyshire et al., 2005; Clark & Moss, 2011; Clark, 2011; Gawler, 2005) and then invite discussion around the child's narrative that accompanies their maps. It is one of a number of techniques associated with community project evaluation and participatory rural appraisal (PRA). Clark's research (2011) in early childhood settings with preschool children has used a type of mapping. With regard to the method, Clark (2011) stated that "the map making was designed [...] for children to work together to build up a map of their immediate environment—their nursery, school or play area-using their own photographs as a starting point" (p. 315). In possession of a digital camera and accompanied by the researcher the children went on a tour of their setting photographing the things that were the most important to them. The children then selected images to print up into an enlarged A4 size. The following day the children were invited to spend time with the researcher building a map of their environment by using a combination of photographs and other modes of communication including role play, model making and drawing.

In another example Punch (2002) used *spider diagrams* as a visual representation of children within their social contexts. In this type of drawing exercise, Punch (2002, p. 53) in her research with older children, used them to identify what helped children in care cope with their circumstances. She invited the children to put the central issue/person in a circle in the middle of the page (by way of an example it could be a picture of the child feeling scared at their move into residential care) then to represent, by lines coming from the centre, all those things/people that help them cope with the transition. The effect is a diagram that looks like a spiders' body with many legs. As noted spider diagrams are a structured form of drawing and other examples include *timelines, Venn diagrams, daily activity schedules/daily routine diagrams, circle maps* often associated with PRA (participatory rapid assessment or participatory rural appraisal). All involve the use of diagrams and drawings to elicit the perspectives and experiences of children and young people. By way of example, the time line can be used to facilitate a child to depict and overview of the different stages of their day, week or to depict transitions and changes in their lives (Gawler, 2005).

Scrapbooks can be used in research as an autobiographical method, helping children explore their identity, their heritage, and their family history. They can also be used to help children make sense of a particular theme or issue. Barber (2011) for example explored the use of autobiographical scrapbooks with children who had a terminal illness to help both the child and their parents review the child's life and address issues relating to death and dying. Also in health related research with young children, Coad (2007) used scrapbooks to ascertain the views of children in hospital regarding the hospital environment and services provided.

Anderson and Balandin (2011) used *storybooks*, with illustrations and interactive pop ups with children aged 7–9 years as part of the feedback process within their research project. Implemented with the aim of addressing the power imbalances and designed to support children's active involvement in the feedback process Anderson and Balandin (2011) found the method engaged research participants well and suggest that it could be rolled out with other groups such as learning disabled adults. In another example McIntosh and Stephens (2012) used the storybook method by inviting children aged 4-9 years to construct a story book around their understanding of illness in order to explore the children's concepts of illness causality within the sociocultural context of their families. Moving away from an emphasis on maturational processes to understanding health and well being the research by McIntosh and Stephens was informed by a socio constructivist approach which informed both the methods used and the analysis of the findings. Young children's understandings of illness and health messages were seen as linked to the social context of the family with the potential for very young children to develop good levels of understanding around illness and health messages.

How Drawing/Writing Methods Are Used

Work by Driessnack (2006) focused on researching experiences of fear in 22 "healthy" children aged 7–8 years old with the recruitment and research being undertaken in the school environment. The method involved an individual interview of one hour long with each child during which they were invited to choose one piece of blank paper and some drawing utensils (from pencils, markers and crayons) and then to think about a time when they were most afraid, to draw it and then when finished to tell the researcher about it. The sessions were audio recorded and transcribed.

Driessnack (2006) subsequently undertook a linguistic analysis of the children's personal narratives comparing the construction of these with normative expectations. She found that young children deviated from the normative personal narrative inventory (which typically consists of six stages) illustrating "how the emotional force of what they were trying to convey influenced the linguistic choices they employed." A thematic analysis of children's stories was also undertaken to reveal commonly held feelings that the children experienced when they were afraid namely: "you're alone"; "you didn't see it coming"; "there is nothing you can do"; and "there is nobody there watching for me." These themes highlighted young children's need to feel more empowered and supported in the situations they had found themselves and this gave rise to a discussion between researcher and child about how the child could "resolve their fear experience" (Driessnack 2006, p. 1429).

In one further example Horstman et al. (2008) used the draw and tell technique was with 38 young children, aged 6–12 years, with cancer to detail their perspectives regarding their care, support needs and services received. Ethics approval was secured and consent was multi-layered as in both parents and children were asked to give their consent for the child to be involved in the study. This safeguard was necessary given that children were recruited while they were still in hospital. The children were at different stages in their treatment programs, from different local hospitals and were interviewed once each either at home and hospital. Children were invited to complete drawings in line with the research questions using prompts and then to reflect on these in the interview encounter. According to Horstman et al. (2008), examples included "think of a child like you who is having medicine and treatment for leukemia. Draw a picture of what that child is doing and thinking" (p. 1007). The study revealed children's perspectives about some of the helpful aspects of cancer care and also some of the practices that children found unhelpful and uncomfortable.

Effectiveness of Draw and Write Methods

Whilst the list is not exhaustive there are three key themes regarding the effectiveness of the draw and write methods that emerge from the research literature. These are the *setting in which the method is used;* the *selection/sampling of the method;* the *safety* of the children and the *skills* of the researcher.

In relation to the *setting* in which the draw and write technique might be used this may influence a child's perception of and reaction to the method. It is possible, for example, that if research is conducted in schools and hospital environments the child may experience the technique either as a test (with a perceived emphasis on accuracy) and/or as a burden (not well enough to concentrate on producing a drawing) as opposed to a supportive framework to express their views and perspectives.

This highlights the importance of the *selection* of the method. In this regard the effectiveness of the method relates to clarity on the part of the researcher about how they intend to use the method—will they use the method to frame, structure and direct children to answer specific questions (for example Driessnack (2006)) or will they use the drawing method to build rapport with a child before moving on to a deeper discussion that may or may not revolve around the production of and discussion about a drawing. Thomson (2007) poses the question "Are methodologies for children keeping them in their place?" Thomson (2007) argues that "employing the polarized, singular and fixed identities of child versus adult" (p. 211) reproduces the assumptions regarding the all-knowing adult and the all-unknowing child. Moving beyond this involves the construction of children as individual identities and the creation of social spaces through which and in which children and adults can have in common similar competence, skills and experience that transcend the usual adult/child divide.

Warming (2012), who carried out ethnographic research in a day care institution in Denmark with children aged 3–12 years (although most were aged 3–6 years) to explore their perspectives as to what constitutes a "good child life," noted that the choice of methods was as much influenced by the needs of the researcher as by the needs of the child. For example, drawings were chosen when the researcher could not find the right words to explain with this being an example of how

> "child-oriented" methods are also oriented toward adults and dominant assumptions of childhood. As such, the use of child-oriented methods without critical reflection may actually reinforce adult representations of children or even restrict understandings of children's experiences and knowledge (p. 92).

If the underlying motivations and purposes regarding method selection are not fully reported the researcher may run the risk of being perceived as being leading in the use of the method and selective in terms of reporting the findings (Backett-Milburn & McKie, 1999; Coates & Coates, 2006; Einarsdottir et al., 2009; Christie et al., 2011). Researcher reflexivity about these issues provides a safeguard in terms of the quality of the study and its findings.

In relation to the *sample of children* an important consideration is what factors drive the choice. The effectiveness of a particular methodology might be hindered or enabled by the number of children involved. However more often than not there is little reporting regarding the rationale for the numbers of children selected to be involved in a study. For example in the research by Horstman et al. (2008) sample selection was based on the requirements of a bigger project seeking the views of all children (aged 4–18 years) receiving cancer care as consumers of that service. In relation to both of the detailed case examples outlined above it is not clear, other than structural constraints (those being the total number of children in a class or a hospital ward), what factors influenced the minimum and maximum number of children selected for the two studies.

While there may be a justification for a study on a sensitive issue affecting young children on the basis that the area has been under researched, the wider issues regarding the *safety* of the children has to be weighed up against the hoped for benefits of the research (Alderson & Morrow, 2011; Powell, 2011; Winter, 2011). No innovative method, no matter how carefully selected, will work well with children where there is a risk of retraumatization following a previously frightening/negative experience for example. In Driessnack's study (2006) the research plan identified appropriate supports for children in case they became upset. In the event no child required the additional support.

A related issue is the *skills* required of the researcher both case examples draw attention to researcher reflexivity (that is the ability of the researcher to identify what influences they bring to bear on the selected research questions, methods, data collection, analysis employed and presentation of the findings) as well as possessing well-developed interpersonal skills within the research process itself. Children require adults who have a genuine interest in their lives, who can listen, question and respond to verbal and nonverbal cues in appropriate and helpful ways, who can empathize, who are warm, friendly and welcoming and who are honest (Alderson, 2008; Winter, 2011).

Researchers therefore require a range of well developed listening, questioning, and responding skills to avoid what Butler and Williamson (1994) noted as children endeavoring "to conceal the problems of their social worlds from adults in order to avoid being 'humiliated' by misunderstanding, misrepresentation and misplaced responses" (p. 305). These skills include the use of closed and of open questions, a nonjudgmental response and the ability to reflect back what has been said, summarize, clarify, paraphrase as well as the ability to make sense of verbal and non verbal cues (O'Kane, 2008; Winter, 2011, 2012a). Researchers recognition and appreciation of the time and effort that the children gave up to take part in the study is critical as is the availability of additional supports for children (via counseling) if required (Driessnack, 2006; Winter, 2011; Powell, 2011).

PHOTOGRAPHIC AND VIDEO METHODS

The use of photographs in research has a long history that is commonly acknowledged as beginning in anthropology with the seminal text by Collier, Collier, & Hall (1967) and is now quite widely used in research within the fields of education, health and social sciences more broadly (Catalina & Minkler, 2010; Barker & Smith, 2012: Prosser & Burke, 2007). In addition to the growth in its use across many fields of enquiry there has been a growth in the terms and processes used as part of the broader photographic method (Plunkett, Leipert, & Ray, 2013). Current research is informed by and supports the view that children make competent photographers (Sharples, Davison, Thomas, & Rudman, 2003) and the benefits are well established (Barker & Smith, 2012) with the method being described as "engaging and interesting to children as it is task centered rather than talk centered [and] does not require verbal or written competency" (p. 92). In the field of early childhood education the use of the disposal camera by young children, who are invited to take photographs of significant places and people in their preschool settings and then to talk about and reflect on them, has been extensively reported upon (Clark & Moss, 2011; Clark, 2005; Cooke & Hess, 2007; Dockett & Perry, 2005, 2005a).

Specific Types of Photographic Method

As noted in Table 14.1 photography is a broad term that encompasses different types of photographic method, ethnographers having used the method extensively since the 1950's. One type of photographic method is *photo elicitation (PE) and/or photo elicitation interviews (PEI's)*. This involves the use of photographs (which can be taken either from a range of sources and selected for an interview) to evoke a memory, stimulate a discussion and elicit data through discussion alone around a particular theme (Harper, 2002; Plunkett et al., 2013; Prosser & Burke, 2011). Plunkett et al. (2013) describe the emergence of *photo novella* as a stage beyond photo elicitation in the use of photographs in research. In this method research participants were given cameras to "document the stories of their lives" (p. 3). Ewald (1985) was one of the pioneers of this type of approach when she taught children in the Appalachians to take pictures of their lives.

According to Plunkett et al. (2013), the work of Wang and Burris (1994, 1997) built upon photo novella and created the iterative process known as *photovoice*. Wang and Burris (1994, 1997) first used photovoice as a community participatory health promotion technique with rural village women in Yunnan province China offering them the opportunity to photograph and record strengths and concerns within their local communities; to explore these on a collective community basis; and to use this to influence policy makers. These three components are now acknowledged as defining the iterative process associated with photovoice (Wang and Redwood-Jones, 2001; Dennis Jr., Gaulochers, Carpiano, & Brown, 2009; Plunkett et al., 2013). Photovoice has since become a technique, often used in research with adults and older adolescents, commonly associated with research in education, sociology, and social geography as well as its field of origin that being health (Catalini & Minkler, 2010).

The *digital photography* method refers to the use of digital cameras as opposed to disposal cameras. The process of applying and using the methodology is similar but digital cameras have the advantage of producing instantly viewable photographs that can also be printed up immediately with the child present (Clark, 2011) thus enhancing children's engagement in the research process. Kullman (2012) has used digital photography to document children's everyday mobilities in relation to their journeys to and from school. Undertaking an ethnographic study on the everyday urban mobility of 23 primary school children aged 7–12 years, Kullman (2012) invited the children to use a digital camera and a digital camcorder to record their journeys the data of which then formed the basis of an interview to explore their journeys in more detail. Through attention to the children's practices of picture-making Kullman (2012) explored how children staged and performed daily mobility practices for the camera, the relational qualities of children's mobilities (sharing cameras, space and experiences with their friends to and from school) and how children incorporated with ease the cameras into associated areas of their daily lives.

Participatory photo mapping (PPM) is a further development within the body of research using photographs version "which unfolds as a four step iterative process" (Dennis Jr. et al., 2009, p. 468). In Stage One people were provided with digital cameras and Global Positioning System (GPS) units with which to take pictures of their community and the use of public space. In Stage Two the photos become the objects of interviews through which individual and collective narratives were attached to the photos. As part of Stage Three the photos were mapped as part of a broader level Geographic Information Systems (GIS) that might include other data (population stats etc) that produced qualitative and quantitative data about health and place with Step Four involving the targeting of messages at policy makers.

The use of *stimulated video recall/video stimulated* methods involves the production of video clips with participants, playback to them to generate discussion and reflection around themes and issues or to analyze more deeply the nature, purpose and quality of interaction. It relies therefore on recall of thought processes behind actions. Research by Theobald (2012) is in this vein but it has distinguished between video stimulated recall and video stimulated accounts. Theobald (2012) has indicated three substantive differences between the approaches: video stimulated recall relies on recall of events whereas video stimulated accounts attend to the interactional matters as the accounts are produced; the context in which the video stimulated account takes place is considered as an interactional matter and therefore forms an important part of the research whereas this is not the primary focus of stimulated video recall; lastly in video stimulated recall the "recall" is taken as fact whereas in video stimulated accounts the account is regarded as a product of interaction and it is these processes that are of importance. Theobald's view is informed by their research (2012) that studied young children's interactions in the playground of an inner city school in South East Queensland, Australia. Phase "A" involved video recordings being taken of children's interactions in the playground and Phase "B" involved children in small groups watching the video clips and discussing them. Using a case study of three children and illustrated by numerous photographic stills of the children in action, Theobald highlighted the intricacies of children's social interactions with each other as they negotiated, aligned and realigned their play activities to fit the evolving agendas of the group members.

The use of *video diaries/participatory video* methods has involved giving children a video camera on which to record their own views or narratives about a particular event, person and situation (Prosser & Burke, 2011). Buchwald, Schantz-Laursen, & Delmar (2009) described how they gathered data from children in Denmark regarding their coping mechanisms in the light of a parent being diagnosed with cancer. The aim of the research was to collate information to help develop cancer care services to affected families. Participants were given a video camera, which they were trained to use. The camera was set up in their home for an agreed period (one month), and children were invited to record entries on a daily basis, as if talking to the researcher, about their thoughts, feelings, and reflections with data being gathered over an extended period as opposed to a one off interview. Children could view their entries and erase unwanted clips. The video was then given to the researcher for analysis. This was part of a three-stage process involving a qualitative interview followed by video diary followed by final interview. These are but two examples of the growing popularity of the video method in research and its multi-faceted usage to aid reflection, participation and/or to make representation (Hawe & Hadfield, 2011).

How Photographic Methods Are Used

Clark-Ibanez (2004) used *photo elicitation interviews* (PEI's) as part of a broader ethnographic study with 55 older school children in two types of elementary school in an urban setting in America. Clark-Ibanez (2004) illustrates, through detailed case studies displaying both the photographs and the narratives, how the importance of the method is not in the photograph per se but in the subjective meanings and narratives that accompany the photograph. The illustrative case studies drew attention to the depth and poignancy of the children's narratives attached to what appear to the "outsider" as mundane, if not boring, photographs. There are different approaches to use of PEI's that involve the researcher taking, organizing and displaying the photographs for an interview or that could involve the research participants in this process as Clark-Ibanez (2004) did. This latter approach is also known as participatory photo interviewing (PPI's) (Jorgeson & Sullivan, 2010)

Jorgensen and Sullivan (2010) used *participatory photo interviews* (PEI's) with 48 children in one private middle school in South Eastern America "to understand how children's competence with information and communication technologies is constructed within the family." The method involved giving children cameras and asking them to photograph themselves or family members at home either working or playing with technology. The pictures were then used in one-to-one interviews to explore deeper meanings. Jorgenson and Sullivan (2010) found that the photographs provided insights that were not accessible by observation but that also they "served as a reminder that children's visual representations cannot be read simply as transparent indicators of underlying dispositions because children are active in the construction of meanings" (p. 215).

While the *photovoice* method is less used with young children, research by Darbyshire et al. (2005) used the method with children, aged 4–12 years regarding their perspectives on physical activity. The research used the technique to encourage young children to take their own photographs of people, places, events, activities that were important to them, that related to the research questions and then supported the children to provide a written commentary about each of the photographs. Darbyshire et al. (2005) found that the photographs (one of several methods they used) provided complimentary to the other methods and produced additional information that did not emerge in the mapping and interviews—for example many children took photographs of trampolines in their back gardens but this theme did not emerge elsewhere and the photographs "also depicted the emotional and exuberant aspects of play that their interview accounts could not" (p. 424).

In other research and as part of an ethnographic study into the experiences of children (aged 7–14 years) living in situations of violence and disease in two Kenyan orphanages, Johnson (2011) employed the *photovoice* method. As part of the project, that ran over several weeks children were trained in the use of the camera and then invited to take two rolls of pictures (the first at three weeks and involving taking pictures of their typical day and the second at 8 weeks and involving taking photographs of things and people that were important to them (Johnson, 2011, p. 147). The children took the pictures in their own time and the ones they put in their journals became the data for the research. Her work highlighted that photovoice not only provided poignant insights into the children's daily lives challenging some of the existing stereotypes regarding the lives of young children in areas affected by violence, poverty, and disease but also provided a photo record of the children's lives—something that they did not normally have.

Serriere (2010) used *digital photography* as a method with preschool children in their school setting to explore their developing social consciousness in their peer group relationships. The researcher took the photographs of the children in their daily interactions, uploaded them on the laptop and invited children to view them in a slide show format to explore what the photograph meant and what was happening. Serriere (2010) called this process "carpet time democracy" as the process of discussion allowed for group ownership of problems and difficulties in peer relationships and agreement within the group as to how the situation might be improved (p. 66).

Robson (2009) used *video* to record the perspectives of young children (aged 3–4 years) regarding their activities in early childhood settings with the aim of exploring children's social relationships and how these shape and inform children's creative thinking. The research involved researcher recorded video data of children's self initiated activities as a start point for reflective dialogues (RD's) between child and researcher about what they were doing and thinking. The value of the video is that it stimulated recall and reflection but is not without its challenges in terms of who chooses the research participants, how confidentiality is maintained, what the impact is on participants, and the process of providing feedback regarding the children's involvement (Hawe & Hadfield, 2011).

Effectiveness of Photographic/Video Methods

In the earlier discussion on draw and write methods the following issues were identified as impacting on method effectiveness namely: the *setting* in which the method was used; the *selection/sampling* of the method and participants; the *safety* and well being of the children as research participants; and the *skills* of the researcher. In this section and based on the review of photographic methods the following issues will be explored: *construction of the child's relationship with technology*; *control* of research process by child/researcher; issues of *confidentiality* and lastly *conveying the findings*. In relation to the *child's relationship with technology* it is commonly accepted that children now have greater opportunities for exposure to and developing familiarity with digital and computer based technology both in school and at home (Hawe & Hadfield, 2011; Jorgenson & Sullivan, 2010). The effectiveness of photographic methods is constrained as well as enabled by a child's relationship with the method and researchers need to confirm and clarify with children that they are comfortable with the technology, that they understand how it is used and that they understand its purpose within the context of the research project in which they are involved (Jorgeson & Sullivan, 2010; Barker & Smith, 2012).

Jorgenson and Sullivan (2010) have pointed out that for some children technology harnesses participation and for others it has fostered passivity and frustration. Furthermore awareness of photographic convention and the reading of researcher expectations about what photographs should be produced have an impact on the data. Context is therefore an all-important consideration. In another example Johnson (2011) recognized that the involvement of children in the research project was affected by the fact that they were unfamiliar with the workings of a camera and that within that particular cultural context (characterized by high levels of political violence, disease and death) photographs were associated with official procedures such as identification and collating documentary evidence of deaths in the area. Johnson (2011) addressed these issues by a process of de-sensitization (walking around for weeks with a camera over her shoulder) and by training the children in the use of the equipment. The basic point for researchers is that the effective engagement of children with a method is contingent on the child's abilities, preferences, degree of comfort with the method as well as wider contextual issues including the time, space, location of the research and the skills of the researcher.

Related to this is the degree of *control* and ownership the child has in the use of the technology, the videos/pictures produced and their inclusion within reported findings. Differing projects have highlighted how far the researcher has been involved in facilitating children to take photographs and video clips. In some studies the researcher has accompanied the child (such as research by Kullman, 2012; Clark, 2010) and in other studies the researcher has taken a back seat allowing the child to take ownership of the camera/video for several days (or maybe a few weeks) (Johnson, 2011). The choice of stills and clips is also differentially controlled by the child with some children having total control over this process and others being invited to consider the photos that they have not included or to jointly choose photos/clips with the researcher (Barker & Smith, 2012). All of the projects emphasize the importance of the researcher reflecting on and being transparent about their influence and direction over the research process and what constructions of childhood and children underpin the project (Balen et al., 2006). The projects mentioned above also highlight the importance of reporting children's narratives regarding the choice and meaning of the photos/clips they have selected (Gallacher & Gallagher, 2008). As Barker and Smith (2012) note this is important as it may not be the photograph itself that is of importance but the intention behind taking it, including it in the portfolio of images for the findings report or excluding it.

A connected issue concerns *confidentiality*. Acknowledging that there may be risks to children's safety and well being by revealing their identity and by attributing to them certain views and perspectives means that researchers have to pay particular attention to maintaining their anonymity which is a particular challenge in the use of photographic and video research methods. Wang & Redwood-Jones (2001) have pointed out that if actual images of children are to be published there is the potential for the exploitation of participants through "use of a person's likeness for commercial benefit" (p. 566). They and others (Barker & Smith, 2012) overcame these obstacles by ensuring that research participants owned the negatives, that they had given consent for the publication of those images and that wherever possible could receive an honorarium for the use of their images.

There is an associated risk in *conveying findings* (in this case the actual images) that negative stereotypes of children and childhood might be reproduced. For example, Johnson (2011) highlighted how the community in which she was located was anxious regarding her presence with a camera because the children had endured the intrusive presence of tourists taking photographs of them which had made them "feel like they were in a zoo" (p. 159). Furthermore some images produced had built on "the iconic image of the starving African child with large, sad eyes and extended bellies [and that while] unforgiving poverty [...] is certainly true, it is only part of the story, and frequently the only one told" (p. 159). Again these issues relate back to the purpose of the project and whether it seeks to add a new dimension to our understanding of children's lives, to confirm what is already known or to transform our thinking. As Jorgenson and Sullivan (2010) have argued "The use of visual methods calls for a complex analytic strategy in which the interpretation of thematic content is intertwined with some awareness of the reactions of children to the research and to the ways they produce their own contexts endogenously."

ARTS BASED METHODS

Knowles and Cole (2008) define arts based research "as the systematic use of the artistic process, the actual making of artistic expressions in all of the different forms of the arts, as a primary way of understanding and examining experience by both researchers and the people that they involve in their studies" (p. 29). Arts based practices are associated with all aspects of the research process, from the research design and collation of data through to interpretation and representation of findings. While what is reported under this section relates to the detailed examination of individual arts-based methods used in the collation of data it is important to note that there is a wide range of research that uses multi-methods in conjunction with each other (Darbyshire et al., 2005; Hemming, 2008; Pascal & Bertram, 2009; Clark, 2011; Clark & Moss, 2011; Gray & Winter, 2011; Christie et al., 2011). For example, the work of Clark (2011, 2011a) and Clark and Moss (2011) is well known for its multi-method approach that incorporates the use of tours, cameras, map making, small focus groups and interviews to gauge children's perspectives about their educational settings.

There are several stated reasons behind the multimethod approach: researchers wish to ensure that the specific strengths of individual children involved in research are recognized and supported; they wish to offer children choice to maximize the chance of the child engaging and feeling comfortable in the research process; they believe that the use of different methods supports children to bring different information to the surface and therefore allows for a deeper level of experience and insight to emerge; and they believe that the use of multimethods keeps children engaged and prevents them becoming bored. The remainder of this section is concerned with the use of arts based methods in the data collection phase and aims to illustrate some of the variety by way of specific detailed case examples that include: researcher initiated role-play; games; and puppets; construction using Lego and construction using shoe boxes. Each is considered in turn.

How Arts-Based Methods Are Used

Role-play is a teaching method used in early childhood and primary education (Rogers and Evans, 2008). Yaacob and Gardner (2012) have used the technique in their sociolinguistic research on multilingualism. In a context where research with children who are multilingual posed particular challenges *researcher initiated role play* (PIRP) was used to explore the perspectives of Malay children, aged 6–7 years, learning to read English. As noted by Yaacob and Gardner (2012) the value of the RIRP was in exploring what children have internalized from their learning experiences and also what they understood and thought about their learning experiences through the modal of play and use of the third person—rather than having to reflect directly on themselves. These benefits are also reflected in the work of Clark and Moss (2011) who, as part of the broader multi-method Mosaic approach, elicited children's perspectives in early childhood settings through role-play using small toy figures (pp. 3, 46).

In their research exploring children's views, aged 3–11 years, about the impact of chronic illness conditions, Christie et al. (2011) developed a *board game* to engage children in a self-report process to determine satisfaction with life or quality of life (QOL). The method developed from the project title Satisfaction in Life for Children with own Report Measures (SILCWORM) and from this title a large silkworm was drawn on a large piece of paper. This was divided into segments with a question relating to each of the 64 questions associated with QOL measure.

The game also had two foam dice that children threw. Similar in principle to the game of snakes and ladders children were invited to count from the die and land on a square on the silk worm. They then picked up the card that related to the square they landed on and were invited to answer the associated question. Their responses were recorded along with the comments of the other participants involved in the game. Once the question had been answered the child colored in the square and at the end of the game the child was allowed to keep the SILCWORM. The board game was successful in helping children describe the effects of living with illness on home, family, friends, school and life in general. The researchers (Christie et al., 2011) stated "the use of a board game emerged as engaging, enjoyable and enabling for children. This allowed open and free-flowing dialogue about their perspectives on a wide range of aspects of their lives" (p. 12).

In their research, Aldiss, Horstman, O'Leary, & Gibson (2009) used *play and puppets* to research the views and experiences of 10 young children aged 4 and 5 years old from three hospitals in London regarding cancer care services. The same research is reported in more detail in Gibson, Aldiss, Horstman, Kumpunen, & Richardson, (2010). A play specialist was recruited to collect data given her expertise in this area. The researchers report that the puppets performed a support role for children and helped children avoid eye contact with the researcher. A second researcher acted as observer and took notes verbatim where possible. Children were asked specific questions in a clear and straightforward way.

Prior to this stage of the research, researchers engaged in a lotto game with the children to put them at ease. The lotto game contained facial expressions, which were also used in the interview so that children could more easily identify their feelings. Examples of questions included "Fizz (the puppet) has been having some special medicines. Have you been having some special medicines? What's it like having your medicines? They found that the children liked to range of toys and games available at the hospital and liked to have the near presence of their parents but rarely mentioned their experiences of being ill and their treatment. The importance of play to the children might reflect the importance placed on play within the hospital context in terms of easing anxiety, providing distraction, an outlet for feelings and tensions, a means of escape.

Pimlott-Wilson (2011) reported on two research projects that used a multi-method approach to access children's perspectives regarding their lives at home, their attitudes towards parental employment and their experiences at school. The children involved were ages 4–16 and methods employed included *construction using Duplo Lego*, drawings of rainbows and clouds as well as collage mood boards. With regards to the use of Duplo Lego Pimlott-Wilson (2011) explained, "basing research encounters around play, a central part of children's cultural experiences, reduces the pressure of a semi-structured interview whilst giving children a tangible focus as they express their opinion" (pp. 136–137).

Children, aged 5–6 years, were given a brief to build a representation of their home and to enact the roles of the people in their home. Duplo figures could be moved in and out of the home and the method enabled children to depict the gendered nature of car travel, child-care and employment. Pimlott-Wilson (2011) reported that key concerns included prejudices, stereotypes regarding Duplo Lego, how far the method distracted children from the task in hand, whether children were hindered through its use by over concern about the accuracy of the model they were constructing, and how to work out when the play moved from the acting out of domestic behaviors to imaginative play (p. 138). It was concluded that the method should be used in conjunction with other methods including prompt pictures. Pictures of the sun and rainbows were used as prompts to report positive feelings and clouds and raindrops to report negative feelings, which were found by Pimlott-Wilson (2011) to be useful "for delving into the feelings and emotions which individuals may find difficult to articulate" (p. 146).

My own specific contribution to innovative methods comes in the form of an arts based method—*construction involving the use of shoeboxes* that were also known as reality boxes (Winter, 2011, 2012a). The concept was based on an idea that I came across at the Childhoods Conference (Oslo, 2005). The reality box was an empty, undecorated shoebox with a lid. On the outside children were invited to construct an image of them that best reflects how they come across to the outside world (their public person). In the inside they constructed images of their thoughts, feelings and perspectives (their private person).

Primarily the inclusion of the shoeboxes was to provide a focus to an interview (depiction of feelings, views and perspectives) and, like the drawing activity, to enable children to "talk whilst doing." This view was informed by my professional and personal experience in which I had noted that children often found it easier to talk if they and I were engaged in an activity such as walking or when I was driving the car. In these dialogues there is mutual listening and responding but the intensity is diluted because the uncomfortable feelings associated with having to make eye contact whilst talking about difficult issues are avoided. As with the drawings the reality boxes were accompanied with the children's narratives and meanings about their boxes. As indicated in Winter (2011, 2012a) the reality boxes were a powerful testament to younger children's views and perspectives; capturing their views in deep, rich, and meaningful ways.

Effectiveness of Arts Based and Multi-Methods

A particular challenge regarding the use of arts based methods relates to the representation of the findings. For example often the real strength lies in having the recorded voice of the child accompanying the artifacts and/or the display (on power point for example) to illustrate their meanings and to ensure the full involvement of the children in the explanation and interpretation of their own data (Christensen, 2004; Alderson & Morrow, 2011; O'Kane, 2008). However using the children's voices to describe their own work can be described as emotive, exploitative (Johnson, 2011; Winter, 2012a) and could breach anonymity. Compromises are often made in the form of the presentation of text-based findings only. A related question is whether more methods and multi-methods make for greater insight into the lives and perspectives of young children or do they just mean more methods. Darbyhsire et al. (2005) contend that:

> Using a variety of research strategies to interest and engage children in the study was both philosophically appropriate and pragmatically valuable. These strategies respected children's agency as social actors and active participants in the creation of their own worlds of meaning. The various approaches complemented rather than duplicated and enabled the expression of different aspects of the children's experiences. The multiple approaches were also successful in depicting the children's worlds in ways that influential adults also found to be credible and valuable. (p. 430)

INTERVIEWS AND FOCUS GROUPS

The interview, until recently, has not been a common method applied in research with young children and therefore its more recent use with younger and younger children has led to its inclusion as an innovative method. Hill et al. (2006) have noted that, in the review of participatory social work research with young children, "Commonly interview studies with children set a lower age limit, below which it is surmised that conversations are unlikely to yield useful data. Typically 7 or 8 years old is used as the cut off" (p. 178). He links these judgments to the influence of narrow Piagetian frameworks, as well as a concern to avoid traumatizing children. Docherty and Sandelowski (1999) argue that historically "because of the belief that children lacked the verbal skills, conceptual abilities, recall and overall narrative competence to convey those experiences, parents, caregivers, and other adults were typically the informants in research focused on children" (p. 177).

More recent research however (Butler & Williamson, 1994; Alderson, 2008; Connolly, 2008; and Clark & Moss, 2011; Winter, 2012b) draws attention to the fact that some younger children communicate well in interview situations. Hill, for example, (2007) states that "straightforward conversation can be very effective using a combination of communication skills including different types of question, reflection and reframing, as well as flexible sensitivity to the nature and communication style of individual children" (p. 180). As these writers have indicated with the right conditions (attention to physical environment, tools), the right support (an adult who conveys empathy, warmth, genuine interest, right tools) young children can be involved in a meaningful way in interviews.

Research studies indicate that young children can choose to engage in the interview with a depth and intensity that is not assumed because of their young age. Irwin and Johnson (2005) and Docherty and Sandelowski (1999) support the view of the competent young children by stating that "Children, even as young as three years old, can give graphic descriptions and have excellent recall of experiences related to adverse events, such as illness and hospitalization" (p. 177). The work of Connolly (2004) reveals the well-developed competencies and capacities of young children. As part of a yearlong ethnographic study of the school experiences of 5–6 year old boys Connolly (2004) undertook small group interviews with the children in the context of the school. Using a semistructured approach the interviews revealed the skills of the children as they negotiated the intricacies, complexities of their social relationships that were intersected by race, class and gender.

How Interviews/Focus Groups Are Used

Looking more closely at the study by Morgan, Gibbs, Maxwell, & Britten (2002), this piece of research used a facilitator, a cofacilitator and a third person observing and taking notes, when undertaking 11 focus groups with 42 children ages 7–11 to explore their experiences of living with asthma. The children were referred through a number of General Practitioner practices and either in mixed groups (between 2–7 in sizes) if there were ages 7–8 years, 8–9 years and separated by gender if aged 10–11 years. The focus groups complimented personal interviews and drawings completed by the children and provided insightful findings.

The use of the method highlighted differences in the perspectives of adults and children regarding asthma. Adults' primary concern was the impact of the asthma on the long term development and health of their child whereas children were happy with their treatment, not worried about their future health but more concerned about dealing with stigma and their medical needs within the school setting. In their work Morgan et al. (2002) illustrate how attention should be paid to the environment (sitting on floor rather than chairs), ground rules (listen to each other, no interruptions), warm up exercises, interspersion of session with games, use of "third persons/objects through which children can conduct role plays/express their views (toys/pen and paper), attention to group dynamics and to the "inclusionary/ exclusionary processes within the group" (p. 105).

These and other studies have revealed that, with or without recourse to supporting arts based materials on offer: some children engaged well in interviews and enjoyed talking in a lot of detail about very sensitive subjects and others spoke in less detail; some were agents in terms of self protection to minimize distress and/or control the pace and depth of the interviews (Backett-Milburn & McKie, 1999; Winter, 2011); and some children can control what was said, when and how; whereas for other children they relied more on action, body language rather than spoken word to express their views (Christensen & James, 2008). Similar themes are evident in the use of focus groups with young children to collate data, where Morgan et al. (2002) highlight that this method was previously thought of as the preserve of adult research participants but, as they illustrate, can be used in a meaningful way with younger children.

Effectiveness of Interviews and Focus Groups

There are common issues related to the effectiveness of undertaking research interviews with young children. These are building *rapport, perceptions of reality* and *recall abilities*. With regards to building *rapport* researchers have considered their position in relation to the child in the research process and have attempted to minimize their adult authority by constructing themselves as the "concerned/interested adult" (Kortesluoma et al. 2003) or "the learner" (Christensen, 2004) or by adopting the "least adult" through practical strategies such as following the children, rapport building, acquiring "access to the group" rituals as first reported by Mandell (1988) and then later reflected in research by Christensen (2004) and Corsaro (2010). Still others have tried to take on the role as "friend" or to construct children as co-researchers/collaborators (Spyrou, 2011) and protagonists (Clark, 2010). Of equal importance is the position adopted by the child (Christensen, 2004; Connolly, 2008; Winter, 2012a).

Perceptions of reality are influenced by social positioning. Children adopt a range of positions throughout the interview ranging from "helper" and "teacher" through to "observer." As social agents they can form collaborative relationships or challenge the status quo (Christensen, 2004; Gallacher & Gallagher, 2008). Winter (2011) illustrated how young children within the structured space of the interview encounter exercised varying degrees of agency—controlling and structuring the depth, pace and content of interview processes by adopting strategies such as deflection, distraction and acting out. Research by Bushin (2008) and MacDonald and Greggans (2008) explored these issues by assessing the benefits and limitations in undertaking interviews within children's family homes. They illustrated, through case studies, how building rapport is contingent on social context and also how children's perceived reality is interdependent with their broader structural and social elements of their lives thus drawing attention to the contingent nature of children's perspectives within a particular time, place and space.

In relation to the concern about children's *recall abilities* and their competence to provide a reliable and accurate account within the context of the interview work by Docherty and Sandelowski (1999) synthesizes "information from contemporary literature on narrative, scripts, and memory in children to show that interview data from children is not less well developed than, but rather different from, data obtained by adults" (p. 178). For example, one area of repeated concern relates to the age at which children can remember past events, for how long and how far back in their personal histories. Docherty and Sandelowski (1999, pp. 178–179) argue that this ability is related to the developing concept of "self" and that begins at roughly the age of two with children beginning to narrate events that have been organized autobiographically in memory. By the time the children are between 3–6 years autobiographical memory can be accurate and stable over time. Young children have also been shown to develop accurate scripts for familiar recurring situations if asked the right type of questions-namely direct questions such as "what-happens-when" or "what-happens-if."

Docherty and Sandelowski (1999) have also addressed issues regarding the content of the interview suggesting that young children may withhold negative experiences because they do not want to "elicit a negative response from the interviewer or others might hear what they say" (p. 180–182) and that there are important considerations regarding the form and number of interviews held. There are mixed findings with some research indicating that the more a young child is interviewed about an issue the more they recall and the converse is the more the child is interviewed the more likely it is that the child will think they have given wrong or incomplete information. They also highlighted that the use of free recall can prove problematic and researchers have found that the use of direct questions is more helpful in engaging children in conversation.

CONTEMPORARY ISSUES REGARDING USE OF QUALITATIVE INNOVATIVE METHODS

As has been highlighted throughout this chapter researchers reflect that the use of innovative methods puts young children at ease, helps them explore their perspectives more freely and openly, plays to their strengths and competencies and helps ameliorate the inherent power imbalances in the researcher-child relationship through opportunities for reciprocity and collaboration. Furthermore children's engagement with these methods produces data not usually accessible and can help children reach "the unrecognized, unacknowledged or "unsayable" stories that they hold" (Leitch, 2008, p. 48). However there is also a growing critique regarding the use of innovative methods (James, 2007; Thomson, 2007; Gallacher & Gallagher, 2008; Holland et al., 2008; Spyrou, 2011; Hunleth, 2011; Ansell, Robson, Hajdu, & Van, 2012; Mand, 2012; Lomax, 2012). What all of these writers have in common as (Ansell et al., 2012) have stated is "the failure of participatory researchers to problematize knowledge production processes" (p. 171) and to critically reflect on the basis of adequate and/or appropriate theoretical frameworks research processes with young children.

Gallacher and Gallagher (2008) through a critical analysis of their own research have argued that within early childhood education research there has been "considerable slippage between pedagogy and research" suggesting that the choice of research methods (including role plays, drawings and the like) with young school aged children has ultimately reflected researchers "expressly taking advantage of children's schooled docility towards such activities" (p. 503). Furthermore they have argued that the reliance on innovative methods has implied that adults must empower children to be social actors and that without these methods children cannot be empowered. An over reliance on a particular set of methods may therefore negate the ways in which children exercise their own social agency in the research process and which may not be connected with the research process *per se*.

Through a critical analysis of their own research, using focus groups with school children, Gallagher (2008) challenged the conception (through the framing of methods) of the "all-knowing adult" and the "incompetent child." The research illustrated how the children exercised their own social agency within the confining structures of the research process by resisting the researchers attempts to impose order and structure and also how the children exercised power over each other through inclusionary and exclusionary practices "within larger webs of power relations—the classroom, the year groups, the school and beyond" (p. 143).

Komulainen's work (2007) has reflected similar themes critiquing the representation of the child voice in research, which has attributed autonomy, rationality and intention to the speaking child and divorced "voice" from its wider social context. Komulainen (2007), from a poststructuralist perspective, has argued for "voice" to be constructed "as social and co-constructed instead of individual, fixed, straightforward, linear or clear" (cited in Spyrou, 2011, p. 152) and for discussion to include researcher assumptions about children within broader institutional, social and structural contexts as these all have enabling and constraining elements in terms of understanding and representing child's voice. Gallacher and Gallagher (2008) have highlighted similar views in relation to the concept of "voice" and the conceptualization of power also from a poststructuralist perspective.

James (2007) has warned against "text positivism" that assumes "that research done with or by children—research including "what children say" is an authentic (and hence unproblematic) representation of children's voices" (p. 263). James (2007) has argued that there is a need for critical and reflexive engagement in relation to issues such as the roles that children's voices take on in research and whether, for example, they run the risk of entrenching prejudices rather than challenging them and whether they capture heterogeneity and individuality or portray children as a homogenous group. Identification of the drivers behind research project is critical. By way of example there might be political imperatives to portray young children as social actors when the findings might be more ambiguous than that.

Spyrou (2011) has drawn together all of the main arguments in this area highlighting the link between researcher reflexivity and increasing "the rigor and creativity of the research process to attain higher quality research in the form of better or more creative research questions, concepts and theories and more ethical approaches" (p. 162). In relation to reflexivity and rigor researchers should take account of the structuring effects of the academic field, their position in the academic field and the effect on one's beliefs and practices and visa versa. Bourdieu's framework is useful here as it attempts to overcome the division between objectivism and subjectivism by arguing that people contribute to the construction of the world and are constructed by it. Bourdieu (1990) writes about researchers' "realist construction" of knowledge (or social reality), which:

> firstly is not carried out in a social vacuum, but that it is subjected to structural constraints; secondly, the structuring structures, the cognitive structures, are themselves socially structured, because they have social origins; thirdly, the construction of social reality is not only an individual enterprise, but may also become a collective enterprise. (p. 131)

Furthermore, and specifically again in relation to rigor there have been concerns about the reliability, generalizability and validity of data collated from young children using innovative qualitative methods (Collingridge & Gantt, 2008; Thyer, 2012). Reliability in qualitative research typically refers to adopting research methods that are accepted by the research community as legitimate ways of collecting and analyzing data. Collingridge and Gantt (2008) have stated, "This concept of reliability differs from the traditional quantitative understanding in that the focus is not on obtaining exactly the same results time and again, but rather on achieving consistent similarity in the quality of the results" (p. 390). Validity means selecting the right method for the given question and applying that method "in a coherent, justifiable, and rigorous manner" (p. 391). High quality standards of rigor in qualitative research (Thyer, 2012) include: adequate description of the data collection methods and frameworks used for analysis; attention to the ways that the trustworthiness of the data was assessed; discussion of alternative explanations; and explanation of authors' philosophical perspectives and conceptual frameworks (p. 123), identifying for example broader traditions such as social constructionism and critical realism.

Generalizability refers to how far the findings from one sample group in a study can be generalized to the wider population and how easy is it to replicate the study. On one level it could be argued that the types of study reported in this chapter could be replicated in the underpinning principles, theoretical/conceptual framework, design, methodology and methods. However what this chapter has shown is that qualitative research involving the use of innovative methods with young children is a complex, dynamic, relational and contingent process where that which we seek to discover—children's meanings, experiences and perspectives, are also contingent in their formation and expression. Accepting this means that we have to accept that there is no one objective truth that research seeks to uncover and place into the public domain but rather that research seeks to illuminate certain aspects or facets of meaning, experience and perspective accepting both their truth and also their contingent nature. As highlighted in this chapter researcher reflexivity on all these aspects adds strength and depth to findings.

CONCLUSION

This chapter has considered the use of innovative qualitative methods in research with young children ages 4–7 years old. The reasons for the emergence of this growing body of research, across a range of disciplines, have been outlined and various methods explored in detail. The effectiveness of specific methods and what factors hinder and enable their use have been considered as having broader debates regarding the reliability, validity, and generalizability of findings using these methods. It is crucial to engage in critical reflection and theorizing as part of the production of research knowledge in this area. It is also crucial to remember the major contribution that has been made to our understanding of children's social worlds through their engagement in research processes that have used innovative qualitative methods. Without these advances the perspectives and experiences of young children would have remained silent and been silenced for much longer.

APPENDIX

THE LEGAL GUARDIAN: Please read the following statements to the child and ask them to draw in the circles if they agree.

The views of children in care

1. I want to take part in Karen's study.

2. The adult looking after me has read a leaflet from Karen with me.

3. If I get fed up I know That I can stop taking part at any time.

4. It's OK for Karen to tape record my chats with her.

5. I know that I can change my mind if I don't want Karen to tape record my chats any more.

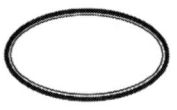

FOR THE LEGAL GUARDIAN TO COMPLETE: I can confirm that I read the above statements to the child and that they understood and agreed with the ones that are marked.

_____   _____   _____

Name   Date

Children's Views about the Letterbox Club

Hello
My name is Karen. I work at Queens University Belfast.

I am doing some work to find out what children who are sent parcels from the Letterbox Club think about it.

Please would you read through this leaflet with your foster carer and have a think about whether you would like to be involved.

PAGE 1

Will people find out what I have said?

If we tape record our meeting I will lock the tape away and only me and one other person who is working with me will listen to the tape. From the tape I will write down what you say and will change your name so nobody knows it is you. I will then erase the tape. I will keep the notes form the tape in a safe place.

Will I get to know the results?
I will keep you up to date with a short report. You can get longer reports too if you want.

Where I work
Karen Winter,
Queens University Belfast,
6, College Park,
Belfast BT7 1LP

Tel: 028 9097 3917
Email: k.winter@qub.ac.uk

Thank you for reading this leaflet!

PAGE 4

What is the research about?

I would like to know about what children think about the Letterbox Club. The main questions I will be asking are:

- What happens when a parcel arrives at your home?
- How often do you read the books or listen to the CD's in the parcel?
- Does anyone help you read the books or use the math's game?
- Is there anything you would like to change?

Who will be in the project?

20 children will be involved. They will all be about your age. I will also talk to your foster carers and some of the staff who run the Letterbox Club.

What will happen to me if I take part?

We will agree where you would like to meet me. I will then come and ask you the questions on this sheet. You can choose who will be at the interview with you, for example your social worker or foster carer. I would like to tape record what we say but only if that is OK with you. I would like to take notes too.

PAGE 2

Could there be problems for me if I take part?

Some children might get worried or bored. If this happens and you want to stop talking or finish our meeting that is fine. You will not get into trouble.

Do I have to take part?

It's up to you if you want to take part or not. Even if you say 'Yes' you can change your mind at any time. You will not be in trouble for changing your mind.

When we are talking you can:

- tell me to stop
- have a break
- tell me if you don't want to talk any more or if you don't want to take part any more

PAGE 3

REFERENCES

Alderson, P. (2000). Convention on the rights of the child: Some common criticisms and suggested responses. *Child Abuse Review, 9*, 439–443.
Alderson, P. (2008). *Young children's rights: Exploring beliefs, principles and practice.* London: Jessica Kingsley.
Alderson, P., & Morrow, V. (2011) *The ethics of research with children and young people: A practical handbook.* London: Sage Publications.
Aldiss, S., Horstman, M., O'Leary, C., & Gibson, F. (2009). What is important to children who have cancer while in hospital? *Children and Society, 23,* 85–98.
Anderson, K., & Balandin, S. (2011). The storybook method: Research feedback with young participants. *Augmentative and Alternative Communication, 27*(4), 279–291.
Ansell, N., Robson, E., Hajdu, F., & Van, L. (2012). Learning from young people about their lives: using participatory methods to research the impacts of AIDS in southern Africa. *Children's Geographies, 10*(2), 169–186.
Backett-Milburn, K., & McKie, L. (1999). A critical appraisal of the draw and write technique. *Health Education Research, 14,* 387–398.
Balen, R., Blyth, E., Calabretto, H., Fraser C., Horrocks, C., & Manby, M. (2006). Involving children in health and social research: 'Human becomings' or 'active beings'? *Childhood, 13*(1), 29–48.
Barber, B. (2011). *An autobiographical scrapbook for terminally ill children: A guide to processing death.* California, Azusa Pacific University (unpublished dissertation thesis).
Barker, J., & Smith, F. (2012). What's in focus? A critical discussion of photography, children and young people. *International Journal of Social Research Methodology, 15*(2), 91–103.
Barker, J., & Weller, S. (2003). "Is it fun?" Developing children centered research methods. *International Journal of Sociology and Social Policy, 23*(1/2), 33–58.
Buchwald, D., Schantz-Laursen, B., & Delmar, C. (2009). Video diary data collection in research with children: An alternative method. *International Journal of Qualitative Methods, 8*(1), 12–20.
Bushin, N. (2008). Interviewing with children in their homes: Putting ethical principles into practice and developing flexible techniques, *Children's Geographies, 5*(3), 235–251.
Butler, I., & Williamson, H. (1994). *Children speak: Children, trauma and social work.* London: NSPCC/Longman.
Catalina, C., & Minkler, M. (2010). Photovoice: A review of the literature in health and public health. *Health Education and Behaviour, 37*(3), 424–451.
Christensen, P. (2004). Children's participation in ethnographic research: Issues of power and representation. *Children and Society, 18*(2), 165–176.
Christensen, P., & James, A. (Eds.). (2008). *Research with children: Perspectives and practices.* NY: Routledge.
Christie, D., Romano, G., Barnes, J., Madge, N., Nicholas, D. B., Koot, H. M., Armstrong, D. F.... Khatun, H. (2011). Exploring views on satisfaction with life in young children with chronic illness: An innovative approach to the collection of self-report data from children under 11. *Clinical Child Psychology and Psychiatry, 11,* 1–11.
Clark-Ibanez, M. (2004). Framing the social world through photo-elicitation interviews. *American Behavioral Scientist, 47*(12), 1507–1527.

Clark, A. (2005). Listening to and involving young children: a review of research and practice. *Early Child Development and Care, 175*(6), 489–505.

Clark, A. (2010). Young children as protagonists and the role of participatory, visual methods in engaging multiple perspectives. *American Journal of Community Psychology, 46*(1–2), 115–123.

Clark, A. (2011). Multimodal map making with young children: Exploring ethnographic and participatory methods special issue. Multimodality and ethnography: Working at the intersection. *Qualitative Research, 11*(3), 311–330.

Clark, A., & Moss, P. (2011a). *Listening to young children: The mosaic approach* (2nd ed.). London: National Children's Bureau.

Clark, A., McQuail, S., & Moss, P. (2003). *Exploring the field of listening to and consulting with young children, Research report 445.* London: Department for Education and Skills.

Coad, J. (2007). Using art-based techniques in engaging children and young people in health care consultations and/or research. *Journal of Research in Nursing, 12*(5), 487–497.

Coates, E., & Coates, A. (2006). Young children talking and drawing. *International Journal Early Years Education, 14*(3), 221–242.

Cocks, A. C. (2006). The ethical maze: Finding an inclusive path towards gaining children's agreement to research participation. *Childhood, 13*(2), 247–266.

Collier, J., Collier, M., & Hall, E. T. (1967). *Visual anthropology: Photography as a research method.* NY: Holt, Rinehart and Winston.

Collingridge, D. S., & Gantt, E. E. (2008). The quality of qualitative research. *American Journal of Medical Quality, 23*(5), 389–395.

Connolly, P. (2004). *Boys and schooling in the early years.* London: Routledge/Falmer.

Connolly, P. (2008). Race, gender and critical reflexivity in research with young children. In: P. Christensen. & A. James (Eds.). *Research with children: Perspectives and practices* (pp. 173–188). London: Routledge.

Cook, T., & Hess E. (2007). What the camera sees and from whose perspective? Fun methodologies for engaging children in enlightening adults. *Childhood, 14*(1), 29–46.

Corsaro, W. A. (2010). *The sociology of childhood. (Sociology for a new century series)* (2nd ed.). Thousand Oaks, CA: Pine Forge Press.

Darbyshire, P., MacDougall, C., & Schiller, W. (2005). Multiple methods in qualitative research with children: More insight or just more? *Qualitative Research, 5*(4), 417–436.

Dennis, S. F. Jr., Gaulochers, S., Carpiano, R. M., & Brown, D. (2009). Participatory photomapping (PPM): Exploring an integrated method for health and place research with young people. *Health and Place, 15*(2), 466–473.

Docherty, S., & Sandelowski, M. (1999). Interviewing children. *Research in Nursing & Health, 22*(2), 177–185.

Dockett, S., & Perry, B. (2005). You need to know how to play safe: Children's experiences of starting school. *Contemporary Issues in Early Childhood, 6*(1), 4–18.

Dockett, S., & Perry, B. (2005a). Children's drawings: experiences and expectations of school. *International Journal of Equity and Innovation in Early Childhood, 3*(2), 77–89.

Dockett, S., & Perry, B. (2007). Trusting children's accounts in research. *Journal of Early Childhood Research, 5*(1), 47–63.

Dockett, S., Perry, B., & Kearney, E. (2012). Promoting children's informed assent in research participation. *International Journal of Qualitative Studies in Education*, 1–27.

Driessnack, M. (2005). Children's drawings as facilitators of communication: a meta-analysis. *Journal of Pediatric Nursing, 20*(6), 415–432.

Driessnack, M. (2006). Draw-and-tell conversations with children about fear. *Qualitative Health Research, 16*(10), 1414–1435.

Driessnack, M., & Furukawa, R. (2012). Arts-based data collection techniques used in child research. *Journal of Special Pediatric Nursing, 17*(1), 3–9.

Einarsdottir, J. (2005). Playschool in pictures: Children's photographs as a research method. *Early Child Development and Care, 175*(6), 523–541.

Einarsdottir, J., Dockett, S., & Perry, B. (2009). Making meaning: Children's perspectives expressed through drawings. *Early Childhood Development and Care, 179*(2), 217–232.

Ewald, W. (1985). *Portraits and dreams: Photographs and stories by children of the Appalachians*. NY: Writers and Readers Publications Inc.

Fox, C., Buchanan-Barrow, E. & Barrett, M. (2007). Children's understanding of mental illness. *Child: Care, Health and Development, 34*(1), 10–18.

Gallacher L. A., & Gallagher M. (2008). Methodological immaturity in childhood research? Thinking through 'participatory methods.' *Childhood, 15*, 499–516.

Gallagher, M. (2008). Power is not an evil: rethinking power in participatory methods. *Children's Geographies, 6*(2), 137–150.

Gardner, S., & Yaacob, A. (2012). Young learner perspectives through researcher-initiated role play. In S. Gardner. & M. Martin-Jones (Eds.) *Multilingualism, discourse, and ethnography* (pp. 241–255). London: Routledge.

Gawler, M. (2005). *Useful tools for engaging young people in participatory evaluation*. Geneva: UNICEF.

Gibson, F., Aldiss, S., Horstman, M., Kumpunen, S., & Richardson, S. (2010). Children and young people's experiences of cancer care: A qualitative research study using participatory methods. *International Journal of Nursing Studies, 47*, 1397–1407.

Gray, C., & Winter, E. (2011). Hearing voices: participatory research with preschool children with and without disabilities. *European Early Childhood Education Research Journal, 19*(3), 309–320.

Hamama, L., & Ronen, T. (2009). Children's drawings as a self-portrait measurement. *Child and Family Social Work, 14*, 90–102.

Harcourt, D., & Einarsdottir, J. (2011). Introducing children's perspectives and participation in research. *European Early Childhood Education Research Journal, 19*(3), 301–307.

Harper, D. (2002). Talking about pictures: a case for photo elicitation. *Visual Studies, 17*(1), 13–26.

Haw, K., & Hadfield, M. (2011) *Video in social science research: Functions and forms*. New York, NY: Routledge.

Hemming, P. J. (2008). Mixing qualitative research methods in children's geographies. *Area, 40*(2), 152–162.

Hill, M. (2007) Participatory methods with children. *Child and Family Social Work, 2*(3), 171–183.

Hill, M., Davis, J., Prout, A., & Tisdall, K. (2006). Moving the participation agenda forward. *Children and Society, 18*(2), 77–96.

Holland, S., Renold, E., Ross, N. I., & Hillman, A. (2008). Power, agency and participation agendas: A critical exploration of young people's engagement in participative qualitative research. *Childhood, 17*(3), 360–375.

Horstman, M., Aldiss, S., Richardson, A., & Gibson F. (2008). Methodological issues when using the draw and write technique with children aged 6 to 12 years. *Qualitative Health Research, 18*(7), 1001–1011.

Hunleth, J. (2011). Beyond *on* or *with*: questioning power dynamics and knowledge production in 'child orientated' research methodology. *Childhood, 18*(1), 81–93.

Irwin, L. G., & Johnson, J. (2005). Interviewing young children: Explicating our practices and dilemmas. *Qualitative Health Research, 15*(6), 821–831.

James, A. (2007). Giving voice to children's voices: Practices and problems, pitfalls and potentials. *American Anthropologist, 109*(2), 261–272.

James, A., & James, A. L. (2004). *Constructing childhood: Theory, policy and social practice*. London: Palgrave Macmillan.

James, A., & Prout, A. (1997). *Constructing and reconstructing childhood: Contemporary issues in the sociological study of childhood*. London: Routledge.

James. A., Jenks, C., & Prout, A. (1998). *Theorizing childhood*. London: Polity Press.

Jenks, C. (Ed.). (1982). *The sociology of childhood: Essential readings*. London: Batsford Academic and Educational.

Johnson, G. A. (2011). A child's right to participation: Photovoice as a methodology for documenting the experiences of children in Kenyan orphanges. *Visual Anthropology Review, 27*(2), 141–161.

Jorgenson, J., & Sullivan, T. (2010). Accessing children's perspectives through participatory photo interviews [43 paragraphs]. *Forum Qualitative Sozialforschung / Forum: Qualitative Social Research, 11(1)*, Art. 8, http://nbn-resolving. de/urn:nbn:de:0114-fqs100189. http://www.qualitative-research.net/index. php/fqs/article/view/447/2890

Komulainen, S. (2007). The ambiguity of the child's 'voice' in social research. *Childhood, 14*(1), 11–28.

Kortesluoma, R., Hentinen, M., & Nikkonen, M. (2003). Conducting a qualitative child interview: Methodological considerations. *Journal of Advanced Nursing, 42*, 434–441.

Kullman, K. (2012). Experiments with moving children and digital cameras, *Children's Geographies, 10*(1), 1–16. .

Leitch, R. (2008). Creatively researching children's narratives through images and drawings. In P. Thomson (Ed.). *Doing visual research with children and young people* (pp. 37–57). London and NY, Routledge.

Lomax, H. (2012). Contested voices? Methodological tensions in creative visual research with children. *International Journal of Social Research Methodology, 15*(2), 105–117.

Lundy, L. (2007). 'Voice' is not enough: Conceptualising article 12 of the united nations convention on the rights of the child. *British Educational Research Journal, 33*(6), 927–942.

MacDonald, K., & Greggans, A. (2008). Dealing with chaos and complexity: the reality of interviewing children and families in their own homes. *Journal of Clinical Nursing, 17*, 3123–3130.

Mand, K. (2012). Giving children a 'voice': arts-based participatory research activities and representation. *International Journal of Social Research Methodology, 15*(2), 149–160.

Mason, J., & Hood, S. (2011). Exploring issues of children as actors in social research. *Children and Youth Services Review, 33*, 490–495.

Mayall, B. (2002). *Towards a sociology for childhood: Thinking from children's lives.* Buckingham: Open University Press.

McIntosh, C., & Stephens, C. (2012). A storybook method for exploring young children's views of illness causality in relation to the familial context. *Early Child Development and Care, 182*(1), 23–33.

Morgan, M., Gibbs, S., Maxwell, K., & Britten, N. (2002). Hearing children's voices: methodological issues in conducting focus groups with children aged 7–11 years. *Qualitative Research, 2,* 5–20.

Morrow, V. (2008). Ethical dilemmas in research with children and young people about their social environments. *Children's Geographies 6*(1), 49–61.

Moschini, L. B. (2005). *Drawing the line: Art therapy with the difficult client.* London: John Wiley and Sons.

Nixon, E., & Halpenny, A. M. (2010) *Children's Perspectives on Parenting Styles and Discipline: A Developmental Approach.* Dublin: Office of the Minister for Children and Youth Affairs.

O'Kane, C. (2008). The development of participatory techniques: Facilitating children's views about decisions which affect them. In P. Christensen. & A. James. (Eds.). *Research with children: Perspectives and practice* (2nd ed.) (pp. 125–155). NY: Routledge Press.

Pascal, C., & Bertram, T. (2009): Listening to young citizens: the struggle to make real a participatory paradigm in research with young children. *European Early Childhood Education Research Journal, 17*(2), 249–262.

Pimlott-Wilson, H. (2011). Visualising children's participation in research: Lego duplo, rainbows and clouds and moodboards. *International Journal of Social Research Methodology, 15*(2), 135–148.

Plunkett, R., Leipert, B. D., & Ray, S. L. (2013). Unspoken phenomena: using the photovoice method to enrich phenomenological inquiry. *Nursing Inquiry, 20*(2), 156–164.

Prosser, J., & Burke, C. (2007) Childlike perspectives through image-based educational research. In: J. G. Knowles & A. Cole. (Eds.), *Handbook of the arts in qualitative research: perspectives, methodologies, examples and issues* (pp. 407–421). London: Oxford University Press.

Prosser, J., & Burke, C. (2011) Image based educational research: Childlike perspectives. *Learning Landscapes, 4*(2), 257–275.

Prout, A., & James, A. (1997) A new paradigm for the sociology of childhood? Provenance, promise and problems. In A. James & A. Prout. (Eds.), *Constructing and reconstructing childhood: Contemporary issues in the sociological study of childhood* (pp. 7–33). London: Routledge.

Punch, S. (2002). Research with children: The same or different from research with adults?' *Childhood, 9*(3), 321–341.

Robson, S. (2009). Producing and using video data in the early years: Ethical questions and practical consequences in research with young children. *Children and Society, 25*(3), 179–189.
Rogers, S., & Evans, J. (2008). *Inside role-play in early childhood education: Researching young children's perspectives.* London: Taylor and Francis.
Rollins, J. A. (2005). Tell me about it: drawing as a communication tool for children with cancer. *Journal of Pediatric Oncology Nursing, 22*(4), 203–221.
Serriere, S. C. (2010). Carpet-time democracy: Digital photography and social consciousness in the early childhood classroom. *The Social Studies, 101,* 60–68.
Sharples, M., Davison, L., Thomas, G., & Rudman, P. (2003). Children as photographers: An analysis of children's photographic behaviour and intentions at three age levels.' *Visual Communication, 2*(3), 303–330.
Spyrou, S. (2011). The limits of children's voices: From authenticity to critical, reflexive representation. *Childhood, 18*(2), 151–165.
Taylor, C., & Coffey, A. (2009). Editorial. Special issue: qualitative research and methodological innovation. *Qualitative Research, 9*(5), 523–526.
Theobald, M. (2012) Video-stimulated accounts: Young children accounting for interactional matters in front of peers. *Journal of Early Childhood Research, 10,* 32–50.
Thomson, F. (2007). Are methodologies for children keeping them in their place? *Children's Geographies, 5*(3), 207–218.
Thyer, B. A. (2012). The scientific value of qualitative research for social work. *Qualitative Social Work, 11*(2), 115–129.
Travers, M. (2009). New methods, old problems: A skeptical view of innovation in qualitative research. *Qualitative Research, 9*(2), 161–179.
United Nations. (1989). *Convention on the Rights of the Child.* Geneva: United Nations.
United Nations. (2005). *General Comment No. 7. 2005. Implementing Child Rights in Early Childhood.* Geneva: United Nations.
United Nations. (2009). *General Comment No. 12 (2009) The Right of the Child to be Heard.* Geneva: United Nations.
Wang, C., & Burris, M. A. (1994). Empowerment through photo novellas: Portraits of participation. *Health Education Quarterly, 21*(2), 171–186.
Wang, C., & Burris, M. A. (1997). Photovoice: Concept, methodology, and use for participatory needs assessment. *Health, Education and Behavior, 24*(3), 369–387.
Wang, C. C., & Redwood-Jones, Y. A. (2001). Photovoice ethics: Perspectives form Flint photovoice, *Health Education and Behavior, 28,* 560–572.
Winter, K. (2011a). *Building relationships and communicating with young children: A practical guide for social workers.* London: Routledge.
Warming, H. (2011b). Getting under their skins? Accessing young children's perspectives through ethnographic research. *Childhood, 18*(1), 39–53.
Winter, K. (2012a). Ascertaining the perspectives of young children in care: Case studies using reality boxes. *Children and Society, 26*(5), 368–380.
Winter, K. (2012b). Understanding and supporting young children's transitions into state care: Schlossberg's transition framework and child-centerd practice. *British Journal Social Work,* First published online: August 16, 2012, doi: 10.1093/bjsw/bcs128
Young, L., & Barrett, H. (2001). Adapting visual methods: action research with Kampala street children. *Area, 33*(2), 141–152.

CHAPTER 15

CASE STUDY RESEARCH
The Child in Context

Susan Hill and Ngaire Millar

Sung Kook said he had three close male friends and they spent most break times playing soccer. He reported that he often had friends over to play at home. His mother said that he had adapted easily to school in Australia because he was so young. She suggested he was learning social skills such as sharing through play and explicit teaching. She said, "I like talking to the other mothers after school" as other parents gave her positive feedback about Sung Kook's achievements. (Millar, 2011 p. 14)

INTRODUCTION

The above vignette, from a case study investigating how young Korean children made cultural transitions to the early years of school in Australia, highlights important reasons for choosing case study research methods in early childhood. The vignette is a brief description that enables the reader to interpret and more fully understand the complex strategies Sung Kook and his mother used as they made important cultural transitions within a real-life context. Compared to other research approaches such as experiments, surveys and histories, case study is a preferred research method when (a) "how" and "why" research questions are posed; (b) the investigator has little control over events; and (c) the focus is on contemporary phenomenon within a real-life context (Yin, 2009, p. 2).

Case study research in early childhood has a rich and very influential history that can be traced back to well know theorists such as Piaget, Freud and Darwin who used case study approaches to explore and to understand children's learning and development in the early years. Case studies have been used in medical research and psychology to understand the development of young children and how children respond in different contexts. In the field of early childhood, case studies of children, families and educational settings have inspired educators and influenced both research and practice. For example, there are memorable case studies of children's learning in a Maori school in New Zealand (Ashton-Warner, 1963). Other notable case studies of young children and their families include children's bedtime stories compiled by Heath (1983) and case studies of children and family literacy practices in Appalachia by Purcell-Gates (1995). Other influential case studies have focused on the quality of early years' learning environments in Britain and these case studies have led to improvement in early years' policy and educators' practices (Pascal & Bertram, 2009). A number of in-depth case studies revealed "why" and "when" certain children succeed against the odds while others fall behind in the British longitudinal study of 3000+ young children performing against the odds (Siraj-Blatchford, Mayo, Melhuish, Taggart, Sammons, & Sylva, 2011).

This chapter considers big picture of what a case study is and what a case study is not. The chapter then explores the similarities and differences between case study and ethnography, different approaches to case study research and types of case studies. Following this, the next section discusses the importance of framing the research questions in case studies and then the range of data collection methods that particularly relate to early childhood case study research. The next section includes ways data may be analyzed and this leads into sections about triangulation, validity and reliability. The chapter concludes with explanations of the various roles of the case study researcher and suggestions for organizing and writing case study reports.

WHAT IS A CASE STUDY?

A case study in educational research is a bounded unit—a person, a group, an institution, or an organization and involves interactions, communications, relationships, and practices between the case and the wider world and vice versa (Hamilton & Corbett-Whittier, 2013). In early childhood, case study research provides the researcher with an opportunity to gain in-depth knowledge of a specific child, or group of children in a particular context such as an early childhood setting. A case study can also be an in-depth investigation of a whole school system, a particular program, a teacher or the development of a child or group of children over a period of time. A case study can focus on an event, such as education professionals working together to investigate a specific experience of childhood (Stake, 2005). While one child, one event or a whole school system may be the focus of a case study it is crucially important for the case study researcher to make decision about the boundaries or the bounded unit of the case study (Hamilton & Corbett-Whittier, 2013). For example, a case study researcher focusing on a four-year-old child learning to read and write at home may consider the bounded unit to include the child's interactions with all family members, the books read, television and other media, plus pencils, crayons, and other tools for representing meaning (Pahl, 2002).

In a case study the researcher explores the bounded unit—a person, a group, an event, an institution, or an organization using multiple research methods and data sources to investigate "the particularity and complexity of a single case, coming to understand its activity within important circumstances" (Stake, 1995, p. xi). The case study researcher seeks to achieve a rich description of the participants' perspectives (Torrance, 2005). To capture the complexity of the case and various participants' perspectives, the case study researcher uses several data collection tools (interviews, observations, reflective journals) as well as different perspectives (child, teacher, parent, researcher) to provide depth understanding of the case and also to provide triangulation to reinforce the legitimacy of the conclusions drawn.

WHAT IS NOT CONSIDERED A CASE STUDY?

A case study is a bounded unit—a child or a teacher—and it involves interactions, communications, relationships and practices between the case and the wider world and vice versa and the general topic like the process of teaching is not considered a case. Also not considered to be case studies are the reasons for a particular innovation or school reform, particular policies or initiatives as these are generalities and not commonly considered a case. General topics like teaching approaches or small group strategies are not considered a case as they are not a bounded system.

CASE STUDIES BRIDGING RESEARCH AND PRACTICE

Early childhood researchers have used case study as a way of conducting and disseminating research to impact upon practice and to refine the way practice is theorized. Often a case can be used by researchers to bridge the work and exchanges between researchers and practitioners as a case can explore a particular context, time and place and conditions that shape teaching and learning involving particular human interactions. In case study research the context, the conditions of teaching and learning are not taken to be background variables but rather lived dimensions that are integral to the teaching-learning event (Freebody, 2003).

CASE STUDIES AND ETHNOGRAPHY—SIMILARITIES AND DISSIMILARITIES

Many beginning researchers puzzle over the similarities and differences between case study research and ethnography as both are qualitative, descriptive approaches to research. There are important distinctions between case study and ethnography. Ethnography is research that involves immersion in a natural setting for an extended period of time. Ethnographies are related to anthropology and focus on a cultural theme whereas case studies focus on in-depth exploration of an actual case. An ethnographer is interested in understanding the shared patterns of culturally influenced behavior of a group whereas a case study researcher is more interested in describing the activities of a group (Creswell, 2012). A case study researcher chooses to focus on a program, event or an activity involving individuals rather than the group as such (Stake, 1995). Unlike an ethnographic study, a case study focuses on one particular instance of educational experience and attempts to gain theoretical and professional insights from a full documentation of that instance (Freebody, 2003). According to Yin (2009) ethnographies usually require long periods of time in the "field" and in contrast "case studies are a form of inquiry that does not depend solely on ethnographic or participant-observer data" (Yin, 2009, p. 15). Further, Yin (2009) writes that it is possible to do a valid and high quality case study using the telephone or the internet, depending on the topic being studied. For example in early childhood, a case study could be compiled using interactive communication technology such as the telephone and internet data to explore topics such as family literacy practices or family participation in early childhood community events.

It is true though that some case study researchers place more attention on cultural practices within a particular case study. For example early childhood case study researchers Dyson and Genishi (2005) focus on children engaged in contemporary events they describe as cultural practices. In fact, the term "ethnographic case studies" can be used too if a case study is designed to understand the case in its sociocultural context and with concepts of culture in mind. This is significant in research with young children if sociocultural perspectives are used to explore how child development is affected by interpersonal relationships and cultural activities (Rogoff, 2003).

While there are differences between case study research—a focus on the case, and ethnographic research—focus on culture, case study researchers utilize many of the data collection sources from ethnography and anthropology including interviews, observations and collection of artifacts such as work samples. Case studies are always situated within a larger context, such as socio-economic, political or geographical settings (Creswell, 2012) and this contextual information is very relevant because case study research does emphasize the importance of social interaction in human activity (Torrance, 2005). In early childhood research, the context of the school, childcare setting, home and the child's interactions with others within these contexts are fundamental to understanding children's worlds.

DIFFERENT APPROACHES AND TYPES OF CASE STUDY

Case study theorists have distinctive orientations towards defining, conducting and interpreting case studies and also there are different types or forms of case studies (Hamilton & Corbett-Whittier, 2013). Stake (1995), a well-known case study theorist likens case study to creating a unique work of art where the case study researcher draws on anthropological and biographical research tools to encourage the readers to interpret the case and thereby form new understandings of their own context and processes. Stake's emphasis on the aesthetic, qualitative and the interpretive nature of case study contrasts sharply with Yin's (2009) more scientific approach. Yin (2009) writes about case study research from a broad social science perspective rather than an education specific one and tends to try to impose quantitative concepts of validity on case study research. Early childhood researchers Dyson and Genishi (2005) have developed case studies of young children, teachers and early childhood settings with particular attention to children's sociocultural understandings. Graue and Walsh (1998) also highlight the importance of researching young children in their local context with attention to many of the practical and ethical concerns of conducting research involving the perspectives very young children.

There are different theoretical orientations to case study research such as the more interpretive and aesthetic case study approach of Stake (1995) and the more positivistic orientation of Yin (2009). There are also distinctions to be made between the nature and purposes of different types of case study, as there are intrinsic, instrumental, collective, theory-led and theory-generating case studies was well as evaluation case studies.

Simons (2009) and Stake (1995) distinguished between three broad types of case study: intrinsic, instrumental and collective. In an intrinsic case study the purpose is to capture the case in its entirety and more fully understand the person, or institution that makes up the case. The researcher seeks to obtain deep understanding of a single case and the intrinsic case study is not designed for generalizability (Stake, 2005). For example an intrinsic case study involving a young child will usually be based on observations and detailed conversations with the child and key adults (Mukherji & Albon, 2010). In the second type, an instrumental case study, the case is chosen to explore an issue or research question to gain insight or understanding (Simons, 2009). The researcher uses instrumental case study to learn about a general phenomenon such as cultural transition, inclusion or young children's transitions from preschool to school (Mukherji & Albon, 2010).

The third type of case study is known as collective case studies where researchers connect several cases together to construct a collective understanding of an issue (Creswell, 2012). One researcher may develop collective case studies to explore an issue or topic (Pahl 2002) or a collaborative team of researchers working within or across institutions can develop collective longitudinal or short term case studies (Millar, 2011; Hill, Comber, Louden, Reid, & Rivalland, 2002). Collective case studies were used by Millar (2011) to investigate Korean children's cultural transition to school in Australia. Data were gathered during semi-structured interviews with four 5-8 year old Korean international students, their mothers and teachers, about their personal experiences and perceptions of the transitions to the early years of school in Australia. To generate the collective case study the data were analyzed and classified into common themes. "Patterns and similarities among individual perceptions were identified" (Millar, 2011, p. 13).

In addition to intrinsic, instrumental and collective case studies, Simons (2009) points out that there can be theory-led case studies and theory-generating case studies. Theory-led can mean exploring a case through a particular theoretical perspective for example in an evaluation case study exploring at the outset what the theory of a particular program is, what it is aspiring to achieve, in order to focus and design the evaluation. Theory-generating case studies are similar to the concept of grounded theory where theory arises from the data itself and this approach often involves exploring several case studies to test to see if the theory holds. For example collective case studies of young children's diverse literacy development in the years before school were linked to the socioeconomic resources in the home and also the pedagogical knowledge of the teachers (Hill et al., 2002).

Further, another type of case study is the evaluation case studies designed to discern the value of a program or project. The evaluation case study has a role of informing decision makers and may be responsive to multiple stakeholders. In evaluation case studies the program commissioners may have a say in what issues are explored and which methodologies are used. Also an evaluation case study may consist of collective case studies or a single case study of an organization such as a school or a school system.

THE RESEARCH QUESTIONS IN CASE STUDY RESEARCH

The research questions in case study research acknowledge the context and the complexity of the particular case under study. The research questions will also have inbuilt assumptions and the researcher's consciousness of underlying theoretic presuppositions. In contrast with more positivistic, experimental research, case study research questions draw attention to issues, problems or concerns linked to political, social historical and personal contexts.

The use of issues to develop research questions helps the researcher see the case in an historical light and recognize the tensions in human interaction. "Issues draw us toward observing, even teasing out the problems of the case, the conflictual outpourings, the complex backgrounds of human concern" (Stake, 1995, p.17). The research questions in an intrinsic or instrumental case study are developed from issues and can evolve as the case study progresses and questions are redefined when unexpected learning occurs. This evolution of research questions as the study progresses is the direct opposite to social science research design based around the testing of hypotheses and fixed research questions. Case study research demands careful planning; however, it is also explorative "Quite often, neither the sites or units of the investigation, nor the precise objects of reasoning, circumstances or core problems are really known at the beginning of the endeavor" (Diefenbach, 2009, p. 877).

An example of an explorative, contextual research question is provided by Ranker (2009) who asked, "What multimodal composing practices did the students import from previous composing events?" (p. 322). The research question was posed to explore the ways three young bilingual boys accessed and combined multimodal resources while composing. In Ranker's (2009) case studies the research questions were used in the overall research design for data collection and analysis of the data collected. The case study of the writing event and the interactions of the three writers enabled the researcher to gain insights into the students' need for social collaboration and the situated nature of composing practices.

The refinement and evolving nature of case study questions is essential in case study research in order to respond to the complexity of the case as it develops. For example, Compton-Lilly (2006) began a case study of a young reader and writer named Devon while she was engaged in Reading Recovery training. The case study explored the literacy development of one child and included data collected from Clay's (2002) Observation Survey, careful lesson notes and running records of the child's reading behaviors. In addition, she collected examples of the child's classroom writing and his Reading Recovery writing journal, plus interviews with Devon and his mother. However, half way through the data collection Compton-Lilly (2006) became aware of issues to do with Devon's identity, race and the connections between literacy in school and out of school. The research questions became more complex, moving from understanding Devon as a reader and writer to creating a much richer portrait concerned with examining how one African-American student's evolving identity, which reflected his media, childhood and cultural resources, intersected with literacy learning and became a tool to support his reading and writing. Compton-Lilly emphasized the importance of Stake's (1995) more aesthetic and interpretation focussed approach to case study and the notion that "the best research questions evolve during the study" (p. 33).

THE CONTEXT, NATURALISTIC, QUALITATIVE RESEARCH AND YOUNG CHILDREN

Renewed interest in naturalistic, contextual and qualitative methods in early childhood research has developed in reaction to narrow, scientific, evidence based research approaches, which usually involve removing participants from their familiar surroundings and placing them in experimental situations. A qualitative approach requires researchers to focus on obtaining participant perspectives in their natural environment. The use of naturalistic settings and context is vitally important in research with young children as obtaining access to children's perspectives, their communication; their views of the world require special approaches to data collection and analysis. As Graue and Walsh (1998) reminds us,

> Who a child is is different on the school bus from in reading group and is different still at the kitchen table. (p. 80)

Case study researchers use qualitative research tools to explore participants' perspectives in natural settings and this usually requires substantial amounts of time spent in early childhood settings schools, education organizations and communities "learning about educational concerns" (Bogdan & Biklen 2003, p. 4). Case study researchers are concerned with revealing assumptions and foregrounding how people negotiate meaning (Bogdan & Biklen, 2003). The researcher seeks to obtain knowledge of participant experiential understanding (Stake, 2005). Case studies of young children, teachers and families may include data which may include "interview transcripts, field notes, photographs, videotapes, personal documents, memos, and other official records" (Bogdan & Biklen 2003, p. 5). Any combination of these data sources may be incorporated in qualitative research with young children to richly represent their perspective of their lives and experiences. For example, in an investigation into how adult-child relationships impacted children's learning Eagle (2012) used a combination of transcripts and observations of video-recorded interactions between the participants during and exploration of children's use of digital technologies.

Case study researchers engaging in research with young children face particular issues due to adult perceptions of children's limited competencies and vulnerability. It has been argued that "biological immaturity is a fact of childhood" (Woodrow, 1999) and this social construct is the basis of much early childhood education policy development and practice. Concepts of young children's vulnerability are closely aligned with adult images of the child and their position in society (James & Prout, 1990). To maintain the idea of vulnerable innocents who need protection adults assume power and control for decision-making on behalf of children. This objectification effectively limits children's capacity to act as social participants who are capable of constructively engaging with issues affecting their own lives (Woodrow, 1999).

In contemporary research a new view of the child as a competent, capable, knowledgeable citizen (Luxford & Smart 2009) with a specific "voice" has emerged. By recognizing and valuing children's perspectives researchers move past the adult oriented research schema (Freeman & Mathison, 2009). This shift in thinking moves researchers away from the notion of doing research "on" children to doing research "with" children. This means researchers should respect and value children's rights which is evident when they develop more participatory and inclusive research strategies (Mukherji & Albon, 2010).

CASE STUDY DATA COLLECTION

Data collection in case study research is linked the initial research questions (Yin, 2009). According to Yin (2009), the basic components of a case study research design should include "the study's question, its propositions, its unit(s) of analysis, the logic linking the data to the propositions and the criteria for interpreting the findings" (Yin, 2008, p. 27). Throughout this chapter case study has been described as a qualitative method which may imply that only qualitative data is incorporated into the research design. In case study research, both qualitative and quantitative data are valuable sources to help the researcher develop a deep analytical understanding of the case (Stake, 2005; Yin, 2009).

During data gathering the researcher is, most likely, going to go out into the field to observe and record the events, behaviors, and processes of a case (Vasconcelos, 2010). The case study researcher will gather a range of sources for evidence when building the case. Documents may include personal items such as children's drawings and artwork, letters, diaries, or public papers such as agendas, memos, written reports. Related research studies on case related topics, media articles, archival records and other physical artifacts could be used. The researcher may include interviews and direct observation along with participant observation (Yin, 2009).

In preparation for data collection the researcher establishes processes for gathering and assessing multiple sources. The researcher then creates a case study database which may include two separate collections—the data sources and the initial written document which will eventually become the final case study report (Yin, 2009). It is crucial to maintain documented evidence and digital technologies are widely used by researchers for this purpose. In addition to personal computers case study researchers use various recording devices such as cellular telephones, digital audio and video recorders (Dyson & Genishi, 2005).

During the early period of preparation the researcher needs to identify the site where data collection will take place. At this stage permissions from the relevant governing bodies will be required. If the research is being undertaken on behalf of an institution, or by a research student, approval from a Human Research Ethics Committee may be required. Education districts may have their own procedures for approving research in childcare centers, preschools and schools. Independent schools may require a personally written letter to the Principal or Director, outlining the research and benefits to the school community. Once the relationship with the site begins the researcher may be in regular contact with administrators (Dyson & Genishi, 2005).

Participant recruitment is the next step after approval has been granted at the site. When working with any human participants, children or adults, the researcher must gain informed consent (Simons, 2005). This involves explaining the purpose of the case study, formally requesting participation, confirming the potential participants will be protected from harm or deception and that their participation will remain confidential. Particular care must be taken when recruiting vulnerable people such as young children (Yin, 2009). Young children's capacity to consent for voluntary participation is subject to consent from a caregiver. However, in ethical research open communication with the child, offering the right to decline to participate or withdraw without prejudice recognizes the child as a competent social actor on their own behalf (Freeman & Mathison, 2009).

The relationship between social science researchers and young children has changed over the years. Governments in many countries now have regulations to protect this vulnerable group. Children are described as vulnerable because they are physically smaller and weaker than adults. They may have less knowledge or experience of researchers and therefore are at risk of manipulation. They are structurally less powerful in political, social and economic circumstances. They are vulnerable because of adult emphasis on developmental theories as a determinant of capacity (Freeman & Mathison, 2009). In response to this raised awareness researchers may choose to seek caregiver consent and child assent to participate in the study. Researchers are also attentive to the risks and benefits for child participants (Freeman & Mathison, 2009).

In due course data gathering begins and the researcher starts working closely with participants using the collection methods described in the original research design or proposal. Two of the main methods used when researching with young children are interviews and observations. Well prepared and documented interviews can be a valuable source of rich data. However, interviews and conversations with young children can cause methodological issues to arise due to the power differential between researcher and participant (Assuncao Folque, 2010). For example, if the question presupposes an answer which is not forthcoming the researcher may press the child to a particular response thereby manipulating the child and potentially placing them at risk of harm. Interviews generally include open-ended questions and are flexible enough for the researcher to gather notes on any unexpected material (Bogdan & Biklen, 2003).

A good interview occurs when the participant is comfortable talking to the researcher and clearly shares personal perspectives (Bogdan & Biklen, 2003). Transcripts of successful interviews yield examples which can be used later in the case study report. Interviews may be designed to gather qualitative or quantitative information. They may be highly structured, like surveys, if the aim is to collect data which will be easy to convert to numbers (Yin, 2009; Mukherji & Albon, 2010). Unstructured interviews might be used if gathering data about children's biographical or life-histories and puppets, props or photographs may be used at times to encourage conversations. In early childhood education research the decision about what type of interview to use is often made based on participant age. In the birth-8 years range semistructured interviews generally suit older children while younger children respond well during unstructured or focus group interviews (Mukherji & Albon, 2010).

Focus group is a type of multiple participant interview and is particularly useful when working with children aged 5–6 years. When conducting focus groups with young children case study researchers recruit children who like each other. The children are encouraged to interact and are comfortable to take part because talking in the group is similar to everyday conversation they have with friends. This interview format is empowering for participants because they become the "experts in their own setting" (Lancaster & Broadbent, 2003 as cited in Mukherji & Albon, 2010, p. 126). However, a note of caution about focus groups with young children. Children's opinions may be influenced by others in their group and the researcher may have difficulty identifying individual children's perspectives due to ambient noise. This could be overcome by posing interview questions when children are seated on the floor at a quiet time during the day (Mukherji & Albon, 2010).

Direct observation is another data collection method which is used during case study research in early childhood education. This method is used to provide additional information when the researcher observes elements which are relevant to the case in the natural setting (Yin, 2009). Direct observation reflects the researcher's perceptions and appraisal of a social and physical environment (Rolfe & Emmett, 2010). During an observation the researcher keeps a precise record of events during a specific situation for analysis and reporting at a later date (Stake, 2005). To document observations of young children's behavior that occur over a period of time in a particular setting the researcher takes a series of field notes. These anecdotal notes present minute details of a specific instance in the child participant's day (Rolfe & Emmett, 2010). For example, the interactions between child and parent at drop-off time in a preschool setting or the process of settling for an afternoon sleep at long day care.

Other sources of data which are of interest to early childhood case study researchers are young children's art and photography. Images generated by children represent their understanding of the social world. Children's drawings and paintings can be seen as "intuitive, representing implicit and subjective knowledge" (Freeman & Mathison, 2009, p. 110). Drawings created during daily activities may be incorporated into the documentation gathered for the case study data base. In most cases when young children's drawings are used in case studies the researcher will elicit the image, from an individual or group, by giving specific direction in the form of a prompt or question (Freeman & Mathison, 2009).

In case study research with young children photographs can be created by the participants as a form of expression or produced by the researcher as an alternate form of prompted visual documentation. In some cases researchers have provided participants with hand-held cameras or video recorders and asked them to record and talk about their photographs to "promote critical dialogue, empowerment, and decision-making" (Hurworth, 2003 as cited in Freeman & Mathison, 2009, p. 122). Visual and audio recording is also used during fieldwork for direct observation and during interviews in preparation for future transcription (Bogdan & Biklen, 2003).

The benefit of recording interviews and observations is the accuracy of the information obtained but the positive aspects are tempered by a number of issues which a researcher should consider prior to using recording devices. An interviewee may be uncomfortable or unwilling to be recorded. Recorded material provides copious amounts of data to analyze and transcribe and a clear management system should be established before data collection begins. The researcher must be certain that using the recording device is not a distraction during the interview. The researcher must still take notes and listen diligently to the interviewee because this is appropriate researcher engagement in the interview process (Yin, 2009).

There is an increasing use of digital recording of data in qualitative research. For instance, Ranker (2009) collected data through audio/video of the focal students' work during composing, audio/video recording of teaching, descriptive analytic field notes, photocopies of the students' writing and informal (audio recorded) discussions with the teacher and students. However, an apparent shift in thinking about images of the child has occurred rapidly in the last few years with their increased use of Information Communication Technologies and access to the internet. Previous notions of children and childhood have changed and now children are described as knowledgeable, competent participants in society who actively construct meaning about the world through exploration and research (Clark, 2007). These developments have led to significant increases in research into how young children use, and learn during interaction, with digital technologies. In a recent project researchers investigated children's perceptions of reading by gathering data during interviews, observations and during the child participants' computer use (Levy, 2009).

Researchers who are interested in young children's experiences with digital technologies are increasingly concerned with developing appropriate contemporary data collection methods. In a case study of a young Punjabi boy's in-school and out-of-school information literacy activities McTavish (2009) used multiple traditional and electronic data sources. She gathered extensive field notes, short video clips and artifacts which included writing samples, drawings, flow charts, projects and photographs. In addition to traditional in class and book based literacy learning the eight year old participant in this study used the family computer to play video games and to read and send text messages via instant messaging. Researchers are recognizing the potential for gathering specific data about young children's computer use (Nielsen, 2010). Rather than making an observation or conducting an interview about how and why a child uses digital technology, researchers are using technology to obtain data—screen grabs and usability software allow researchers to "capture" still or moving images and audio on a computer screen in real time. Using new technology for data generation may lead to child participants having a clearer "voice." They will have the opportunity to develop a youth–adult partnership with the researcher (Freeman & Mathison, 2009).

WAYS DATA MAY BE ANALYZED

This section describes analysis and interpretation of data collected in intrinsic and instrumental case studies. The approach used in data analysis and interpretation will be determined by the nature of the case study, the focus of the research questions and the particular curiosity of the case researcher. In this section on data analysis and interpretation the importance of naturalistic generalizations will be explored. Case study research is about making cases understandable to the reader and naturalistic generalizations in case studies provide enough raw data so that readers can consider their own alternative interpretations.

Analysis and interpretation highlight the major differences between qualitative case study research and quantitative research. "At no point in naturalistic case study research are the qualitative and quantitative techniques less alike than during analysis" (Stake, 1995, p. 75). The qualitative researcher concentrates on the instance or the event trying to pull it apart, to analyze the elements, look for patterns and then put it back together more meaningfully using analysis and synthesis in direct interpretation. In contrast, the quantitative researcher seeks a collection of aggregated instances and expects that relevant meanings will emerge. An example of interpretation of an instance occurred in a classroom observation of Sean, in the 100 children go to school research project (Hill, Comber, Louden, Reid, & Rivalland, 2002). Sean was seated at a table drawing, when he jumped and hid under the table when there was a loud banging noise in the classroom. This observation of this instance led to questions such as—How often does this happen? What does this behaviour mean? Does this happen at home and at school? How may this behavior connect with his difficulties in early literacy?

In case study research there is no particular moment when analysis and interpretation begin. Analysis occurs when the case researcher gives meaning to first impressions as well as the final compilation. By acknowledging that case studies are not used for generalizations researchers can identify emergent themes as issues that are clarified during analysis (Vasconcelos, 2010). Researchers may set aside several weeks for analysis of study data but analysis should not be seen as separate from the everlasting efforts to make sense of things. Stake (1995) uses two metaphors to communicate the meaning of analysis and interpretation in case study research. One is the process of awareness of meaning when meeting an old friend you have not seen for years. At first you don't recognize them then suddenly the face fits a pattern we recognize, then we wonder why we didn't recognize them in the first place. The second metaphor is meeting strange phenomena and puzzling the meaning as in the understanding of a complex poem which can only be understood after multiple rereadings, complete immersion in the words of the poem, analysis of words and phrases until finally some insight into the meaning of the poem becomes clearer.

The search for meanings usually involves a search for patterns. Patterns can occur when observing documents, in observations and in interviews and they can be coded and the case researcher can aggregate the frequencies. Sometimes the patterns will be known in advance and linked to the research questions and sometimes the patterns will emerge from the data analysis (Yin, 2009). Case study researchers may work in two ways to reach new meanings to find patterns—direct interpretation of the individual instances and through aggregation of instances. The case study worker sequences the actions, categorizes the properties and makes tallies in an intuitive aggregation. "Each researcher needs, through experience and reflection, to find the forms of analysis that work for him or her" (Stake, 1995, p. 77).

The search for patterns can involve filtering, and assessing the relevance of a large amount of data. Experienced qualitative researchers such as Stake (1995) and Wolcott (2009) suggest that data requires constant winnowing or sieving to discover the finest data, or essences or examples in context before moving on to deeper analysis. The avalanche of data available from video and audio recording may contain so many examples of an event that the researcher is required to engage in very careful in depth analysis. Yin (2009) explains that using pattern-matching logic can help strengthen the internal validity of a case study.

Naturalistic generalizations are important in case study research as the reader is expected to make generalizations to other experiences, to other cases or adjust their previous learning to more fully understand an issue or an event. The ways to assist the reader in making naturalistic generalizations is to provide vicarious experience through personal accounts, describing sensory experiences and this may be achieved through a narrative account, a story or a chronological time line. Creating vicarious experiences by emphasizing time, place and persons are the first three major steps in naturalistic generalizations (Stake, 1995). Naturalistic generalizations also support the validity of the case study by including information the reader may be familiar with so they can detect researcher bias and importantly how triangulation was carried out and how efforts were made to confirm or disconfirm major assertions made by the case researcher.

The process of data analysis is discussed by Pahl (2002) and Pahl and Allen (2011) when analyzing children's meaning making at home. Pahl (2002) created case studies of three young children, viewing each child as a shifting unit whose meaning making both coexisted and pulled away from the home and the child's parents and the parental voice. Pahl (2002) coded 18 months of observation and interview data using thematic coding generated from the data and established patterns using the meaning structures arising from the home. She went back to the homes over time for more information on the particular cultural objects and meaning making in the homes finding that meaning making was culturally specific with localized meanings not recognized in the formal school context. In later research Pahl and Allen (2011) brought data back to the children and recorded the children's reactions for further data collection and analysis. The children looked at the data in this project and further interpretations were gathered by the researcher. Pahl and Allen worked as coresearchers and met for two hours each week to reflect on the data set. These reflective conversations were vital for the data analysis process and meant that the research was subjected to a continual process of investigator triangulation.

VALIDITY, RELIABILITY, AND THE IMPORTANCE OF TRIANGULATION

The concepts of reliability, internal validity, external validity and the concept of objectivity stem from the concept of quantitative, positivistic approaches to research in education. Qualitative researcher, Wolcott (1994) argues against the use of the terms "validity" and "reliability" as used in quantitative research. Stake (1995) argues that case study researchers have ethical obligations to minimize representations and misunderstanding and used various protocols of data source triangulation, theory triangulation, investigator triangulation, methodological triangulation and member checking to ensure that case studies are validated for the reader. These elements all merge to offer "as sound a representation of the field of study as the research methods allow" (Edwards, 2010, p. 162).

Case study researchers working in the area of early childhood need to make their reports credible, trustworthy and authentic. Credibility in a case study is based on the researcher's skill in appealing to the reader's experience and the actual situation described as the basis for validity. The reader should comprehend enough about the methods of the research that the study might be replicated (Wiersma & Jurs, 2009). In addition, the concept of "authenticity" is vitally important in the early childhood research field as this includes criteria such as fairness, respecting the participant's perspective and empowering them to act (Mukherji & Albon, 2010).

Guba and Lincoln (1989) have used the terms "trustworthiness" and "authenticity" for case validity. To develop trustworthiness the concepts of credibility, transferability, dependability and confirm-ability must be evident in a case report. In case study research in early childhood democratic research processes are important for validity and this includes giving voice to young children and reciprocity between the researcher and the participants. Case study research is not a quick collection of quantitative test data with young children with no apparent benefit to the children.

Triangulation is used in case study research to increase the validity and the reliability of the study by cross checking the researchers' interpretation of meaning. "The term triangulation originally comes from the application of trigonometry to navigation and surveying" (Bogdan & Biklen, 2003, p. 107). It suggests that to establish validity researchers must use more than one source of information. This is similar to celestial navigation, where a navigator uses at least three stars in the sky in the morning and early evening to triangulate the location of a ship at sea. The use of one star as a reference point is not enough as the navigator has to cross check the position of the ship with the position of the star to gain a more accurate reading (Stake, 1995). In triangulation in case study research we "assume the meaning of an observation is one thing, but additional observation gives us ground for revising our interpretations" (Stake, 1995, p. 110).

Triangulation in case study research involves employing protocol or procedures that go beyond simple repetition of data gathering to a deliberate effort to find the validity of the data observed. The following section explains data source triangulation, investigator triangulation, theory triangulation, methodological triangulation and member checking (Stake 1995; Denzin 1989; Simons 2009).

Data source triangulation occurs when the researcher looks to see if the phenomena or case remains the same at other times, or in other spaces, or in interactions with other people. During data triangulation the researcher uses a variety of data sources (Edwards, 2010).

Investigator triangulation occurs when a colleague, critical friend or research team member observes the same phenomena and comments on their perceptions or interpretations of the phenomena or event. It involves collaboration between several researchers (Edwards, 2010). If it is not possible for the team member to observe the same event then sharing observations or field notes with a colleague and then recording or noting their alternative or similar interpretations can take place.

Theory triangulation occurs when another investigator compares data. No one investigator ever interprets things exactly the same. This process may combine perspectives from several researchers when interpreting a single set of data (Edwards, 2010). "For example, one investigator, intentionally, or unintentionally, is more the behaviorist, another is more the holistic" (Stake, 1995, p. 113) to the extent that the two researchers agree on meaning–the interpretation is triangulated. Methodological triangulation is commonly used in case study research as it has to do with using multiple methods to collect data on an event, issue or phenomena such as observation, interview and document review (Edwards, 2010). Member checking is the final triangulation procedure discussed here and it is often the most confronting form of triangulation because it has to do with inviting those who are participants, perhaps teachers or parents, to review drafts or transcripts of interviews or written descriptions of actions (Stake, 1995). The case study researcher may have interpreted the actions of young child in ways the teacher or parent may agree with or disagree with. The researcher's perspectives of the event may be corrected or additional information may be provided at the member checking phase. The researcher may change the wording of a draft, or decide to remove sections of a draft. Sometimes the participant will carefully read the draft and write comments at other times there will be little forthcoming.

The reliability and validity of case study research is enhanced through data source triangulation, theory triangulation, investigator triangulation, methodological triangulation and member checking to ensure that case studies are validated for the reader. In early childhood case researchers need to make the research credible, trustworthy and authentic in their representations of children and early childhood settings.

THE VARIOUS ROLES OF A CASE STUDY RESEARCHER

There are various roles that can be taken in case study work with children and these roles relate to the specific context. The context of the research includes not only the physical aspect of conducting the fieldwork but also the conditions brought to the project such as personal histories, relationships with children and the particular perspective taken in the project. The researcher may be the teacher, a collaborative research partner, participant observer or a more removed, distanced observer. Whatever the researchers' role, case study researchers require very effective interpersonal skills to help them interact positively with others to work together toward a common goal. These skills include a capacity to ask good questions, listen carefully to responses and interpret answers. A case study researcher should be "adaptive and flexible" while keeping a "firm grasp of the issues being studied" (Yin, 2009, p. 69). Overall, the good case study researcher works carefully to define target behaviors through observer training in order to increase their objectivity (Rolfe & Emmett, 2010).

One important role of a case study researcher is to use effective interview techniques which stimulate detailed and meaningful transcripts. A good interviewer displays interest in the subject by using body language such as nodding the head and suitable facial expressions (Bogdan & Biklen, 2003). The case study researcher must also be able to make decisions about what to include in data analysis and the written report. What is left out is as significant as what is left in when presenting the case study to the reader. According to Platt (2007) the role of the case study researcher is to strike a balance between the need to limit work to a problem of viable scope and the need to take into account sufficient of the context of the case.

Case study research may be conducted by teachers in their own classrooms with familiar children in a known setting. Case studies are also prepared by researchers who only enter a setting for a prescribed period of time (Freeman & Mathison, 2009). How each early childhood researcher presents to potential and consenting participants will impact on how they may establish sound working relationships which, in turn, may alter the effectiveness of the data collection process. Therefore, researchers are recommended to engage in self-reflexivity to explore personal "assumptions about children because decisions about how to seek access and relate within the research context are influenced by what we expect of children" (Freeman & Mathison, 2009, p. 58).

WRITING THE CASE STUDY REPORT

A case study report does not have a standard format. In the absence of specific writing guidelines a researcher may find composing the report quite challenging. This can be an unforeseen experience for the novice case study researcher but organizing the report structure in the data collection and analysis stage will help ward off procrastination during the intense composition period at the end of the study (Yin, 2009). To assist with decision-making about the report structure the following paragraphs suggest two structural alternatives.

Stake (2005) suggests beginning the case study report with an entry vignette to provide readers with come contextual information. This is followed by issue identification, purpose and method of study to explain how the case study began and evolved in the early stages. Next Stake suggests including an executive narrative, description to define the case and contents. At this point key issues can be developed to explain complexity. In this section the researcher may refer to other research and personal understandings of the case. Descriptive detail, documents, quotations and triangulating data are then followed by assertions and a closing vignette (Stake, 2005, p. 123).

In contrast to the guidelines described above, Mac Naughton and Rolfe (2010) suggest a more formal structure for the case study report. This example begins with the title of the research project followed by researcher name, qualifications and institutional affiliation. Next will be acknowledgements and then an abstract which includes a summary of the research question, methods and findings. The main body of the report will include an introduction, method, results and summary. The document is completed with a reference list and appendices (Mac Naughton & Rolfe, 2010, pp. 31–32).

An important section in a research report is the literature review. This section provides the reader with a critical review of journal articles, books, and other documents that describes the past and current state of information relating to the study (Creswell, 2012). The literature review is used to explain how the study augments existing research. In qualitative reports, such as case studies, the literature review may be placed at the beginning or end of the document. Sometimes the literature review is incorporated at the end of the report to compare and contrast with the major findings (Creswell, 2012).

CONCLUSION

Case study in early childhood research foregrounds the importance of the child in context. The case is bounded unit—a person, a group, an institution or an organization and involves interactions, communications, relationships and practices between the case—always with the broader context in mind. The case study researcher employs multiple data collection methods to develop a detailed description of the case. Important in developing case study research are consideration of different approaches to case study research and types of case studies. Also important the types of research questions in case studies and the range of data collection methods that particularly relate to early childhood case study research. The concepts of validity and reliability are linked to many different ways to check for trustworthiness and credibility through the process of triangulation.

This chapter began with a vignette from a unique case study of Korean children studying at an Australian school. The case study of four young Korean children revealed the importance of interpersonal relationships in cultural adjustment for international students. The children were all invited to homes of Australian students for social gatherings and developed positive relationships with their class teachers. The mothers said that strong friendship groups were "crucial to their children's academic success" (Millar, 2011).

These results, along with a wide range of other important findings relevant to early childhood education, were brought to the foreground through case study methods. Using semistructured interviews, observations, work samples, and careful triangulation for validity enables the evidence to emerge. The same results would not have been possible in an experimental, survey based or strictly quantitative study. Language rich descriptions in this case study presented a case that was rich in details and may inform education policy and practice in the future.

REFERENCES

Ashton-Warner, S. (1963). *Teacher*. New York, NY: Simon and Schuster.
Assuncao Folque, M. (2010). Interviewing young children. In G. MacNaughton, S. A. Rolfe, & I. Siraj-Blatchford (Eds.), *Doing early childhood research: International*

perspectives on theory and practice (2nd ed., pp. 239–260). Maidenhead, Berkshire, England: McGraw-Hill/Open University Press.

Bogdan, R. C., & Biklen, S. K. (2003). *Qualitative research for education: An introduction to theory and methods* (4th ed.). Boston, MA: Allyn and Bacon.

Clark, A. (2007). A hundred ways of listening: Gathering children's perspectives of their early childhood environment. *Young Children, 62*(3), 76–81.

Clay, M. M. (2002). *An observation survey of early literacy achievement* (2nd Rev. ed.). Auckland, NZ: Heinemann.

Compton-Lilly, C. (2006). Identity, childhood culture and literacy learning: A case study. *Journal of Early Childhood Literacy, 6*(1), 57–76.

Creswell, J. W. (2012). *Educational research: Planning, conducting, and evaluating quantitative and qualitative research* (4th ed.). Upper Saddle River, NJ: Pearson/Merrill Prentice Hall.

Denzin, N. K. (1989). *The research act: A theoretical introduction to sociological methods*. Englewood Cliffs, NJ: Prentice Hall.

Diefenbach, T. (2009). Are case studies more than sophisticated storytelling? Methodological problems of qualitative empirical research mainly based on semi-structured interviews. *Quality & Quantity, 43*(6), 875–894.

Dyson, Haas, A., & Genishi, C. (2005). *On the case: Approaches to language and literacy research*. New York, NY: Teachers College Press.

Eagle, S. (2012). Learning in the early years: Social interactions around picturebooks, puzzles and digital technologies. *Computers & Education, 59*, 38–49.

Edwards, A. (2010). Qualitative designs and analysis. In G. MacNaughton, S. A. Rolfe, & I. Siraj-Blatchford (Eds.), *Doing early childhood research: International perspectives on theory and practice* (2nd ed., pp. 155–175). Maidenhead, Berkshire, England: McGraw-Hill/Open University Press.

Freebody, P. (2003). *Qualitative research in education: Interaction and practice*. Thousand Oaks, CA: Sage.

Freeman, M., & Mathison, S. (2009). *Researching children's experiences*. New York, NY: Guilford Press.

Graue, M., & Walsh, D. (1998). *Studying children in context: Theories, methods & ethics*. Thousand Oaks, CA: Sage.

Guba, E. G., & Lincoln, Y. S. (1989). *Fourth generation evaluation*. Thousand Oaks, CA: Sage.

Hamilton, L., & Corbett-Whittier, C. (2013). *Using case study in education research*. Thousand Oaks, CA: Sage.

Heath, S. B. (1983). *Ways with words: Language, life, and work in communities and classrooms*. New York, NY: Cambridge University Press

Hill, S., Comber, B., Louden, W., Reid, J., & Rivalland, J.A. (1998). *100 children go to school: Connections and disconnections in literacy development in the year prior to school and the first year of school*. Canberra: Department of Employment, Education, Training and Youth Affairs, DEETYA.

Hill, S., Comber, B., Louden, W., Reid, J., & Rivalland, J. A. (2002). *100 children turn 10: A longitudinal study of literacy development from the year prior to school to the first 4 years of school* (Vols. 1–2). Canberra: Department of Science, Education and Training, DEST.

James, A., & Prout, A. (1990). *Constructing and reconstructing childhood: Contemporary issues in the sociological study of childhood*. London: Falmer Press.

Levy, R. (2009). "You have to understand the words... but not read them": Young children becoming readers in a digital age. *Journal of Research in Reading, 32*(1), 75–91.

Luxford, H., & Smart, L. (2009). *Learning through talk: Developing learning dialogues in the primary classroom*. New York, NY: Routledge.

Mac Naughton, G., & Rolfe, S. A. (2010). The research process. In G. MacNaughton, S.A. Rolfe & I.Siraj-Blatchford (Eds.), *Doing early childhood research: International perspectives on theory and practice* (2nd ed., pp. 13–34). Maidenhead, Berkshire, England: McGrawHill/Open University Press.

McTavish, M. (2009). "I get my facts from the Internet: A case study of the teaching and learning of information literacy in-school and out-of-school contexts." *Journal of Early Childhood Literacy, 9*(1), 3–28.

Millar, N. (2011). Korean children's cultural adjustment during transition to the early years of school in Australia. *Australian Journal of Early Childhood, 36*(3), 10–18.

Mukherji, P., & Albon, D. (2010). *Research methods in early childhood: An introductory guide*. Thousand Oaks, CA: Sage.

Nielsen, J. (2010). *Children's websites: Usability issues in designing for kids*. Retrieved from http://www.useit.com/alertbox/children.html.

Pahl, K. (2002). Ephemera, mess and miscellaneous piles: Texts and practices in families. *Journal of Early Childhood Literacy, 2*, 145–166.

Pahl, K., & Allan, C. (2011). "I don't know what literacy is": Uncovering hidden literacies in a community library using ecological and participatory research methodologies with children. *Journal of Early Childhood Literacy, 11*(2), 190–213.

Pascal, C., & Bertram, T. (2009). Listening to Young Citizens: The Struggle to Make Real a Participatory Paradigm in Research With Young Children. *European Early Childhood Research Journal, 17*(2), 249–262.

Platt, J. (2007). Case study. In W. Outhwaite & S. P. Turner (Eds.), *The Sage handbook of social science methodology* (pp. 100–118). Thousand Oaks, CA: Sage.

Purcell-Gates, V. (1995). *Other people's words: The cycle of low literacy*. Cambridge, MA: Harvard University Press.

Ranker, J. (2009). Redesigning and transforming: A case study of the role of semiotic import in early composing practices. *Journal of Early Childhood Literacy, 9*, 319–347.

Rolfe, S. A., & Emmett, S. (2010). Direct observation. In G. MacNaughton, S. A. Rolfe, & I. Siraj-Blatchford (Eds.), *Doing early childhood research: International perspectives on theory and practice* (2nd ed., pp. 309–325). Maidenhead, Berkshire, England: McGraw-Hill/Open University Press.

Simons, H. (2005). Ethical responsibility in social research. In B. Somekh & C. Lewin (Eds.), *Research methods in the social sciences* (pp. 56–63).

Simons, H. (2009). *Case study research in practice*. Thousand Oaks, CA: Sage.

Siraj-Blatchford, I., Mayo, A., Melhuish, E., Taggart, B., Sammons, P., & Sylva. K. (2011). *Performing against the odds: developmental trajectories of children in the EPPSE 3–16 study*. London: Department for Education. Retrieved from https://www.education.gov.uk/publications/standard/publicationDetail/Page1/DFE-RB128

Rogoff, B. (2003). *The cultural nature of human development.* New York, NY: Oxford University Press.

Stake, R. (1995). *The art of case study research.* Thousand Oaks, CA: Sage.

Stake, R. (2005). Qualitative case studies. In N. K. Denzin & Y. S. Lincoln (Eds.), *The Sage handbook of qualitative research* (3rd ed., pp. 443–466). Thousand Oaks, CA: Sage.

Tedlock, B. The observation of participation and the emergence of public ethnography. In N. K. Denzin & Y. S. Lincoln (Eds.), *The Sage handbook of qualitative research* (3rd ed., pp. 467–481). Thousand Oaks, CA: Sage.

Torrance, H. (2005). Case study. In B. Somekh & C. Lewin (Eds.), *Research methods in the social sciences* (pp. 33–40). Thousand Oaks, CA: Sage.

Vasconcelos, T. (2010). Case study. In G. MacNaughton, S. A. Rolfe & I. Siraj-Blatchford (Eds.), *Doing early childhood research: International perspectives on theory and practice* (2nd ed., pp. 327–343). Maidenhead, Berkshire, England: McGraw-Hill/Open University Press.

Wiersma, W., & Jurs, S. G. (2009). *Research methods in education: An introduction.* (9th ed.). Boston, MA: Pearson.

Wolcott, H. F. (1994). *Transforming qualitative data: Description, analysis and interpretation.* Thousand Oaks, CA: Sage.

Wolcott, H. F. (2009). *Writing up qualitative research.* Los Angeles: Sage.

Woodrow, C. (1999). Revisiting images of the child in early childhood education: Reflections and considerations. *Australian Journal of Early Childhood, 24*(4), 7–12.

Yin, R. K. (2009). *Case study research: Design and methods* (4th ed.). Thousand Oaks, CA: Sage.

CHAPTER 16

ACTION RESEARCH WITH CHILDREN

Kylie Smith

INTRODUCTION

There are many approaches to action research. Reason and Bradbury (2008) describe the diversity of action research models as a "family of approaches" (p. 1). However, there is a core purpose to all of these approaches, which is participation. Action research is about researching *with* others rather than *about* others within individual contexts in the every day. Cohen and Manion (1994) support this understanding in their definition of action research as:

> ...a small-scale intervention in the functioning of the real world and a close examination of the effects of such an intervention. (p. 186)

The focus of action research is about change, however, for some approaches to action research, the key aim is changing to create more socially just thinking and practice. As seen in Kemmis and McTaggart's (1988) in their definition:

> Action research is a form of collective self-reflective inquiry undertaken by participants in social situations in order to improve the rationality and justice of their own social or educational practices, as well as their understanding of these practices and the situations in which these practices are carried out. (p. 5)

Action research supports spaces to illuminate the gaps and separations between valid (theoretical/ academic) knowledges and the invalid questions of practitioners and researchers about those knowledges and their effects. It is important to note that action research is sometimes called practitioner research; however, there are distinctions between action research and the everyday practices or actions of the teacher. In action researcher there is a more systematic collecting and recording of evidence (data) with critical reflections interfacing with this. Kemmis and McTaggart (1992) also argue that in action research, the "researcher" is posing a problem to improve understandings and create change, and is not just attempting to solve it.

CHARACTERISTICS OF ACTION RESEARCH

There are diverse suggestions on the key characteristics of action research. As previously noted general consensus is that action research is collaborative and participatory (Hult & Lennung, 1980; McKernan, 1991; MacNaughton & Hughes, 2009; Reason & Bradbury, 2008). Other characteristics of action research are:

- Challenges taken for granted truths to create frame breaking ideas and knowledge (Cohen, Manion, & Morrison, 2011; MacNaughton & Hughes, 2009; Smith, 2003)
- Allows participants to critically reflect on theory and practice through a collaborative educational approach (Carr & Kemmis, 1986; Kemmis & McTaggart, 1988; MacNaughton, 2001; MacNaughton & Hughes, 2009)
- Allows participants to identify an issue and then alter practice to improve what is happening in the classroom setting (Cohen, Manion, & Morrison, 2011; Kemmis & McTaggart, 1988; MacNaughton & Hughes, 2009)
- Investigates a problem through a collaborative cycle of planning, acting, observing and reflecting (Carr & Kemmis, 1986; Kemmis & McTaggart, 1988; Kemmis & Wilkinson, 1998)
- Allows participants to critically analyze and become political by challenging current practice that has been institutionalized within their profession (Cohen, Manion, & Morrison, 2011; MacNaughton, 2001, 1996; MacNaughton & Hughes, 2009)

- Records changes in activities and practice, language and discourse, social relationships and forms of organization (Kemmis & McTaggart, 1988; MacNaughton, 2001; Montessori & Ponte, 2012)

Furthermore, when I investigated literature on action research, my visions about researching *with* children were listed as key characteristics of action research by many authors as follows (e.g., Cohen, Manion, & Morrison, 2011; MacNaughton & Hughes, 2009; McNiff, 2002). Action research has been argued as a powerful tool for change that supports a focus at the local level (Cohen, Manion, & Morrison, 2011). It can be used within a variety of settings to support people to investigate a question or problem related to a multitude of areas such as learning processes, evaluation and assessment, professional development, curriculum, pedagogy, management, administration and philosophies, values, and attitudes (Cohen, Manion, & Morrison, 2011). Individual people or groups can undertake action research and change can occur for individuals as well as the change of the culture of a group. There is a large body of action research within education in areas in primary, secondary and higher education. Within the early childhood research there is a growing body of work (e.g., Gillberg, 2011; Hawkins, 2007; Pacini-Ketchabaw & Berikof, 2008; Walton, 2011). With the influence of Children's rights and sociology of childhood, researchers are increasingly drawn to participatory research methodologies that recognize children's agency, children as current (rather than future) citizens in the world and that children are researched with rather than researched on (Brooker, 2011; Pascal & Bertram, 2009; Pinter & Zandian, 2012).

Moreover, my literature review on my research topic on early childhood observational practices clearly showed that there was a gap in professional literature about the theoretical, political, social and historical construction of observation (see Smith, 2003). I wanted to be able to research *with* participants so that the information that emerged from the research supported day-to-day practices and challenged the binary between theory and practice. Thus, I believed action research as a methodology would support these processes and assist my fellow research participants and myself to build an early childhood research community.

This chapter will draw on my first experience in action research with children during my research to explore the aims, processes, benefits, and limitations of action research as a methodology. As a doctorial student who was new to research I began to explore different methodologies. I knew I wanted a methodology that involved:

- Researching *with* people rather than about people
- Research that was relevant and accessible to the people I would be working with

- Research that worked to support change in early childhood practice that would be supportive and useful to participants' daily lives
- Research that involved critical reflection to support my coresearchers (educators or children and families) and I, to make visible and question why we act and speak within particular discourses
- Research that empowered participants to share their lived experiences, history, culture, class, race, gender and sexuality, and for those experiences and related knowledge to be recognized as intricate, shifting and diverse parts of how data is documented and recognized
- Research that would promote and support social justice

In what follows I examine the processes in the cycles of action research *with* children in early childhood settings.

LIMITATIONS OF ACTION RESEARCH AS A METHODOLOGY

All research methodologies have their limitations. Action research can be limiting, as it is contextual and local. This means that findings from action research cannot be generalized. Taylor (2010) argues that this should be seen as a strength rather than a limitation as it means the knowledge is not used as a normalizing a standard that can restrict the diversity and silence the complexity of communities. Another, element of action research that could be seen as a limitation is its cyclical process, which means that an action research project has to be ongoing, and as a first time researcher it can be hard to see when to stop. I would advise those who are engaging in an action research project for the first time to have a clear time frame including how many cycles you will undertake. It is important to make sure you have time to analyze and write up the findings of your research and not get lost in the momentum of the research.

Action research is about creating change. This can become tricky when you are working with research participants/co-researchers who don't want to change or struggle with the implications of change. It can be particularly confronting when engaging with critical reflection and you identify that your knowledge/practice silences or oppresses individuals and groups. Despite all these limitations I decided to engage with action research to support research *with* children for social change in early childhood observational practices.

PROCEDURES FOR ACTION RESEARCH

Action research is a cyclical process that creates change through participatory methods. The key features of action research positions research as a social process, participatory, practical and collaborative, emancipatory, critical, recursive, reflexive, and dialectical (Assuncao Folque, 2010; Kemmis & Wilkinson, 1998; Reason & Bradbury, 2008; MacNaughton & Hughes, 2009; McNiff, 2002; Perry, 2012). Different action researchers describe the action research cycles in diverse ways however there are key principles that guide the phases in the cycles—thinking, doing and changing (Cohen, Manion, & Morrison, 2011; MacNaughton & Hughes, 2009).

Drawing on the work of Ferguson (2012), MacNaughton and Hughes (2009), Kemmis and McTaggart (1982), I identified five phases in my approach to action research as illustrated in Figure 16.1.

Phase 1: Choosing to change

Below I examine the different phases with the use of narratives from my study to show how this unfolded in my research.

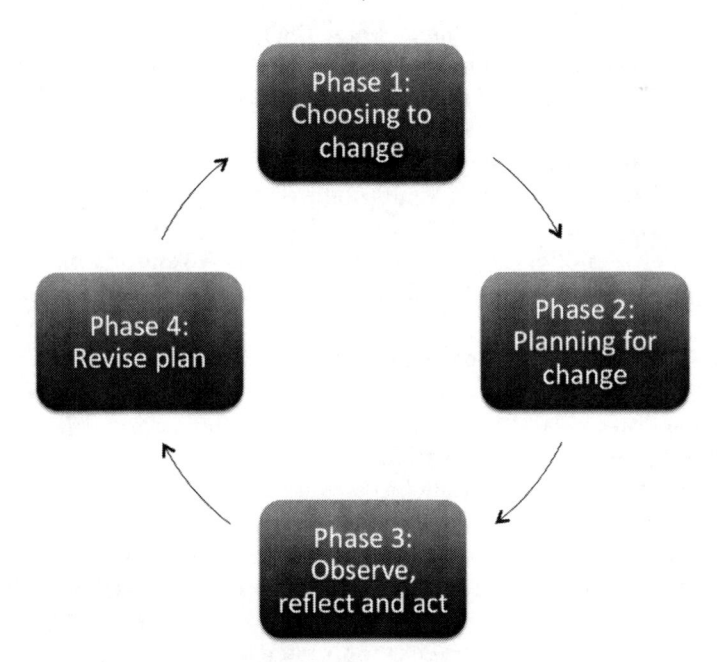

Figure 16.1 Four phases of action research. Adapted from the work of Ferguson (2012), MacNaughton and Hughes (2009), Kemmis and McTaggart (1982).

Authors such as, MacNaughton and Hughes (2009) and McNiff (2002) recommend action researchers to choose a topic and to create or ask a question with the desire to create a change in theory and in practice. My experience with action research was triggered by the following quote:

> Action research begins with hopes, dreams and desires. (MacNaughton & Hughes, 2009, p. 5)

My hopes were to create social change in how children are seen and assessed in the everyday early childhood classroom. My dreams were and continue to be that children's gender, culture, race, and class will be understood and represented in respectful ways through observation and assessment processes. My desires were for children to be empowered to have a voice in this process and that adults would listen in ethical and respectful ways and that this will continue in the classroom after the research was concluded. Hence, my research question was: How can I reconceptualise observation in the early childhood setting?

Phase 2: Planning for Change

During the planning for change phase the researcher needs to first identify their approach to action research, collate a literature review, explore ethical considerations, and plan for rigour and validity in the study.

Identify the Approach to Action Research

As I had mentioned earlier, although there are many approaches to action research (See Cohen, Manion and Morrison, 2011), it is important to decide on a model based on your "aims and intentions, the focus of the change, principles and processes, and the theoretical foundations" (MacNaughton & Hughes, 2009, pp. 38–39). For example, Cohen, Manion, and Morrison, (2011) drawing on the work of Grundy (1987) identify and describe three designs of action research—*technical* action research, *practical* action research, and *emancipatory* action research. *Technical* action research is designed to work on ensuring existing situations or ideas to be more effective. This model as termed by Schon (1987) is an action research process where the researcher undertakes "reflection in action." *Practical* action research too supports teacher–researcher reflection of current pedagogical practices, and is in line with Schon's (1987) idea of "reflection on action." On the other hand, *emancipatory* action research has a political agenda which seeks to unpack how power circulates to repress, silence, dominate, and control to create more socially just environments, practices and/or systems.

My experiences with identifying the approach to action research. I chose to undertake *emancipatory* action research, which is based on the principles of critical theory (MacNaughton, 2000). Critical theory emerged from the Frankfurt School of sociological and philosophical inquiry in the 1920s (Bloch, 1992; Fay, 1987; Held, 1980; Ward, 1996). Critical theorists argue that the oppressed, whether that is through class, gender, sexuality, color, or ethnicity, should have the opportunity and right to fully participate within society (Freire, 1970; Giroux, 1995; Usher & Edwards, 1994). Giroux (1995) notes that critical theory within educational pedagogy supports a cultural practice that enables teachers and students to engage with education as a political, economic, and social activity. It acknowledges and respects diversity and in doing so supports the visibility and operation of multiple discourses. Further, these multiple discourses can be used to trouble, question, and resist traditional modern discourses. Giroux (1995) calls the diverse discourses that bring a counter text to traditional understandings of the world "border pedagogy" (p. 44). Within critical theory, border pedagogy can be used to map, decentre, and rewrite cultural politics in order to transform and emancipate the individual (Diaz Soto, Hixon, & Hite, 2010; Giroux, 1995; MacNaughton, 2005; Robinson, 2013). This resonated for me as children's perspectives are often missing in early childhood observations. Through the influence of observation tools such as pedagogical documentation and learning stories more educators are recording children's dialogue in observations. However, I felt that this dialogue is often selected by the educators and children are rarely invited to select their texts or to interpret the meanings they place on their conversation and play (Smith, 2003, 2007).

Literature Review

After choosing your approach to action research, researchers should begin to collate their literature that reflects their topic and approach. The literature review or reconnaissance helps you to understand what people have written about, thought, and spoken about your topic and where the gaps are.

My experiences with undertaking literature review. When undertaking your literature review, record what types of materials you are using e.g., primary research articles, policy documents, professional development literature); the date of publication (which helps to see how ideas may have shifted or changed over time); and the country of origin (this can provide geographical and cultural context). Especially for me it became critical to ask, who the research participants are and who has not been involved in understanding the topic of investigation (this helps highlight the gaps and whose view is missing). MacNaughton and Hughes (2009) provide guiding questions to support you to review your literature when you have finished:

- What do I know now about my research topic?
- What more do I need to know about it?
- How do I find out more about it?
- What are the most important questions about my research question?
- How can I use the results of my literature review to create change (alone or with others) through my action research project? (p. 57).

Ethical Considerations

Informed consent from participants and in the case of children their guardian/parent is a starting point. You will also need to consider what will be put in place in the classroom where a teacher or child do not take part in the research and that they are not disadvantaged by this (for example they do not miss out on an activity or part of the curriculum).

My experiences with ethical considerations. At the onset of this research I acknowledged that young children were competent meaning makers who have valid and important knowledge and can be active researchers (MacNaughton & Smith, 2008; Assuncao Folque, 2010, Clark, 2010). There has been a continuing growing body of work within the sociology of childhood that articulates and advocates children as active citizens who have the right and the capacities to contribute to research and that adult researchers should research *with* rather than *about* children (Woodhead & Faulkner, 2008; MacNaughton & Smith, 2008; Clark, 2007, 2010; Goulart & Roth, 2010; Smith, 2009). Christensen and James (2000) wrote:

> We need to treat children] as social actors in their own right in contexts where, traditionally, they have been denied those rights of participation and their voices have remained unheard. (p. 2)

Ethically working with children as researchers was a core principle in my research. For me, action research fits as an ethical methodological approach, as researching *with* children called for the researchers to engage with issues of power, relationships, knowledge, and participation (MacNaughton & Hughes, 2009; Clark, 2010). This meant that throughout the research I had to consciously continue to critically reflect on questions that allowed me to explore how power, knowledge, relationships, and participation operated and circulated within and through the action research cycles, data collection and analysis between the children and myself and between the children and other adult researchers. I share below some of the questions that supported me to do this:

- In whose best interest am I doing this research?
- Whose questions am I exploring and why?
- Who decides on the data I am collecting?
- How am I supporting children to collect and analyze data that they see as important?
- Whose voice is privileged and who is silent in our research meetings?

In my action research practice, ethical engagement meant that while parents had signed consent forms, I always asked children if they wanted to be part of the research and asked their permission to record or document conversations and interaction at each point of data collection. Where children's responses were "no" to collecting data, I would not turn on the video or audio record without question (even when the most amazing events were unfolding or intriguing conversations were taking place that seemed perfect for my research!). I would also read back transcribed conversations and events to the children to ask permission to use their dialogue and ask them if they wanted anything added or changed. I would also ask children if I could copy any artwork and return the original work to the children recognizing their ownership (MacNaughton & Smith, 2008).

Rigour and Validity

Planning for rigour and validity is an important component of this phase of the action research cycle. Ensuring validity in qualitative research can take many forms. Unlike quantitative research, validity in my research was not based on the same fundamental objective that ensured data and its analysis were *objective* and *true*. I considered how Silverman (1993) cautioned that methods of validity should be reconsidered. He argued that rather than looking at validity qualitative researchers should consider what he calls "subtle realism." The three principles of subtle realism he described are:

1. Validity is identified with confidence in our knowledge but not certainty.
2. Reality is assumed to be independent of the claims that researchers make about it.
3. Reality is always viewed through particular perspectives; hence our accounts represent reality they do not reproduce it (Hammersley cited in Silverman, 1993, p. 155).

These principles begin to trouble the "scientific truths" that create answers and certainty found in modern discourses and that introduce space for skepticism in reproducing current *fact* about the social world. Action research and postmodern theories created multiple possibilities within my research that could not be predicted. Therefore, the methods of validity that I wanted to use were multiple and changing so that they remained relevant to the context in which I was researching. To include this form of validity I used Lather's (1993) validation of "rhizomatic validity" as follows.

Patti Lather (1993) proposes the use of what she calls "rhizomatic validity" to make visible the complexity and multiplicity of discourses rather than a method of validity that verifies a singular positivist statement of truth or fact. She describes rhizomatic validity as a validity that is emancipatory in nature because it examines strategies, social relations, tensions, and political agendas to inquire and problematised text. At each stage of the research rhizomatic validity considers disruptions and anomalies within the data and highlights the interwoven, layers, twists, turns, intersections, and juxtapositions of text and the multiplicity and complexity of the discourses (Lather, 1993). I, therefore, regarded rhizomatic validity as an appropriate approach to add validity to my research.

The understanding of validity in modern research discourses is a belief that it is possible to prove the true singular value of data. Within this modern research discourse the emphasis on validity is to reach a consensus about what data and knowledge are valid and important, often with little say by the participants (Campbell, 2001; Lather, 1994, MacNaughton & Hughes, 2009; Taylor, 2010). However, the rhizomatic validity sits within postmodern research discourses where validity creates spaces for multiple readings of the data by multiple people (including participants) and sources (Ryan & Campbell, 2001).

My experiences with rigour and validity. Having chosen an emancipatory action research model, I further chose "rhizomatic validity" (Lather, 1993), that included multiplicity and complexity of discourses and supported the inscription of new understandings and meanings within discourse and the effects for practice. I considered validity criteria in my research as follows:

- Locating institutionalized and local context of epistemological ideas and understandings. Firstly, this supported my endeavour to ensure the validity of the research by identifying and describing what currently informs observation theory and practice for participants and within early childhood education. Secondly, it provided a base to theorize these understandings and ideas and identify when change occurred.
- Ensuring the focus problem/question was authentic and relevant to the service and individual participants. This was to maintain the progression of the research and the collection of data to be driven by the question. This was intended to keep the research focused and contained.
- Documenting the processes of the research methodically and rigorously. This was intended to ensure validity as it marked visible the processes and documentation of the research. The cyclical process

of planning, acting, observing, and critical reflection supported this. It provided a "checks and balance" process of working within a complex and "messy" process with a group of people.
- Making sure the epistemology was trustworthy and multiple (Campbell, 2001, Kemmis & McTaggart, 1988; MacNaughton, 1996; Silverman, 1993). Validity of the research was seen through the identification of understandings and ideas represented in multiple forms of data (interviews, journals, video recordings of children and teachers interacting, dialogue, and children's artwork). This was then identified as trustworthy with the intersection of theory and critical reflections of the research participants.
- Being receptive to changes that were reasonable and practical that occurred as a result of questions rose through the research process. This was intended to ensure that the ethics of action research as a collaborative process was ensured. Although it has been widely acknowledged that action research is change inducing, I further elaborate on why such changes became critical to my action research.
- "Changes were catalytic" (Campbell, 2001, p. 86), as changes become the force of reflection and revised action. This assisted the validity of my action research, as it allowed us, as researchers to identify why change had occurred in order to critically engage in the effects of these changes.
- Changes were problematised so that participants critically engaged in debate, reflected and negotiated questions that emerge and how changes occurred in practice. This was intended to ensure that research participants had a voice in the research process. Further, problematising change provided opportunities for adults and children to theorize and make visible what had happened and the effects of this change for theory and practice.

Phase 3: Observe, Reflect, and Act

During the observe, reflect, and act phase of the action research cycle researchers will form their action research group, observe to gather baseline data and reflect on what is currently happening in practice and, how and why you and your research group understands this.

Form Your Action Research Group
When forming a collaborative research group, McNaughton and Hughes (2009) argue that it is important to consider three broad themes "culture, participation and diversity" (p. 138). When considering the culture of the group, it is important to explore the members' histories and experiences

and how these have shaped their identities and the impact on how individuals understand and interpret your research topic. It is important to take time to discuss and debate with the group goals and procedures for your action research meetings. How members can participate in the action research project should also be discussed physically such as attending meetings and undertaking a reflective journal. Equally, the ethical considerations for participating or the rules for engagement in dialogue need to be established and agreed to by the group. Issues such as:

- Listening to new ideas when they may be challenging
- The difference between debate and interruption
- Protocols for "fair play" (MacNaghton & Hughes, 2009, p. 140)

My experiences with forming a research group. In my literature review, I identified that children rarely had a voice in observation and assessment of their own learning and development. At the time of this research I was working full time as the director and kindergarten teacher in an Australian inner urban long child care and kindergarten service and studying part time. After a great deal of reflection and ethical troubling about where to undertake my research, I invited the children, families, and educators in my classroom (Spider Room) to form an action research group to be able to research *with* me.

Observation—Gather Baseline Date

This is where you need to decide how you are going to collect data and document. Data and documentation are not the same. MacNaughton and Hughes (2009) clearly define the difference between data and documentation. They note:

> Data is information that researcher gather deliberately and systematically to answer their research question. It can take a variety of forms including numbers, words, images and/or sounds; and it can be collected in a variety of media, including handwritten field notes, questionnaires, checklists, photographs, video- or audio-recordings. Documentation is the process by which researchers record and organize their data for interpretation. (MacNaughton and Hughes, 2009, p. 150)

My experiences with gathering base line data. The children and I collected data during the project. I invited children to participate in the research in a variety of ways including:

- Audio-taping and video-taping of their play, conversations, and meetings with each other and the early childhood educators in Spider room

- Drawings and writing in individual journals
- Artwork and written dialogue

Drawing and artwork were particularly important as a tool for children where English was their second or third language or where there were delays in language development to express their views and opinions.

Reflection

Critical reflection helps to create questions about taken for granted truths or dominant ideologies. It encourages the researcher to explore how power circulates within dominant ideologies to silence or oppress people, knowledge. and practice (Montessori & Ponte, 2012; Roche, 2011). This can be a daunting task as it asks the researcher/ educator/ child/parent to shift their gaze from the familiar or usual. Further, it asks educators to look deeply into why they understand what they do and where these understandings come from. bel hooks (2010) describes critical thinking as:

> ...a way of approaching ideas that aims to understand core, underlying truths, not simply that superficial truth that may be most visible. (p. 9)

Questions that can support critical reflection are:

- Who has a voice in these practices or ideas and why?
- Who is silent and why?
- Who benefits from my understandings?
- How and why do they benefit?

My experiences with reflection. The processes of revisiting and problematising understandings of observation took place between children, parents, early childhood professionals, and me. Critical reflections occurred during group meetings but also during individual reflection in journals. Our revisiting and reflections took place after observing the changes that had taken place in observational practices in the classroom (Spider room). The methods we used to do this were:

- Group meetings between children and early childhood educators and the researcher
- Meetings between the early childhood educators and the researcher
- Group and individual projects with children, parents, and early childhood educators
- Reflections in group and individual children's journals by families, children and early childhood educators

This work occurred in the day-to-day workings of the room. However, meetings and reflections would be postponed or stopped where it may have disrupted the needs of the children, families, and educators. I discuss this key phase that became central to my study and my future work with children, families, and educators as follows.

My experiences with this key phase–Observe, reflect and act. To examine what the process of observe, reflect, and act looks like in action research, I will share a piece from my research called "Fighting Games." I have used a data set drawing on research dialogue with child researchers Donald, Madeline, Shan Yu, Damien, and Joel, and educator researcher Gemma. On February 2000, Gemma (educator researcher who worked full time in Spider room) and I were in the backyard observing the children's play. The games that were being played seemed to continually be violent with hitting, kicking, pushing, and blocking. These games seemed to be played regularly both inside in the classroom and outdoors. On numerous occasions I reverted into my modernist teacher's role as the rational person with expert knowledge and either explained that "*fighting games hurt people*" or asked children "*what have we talked about fighting games?*" Children were able to strategically and politically step into my rational discourse and parrot the words I wanted to hear, and these were my dispositional ideas that I had exchanged in the past with them. Donald told me:

Donald: Fighting games hurt people.

Or Madeline who replied:

Madeline: You don't like guns because they hurt people and that's sad.

I would ask children to find a "different" or "new" game, activity, or storyline and if they were unable to do this I would redirect them into a new activity or space. My impotency and frustration of not being able to change the violent games and behaviors lead to an episode that I call "Tell me what you like about fighting games?"

After seeing what was happening outside Gemma (an educator working in Spider room) and I decided that we would have a meeting with the Spider room children so that the children could talk about their behavior and storylines. The 15 children were asked to come inside and sit down for a "Spider room meeting," which was a regular part of the day. Gemma recorded the conversations through note taking in the room journal and I began the conversation. This conversation began very different to any other meeting that I had participated in with the children. Rather than having a clear message or skill that I wanted to teach the children, I started the conversation with a question. This started the action research process of reconnaissance where I opened up the investigation and identification of current institutional and local discourses of fighting games *with* children. The episode unfolded as follows:

> **Kylie:** Tell me what you like about fighting games?

Silence in the room.

> **Kylie:** Gemma and I don't understand what you like about fighting games. We just don't get it. I feel like I just nag and rant and rave about fighting games and you all know I don't like fighting games because it hurts people. But you keep playing the games. I don't understand just tell me what you like so that I can understand. I just don't get. And Gemma doesn't get it either.

Donald replied:

> **Donald:** We just like hitting and fighting.
> **Shan Yu:** Yeah.
> **Damien:** Yeah.
> **Joel:** Yeah.
> **Shan Yu:** And we just get them. We get the baddies.
> **Donald:** Yeah like Scar (character from The Lion King movie).

The children continued to talk over the top of each other trying to explain their ideas and understandings of fighting. It felt like opening a floodgate. I just kept thinking, "Where is this coming from?" I thought that they were fighting for the sake of fighting but this was a far more complex action. Later I was able to recognize this as the expression of multiple discourses of the child. At this point it was lunchtime and like most fractured events in many classrooms, we had to stop the conversation. However, Gemma and I agreed that we would invite children to the drawing table the next day to talk further and/or draw about their ideas. An example of this is when I spoke with Donald:

> **Kylie:** Tell me what do you like about fighting games? When you play fighting games what sort of things do you do?
> **Donald:** Fight.
> **Kylie:** Fighting. So what sort of fighting? How do you fight?
> **Donald:** Punching bag fighting.
> **Kylie:** Punching bag fighting. What else? Do you use any other part of your body?
> **Donald:** Fighting baddies.
> **Kylie:** What sort of things are baddies?

Donald: They get meanies.
   Kylie: They get meanies. What sort of things do they do if they are mean?
Donald: They fight.
   Kylie: They fight. And so when they fight what do they do?
Donald: (silent).
   Kylie: What do meanies do when they fight?
Donald: They stop the goodies.
   Kylie: They stop the goodies. So who are the goodies?
Donald: They're the good guys.
   Kylie: What do the good guys do?
Donald: They fight the baddies.
   Kylie: O.k. and where do you learn about fighting?
Donald: At the movie...
   Kylie: Can you tell me are there fighting games at the centre?
Donald: (nods no).
   Kylie: No! There are no fighting games at the centre? So you never fight here?
Donald: (nods no).
   Kylie: What about the other children here do they play fighting games?
Donald: (nods yes).
   Kylie: They do?
Donald: (nods yes).
   Kylie: What sort of games do they play?
Donald: They play hide and seek games.
   Kylie: OK so what do you do? Do you play hide and seek and then what do you do?
Donald: Fight.
   Kylie: And then you fight?
Donald: (nods yes).
   Kylie: And what do you do... what sort of games do you play? What sort of um who do you become when you become the fighting person?
Donald: Malcolm.
   Kylie: You become Malcolm?
Donald: (nods yes).
   Kylie: Does Malcolm do fighting?
Donald: (nods yes).
   Kylie: He does. Who else does fighting?
Donald: Isabel.
   Kylie: Isabel does fighting?
Donald: (nods yes).

Multiple Reflections and Rhizomatic Validity

To reflect on and analyze your data you need to draw on theories that will help you to deepen and broaden your understandings of the data and specifically you want to draw on theories that will challenge your understandings and create alternative views of your topic and/or the world. The theories you draw on will be different for different people. Asking yourself what your research agenda is and what you want to change will help you to decide. Foucault (1977) believed concepts such as observation could substantiate as "true" social expectations and norms as "true" through continual reinforcement and positioning of people in appropriate ways. This is evident when he wrote:

> Through hierarchized, continuous and functional surveillance, disciplinary power became as "intergrated" system, linked from inside to the economy and to the aims of the mechanism in which it is practiced. (Foucault, 1977, p. 177)

From this perspective developmental observation acts as a form of disciplinary power. The child is placed under surveillance, is regulated and normalized using techniques of measurement, classification, categorization, and assessment.

My experiences *with* multiple reflections and rhizomatic validity. I drew on poststructural theories to support my reflections to support multiple reflections on and analysis of my data. I was drawn to theories that helped me explore multiple truths about the child and how power circulated within and through discourses of observation.

In talking about his understandings and desires in fighting games, Donald was able to begin to reflect and talk about issues of fighting and raise his understandings of Isabel and Malcolm in fighting games and provided insight into storylines that supported inclusion and exclusion in play and relationships. This also made me step back and think about the complexity of children's lives. It made me question how observation as a process of me looking and assessing the child provided a singular and superficial image of the child. Using my gaze alone provided a glimpse of the surface of a terrain that was and is multilayered and diverse. Previous educators' observations of Donald using a developmental lens to analyze these observations understood Donald's participation in fighting as his lack of understanding of the rules and expectations of the room—no fighting games. Donald's participation was seen and assessed as his need to develop further social skills and language skills to be able to negotiate and navigate play with others that involved talking about ideas and understandings without the use of hitting and kicking. One of the observations written by an educator researcher in 1999 about Donald was:

Donald has difficulty in taking turns. When he becomes impatient waiting for a turn he often pushes children aside or snatches objects. When dealing with a difficult situation Donald will push, hit or kick out at other children or cry rather than verbally discuss the problem.

However, when Donald explained his understandings, his interpretation of the observation of fighting games it was related to what he saw in movies and his play with other children, this assessment was troubled. I began to question how developmental observation was informing my understandings of Donald. In particular, who Donald was, and why he behaved in certain ways. For example, Donald explained his understandings of good revisiting evil using the concept of goodies versus baddies. He talked about fighting as a way to protect people from "baddies." Donald knew the rules and expectations of Spider room. He could tell me clearly that I "didn't like fighting games because they hurt people." Donald's words provided a different gaze. Glimpses of the child as socially, politically, and historically constructed that Weedon's (1987) writing had introduced to me began to flash before me. In this conversation Donald talked about "goodies" and "baddies" as an understanding of good versus evil. This understanding can be traced back historically to popular culture text such as fairy tales like Snow White and Cinderella. Donald referred to the "movies" as a source of information about fighting games. Donald was not alone in this meaning making. All 15 children were able to talk about or draw their ideas about fighting games and social construction the "goodies" fighting "baddies" to protect the weak, innocent, and young.

When I reanalyzed Donald's dialogue about "goodies" and "baddies" there were questions that were raised for me about the discourses that were silent in my assessment of him in February 2000. Some of these questions include:

- What discourses do children learn through media and popular culture?
- How do children's stories, videos, movies and computer games represent ideas of good over evil and fighting the "baddies" to protect the young and fragile?
- When I ask children to find a different game to play instead of fighting games is it possible?
- What access do children have to different storylines that represent fair and equitable discourses?
- How do children take up storylines to gain access to friendship groups?

Phase 4: Revise Plan

This is where the researcher is required to draw conclusions about your action research project in relation to what changes have occurred to thinking, reflecting, and acting and what that has told you or what it hasn't told you about your research question and what new questions you have (MacNaughton & Hughes, 2009). At this point, it is important to decide if you have explored your question to the point that you are ready to draw conclusions from your data and share the key learning from your research or if you return to the first phase and create a new change process.

My experiences with revising my action research plan. Through critical reflection I began to rethink how I might listen and respond differently to children's ideas and knowledge. By asking a question such as "Tell me what you like about fighting games?" I was able to give myself permission to not have to be the "expert teacher" with all the answers but more importantly I was able to open up a space to support children to talk differently. How had my "no fighting game" stance in the classroom silence issues and ideas that children had? How had this stance made conversations about fighting and violence taboo? How did children then "cover up" their knowledge to avoid the risk of my displeasure? What other knowledges had I silenced?

The children, Gemma, and I began to plan what action could be taken to improve current practice and develop further epistemological understandings. This was done through creating space for children to talk further about their ideas and use art materials to share their thoughts and feelings with the educators, parents, and between themselves. This created an energy within the room that was in some moments filled with excitement (the children were able to talk about ideas that had been continually silenced), in other moments urgency and caution (the children worried that Gemma and I would "change the rules" again and not allow the fighting conversations), and at many points celebratory energy (children who were often positioned as delayed in development, skills, and knowledge and/or deviant in behaviors were seen by adults and children as experts, teachers, researchers, and critical friends). Children and adults began to collaborate on activities differently as children were the drivers of conversations and activities. For example. Lauren (child researcher) called Gemma over to the painting area and asked her to document her ideas as she painted:

> The world would look nice if there were only goodies in it and there wouldn't be any Hurt or any killing or anything Broken. There would be lots of pretty colours and everyone will feel happy and safe. They will laugh. Well sometimes. They try to be friendly and the world looks pretty and peaceful. There will be cats and dogs and little parrots and grass and sky and flowers and people. That's my favourite things if it's peaceful because it feels nice.

George drew a picture of a "baddie" (see Picture 16.1) and explained:

> They sometimes the goodies have too much power and they just give up on the battle of fighting and they can save some power for the next battle just in case. Goodies can turn into baddies if they want to. They start fighting with the goodies and not fighting with the baddies.

The children also drew images of what a "goodie" looked liked as seen in Picture 16.2 of the Goodies/baddies table.

These conversations and artifacts created large conversations about the social context of people who are good and bad and what role we play to support these people. Questions discussed were:

1. What does a baddie look like?
2. What does a goodie look like?
3. What do baddies and goodies do to make them this way?
4. Can a baddie ever be a goodie and can a goodie ever be a baddie?
5. What could we do to help people rather than "kill," punch or hurt them? Families were also part of these conversations.

Picture 16.1 George's "baddie."

Picture 16.2 Goodies/baddies table.

My experiences with revise plan—Implementing change *with* children. Moving into the next phase of action research the children, Gemma (a teacher) and I in conversation with families, began to implement change in the planning processes within the program. Gemma and I began this by asking the children what activities and materials they would like to have in Spider room. This required Gemma and I to share power, knowledge, and expertise in the classroom and in the research with children. It required us to walk an ethical tightrope to balance children's families' and educators ideas. This required me to remind myself through critical reflection that action research is about emancipation and collaboration as well as taking political risks for social change. I asked myself several questions:

1. How will I react if children ask for activities that I don't agree with?
2. Will children's ideas be enacted only if they fit in with what I deem as appropriate?
3. How will I need to acknowledge my subjectivity and the biases attached to this when supporting children's ideas?
4. What if I don't want to hear what children have to say?

So with caution I met with the children and invited them to participate in planning Spider room with Gemma and me. One of the first requests was for superheros. Previously to this project my first and immediate response would have been to say, "No!" However, I asked myself:

1. Why can't we have superheros in the room? We had banned home toys from the center but children had circumvented this in powerful and strategic ways by bring in their back packs with superheros and popular culture icons on them. Further, they wore tops, socks, pants, and underwear or dress ups representing these images and used them to support their ideas and gain entry into play.
2. How could we introduce superheros into the room? Rather than coming up with reasons or excuses for not having an activity I began to flip the issue over to create a question to reflect on to consider what might be possible.

This time, rather than coming up with an answer, I posed the question to the children: How could we introduce superheros into Spider room? The reaction of the children reminded me of the day that I asked the children to tell me about fighting games. Children spoke over each other in their excitement to share their ideas and imagine the possibilities. Gemma's role was to document the ideas, my role was to support everyone to have a turn to share their ideas and the children's role was to lead the conversations using their expertise about superheros. The children identified a space in the room that could be used for the activity, they decided what the rules would be in using the toys and sharing the space and were able to instruct me on the superheros that were needed and where I need to go to buy these items. Due to my subjectivity, guns were still an issue for me and no guns in the center was still a "bottom line" for me. When I raised the issue of guns with the children they carefully explained the different powers of the superheros to me and assured me that there would be no guns and explained to me that if for some reason the superheroes did have guns I could keep them in my office and they wouldn't use them.

Over the weekend, I shopped for superheros at the store the children had directed me to. On the Monday morning, I set the dolls in the area nominated. With great anticipation children arrived and waited patiently throughout the day to use the space. The area created an opportunity to continue conversations *with* children to learn about their ideas and understandings.

LESSONS LEARNT AND FUTURE RESEARCH

Throughout my research I learnt some valuable lessons about action research with children. Firstly, it was important that I kept my research question in the foreground of my research (on a pin board next to my computer). Throughout the cyclical process new data and knowledge emerged, and it was easy to be seduced by new topics to share and go off into a variety of directions. My advice, therefore, is important to being open and courageous to question and seek new knowledge, yet keep these within the overarching research question. My supervisor always reminded me that there is my life's work and there is my research. It is impossible to study everything in one study.

Secondly, action research usually unfolds in unexpected ways with twists and turns that you may never expect but that does not mean that there are not clear processes and structures within action research. Action research methodologies have been critiqued as being unstructured and random, however, I feel otherwise. In my research, it was important for me to be clear of the cyclical processes as a way to be systematic in my data collection and to support the participation of my coresearchers, which still allowed spaces for new contradictions and unpredictabilities.

Thirdly, I learnt firsthand the importance of inviting children to be coresearchers. My coresearchers demonstrated that they were competent meaning makers and provided invaluable insights and catalytic moments that created new knowledge about how I see and assess children through observation in the everyday classroom. I will continue to invite children to research with me in the future and hope to develop research questions with them. In this research, despite the fact that I came, in with my own research question, which positioned my research as researching *on* children the action research process supported the children to share their own reflections, insights, and questions which shifted the research to a process of researching *with* children.

Finally, I learnt that critical reflection was an important tool in action research to create opportunities for deeper thinking. Critical reflection was vital in supporting Gemma and me to recognize the subjectivity of our gaze. Recognition of the observer's subjectivity and how that influenced the gaze was a difficult terrain to traverse. Recognizing the subjectivity of my gaze meant that I had to acknowledge that while my intent was to operate in fair and equitable ways I could not operate outside who I was as a white, working class, and Catholic female. Further, I operated within a patriarchal society that privileged white, middle class, male society. With the support of audio-taped and video-taped episodes of children's play in Spider room, children's dialogue and artwork, and my own written observations of these episodes I was able to recognize how these understandings of myself and the world privileged particular children in Spider room while marginalizing other children such as Donald. The whiteness of my gaze had seen and assessed children in white, working class, and Catholic female understandings, which positioned children such as Donald as delayed and deviant. By recognizing my subjectivity I was able to move to a different understanding of observation. I recognized that observation was not just about seeing and assessing the child but also seeing and assessing yourself as the observer.

I had to consider what my subjectivity brought to bear on my gaze. When the observer critically reflects within while observing others their subjectivity can be made visible and recorded juxtaposed with what is written and interpreted about the child.

Meetings to plan and to revisit audio, video, art, children's dialogue, transcriptions and journals also supported the process of critical reflection. These meetings provided time and space to think about what was happening for children in the classroom and how we had observed the situation or behavior. Further it allowed a forum for participants to raise questions about their subjectivity, language, and practice and the effects for observation and equity.

Critical reflection also created treacherous paths for travel during the research. Critical reflection opened space for me to recognize my subjectivity and the effect of this on how I practiced as not only a researcher but an early childhood professional in Spider room. On the one hand, this supported change in how I recognized myself as an observer and how I considered social justice in seeing and assessing the child. However, it was also personally confronting because it effected how I recognized myself. I was and continue to be committed to equity and social justice yet critical reflection illuminated the times that I operated in racist, sexist, and classist ways in how I saw and assessed the child and the parent. This was emotionally difficult to deal with. I thought that I could be the rational researcher, the rational director, and the rational early childhood professional. I had to reconsider my own identity and the political, historical, and social construction of who I am.

A space in the foyer of the center became a "gallery" where children's artwork was displayed. This space became a community reflection space where children could reflect with each other and with their families and educators and educators also used it as a space to reflect on themselves as teachers and illuminate the observation discourses they were navigating. The "Goodies/baddies" table (as illustrated above) created a "catalytic" moment for me when I began to reflect on how for me the notion of "goodies" and "baddies" reflected how my observations framed how I unconsciously labelled children as "goodies" and "baddies." I began to ask myself the questions that I had asked the children:

1. What do baddies and goodies do to make them this way?
2. Can a baddie ever be a goodie and can a goodie ever be a baddie?

I thought about how Donald had been labelled as difficult—"*baddie*"— through our observations. Did he ever get to be a *"goodie"*—successful, expert, leader? I began to recognize the power of observation and how it can silence and marginalize children. Through listening to Donald and other children's knowledge, I began to get different insight into the multiplicity of children and gain new insight into who I was.

Critical reflection created a forum for dialogue. Juxtaposed to this were the use of discourse analysis and the discursive positioning of knowledge. This created questions about what constituted valid knowledge and the mapping of intersections of this knowledge and regimes of truth. When Gemma and I began to raise questions about what troubled, how and why we practiced observations, and our concerns of the effects of this we began to trouble the discourses of the expert rational teacher. We also began to discuss discourses that drew us to intersections of "regimes of truth" that supported understandings of the irrational nurturing parent and the parent as the apprentice (Foucualt, 1977). Gemma and I began to ask questions and have conversations *with* children rather than "teach" the children. This created spaces for children to consider, reflect, and share their own ideas and experiences. And for the adults and other children to recognize these ideas as important

MY CONTINUED TENSIONS AND CHALLENGES OF UNDERTAKING ACTION RESEARCH WITH CHILDREN

The intent of our strategies and the effects of these for each of the participants was not always the same. One of the biggest tensions for me was that this was my doctoral work and as such at the end I obtained a PhD. While I acknowledged the children in my thesis they didn't obtain the same or even similar credit for the work that they contributed to. I reconcile to this, by believing that they were intrinsic in creating social change in their classroom and they received the benefits of this through being seen and assessed by educators in what I believe as multiple and fairer ways. I believed that they constructed their own observations and had a voice in contributing to their assessment; and they were able to coconstruct their curriculum during and after the project.

One of the other dilemmas for me in this research was that I came to the center with my research question. This meant that while the project was a social process, participatory, practical and collaborative, emancipatory, critical, recursive, reflexive, and dialectical it was framed around my research topic and questions. Further, investigation is required to consider how we develop research questions *with* children prior to entering the research. This is particularly important given the processes involved in gaining ethics approval from our University's Human Subjects and Ethics Committee where it is a requirement to identify your research question as part of your application prior to entering into the research.

I also continue to struggle with questions about technology and ways it might support the children's participation in research. If I had given children a video recorder, audio-tape recorder, and cameras what might they have recorded and marked as valid and important? The children operate within and through discourses that I do not necessarily see or acknowledge that I am part of. Hence, what the children might record in the day-to-day operation of Spider room I might not even know existed or have seen as important in the same way the children might.

CONCLUSION

MacNaughton and Hughes (2009) state:

> To be effective (and reflective) researchers, we should constantly challenge our "will to truth" with a "will to know." (p. 104)

Our action research project worked to support social change in how children were seen and assessed through observational practices in Spider room. Action research with children acknowledged children as social actors and competent meaning makers. Through artwork, dialogue, journaling, and critical reflection children were able to challenge discourses that placed educators as experts who can understand a singular truth about who the child is and what their behaviors mean to create other, multiple understandings of the child. Children supported teachers to reflect on how children can be treated unfairly. Children began to have opportunities to talk about their ideas and experiences instead of engaging with topics that are always being driven by adult understandings and agendas. As a research community we resisted truths about right and wrong ways to observe, rather in the pursuit of multiple knowledges we explored and illuminated the effects of different observational practices and theories. This created "new" fairer ways of "knowing" children and ourselves as observers. This was done through sharing power, knowledge, and participation *with* children, which provided opportunities for children to share local knowledge and be coresearchers engaging with new knowledge and coconstructors in creating change in observational theory and practice. I would like an opportunity to conduct further action research in diverse early childhood classrooms to inquire how this might be similar or different for children living in different communities within Australia and internationally.

The experience of undertaking action research *with* children has further fuelled my hopes, dreams, and desires to support children's authentic participation in research. Change is not "forever" which is why action research is such a powerful methodology as it acknowledges the shifting and changing nature of the operation of relations of power/ knowledge. Action research supports the troubling of "truths"—for me in this project the troubling of the "knowable" child through observation and the troubling of the "expert" adult observer.

REFERENCES

Assuncao Folque, M. (2010). Action research. In G. MacNaughton, S. A. Rolfe, & I. Siraj-Blatchford (Eds.), *Doing early childhood research: International perspectives on theory and practice.* (pp. 239–260). Crows Nest: Allen & Unwin.

Bloch, M. N. (1992). Critical perspectives on the historical relationship between child development and early childhood education research. In S. A. Kessler & B. B. Swadener (Eds.), *Reconceptualizing the early childhood curriculum* (pp. 3–20). New York, NY: Teachers College Press.

Brooker, L. (2011). Taking children seriously: An alternative agenda for research? *Journal of Early Childhood Research, 9*(2), 137–149.

Campbell, S. (2001). *A social justice disposition in young children.* Unpublished doctoral dissertation, The University of Melbourne, Melbourne, Victoria, Australia.

Carr, W., & Kemmis, S. (1986). *Becoming critical: Knowing through action research.* Geelong: Deakin.

Cohen, L., & Manion, L. (1994). *Research methods in education* (4th ed.). London: Routledge.

Cohen, L., Manion, L., & Morrison, K. (2011). *Research methods in education* (7th edition). New York, NY: Routledge.

Christensen, P., & James, A. (2000). Subjects, objects or participants? In P. Christensen & A. James (Eds.), *Research with children: perspectives and practices* (pp. 1–9). New York, NY: Falmer Press.

Clark, A. (2010) Young children as protagonists and the role of participatory, visual methods in engaging multiple perspectives. *American Journal of Community Psychology, 46,* 115–123.

Clark, A. (2007). Views from inside the shed: young children's perspectives of the outdoor environment. *Education, 35*(4), 349–363.

Diaz Soto, L., Hixon, S., & Hite, S. (2010). Diversity, linguistics, and the silencing of social justice in education and care. In G. Cannella & L. Diaz Soto (Eds.), *Childhoods* (pp. 215–230). New York, NY: Peter Lang.

Fay, B. (1987). *Critical social science.* Oxford: Cornell.

Ferguson, P. (2012). Breaking down barriers in building teacher competence. *Action Learning and Action Research Journal (ALARJ), 18*(1), 68–84.

Freire, P. (1970). *Pedagogy of the oppressed.* London: Penguin.

Foucault, M. (1977). *Discipline and punish: The birth of the prison.* London: Penguin.

Gillberg, C. (2011). A narrative of an action research study in preschool: choice points and their implications for professional and organisational development. *Educational Action Research, 19*(2), 137–152.

Giroux, J. (1995). Border pedagogy and the politics of postmodernism. In P. McLaren. (Ed.), *Postmodernism, postcolonialism and pedagogy*. (pp. 37–64). Albert Park: James Nicholas.

Goulart, M. I. M., & Roth, W.-M. (2010). Engaging young children in collective curriculum design. *Cultural Studies of Science Education, 5*(Brazil), 533–562.

Grundy, S. (1987). *Curriculum: Product or praxis*. New York, NY: Falmer.

Held, D. (1980). *Introduction to critical theory Horkheimer to Habermas*. Berkley: University of California.

Hawkins, K. (2007). The story so far... the use of children's literature in facilitating preschoolers awareness of, and sensitivity to social justice issues. *ARECE Conference*. Monash University, Melbourne, Melbourne, Victoria, Australia.

hooks, b. (2010). *Teaching critical thinking: practical wisdom*. New York, NY: Routledge.

Hult, M., & Lennung, S. (1980). Towards a definition of action-research: A note and bibliography. *Journal of Management Studies, 17*(2), 241–250.

Kemmis, S., & McTaggart, R. (1988). *The action research planner* (2nd ed.). Victoria: Deakin University.

Kemmis, S., & McTaggart, R. (1992). *The action research planner* (3rd ed.). Victoria: Deakin University.

Kemmis, S., & Wilkinson, M. (1998). Participatory action research and the study of practice. In B. Atweh, S. Kemmis, & P. weeks (Eds), *Action research in practice: Partners for social justice in education* (pp. 21–36). London: Routledge.

Lather. P. (1994). Fertile obsession: Validity after poststructuralism. In A. Gitlin (Ed.), *Power and method: Political activism and educational research* (pp. 36–60). London: Routledge.

Lather. P. (1993). Fertile obsession: Validity after poststructuralism. *The Sociological Quarterly. 34*(4), 673–693.

MacNaughton, G. (2005). *Doing Foucault in early childhood studies*. London: Routledge.

MacNaughton, G. (2001). Action research. In G. MacNaughton, S. A. Rolfe, & I. Siraj-Blatchford (Eds.), *Doing early childhood research: International perspectives on theory and practice* (pp. 208–223). Crows Nest: Allen & Unwin.

MacNaughton, G. (1996). Research for quality: A case for action research in early childhood services. *Australian Early Childhood Journal. 21*(2), 29–33.

MacNaughton, G., & Hughes, P. (2009). *Doing action research in early childhood studies: a step by step guide*. Maidenhead: Open University Press.

MacNaughton, G., Hughes, P., & Smith, K. (2008) Children challenging adults: The Yarra Valley Project. In G. MacNaughton, P. Hughes, & K. Smith (Eds.), *Young children as active citizens: principles, policies and pedagogies* (170–192). London: Cambridge Scholars Publishing.

MacNaughton, G., Davis, K., & Smith, K. (2009) Exploring "race-identities" with young children: making politics visible. In MacNaughton, G. M. & Davis, K. (Eds), *Race and early childhood education: An international approach to identity, politics, and pedagogy* (pp. 31–48). Newcastle: Palgrave MacMillan.

MacNaughton, G., & Smith, K. (2008). Engaging ethically with young children: principles and practices for listening and responding with care. In G.

MacNaughton, P. Hughes, & K. Smith (Eds.), *Young children as active citizens: principles, policies and pedagogies* (31–43). London: Cambridge Scholars Publishing.

McKernan, J. (1991). *Curriculum action research*. London: Kogan Page.

McNiff, J. (2002). *Action research: Principles and practice*. London: Routledge Falmer.

Montessori, N. M., & Ponte, P. (2012). Researching classroom communications and relations in the light of social justice. *Educational Action Research, 20*(2), 251–266.

Pacini-Ketchabaw, V., & Berikof, A. (2008). The politics of difference and diversity: from young children's violence to creative power expressions. *Contemporary Issues in Early Childhood, 9*(3), 256–264.

Pascal, C., & Bertram, T. (2009). Listening to young citizens: The struggles to make real a participatory paradigm in research with young children. *European Early Childhood Research Journal, 17*(2), 249–262.

Perry, R. (2012). Facilitated action research: Ehancing the teaching of classroom drama. *Action Learning and Action Research Journal, 18*(1), 5–34.

Pinter, A. & Zandian, S. (2012). "I thought it would be tiny little one phrase that we said, in a huge big pile of papers": Children's reflections on their involvement in participatory research. *Qualitative Research*, 1–16. Available online: http://qrj.sagepub.com/content/early/2012/11/27/1468794112465637

Reason, P., & Bradbury, H. (2008). Introduction. In P. Reason & H. Bradbury (Eds.), *The Sage handbook of action research* (pp. 1–10). London: Sage.

Roche, M. (2011). Creating a dialogical and critical classroom: reflection and action to improve practice. *Educational Action Research, 19*(3), 327–343.

Robinson, K. (2013). *Innocence, knowledge, and the construction of childhood*. Milton Park: Routledge.

Ryan, S., & Campbell, S. (2001). Doing research for the first time. In G. MacNaughton, S. A. Rolfe, & I. Siraj-Blatchford (Eds.), *Doing early childhood research: International perspectives on theory and practice*. (pp. 56–63). Crows Nest: Allen & Unwin.

Schon, D. (1987). *Educating the reflective practitioner*. San Francisco, CA: Jossey-Bass.

Silverman. D. (1993). *Interpreting qualitative data: Methods for analysing talk, text and interaction*. London: Sage.

Smith, A. (2009). Child participation in the early years of education. *Educating Young Children, 15*, 39–41.

Smith, K. (2007) Fairytales and fantasies: The early childhood curriculum truths and their effects for seeing and assessing children. *International Journal of Equity and Innovation in Early Childhood, 5* (1), 58–68.

Smith, K. (2003). *Reconceptualising observation in the early childhood curriculum*. Unpublished PhD Thesis, The University of Melbourne, Melbourne, Victoria, Australia.

Taylor, L. (2010). Action research. In G. MacNaughton, S. A. Rolfe, & I. Siraj-Blatchford (Eds.), *Doing early childhood research: International perspectives on theory and practice* (pp. 291–308). Crows Nest: Allen & Unwin.

Usher, R., & Edwards, R. (1994). *Postmodernism and education*. Chatham: Routledge.

Walton, J. (2011). A collaborative inquiry: "How do we improve our practice with children?" *Educational Action Research, 19*(3), 297–311.

Ward, G. (1996). *Theology and contemporary critical theory.* Ipswich, Suffolk: MacMillan.
Weedon, C. (1987). *Feminist practice & poststructuralist theory.* Cambridge: Blackwell.
Woodhead, M., & Faulkner, D. (2008). Subjects, objects, or participants? In P. Christensen & A. James (Eds.), *Research with children: Perspectives and practices* (pp. 10–39). London: Falmer Press.

CHAPTER 17

MICROETHNOGRAPHIC RESEARCH IN EARLY CHILDHOOD EDUCATION

John A. Sutterby

INTRODUCTION

Selecting Microethnography

Microethnography is a research methodology that has been used to conduct research in early childhood environments with both adults and children. Historically, microethnography is a relatively recent methodology as it was first developed in the 1960s and 1970s. Microethnography draws its roots from ethnography and the research methods developed in the fields of anthropology, psychology and sociology. The central focus of microethnography is on communicative interactions in particular settings (LeBaron, 2006).

Researchers in early childhood considering using microethnography will focus on the uses of language and communication in particular social settings. Research questions which lend themselves to microethnography are ones that involve examining communication in settings such single classrooms. In addition, the researcher will want to investigate the cultural context of the setting selected for research. In early childhood, the setting might be a classroom, a parent-teacher conference, or it may be a situation such as pick up and drop off at a school or child care facility. Finally, researchers using microethnography as a research method will need to make a decision about how to use technology in order to collect samples of language and communication in that setting.

The goal of this chapter is to help researchers better understand microethnography and when and how to use the methodology in early childhood settings. This chapter will focus on the relationship between ethnography and microethnography, the historical roots of microethnography and the philosophical traditions of microethnography. Secondly this chapter will outline the process of conducting a microethnographic research study, including issues of validity and reliability, the research tools used in microethnography and the process of data analysis in microethnography. Finally, this chapter will discuss a number of microethnographic studies conducted in early childhood settings.

Ethnography

Ethnography can be defined as a methodology which seeks to better understand society and culture through close engagement within the setting. The assumption is that in order to understand a society or culture, the researcher must become immersed in the environment (Hobbs, 2006). Ethnography in the field of anthropology originally was developed with a particular set of research tools and training and with the perspective that a researcher as a neutral, objective, outside observer in the setting. That perspective has evolved over the last few decades to where ethnography is undertaken by researchers from many different perspectives and many approaches to methodology (Denzin & Lincoln, 2005a; 2005b).

What is meant by ethnography as a research method has been muddied recently, Denzin & Lincoln suggest, "it is no longer possible to take for granted what anyone means by *Ethnography*" (2005b, p. xvi). Wolcott (1999) would add, "Imagine a group of ethnographers meeting today and agreeing on *anything*, let alone a definition limiting ethnography to 'descriptive accounts of nonliterate peoples'" (p. 9). Postmodern and post-structuralist influences on the field of ethnography have changed how researchers approach the setting and participants, the methodology, what is seen as data and how data in analyzed.

Many ethnographic researchers conducting research today carefully consider their role in the research process, the ethics of the research process and the politics of the research process (Jupp, 2006; Wolcott, 1999; Denzin & Lincoln, 2005a; Deyhle, Hess & LeCompte, 1992). Ethnography is a way to research the more complex social and cultural aspects of human interaction. As Erickson (1992) describes it, ethnography is a way to see "inside the "black boxes" of ordinary life in educational settings" (p. 202).

Ethnography has been used to investigate early childhood care settings. Child care settings are viewed as a being a particular cultural context. As Buchbinder, Longhofer, Barrett, Lawson & Floersch (2006) state, "The child care center is a site for everyday practices where cultural values, government policies, family systems, and practice theories are integrally combined" (p. 46). Buchbinder et al., classify ethnographic studies in early childhood into four categories or perspectives. They identify a care-giver perspective, a mother perspective, a child-centered perspective and a societal perspective. They suggest that ethnography in child care settings can help researchers better understand the micro and macro processes that occur within these settings.

DEFINITION OF MICROETHNOGRAPHY

Microethnography has grown out of the field of ethnography as a method to closer examine the communicative practices in particular cultural settings. It incorporates many ethnographic methods, but adds a focus on language and communication. Microethnography in early childhood settings looks at communicative practices that occur in early childhood. These communicative events can be between adults and children, between children or between adults, for example mothers and teachers. Like with the definition of the method of ethnography there is some confusion about what actually occurs in a microethnographic study.

Microethnography falls under the interpretivist approach to research. Interpretivist approaches come out of the field of anthropology, which emphasize understanding behavior from cultural traditions. Interpretivist traditions look at sense making in interactions. Discourse or conversational analysis is the method of coming to an understanding of what has occurred in a communicative interaction event (Wetherell, 2006). Microethnography is also often used to study cross cultural interactions in that it can help identify where cross cultural miscommunication occurs (Bloome, Carter, Christian, Otto, & Shuart-Faris, 2005).

There are also some differences in the definition of microethnography. Some define microethnography as simply a smaller version of an ethnography. For example Gerrish and Lacey (2010) say microethnographies "are small scale studies into a single social situation" (p. 172). They suggest this methodology is simpler and less time consuming than ethnography. They write, "Novice nurse researchers often choose a microethnography as it makes fewer demands on their time than macro-ethnography and seems more immediately relevant to the world of the nurse" (p. 172). Kim (2006) mirrors this, writing, "Microethnography has a smaller scope and focus than ethnography. It examines discrete events or small units of particular behaviors in a social setting with little immediate concern for the culture as a whole... The underlying assumption of microethnography is that cultural ethos and beliefs are reflected in selected aspects of human interaction and thus they are identifiable" (p. 39).

Garcez (1997), drawing on the work of Erickson (1992) and others who were seminal in the development of the methodology of microethnography, describes it as a method which is concerned with "face-to-face interactional engagements constituting societal and historical experience" (p. 187). Thus in this case microethnography is seen as a method specific to communication, rather than as just a mini-ethnography. Methodologically, examining face-to face interactions relies on the analysis of video or audio recordings of interactions (Garcez, 1997; Anthrostrategist, 2012).

Au and Mason (1982) also use microethnography as a research method. They focus on the interaction event between communicators as most significant and base their data collection technique on the collection of videotapes and careful analysis of the videotape to better understand interactions. They write, "In the microethnographic study of classroom behavior, an event is videotaped and then carefully analyzed to determine its social organizational features" (p. 2). Unlike the definition of microethnography as a scaled down, simpler ethnography, Au and Mason see this method as much more painstaking. "Since conducting such fine-grained analyses is extremely time-consuming and painstaking, thought should be given to exactly what the unique contributions of this research approach are" (p. 3).

On the other hand, not all microethnographic researchers see technology for data collection in a microethnography as critical. Stokrocki and White (1995) define microethnography as, "the description, analysis, and interpretation of a slice of everyday life" (p. 52). In their microethnography, audio and video data were not collected. The researchers were unable to get usable audiotapes of the participants in their study so they fell back to using field notes, document analysis, and informal interviewing. They also included time sampling of events as part of their data collection process.

Critical ethnography has traditionally been used to critique modern society; it has also been used to critique positivist research paradigms. Critical ethnography has also informed political movements as a result of their investigations (Foley & Valenzuela, 2005). Critical microethnography is a form of microethnography which uses a critical lens to examine unjust or discriminatory practices. For critical ethnography, the participants are seen as having agency along with the researcher. Critical microethnography in schools examines the experiences of marginalized students and how the educational environment determines what is being learned (Pane & Rocco, 2009).

For the purposes of this chapter, the definition of microethnography will follow more of the Erickson (1992, 2004) model. This includes the process of using ethnographic method; for example, participant observation, field notes, and formal and informal interviews (Pane & Rocco, 2009). In addition, the definition will focus on interactional events in a cultural setting. These interaction events will involve some sort of technological recording of interactions in selected settings. These recorded interactions are analyzed for themes based on some sort of discourse microanalysis.

ROOTS OF MICROETHNOGRAPHY

Microethnography is a method which can be used in many contexts including early childhood education. Microethnography, as a form of ethnography focuses on similar issues as ethnography but with a much narrower focus. Microethnographic research focuses on the interactions of people in particular naturalistic settings. This focus on interaction involves both verbal and nonverbal interactions (LeBaron, 2006). An analysis of discourse patterns and interactions is one of the main uses of microethnography within an ethnographic framework (Popescu, 2010).

Microethnography has its roots in five areas of research; context analysis, ethnography of communication, presentation of self, conversational analysis and discourse analysis. Context analysis is the examination of verbal and nonverbal behavior during an interaction. Context analysis draws from the field of anthropology and the view that linguistic interactions cannot be understood outside of their specific contexts (McDermott & Roth, 1978).

Ethnography of communication examines communication interactions from a cultural perspective. Ethnography of communication looks at communication; however it generally did not use technology, but looked at communication in a community from a more global view or holistic view (Watson-Gegeo, 1997). Carbaugh (2005) uses ethnography of communication to examine intercultural communication in a variety of settings. For example, he and a colleague examine the role of speaking and silence in Finnish-USA American communication. Although, not specifically described as an ethnography of communication, many of the works of Vivian Paley like, *You Can't Say You Can't Play* (1993), and *The Boy Who Would be a Helicopter* (Paley, 1991) would be examples of this type of ethnography in early childhood settings.

Presentation of self looks at interactions as rituals of display of the self or concealment of the self. Presentation of self draws on the work of Goffman (1959) who described how people give performances of themselves in everyday conversations. Goffman drew on participant observation as a key data collection tool. Corsaro's (2003) work in examining children's culture from a participant observer status is an example from early childhood education of this type of research perspective. Corsaro took a role on the playground which he used to gain a better understanding of how communication and social roles were developing on the playground.

Conversational analysis looks at sense making by the participants in a communication interaction. It is seen as an improvisational act between the interactors. Conversational analysis uses audio or video recorded conversations in naturalistic settings. Conversational analysis is based on turn taking in conversation as two (or more) speakers negotiate the process of communication (Greco, 2006). Sawyer (1997), looks at pretend play conversations for children as an improvisational activity, he examined how children's conversations are developed and maintained and how they become more complex as children mature.

Finally, power relationships are examined as part of interactional patterns between interactors. These power relationships in interactions have been investigated by a number of researchers such as Bourdieu, Foucault, Habermas, and Bakhtin. They have been exploring how are power relationships reproduced through language and action (Erickson, 1992; Bloome et al. 2005). Power relationships in early childhood microethnography may examine how society frames the play activities of children from diverse linguistic backgrounds (Riojas-Cortez, 2001) or how families with children with special needs are treated by the school system (Mutua, 2001).

Although the above mentioned methodological approaches; context analysis, ethnography of communication, perception of self, conversation analysis and analysis of power relationships have been used in various research fields, they all are part of the development of the tradition of micro analysis of interactions. Erickson describes how these five areas of research methodology have come together into the research method we call microethnography (Erickson, 1992).

THE PROCESS OF MICROETHNOGRAPHY

Conducting a microethnography in early childhood involves making a number of choices. Like many qualitative methods, researchers decide what methods they want to use in the research process. Choices may include what framework for validity is going to be followed, what tools for data collection are going to be used. How the data collection process will be ordered, and how the data will be analyzed. This will involve the researcher deciding where to position herself in the research setting, for example as a friendly observer or as an active conversational partner, as in Opie's (1994),

The People on the Playground. The researcher will also need to decide what technology to use for data collection, for example, hand held video recorders vs. a fixed location for video recording. Of course the researcher will also need to find a setting for research, like a classroom, which will help him answer the research question.

Validity in Microethnography

Microethnography falls under the category of qualitative research. Validity in qualitative research has been an area of discussion for decades (Cho & Trent, 2006). The construct of validity has evolved over time and continues to evolve as researchers examine this concept. Generally, it appears that the theoretical model many researchers are working from is that the researcher needs to decide what type of validity is being sought (Saukko, 2005; Cho & Trent, 2006; Ellis, 2003). Traditional conceptions of validity have focused on trying to accurately depict reality. More recently the focus has been on the interactional process between the researcher and the other being researched (Saukko, 2005). Cho & Trent (2006) suggest two approaches to validity, transactional and transformational. They discuss the concept of transactional validity, which involves techniques such as member checking and triangulation as part of the process in order to add integrity to the research. On the other hand, they suggest transformational validity is not based on the techniques employed by the researcher, but by the self-reflection of the researcher involved in the research process. Ellis (2003) discusses ethnographic validity in terms of how it is seen by the researcher, how it impacts the research participants and how readers of the research are engaged.

The microethnographic researcher, like other qualitative researchers, can approach the concept of validity from many different perspectives. Early microethnographic researchers have focused on transactional validity, as they focused on the fidelity of the recording process of the language interaction, for example, LeBaron (2006), describes a process of listening and relistening to the recordings in order to be able to truthfully present the research data. Bloome et al. (2005), take a more transformational approach to microethnography as they examined the positioning of the researcher and the relations of power in language and literacy discourse in the classroom. Early childhood microethnographic researchers will have to make a decision about how they want to approach the concept of validity in their research design. Will the researcher focus on the integrity of the research process and data analysis or will the researcher focus on the reflection on the research process itself?

Audio/Video Data Collection Tools for Microethnography

Microethnography uses technological means like audio and video equipment to capture the details of the interaction events. Access to video or audio files allows for repeated viewing/listening to the events for analysis which is an important technique in microethnography. Microethnography became possible with the development of technological tools to capture audio and video. More recently, advances in digital technologies for both audio and video have made the collection of data even easier than before (Le Baron, 2006).

Film has been used for decades as a data collection tool; however the limitation on the length of film only allowed for observations of around an hour (Erickson, 1992; Rosenstein, 2002). Microethnography has been greatly enhanced with major technological advances in the ability to collect video images and audio. Video and audio files allow for extensive reviewing and careful analysis that is not possible when a researcher is in the moment during research. In addition, video allows for sharing of events with the participants (Baker, Green, & Skukauskaite, 2008). Video recording allows for interpretation of physical actions along with dialogue. Nonverbal communication is an important aspect which gives context to the transcript of the conversation. Movements, gestures, body language, and facial expressions can be interpreted examining video data (Rosenstein, 2002; Baker, Green, & Skukauskaite, 2008; Dufon, 2002).

When using audio or video recordings with young children it is important to note that there are some important concerns to take into consideration. First, audio and video recordings can expose the identity of research participants in that they are relatively permanent and may require special approval from Institutional Review Boards (Baker, Green, & Skukauskaite, 2008). Secondly, video and audio recordings can be intrusive in educational settings. Children are aware that they are being monitored and the presence of a microphone or audio camera can lead to children "acting out" for the microphone or audio camera (Sutterby, 2002). The research will need to evaluate these choices when deciding what technological tool to use for data collection.

Using Ethnographic Methods in Microethnography

Microethnography also uses many of the same tools of ethnography. These tools may include participant observation, field notes, reflective journaling, formal and informal interviewing and artifact analysis. These traditional qualitative data collection techniques allow for a richer description of the setting and events. They also aid in the interpretation of data as the researcher constructs the research narrative.

Participant observation involves for obvious reasons two factors, observation and participation. The idea is that the researcher is becoming involved in some way in the research setting. The participant observer acknowledges to a certain extent that the observer is part of the setting and has an impact on what goes on there. The ethnographic researcher thus needs to decide where the balance is between participation and observation (Wolcott, 1999). Researchers in early childhood settings may need to decide what role they are going to take in the classroom. Adult researchers in these settings have an obligation to act as a caregiver in that if there is a risk of injury to a child then they will need to intervene. On the other hand, researchers may decide not to intervene in cases where children break classroom rules (Sutterby, 2002).

Field notes or field journals are the recorded thoughts, feelings, memories and details about the observed experience (Pane & Rocco, 2009). Although many ethnographic researchers collect field notes, the notes themselves are not meant to be exact details of an event, they are meant more to give impressions for further reflection (Ellis, 2003). Field notes are also an expression of what the researcher has decided to focus on in field work. Field notes may involve recording the most significant events or a more systematic attempt to collect all the possible data (Wolfinger, 2002). Field notes in microethnography are meant to help fill out the details of the transcriptions of the video or audio recordings (Pane & Rocco, 2009).

Reflection and reflective journaling are another source of information in microethnographic research. Reflection and reflective journaling usually involves recording observations, ideas, insights, emotions and other details which occur during the research process. Reflexivity is important in the qualitative research process because the researcher is acting as the instrument of the research. Reflection by the researcher serves several purposes. In the microethnography it becomes part of the validation process of the research. Reflection may also expose questions of ethics, like the power relationships between the researcher and participants or the conscious decision not to record a particular event (Jupp, 2006; Wolcott, 1999; Ellis, 2003).

Interviewing can be used in microethnography in certain cases. Interviewing in microethnography is not the central focus of inquiry in that microethnography involves data collection in naturalistic settings (LeBaron, 2006). Interviewing can be an additional source of data in that it can help explain interactional events. For example, participants may be shown a video recording of an event and then the researcher could ask the participant what is happening. Erickson (1992) suggests that interviews can help identify, "special local identities, attitudes, and customs" (p. 221) that may be part of a particular local culture which will shed light on local interaction patterns. Stokrocki & White (1995) in their study of art education in the Navajo community had to rely on interviews of participants along with document analysis due to the inaudible nature of the participants on audio recordings.

Artifact analysis also is a part of microethnography in that documents can shed light on insider knowledge. In addition artifacts can become part of the data available that might not be identifiable during the video or audio taping process. Special education referral forms can shape how participants in the referral of students for special education are identified. Knotek (2003) and Bennet (1988) both looked at the forms used in the referral of children to special education for minority students. These forms contained notes and other information which impacted the participants' decision making processes.

RESEARCH PROCESS IN MICROETHNOGRAPHY

LeBaron (2006) describes aspects of the research process for microethnography. The first step in the research process is that the researcher needs to select a setting which will help address the research question. The setting is a specific site where people come together for a naturalistic interactional activity. The importance of the setting is that particular types of interactions occur in particular settings. Courtrooms will have different interactions than classrooms for example. Kim (2012) and Riojas (1998) selected early childhood classrooms for their studies, while Knotek (2003) focused on the setting of the family school interface for special education.

LeBaron (2006) notes the second aspect of microethnographic research is to "collect naturally occurring data" (p. 178). The data collected should be as near as possible to what would have occurred without the presence of the data collection equipment. In early childhood classrooms this may mean locating a microphone in an unobtrusive location or using a small hand held video camera. A third aspect of microethnographic research is the repeated viewing of or listening to the data. Viewing the data over and over again allows the researcher to examine the significant details of an event which would not be noticed in a typical observation based solely on the memory of the researcher. LeBaron also recommends digitizing data in order to facilitate computer analysis of the data.

According to Erickson (1992), data collection in microethnography generally begins with participant observation. Pane & Rocco (2009) call this passive observation. Participant observation allows the researcher to get a general sense of the typical events that occur in a particular setting. It is also helpful to have some observations of the participants outside the setting.

Once patterns have been established at the setting the researcher then begins to narrow focus onto more selective videotaping or audio recording. In early childhood settings the researcher may take some time in the classroom to observe and interact with the children, before deciding where to place microphones or video cameras. Background noise and blind spots can impact the quality of the data collected.

At this point the researcher needs to decide what is going to be the area of focus. "Decisions about what to record and how to record it...are not neutral. They are research decisions that should be informed by the overall conduct of participant observation in the study" (Erickson, 1992, 207). Riojas (1998) for example selected to focus her attention on children's socio dramatic play. She followed the children using a portable video camera to the centers in the classroom where the dramatic play was taking place. McGrath (2007) on the other hand focused on the interactions of parents and teachers during pick up and drop off of children at an early childhood center. Sutterby (2002) used a microphone and audio recording device placed near the play centers in the classroom, rotating centers until all of the centers had been recorded at least once. Kim (2012) used videotaping to capture story reading and story writing in kindergarten classroom's that included children who were deaf. Kim suggested the activity to the teacher as a way of eliciting oral and written narratives.

Data analysis in microethnography occurs during and following the collection of data. Ethnographic notes, reflective journals and other data sources are analyzed for themes. Electronic notes such as audio or video files of interactions as well as interviews are transcribed. Pane and Rocco (2009) calls this the reconstructive data analysis of the primary record.

Erickson (1992) relates a five stage process when approaching microanalysis of video and audio data. The first stage of data analysis is looking over or reviewing the whole event. Examining a video recorded event would involve looking at the event from start to finish. While reviewing the recorded event the researcher continues to take field notes. These notes will include when events occur and any special events which might have occurred during this initial viewing. This also helps to put boundaries around an event. This is more of a holistic process that takes place before the video recording is broken down into smaller units (Pane & Rocco, 2009).

Smaller units of data are selected at this point. The researcher will need to decide what the boundaries of an event are. Boundaries are socially constructed starts and ends to an event. Stories will be bounded by specific linguistic phrasing, for example. A story will have a beginning introduction, like once upon a time, and a conclusion, and they lived happily ever after, which mark the beginning and end of the story. Researchers have to carefully observe the collected data in order to identify the specific boundaries as they may differ across educational and cultural contexts (Bloome, et al., 2005).

The second stage of analysis begins once boundaries have been established around an event. Erickson (1992) suggests there are three general phases to an event which are what he calls, "getting started, a phase of main instrumental focus, and a phase of winding up on the way to the next event" (p. 218). The second phase of data analysis involves identifying when these shifts occur.

The third phase of data analysis involves looking in greater detail at the events of the interaction. In this stage the level of participation of each participant is examined. This may involve for example, one main speaker and several listeners who participate through nonverbal responses such as head nodding (Erickson, 1992). Later the speaker may receive a number of responses. Recently at a conference I presented at, I noted at some points there were many participants engaged through focused attention, at other points participants were responding to questions, and at other points there was communication between the participants themselves, finally some participants were engaged primarily with electronic devices.

The fourth stage of data analysis involves the development of some sort of discourse or conversational analysis structure. Transcript analysis involves a number of conventions to demonstrate actions like pauses, rising tone of voice, and who is talking. These transcript notes may differ depending on the researcher.

Some of the transcript notes from Pane & Rocco (2009):

(.) Short pause
\>fast< Noticeably faster talk
<slow> Noticeably slower talk

Transcript notes from Bloome et al. (2005)

XXXX Undecipherable
I Short pause
III Long pause
Student Unknown student talking
Students Many students speaking at once

Erickson (1992) suggests that this level of analysis begins to illustrate cross cultural differences in communication as speakers from different cultural groups respond in different ways during the interaction event.

The fifth level of analysis according to Erickson (1992) involves looking over the entire "corpus of recordings" (p. 220) to identify patterns of interactions such as the use of humor. It also serves to identify typical and atypical cases. The identification of patterns in the analysis suggests what are typical conversation events at the same time the researcher can identify unusual cases. Additional inquiry may be required to identify why the unusual cases differed from the usual pattern of interaction.

This describes one method of analyzing data; however, different levels and methods of microanalysis have been developed to examine microethnographic data. Pane and Rocco (2009) for example have six levels of coding for their critical microethnography. Overall, data analysis for microethnography will follow similar patterns in that they move from the general to the specific. They also move from the typical to identifying the atypical.

The final step in microethnography involves preparing a manuscript based on the data sources. Writing up microethnography involves using transcripts of what has occurred and possibly screen grabs of events. These events may be reinforced with field notes, interviews or artifact analysis depending on the qualitative data gathered in the data collection process (LeBaron, 2006). In the future, the possibility exists for including actual video or audio recordings embedded in research articles to allow the reader to view the recording and evaluate the researchers' interpretation themselves.

ETHICS OF MICROETHNOGRAPHY

Ethics in research methods became codified in the 1970s and 1980s with the publication of documents such as The Belmont Report. These codes set out to define the limits of ethical research. The four major components of ethics in research are informed consent, avoidance of deception, privacy and confidentiality and accuracy of data. Ethical issues in research are overseen by Institutional Review Boards which review research protocols. Qualitative researchers generally take on additional ethical considerations beyond what is found in ethical codes (Christians, 2005). Microethnography in research with young children also presents ethical issues, some of the issues that researchers should consider when conducting a microethnography with children include; reciprocity, research outcomes, story ownership, and consent of young children in research.

Reciprocity is one way microethnographic researchers try to benefit the research participants. The researcher usually gains some benefit from research, a research publication, or possibly a promotion. Reciprocity demonstrates respect for the research participants' effort in the research process. Reciprocity in research with children may take many forms, for example some sort of compensation for their time. Reciprocity may involve being taken seriously by the researcher and being respected throughout the research process. Reciprocity may also involve the researcher giving something back to the community (Freeman & Mathison, 2009). Bower and Griffin (2011) describe how important reciprocity is for them as part of the research process. The lead researcher "would often assist with tasks within the school or on activities such as assembling fundraiser packets, assisting with grant applications and interventions, and researching resources that may be available to the school" (p. 80).

Another point of ethical consideration is looking at what is the ultimate outcome of the research. The question is; how will this research impact the participants in the research study as well as the society at large? In critical microethnography an attempt is made to direct the focus of research on discriminatory classroom practices. The researcher conducting a critical microethnography should try to examine themselves within the culture. They should examine how they contribute to culture and how examining classroom culture may lead to improvements in classroom culture overall (Pane & Rocco, 2009).

Ethics of Story Ownership

Ethics of microethnography can also be seen in terms of who "owns" the story. As Denzin & Lincoln point out, "We do not 'own' the field notes we make about those we study. We do not have undisputed warrant to study anyone or anything. Subjects may challenge how they have been written about, and more than one ethnographer has been taken to court" (2005, p. xvi). Videotaping, which is an important aspect of microethnography, can have ethical implications as to who owns the rights to the video files and how they can be used.

> The issue of ownership is complex in all research. Does the videotaped data belong to the subject/object of the video or to the researcher? Often, the object of the research would like to use the video for documentation, publicity, fund raising, or other purposes. Where can the video be shown? Can the researcher show it at will to colleagues at conferences or to students during lectures? To which audiences does a waiver apply? (Rosenstein, 2002, p. 9)

This especially applies to microethnographic research where footage of a study is relatively permanent. An agreement should be made before videotaping begins on what will be the ultimate destination of all recordings and how they will be used. This is also important when working with young children who may have permanent video files created of them where they do not have the opportunity to provide informed consent due to their minor status. Important questions should be answered before the research process such as, how long will video files of participants as children exist and how much control of these files will they have as adults?

Microethnography also presents some unique ethical issues due to the nature of the data collection. Technological collection of data through audio and or video tape is a relatively exact reproduction of events. It can be difficult to mask events and participants enough to guarantee anonymity. Thus there is a possibility of embarrassment or even risk of damage in the recounting of ethnographic events (Erickson, 1992).

Ethical Issues in Research With Children

Conducting a microethnography with children presents ethical challenges for the researcher. Children have traditionally been viewed as objects or subjects of research. More recently researchers are beginning to see children as more active participants in the research process. Young children under current guidelines cannot consent to participate in research, consent is generally only granted to parents or guardians. The minors assent to participate in research varies in age depending on the Institutional Review Board, with ages ranging between six and 15 years of age (Kon, 2006).

This inconsistency is due to differences in beliefs about what decisions children are capable of making in regards to research. Generally, the idea of assent relies on what researchers believe is developmentally appropriate for children. Differences also exist in the belief that active assent be required rather than a lack of dissent (Kon, 2006). Researchers working in the area of microethnography with young children will need to carefully consider how to show respect of young children to make their own decision about whether to participate in the research process.

Finally, when researching with young children, the researcher has to have an understanding that there are adult-child power differences that can impact the research process. Children, especially young children may defer to adults and agree to participate in research out of fear of punishment rather than assenting freely. In addition, in researching with young children, adults are by definition outsiders to the participants. We may have been children once, but we no longer are and thus may not really understand the perspectives of child participants (Freeman & Mathison, 2009; David, Tonkin, Powell & Anderson, 2005).

MICROETHNOGRAPHIC RESEARCH IN EARLY CHILDHOOD SETTINGS

Microethnography has been used in a variety of settings to better understand the interactions that occur in these settings. Sometimes these interactions are between adults, between adults and children, and sometimes between children. It has also been used in cross cultural research to better help understand cultural communication. Microethnography has also been used in research in specific settings such as special education (Kim, 2012; Murray, Anderson, Bersani & Meseros, 1986), and bilingual education (Riojas-Cortez, 1998; Sutterby, 2002). Microethnography has also been used to investigate home school relationships in both public elementary schools and in child care (Bennett, 1988; McGrath, 2007).

Home-School Relationships

McGrath (2007) conducted a microethnography of early child care and the relationships between parents and teachers. She found that three factors; power, trust and partnership defined that relationship. The power relationship was defined that parents, typically mothers came from a higher socioeconomic status than the teachers, however in order to get information about the events at school, they had to rely on the teachers for information. Parents had to meet the teachers in their work environment. On the other hand, parents had access to the director and used that access to undermine the authority of the teachers. Trust was a second dynamic in the parent teacher relationship in that the parents had to trust the teachers to take care of their children's best interests.

Because of issues of power and trust, the child care educators' attempts to develop parent teacher partnerships was problematic. An additional factor in this relationship was the role of the child and how the child created a dynamic between parent and teacher. In this case, the observations afforded by microethnography allowed the researcher to more closely examine the meanings behind parent teacher interactions.

Bower and Griffin (2011) used microethnographic methods as part of their case study of an elementary school. They investigated how parental involvement played out in a high-minority, high-poverty elementary school. They found that the school's traditional methods of reaching out to parents were not having much success. Notes home and invitations to parent events did not engage the parents. Differences in cultural communication also caused miscommunication at school events and meetings. The lack of reciprocal communication at the school led to frustration on the part of the school staff, who essentially gave up on parental involvement at school. The researchers suggest that the school needs to reevaluate the ways that they are trying to engage parents as the traditional methods were not proving to be effective. They felt that relationship building would go a long way toward improving parent involvement at the school.

Microethnography is an interpretivist approach in that it attempts to understand the meaning behind certain behaviors. This research method has been used in areas like special education where researchers have examined the processes of referring children for special education evaluation and assessment. This research has examined teacher interviews, referral forms and examined video tape to examine differences between children who were referred for special education and those who were not. The use of microethnographic methods allowed researchers to identify the complexities involved in the referral process (Jacob, 1990).

Bennett (1988) used microethnographic methods to investigate how Hispanic parents of deaf children were engaged in their children's schooling. He investigated one particular family and followed them through the process of getting into school. He also looked into the unequal relationships which occurred between the educational staff and the families of the deaf children. They found that the relationship between these groups was one "of struggle and contradiction" (p. 126). The parents in this study felt that if they complained about staff than their child would suffer. Bennett makes a conclusion at the end, that the struggle with the school was one where the school was trying to impose a particular pattern of interaction on the families which was not congruent with their cultural expectations. Because of the power disparity the families were unable to challenge the schools hegemonic practices.

Another microethnography in special education (Knotek, 2003) investigated the over referral of African American children to special education. This study also used a framework of power relationships between the school staff and their identification of students. The themes which emerged from the analysis of the data suggested that the evaluation teams had negative attitudes towards the families, and these attitudes influenced the referral process. Knotek found a confirmatory bias in the referral of low socioeconomic status children to special education despite attempts to have an objective process.

In addition, there was a concern that not all members of the evaluation team were of the same status. Higher educated members for example, had more control over the referral process. Thus many teachers did not speak up in the team meetings and went along with the recommendations of the higher status members. This also led to less than objective decision making for the children who were being evaluated (Knotek, 2003).

Examining Young Children's Understandings

Dyson (1998) conducted a microethnography in a third grade classroom. One important aspect of classroom interactions that occurred during the study was the use of authors' theatre. Dyson focused on the stories the children composed for the readers' theater. Children's popular culture themes, like Men, were part of the stories in the classroom. The stories which the children drew from popular media culture often made adults uncomfortable as the stories represented traditional views of power and gender. On the other hand, Dyson concludes that the children's stories based on popular media allow them to take on powerful roles. She recommended that instead of banning these stories, teachers should instead incorporate them into the classroom culture (Dyson, 1998).

Another ethnography that examined stories in the classroom focused on the language skills of children who are deaf (Kim, 2012). Kim videotaped kindergarten children who are deaf in two different classroom settings during storytelling and story writing time. She examined an inclusion classroom and a state school classroom. She found that children used many affordances in order to participate in literacy events. However, she also found that in the inclusion school, the formal literacy assessment limited the resources that the children could draw upon. In the state school she found that children often used ASL rather than English structures in their literacy activities. She suggests that the educational context is important in understanding how children's literacy skills develop and that educators should be cautious in interpreting student outcomes without understanding the educational context of the child.

Chami-Sather & Kretschmer (2005) used microethnographic methods to analyze the discourse and interactions of two groups of young children from different cultures. They analyzed the discourse of Lebanese Arabic children in comparison with American children. They found that the Lebanese children tended to engage more quickly during the discussion portion of the interactions and engaged in more interruptions and scaffolded the other children's conversation more frequently. They felt these differences in interaction patterns reflected the societal interaction patterns of the community.

Riojas-Cortez (2001) used microethnographic methods to investigate the dramatic play behaviors of young bilingual children from a Mexican American background. Her microethnography looked at cultural traits in a preschool classroom in dramatic play, at a small rural elementary school. She also conducted parent interviews on the children's cultural themes. Some of the cultural themes included child care, household care, family values, entertainment, friendship, travel/geography, popular TV, education, economics, scientific knowledge, ranching and farming, construction.

Microethnography allowed a closer examination of culture during play. Riojas-Cortez found that the children in her study used their funds of knowledge to create dramatic play episodes that were unique to the culture of the area. The funds of knowledge that children drew from included their language resources like Spanish and code switching. The children also displayed their values and beliefs in their play, like what were appropriate sleeping arrangements in a household based on the teaching of their parents. The children also engaged in dramatic play around household chores and discussed ideas like the value of education. Again, microethnographic research methodologies contributed significantly to this research as Riojas-Cortez was able to explore in depth the experiences that the children brought to the school setting from home during dramatic play (Riojas-Cortez, 2001).

Sutterby (2002) engaged in a microethnographic study of a prekindergarten dual language immersion classroom. He used audio recording of the children's play to better understand the negotiations and interactions of the children. His analysis suggested that different settings were more supportive of cross-linguistic interactions than others. Dramatic play for example was difficult for children from different language backgrounds. Language neutral areas included sand and water play which required little co-construction of play. Games and other structured activities allowed for more cross-linguistic interactions. Although the goal of the dual language program was to encourage bilingual and bicultural development, the lack of interactions across language groups limited the reaching of these goals.

CONCLUSION AND SUMMARY

This chapter has situated microethnography within the field of ethnography. Microethnography is a research method which focuses on specific settings. Microethnography also is used to focus on specific communicative events. In order to conduct microethnography researchers usually rely on some form of audio or video recording to collect data. Video recording is often preferred in that it also captures nonverbal responses such as head nods and body language. If audio recording is the primary method of data collection, then field notes are used to fill out the details of the interactive events.

Microethnographic research uses many of the same tools as ethnography; these tools include participant observation, field notes, reflective journaling, interviews and artifact analysis. The process of research generally begins with a more global holistic view of the setting and then a narrower focus is taken on the naturalistic events which occur in the setting. The analysis of the data generally follows some sort of discourse or conversational analysis of the video and transcripts.

Microethnographers should have a high standard of ethics when conducting this research. The participants in microethnography are being observed in a naturalistic setting and so there is the possibility of them being harmed by the research process either through embarrassment or by having some aspect of their lives exposed. Microethnographers often take into consideration the time of the participants and try to have some benefit for the participants.

Microethnography as a method has been used by a number of researchers in the area of early childhood education. It has been used to examine interactions between adults, between adults and children and to examine the worlds of children's interactions. Microethnography has been used in to examine these interactions in naturalistic settings. These interactions are recorded using either audio or video to allow for reexamination of events frame by frame and over and over again in order to better understand both the verbal and nonverbal communication.

Microethnography has been used to examine cross-cultural differences in communication in early childhood settings as well as in particular placements such as special education. Microethnography also is being used to investigate issues of power and struggle as in the cases of Bennett (1988) and McGrath (2007). Special education research in early childhood appears to be drawn to microethnography due to the nature of the individual context of special education.

Overall microethnography is a painstaking process of conducting research. However, the benefits of examining these interactional experiences can help us better understand human communication. This research in educational environments can also be important in better understanding the interactions that go in inside classrooms or in home school communication. Miscommunication across cultures can lead to conflict and poorer educational outcomes. A better understanding how these miscommunications occur will help educators avoid these errors. Microethnography is the kind of methodology that will us better understand the link between culture and communication.

REFERENCES

Anthrostrategist (2012). *Doing microethnography*. Retrieved from http://anthrostrategy.com/2012/06/24/doing-microethnography/.

Au, K., & Mason, J. (1982). *A microethnographic approach to the study of classroom reading instruction: Rationale and procedures*. Technical Report No. 237. Cambridge, MA: Bolt, Beranek and Newman.

Baker, W. D., Green, J. L., & Skukauskaite, A. (2008). Video-enabled ethnographic research: A micro ethnographic perspective. In Walford, G. (Ed.), *How do you do educational ethnography* (pp. 76–114)? London: Tufnell Press.

Bennett, A. T. (1988). Gateways to powerlessness: Incorporating Hispanic deaf children and families into formal schooling. *Disability, Handicap & Society*, 3(2), 119–151.

Bloome, D., Carter, S., Christian, B., Otto, S., & Shuart-Faris, N. (2005). *Discourse analysis and the study of classroom language and literacy events: A microethnographic perspective.* Mahwah, NJ: Lawrence Earlbaum and Associates.

Bower, H., & Griffin, D. (2011). Can the Epstein model of parent involvement work in a high-minority, high poverty, elementary school: A case study. *Professional School Counseling, 15*(2), 77–87.

Buchbinder, M., Longhofer, J., Barrett, T., Lawson, P., & Floersch, J. (2006). Ethnographic approaches to child care research. *Journal of Early Childhood Research, 4*(1), 45–63.

Carbaugh, D. (2005). *Cultures in conversation.* Mahwah, NJ: Lawrence Erlbaum Associates.

Chami-Sather, G., & Kretschmer, Jr., R. R. (2005). Lebanese/Arabic and American children's discourse in group-solving situations. *Language & Education: An International Journal, 19*(1), 10–31.

Cho, J., & Trent, A. (2006). Validity in qualitative research revisited. *Qualitative Research, 6*(3), 319–340.

Christians, C. (2005). Ethics and politics in qualitative research. In N. Denzin & Y. Lincoln (Eds.) *The Sage handbook of qualitative research* (3rd ed., pp. 139–164. Thousand Oaks, CA: Sage Publications.

Corsaro, W. (2003). *We're friends right? Inside kids' culture.* Washington DC: Joseph Henry Press.

David, T., Tonkin, J., Powell, S., & Anderson, C. (2005). Ethical aspects of power in research with children. In A. Farrell (Ed.) *Ethical research with children* (pp. 124–137). Maidenhead, England: Open University Press.

Denzin, N., & Lincoln, Y. (2005a). Introduction: The discipline and practice of qualitative research. In N. Denzin & Y. Lincoln (Eds.) *The SAGE handbook of qualitative research* (3rd ed., pp. 1–32) . Thousand Oaks, CA: Sage Publications.

Denzin, N., & Lincoln, Y. (2005b). Preface. In N. Denzin & Y. Lincoln (Eds.) *The SAGE handbook of qualitative research* (3rd ed., pp. ix–xix). Thousand Oaks, CA: Sage Publications.

Deyhle, D., Hess, A., & LeCompte, M. (1992). Approaching ethical issues for qualitative researchers in education. In M. LeCompte, W. Millroy, & J. Preissle (Eds.) *The handbook of qualitative research in education* (pp. 597–641). New York, NY: Academic Press.

DuFon, M. (2002). Video recording in ethnographic SLA research: Some issues of validity in data collection. *Language Learning & Technology, 6*(1). 40–59.

Dyson, A. (1998). Folk processes and media creatures: Reflections on popular culture for literacy educators. *Reading Teacher, 51*(5), 392–402.

Ellis, C. (2003). *The autoethnographic I: A methodological novel about autoethnography.* Walnut Creek, CA: Altamira Press.

Erickson, F. (1992). The interface between ethnography and microanalysis: Intellectual antecedents and aims of microanalysis. In M. LeCompte, W. Millroy, & J. Preissle (Eds.), *The handbook of qualitative research in education* (pp. 202–225). New York, NY: Academic Press.

Erickson, F. (2004). *Talk and social theory: Ecologies of speaking and listening in everyday life.* Cambridge, UK: Polity Press.

Foley, D., & Valenzuela, A. (2005). Critical ethnography: The politics of collaboration. In N. Denzin & Y. Lincoln (Eds.), *The SAGE handbook of qualitative research* (3rd ed., pp. 217–234). Thousand Oaks, CA: Sage Publications.

Freeman, M., & Mathison, S. (2009). *Researching children's experiences.* New York, NY: The Guildford Press.

Garcez, P. (1997). Microethnography. In N. Hornberger & D. Corson (Eds.), *Encyclopedia of language and education, vol. 8: Research methods in language and education* (pp. 187–196). Amsterdam: Kluwer Academic Publishers.

Gerrish, K., & Lacey, A. (2010). *The research process in nursing* (6th ed.). Hoboken, NJ: Wiley, John & Sons.

Goffman, E. (1959). *The presentation of self in everyday life.* Indianapolis, IN: Bobbs-Merrill.

Greco, L. (2006). Conversation analysis. In V. Jupp (Ed.), *The SAGE dictionary of social research methods* (pp. 42–43). Thousand Oaks, CA: Sage Publications.

Hobbs, D. (2006). Ethnography. In V. Jupp (Ed.), *The Sage dictionary of social research methods* (pp. 101–102). Thousand Oaks, CA: Sage Publications.

Jacob, E. (1990). Alternative approaches for studying naturally occurring human behavior and thought in special education research. *Journal of Special Education, 24*(2), 195.

Jupp, V. (2006). Reflexivity. In V. Jupp (Ed.) *The SAGE dictionary of social research methods* (pp. 258–259). Thousand Oaks, CA: Sage Publications.

Kim, M. (2006). *An ethnographic study of the culture of a third grade ESL class: ESL education for whole child development.* Unpublished doctoral dissertation, Indiana University.

Kim, M. (2012). Intertextuality and narrative practices of young deaf students in classroom contexts: A microethnographic study. *Reading Research Quarterly, 47*(4), 404–426.

Kon, A. (2006). Assent in pediatric research. *Pediatrics, 117*(5), 1806–1810.

Knotek, S. (2003). Bias in problem solving and the social process of student study teams. *Journal of Special Education, 37*(1), 2–14.

LeBaron, C. (2006). Microethnography. In V. Jupp (Ed.) *The SAGE dictionary of social research methods* (pp. 177–179). Thousand Oaks, CA: Sage Publications.

McDermott, R. P., & Roth, D. R. (1978). The social organization of behavior: Interactional approaches. *Annual Review of Anthropology, 7,* 321–345.

McGrath, W. (2007). Ambivalent partners: Power, trust, and partnership in relationships between mothers and teachers in a full-time child care center. *Teachers College Record, 109*(6), 1401–1422.

Murray, C., Anderson, J., Bersani, H., & Mesaros, R. (1986). Qualitative research methods in special education: Ethnography, microethnography, and ethology. *Journal of Special Education Technology. 7*(3), 15–31.

Mutua, N. (2001). Policied identities: Children with disabilities. *Educational Studies 32*(3), 289–300.

Opie, I. (1994). *The people on the playground.* New York, NY: Oxford University Press.

Paley, V. (1991). *The boy who would be a helicopter.* Cambridge, MA: Harvard University Press.

Paley, V. (1993). *You can't say you can't play.* Cambridge, MA: Harvard University Press.

Pane, D. M., & Rocco, T. S. (2009). Critical microethnography: The search for emancipatory methods [101 paragraphs]. *Forum Qualitative Sozialforschung / Forum: Qualitative Social Research, 10*(2), Art. 12, Retrieved from http://nbn-resolving.de/urn:nbn:de:0114-fqs0902129.

Popescu, C. (2010). The role of (micro)ethnography in classroom research. *Petroleum—Gas University Of Ploiesti Bulletin, Philology Series, 62*(2), 9–16.

Riojas, M. (1998). *A microethnography of Mexican American children during socio dramatic play in a preschool classroom.* Unpublished doctoral dissertation. Austin, TX: University of Texas at Austin.

Riojas-Cortez, M. (2001). Preschoolers' funds of knowledge displayed through sociodramatic play episodes in a bilingual classroom. *Early Childhood Education Journal, 29*(1), 35–40.

Rosenstein, B. (2002). Video use in social science research and program evaluation. *International Journal of Qualitative Methods, 1*(3), 1. Retrieved from http://www.ualberta.ca/~ijqm.

Saukko, P. (2005). Methodologies for cultural studies: An integrative approach. In N. Denzin & Y. Lincoln (Eds.), *The SAGE handbook of qualitative research* (3rd ed., pp. 343–356). Thousand Oaks, CA: Sage Publications.

Sawyer, K. (1997). *Pretend play as improvisation: Conversations in the preschool classroom.* New York, NY: Psychology Press.

Stokrocki, M., & White, I. (1995). A microethnographic study of a novice, bicultural, elementary art teacher: Context, competencies, and concerns. *Visual Arts Research, 21*(1), 51–62.

Sutterby, J. (2002). *Todos somos amigos:* Unpublished Doctoral Disseration. Austin, TX: University of Texas at Austin.

Watson-Gegeo, K. (1997). Classroom ethnography. In N. Hornberger & D. Corson (Eds.), *Encyclopedia of language and education, Vol. 8: Research methods in language and education* (pp. 135–144). Amsterdam: Kluwer Academic Publishers.

Wetherell, M. (2006). Interpretive repetoires. In V. Jupp (Ed.) *The SAGE dictionary of social research methods* (pp. 153–155). Thousand Oaks, CA: Sage Publications.

Wolcott, H. (1999). *Ethnography: A way of seeing.* Walnut Creek, CA: Altamira Press.

Wolfinger, N. (2002). On writing fieldnotes: Collection strategies and background expectancies. *Qualitative Research, 2*(1), 85–95.

CHAPTER 18

PRESCHOOLERS' SELECTIVE LEARNING FROM ADULTS

Lessons for Research Methods in Early Childhood Education

Kathleen H. Corriveau and Julie Dwyer

One of the missions in early childhood education is to provide young children with an opportunity to learn new epistemic and social information—and to prepare young children with the skills needed for a lifetime of successful learning. As such, an important task for children during the early childhood years is to determine how to acquire knowledge in an accurate and efficient manner. When children are learning new information about the world, they have two sources available to them: they can rely on their own, first-hand observations, or they can rely on the information provided by other people. In many educational situations, children have access to both types of information, such as in a lesson on gravity that allows young children to both experience the effects of gravity on falling objects and to hear scientific information about gravity from the classroom teacher, a trusted source. But there are many instances where the information they have about the world can only be learned from others. In those instances, do children believe everything they see and hear?

Although a rich history of research has documented how children learn from first-hand observation (Gopnik & Meltzoff, 1998; Rousseau, 1762/1957; Piaget, 1923/2002) and experiential learning (Duckworth, 2006), the systematic investigation of children's learning from the teacher as a source of information has been relatively understudied. In part, this may have been because of the notion that children are born as a blank slate, and learning is based on experience and perception. If young children are simply sponges soaking up information, then they should learn the new information, regardless of the characteristics of the speaker. Nevertheless, early childhood practitioners have long emphasized the importance of teacher–child relationships in promoting student learning and positive student outcomes (Hamre & Pianta, 2005). Positive relationships help to promote learning, whereas negative relationships are problematic for learning. In this chapter we discuss new research suggesting that, contrary to the Rousseau-Piaget tradition in psychology and the experiential learning tradition in early childhood education, a distrust of the testimony provided by others and a privileging of first-hand knowledge over all other sources may be problematic for healthy learning in early childhood (Harris & Corriveau, 2011). Trust in the claims made by other people is warranted, particularly when it provides children with access to expert information that has been accumulated over generations.

This chapter outlines methodology we have used when exploring preschoolers' selective trust in particular informants. In Part I, we provide a theoretical background to our research question and a rationale for our choice of method to study children's selective trust. The remainder of the chapter is divided into three parts, based on new research exploring two cues young children use when selecting amongst potential informants. In Part II, we discuss how we modified the selective trust paradigm to investigate children's use of prior accuracy when deciding from whom to learn. That is, are children sensitive to the fact that if an informant has previously been a reliable source, she is likely to be a credible source for new information? In Part III, we discuss how we modified the selective trust paradigm to investigate children's use of social group cues when selecting amongst potential informants. If children do not have access to information about a person's prior history of reliability, will they use social information to select amongst informants? Finally, in Part IV, we seek to bring together the methodologies from these various studies. We suggest four points that researchers should be cognizant of when designing, analyzing, and interpreting data from preschool subjects. Although we have focused on children's selective trust, we anticipate that the lessons learned from our work with children will be useful to a broad range of researchers working with preschoolers using behavioral measures.

Throughout this chapter we focus on the decisions we made when designing our experiments, analyzing our data, and interpreting our findings with respect to classroom learning. We hope the novice researcher will pay particular importance to how we chose to use developmentally-appropriate behavioral methods to systematically unpack exactly how young children determine whether or not an informant (such as a teacher) is trustworthy. Although the focus of this chapter is on children's trustworthy decisions, we believe this method is flexible enough to be of use to researchers interested in a variety of questions pertinent to early childhood education.

PART I: CHILDREN'S SELECTIVE TRUST

Children's ability to be selective in their choice of informant is important because much of what children come to know has to be learned on the basis of what other people tell them rather than via first-hand observation. For example, when learning about domains such as history, science and religion, it is difficult for children to gather the relevant information from their day to day observations of the world. Thus, children must rely on the information provided by others (Harris & Koenig, 2006). Consider learning about the shape of the Earth. Although one could conceivably learn that the Earth is a sphere from observing the planet at a distance from space, it is highly unlikely that most children will have that experience. In fact, most observable data about the shape of the Earth that we encounter on a daily basis indicates that it is flat. To learn that Earth is a sphere, children must rely on parents and teachers to supply them with relevant information. Indeed, even when learning about more mundane aspects of life, such as what to expect from a visit to a restaurant, children are reliant on critical information from others. They are generally not able to deduce, simply from observation, which artifacts (e.g., the cash register) or individuals (e.g., the chef, the wait staff) are highly important aspects of eating in a restaurant. They rely on more expert others to acquire this information. Their selective trust in particular informants is likely to provide a useful filter against misleading information—even if this filter is far from infallible.

It is interesting to note that such trust in the information provided by other people is in contrast with the views held by a developmental psychologist whose work will be familiar to early child educators: Jean Piaget. Piaget (1923/2002) promoted active exploration and observation in order to achieve knowledge, and asserted that children who learned on the basis of other people's testimony were prone to "verbalism," a superficial rather than a deep understanding of the phenomenon in question. A similar approach, based on the Piagetian notion of cognitive autonomy, can be seen in contemporary educational settings in the form of inquiry-based approaches to learning. Educators adopting this approach view the role of the teacher as facilitative in nature rather than as arbiters of knowledge; the teacher guides children through the scientific processes of posing questions, observing, hypothesizing, investigating, and making inferences based on their findings (French, 2004).

When children judge the accuracy of an informant, they can think about trustworthiness from both an epistemic and an interpersonal point of view. That is, we expect a trustworthy source to act in a thoughtful, sensitive fashion. For example, we expect them to keep their promises, to provide help and solace when asked to do so and to be discreet if we confide in them. Quite a large body of research has investigated young children's developing understanding of interpersonal trust in friendships with peers and adults (e.g., Rotenberg, 2010). By contrast, it has only been in the past 10 or so years that researchers have systematically explored children's developing understanding of informant trustworthiness from an epistemic stance. As adults, we are often aware of our own lack of expertise or information on a given topic and we turn to others for guidance. For example, we seek information about medical, financial, and culinary matters. Yet we also recognize that individuals differ in the extent to which they provide accurate information: some informants are more trustworthy than others—in this epistemic sense. In this chapter, we describe how we used experimental methods with forced-choice questions to study a particular psychological question. Specifically, we focus on the methodology we used to study two potentially related but different aspects of trust—children's judgment of informant accuracy (epistemic trust) and children's use of social cues when gauging trustworthiness (social group trust). Note that although we focus on how this method is used to study children's selective trust, we believe that using an experimental forced-choice design is a potentially powerful means to discerning early biases in young children's learning. Although this method may be seen by classroom instructors as "removed" from the day-to-day aspects of teaching and learning, we believe that using experimental methods allows for researchers to uncover specific aspects of the way children learn, that can, in turn, inform classroom practice. We hope that novice researchers pay particular attention to the fact that we consider the age of the child and concomitant cognitive and language capabilities when designing our tasks.

It could be argued that social group trust and epistemic trust are simply two different aspects of the same package. For example, if we are prepared to share private information with someone—to trust them interpersonally—we are also often willing to act on the advice that they offer—to trust them epistemically. The image of the trusted babysitter typically includes both social and epistemic aspects. From a child's perspective, a babysitter is a person in whom they can confide, but also is a person the parents can trust to make developmentally-appropriate decisions with regards to the child's safety. Yet sometimes we do not need to pay attention to both interpersonal and epistemic aspects of an individual. For example, when making decisions about what brand of toy to purchase for a young child, we care only about the company's safety record, and not at all about their philanthropic endeavors. By contrast, when making decisions about which children to invite over after school, we care only about whether or not the child is nice, and not at all about the child's rank in school. Thus, although there are plenty of occasions in the life of a young child where the social and epistemic aspects of trust overlap, there are certainly cases where reliance on both is contingent rather than necessary. The two dimensions of trustworthiness are empirically separable. We consider these dimensions in Parts II and III.

There are several methods we could have used to research how children use adults as sources of information. For example, we could have observed classrooms to determine general characteristics of early childhood educators. However, how would we know that we had captured all of the important trustworthy characteristics, and how would we link those characteristics to children's perceptions of trustworthiness? We also could have observed teacher-child interactions in early childhood settings. But observation alone would not allow us to discern to what extent a child views her teacher as an accurate source of information and on what basis she is making those decisions. Alternatively, we could have designed surveys asking children to rate particular teacher characteristics. However, a good amount of social psychological research has indicated that people's predictions of what they *think* is important does not always coincide with how they *actually behave* in real-world situations (e.g., Gilbert, Pinel, Wilson, Blumberg & Wheatley, 1998).

Thus, although the methods described above can be useful for answering many questions pertaining to early childhood, the most appropriate method for our research question was using a behavioral approach where we worked with children one-on-one in an experimental setting. Note that it might be surprising for some early childhood educators to think about conducting research important for classroom learning by going *outside of the classroom*. We acknowledge that although the carefully-controlled conditions we used in our experiments may increase the internal validity of our findings, such conditions may not be the reality in a messy, busy, real-world classroom (thereby calling the external validity of our findings into question). Nevertheless, we believe those pristine conditions allow us to systematically unpack exactly what children are doing when they are making such learning decisions. Further research can build on these findings, moving methodically from a laboratory environment to the more complex early childhood classroom. As the reader will see in the following sections, our findings are extremely reliable (both within a child and across multiple research groups) and have high internal validity. We describe our method in more detail below.

PART II: CHILDREN'S USE OF (IN)ACCURACY WHEN MONITORING INFORMANTS

Primary caregivers and other family members are typically children's earliest and primary source of information about the world. As children begin to enter the world of preschool education and eventually move into more formal schooling, early childhood teachers become another important fount of knowledge for children about any number of domains. Traditionally, it has been taken for granted that young children unflinchingly view both their primary caregivers and teachers as inherently trustworthy and reliable sources of information. However, there is recent evidence that children as young as three are surprisingly discerning in their attribution of trustworthiness to adults around them (e.g., Harris, 2007). In this section, we describe one method a young child could use to select amongst informants—namely, whether or not the informant's statement is consistent with the child's own past experience. If the informant's statement is consistent with past experience, the child can mark this informant as "accurate" and choose to turn to this informant in future learning scenarios; if not, the child can mark the informant as "inaccurate" and refrain from learning future information provided by this speaker. In this manner, children would be evaluating informants using the same heuristics used to evaluate first-hand observation. Below, we review the method used to initially explore children's use of prior accuracy when selecting amongst informants. We then discuss more recent work exploring how and why children use accuracy as a cue to future trustworthiness.

The earliest studies exploring children's use of prior accuracy when selecting amongst informants compared children's selective preference for learning from the previously accurate informant over the previously inaccurate informant (Clément, Koenig, & Harris, 2004; Koenig, Clément, & Harris, 2004; Koenig & Harris, 2005). These studies used word learning as the dependent measure because of the mutual exclusivity properties in word learning (Merriman & Bowman, 1989). Specifically, at least in very early word learning, young children are biased to assume a word only has one primary label (Markman, 1992), and that label is shared across multiple speakers. Thus, when two informants offer conflicting labels for an object, the child can readily interpret this interaction and think about one informant as being "accurate" or "trustworthy" and the other informant as being "inaccurate" or "untrustworthy." Word learning allows children to utilize the Gricean maxims of quality and relevance (Grice, 1975). That is, children expect their interlocutors to provide accurate (truthful) and relevant information, and are surprised when they do not do so. A violation of these Gricean maxims suggests that the interlocutor may not be a good pragmatic partner.

In the early selective trust studies, 3- and 4-year-old children were asked to judge the relative trustworthiness of two different informants—one who is accurate, and one who is inaccurate (Clément, Koenig, & Harris, 2004; Koenig, Clément, & Harris, 2004; Koenig & Harris, 2005;). In a training or familiarization phase, both informants labeled familiar objects with familiar labels, thus demonstrating consistent accurate or inaccurate behavior. Then, in a test phase, the informants labeled novel objects with conflicting novel labels. The dependent measures were the extent to which children chose to ask the previously accurate informant for help, and the extent to which they chose to endorse her novel label as accurate.

For example, in Koenig and Harris (2005), 3- and 4-year-old children were introduced to the informants in two phases. In a training phase, children watched a video in which two informants were asked by an interviewer to label familiar objects with familiar labels. For example, when viewing a cup, the interviewer would ask, "Can you tell me what this is called?" One informant would say "That's a cup" and the other informant would say "That's a plate." The experimenter then turned to the child, and asked, "What do you think it's called?" Children's responses were recorded, and no feedback was given in the case of incorrect answers. This was repeated over three successive trials. Importantly, at the end of this phase, children were asked to explicitly judge the relative accuracy of the two informants. The experimenter pointed to a still shot of the two informants and asked, "Which of these two girls was better at saying the names of these things?" This explicit judgment question allowed the researchers to determine whether or not young children were tracking the consistent accurate and inaccurate responses and using that information to determine who was "better" at the task.

In designing this procedure, there were three possible methods the investigators could have used to expose children to the two informants. First—and perhaps most obvious—investigators could have chosen to present the two informants to the child live. This is perhaps the most real-world scenario, but live presentation with young children has multiple drawbacks. First, from a practical point of view, it requires that three researchers (at a minimum) are present for every testing session. This is more difficult to schedule than if only one researcher was needed for each testing session. Moreover, the inclusion of these additional researchers opens the possibility for greater experimenter error across the study's lifetime. Finally—and perhaps most importantly—live presentation requires the preschooler to interact with three unknown researchers, which may be overwhelming to young children, and may yield less verbal information than if the child interacted with one researcher.

An alternative method is used by Clément et al. (2004). Here, the experimenter presents the child with two puppets, who each interact with the child (through the experimenter), providing accurate and inaccurate information. This decreases the number of people in the room, but from a theoretical point of view comes with substantial drawbacks. Specifically, it could be the case that young children think about puppets in a fantasy-based context, and therefore do not monitor puppet sources in the same manner as they do for human sources. There is some research to suggest that this may be the case. Moreover, the excellent work on children's imagination and pretend play in the last 20 years suggests that children often display more sophisticated reasoning strategies in a fantasy context than they do in an analogous nonfantasy context (e.g., Dias & Harris, 1988, 1990; Sobel & Lillard, 2002; Sobel, 2006). Thus, although more practical, the inclusion of puppets leaves researchers open to possible critiques on the robustness of the design.

A third method is to present young children with static images or video stimuli to incorporate visual and auditory information. This is the method that was used by Koenig, Clément & Harris (2004) and Koenig & Harris (2005). Here, the experimenter presents a video to the child, pausing the video at designated points to ask experimental questions. Video stimuli offer substantial benefits from a design perspective. First, video presentation allows for relative standardization of the procedure, ensuring that all children are exposed to the same informant characteristics. For example, in the Koenig & Harris (2005) study, children can be presented with different video stimuli during the training period (varying informant accuracy), but all children can be shown the same video stimuli during the test period. Thus, researchers can infer that children's selective preference for one informant's novel label is related to her prior accuracy. Second, video presentation allows researchers to control the pace of the testing session. That is, the experimenter can wait to start the video until the preschooler is attending to the stimuli. This is especially important when working with young children, as executive functioning is rapidly developing at this age (Carlson, 2005). Despite these substantial benefits, there are some limitations when interpreting the findings from experiments using video stimuli. Specifically, researchers may be questioned as to whether children will behave similarly in real-life scenarios than they do when attempting to acquire information from a video source. Indeed, past research has suggested that young children learn more readily from live informants than they do from video (Anderson & Pempek, 2005). These findings actually suggest that the importance of selectively learning from real teachers in real classrooms may be *underestimated* in research investigating children's selective learning from a person on video. Thus, we believe the benefits of video presentation with young children far outweigh the potential limitations in interpretation.

A second design choice warrants discussion. In all three of the initial studies exploring children's selective trust, the dependent measures were forced-choice questions. In a test phase (consisting of four trials), children were presented with a novel object and asked who they would like to ask to learn the name of the object (informant 1 or informant 2). After the two informants labeled the object, children were invited to say what they thought the object was called (label 1 or label 2). The use of forced choice questions with young preschoolers is critical as a measure of children's selective trust. Although it would have been possible (and likely very interesting) to ask children open-ended "why" questions in this context, the quality of these responses has the potential to be influenced by any number of unmeasured variables (e.g., individual verbal ability, personality traits, etc.). For example, asking an open-ended "why" question puts demands on both a child's receptive and expressive language capabilities. Not only does a child have to comprehend the question being asked, but she must craft a contingent response that accurately communicates her attribution of trustworthiness of a source. Given the complexity of comprehending and responding to open ended questions, a highly verbal child (both receptively and expressively) and a less verbal child who were each equally accurate in their attribution of trustworthiness would likely give very different answers when asked "why?". For this reason, in these studies, the use of forced choice questions was preferable to open-ended questions as a source of information regarding very young children's understanding. The questions used here allowed children to respond *either* verbally (e.g., "It's a wug") *or* by pointing to one of the two informants. Although forced-choice questions do require children to use their receptive language capacities to understand the question being asked, this method of questioning at least removes the confound of differing expressive verbal abilities between subjects. Despite having only forced-choice questions, data could be analyzed using parametric statistics (ANOVAs and t-tests) because children's responses to these two questions (children were asked "Who do you want to ask?" and "What do you think this is called?") were scored as 1 if they chose the previously accurate informant or 0 if they chose the previously inaccurate informant. These scores were then summed across the multiple trials (3 or 4, depending on the study). Thus, the researchers could create a semicontinuous dependent variable. For example, in a study that had two questions per trial and three test trials, a child could have a "total trust score" between 0 and 6. Thus, the dependent variable (children's "scores") is now semicontinuous, ranging from 0 to 6.

Note that it is only appropriate to collapse across the two types of questions ("Who do you want to ask?", "What do you think this is called?") when the questions being combined address the same construct (e.g., construct validity). To ensure that this was the case, most researchers conduct correlations of the questions prior to collapsing across both questions (e.g., Corriveau, Kinzler & Harris, 2013).

As an alternative analysis strategy, the individual questions could have been analyzed separately with nonparametric statistics (chi-square or McNemar's test for change), but parametric statistics are preferred in quantitative analysis, as they are more robust to Type II error (Kirk, 1969). Some studies have analyzed the data from selective trust paradigms using both parametric and nonparametric statistics, yielding similar results (see, for example, Sobel & Corriveau, 2010). Thus, we suggest that, although the sum of these categorical, forced-choice questions is only semicontinuous, current research has supported the use of parametric statistics. Therefore, this particular design allows for the most flexibility in child responses (using forced-choice questions with either verbal or nonverbal responses) while still allowing for parametric statistics.

We do want to emphasize the importance of carefully considering the number of test trials. It is often the case in early childhood research that studies include only one trial—or at best a very small number of test trials. We urge researchers to consider designs such as the one presented here that allows for a measure of reliability within the child (how they systematically respond to the forced-choice questions) but also acknowledges developmental limitations in preschoolers' attentional capabilities.

Taken together, the results of these initial investigations into children's accuracy are relatively straightforward in their interpretation. Overall, both 3- and 4-year-olds proved to be remarkably good at monitoring, predicting and utilizing the difference between the two informants (Clément et al., 2004; Koenig et al., 2004; Koenig & Harris, 2005). Thus, in answering the explicit judgment questions, children reliably picked out the informant who was "not very good" at answering the questions. When given an opportunity to ask for information, they preferred to turn to the knowledgeable as opposed to the ignorant informant. Finally, when given an opportunity to endorse the name supplied by one informant or the other, they tended to endorse the name supplied by the knowledgeable informant—although this selective pattern of endorsement was significant for 4-year-olds but not for 3-year-olds (Koenig & Harris, 2005). These results imply that children rapidly form an assessment of the knowledge of one informant as compared to another. A considerable body of research suggests that children rarely use trait terms to describe and explain people's actions until middle childhood (Yuill, 1993; Liu, Gelman & Wellman, 2007). By contrast, these findings suggest that in the domain of epistemic reliability, at least, preschoolers quickly detect regularities in the behavior of people they have just met and they use those regularities to anticipate people's future behavior.

Despite this relatively straightforward interpretation, several questions remain. First, do task demands account for the reason for the developmental difference between 3- and 4-year-olds in this task? Second, how long do children retain a bias for learning from a previously accurate over a previously inaccurate informant? Third, are children building up trust in an accurate informant, or decreasing trust in an inaccurate informant? We investigated these questions in a series of studies. Below, we systematically walk through our thought process in design, analysis and interpretation.

How Can We Interpret the Developmental Difference Between 3- and 4-Year-Olds?

In the Koenig & Harris (2005) study, 4-year-olds—but not 3-year-olds—selectively endorsed the label provided by the previously accurate informant. What is the reason for this developmental difference? To explore this question, we designed a series of experiments to test two separate hypotheses about the differences between 3- and 4-year-old children (Pasquini, Corriveau, Koenig, & Harris, 2007, Experiment 1). We outline each of these hypotheses below, to show the relationship between our research question and our design approach.

Koenig and Harris (2005) suggested that 3-year-olds' inferior performance when choosing between accurate vs. inaccurate speakers might be explained in terms of their limited understanding of false belief. Three-year-olds typically lack the ability to represent the false beliefs that underlie mistaken utterances and actions (Wellman, Cross, & Watson, 2001). For example, when given a box of Band-Aids, children will predict there will be bandages inside. They will subsequently be shown that the box actually contains something unexpected (for example, candles) and then asked what they had originally thought was inside. Three-year-olds typically claim that they had thought there would be candles—even though they had previously said they thought there would be bandages. Four-year-olds, on the other hand, are more likely to claim that they did not have knowledge of the unexpected event (Gopnik & Astington, 1988). Based on this inability to understand and incorporate false information, 3-year-olds may not know how to interpret an informant who consistently misnames objects because they do not yet understand the false beliefs that may motivate them (Gopnik & Astington, 1988; Wellman et al., 2001). To determine if selective trust is associated with an understanding of false beliefs, we included a standard assessment of false belief understanding like the example mentioned above. If performance on this task is predictive of selective trust after controlling for age, this would support the proposal that selective trust depends on children's ability to attribute mistaken utterances to false beliefs.

An alternative explanation for 3-year-olds' inferior performance is that despite some ability to interpret misnaming, 3-year-olds found it difficult to differentiate and keep track of the accurate versus the inaccurate informant. On this hypothesis, 3-year-olds might show selective trust if the difference between the two informants were more obvious or salient. To test this hypothesis, we modified the Koenig & Harris (2005) procedure in the following ways (Pasquini, Corriveau, Koenig, & Harris, 2007). First, we kept the position of the informants (left side or right side) fixed within informants, although this was varied across subjects. In the Koenig & Harris (2005) training trials, the location of the two informants was not fixed. Thus, on trial 1, the accurate informant may be on the left-hand side of the screen, but on trial 2, she may be on the right-hand side. This was a purposeful decision, as successful extraction of the informant characteristic (accuracy) could not be explained by a simple side-bias. Nevertheless, it made the task much more difficult for young children, as they first needed to search for and locate the accurate informant before they could update their representation of her with the new labeling information. Because monitoring which person had provided which information (source monitoring) is still developing in preschool (Gopnik & Graf, 1988), we wanted to remove that demand from the task to focus solely on accuracy monitoring. Second, to help the child explicitly remember the two informants, the experimenter referred to each informant by the color shirt she was wearing and used this name during each trial. This allowed the subjects to have an explicit label for both informants. Third, we increased the amount of exposure to each informant by increasing the number of familiar objects that each informant labeled (from 3 to 4). By making these three modifications to the task, we anticipated that it would be easier for young children to keep track of which informant had been previously accurate—and to use that information when deciding from which informant to learn novel labels.

We found that both 3- and 4-year-olds were able to selectively ask for information from and endorse the information provided by the previously accurate informant (over the previously inaccurate informant; Pasquini, Corriveau, Koenig, & Harris, 2007, Experiment 1: 100%-0% condition). Thus, 3-year-olds' chance-level performance in Koenig & Harris (2005) may have been due to the difficult task demands—and not because they were unable to selectively monitor for accuracy information. Nevertheless, there was still an age difference between the 3- and 4-year-olds, with 3-year-olds choosing the previously accurate informant 68% of the time, and 4-year-olds choosing her about 86% of the time, on average. Thus, the earlier conclusions of Koenig and Harris (2005) do stand, but with important qualifications. Although, as they claimed, selective trust improves between the ages of 3 and

4, this is not because 3-year-olds are incapable of selective trust. So long as the two informants can be easily discriminated and children have enough exposure to them, 3-year-olds display selective trust.

We were also interested in examining false belief understanding as a potential mechanism underlying the development of selective trust between the ages of 3 and 4. We found that 4-year-olds outperformed 3-year-olds on the false belief task, with 3-year-olds performing significantly below chance and 4-year-olds performing at chance levels. However, correlation analyses controlling for age did not detect a relationship between false belief understanding and success in the test trials. Furthermore, children who answered every false belief question incorrectly were still above chance in demonstrating selective trust, indicating that selective trust does not require an understanding of false belief.

However, if false belief does not explain the age difference in performance between 3- and 4-year-olds, what does? We were able to improve 3-year-olds' performance by reducing task demands in the procedure, but we were unable to eliminate these age differences completely. One hypothesis is that the strategy used by the two age groups to solve the task is different. A second question in Pasquini et al. (2007) was whether children would monitor for accuracy and inaccuracy under less certain conditions (e.g., one informant was mostly correct, but made an error). Four-year-olds were sensitive to relative accuracy and inaccuracy information, selectively preferring to learn from an informant who was correct on 75% of trials, but incorrect on 25% over an informant who was correct on 25% of trials, but incorrect on 75% of trials (Pasquini et al., 2007; Experiment 2). By contrast, 3-year-olds performed at chance when judging between two informants who both had erred at least once. Based on these findings, we might infer that 3-year-olds are more sensitive to inaccuracy information when judging between informants, whereas 4-year-olds are sensitive to both accuracy and inaccuracy information (note that we come back to this question later on p. 613). More research is needed to determine just what—if anything—3-year-olds are learning from an inaccurate source. Findings could have implications for developing educational interventions and informing ideal teacher-child interactions with young children at different ages.

How Long Do Children Trust an Accurate Source?

In the studies described above, children were asked to select amongst sources immediately following their accurate and inaccurate claims. Thus, although we had interpreted that children access and use accuracy-related information in a trait-like manner, a trait-based interpretation would predict that children's memory for accurate and inaccurate sources should remain stable over time. However, as mentioned above, it would be surprising if young preschoolers are able to make a behavior-to-trait evaluation, as this is usually quite difficult for them (Liu, Gelman & Wellman, 2007, but see Fusaro, Corriveau, & Harris, 2011).

To investigate children's memory for, and use of, accuracy information, we showed 3- and 4-year-old children the same videos in which one informant consistently labeled objects accurately and the other informant labeled objects inaccurately (Corriveau & Harris, 2009a). Immediately following this accuracy information, we assessed children's preference for the two informants in test trials. We also tested children's preference for the two informants following a delay. Specifically, half of the preschoolers were visited four days later and shown only novel label trials. The other half of the preschoolers were visited 1 week later (Corriveau & Harris, 2009a, Experiment 2). To introduce the second testing session, the experimenter presented a still shot of the two informants and asked children if they remembered watching a movie about the two informants. She said that the two informants would provide more labels for some more "funny-looking things," and invited children to endorse one of the two labels. If children remembered the informants' differential accuracy and continued to make attributions on the basis of that memory, they should exhibit a preference towards the more accurate informant not just immediately but 4 days and even one week later. By contrast, if children did not remember the differential accuracy, they should perform at chance levels in their preference for asking and endorsing information from both speakers.

We chose to include both 3- and 4-year-olds in this study because it is plausible that 4-year-olds but not 3-year-olds would be able to retain the accuracy information and selectively prefer the previously accurate informant after a delay of several days. Recall that in some experimental setups, 3-year-olds had difficulty selectively endorsing the previously accurate informant even with no delay (Koenig & Harris, 2005). In this study, we used the Pasquini, Corriveau, Koenig, & Harris (2007) modifications to the procedure, in the hopes that 3-year-olds would be able to track accuracy information even after a delay.

We found that both 3- and 4-year-olds were able to retain information about the trustworthiness of the informants, and selectively chose to endorse the information provided by the previously accurate informant. Both age groups of children demonstrated a preference for learning from the previously accurate informant at rates significantly greater than chance, both after a 4-day delay, and after a 1-week delay (Corriveau & Harris, 2009a).

Not only did children require minimal exposure to the differential accuracy of the two informants, they retained and used that information in a relatively stable fashion. Thus, in both age groups selectivity was evident after one week even though the absolute strength of that selectivity was less marked than on initial testing. Note that children were given no further exposure to informants' relative accuracy during the one-week delay and they were never questioned about informants' relative accuracy until the end of the experiment. These findings suggest that children not only formed a rapid initial impression of the two informants, but also continued to rely on that impression. Preschoolers' ability to spontaneously form such impressions is particularly striking given the experimental context. They were not provided information about why the inaccurate informant was incorrect, yet they viewed her as inaccurate.

Future research should explore how much exposure is necessary to generate a stable trait-like representation of accuracy and inaccuracy. Some recent findings suggest that children make trait-like judgments following only one familiarization trial demonstrating informant accuracy and inaccuracy (Fusaro, Corriveau & Harris, 2011). In addition, data from adults suggests that brief initial impressions (as brief as 2 seconds exposure) are subsequently retrieved in a relatively automatic fashion. Thus, on re-exposure to individuals previously associated with distinctive behaviors, adults retrieve that information even when making other, distinct judgments about that individual (Todorov, Gobbini, Evans, & Haxby, 2007; Todorov & Ullman, 2002, 2003). In future research, it will be interesting to determine both how little exposure is necessary for young children to form a lasting impression about an informant and whether they are prone to the same type of automatic retrieval. Moreover, although the delay length was relatively long in the Corriveau & Harris (2009a) study, future research could explore the limits of children's explicit memory for and use of previous accuracy over longer periods of time.

Do Children Monitor for Accuracy or Inaccuracy?

Despite the robust evidence that preschoolers are able to track and selectively choose to learn from a previously accurate source, the exact basis for such a choice is unclear. In all the experiments described above, one informant was accurate all of the time whereas the other informant was inaccurate all of the time. To test whether children monitor for accuracy or inaccuracy in informants—or both—we manipulated the earlier study design by presenting children with accurate, inaccurate, or neutral informants (Corriveau, Meints, & Harris, 2009). We predicted that children might adopt at least three different strategies in tracking relative accuracy. First, they might take an informant's accuracy for granted but track and remember an informant's inaccuracy. Thus, preschoolers would adopt a stance of default trust but withdraw that default trust when they detect error. This simple model explains the above results by assuming that children come to mistrust an informant who is consistently or mostly inaccurate.

A second possibility is that children do the reverse. They do not take accuracy for granted. Instead, they track informants' claims for truth and take notice whenever accurate claims are made. More specifically, they build up trust in an informant who proves to be consistently or mostly accurate. This strategy is consistent with the possibility that children might register the fact that an informant has erred but keep no record of that error. For example, they might notice when an object has been misnamed—a sensitivity that is displayed by toddlers of 16 months (Koenig & Echols, 2003)—but fail to characterize the speaker as in any way untrustworthy. Again, this model explains all recent results but it does so by emphasizing the accumulation of trust as opposed to mistrust.

A third possibility is that children monitor concurrently for both truth and falsity. Not only do they accumulate trust in informants who produce true claims, they accumulate mistrust in those who make false claims. This model explains the findings reported so far by assuming that earlier studies were optimally, albeit inadvertently, designed to provoke preschoolers into maximal differentiation between the two informants with the accurate informant eliciting trust and the inaccurate informant eliciting mistrust.

Of these three strategies, the first would appear to be the simplest and most plausible. After all, obvious inaccuracy in communication is the exception rather than the rule especially in the context of adult-child communication. Accordingly, it makes sense that children would bring to any unfamiliar interlocutor an expectation that he or she will be informative and accurate. It seems more plausible that children bring a stock of trust to each new encounter, but nevertheless notice and record signs of untrustworthiness.

In order to assess whether 3- and 4-year-olds use any of the three strategies just described, we designed an experiment that retained many of the features of earlier studies but the initial video familiarization period with the two informants was systematically varied (Corriveau, Meints, & Harris, 2009). We presented children with three separate conditions (between-subjects). First, in the Accurate-Inaccurate condition, we used the standard procedure where one informant was consistently accurate in naming objects and one informant was consistently inaccurate. Second, in the Accurate-Neutral condition, a consistently accurate informant was included but the second informant made only neutral remarks (e.g., "Let me take a look at that") that could not be easily evaluated for their truth. Third, in the Inaccurate-Neutral condition, a consistently inaccurate informant was paired with a neutral informant.

If children monitor for inaccuracy, they should bring default trust to each unfamiliar informant, but come to mistrust an informant who proves inaccurate. Hence, they should display selective trust in the Accurate-Inaccurate and Inaccurate-Neutral conditions, because in each of those conditions one of the two informants makes false claims. By contrast, in the Accurate-Neutral condition, neither informant makes a false claim so that both informants should retain children's default trust. On the other hand, if children build up trust on the basis of accuracy, ignoring inaccuracy, they should display selective trust in the Accurate-Inaccurate and Accurate-Neutral conditions but not in the Inaccurate-Neutral condition, where neither informant provides any evidence of accuracy. Finally, if children are sensitive to both accuracy and inaccuracy, they should display selective trust across all three conditions. Moreover, selectivity might be especially marked in the Accurate-Inaccurate condition because children would have a double opportunity to evaluate the two informants, i.e., to simultaneously build up trust in the accurate informant and to reduce trust in the inaccurate informant.

The results from the study by Corriveau, Meints, and Harris (2009) indicate that children's pattern of trust varied both by condition and age (see Figure 18.1). In the Accurate-Inaccurate condition, both age groups were more likely to trust the accurate informant although this effect was stronger for 4-year-olds than 3-year-olds. This finding is consistent with previous studies showing that when they meet two unfamiliar informants, both 3- and 4-year-olds trust an accurate informant rather than an inaccurate informant

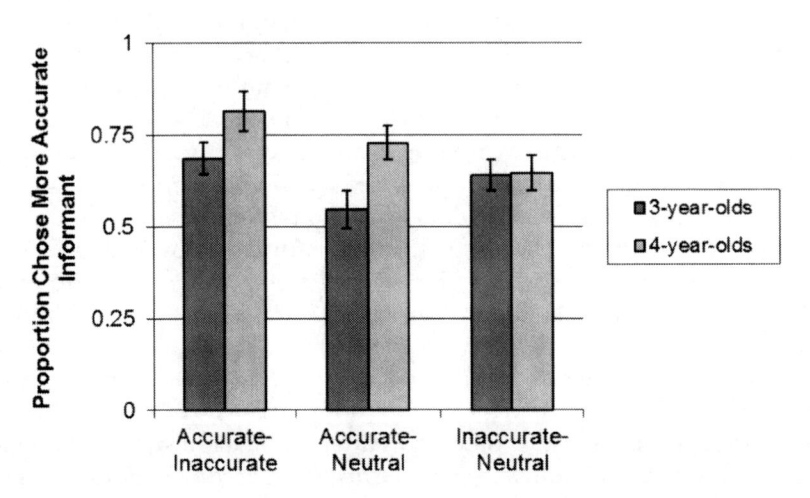

Figure 18.1 Proportion of choices directed at the more trustworthy informant by age (3-year-olds, 4-year-olds) and condition (Accurate-Inaccurate, Accurate-Neutral, Inaccurate-Neutral). Figure adapted from Corriveau, Meints & Harris (2009).

and that the effect is more robust among 4-year-olds than 3-year-olds (e.g, Clément, Koenig, & Harris, 2004; Corriveau & Harris, 2009a,b; Koenig, Clément, & Harris, 2004; Koenig & Harris, 2005). In the Inaccurate-Neutral condition, both age groups were likely to trust the neutral informant more than the inaccurate informant and did so to the same extent. In the Accurate-Neutral condition, only the 4-year-olds were selective, showing greater trust in the accurate informant. Three-year-olds, were indiscriminate between the two informants.

A simple and plausible explanation for this pattern of results is that 3-year-olds monitor for inaccuracy but not for accuracy. Errors reduce their trust in an informant but accuracy does not increase it. Thus, in the two conditions where one of the two informants clearly made errors (Accurate-Inaccurate; Neutral-Inaccurate), 3-year-olds preferred to trust the informant who had not been inaccurate. By contrast, 4-year-olds monitor for both inaccuracy and accuracy. Inaccuracy reduces their trust in an informant but, in addition, accuracy increases it. Thus, when both cues are available, as in the Accurate-Inaccurate condition, their differentiation between the two informants is maximized; when only one cue is available, they are selective but less markedly so. This interpretation that young children first monitor for inaccuracy, and only later monitor for accuracy is consistent with the results from Corriveau, Meints & Harris (2009), as well as from Pasquini et al. (2007; Experiments 1 & 2) and Koenig & Jaswal (2011).

How can we account for the change in strategy between 3 and 4 years? More specifically, why do 4-year-olds but not 3-year-olds trust an accurate over a neutral informant? As we mention above, one hypothesis is that this shift is related to children's developing understanding of theory of mind. Yet, as mentioned above, recent evidence shows that false belief understanding is not necessary for children to display selective trust in an accurate as compared to an inaccurate informant (Pasquini et al., 2007).

One way to reconcile these findings is to suggest the following two stage hypothesis concerning the development of accuracy monitoring. First, even in the absence of false belief understanding, preschoolers can monitor for inaccuracy and accumulate mistrust in an informant who makes inaccurate claims. This is consistent with the results obtained by Pasquini et al. (2007) and by Corriveau, Meints & Harris (2009). Three- and 4-year-olds show a similar level of differentiation between an inaccurate and a neutral informant. Nevertheless, by 4-years of age, children realize that accurate claims should not be taken for granted—informants can and sometimes do make false claims. Thus, they not only accumulate mistrust in an inaccurate informant, they also accumulate trust in an accurate informant. The availability of this double strategy to 4-year-olds implies that even if selective trust is displayed by 3-year-olds, discrimination between a consistently accurate and a consistently inaccurate informant should be stronger among

4-year-olds. This predicted age difference corresponds to the pattern of results obtained by Pasquini et al. (2007) as well as Corriveau, Meints & Harris (2009). This is a hypothesis that could be explored experimentally in future research.

Summing Up: What Have We Learned From Accuracy Monitoring?

Summing up the findings so far, it appears that preschoolers are quite sensitive to variation between informants in their trustworthiness. If one informant is consistently accurate, but the other is either consistently ignorant or inaccurate, 4-year-olds display selective trust. They appropriately judge one informant to be better at answering questions; they anticipate how each informant will describe an unfamiliar object; they seek information from the more reliable informant; and they selectively endorse the information that they receive from that informant. Three-year-olds display the same pattern when confronted by a knowledgeable as compared to an ignorant informant. They are less selective when differentiating between informants in terms of their relative accuracy. Nevertheless, when given repeated evidence of the accuracy of one informant and the inaccuracy of the other, 3-year-olds are also selective. We suggest that the age change in this selectivity is not linked to their improvement on false belief tasks. By contrast, we suggest that the age change may be due to an increased awareness that accuracy-monitoring is useful in addition to the inaccuracy-monitoring that appears to be present at earlier ages. This increased awareness of accuracy-monitoring potentially allows young children to develop concepts of expertise (Danovitch & Keil, 2004; Lutz & Keil, 2002; Keil, Stein, Webb, Billings, & Rozenblit, 2008). There is some evidence that, at least by the age of four, young children recognize the importance of the domain of knowledge when making inferences about expertise. For example, they infer that accurate object labelers will be accurate when providing novel object function information (e.g., Birch, Vauthier, & Bloom, 2008; Koenig & Harris, 2005; Kinzler, Corriveau & Harris, 2011). Future research should focus on 4-year-olds' developing understanding of the importance of accuracy-monitoring and the connection between accuracy-monitoring and the development of expertise.

It is important to acknowledge that the majority of the studies reviewed above have focused on word learning as the dependent variable. We mentioned above why we chose to focus on word learning as an initial way to explore children's selective biases for one informant over another (most notably because word learning allows us to take advantage of children's knowledge of mutual exclusivity). Because we know that early vocabulary is highly related to later achievement and school success (National Reading Panel, 2000; Scarborough, 1998; Sénéchal, Oulette, & Rodney, 2006), it is very important to understand what information children are using during word learning so educators and educational researchers can provide children with the optimal environment for vocabulary acquisition. Nevertheless, it is plausible that children use different strategies when learning about different and more complex phenomena. For example, if children are asked to decide which explanation or argument is correct, would they still rely on prior accuracy? Situations where a child is presented with an explanation or argument abound in an early childhood classroom, ranging from explanations by the teacher about how to care for a classroom pet to an argument presented by the teacher about the importance of eating healthy foods each day. However, to date relatively little research has explored preschoolers' use of accuracy and inaccuracy when monitoring in other domains besides word learning (Brosseau-Liard & Birch, 2010; Mascaro & Sperber, 2009; Fusaro, Corriveau, & Harris, 2011; Ganea & Harris, 2010; Koenig & Harris, 2005; Ma & Ganea, 2010)—and most of these studies include a measure of word learning as a comparison. Future research should explore preschoolers' use of accuracy monitoring when making these more complex decisions.

PART III: CHILDREN'S USE OF SOCIAL GROUP CUES WHEN MONITORING INFORMANTS

In Part II, we discussed evidence suggesting that by the age of four—and in some cases by the age of three, children already possess sophisticated strategies to selectively choose amongst informants on the basis of prior accuracy. We presented a relatively simple experimental paradigm to test this question and explained our subsequent modifications of this paradigm in order to systematically explore 3- and 4-year-olds' strategies when determining from whom to learn. In Part III, we again explain our modifications to the paradigm in order to explore how young children use social group information to judge between and across informants. We focus on social group information because prior epistemic information is unlikely to be the only cue young children use to judge informant trustworthiness. We believe this is true for two reasons.

First, we ended Part II by suggesting an important age change in how 3- and 4-year-olds judge informant accuracy, suggesting that 3-year-olds use inaccuracy information only, but 4-year-olds use inaccuracy and accuracy information. If this were the only information young children were using to select amongst informants, this would promote the following counterintuitive prediction. Suppose a child is asked to learn from their mother (someone they have had a rich history of information about prior accuracy and inaccuracy) or from a stranger (someone they have no history of information about). Although it is likely that the child's mother has provided more accurate information than inaccurate information over the child's lifetime, it is also likely that she has made at least one mistake in her claims. This single inaccurate claim might mark her as an inaccurate source—at least in the case of a 3-year-old child. Thus, our accuracy and inaccuracy model would predict that a 3-year-old child would turn to a stranger over their mother for information. Yet we know that even from infancy, young children are surprisingly selective in whom they turn to for emotional support (Ainsworth et al., 1978). Thus, it would seem fairly implausible that they do not take into account emotional familiarity when making informant decisions.

There is a second reason why it might make sense to think beyond prior accuracy when asking how young children select amongst informants. There are many instances when children do not have access to prior accuracy information—especially in the particular domain of knowledge where children are trying to learn novel information. This would be especially true when acquiring cultural practices and conventions that are not true or false in any straightforward, factual sense. Nevertheless, these cultural conventions are likely to be favored by members of a given culture. For example, in some cultures head-shaking means "no" and in others, it means "yes." How do children maximize the likelihood that what they learn is representative of the cultural group to which they belong? A prior accuracy model would predict that children would perform at chance when selecting amongst unknown individuals—even if one informant is culturally prototypical-acting or talking in ways that reflect the surrounding culture. Yet, there is substantial evidence that preschool children do select amongst unknown individuals when making social judgments, choosing the culturally prototypical individual over the less-prototypical one. For example, they prefer to look more at a toy presented by an informant who speaks the same language as they do over an informant who speaks a foreign language or speaks with a foreign accent (Kinzler, Dupoux, & Spelke, 2007). In addition, they prefer to share more with a child of their same gender, age, or race (Shutts, Banaji & Spelke, 2010), and with a puppet who has friends over a puppet who does not have friends (Olson & Spelke, 2008). They even prefer to socially engage with lucky individuals over unlucky individuals—even though there is absolutely no epistemic rationale for that choice (Olson, Dweck, Banaji, & Spelke, 2006). Taken together, these data suggest that children do make social judgments on the basis of nonepistemic information. Below, we ask whether preschoolers use social group information when making decisions not only about who to socially interact with but also when deciding from whom to learn. We first discuss how we have designed experiments to test whether or not children use informant familiarity when making novel learning decisions. Next, we discuss how children weight informant familiarity and prior accuracy. Finally, we discuss how children use social group information when making trustworthy decisions.

Informant Familiarity

As mentioned above, although the accuracy-inaccuracy model would predict that children would make trustworthy judgments based on relative accuracy (in the case of 4-year-olds) and absolute inaccuracy (in the case of 3-year-olds), it seems likely that young children, like adults, take into account whether or not an informant is known to them. Even before birth, neonates recognize and respond to their mother's voice (Kisilevsky & Hains, 2011; Kisilevsky, Hains, Brown et al., 2009). Their heart rate increases when they hear their mother's voice, and decreases when presented with a stranger's voice, suggesting a preference for listening to mother. Similarly, infants prefer to look at mother's face over a stranger's face (e.g., Pascalis, de Schonen, Morton, Deruelle & Fabre-Grenet, 1995) and prefer infant-directed speech spoken in their native language with a native accent over speech spoken in a foreign language or foreign accent (Kinzler, Dupoux & Spelke, 2007). Based on a large body of literature, we know that young children use this knowledge of the familiar when making socioemotional decisions (Ainsworth et al., 1978). At question here is whether or not they use this same preference for the familiar when they are learning new information. If the goal is simply to learn accurate information about the world, it may be the case that young children do not take into account a speaker's familiarity. However, if the goal is to learn accurate information *relevant to one's own culture* it is likely that they will consider how familiar the source is when learning novel information, both when the information is truth-based (such as learning the correct label for a given referent) and convention-based (such as learning how the particular culture uses a given tool). Below, we describe how we have probed preschoolers' selective preference for someone they know, over someone they do not know, and for someone who talks like them over someone who does not.

Learning from a Familiar Source: The Case of Teachers and Parents

To test whether preschoolers prefer to learn from a familiar source over an unfamiliar one we showed children a film of two preschool teachers labeling novel objects with novel labels and providing novel functions for novel objects (Corriveau & Harris, 2009b). The preschool teachers were working at different sites of the same preschool, so had experience with children in their own center only. Importantly, although neither preschool teacher had any interaction with the children from the other center site, both teachers received the same center-based training and employed the same pedagogical philosophy. This allowed for an ideal scenario wherein the relative preference for Teacher A from Site A should be similar for the preference for Teacher B in Site B; however the preference for Teacher A should differ depending on whether the participants were from Site A or from Site B. As a further probe of the child's relationship with the familiar teacher, we asked the two teachers to rate their relationship with each child in their care using the Student–Teacher Relationship Scale—Short Form (Pianta, 2001). We anticipated that children exhibiting a more close and/ or a less conflictual relationship with the familiar teacher might be especially prone to seek and endorse information from her as opposed to the relatively unfamiliar teacher. By contrast, children who exhibited a more conflictual relationship with the familiar teacher might be less prone to view her as a good source of information, and may even display a preference for the unknown stranger. All children were shown 4 novel object trials where the two teachers provided different novel labels for the novel objects and 4 novel function trials where the two teachers provided different novel functions for the novel objects. We chose to present children with both novel objects and novel functions for two reasons. First, we wanted to have more trials to determine if children's trust in a familiar informant when learning novel information increased over time. We found that young children's selective preference was similar across all 8 trials. Given that young children have hundreds (if not thousands) of experiences learning from their preschool teacher over the course of a school year, it is unsurprising that an additional eight experiences did not make a significant impact on children's selective preference. Second, we wanted to generalize trust in a familiar informant beyond novel word labels. Object functions are arguably more about social conventions than word labels (although one could make the argument that labels for given objects vary across cultural groups—think about the US variation in what is called "soda"), and thus children might prefer to learn from a familiar informant at greater rates than in novel object label trials. Again, although we had predicted that we may see a difference between object label and object function trials, we found that the magnitude of children's preference for the familiar informant did not vary across trial type.

Figures 18.2a and 18.2b display 3-, 4-, and 5-year-old children's preference for Teachers A and B in Sites A and B (collapsed across novel label and novel function trials). There are several findings of interest to note here. First, as anticipated, all three age groups display a selective preference

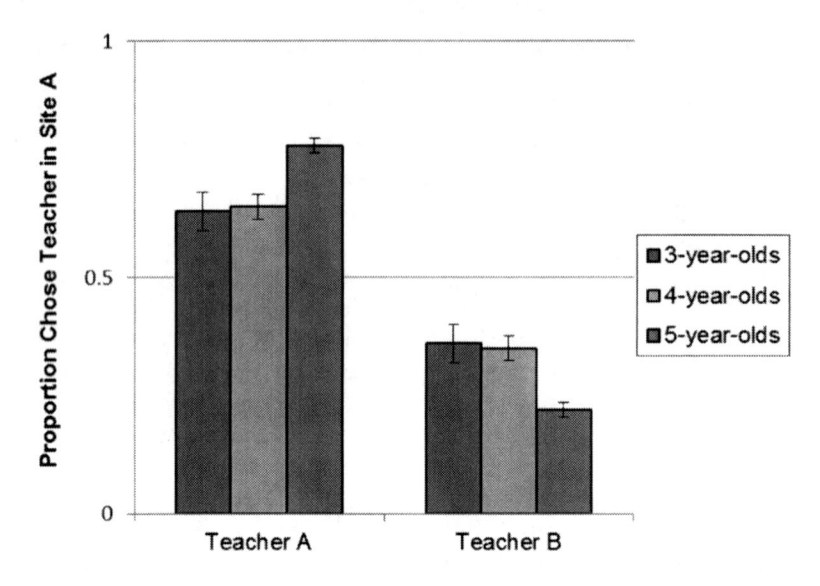

Figure 18.2a Proportion chose Teachers A and B by age (3, 4, 5 years) at Site A. Figure adapted from Corriveau & Harris (2009b).

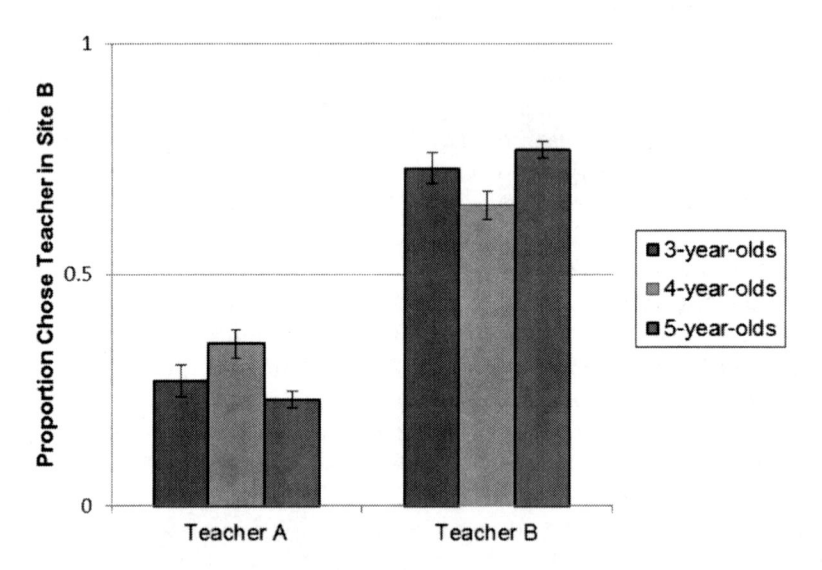

Figure 18.2b Proportion chose Teachers A and B by age (3, 4, 5 years) at Site B. Figure adapted from Corriveau & Harris (2009b).

for the familiar teacher, dependent on site. Second, there is relatively no change in selective preference. Thus, children's preference for the familiar starts early, and is relatively stable across this developmental period. Finally, the relative preference for Teacher A in Site A was similar to the preference for Teacher B in Site B. Thus, because we carefully controlled the study design, we can be confident that children's preference for the familiar demonstrates a true familiarity preference, independent of individual speaker characteristics.

Recall that we had also predicted that children's preference for their familiar teacher would vary based on that teacher's rating of her closeness to the individual students. To our surprise, we did not find that this was the case. One plausible interpretation of this finding is that familiarity—and not emotional relationship—is the largest predictor of children's selectivity. However, both teachers were experienced preschool workers with a stable history of employment at the respective facilities. Hence, they had probably established relatively close relationships with most, if not all, of the children in their care. Indeed, scrutiny of the scores for the group of children at each preschool confirms that scores were concentrated in the upper and lower half of the scales for closeness and conflict, respectively. Thus, neither teacher reported having a distant relation to any child in her care. It remains to be seen if this selective preference would be present in a lower quality preschool classroom where teachers displayed less positive relationships with students. Indeed, it is in these classrooms where we might see less effect of familiarity, both because of the potential interaction between familiarity and emotional relationship and the high rates of teacher-turnover in these classrooms (Barnett, 2003). A second plausible interpretation is that we should have explored the relationship in the reverse—that is, we should have asked *children* to rate their closeness to their teacher. From a methodological point of view, we had chosen to ask teachers to rate their relationship with their students for two reasons: (a) adult ratings are somewhat less subjective than child ratings, and (b) by having only one rater we were able to ask the teacher to think about her relationship with the students *relative to each other*. Nevertheless, it is plausible that child closeness ratings could have uncovered meaningful differences. Future research could explore child closeness and the relationship between closeness and selective learning.

To further explore the relationship between children's preference for the familiar and their emotional relationship with the familiar caregiver, we explored children's preference for their mother over an unfamiliar stranger (Corriveau, Harris, Meins et al., 2009). The mother–child attachment had been measured for each mother-child dyad at 15 months using the Strange Situation procedure (Ainsworth et al., 1978). Thus, we were able to explore how children's preference for the familiar informant (their mother) might vary with attachment security. It could be the case that we would replicate the Corriveau & Harris (2009b) finding with preschool teachers. Under that hypothesis, familiarity—and not emotional relationship—was the most important cue for young children. Thus, we would anticipate that all attachment classifications would display similar levels of preference for their mother in a novel learning task. Alternatively, emotional relationship might play a larger role in children's learning strategies. Under this hypothesis, we would anticipate that preference for mother would vary across attachment classifications.

We tested 4-year-old children on the same novel function and novel object task used in Corriveau & Harris (2009b). As in Corriveau & Harris (2009b), preliminary analysis revealed that children performed similarly with respect to both object names and object functions. Accordingly, Figure 18.3 (Novel Objects tasks) displays the proportional scores calculated with object name trials and object function trials combined across attachment classification (insecure-avoidant, secure, insecure-ambivalent). Inspection of Figure 18.3 reveals that insecure-avoidant children showed no systematic preference for their mother in the Novel Objects task. By contrast, secure children and insecure-ambivalent children displayed more reliance on the mother, systematically accepting information from her in the Novel Objects task. This suggests that in general, most children selectively prefer to learn from their mother, with the exception of insecure-avoidant children.

How might we interpret such a pattern of results? Recall from attachment theory that insecure-avoidant children are classified based on their avoidance of interaction with a caregiver (Ainsworth et al., 1978). Thus, it seems plausible that these children would display relatively autonomous interaction with the environment, perhaps choosing to rely more on their own experience than on information provided by others.

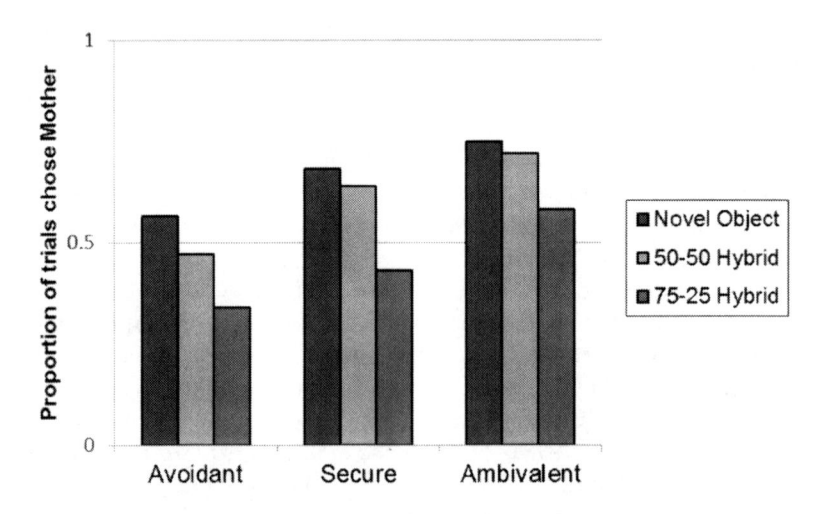

Figure 18.3 Proportion of trials on which children chose their mother by task (Novel Objects, 50–50 Hybrids, 75–25 Hybrids) and attachment group (Insecure-Avoidant, Secure, Insecure–Ambivalent). Figure adapted from Corriveau, Harris, Meins et al. (2009).

We were able to test children again when they were five years old (at 61 months). This allowed us to explore two related questions. First, was children's preference for their mother in a novel learning task stable over time and across attachment classifications? Second, would children's preference for their mother vary if her answer was in conflict with the available perceptual evidence? To answer both of these questions, children completed two further object naming tasks involving unfamiliar stimuli. Our stimuli were animal hybrids, similar to those used by Jaswal (2004; see Figures 18.4a and b for examples). We chose to employ hybrid pictures to make the stimuli seem less novel than unfamiliar objects, but still be able to control the amount of background knowledge the child could bring to a particular picture. For example, one task (50–50 Hybrids) was analogous to the task administered when children were 4 in that there was truly no right or wrong answer. Here, a hybrid might be 50% cow and 50% horse (see Figure 18.4a). In the other task (75–25 Hybrids), a hybrid might be 75% bird and 25% fish (see Figure 18.4b). Here, one informant's response would be in conflict with the child's perceptual experience and the other informant's response

Figure 18.4a Examples of 50–50 Hybrids (Cow-Horse).

Figure 18.4b Examples of 75–25 Hybrids (Bird-Fish).

would be in concord with the experience. This allowed us to contrast perception with familiarity. To do that, the child's mother always provided the label accounting for 25% of the hybrid (e.g., "fish") whereas the stranger provided the label accounting for 75% of the hybrid (e.g., "bird"). Thus, if the child selectively chose the mother on the 75–25 Hybrids, it would suggest that the child was "forgiving" the labeling error that the mother had made, and privileging familiarity over perceptual experience. By contrast, if the child selectively chose the stranger on these trials, it would suggest that the child was privileging perceptual experience over familiarity.

Figure 18.3 (50–50 Hybrids, 75–25 Hybrids) displays children's selective preference for their mother by attachment classification. Two findings warrant attention. First, we replicated the pattern of responses by attachment type in the 50–50 Hybrids task. Insecure-avoidant children performed at chance, whereas securely attached and insecure-ambivalent children selectively preferred to learn from their mother. This suggests that children's learning style is relatively stable over time—at least in the preschool years. Second, all children reduced their preference for the information provided by their mother when her testimony was in conflict with perceptual evidence. Insecure-avoidant and securely attached children selectively preferred the information provided by the stranger (which was consistent with perceptual evidence). By contrast, insecure-ambivalent children showed no selective preference for either informant.

One way to interpret these findings is that, in gathering information, insecure-avoidant children may favor a strategy of self-reliance—they accept information from an informant that is consistent with their own autonomous observation. By contrast, insecure-ambivalent children prefer to rely on a familiar caregiver. Secure children display more flexibility, sometimes adopting a self-reliant strategy and sometimes relying on a familiar caregiver. Consistent with their persistent instability from infancy through the preschool years, disorganized children showed the least consistency in their responses.

Learning from a Familiar-Sounding Source: Informant Syntax and Accent

Although the studies above lend credence to the possibility that young children prefer to learn from known individuals over unknown ones, the question remains why they might do so. We had speculated above that one reason for learning from familiar individuals is a history of positive emotional relationship with her. A separate reason might be that the familiar individual *sounds like* a credible source. That is, regardless of her accuracy or inaccuracy, her language marks her as a member of the same cultural group as the child, thus allowing the child to make an inference as to whether or not she will provide relevant cultural information. Below, we review two separate paradigms to explore this possibility. Note here that we exposed children to previously unfamiliar informants who differ in the way they communicate, thus allowing us to isolate the influence of linguistic factors on children's trust.

First, we asked whether children would prefer to learn from someone who spoke using a relatively complex syntactic structure (passive voice) over someone who used less-complex syntax (active voice; Corriveau, Pickard, & Harris, 2011). In a first, *initial phase*, we presented static pictures of a child performing a familiar action (for example, walking a dog) and asked 4-year-olds to "say what is going on in the picture." All 4-year-olds used active voice when constructing a sentence (e.g., "He's walking the dog"). In a second, *familiarization phase*, we showed children four trials. In each trial, children watched a video where two informants described an action in a picture, but one used active voice (e.g., "The little girl picked up the flower" and the other used passive voice (e.g., "The flower was picked by the girl"). The experimenter repeated the two sentences and asked the child "what would you say?" Note here that we controlled for sentence length and verb tense, such that any preference for the informant would be due to syntactic construction. Children showed no preference for either informant during this phase. Finally, in a third, *test phase*, children received 4 trials where the two informants provided conflicting novel labels for novel objects (e.g., "That's a wug" "That's a dax") and 4 trials where the two informants provided conflicting novel verb constructions for novel actions (e.g., "Yesterday he mung" "Yesterday he mang"). Children were asked to endorse the labels and verbs from one of the two informants. Figure 18.5 displays children's preference for the passive informant on novel label trials and novel verb trials. Inspection of Figure 18.5 reveals a difference in children's preference for the informant based on the child's socioeconomic status. Children who qualified for free lunch (Low-SES) showed a selective preference for learning from the informant who spoke using active voice. By contrast, children who did not qualify for free lunch (Mid-SES) showed a selective preference for learning from the informant who spoke using passive voice. Importantly, the two groups of children did not differ on a post-test measure of syntactic competence or on a measure of receptive vocabulary.

What can we make of these findings—and why is it that some children show preferences based on sentence construction? We argue that linguistic exposure may play a large role in what children look for in a competent speaker. This becomes an important question once children reach school, as the teacher—and the books they read—will most often use passive-voice construction. If lower socioeconomic status children come to the classroom with a bias against passive-voice, this could have a deleterious effect on their

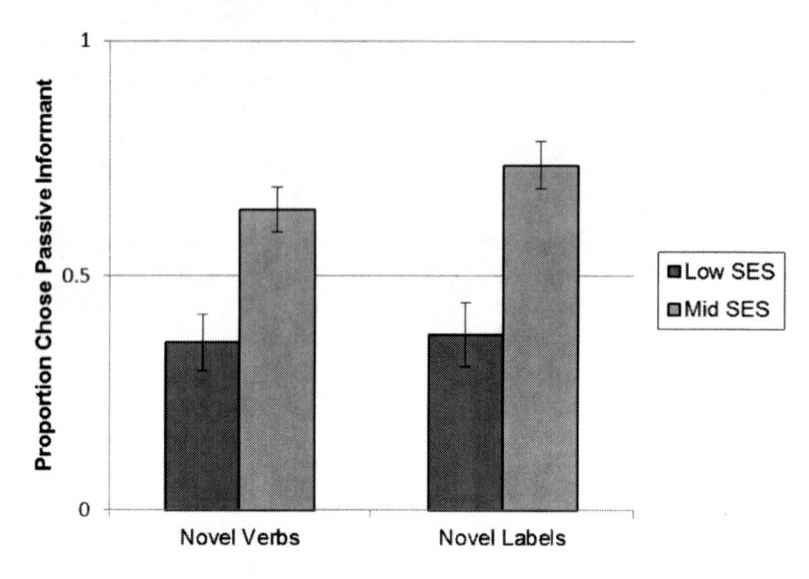

Figure 18.5 Proportion of times children chose the speaker using passive-voice sentence construction by socioeconomic status (Low SES: qualified for free lunch; Mid SES: did not qualify for free lunch). Figure adapted from Corriveau, Pickard & Harris (2011).

learning and place them at an even greater disadvantage beyond the other effects of living in poverty. One possible mechanism for increasing exposure to passive-voice construction for all children is exposure to books. Future research should explore the possibility of including an intervention surrounding book exposure and trust in syntactic structure.

A second way that children could show biases based on language is informant accent. As adults, we all have the experience of listening to a foreign—or regional—accent and judging the speaker based solely on how he sounds. Do young children also make similar judgments? And if so, would they selectively prefer to learn from someone who speaks *like them*, over someone who does not? To explore this question, we focused on monolingual 3- 4- and 5-year-olds (Kinzler, Corriveau & Harris, 2011; Corriveau, Kinzler & Harris, 2013). In an induction phase, half of the children watched a video where two speakers spoke the first four sentences from H.A. Ray's *Curious George* ("This is George. He lived in Africa. He was a good little monkey, but always very curious. One day, George met a man."). One informant spoke with a native, English accent. The other informant spoke with a non-native Spanish accent. The other half of the children watched as the two informants spoke the first few lines of Lewis Carroll's *Jabberwocky* ("Twas brillig and the slithy toves did gyre and gimble in the wabe. All mimsy were the borogroves. And the mome raths outgrabe."). We chose to use two different passages in the induction phase to see if children were sensitive to whether or not the speakers said something with semantic content (Curious George) or was nonsense (Jabberwocky). Both informants were bilingual speakers of English and Spanish, and were filmed speaking with a native and foreign accent, so as to rule out other speaker characteristics.

To test whether or not children were sensitive to speaker accent, we next employed the standard familiarization period used with familiar teachers (Corriveau & Harris, 2009b). Children received 4 trials where the two informants provided novel functions for novel objects (we did not use novel label trials here because we wanted to limit the amount of linguistic exposure to the two speakers). The experimenter pantomimed both functions and then gave the object to the child and asked the child to "show me what this is for." Figure 18.6 displays children's preference for the informant speaking with a native English accent and the informant speaking with a non-native Spanish accent. Inspection of Figure 18.6 reveals that children selectively preferred to learn from the speaker with the native accent, both when she spoke Curious George, and also when she spoke Jabberwocky.

We believe these data have implications for initial biases in classroom learning. There is often a mismatch between the child's accent and the

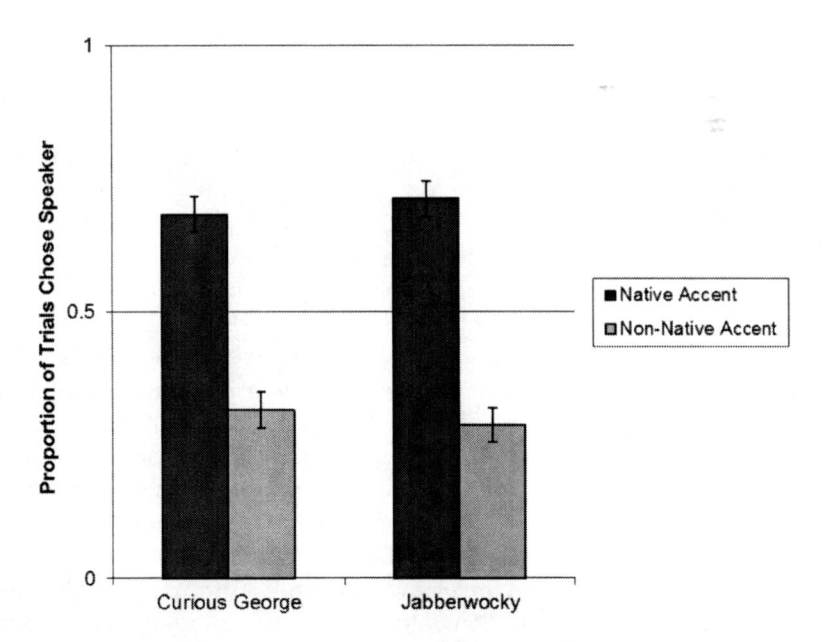

Figure 18.6 Proportion of trials children chose the informant with the native English accent or the non-native Spanish accent by training type (Curious George passage, Jabberwocky passage). Figure adapted from Kinzler, Corriveau & Harris (2011).

teacher's accent. How might this affect children's subsequent trust in her? There are a few important caveats to the extent to which we can make inferences based on these data. The current set of studies focused on monolingual English-speaking children. Although a range of ethnicities were represented, the children were for the most part Caucasian. Thus, future research could extend this work in two important ways. First, research should focus on how bilingual children use accent information when learning from informants. It could be the case that they show a selective preference for the familiar language spoken in their own home. It is likely that their parents speak English with a non-native accent, thus making it more likely that bilingual children would prefer to learn from a non-native, foreign accent. However, it is equally plausible that bilingual children might show a preference for learning from the accent of the majority dominant culture—the native accent. Similarly, studies could focus on monolingual minority students. Minority students may show a selective avoidance for the native-accent speaker simply because they view a native accent as the outgroup. By contrast, minority students may display a pattern of results similar to the data discussed above (Corriveau, Kinzler, & Harris, 2013; Kinzler, Corriveau, & Harris, 2011), selectively preferring the speaker with a native accent.

Monitoring Accuracy and Familiarity

In the preceding sections, we have made the case that young children monitor for two types of information: informant familiarity and prior accuracy. How do they weight these two cues? Based on the findings from Corriveau, Harris, Meins et al. (2009), we might anticipate that, on average, children's preference for the familiar can be easily modified based on accuracy information. When the child's mother provided a label that was in conflict with the child's perceptual knowledge (in the 75–25 Hybrids task), most children abandoned their preference for their mother. Nevertheless, children did not completely abandon their preference for her—and, in the case of insecure-ambivalent children, they did not display a selective preference in either direction. An equally plausible alternative is that children monitor an informant over an extensive period, generally creating a deep reservoir of trust in the reliability of the person's claims. A short-term display of inaccuracy on the part of this familiar informant might have little impact on this reservoir. Thus, although previous findings have clearly shown that preschoolers—especially 4-year-olds—come to mistrust an inaccurate informant, this might apply only to unfamiliar informants and not to familiar informants.

We explored how children weight informant accuracy and familiarity in two separate studies exploring relative preference for a familiar preschool teacher (Corriveau & Harris, 2009b) and relative preference for an informant who speaks with a native accent (Corriveau, Kinzler, & Harris, 2013). Both studies employ the same 3-part paradigm. The *pretest trials* were discussed in the previous sections and were designed to provide a baseline level of trust based on familiarity. Two informants, varying in familiarity (or in linguistic familiarity), provide novel labels or functions for unfamiliar objects. The *accuracy training trials* were analogous to the training or familiarization trials discussed in Part II. Across 4 trials, one informant provided accurate labels for known objects whereas the other informant provided inaccurate labels. Importantly, for half of the children, the accurate informant was also familiar; for the other half of the children, the inaccurate informant was familiar. Finally, in 4 *posttest trials* the two informants again provided novel labels for novel objects. Thus, we were able to explore how children's preference for a familiar informant is modified based on accuracy information.

We find that children's relative weighting of familiarity and accuracy varies with age. Three-year-olds in both studies (Corriveau & Harris, 2009b; Corriveau, Kinzler, & Harris, 2013) maintain their preference for the familiar, or familiar-sounding individual—regardless of her accuracy. By contrast, 5-year-olds modify their preference based on accuracy information. Thus, for younger children, familiarity acts as a buffer or protective factor against a relatively short (4 trials) burst of inaccuracy. For older children, accuracy has more importance. It remains to be seen how much of a protective factor familiarity is for younger children. Future research could modify the length of inaccuracy or the type of errors to explore this relationship.

Monitoring Across Sources: Children's Use of Consensus

When monitoring for accuracy or for familiarity children match how a person looks or sounds—or what they say—with the child's existing knowledge about the world. Nevertheless, there are instances when children are asked to make judgments about beliefs or practices that are quite unfamiliar to them—practices that children cannot gauge for cultural representativeness. In these circumstances, how can young children optimize the likelihood that a potential informant is providing information that is culturally typical rather than marginal or deviant? One strategy that children might adopt is to behave like sociologists—to look for signs of consensus or dissent among a group of potential informants.

Children's use of consensus information as a potential knowledge source has now been explored across several studies (Chen, Corriveau, & Harris, 2011, 2013; Corriveau, Fusaro, & Harris, 2009; Corriveau & Harris, 2010; Corriveau, Kim, Song, & Harris, 2013; Fusaro & Harris, 2008). Below, we review three paradigms that have been used to explore how children monitor across information sources. We hope that by walking through the methods used we can stimulate more interest in children's monitoring for social group membership, as we believe this is an important area for future research.

In one paradigm that we now think of as consensus, children were presented with a video depicting two informants—similar to previous studies—and two bystanders (Fusaro & Harris, 2008). As in previous studies, children watched 4 trials where the two informants provide conflicting novel labels for novel objects. However, the claims made by one informant elicit approval (smiling and head nodding) from bystanders whereas the claims made by the other elicit disapproval (frowning and head shaking). The question was whether preschoolers would use these bystander reactions to moderate their trust in the novel claims made each informant. The results indicate that 4-year-old children overwhelmingly endorsed the speaker who had attracted bystander approval rather than disapproval on just over 90% of the trials. By implication, children noticed, and were influenced by, the reactions of the bystanders in what was an otherwise ambiguous situation because the objects themselves offered no clue as to which of the conflicting names was correct.

In the next phase of the study (Fusaro & Harris, 2008), the two bystanders withdrew and the two informants continued to provide conflicting names for novel objects. Overall, 4-year-olds continued to place more trust in the informant who had previously attracted bystander assent—even when the bystanders themselves were no longer present.

There were two ways to interpret these findings. First, it could be that children were marking the two informants as accurate and inaccurate based on bystander information. However, an alternative interpretation is that children were marking the two informants as positive or negative—and not thinking about the positivity or negativity in epistemic terms. To test this hypothesis, we developed a different paradigm (Corriveau, Fusaro, & Harris, 2009). Instead of head nodding and head shaking, agreement and disagreement was conveyed in a more tacit fashion (Corriveau, Fusaro & Harris, 2009; Chen, Corriveau, & Harris, 2011, 2013).

Three and 4-year-olds watched as four informants were invited to indicate which of a set of objects was, for example, "a modi." Three of the four informants all silently pointed to the same object but a lone dissenter pointed to a different object. Asked for their judgment, both 3- and 4-year-olds typically agreed with the majority verdict rather than with the lone dissenter. This bias was not as strong as the one observed in the previous experiment but it was significant for each age group (3-year-olds: 67%; 4-year-olds: 70%; Corriveau et al., 2009, Study 1).

In the next stage of the experiment, two of the majority of three left the room. The remaining member of the majority and the lone dissenter supplied conflicting names for additional, novel objects. Both 3- and 4-year-olds were more likely to endorse the names supplied by the previous member of the majority as opposed to the lone dissenter. Note that no signs of liking or disliking had been expressed toward either informant. In the initial induction phase, the four adults had simply pointed wordlessly and with a neutral facial expression. Therefore, if the member of the consensus elicited more trust in the second stage of the study, it was because children had noted that her behavior was more typical.

However, an alternative interpretation warrants investigation. Specifically, children could have selectively preferred the consensus not because they were in agreement, but because they had more hands pointing towards the referent, alerting subjects to attend more to that referent. Therefore, we repeated the method described above with a consensus of two adults and a dissenting adult (Corriveau, Fusaro & Harris, 2009, Study 2). Importantly, in the 2-person consensus, both informants pointed with one hand, but the dissenter pointed to the referent with both hands. Thus, both referents had equal attention, but one referent was recommended by the consensus, whereas the other was endorsed by the dissenter. As before, in the induction phase, children were more likely to endorse information provided by the informants who were in agreement. In addition, when one of the two left, children were more likely to trust the remaining member of the pair than the lone dissenter. By implication, children's sensitivity to a consensus is acute. Two people in agreement override a single other.

In another series of studies we have asked whether the composition of the consensus was important to children. Specifically, children in the United States and Taipai, Taiwan either saw a consensus composed of own-race members, or they saw a consensus composed of other-race members (Chen, Corriveau, & Harris, 2011, 2013). Although children in all conditions across locations selectively preferred the referent endorsed by the consensus when the consensus was present, we found that their preference for the individual member of the consensus weakened in the follow-up test phase when the consensus was not present. By implication, when children meet informants who come from a different group, they are less attentive to any consensus that they form. This makes sense if children look to members of a consensus for guidance about the norms that prevail in their own group. Future work is needed here to unpack just how important group membership is when assigning trait-based information.

Finally, we describe a third consensus-based paradigm (Corriveau & Harris, 2010; Corriveau et al., 2013). We asked whether children would show a preference for consensus information if consensus information directly conflicts with perceptual experience. Here, we borrowed from the Asch line-length paradigm used in adult social psychology (Asch, 1956). We presented preschoolers with 3 lines and asked them to judge which line was "big." Then, we showed them four test trials. In each trial, children watched a video of three informants who all pointed to a smaller line as the "big line." Again, we asked children to tell us which line they thought was largest. Here we found remarkable similarity in deference levels in preschoolers as in adults (30% of children deferred, vs. 33% of adults). Moreover, as with adult research (Bond & Smith, 1996) we find that Asian-American preschoolers display greater deference levels than Caucasian-American preschoolers. Whereas 30% of Caucasian-American preschoolers deferred to the consensus, about 60% of Asian-American children deferred (Corriveau & Harris, 2010). In a follow-up study we explore this finding in greater depth by recruiting first- and second-generation Asian-American preschoolers. We find that rates of deference are greatest among first-generation preschoolers, and are relatively similar across second-generation Asian-American and Caucasian-American preschoolers.

One other methodological manipulation warrants attention in the Corriveau et al. (2013) study. For half the children, the experimenter watched while the child made their judgment about the line length. The remaining half of the children made their judgment in private. When children made their judgment privately we find no effect of cultural group. This is a finding that has been reported in adults, but to our knowledge, has not been reported with young children. We hope that future research can be generated around this topic as we believe this is an important issue to consider in early childhood assessment.

PART IV: DISCUSSION AND GENERAL SUGGESTIONS FOR RESEARCH IN EARLY CHILDHOOD EDUCATION

In this chapter, we have outlined a very simple experimental method we have used to explore children's learning preferences when learning from particular sources of information. We have presented children with two informants who differ across one dimension (e.g., accuracy, familiarity, group membership) and asked children which informant they would like to learn from. We believe that these findings have implications for what happens in real-life classroom settings. Importantly, if the goal in early childhood education is to provide the best learning environment for the child, it is critical that the classroom teacher—and for that matter, the child's parent—is seen as a credible source when learning new information.

We want to highlight the fact that although much of the work presented in this chapter has occurred in relatively sterile, lab-based experiments, we believe the findings can be applied to early childhood education. As we hope we have shown in this chapter, because we conducted these studies in a very controlled experimental setting we were able to systematically determine which cues are important for young children when determining informant trustworthiness. If we had simply "jumped in" and started researching these questions in an authentic classroom, our findings would have been arguably more noisy, and the conclusions we could have drawn would have been more tempered due to compromised internal validity. The lab-based findings presented in this chapter represent a starting point from which educational researchers and educators can base further research and classroom instruction.

Based on these findings, what recommendations might we make for classroom teaching? We have argued that children use two—or maybe three—separate cues when determining informant credibility. In Part II, we demonstrated that children first focus on informant *inaccuracy*, selectively avoiding an informant who has been previously inaccurate. By the age of four, children also focus on informant *accuracy*—systematically building up trust based on an informant's previous accurate claims. Given the bias against inaccurate informants—especially at young ages—we suggest that classroom teachers recognize how children might interpret inaccurate claims. This is not to say that teachers should ever willingly provide inaccurate information. However, teachers should be aware of how children seem to interpret inaccurate information, even if it is presented in a playful, humorous way.

In Part III, we first showed data indicating children's preference for an informant who is familiar to them, and then turned to children's preference for information that is met with group consensus over information that is met with dissent. We might consider these cues as part of an overarching ability for children to monitor the credibilty of sources based on social group information. That is, children ask whether an informant is "like me," and make subsequent decisions about trustworthiness based on their answer (Meltzoff, 2007). How can we apply that to early childhood settings? First, based on the available research it seems that children respond better to indiviudals who are familiar, warm, and emotionally available. Although this is hardly a new recommendation in the field of early childhood, perhaps it is one worth revisiting given the high rates of teacher-turnover prevalent in many early childhood settings. his is particularly true in early childhood settings serving the most at-risk children (Barnett, 2003)—the very settings where we we might see the most benefit from the stable, familiar, warm interaction of high-quality teachers on children's learning. These suggestions come with a large caveat, however. Few of the studies mentioned above have explored a wide range of ethnicities, nor have they explored a wide range of socioeconomic statuses (but see, Corriveau, Harris, Meins et al., 2009). Future research should look more specifically if children from minority backgrounds show similar preferences when learning from particular sources of information.

Second, it seems that children prefer to learn from the group. This is important information for early childhood teachers to consider. Children come to preschool possessing knowledge across multiple domains. It is likely that this information may have been met with agreement across several sources (e.g., picture books, television, etc.), or multiple informants (e.g., parents, friends), or both. When children arrive at school, it is very possible that their preschool teacher may provide information that is at odds with this prior knowledge they acquired previously through consensus. Based on the results described above, children may have difficulty updating their prior knowledge with new information from a single informant (i.e., their teacher) when her information is not in accord with children's consensus-based prior knowledge. Overall, we believe research exploring children's selective trust in informants has great potential for helping to shape early childhood classrooms. We hope future research will help to elucidate just how and why we can transfer this work to the classroom.

Finally, we offer four recommendations for research in early childhood that we hope will be helpful for researchers.

First, it is important to ensure that the method used is appropriate for the age group in question. In this chapter, we have provided an overview of research on preschoolers (3-, 4-, and 5-year-olds). Thus, most of our measures employ forced-choice questions (instead of open-ended responses) in order to control for some of the variability associated with open-ended responses. As we state above, that is not to say that open-ended reponses are not a valuable source of information from preschool subjects (and indeed, we both utilize open-ended responses in some study designs). Nevertheless, it is important to use both types of dependent measures in parallel, or to be aware of how individual differences in verbal ability might play a role in children's responses. Similarly, we have carefully outlined several procedural decisions we made to test preschoolers' preference for one informant over another—in part to control for other individual differences in attention and memory. Specifically, the use of video stimuli allowed us to ensure the child's attention during testing as well as to reduce the heightened anxiety associated with testing with multiple adult experimenters who are strangers to the child. Moreover, carefully controlling our informant stimuli allowed us to make inferences about children's trust in a particular cue independent of specific informant characteristics.

Second, it is important for researchers to begin thinking about the analysis plan during the earliest stages of the the design process. In the studies above we tried to be explicit about the hypotheses we were trying to test, including the hypothesis we anticipated and any alternative hypothesis. We were then able to design multiple conditions in order to systematically tease apart these alternative hypotheses. Without thinking carefully through the research process from the design phase to analysis beforehand, researchers run the risk of producing spurious (at best) or invalid findings (at worst).

Third, be open to unexpected findings. One of us (KC) is now actively exploring within- and between-culture variability in children's learning as a result of an unexpected—but consistent—difference between Caucasian-American and Asian-American preschoolers in the manner that they deferred to adult informants. It is important to not ignore those findings and to be willing to systematically explore whether or not they are robust across multiple experiments.

Fourth, we have found that some of the most exciting research occurs in true partnership with early childhood educators. We have found the experience of talking, reflecting, and collaborating with professionals in the field provides a unique insight into the important questions on practitioners' minds and helps us to interpret what our results mean for early childhood classrooms. Early childhood educators can serve as a rich source of information in terms of everyday classroom occurrences, and can often highlight unexpected difficulties or strengths that they have seen over time in children's learning.

REFERENCES

Ainsworth, M. D. S., Blehar, M. C., Waters, E., & Wall, S. (1978). *Patterns of attachment: A psychological study of the strange situation.* Hillsdale, NJ: Erlbaum.

Ainsworth, M. D. S (1992). A consideration of social referencing in the context of attachment theory and research. In. S. Feinman (Ed.), *Social referencing and the social construction of reality in infancy* (pp. 349–367). New York, NY: Plenum Press.

Anderson, D. R., & Pempek, T. A. (2005). Television and very young children. *American Behavioral Scientist, 48,* 505–522.

Asch, S. E. (1956). Studies of independence and conformity. A minority of one against a unanimous majority. *Psychological Monographs, 70,* 1–70.

Barnett, W. S. (2003). Low wages = Low quality: Solving the real preschool teacher crisis. *NIEER Preschool Policy Matters, 3.* New Brunswick, NJ: NIEER

Birch, S., Vauthier, S., & Bloom, P. (2008). Three- and four-year-olds spontaneously use others' past performance to guide their learning. *Cognition, 107,* 1018–1034.

Bond, R., & Smith, P. B. (1996). Culture and conformity: A meta-analysis of studies using Asch's (1952b, 1956) line judgment task. *Psychological Bulletin, 119,* 111–137

Brosseau-Liard, P. E., & Birch, S. A., (2010). "I bet you know more and are nicer too!": What children infer from others' accuracy. *Developmental Science, 13,* 772–778.

Chen, E. E, Corriveau, K. H., & Harris, P. L. (2011). Children are sociologists. *Anales de Psycologia, 27,* 625–630.

Chen, E. E., Corriveau, K. H., & Harris, P.L. (2013). Children trust a consensus composed of outgroup members—but do not retain it. *Child Development, 84,* 269–282.

Carlson, S. M. (2005). Developmentally sensitive measures of executive function in preschool children. *Developmental Neuropsychology, 28,* 595–616.

Clément, F., Koenig, M., & Harris, P.L. (2004). The ontogenesis of trust in testimony. *Mind and Language, 19,* 360–379.

Corriveau, K. H., Fusaro, M., & Harris, P. L. (2009). Going with the flow: Preschoolers prefer non-dissenters as informants. *Psychological Science, 20,* 372–377.

Corriveau, K. H., & Harris, P. L. (2009a). Choosing your informant: weighing familiarity and recent accuracy, *Developmental Science, 12,* 426–437.

Corriveau, K. H., & Harris, P. L. (2009b). Preschoolers continue to trust a more accurate informant 1 week after exposure to accuracy information. *Developmental Science, 12,* 188–193.

Corriveau, K. H., & Harris, P. L. (2010). Preschoolers (sometimes) defer to the majority in making simple perceptual judgments. *Developmental Psychology, 46,* 437–445.

Corriveau, K. H., Harris, P. L., Meins, E., Ferneyhough, C., Arnott, B., Elliott, L., Liddle, B.... de Rosnay, M. (2009). Young children's trust in their mother's claims: Longitudinal links with attachment security in infancy. *Child Development, 80,* 750–761.

Corriveau, K. H., Kim, E., Song, G., & Harris, P.L. (2013). Young children's deference to a consensus varies by culture. *Journal of Cognition and Culture, 13,* 267–381.

Corriveau, K. H., Kinzler, K. D., & Harris, P. L. (2013). Accuracy trumps accent in children's endorsement of object names. *Developmental Psychology, 49,* 470–479.

Corriveau, K. H., Meints, K., & Harris, P. L. (2009). Early tracking of informant accuracy and inaccuracy. *British Journal of Developmental Psychology, 27,* 331–342.

Corriveau, K. H., Pickard, K., & Harris, P. L. (2011). Preschoolers trust particular informants when learning morphology. Paper presented at the biannual Society for Research in Child Development, Montreal, Canada.

Danovitch, J. H., & Keil, F. C. (2004). Should you ask a fisherman or a biologist?: Developmental shifts in ways of clustering knowledge. *Child Development, 75,* 918–931.

Dias, M., & Harris, P. L. (1988). The effect of make-believe play on deductive reasoning. *British Journal of Developmental Psychology, 6,* 207–221.

Dias, M., & Harris, P. L. (1990). The influence of the imagination on reasoning by young children. *British Journal of Developmental Psychology, 8,* 305–318.

Duckworth, E. (2006). *The having of wonderful ideas and other essays on teaching and learning* (3rd ed.). New York, NY: Teachers College Press.

Fusaro, M, Corriveau, K. H., & Harris, P. L. (2011). The good, the strong, and the accurate. Preschoolers' evaluations of accurate and strong informants. *Journal of Experimental Child Psychology, 110,* 561–574.

Fusaro, M., & Harris, P. L. (2008). Children assess informant reliability using bystanders' non-verbal cues. *Developmental Science, 11,* 771–777.

French, L. (2004). Science as the center of a coherent, integrated early childhood curriculum. *Early Childhood Research Quarterly, 19,* 138–149.

Ganea, P. A., & Harris, P. L. (2010). Not doing what you are told: Early perseverative errors in updating mental representations via language. *Child Development, 81,* 457–463.

Gilbert, D. T., Pinel, E. C., Wilson, T. D., Blumberg, S. J., & Wheatley, T. (1998). Immune neglect: A source of durability bias in affective forecasting. *Journal of Personality and Social Psychology, 75,* 617–638.

Gopnik, A., & Astington, J.W. (1988). Children's understanding of representational change and it's relation to the understanding of false belief and the appearance-reality distinction. *Child Development, 59,* 26–37.

Gopnik, A., & Graf, P. (1988). Knowing how you know: Children's understanding of the source of their knowledge. *Child Development, 59,* 1366–1371.

Gopnik, A., & Meltzoff, A. (1998). *Words, thoughts & theories.* Cambridge, MA: MIT Press.

Grice, H. P. (1975). Logic and conversation. In P. Cole & J. Morgan (Eds.) *Syntax and semantics, 3: Speech acts* (pp. 41–58). New York, NY: Academic Press.

Hamre, B. K., & Pianta, R. C. (2005). Can instructional and emotional support in the first-grade classroom make a difference for children at risk of school failure? *Child Development, 76,* 949–967.

Harris, P. L. (2007). Trust. *Developmental Science, 10,* 135–138.

Harris, P. L., & Corriveau, K. H. (2011). Young children's selective trust in informants. *Philosophical Transactions of the Royal Society B, 366,* 1179–1187.

Harris, P. L., & Koenig, M. (2006). Trust in testimony: How children learn about science and religion. *Child Development, 77,* 505–524.

Jaswal, V. K. (2004). Don't believe everything you hear: Preschoolers' sensitivity to speaker intent in category induction. *Child Development, 75,* 1871–1885.

Keil, F. C., Stein, C., Webb, L., Billings, V. D., & Rozenblit, L. (2008). Discerning the Division of Cognitive Labor: An emerging understanding of how knowledge is clustered in other minds. *Cognitive Science, 32,* 259–300.

Kinzler, K. D., Corriveau, K. H., & Harris, P. L. (2011). Preschoolers' use of accent when deciding which informant to trust. *Developmental Science, 14,* 106–111.

Kinzler, K. D., Dupoux, E., & Spelke, E. S. (2007). The native language of social cognition. *Proceedings of the National Academy of Sciences, 104,* 12577–12580.

Kirk, R. E. (1969). *Experimental Design: Procedures for the Behavioral Sciences.* Belmont, CA: Brooks Cole Publishing.

Kisilevsky, B. S. Hains, S. M. J., Brown, C. A., Lee, C. T., Cowperthwaite, B, Stutzman, S. S. , Swansburg, M. L....Wang Z. (2009). Fetal sensitivity to properties of maternal speech and language. *Infant Behavior and Development, 32*(1), 59–71.

Kisilevsky, B. S., & Hains, S. M. J. (2011), Onset and maturation of fetal heart rate response to the mother's voice over late gestation. *Developmental Science, 14,* 214–223.

Koenig, M., Clément, F., & Harris, P. L. (2004). Trust in testimony: Children's use of true and false statements. *Psychological Science, 10,* 694–698.

Koenig, M. A., & Echols, C. H. (2003). Infants' understanding of false labeling events: the referential role of words and the people who use them. *Cognition, 87,* 181–210.

Koenig, M., & Harris, P. L. (2005). Preschoolers mistrust ignorant and inaccurate speakers. *Child Development, 76,* 1261–1277.

Koenig, M. A., & Jaswal, V. K. (2011). Characterizing children's expectations about expertise and incompetence: Halo or pitchfork effects? *Child Development, 82,* 1634–1647.

Liu, D., Gelman, S. A., & Wellman, H. M. (2007). Components of young children's trait understanding: behavior-to-trait inferences and trait-to-behavior predictions. *Child Development, 78,* 1543–1558.

Lutz, D. J., & Keil, F. C. (2002). Early understanding of the division of cognitive labor. *Child Development, 73,* 1073–1084.

Ma, L., & Ganea, P. A. (2010). Dealing with conflicting information: Young children's reliance on what they see versus what they are told. *Developmental Science, 13,* 151–160.

Markman, E. M. (1992). Constraints on word learning: Speculations about their nature, origins and domain specificity. In M. R. Gunnar, & M. P. Maratsos (Eds.), *Modularity and constraints in language and cognition: The Minnesota symposium on child psychology* (pp. 59–101). Hillsdale, NJ: Erlbaum.

Mascaro, O., & Sperber, D. (2009). The moral, epistemic, and mindreading components of children's vigilance towards deception. *Cognition, 112,* 367–380.

Meltzoff, A. N. (2007). 'Like me': A foundation for social cognition. *Developmental Science, 10,* 126–134.

Merriman, W. E., & Bowman, L. L. (1989). The mutual exclusivity bias in children's word learning. *Monographs of the Society for Research in Child Development, 54,* 1–132.

National Reading Panel (2000). *Teaching children to read: An evidence-based assessment of the scientific literature on reading and its implications for reading instruction.* Washington, DC: US Department of Education.

Olson, K. R., Banaji, M. R., Dweck, C. A., & Spelke, E. S. (2006). Children's bias against lucky vs. unlucky people and their social groups. *Psychological Science, 17,* 845–846.

Olson, K. R., & Spelke, E. S. (2008). Foundations of cooperation in preschool children. *Cognition, 108,* 222–231.

Pasquini, E. S., Corriveau, K., Koenig, M., & Harris, P. L. (2007). Preschoolers monitor the relative accuracy of informants. *Developmental Psychology, 43,* 1216–1226.

Pascalis, O. de Schonen, S., Morton, J., Deruelle, C., & Fabre-Grenet, M. (1995). Mother's face recognition by neonates—a replication and an extension. *Infant Behavior and Development, 18,* 79–85.

Piaget, J. (1923/2002). *The language and thought of the child.* New York, New York, NY: Routledge.
Pianta, R. (2001). *Student-teacher relationship scale—short-form.* Lutz, FL: Psychological Assessment Resources, Inc.
Rotenberg, K. J. (2010). *Interpersonal trust during childhood and adolescence.* Cambridge, UK: Cambridge University Press.
Rousseau, J-J. (1762/1957). *Emile.* New York, NY: Dutton.
Scarborough, H. S. (1998). Early identification of children at risk of reading disabilities: Phonological awareness and some other promising predictors. In Shapiro, Accerdo, & Capute (Eds.), *Specific reading disability: A view of the spectrum* (pp. 75–199). Timoniuum, MD: York Press.
Sénéchal, M., Ouelette, G., & Rodney, D. (2006). The misunderstood giant: On the predictive role of early vocabulary to future reading. In D. K. Dickinson & S. B. Neuman (Eds.), *Handbook of early literacy research* (Vol. 2, pp. 173–182). New York, NY: The Guilford Press.
Shutts, K., Banaji, M. R., & Spelke, E. S. (2010). Social categories guide young children's preferences for novel objects. *Developmental Science, 13,* 599–610.
Sobel, D. M. (2006). How fantasy benefits young children's understanding of pretense. *Developmental Science, 9,* 63–75.
Sobel, D. M., & Corriveau, K. H. (2010). Children monitor individuals' expertise for word learning, *Child Development, 81,* 669–679.
Sobel, D. M., & Lillard, A. S. (2002). Young children's understanding of pretense: Do words bend the truth? *Developmental Science, 5,* 87–97.
Todorov, A., Gobbini, M. I., Evans, K. K., & Haxby, J. V. (2007). Spontaneous retrieval of affective person knowledge in face perception. *Neuropsychologia, 45,* 163–173.
Todorov, A., & Uleman, J. S. (2002). Spontaneous trait inferences are bound to actors' faces: Evidence from a false recognition paradigm. *Journal of Personality and Social Psychology, 83,* 1051–1065.
Todorov, A., & Uleman, J. S. (2003). The efficiency of binding spontaneous trait inferences to actors' faces. *Journal of Experimental Social Psychology, 39,* 549–562.
Wellman, H. M., Cross, D., & Watson, J. (2001). Meta-analysis of theory-of-mind development: The truth about false belief. *Child Development, 72,* 655–684.
Yuill, N. (1993). Children's understanding of traits. In M. Bennett (Ed.), *The development of social cognition: The child as psychologist* (pp. 87–110). New York, NY: Guilford.

CHAPTER 19

CONDUCTING HISTORICAL RESEARCH IN EARLY CHILDHOOD EDUCATION

Sue C. Wortham

INTRODUCTION

To understand early childhood education one needs to learn about its history. The education of young children can be traced back to the Hebrews in Christian and Jewish history when Hebrews lived as roaming tribes and taught their young children through family religious rituals beginning in infancy. Other cultures and religions have similar histories (Cubberley, 1920).

The focus of this chapter is how to conduct historical research in early childhood education in the United States. The education of young children in the United States began soon after the first permanent settlements were established in the colonies prior to the American Revolution. From the beginning of these first educational endeavors, the education of young children was influenced by European immigrants who traveled to the United States to begin a new life. The history of early childhood education cannot be separated from the history of early childhood. How, when, and where very young children experienced the early years cannot be separated from how they were educated. The time and place of a child's early years have a strong relationship with the educational settings and types of early childhood education. Culture, family routines, religion, social and economic factors, and types of opportunities for learning all affect the possibilities for early education (Kagan, 1984).

A child's early life resembles the pieces of a puzzle. Many different pieces make up the whole of the child's life and experiences. The task of the historical researcher is to find as many pieces of the child's life as possible to compose a rich picture of children and their learning experiences both in and out of an educational setting. Likewise the researcher tries to find many sources related to a topic to form a complete picture of a period in history.

THE NATURE OF HISTORICAL RESEARCH IN EARLY CHILDHOOD EDUCATION

Historical research is the process of searching for clues that explain the mosaic of the young child's life and education. This type of research is very different from educational research in that it expands our understanding of the history of early childhood education from a variety of kinds of resources. This contrast with educational research will be explained later.

History relates to the nature of some element of life and how it changes over time. Historical research is the study of a topic of interest to develop a comprehensive understanding from the many changes related to the topic as time has passed. The types of historical topics that can be studied are almost infinite. If the historical researcher wants to understand the nature of early childhood, he includes the relevant factors of childhood in different periods of history. Some of the elements include social and economic conditions of the period, the role of the family and community, and life situations for different groups of children. For example, life for families in the 1930s was strongly influenced by the Great Depression that lasted over two decades in the United States. Conditions for families and children were impacted by unemployment, a lengthy drought during the period, and limited financial resources for early education. Each historical period in a country has direct and indirect relationships with the conditions during those times (Wortham, 2002).

HISTORICAL RESEARCH AS A TREASURE HUNT

Historical research is a treasure hunt. As the researcher seeks items of information, there may be some surprises. Information can emerge in unusual forms. Many years ago I conducted research on African Americans in Texas when the state was an independent nation after the revolution to separate Texas from Mexico. African Americans escaped to Texas from their masters in the south and reestablished themselves as free citizens in Texas (Billington, 1950). One of the best sources of information about the topic could be found in the Texas archives at the University of Texas at Austin. I worked in the archives for many months to find primary information about free blacks that lived in Texas during that period. The search that began with a bit of information on a file card might end with a box with various papers and newspaper cuttings, or the tax records of an African American farmer. One of the most surprising items was a small velvet purse decorated with fringe. Inside it had folded pieces of paper with the records of three slaves who had been freed and moved to Texas (Wortham, 1970).

PRIMARY AND SECONDARY RESEARCH RESOURCES

The little purse was an example of a primary historical artifact. There are two types of research sources: primary and secondary: Primary resources are the original items of information that are located. Secondary resources are information about a topic that has been published in some form from earlier research. Primary research is preferred; however, there is more secondary information available on many historical topics.

Frederich Froebel and Jean Jacques Rousseau were two early writers on the nature of early childhood and learning. Their own writings are primary resources to learn about their work. One can read about Frederick Froebel's first kindergarten in Germany and his philosophy and curriculum (Froebel, 1899; Kilpatrick, 1916). Many published accounts of the history of early childhood education include pictures of the gifts and occupations (McCarthy & Houston, 1980; Spodek, 1973; Wortham, 2002). The pictures and written information are secondary resources about gifts and occupations. A researcher can also see a set of the original gifts and occupations and other training materials for the Froebelian curriculum in the Archives of the Association for Childhood Education International. This primary resource is located in the main library of the University of Maryland in Silver Springs, Maryland.

Froebel is credited with establishing kindergartens for young children based on his book, *Education of Man* (1899. He formulated the kindergarten system with emphasis on the use of gifts and occupations through play (Smith, 2012). Rousseau was considered to be an educational leader, but best known as a philosopher. Although he was a prolific writer, his book, *Emile* (1911), focused on the nature of childhood and the education of the young child. *Emile* is available in several English translations (Bloom, 1991;

Dent, 1988; Rousseau, 1911). Additional information about Rousseau can be found online (Delaney, 2005; Doyle & Smith, 2007).

The historical researcher in early childhood education has both primary and secondary sources from which to construct a picture of early efforts to establish kindergartens in the United States. There are also online resources that can be used to add to earlier information in published volumes.

INTERPRETATION AND REVISION OF HISTORICAL RESEARCH

The historical researcher seeks to interpret periods in history. After gathering information over a period of time the writer then seeks to give an explanation of the period so that the reader can benefit from the lessons of history. The interpretation might have as its purpose to help readers to better understand what happened in the past. As new information evolves over time, different interpretations may be proposed. This is the process of revision in historical research. New information has led to a new understanding of the history of the period.

There are many examples of interpretation and revision in the history of early childhood education. Like other elements of education, the nature of early childhood and early childhood education evolved and was reinvented over time to the present. Again, the example of the work of Rousseau and Froebel served as the beginning of the development of curriculum and learning experiences for children under the age of six. Examples of primary and secondary sources about these pioneers were provided in previous discussions. Primary and secondary resources can direct the researcher to more resources to explore.

In the sections that follow the establishment of early childhood education is traced from the days of original settlement up to 1900. The early years of settlement and the kindergarten movement will be explored. Later, during the early decades of the twentieth century, the advent of new understandings about child development transformed education, including preschool education. The child study movement, progressive education movement, and many other factors led to revisions in how children develop and learn and revisions in how early childhood educators viewed early childhood education.

THE EARLY YEARS OF SETTLEMENT TO 1900

In the early years of settlement prior to the American Revolution and westward expansion after the Revolution, the first educational institutions in the young country were for higher education. Next, secondary schools were established. Public schools initiated for elementary education were the last to be organized. The first efforts at education for elementary age children were informal and based in a home or community building. Well-to-do families sent their children to subscription schools that were financed through taxes and subscriptions (fees). Families who could not afford subscription schools hired a mother or other female in the community to teach students in homes that were called Dame Schools (Gross & Gross, 1976; Gulliford, 1984; Weber, 1969). Although there were no programs specifically for preschool children, children under six often attended Dame Schools where they learned biblical scriptures, the alphabet, and practical household skills with their older siblings.

The first formal elementary schools were established on a large scale during the westward expansion and at first used learning materials imported from England and Europe. Sunday Schools were frequently the first schools established in a new community; as a result, Sunday school materials were sometimes provided for frontier schools. The American Sunday Union produced education materials developed from the Sunday School Movement in England. (Lynn & Wright, 1971). These first schools on the western frontier were one-room schoolhouses that were built and controlled locally (Gulliford, 1984).

Interpretation of History From Early Settlement to 1900

Resources for early childhood education during the early years of settlement and westward expansion include both primary and secondary sources. The Library of Congress has early primers from the American Sunday School Union as well as early textbooks developed for beginning primary students in this country. State historical archives have records for the history in their state. Historical societies are active in most states and have collections of photos and materials from the first years of elementary education. Similar original materials from the period are located in the Association for Childhood Education archives at the University of Maryland Main Library in Silver Springs, Maryland.

Based on these early resources and others, the researcher could interpret that early attempts at schooling did not focus on preschool children. They were taught passages from the Bible and their learning experiences were mostly designed for older children. It was not until after the Civil War that the influences of Froebel, Rousseau, and others affected the initiation of education designed for preschool children. It was the introduction of kindergarten into the United States that added the focus on early education that started early childhood education as a movement in the United States.

THE KINDERGARTEN MOVEMENT IN THE UNITED STATES

German settlers introduced kindergartens in the United States. Kindergartens were established on a large scale in the United States between the end of the Civil War and the beginning of the twentieth century. The expansion of public schools and concerns for children of the poor, especially recent immigrants impacted the establishment and expansion of kindergartens. Most of the first kindergartens were private; however, advocates of the kindergarten movement encouraged the inclusion of kindergartens in public schools. At the same time, philanthropic individuals and organizations established kindergartens to serve immigrant children in poverty areas of big cities (Weber, 1984).

During this same period, Rousseau's influences on the nature of young children resulted in a change in attitudes toward young children. The belief that education must permit the goodness of the child to unfold replaced the Puritan belief in the child as sinner. These three factors, the wave of immigration, a new understanding of childhood and the introduction of the kindergarten resulted in a major period of growth in early childhood education. By 1880 there were almost 400 kindergartens in the United States. As the philanthropic movement declined toward the end of the nineteenth century, the kindergartens they established were absorbed into public schools.

Training schools were established for kindergarten teachers (Weber, 1969). In 1892 a small group of kindergarten educators organized their own advocacy group at a conference of the National Education Association that was later to become the International Kindergarten Union (IKU) (Wortham, 2002).

The child-study movement, progressive trends in education, and conflicts between followers of Froebel and progressive movement leaders seeking to improve preschool education fueled new influences in early childhood education. The nursery school movement had also been established to serve young immigrants. The field of early childhood education had become larger and more complex with many of the early childhood educators becoming leaders. African American and Native American children were taught in separate schools. The early childhood education movement was part of an era of education reform as consolidated urban schools replaced one-room schoolhouses (Cremin, 1961, 1988).

Interpretation of the Kindergarten Movement in the United States

By the time that kindergartens were first established before 1890, the professional community had many resources for training prospective teachers in Froebelian methods. Early childhood educators could attend professional meetings, educational conferences, and read articles and books related to the subject. The historical researcher of the period can access these same sources for important information. When beginning a search a one starting point could be an older history, *The Kindergarten. Its Encounter with Educational Thought in America (Weber, 1969)*. The bibliography for each chapter in this book lists resources that are organized by original writings (primary resources), interpretive writings (secondary resources) and articles and addresses. This early volume on the history of early childhood education, especially the kindergarten movement, points the way to using more recent publications for comprehensive information on the period. Weber's books have been followed by more recent histories on early childhood education (Beatty, 1995; Hinitz, 2002; Lascarides & Hinitz, 2011). Contemporary sources can also be accessed online. For example, a search on the history of the kindergarten as a topic results in articles such as *Kindergarten*. (Encyclopedia of Children and Childhood in History and Society, 2002) and *Kindergarten* (Watson, 1997). They include summaries of the kindergarten movement and Froebel's work. Similar websites are available for most topics desired for a historical search.

EARLY CHILDHOOD EDUCATION REFORM FROM 1900 TO 1950

Shortly after the International Kindergarten Union was organized in 1892, it became a center of educational reform in the United States. The rise of the progressive movement and its focus on child-centered experiences and a curriculum based on the real life of the child was in conflict with the Froebelian methods that were teacher directed and used prescribed activities. The issue came to a head at the 1900 meeting of IKU when advocates of the conflicting methods engaged in arguments in support of their view. Advocates of both positions were leaders in early childhood education. The opposing presentations by such leaders as Alice Temple, Patty Smith Hill, Susan Blow, and Lucy Wheelock were shocking to the participants at the conference (Weber, 1969; Wortham, 2002). The controversy continued through decades, but slowly the progressive movement grew in strength with a new evolving curriculum with opportunities for child-initiated activities. During the same period the scientific method of measuring learning and the effects of information from the child study movement (Hall, 1883) also added to the complexity of the best programs for preschool children. Preschool educators were introduced to thematic curriculum involving projects from John Dewey's work (Dewey, 1899; Ratner, 1939) and continuing availability of new materials and strategies (Benjamin, 1964). Between 1900 and 1950 these advances were examined and implemented until a new era of influences again impacted the course of early childhood education.

Interpretation of Early Childhood Education Reform from 1900 to 1950

Resources for historical research are extensive for this period of educational reform and revision. There were many leaders in preschool education and opportunities for presenting their views and ideas were abundant. Early childhood educators of the period were able to present papers at conferences, publish journal articles, and write books about their work (Snyder, 1972). As early childhood educators adopted progressive methods in their work, they could also present, publish, and serve as leaders in the training of new teachers. These materials can be found in university collections, early childhood education journals such as *Childhood Education (ACEI)* and *Young Children* (NAEYC) and many other published resources in electronic and hard copy forms.

The historical researcher has almost unlimited access to primary and secondary sources through original writings by growing numbers of authors addressing different elements of reform. The evolution of the child study movement included it expansion to various universities across the country. A researcher can follow the work of Arnold Gesell (1925) and his students in their work to establish developmental norms of development. John Dewey's work and the implementation of project work in preschool and primary settings were widely published in early childhood publications. The history of early childhood in the period was a combination of many movements that complemented or challenged each other.

In this section of the chapter we have reviewed the development of early childhood education beginning with the settlement of the original colonies to the reform that extended to 1950. Again, discussions were necessarily brief and some topics were not addressed. The education of minority children and children with disabilities is an example. No attention was given to the establishment and expansion of the National Association for the Education of Young Children and other organizations related to preschool education and educators.

The next section will address the differences between historical research and educational research. Specific steps in conducting historical research will be presented in the final part of the chapter.

HISTORICAL RESEARCH AND EDUCATIONAL RESEARCH COMPARED

There are some common characteristics between historical and educational research. First they both start with some type of problem or question. Second, they both conduct a search of available information on the problem or question. Third, they both establish hypotheses or questions about the topic to be studied.

After the first three steps the two types of research diverge in their methods. Educational research follows a series of steps to investigate the topic. Some element of education is studied through data gathering that includes who the participants will be in the study, procedures for selecting the participants, methods of collecting data, and procedures for data collection. Finally the data is analyzed for quantitative or qualitative results and the results of the study are reported. In educational research the steps in research always follow the same sequence. The format remains the same regardless of the many varieties of studies conducted. The evaluation of educational research leads to discrete findings related to the research study that included implications and limitations of the findings (Creswell, 2011; Johnson & Christiansen, 2004; Tuckman, 1999).

The conduct of historical research follows a different process from educational research. Rather than conducting a study on an educational issue or question, the historian spends the most time and effort searching and organizing information about a topic. Both primary and secondary resources are consulted to construct a complete picture of the time sequence and interrelationships between factors related to the topic. Unlike educational research where a study of a question or issue produces quantifiable data to determine study's effect, the historical researcher uses primary and secondary sources to collect information and then interprets the findings to provide a comprehensive, detailed picture of the topic during the time period studied. (Busha & Harter, 1982).

Unlike educational research, the historian interprets the findings from the search for information subjectively. The historian is creative and interpretation includes the historian's interests, values, and training. Moreover, it is difficult to use quantitative methods because available historical data is frequently incomplete. However, quantitative research does help develop a picture of the realities of schooling in the past (Kaestle, 1997).

654 ▪ S. C. WORTHAM

Because the educational historian's work is personally focused, objectivity is difficult to achieve. The historian's role is to be neutral or disinterested; however, during some historical periods, opposite views have prevailed. One issue in American history was the origins of the Civil War. There were opposing views on why the war started. More recently, educational historians have been unable to reconcile some interpretations of history and have abandoned objectivity to individual perspectives based on the historian's background and interest in history (Novick, 1988). This issue can be recognized in the treatment of the history of childhood and childhood education. The interpretation of information depends on the population of children and the nature of education they received. The Native American child and African American child lived differently and were educated differently than the middle class, mainstream child in different periods of history (Wortham, 2002). The historian's interpretation of these educational differences can vary based on individual perceptions. These factors should be kept in mind when addressing the information in the next section.

THE CONTEXTS OF HISTORICAL RESEARCH IN EARLY CHILDHOOD EDUCATION

When one considers what is important to know about early childhood education, there are four possible major themes including the following:
Historical Themes in Early Childhood Education

1. The history of childhood
2. The history of developmental theories
3. The history of curriculum development and instruction

The four themes do not exhaust the possibility of other themes, but many topics that have been studied in the past fall within these four categories in some manner. The four categories reflect the content of early childhood teacher preparation textbooks. Although some texts only focus on contemporary thought and practices, many textbooks give historical background information on the context of an advance or change in an educational topic. Many times an issue in early childhood education can be better understood if the historical perspective is known. As a subset of the four possible themes, there is an extensive list of possible topics to be studied. Following is a partial list of sample topics that might be of interest.
Possible Topics for Early Childhood Education History

1. Technology in early childhood education
2. Inclusion in early childhood programs

3. Multicultural curriculum
4. Developmentally appropriate curriculum
5. Assessment of young children
6. Play in early childhood education
7. Professional and social status of the early childhood educator

A history of the topic being studied should fill a need. Perhaps there are questions that can be answered through an historical survey. Fortunately we have ample materials on early childhood education that include an historical perspective. For example, there has been a changing view of the use of technology in preschool classrooms. When computers were introduced to schools in the latter part of the twentieth century, there were many concerns about the danger of providing them to preschool children. Questions were asked about how developmentally appropriate computers were for preschool children (Cuffaro, 1984; Dutton & Dutton, 1988; National Science Foundation, 1983; Papert, 1980). How much were young children able to understand about using a computer (Clements, 1985; Haugland & Shade, 1988)? There were interviews with developmental specialists to determine what was best for young children. Now in the second decade of the twenty-first century, those concerns or discussions seem quaint. Children are growing up with mobile phones, computer games, and wireless tablets. Three-year-old children can play "Angry Birds" on a parent's cell phone. A first-grader can supply passwords for the family's computer programs, and small children flying to distant destinations are quietly sitting in their seats with their own electronic tablets, cell phones, and games.

It is interesting to look back at the issues about the use of technology with preschoolers when computers were first introduced and trace the history to the present time to understand how the acceptance of electronic devices has changed over the years. However, the issue of the dangers of the practice of giving preschool children electronic devices still exist. One concern is that home computer furniture is not set up properly for physical needs of young children. Another concern is that parents might use computers as a baby sitter (Education.com, 2012). A more recent issue is how children should be using computers and the most appropriate age to introduce computers to children (three-years-old) (Haugland, 1999).

The reality that preschool children are fascinated with all things electronic and quickly learn to use them at home demonstrates a new facet on how young children develop, learn, and play in their world today. It is no longer a matter of should young children be doing this type of activity. It is a reality in their lives and we need to understand what we can learn from the phenomenon. We can encourage preschool children in using electronic devices and still be sensitive to possible problems they might encounter when used excessively or improperly.

HOW TO CONDUCT HISTORICAL RESEARCH IN EARLY CHILDHOOD EDUCATION

Historical research follows a definite sequence of steps. The historial writer must determine what they want to know about early childhood education. How will an historical perspective help them to answer their questions? Interest in early childhood education can be traced back several centuries to the earliest thinkers about the nature of childhood and how they believed very young children should be educated. Froebel's concept of early childhood education as a child's garden was adopted around the world. In many countries contemporary early childhood programs are still referred to as kindergartens regardless of how they have evolved using changing influences over the years (Kang, Lee, & Hong, 2013; Sandell & Klypa, 2013; Stegelin & Cecconi, 2013). In Chile the title of preschool programs is "Jardin Infantil." Thus, early childhood programs in many parts of the world refer back to Froebel and Pestalozzi, although their programs may now be very different. The answers to historical writer's interests or questions are found by following the steps described next.

1. Select a Research Topic

State what you want to know about a topic. The question might be: "How did Froebelian kindergarten evolve into progressive kindergartens in the United States?" The topic then might be titled, "The Evolution of Frobelian Kindergartens into Progressive Kindergartens." Once the topic has been established, the historical writer is ready to define the nature of the historical project.

Determine the scope of the project. It is important next to define the parameters of the project. Will the researcher write a journal article, a chapter in a book, or perhaps a book? The amount of information that can be used will vary according to the scope of research the writer wants to do on the topic.

Develop an outline of the research. The scope of the project helps determine the outline of the research report. How will the report be organized? How will the topic be introduced? Why was the topic selected? How will understanding the sequence of one type of kindergarten to another help readers understand the nature of the evolution of early childhood education? Develop a draft of an outline for what you want to learn from your research.

2. Determine Possible Resources for Your Research Topic

The writer is now ready to look for information to develop the research project. All types of resources will be used to collect information relevant to the topic. The first search will be to find primary sources.

Search primary sources. Original sources of information are the strongest evidence in a research project. For example, seeing Froebel's gifts and occupations discussed earlier is more impressive than written descriptions of how they were used in his curriculum. Both together provide a complete picture of his learning materials. Original writing by Froebel, John Dewey, and later early childhood leaders such as Patty Smith Hill, Anna Bryan, and Margaret Nauman, who established the Walden School based on the psychoanalytic theories of Freud (Lascarides & Hinitz, 2011, p. 303) and Jung (Hinitz, 2002, p. 43), are just a few whose own writings inform the topic.

Such primary sources of information can be found in organizational archives and other national and state records. The Association for Childhood Education International and The National Association for the Education of Young Children have extensive archives that date back to the origins of the organizations. Early publications and records from these organizations will include writing by early leaders in the early childhood education movement in the twentieth century.

Another source is to locate current early childhood leaders or organizations who may have a link to earlier periods in history. For example, the Gesell Institute should have information that dates back to the early work on Gesell's norms for development. Descendents of the early leaders can also have important information and artifacts. A niece of Patty Smith Hill's nephew lived near me several years ago. She contacted me and invited me to her home to see some of Patty Smith Hill's school furniture and teaching materials. Reading about Patty Smith Hill's work in kindergarten development could not equal seeing some of her children's furniture and her teaching materials.

Search secondary resources. It is much easier to locate secondary resources, particularly in early childhood education. Professional journals such as *Young Children, Childhood Education,* and *Early Childhood Education Journal* often have articles that address the history of early childhood education. Professional Early Childhood Research journals such as the *Childhood Education Journal of Research, History of Education Quarterly,* and *History of Education Society* also can have relevant articles.

Professional textbooks, internet publications, articles in major news magazines, and newspapers are other sources of historical information. These are slowly being supplanted with electronic news outlets, search engines, television documentaries, and other televised specials on historical topics.

3. Conduct a Literature Review

The major effort in history research is to gather available information, also known as a literature review. Study the topic to be researched and determine a time frame to be used for the investigation. Check the internet for resources relevant to your topic. Look for published information in books, journals, and other printed sources. Keep in mind how you might locate some primary sources. As you begin to collect resources you can use the following process to organize the information.

Taking notes. If you have copies of the sources you are searching, underline the relevant material. Write notes electronically or by using a file card about key information that fits the topic. If using file cards, use a separate card for each source. Put the correct citation information at the top of the card. Underneath the citations, indicate which topics in your study are addressed in that particular source. You can indicate page numbers in the source, if needed. Add information as a document on the computer if additional space is needed for notes.

Notes can be written and organized electronically using software programs. There are many programs available that can be used for historical research. MicrosoftOneNote (http://office.microsoft.com/en-us/onenote/), Zotero (http://www.zotero.org/), and Evernote (http://www.evernote.com/e/n/) are three of many possible programs that can be used. An online guide to taking notes can be found at Note-Taking (http://edutechwiki.unige.ch/enNote_taking. Several methods of taking and organizing notes are included on this website.

Organizing notes. The accumulation of information from many sources can now be inserted into the original project outline according to the categories and subtopics in the project. The notes taken during source collection are organized according to where they fit into the outline. As the search continues, look for other search possibilities within the material being studied. Works cited in the context of the material or references at the end of a document can be very informative. Searching additional sources will help verify information and strengthen the validity of the written report (Cronon, 1988).

Once a sufficient amount of information or data has abeen collected, the writer can begin organizing the information to match the research outline. Gaps in information indicate that additional work is needed, or that there is not enough information to use in the study.

If the research project is large and spans a long period of time, chapters can be developed for the time periods. In the case of multiple chapters, the citations of sources and data are recorded and organized for each chapter.

At the end of the information collection process, the writer can revise and expand the project outline to accommodate new, unexpected information that informs the research purpose.

Evaluate the data. As the writer approaches the writing process, it is time to evaluate the quality and professionalism of the sources. Eliminate any resources that are not scholarly in nature, particularly from electronic sources. Although leaders in early childhood education do write for electronic publications, some electronic sources may lack careful research. For example, a search using key words, *early childhood education research*, produced an article that proposed that early childhood education in the United States began with the organization of the National Association for the Education of Young Children. Because early childhood education in the United States originated with the kindergarten movement in the nineteenth century, and NAEYC was first organized as the National Association for Nursery Education (NANE) in 1929, this statement indicates a lack of knowledge on the part of the writer and little effort to look for more accurate information (NAEYC, undated).

Use multiple sources to reflect the veracity of your information. If several credible authors present similar information about a topic, it is more likely to be reliable. Once the historical writer is comfortable with the content of search resources and information, writing the report can begin.

4. Prepare the Historical Report

The historical report is written in much the same manner as other narratives. For an article or a chapter, the beginning section is an introduction that includes the purpose of the research and how the history project will be discussed. The topics of the report are introduced and the author's reason for selecting the topic are included. Also included are the author's view of the relevance of the research study.

In the body of the report the historian discusses relevant information what the data reveals about the original research questions. The writer discusses what happened in the past or within periods of the past. The question of what happened and why are explained. The history also reveals the consequences of what happened. The notes taken during the data collecton process and citations of sources are organized to support the narrative. When each hypothesis or question has been discussed with suppporting references, a conclusion is written. In the conclusion the writer again states the questions, reviews the research and findings, and summarizes how the purpose for the research was accomplished.

When the report is completed, a reference list is added at the end. If footnotes have been used, they are listed as a separate section. To construct the reference list, the reference cards are now put into alphabetic order and listed. If the report is in the form of a book, the references might be listed at the end of each chapter or reported in one master list at the end of the book.

Writers who use electronic programs to write papers and organize citations into a bibliography can develop a reference list much more efficiently than using file cards. For example, Microsoft Office Word has a "Manage Resources" tab under "References" to achieve this process (http://aps.brepolis.net/bbih/manual).

CONCLUSION

Historical research answers questions about how the present is informed by the past. When conducting research in early childhood education, we learn how things happened that influenced how we approach early childhood programs today. There are two ways to understand the effect of history on early childhood education. One influence is the cumulative effect of history and the other is the revisionist effect of history.

When we study the changes in classroom arrangement and orgnization of materials used by the children since the first early childhood programs were introduced in the United States, we can see that some characteristics continue from one period to another. Child-sized furniture has changed in how it is constructed, but the tradition continues with newer furniture design using a variety of new materials. The use of art materials has continued over the historical periods. The inclusion of paints, brushes, easels, crayons, and modeling clay have been accepted creative materials throughout other program changes. Other curriculum concerns such as attention to large motor and fine motor skills during the school day are still present. Many practices used in Froebelian schools in the 18th century are part of the early childhood programs today.

Another effect of history is revision. The revision of history was discussed early in the chapter. Many practices used in early school programs have been revised as new information has become available. One example is Froebel's gifts and occupations. The activities recommended for Froebelian classrooms stressed fine motor skills and very small materials. Children learned to weave complex patterns using paper. Concrete materials were very small. During the progressive period as the result of the child study movement, it was found that children needed to have larger materials that required use of the large muscles of the body. Thus small construction blocks in the Froebelian classroom evolved into large building blocks in classrooms in the twentieth century. Small motor skills are still exercised using jigsaw puzzles and small construction toys such as Legos. We have learned to improve how we introduce learning experiences for children, but some things have been continuous in some form over time.

The focus in this chapter has been on how to conduct historical research in early childhood education. The strategies to conduct history have been introduced as well as how to collect and report historical information. Unlike educational research that follows prescribed methods and steps, historical research is more flexible and open-ended in how data is collected and reported. Educational research often is used to seek improved teaching methods in the classroom. Historical research is used to find out what happened in the past and why it is important to know that information. The early childhood education historian seeks to determine what lessons we can learn about curriculum, environment, and other elements of the preschool program so that we can learn from history and change accordingly.

We can consider the pros and cons for conducting historical research. There are strengths and limitations that are realistic when considering using this research tool. Following are some strengths and limitations:

Strengths

- Provides a comprehensive picture of historical trends
- Uses existing information
- Provides evidence of ongoing trends and problems

Limitations

- Time-consuming
- Resources may be hard to locate
- Resources may be conflicting
- May not identify cause of a problem
- Information may be incomplete, obsolete, inconclusive, or inaccurate
- Data is restricted to what already exists (HD.gov., 2009, p 2).

How does history influence the way we conduct early childhood programs today? History helps us to understand what we should be doing today and how we have come to that conclusion. And finally, historical research provides opportunities to find information we might not have expected. Is there anything more important than learning about Maria Montessori and how she came to design the materials she used in in her classrooms for disadvantaged children? How are Montessori materials used today? How has their use changed over two centuries? These questions become an adventure to answer and the search will change our perspective about early childhood education and why we do what we do with very young children.

APPENDIX

Lists of Resources for Historical Research in Early Childhood Education

Current Histories of Early Childhood Education
Beatty, B. (1995). *Preschool education in America. The culture of young children from the colonial era to the present.* New Haven, CT: Yale University Press.
Beatty, B. (2012) The debate of the young 'disadvantaged child': Preschool intervention, developmental psychology, and compensatory education in the 1960s and early 1970s. *Teachers College Record, 114*(6).
Hinitz, B. F. (Ed). (2013). *The hidden history of early childhood education and care.* New York, NY: Routledge.
Kammerman, S. B. (2006). *A global history of early childhood education and care.* Paper commissioned for the EFA Global Monitoring Report 2007, Strong foundations: Early childhood care and education. Contact efareport@unesco.org.
Lascarides, V. C., & Hinitz, B. (2011). *History of early childhood education.* New York, NY: Taylor & Francis.

Examples of Histories of Childhood

Aries, P. (1962). *Centuries of childhood. A social history of family life.* New York, NY: Vintage Books.
Avery, G. (1965). *Nineteenth century children. Heroes and heroines in English children's stories.* London: Hodder & Stoughton.
Grotberg, E. H.(Ed.). (1976). *200 Years of children.* Washington, DC: U.S. Department of Health, Education, and Welfare; Office of Human Development; Office of Child Development.
Kamm, A., & Lean, A. (Eds.). (1985). *A Scottish childhood.* Glasgow: Collins in association with Save the Children Fund.
Marcus, I. G. (1996). *Rituals of childhood. Jewish acculturation in medieval Europe.* New Haven and London: Yale University Press.
Pettigrew, J. (1991). *An Edwardian childhood.* Boston: Little, Brown and Co.
Shein, M. (1992). *The Precolumbian child.* Culver City, CA: Labyrinthos.

REFERENCES

Beatty, B. (1995). *Preschool in America. The culture of young children from the colonial era to the present.* New Haven, CT: Yale University Press.

Benjamin, H. R. (1964). John Dewey's influence on educational pracctice. In D. E. Lawson & A. E. Lean (Eds.), *John Dewey and the world view.* Carbondale, IL: Southern Illinois University Press.

Billington, R. A. (1950). *Westward expansion: A history of the American frontier.* New York, NY: Macmillan.

Bloom, A. (1991). Introduction to Rousseau, J. J. (1762) *Emile.* London: Penguin.

Busha, C., & Harter, S. P. (1982). *Research methods in librarianship: Techniques and interpretations.* New York, NY: Academic Press.

Clements, D. H. (1985). *Computers in early and primary education.* Upper Saddle River, NJ: Prentice Hall.

Cremin, L. A. (1961). *The transformation of the school.* New York, NY: Knopf.

Cremin, L. A. (1988). *American education: The metropolitan experience 1876–1980.* New York, NY: Harper & Row.

Creswell, J. W. (2011). *Educational research: Planning, conducting, and evaluating quantitativeand qualitative research.* (2nd. ed.). Upper Saddle River, NJ: Pearson.

Cronon, W. (1988). Learning to do historical research. A primer for environmental historians and others. Retrieved from http://www.Williamcronon.net/resarching

Cubberley, E. P. (1920). *Readings in the history of education.* Boston: Houghton Mifflin.

Cuffaro, H. M. (1984). Microcomputers in education: Why is earlier better? *Teachers College Record, 85,* 559–568.

Dent, N. J. H. (1988). *Rousseau: An introduction to his psychological, social, and political theory.* Oxford: Basil Blackwell.

Dewey, J. (1899). *The school and society.* Chicago: University of Chicago Press.

Dutton, W. H., & Dutton, A. (1988). *Mathematics children use and understand.* Mountain View, CA: Mayfield.

Education.com (2012). Computers in preschool: Hurting or helping? Retrieved from http://www.education.com/magazine/article/preschoolers-computers

Encyclopedia of Children and Childhood in History and Society. (2002). *Kindergarten.* Retrieved from www. Facs.org/childhood/KeMe/kindergarten.html

Froebel, F. (1899). *Education of man.* New York, NY: Appleton.

Gesell, A. (1925). *The mental age of the child.* New York, NY: Macmillan.

Gross, R., & Gross, B. (1976). Lifelong learning. In E. H, Grotberg (Ed.), *200 years of children* (pp. 178–187). Washington, DC: U.S. Government Printing Office.

Gulliford, A. (1984). *Amerian's country schools.* Washington, DC: The Preservation Press.

Hall, G. S. (1883, May). The contents of children's minds. *The Princeton Review, 11,* 249–253.

Haugland, S. W. (1999). What role should technology play in young children's learning? *Young Children, 54,* 26–31.

Haugland, S. W., & Shade, D. D. (1988). Developmentally appropriate software for young children. *Young Children, 43,* 37–43.

HD.gov (2009). Methods historical research. Retrieved from http://www.hd.gov/HDdotGov/detail.jsp?ContentID-330

Hinitz, B. (2002) Margaret Naumburg and the Walden School. In A R. Sadovnik, & S. F. Semel (Eds.), *Founding mothers and others: Women educational leaders during the progressive era* (pp. 37–59). New York, NY: Palgrave.

Johnson, B., & Christiansen. L. B. (2004). *Educational research: Quantitative, qualitative, and mixed approaches* (2nd ed.). Boston: Allyn & Bacon.

Kaestle, C. F. (1997). Recent methodological developments in the history of American education. In R.M. Jaeger, (Ed.), *Complementary methods for educational research*, (2nd ed, pp. 114–131). Washington, DC: American Education Researcu Association,.

Kagan, J. (1984). *The nature of the child.* New York, NY: Basic Books.

Kang, S. Y., Lee, G. L., & Hong, S. (2013). Preserving cultural heritage in kindergartens in Korea. In S. C. Wortham (Ed.), *Common characteristics and unique qualities in preschool programs. Global perpectives in early childhood education* (pp. 67–74). Dordrecht, Heidelberg, London: Springer.

Kilpatrick, W. H. (1916). *Froebel's kindergarten principles critically examined.* New York, NY: Macmillan.

Lascarides, V. C., & Hinitz, B. (2011). *History of early childhood education.* New York, NY: Taylor & Francis.

Lynn, R. W., &Wright, E. (1971). *The big little school.* New York, NY: Harper & Row.

McCarthy, M. A., & Houston, J. P. (1980). *Fundamentals of early childhood education.* Cambridge, MA: Winthrop Publishers.

National Association for the Education of Young Children. (no date). *Our history.* Retrieved from http://www.naeyc.org/about history

National Science Foundation. (1983). *Educating America for the 21st century: A report to the American people and the National Science Board.* Washington, DC: Author.

Novick, P. (1988). *That noble dream: The objectivity quesstion in American history.* New York, NY: Cambridge University Press.

Papert, S. (1980). *Mindstorms: Children, computers, and powerful ideas.* New York, NY: Basic Books.

Ratner, J. (Ed.) (1939). *Intelligence in the modern world. John Dewey's philosophy.* New York, NY: Random House.

Rousseau, J. J. (1911). *Emile.* London: J. M. Dent & Sons.

Sandell, E. J., & Klypa, O. V. (2013). Kindergarten in Russia's Far East. In S.C. Wortham (Ed.) *Common characteristics and unique qualities in preschool programs. Global perspectives in early childhood education,* (pp. 57–66). Dordrecht, Heidelberg, London: Springer.

Smith, M. K. (2012). *Frederich Froebel.* Retrieved from http://www.infed.org/thinkers/etfroeb.htm

Spodek, B. (1973). *Early childhood education.* Englewood Cliffs, NJ: Prentice-Hall..

Snyder, A. (1972). *Dauntless women in childhood education.* Olney, MD: Association for Childhood Education Internationl.

Stegelin, D., & Cecconi, L. (2013). Kindergarten environments in Reggio Emilia, Bologna, Modena, and Parma, Italy in Search of Quality. In S. C. Wortham (Ed.), *Common characteristics and unique qualities in preschool programs educating the young* (pp. 47–54). Dordrecht, Heidelberg, London: Springer.

Tuckman, B. W. (1999). *Conducting educational research* (5th ed.). Ft. Worth, TX: Harcourt Brace College Publishers.

Watson, B. (1997). *Kindergarten.* Retrieved from www.froebelweb.org/folkind.html
Weber, C. (1969). *Early childhood education: Perspectives on change.* Worthington, Ohio: Charles A. Jones.
Weber, C. (1984). *Ideas influencing early childhood education* New York, NY: Teachers College Press.
Wortham, S. C. (1970, May). *The role of the Negro on the Texas frontier (1821–1836).* Unpublished Master's thesis. San Marcos, TX: Southwest Texas State University.
Wortham, S. C. (2002). *Childhood 1892–2002* (2nd ed). Olney, MD: Association for Childhood Education International.

CHAPTER 20

PAST AS PROLOGUE

Doing Historical Research in Early Childhood Education

Edna Runnels Ranck

> A large, convincing, body of research in psychology, economics and neuroscience points to the importance of the early years in producing successful outcomes for the advantaged and in accounting for social pathologies found among the disadvantaged. This research should cause us to rethink policies focused on human development. (Heckman, 2007, p. 3)

Interest in the lives of young children and their education and care is expected of parents, early education program professionals, teacher educators, pediatricians, and child advocates. Over recent decades, however, heightened investigations in the field of early childhood education and a commitment to understand societal responses to the needs of young children have emerged from economists, public policymakers, university professors, health professionals, and historians. The widening awareness of and interest in young children's lives in the United States and elsewhere is represented by the following data reports that reflect an expanding awareness of young children.

- The number of children in care and educational programs outside the home. The most recent U.S. Census data report that nearly 11 million children under age five with working mothers are in some type of regular child care arrangement every week (NACCRRA, 2012a).
- The number of states providing prekindergarten classes in public schools and the federal funding levels. Thirty-nine of 50 states provide four-year-old prekindergarten classes in public schools; 24 of these states also serve three-year-olds in pre-K classes. Eleven states do not offer prekindergarten classes. The total state preschool spending, including TANF and ARRA funds directed toward preschool at the states' discretion is $5,492,133,988.00. (Barnett, Carolan, Fitzgerald, & Squires, 2011).
- The number of workers (teachers, assistant teachers, teacher aides) in the early childhood education field. The U.S. Bureau of Labor Statistics estimates the size of the formal child care workforce at 1.25 million. Women compose 94.7% of this segment of the workforce. One of the most compelling statements connected to these figures is that "many child care providers lack the education and training necessary to provide quality child care" (NACCRRA, 2012b).

For the historian of early childhood education, these data signify the changing work lives of fathers and mothers, the entry of ever younger children in public school systems, and the development of stronger professional requirements for entering and remaining in the field of early childhood education, all potential topics of historical research.

PART ONE: HISTORICAL CONTEXT

Purpose

Early childhood education programs and services for young children are critically important for American families and society in the twenty-first century. Concerned citizens need to know how such programs and services have been introduced and implemented in the past, including the eighteenth, nineteenth, and twentieth centuries, and how educators can continue to build the body of knowledge that will continue expanding the story of early childhood education in this country. The chapter will claim that doing historical research in early childhood education is essential to formulate the policies and practices necessary to produce successful citizens.

Part I, Historical Context, presents the steps a historian of early childhood education will take to research, write, and disseminate a historical document. Early education conditions are identified and questions are asked. Models of doing general history, educational history, and early childhood history are described and lessons learned from the historical record are given. Appendixes offer an overview of researching and writing history that references Rael, 2004, and Storey, 2009; noting the characteristics of an early childhood historian; handling details that differ among sources; and listing caveats for the historical researcher in early education.

Part II, Historical Content, introduces the tools of the historian's toolbox: selecting a style manual, locating and using primary, secondary, and tertiary sources; locating archives, libraries, historical societies, and finding Internet resources. Guidelines gleaned from researching the chapter, together with recommendations for future historical research projects, conclude Part II.

Questions addressed in the chapter and the section in which they are addressed follow:

- What is the purpose of conducting historical research? What is the difference between history and historiography? *Part I and Appendix A*
- Who are general and educational historians about whom the historian should know and whose publications should be read? Who are some early childhood historians whose works should be known and read by the historian for the purpose of becoming widely knowledgeable about the historical nature of early childhood education? *Part I*
- What are the typical sources used by the historian, where are they found, and what are the guidelines for selecting and judging the quality of sources to be referenced? *Part II*
- What future research topics are recommended for the early childhood research historian? *Part II*

Models of Historiography

The books introduced here are models of "doing history" or thinking about how to do history. The reader will want to question the contents of each book to determine the author's point of view, the major ideas, and the omitted topics. Does the book honor the subject appropriately? Does it present all sides of the main issue it addresses? Does it reflect a thorough investigation of its main issue? Three groups of educational historians are represented: General historians who, as a rule, do not do educational research; educational historians who, as a rule, do not do early childhood education historical research; and early childhood historians who represent the field in various styles.

General Historians

Each selection features a brief biographical sketch of the author, cites a book, and provides a brief report of the publication's content. The general historians were selected to show an approach to handling the how-to features of doing history; they looked behind the obvious data and found the "messiness" of them. The selected authors are Eric Foner, Carl F. Kaestle, Mark T. Gilderhus, and Jacques Barzun and Henry F. Graff. Other general historians whose works should be known and read by early childhood historians are Bernard Bailyn, 1960; Marc Bloch, 1953; Peter Novick, 1988; and Fritz Stern, 1972. Locate additional book titles by searching each name on an Internet search engine.

Eric Foner (2002)

Who owns history? Rethinking the past in a changing world. Born in New York (Long Island) in 1943; a graduate of and a professor at Columbia University, and other universities; best known for his work on the Civil War (his book on Reconstruction after the Civil War took over 10 years to research and write; he had anticipated three years.

"Who owns history? Everyone and no one—which is why the study of the past is a constantly evolving, never-ending journey of discovery" (p. xix). The essays on his life emphasize the chance aspects of life and, therefore, of history. Foner marks the difference between the viewpoints of history held by professors of history and by the broader public. While historians keep searching for more data on which to expand knowledge, many in the public arena look at reinterpretation "with suspicion and negativity." He reminds the reader that selecting some facts and ignoring others is a way of reinterpreting the past, and that "truth exists...as a reasonable approximation of the past" (p. xvii). Some have difficulty with the idea that history is *not* simply facts and figures, that it is *not* somehow based on real truth. Foner's point: history is interpretation, but done systematically and with great care.

Kaestle, C. F. (1992, Fall)

Standards of Evidence in Historical Research: How Do We Know When We Know? Professor of Education, History, and Public Policy, Brown University; as of 2005, author of five books and numerous articles. A copy of this article was downloaded by the Smithsonian Institution library from JSTOR, a subscription database, and mailed on January 15, 2013. As the *History of Education Quarterly* does not make available issues before 2001, I needed a library to access it. After 10 days, the article I received was missing three pages. The librarian disregarded policy and emailed the full article. The experience is a reminder to allow sufficient time to receive requested information from an outside source.

Kaestle sparks curiosity with the title of the article. His brief effort to help colleagues know when they have spied the truth is helpful, in part to understand how historians viewed the problem at the end of the twentieth century.

Kaestle viewed the historical profession as "fragmented, ideologically diverse, and somewhat relativistic..." (p. 361). Examples from a historical subject are used to ask: What are the implicit standards for defining truth? The accepted fact is that "the more certainty [there is] about a historical "fact," the more trivial it is apt to be. And the more significant [the fact], the less certain" (p. 363). "Historical truths are social truths," thus dissent happen. Over time, with sufficient and varied studies that are compared and written about, some generalizations emerge. Kaestle's view: [History] is "messy" with murky evidence that is "frustrating and necessary"—the historian's job is to "set questions, agendas, share tentative hypotheses, and get ready to move" (p. 366). Multiple levels of analysis, synthesis of claims that disagree, and reinforcement occurs across time and space; to know for sure is never absolute and a tentative conclusion is always subject to rejection and revision.

Gilderhus, M. T. (2007)

History and Historians: A Historiographical Introduction. (6th ed.). Professor of history at Texas Christian University in 2007; research interest in U.S. diplomatic and military history and historiography; book is now available in a seventh edition.

The book is "an introduction to some of the main issues and problems in historiography, philosophy of history, and historical method" (p. iv). As definitions and descriptions of historical events and ways of thinking emerge, Gilderhus offers a basic guide for understanding aspects of historical research that have evolved over time. Its brevity is an introduction to refresh memory and knowledge about historical beliefs and practices. He relates history to civic responsibility; as a way to gain self-knowledge and to levy sanctions on unethical or immoral actions; as a learning experience to avoid future errors; and, most importantly, to tell the truth about the past in the present and to the future (pp. 4–6). The historian must decide what the past means for the present: "Among other things, history involves its practitioners in an ongoing and sometimes unresolvable debate over the meaning of human experience" (p. 10). Gilderhus explores key aspects of history by examining a range of publications, by doing historiography. Chapters on culture wars and postmodernism offer a brief description of recent historical research and a helpful list of readings.

Barzun, J. and Graff, H. F. (2004)

The modern researcher. (6th ed.). Belmont, CA: Wadsworth Centage Learning. Both professors of history at Columbia University (Barzun in Modern Cultural and Graff in American Political and Diplomatic. Barzun died in October 2012 at age 104; Graff is professor emeritus. This book is "a guide to the necessary steps from inquiry to communication."

First published in 1957, *The Modern Researcher* holds a unique place in research literature, including creating the historical record. Surviving to its sixth edition lends it credibility. This author recommends it to early childhood education historians for two reasons: (1) It is a companion to any style manual and strives to be instructive by providing numbered lists throughout the book (1961) to guide research, including Internet and regular Library sources; and (2) its readability in the face of complex material, such as the chapter "Handling Ideas" (pp. 101–116), and the follow-up information about "truth, causes, and conditions" harboring a section on "evidence" (pp. 117–148). While this book is grounded in philosophy, the longevity of both authors lends a rich source of information in its own right.

The lessons learned from the general historians will be combined with those from the remaining historians covered below. In addition to choosing books for further reading, the historian can also track new histories in newspapers and journals. The *New York Times* and the *Washington Post* publish book review in their dailies and on Sundays in special sections. The American *History of Education Quarterly* includes book reviews in each issue. In this way, the historian follows the guideline of reading widely and deeply and keeps up with advances in historical research.

Education Historians

In addition to the historians cited above, a number of historians of education support concerns frequently expressed by leaders in early childhood education. None of the following authors specializes in early childhood, but the books address pertinent issues. All were written by academic historians, educators, or educational advocates. The selected authors are Irwin Garfinkel, Jennifer L. Hochschild, Sara S. McLanahan, Sonya Michel, and Judith Sealander. Other education historians whose publications the early childhood historian should know are Lawrence Cremin, 1961, and John Dewey, 1902, 2001, both affiliated with Teachers College, Columbia University, and each of whom published numerous, well-respected volumes on education.

Garfinkel, I., Hochschild, J. L., and McLanahan, S. S. (1996)

Social policies for children. The eight chapters address a range of services provided for young American children, of which one speaks about early childhood: "Child Care: The Key to Ending Child Poverty" by Barbara R. Bergmann illustrates as do many early childhood histories, that child care for children in poverty is viewed as the means by which significant governmental appropriations can reduce poverty. Thus, the programs also support employed parents as well. Differences of opinion among those attending the conference out of which the chapters came were cited in the introductory chapter; the viewpoints varied pro and con, as positions on government-funded early childhood education programs have for centuries (pp. 17–19).

Sonya Michel (1999)

Children's interests/mothers' rights: The shaping of America's child care policy. Michel's study presents an in-depth review of the status of child care in the United States from its years in the early decades of the nineteenth century until the late 1990s. This book, like that of Barbara Beatty described in the next section, began as a doctoral dissertation (Brown University) "where I first learned that social policy had a history" (p. 395). The author of this chapter found Michel very helpful in revising a conference paper on early education policy during the Eisenhower administrations for a book chapter (Ranck, 2013). Its thoroughness demonstrates the historical process over time in which many writers on early childhood education move from discussing World War II support for child care to the Head Start program in the mid-1960s, completely omitting policy references from the 1950s. Michel makes connections between women's and children's public policies addressed during Dwight Eisenhower's administrations, using reports from the National Manpower Council: *Womanpower: A Statement by the National Manpower Council with Chapters by the Council Staff* (1957) and *Work in the Lives of Married Women: Proceedings of a Conference on Womanpower* (1958). These volumes, largely devoid of representatives from the field of early childhood education, struggle to agree about the role of working mothers in America.

Judith Sealander, J. (2003)

The failed century of the child: Governing America's young in the twentieth century. A professor of history at Bowling Green State University. Michel and Sealander's books focus on timeframes spanning centuries. Choosing to emphasize a specific time period is crucial to historical research, but the historian must also provide a context that introduces the era before and lists the influences continuing into the future. Public policies combined with research quantification compound the efforts to understand the connections between government and children, and often fails to see the interwoven relationships among children's welfare, work, education, and health, the central headings for the book's four parts.

Sealander cites briefly a major publication for the twentieth century: *The Century of the Child* by Ellen Key. Written in Sweden in 1900 and published in the United States in 1909, Key addressed the rights of children, the role of women, education, homelessness, "soul murder in the schools," religious education, child labor, and the crimes of children (1909). Sealander writes that in spite of Key's modern ideas about rearing children, the "centrality of children's welfare in the twentieth century's progress" was limited: "Nowhere did this [major change] really happen, certainly not in the United States" (p. 1).

Key's thinking and especially her book title reappeared in 2012 as the impetus for a major exhibition on children and design at the Museum of Modern Art in New York City, inspired in part by Key's position on design and childhood. The curator of the exhibition and coauthor of its catalog wrote: "Despite being ubiquitous and the focus of intense concern and profound thought, children remain one of the most underevaluated subjects in the historical analysis of modern design" (Kinchin & O'Connor, 2012, p. 16). Several pages later a section titled "The Kindergarten Movement: Building Blocks of Modern Design" quotes the writings of Friedrich Froebel. The MoMA exhibition was an example of an unexpected early childhood historical event. The MoMA exhibition also suggested enumerable research: public policy and childhood, caveats about rearing children in the next 100 years, and the world of art and design throughout the world.

Early Childhood Education Historians

The existence of books and journal articles on the history of early childhood education does not mean that all or even most early childhood professionals will read and reflect on them. Judging by the publication dates of the material selected for review in this chapter, the historical writing about early childhood education appears to have increased in recent decades. It is interesting to note that the limited survey that follows and that was chosen for variety, subject, and style, could be divided into six categories.

Basic Early Childhood Education Histories

In *Past Caring: A History of U.S. Preschool Care and Education for the Poor, 1820–1965*, **Emily D. Cahan** (1989). provided a brief monograph describing the efforts of two centuries to address issues of poverty by providing child care and education programs to poor families. Cahan described a two-tier system established in the nineteenth century for the care and education of the child below compulsory school attendance from poor families. Kindergartens and nursery schools had been designed largely for the education and socialization of young children from middle-income families. For low-income families, however, day nurseries and child care programs were offered, often with poorer quality programming and a strong negative stigma attached. "Historically, differences in quality of child care have been associated with differences in socioeconomic class...we must remain mindful of the historical persistence of a tiered system of child care and education" (p. 50).

Barbara Beatty (1995) expanded her doctoral dissertation at the Harvard Graduate School of Education into *Preschool Education in America: The Culture of Young Children from the Colonial Era to the Present*. In the deceptively simple opening sentences of the Preface, Beatty drafts a key question: "This is the story of how Americans came to think that young children should have access to preschool education outside the home...more specifically, this is a history of policy and pedagogy in American preschool education. Why...is no provision made for universal preschool education in the United States today" (p. ix)? Beatty traces with great attention to detail and depth how infant schools, kindergartens and nursery schools—preschool programs—for children between the ages of three- and five-years-of age came into being in the first half of the nineteenth century, as well as the relationship between children's culture and women's culture. The author carefully identifies the sub-topics that are not covered (pp. x–xi) and explains why it took years to research and write the book: "...I enjoy spending time in libraries and archives and kept unearthing more treasures I wanted to include" (p. xiv–xv).

Maris A. Vinovskis (2005) in *The Birth of Head Start: Preschool Education Policies in the Kennedy and Johnson Administration,* comments on Beatty's limited attention to Head Start's origins (p. 2). Vinovskis's book itself covers in detail the complex policies that evolved during the early years of Head Start, giving it a "top-down" review of people and policies that created a huge program for poor children largely under the age of five years. He cites several of Edward Zigler's earlier books as valuable and "insightful personal reflections and scholarly analyses" derived from "his Washington experiences and his extensive relationships with other key participants" (p. 2). See the section 5 below on "Biographical Histories" for additional information about Zigler's role in the creation and development of Head Start.

Another Head Start-related publication is **Jon N. Hale's** article in *History of Education Quarterly* gives a "bottom-up" historical account of the start and growth of Head Start in Mississippi (Hale, 2012). Hale's article is also referenced below in Appendix A in connection with the definition of historiography.

Mixed Histories: Based on the Timeframes Covered and the Amount and Source of Subject Matter Included

Samuel J. Braun and **Esther P. Edwards** (1972): *History and Theory of Early Childhood Education* links excerpts from much older publications, much like a shorter version of the Bremner documentary history cited below in Part II. Citations for the original documents are provided for each entry. Other helpful features are a section on approaches to learning with entries by Constance Kamii and Barbara Biber, noted early childhood educators and researchers, and a series of appendices by Margaret McMillan, Lawrence K. Frank, James L. Hymes, Jr., Gwen Morgan and Bettye Caldwell (the latter two are retired and live in Massachusetts and Arkansas, respectively).

James L. Hymes, Jr., (1991) and D. Keith Osborn, (1991) both contributed significantly to the field of early childhood education, Hymes during World War II and Osborn at the beginning of Head Start. Each wrote a history of early childhood education that surveys different time periods: Hymes's *Twenty Years in Review: A Look at 1971–1990* records a wide range of political, social, and professional events as a summary of annual reports beginning in 1971. It reflects his role in the growth of the field during a time of intense expansion of ideas and policies revolving around early childhood. All but the first four annual reviews provide end-of-chapter notes. No Internet websites or e-mail addresses are listed for any chapter. Although *Twenty Years in Review* is a personal accounting of each of the 20 years, the status of the author and the collegial offers of information assure relative reliability. Both authors took advantage of their professional and biological longevity and recalled from memory, notes, and contributions from colleagues a broad range of details about the field of early education during the selected timeframes. What these publications lack in depth is made up for in references to aspects of early childhood education from the fifteenth century through most of the twentieth century.

D. Keith Osborn's *Early Childhood Education in Historical Perspective* in its third edition begins in prehistory millions of years BC and continues through the date of publication. (Present-day style manuals use CE and BCE for Common Era and Before Common Era; Osborn used BC and AD to date events.) Osborn's Name and Subject Indexes are backed up by an extensive list of References. It offers the reader both a wide-ranging survey of the growth and development of the field of early childhood education as well as links to many original historical and research publications. Some entries are quite extensive, while others are brief. The historian can find some unexpected information among the various sections, including references to events that occurred during the 1950s, a decade often ignored by early childhood educators and historians.

Elizabeth Palmer Peabody's letters were edited in 1984 (Ronda). One of the pioneers featured in *Dauntless Women in Childhood Education* (Snyder, 1992), Peabody exchanged letters with family, colleagues, and friends in a "vast correspondence" now located in numerous archives and depositories (p. xvii–xviii). Among the people receiving letters on the subject of Froebel, early childhood education, and the kindergarten were Horace Mann, Jr., Henry Wadsworth Longfellow, William Lloyd Garrison, William T. Harris, A. Bronson Alcott, Louisa May Alcott, and her sister, Mary Peabody Mann (pp. viii–ix). Peabody also trained kindergarten teachers and wrote about the Froebelian kindergarten as it took shape in the United States (Peabody, 1888).

Profiles in Childhood Education, 1931–1960 (Association for Childhood Education, 1992) and Agnes Snyder's *Dauntless Women in Childhood Education, 1856–1931* (1972) cover the lives of people, 32 women and five men, who contributed to early childhood education during two centuries. Published by the Association for Childhood Education International (ACEI), the oldest early childhood professional organization in the United States, the books are unique in that Agnes Snyder who worked with Patty Smith Hill, a major figure in early childhood education, also wrote about her. Snyder herself was included in the *Profiles* book and also had extensive access to the ACEI archives. The organizations represented in the archives located at the University of Maryland include the International Kindergarten Union (IKU), beginning in 1892, the National Council of Primary Education that merged with IKU in 1931 to become the Association for Childhood Education (ACE), and ACEI itself. Information for accessing the ACEI archives is provided in Part II, *Historical Content.* Access to primary sources in *Dauntless Women* with its footnotes, references, and index is balanced by *Profiles* with none of these resources, but with a record of taped interviews listing the subject's name, the name of the interviewer, and the interview date. The entries in *Profiles* were reprinted from volumes 61–68 of the ACEI journal *Childhood Education*, a quarterly journal still in print.

History of Early Childhood Education coauthored by V. Celia Lascarides and Blythe F. Hinitz (2000; 2011 in paper) is a lengthy record of early childhood dating from antiquity and ending just prior to publication. The 24 chapters, four appendixes, and 15 figures cover the beginnings of early childhood education (Part I), an account of the subject in the United States (Part II), and accounts of diverse populations in America (Part III—Native Americans, Black Americans, Asian Americans, Hispanic Americans, bilingualism, selected overseas programs, and early childhood professional organizations (Contents, pp. vii–xiii). The roots of the extensive book are in a paper the authors presented at a European conference in conjunction with other early childhood colleagues that reported on a 1987 survey designed to "...to find out if there was a base of historical knowledge among enrolled students in four-year programs in early childhood education [in America]" (Salimova & Johanningmeier, 1993, p. 264). Students (236) so enrolled were found to "have knowledge of the history of early childhood education (concepts, ideas, trends)" (p. 275). The findings also reported "...a lack of a core knowledge taught to students" (p. 276).

In 1981, Jean Simpson produced a doctoral dissertation in which she conducted oral interviews with African-American early childhood education educators. The study was continued and expanded later to include video-taped interviews with other African American leaders. (Simpson, 1981). Presentations on selected interviewees have been given at the History Seminar held during annual conferences of the National Association for the Education of Young Children (NAEYC), and Oneida Cockrell, a Chicago interviewee, was featured in an "Our Proud Heritage" column" in *Young Children* (Simpson, 1981, 2012).

Organizational Histories

While susceptible to being friendly history, organizational histories nevertheless offer a compilation of primary sources and a narrow view of the field of early education, both over a given time period as well as at a particular time, a snapshot as it were. The contents can include not only a timeline of important events, but also often provide a parallel list of events throughout the field of early childhood education (NAEYC, 2001; NAFCC, 2007). An organization's accomplishments are a platform on which the organization will continue moving forward into its unknown future. In addition, a compilation of board presidents and members; agency staff; dates, themes, speakers, and locations of regular conferences; and a survey of strategic plans over time also demonstrates organizational growth and development (NAEYC, 2001; NAFCC, 2007; NARA, 2006; Ranck, 1997 (NACCRRA); Wortham, 1992 (ACEI).

Biographical Histories: Books Written by Authors Who Experienced What They Wrote About

- Polly Greenberg (1969) worked for the federal government at the time Head Start was established in 1965, and also spent time helping to implement the Child Development Group of Mississippi (CDGM). *The Devil Has Slippery Shoes: A Biased Biography of the Child Development Group of Mississippi* (its 700 pages are one-half of what Greenberg submitted to the publisher) is an intense book with a steadfast message transmitted from the past to the future: "This is intended to be the biography of the beginning of one group's search for a way to overcome the discouragingly formidable weave of economic, educational, psychological, racial, social, and political obstacles that lurk between people and their modest dream. It is neither a comprehensive nor a neutral biography" (p. xii). Published only four years after Head Start began, it speaks of history-in-the-making events that occurred from the top-down (Washington, D.C.) and from the bottom-up (Mississippi).
- Edward Zigler, a major voice in American early childhood education both as a child development researcher at Yale University and from the beginnings of Head Start in 1965, has written many books about

the federally-funded program, usually based in part on his multiple roles at its inception and throughout its continued development. In *The Hidden History of Head Start* (Zigler & Styfco, 2010) brings to a close his role in one of the strongest early childhood education experiences in the United States. His closing words are thoughtful: "... I step back from my nearly half-century involvement with America's Head Start program. Its history has been bold, illuminating, agonizing, and filled with potholes. A grasp of the successes as well as failures of the past will hopefully guide the next generation of Head Start's supporters and leaders in building a stronger, continuously better program" (p. 351). Vinovskis (2005) provides another historical version of Head Start's tumultuous beginning; it is a top-down, parallel view of Head Start's history. It is also to be compared with a bottom-up description of part of the Head Start story (Hale, 2012).

Absence of Historical Research: When Publications Are Dominated by Empirical Research or History Is Ignored

A historian conducting a literature search for documents and publications available for research may find gaps in the literature, either in terms of topics covered or of historical omissions. The historian may want to determine how to fill or correct the gaps and omissions; one research omission in early childhood has been historical research itself.

Early Childhood Education Child Development Research. The National Association for the Education of Young Children (NAEYC) has published many types of books for the early childhood education profession, including three volumes of child development research studies (Hartup, 1972; Hartup & Smothergill, 1967; Moore & Cooper, 1982). The research reviews were designed in part for classroom practitioners working with preschool children. Historical research was not included or referred to in these volumes.

In 1986, NAEYC introduced the *Early Childhood Research Quarterly*. The first article in volume 1, number 1, on page 1 was titled "The Past, Present, and Future for the Early Childhood Education Researcher" by Millie Almy (1986). Subsequent volumes through Volume 11 produced 44 issues with over 400 articles; of that number, only four more articles labeled as historical appeared. By observing gaps in the historical record, the historian can call attention to the omissions or submit an article to meet the need for contributions to historical research.

To its credit, NAEYC has contributed a growing number of early childhood education historical initiatives:

1. For NAEYC's 75th anniversary in 2001, the organization issued a publication containing the 50th anniversary article originally published in 1976, a timeline for NAEYC and the field of early childhood education, articles related to the anniversary, and lists of annual conferences, past presidents, and Governing Board members (2001).
2. The NAEYC Annual Conference has offered a version of the History Seminar since 1973, starting with one presentation for one hour through 2012 with 23 presenters giving 20 presentations from 8:30am to 4:30pm (2012). A full listing of all the presentation titles and presenter names is available from this author at the e-mail address in the References (Ranck, 2012).
3. In 2009, NAEYC introduced a regular column in the journal *Young Children* titled "Our Proud Heritage." Seven history-themed columns appeared in 2010–2012. Thus, it appears that NAEYC with a limited interest in historical publications in the past has expanded its offering of historical information to members and advocates.

Harvard Family Research Project. In 2004, the Harvard Family Research Project, Harvard Graduate School of Education, published a report titled *Early childhood programs and evaluation* (Weiss, 2004). The Harvard University-sponsored program placed the start of the field of early childhood education in 1965. The series of articles written by well-known researchers and authors began its first article by stating: "The field of early childhood is entering middle-age. Its infancy began in 1965 with the country's first and only federally-funded program—Head Start" (p. 2). Another article opened with a similar sentence: "Early childhood programs have been a part of the nation's social policy landscape for decades. Beginning with the establishment of Head Start and the Handicapped Children's Early Education Program in the 1960s and extending into the debates over early care and education in the 2000s, the call for public investment has been impassioned and the demand for accountability has been persistent" (p. 3). As noted above in books by Cahan, Beatty, Michel, and Sealander, calls for investment and demands for accountability have been issued in the United States, not for decades, but for centuries, beginning with infant schools and public and private kindergartens in the early-to-mid-nineteenth century, and continuing throughout the twentieth and into the twenty-first centuries. This otherwise informative report would have been stronger and more accurate with a brief and accurate statement about earlier experiences linking poverty with early childhood programs in the United States.

Historical Observations from an Early Childhood Leader. Bettye Caldwell, a retired early childhood researcher and professor, has promoted the study and dissemination of historical data in the early childhood education field more than once. In the Foreword to *Past Caring* (Cahan, 1989),

Caldwell expresses regret at the lack of knowledge of the historical roots of early childhood by the more recent professionals in the field. Caldwell ends the Foreword with these words: "Those concerned with early childhood programs should be aware of the way in which theory, knowledge, and social relevance are melded in the past and the present. It is hoped that these aspects of the field's history... will be equally visible in the future" (Caldwell, 1989, p. xi).

In 2009, in part at Caldwell's recommendation, the column "Our Proud Heritage" was initiated by NAEYC in its practitioner journal *Young Children* (D. Koralek, personal communication to the author, February 24, 2009). The column on early childhood education history was published three times in 2010, and twice each in 2011 and 2012. The next two columns will appear in May and November 2013. Sufficient columns have been submitted to meet the publication schedule through 2016. For "Our Proud Heritage columns published on early childhood education topics, see (http://www.naeyc.org/yc/columns/ourproudheritage)

Lessons Learned From General, Educational, and Early Childhood Educational Historians

Historians of early childhood education select subjects on which to write and publish for various reasons: an authorial interest in children and their role in a nation's growth and development; policies and practices at multiple levels of government; and theories of child development, health, welfare, and especially education. The books featured in these examples represent the results of intense and thorough research. Reading these and other authors reward the historian with heightened awareness, knowledge, and reflection skills and experiences needed for researching and writing historical publications. A summary of the impact of the authors follows as a guide to the current early childhood historian.

- Authors have read widely, located sources that are then referenced, distinguished between history and historiography, and studied sources extensively and intensively. Sources have been shared in endnotes and references, and have provided the reader with information for selecting a single topic or a range of subjects.
- Authors have distinguished between objectivity and appropriate subjectivity, correcting for personal bias and potential conflicts of interest. Authors have re-assessed evidence and offered re-interpretations to the present & for the future. The early childhood historians formed a bridge between the *historical context of available documents* to read and the *historical content available* to acquire.

- Authors have experienced and shared a passionate involvement with historical sources, knowing it takes time to search and find all essential sources.
- Authors in education and early childhood have recognized the practice of using young children's education and caregiving programs to address poverty in communities and nations, numerous references made available to a new historian. Authors have also addressed modern issues: gender, race, immigration, health, how children learn, and recognizing conflict and controversy over resolving problems.
- Front-of-the-book and back-of-the-book sections though similar among all the books, play a particularly useful role in books of historical research. The brief sections convey the historian's depth of feeling about and some of the difficulties of doing history .
- Books examine old and new evidence and come to new conclusions and recommendations. Frustration is experienced: historians echo "Dory" in *Finding Nemo:* "Just keep swimming!"
- Doing history provides a landscape for the new generation to observe and on which to conduct research to contribute to the next generation of knowledge.
- The authors represented a range of styles, topics, and time periods. A link may have been disconnected or have become an erratic conclusion. The new historian will review the .literature by reinterpreting, revising, and reporting out at a different time and place.
- The early childhood historian with roots in the past experience of educating young children follows up by doing history to re-evaluate the past and move on to the future. All the publications identified in this chapter are part of a "cloud of witnesses" who have written it down to become for those in the present a home, a heritage, and a history.

PART TWO: HISTORICAL CONTENT

To become part of the historical context, the early childhood historian requires a well-chosen subject and sufficient numbers of sources to write and publish a research paper, report, thesis, dissertation, an article or a book. The sources are the documents, artifacts, and electronic sources from which the author will gather data, analyze the collected information, and formulate an interpretation composed of findings, conclusions, implications, and recommendations. The materials described in Part II, *Historical Content,* are comprised of publication style manuals and primary, secondary, and tertiary sources.

Preparation for Publication

The historian who seeks to become a published author must agree to practices required for publication. Selecting a well-known publication style manual (or the one the publisher requests) is the first step. Two often used by historians and educators are:

- American Psychological Association. (2010). *Publication Manual of the American Psychological Association.* (6th ed.). Washington, D.C.: Author.
- Turabian, K. L. (2007). *A manual for writers of research papers, theses, and dissertations.* (7th ed.). Chicago: University of Chicago.

In addition to a wide range of writing styles and requirements for citing references or creating a bibliography, publication manuals also include information about illegal writing practices. The *APA Publication Manual* describes the ethical standards to be met by authors and provides an Ethical Compliance List (p. 20) for the author to follow. The signed document required of prospective authors, "Compliance with Ethical Principles Form," is shown in the *APA Publication Manual* and references the APA Ethical Principles and the website from which it may be downloaded and printed (pp. 233–234). Among ethical issues an author must be aware of are plagiarism and self-plagiarism (pp. 15–16). To avoid plagiarism, the author must "not claim the words and ideas of another as their own; they give credit where credit is due" (p. 15). Writers often wonder why an author would commit plagiarism. It happens even with fact-checkers; a recent column by the ombudsman of *The Washington Post* testifies to the reality of plagiarism, even in the headline of the column: "Using someone else's words—again" (Pexton, 2013). To guard against errors and unethical practices, the historian must become familiar with the style manual selected; owning a copy of the current edition is recommended.

An equally useful resource similar to style manuals but giving much more information is in the *Handbook of Complementary Methods in Education Research* edited by Judith Green, Gregory Camilli, and Patricia B. Elmore (2006). The third edition of the handbook produced by the American Educational Research Association (AERA) has two chapters on historical research: John L. Rury, "Historical Research in Education" (pp. 323–332), and Annette Henry, "Historical Studies: Groups/Institutions" (pp. 333–356). The front-end materials provide "an ethnographic framework to make visible the underlying thinking and logic of each [research] tradition from the perspective of the authors." The survey of educational research methods across 46 chapters is composed of elegant examples of high-level research in education. The introductory sections in the front of the book are available on line; find the site on http://www.amazon.com or on another search engine by entering the book title in the search box and following the prompts. Check a bookstore or local or academic library for a copy of the book itself.

Sources

Sources from which research is conducted are usually sorted into three main categories: **primary, secondary,** and **tertiary sources.** Part II, *Historical Content,* reverses the order in which the three categories are discussed, beginning with tertiary or the third level of sources, continuing with secondary sources, and ending with primary sources. Although each category of sources has its specific research purposes, the historian gives main emphasis to primary sources, deciding whether to focus on the "top-down" or "bottom-up" style or to select documents from both groups.

Tertiary Sources

The purpose of tertiary sources is to provide introductory and background information as well as an overview of the subject matter addressed. Used properly, these publications offer a rich source on which the early childhood education historian can build research. They are in no way intended to be the only publications used and should, in fact, lead the historian to numerous other, more detailed sources. These examples are listed alphabetically by author and should be sought in libraries, public and academic; new and used book stores; and online sources. The early childhood education historian should keep a look-out for these and all types of publications to add to a personal library; specific locations for purchasing items for a personal library is given below. The use of brief descriptions of many topics and the compilation of bibliographical sources serve to point the historian toward numerous primary and secondary sources. For the purposes of retrieval of referenced documents, the historical researcher must use exceptional care in providing exact citations so that readers can find and use the cited document. Examples of citing the exact retrieval information from printed documents or off the Internet are provided below. Full citations for these three sources are in the References.

Richard H. Bremner, (Ed.) 1971

Children and Youth in American: A Documentary History, (Three volumes in five books). This helpful series offers selected child- and youth-related documents from 1600 until the publication of the third volume (Volume 2 consists of Parts 1–6 and Parts 7–8 in two books covering the years 1866–1932).

Search a library's reference section for this and similar documents. *From time to time, books are available at reduced prices. This author's copies of Bremner's Volume II were purchased from the Harvard University Press, 1981, for $5.00. The original price for Volume II (two books) was $40.00.* While many documents are relevant to a variety of child-related studies, some early childhood-specific documents include The Children's Charter from 1930 and examples in Kindergarten Instruction from the nineteenth and early twentieth centuries.[1]

The historian will also note that in Part Three, III, *Issues in Child Care*, pp. 398–438, the topic of child care refers to foster care and welfare services as *substitute care* for dependent children, rather than child day care as *supplemental care* for working parents as the term is used today.

Rebecca S. New and Moncrieff Cochran (Eds.) 2007

Early Childhood Education: An International Encyclopedia, 4 volumes. This encyclopedia "is unique in form and contents, providing in four volumes a compilation of understandings, controversies, theories, policies, and practices in early childhood education as currently found in the United States and 10 other nations around the world" (p. xix). Its planned audience is diverse: "...undergraduate and graduate students of education, child development, social policy, and cross-cultural studies; parents and teachers of young children in the United States and abroad; scholars—national and international; program administrators; policy makers and analysts; and the general public" (p. xix). It is intended not only to address a particular period of time in the history of the field, but also "to present the *status quo* of early childhood education...as a catalyst for continued debate about and engagement in future actions and advocacy on behalf of young children's early learning and development" (pp. xix–xx). The entry on Susan Elizabeth Blow (1843–1916; see Appendix B in this chapter) is a short introduction to her life, but offers limited entries in *Further Readings*. In other entries, many more listings under *Further Readings* are provided. Note that the entry for the Child Development Group of Mississippi (CDGM) was written by Polly Greenberg, the author of *The Devil Has Slippery Shoes* (Greenberg, 1969).

Richard A. Shweder (Ed.) 2009

The child: An encyclopedic companion from birth to adolescence. In addition to its over 1,100 pages with its 41 "Imagining Each Other Essays," the range of multicultural topics is broad and are prepared by numerous contributors from higher education, professional organizations, and similar institutions. The provocative introduction outlines the knowledge summarized in quantities of individual research from many places on our planet. The entry for "Head Start" written by Edward F. Zigler, Yale University, manages to summarize his vast knowledge of Head Start into less than two pages.

The list of references for further reading includes two of Zigler's books and the Website addresses of the federal Office of Head Start and the National Head Start Association (NHSA).

Secondary Sources

Many books, book chapters, journal articles, organizational reports, films, and newspaper articles form the backbone of secondary sources and play a vital role in conducting historical research. Among the purposes of secondary sources are: confirmation of basic information, follow-ups to bibliographic references, presentations of particular points of view, confirmation of positions supported and rejected, an expanded perception, and making historical research intentional. The early childhood education historian will use many secondary sources and in some instances, rely heavily on their content. The early childhood historian is, in fact, building on the contents of previous publications and seeking to add to the professional literature and historical account of early childhood education. Some secondary sources provide a particularly robust foundation of information and interpretation. The entries described under Models of Historiography are secondary sources and highly useful to the historian. Acquiring the secondary sources, while not as difficult as locating primary sources, may still be problematic. This section strives to identify where early childhood education-related books can be located, how the reader can obtain them by borrowing or buying the items, and how to use the Internet to search for journal articles.

Books may be borrowed from public and academic libraries. To borrow books from a *public library*, a membership card will be necessary, usually at little or no cost to residents of the municipality that operates the library system. Learn about and use the Interlibrary Loan system for your region. For *academic libraries*, check with the academic library or libraries in your city or region to learn if nonuniversity residents are allowed to use the library and what restrictions apply. If the institution has a school of education, access to the library will be fruitful. In the past, residents of a state had access to the *state library* from which books could be borrowed by mail. Contact the state library online and find out what procedures are to be followed. Go online to determine if the Smithsonian Institution Libraries or the Library of Congress can be of assistance in doing research. Both institutions have websites: http://library@si.edu or http://www.loc.gov.

Books may be purchased at a variety of locations. *Chain and local independent book stores* are available to many researchers. Stores like Target or K-mart often have book sections. Another source is a *used book store* where locating a low-cost book may prove successful if regular visits and extra time to search for a particular book are implemented. Locate used books stores in the area by searching for them online. *Nonprofit organizations* often schedule used books sales. Arrange to get on e-mail and mailing lists for announcements at libraries, churches, university and colleges, public and private schools, organizations that serve children, and similar groups. Watch for signs posted in libraries, near churches and schools, and at Y organizations announcing book sales. Personal yard sales are also a source of used books. Early childhood education conferences with exhibitors usually host publishers who often reduce prices and waive shipping costs.

Online sources of books are expanding and short delivery times and reduced prices for new and used books make ordering attractive and easy. Two well-known and reliable online book sources are www.amazon.com and www.books.google.com. Others are available on search engine directories; go to www.thesearchenginelist.com and scroll to "books."

A historian should gradually build a *professional library*. Obtain or have book shelves built. Organize the books purchased at the locations described above and use a logical system of placing books on shelves alphabetically by author (keep a list to which new volumes are added), by subject matter, or by another system that lets you locate the book immediately. In addition to books, journals, films (videos and DVDs), and CDs can be added to the collection.

Motion Pictures

In today's world of screens, citing films and other recorded material is increasingly common. The APA *Publication Manual* has instructions for the appropriate formats for a motion picture, a music recording, a video or DVD, a podcast, a single episode from a television series (2010, pp. 209–210). Films owned by an individual are usually in the DVD format that must be played on an electric or battery-operated player designed especially for that purpose. Older films may require a player for that format. Films can also be shown on some computers and hand-held smartphones and tablets.

Journals

Professional journals offer relevant, current professional material to the early childhood historian. Some professional organizations include a journal in the price of membership. If the historian is a member of at least one early childhood professional organization, that journal will be available on a bi-monthly or quarterly schedule. Some journals are available to the nonsubscriber online; some journals offer free copies, others charge a fee. . The journals of interest to early childhood historians listed below are all from the United States unless otherwise indicated. Go online to obtain subscription and ordering instructions. Some journals offer an abstract and a few pages from the article. The partial list of early childhood journals includes:

- *American Historical Association* http://www.historians.org/pubs/free/journals/browse.cfm?group=gtol
- *Childhood Education, a journal of the Association for Childhood Education International—www.acei.org* for membership and subscription information
- *Early Childhood Research Quarterly*—http://www.journals.elsevier.com/early-childhood-research-quarterly/# or http://www.sciencedirect.com/science/journal/08852006
- *Educational Researcher*—American Educational Research Association–www.aera.net http://www.sagepub.com/journals/Journal201856
- *History of Education Quarterly*—cs-journals@wiley.com. HEQ is a benefit for members of the History of Education Society; members are also able to download and print out articles back through 2001. Copies of articles in issues prior to 2001 may go through www.worldcat.org.
- *Journal of Early Childhood Research*—http://ecr.sagepubcom/
- *History of Education: Journal of the History of Education Society*—Great Britain http://www.tandfonlilne.com/loi/thed20 (Great Britain)–Routledge/Taylor and Francis Group (tandfonline.com); Special Issue: Early Years Education: Some Froebelian Contributions, Volume 35, Issue 2, 2006.
- *Paedagogica Historica*—http://www.tanfonline.com/doi/full/10.1080/00309230.2011.644568; Special Issue: Discoveries of childhood in history, Volume 48, Issue 1, 2012.
- *Young Children*-a National Association for the Education of Young Children (NAEYC) journal published five times a year—http://www.naeyc.org/yc

Primary Sources

Locating and using primary sources are among the most exciting and demanding aspects of doing research, including that for early childhood education. The sources are "primary" not because of importance or are to be used first, but because they "originated in the time period [the historian] is studying" (Storey, 2009, p. 26). Primary sources actually come from the time being researched. Primary sources represent the people who were there, who lived in another time, and who recorded stories, often without realizing history was being crafted. Thus, the initial clue to a primary source is the source of the document and its date. Without a date, a document's future usefulness is compromised, if not entirely lost. Historians are reminded to date their notes and rough drafts with the month, day, and year.

The second thing to know about primary sources is the types of documents. Primary sources can be documents, films, music recordings, and art objects. Most primary sources used in early childhood research are printed documents, although art objects, clothing, and toys and games may be included. Print sources come from government, organizational, and personal documents.

Government documents are made up of the constitutions, amendments, statutes (laws), bills, regulations and standards, resolutions, forms, hearing testimony, *Code of the Federal Register* volumes, Congressional and departmental publications, correspondence, licenses, internal policy documents, speeches, court decisions, meeting notes, reports, newsletters, and patents.

Organizational documents refer to constitution and by-laws, policy documents (staff, board, and clients), public announcements and publicity materials, board and staff meeting agendas and minutes, correspondence, conference programs, speeches, position papers, original publications-newsletters, periodicals, special and occasional reports-accreditation documents and awards, original photographs, contracts, budget documents, media reports, published articles about the organization; and oral history recordings; Note: The list cites documents that child care programs often have or should have in their files; early childhood historians should determine which child care programs have archives (Ranck, 1995).

Individual documents include wills, licenses, contracts, mortgages, receipts, diaries and journals, correspondence, oral history recordings, audiovisual tapes and disks, and published documents if owned by the individual (copyright).

Oral histories have been recorded on audio tape or disk, video recordings and movie films of people who lived through the times under examination. Watching a film or listening to a recording of a person who has been dead a long time is meaningful. Today, access to sound and visual recordings is easily available and can be used until new technologies come on the market and the equipment used to play the recordings becomes obsolete. The historian who creates or owns recordings should plan transfers to current technology.

Resources to guide the creation and use of oral histories are available: (Copeland, 1986; Eick, 2011; Hymes, 1991; *Profiles in Childhood Education, 1931–1960*, 1992; Ross, n.d.; Simpson, 1981; Sommers, 2009. Simpson's dissertation on African American early childhood educators has demonstrated the use of oral history material in other ways (1981): at regional seminars in Washington, DC, of an international early childhood education organization; as presentations at the History Seminar held at National Association for the Education of Young Children (NAEYC) annual conferences; and as the basis for an "Our Proud Heritage" column in *Young Children* (Simpson, 2012).

How Are Primary Sources Reported?

Instructions for using and citing primary sources are in style manuals. The historian should obtain all necessary use permission.

690 ■ E. R. RANCK

Internet Sources

Publications from the past are sometimes available online to be downloaded and printed at no cost. The early childhood historian will want to spend time using Internet search engines to locate relevant historical documents and their physical or online locations. For example, a book by Frederich Frobel was translated by Susan Blow and published in the International Education Series in 1897s (Blow, 2004).

Criticism of All Primary Sources

Primary sources must be assessed critically as with any document used in research. The historian must not only select the facts to examine for a particular study, but also judge the evidence based on accuracy, authenticity, reliability, and validity. See Appendix A, *An Overview of Writing History* for more information cited in Storey, 2009, and Rael, 2004.

Archives and Libraries

Many educational primary sources are housed in archives, in state and local historical societies, and special collections in academic or public libraries. Locating and accessing such repositories takes time and often requires travel to archives in obscure and remote locations. Furthermore, reviewing and organizing quantities of paper from years ago requires resources in terms of reviewers, resources to pay a salary, and the space in which to store materials that then can be used for formal research. In fact, stories abound about historians discovering uncataloged boxes of primary documents: David McCullough found the Roebling family papers about the building of the Brooklyn Bridge (from a speech heard at the first National Book Festival, Library of Congress, Washington, DC, September 9, 2001); Eric Foner came across boxes of correspondence from the Reconstruction period in the state archives of South Carolina when he went to teach there (2002, p. 15); and in 1912, two graduate students discovered in an academic basement at Drew University, papers from a 50-year-old conference involving Martin Heidegger, a German philosopher who lived during World War II (Hann, 2013).

At least two archives specifically for early childhood education organizations have been identified: The archives for the Association for Childhood Education International (ACEI) and for the National Association for the Education of Young Children (NAEYC).

The Association for Childhood Education International (ACEI) began as the International Kindergarten Union (IKI) in Saratoga Springs, NY, in 1892. The archives include documents from IKU and ACEI, as well as the National Council of Primary Education (NCPE) that merged with IKU in 1931 to become the Association for Childhood Education (ACE).

The combined ACEI archives are located at the Archives and Manuscripts Department, University of Maryland Libraries, Hornbake Library. To contact the Special Collections, Hornbake Library, College Park, MD 20742, phone 301-405-9212 or go to the website at http://www.lib.umd.edu/special. "The inclusive dates for the materials are 1807–1986. Also included are a broad range of document types from operating records to publications, audio-visual materials, and three-dimensional objects such as toys. Among the many subjects addressed in the collection are early childhood curriculum, teacher education, the history of prekindergarten and kindergarten education, and the development of preschool education in countries other than the United States. There are also several unprocessed accessions for which preliminary inventories are available" (Anne Bauer, personal communication, January 15, 2013). An ACEI staff member identified a "lengthy document" titled "Guide to the Archives of the Association for Childhood Education International" (Sheri Levin, personal communication, April 12, 2012). For other ACEI archives information, visit http://digital.lib.umd.edu, enter "Education" on the Browse search, and enter the dates "1807" to "1986." Scroll through documents. To obtain the full link to the ACEI archives, go to http://www.acei.org.

The **NAEYC archives** are located at the Special Collections Department, University Archives, Room 309, Cunningham Memorial Library, Indiana State University, Terre Haute, IN 47809. Contact Dennis Vetrovec at Dennis.Vetrovec@indstate.edu, 812-237-4205. The historian may request a list of documents available. Copies of the National Association for Nursery Education (NANE) (between 1926 and 1964) and NAEYC journals are available at the NAEYC headquarters in Washington, DC; contact http://www.naeyc.org for further information.

To find out the status of archives for other national and international early childhood education organizations, go to the following websites for lists of early childhood education professional organizations:

- National organizations—http://www.naeyc.org/links
- International organizations—http://www.naeyc.org/node/109
- Exchange Press, publisher and conference sponsor primarily serving early childhood center-based programs and advocates, lists international organizations as well—http://www.childcareexchange.com/ece_orgs/index.php.

Contact the organizations of interest and identify a contact person or use the online "Contact us" form to send an e-mail query or an online request to determine if the organization has a formal archives. Ask the following questions: Where is the archives? Who is the contact at the archives? Is a directory of available documents available for review? Who is eligible to use the archives? Are visits to be scheduled in advance? What is the process by which to submit a request to access the archives? Are there any financial charges applicable? Expect to spend more time in archives than planned.

Libraries

Universities with schools or colleges of education are likely to have special collections or substantial resources for research purposes. Contact relevant institutions and determine the status of their archival capacity. As an example, the Gottesman Libraries at Teachers College, Columbia University, New York City have Special Collections containing early childhood educational resources. Go to http://library.tc.columbia.edu/support to learn more about the contents and access information.

Vast national organizations (Smithsonian Institution Libraries (www.library.si.edu), the Library of Congress (www.loc.gov/about/history.html; and the National Archives of the United States (http://www.archives.gov/dc-metro/Washington/ have many collections and available resources. To use any Washington, D.C.-based resources, spend some time on their well-designed websites to learn what is available and how best to access the documents and services.

State Historical Societies

Investigate the historical society for your state and for any state that relates to your research topic. For example, to obtain information about Susan Blow (1843–1916) who lived and worked in Missouri, I contacted and was helped by The State Historical Society of Missouri (http://shs.umsystem.edu/historicmissourians/name/b/blow/index.html).

Internet

Go to Amazon.com (www.amazon.com), Google (www.books.google.com, and to search engines; enter www.thesearchenginelist.com and scroll to "books." Learn about and how to access JSTOR, EBSCO Host, and ProQuest (Storey, 2009, p. 15). Some are accessible by subscription only, but can be obtained from local libraries through Interlibrary Loan arrangements.

GUIDELINES FOR HISTORIANS OF EARLY CHILDHOOD EDUCATION

Guidelines for doing early care and education historical research are similar to those used to conduct any type of historical research. With practice and experience the historian gains skills for and knowledge about carrying out successful historical research projects. Internalize the guidelines for researching and writing historical publications. These guidelines summarize the processes under which the early childhood research historian works to produce new information for the field of early childhood education. The guidelines fall into three categories.

ENGAGE COLLEAGUES AND DEAL WITH FRUSTRATIONS

1. Network with colleagues, engage a mentor, join and participate in one or more professional organizations.
2. Develop a love of learning and realize your passion for doing historical research. Build a professional library of books, journals, and films.
3. Request comments from colleagues and work at resolving difficulties and disagreements. Look at all sides of a conflict and balance out the issues; often, the answer is "it is both!"
4. Observe the world constantly and include children, using eyes, ears, nose, mouth, and skin (touch): Children interact constantly with persons and objects in their environment, beginning at birth; children are cared for and educated simultaneously and at all times, feeling presence and absence; children respond optimally to people who are positively intentional, passionate, informed, prepared, committed, and wise, and who provide them with appropriate relationships, equipment, supplies, and materials. The historian would do well to mimic the child.

KNOW THE EARLY CHILDHOOD EDUCATION FIELD AND READ WIDELY AND DEEPLY

1. Keep a journal in which every page is dated with the month, day, and year. Jot down ideas, book titles, film names, and significant events.
2. Practice crafting good questions about everything and enter the answers when they appear.
3. Guard against a biased opinion and use hard data and evidence on which to make decisions for action.
4. Recognize the influences on authors and on decisions made.

DO HISTORY BY PLANNING ACTIONS ON WHAT IS READ AND WRITTEN

1. Identify the gaps in what is read and recognize the limits on objectivity.

2. Assess an author's use of data, the pro and con decisions made, and the overt and covert values espoused.
3. Track all sources—primary, secondary, and tertiary—as open-ended until resolved, and double-check facts, inferences, and conclusions before making recommendations for action. Read what has been written more than once. Edit the document with care: check spelling, select the 'right' word, ensure noun and verb agreement, and use active verbs. Consult the selected style manual as needed.
4. Beware of "unexamined, underlying assumptions" and address them until they are no longer any of the three (Gwen Morgan, Wheelock College, in personal conversations through the years).

RECOMMENDED FUTURE RESEARCH PROJECTS

Throughout the process of writing this chapter, names and topics have surfaced with a hovering question mark. The experiences signal the possibility of more research. The following topics suggest interesting historical research projects for the future; suggested starting points for research are included.

- Who was the first person to open a kindergarten in the United States? The word "first" in a sentence can be misread and convey incorrect information. How were Susan Blow, Elizabeth Peabody, Margarethe Schurz, and Caroline Frankenburg first with kindergartens in the nineteenth century? *Start with Barbara Beatty, 1995; and Agnes Snyder, 1972.*
- What has been the influence of William James on the field of early childhood education? The name of this renowned philosopher and psychologist has been linked in some way with Patty Smith Hill, G. Stanley Hall, Elizabeth Peabody, and Lucy Sprague Mitchell. *Start with* Lucy Sprague Mitchell: The Making of a Modern Woman, *Joyce Antler, 1987;* The Thought and Character of William James, *Ralph Barton Perry, 1935.*
- Do we know how many early childhood history books have been written in the United States since the second half of the nineteenth century? Has the number grown or shrunk at various time? Conduct an inventory of early childhood education historical documents by year within set dates to determine the answers. Include parenting books, early childhood professional books, curriculum materials and books not overtly about early childhood education, but that include references to the field. *Start with Braun & Edwards, 1972.*

- How has the Froebelian kindergarten influenced early education programs in American Roman Catholic parochial schools? *Start with a history of American religious education and locate a study on early education in Roman Catholic elementary schools. Include Lascarides & Hinitz, 2000, and Braun & Edwards, 1972.*
- Who was Felix Adler? Adler founded the Ethical Culture Society and School, New York City; his name appears in the indexes of early childhood books listed here. *Start with references in Bremner, Volume 11, Part 5; Snyder, 1972; D. Keith Osborn, 1991; and Lascarides & Hinitz, 2000.*

CONCLUSION

The journey captured in this chapter came from examining multiple sources revolving around early childhood education and the conduct of historical research. Examples of various sources were identified: primary sources (a conference program, a conference presentation hand-out, personal communications); print and Internet secondary sources (journal articles, book chapters, books in different styles and formats, a newspaper article, dissertations, a style manual, a confer early childhood organizational histories, a volume of letters, museum catalogs, a university newsletter; three tertiary sources that provided background data. Each volume and document selected helped craft this document. Its purpose, among others, is to help early childhood educators become historians, to understand their place in the continuum of history and to contribute to the body of knowledge already available to persons who want to work and play with young children. The chapter closes with the last paragraph from William Storey's *Writing History* (2009):

> Keep the Rules in Mind, but Enjoy Your Writing. Writing history can be difficult, but most historical writers consider themselves to be quite privileged. Research and writing can be both exhilarating and plodding, but the end result is almost always worth the effort. (p. 119)

NOTE

1. *The Children's Charter,* 1930, is located in the U.S. Children's Bureau's *The Story of the White House Conferences on Children and Youth* (Washington, 1967), pp. 11–12. In Bremner, it is in Volume II, 1866–1932, Part One, II, C, pp. 106–108. *Kindergarten Instruction:* The opening entry is from a book by Mary P[eabody] Mann and Elizabeth P. Peabody, *The Moral Culture of Infancy and Kindergarten Guide,* 4th ed. (New York, 1870, first published in 1863), pp. 55–57 and pp. 32–34. In Bremner, it is in Volume II, 1866–1932, Part Eight, VI, C, pp. 1452–1454. Other kindergarten documents appear on pp. 1454–1462).

APPENDIX A

An Overview of Writing History

Doing historical research in early childhood education should result in a published written document that will contribute and add to the historical literature of the field of early childhood education. A well-researched document must also be well-written; this appendix summarizes the writing process for historical research by referring to two recent and relevant publications:

- *Writing History: A Guide for Students* by William Kelleher Storey and published in its third edition by Oxford University Press in 2009, is available in libraries and can be purchased from bookstores and online booksellers. From its origins in a writing program directed by the author as an undergraduate at Harvard University, the guide has broadened its scope and the author is now a professor of history at Millsaps College in Mississippi. The book's qualities-Harvard roots, author's professorship in history, third edition, and solid publisher-indicate a reliable source. The book is available at low cost.
- *Reading, Writing, and Researching for History: A Guide for College Students* by Patrick Rael, an associate professor of history at Bowdoin College, is an online PDF document available for downloading and printing. Copyrighted in 2004, it is available at http://academic.bowdoin.edu/WritingGuides/. The characteristics of the document-associate professor author, durability on the Internet, caliber of the college-make it a reliable source.

Other guides for historical research and writing history include Barzun and Graff, 2004, and Rury, 2006. *The Modern Researcher*, in a sixth edition, was written by two former Columbia professors of history, and is highly readable. Rury's publication, Historical Research in Education, is one of 46 chapters in the *Handbook of Complementary Methods in Education Research* (Green, Camilli & Elmore, 2006). The reader will use a style manual in which research guidelines are prominent (American Psychological Association, 2010; Turabian, 2007).

This appendix summarizes Storey and Rael's works on writing history. The subjects covered by both are crafting a statement of purpose; reading for data and historical background; forming questions and stating an argument; selecting, locating, and interpreting primary, secondary, and tertiary sources; writing a narrative that is free from bias; and recording citations properly (following a style manual format) and accurately (providing the full content cited).

Storey's historical research is based on sources and people: "...The only way to write history is to engage with source materials and other writers" (2009, p. 3). The key act is deceptively simple: "Writing history is about making decisions" [about] "topics that shed light on contemporary problems... and to seek cause of change over time" (pp. 1–2). History is more than recounting chronology; it is interpretation: "Historians collect facts, but they also select and arrange them—and some are ignored" (p. 30). Storey confirms the guideline about reading widely and deeply: "Good writing starts with careful reading. While...reading, look for conflicts" (p. 3). Another focus emphasizes identifying an issue (conflict), examining authors' position (evidence), and concluding the results of research (interpretation).

Rael's monograph has as a main emphasis the actual writing of the document. His paper-writing checklist includes the introduction, paragraph structure, argumentation, quotations and citation, style, and editing. Counsel to students includes three further steps:

1. Finding a historical problem worth addressing
2. Locating a set of primary historical sources
3. Putting the information together and producing knowledge (2004, pp. 5–6).

Definitions of History and Historiography Follow

The authors introduced in Part I, *Historical Context*, also present types of historical research and writing. Historical research is shaped by definitions from the *Random House Unabridged Dictionary*, 2d edition:

- *History*. 1. The branch of knowledge dealing with past events; 2. A continuous systematic narrative of past events as relating to a particular people, country, period, person, etc., usually written; 3. The aggregate of past events; 4 and 5. The record of past events; one notable for important, unusual, or interesting events; and 6. Acts, ideas, or events that will or can shape the course of the future.
- *Historiography*. 1. The body of literature dealing with historical matters; histories collectively; 2. The body of techniques, theories, and principles of historical research and presentation; methods of historical scholarship; 3. The narrative presentation of history based on a critical examination, evaluation, and selection of materials as primary and secondary sources and subject to scholarly criteria; and 4. An official history (of an organization, a person, a city, etc.

Examples of Doing History Are Helpful

To show the distinction between history and historiography, Jon N. Hale defines the difference in a recent article in *History of Education Quarterly* titled "The Struggle Begins Early: Head Start and the Mississippi Freedom Movement."

> This history begins with the people across Mississippi who *initially* implemented federal funds, controlled the direction of Head Start, and adapted it to the needs of the local community. The article builds upon the historiography that grounds the history of Head Start in the Freedom Movement." (p. 510)

Using a segment of the historiography of Head Start, Hale wrote about the development of Head Start in Mississippi (Hale, 2012).

Both Hale's article and Jean Simpson's research on African American early childhood professionals (1981) are examples of "bottom-up" historical research as opposed to "top-down" histories that have recorded the lives of highly-visible presidents, kings and queens, and organizational leaders and whose events have dominated accounts of the past. Examples include Eric Foner's *Reconstruction* (2002, pp. 15–16) and Marten's account of how the Civil War affected children (1998). Howard Zinn, a leader in the bottom-up rendering of history, edited with Anthony Arnove, a book titled *Voices of a People's History of the United States* (Zinn 2009): "testimonies to living history...left by the [little] people who make history happen but who usually are left out of history books...." Children fall into a category of being "left out of history books" except when studies based on groups of anonymous children are created. Evidence from real children such as drawings, toys, and made objects are often discarded, and children do not write major documents until well out of childhood. Historians like Hale, Simpson, and Marten have found other sources of information about children and their lives (Ranck, 1986, p. 19).

Tracking multiple ideas, thoughts, and sources requires engagement among the components to produce notes from which written drafts are composed that become an addition to the historical record. The sources begin with existing print and online documents published by general, educational, and early childhood education historians prepared by education and experience to be historians. Every historian must also approach each new book to allow engagement.

- Start by reading the material on the jacket. What art work was selected? Does it reflect the thought in the book itself? Does the writing on the flaps capture the themes and big questions? Who was invited to contribute a promotional statement about the book?

- Read the front of the book: dedication, preface, foreword, notes on previous editions, acknowledgements, introduction, and table of contents. What are the big ideas and questions addressed in the book? Who wrote the foreword, to whom is the book dedicated, and who is acknowledged for what? How does the introduction and Chapter 1 (often the same) reflect on the outline captured in the table of contents?
- Read the back of the book: the endnotes or footnotes, appendixes, references, and index: What works are cited in the notes, what are the topics of the appendixes, and who is included in the references? What are the main entries emphasized by the author?

Rael instructs on how to read a book: STAMP it! The letters stand for Structure, Thesis, Argument, Motives, and Primaries (pp. 14–15). Each word introduces a set of questions by which the reader probes the contents of the book and with the answers, is then able to evaluate and incorporate the book into the reader's research project. The questions are designed for deep analysis and clearly expect the reader/historian to spend time and energy reading the book. In addition, Rael offers three more questions for the reader to ask the book: What does the author say? Why does the author say it? Where is the author's argument weak or vulnerable (p. 15).

A historian's life is like a series of doors opening one after the other, each door leading to something new: documents and publications written years ago, a resource now available in print or online, or a heretofore undiscovered box of primary sources. As the appeal of the history of early childhood education emerges, awareness of history's complexity expands. No matter how much reading, interviewing, and searching for data are accomplished, more is or could be available. Some early childhood professionals believe a lack of interest in and knowledge of history and the historical record mars the effectiveness of the field; thus it is important to define, research, and publish the history of early childhood.

APPENDIX B

Some Characteristics of an Early Childhood Education Historian.

Conducting historical research in early childhood education benefits from the conditions and events that have shaped the life of the writer. Eric Foner (2002) describes in a series of essays produced over a period of nearly 20 years "how the context within which a historian lives and writes affects one's choice of subject and approach to the past" (p. xviii). The intent of this appendix is to share experiences and practices that have contributed to my evolving role as a historian in the field of early childhood education. The information falls into three categories.

- Reflecting on a life-long experience and building an educational background.
- Establishing a career that deepens and broadens one's education and experience.
- Keeping up with current events, professional developments, and connections with a network of family, friends, and colleagues.

That learning is life-long keeps a person able to make a difference in the lives of children and adults in the family and the wider community. The family members, the schools, the religious contacts, the community or communities lived in, and the national and international situations lived through, and the later family, friends, and colleagues all contribute to the end product. My life lived as an only child with paternal grandparents and relatives living next door on both sides was what came to be known in the 1960s as the "extended family."

My elementary education in a small town in Maine featured mixed-age classes. Parental attitudes toward education and four women who had been teachers—my mother, my grandmother, and two aunts—provided a climate for excellence in which I thrived and maintained through graduate school. I gave my first public speech when I was four-years-old; a copy of the four-line poem given at a church Christmas program is still in my baby book. Friends met in first grade were the ones I shared a desk with, took Brownie Scout hikes with, and finished fifth grade with. Those relationships helped create a self-image that says a difference can be made in the world.

I had experienced the Great Depression and all of World War II by the time I was 10. Before that age, I recycled, turned off lights, and saved money; I had my own checking account at age eight. When my parents and grandparents sold our homes and journeyed south, I found a new world. Viewing the sunrise behind the New York City skyline after living in a town with a population of fewer than one thousand left a permanent image. Years later, I traveled to graduate school in the city, seeing the same skyline every week. In between, I lived in South Florida and New York State; finished college with a major in political science, including history courses; married and had children; finished theological school where studying the Old and New Testaments taught me content analysis of documents; and began a career in early childhood education, based largely on my work as a church school kindergarten teacher. I learned about the connection between political science and early childhood education years later, following up with a graduate degree for which I wrote a dissertation on state public policy and early childhood education licensing laws and regulations'

- Professional development and current events. An educational historian must maintain a balanced connection between professional activities and current events at the local, state and national levels. Some will branch out into international interests. Thus, a historian must be a member of at least one professional organization, with the option of belonging to as many as time allows; and must subscribe to one or more journals, often acquired as a membership benefit. I belong to professional organizations that focus on national and international early childhood education in center-based programs and family child care homes, teacher education, and child care regulations; each has a print or an online journal that comes with the membership. I also receive the *History of Education Quarterly* and have written or contributed to the published histories of five leading early childhood organizations. My publications have focused on history in 1986, 1990, 1995, 1997, 1998, 1999, 2007, 2012 and 2013.
- In addition, a historian must also keep up with events in the wider world; early childhood takes place in the context of community, state, province, nation, and world. Newspapers need to be read daily in print or electronically, and relevant articles need to be clipped or printed and filed. I read regularly to two newspapers and five journals from nonearly childhood organizations.
- Committing to a dynamic and demanding career represents great effort. An early childhood professional must periodically review professional characteristics (Colker, 2008). Colker's list of early childhood teacher characteristics highlights a passion about children and teaching, perseverance, risk taking, pragmatism, and patience. Career building looks toward acquiring credentials, education, and skills, and the knowledge needed to know what is needed.
- Connecting with a network of colleagues and friends. Relationships are the key standard for early childhood program accreditation.

Colleagues hire you, promote you, give you a heads-up for a position or grant opportunity that will help you move ahead. Mentors and coaches are the people to whom you turn for help. Of the 11 paid jobs and five volunteer positions I have had since college, with one exception, I have been invited to apply for or informed about positions by a colleague. An established career nurtures growth and development, and established, meaningful relationships make all the difference in life.

APPENDIX C

When Data Disconnect: How to Handle Historical Details that Disagree

When Data Disagree

The historian must ask one question of historical primary and secondary sources, is it true? A research historian's goal is to use accurate and authentic information; missing or conflicting data raise problems. When problems arise, historian must seek additional sources, track warring facts to ultimate conclusions, provide a written explanation of the difficulty, or omit the citation. Appendix C addresses three conflicting stories from the life of **Susan E. Blow** (1843-1916), a strong American advocate for kindergarten as conceived and introduced by Friedrich Froebel (1782-1852) in Germany in the early nineteenth century. Blow introduced the first public kindergarten in St. Louis in 1873; designed training programs to prepare future kindergarten teachers; and as a prolific writer and speaker, traveled extensively throughout the United States and studied with Froebel's successors in Europe. Among sources about Susan Blow are three about which confusion appears to prevail:

- The date of the day she died;
- The dates when she taught at Teachers College, Columbia University in New York City;
- Listings of her publications.
- Date of Death. Susan Blow's date of death is reported in primary and secondary historical sources as March 26, 1916 (Lascarides & Hinitz, 2000, p. 246; *The New York Times, 1916;* the *St. Louis Post Dispatch* on three consecutive days, 1916; Snyder, 1972, p. 84). A journal article (Harris, 1983) gave only the year of her death as did an online chronology (Retrieved from http://www.womanphilosophers.com/Susan-Blow.html. In a Wikipedia listing, however, the date on Blow's gravestone is given as March 27, 1916 (Retrieved from http://en.wikipedia.org/wiki/Susan_Blow). The March 27, 1916, date appeared only on Wikipedia, an online resource open to input and thus subject to biased and incorrect information and to be cited with care (Storey, 2009, pp. 11–12). To resolve the discrepancy, an online request was sent to The State Historical Society of Missouri in Columbia, MO, on January 14, 2013. Retrieved from http://shs.umsystem.edu/historicmissourians/name/b/blow.html. Within an hour a manuscript specialist for photographs e-mailed a link to www.findagrave.com. Although the biography accompanying

the photograph gives the March 26, 1916, date, the gravestone in the color photograph clearly shows the date of death as March 27.
- Time at Teachers College. Susan Blow's teaching experience at Teachers College, Columbia University, has been reported as 1896–1916 and also as 1905–1909 (Lascarides & Hinitz, 2000, p. 246). It becomes apparent when time periods are compared that the longer period of time includes a series of lectures given at Teachers College among those she gave in many American cities (Snyder, 1972, pp. 76–77; http://www.woman-philosophers.com/Susan-Blow.html.). At Teachers College, Blow's name is also linked to Patty Smith Hill (1868–1946), a rising voice in the expanding kindergarten movement in the United States at the end of the nineteenth century. Both women were leaders of the International Kindergarten Movement (IKU), established in 1892, whose well-archived records reflect the growing differences between Froebelian-influenced kindergartens (Blow's position) and those connected to the emerging child study movement led by G. Stanley Hall (Hill's viewpoint). James Earl Russell, dean of Teachers College, invited Blow and Hill to team-teach courses on kindergarten education. Thus, the differing dates: after Blow completed lectures at Teachers College beginning in 1896, she then taught the courses with Hill from 1905 to 1909.
- Blow's Publications. Blow's experience in the development of the kindergarten in the St. Louis school system and her national lectures led to numerous publications. Wikipedia, apparently summarizing the data, lists four publications produced between 1894 and 1908 (Retrieved from http://en.wikipedia.org/wiki/Susan_Blow). However, Agnes Snyder reports three additional publications appearing between 1890 and 1895 (Snyder, 1972, p. 80), and cites a bibliography of over 108 documents and other publications written about her (p. 79n.) In Lascarides and Hinitz (2000), Blow's translations of Froebel's works are highlighted with references; however, none of the references refer specifically to the International Education Series. Still other Blow publications are listed in a selected chronology retrieved from http://www.women-philosophers.com/Susan-Blow.html. Yet another Internet reference cites her 1895 translation of Friedrich Froebel's *Mother Play* from the original German into English, but assigns it to the wrong volume (retrieved from http://froebelweb.org/images/blow.html). Blow's translation of Froebel's *Mother Play* is in volume 31, not volume 11, in the International Education Series published by William Torrey Harris, a St Louis colleague of Blow and a reliable educator in the late nine-

teenth and early twentieth centuries. The Wikipedia print-out also provides a reference to the *Mother Play* publication.

Tracking conflicting online material reflects the problem of limited time on a research quest. A comparison of all websites linked to Susan Blow would be more effective. Suspicious or incorrect data would be deleted. Historians must allow sufficient time to locate reliable sources, to contact unknown archivists and librarians, to follow-up queries to websites, and to continue searches. Locating answers to questions can be tedious and time-consuming, but it is part of the exciting detective work required in historical research.

APPENDIX D

Caveats for Early Childhood Education Historians

The early childhood education historian must guard against situations that can complicate research and writing. For example, historians committed to the use of primary sources must also pay attention to helpful secondary sources. The characteristics of strong secondary sources represented in many of the examples allow the historian to maintain continuous connections to all aspects of the field of early childhood education.

- Biographical History. Be aware of authors who wrote books about the times and events in which they lived, worked, and participated. Polly Greenberg and Edward Zigler published books cited in Part I about the creation of Head Start: Greenberg (1969) in Washington and Mississippi in the mid-1960s, and Zigler (Zigler & Styfo, 2010) in several positions in the Federal government offices responsible for establishing and implementing Head Start policies. Authors who write such books should provide disclaimers when needed.
- Searching Indexes for Early Childhood Entries. Early childhood education topics are often found under multiple headings in both older and recent indexes; the historian must inspect indexes for the various examples of terminology and to ensure all topics are reviewed. The topics include early childhood education, early childhood development, day nurseries, day care centers, child care centers, child development centers, family day care and family child care homes, Early Head Start, Head Start, infant/toddler programs, nursery schools, preschools, kindergartens, prekindergartens, pre-K, school-age and before/afterschool programs.
- Program Sponsors. Except for Head Start and military child development programs, the United States has had no systems of early childhood education. Historians of the field must know the types of early childhood sponsors that operate, often in the same geographical region: private nonprofit, for-profit, proprietary, corporate, faith-based institutions, public and private schools, higher education institutions, and governments. Early childhood program regulations exist in every state, and in the military and some municipalities. The licensing content varies widely among entities.
- Professional Organizations. The historian must identify the wide range of professional organizations that serve the field. For lists of early childhood professional organizations, go to the National Association for the Education of Young Children (NAEYC), http://www.naeyc.org/links (national organizations) and http://www.

naeyc.org/node/119 (international organizations), as well as Exchange Press (http://www.childcareexchange.com/ece_orgs/index.php. Early childhood-related books often have a section titled Abbreviations which feature lists of organizations. Two sources of lists are Lascarides and Hinitz (2000), pp. xxiii–xxvi, and Sonya Michel (1999), pp. ix–x. Other groups operate as well: child care is an interest of the National Association of Regulatory Administration (NARA) at www.nara-licensing.org, as it is of the World Forum Foundation (http://www.worldforumfoundation.org.

- International Early Childhood Education. Early childhood and its research topics have become linked to other fields of study: women's studies, child health studies, family and educational policy, and work and family initiatives. International interests in the field belong to the United Nations (http://www.unesco.org) and http://www.unicef.org), the World Bank (http://www.worldbank.org, and the Organization of American States (http://www.oas.org. The World Organization for Early Childhood Education (OMEP) was established in Europe in 1948, to give voice for young children at the United Nations. OMEP has over 70 national committees (chapters) and is presently headquartered in Sweden. Its webpage is http://www.omep.org.gu.se/.

- Trends, Patterns, and Changing Issues. The early childhood education historian must maintain constant awareness of how early childhood education is growing and developing. Historians have learned to attend to the history of the kindergarten as it moved across space and time, beginning in the nineteenth century with Frederich Froebel in Germany and continuing his influence in Europe and the United States (Brosterman, 1997; Bultman, 2001; Foebel, 1985; Pilto, 2011; Rubin, 2002; Wright, 1957). Its continuation was highlighted by authors whose publications are still available today: Susan Blow (Harris, 1983); Cooper, 1893; William Torrey Harris, 1880, in Bremner, 1971; Hill, 1941, in Braun & Edwards, 1972; von Marenholtz-Bülow, trans. by Mary Peabody Mann, 1895/2007); Peabody, letters in the 1880s, in Ronda, 1984).

- A special issue of the American *History of Education Quarterly* presented six articles and three commentaries on the international spread of kindergartens and nursery schools (Nawrotzki, 2009). The Preface titled "New Perspectives on Preschooling: The Nation and the Transnational in Early Childhood Education" describes the perspectives in the articles that show how crooked runs the historical record in early childhood education.

REFERENCES

Almy, M. (1986). The past, present, and future for the early childhood education researcher. *Early Childhood Research Quarterly, 1*(1), 1–13.

American Psychological Association. (2010). *Publication manual of the American Psychological Association.* (6th ed.). Washington, DC: Author.

Antler, J. (1987). *Lucy Sprague Mitchell: The making of a modern woman.* New Haven and London: Yale University Press.

Association for Childhood Education International (ACEI). (2013). *Archives of International Kindergarten Union, National Council of Primary Education, Association for Childhood Education and Association for Childhood Education International.* Special Collections, University of Maryland Libraries, College Park, MD.

Association for Childhood Education International. (1992). *Profiles in childhood education, 1931–1960.* Wheaton, MD: Author.

Bailyn, B. (1960). *Education in the Forming of American Society.* New York, NY: W.W. Norton & Company, The Norton Library.

Barnett, W. S., Carolan, M. E., Fitzgerald, J., & Squires, J. H. (2011). *The state of preschool 2011: State preschool yearbook.* Retrieved from http://www.nieer.org/yearbook.

Barzun, J., & Graff, H. E. (2004). *The modern researcher.* (6th ed.). Belmont, CA: Wadsworth Cengage Learning.

Beatty, B. (1995). *Preschool education in America: The culture of young children from the colonial era to the present.* New Haven and London: Yale University Press.

Bloch, M. (1953). *The historian's craft.* New York, NY: Vintage Books, a division of Random House.

Blow, S. (n.d.) *Retrieved Internet resources.* Obituary notice and death date: Retrieved from http://www.slpl.org/slpl/gateways/article240117800.asp (*St. Louis Post-Dispatch,* March 28, 16, p. 18); *New York Times,* March 29, 1916 (no page available); http://en.wikipedia.org/wiki/Susan_Blow; http://www.woman-philosophers.com/Susan-Blow.html; publications: Retrieved from http://froebelweb.org/images/blow.html

Blow, S. E. (2004). Symbolic education: A commentary on Froebel's "Mother Play." In W. T. Harris (Ed.), *International Education Series,* XXVI. To view online, go to http://www.amazon.com, enter title in search box and click on Go. Original published 1897.

Braun, S. J., & Edwards, E. P. (1972). *History and theory of early childhood education.* Belmont, CA: Wadsworth Publishing.

Bremner, R. H. (Ed.). (1971). *Children and youth in America: A documentary history.* Three volumes in five books. Cambridge: Harvard University Press.

Brosterman, N. (1997). *Inventing kindergarten.* New York, NY: Harry N. Abrams, Inc., Publishers.

Bultman, S. (2001). *The Froebel kindergarten philosophy.* Retrieved from http://www.froebelfoundation.org/philosophy.html.

Cahan, E. D. (1989). *Past caring: A history of U.S. preschool care and education for the poor, 1820–1965.* New York, NY: Columbia University, School of Public Health, National Center for Children in Poverty.

Caldwell, B. M. (1989). Foreword. In E. D. Cahan, *Past caring: A history of U.S. preschool care and education for the poor, 1820–1965,* pp. vii–xi. New York, NY: National Center for Children in Poverty, Columbia University.

Colker, L. J. (2008, March). Twelve characteristics of effective early childhood teachers. *Young Children, 63*(2), 68–73.

Cooper, S. B. (1893). The kindergarten in its bearings upon crime, pauperism, and insanity. In Committee on the History of Child Saving Work, *History of child saving in the United States* (pp. 89–98). Boston: Geo. H. Ellis.

Copeland, M. L. (1986, Fall). Oral history as a vehicle for teaching issues in day care. *Newsletter "Oral History in the Classroom,"* p. 1. Address: New Jersey Historical Commission, *Resources for Oral History,* 113 West State Street, CN 305, Trenton, NJ 08625.

Cremin, L. A. (1961). *The transformation of the school: Progressivism in American education 1876–1957.* New York, NY: Vintage Books, a division of Random House.

Dewey, J. (2001). *The school and society* [original published 1915], pp. 5–101, and *The child and the curriculum* [original published 1902], pp. 103–123. Mineola, NY: Dover Publications. [Both works in one volume].

Eick, C. (2011, May). Oral histories of education and the relevance of theory: Claiming new spaces in a post-revisionist era. *History of Education, 51*(2), 158–183.

Foner, E. (2002). *Who owns history? Rethinking the past in a changing world.* New York, NY: Hill and Wang, a division of Farrar, Straus & Giroux.

Froebel, F. W. (1985). *Pedagogies of the kindergarten or, his ideas concerning play and playthings of the child* (J. Jarvis, Trans.). New York, NY: D. Appleton. [Original work published 1887].

Garfinkel, I., Hochschild, J. L., & McLanahan, S. S. (Eds.). (1996). *Social policies for children.* Washington, DC: The Brookings Institution.

Gilderhus, M. T. (2007). *History and historians: A historiographical introduction.* (6th ed.). Upper Saddle River, NJ: Pearson Prentice Hall.

Green, J. L., Camilli, G., & Elmore, P. B. (Eds.). (2006). *Handbook of complementary methods in educational research.* (3rd ed.). Washington, DC. American Educational Research Association.

Greenburg, P. (1969). *The devil has slippery shoes: A biased biography of the Child Development Group of Mississippi.* London: The Macmillan Company.

Hale, J. N. (2012, November). The struggle begins early: Head Start and the Mississippi Freedom Movement. *History of Education Quarterly, 52*(4), 506–534.

Hann, C. (2013, Winter). Heidegger exposed. *Drew Magazine,* 12–17.

Harris, N. (1983). Preserving kindergarten history: The Carondelet Historic Center and Susan E. Blow. *Childhood Education, 59*(5), 336–338. Retrieved from http://dx.doi.org/10.1080/00094056.1983.10520613.

Hartup, W. W., & Smothergill, N. L. (Eds.) (1967). *The young child: Reviews of research.* Washington, DC: National Association for the Education of Young Children.

Hartup, W. W. (Ed.). (1972). *The young child: Reviews of research, Vol. 2.* Washington, DC: National Association for the Education of Young Children.

Heckman, J. (2007, June 23). *Investing in disadvantaged young children is good economics and good public policy.* Testimony before the Joint Economic Committee, U. S. Congress. Chicago: University of Chicago.

Hill, P. S. (1941). Kindergarten, in *American Educators' Encyclopedia*, pp. 1948–1972. Lake Bluff, IL: The United Educators. In S. J. Braun & E. P. Edwards, *History and theory of early childhood education* (pp. 73–78). Belmont, CA: Wadsworth Publishing.

Hinitz, B. F. (Ed.). (2013). *The hidden history of early childhood education*. New York, NY: Routledge.

Hymes, Jr., J. L. (1991). *Twenty years in review: A look at 1971–1990*. Washington, DC: National Association for the Education of Young Children.

Kaestle, C. F. (1992, fall). Standards of evidence in historical research: How do we know when we know? *History of Education Quarterly, 32*(3), 361–366.

Key, E. (1909). *The century of the child*. New York, NY: G. P. Putnam's Sons.

Kinchin, J., & O'Connor, A. (2012). *Century of the child: Growing by design 1900–2000*. New York, NY: Museum of Modern Art.

Lascarides, V. C., & Hinitz, B. F. (2000). *The history of early childhood education*. New York, NY: Falmer Press, a member of the Taylor & Francis Group. Published in paperback 2011.

Lascarides, V. C., & Hinitz, B. (1993). Survey of important historical and current figures in early childhood education, In K Salimova & E. V. Johanningmeier (Eds.), *Why should we teach history of education?* Moscow: International Academy of Self-Improvement.

Marten, J. (1998). *The children's Civil War*. Chapel Hill & London: University of North Carolina Press.

Michel, S. (1999). *Children's interests/Mothers' rights: The shaping of America's child care policy*. New Haven: Yale University Press.

Moore, S. G., & Cooper, C. R. (Eds.). (1982). *The young child: Reviews of research, Vol. 3*. Washington, DC: National Association for the Education of Young Children.

NACCRRA. (2012a). U.S. Census Bureau, 2011. *Capital connection guidebook, 112th Congress, 2nd session*. Washington, DC: Author. Now Child Care Aware America. Retrieved from http://www.census.gov/hhes/childcare/data/sipp/2010/tables/html.

NACCRRA. (2012b). U.S. Department of Labor, Bureau of Labor Statistics, 2011. *Capital connection guidebook, 112th Congress, 2nd session*. Washington, DC: Author. Now Child Care Aware America. Retrieved from http://bls.gov/cps/cpsa2010.pdf.

National Association for the Education of Young Children. (2012). *Final Program: Atlanta*. Washington, DC: NAEYC.

National Association for the Education of Young Children. (2001). *NAEYC at 75: 1926–2001-Reflections on the past-challenges for the future*. Washington, DC: Author.

National Association for Family Child Care. (2007). *NAFCC @ 25, 1982–2007-Preserving our past, enhancing our present, inspiring our future*. Salt Lake City, UT: NAFCC.

National Association for Regulatory Administration. (2006). *In celebration of NARA: Consumer protection through prevention-30 years*. Atlanta: NARA.

National Manpower Council. (1957). *Womanpower: A statement by the NMC with chapters by the Council staff*. New York, NY: Columbia University Press.

National Manpower Council. (1958). *Work in the lives of married women: Proceedings of a conference on womanpower.* Held October 20–25, 1957, at Arden House, Harriman Campus of Columbia University.

Nawrotzki, K. D. (2009, May). *Prefac155-e:* New perspectives on preschooling: The nation and the transnational in early childhood education. *History of Education Quarterly, 45*(2), 155.

Novick, P. (1988). *That noble dream: The objectivity question.* Cambridge: Cambridge University Press. Partially retrieved from http://www.amazon.com/That-Noble-Dream-Objectivity/dp/052137454#reader_052137454

Osborn, D. K. (1991). *Early childhood education in historical perspective.* (3rd ed.). Athens, GA: Daye Press.

Peabody, E. (1888). *Lectures in the training schools for kindergartners.* Boston: D. C. Heath.

Perry, R. B. (1935). *The thought and character of William James.* 2 vols. Boston: Little, Brown.

Pexton, P. B. (2013, January 20). Using someone else's words—again. *The Washington Post,* Section A, 23.

Pilto, C. (2011). The Steins build: Le Corbusier's villa Stein-deMonzie, Les Terrasses. In *The Steins collect: Matisse, Picasso, and the Parisian Avant Garde* (pp. 167–175). New York, NY: Metropolitan Museum of Art.

Rael, P. (2004). *Reading, writing, and researching for history: A guide for college students.* Brunswick, ME: Bowdoin College. Retrieved from http://academic.bowdoin.edu/WritingGuides/

Ranck, E. R. (2012). *Celebrating the NAEYC History Seminar: A historical chronology, 1973–2012.* Unpublished list of History Seminar presenters and topics available from the author at edna.ranck@verizon.net.

Ranck, E. R. (1995, November). Do Will you remember? Taking a child care program's past into the future-Building an archival system for your program. *Exchange,* Issue 106, 91–95.

Ranck, E. R. (2013). Early care and education in the 1950s: The thorny path when public issues confront passionately-held beliefs. In B. F. Hinitz, (Ed.), *The hidden history of early childhood education* (pp. 98–139). New York, NY: Routledge.

Ranck, E. R. (1990, October). *Emerging policies for children: The surprising Eisenhower legacy for early education and child care.* (Unpublished paper presented at a symposium honoring Dwight D. Eisenhower's centennial year). Gettysburg: PA: Gettysburg College. A revised version will be published in Hinitz, 2013).

Ranck, E. R. (1999, February). Gender issues in preparing a professional workforce: New views of women's work in early care and education. *Child and Youth Care Forum, 28*(1), 59–67.

Ranck, E. R. (1998, March). Highlights and lowlights of the past two decades. *Exchange,* Issue 120, 12–16.

Ranck, E. R. (1997). NACCRRA at 10: A commemorative history of the National Association of Child Care Resource and Referral Agencies. Washington, DC: NACCRRA.

Ranck, E. R. (1986). *The politics of childhood: The historical development of early childhood education licensing laws and regulations in New Jersey, 1946–1972.* (Unpublished dissertation). Teacher College, Columbia University, New York, New York.

Ranck, E. R. (2007). Susan Isaacs. In R. S. New & M. Cochran, (Eds.), *Early childhood education: An international encyclopedia, 2*, (pp. 459–461). Westport, CT: Praeger.

Ranck, E. R. (2001). Timeline of early care and education. In *NAEYC at 75: 1926–2001—Reflections on the past, challenges for the future* (pp. 5–32). Washington, DC: National Association for the Education of Young Children.

Ronda, B. A. (Ed.). (1984). *Letters of Elizabeth Palmer Peabody: American renaissance woman*. Middletown, CT: Wesleyan University Press.

Ross, M. (n.d.) *Three documents: 1) What is oral history? 2) Basic techniques for oral history interviewing. 3) Sequence of oral history functions*. College Park, MD: University of Maryland, Department of History.

Rubin, J. S. (2002). *Intimate triangle: Architecture of crystals, Frank Lloyd Wright, and the Froebel kindergarten*. Huntsville, AL: Polycrystal Book Service.

Rury, J. L. (2006). Historical research in education. In J. L. Green, G. Camilli, & P. B. Elmore (Eds.), *Handbook of complementary methods in educational research* (3rd ed., pp. 323–332). Washington, D. C.: American Educational Research Association.

Salimova, K., & Johanningmeier, E. V. (1993). *Why should we teach history of education?* Moscow, Russia: The Library of International Academy of Self-Improvement.

Sealander, J. (2003). *The failed century of the child: Governing America's young in the twentieth century*. Cambridge: Cambridge University Press.

Shweder, R. A. (Ed.). (2009). *The child: An encyclopedic companion-From birth through adolescence*. Chicago: University of Chicago Press.

Simpson, J. (1981). *A biographical study of Black educators in early childhood education*. [Unpublished dissertation]. The Fielding Institute, Santa Barbara, CA.

Simpson, J. (2012, November). Oneida Cockrell: A pioneer in early childhood education. *Young Children, 67*(5), 58–61.

Snyder, A. (1972). *Dauntless women in childhood education, 1856–1931*. Washington, DC: Association for Childhood Education International.

Storey, W. K. (2009). *Writing history: A guide for students*. (3rd ed.). New York, NY: Oxford University Press. [Now in its 4th edition].

Turabian, K. L. (2007). *A manual for writers of research papers, theses, and dissertations*. (7th ed.). Chicago: University of Chicago.

Vinovskis, M. A. (2005). *The birth of Head Start: Preschool education policies in the Kennedy and Johnson administrations*. Chicago: University of Chicago Press.

Von Marenholtz-Bŭlow, B. (1895/2007). *How kindergarten came to America: Friedrich Froebel's radical vision of early childhood education*. (Trans. from the German by Mrs. Horace [Mary] Mann). New York, NY: The New Press.

Weiss, H. (Ed.). (2004, Summer). Early childhood programs and evaluations. *The evaluation exchange, 10*(2), 1–29. [Harvard Family Research Project, Harvard Graduate School of Education, Harvard University]

Women in Military Service for America Memorial Foundation. Oral history-Collecting oral history. [Online webpage]. Retrieved from http://www.womensmemorial.org/H&C/Oral_History/ohhowto.html.

Wortham, S. (1992). *Childhood: 1892–1992*. Wheaton, MD: Association of Childhood Education International. [Now in its 2nd edition].

Wright, F. Ll. (1957). A testament. In B. B. Pfeiffer (Ed.), *Frank Lloyd Wright: Collected writings,* (pp. 155–225). New York, NY: Rizzoli International

Zigler, E., & Styfco, S. J. (2010). *The hidden history of Head Start.* New York, NY: Oxford University Press.

Zinn, H., & Arnove, A. (Eds.). (2009). *Voices of the people's history of the United States.* (2nd ed.). Retrieved from http://www.sevenstories.com/book/?GCOI=58322100808900

PART III

THE RESEARCH PROCESS:
FROM CONCEPTUALIZATION TO PUBLICATION

CHAPTER 21

METHODS FOR DEVELOPING SCIENTIFIC EDUCATION

Research-Based Development of Practices, Pedagogies, Programs, and Policies[1]

Douglas H. Clements and Julie Sarama

Many types of studies contribute to the field of education. But too few, in our opinion, go to the heart of the educational enterprise—developing scientifically based practices, pedagogies, programs, and policies. Whether developed for children or their teachers, these are the main malleable factors that affect the quality of children's educational experiences. In this chapter, we describe why be believe that this type of research-and-development program should take precedence in early childhood education and then describe a framework for such a program.

WHY DO WE NEED RESEARCH-BASED DEVELOPMENT OF PRACTICES, PEDAGOGIES, PROGRAMS, AND POLICIES?

What directly affects the quality and effectiveness of young children's experiences in the classroom? Teachers do, including their practices and pedagogical strategies (Darling-Hammond, 1997; Ferguson, 1991; National Research Council, 2001; Schoen, Cebulla, Finn, & Fi, 2003). In addition, programs or curricula for children have a substantial impact on teachers and their practices and on what children experience and learn (Goodlad, 1984; Grant, Peterson, & Shojgreen-Downer, 1996; National Research Council, 2009; Whitehurst, 2009). Similarly, professional development practices (e.g., workshops) and programs (e.g., certifications, degrees) affect teachers (Darling-Hammond, 1997; Ferguson, 1991; National Research Council, 2001; Sarama & DiBiase, 2004; Schoen, et al., 2003). (Indeed, a combination may be best. Top-down imposition of a new curriculum with limited professional development and support, for example, may have limited influence on teachers' beliefs and practices, Stein & Kim, 2009.)

However, the quality of all these varies widely and does not show steady improvement year to year (Early, et al., 2005; Goodlad, 1984; National Research Council, 2009). A major reason is that practices, programs, and the policies that should support them are rarely developed or evaluated and revised following systematic, much less scientific, research methods (Clements & Battista, 2000; Davidson, Fields, & Yang, 2009). We begin by defining what we mean by scientific research.

Science includes the observation, description, analysis, hypothesizing, experimental investigation, and theoretical explanation of phenomena. Scientific knowledge is accepted as more reliable than everyday knowledge because the way in which it is developed is explicit and repeatable. "Our faith [in it] rests entirely on the certainty of reproducing or seeing again a certain phenomenon by means of certain well defined acts" (Valéry, 1957, p.1253, as quoted in Glasersfeld, 1995). Scientific method, or research, is disciplined inquiry (Cronbach & Suppes, 1969). The term "inquiry" suggests that the investigation's goal is answering a specific question. The term "disciplined" suggests that the investigation should be guided by concepts and methods from disciplines and connected to relevant theory in those disciplines, and also that it should be in the public view so that the inquiry can be inspected and criticized. The use of research methods, and the conscientious documentation and full reporting of these processes—data collection, argumentation, reasoning, and checking for counterhypotheses—distinguishes disciplined inquiry from other sources of opinion and belief (Cronbach & Suppes, 1969; National Research Council, 2002; Shulman, 1997).

Science does not, however, produce the "truth" or a single correct view. It provides reliable ways of dealing with experiences and pursuing and achieving goals (Glasersfeld, 1995). It involves the process of progressive problem solving (Scardamalia & Bereiter, 1994). Thus, the goal for scientific methods of research and development cannot be to develop a single "ideal" (practice, pedagogy, program, or policy—hence referred to as *products*), but rather dynamic problem solving, progress, and advancement beyond present limits of competence (Dewey, 1929; Scardamalia & Bereiter, 1994; Tyler, 1949). Ironically, another implication is that educational products should be based on research—as defined here. Given that traditions, social interactions, and politics have strong effects on education, the checks and balances of scientific research are essential to progress.

Still, does that not limit the creativity of researchers, developers, and teachers? Somewhat ironically, we believe the opposite. Scientific knowledge is necessary but not sufficient, for the continued development of high-quality educational products. More than 120 years ago, William James made this same argument, speaking of the young science of his own time, psychology.

> You make a great, a very great mistake, if you think that psychology, being the science of the mind's laws, is something from which you can deduce definite programmes and schemes and methods of instruction for immediate classroom use. Psychology is a science, and teaching is an art; and sciences never generate arts directly out of themselves. An intermediary inventive mind must make the application, by using its originality. (James, 1892/1958, pp. 23–24)

James argues that scientific knowledge is applied artfully to create teaching products. Such research-to-practice methods are included in our framework. However, this method used alone is incorrect in its presumptions (that extant research is a sufficient source for development of products), insensitive to changing goals in the content area (new standards are created at a fast pace that research cannot comprehensively address), and unable to contribute to a revision of the theory and knowledge on which it is built (i.e., it is inherently conservative, evaluating "what is")—the second critical goal of scientific research and development. In contrast, research should be present in all phases of the creative or development process.

In this way, the framework is mainly about researcher-developers (which includes some teachers, of course), but before we leave this section, let's address whether such a scientific approach denies professionalism and creativity to classroom teachers. Again, we claim it promotes them—in scientists, developers, and teachers. One reason is that professionals such as doctors and teachers share a scientific knowledge base; that is, as all professionals, they share scientific guidelines of systematic, rather than idiosyncratic, practice. Such systematic practice is more effective and amenable to scientifically based improvement than private, idiosyncratic practice (Raudenbush, 2009). This is *not* to say that teachers should deliver "scripted" lessons with little or no interpretation. Rather, it is to argue that their creativity should be in building upon the research foundation, using the resources of science (and that wisdom of expert practice not yet studied), to create environments and interactions that promote their children's development and learning. It does mean that many of us hold notions of teacher creativity that may benefit from a revision. As a personal example, when one of us (Clements) taught kindergarten, all the early childhood educators around him believed that "creative teachers" made up all their ideas and made all their materials. I too believed, then, that if I copied an idea or game that another successful teacher used, I was "less creative." Such thinking erects an unfortunate barrier to the spread of the most effective practices and programs. Instead, we believe, teachers' creativity is best used to use and imaginatively apply the best of the resources of science and the wisdom of expert practice.

All this is not to say that scientific programs cannot be outperformed (e.g., by a talented, idiosyncratic teacher). James had more to say on this matter.

> The science of logic never made a man reason rightly, and the science of ethics (if there be such a thing) never made a man behave rightly. The most such sciences can do is to help us catch ourselves up and check ourselves, if we start to reason or to behave wrongly; and to criticize [sic] ourselves more articulately after we have made mistakes. A science only lays down lines within which the rules of the art must fall, laws which the follower of the art must not transgress; but what particular thing he shall positively do within those lines is left exclusively to his own genius. One genius will do his work well and succeed in one way, while another succeeds as well quite differently; yet neither will transgress the lines.... And so everywhere the teacher must agree with the psychology, but need not necessarily be the only kind of teaching that would so agree; for many diverse methods of teaching may equally well agree with psychological laws. (James, 1892/1958, p. 24)

Thus, there are several approaches, but each should be consistent with what is known about teaching and learning. Those that appear successful, such as our talented teacher's, should be documented, investigated as to why the approach is successful, and added to the research literature. Without such research methodologies, the talented teacher's practices and materials will be limited in their contribution to the myriad teachers and researcher-developers who come after.

This is also not to say that all research should be scientific. Other types of research may make serious contributions, such as narrative (Bruner, 1986), or humanistic (Schwandt, 2002) perspectives, historical research (Darling-Hammond & Snyder, 1992), aesthetic approaches (Eisner, 1998), or literary criticism (Papert, 1987), just to name a few. Such approaches complement the scientific research methods described here. Of course, no single scientific finding or set of findings should dictate pedagogy. Consistent with James, John Dewey stated the following.

> No conclusion of scientific research can be converted into an immediate rule of educational art. For there is no educational practice whatever which is not highly complex; that is to say, which does not contain many other conditions and factors than are included in the scientific finding. Nevertheless, scientific findings are of practical utility, and the situation is wrongly interpreted when it is used to disparage the value of science in the art of education. What it militates against is the transformation of scientific findings into rules of action. (Dewey, 1929, p. 19)

Consistent with Dewey's formulation, our framework for research-and-development rejects strict "rules" but values scientific research for its practical, and political, utility.

In summary, scientific knowledge is valued because it offers reliable, self-correcting, documented, shared knowledge based on research methodology (Mayer, 2000; National Research Council, 2002). Education is a design science (Brown, 1992; H. A. Simon, 1969; R. Walker, 2011; Wittmann, 1995) and knowledge created during research-and-development should be both generalized and placed within a scientific research corpus, peer reviewed, and published. However, this is not a deterministic science and certainly not one limited to (although it includes) quantitative experiments (Dewey, 1929). As the framework presented here will make clear, many research methodologies, mostly qualitative, are used to produce research-based education.

EARLY ATTEMPTS TO BASE EDUCATION ON RESEARCH

Research, especially psychological research from the time of William James on, has played a substantial role in education, especially in early childhood (Clements, 2008b). However, its role has been less to produce practical materials for teaching, than to interpret the phenomena of early education (Ginsburg, Klein, & Starkey, 1998). As stated previously, this is important, but indirect. We believe that most of the ways that development might be based on research should be employed. We next describe a small number of early attempts to base product development on research.

Early efforts to write research-based teaching approaches and materials often were grounded in the broad philosophies, theories, and empirical results on learning and teaching. For example, in early childhood, early applications of Piaget's theories often led to suggestions that children be to perform accurately on Piagetian clinical tasks. Other incorporated materials directly adapted from those tasks (Forman & Fosnot, 1982; Kamii, 1973). These were not particularly successful. Even detailed analyses of Piagetian research failed to guide the development of programs or curricula in directly useful ways (Duckworth, 1979).

Others based their educational programs on Piaget's constructivist foundation. For example, Duckworth encouraged teachers to create environments in which children would "have wonderful ideas" (Duckworth, 1973). Such programs have been arguably more successful, although the interpretations varied widely (Forman, 1993). Indeed, the programs were distinct. The broad philosophy and theory, unsurprisingly, leaves much room for interpretation and provides little specific guidance for teaching or the development of materials.

In summary, the research-to-practice model has a less than stellar historical record (Clements & Battista, 2000; Gravemeijer, 1994b). As stated previously, it also is limited in its contribution to either theory or practice (Clements, 2007, 2008b). The alternative we propose here is less about new research approaches or practices, and more about a specific framework for synthesizing those that have been used successfully into a complete scientific research-and-development system for designing and evaluating educational products.

A COMPREHENSIVE FRAMEWORK FOR RESEARCH-BASED EDUCATION

We developed a comprehensive framework detailing the methods used to create and evaluate research-based practices, pedagogies, and programs (with implications for policies) so we could contribute to both theory and practice. First, we established goals based on the belief that any valid scientific development product should address two basic issues—effect and conditions—in three domains, practice, policy, and theory, as diagrammed in Figure 21.1.

To achieve these goals, researcher-developers must build on previous research, structure and revise the nature and content of components in accordance with models of children's thinking and learning in a domain, and conduct formative and summative evaluations in a series of progressively expanding social contexts. These form the categories of research-and-development activity that define our framework. These categories include ten phases of such activity that warrant claiming that a product is based on research (Clements, 2007; Sarama & Clements, 2008). The categories and phases involve a combination of research methods; no single method would be adequate. For example, design experiments (Brown, 1992; Cobb, Confrey, diSessa, Lehrer, & Schauble, 2003; Ruthven, Laborde, Leach, & Tiberghien, 2009; The Design-Based Research Collective, 2003; R. Walker, 2011), developed as a way to conduct formative research to test and refine educational designs

	Practice	Policy	Theory
Effects	Is the intervention effective in helping children achieve specific learning goals? Are the intended and unintended consequences positive? (6–10)* Is there credible documentation of both a priori research and research indicating the efficacy of the approach as compared to alternative approaches? (all)	Are the goals important (e.g., to meeting standards)? (1, 5, 10) What are the effect sizes? (9, 10) What effects does it have on teachers? (10)	Why is the intervention effective? (all) What were the theoretical bases? (1, 2, 3) What cognitive changes occurred and what processes were responsible? That is, what specific components and features account for its impact and why? (4, 6, 7)
Conditions	When and where? Under what conditions is the intervention effective? (Do findings generalize?) (8, 10)	What are the support requirements (7) for various contexts? (8–10)	Why do certain conditions change the effectiveness? (6–10) How do specific strategies produce previously unattained results and why? (6–10)

Note: Numbers in parentheses refer to the phases of the Framework described in the following sections.

Figure 21.1 Goals of research and development (adapted from Clements, 2007).

(Collins, Joseph, & Bielaczyc, 2004) are central, but are usually limited to pilot testing (Fishman, Marx, Blumenfeld, Krajcik, & Soloway, 2004; National Research Council, 2004, p. 75), put too little focus on the development of curricula, and do not address the full range of questions (Clements, 2008a; R. Walker, 2011). Our work is based on the assumption that all appropriate methods should be synthesized into a coherent, complete framework for research and development, as described in Figure 21.2 (see Clements, 2007, for a full description). (Space prohibits describing the work of many researcher-developers from which this framework was abstracted, but see citations and descriptions of their work in Clements, 2002, 2007, 2008b; Clements & Battista, 2000; Sarama & Clements, 2008.)

DESCRIPTION AND APPLICATION OF THE FRAMEWORK

In this section, we describe the categories and phrases of the Framework in more detail. We also briefly illustrate its application using our instantiation of it developing and evaluating the *Building Blocks* early childhood mathematics curriculum and the TRIAD model of intervention at scale.

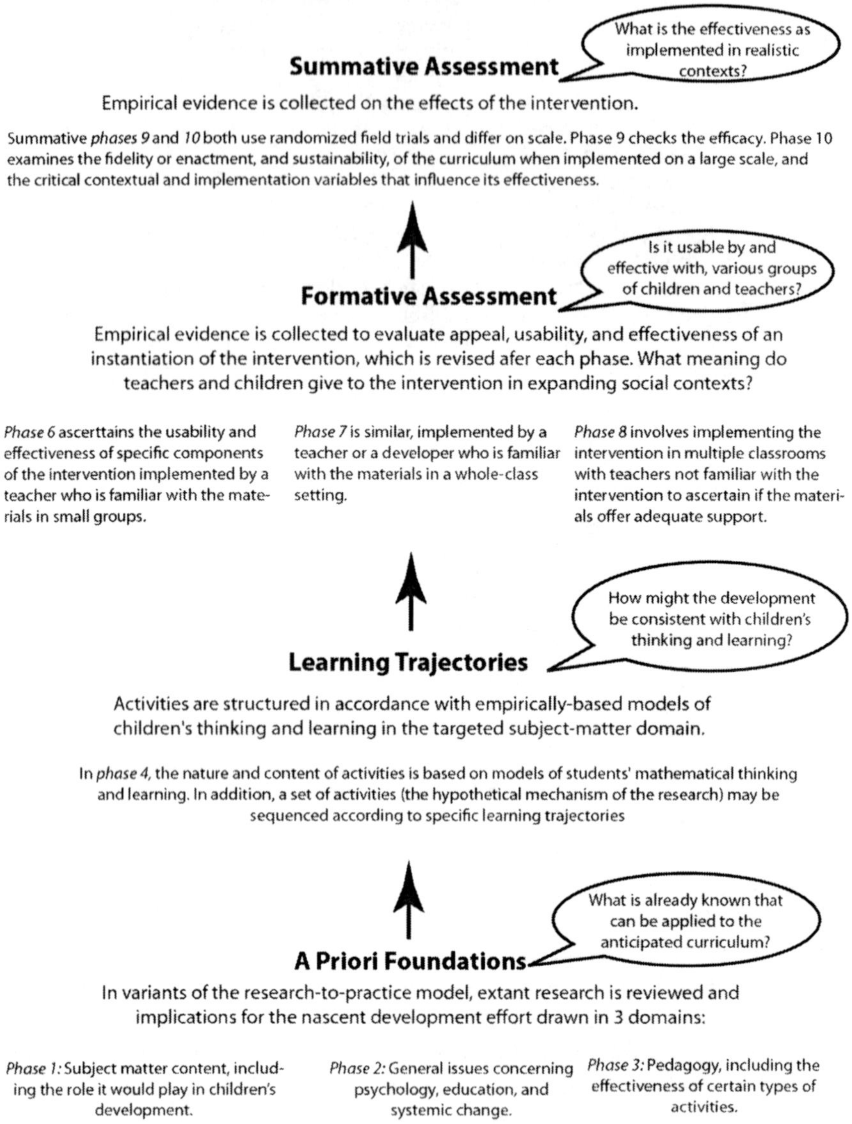

Summative Assessment — *What is the effectiveness as implemented in realistic contexts?*

Empirical evidence is collected on the effects of the intervention.

Summative *phases 9* and *10* both use randomized field trials and differ on scale. Phase 9 checks the efficacy. Phase 10 examines the fidelity or enactment, and sustainability, of the curriculum when implemented on a large scale, and the critical contextual and implementation variables that influence its effectiveness.

↑

Formative Assessment — *Is it usable by and effective with, various groups of children and teachers?*

Empirical evidence is collected to evaluate appeal, usability, and effectiveness of an instantiation of the intervention, which is revised afer each phase. What meaning do teachers and children give to the intervention in expanding social contexts?

Phase 6 ascerttains the usability and effectiveness of specific components of the intervention implemented by a teacher who is familiar with the materials in small groups.

Phase 7 is similar, implemented by a teacher or a developer who is familiar with the materials in a whole-class setting.

Phase 8 involves implementing the intervention in multiple classrooms with teachers not familiar with the intervention to ascertain if the materials offer adequate support.

↑

Learning Trajectories — *How might the development be consistent with children's thinking and learning?*

Activities are structured in accordance with empirically-based models of children's thinking and learning in the targeted subject-matter domain.

In *phase 4*, the nature and content of activities is based on models of students' mathematical thinking and learning. In addition, a set of activities (the hypothetical mechanism of the research) may be sequenced according to specific learning trajectories

↑

A Priori Foundations — *What is already known that can be applied to the anticipated curriculum?*

In variants of the research-to-practice model, extant research is reviewed and implications for the nascent development effort drawn in 3 domains:

Phase 1: Subject matter content, including the role it would play in children's development.

Phase 2: General issues concerning psychology, education, and systemic change.

Phase 3: Pedagogy, including the effectiveness of certain types of activities.

Figure 21.2 The Framework for Comprehensive Research and Development.

A Priori Foundations

In this category, established research review procedures (e.g., Galvin, 2009; Light & Pillemer, 1984) and content analyses (National Research Council, 2004) are employed to garner knowledge concerning the specific subject matter content, including the role it would play in children's development (*phase 1*); general issues concerning psychology, education, and systemic change (*phase 2*); and pedagogy, including the effectiveness of certain types of environments and activities (*phase 3*).

Phase 1: Subject Matter A Priori Foundation

Developing goals is a complex process, not all of which, perhaps most of which, is not amenable to scientific investigation. Societal-determined values and goals are substantive components of any program (Hiebert, 1999; National Research Council, 2002; Schwandt, 2002; Tyler, 1949). Creating goals requires a cooperative process among the many legitimate direct and indirect stakeholders (van Oers, 2003). The array of advice from a wide variety of such stakeholders involved in such large-scale projects as those in the domain of mathematics, the *Principles and standards for school mathematics* (National Council of Teachers of Mathematics, 2000) and *Common Core State Standards* (CCSSO/NGA, 2010) illustrate this point. For example, subject matter experts and their organizations evaluated whether these goals included those concepts and procedures that play a central role in the domain (cf. content analyses in National Research Council, 2004). Nevertheless, scientific procedures help identify subject-matter content that is valid within the discipline and makes a substantive contribution to the development of children in the target population. That is, concepts and procedures of the domain should build from the children's past and present experiences (Dewey, 1902/1976) and be generative in children's development of future understanding (Clements, Sarama, & DiBiase, 2004).

In our *Building Blocks* project, (Clements & Sarama, 2007a), we built our goals upon the results of a large conference we organized (funded by NSF and the ExxonMobil Education Foundation) that involved representatives from state departments of education and from the U.S. Department of Education, mathematicians, mathematics and early childhood educators (pre-K to university) and researchers, childhood policy makers, and developers. This was preceded and followed by extensive research reviews (for a full report, which also influenced the Curriculum Focal Points and Common Core, see Clements, et al., 2004). We vetted the specific goals for our project to an advisory board consisting of members of these same groups. As an example, we determined that the competence of subitizing is crucial to young's children's mathematical development (Clements, 1999; Clements & Conference Working Group, 2004). Subitizing, the ability to recognize and name the numerosity of a group quickly (from the Latin "to arrive suddenly"), is the earliest developing quantitative, or numerical, ability (Sarama & Clements, 2009). It also contributes to many other competencies, such as counting and arithmetic (Baroody, 1987; Clements, 1999; Fuson, 1992; Sarama & Clements, 2009).

Phase 2: General A Priori Foundation

In this phase, philosophies, theories, and empirical results on teaching and general educational issues are reviewed for their applicability to the product. Researcher-developers might start from an Ausubelian, Piagetian, or general constructivist perspective and proceed in any of several directions (Forman, 1993; Lawton, 1993). In addition, theory and research offer perspectives on children's and teachers' experiences with similar products. For our own part, we used theory and research on early childhood learning and teaching (Clements, 2001; National Research Council, 2001), to decide that the basic approach of *Building Blocks* would be finding the mathematics in, and developing mathematics from, children's activity. The materials were designed to facilitate children's extending and mathematizing their everyday activities, such as building blocks, art projects, stories, songs, and puzzles.

Phase 3: Pedagogical A Priori Foundation

In this phase, research relevant to creating specific types of educational environments and activities is reviewed. Intuition of practitioners—the art of teaching—is also garnered as much as possible by viewing patterns of promising practice (Dewey, 1929; Hiebert, 1999).

> A science only lays down lines within which the rules of the art must fall, laws which the follower of the art must not transgress; but what particular thing he shall positively do within those lines is left exclusively to his own genius... many diverse methods of teaching may equally well agree with psychological laws. (James, 1892/1958, p. 24)

Note that James treats research only as providing a priori foundations. Our framework uses research in this way, but considers this just a beginning.

Building Blocks pedagogical foundations were based on the same body of research (e.g., National Research Council, 2001), including a wide range of grouping (whole group, small group, individual) and teaching strategies (from the design of the entire environment to explicit instruction to centers and "teachable moments" during play). As just one example, for a minor, but important, component of the curriculum, we consulted empirical data on features that appeared to make computer programs motivating (Escobedo & Evans, 1997; Lahm, 1996; Shade, 1994) and effective (Childers, 1989; Clements & Sarama, 1998; Lavin & Sanders, 1983; Murphy & Appel, 1984; Sarama, Clements, & Vukelic, 1996).

Learning Model, Learning Trajectories

This phase differs from phase 3 in the focus on the children's thinking and learning, rather than teaching strategies alone, in the greater degree of specificity, and in the iterative nature of its application. That is, in practice, models are usually created or refined along with the development of instructional tasks, using, clinical interviews, teaching experiments, and design experiments.

Phase 4: Structure According to Specific Learning Trajectories

Learning trajectories are found or developed to form the core of the product, especially for a curriculum or teaching sequence (M. A. Simon, 1995). Learning trajectories are based on the idea that children follow natural *developmental progressions* in learning and development. As they learn to crawl, then walk, then run, then run, skip, and jump with increasing speed and dexterity, they follow natural developmental progressions in learning in other domains. Learning trajectories built upon natural developmental progressions and empirically based models of children's thinking and learning are more mature in some areas, such as literacy (e.g., progressions within phonemic awareness and alphabet recognition, as well as movement from these to early graphophonemic analysis, Anthony, Lonigan, Driscoll, Phillips, & Burgess, 2003; Brice & Brice, 2009; Justice, Pence, Bowles, & Wiggins, 2006; Levy, Gong, Hessels, Evans, & Jared, 2006) and mathematics (Carpenter & Moser, 1984; Case, 1982; Griffin & Case, 1997), but are also developed in science (Hmelo-Silver & Duncan, 2009; National Research Council, 2007), albeit less for the earliest years (Brenneman & Gelman, 2009), and in social-emotional development (e.g., Bredekamp, 2014). Sometimes different names are used (e.g., "learning progressions") and some describe developmental progressions, but not instructional suggestions. However, they share a family resemblance and each can be used to serve the purposes of research and development as proposed here.

We believe that much of the educational potential of learning trajectories lies in their ability to connect developmental progressions to the educational environment and to teaching. We define learning trajectories as "descriptions of children's thinking and learning in a specific domain, and a related, conjectured route through a set of instructional tasks designed to engender those mental processes or actions hypothesized to move children through a developmental progression of levels of thinking, created with the intent of supporting children's achievement of specific goals in that domain" (Clements & Sarama, 2004b, p. 83). Thus, in our view, complete learning trajectories have three parts: a *goal*, a *developmental progression* or path along which children develop to reach that goal, and a set of recommendations for *educational environments and activities*, matched to each of the levels of thinking in that path that help children develop ever higher levels of thinking.

The product of this stage is a well-developed cognitive model of children's learning as expressed in learning trajectories. Ideally, such models specify knowledge structures, the development of these structures, mechanisms or processes of development, and developmental progressions of nascent learning trajectories that specify hypothetical routes that children might take in achieving the goal (Sarama & Clements, 2009, presents detailed cognitive models not included here).

As an example, our synthesis of research for the *Building Blocks* project created a first draft of a developmental progression for subitizing. We chose to illustrate the subitizing learning trajectory in this chapter due to its simplicity[2] (i.e., learning trajectories for other topics are longer and more complex). Although there are several features, the basic characteristics are the number of objects and the development of the type of subitizing. First, of course, very young children begin very small numbers—one or two. They slowly develop the ability to subitize larger numbers. Second, the type of subitizing develops from perceptual subitizing to conceptual subitizing. Perceptual subitizing involves recognizing a number of objects without consciously using other mental or mathematical processes and then naming it. This is limited to sets of up to 4 to 6 objects. Conceptual subitizing plays an advanced organizing role, as seeing "10" on a pair of dice by recognizing the two collections (via perceptual subitizing) and consciously composing them. These advancements can be seen in Figure 21.3, which illustrates a portion of this learning trajectory. The left column names and describes each level of thinking in the developmental progression; examples of behaviors are shown in a smaller font (from Sarama & Clements, 2009, which also describes cognitive science descriptions of mental components and processes not included here). We used clinical interviews to check that developmental progression. A simple example of a revision these engendered was a differentiation between the perceptual subitizer to 5 and the conceptual subitizer to 5, which did not exist in the original version.

We then used research reviews and targeted teaching experiments to design the initial instructional activities. The right column of Figure 21.3 provides examples of the types of environments and activities that help children construct that level of thinking (from Clements & Sarama, 2009). These involve informal interactions (e.g., see the first level) and intentional activities. As an example of the latter, a simple, enjoyable "snapshots" game is played at many levels, starting with "Perceptual Subitizer to 4." The activity is introduced by talking about cameras, and having "our eyes and mind take snapshots" like cameras. The teacher covers, say, three counters with a dark cloth. She reminds children to watch carefully to take a "snapshot," then uncovers the counters for two seconds only. Children show how many counters they saw with their fingers. Once they have seen all responses, teachers ask children to whisper to each other how many counters they saw. The teacher then uncovers the counters to check answers, and so forth.

Methods for Developing Scientific Education ▪ **729**

Developmental Progression	Instructional Activities
Small Collection Namer Names groups of 1 to 2, sometimes 3. 　Shown a pair of shoes, says, "Two shoes."	Gesture to a small group of objects (1 or 2, later 3 when the children are capable). Say, "There are two balls. Two!" When the children are able, ask them how many there are. This should be a natural part of interaction *throughout* the day. Name collections as "two." Also include non-examples as well as examples, saying, for instance, "That's not two. That's three!" Or, put out three groups of 2 and one group of 3 and have the child find out "the one that is not like the others." Talk about why.
Maker of Small Collections Nonverbally makes a small collection (no more than 4, usually 1–3) with the same number as another collection. Might also be verbal. 　When shown a collection of 3, makes another collection of 3.	Ask children to get the right number of crackers (etc.) for a small number of children. Lay out a small collection, say 2 blocks. Hide them. Ask children to make a group that has the same number of blocks as your group has. After they have finished, show them your group and ask them if they got the same number. Name the number. *In this and every other level, continue to name collections throughout the day.* "Would you please put those *four* books on the shelves?" Ah, *three* beautiful flowers." "Nice design of *five* squares you made!"
Perceptual Subitizer to 4 Instantly recognizes collections up to 4 briefly shown and verbally names the number of items. 　When shown 4 objects briefly, says "four."	Play "Snapshots" (see the text). At this level, play with collections of 1 to 4 objects, arranged in a line or other simple arrangement, asking children to respond verbally with the number name. Start with the smaller numbers and easier arrangements, (the top row of dots) moving to others as children become competent and confident.

Figure 21.3 A learning trajectory for subitizing—sample levels (adapted from Clements & Sarama, 2009; Sarama & Clements, 2009).

730 ■ D. H. CLEMENTS and J. SARAMA

Developmental Progression	Instructional Activities
	Play "Snapshots" on the computer. (a) Children see an arrangement of dots for 2 seconds. (b) They are then asked to click on the corresponding numeral. They can "peek" for 2 more seconds if necessary. (c) They are given feedback verbally and by seeing the dots again.
Perceptual Subitizer to 5 Instantly recognizes briefly shown collections up to 5 and verbally names the number of items. Shown 5 objects briefly, says "5."	Play "Snapshots" on or off the computer with matching dots to numerals with groups up to and including five. Play "Snapshots" with dot cards, starting with easy arrangements, moving to more difficult arrangements, as children are able.

Figure 21.3 (continued)   A learning trajectory for subitizing—sample levels (adapted from Clements & Sarama, 2009; Sarama & Clements, 2009).

Developmental Progression	Instructional Activities
Conceptual Subitizer to 5 Verbally labels all arrangements to about 5, when shown only briefly. "5! Why? I saw 3 and 2 and so I said 5."	Use different arrangement the various modifications of "Snapshots" to develop conceptual subitizing and ideas about addition and subtraction. The goal is to encouraging students to "see the addends and the sum as in 'two olives and two olives make four olives'" (Fuson, 1992, p. 248).
Conceptual Subitizer to 10 Verbally labels most briefly shown arrangements to 6, then up to 10, using groups. "In my mind, I made two groups of 3 and one more, so 7."	Play "Snapshots" on or off the computer with matching dots to numerals. The computer version's feedback emphasizes that "three and four make seven."

Figure 21.3 (continued) A learning trajectory for subitizing—sample levels (adapted from Clements & Sarama, 2009; Sarama & Clements, 2009).

The goal, developmental sequence, and instruction make up the complete learning trajectories. Learning trajectories such as these formed the skeleton of the nascent *Building Blocks* product.

Evaluation

The remaining six phases, in the third category, *evaluation*, involve collecting specific empirical evidence in marketing, formative, and summative evaluations. The goal is to evaluate the attractiveness, usability, and efficacy of the product, even if it is still in draft form.

Phase 5: Market Research

Market research is consumer-oriented research. Often, it is *not* done scientifically. For example, publishers may create prototype materials that are presented to "focus groups" in a geographically balanced sample of sites, along with general questions about what they are looking for. Identities and results are hidden—parting with the scientific criterion that methods and results should be in the public view so that the inquiry can be inspected and criticized.

In contrast, collecting useful information about goals, needs, usability and probability of adoption and implementation is important for dissemination and adoption (Tushnet et al., 2000). Our framework includes market research that is scientific; that is, fully grounded in the disciplines, is in the public view, conscientiously documented, and fully reported (Jaeger, 1988). Such market research is conducted at several points in the developmental cycle, from the beginning, as a component of the *A Priori Foundations* phases, and through the last phase of planning for diffusion (Rogers, 2003). We worked with 35 teachers in developing the *Building Blocks* products, and reached out to hundreds of others for advice.

Formative Evaluation

The following three phases involve repeated cycles of design, enactment, analysis, and revision (Clements & Battista, 2000), with increasing grain size of the populations and the research variables. The goal is to discover whether the product is usable by, and effective with, various children and teachers.

In formative *phases 6 to 8*, researchers seek to understand the meaning that both children and teachers give to the product in progressively expanding social contexts. For example, researchers assess the ease of use and efficacy of the parts and attributes of the product as implemented first by a teacher who is familiar with the materials, working with small groups of children *(phase 6)* and, later, whole classes *(phase 7)*. Later, similar studies are conducted in cooperation with a more diverse group of teachers *(phase 8)*. Methods include interpretive work using a mix of model testing and model generation strategies, including design experiments, microgenetic, microethnographic, and phenomenological approaches *(phase 6)*, classroom-based teaching experiments and ethnographic participant observation *(phase 7)*, and these plus content analyses when appropriate *(phase 8)*. The product is refined based on these studies, especially including issues of support for teachers.

Phase 6: Formative Research: Small Group

This phase involves intensive pilot testing with individuals or small groups of children, often focusing only on one section of the product at a time. Scientific approaches include design experiments, as well as grounded theory, microgenetic, microethnographic, and phenomenological approaches (Siegler & Crowley, 1991; Spradley, 1979; Steffe, Thompson, &

Glasersfeld, 2000; Strauss & Corbin, 1990). The objects of these studies is to gain understand of the meaning that children give to the product or the instantiation of the product (e.g., see Lincoln, 1992).

The focus is on the congruity between the actions of the children and the learning model or learning trajectory. If there is a mismatch, then some aspect of the learning trajectory is changed. (This is an advantage of the Framework compared to traditional formative and summative evaluations, which often do not connect to theory and do not typically create new theories, cf. Barab & Squire, 2004.) For example, one asks whether the children use the objects provided (e.g., manipulatives, tables or graphs, software tools or features) to perform the actions they are designed to engender, either spontaneously or with prompting from the teacher (if the later, what type of prompting)? Using the cognitive and learning trajectories as guides, and the tasks as catalysts, the researcher-developer creates more refined models of the thinking and especially the learning of children and particular children or groups of children. At the same time, the researcher-developer describes what elements of the teaching and learning environment, such as teaching strategies or "moves," appear to contribute to learning (D. F. Walker, 1992). The ultimate goal is to connect children's learning processes with specific characteristics of the environment and the teacher's actions, and thus begin to describe the competencies that are expected of the teacher to be effective.

As in all phases, but especially here, equity is a concern (Confrey, 2000). Convenience samples are often inadequate. For example, a product cannot be effectively designed for "all children" or specifically at-risk children if the field testing is done in affluent schools. It is not uncommon to see evaluations in which sites are selected through advertisements, often resulting in samples mostly of white, middle-income, suburban populations.

This may be the most intensive phase of cycling the research and design processes, sometimes as quickly as every twenty-four hours (Burkhardt, Fraser, & Ridgway, 1990; Clements & Sarama, 1995). Refined or newly created activities or approaches might be developed one night and tried the next day. Several classrooms may also be used so that revised lessons can be tested in a different classroom, with one staggered to be from one to five days behind the other in implementing the product (Flagg, 1990). Not only are these activities challenging, but it is easy to fail to perform the necessary documentation that will permit researchers to connect findings to specific revisions of the product. Field notes, audiotapes, and videotapes can help. Computer programs are available that allow researchers to transcribe, code, and analyze such recordings. Technology can also assist in documenting children's ongoing activity, as in solution-path recording (Gerber, Semmel, & Semmel, 1994; Lesh, 1990). Stored solution paths can be re-executed and examined by the teacher, child, or researcher. Such documentation should be used to evaluate and reflect on those components of the design that were based on intuition, aesthetics, and subconscious beliefs.

Although this phase includes a model-testing approach, there remains significant adaptation to children's actions and their own creative responses to the product. For example, their free exploration of environments and materials may be encouraged and observed before the introduction of any structured activities. As previously stated, one of the beneficial, albeit challenging, features of the proposed research-and-development is that it studies what *could be*, in contrast to traditional research, which usually to investigates *what is*. The Framework provides an alternative to research that allows, or even encourages, unfortunate confirmation bias and, instead, attempts to invent ways to produce previously unattained results (Greenwald, Pratkanis, Leippe, & Baumgardner, 1986; Sarama & Clements, 2009, see pp. 363–364 for a description of the problems with confirmation bias in early childhood research).

In summary, research in this phrase has much to offer. Using the learning trajectories as a guide, and the tasks as a catalyst, the researcher-developer creates more refined models of particular children and groups of children. Researchers also learn about the value of various characteristics of the teaching and learning environments, many of which will emerge from interaction of the teacher-developer and the child.

As an example from our *Building Blocks* project, the "snapshots" activities from our first instructional sequence did *not* include a second look—another "peek." We found that young children often needed that repeated exposure to attend, build the image, and generate the quantity. Without such mental activity, some did not progress through the learning trajectory. Therefore, we built it into whole and small group activities, as well as the software (see the blue "Peek" button in the software screens).

As another example, we originally planned an entire separate, related learning trajectory dealing with numerosity estimation. That is, following the subitizing activities in which children named exact quantities, we asked children to estimate the amount in larger sets. We tried a variety of sequences and activities but eventually abandoned this learning trajectory, because children's estimation abilities did not improve. We hypothesized that until exact quantities are well-established, benchmarks for numerosity estimation are too weak to justify the time spent on this learning trajectory in the earliest years. As disappointing as the results seemed at the time (we spent so long developing this learning trajectory!), research at this phase potentially saved many teachers and children from wasting their time on unproductive instructional activities.

One final type of work at this phase is significant. Given the importance yet paucity of child-designed projects, provision for such self-motivated, self-maintained work should not be ignored. Open-ended activities using

Methods for Developing Scientific Education ▪ **735**

the objects and actions should therefore be a part of the design so that the environment can be a setting in which children think creatively. Design activity on the part of children is one for that to happen. In geometry, such activity can be generated, with children producing interesting, relevant, and aesthetically attractive designs (e.g., see Clements & Sarama, 2009). In comparison, design activity with small sets of objects seems difficult or impossible. In our present work, however, we used Donald Crews' book, *10 Black Dots*, as a starting point, and encouraged children to make their own design with small numbers of black dots. This has been successful.

Phase 7: Formative Research: Single Classroom

Teachers are involved in all phases, but this phase includes a special emphasis on the process of *enactment* (Ball & Cohen, 1996; Dow, 1991; Snyder, Bolin, & Zumwalt, 1992). For example, a goal of the product may be to help teachers interpret children's thinking about the goals or content they are designed to teach; support teachers' learning of the goals and content; and provide support for representing that content (Ball & Cohen, 1996), often in the 100 languages of children (Edwards, Gandini, & Forman, 1993). So, this phase contains two research foci. Classroom-based teaching experiments are used to document and evaluate child development, to understand how children think in learn in a classroom implementing the product (Clements, Battista, Sarama, & Swaminathan, 1996; for examples, see Clements, Battista, Sarama, Swaminathan, & McMillen, 1997; Gravemeijer, 1994a; Pinar, Reynolds, Slattery, & Taubman, 1995). Field notes and often videotapes are used so that children's performances can be examined, often repeatedly, for evidence of their interpretations and learning.

The second focus is on the entire class, as the researchers seeks information about the usability and efficacy of the product. Ethnographic participant observation may used to examine the teacher and children as they interact to build the classroom cultures and learning environments(Spradley, 1980). Observations are on how teachers and children use the materials, how the teacher guides children, what attributes of these interactive environments emerge, and, of course, how these processes are connected to both intended and unintended child outcomes.

During this phase the class may be taught either by a team including one of the researcher developers and the teacher, or by a teacher familiar with and intensively involved in product's development. The goal is to observe learning in the context produced by teachers who can implement the product with high fidelity, consistent with the developers' vision (in contrast to observing how the product is implementing in classrooms in general, which is one focus of the following phase. "High fidelity" does not necessary following a script. Many pedagogical approaches are not implemented with fidelity to the creator's vision without creative and adaptive enactment. In other words, the philosophy of the product and of the researchers influence the interpretation of fidelity on a continuum from compliance to the creative implementation and adaptation of an individual of particular educational vision.

Whatever the position along this continuum, this phase seeks "super-realization" (Cronbach et al., 1980)—a painstaking assessment of what the product can accomplish "at its best." This usually implies frequent meetings of teachers and researchers. Video and written records can serve both as research evidence and useful "existence proofs" that are effective complements to other research data for researchers, and especially practitioners and policy makers. The end results of these efforts is a better-developed draft of the product, along with measures of child outcomes and fidelity of implementation (Snyder et al., 1992).

As stated, this pilot test stage involves teachers working closely with the researcher-developers. The class is taught either by a team including one of the researcher-developers and the teacher, or by a teacher familiar with and intensively involved in curricula development. The *Building Blocks* project included several tests of learning trajectories (e.g., the full subitizing learning trajectory) in this phase (e.g., Clements & Sarama, 2004a).

Phase 8: Formative Research: Multiple Classrooms

Building on the previous phase, here several classrooms are observed for information about the efficacy and ease of implementation of the product. The focus turns more to conditions under which the product is more or less effective, and how it might be altered or complemented to better serve any conditions in which it was not as effective. Too often, innovative materials provide less support for teachers relative to their need; that is, because the approach is new, more support is needed. The first of three main research questions for this phase, then, is whether the supporting materials are adequate in supporting multiple contexts, modes of instruction (e.g., whole groups, small groups, centers, incidental and informal interactions), and styles of management and teaching. Addressing this question goes beyond evaluating and increasing a product's effectiveness—by employing strategies of condition seeking, it extends the research program's inoculation against the unfortunate phenomenon that we mentioned previously, confirmation bias (Greenwald et al., 1986). That is, by trying to fail (e.g., finding contexts or populations for which the product is less successful), researchers identify the limiting, necessary, and sufficient conditions and may learn how to be successful (often where few were successful previously). In so doing, they extend theory, effectiveness, and guidance to future design and empirical research work. Collaborative work with others, especially those not previously involved in the development (and thus not ego-involved in the product) can also help.

A second question is whether the product supports teachers if they desire to learn more about their children's thinking and then teach them differently. A third question asks which contextual factors support productive adaptations and which allow lethal mutations (Brown & Campione, 1996) and why, as well as how, the product might be changed to facilitate the former, which are especially valuable for formative assessment, and eliminate the latter. As learning trajectories in curricula or programs are actually *hypothetical* learning trajectories (M. A. Simon, 1995) that must be realized or coconstructed in each classroom, so too is a product a hypothetical path to teaching and learning that is sensitive to local contexts (Herbst, 2003). Modification are not expected to make products "fool-proof" but rather support is provided for as wide a variety of contexts as possible.

Ethnographic research (Spradley, 1979, 1980) is again important in this phase, because teachers may agree with the product's goals and approach but their implementation of these may not be consistent with the researcher developers' vision (Sarama, Clements, & Henry, 1998). This phase should determine the meaning that the various materials have for both teachers and children. Professional development approaches and materials may be created, or revised, based on this research evidence, and assessment instrumentals for the future summative evaluations may be revised and validated. In addition, qualitative methods may uncover previously ignored factors (variables) that provide a better *explanation* for a product's effects and indicate what design features may provide a more efficacious product. Finally, another set of content analyses may inform revisions to the product before summative evaluations begin, ideally conducted by multiple experts from different perspectives using approved procedures (National Research Council, 2004). Our work at these levels is too extensive to summarize here (but see Clements & Sarama, 2004a, 2006; Sarama, 2004).

Summative Evaluation

In these final two phases, researchers determine the effectiveness of the product, now in its complete form, as it is implemented in realistic contexts. Summative phases 9 and 10 *both* use cluster randomized field trials. They differ in scale. That is, phase 10 involves a few classrooms, whereas phase 10 examines the fidelity or enactment, and sustainability, of the product when implemented on a large scale, and the critical contextual and implementation variables that influence its effectiveness.

In both phases, experimental or carefully planned quasi-experimental designs, incorporating observational measures and surveys, are useful for generating political and public support, as well as for their research advantages. The main such advantage is the experiments provide the most efficient and least biased designs to assess causal relationships (Cook, 2002). In addition, qualitative approaches continue to be useful for dealing with the complexity and indeterminateness of educational activity (Lester & Wiliam, 2002). This mixed methods approach, synthesizing the two approaches, is a powerful pairing.

The cluster randomized design requires that the product is well described and able to be implemented with fidelity. Also, the curricula or practices used in the comparison classrooms should be fully and explicitly described, and ideally selected on a principled basis. To do so, the quantity and quality of the environment and teaching must be measured in all participating classrooms. Experiments should be designed to have greater explanatory power by connecting specific processes and contexts to outcomes so that moderating and mediating variables are identified (Cook, 2002). Finally, if quasi-experiment designs only are possible, careful consideration of bias must be conducted to ensure comparability (e.g., of children, teachers, and classroom contexts, National Research Council, 2004).

Phase 9: Summative Research: Small Scale

In this phase, researchers evaluate what can actually be achieved with typical teachers under realistic circumstances (Burkhardt et al., 1990; Rogers, 2003). In a few classrooms, from about 4 to about 10, researchers conduct pre- and posttest cluster randomized experimental designs using measures of learning. As stated, experiments are conducted in to complement methodologies previously described. Qualitative work is stronger if conducted within the context of a randomized experiment. For example, if teachers volunteer to implement the product in a quasi-experimental design, neither quantitative nor qualitative techniques alone will easily discriminate between the effects of the implementation of the product and the teachers' dispositions and knowledge that led to their decisions to volunteer.

Surveys and interviews of teacher participants also may be used to compare data collected before and after they have used the product, as well as to collect such data as teacher's background, professional development, and resources. The combined interpretive and survey information also evaluates whether supports are viewed as adequate by teachers and whether their teaching practices have been influenced. Do before-and-after comparisons indicate that they have learned about children's thinking in specific subject matter domains and adopted new teaching practices? Have they changed previous approaches to teaching and assessment of the subject matter?

Such research is similar to, but differs from, traditional summative evaluations. A theoretical frame is essential; comparison of scores outside theory, permitted in traditional evaluation, is inadequate. A related point is that the comparison curriculum or practices must be selected deliberately, to focus on specific research issues. Further, connecting the product's objects and activities and the processes of enactment, including all components of the implementation, to the outcomes is important for theoretical, development, and practical reasons. Variables from the broader data collected should be linked to child outcomes. Links also should be made across experimental and comparison classrooms. Without such, there is an inadequate basis for contributing to theories of learning and teaching in complex settings, guiding future research as well as implementations of the product in various contexts. Finally, statistical analyses performed on the appropriate unit of analysis, often the classroom or school, should allow making those connections (National Research Council, 2004) and provide estimates of the efficacy of the product expressed as effect sizes.

The first summative (phase 9) evaluation of *Building Blocks* resulted in significant differences, with effect sizes of 1.71 for number and 2.12 for geometry (Cohen's d, Clements & Sarama, 2007b). Effect sizes of the first of two large-scale evaluations (*phase 10*) ranged from .46 (compared to another research-based curriculum) to 1.11 (compared to a "home grown" control curriculum). Achievement gains of the experimental group were thus comparable to the sought-after 2-sigma effect of individual tutoring (Bloom, 1984).

Phase 10: Summative Research: Large Scale

Commonly known is the "deep, systemic incapacity of U.S. schools, and the practitioners who work in them, to develop, incorporate, and extend new ideas about teaching and learning in anything but a small fraction of schools and classrooms" (see also Berends, Kirby, Naftel, & McKelvey, 2001; Cuban, 2001; Elmore, 1996, p. 1). Thus, with any product, but especially one that differs from tradition, evaluations must be conducted on a large scale (after considering issues of ethics and practical consequences, see Lester & Wiliam, 2002; Schwandt, 2002). Such research should use a broad set of instruments to assess the impact of the implementation on participating children, teachers, program administrators, and parents, as well as document the fidelity of the implementation and effects of the product across diverse contexts (from Clements, 2007). That is, unlike the treatment standardization necessary to answer the questions of previous phases, here it is assumed that implementation fidelity will vary (often widely, with research indicating that people who take advantage of all program components are more likely to benefit, Ramey & Ramey, 1998), with the questions centering around the product's likely effects in settings where standard implementation cannot be guaranteed (Cook, 2002).

A related goal is to measure and analyze the critical variables, including contextual variables (e.g., settings, such as urban/suburban/rural; type of program; class size; teacher characteristics; child/family characteristics) and implementation variables (e.g., engagement in professional development opportunities; fidelity of implementation; leadership, such as principal leadership, as well as support and availability of resources, funds, and time; peer relations at the school; "convergent perspectives" of the researcher developers, school administrators, and teachers in a cohort; and incentives used) (Berends et al., 2001; Cohen, 1996; Elmore, 1996; Fullan, 1992; Mohrman & Lawler III, 1996; Sarama et al., 1998; Weiss, 2002). A randomized experiment provides an assessment of the average impact of exposure to a product. A series of analyses (e.g., hierarchical linear modeling, or HLM, that provide correct estimates of effects and standard errors when the data are collected at several levels; that is, repeated observations nested within individual children, children nested within classrooms) relate outcome measures with a set of target contextual and implementation variables, critical for identifying moderating and mediating variables (appropriate units of analysis—such as the class—should be defined and should be identical to the unit used for random assignment). Ideally, because no set of experimental variables is complete or appropriate for each situation, qualitative inquiries supplement these analyses. From the wide breadth of documents, including field notes, theoretical notes (methodological and personal journals), drafts of research literature syntheses, and the like, researchers conduct iterative analyses, to determine the significant meanings, relationships, and critical variables that affect implementation and effectiveness (Lincoln & Guba, 1985) and thus meaningfully connect implementation processes to learning outcomes.

Finally, summative evaluations are not complete until two criteria are met. First, the product must be sustained and evaluated in multiple sites for more than two years, with full documentation of the contextual and implementation variables, including practical requirements, procedures, and costs (Berends et al., 2001; Bodilly, 1998; Borman, Hewes, Overman, & Brown, 2003; Fishman et al., 2004; Fullan, 1992). Second, evaluations must be confirmed by researchers unrelated to the developers of the product (Darling-Hammond & Snyder, 1992), with attention given to issues of adoption and diffusion of the product (Fishman et al., 2004; Rogers, 2003; Zaritsky, Kelly, Flowers, Rogers, & O'Neil, 2003). The large expense and effort involved in meeting these criteria is another reason that previous evaluation phases should be employed first; only effective program should be scaled up.

Given this variety of possibilities, claims that a product is based on research should be questioned to reveal the nature and extent of the connection between the two, including the specific phases used of the ten described and the results obtained with each.

We built a new model to scale up. The TRIAD (Technology-enhanced, Research-based, Instruction, Assessment, and professional Development) model has the goal of increasing math achievement in young children, especially those at risk, by means of a high-quality implementation of the *Building Blocks*, with all aspects of the curriculum—mathematical content, pedagogy, teacher's guide, technology, and assessments—based on a common core of learning trajectories. For example, we performed a "gold standard" Randomized Cluster Trial (RCT) in three states. Forty-two schools serving low-resource communities were randomly selected and randomly assigned to three treatment groups using a randomized block design involving 1,375 preschoolers in 106 classrooms. Teachers implemented the intervention with adequate fidelity. Pre- to posttest scores revealed that the children in the TRIAD/*Building Blocks* group learned more mathematics than the children in the control group (effect size, g = 0.72, Clements & Sarama, 2007b). They also developed better language competencies (e.g., effect sizes ranging from .16 to .36, Sarama, Lange, Clements, & Wolfe, 2012).

CONCLUSIONS AND IMPLICATIONS

In this final section, we describe ramifications of our Framework. First, theoretical purity is less important than a consideration of all relevant theories and empirical work. The complexity of the field often creates a Babel of disciplines (Latour, 1987) in which the lack of communication prevents progress. This is one conceit researcher developers can ill afford. Instead, they must meld academic issues and practical teaching demands no less than a serious consideration of what researchers and teachers from other philosophical positions experience and report. This does not imply inconsistent positions. It does imply that overzealous applications (often misinterpretations and overgeneralizations) can limit practical effectiveness. As merely one illustration, constructivism does not imply that practice is not necessary and does not dictate specific pedagogical practices (Clements, 1997; M. A. Simon, 1995).

Second, particular research designs and methods are suited for specific kinds of investigations and questions, but can rarely illuminate all the questions and issues in a line of inquiry (cf. National Research Council, 2002, p. 4; 2004). This is why different methods are used in various phases of the Framework (Clements, 2007). For example, although iterating through one or two of the phases *might* lead to an effective product and high-quality research, this would not meet all the goals of an integrated research and development program. As a simple example, the curriculum might be effective in some settings, but not others, or it might be too difficult to scale up. Moreover, we would not know *why* the curriculum is effective.

Third, the Framework is resource intensive. Some might argue that using multiple stages and phases are logistically or practically infeasible. Just producing satisfactory evaluation data (National Research Council, 2004) is costly. Consider, with the hundreds of millions of dollars undoubtedly spent on developing and testing products without it impracticable to use the proposed framework? We argue, paradoxically, that it is impractical to spend such sums without using it.

Fourth, the education community should support and heed the results of research frameworks such as the one proposed. Given the grounding in both comprehensive research and classroom experience, the curricular products and empirical findings of such integrated research and development programs should be implemented in classrooms. Researcher developers should follow models and base their development on the findings and lessons learned from these projects. Administrators and policy makers should accept and promote curricula based upon similar research-based models. Educators at all levels should eschew software that is not developed consonant with research on children's learning and that does not have the support of empirical evaluation. This would eliminate much of what is presently used in classrooms. This is a strong position, but one that may avoid a backlash against the use of computers in education, and the use of innovative curricula in general, and that will, we believe, ultimately benefit children.

Fortunately, the design models discussed here, with their tight cycles of planning, instruction, and analysis, are consistent with the practices of teachers who develop broad conceptual and procedural knowledge in their children (Cobb, 2001; Lampert, 1988; M. A. Simon, 1995; Stigler & Hiebert, 1999). Therefore, the product and findings are not only applicable to other classrooms but also support exactly those practices.

Fifth, and in a similar vein, universities should legitimize research programs such as these. There is a long history of bias against design sciences.

> As professional schools, including the independent engineering schools, are more and more absorbed into the general culture of the university, they hanker after academic respectability. In terms of the prevailing norms, academic respectability calls for subject matter that is intellectually tough, analytic, formalizable, and teachable. In the past, much, if not most, of what we knew about design and about the artificial sciences was intellectually soft, intuitive, informal, and cookbooky. Why would anyone in a university stoop to teach or learn about designing machines or planning market strategies when he could concern himself with solid-state physics? The answer has been clear: he usually wouldn't. (H. A. Simon, 1969, pp. 56–57)

In particular, the more that schools of education in prestigious research universities "have rowed toward the shores of scholarly research the more distant they have become form the public schools they are bound to serve" (Clifford & Guthrie, 1988, p. 3). This is a dangerous prejudice, and one that we should resist. Education might be seen largely as a design science, with a unique status and autonomy (Wittmann, 1995). "Attempts to organize...education by using related disciplines as models miss the point because they overlook the overriding importance of creative design for conceptual and practical innovations" (Wittmann, 1995, p. 363). The converse of this argument is that universities benefit because the approaches described here will prove practically useful, they will legitimize academic research per se.

In summary, traditional research is conservative; it studies "what is" rather than "what could be." When research is an integral component of the design process, when it helps uncover and invent models of children's thinking and builds these into a creative product, then research moves to the vanguard in innovation and reform of education.

NOTES

1. This paper was supported in part by the Institute of Educational Sciences (U.S. Department of Education) under Grants No. R305K05157 and R305A110188 and by the National Science Foundation, under grant No. DRL-1020118 and by the James C. Kennedy Institute for Educational Success and the Marsico Institute for Early Learning and Literacy at the Morgridge College of Education. Any opinions, findings, and conclusions or recommendations expressed in this material are those of the authors and do not necessarily reflect the views of the funding agencies.
2. Rather, subitizing is amenable to a simple presentation. A complete account, including the multiple theories and studies on the innate processes that underlie it, the role of learning and development (including language) and so forth, would be chapter or even book length (Sarama & Clements, 2009). Not discussed here, but represented somewhat is Figure 3, are such features as arrangement of objects and even the type of object (visual, auditory, etc.) that can be subitized. Thus, none of this is actually "simple," merely simplified for our purposes here.'

REFERENCES

Anthony, J. L., Lonigan, C. J., Driscoll, K., Phillips, B. M., & Burgess, S. R. (2003). Phonological sensitivity: A quasi-parallel progression of word structure units and cognitive operations. *Reading Research Quarterly, 38*(4), 470–487.

Ball, D. L., & Cohen, D. K. (1996). Reform by the book: What is—or might be—the role of curriculum materials in teacher learning and instructional reform? *Educational Researcher, 25*(9), 6–8; 14.

Barab, S., & Squire, K. (2004). Design-based research: Putting a stake in the ground. *The Journal of the Learning Sciences, 13*, 1–14.

Baroody, A. J. (1987). *Children's mathematical thinking.* New York, NY: Teachers College.

Berends, M., Kirby, S. N., Naftel, S., & McKelvey, C. (2001). *Implementation and performance in New American Schools: Three years into scale-up.* Santa Monica, CA: Rand Education.

Bloom, B. S. (1984). The 2-sigma problem: The search for methods of group instruction as effective as one-to-one tutoring. *Educational Researcher, 13*, 4–16.

Bodilly, S. J. (1998). *Lessons from New American Schools' scale-up phase.* Santa Monica, CA: RAND Education.

Borman, G. D., Hewes, G. M., Overman, L. T., & Brown, S. (2003). Comprehensive school reform and achievement: A meta-analysis. *Review of Educational Research, 73*, 125–230.

Bredekamp, S. (Ed.). (2014). *Effective practices in early childhood education: Building a foundation* (2nd ed., revised ed.). Upper Saddle River, NJ: Pearson Education.

Brenneman, K., & Gelman, R. (2009, April). *Supporting and assessing scientific reasoning in young children.* Paper presented at the Biennial meeting of the Society for Research in Child Development, Denver, CO.

Brice, A. E., & Brice, R. (2009). *Language development: Monolingual and bilingual acquisition.* Boston, MA: Allyn & Bacon.

Brown, A. L. (1992). Design experiments: Theoretical and methodological challenges in evaluating complex interventions in classroom settings. *The Journal of the Learning Sciences, 2*(2), 141–178.

Brown, A. L., & Campione, J. C. (1996). Psychological theory and the design of innovative learning environments: On procedures, principles, and systems. In R. Glaser (Ed.), *Innovations in learning: New environments for education* (pp. 289–325). Mahwah, NJ: Erlbaum.

Bruner, J. (1986). *Actual minds, possible worlds.* Cambridge, MA: Harvard University Press.

Burkhardt, H., Fraser, R., & Ridgway, J. (1990). The dynamics of curriculum change. In I. Wirszup & R. Streit (Eds.), *Developments in school mathematics around the world* (Vol. 2, pp. 3–30). Reston, VA: National Council of Teachers of Mathematics.

Carpenter, T. P., & Moser, J. M. (1984). The acquisition of addition and subtraction concepts in grades one through three. *Journal for Research in Mathematics Education, 15*, 179–202.

Case, R. (1982). General developmental influences on the acquisition of elementary concepts and algorithms in arithmetic. In T. P. Carpenter, J. M. Moser, & T. A. Romberg (Eds.), *Addition and subtraction: A cognitive perspective* (pp. 156–170). Hillsdale, NJ: Erlbaum.

CCSSO/NGA (2010). *Common core state standards for mathematics.* Washington, DC: Council of Chief State School Officers and the National Governors Association Center for Best Practices.

Childers, R. D. (Cartographer). (1989). *Implementation of the Writing to Read instructional system in 13 rural elementary schools in southern West Virginia. 1988–89 annual report.*

Clements, D. H. (1997). (Mis?)Constructing constructivism. *Teaching Children Mathematics, 4*(4), 198–200.

Clements, D. H. (1999). Subitizing: What is it? Why teach it? *Teaching Children Mathematics, 5*, 400–405.

Clements, D. H. (2001). Mathematics in the preschool. *Teaching Children Mathematics, 7*, 270–275.

Clements, D. H. (2002). Linking research and curriculum development. In L. D. English (Ed.), *Handbook of international research in mathematics education* (pp. 599–636). Mahwah, NJ: Erlbaum.

Clements, D. H. (2007). Curriculum research: Toward a framework for 'research-based curricula'. *Journal for Research in Mathematics Education, 38*, 35–70.

Clements, D. H. (2008a). Design experiments and curriculum research. In A. E. Kelly, R. A. Lesh & J. Y. Baek (Eds.), *Handbook of innovative design research in science, technology, engineering and mathematics (STEM) education* (pp. 761–776). Mahwah, NJ: Erlbaum.

Clements, D. H. (2008b). Linking research and curriculum development. In L. D. English (Ed.), *Handbook of international research in mathematics education* (2nd ed., pp. 589–625). New York, NY: Taylor & Francis.

Clements, D. H., & Battista, M. T. (2000). Designing effective software. In A. E. Kelly & R. A. Lesh (Eds.), *Handbook of research design in mathematics and science education* (pp. 761–776). Mahwah, NJ: Erlbaum.

Clements, D. H., Battista, M. T., Sarama, J., & Swaminathan, S. (1996). Development of turn and turn measurement concepts in a computer-based instructional unit. *Educational Studies in Mathematics, 30*, 313–337.

Clements, D. H., Battista, M. T., Sarama, J., Swaminathan, S., & McMillen, S. (1997). Students' development of length measurement concepts in a Logo-based unit on geometric paths. *Journal for Research in Mathematics Education, 28*(1), 70–95.

Clements, D. H., & Conference Working Group (2004). Part one: Major themes and recommendations. In D. H. Clements, J. Sarama & A.-M. DiBiase (Eds.), *Engaging young children in mathematics: Standards for early childhood mathematics education* (pp. 1–72). Mahwah, NJ: Erlbaum.

Clements, D. H., & Sarama, J. (1995). Design of a Logo environment for elementary geometry. *Journal of Mathematical Behavior, 14*, 381–398.

Clements, D. H., & Sarama, J. (1998). *Building Blocks—Foundations for Mathematical Thinking, Pre-Kindergarten to Grade 2: Research-based Materials Development* [National Science Foundation, grant number ESI-9730804; see http://www.gse.buffalo.edu/org/buildingblocks/%5D. Buffalo: State University of New York at Buffalo.

Clements, D. H., & Sarama, J. (2004a). Building Blocks for early childhood mathematics. *Early Childhood Research Quarterly, 19*, 181–189.

Clements, D. H., & Sarama, J. (2004b). Learning trajectories in mathematics education. *Mathematical Thinking and Learning, 6*, 81–89.

Clements, D. H., & Sarama, J. (2006). *Final report of building blocks—Foundations for mathematical thinking, pre-kindergarten to grade 2: research-based materials development* (NSF Grant No. ESI-9730804). Buffalo: State University of New York at Buffalo.

Clements, D. H., & Sarama, J. (2007a). *Building Blocks—SRA Real Math Teacher's Edition, Grade PreK.* Columbus, OH: SRA/McGraw-Hill.

Clements, D. H., & Sarama, J. (2007b). Effects of a preschool mathematics curriculum: Summative research on the *Building Blocks* project. *Journal for Research in Mathematics Education, 38*, 136–163.

Clements, D. H., & Sarama, J. (2009). *Learning and teaching early math: The learning trajectories approach.* New York, NY: Routledge.

Clements, D. H., Sarama, J., & DiBiase, A.-M. (2004). *Engaging young children in mathematics: Standards for early childhood mathematics education*. Mahwah, NJ: Erlbaum.
Clifford, C. J., & Guthrie, J. W. (1988). *Ed school: A brief for professional education*. Chicago, IL: The University of Chicago Press.
Cobb, P. (2001). Supporting the improvement of learning and teaching in social and institutional context. In S. Carver & D. Klahr (Eds.), *Cognition and instruction: Twenty-five years of progress* (pp. 455–478). Mahwah, NJ: Erlbaum.
Cobb, P., Confrey, J., diSessa, A., Lehrer, R., & Schauble, L. (2003). Design experiments in educational research. *Educational Researcher, 32*(1), 9–13.
Cohen, D. K. (1996). Rewarding teachers for student performance. In S. H. Fuhrman & J. A. O'Day (Eds.), *Rewards and reforms: Creating educational incentives that work* (pp. 61–112). San Francisco, CA: Jossey Bass.
Collins, A., Joseph, D., & Bielaczyc, K. (2004). Design research: Theoretical and methodological issues. *Journal of the Learning Sciences, 13*(1), 15–42.
Confrey, J. (2000). Improving research and systemic reform toward equity and quality. In A. E. Kelly & R. A. Lesh (Eds.), *Handbook of research design in mathematics and science education* (pp. 87–106). Mahwah, NJ: Erlbaum.
Cook, T. D. (2002). Randomized experiments in educational policy research: A critical examination of the reasons the educational evaluation community has offered for not doing them. *Educational Evaluation and Policy Analysis, 24*, 175–199.
Cronbach, L. J., Ambron, S. R., Dornbusch, S. M., Hess, R. D., Hornik, R. C., Phillips, D. C., et al. (Eds.). (1980). *Toward reform of program evaluation: Aims, methods, and institutional arrangements*. San Francisco, CA: Jossey-Bass.
Cronbach, L. J., & Suppes, P. (Eds.). (1969). *Research for tomorrow's schools: Disciplined inquiry for education*. New York, NY: Macmillan.
Cuban, L. (2001). *Oversold and underused*. Cambridge, MA: Harvard University Press.
Darling-Hammond, L. (1997). *The right to learn: A blueprint for creating schools that work*. San Francisco: Jossey-Bass.
Darling-Hammond, L., & Snyder, J. (1992). Curriculum studies and the traditions of inquiry: The scientific tradition. In P. W. Jackson (Ed.), *Handbook of research on curriculum* (pp. 41–78). New York, NY: Macmillan.
Davidson, M. R., Fields, M. K., & Yang, J. (2009). A randomized trial study of a preschool literacy curriculum: The importance of implementation. *Journal of Research on Educational Effectiveness, 2*, 177–208.
Dewey, J. (1902/1976). The child and the curriculum. In J. A. Boydston (Ed.), *John Dewey: The middle works, 1899–1924. Volume 2: 1902–1903* (pp. 273–291). Carbondale, IL: Southern Illinois University Press.
Dewey, J. (1929). *The sources of a science of education*. New York, NY: Liveright Publishing Corp.
Dow, P. B. (1991). *School house politics*. Cambridge, MA: Harvard University Press.
Duckworth, E. (1973). The having of wonderful ideas. In M. Schwebel & J. Raph (Eds.), *Piaget in the classroom* (pp. 258–277). New York, NY: Basic Books.
Duckworth, E. (1979). Either we're too early and they can't learn it or we're too late and they know it already: The dilemma of "applying Piaget." *Harvard Educational Review, 49*, 297–312.

Early, D., Barbarin, O., Burchinal, M. R., Chang, F., Clifford, R., Crawford, G., et al. (2005). *Pre-Kindergarten in Eleven States: NCEDL's Multi-State Study of Pre-Kindergarten & Study of State-Wide Early Education Programs (SWEEP)* Chapel Hill, NC: University of North Carolina.

Edwards, C., Gandini, L., & Forman, G. E. (1993). *The hundred languages of children: The Reggio Emilia approach to early childhood education.* Norwood, N.J.: Ablex Publishing Corp.

Eisner, E. W. (1998). The primacy of experience and the politics of method. *Educational Researcher, 17*(5), 15–20.

Elmore, R. F. (1996). Getting to scale with good educational practices. *Harvard Educational Review, 66*, 1–25.

Escobedo, T. H., & Evans, S. (1997). A comparison of child-tested early childhood education software with professional ratings. Paper presented at the March 1997 meeting of the American Educational Research Association in Chicago, Illinois.

Ferguson, R. F. (1991). Paying for public education: New evidence on how and why money matters. *Harvard Journal on Legislation, 28*(2), 465–498.

Fishman, B., Marx, R. W., Blumenfeld, P. C., Krajcik, J. S., & Soloway, E. (2004). Creating a framework for research on systemic technology innovations. *The Journal of the Learning Sciences, 13*, 43–76.

Flagg, B. (1990). *Formative evaluation for educational technology.* Hillsdale, NJ: Lawrence Erlbuam Associates.

Forman, G. E. (1993). The constructivist perspective to early education. In J. L. Roopnarine & J. E. Johnson (Eds.), *Approaches to early childhood education (2nd ed.)* (2nd ed., pp. 137–155). New York, NY: Merrill.

Forman, G. E., & Fosnot, C. T. (1982). The use of Piaget's constructivism in early childhood education programs. In B. Spodek (Ed.), *Handbook of research in early childhood education* (pp. 185–211). New York, NY: The Free Press.

Fullan, M. G. (1992). *Successful school improvement.* Philadelphia, PA: Open University Press.

Fuson, K. C. (1992). Research on whole number addition and subtraction. In D. A. Grouws (Ed.), *Handbook of research on mathematics teaching and learning* (pp. 243–275). New York, NY: Macmillan.

Galvin, J. L. (2009). *Writing literature reviews: A guide for students of the social and behavioral science* Glendale, CA: Pyrczak Publishing.

Gerber, M. M., Semmel, D. S., & Semmel, M. I. (1994). Computer-based dynamic assessment of multidigit multiplication. *Exceptional Children, 61*, 114–125.

Ginsburg, H. P., Klein, A., & Starkey, P. (1998). The development of children's mathematical thinking: Connecting research with practice. In W. Damon, I. E. Sigel, & K. A. Renninger (Eds.), *Handbook of child psychology. Volume 4: Child psychology in practice* (pp. 401–476). New York, NY: John Wiley & Sons.

Glasersfeld, E. v. (1995). Radical constructivism: A way of knowing and learning.

Goodlad, J. I. (1984). *A place called school: Prospects for the future.* New York, NY: McGraw-Hill.

Grant, S. G., Peterson, P. L., & Shojgreen-Downer, A. (1996). Learning to teach mathematics in the context of system reform. *American Educational Research Journal, 33*(2), 509–541.

Gravemeijer, K. P. E. (1994a). *Developing realistic mathematics instruction.* Utrecht, The Netherlands: Freudenthal Institute.

Gravemeijer, K. P. E. (1994b). Educational development and developmental research in mathematics education. *Journal for Research in Mathematics Education, 25,* 443–471.

Greenwald, A. G., Pratkanis, A. R., Leippe, M. R., & Baumgardner, M. H. (1986). Under what conditions does theory obstruct research progress? *Psychological Review, 93,* 216–229.

Griffin, S., & Case, R. (1997). Re-thinking the primary school math curriculum: An approach based on cognitive science. *Issues in Education, 3,* 1–49.

Herbst, P. G. (2003). Using novel tasks in teaching mathematics: Three tensions affecting the work of the teacher. *American Educational Research Journal, 40,* 197–238.

Hiebert, J. C. (1999). Relationships between research and the NCTM Standards. *Journal for Research in Mathematics Education, 30,* 3–19.

Hmelo-Silver, C. E., & Duncan, R. G. (2009). Learning progressions (special issue). *Journal of Research in Science Teaching, 46*(6), 605–737.

Jaeger, R. M. (1988). Survey research methods in education. In R. M. Jaeger (Ed.), *Complementary methods for research in education* (pp. 303–340). Washington, DC: American Educational Research Association.

James, W. (1892/1958). *Talks to teachers on psychology: And to students on some of life's ideas.* New York, NY: Norton.

Justice, L. M., Pence, K., Bowles, R. B., & Wiggins, A. (2006). An investigation of four hypotheses concerning the order by which 4-year-old children learn the alphabet letters. *Early Childhood Research Quarterly, 21,* 374–389.

Kamii, C. (1973). Pedagogical principles derived from Piaget's theory: Relevance for educational practice. In M. Schwebel & J. Raph (Eds.), *Piaget in the classroom* (pp. 199–215). New York, NY: Basic Books.

Lahm, E. A. (1996). Software that engaged young children with disabilities: A study of design features. *Focus on Autism and Other Developmental Disabilities, 11*(2), 115–124.

Lampert, M. (1988). *Teaching that connects students' inquiry with curricular agendas in schools. Technical Report.* Cambridge, MA: Educational Technology Center, Harvard Graduate School of Education.

Latour, B. (1987). *Science in action.* Cambridge, MA: Harvard University Press.

Lavin, R. J., & Sanders, J. E. (1983). *Longitudinal evaluation of the C/A/I Computer Assisted Instruction Title 1 Project: 1979–82:* Chelmsford, MA: Merrimack Education Center.

Lawton, J. T. (1993). The Ausubelian preschool classroom. In J. L. Roopnarine & J. E. Johnson (Eds.), *Approaches to early childhood education* (2nd ed., pp. 157–177). New York, NY: Merrill.

Lesh, R. A. (1990). Computer-based assessment of higher order understandings and processes in elementary mathematics. In G. Kulm (Ed.), *Assessing higher order thinking in mathematics* (pp. 81–110). Washington, DC: American Association for the Advancement of Science.

Lester, F. K., Jr., & Wiliam, D. (2002). On the purpose of mathematics education research: Making productive contributions to policy and practice. In L. D.

English (Ed.), *Handbook of International Research in Mathematics Education* (pp. 489–506). Mahwah, NJ: Erlbaum.

Levy, B. A., Gong, Z., Hessels, S., Evans, M. A., & Jared, D. (2006). Understanding print: Early reading development and the contributions of home literacy experiences. *Journal of Experimental Child Psychology, 93*(1), 63–93.

Light, R. J., & Pillemer, D. B. (1984). *Summing up: The science of reviewing research.* Cambridge, MA: Harvard University Press.

Lincoln, Y. S. (1992). Curriculum studies and the traditions of inquiry: The humanistic tradition. In P. W. Jackson (Ed.), *Handbook of research on curriculum* (pp. 79–97). New York, NY: Macmillan.

Lincoln, Y. S., & Guba, E. G. (1985). *Naturalistic inquiry.* Newbury Park, CA: Sage.

Mayer, R. E. (2000). What is the place of science in educational research? *Educational Researcher, 29*(6), 38–39.

Mohrman, S. A., & Lawler III, E. E. (1996). Motivation for school reform. In S. H. Fuhrman & J. A. O'Day (Eds.), *Rewards and reform: Creating educational incentives that work* (pp. 115–143). San Francisco: Jossey-Bass.

Murphy, R. T., & Appel, L. R. (1984). *Evaluation of writing to read.* Princeton, NJ: Educational Testing Service.

National Council of Teachers of Mathematics (2000). *Principles and standards for school mathematics.* Reston, VA: Author.

National Research Council (2001). *Eager to learn: Educating our preschoolers.* Washington, DC: National Academy Press.

National Research Council (2002). *Scientific research in education.* Washington, DC: National Research Council, National Academy Press.

National Research Council (2004). *On evaluating curricular effectiveness: Judging the quality of K–12 mathematics evaluations.* Washington, DC: Mathematical Sciences Education Board, Center for Education, Division of Behavioral and Social Sciences and Education, The National Academies Press.

National Research Council (2007). *Taking science to school: Learning and teaching science in grades K–8.* Washington, DC: National Academy Press.

National Research Council (2009). *Mathematics in early childhood: Learning paths toward excellence and equity.* Washington, DC: National Academy Press.

Papert, S. (1987). Computer criticism vs. technocentric thinking. *Educational Researcher, 16*(1), 22–30.

Pinar, W. F., Reynolds, W. M., Slattery, P., & Taubman, P. M. (1995). *Understanding curriculum: An introduction to the study of historical and contemporary curriculum discourses.* New York, NY: Peter Lang.

Ramey, C. T., & Ramey, S. L. (1998). Early intervention and early experience. *American Psychologist, 53*, 109–120.

Raudenbush, S. W. (2009). The Brown legacy and the O'Connor challenge: Transforming schools in the images of children's potential. *Educational Researcher, 38*(3), 169–180.

Rogers, E. M. (2003). *Diffusion of innovations* (5th ed.). New York, NY: The Free Press.

Ruthven, K., Laborde, C., Leach, J., & Tiberghien, A. (2009). Design tools in didactical research: Instrumenting the epistemological and cognitive aspects of the design of teaching sequences. *Educational Researcher, 38*(5), 329–342.

Sarama, J. (2004). Technology in early childhood mathematics: *Building Blocks™* as an innovative technology-based curriculum. In D. H. Clements, J. Sarama, & A.-M. DiBiase (Eds.), *Engaging young children in mathematics: Standards for early childhood mathematics education* (pp. 361–375). Mahwah, NJ: Erlbaum.

Sarama, J., & Clements, D. H. (2008). Linking research and software development. In G. W. Blume & M. K. Heid (Eds.), *Research on technology and the teaching and learning of mathematics: Volume 2, cases and perspectives* (Vol. 2, pp. 113–130). Charlotte, NC: Information Age.

Sarama, J., & Clements, D. H. (2009). *Early childhood mathematics education research: Learning trajectories for young children.* New York, NY: Routledge.

Sarama, J., Clements, D. H., & Henry, J. J. (1998). Network of influences in an implementation of a mathematics curriculum innovation. *International Journal of Computers for Mathematical Learning, 3,* 113–148.

Sarama, J., Clements, D. H., & Vukelic, E. B. (1996). The role of a computer manipulative in fostering specific psychological/mathematical processes. In E. Jakubowski, D. Watkins & H. Biske (Eds.), *Proceedings of the 18th annual meeting of the North America Chapter of the International Group for the Psychology of Mathematics Education* (Vol. 2, pp. 567–572). Columbus, OH: ERIC Clearinghouse for Science, Mathematics, and Environmental Education.

Sarama, J., & DiBiase, A.-M. (2004). The professional development challenge in preschool mathematics. In D. H. Clements, J. Sarama, & A.-M. DiBiase (Eds.), *Engaging young children in mathematics: Standards for early childhood mathematics education* (pp. 415–446). Mahwah, NJ: Erlbaum.

Sarama, J., Lange, A., Clements, D. H., & Wolfe, C. B. (2012). The impacts of an early mathematics curriculum on emerging literacy and language. *Early Childhood Research Quarterly, 27,* 489–502.

Scardamalia, M., & Bereiter, C. (1994). Computer support for knowledge-building communities. *The Journal of the Learning Sciences, 3,* 265–283.

Schoen, H. L., Cebulla, K. J., Finn, K. F., & Fi, C. (2003). Teacher variables that relate to student achievement when using a standards-based curriculum. *Journal for Research in Mathematics Education, 34*(3), 228–259.

Schwandt, T. A. (2002). *Evaluation practice reconsidered.* New York, NY: Peter Lang.

Shade, D. D. (1994). Computers and young children: Software types, social contexts, gender, age, and emotional responses. *Journal of Computing in Childhood Education, 5*(2), 177–209.

Shulman, L. S. (1997). Disciplines of inquiry in education: A new overview. In R. M. Jaeger (Ed.), *Complementary methods for research in education* (Vol. 2, pp. 3–29). Washington, DC: American Educational Research Association.

Siegler, R. S., & Crowley, K. (1991). The microgenetic method: A direct means for studying cognitive development. *American Psychologist, 46,* 606–620.

Simon, H. A. (1969). *The sciences of the artificial.* Cambridge, MA: The M.I.T. Press.

Simon, M. A. (1995). Reconstructing mathematics pedagogy from a constructivist perspective. *Journal for Research in Mathematics Education, 26*(2), 114–145.

Snyder, J., Bolin, F., & Zumwalt, K. (1992). Curriculum implementation. In P. W. Jackson (Ed.), *Handbook of research on curriculum* (pp. 402–435). New York, NY: Macmillan.

Spradley, J. P. (1979). *The ethnographic interview.* New York, NY: Holt, Rhinehart & Winston.
Spradley, J. P. (1980). *Participant observation.* New York, NY: Holt, Rhinehart & Winston.
Steffe, L. P., Thompson, P. W., & Glasersfeld, E. v. (2000). Teaching experiment methodology: Underlying principles and essential elements. In A. E. Kelly & R. A. Lesh (Eds.), *Handbook of research design in mathematics and science education* (pp. 267–306). Mahwah, NJ: Erlbaum.
Stein, M. K., & Kim, G. (2009). The role of mathematics curriculum materials in large-scale urban reform. In J. T. Remillard, G. M. Lloyd & B. A. Herbel-Eisenmann (Eds.), *Mathematics teachers at work: Connecting curriculum materials and classroom instruction* (pp. 37–55). New York, NY: Routledge.
Stigler, J. W., & Hiebert, J. C. (1999). *The teaching gap: Best ideas from the world's teachers for improving education in the classroom.* New York, NY: The Free Press.
Strauss, A., & Corbin, J. (1990). *Basics of qualitative research: Grounded theory procedures and techniques.* Newbury Park, CA: Sage.
The Design-Based Research Collective (2003). Design-based research: An emerging paradigm for educational inquiry. *Educational Researcher, 32*(1), 5–8.
Tushnet, N. C., Millsap, M. A., Abdullah-Welsh, N., Brigham, N., Cooley, E., Elliot, J., et al. (2000). *Final report on the evaluation of the National Science Foundation's Instructional Materials Development program.* Arlington, VA: National Science Foundation.
Tyler, R. W. (1949). *Basic principles of curriculum and instruction.* Chicago: University of Chicago Press.
van Oers, B. (2003). Learning resources in the context of play. Promoting effective learning in early childhood. *European Early Childhood Education Research Journal, 11*, 7–25.
Walker, D. F. (1992). Methodological issues in curriculum research. In P. W. Jackson (Ed.), *Handbook of research on curriculum* (pp. 98–118). New York, NY: Macmillan.
Walker, R. (2011). Design-based research: Reflections on some epistemological issues and practices. In L. Markauskaite, P. Freebody & J. Irwin (Eds.), *Methodological choice and design: Scholarship, policy and practice in social and educational research* (pp. 51–56). New York, NY: Springer.
Weiss, I. R. (2002, April). *Systemic reform in mathematics education: What have we learned?* Las Vegas, NV.
Whitehurst, G. J. (2009). *Don't forget curriculum.* Washington, DC: Brown Center on Education Policy, The Brookings Institution.
Wittmann, E. C. (1995). Mathematics education as a 'design science'. *Educational Studies in Mathematics, 29*, 355–374.
Zaritsky, R., Kelly, A. E., Flowers, W., Rogers, E., & O'Neil, P. (2003). Clinical design sciences: A view from sister design efforts. *Educational Researcher, 32*(1), 32–34.

CHAPTER 22

RE-EXAMINING THE LITERATURE REVIEW

Purposes, Approaches, and Issues

Mary Renck Jalongo and Kelly Heider

The word "review" means, quite literally, to see again. In academic contexts, the process of reviewing goes beyond a mere retrospective to offer a synthesis and critical reappraisal of the scholarly work published thus far on a particular topic (Cooper, 1998; Mertler & Charles, 2005). The general characteristics of a high-quality literature review are "appropriate breadth and depth, rigor and consistency, clarity and brevity, and effective analysis and synthesis" (Hart, 1998, p. 1). For scholars in general, and the early childhood field in particular, the material under review must consist of authoritative sources—the theory, research, and professional wisdom that have been subjected to peer review and published in widely-respected outlets (Barnes, 2005; Ngai & Wat, 2002).

Webster and Watson (2002) defined an effective literature review as one that "creates a firm foundation for advancing knowledge. It facilitates theory development, closes areas where a plethora of research exists, and uncovers areas where research is needed" (p. 13). Expectations for the literature

Handbook of Research Methods in Early Childhood Education, pages 753–781
Copyright © 2015 by Information Age Publishing
All rights of reproduction in any form reserved.

review do not stop there, however. The quality of the writing also enters into the work of reviewing because it is a narrative essay (Merriam, 2009) that takes a point of view (Reuber, 2011) and presents a coherent synthesis of the literature in discursive prose (Notar & Cole, 2010). Two former editors of the American Education Research Association publication, *Review of Educational Research*, used the metaphor of a stone wall to explain the interdependence of research and the work of reviewing:

> The scholarly literature in education... is like a wall that is built one stone at a time, each stone filling a hole previously unfilled, each one mortared and connected to those that came before and after it, each one providing a support for the subsequent ones, and each one being supported by those that came before... The review article attempts to describe the wall itself and to discover its mortar, its architecture, and design; the wall's place in the architecture of the larger structure; its relation to the other elements in the structure; its significance, purpose, and meaning in the larger structure. (Murray & Raths, 1994, p. 197)

A successful review of the literature in early childhood education uses a collection of carefully selected sources to arrive at "big picture" understandings of a topic that will advance thinking and promote more enlightened perspectives on the care and education of the very young.

Just as metacognition is often defined as thinking about one's own thinking, writing a review on reviewing the literature is a challenging intellectual undertaking (Swales, 2009). Our goal for this chapter is not only to produce a helpful resource suited for a research handbook but also to exemplify a high-quality literature review in the process. Generally speaking, the literature about literature reviews is essentially of three types: (1) qualitative approaches that investigate the conceptualization processes undergirding literature reviews; (2) quantitative approaches that use statistical formulas and effect sizes in empirical studies as a foundation for the literature review, and (3) professional wisdom from various gatekeepers involved in assessing literature reviews, such as dissertation advisors and journal editors. In conducting the review for the chapter, we relied on articles published in leading professional journals across the social science disciplines, books and chapters published by scholarly publishers, and research textbooks and textbook chapters that had survived to at least a second edition. For the articles, we focused on the past decade but also conducted a "backward search" that consisted of reading the "references of the references" yielded in the search and searching the previous work of the authors (Levy & Ellis, 2006; Webster & Watson, 2002).

HIGHER-ORDER THINKING AS A THEORETICAL BASE

Successful reviews rely on interaction between the qualities of the database and the capabilities of the reviewer. In terms of the qualities of the database,

- How appropriate it is for the reviewer's topic?
- Does it allow the researcher to conduct an advanced, Boolean[1] search?
- Does it allow the researcher to limit his/her searches to peer-reviewed journals?
- Does it provide a high-quality thesaurus?
- Is there depth to its subject indexing?
- Does it provide access to "high-impact" journals? (The impact factor, created by Eugene Garfied [1987] is the average number of citations per paper published in a journal during the two preceeding years.)
- Does it allow the researcher to conduct a "cited reference search" (i.e., a search for articles that have cited a previously-published work)?

The capabilities of the reviewers, include their

- Information literacy, defined as "a set of abilities requiring individuals to recognize when information is needed and have the ability to locate, evaluate and use effectively the needed information" (Association of College and Research Libraries, 2000, p. 2);
- Ability to understand the methodological qualities of studies;
- Willingness to invest time and mental energy;
- Capacity for processing a huge amount of material;
- Attention to details and accuracy;
- Ability to form a mental landscape of the literature;
- Tolerance for ambiguity when coping with an unstructured problem; and
- Commitment to contribute (Lather, 1999) to the "body of knowledge" (BoK), defined as the cumulative, research-supported knowledge achieved by "building on each other's [research] results" (Iivari, Hirschheim, & Klein, 2004, p. 314).

Limitations in the resources or in the reviewers diminish the potential for positive interaction and affect the quality of the review. To illustrate, in preparation for the candidacy exam, a student indicated that she wanted to study "student teachers' professional growth" and the role of the classroom teachers to whom they were assigned but had difficulty locating resources. It was not until a faculty member suggested that she look into the Professional Development Schools literature that the student found the research strand that would enable her to produce a literature review. Thus, the interpersonal support, the available resources, and the characteristics of the reviewer all interact in ways that influence a literature review.

There is little question that higher order thinking skills are demanded in order to produce a high quality review of the literature (Fisher, 2004). Originally set forth in Benjamin Bloom and his associates' (1956) *Taxonomy of Educational Objectives: Handbook I, The Cognitive Domain*, these skills are:

- Analysis—the ability to perform mental operations such as comparing/contrasting, categorizing, and differentiating. Applied to reviewing, this would involve such things as assembling the data, identifying major works, making lists of authors/citations, or arranging information chronologically.
- Synthesis—the capacity to combine and generate something original. Applied to reviewing, this would involve such things as outlining, mapping, and identifying strands or themes in the data. (See Sciplore, 2010).
- Evaluation—the practice of supporting ideas with evidence, appraising/critiquing the literature, and summarizing the implications. Applied to reviewing, this would involve weighing the evidence, using it to support a complex argument, and applying accepted argument patterns (e.g., analogy, sample to population, cause and effect) to the assembled evidence (Hart, 2008; Fisher, 2003).

For the remainder of this chapter, six themes were used to synthesize the material:

1. The purposes that literature reviews serve for various stakeholders in the early childhood field
2. Broad categories of literature reviews and the theoretical underpinnings of each type
3. Major mistakes in reviewing the literature and ways to avoid them
4. Human and online resources that support the skills of reviewing
5. Writing reviews with an eye toward publication
6. The future of reviewing

PURPOSES OF THE LITERATURE REVIEW

Much of the writing about the literature review is aimed at contextualizing a piece of original research in the context of the work that antedates it—a practice that is commonly referred to as finding a gap in the extant research (e.g., Bettany-Saltikov, 2010; Blaiki, 2007; Creswell, 2003; Notar &

Cole, 2010; Reuber, 2011). What is frequently overlooked in discussions of literature reviews is that they differ, depending upon their purposes, audiences, and authors. For example, a literature review could take the form of Chapter 2 for a dissertation that is written by a novice researcher. Another literature review could be more of a "translation" of the research, written with newcomers to the early childhood field in mind, such as a college-level textbook written by a teacher/scholar. Yet another literature review might be the background section of a research protocol submitted to a university Institutional Review Board that was written by a leading researcher. Each of these literature reviews has a different audience and, therefore, a somewhat different purpose. In the case of a Chapter 2 for a dissertation, the goal is to convince the dissertation committee that the candidate is sufficiently conversant with the literature to earn the degree and conduct independent research. In the case of the introductory textbook, the goal is to be true to the theory and research, yet make it understandable to beginners. Finally, in the case of the research protocol, the purpose is to show the diverse membership of an institutional review board, most of whom probably are outside the researcher's field, that their colleague's plan reflects respect for human subjects while making an original and significant contribution to the field. Figure 22.1 highlights six purposes for reviews identified by Neuman (2009) and applies them to the early childhood field.

Another key aspect of literature reviews is that they have different outcomes for different consumers of the scholarly literature. Most of what is written about literature reviews tends to focus on potential benefits for those seeking to conduct research, whether novice or experienced, and includes such things as:

- Contributing to a well-stocked mind that can yield new insights
- Establishing a solid foundation and theoretical framework for original research
- Identifying fruitful directions for further research
- Saving time, effort, and resources by informing researchers about what has been studied previously and with what level of success
- Enabling researchers to situate their work within in the larger context, thereby making the nature of their original contribution clear
- Providing researchers from different disciplinary backgrounds with a way to study an issue from multiple perspectives (Hart, 1998; Merriam, 2009; Pan, 2004; Ridley, 2008; Trainor & Graue, 2012; Webster & Watson, 2002)

Yet, in a field as diverse as early childhood education, outcomes of literature reviews that extend beyond those afforded to established researchers need to be considered. Two important categories of consumers are college

self-study
increases the reader's confidence in writing about the topic
Example: a textbook author reads extensively on a new topic recommended by a reviewer as part of the revision process

context
supplies "big picture" framing for the review
Example: a doctoral student uses the review to identify a gap in the research

historical
traces the development of an issue over time
Example: a professor studies the history of child protection to prepare for a lecture on contemporary legislation

theoretical
compares how different theories address an issue
Example: an author of a practical article on children's literature reviews reader response theories

methodological
reviews other studies--even those outside the discipline--that use similar methods
Example: A researcher searches for studies that used focus group interviews

integrative
supplies a "state of the art" on a given topic
Example: An author writes a practical article about young children on the Autism Spectrum

Figure 22.1 Multiple purposes for the literature review. Adapted from Neuman, 2009.

students and practitioners working with children and families. For college students, particularly those enrolled in teacher preparation programs or in master's degree programs for experienced teachers, the high-quality literature review can supply authoritative definitions of key terminology and discussion of relevant constructs, challenge their assumptions, quickly orient them to a topic of relevance, and lead them to the resources necessary to complete their assignments. Reading and understanding a well-fashioned literature review also simulates participation in the professional dialogue as students "think along" with the writer of the review and interrogate the text by writing comments or questions in the margins. Such practice enables students to see how they might enter into those important discussions, both during class and beyond. A balanced literature review offers many important benefits to those who are not enrolled in formal study as well. For the early childhood practitioner responsible for the care and education of the very young, a high-quality literature review can surmount the obstacle of attaining sophisticated research skills, save the time of conducting a review, resolve some pedagogical puzzle, promote professional development on a topic or issue of interest, and locate authoritative support when a controversy surfaces in the workplace. When literature reviews are published and widely disseminated, they serve the additional purpose of transcending geographic boundaries, furthering intercultural understanding, and promoting interdisciplinary approaches to research.

TYPES OF REVIEWS

In their analysis of the literature on literature reviews, Notar and Cole (2010) conclude that there are at least four main types of literature reviews: (1) integrative reviews, (2) systematic reviews, (3) meta-analyses, and (4) qualitative reviews. Figure 22.2 includes the four approaches, offers an example from the early childhood field, and highlights the strengths/limitations of each.

As Machi and McEvoy (2008) observe,

> Doing a literature review is a complex project for even the most advanced researcher, especially if learning how to compose a literature review has been by trial and error. To become successful at this craft, researchers need many skills. They need a way to narrow the research topic and to focus on their literature search, and they need the tools necessary to negotiate the myriad books, periodicals, and reports about their topic. (p. ix)

Such challenges can lead to mistakes, both unintentional and intentional.

MAJOR MISTAKES IN REVIEWING

The pitfalls of literature review for novices are legion. Novices may, for example, be unaware of the quality of various sources, rely exclusively on an online search with narrow parameters, fail to use the appropriate search terms, ignore work outside their disciplinary specialty, neglect to exhaust all authoritative sources, and become overwhelmed by the sheer number of resources on a topic (Levy & Ellis, 2006). An admixture of procrastination

Type of Review	Integrative	Systematic	Meta-Analytic	Qualitative/Interpretive
Definition				
Primary Purpose	To demonstrate mastery of a corpus of theory, research, and professional wisdom in the literature by synthesizing and critiquing it	To make an informed decision based on an exhaustive review of empirical studies on a narrowly defined topic	To persuade, using the weight of quantitative evidence as support	To supply one person's interpretation of a diverse body of literature and to promote further reflection and varied perspectives
ECE Example	A review article published in *Young Children* or *Childhood Education* to inform educators about a timely topic	A review used to decide which assistive technology tool is most appropriate to support a child with a specific auditory impairment	A meta-analysis article published in *Review of Educational Research*	An article on a controversial topic published in *Teachers College Record* that is designed to stimulate professional dialogue
Strengths	Distills a wide-ranging topic into its essence and the whole is more than the sum of its parts	Provides an "audit trail" evidence-based guidance	Produces a "state of the art" document with statistically significant findings as the foundation	Identifies themes and strands in the literature that are fruitful for advancing thinking in the field
Limitations	May deteriorate into a rehash of existing work	May overlook relevant work within or outside the field through the narrow scope set at the start	May seem more absolute in its answer to the question than is warranted; deliberately ignores qualitative research findings	May be less persuasive to decision-makers seeking facts and figures
Resources	Barnes, 2005; Edgemon, Wiley, Jablonski & Lloyd, 2006; Levy & Ellis, 2006; Torraco, 2005; Webster & Watson, 2002; Whittemore & Knafl, 2005	Aveyard, 2011; Bettany-Saltikov, 2010; The Cochrane Collaboration, 2012; Garrard, 2011; Jesson, 2011; McKibbon, 2006; Tranfield, Denyer & Smart, 2003; Torgerson, 2003	Frankel & Wallen, 2009; Sciplore, 2010	Eisenhart, 2009; Gay, Mills, & Airasian, 2006

Figure 22.2 Four main types of literature reviews.

and panic sometimes leads to deliberate unethical actions such as plagiarizing from published sources or purchasing a ready-made review paper. Figure 22.3 summarizes the worst mistakes in conducting a literature review and ways to avoid them.

Another major impediment to the successful literature review is simplistic, linear conceptualizations of the process of reviewing. In Bruce's (1994) study of students' approaches to the literature review, their ideas about reviewing varied widely. They were, from lowest level of conceptualization to highest:

- *List*—a collection of references without in-depth knowledge of content
- *Search*—an emphasis on the strategies for locating relevant materials
- *Survey*—a representation of immersion in the knowledge base
- *Vehicle for learning*—the reviewer interacts with material and is influenced by it
- *Research facilitator*—the literature review shapes the reader's thinking and guides original research
- *Report*—a synthesis/final representation of the researcher's interaction with and evaluation of the literature

Therefore, as a first step, reviewers need to view a literature review as a high-level conceptualization task that is recursive, rather than linear. The "literature universe" of the field of early childhood education is comprised of diverse, interdisciplinary work including psychology and educational psychology, literacy and linguistics, neuroscience, child development, medicine, special education, physical education, family studies, and more; this can make it particularly challenging to access the best sources for a particular topic. If, for example, a student wanted to conduct research on military families who have a young child with special needs, some of this information would be found in articles about geographic relocation, statistics on the provision of special education services in different states and countries, discussions on the effects of parental absences on young children, and the policies of various branches of the armed service—to name a few. A practical situation such as this one helps to explain why librarians Boell and Cecez-Kecmanovic (2010) have conceptualized reviewing as a hermeneutic cycle in which the tasks of searching, sorting, selecting, acquiring, reading, identifying, and refining are interconnected and ongoing; the reviewer can re-enter the cycle at any of these points as needs for information on new topics surface, the need to dig deeper or wider on an aspect of a topic emerges, or new insights are acquired.

Plagiarism	Errors of Fact	Inadequate Sources	Listing	Weak Argument
• take notes carefully and devise a system for differentiating between your ideas and those of others • document all sources in complete, correct bibliographic style throughout the process from note-taking to final manuscript • create an annotated bibliography and maintain copies of the original source material • consider submitting your work to Turnitin, a Web-based plagiarism detection service, to get a similarity score with published work • particularly for students studying in a different country, realize that definitions for plagiarism vary from one culture to another	• use primary sources rather than relying on someone else's interpretation • take the time to double check everything • present a balanced view and include conflicting findings • for major studies, include a detailed description of the findings	• select scholarly sources (reputable, refereed publications) rather than popular sources • work with an academic librarian to identify appropriate databases, develop effective search strategies, and evaluate potential sources • discuss your idea with an expert in the field • read widely and well	• avoid boring lists in which each paragraph begins with a name and a date • chunk information and strive for meaningful synthesis • compare, contrast, and critique rather than merely report • cluster minor studies with similar findings together • pay attention to writing style, not just content, when reading; strive to emulate this style	• use authoritative definitions from the professional literature (rather than the dictionary) • supply concise examples to illustrate key points • use an "assert, then support" strategy that backs up ideas with evidence • read more about the common fallacies in logical arguments—and how to avoid them

Figure 22.3 Ways to avoid major mistakes in reviewing. *Sources:* Bloomberg & Volpe, 2008; Blum & Muirhead, 2005; Fink, 2009; Hart, 2001; 2008; Laband & Piette, 2000; Levy & Ellis, 2006; McMillan & Schumacher, 2010; Mertler & Charles, 2005; Muirhead, 2004; Notar & Cole, 2010; Petticrew & Roberts 2006; Randolph, 2009; Steward, 2004; Swales & Lindemann, 2002; Torgerson 2003; Zinsser, 2001.

HUMAN AND ONLINE RESOURCES TO SUPPORT REVIEWING

After reviewers understand the cyclical nature of the literature review, they can begin to direct their attention to searching for resources. Online periodical databases offer access to the largest amount of current, scholarly information in the field of early childhood education. Of course, academic libraries pay to subscribe to these databases and, therefore, a reviewer's access to certain databases depends upon his/her access to an academic library as well as that academic library's budget. Most large academic libraries, however, subscribe to hundreds of online periodical databases, providing reviewers with a wealth of information but making it very difficult to know where to begin. Recommendations for scholars at this stage follow.

Selecting and Narrowing the Topic

Research interests often emanate from professional experience, suggestions from experts, the academic journals, and the media (Machi & McEvoy, 2008). Selecting a focus for the literature review also is dependent upon the writer's role. Students should begin by referring to the course syllabus because faculty may have identified a list of topics or, topics may be suggested by the subjects to be covered in the course, the recommended readings, and the table of contents and references in the required and recommended textbooks. One advantage of using these materials as a starting point is that they supply the reviewer with the professional terminology that would be helpful in conducting a search. For example, if a student is interested in learning more about autism in young children, descriptors such as autism spectrum disorder (ASD), pervasive developmental disorders, and Asperger's syndrome might be useful. Following this procedure also enables the student to generate a list of possibilities that could be discussed with the instructor. If the reviewer has a free choice of topic, then the best advice is to select a subject that holds great interest for the writer, is timely, and has a sufficient body of research on which to base the review.

One of the challenges inherent in selecting a topic, is narrowing it sufficiently to treat the subject adequately within the page limit range that has been specified. To illustrate, "infant/toddler development" would be an encyclopedia or a book; it would need to be much more specific in order to conduct a meaningful review. At this point, the reviewer needs to decide what particular aspect of infant/toddler development is of most interest; however, if a topic such as literacy is the choice even that may be too broad to treat adequately in a short piece of writing. Further narrowing might take the topic to vocabulary growth during the infant/toddler years. Now the topic is sufficiently narrow to search and write an 8–10 page paper for a class assignment.

Doctoral candidates who are conducting a literature review for the traditional Chapter 2 of a dissertation have a different challenge where conducting the literature review is concerned. Their review needs to provide background on many different clusters of information related to the study's purpose and focus. If a doctoral student is conducting an interview study of children, parents, and teachers in Title I Reading Programs, then some of the areas will be on the topic (e.g., children's literacy development, research on reading difficulties, the history of Title I) and some on the method (e.g., qualitative research, interviewing techniques, using *NVivo* for data analysis). Equally important is the theoretical base, which is discussed in the next section.

Finding a Theoretical Base

For doctoral candidates and college/university faculty seeking to publish, there will be an expectation that the writer identify and describe a theoretical base to serve as a conceptual framework for the review of the literature. A first step in understanding how theory "frames" the review is with a metaphor. Picture, in your mind's eye, a mansion on a hilltop with many windows on each side. It is not possible to look out of all of the windows and take in all of the views simultaneously; rather, it is necessary to choose a particular window and allow it to frame the perspective. This does not mean that the author is unaware that there are other viewpoints, only that she or he makes it clear which perspective was selected and why. Theory functions in much the same way; although it limits in some ways, it also provides a focal point that helps to structure the review. To illustrate, if a doctoral candidate were interested in parent/family involvement in early childhood education programs that topic has an extensive body of literature associated with it. Narrowing the topic might lead to a focus on parent/family involvement in kindergarten. Based on practical experiences, the candidate concludes that some of the efforts to "involve" parents and families of young children have failed because they do not respect what families know and do in support of children; rather, they presume that the only way to help young children is to require that parents/families push the child to complete drill and practice types of activities at home, as designated by the teacher. The reviewer in this case finds a theory, social capital theory, with relevance for the study. In a nutshell, social capital theory takes the stance that, in every person's life, there is a range of resources that is intellectual, economic, cultural, and institutional in nature (Li, 2004). These resources are referred to as capital because, like personal wealth or the natural resources of a country, they are not equally distributed and allocated. Use of the resources depends on an individual's circumstances in society, access to resources, and ability to elicit appropriate support. This leads to the concept of "funds of knowledge" as described in the work of Moll, Amanti, Nett, & Gonzales (1992). From this perspective, family involvement is successful when it is respectful of what families know, approaches families from a strengths (rather than deficits) orientation, recognizes that families understand their child in ways that others cannot, affirms their expressions of care and concern for their child, and acknowledges that support for learning often is rooted in everyday experiences rather that school-like tasks (Dunst, Raab, Trivette & Swanson, 2010; Hanson & Lynch, 2010). Clearly, using this theory as the "base of operations" for the literature review suggests some ways of organizing the review into themes or strands that would be missed in the absence of a firm grounding. When reviewing the literature for a dissertation or a professional journal article, it is vital to identify the theoretical base early in the process. This does not mean that the review will be biased and ignore other research. It does mean that the researcher will make the theoretical stance clear to the reader instead of pretend that all research literature is equally pertinent for the study that is planned. If a quantitative study is planned, quantitative research is, by definition, a test of a theory; without a theory, there is no study.

Theory plays a somewhat different role in qualitative research where it serves as a tool for reflection. At times, the qualitative researcher seeks to use the data to allow a theory to "bubble up" from the data related to a specific situation in a particular context, referred to as a grounded theory study. Whether a study used qualitative, quantitative, or mixed-method approaches, identifying a suitable theoretical base is a major stride forward in conducting the review for original research such as the dissertation.

Choosing Appropriate Research Tools

The first step in choosing appropriate research tools is to visit the database page on an academic library's website. "Even though the databases are grouped by subject and there are links to scope and coverage notes, (users) often do not choose the correct database for their research topic" (Chapman, Pettway, & Scheuler, 2002/2003, p. 368). Many users tend to click on the first full-text database they see and neglect to consider its appropriateness, currency, or coverage. Therefore, it is important that reviewers spend time familiarizing themselves with the database page—paying close attention to subject groupings and database descriptions.

Public search engines, such as Google Scholar, are also excellent research tools for conducting literature reviews. "An important feature of Google

Scholar is that researchers can use it to trace interconnections among authors citing articles on the same topic and to determine the frequency with which others cite a specific article, as it has a *cited by* feature" (Noruzi, 2005, p. 170). Unlike periodical databases, Google Scholar provides researchers with access to documents posted on the Web. "Since several authors post preprints to their Web sites much earlier than the articles appear in printed journals, researchers may find more current information than they would through commercial databases" (Noruzi, 2005, p. 174).

Despite providing access to current information through a user-friendly interface, Google Scholar has its disadvantages. Searches conducted through this search engine can sometimes lead researchers to resources that are not considered scholarly, such as PowerPoint presentations, technical reports, and library guides. Also, Google Scholar provides links to journal articles that are not free; resulting in researchers paying for articles they may be able to access free-of-charge through their academic libraries' database subscriptions. Therefore, it is important that researchers use Google Scholar in conjunction with a variety of periodical databases in order to conduct a thorough and cost-effective search of relevant literature.

After reviewers have identified several possible tools for their research, the next step is to begin accessing these databases to search for sources.

Searching for Sources

The Association of College and Research Libraries [ACRL] (2000) stresses the importance of search strategies that enable scholars to access resources effectively and efficiently. The ACRL suggests:

1. Developing a research plan appropriate to the investigative method
2. Identifying keywords, synonyms, and related terms for the information needed
3. Selecting controlled vocabulary specific to the discipline or information retrieval source
4. Constructing a search strategy using appropriate commands for the information retrieval system selected (e.g., Boolean operators, truncation, and proximity for search engines; internal organizers such as indexes for books)
5. Implementing the search strategy in various information retrieval systems using different user interfaces and search engines, with different command languages, protocols, and search parameters
6. Using investigative protocols appropriate to the discipline. (pp. 9–10)

For example, if a reviewer is interested in researching diversity and inclusive practices in early childhood education, formulating a research question is the first step. According to Agee (2009), "good questions do not necessarily produce good research, but poorly conceived or constructed questions will likely create problems that affect all subsequent stages" of the research process (p. 431). Research questions typically emanate from a problem that a reviewer identifies through professional literature and/or experience (Meadows, 2003).

Perhaps the reviewer has read or observed that early childhood educators are not being trained to implement inclusive practices in their classrooms. As a result, he/she might ask, "How can teacher preparation programs educate preservice teachers to embrace diversity and institute inclusive practices in early childhood education?" After developing a research question, the reviewer should identify keywords which will be used to construct a search string. In the aforementioned research question, possible keywords include: *teacher education, inclusion, diversity,* and *early childhood.* Therefore, the reviewer's search string (in an advanced search using Boolean operators) might read, "teacher education" AND "diversity" AND "inclusion" AND "early childhood." Limiters may also be used to narrow a search. For instance, the review might be limited by date (e.g., the last five to ten years) or by journal type (e.g., scholarly, peer-reviewed journals). After examining the result list produced by a search, the reviewer may find that the search string needs to be modified because the search produces an overwhelming amount of hits, too few hits, or articles that are not answering the research question.

Locating Search Terms and Additional Sources

The following database tools may be used to locate more appropriate search terms or additional articles:

- *Database-suggested search terms*—These words pop up as users type search terms in the search boxes. They represent the most commonly-searched terms in relationship to the term the user is typing. For instance, if the reviewer were to begin typing "early childhood" into a search box, he/she would also be presented with the terms *early childhood development, early childhood education, early childhood special education,* and *early childhood teacher.* By using one of these suggested terms, the user may access more relevant articles.
- *Thesaurus*—This is a list of the preferred subject terms used by the database; the thesaurus also suggests related terms and broader or narrower subject headings. Based on the search string "teacher education" AND "inclusion" AND "early childhood," the thesaurus might list preferred subject terms such as *teachers—training of,* re-

lated terms such as *students with disabilities,* broader subject headings such as *classrooms,* and narrower subject headings such as *teachers—attitudes.* Using one or several of these terms may help the reviewer broaden or narrow a search.

- *Subject headings/descriptors/keywords*—This is the controlled vocabulary listed in the record of an article. A *controlled vocabulary* is a carefully-selected list of words and phrases which is used to classify information so that it can be more easily retrieved from a database. By examining the controlled vocabulary assigned to specific articles, reviewers may find more appropriate search terms.
- *Links to similar articles*—This feature enables users to view a new list of articles that have the same subject headings/descriptors/keywords as the article they are currently viewing. Sometimes this link is identified with the words "Find Similar Results" and, by pursuing this, that one "perfect" article located by the reviewer can snowball into several more.

According to Horsley, Dingwall, and Sampson (2011), "another commonly applied strategy is the checking of reference lists of papers and reports already retrieved to identify additional, potentially relevant records" (p. 2). By checking the reference lists of articles in a database result list, reviewers can also trace the history of a theory or argument back to its original source; a strategy that is particularly important for scholars conducting academic research.

Differentiating Between a Research Review and a Research Report

After a variety of suitable articles have been identified, the reviewer needs to distinguish between published literature reviews and reports of empirical research. Although journal articles that present a review of literature summarize and synthesize the work of leading experts in a given field, they do not provide the researcher with a detailed understanding of the methods, limitations, and results of cited studies. To get this information, researchers must locate cited authors' original research reports.

Both research reviews and research reports are published in scholarly journals, and some databases allow researchers to limit their search by document type. When this type of limiter is not available, users can distinguish a research report from a research review with one quick glance. Empirical research reports will contain, at the very least, the following sections:

- Introduction
- Literature Review
- Methodology

- Results
- Discussion
- Conclusion
- References

In addition, the abstract of an empirical research report will mention a study, an observation, an analysis, or a number of participants or subjects (University of La Verne, 2012).

Evaluating Sources

After categorizing the articles as reports of original research or reviews of published research, the researcher must critically evaluate those sources for their "reliability, validity, accuracy, authority, timeliness, and point of view or bias" (ACRL, 2000, p. 11). By comparing information from various sources, the reviewer can begin to determine the value of the information, verify the information or identify contradictions, and integrate new information with previous knowledge. Reviewers may critically evaluate a scholarly resource by asking themselves the following questions:

1. Who is the author of the material?
2. When was the information published?
3. Is the material published in an academic article, a newspaper or a textbook?
4. How relevant is the material to the reviewer's research question(s)?
5. What is the author's overall purpose? What led the author to his/her hypotheses?
6. What methods were utilized by the author and why?
7. What results were obtained?
8. Were hypotheses supported?
9. What were the author's conclusions/recommendations?
10. Does the author provide a detailed list of references/bibliography?
11. Has the article, book or website been cited or referred to by other authors? (Lawlor & Gorham, 2004, p. 17)

Working With the Academic Librarian

Despite the reviewer's best attempts at choosing appropriate resources, searching for articles, and evaluating sources, roadblocks may surface. For instance, what should a reviewer do if the database he/she is using does not provide a full-text link to an article? What if the reviewer is having trouble finding any relevant articles that answer his/her research questions? What if the reviewer lacks the basic technology and information literacy skills required to choose appropriate databases, search for articles, or evaluate sources?

Academic librarians have the knowledge and skill to help reviewers overcome these obstacles and connect them with the scholarly resources they need to develop a high-quality literature review. Today, academic librarians are accessible to users in a variety of settings. Although they are still available at reference desks in many colleges and universities, academic librarians are more accessible than ever before (Aguilar, Keating, Schadl, & Reenen, 2011). They can be consulted through virtual services such as electronic reference forms, chat reference, and those found on Facebook and Twitter accounts. In addition, academic librarians are creating wikis, blogs, YouTube videos and LibGuides that teach library users basic and advanced information literacy skills they need to locate, access, and use information effectively. Academic library websites are the gateway to these services.

Another growing trend in academic librarianship is the embedded librarian. Embedded librarians are hired to serve as liaisons between their academic libraries and certain colleges or departments. Such programs can improve the library's relationship with faculty and students; shape a more relevant collection of print, media, and electronic resources that meets curriculum, instruction, and research needs; create opportunities for college/university library collaboration through new programs, team-teaching, and scholarly endeavors; and, most importantly, improve the quality of teaching and learning (Heider, 2010). "Embedded librarianship focuses on the user and brings the library and the librarian to the user, wherever they [sic] are—office, laboratory, home, or even on their mobile device" (Kesselman & Watstein, 2009, p. 383). Embedded librarians often have offices in the college or department(s) they serve, making it easier for students to consult with them in person regarding concerns or difficulties they are experiencing with research. In addition, many librarians have formed collaborative relationships with faculty who teach online courses. These relationships have led to librarians becoming embedded in course management systems such as Blackboard, Moodle, and D2L. "Providing academic resources to students working on course-related assignments within their online learning space enables the embedded librarian to work efficiently by customizing materials and tools available from the university library system and making them available immediately to all registered students" (Tumbleson & Burke, 2010, p. 973).

If a student or faculty member is having difficulty conducting a review of the literature, then the first step is to determine if his/her university has an embedded librarian program. Academic library's websites can be very helpful in directing students to librarians who have expertise or experience with research in certain fields (e.g., early childhood education). If such a person exists, the next step is contacting this librarian to set up a consultation, either in person or online. There are many benefits for students who have access to an embedded librarian. "Whether the student is enrolled in a traditional, off-campus, hybrid, or online course, students are directed to the best library database, electronic collections, and titles as well as given instruction in developing research strategies" (Tumbleson & Burke, 2010, p. 973). Unfortunately, not everyone seeking to review the literature will have access to a librarian who can guide them through the process of conducting a literature review. So, where can these reviewers go for help?

Technology Resources for Reviewers

Fortunately, there are many helpful resources on conducting literature reviews available online as highlighted in Figure 22.4.

When to Quit

Thus, the question arises: "At what point should the process of gathering additional relevant literature end?" Leedy and Ormrod (2012) noted that one common rule of thumb is that the search is near completion when one discovers that new articles introduce arguments, methodologies, findings, authors, and studies with which the reviewer is familiar already. In sum, as Webster and Watson (2002) observed, "you can gauge that your review is nearing completion when you are not finding new concepts in your article set" (p. 16). The next step in the process is drafting the review (Randolph, 2009).

WRITING THE REVIEW

As Reuber (2011) points out,

> It is important to recognize that *doing* a literature review is different from *writing* a literature review. *Doing* a literature review is ongoing and should be wide ranging to allow you to gain and maintain a wide and up-to-date understanding of your subject area and the areas that relate to it, even tangentially. However, *writing* a literature review needs to be tightly focused and purpose driven... this means that while much of the prior research you have read will contribute to your understanding of a field, only a subset of it is likely to be included in the literature review of any one individual paper submitted for publication. (p. 106)

Students are sometimes surprised to learn that the literature reviews that earned an "A" at a previous level of study—for example, a doctoral student

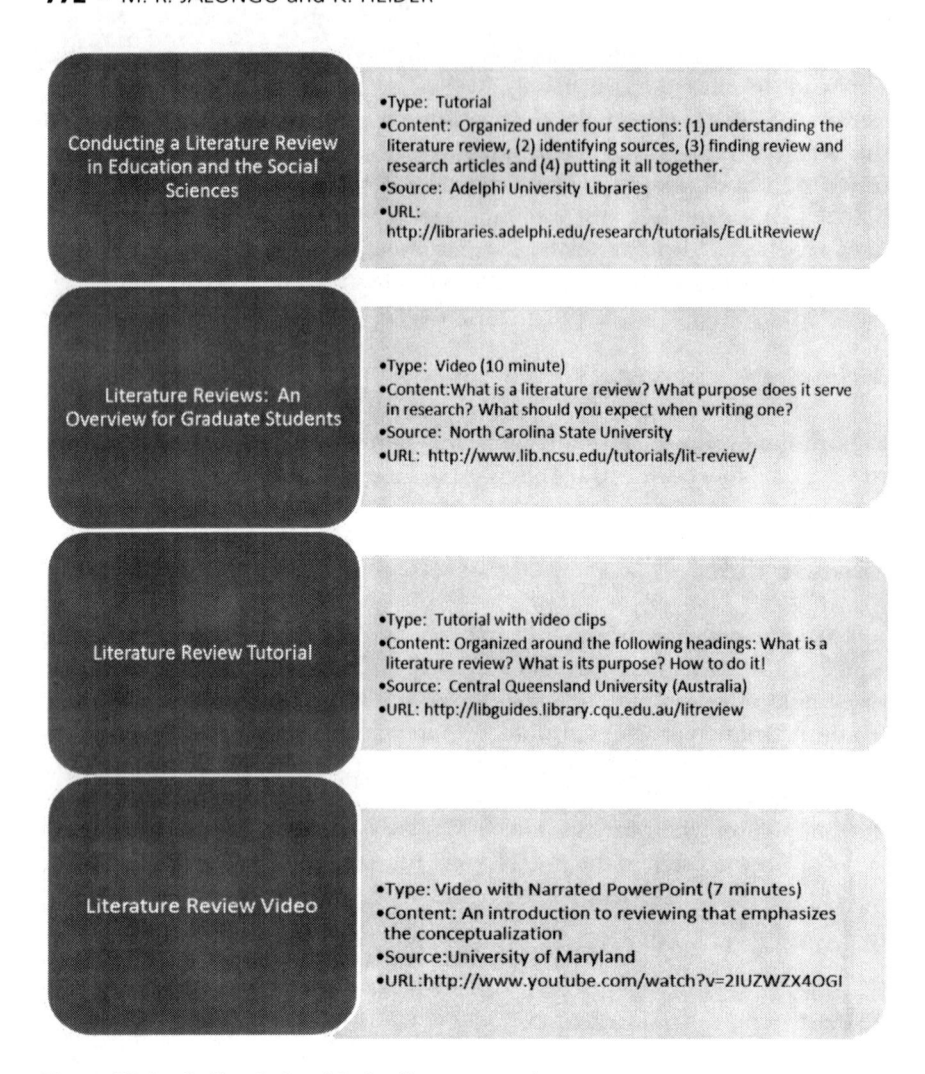

Conducting a Literature Review in Education and the Social Sciences
- Type: Tutorial
- Content: Organized under four sections: (1) understanding the literature review, (2) identifying sources, (3) finding review and research articles and (4) putting it all together.
- Source: Adelphi University Libraries
- URL: http://libraries.adelphi.edu/research/tutorials/EdLitReview/

Literature Reviews: An Overview for Graduate Students
- Type: Video (10 minute)
- Content: What is a literature review? What purpose does it serve in research? What should you expect when writing one?
- Source: North Carolina State University
- URL: http://www.lib.ncsu.edu/tutorials/lit-review/

Literature Review Tutorial
- Type: Tutorial with video clips
- Content: Organized around the following headings: What is a literature review? What is its purpose? How to do it!
- Source: Central Queensland University (Australia)
- URL: http://libguides.library.cqu.edu.au/litreview

Literature Review Video
- Type: Video with Narrated PowerPoint (7 minutes)
- Content: An introduction to reviewing that emphasizes the conceptualization
- Source: University of Maryland
- URL: http://www.youtube.com/watch?v=2IUZWZX4OGI

Figure 22.4 Online help with the literature review.

writing a master's student type of literature review—will not suffice. The same holds true for making the transition from a class paper to a publishable literature review; what typically was acceptable as an assignment will not be publishable. Class papers and publishable articles differ from student work along several key dimensions of writing.

- Purpose: The student writer is expected to demonstrate familiarity with the field, collect a sufficient number of resources for the bibliography, and fulfill course requirements; the published author

is expected to make an innovative contribution to the field and to inform, enlighten, persuade, or some combination of these so that readers will choose to read, duplicate, and cite the work.
- Audience: Student writing often is for one faculty member who is likely to be interested in and knowledgeable about the topic (and obligated to read it); published writing has a large audience of unknown professional colleagues who have varying levels of interest in and familiarity with the content (and are free to read something else).
- Voice: Student writing pays homage to the leaders in the field and is relatively silent; a published author is expected to enter into the professional dialogue and speak authoritatively.
- Organization: Student writing typically consists of page after page of unbroken text, often loosely organized; published writing is tightly structured and the organization is tailored to the specific outlet; it also makes use of visual material (e.g., headings, figures, tables, graphs, examples, illustrations) to break up the text as appropriate.
- Focus: Student writing generally results in superficial treatment of broad topics deemed important by the instructor while published writing has a clear focus on a topic that can be adequately addressed in a short manuscript (Jalongo, 2002).

Given these vast discrepancies, the best advice for scholars is to make the intended publication outlet their "textbook"; in other words, to study the purpose, audience, style, voice, organization, and focus represented in published work rather than relying on their past experiences with writing (Natriello, 1996). Making the transition from beginning writing to published writing will place a high demand on the writer's ability to use higher-order thinking skills of analysis, synthesis, and evaluation. Peer reviewers for professional journals expect a publishable review to go beyond mere reporting and advance thinking in the field. An important part of that process is selecting a topic and focus.

THE PUBLICATION POTENTIAL OF REVIEWS

Expectations for a comprehensive literature review sometimes are steeped in tradition and more grounded in what professors remember from their own doctoral studies than centered on what is best for students. Nationally, the Council of Graduate Schools (2011) notes that no more than 75% of the doctoral students who achieve candidacy ultimately complete the degree. Evidently, the need to produce a wide-ranging, exhaustive review of the literature is one place where doctoral candidates frequently falter. In a focus group study of 272 faculty members in 74 departments across ten disciplines at nine research universities, respondents were asked to characterize key components of dissertations at four different quality levels—outstanding, very good, acceptable, and unacceptable (Lovitts, 2008). Collectively, this group had 6,129 years of experience, had chaired approximately 3,470 dissertations, and had served on about 9,890 dissertation committees. Many of the markers of quality mentioned had to do with the literature review. In the outstanding category, some commonly mentioned attributes were: synthesizes the literature well and is interdisciplinary; connects components in a seamless way; exhibits mature, independent thinking; has a point of view and a strong, confident, independent, and authoritative voice; displays a deep understanding of a massive amount of complicated literature; and presents an argument that is focused, logical, rigorous, and sustained. By way of contrast, dissertations in the "Acceptable" category were described as: somewhat pedestrian and not very original, significant, exciting, or interesting; a chore to read; and knows the literature but is not critical of it or does not discuss what is important. In the "Not Acceptable" group, inadequacies of the literature review were glaring: contains errors or mistakes; plagiarizes or deliberately misreads or misuses sources; does not understand or misses relevant literature; and has a weak, inconsistent, self-contradictory, unconvincing, or invalid argument.

A hotly-debated issue in reviewing the literature is whether a wide-ranging review is the best approach. Is it feasible, through a more focused review, to accomplish the four objectives of a literature review identified by Neuman (2009)—(1) demonstrating a familiarity with a body of knowledge and establishing credibility, (2) showing the path of prior research and how a current project is linked to it, (3) integrating and summarizing what is known in an area, and (4) learning from others and stimulating new ideas. Some argue for a focused review (Maxwell, 2006) while others contend that a narrower scope is less scholarly and less likely to result in original insights (Boote & Beile, 2005; Beile & Boote, 2006). Nevertheless, some consideration needs to be given to the long-term outcomes of literature reviews produced by graduate students. As many journal editors will attest, referring to a manuscript as "thesis or dissertation style" is a prime reason for rejection (Hartman, Montagnes, & McMenemy, 2003; Luey, 2002, 2007). This raises the question of whether assignments—including the traditional dissertation—have outlived their usefulness.

In some regions of the world, notably the United Kingdom (Badley, 2009), Scandinavian countries, and North America (e.g., Vanderbilt University, Utah State University, University of Alberta, Canada, and DePaul University) institutions have challenged the assumption that students should generate reams of writing that would need to be completely restructured and rewritten in order to be publishable. In response, they have given doctoral students the option of a multipaper dissertation; in other words, published work in peer-reviewed scholarly publications *is* the dissertation (Duke & Beck, 1999; Thomas, Nelson & Magill, 1986). The assumption here is that "if students publish in their formative years, they are more likely to do so as established academics or informed professionals in their chosen careers" (Kamler, 2008, p. 292). Questions persist about what form the literature reviews that are required of graduate students should take. In any case, a literature review has far greater potential as a publication when it exemplifies a high level of conceptualization, sets forth a logical argument, and is grounded in inquiry. Indeed, Machi and McEvoy's (2008) book, *The Literature Review*, states that a fundamental stance of inquiry and openness to discovery and learning is the single, most important aspect of literature reviews. They describe the "inquiring researcher" as one who knows how to set aside personal biases, comes to the research with an open mind, is capable of seeing both the details and the big picture, weighs all the evidence for veracity and value, proceeds with diligence, reflects deliberately and continually, and works ethically.

CONCLUSION: THE FUTURE OF REVIEWING

Each time the communication environment is modified by technological advances, it changes our interests (what we think about), it changes the symbols and tools we use (what we think with), and it alters the nature of our communities (how we interact) (Innis, 1951). Whether it is the introduction of the clay tablet or an electronic one, the communication environment is forever changed. Although instant access to information has changed the communication environment for scholars in many positive ways, it also can facilitate academic dishonesty in scholarly writing and publishing, including plagiarism, purchasing papers, and "salami science" (shaving many pieces from one piece of work). A more fundamental question has to do with why people would make these bad decisions and take the associated risks in the first place. Perhaps enabling students to see a real purpose for a literature review and supporting them in producing more skillful literature reviews may be one way to counteract such acts of desperation. If, for example, graduate students were carefully guided in producing literature reviews with greater publication potential then their work could have practical value that extends beyond completing class assignments and program requirements. Such issues also have to be considered in the long term. Ordeals associated with the literature review surely can have the unintended effect of causing former students and current faculty members to avoid writing and, therefore, erode the goals of scholarship.

Misconceptions about reviewing are another issue that merits close attention. Too often, novice and experienced researchers assume that they know how to review; doctoral students may believe that they "learned that already" during their master's degrees programs, faculty that they mastered it during their doctoral programs, and so forth. Yet literacy in general, and information literacy in particular, are moving targets. Back when students and researchers were almost entirely reliant on brick/mortar libraries and print sources, it was not unusual to seize upon the opportunity to physically return to a library where the researcher had used the resources extensively (e.g., a former doctoral student returning to use the library of the degree-granting institution). The fact that much of what we need to use is now in digital form does not obviate the need for that familiarity, however. Each academic institution has its own nuances, and scholars would be wise to attend a real or virtual orientation periodically to update their skills. Graduate program faculty definitely should not assume that all of their students are fully oriented to search processes in general or the ones specific to their institution; they also should not assume that their students or even themselves have completely mastered all of the skills of reviewing, given the constantly changing nature of search strategies and the controversies about various types of reviews (e.g., focused vs. wide ranging approaches). In a study of 33 dissertation advisors' practices in preparing doctoral candidates to review the literature, Zaporozhetz (1987) found that professors ranked the traditional Chapter 2 the lowest of the five dissertation chapters, both in terms of their expertise and the amount of time they invested; they assumed that their advisees already would have doctoral-level reviewing skills when some of them did not. This led the researcher to conclude that explicit instruction in the work of reviewing—on par with research methodology instruction for doctoral candidates—was necessary. Even vastly-experienced authors sometimes need advice concerning how to conduct the review, data bases outside the usual choices, or the latest technological advances.

We began this chapter with a definition of the literature review and used higher-order thinking skills to form a foundation for the chapter. Then, we examined overarching purposes for literature reviews and proposed a typology for literature reviews that includes their theoretical foundations. Next, we offered research-based advice on the process of conducting reviews and discussed both human resources and technological advances for those engaged in the work of reviewing. Finally, we discussed described ways to enrich and enlarge the work of reviewing that plays such a pivotal role in various scholarly endeavors. If the literature review in early childhood education is to transcend its reputation as high-stakes homework and realize its potential to truly *re*view—to see anew, with fresh eyes, and improved perspectives—then everyone engaged in the process, including students, teachers, faculty members, librarians, readers, peer reviewers, and editors will need to be fully socialized into the values of scholarship and committed to the advancement of the field.

NOTE

1. George Boole, an English mathematician in the nineteenth century, developed "Boolean Logic" in order to combine the truth values, true or false, of individual algebraic formulas. Boolean searching combines certain concepts and excludes certain concepts using the words AND, OR, and NOT.

REFERENCES

Agee, J. (2009). Developing qualitative research questions: A reflective process. *International Journal of Qualitative Studies in Education, 22*(4), 431–447.
Aguilar, P., Keating, K., Schadl, S., & Van Reenen, J. (2011). Reference as outreach: Meeting users where they are. *Journal of Library Administration, 51*(4), 343–358.
Association of College and Research Libraries [ACRL]. (2000). *Information literacy competency standards for higher education.* Chicago, IL: American Library Association.
Aveyard, H. (2011). *Doing a literature review in health and social care: A practical guide.* New York, NY: Oxford University Press/McGraw Hill.
Badley, G. (2009). Publish and be doctor-rated: The Ph.D. by published work. *Quality Assurance in Education, 17*(4), 331–342.
Barnes, S. J. (2005). Assessing the value of IS journals. *Communications of the ACM, 48*(1), 110–112.
Beile, P., & Boote, D. N. (2006). On "literature reviews of, and for, educational research": A response to the critique by Joseph Maxwell. *Educational Researcher, 35*(9), 32–35.
Bettany-Saltikov, J. (2010). Learning how to undertake a systematic review: Part 1. *Nursing Standard, 24*(50), 47–56.
Blaiki, N. (2007). *Approaches to social enquiry.* Cambridge, UK: Polity Press.
Bloom, B. S. (1956). *Taxonomy of educational objectives: Handbook I, The cognitive domain.* New York, NY: David McKay & Co.
Bloom, B. S. (1984). *Taxonomy of educational objectives.* Boston, MA: Allyn & Bacon. (originally published in 1956).
Bloomberg, L. D., & Volpe, M. (2008). *Completing your qualitative dissertation: A roadmap from beginning to end.* Thousand Oaks, CA: Sage.
Blum, K., & Muirhead, B. (2005). The right horse and harness to pull the carriage: Teaching online doctorate students about literature reviews, qualitative, and quantitative methods that drive the problem. [Online] Retrieved from: http://www.itdl.org/Journal/Feb_05/article03.htm
Boell, S. K., & Cecez-Kecmanovic, D. (2010). Literature reviews and the hermeneutic circle. *Australian Academic & Research Libraries, 41*(2), 129–144.

Boote, D. N., & Beile, P. (2005). Scholars before researchers: On the centrality of the dissertation literature review in research preparation. *Educational Researcher, 34*(6), 3–15.

Bruce, C. S. (1994). Research students' early experiences of the dissertation literature review. *Studies in Higher Education, 19*(2), 217–230.

Chapman, J. M., Pettway, C. K., & Scheuler, S. A. (2002/2003). Teaching journal and serials information to undergraduates: Challenges, problems and recommended instructional approaches. *Reference Librarian, 38*(79/80), 363–382.

The Cochrane Collaboration (2012). Cochrane reviews. Retrieved from http://www.cochrane.org/cochrane-reviews

Cooper, H. M. (1998). *Synthesizing research: A guide for literature reviews* (3rd ed.). Thousand Oaks, CA: Sage.

Council of Graduate Schools (2011). Ph.D. completion project. Retrieved from http://www.cgsnet.org/Default.aspx?tabid=157

Creswell, J. W. (2003). *Research design: Qualitative, quantitative, and mixed methods approaches* (2nd ed.). Thousand Oaks, CA: Sage.

Duke, N. K., & Beck, S. W. (1999). Education should consider alternative formats for the dissertation. *Educational Researcher, 28*(3), 31–36.

Dunst, C. J., Raab M., Trivette, C. A., & Swanson, J. (2010). Community based everyday child learning opportunities. In R. A. McWilliam (Ed.). *Working with families of children with special needs* (pp. 60–92). New York, NY: Guilford Press.

Edgemon, E. A., Wiley, A. L., Jablonski, B. R., &. Lloyd, J. W. (2006). *Conducting integrative reviews of special education research: Overview and case study.* Cambridge, England: Emerald Group Publishing Limited.

Eisenhart, M. (2009). On the subject of interpretive reviews. *Review of Educational Research, 68*(4), 391–399.

Fink, A. (2009). *Conducting research literature reviews: From the internet to paper.* Thousand Oaks, CA: Sage.

Fisher, A. (2003). *The logic of real arguments.* Cambridge, England: Cambridge University Press.

Fisher, A. (2004). *Critical thinking: An introduction.* Cambridge, England: Cambridge University Press.

Frankel, J. R., & Wallen, N. E. (2009). *How to design and evaluate research in education.* New York, NY: McGraw-Hill.

Garfield, E. (1987). Reviewing review literature. Part 1, Definitions and uses of reviews. *Current Contents, 18*(4), 5–8.

Garrard, J. (2011). *Health sciences literature review made easy: The matrix method* (3rd ed.). Sudbury, MA: Jones & Bartlett.

Gay, L. R., Mills, G. E., & Arasian, P. (2006). *Educational research: Competencies for analysis and application.* (8th ed.). Upper Saddle River, NJ: Pearson.

Hanson, M. J., & Lynch, E. W. (2010). Working with families from diverse backgrounds. In R. A. McWilliam (Ed.)., *Working with families of young children with special needs* (pp. 147–174). New York, NY: The Guilford Press.

Hart, C. (1998). *Doing a literature review: Releasing the social science research imagination.* Thousand Oaks, CA: Sage.

Hart, C. (2001). *Doing a literature search: A guide for the social sciences.* London, England: Sage.

Hart, C. (2008). Literature reviewing and argumentation. In G. Hall & J. Longman (Eds.), *The postgraduate's companion*. London, England: Sage.

Hartman, E., Montagnes, I., & McMenemy, S. (Eds.). (2003). *The thesis and the book: A guide for first-time academic authors*. Toronto, Canada: University of Toronto Press.

Heider, K. L. (2010). Ten tips for implementing a successful embedded librarian program. *Public Services Quarterly, 6*(2/3), 110–121.

Horsley, T., Dingwall, O., & Sampson, M. (2011). Checking reference lists to find additional studies for systematic reviews. *Cochrane Database of Systematic Reviews, 2011*(8), Article MR000026.

Iivari, J., Hirschheim, R., & Klein, H. K. (2004). Towards a distinctive body of knowledge for information systems experts: Coding ISD process knowledge in two IS journals. *Information Systems Journal, 14*(4), 313–342.

Innis, H. (1951). *The bias of communication*. Toronto, Canada: University of Toronto Press.

Jalongo, M. R. (2002). *Writing for publication: A practical guide for educators*. Norwood, MA: Christopher-Gordon.

Jesson, J. K. (2011). *Doing your literature review: Traditional and systematic techniques*. Thousand Oaks, CA: Sage.

Kamler, B. (2008). Rethinking doctoral publication practices: Writing from and beyond the thesis. *Studies in Higher Education, 33*(3), 283–294.

Kesselman, M., & Watstein, S. (2009). Creating opportunities: Embedded librarians. *Journal of Library Administration, 49*, 383–400.

Laband, D. N., & Piette, M. J. (2000). Perceived conduct and professional ethics among college economics faculty. *American Economist, 44*(1), 24–34.

Lather, P. (1999). To be of use: The work of reviewing. *Review of Educational Research, 69*(1), 2–7.

Lawlor, J., & Gorham, G. (2004). Dublin Institute of Technology, Faculty of Tourism & Food: The reference handbook. Retrieved from: http://remus.dit.ie/DIT/tourismfood/hospitality/Reference.pdf

Leedy, P. D., & Ormrod, J. E. (2012). *Practical research: Planning and design* (10th ed.). Boston, MA: Addison-Wesley/Pearson.

Levy, Y., & Ellis, T. J. (2006). A systems approach to conduct an effective literature review in support of information systems research. *Informing Science Journal, 9*, 181–212.

Li, J. (2004). High abilities and excellence: A cultural perspective. In L. V. Shavinina & M. Ferrari (Eds.), *Beyond knowledge: Extracognitive aspects of high ability* (pp. 187–208). Mahwah, NJ: Erlbaum.

Lovitts, B. E. (2008). The transition to independent research: Who makes it, who doesn't, and why. *The Journal of Higher Education, 79*(3), 296–325.

Luey, B. (2002). *Handbook for academic authors* (4th ed.). New York, NY: Oxford University Press.

Luey, B. (2007). *Revising your dissertation: Advice from leading editors*. Berkeley, CA: University of California Press.

Machi, L. A., & McEvoy, B. T. (2008). *The literature review: Six steps to success*. Thousand Oaks, CA: Corwin Press.

Maxwell, J. A. (2006). Literature reviews of, and for, educational research: A commentary on Boote and Beile's "Scholars before Researchers." *Educational Researcher, 35*(9), 28–31.

McKibbon, K. A. (2006). Systematic reviews and librarians. *Library Trends, 55*(1), 202–215.

McMillan, J. H., & Schumacher, S. (2010). *Research in education: Evidence-based inquiry.* (7th ed.). Upper Saddle River, NJ: Pearson.

Meadows, K. A. (2003). So you want to do research? 2: Developing the research question. *British Journal of Community Nursing, 8*(9), 397–403.

Merriam, S. B. (2009). *Qualitative research: A guide to design and implementation.* San Francisco, CA: Jossey-Bass.

Mertler, C. A., & Charles, C. M. (2005). *Introduction to educational research.* (5th ed.). Boston, MA: Pearson.

Moll, L. C., Amanti, C., Neff, D., & Gonzalez, N. (1992). Funds of knowledge for teaching. *Theory Into Practice, 31,* 132–141.

Muirhead, B. (2004). Literature Review Advice. [Online] Retrieved from http://www.itdl.org/journal/Feb_04/article06.htm

Murray, F., & Raths, J. (1994). Call for manuscripts. *Review of Educational Research, 64*(2), 197–200.

Natriello, G. (1996). Lessons for young scholars seeking to publish. *Teachers College Record, 97*(4), 509–517.

Neuman, W. L. (2009). *Social research methods: Qualitative and quantitative approaches* (7th ed.). Boston, MA: Allyn and Bacon.

Ngai, E. W. T., & Wat, F. K. T. (2002). A literature review and classification of electronic commerce research. *Information & Management, 39*(5), 415–429.

Noruzi, A. (2005). Google Scholar: The new generation of citation indexes. *Libri, 55*(4), 170–180.

Notar, C. E., & Cole, V. (2010). Literature review organizer. *International Journal of Education, 2*(2), E2. Retrieved from www.macrothink.org/journal/index.php/ije/article/view/319

Pan, M. L. (2004). *Preparing literature reviews: Qualitative and quantitative approaches.* (2nd. ed.). Glendale, CA: Pyrczak.

Petticrew, M., & Roberts, H. (2006). *Systematic reviews in the social sciences: A practical guide.* Oxford, UK: Blackwell Publishing.

Randolph, J. J. (2009). A guide to writing the dissertation literature review. *Practical Assessment, Research & Evaluation, 14*(13), 1–13.

Reuber, A. R. (2011). Strengthening your literature review. *Family Business Review, 23*(2), 105–108.

Ridley, D. (2008). *The literature review: A step-by-step guide for students.* Thousand Oaks, CA: Sage.

Sciplore (2010). How to write a thesis (Bachelor, Master, or PhD) and which software tools to use. Retrieved from http://sciplore.org/2010/how-to-write-a-phd-thesis/

Steward, B. (2004). Writing a literature review. *British Journal of Occupational Therapy, 67*(11), 495–500.

Swales, J. M., & Lindemann, S. (2002). Teaching the literature review to international graduate students. In A. M. Johns (Ed.), *Genre in the classroom: Multiple perspectives* (pp. 105–120). Mahwah, NJ: Lawrence Erlbaum.

Swales, J. W. (2009). *Telling a research story: Writing a literature review*. Ann Arbor, MI: University of Michigan Press/ESL.

Thomas J., Nelson, J., & Magill, R. (1986). A case for an alternative format to the thesis/ dissertation. *Quest, 38*, 116–124.

Torgerson C. (2003). *Systematic reviews*. London, UK: Continuum.

Torraco, R. J. (2005). Writing integrative literature reviews: Guidelines and examples. *Human Resource Development Review, 4*(3), 356–367.

Trainor, A. A., & Graue, E. (Eds.). (2012). *Reviewing qualitative research in the social sciences: A guide for researchers and reviewers*. New York, NY: Routledge.

Tranfield, D., Denyer, D., & Smart, P. (2003). Towards a methodology for developing evidence-informed management knowledge by means of a systematic review. *British Journal of Management, 14*, 207–222.

Tumbleson, B. E., & Burke, J. J. (2010). When life hands you lemons: Overcoming obstacles to expand services in an embedded librarian program. *Journal of Library Administration, 50*(7/8), 972–988.

University of La Verne. (2012). What is an empirical article? Retrieved from http://library.laverne.edu/empirical-research.php

Webster, J., & Watson, R. T. (2002). Analyzing the past to prepare for the future: Writing a literature review. *MIS Quarterly, 26*(2), 13–23.

Whittemore, R., & Knafl, K. (2005). The integrative review: Updated methodology. *Journal of Advanced Nursing, 52*(5), 546–553.

Zaporozhetz, L. E. (1987). *The dissertation literature review: How faculty advisors prepare their doctoral candidates* (Unpublished doctoral dissertation). University of Oregon, Teacher Education, Eugene, OR.

Zinsser, W. (2001). *On writing well: The classic guide to writing nonfiction* (25th anniversary ed.). New York, NY: Quill.

CHAPTER 23

READING AND INTERPRETING EARLY CHILDHOOD RESEARCH[1]

Angela C. Baum and Paula McMurray-Schwarz

Scientific inquiry provides a forum to facilitate the ongoing process of questioning and evaluating practice, presents informed practice based on available data, and innovates new practices through research and experimental learning. (Hudson-Barr, 2004, p. 70)

Early childhood professionals engage in reading published research for a variety of purposes. Whether reading to learn more about a topic, to explore innovative strategies for practice, or to build a strong rationale for a new research project, reading research is an important activity for those in the early childhood field. For some, however, the task of reading published research may be a challenging undertaking. The language used in research writing is often technical and the methods used to gather and analyze data may be complicated. The purpose of this chapter is to make the experience of reading research more manageable. This chapter delineates the sections of a typical research manuscript, describes the purpose of each section, and identifies practical strategies for developing clear interpretations and understandings of the research. In addition, this chapter aims to support readers as they become wise consumers of research, preparing them

Handbook of Research Methods in Early Childhood Education, pages 783–800
Copyright © 2015 by Information Age Publishing
All rights of reproduction in any form reserved.

to engage in basic evaluation by identifying important points and questions to consider while reading.

WHY IS READING RESEARCH IMPORTANT?

Research Provides a Foundation for Further Investigation

Reading published research plays a critical role in the design and implementation of new research. Researchers often begin their investigations by first becoming familiar with the existing research base on a specific topic, which provides an important foundation for their work. Understanding the results of previous studies helps researchers clearly identify a topic of interest and fine-tune their research questions and/or hypotheses (Salkind, 2012). In addition, researchers use existing research to build a rationale for their own work and to justify its necessity and potential impact within the field. Researchers also rely on the work of others to help them make decisions about their own work, such as which populations to study, which methods of research to employ, and which data analysis strategies to use. Finally, researchers continue to rely on previous research at the conclusion of their study to situate their results and recommendations within the field, highlighting the unique contributions that their findings make to the current knowledge base on that topic.

Research Informs Practice

In addition to establishing a foundation for new research investigations, published research supports early childhood professionals as they make daily decisions about their work with, or on behalf of, young children. Consider the following example. In an article written by Cryer et al. (2005), the authors describe their study examining the ways in which infants and toddlers reacted as they transitioned to a new classroom. Results of their investigation suggest that infants and toddlers may experience increased stress during these transitions. Early childhood professionals, in a variety of roles, may find reading this research article beneficial. For example, in an effort to reduce stress and ensure high quality care for very young children, the director of a child care center might draw on these results to provide a rationale for implementing continuity of care (Program for Infant/Toddler Care, 2008) in her center. In another case, after reading this article, a toddler teacher might engage in teacher research (Stremmel, 2002), systematically collecting data to document whether or not children who have recently transitioned into his classroom display signs of stress and then, depending on his findings, advocate for fewer classroom transitions in his center or explore techniques to reduce any stress experienced by the children in his care. Additionally, a teacher educator might integrate the content of this study into a course she teaches on infant/toddler care and development to help illustrate important aspects of child care quality. Finally, a researcher might use this study to conduct additional investigations of this nature utilizing a larger, more diverse sample or to design an investigation that follows children over a long period of time to ascertain the impact of classroom transitions on children's later development (Cryer et al., 2005). While the professionals described in this example function in different roles in early childhood education, each may find that the practice of reading research has a meaningful influence on their work.

In the sections that follow, information typically included in a research article is described. Guidance will be provided to help readers of research understand the purpose of each section and the important points to consider when making initial judgments about the usefulness or quality of the information presented in the article. The material presented in this chapter is meant to be practical in nature and to provide early childhood professionals with basic information to assist them in the important task of reading research.

THE RESEARCH ARTICLE

Author and Journal

While the first thing readers will notice about a research article is the title and how the topic is related to their work, there is additional information that readers should consider, including what is known about the author(s), the author's affiliation, the journal in which the article was published, the date of publication, and any organizations that may have funded the research. While this may seem somewhat straightforward or unremarkable, it can provide the reader with valuable insight related to the nature and quality of the research.

First, readers should notice the authors of the manuscript, whose names appear in the order of their contribution to the research. As readers review this information, it is important to consider other work they have read by the authors. This provides a history of the authors' professional interests and the evolution of their work on this subject, which helps to establish the authors' expertise. In addition, readers should note the authors' affiliation, which is usually an institution (APA, 2010). Knowing whether the authors' institution is designated by the Carnegie Foundation[2] as having very high or high levels of research activity can provide valuable information related to the kind of support the authors receive to conduct research. At institutions that value and support research activity, authors are likely to be given more financial support and time to pursue their scholarly agendas, allowing them to more fully develop their knowledge and skills as researchers. Additionally, the Author Note (often located at the bottom of the first page of an article) may include the lead author's contact information, which may be valuable if the article proves to be important to the reader's research agenda or practice. The Author Note may also include departmental affiliation, acknowledgements, and/or disclaimers for perceived conflict of interest (APA, 2010).

When noting the author's affiliation, it is useful to look at whether or not they are associated with any particular interest group such as the U.S. Department of Education, National Institutes of Health (NIH), or other governmental agencies, as well as private foundations such as the Bill and Melinda Gates Foundation. It is also important to note who published the research journal. This information provides a way to identify any possible source of bias or conflict of interest in the research study. As mentioned previously, it is appropriate for the authors to include, in the Author Note, disclaimers associated with the agency that funded the study (APA, 2010). This disclaimer may include a statement explaining that the research reported in the article does not reflect the views of the organization that sponsored the research study. Without this disclaimer, the reader should be aware of any possible bias contained in the article. According to Crosser (2005), readers must be aware of the fact that an organization may not publish findings that are contrary to their mission or may report findings reflecting their political priorities or policies. While affiliation with a particular interest group or organization does not automatically discredit or reduce the validity of the study, it is important information to consider as readers make decisions about the applicability of the findings.

Readers should also consider the reputation of the journal in which an article is published and the date of the publication. The status of a research journal is based, in part, on whether the articles are peer-reviewed or refereed. This process involves a blind review of submitted articles by two or more peers who have expertise on the subject or have related research agendas. Another process of review involves a critique by an approved panel of independent experts through a comparably rigorous, objective, and scientific process (Edyburn, 2009). A peer-reviewed journal is generally considered to be of higher status and garners more respect in the field of study than a nonpeer-reviewed journal. According to Andrade (2011), the peer review process helps improve the quality of an article and potentially correct biases. The review process can take six months to over a year, depending on the speed at which articles are distributed to reviewers and how much time they have to respond with their evaluation of the article. More recently, this process has been streamlined with the use of online systems that allow for quick turnaround times. Some journals publish the date when each article was first received by the journal editor, when revisions were submitted, and when it was accepted for publication. A short time frame between first submission and acceptance may mean that the article required few revisions. The date of publication also indicates the timeliness of the research and can help the reader place it within a group of similar articles. Information about the length of time from submission to publication may be of particular interest to the reader if, in the future, he or she decides to submit a manuscript to the same journal for possible publication.

Another aspect of the journal that warrants consideration is its acceptance rate. The acceptance rate of the journal refers to how many articles are accepted for publication from a pool of articles that were submitted to the journal editor in a specified amount of time. For example, a journal may have a 21% acceptance rate, which means that 21 out of 100 articles received were eventually published in the journal. A low acceptance rate means that the journal is highly selective and that research published in the journal may be well-respected within a field of study. Details regarding acceptance rate are available on the journal's website or in a variety of citation indices.

The Abstract

The main purpose of the abstract, considered by some to be the most important paragraph in an article, is to provide the reader with a general understanding of what the article is about (APA, 2010; Feldt & Moore, 1999). An abstract provides a brief, usually 100–150 words, comprehensive overview or summary of the purpose of the study. It gives the reader a broad understanding of the context of the study and often contains information regarding the problem, questions or hypotheses, participants, methods used to conduct the research, and the main findings of the project (Hudson-Barr, 2004; Saracho, 2013). The abstract provides a manageable way to quickly decide if there is value in reading the article in its entirety, if the article is relevant to the reader's work, and of sorting articles for a literature review (APA, 2010; Edyburn, 2005). Also, the abstract will identify whether the article is original research or if it is a literature review on a specific topic (Bogucka & Wood, 2009).

After reading the abstract, readers should ask themselves, "Does this article provide the information that I am searching for in relation to my practice, research, or interests?" If the answer is yes, the reader should move forward and read the article in its entirety by first breaking it down into smaller sections, each of which is described below (Feldt & Moore, 1999). An important point to keep in mind is that reading the abstract should never substitute for reading the complete article. Readers should not rely on information in the abstract as the final word on the topic. It is important to read the full article in an effort to obtain a clear picture of what the author is trying to communicate and for the reader to make personal judgments about the importance or quality of the research findings. In essence, an abstract is an important tool that can save readers the frustration of investing precious time in reading a full article (Bogucka & Wood, 2009), only to find that it doesn't really provide the information sought. When critiquing the abstract, readers should consider the following questions: Does the abstract accurately match the headings of the article? Does it provide a nonevaluative description of the study? Is it coherent, readable, and concise (APA, 2010)?

The Introduction

Following the abstract, the main body of the research article begins with an introduction, including the literature review. This introductory section typically identifies the problem being studied, provides an explanation or rationale for the author's research project, and may briefly describe the processes undertaken by the author (Saracho, 2013). In this section, the author should explicitly state why the problem deserves new research (APA, 2010). This is usually followed by a statement of the purpose or rationale of the research study (Hudson-Barr, 2004).

Additionally, the author will provide a summary of the most recent and pertinent work related to the current study. This description of literature includes a brief overview of studies related to the author's subject and makes explicit the theoretical model for the study. Laramee (2011), states that this includes a description of mature areas versus new directions for this line of research, including unsolved problems. Readers should evaluate whether the author emphasized pertinent findings, relevant methodological issues, and major conclusions from previous literature (APA, 2010). This is done to provide a framework for the current study, identifying the gaps in a line of related research studies, and a reason for the topic to be explored (Edyburn, 2005; Hudson-Barr, 2004). In addition, the citations in this section provide resources to locate more information on the topic (Edyburn, 2005). Put simply, in the review of literature, the author explains what is already known about the topic and what is not yet addressed in an effort to describe the concept for the present study and to lay the foundation for the next logical step of exploration (Hudson-Barr, 2004; Laramee, 2011). The "next step" is the purpose or the unique contribution of the current study (Edyburn, 2005) and explicitly describes how it relates to the preceding literature (Laramee, 2011). Hudson-Barr (2004) states that if the gap between the known and unknown is too large, the author will select only a portion of the problem to address in the current study.

While reading this section of the article, it is important to note the theoretical framework or perspective for the study and operational definitions/terminology (Hudson-Barr, 2004). The theories used in previous research and how they relate to the current study provide a context for the research being described in the article (Edyburn, 2005). Operational definitions provide the reader with working knowledge of the constructs used in past research as well as in the current study. In other words, how is the author defining constructs and terms? Are these terms clearly articulated or are they confused by professional jargon? Readers should be able to understand the author's perspective or lens and see how the research report fits with others in the same field of study. Is this study a new piece of the puzzle that fills a gap in the literature or is it a replication of previous research studies? The author should clearly identify the variables or constructs used in previous research studies and link them to what will follow in the current article.

It is common for this section to include, often toward the end, the research questions or hypotheses that the author is attempting to explain in the article (Hudson-Barr, 2004). The research objectives, questions, or hypotheses explain the author's approach to solving the problem described earlier in the introduction (APA, 2010). The author should describe how these hypotheses or questions were derived from theory or logically related to previous literature in the field of study (APA, 2010). Explaining how the research design allows inferences to be drawn from the data and answer the research questions or examine the hypotheses is an important element in the introduction of the research manuscript (APA, 2010). For those reading the article with the primary purpose of gathering information on a topic of interest as opposed to developing a foundation for their own research project, Hudson-Barr (2004) suggests that it may be possible to skim this section to identify the big ideas, but reminds readers that the primary task is to identify the research questions or hypotheses.

In summary, after completing this section, readers should be able to answer the following questions: Why is this topic important to explore? What is currently known about this topic? How does this study relate to previous work? What are the research objectives, questions or hypotheses? What is the author trying to accomplish, i.e., what are the theoretical and practical implications of the study? (APA, 2010). According to Edyburn (2005), readers might also consider: Do I agree with the author's critique of previous literature? Are there notable omissions? Are the research questions derived from what is already known and what is yet to be considered? Am I convinced of the need for this study? Is the research related to my interests?

Methods and Procedures

Once the research questions are established and justified, the author must decide how to proceed in answering those questions. It is important that the research methods and procedures are clearly explained, allowing the reader to make decisions regarding the quality and applicability of the author's findings. Did the author use the best possible methods to gather the data? Do the findings of the study seem to be applicable to other situations? This section of the research article is often divided into several subsections, including the participant characteristics, sampling procedures, sample size, measures, and research design. If these specific details are omitted from the published article, those who want to replicate the study or conduct a similar study, can contact the author to inquire about the missing information (Hudson-Barr, 2004). Due to the technical nature of data collection and analysis procedures, the Methods section may be one of the most difficult sections in the research article to read and understand, especially for beginning researchers or practitioners (Edyburn, 2005). For those with less interest in the specific details related to the methods and procedures employed in the study, Bogucka & Wood (2009) suggest that a possible order for reading research articles could be ADIR(M); Abstract, Discussion, Introduction, Results, and Methods, with the Methods section being optional.

Participant Characteristics

In order to generalize findings, make comparisons across replicated studies, and to use the information to synthesize research for literature reviews, the author must clearly and thoroughly describe the characteristics of the participants (APA, 2010). Significant characteristics are demographic variables related to age, socioeconomic status, sex, ethnic and/or racial group, occupation, religious affiliation, state of residence, income, marital status, and any other participant characteristics that are relevant to the study. After reading the description, readers should note if there are any pertinent participant characteristics missing. In addition, readers should be aware of the participant eligibility and exclusion criteria and if there were any restrictions based on demographics (APA, 2010). Of particular interest in this section is how these participant characteristics might influence the interpretation of the results and to what degree the results can be generalized to other populations for both the purposes of research and practice. For readers who are researchers, identifying the participant characteristics has implications for the participants that they select to replicate the study or to fill a gap in the literature by selecting different participants. A practitioner reading the article should note the participant characteristics in order to assess whether the results apply to his or her classroom.

Sampling Procedures and Sample Size

Another important consideration in the Methods section of the article is how the participants were selected for the study (Edyburn, 2005). If the participants were randomly selected, then the results of the study should be more easily generalized to other similar populations. In addition, the number of participants who were recruited and participated in the study and the number of participants that volunteered for the study should be reported (APA, 2010; Hudson-Barr, 2004). Participants who were invited to participate based on the use of a random sampling method may be different from those that volunteered for the study or received compensation in exchange for their participation, which may influence how the results should be interpreted. For example, if the author offered participants money to compensate them for completing a survey, then could the money have impacted the participants' level of involvement? It is important that the author transparently describes this component of the study so that the reader can consider its potential impact.

It is also important to note the setting or location in which the data were collected, as well as whether the study was approved by an institutional review board (APA, 2010; Hudson-Barr, 2004). In addition, the response rate in survey research is important to consider. The higher the response rate the better return the author had on his or her completed surveys.

The size of the sample, or the number of the participants, including a description of how the final sample differs from the target population should be clearly described, because conclusions and interpretations of the results should not go beyond what the sample would merit (APA, 2010; Edyburn, 2005). The author may also discuss the power or precision of any inferential statistical tests used to analyze data considering the size of the sample (APA, 2010). Readers should ask, "Am I confident that the sample size and their characteristics are sufficient to represent the population described in the study?"

Measures

This section describes the constructs measured in the research study and the instruments or strategies used to collect the data. The constructs must be explicitly defined by the author. Data collection methods or strategies may include but are not limited to questionnaires, interviews, or observations and the author should describe whether the instruments were developed specifically for the study or adapted from those developed and used in previous research on the topic. Also, the author should describe how he or she enhanced the quality of these measurements, including providing training for the assessors or conducting multiple observations (APA, 2010). Instruments that were used, including their psychometric properties and cultural validity should also be explained in this section of the article (APA, 2010). Reporting how the data were coded, and the reliability (same results over time) and validity (measures what it is supposed to measure) of the instruments are essential to understanding the research measures (Edyburn, 2005; Edyburn, 2009; Hudson-Barr, 2004). In essence, the author should demonstrate "that the right data were collected from the right subjects in the right manner" (Hudson-Barr, 2004, p. 71).

Research Design

According to APA (2010), the description of the research design should include the answers to the following questions: Were the participants in an experimental condition or were they observed naturalistically? If there were multiple conditions, how were subjects assigned to each condition, through random assignment or some other selection procedure? Was the study a between-subjects design or a within-subjects design? Additionally, the research design should include a description of how the data were analyzed (Edyburn, 2005).

There are different ways to report research results depending on the research design (APA, 2010). Regardless of the type of design utilized, the author must thoroughly describe the "who, what, when, where, and how" of the study to allow for replication or opportunity to build on the findings (Edyburn, 2005; Edyburn, 2009). Typically, quantitative or qualitative methods, a combination of both, or multiple methods are used to collect data on a specific construct. It is beyond the scope of this chapter to describe the specifics of research design; therefore, it is advised to refer to other chapters in this book, additional texts addressing research methodology in the field of education, and the APA (2010) Publication Manual for specific descriptions of various methods.

In sum, after reading this section of the article, readers should ask: Were the appropriate participants chosen in the most appropriate manner? Did the author select the appropriate variables or constructs to measure? Did the procedures make sense? Were the data collection procedures and analysis logical (Hudson-Barr, 2004)?

Analyses, Results, and Findings

After describing the methods and procedures used to gather data, the next step is to explain processes used to analyze the data. The purpose of this section is to summarize the data analyses strategies and results in an effort to justify the author's conclusions (APA, 2010). There are countless ways to analyze data, and depending on the type of data collected, the methods used to collect data, and the overall purpose of the study, analysis strategies can range from complex statistical analyses and techniques to qualitative approaches involving massive amounts of narrative text to read and reread in order to identify common themes and patterns. Entire classes are devoted to these strategies and it is beyond the scope of this chapter to delve into the specific details of data analysis. Writers of research are advised to write these sections assuming that the reader has a professional knowledge of data analysis technique (APA, 2010). In reality, readers of research bring varying levels of knowledge and expertise with them to the task of reading data analysis.

For those with limited training or experience in research methodology or data analysis, this is one point in reading a research article when readers may be tempted to give up. The details of data analysis can be complicated and it may take years of specialized training to fully understand various analysis strategies. The goal of this chapter, however, is to encourage readers to continue reading, even if the information in this section seems confusing. Readers may ask, "How can I develop confidence in the author's findings if I don't understand the processes used to analyze the data?" This is a valid question and may inspire the reader to pursue some additional training in the area of data analysis. Some readers, however, may not be interested in enrolling in a statistics course. However, this does not mean that one can't read research articles and benefit from them.

There are other ways to evaluate the quality of data analysis. One way is to examine the medium in which the article is published. Often there are measures in place to ensure that the analysis procedures are solid before the article is published (Hudson-Barr, 2004). For example, as described previously, articles appearing in peer reviewed journals are not published until they have been reviewed by a panel of experts and an editor. If there are questions related to the appropriateness or use of a specific analysis technique, it is likely that the issue will be addressed before it is even in print. This is not a fail-proof method, of course, but it should instill confidence in the reader that the article has most likely been reviewed by someone who has expertise in the area.

More experienced readers will likely view the analysis and results section of a research article through a different, more critical lens than the novice reader. As stated previously, it is beyond the scope of this chapter to provide all of the information the reader will need to read, interpret, and understand data analysis in all the research read. Instead, the information presented here is intended to give the reader a general place to begin the process of considering the meaning and value of the research that is read. It is recommended that readers of research utilize experts in the areas of data analysis, if needed, or additional resources, such as the other chapters in this book, as a guide to deeper understanding of high quality data analysis techniques.

One thing to consider is the appropriateness of the techniques or strategies used to manage and analyze the data that were collected. Readers should feel confident that the strategies used are appropriate for the data collected, purpose of the research study, and the characteristics of the sample. For example, did the author select the appropriate statistical test to use? If qualitative data analysis strategies are employed, are these processes suitable for the data that were collected and the research questions asked? Did the author conduct their selected analysis strategies correctly? Did the author use data analysis software to aid them in the process? In short, the reader should believe that the analysis techniques in use were appropriate for the task at hand and that the author used them in accurate ways.

Once the reader understands the analysis techniques used by the author, he or she can begin to make judgments regarding the integrity of the findings and whether or not the results of the study are convincing. Depending on the processes used, readers can be convinced of the author's findings in a variety of ways. For example, if the author reports the use of an inferential test of statistical significance, such as a t-test or analysis of variance, the reader should pay attention, in part, to whether the results are significant and at what level. If the study was conducted within a qualitative paradigm, using methods such as ethnography, case study, or focus groups, the reader should be convinced that the evidence provided supports the author's findings (Denzin & Lincoln, 2011, Maxwell, 1992). In other words, the author must describe evidence that is "good enough" to convince the reader of the findings' integrity (Altheide & Johnson, 2011). This evidence might include, among other things, a thick description (Geertz, 1973), an adequate number of data excerpts, or address measures of trustworthiness (Lincoln & Guba, 1985). To reiterate a previous point, the examples described here are not meant to provide an exhaustive description of possibilities in need of consideration. The examples are just that—examples—individual readers must decide for themselves which questions to ask, which enables them to develop confidence in the findings presented in individual research articles.

Readers of research should also carefully consider the way in which the author presents or displays the data. For example, many articles include tables, graphs, or charts to communicate information about the findings that can be more efficiently detailed in graphical format. In addition, these data display methods can help the reader make better sense of a large amount of data or data that are especially complex. When reading tables, the reader should pay close attention to the ways in which the tables are constructed, and read all titles and notes for important information about the data being presented. One may be tempted to skim the results section of an article, hoping to obtain an overview of the main findings by focusing primarily on information presented in tables or graphs. It is important, however, to read both text and tables completely and thoroughly. A table is not designed to duplicate the information in the text, but is provided as a supplement that may clarify or add to the information presented in narrative form (APA, 2010).

In sum, when reflecting on this section of the article, readers should be able to identify strategies used to analyze the data, make judgments about the appropriateness of these strategies, develop a sense of confidence in the author's findings, and evaluate the way in which the author presented his or her results to the reader.

Discussion, Interpretations, and Implications

After a thorough discussion of procedures, analyses, and results, authors will offer their interpretations and explanations as to what their research findings mean for early childhood professionals. This may take many different forms, but many times these sections are titled "Discussion" or "Implications." Many readers find this to be the most interesting and beneficial portion of the article, in which the author examines his or her analysis and offers interpretations and explanations as to what the results might mean. Most likely, the author will explain how the findings relate to the original purpose of the research study and describe how, if at all, the findings provide answers or insights into the original research questions or hypotheses (APA, 2010). In many cases, the author will also relate the findings back to the literature review and explain how these findings can be situated within the existing literature. A good example of this can be found in a portion of the article written by Tang, Dearing, and Weiss (2012) in which they examined the impact of early childhood teachers, who were fluent in both Spanish and English, on children's literacy. In their literature review, the authors laid the foundation for their investigation, in part, by citing research that described a positive association between family involvement and children's achievements. In addition, they cited literature calling for more early childhood teachers who are fluent in both Spanish and English. After completing their study, Tang and colleagues found that in classrooms in which teachers spoke both Spanish and English, families whose home language was Spanish were more involved in school activities. In their discussion section, the authors then brought the reader back to their literature review, stating that the findings of their research further substantiate the recommendation for more early childhood teachers to become fluent in Spanish and English and that this might encourage families who speak Spanish to become more involved in their child's classroom experiences, thus having a positive impact on the achievement of their children.

The "Discussion" or "Implications" section of a research article will also likely include the authors' suggestions or recommendations, based on their findings, which are useful for the reader when incorporating the research into his or her work with young children. For example, in one study designed to examine the necessity of assessing toddler's book knowledge in order to support their developing literacy skills, the author recommends that teachers assess toddlers' book knowledge by informally observing them during frequent book reading opportunities and then suggests several specific strategies for doing so (Lee, 2011).

Recommendations for others wishing to engage in this line of research may be included in this section, as well. A study conducted by Nicholson and Reifel (2011) illustrates this point. In concluding their account of a study exploring child care teachers' perceptions of their training experiences, the authors suggested the need for future research to further explore the ways in which early childhood teachers learn from one another as a way to better understand how to support the improvement of their child care practices. Many times, the results of a research study generate many new questions in need of exploration. Reading the conclusion will frequently offer new ideas for readers to explore, often with some suggestions about where to begin and how to proceed.

In addition to offering interpretations and recommendations, authors will often describe any limitations that should be considered when reading this research and address any alternative explanation of the results (APA, 2010; Hudson-Barr, 2004). This information is useful for the reader in that it helps to identify any variables or circumstances that may have directly or indirectly influenced the outcome of the study. For example, there may be variables for which the authors were unable to control that may have, in some way, influenced the results of the analyses. In addition, the author may caution the reader to keep specific information in mind either when interpreting the results of the study or generalizing the information to another population. For example, if the sample size studied is small or the participants homogeneous, authors might recommend that readers do not overgeneralize to larger or more diverse populations. In fact, they may recommend that future studies looking at this topic utilize larger or more diverse populations.

Generally, the authors will conclude this section with a concise description of the importance of their findings, leaving the reader with a clear idea of what the authors believe to be the unique contributions of their research. In conclusion, Edyburn (2005) suggests that readers ask the following questions about the conclusions presented in this section of the article: What were the major findings of this study? What limitations may have impacted the findings? Based on the results of this study, what additional research is needed? What are the implications for practice?

REFERENCES

The reference list can serve as a valuable resource for readers of research and should be given more than just a passing glance. Beyond the obvious purpose of providing the reader with publication details about the works cited in the article and how to locate them (APA, 2010), readers can gather other important information from the reference list. First, readers should pay close attention to the names that are cited in the reference list. Are those listed considered to be leaders in their area of expertise? Are there experts whose work is not included that should be considered when exploring this topic? This information can help the reader make judgments about the completeness of the information included the article and whether or not the reader should engage in additional research to consider the topic in a more comprehensive way. The publication date of the referenced work is another important point for readers to consider. Readers should feel confident that the works cited in the article reflect the most current perspectives within the field. Exceptions to this point may occur when works that are considered to be "classic" are cited.

For individuals designing and conducting research, the reference list can serve as an important tool to aid in the process of locating additional articles related to one's own research project. This strategy can supplement searches done on databases available through libraries or other search engines. The reference list will often lead readers to additional work that may have been overlooked through other means of information gathering.

SUMMARY AND CONCLUSION

Early childhood professionals are required to be aware of current advances in the field of education, which involves reading, evaluating, and utilizing research. Reading research is critical to their work whether they are researchers, practitioners, policymakers, or teacher educators. This article provides information that can serve as a first step in utilizing research as a means of strengthening their work with, or on behalf of, young children and their families. In closing, the following list provides a summary of questions to consider while reading research and is designed to serve as a guide in thinking about the process of reading and interpreting early childhood research.

Author and Journal

- What is known about the authors and their affiliations?
- Are the authors or publishers associated with any special interest groups?
- Is the journal considered to be of high quality?

The Abstract

- What information is provided in the abstract?
- Would it be beneficial to read this article in its entirety?

The Introduction

- What does a review of existing literature reveal about the topic being studied?
- What is the purpose of this study?
- Does the review of literature provide a solid rationale for the current study?
- What are the research questions/hypotheses?

Methods and Procedures

- Who are the participants in the study? What are their characteristics?
- How were the participants selected for the study?
- Is the sample size sufficient to justify the authors' findings?
- What measures or instruments were used to collect data? How were these measures implemented?
- What is the research design of the study?
- Is sufficient detail provided in order for someone to replicate the study, if desired?

Analyses, Results, and Findings

- How did the authors analyze the data?
- Did the authors select the appropriate tools for analysis?
- Did the authors use the analysis tools correctly?
- Is there confidence in the authors' account of the results/findings?
- What information can be gained from the tables or other graphical presentations included in the article?

Discussion, Interpretations, and Implications

- How did the authors interpret the results?
- Are there limitations to consider when evaluating the findings of this research?
- What new questions were generated based on this research?
- What unique contributions does this research make to the field of study?
- What does this research mean for future research or practice?

References

- Are the leading experts in the field represented in the reference list?
- Are the references current in relation to the research done on this topic?
- Are there articles listed that should be located for further information?

NOTES

1. This chapter is based on an article previously published in *Early Childhood Education Journal.* See Baum, A. C. and McMurray-Schwarz, P. (2007).
2. For more information about the Carnegie Foundation for Advancement of Teaching and the Carnegie Classification of Institutions of Higher Education please refer to their website at www.carnegiefoundation.org.

REFERENCES

American Psychological Association (APA) (2009). *Publication Manual of the American Psychological Association* (6th ed.). Washington, DC: American Psychological Association.

Altheide, D. L., & Johnson, J. M. (2011). Reflections on interpretive adequacy in qualitative research. In N. K. Denzin & Y. S. Lincoln (Eds.), *The SAGE handbook of qualitative research* (pp. 581–594). Thousand Oaks, CA: Sage.

Andrade, C. (2011). How to read a research paper: Reading between and beyond the lines. *Indian Journal of Psychiatry, 53*(4), 362–366.

Baum, A. C., & McMurray-Schwarz, P. (2007). Research 101: Tools for reading and interpreting early childhood research. *Early Childhood Education Journal, 34*(6), 367–370.

Bogucka, R., & Wood, E. (2009). How to read scientific research articles: A hands-on classroom exercise. *Issues in Science and Technology Librarianship, 59*, 1–9.

Crosser, S. (2005). *What do we know about early childhood education? Research based practice.* New York, NY: Thomson Delmar Learning.

Cryer, D., Wagner-Moore, L., Burchinal, M., Yazejian, N., Hurwitz, S., & Wolery, M. (2005). Effects of transitions to new child care classes on infant/toddler distress and behavior. *Early Childhood Research Quarterly, 20*(1), 37–56. doi: 10.1016/j.ecresq.2005.01.005.

Denzin, N. K., & Lincoln, Y. S. (2011). The discipline and practice of qualitative research. In N. K. Denzin & Y. S. Lincoln (Eds.), *The SAGE handbook of qualitative research* (pp. 1–25). Thousand Oaks, CA: Sage.

Edyburn, D. L. (2005). How to read a special education technology research article. *Journal of Special Education Technology, 20*(2), 47–49.

Edyburn, D. L. (2009). Using research to inform practice. *Special Education Technology Practice, 11*(5), 21–28.

Feldt, R. C., & Moore, R. E. (1999). Learning how to read empirical research articles: An application of a modified version of SQ3R. *Reading Improvement, 36*(3), 102–108.

Geertz, C. (1973). Thick description: Toward an interpretive theory of culture. In C. Geertz (Ed.). *The interpretation of cultures* (pp. 3–30). New York, NY: Basic Books.

Hudson-Barr, D. (2004). How to read a research article. *Journal for Specialists in Pediatric Nursing, 9*(2), 70–72.

Laramee, R. S. (2011). How to read a visualization research paper: Extracting the essentials. *IEEE Computer Graphics and Applications, 31*(3), 78–82.

Lee, B. H. (2011). Assessing book knowledge through independent reading in the earliest years: Practical strategies and implications for teachers. *Early Childhood Education Journal, 39*(4), 285–290.

Lincoln, Y. S., & Guba, E. G. (1985). *Naturalistic inquiry.* Beverly Hills, CA: Sage.

Maxwell, J. (1992). Understanding and validity in qualitative research. *Harvard Educational Review, 62*(3), 279–301.

Program for Infant/Toddler Care, "PITC's Six Program Policies" (2008). Retrieved from http://www.pitc.org/pub/pitc_docs/138?x-r=disp.

Nicholson, S., & Reifel, S. (2011). Sink or swim: Child care teachers' perceptions of entry training experiences. *Journal of Early Childhood Teacher Education, 32*(1), 5–25.

Salkind, N. J. (2012). *Exploring research.* (8th Ed.). Boston, MA: Pearson.

Saracho, O. (2013). Writing research articles for publication in early childhood education. *Early Childhood Education Journal, 41*(1), 45–54.

Stremmel, A. J. (2002). Teacher research: Nurturing professional and personal growth through inquiry. *Young Children, 57,* 62–70.

Tang, S., Dearing, E., & Weiss, H. B. (2012). Spanish speaking Mexican-American families' involvement in school based activities and their children's literacy: The implications of having teachers who speak Spanish and English. *Early Childhood Research Quarterly, 27*(2), 177–187.

CHAPTER 24

ELEMENTS IN WRITING SCIENTIFIC RESEARCH PUBLICATIONS

Olivia N. Saracho

INTRODUCTION

Scholarly productivity in peer-reviewed research journals strongly affects hiring, tenure, and promotion decisions (Martínez, Floyd, & Erichsen, 2011). Research universities use research publications to make decisions concerning salary, promotion, and tenure (Nihalani & Mayrath, 2008). Thus, publishing becomes the major responsibility of tenure-track professors. The expectation for scholars to publish their research has become a universal pressure in academia. High publication rates indicate the performance of both the individuals and institutions. In spite of the publication requirement to publish, academic publication productivity continues to be low (McGrail, Rickard, & Jones, 2006). When academics lack the framework or formal structure to continue with their writing, they discontinue their productivity (Morss & Murray, 2001). Novice researchers need assurance, professional support, and encouragement (Baldwin & Chandler, 2002) to develop their writing skills. Many academics are afraid and anxious about writing (Lee & Boud, 2003), misinterpret the writing and

Handbook of Research Methods in Early Childhood Education, pages 801–817
Copyright © 2015 by Information Age Publishing
All rights of reproduction in any form reserved.

publication approach, and develop emotional difficulties (e.g., a fear of rejection, fear of competition). Some are unsure of which ideas are worth publishing (Dies, 1993) whereas those with important ideas doubt that they have the writing ability (Grant & Knowles, 2000). Several researchers are prolific writers, but some novice researchers have trouble with the writing and publication process.

Writing for publication involves a well developed level of writing skills; but many academics lack the knowledge on how to become productive writers, especially those novice researchers who did not receive this type of preparation in their graduate courses (Murray & Newton, 2008). The graduate students' extensive writing experience did not include the preparation to publish professionally. Since most graduate students did not have the advantage of enrolling in a formal course in writing for publication, they implemented their professors' writing style. Afterward as beginning researchers, they used their educational readings to imitate those authors' writing style as well as all their flaws, which led them to generate consistent and systematic mistakes (Day & Sakaduski, 2011). Most of their learning about writing for publication was based on a twist of fate and relying on influential advisers to substantially help novice researchers through the publication path. However, advisers assumed that the most competent graduate students would develop their publication skills and be able to publish on their own (Jalongo, 2013).

How to write research publications is ambiguous. Many authors have written standard conventional texts on how to write for publication. Unfortunately, such texts neglect to specify the actual techniques that novice researchers must know to be able to publish (Murray & Newton, 2008). Researchers without this knowledge tend to encounter difficulties in writing a research article (Derntl, 2011). A publishable manuscript needs to be well written and provide details of the original research based on specific requirements on how to write and publish a scientific research report (Day & Sakaduski, 2011).

The purpose of this article is to describe the process of manuscript preparation in such a way that it can serve as a guide for inexperienced researchers in all disciplines. Finally, it describes the publication process. Since journals differ in their requirements, it is impossible to provide recommendations that are universally acceptable. Therefore, general basic standards that most journals from different disciplines accept will be provided.

A VALID AND ACCEPTABLE RESEARCH PUBLICATION

Researchers, students, authors, editors, and all others involved need to know the requirements of a well-*written* and *published* study that describes *original* research results. There are certain requirements on *how* the paper is written and published. The process, content, style, and development of the publication have equal importance. A study that is published in the appropriate research journal (e.g., peer-reviewed journal in the appropriate field) is considered a *valid publication* and is referred to as a scientific research publication. Studies that are published in newspapers, proceedings, newsletters, conference reports, internal reports, newspapers, or anywhere else are not considered a scientific publication. In addition, government reports, conference proceedings, institutional bulletins, and other ephemeral publications do not meet the criteria of a scientific publication (Day & Sakaduski, 2011). According to the Council of Biology Editors (CBE):

> An acceptable primary scientific publication must be the first disclosure containing sufficient information to enable peers (1) to assess observations, (2) to repeat experiments, and (3) to evaluate intellectual processes; moreover, it must be susceptible to sensory perception, essentially permanent, available to the scientific community without restriction, and available for regular screening by one or more of the major recognized secondary services (Council of Biology Editors Newsletter, 1968, pp. 1–2) such as educational abstracts, databases, and indices.

To update this definition, an ad hoc committee was charged to revise and renew the term "scientific publication." The committee members considered the definition that was published in the 1968 newsletter. The ad hoc committee determined that the original definition had insight, accuracy, and meticulousness; therefore, the Board and the Committee recommended that the definition by the Council of Biology Editors (1968) be used as a present interpretation of a scientific research publication (Stegemann & Gastel, 2009).

Writing a research study in a scientific style can be challenging. It may be threatening to both novice researchers and some experienced researchers. However, if they follow a reasonable and methodical process, they can lessen this emotion (Cunningham, 2004).

STANDARD STRUCTURE OF A PUBLISHABLE MANUSCRIPT

Researchers need to keep records of their work for themselves, the readers, and peer researchers who expect a standard form, language, and style when they read a research study. They need to communicate their research clearly and concisely (Johansson, 2004). Studies need to follow a set of principles in presenting a body of scientific information in a rationally smooth and logical manner. The following sections describe the structure of the research publication.

The standard structure of a scientific research report includes a title, an abstract, and four sections that consist of introduction, methodology, results, and discussion (IMRaD). According to Johansson (2004), the IMRaD format is structured in the following way:

Introduction: *What* question was studied and why?
Methodology: *How* was the problem studied?
Results: *What* were the findings?
   and
Discussion: *What* do these findings mean?

In a few words, IMRaD is the format that researchers use in reporting their research. It provides an appropriate and comprehensive description of a research study to help readers determine *what* is known, *what* is not known, and *why* the study was carried out (Introduction); *who* were the subjects, *what* were the materials/instruments and procedures, and *how* were the results determined based on the materials/instruments and procedures (Methodology); *what* was discovered (Results), and *what* is the significance and meaning of the study (Discussion) (Todorovic, 2003). Table 24.1 provides a summary of each section that develops in sequential order throughout the research manuscript. For example, the introduction is followed by the methodology, after that the results, and lastly the discussion (Sharp, 2002). Additionally, conclusion, references, appendices, and acknowledgments are part of the manuscript.

Title

Since readers typically read the title first to determine if the study is relevant to their research, it must provide them with accurate information. In addition, electronic indexing services seriously rely on the description in the title to guide readers in searching for any related literature. Day and Sakaduski (2011) state that an appropriate title contains "... the fewest possible words that adequately describe the contents of the paper" (p. 9) and the sixth edition of the American Psychological Association's (APA, 2010) style manual establishes a limit of 12 words on article titles. A long title usually contains an excessive amount of *wasted words* like titles that begin with "Investigations on..." On the other hand, short titles are very general and unclear. For instance, the title, "Writing Reports" needs more information about the study. As a result, every word in the title must be meticulously chosen, be associated to other words, and appropriately arranged. Peat, Elliott, Baur, and Keena (2002) propose that acceptable titles should (a) establish the manuscript's key problem; (b) begin with its topic; (c) be accurate, understandable, explicit, and complete; (d) avoid using abbreviations; and (e) be of interest to readers. For example,

TABLE 24.1 Components of a Scientific Research Publication

Component	Content
Title	Helps the reader understand the nature of the research study and determine if they wish to read it
Abstract	Provides a complete but concise description of the study – Gives a brief summary using a word limit that usually ranges between 200 to 300 words – Includes key words for index listing and on-line search for databases
Introduction	Uses brief descriptions of previous related studies to support the current research – Provides a theoretical framework to justify the need for the current research study – Concludes with the hypotheses or research questions and the purpose of the study
Methodology	Describes everything that is needed to replicate the study such as it: – Explains and justifies the methodology used – Describes, procedures, materials, measures, analyses, and subjects used (including ethics and consent) – Describes and justifies the sample size calculation – Describes and justifies the statistics used to analyze the data
Results	Describes all findings (including significant, negative, and nonsignificant results) – Complements the description of the outcomes with appropriate tables, graphs, and figures
Discussion	Emphasizes the major findings and compares them with findings from previous related studies – Discusses any limitations of the study – Provides recommendations for future research and practice
References	Provides complete references that were cited in the text – Uses the current edition of the APA style to cite references in text and to list them in the references' section

Note: Adapted from Cunningham's (2004) original table.

Saracho, (2008) examined a family literacy intervention program to document the literacy experiences of 25 fathers and their five-year-old children. Such intervention program was designed to assist fathers to promote their children's acquisition of literacy. She found that the fathers who learned literacy strategies and activities were able to contribute to their children's literacy development. The title of this article was "Fathers and young children's literacy experiences." In a different study, Saracho (1992) investigated the relationship between 300 three- to five-year-old children's cognitive style and their social play and the relationship's implications for creativity. She tested their cognitive style (field dependence independence) and recorded their play behaviors in relation to their cognitive style and creativity. A repeated measures multivariate analysis of variance indicated that children played differently based on their cognitive style and creativity. The title of this article was, " Preschool Children's Cognitive Style and Play and Implications for Creativity."

Abstract

Abstracts are at the beginning of the manuscript. Typically, readers only read the abstract to identify studies in a specific area. Also other researchers may only use the abstracts to determine their relevance to their study. Therefore, the information in the abstracts is of critical importance. Researchers need to check and make sure that their abstract provides a brief and comprehensive summary that matches the text of the manuscript (Sharp, 2002). Since abstracts summarize the whole study in one paragraph, it is important how the abstract is written, which means that the abstract briefly describes the content in the manuscript.

Abstracts are restricted to a word count that ranges between 200 and 300 words or less. Since the word count limits the amount of information in the abstract, it is essential that the abstract provides a comprehensive summary. Thus, abstracts provide a brief but complete information in a well organized, well written, and clearly understood style. They offer a comprehensive aspect of the study by describing its purpose, methodology, major results, and conclusions. An abstract must stand on its own and be independent of the manuscript to guide researchers to instantly determine if the study is relevant to their research (Selvanathan Udani, Udani, & Haylett, 2006). Boxes 24.1 and 24.2 provide examples of an abstract. In the first example, Saracho (1983) investigated the significance of matching the cognitive styles of first and third-grade students to their teachers in relation to both the teachers' perceptions of their students' academic competence based on the students' sex and grade level. In the second example, Saracho (2010) examined a literacy program for Hispanic fathers and their children.

Journal editors generally ask researchers for key words that describe or classify their study. These key words are included in the manuscript's title page (Sharp, 2002), although journals usually include them below the abstract. Sometimes readers look at the key words to determine the relevance to their study. Thus, this increases the abstract's importance. For example, for this chapter key words may consist of *writing research studies, developing research manuscripts,* and/or *scholarly writing.*

Introduction

The introduction critically reviews and analyzes findings of relevant studies to provide a justification for the researcher's study. These related studies provide

> **BOX 24.1   ABSTRACT**
>
> **FIRST EXAMPLE**
>
> The study investigated the significance of matching the cognitive style of first- and third-grade students to their teachers. The Articulation of the Body-Concept Scale was administered as a measure of cognitive style to 20 first- and 20 third-grade female teachers and a sample ($n = 480$) of six boys and six girls for each teacher. Teachers ranked their students according to their judgment of the students' academic competence. Discrepancy scores were obtained based on the degree to which teachers differed in ranking their students in comparison to rankings on the Comprehensive Tests of Basic Skills. A repeated measures analysis of variance indicated statistically significant main effects for grade level and a statistically significant interaction among the cognitive styles of teachers in ranking their matched and mismatched students according to sex in relation to the students' academic achievement scores (Saracho, 1983, p. 184).
>
> From Saracho, O.N. (1983). Relationship between cognitive style and teachers' perceptions of young children's academic competence. *Journal of Experimental Education, 51*(4), 184–189.

> **BOX 24.2   ABSTRACT**
>
> **SECOND EXAMPLE**
>
> This study examined a language and cultural literacy program for Hispanic fathers to promote their children's literacy development. This study had two phases: (a) training the teachers, and (b) educating the fathers. The results indicated that the fathers learned how to promote their Hispanic children's literacy development using their family's language, culture, interests, and experiences. Fathers differed in their use of language, culture, literacy strategies, literacy experiences, and responses to the literacy program (Saracho, 2010, p. 281).
>
> From Saracho, O. N. (2010). A culturally responsive literacy program for Hispanic fathers and their children. *Journal of Hispanic Higher Education, 9*(4), 281–293.

a theoretical framework and support the researcher's research questions/hypotheses and methodology including their choice of qualitative, quantitative, or mixed methods procedures. The introduction includes (a) the research questions or hypotheses and the way they will be addressed, (b) the purpose of the study, (c) the materials/instruments and procedures that were used to conduct the study, (d) the expected outcomes, and (e) the rationale (including the theoretical framework) that influenced the research questions/ hypotheses. The introduction should be approximately one-fourth of the complete length of the manuscript (Udani, Selvanathan, Udani, & Haylett, 2007). Box 24.3 provides an example of research questions from an early childhood education study while Box 24.4 provides an example of the purpose of the study.

Methodology

Researchers can keep a journal to record all of the study's information and results to make it easy to write a comprehensive description about the study. The description provides specific information that assists researchers

---

BOX 24.3 RESEARCH QUESTIONS

The following research questions can be used with the study that is summarized in Saracho's (1983) abstract.

- What are the effects of the teachers' cognitive styles (more field dependent or more field independent) on their students' standardized achievement scores?
- Are there differential effects for grade levels or for students who match or fail to match the teachers' cognitive styles?

BOX 24.4 PURPOSE OF THE STUDY

Several studies on parents' reading to children have examined the use of storybooks, but the genre of the books being read has usually been ignored (Anderson, Anderson, Lynch, & Shapiro, 2004). A few studies (e.g., Bus, van IJzendoorn, & Pellegrini, 1995, Torr, 2007) have examined the parents reading stories to their children in relation to two genres (information and narrative texts). The present study expanded that number of genres. Its purpose was to examine the frequency and nature of story reading at home and their selection of children's literature books, the parents' perceptions about literacy, and their literacy involvement in their home environment. The results from studies on shared book reading between parents and children were used to develop a plan for parents to learn to effectively read stories to their children. It also attempted to identify the literacy experiences that parents shared with their children (Saracho & Spodek, 2010, p. 402).

From: Saracho, O. N., & Spodek, B. (2010). Families' selection of children's literature books. *Early Childhood Education Journal, 37*(5), 401–409.

to understand and duplicate the study. It also cites any procedures that were used and modified from related studies. Finally, the analyses (e.g., statistical methodology, software package) of the data are explained (Udani et al., 2007). The methodology section describes the (a) scientific procedures; (b) subjects, measures, materials, and equipment; and (c) procedures that were used in the study. Briefly, it defines the sources of evidence and the analyses of the data (Maloy, 2001). The following boxes provide examples of some of the methodology (See Box 24.5 for subjects, Box 24.6 for measures, Box 24.7 for materials, and Box 24.8 for procedures).

BOX 24.5 SUBJECTS

The subjects were 1276 children from Head Start, child-care, nursery school, and university early childhood centers located in California, Maryland, Pennsylvania, and Texas. Sixty classrooms were used, with the enrollment ranging between 20 and 25 children per classroom. To control for age and sex differences, children were randomly selected from these classrooms to include an equal number from each age and sex group. Specifically, there were 424 three-year-olds (212 girls, 212 boys), 424 four-year-aids (212 girls, 212 boys) and 428 five-year-olds (214 girls, 214 boys). Thus, the sample selection was diverse (e.g., different geographic areas, ethnic groups, and socioeconomic levels). Children were selected from classrooms where teachers volunteered to participate in the study. Permission was also solicited from the children's parents and only subjects with parental permission were selected (Saracho, 1996, p. 867).

From: Saracho, O. N. (1996). The relationship between the cognitive style and play behaviors of 3 to 5-year-old children. *Personality and Individual Differences, 21*(6), 863–876.

BOX 24.6 MEASURES

Two measures were used in the study: (a) the Preschool Embedded Figures Test (PEFT) to assess cognitive style and (b) the Play Rating Scale (PRS) to record the children's play behaviors. Because children engaged in the play of their choice, the observations in the PRS were assumed to represent a better indicator of children's play than would children's verbal comments about their play (Saracho, 1992, pp. 36–37). Descriptions of these measures as well as their reliability and validity estimates are described in the sections that follow.

From: Saracho, O. N. (1992). The Relationship between Preschool Children's Cognitive Style and Play: Implications for Creativity. *The Creativity Research Journal, 5*(1), 35–47.

> ### BOX 24.7   MATERIALS
>
> A variety of materials were used in the family literacy program including children's books, family photographs, comic strips from the newspapers, magazine pictures, and items from the home environment. Children's books were those that were appropriate for the family's children such as young children's interests and concerns. Family photographs, comic strips, and magazine pictures that encouraged storytelling were used to create stories. Objects from the home environment that could be used in an activity to extend a story from the children's books were also used (Saracho, 2000b, p. 136).
>
> From Saracho, O. N. (2000b). Enhancing young children's home literacy experiences, *International Journal of Early Childhood Education, 5,* 135–141.

> ### BOX 24.8   PROCEDURES
>
> Kindergarten pupils were individually administered the PEFT to determine their cognitive style, selecting only those kindergarten pupils representing the top third (FD) and the bottom third (FI) scores in the PEFT. They were identified as FD or FI. Then these kindergarten pupils were individually interviewed using the FDIC Scale to obtain their descriptions of their preferred teacher. Scores for the 10 statements in the FDIC Scale were obtained for each pupil. Though many researchers avoid specifying the characteristics related to being rated as a good teacher, Dor-Shave and Peleg (1989) show that pupil behavior is a reliable measure of 'goodness' as seen from the kindergarten pupils' point of view. In addition, Renninger and Snyder (1983) found that young children are sensitive to differences related to the teachers' FDI cognitive style including their enjoyment and interaction with the FD and FI teachers (Saracho, 2001, p. 202).
>
> From: Saracho, O. N. (2001). Cognitive style and kindergarten pupils' preferences for teachers, *Learning and Instruction, 11,* 195–209.

Sources of Evidence

The methodology section provides details concerning the study's sources of evidence, data, and experimental materials that were used to respond to the research questions, hypotheses, or problem. Sources of evidence include measures, materials, subjects, research sites, groups, events, and/or any other components that are part of the study. The characteristics, procedures, and basis for their selection need to be described and justified to help researchers replicate the study.

In addition, the methodology section describes and justifies the data, empirical materials, and procedures that were use. Data are gathered across cases or units of research analyses using participant and nonparticipant observations; unstructured or semi-structured interviews; documents and other artifacts; audio- or video-recordings; and standardized measures which may include surveys, tests, structured interview protocols, and categorical demographic information (American Educational Research Association, 2006).

Data Analyses

Since researchers frequently collect more data than they need, it is important that they only select the data and analyses (e.g., analyses of variance, factor analyses) that address their research questions or hypotheses. The data analyses are justified and described in detail to help researchers understand the data analyses, processes, outcomes, and assumptions that are required in the specific methods (e.g., content analysis, discourse or text analysis, deliberation analysis, time use analysis, network analysis, event history analysis). The analyses and report of the results concentrate on the research questions/hypotheses to justify them or conclusions that emerge from the research (American Educational Research Association, 2006). See Box 24.9 for an example of analysis.

BOX 24.9   ANALYSIS

The design of the study involved two blocking factors, grade level (second and fifth) and cognitive style of classroom teacher (field dependent and field independent). In addition, there were repeated measures per classroom for matched and mismatched children. Since pre-CTBS and post-CTBS scores were available, the techniques of analysis of covariance (ANCOVA) were utilized, with the pre-CTBS scores serving as the covariate.

In the initial analyses of the data, separate means for males and females were computed per classroom. However, all effects associated with sex were nonsignificant (for ease of presentation, the sex variable was omitted from the current discussion).

From: Saracho, O.N., & Dayton, C.M. (1980). Relationship of teachers' cognitive styles to pupils' academic achievement gains. *Journal of Educational Psychology, 72*(4), 544–549.

Results

The results section needs to be brief but comprehensible. It provides a brief explanation (a sentence or two) about the study and discusses only those findings that relate to the hypotheses/research questions based on the data (Maloy, 2001). Since researchers usually obtain more data than they can publish, they need to reduce their presentation of the results and only report those that are relevant to their hypotheses/research questions. Readers are not interested in raw data. However, the raw data must be stored, because interested researchers (e.g., journal editors, referees, journal readers) may ask to check the raw data (Sharp, 2002). See Box 24.10 for an example of results.

Researchers need to discuss their results based on their research questions/hypotheses. Presenting unrelated data, tables, and analyses will disregard the purpose of the study. If only a small number of results are significant, the results should be discussed in the text of the manuscript. However, major findings that use multiple data points can clearly communicate their meaning when they are displayed in tables or figures. In addition, they need to be summarized in the text. Each finding does not need a separate table or figure. The results' section discusses a few statistical outcomes or provides a straightforward explanation of the findings in the text instead of displaying them in a table or figure. The information in the text about the findings needs to refer to the tables and figures in relation to the hypotheses/research questions. In addition, the results section integrates statistical parameters

---

BOX 24.10 RESULTS

To understand the patterns in the kindergarten pupils' responses more precisely, means and standard deviations for FD and FI kindergarten pupils' preferences for selecting the teachers' FDI characteristics are displayed in Table 3, the FD and FI kindergarten pupils' rankings of their preferred FDI characteristics are presented in Table 4, and the univariate and multivariate F ratios are revealed in Tables 5–7. The kindergarten pupils' responses to the FDI descriptions were significant at the 0.0001 level for the multivariate F values (Table 5) and Wilks' Lambda Criterion (Table 6). Significant univariate F ratios can be observed in Table 7. Significant interactions were found for

1. The kindergarten pupils' preferences based on their cognitive style, total score for the FDI characteristics, and individual scores for each FDI characteristic and
2. The total score for the FDI characteristics and individual scores for each FDI characteristic.

Thus, the characteristics preferred by FD and FI kindergarten pupils consist of:

1. Teachers with FD characteristics received higher ratings.
2. FD kindergarten pupils preferred FD teachers (a FD match).
3. FI kindergarten pupils preferred FI teachers (a FI match) (Saracho, 2001, p. 203)

From: Saracho, O. N. (2001). Cognitive style and kindergarten pupils' preferences for teachers, *Learning and Instruction, 11*, 195–209.

that reinforce the reported findings. Tables with considerable amounts of data should be avoided. A graphical interpretation provides a better interpretation; therefore, some researchers use a graph rather than a table to communicate their findings. It is important that the titles, tables, and figures are self-explanatory without referring to the text (Cunningham, 2004).

Discussion

The discussion section provides a critical analysis, comparison, and discussion of the results in relation to the research problem, research questions/hypotheses, and methods. The outcomes in the study are compared to those in related studies. In this section, researchers discuss how (a) they interpreted the data, (b) the research questions or hypotheses are accepted or rejected, and (c) the outcomes are compared to those of previous studies. They also explain the study's limitations and suggest ways to decrease these limitations (Udani et al., 2007). Researchers interpret the most important outcomes including (a) the patterns, principles, and relationships that are found in the outcomes; (b) how the study's outcomes support or disagree with the outcomes found in related studies; (c) explanations for any agreements, inconsistencies, or exclusions; and (d) recommendations for future research that might focus on eliminating the study's limitations. In addition, researchers explain the theoretical implications, practical applications, techniques that can be used in different situations, and in what ways the study's outcomes offer a better understanding of the area under study. These interpretations lead to the conclusions that (a) are comprehensive descriptions with appropriate evidence for each conclusion and (b) discuss possible reasons for the expected and unexpected outcomes. Researchers need to discuss their assessment of any agreement, contradiction, knowledge gap, and possible outcomes that lead the manuscript to the conclusion (Maloy, 2001).

Conclusion

Several researchers add a conclusion to summarize the results. It begins with a basic presentation that is short and to the point of the most important findings. The researchers use related studies to justify the importance of their results. They compare the results of other related studies to determine the significance of the study's outcomes (Maloy, 2001). Then researchers finish this section with four or five most important conclusions, which can be displayed by means of bullet points to provide the maximum effects (Cunningham, 2004). Sometimes researchers provide their recommendations for future studies as part of their conclusion.

References

Published studies that justify and support the researcher's study are discussed and referenced in the manuscript to propose a basis for the study. Therefore, references must be accurate sources of information. References are cited in the text and are listed in alphabetical order at the end of the manuscript (Derntl, 2011). Many styles of referencing are available, but the majority of journals expect for authors to use the guidelines from the latest edition of the *American Psychological Association (APA,* 2010) style. In developing a manuscript, authors follow these guidelines for the references section and the text in the manuscript.

Appendices

The appendices section contains information that can assist readers to understand the study's procedures and results. For instance, Saracho and Spodek (2010) examined the families' preference of children's literature books for joint story reading. They found that families chose children's literature books that were developmentally appropriate and were based on the children's interests, concerns, and age group. Saracho and Spodek (2010) displayed the books that the families selected in an appendix at the end of the article, while Saracho (2000a) included the Family Literacy Questionnaire that she used to survey the families' perceptions of their contributions to promote their young children's acquisition of literacy.

Acknowledgements

Some researchers receive support when they conduct research and/ or develop the manuscript. Researchers usually acknowledge anyone who provided assistance, which ranges from receiving financial assistance, help with empirical methods, to individuals who offered comments and advise on the final manuscript. Box 24.11 provides an acknowledgement for financial support.

BOX 24.11   ACKNOWLEDGEMENTS

This research was supported by the General Research Board at the University of Maryland. The opinions expressed in this article do not reflect the positions, policy, or endorsement of the University (Saracho, 1983, p. 189).

Saracho, O.N. (1983). Relationship between cognitive style and teachers' perceptions of young children's academic competence. *Journal of Experimental Education, 51*(4), 184–189.

FINAL COMMENTARIES

Writing scientific research publications is as complicated as designing and conducting studies. Developing a manuscript requires clear and accurate thinking to be able to articulate a clear understanding about the study. Also when writing the manuscript, researchers need to select the journal that is most appropriate for their manuscript and follow the journal's guidelines in writing the manuscript. The journal's website provides this information and describes the journal's background and target audience. This information assists researchers to select the most appropriate journal for their study. For example, Table 24.2 presents the journals in early childhood

TABLE 24.2 Early Childhood Education Journals

Early Childhood Education Journal	• Examines early childhood education issues, trends, policies, and practices • Supports points of view and practical recommendations
Early Child Development and Care	• Publishes studies on all facets of early child development and care • Includes descriptive and evaluative articles on social, educational and preventive medical programs for young children, experimental and observational studies, critical reviews and summary articles
Journal of Research in Childhood Education Affiliated with the Association for Childhood Education International (ACEI)	• Publishes articles that advance knowledge and theory for the education of children (birth through early adolescence) • Includes reports of empirical research, theoretical articles, ethnographic and case studies, participant observation studies, and studies using data collected from naturalistic settings. • Has cross-cultural studies and international concerns
Early Education and Development (EE&D)	• Publishes articles that focus on educational and preschool services • Publishes studies on children and their families • Includes implications for practice of research and solid scientific information
Early Childhood Research Quarterly (ECRQ) Affiliated with the National Association for the Education of Young Children (NAEYC)	• Publishes empirical research (quantitative or qualitative) on early childhood development, theory, and educational practice
Early Childhood Research & Practice (ECRP)	• First open-access, peer-reviewed, bilingual Internet journal in early childhood education and care
Journal of Early Childhood Research	• Offers an international forum for empirical research on learning and development in early childhood • Includes policymakers and practitioners working in fields related to early childhood

education that are most widely used. However, numerous productive researchers publish in journals outside their discipline, although they still are making valuable contributions to their field (Martínez et al., 2011).

When preparing a research study for publication, researchers need to follow the selected journal's guidelines and the standard structure in framing the research report that was discussed in this article. Both emerging and productive researchers need to continue to follow the guidelines of writing and publishing a research article. They usually are required to make revisions. Even productive researchers encounter writing problems and dread revising the manuscript. Still they enjoy the feeling of satisfaction and achievement when their manuscript is accepted for publication. When researchers see their research in print, all their work seems worthwhile (Martínez et al., 2011).

REFERENCES

American Educational Research Association. (2006). Standards for reporting on empirical social science research in AERA publications. *Educational Researcher, 35*(6), 33–40.

American Psychological Association. (2010). *Publication Manual of the American Psychological Association* (6th ed.). Washington D. C.: American Psychological Association.

Baldwin, C., & Chandler, G. E. (2002). Improving faculty publication output: The role of a writing coach. *Journal of Professional Nursing, 18*(1), 8–15.

Council of Biology Editors (November, 1968). Proposed definition of a primary publication. *Council of Biology Editors Newsletter,* 1–2.

Cunningham, S. J. (2004). How to write a paper. *Journal of Orthodontics, 31*(1), 47–51.

Day, R., & Sakaduski, N. (2011). *How to write and publish a scientific paper.* Westport, CT.: Greenwood Press. Link to book:

Derntl, M. (2011). *Basics of research paper writing and publishing.* Unpublished manuscript, RWTH Aachen University.

Dies, R. R. (1993). Writing for publication: Overcoming common obstacles. *International Journal of Group Psychotherapy, 43*(2), 243–249.

Grant, B., & Knowles, S. (2000). Flights of imagination: Academic women be(com)ing writers. *International Journal for Academic Development, 5*(1), 6–19.

Jalongo, M. (2013). Getting on the conference program and writing a practical article: templates for success. *Early Childhood Education Journal, 41*(1), 13–23.

Johansson, R. (2004). How to write a scientific text: Lecture Notes. Retrieved from http://www.infra.kth.se/courses/1U1030/LectureNotes_A.pdf

Lee, A., & Boud, D. (2003). Writing groups, change and academic identity: Research development as local practice. *Studies in Higher Education, 28*(2), 187–200.

Maloy, S. (2001). *Guidelines for writing a scientific paper.* University of California, Irvine. Retrieved from http://www.marshfieldclinic.org/proxy/mcrf-admin-oswp-rm-guidelines_for_writing_a_scientific_manuscript.1.pdf

Martínez, R. S., Floyd, R. G., & Erichsen, L. (2011). Strategies and attributes of highly productive scholars and contributors to the school psychology literature: Recommendations for increasing scholarly productivity. *Journal of School Psychology, 49,* 691–720.

McGrail, M. R., Rickard, C. M., & Jones, R. (2006). Publish or perish: A systematic review of interventions to increase academic publication rates. *Higher Education Research & Development, 25*(1), 19–35.

Morss, K., & Murray, R. (2001). Researching academic writing within a structured programme: Insights and outcomes. *Studies in Higher Education, 26*(1), 35–42.

Nihalani, P. K., & Mayrath, M. C. (2008). Publishing in educational psychology journals: Comments from editors. *Educational Psychology Review, 20,* 29–39.

Peat, J., Elliott, E., Baur, L., & Keena, V. (2002). *Scientific writing—Easy when you know how.* London: British Medical Journal (BMJ) Books.

Saracho, O.N. (1983). Relationship between cognitive style and teachers' perceptions of young children's academic competence. *Journal of Experimental Education, 51*(4), 184–189.

Saracho, O. N. (1992). The relationship between preschool children's cognitive style and play: Implications for creativity. *The Creativity Research Journal, 5*(1), 35–47.

Saracho, O. N. (1996). The relationship between the cognitive style and play behaviors of 3 to 5-year-old children. *Personality and Individual Differences, 21*(6), 863–876.

Saracho, O. N. (2000a). Assessing the families' perceptions of their young children's acquisition of literacy. *Early Child Development and Care, 161,* 83–91.

Saracho, O. N. (2000b). Enhancing young children's home literacy experiences, *International Journal of Early Childhood Education, 5,* 135–141.

Saracho, O. N. (2001). Cognitive style and kindergarten pupils' preferences for teachers, *Learning and Instruction, 11,* 195–209.

Saracho, O. N. (2008). Fathers and young children's literacy experiences. *Early Child Development and Care, 178*(7/8), 837–852.

Saracho, O. N. (2010). A culturally responsive literacy program for Hispanic fathers and their children. *Journal of Hispanic Higher Education, 9*(4), 281–293.

Saracho, O. N., & Dayton, C. M. (1980). Relationship of teachers' cognitive styles to pupils' academic achievement gains. *Journal of Educational Psychology, 72*(4), 544–549.

Saracho, O. N., & Spodek, B. (2010). Families' selection of children's literature books. *Early Childhood Education Journal, 37*(5), 401–409.

Selvanathan, S. K., Udani, R. D., Udani, S. D., & Haylett, K. R. (February, 2006). The art of the abstract. *Student: British Medical Journal, 14,* 70–71.

Sharp, D. (2002). Kipling's guide to writing a scientific paper. *Croatian Medical Journal, 43*(3), 262–67.

Stegemann, S., & Gastel, B. (2009). Council Classics: What constitutes primary publication? *Science Editor, 32*(2), 57–58.

Todorovic, L. (2003). Original (scientific) paper: The IMRAD layout. *Archive of Oncology, 11*(3), 203–205.

Udani, R.D., Selvanathan, S. K., Udani, S. D., & Haylett, K. R. (2007, November). Writing up your research, *Student: British Medical Journal, 15,* 406–408.

CHAPTER 25

WRITING FOR PUBLICATION ON RESEARCH WITH YOUNG CHILDREN

Nancy Dixon

WHY PUBLISH

The Issues

Providing the best possible educational experiences for young children remains a challenge in educational systems throughout the world (Moreno, 2008; Peralta, 2008). Many different people have a stake in the quality of early education, including teachers, educational system leaders and managers, child development specialists, psychologists, policy makers, researchers, and families (Jalongo, 2013b). All these stakeholders need to know about and be able to use new knowledge based on high-quality research studies about what works best under what circumstances to enhance the quality of early childhood education.

The spread of good practice in early childhood education, based on research evidence from well-designed studies, is dependent on new knowledge being accessible in professional journals. In turn, journals' publication of new knowledge depends on the people who are carrying out research to submit what they have learned for publication (Saracho, 2013). Research findings that remain unpublished and lessons learned that are not shared with colleagues in the field are unlikely to benefit the education of young children.

People who do not develop experience writing for publication can think that the process is daunting, takes time, and can be risky (Dixon, 2001; Gargiulo, Jalongo, & Motari, 2001; Gump, 2010); experienced educational researchers know the work involved in writing for publication and have developed the skills needed. Traditionally, graduate students in early childhood education research learn research skills and carry out research as part of their doctoral training. However, given the competing demands on doctoral students, being formally supported to develop writing for publication skills may not have as much emphasis in academic programs (Jalongo, 2013a; Kamler, 2008).

Carrying out research studies and sharing the findings of the studies go hand in hand as professional activities; therefore, the skills involved in carrying out a research study and communicating about the research really should be developed simultaneously (Lee, 2010). Writing a journal article on a research study brings absolute focus on the importance of the research to the field and key messages about the research to be communicated to colleagues. The discipline of explaining a research study concisely could help a doctoral student in clarifying the background to the research, the justification for the research methodology, and the importance of the research findings.

First-time authors sometimes think their work is on a "common" subject that everyone is familiar with, so the work won't be important to a journal (Dixon, 2001). However, common subjects in early childhood education affect many educational settings; therefore, additional knowledge of what works to improve day-to-day educational experiences and outcomes for young children may be of interest to many others. Researchers also sometimes think that because a research study did not go perfectly, or the hypotheses established for the study were not confirmed, the work is not good enough for publication. Again, others may benefit from learning about the problems experienced and the possible "failure" of an hypothesized intervention is important knowledge for the field.

The Benefits

There are a number of specific benefits of writing about a research study for publication that usually justify the time and work involved, including the following (Amodei, Jalongo, Myers, Onchwari, & Gargiulo, 2013; Dixon, 1999; Murray, 2009):

- The work being reported may result in improvements in one or more aspects of early childhood education that will benefit young children because your work can influence professionals working in the field.
- Lessons learned from a research study may be useful to people working in other educational settings.
- The work may suggest areas for further research or development or debate among colleagues interested in the same or a similar issue.
- Publication may lead to identifying or forming a network of people who are interested in the same subject or method reported or who are doing similar work.
- Publication may contribute to gaining recognition for you and your colleagues, students, or institution.
- Others are able to review the work and provide helpful feedback or suggestions or share experiences with the same or a related approach.

For those who intend a career in early childhood education research, having research "outputs," as demonstrated by journal publications, is essential for professional credibility, career advancement, and professional forms of recognition as well as personal satisfaction (Amodei et al., 2013). Publications also provide evidence of a researcher's scholarship and facilitate communication with colleagues in the early childhood research community (Hagel, 2011). Finally, in early childhood research, research publications can raise the status of the profession and make a contribution to the field (Amodei et al., 2013).

The experience of writing for publication is valuable for an author in the following ways:

- Preparing a paper for publication is a learning experience that will build or enhance useful skills, including logical thinking and communication.
- Going through the process, especially for the first time, will demystify what's involved in publication and make successive papers much easier to prepare.
- Publication will minimize the possibility that others could take credit for your work or ideas.

PERSONAL ATTITUDES AND BEHAVIORS AND EVIDENCE-BASED PUBLISHING

Potential authors sometimes put themselves off writing at the start, particularly if they haven't submitted an article for publication previously, or even if they have, but they don't feel comfortable with the process. It is important to take time before beginning to work on a publication to identify and manage your personal attitudes and behaviors. Some thoughts that people have about writing for publication are in Table 25.1 (Amodei, et al., 2013;

TABLE 25.1 Possible Personal Attitudes and Behaviors About Writing for Publication and How to Respond to Them

Personal Attitude or Behavior About Writing for Publication	What You Can Do About It
"I am too busy, I don't have time."	• Everybody has the same amount of time; the issue is how to use time. • Plan the writing to see how much time it really will take. • Allocate small chunks of time to do one part of an article at a time rather than trying to do it all at once. • Don't allow interruptions in your dedicated writing time.
"I am not well connected so I don't have any hope of success."	• Journal editors want good publications regardless of "connections" of the author. • Approach a research supervisor or senior colleague to work with you on producing the article.
"I am only a teacher (graduate student, researcher, etc.)."	• You are likely to be the "closest" to the subject you want to write about, and that will show in your publication if you write it well.
"My first attempts weren't successful; I guess I'm not a good writer."	• Writing is a learned skill. If you know what you are doing when you start to write for publication, you have a greater chance of success.
"Who would want to read about what I have done?"	• Anybody who works in a similar setting or has experienced a similar situation may be interested, particularly if they have thought about the same subject.
"I am not a writer; I don't write well."	• Decide for yourself that you will meet the personal challenge and improve your writing. Until you commit to learning how, you'll waste time.
"I don't know where to submit my manuscript."	• Do your homework. Find journals related to your work (see Appendix) and their requirements and expectations.
"I am waiting to hear back from the journal."	• Journal review processes are time consuming. Develop another idea for publication and work on another manuscript in the meantime.
"The article I submitted was rejected."	• Get over the "rejection." Many manuscripts submitted to scientific journals are not accepted as they are submitted. Use the feedback from the journal to amend your manuscript and resubmit it or submit it immediately to another journal. • If it turns out that your research is flawed, accept any flaws and write the manuscript openly acknowledging them. • If your study is seriously flawed, you may need to abandon your publication goal and apply what you learned to your next project.

Gargiulo, Jalongo, & Motari, 2001; Jenkins, 2002; Murray, 2009). Check if any of these apply to you and what you can do about it before you proceed.

Writing for publication skills traditionally have been learned primarily from senior academic staff giving advice and guidance to students. Also, publishers provide guidance for authors in their journal issues or on their websites. Journal publication is a field in which there has been surprisingly little research to provide a scientific evidence base on what makes up good practice in preparing a report on research for publication (Jalongo, 2013b). Findings of available research studies on journal publication could be helpful to new authors, along with practice guidance from experienced authors.

WHAT TO WRITE

If you have carried out a substantial research study, you probably want to write about the study. However, journal editors are interested in other types of publications and there may be other opportunities through which you can gain experience in describing your work.

Submit a Review

If you have completed a systematic or narrative review or a review of methodology in establishing the background for your research study, and the review is well executed and extensive, you could consider submitting the review itself for publication (Hoot & Szente, 2013). If you decide to submit a review for publication, check that you meet a journal's requirements for a review.

Submit a Conference Paper or Poster

State, regional, and national associations offer opportunities to present papers or posters on research studies. It may be easier to gain experience explaining a research study through giving a 10–minute presentation on your work at a conference. An alternative is to submit a poster. Both paper and poster submissions are helpful to inexperienced writers because they require focus on the most important points you want to get across. If you can communicate these important points in a short presentation or a poster, it is easier to elaborate on your ideas for a journal article. You can follow templates for conference proposals to prepare a submission (Jalongo, 2013a).

HOW TO THINK ABOUT WHAT JOURNAL EDITORS WANT

Define Your Ideal Readers

Thinking about the research you have done, consider who might be interested in your work. Start with groups of people that can identify with your subject, the setting for your work, or the method you used. Also, think about people who would be interested, if only they knew about your work. Then develop a mental profile of the types of people who have come to your mind. Use the questions in Table 25.2 about your potential target readers to help you imagine them (Dixon, 2001).

Most of your readers will want to learn details about your work. They will be interested in why you carried out the work, an overview of previous research on your subject and how your study relates to previous research, the approach and methods you used, the findings and how you interpret them, and the conclusions. Others may be more interested in having only a summary of the research and a detailed explanation of the implications of implementation of your research findings from policy or practical classroom perspectives. Thinking about who you really want to know about your work will help you select a journal.

TABLE 25.2   Potential Target Readers and What You Know About Them

Potential Target Readers and What You Know About Them

- Who are the main groups of people interested in your subject and your work, for example, people who work in the same setting or people who have tried to use the methodology you used?
- Who else might be interested, for example, people who are interested in research in this field, who are teachers of young children, who teach at an academic level, or who need to make policy about your subject?
- What is likely to be the background of the main readers of a publication about your work and the backgrounds of other potential readers? What could be their jobs?
- What will interest your readers in your publication? What is the main point that might interest the readers you have identified?
- How much experience are the readers likely to have with your subject?
- Are the readers likely to be familiar with the setting or circumstances in which you carried out the work you intend to write about?
- Why should the readers read the paper? What do you think they should learn about your work?
- What would you like your readers *to do* as a result of reading your publication? Are there practical implications of your study findings that can be applied in particular settings? Is there a need for further research, and if so, on what aspects of the subject?

Select Your Journal and Know What Your Journal's Editor Wants

When you have defined for yourself the types of people who may be interested in your research, often you have identified the journal or journals to target. Read articles in journals you have selected to help you decide on the first journal to which you will submit your article.

All professional journals have rules about submissions that specify that the same paper cannot be submitted to two journals at the same time. If you have selected two or more possible journals to submit to, rate them in accordance with your judgment about which journal might be most likely to be interested in your work, and submit your article to the journal you rated as your highest priority. If your first-choice journal does not accept your paper, you can try other journals in turn.

Occasionally, when a research study uses a complex design or has several stages, authors consider sending a paper on one aspect of the research, such as an innovative use of a methodology or tool, to one journal, and another paper on a different aspect of the research, such as the practical implications of implementation of the research findings, to another journal (Hoot & Szente, 2013). This situation can occur when describing all aspects of a research study would exceed a journal's requirements for length of a single article. If you think of taking this approach, you have to inform both journals of both submissions. This approach may be acceptable to journal editors if the papers present completely different aspects of the research or if the journals attract different readers.

Some of the journals that publish research in early childhood education are in the Appendix (Amodei et al., 2013). Information is provided on the peer review status of the journal; the number of issues published each year; the professional organization publishing the journal, where applicable; and a brief description of the type of work the journal is interested in publishing. When a journal identifies itself as peer reviewed, your article will be sent to people who are regarded as expert in the field for their views about your article. Reviewers are given a series of questions to answer for the journal editor and are asked to advise the editor on the quality of the submission.

Consider Electronic Versus Print Journals

Many well-established scientific journals publish both paper and electronic versions, and some journals publish online only. Electronic versions of journals can include more extensive information about research studies, such as detailed findings or the results of testing methodologies or tools.

Electronic journals can provide completely free access, provide free back issues, or require payment for access to a journal article. It is estimated that over 6,000 scientific journals are now open access (OA), which means that the journal content is freely available online without any hindrance (Laakso et al., 2011).

The major advantages to authors of electronic publishing are as follows (Morris, 2006):

- Many researchers are more and more reliant on accessing material online. Print-only journals not accessible online, therefore, may have a lower profile to people who prefer accessing material electronically.
- An online journal can attract international readers, and therefore, possibly expand an author's potential network of people interested in the same or related research.
- Online journals tend to be published somewhat faster than print journals because publication does not involve printing, binding and dispatching copies of journal issues.
- Because of the lack of a page (and cost) limitation, journal editors are willing to publish longer articles in an electronic journal.
- Journal articles that are approved for publication may be made available electronically prior to an entire electronic journal issue being available.
- Online journals have advantages for readers, including the ability to search for articles across journal issues and journals and to use electronic links to references in articles.
- For journal staff, online publication normally offers advantages of reduced cost of journal production and the ability to streamline working practices involving the review and production of manuscripts.

For journal authors, a perceived disadvantage of publishing in an electronic journal is concern that academic institutions and researchers may not recognize an electronic journal as credible, particularly in consideration of an academic's research performance (Morris, 2006). However, many online-only journals are now indexed and peer reviewed, and high-profile scientific journals are innovators in electronic publishing. Therefore, concern about the reputation of electronic journals is rapidly changing.

Questions have been raised about the impact of articles published in open access journals in particular. In a controlled study of OA publishing, researchers randomly made some journal articles freely available and kept others available by subscription only (Davis, Lewenstein, Simon, Booth, & Connolly, 2008). The objective was to determine if increased access to journal articles results in more article downloads and citations. The researchers found that in the year after the articles were published, open access articles were downloaded more than subscription-based articles, but they were no more likely to be cited than subscription-based articles.

In another study, Björk & Solomon (2012) compared the impact factors of 610 open access journals and over 7,000 subscription journals. Citation rates for subscription journals were about 30% higher than for OA ones; however, the difference was largely due to a higher share of older OA journals. When journals disciplines, age of the journal, and countries of publication were compared, the differences disappeared except for journals started before 1996. Open access journals funded by article processing charges were on average cited more than other journals. In medicine and health, OA journals founded in the last 10 years received on average as many citations as subscription journals launched during the same time (Björk & Solomon, 2012).

Whether or not the journal is electronic or open access shouldn't affect your decision to submit a paper to the journal. If a journal is suitable for publishing your work, and the journal has a peer review process in place for all research papers, you should consider it.

Decide If Journal Prestige Is important

Academic researchers and institutions may be interested in the ranking or rating of a journal as a basis for deciding whether or not to submit a research paper for publication. An easy way to check how widely a journal is recognized is to look at indexes of journals to see if the journal you are interested is included. Journal indexes in which educational research articles might appear include the following: EBSCO Academic Search Complete, Gale Academic OneFile, ProQuest Central, ERIC (Education Resources Information Center), PsycINFO, Web of Science, DOAJ (Directory of Open Access Journals), Google Scholar, or WorldCat.

A number of methods are available to rank or rate scientific journals, which are referred to as journal metrics. The diverse measures have been developed to attempt to respond to variations in publication practices in different subject fields and create "a level playing field" for ranking journals across fields of work. The measures include: impact factor, the SJR, SNIP, the H-index, and the Eigenfactor. The metrics are explained in Table 25.3 (Bergstrom, 2007; Garfield, 2005; González-Pereira, Guerrero-Bote, & Moya-Anegón, 2009; Hirsch, 2005; Moed, 2010).

A journal's ratings are normally available on the journal's website. Journals publishing early childhood educational research may not be directly comparable because they use different measures.

TABLE 25.3 Types of Journal Metrics

Metric	Explanation
Eigenfactor	A rating of the total importance or influence of a journal. A journal is considered to be influential if it is cited often by other influential journals. The Eigenfactor methodology is based on network analysis and information theory. Within a "network" of scholarly articles connected through citations, the method uses information on citations, as tallied by Thompson Scientific's Journal Citation Reports (JCR), to calculate the Eigenfactor.
H (Hirsch)-index	A measure of both the productivity and impact of the published work of a scholar. The index is based on the set of the author's most cited papers and the number of citations that they have received in other publications.
Impact factor	A measure of the frequency with which the "average article" in a journal has been cited in a particular year or period, usually calculated by dividing the number of current year citations to the source items published in that journal during the previous two years. Journal impact factors range from less than 1 to over 50. Impact factors from 1 to 3 are typical for fields of research that are highly focused with relatively few researchers working in the field. For example, the currently available five-year impact factor for the *Early Childhood Research Quarterly* is 2.610.
Scimago Journal Rank (SJR)	A size-independent measure aimed at measuring the current "average prestige per paper" of journals. Relative scores are assigned to all the journals in a subject field. A journal transfers its own status to another journal through citing it. A citation from a journal with a relatively high SJR is worth more than a citation from a source with a lower SJR.
Source-Normalized Impact per Paper (SNIP)	A ratio of a journal's citation count per paper and the citation potential in its subject field. It is intended to enable direct comparisons of sources in different subject fields. It takes into account the frequency at which authors cite other papers in their reference lists, the speed at which citation impact matures, and the extent to which the database used in the assessment covers the field's literature.

Finally, you may want to consider a journal's acceptance rate, that is, the percentage of articles submitted for publication that is published in the journal. A journal's time to decision to publish also may be important. In early childhood education, journal acceptance rates for journals that publish their rates may be from 10% to more than 33% (Amodei et al., 2013).

HOW TO DECIDE ON AUTHORSHIP

Clarify Authorship

If you are writing about research that you have designed and carried out on your own, you may want to be the only author of an article about your research. But if you are publishing for the first time or you have shared the research work with others in any way, you may need to plan for one or more additional authors.

The subject of authorship of research papers is complex, and journals vary in their requirements on authorship. Terms relating to authorship may include author, contributor, or guarantor. The terms are explained in Table 25.4 (American Educational Research Association, 2006, 2009; American Psychological Association, 2010; Osborne & Holland, 2009). Journals may require a statement from the authors explaining who has contributed what to the study being described in a paper and who is responsible for the overall content of the paper.

Planning Authorship for Doctoral or Student Research

If a student has carried out the research being published, for example, for a thesis or dissertation, there should be discussion about authorship throughout the process of documenting the research (APA Science Student Council, 2006). Research advisors or colleagues who meet the definition of an author may be named authors (Hoot & Szente, 2013).

A graduate student could start out with the expectation that a research project being carried out will be submitted for publication, which happens in some other countries, for example (Lee, 2010). The student could initiate a discussion about publication and authorship with a research advisor, including who might be authors, who will do what work on an article, and

TABLE 25.4   Authorship-Related Terms

Term	Explanation
Author	Someone who has made a primary or substantive creative contribution to an intellectual product and holds primary responsibility for the data, concepts, and interpretation of results. Some journals add that an author is also someone who drafts the article or revises it critically for important intellectual content and approves the version to be published.
Contributor	Someone who made a contribution to the work being described but whose contribution is not at the level of the authors. Contributors may have carried out any of the following roles: procured funding for the work (but were not involved in carrying out the work); researched published literature reviewed as part of the research; reviewed and/or edited a manuscript; or carried out administrative work relating to gathering or checking data. It is customary to name contributors and briefly describe their contributions at the end of an article; this practice is sometimes referred to as acknowledgements.
Guarantor	Someone who accepts full responsibility for the conduct of the study, had access to the data, and controlled the decision to publish. Journals require guarantors in some field of research such as medicine.

the possible sequence of authors' names on an article. Authorship order should be decided by the magnitude of the contribution to the research rather than by the status of individuals involved (Osborne & Holland, 2009). Agreement concerning authorship may change, including adding or deleting authors or rearranging the sequence of authors' names. The changes in authorship may happen because of changes in who carried out the work or additional expertise provided (Osborne & Holland, 2009).

HOW TO DECIDE WHAT TO WRITE

The Content

If you are writing about a research study, journal editors generally have agreed to a structure for reports on research. The main parts of a research paper and what should be included in each part are explained in Table 25.5 (American Educational Research Association, 2006; Saracho, 2013). The structure is highly similar to most universities' requirements for a doctoral thesis or dissertation on research. Therefore, a well-executed research study completed as a doctoral candidate can be used as the basis for writing a journal article.

TABLE 25.5   Main Parts of A Research Article Explained

Main Part of a Research Article	Explanation
Purpose of the research	A specific statement of the problem, question, or issue the research addresses, or the hypotheses tested through the research
Background to the research (Introduction)	How the research relates to previous and existing knowledge about the subject, including an accurate description of current research on the subject
Setting or context	The setting in which the research was carried out, including key characteristics of the participants in the research so that readers can decide if findings from the research could potentially be transferable to other settings involving other children
Design and methods	Exactly how the research study was carried out, including detailed descriptions of any interventions used and exactly how they were used and the methods used to collect and analyse data, including statistical tests used
Findings (results)	The presentation of the data analysis and interpretation of the data
Analysis (discussion)	How the findings of the study relate to the purpose or hypotheses for the research, and also to the findings of previous research
Conclusion	The implications of the research findings, including whether or not they can be generalized or if further research is indicated by the findings

Ethics considerations relating to your research study also will need to be described (American Educational Research Association, 2006).

The Requirements

For the journal or journals you have selected, find the guide for authors on the journal websites or in a recent issue of the journals. The description is what a journal editor wants from authors in terms of contents to be provided, any limitations on length, the format for graphics including tables, and the style for references.

Some journals request that reports of research studies are between 2,500 and 3,500 words. Specifications for length of journal articles relate to how many pages the journal prints in each issue, which in turn is related to the cost of printing and distribution of journals, and in turn to subscription fees.

Journal staff members do the first screening of submissions to the journal to determine if the journal's requirements have been met. If they have not been met, the submission will be rejected, whatever its quality (Hoot & Szente, 2013). Some journals may invite authors to resubmit the article in strict conformance with the journal's requirements, but others may not.

HOW TO GET READY TO WRITE

Be a Hunter Not a Gatherer in Your Approach

When people have to write a paper, they seem to have one of two work styles: gatherer or hunter (Dixon, 1999, 2001, 2011). A gatherer collects all available material that might be relevant to the paper, reads all the material gathered, sifts through and uses the material to organize ideas for the paper, and then begins to write. Gathering behavior is appropriate if you are writing a literature review, for example. It is the behavior that students learn as part of their formal education. However, gathering behavior is not appropriate for all writing, because it does not encourage defining a writer's intended readers and journals or being clear about the key messages a writer wants to convey and the most effective way to convey the ideas.

Many experienced writers tend to use the hunter style of writing. They are clear about whom they are writing for. They know the specifications their writing has to meet. They know why the article they are writing is needed. They devise an outline that meets the readers' and journal editors' specifications, and then they gather only the material they need to fill in the outline. They organize their ideas logically to get across key messages. They get their ideas down quickly and test to confirm the ideas are clear.

They edit their writing, maybe a couple of times, to end up with the clearest possible writing about their work.

Translate the Requirements into the Work to be Done

When you know the specifications for your article, highlight especially these requirements: the length of the article in words or pages; the main parts that are required by the journal; and tables, figures, or illustrations you might include. Convert the intended length of the article into a measure you can easily relate to, for example, pages of text.

For example, if you normally write text using a standard word processing package, note the number of words that fit on one of your typical text pages, given the font size and line spacing you usually use. Compare the font size and line spacing you use with the journal's requirements. Convert a page of your usual text to a page that meets the journal specifications and then estimate the number of text pages needed for your article. For example, if you are aiming to write 3000 words, and you learn that a page formatted according to the journal requirements has about 250 words, you know that you need to write 12 pages of text.

Then, estimate the amount of time it takes you to compose one page of text, assuming you are working to an outline of what you are writing. Some sections of your paper may be easier to write than others. Spend an hour or two drafting what you consider to be easy-to-write and hard-to-write text. Then calculate an average time to draft one page. If it takes you a half-hour to draft one page, you know you need about 6 hours to develop the first draft of your article. You can now allocate your time appropriately to meet any deadline you are working to. You can set aside an hour or two a day for a few days. The point is that at the end of your allocated time, you should have a complete very rough draft of your article.

HOW TO DEVELOP AN OUTLINE OF WHAT YOU WILL WRITE

Use Your Own Learning Style

People learn scientific writing skills using different approaches. For some people, just getting text down in the way it occurs to you is a way to start. You can later organize what you have rough drafted and continue to refine the ideas and the text until you have a complete rough draft. Another technique new writers can use is to ask a friend to carry out an interview with you about your research, as if the friend is a journalist reporting on your research. Record your interview and transcribe it. Then, use your answers in the interview as a basis for organizing and drafting an article on your research. Another approach is to set out draft answers to specific questions about your research.

Do the Thinking First

The most important work in preparing a paper is often the hardest: Think very clearly about exactly what you want to say to your readers. Don't start to write until you have finished thinking about the key messages you want to get across. Start by thinking about the answers to the key questions in Table 25.6 (Dixon, 2001, 2011).

For each of the questions in Table 25.6, write *one complete sentence*. People often make single word or phrase or bullet point notes for each question, but that isn't enough to help you formulate your outline. The formal sentence structure of a subject and a predicate prompts you to draw out the key ideas you need to include in the paper. Skip any questions that are not directly relevant to your work or that would mean exact duplication of a previous answer.

When you have written ten complete sentences, you now have the framework or outline for your paper. The sentences can become topic sentences for the first paragraph in each section of your paper. Each topic sentence

TABLE 25.6 Key Questions to Structure the Content of a Paper

Questions to Answer to Develop an Outline for a Paper

- Why did I (or we) set out to do the work I am writing about—what is the background that led to the work being done?
- Why am I writing about it—what do I want to achieve through publication of the work?
- What does available published evidence say about the subject I am writing about? Refer to conclusions of any reviews published, other research studies published, expert opinion, or literature, as appropriate.
- What was happening in our own setting that prompted me (us) to carry out the work? Describe what about the situation in your research setting prompted you to think about the work.
- What did I (or we) do in carrying out the work? Refer to the nature of the work you carried out, for example, qualitative research study, before–after change study, etc.
- How did I (or we) do it? Describe the specific approach or method you used.
- What did I (or we) show through what I (or we) did? What was (were) the major finding(s)?
- What did I (or we) learn by doing what we did? What lessons would I (or we) like others to learn from our work?
- What did I (or we) do next or plan to do next with what I (or we) have learned if anything?
- What are the benefits of what I (or we) did for other researchers, teachers, parents, education program developers or administrators, policy makers or any others?

summarizes and organizes the main ideas in a paragraph, keeps you focused on what you want to say, and helps readers understand your ideas. The topic sentences you write also will be helpful later when you write the abstract for your paper.

After you have drafted the ten sentences, review each sentence carefully. Check if the meaning of each sentence is as clear as it can be. Add any ideas that occur to you as you are reviewing your draft sentences. When you are satisfied with your key sentences, decide on the one or two key points you really want to get across to readers. Be sure these points are clear in your key sentences, and amend or rewrite the sentences as needed to draw out your key or main points.

Arrange Your Content into Main Parts

When you are happy with your sentences and you have identified the one or two key ideas you want to communicate clearly to your readers, you can arrange your work into the main parts of your paper and develop a more complete outline of your content. Table 25.7 illustrates how your sentences can relate to the main parts of a paper.

Plan the Work of Writing the Paper

When you have laid out how your key sentences relate to the main parts of your paper and your content outline, you can plan the remaining work. Work backwards from the total word limit for your article. Allocate an

TABLE 25.7 Arranging Topic Sentences Into Main Parts of a Paper

Main Part	Answers to Key Questions
Purpose or rationale	Why you did what you did and why you are writing about it
Background	What available evidence says
Setting or context	What was happening in the setting or situation that prompted you to do the work you are describing
Design and methods	Exactly what you did and how you did it
Findings	What you showed through what you did
Analysis (sometimes called Discussion)	What you learned from what you did and what you did about it, if anything
	What you will do next or plan to next, if anything, and the next steps for the work
Conclusion	What are the benefits of what you did, including possible benefits for people working in similar and other settings

approximate number of words to be written for each of your article's main parts. The section on participants in a research study may have a few words compared to the discussion section, for example. This tactic avoids wasting time writing too much on individual parts, such as the rationale or background to the work, and not writing enough on the analysis.

For example, suppose you are intending to write a paper that has a total word count of 3,000 words. You might decide that, given the content you have outlined, you will allocate the word count as follows: 300 words for the purpose, background and rationale; 500 for the review of existing evidence; 250 for the context or setting for your work; 500 for the methodology; 600 for the findings; 500 for the analysis or discussion; and 350 for the conclusion. You can convert the number of words to number of pages you need to draft for each section and manage your time accordingly. For example, you could allocate two of your "writing hours" to draft the findings section.

There are no rules about the sequence in which the parts of a journal article are drafted. Some people find it easier to start at the beginning with the background and work through the sections in sequence. Others find it easier to start with the subjects and methodology section, or the findings. As long as all the parts eventually flow logically from one to the other, it doesn't matter where you start.

As you are allocating the preliminary number of words to each part of your paper, consider where you can use tables, diagrams, graphs, charts, or other illustrations to present findings or other information. Some authors prefer to plan and prepare tables, diagrams, or illustrations before writing text for the relevant sections of a paper, so that they know the main points the text needs to make about the content of the graphics. This approach makes it easier to write the text on research findings.

Do the Writing

Use the thinking about the contents, key ideas, and graphics for your paper to write a first draft. There is a useful maxim for authors, especially new authors: First get it down and then later get it right. After you have completed the first draft, you can work on perfecting the exact wording of a paragraph or section of the paper. Fretting over one particular idea or section at the first draft stage wastes time and is not productive, particularly if you are a person who doesn't especially enjoy the process of writing.

As you are drafting, be careful to note your references in the text. Most journals that publish research in early childhood education require the use of the APA style for references (American Psychological Association, 2010). Although you needn't format the references exactly correctly when you are producing your first draft, it is important that you record your references carefully as you work. It is difficult and a waste of your time to have to find references sometime later for text you have written.

As you are working on the data collection and analysis methods and findings or results of the research, explain briefly why you selected the statistical techniques you used for analysis. Prepare any tables, graphs, or other illustrations of the findings accurately and completely, and number and title them correctly. Then, draft text around the tables, graphs, or illustrations. Refer to the *Publication Manual of the American Psychological Association* (American Psychological Association, 2010) for detailed guidance on the presentation of statistics.

Consider Your Writing Style

Read articles in your target journals and any instructions the journals provide on writing style. In the past, scientific publishing was dominated by sentences composed in passive rather than active voice. For example, "The research study was carried out by a team of students" is in passive voice; "A team of students carried out the research study" is in active voice. Modern journals now prefer easily readable sentence structure with approximately 20 or fewer words in each sentence, and for ideas to be expressed in active voice.

HOW TO CHECK YOUR DRAFT

There are five checks to make on the draft of your paper: the journal submission requirements, standards for publication about research, the clarity of your writing, the accuracy of the presentation of your data, and your writing style.

Recheck Journal Requirements and Standards for Publishing Research

First, when your first draft is completed, recheck the requirements for authors for the journal you are targeting, and make sure you have followed all the journal's directions. Journal editors are not forgiving of an author's failures to follow the journal's requirements.

Next, if you are writing about a research project in early childhood education, check if the presentation of your work is consistent with standards for reporting on research in education. There are two sets of standards, one on empirical social science research and one on humanities-oriented research (American Educational Research Association, 2006, 2009). These standards

TABLE 25.8 Subjects of Standards for Reporting on Research in Educational Research Publications

Subjects of Standards for Reporting on Empirical Social Science Research	Subjects of Standards for Reporting on Humanities-Oriented Research
Problem formulation	Significance of the topic
Design and logic	Methods
Sources of evidence	Conceptualization
Measurement and classification	Substantiation
Analysis and interpretation	Coherence
Generalization	Quality of communication
Ethics	Ethics

are a guide for checking on your manuscript at the preparation stages, and journal editors also use the standards in their review of submissions for publication. Table 25.8 provides a summary of subjects covered by the standards.

Edit Your Draft

Finally, edit your draft. If you are not an experienced author, plan to edit your own work at least two or three times. Have a break between edits so that you have a fresh view of your paper before you start on the next edit. Use the key points in Table 25.9 to improve the writing in your draft (Dixon, 2011).

Check Your Data Presentation and Your Writing Style

Double-check all the data, the calculations and the values obtained from application of statistical tools that are presented in your article for accuracy and clarity of presentation. Along with editing your text, check that most of your sentences are as short as possible without losing meaning and in active voice. Check on any other elements of style that the journal you are writing for has established.

WRITE THE ABSTRACT, IDENTIFY KEYWORDS, AND DEVELOP THE TITLE

The Abstract

The purpose of an abstract is to provide a summary description of a paper. The abstract is important because it often is the basis for journal

TABLE 25.9   Key Points on Improving Your Writing

Practical Advice on Writing Style

1. Simplify—rather than complicate—your writing
   - Use the shortest words possible, without compromising meaning, throughout your text. For example, use "some" rather than "a number of," "now" not "at the present time," or "indicate" not "give an indication of."
   - Use active rather than passive voice to the extent possible. For example, "The children played the game" not "The game was played by the children." The use of passive voice makes it much harder for readers to understand what you are saying.
   - Look for inappropriate uses of words and change them. For example, a phrase such as "This paper discusses..." is not appropriate because a paper cannot talk; try "This paper presents..." "Last month saw an increase in..." is not appropriate because months can't see, and also the sentence is passive.
   - Try to have each sentence consist of no more than 20 to 25 words.
   - Try to limit each paragraph to no more than 6 sentences.
   - Delete unnecessary punctuation, especially commas that aren't needed.
   - Find any jargon words and replace them.
   - If you are writing for an international journal, find any words, phrases, acronyms, or organizations that require explanation for someone who works in another country.

2. Review the structure of your paper and the headings you used.
   - Check if each part of your paper is clear as a separate section.
   - Rewrite and rewrite each of your paragraphs until you think your paper describes your ideas in the clearest, simplest way possible.

3. Recheck the overall meaning. Decide:
   - Have you communicated your most important ideas clearly?
   - Is what you hope readers will get from reading your paper stated as clearly as possible?

staff and readers deciding whether or not to read the paper. Some journals prescribe the format of an abstract; for example, for a research report, a journal may require that the following be described: the purpose of the research; the design or methodology; the main findings; and the conclusions drawn. Use the topic sentences created to outline the paper as the basis for the abstract.

Check that the abstract drafted is an accurate reflection of the content in the article and tells the complete story of what is in the article. The journal normally sets a word limit for an abstract, usually between 100 and 250 words.

Keywords

Search engines for published literature use keywords as a basis for finding papers for people searching for literature. Normally, a journal asks the author to identify three to six keywords to be used for this purpose. Choose words or phrases that describe the subject of the paper. Publication databases often have directories of keywords, such as the ERIC Thesaurus, and the directories also can suggest keywords for an article.

The Title

The title of a paper should accurately express what the paper is about and should be self-explanatory. It needs to attract potential readers; people scanning literature searches can use journal article titles as the basis for deciding whether or not to access an article.

Current good practice in journal publication is that the title of a research paper should include the research method used; a short description of the subject of the research and, if relevant, the setting in which the research was carried out. Avoid vague words in titles such as "an investigation of" because the term does not adequately inform potential readers about the research method. Potential readers may make selections of articles to read if the title contains specific terms such as "qualitative study" or "randomized controlled trial."

Experienced authors advise that a journal article title should use as few words as possible. However, research on journal titles in medicine could be considered. Jacques and Sebire (2010) identified the top and bottom 25 articles in three medical journals in terms of citations of articles published in 2005. For each article, they collected data on title word counts, title structure, and specific title words appearing most frequently in each group and compared the frequencies statistically. The most frequently cited journal articles had more words in the title, used a title with two components separated by a colon, and used descriptors of research studies, such as the words randomized, controlled, meta-analysis, or case-control.

HOW TO CHECK YOUR LAST DRAFT

When you are satisfied with your draft, there are two final checks you can make on your paper before submitting it to a journal: special checklists that may be relevant to the type of research or paper you are submitting; and feedback from colleagues.

Use Special Checklists

Checklists are available for different types of research articles and they can help to verify that you have covered everything in your paper that your readers and journal editors would expect. Many of the internationally used special checklists were developed for application in healthcare and medical research (Clark, 2003; Davidoff, Batalden, Stevens, Ogrinc, & Mooney, 2008; Moher, Liberati, Tetzlaff, Altman, & The PRISMA Group, 2009; Schulz, Altman, Moher, & CONSORT Group, 2010; Stroup et al., 2000); however, they are valuable for assessing research in any field. A summary of these special checklists is in Table 25.10.

Ask Colleagues for Feedback

When you have done all the checking of your article that you can and you think you have the clearest possible manuscript, ask one or more colleagues who have not been involved in the work to read your paper (Hoot & Szente, 2013). Be specific about your directions to colleagues; don't just ask them to let you know what they think. Ask your colleagues to tell you the following:

- The three most important points made in the paper
- Every idea or sentence in the paper that is not entirely clear

TABLE 25.10 Guidance for Publishing Different Types of Research Papers

Nature of Research Being Reported	Guidance
Randomized controlled trial	CONSORT (Consolidated Standards of Reporting Trials) statement www.consort-statement.org
Qualitative research study	RATS guidelines RATS stands for: Relevance of study question Appropriateness of qualitative method Transparency of procedures Soundness of interpretative approach www.biomedcentral.com/info/ifora/rats
Systematic review	PRISMA (Preferred Reporting Items for Systematic Reviews and Meta-Analyses) guidelines www.prisma-statement.org
Meta-analysis of observational studies	MOOSE (Meta-analysis of Observational Studies in Epidemiology) guidelines www.consort-statement.org
Quality improvement research or project	SQUIRE (Standards for Quality Improvement Reporting Excellence) www.squire-statement.org

- If your tables, charts, graphs, or diagrams were entirely clear and helpful
- If statistics you presented were explained carefully and are clear
- What you could improve in the paper

It is sometimes tempting to disregard comments made by colleagues, thinking they are being picky or they don't understand work in your field. Often, colleagues' feedback is representative of how readers will respond to your writing. If colleagues don't pick out the most important points you wanted to make, or find that something is unclear, rewrite your paper as needed to respond to their points.

HOW TO PREPARE FOR THE JOURNAL'S REVIEW PROCESS

Journals usually describe on their websites the processes they follow to review a submission. The websites also may tell you the usual timeframes for review of your submission so that you know when to expect a decision from the journal.

The Journal Review Process

Normally, there is a two-stage review process. In the first stage, the journal's staff consider if the paper submitted is consistent with the journal's aims and scope and instructions to authors, and if it is of sufficient quality to merit publication in the journal. The journal's staff also will consider whether or not there are likely to be any special issues related to the paper such as an assurance of appropriate consent of participants in a research study or potential competing interests of the author. If the journal's staff concludes that a paper submitted is not consistent with the aims and scope of the journal or is not sufficiently well written, the paper will be returned to the author directly.

In the second stage, if the paper submitted passes the screening process used by the journal's editorial staff, the editor will forward the paper for peer review, with questions to be considered by each reviewer. Deadlines are set for peer reviewers and journals consider carefully reviewers' comments on a paper. The peer review process tends to flag parts of a paper where the structure, content or meaning is not entirely clear or where the content is inconsistent with other research on the subject and the paper has not acknowledged or explained the inconsistency. The process is designed to improve the quality of papers published.

Guidance to Peer Reviewers

Each journal provides guidance to its peer reviewers on how to carry out the review of an article. Questions that journal editors might ask peer reviewers to consider are in Table 25.11.

Identity of Peer Reviewers

Traditionally, the journal peer review process has been double-blinded. The peer reviewers are not informed of the authors' identities and the authors do not know who the peer reviewers are. A randomized trial of open versus anonymous peer review of articles submitted to a medical journal demonstrated that asking peer reviewers to consent to being identified to the authors had no important effect on the quality of the review, the recommendation regarding publication, or the time taken to review (van Rooyen, Godlee, Evans, Black, & Smith, 1999). However, reviewers

---

TABLE 25.11 Possible Questions for Journal Peer Reviewers

Journal Peer Reviewer Questions About a Submission on a Research Project

Overall
- Is the article important to the field?
- Will the article help readers to make better decisions about practice and, if so, how?
- Will the article add to existing knowledge? Is the potential addition to existing knowledge sufficient to justify publication?
- Does the article read well and make sense?
- Does the article have a clear message?

For a Research Study
- Is the research question clearly defined and appropriately answered?
- Is the overall design of the study appropriate and adequate to answer the research question?
- Are the participants in the research study adequately described, along with inclusion and exclusion criteria? How representative of children for whom this evidence is relevant are the participants?
- Are the methods adequately described? Are the measures used in the research clear?
- Was the study ethical in its conduct?
- Do the results answer the research question? Are the results credible and well presented?
- Are the interpretation of the findings and the conclusions warranted by and sufficiently derived from the data collected? Are the findings discussed in relation to previous research findings? Is the message clear?
- Are the references up to date and relevant? Are there any glaring omissions from the references?
- Does the abstract or summary reflect accurately what the paper says?

who were randomized in the group to be asked to be identified were 12% more likely to decline to review than reviewers randomized to remain anonymous (35% vs. 23%).

The Editor's Decision Options

Following the peer review process, the journal's editor makes a decision about publication of the paper based on the comments of the reviewers. The editor's options normally are to: accept the paper as it was submitted; accept the paper if minor amendments are made; recommend that the paper be substantially revised and resubmitted; reject the paper with reasons provided; or recommend submission of the paper to another type of publication (Amodei et al., 2013). If a reviewer or the editorial staff identify one or more issues with the paper as submitted, but the journal wants to publish the paper if the amendments can be made, the journal's editor provides specific information about the reviewers' comments or parts of the paper that require revision, and invites the author to submit a revised version of the paper with a deadline for resubmission.

Responding to a Journal's Editor

It is easy to react emotionally to reviewers' or to a journal editor's comments about your article. Put aside your feelings and appreciate that the people who have read your paper are relying only on the paper to inform them about your work. They are not being critical of you as a researcher or a professional; they are merely saying that there are some points they would like to have clarified.

Unless a request for amendment would make content in the paper factually incorrect, it is good practice for an author to make amendments to an article that accommodate reviewers' comments as completely as possible. Should you take issue with a specific request for amendment on the basis that the requested amendment would be factually incorrect, submit a full explanation with supporting information, justifying your view.

SUMMARY

People who are responsible for and involved in early childhood education need to know about what research has shown to work best under what circumstances in order to enhance the quality of early childhood education. The spread of good practice in early childhood education is dependent on new knowledge being accessible in professional journals, and in turn, on researchers submitting their work for publication. Carrying out research and writing about it should be skills that students develop simultaneously.

There are a number of recognized benefits of publication. However, the writing and journal submission processes can be daunting to students and inexperienced authors. There is little research evidence available to guide authors on what makes a successful journal publication. Inexperienced authors and students can benefit from noting the limited research evidence available on writing for scientific journals and using a structured approach to writing a paper on a research study. Keys to preparing a paper on research with young children include the following:

- Decide on the people who would be interested in learning about your research, and the journal or journals they are likely to read.
- Be clear about the requirements for submissions to journals in which you are interested.
- Write one-sentence answers to key questions about your research, and use them as topic sentences of sections of the paper.
- After drafting a paper, check that you have met journal requirements and standards for reporting research, and edit the paper to ensure that every idea is as clearly and simply expressed as possible.
- Write the abstract, keywords and title for the paper after you have edited the first draft.
- Check a second draft of the paper against checklists for reporting on specific types of research papers and ask for specific feedback on your draft from colleagues.
- Submit your paper to the journal selected and be prepared to respond to the editor's response.

APPENDIX
Journals That Publish Research in Early Childhood Education

Publication Interests of Journals That Publish Research in Early Childhood Education

Australasian Journal of Early Childhood
Peer reviewed, four issues per year, published by Early Childhood Australia (ECA)
Includes research-based articles that are designed to impart new information and encourage the critical exchange of ideas among early childhood practitioners, academics and students
http://www.earlychildhoodaustralia.org.au/australian_journal_of_early_childhood/about_ajec.html

Childhood Education
Six issues per year, published by Association for Childhood Education International (ACEI)
Focuses on the learning and well-being of children around the world from birth through age 13, highlighting various perspectives on innovative classroom practices from around the world; cutting-edge concepts for education delivery; innovative schooling models; child growth and development theory; timely and vital issues affecting education, children, and their families; and research reviews from varied countries and advocacy- and policy-oriented organizations and academic institutions
http://www.acei.org/childhood-education

Contemporary Issues in Early Childhood
Four issues per year, published by Symposium Journals
Includes reports of research from a variety of paradigms; articles about research, literature reviews, and theoretical discussions; book reviews; colloquia and responses or critiques; and invited commentaries
http://www.wwwords.co.uk/ciec/

Dimensions of Early Childhood
Peer reviewed, three issues per year, published by Southern Early Childhood Association (SECA)
Includes articles and information of interest to early childhood professionals and translates "research into practice," making the latest research and early childhood data accessible to teachers and people working in early childhood classrooms
http://www.southernearlychildhood.org/publications.php

Early Child Development and Care
Peer reviewed, 12 issues per year, published by Routledge
Provides English translations of work in this field that has been published in other languages and original English papers on all aspects of early child development and care: descriptive and evaluative articles on social, educational and preventive medical programs for young children, experimental and observational studies, critical reviews and summary articles
http://www.tandfonline.com/action/journalinformation?show=aimsScope&journalCode=gecd20

Early Childhood Education Journal
Peer reviewed, six issues per year, published by Springer
Includes articles covering curriculum, childcare programs, administration, staff development,

family-school relationships, equity issues, multicultural units, health nutrition, facilities, special needs, employer-sponsored care, infant and toddler programs, child development, and advocacy. Areas of emphasis are: international studies, educational programs in diverse settings, projects demonstrating inter-professional collaboration, qualitative and quantitative research, case studies, theory, research, and practice relating to professional development, and family support and community action programs
http://www.springer.com/education+%26+language/learning+%26+instruction/journal/10643

Early Childhood Research and Practice
Peer reviewed, two issues per year, published by Early Childhood and Parenting (ECAP) Collaborative at the University of Illinois at Urbana-Champaign
Publishes research reports, literature reviews, essays, interviews, reflections, and commentary on emerging trends and issues by scholars and practitioners from around the world. Areas of emphasis include classroom practice, curriculum, ethics, teacher preparation, higher education, policy, and parent participation
http://ecrp.illinois.edu/

Early Childhood Research Quarterly
Peer reviewed, four issues per year, published by the National Association for the Education of Young Children (NAEYC)
Publishes predominantly empirical research (quantitative or qualitative methods) on issues of interest to early childhood development, theory, and educational practice (birth through 8 years of age). Occasionally publishes practitioner and/or policy perspectives, book reviews, and significant reviews of research and work that has social, policy, and educational relevance and implications and work that strengthens links between research and practice
http://www.journals.elsevier.com/early-childhood-research-quarterly/

Early Education and Development
Peer reviewed, eight issues per year, published by Routledge
Serves as a connecting link between the research community in early education and child development and school district early education programs, daycare systems, and special needs preschool programs
http://www.tandfonline.com/action/journalinformation?show=aimsScope&journalCode=heed20

Early Years: An International Research Journal
Peer reviewed, four issues per year, published by the Association for the Professional Development of Early Years Educators (TACTYC)
Publishes research papers and scholarly critiques on all issues associated with early childhood education and care. Overall approach is international and multi-disciplinary, aiming to broaden the cross-national debate by representing a wide range of perspectives from different countries, different disciplines and different research methodologies and paradigms
http://www.tandfonline.com/action/journalinformation?show=aimsScope&journalCode=ceye20

Education 3–13: International Journal of Primary, Elementary and Early Years Education
Peer reviewed, six issues per year, published by Association for the Study of Primary Education (ASPE)
Publishes articles on high quality research and analysis of practice relating to children aged 3–13 years, both in the UK and internationally, that will help to develop policy and practice in primary education and will also assist practitioners by providing helpful and

stimulating ways of viewing what they do or might do
http://www.tandfonline.com/action/journalinformation?show=aimsScope&journalCode=ciey20

European Early Childhood Research Journal

Peer reviewed, four issues per year, published by European Early Childhood Education Research Association (EECERA)

Publishes papers that have a clear application to early childhood education and care policy and practice and seeks to provide a common forum for shared issues in early childhood education research, and, on occasion, to provide a forum for controversy in the discussion of such issues. Includes reports of research in progress, discussion of conceptual and methodological issues and review articles
http://www.tandfonline.com/action/aboutThisJournal?show=aimsScope&journalCode=recr20

International Journal of Early Childhood

Peer reviewed, three issues per year, published by l'Organisation Mondiale pour l'Education Préscolaire

Contributes to an international and critical scientific debate about research and practice in the field of early childhood with an emphasis on children's rights and general position in society and their education all over the world. Includes theoretical and empirical articles addressing key issues in early childhood on diverse topics, from different disciplines and perspectives, and with various research methodologies, which will be of interest to researchers and practitioners internationally
http://www.springer.com/education+%26+language/journal/13158

International Journal of Early Years Education

Peer reviewed, four issues per year, published by Routledge

Provides a forum for researchers and practitioners to debate the theories, research, policy, and practice that sustain effective early years education worldwide. Offers a comparative perspective on early years research and major new initiatives in the care and education of young children
http://www.tandfonline.com/action/journalinformation?show=aimsScope&journalCode=ciey20

International Journal of Early Childhood Education and Care

Two issues per year, National Child Development Research Center, Sultan Idris Education University, Malaysia

Publishes research on children, childhood and early childhood education across various social and cultural contexts and contributes to the international debate on early education. The journal covers topics such as multicultural issues, children's learning and sustainable development, recent issues in early childhood education and care and curriculum questions. The journal places considerable emphasis on the child's right to education and care.
http://www.noodls.com/viewNoodl/12698986/universiti-pendidikan-sultan-idris/international-journal-f-early-childhood-education-and-care

International Research in Early Childhood Education

Peer reviewed, two issues per year, published by Monash University Education

Publishes articles about the field of early childhood education and its international contexts, matters relevant to debate within the field in local and regional contexts, issues arising from interdisciplinary relationships between early childhood education and other fields, such as post-developmental approaches to psychology, socio-cultural/cultural environmental science and globalisation, refugee studies, international policy studies, feminism and queer studies, space and place, and post-structuralist research http://www.education.monash.edu.au/research/irecejournal/about.html

Journal of Early Childhood Research
Peer reviewed, three issues per year, published by Sage Journals
Provides an international forum on childhood research, bridging cross-disciplinary areas and applying theory and research within the professional community
http://ecr.sagepub.com/

Journal for Early Childhood Teacher Education
Peer reviewed, four issues per year, published by the National Association of Early Childhood Teacher Educators (NAECTE)
Provides a forum for consideration of issues and for exchange of information and ideas about research and practice in early childhood teacher education. Includes research reports, position papers, essays on current issues, and reflective reports on innovative teacher education practices
http://www.tandfonline.com.action/journalinformation?show=aimsScope&journalCode=ujec20

Journal of Early Intervention
Peer reviewed, four issues per year, published by The Division of Early Childhood (DEC) of the Council for Exception Children and Sage Journals
Includes articles related to research and practice in early intervention for infants and young children with special needs and their families. Early intervention is broadly defined as procedures that facilitate the development of infants and young children who have special needs or who are at risk for developmental disabilities
http://www.dec-sped.org/Journals

Journal of Research in Childhood Education
Peer reviewed, four issues per year published by the Association for Childhood Education International (ACEI)
Features articles that advance knowledge and theory of the education of children, infancy through early adolescence. Reports empirical research, theoretical articles, ethnographic and case studies, participant observation studies, studies deriving data collected from naturalistic settings, cross-cultural studies, and studies addressing international concerns
http://www.acei.org/jrce.html

Pastoral Care in Education: An International Journal of Personal, Social and Emotional Development
Peer reviewed, four issues per year, published by the National Association of Pastoral Care in Education
Publishes on contemporary issues such as current developments in the curriculum, including citizenship; health, social and moral education; managing behavior; whole school approaches; school structures; and issues of care such as school exclusion, bullying and emotional development
http://www.tandfonline.com/action/Journalinformation?show=aimsScope&journalCode=rped20

Topics in Early Childhood Special Education
Peer reviewed, four issues per year, published by Hammill Institute on Disabilities and Sage Journals
Focuses on information that will improve the lives of young children with special needs and their families by helping professionals improve service delivery systems for preschool children with special needs
http://tec.sagepub.com/

Young Children
Peer reviewed, five issues per year, published by National Association for the Education of Young Children (NAEYC)
Publishes relevant research-based articles organized around themes important to the early childhood education field and focused for practitioners
http://www.naeyc.org/yc/about

Young Exceptional Children
Peer reviewed, four issues per year, published by the Division of Early Childhood (DEC) of the Council for Exceptional Children and Sage Journals
Provides a practical resource designed for teachers, administrators, therapists, family members and others who work with young children with special needs
http://www.dec-sped.org/Journals

Note: The information in this table was obtained from the journal websites provided at the time of publication.

REFERENCES

American Educational Research Association. (2006). Standards for reporting on empirical social science research in AERA publications. *Educational Researcher, 35*(6), 33–40.

American Educational Research Association. (2009). Standards for reporting on humanities-oriented research in AERA publications. *Educational Researcher, 38*(6), 481–486.

American Psychological Association. (2010). *Publication Manual of the American Psychological Association.* (6th ed.). Washington DC: American Psychological Association.

Amodei, M. L., Jalongo, M. R., Myers, J., Onchwari, J., & Gargiulo, R. M. (2013). Survey of publication outlets in early childhood education: Descriptive data, review processes, and advice to authors. *Early Childhood Education Journal, 41*(2), 115–123.

APA Science Student Council. (2006). A graduate student's guide to determining authorship credit and authorship order. Retrieved from http://www/apa.org/science/leadership/students/authorship-paper.aspx

Bergstrom, C. (2007). Eigenfactor: Measuring the value and prestige of scholarly journals. *College & Research Libraries News*, 314–316. Retrieved from http://crln.acrl.org/content/68/5/314.full.pdf+html?sid=b4733b01-152c-4e87-b9eb-2610afd25a72

Björk, B. C., & Solomon, D. (2012). Open access versus subscription journals: A comparison of scientific impact. *BMC Medicine, 10,* 73.

Clark, J. P. (2003). How to peer review a qualitative manuscript. In F. Godlee & T. Jefferson (Eds.), *Peer review in health sciences.* (2nd ed., pp. 219–235). London: BMJ Books. Retrieved from http://www.biomedcentral.com/authors/rats

Davidoff, F., Batalden, P., Stevens, D., Ogrinc, G., & Mooney, S. (2008). Publication guidelines for quality improvement in health care: evolution of the SQUIRE project. *Quality and Safety in Health Care, 17* (supplement 1), i3–i9.

Davis, P., Lewenstein, B. V., Simon, D. H., Booth, J. G., & Connolly, M. J. L. (2008). Open access publishing, article downloads, and citations: Randomised controlled trial. *British Medical Journal, 337*, a568.

Dixon, N. (1999). *Writing about a clinical project for a report or for publication.* Romsey, England: Healthcare Quality Quest.

Dixon, N. (2001). Writing for publication—a guide for new authors. *International Journal for Quality in Health Care, 13*(5), 417–421.

Dixon, N. (2011). Writing for publication for the first time—try the hunter style. *International Journal of Physiotherapy and Rehabilitation, 1*(2), 38–45.

Garfield, E. (2005, September). *The agony and the ecstasy—The history and meaning of the journal impact factor.* Paper presented at the International Congress on Peer Review and Biomedical Publication, Chicago, IL. Retrieved from http://garfield.library.upenn.edu/papers/jifchicago2005.pdf

Gargiulo, R., Jalongo, M. R., & Motari, J. (2001). Writing for publication in early childhood education: Survey data from editors and advice to authors. *Early Childhood Education Journal, 29*(1), 17–23.

González-Pereira, B., Guerrero-Bote, V. P., & Moya-Anegón, F. (2009). The SJR indicator: A new indicator of journals' scientific prestige. Retrieved from http://www.scimagojr.com/

Gump, S. E. (2010). Publishing pedagogies for the doctorate and beyond (review). *Journal of Scholarly Publishing, 41*(4), 496.

Hagel, P. (2011). Writing for publication about student learning, teaching or professional practice in higher education. Retrieved from http://www.deakin.edu.au/herg/resources/herg-guides.php

Hirsch, J. E. (2005). An index to quantify an individual's scientific research output. *Proceedings of the National Academy of Sciences, 102*(46), 16569–16572.

Hoot, J. L., & Szente, J. (2013). Avoiding professional publication panic: Advice to new scholars seeking to publish in the field of early childhood education. *Early Childhood Education Journal, 41*(1), 5–11.

Jacques, T. S., & Sebire, N. J. (2010). The impact of article titles on citation hits: an analysis of general and specialist medical journals. *Journal of the Royal Society of Medicine Short Reports, 1*(1/2). Doi: 10.1258/shorts.2009.100020

Jalongo, M. R. (2013a). Getting on the conference program and writing a practical article: Templates for success. *Early Childhood Education Journal, 41*(1), 13–23.

Jalongo, M. R. (2013b). Professional wisdom and writing for publication: Qualitative interviews with editors and authors in early childhood education. *Early Childhood Education Journal, 41*, 65–79.

Jenkins, D. B. (2002). Writing for publication: Overcoming the barriers that block us. *Mid-Western Educational Researcher, 15*(1), 31–32.

Kamler, B. (2008). Rethinking doctoral publication practices: Writing from and beyond the thesis. *Studies in Higher Education, 33*(3), 283–294.

Laakso, M., Welling, P., Bukvova, H., Nyman, L., Björk, B., & Hedlund, T. (2011). The development of open access journal publishing from 1993 to 2009. *Public Library of Science* (June 13), 6(6), e20961.

Lee, A. (2010). When the article is the dissertation: Pedagogies for a PhD by publication. In C. Aitchison, B. Kamler, & A. Lee (Eds.), *Publishing pedagogies for the doctorate and beyond* (pp. 12–29). NY: Routledge.

Moed, H. F. (2010). Measuring contextual citation impact of scientific journals. *Journal of Informetrics, 4*(3), 265–277.
Moher, D., Liberati, A., Tetzlaff, J., Altman, D. G., & The PRISMA Group. (2009). Preferred reporting items for systematic review and meta-analyses: The PRISMA statement. *British Medical Journal, 339,* b2535.
Moreno, T. (2008). Editorial. *Early Childhood Matters, 110,* 1–2.
Morris, S. (2006). *Getting started in electronic journal publishing* (5th ed., pp. 1–7). Retrieved from International Network for the Availability of Scientific Publications web site.
Murray, R. (2009). *Writing for academic journals* (2nd ed.) Maidenhead, England: Open University Press.
Osborne, J. W., & Holland, A. (2009). What is authorship, and what should it be? A survey of prominent guidelines for determining authorship in scientific publications. *Practical Assessment, Research & Evaluation, 14*(15). Retrieved from http://pareonline.net/pdf/v14n15.pdf
Peralta, M. V. (2008). Quality: Children's right to appropriate and relevant education. *Early Childhood Matters, 110,* 3–12.
Saracho, O. N. (2013). Writing research articles for publication in early childhood education. *Early Childhood Education Journal, 41*(1), 45–54.
Schulz, K. F., Altman, D. G., Moher, D., & CONSORT Group. (2010). CONSORT 2010 Statement: Updated guidelines for reporting parallel group randomized trials. *Annals of Internal Medicine, 152,* 726–732. Epub 2010 Mar 24.
Stroup, D. F., Berlin, J. A., Morton, S. C., Olkin, I., Williamson G. G., Rennie, D., ... Thacker, S. B. (2000). Meta-analysis of observational studies in epidemiology: A proposal for reporting. Meta-analysis of Observational Studies in Epidemiology (MOOSE) group. *Journal of the American Medical Association, 283*(15), 2008–2012.
Van Rooven, S., Godlee, F., Evans, S., Black, N., & Smith, R. (1999). Effect of open peer review on quality of reviews and on reviewers' recommendations: a randomised trial. *British Medical Journal, 318*(7175), 23–27.

FURTHER READING

Albers, C. A., Floyd, R. G., Fuhrmann, M. J., & Martinez, R. S. (2011). Publication criteria and recommended areas of improvement within school psychology journals as reported by editors, journal board members, and manuscript authors. *Journal of School Psychology, 49*(6), 669–689.
Floyd, R. G., Cooley, K. M., Arnett, J. E., Fagan, T. K., Mercer, S. H., & Hingle, C. (2011). An overview and analysis of journal operations, journal publication patterns, and journal impact in school psychology and related fields. *Journal of School Psychology, 49*(6), 617–647.
Körner, A. M. (2008). *Guide to Publishing a Scientific Paper.* NY: Routledge.
Rafanello, D. (2006). Publish your writing: Sharing your ideas with the early childhood community. *Exchange,* November/December, 68–71.
Wellington, J. (2003). *Getting Published. A guide for lecturers and researchers.* London: Routledge.

Although the following articles use clinical chemistry examples, they are unique in explaining ways to present an introduction, methods and statistics in professional journals:

Annesley, T. M. (2010). Bars and pies make better desserts than figures. *Clinical Chemistry, 56*(9), 1394–1400.
Annesley, T. M. (2010). "It was a cold and rainy night": Set the scene with a good introduction. *Clinical Chemistry, 56*(5), 708–713.
Annesley, T. M. (2010). Put your best figure forward: Line graphs and scattergrams. *Clinical Chemistry, 56*(8), 1229–1233.
Annesley, T. M. (2010). Who, what, when, where, how, and why: The ingredients in the recipe for a successful methods section. *Clinical Chemistry, 56*(6), 897–901.

Also, see the January 2013 special issue of the *Early Childhood Education Journal* on Writing for publication.

ABOUT THE CONTRIBUTORS

Angela C. Baum received her PhD in Early Childhood Education from Iowa State University. She is an Associate Professor of Early Childhood Education in the Department of Instruction and Teacher Education at the University of South Carolina. Her expertise lies in the areas of early childhood teacher preparation and professional development. She is currently engaged with the South Carolina Department of Social Services on several child care quality initiatives. She actively presents, at both the state and national level, on topics related to the preparation of early childhood professionals. Her work has been published in journals such as *Young Children, Journal of Early Childhood Teacher Education, Early Childhood Education,* and *Action in Teacher Education.*

Rosanne Burton Smith is Honorary Research Associate in the School of Psychology at the University of Tasmania in Tasmania Australia, since 1989. Previously she taught at the Goroka campus of the University of Papua New Guinea (1988) and held positions as a practicing psychologist in the UK, New Zealand, and Papua New Guinea. Current research interests include peer relationships, disability issues, gender differences and body image.

Rosanne obtained her PhD in psychology from the University of Tasmania. She also holds a Masters degree in educational psychology from the University of Exeter UK. Her professional activities include several years working as a psychologist in Papua New Guinea in the fields of educational and occupational psychology; and later in the UK and New Zealand in the area of developmental disabilities. Rosanne's teaching and research interests cover psychological assessment; developmental issues such as childhood anxiety and the effects of divorce on minors; gender differences in children's peer relationships; and body image and dietary behaviour in adolescents and young adults. Rosanne has taught at both undergraduate and postgraduate levels in the School of Psychology University of Tasmania since 1989. She retired from full-time teaching and research activities in 2007, but continues at the School in a voluntary capacity

Helen Cameron is a retired academic who has current Adjunct Senior Research Fellow status in the School of Psychology, Social Work & Social Policy, within the University of South Australia. Her research and academic publications focus on counselling and interviewing both children and adults, families and children in poverty, images of social workers, aspects of undergraduate and postgraduate education, housing and mental health, monitoring and addressing aggression and road rage. She is also a published poet. She currently has several PhD students under her supervision. She lives in the regional seaside town of Victor Harbor in South Australia.

Kathy Charmaz is Professor of Sociology and Director of the Faculty Writing Program at Sonoma State University. She has written, co-authored, or co-edited nine books including *Good Days, Bad Days: The Self in Chronic Illness and Time*, which received awards from the Pacific Sociological Association and the Society for the Study of Symbolic Interaction, and *Constructing Grounded Theory: A Practical Guide through Qualitative Analysis*, which received a Critics' Choice award from the American Educational Studies Association and has been translated into Chinese, Japanese, Polish, and Portuguese. Her recent multi-authored books are *Five Ways of Doing Qualitative Analysis: Phenomenological Psychology, Grounded Theory, Discourse Analysis, Narrative Research, and Intuitive Inquiry* and *Developing Grounded Theory: The Second Generation*. Dr. Charmaz gives professional development workshops on qualitative methods and writing for publication across the globe.

Douglas H. Clements is Kennedy Endowed Chair in Early Childhood Learning and Professor at the University of Denver. Previously a kindergarten teacher for five years and a preschool teacher for one year, he has conducted research and published widely in the areas of the learning and teaching of early mathematics and computer applications in mathematics education. His most recent interests are in creating, using, and evaluating a research-based curriculum and in taking successful curricula to scale using technologies and learning trajectories. He has published over 120 refereed research studies, 18 books, 70 chapters, and 275 additional publications. His latest books detail research-based learning trajectories in early mathematics education: *Early childhood mathematics education research: Learning *trajectories for young children* and a companion book, *Learning and teaching early math: The learning trajectories approach* (Routledge).

Dr. Clements has directed 20 projects funded by the National Science Foundation (NSF) and the U.S. Dept. of Educations, Institute of Education Sciences (IES). Currently, Dr. Clements is Principal Investigator on two large-scale randomized cluster trial projects (IES). He is also working with colleagues to study and refine learning trajectories in measurement (NSF). Two recent research projects have just been funded by the NSF. Clements is PI on the first, *Using Rule Space and Poset-based Adaptive Testing Methodologies to Identify Ability Patterns in Early Mathematics and Create a Comprehensive Mathematics Ability Test*, which will develop a computer-adaptive assessment for early mathematics. Clements is co-PI on the second, *Early Childhood Education in the Context of Mathematics, Science, and Literacy*, developing an interdisciplinary preschool curriculum.

Dr. Clements was a member of President Bush's National Math Advisory Panel, convened to advise the administration on the best use of scientifically based research to advance the teaching and learning of mathematics and coauthor of the Panel's report. He was also a member of the National Research Council's Committee on Early Mathematics and co-author of their report. He is presently serving on the *Common Core State Standards* committee of the National Governor's Association and the Council of Chief State School Officers, helping to write national academic standards and the learning trajectories that underlie them. He is one of the authors of NCTM's *Principles and Standards in School Mathematics* and *Curriculum Focal Points*. See http://portfolio.du.edu/dclemen9.

Chonika Coleman-King is Assistant Professor of Theory and Practice in Teacher Education at the University of Tennessee. Her research and teaching focus on urban-multicultural issues in education. She is particularly interested in the identity development of Black American and Afro-Caribbean students and their experiences in U.S. schools. Currently, she is completing a manuscript for a book entitled, *The (Re-)Making of a Black American: Tracing the Racial and Ethnic Socialization of Caribbean American Youth*. She has also published on the topic of multimodal literacy instruction for students from immigrant backgrounds (with Kathy Schultz).

Gabrielle Coppola is a researcher at the *Department of Neuroscience and Imaging*, University "G. D'Annunzio" of Chieti-Pescara, Italy. She completed her PhD study at the Department of Psychology of the University of Bari, and received Post-doctoral training at the Department of Human Development & Family Studies, Auburn University, USA. Her research focuses on attachment processes throughout the life span and social development in the first years.

Kathleen H. Corriveau is an Assistant Professor of Human Development in the School of Education at Boston University, where she is the director of the Social Learning Lab. She earned a ScB in Cognitive Neuroscience from Brown University a MPhil in Education from the University of Cambridge, and a doctorate in Human Development and Psychology from Harvard University. Her research interests are broadly in social cognitive development, with a specific focus on children's learning from others. She is on the editorial boards of the *Journal of Experimental Child Psychology* and the *Journal of Cognition and Development and Developmental Psychology* and has published in major psychological and educational journals such as *Psychological Science, Developmental Psychology,* and *Child Development.*

Nancy Dixon teaches doctors and other healthcare professionals who are in professional training programs how to write for publication about research and quality improvement studies. She has written guidance on writing for publication and has served as editor of a journal on quality in healthcare. She also is the author or co-author of a number of technical books in the field of quality and safety in healthcare.

Carl J. Dunst, PhD, is a Research Scientist, Orelena Hawks Puckett Institute, Asheville and Morganton, North Carolina. His research has included the meta-analyses of evidence-based early childhood intervention practices and evidence-based family systems intervention practices, and the methods and procedures for promoting early childhood intervention practitioners' use of evidence-based practices with fidelity as part of routine home-based and center-based interventions. His recent research and practice has focused on the applicability of implementation sciences for understanding the relationships between professional development practices and early childhood practitioners' sustained use of evidence-based intervention practices.

Julie Dwyer is an Assistant Professor of Education in the Early Childhood Department at Boston University. Dr. Dwyer holds an M.Ed. in Language and Literacy from Harvard University and a PhD in Language, Literacy, and Culture from the University of Michigan. Her research focuses on early language and literacy learning and teaching, with a particular focus on vocabulary development and instruction and the interplay between conceptual knowledge and vocabulary development. She is on the editorial board of *Reading Research Quarterly* and the *Journal of Literacy Research* and has presented at local and national reading and educational research conferences on vocabulary development and instruction in early childhood settings. She has also published in *Reading Research Quarterly, Early Childhood Research Quarterly, The Reading Teacher,* and *Early Childhood Education Journal.*

Richard Faldowski is an Associate Professor in the Department of Allied Health Sciences at the University of North Carolina at Chapel Hill. He received his PhD in 1995 in quantitative psychology with a minor in cognitive science from the L.L. Thurstone Psychometric Laboratory at the University of North Carolina at Chapel Hill. Prior to coming to UNC-CH, Dr. Faldowski was on the faculty of the University of North Carolina at Greensboro and the Medical University of South Carolina. He is a quantitative psychologist with dual research foci on quantitative methods and context-sensitive treatment and prevention programs for children and families placed at risk of adverse developmental outcomes by health, poverty, abuse, and other psychosocial circumstances. He is the principal investigator for the South Carolina site in the (U.S.) national evaluation of Early Head Start, and has extensive methodological consultation experience on a host of behavioral and medical research projects. He has long-standing interests in understanding and modeling developmental processes and reciprocal influences between collective and individual aspects of social phenomena. Currently, Dr. Faldowski is on the editorial boards of *Integrative Psychological & Behavioral Science* and *Developmental Psychobiology*.

Heidi Gazelle is Senior Lecturer (equivalent to Associate Professor in North America) in Developmental Psychology in the Melbourne School of Psychological Sciences at the University of Melbourne, Australia. Her 2002 PhD from the University of Illinois at Urbana-Champaign won the 2003 Division 7 (Developmental) American Psychological Association Dissertation Award. She held a postdoctoral fellowship at the Center for Developmental Science at the University at North Carolina at Chapel Hill from 2002 to 2004. She subsequently directed the longitudinal study *Multiple Trajectories in Anxious Solitary Youth*, funded by an NIMH K01 Career Award, while at the University of North Carolina at Greensboro. Her programmatic line of research emphasizes the interaction between the vulnerabilities and strengths of anxious solitary children and the risks and supports available in their interpersonal environments; guided by a holistic, interactionist child by environment perspective. Together with Ken Rubin, she is editor of the *New Directions for Child and Adolescent Development* monograph *Social Anxiety in Childhood: Bridging Developmental and Clinical Perspectives* (2010). She currently serves on the editorial boards of *Child Development* and the *International Journal of Behavioral Development*.

J. Amos Hatch is Professor of Theory and Practice in Teacher Education at the University of Tennessee. He has published widely in the areas of early childhood education, qualitative research, and teacher education. He served co-executive editor of *Qualitative Studies in Education* from 1991 to 1996 and the *Journal of Early Childhood Teacher Education* from 2008 to 2012.

He has written or edited a number of books, including *Teaching in the New Kindergarten* (Thompson, 2005), *Early Childhood Qualitative Research* (Routledge, 2007), and (with Susan Groenke) *Critical Pedagogy and Teacher Education in the Neoliberal Era* (Springer, 2009).

Kelly Heider is an associate professor at Indiana University of Pennsylvania (IUP) where she serves as an embedded librarian in the College of Education and Educational Technology. In 2012, she received the Lloyd W. Briscoe Award for outstanding service to students in IUP's Department of Professional Studies in Education. Before joining the faculty at IUP, Kelly was a public school teacher for the Burrell School District where she taught middle and high school English, worked as a library media specialist, and served as chair of the library department. Her research interests include embedded librarianship, information literacy, the integration of technology and curricula, and service-learning programs. She currently coordinates a service-learning program for students enrolled in IUP's Early Childhood—Special Education Program. Kelly has published several journal articles in Springer's *Early Childhood Education Journal* and has presented at numerous international conferences sponsored by organizations such as the Association for Childhood Education International and the Society for Information Technology and Teacher Education.

Susan E. Hill, Associate Professor of Early Childhood, School of Education, University of South Australia. Her research interests are early literacy development, family literacy and case study research methodology.

Mary Renck Jalongo is a professor at Indiana University of Pennsylvania where she earned the university-wide outstanding professor award and coordinates the Doctoral Program in Curriculum and Instruction. As a classroom teacher, she worked with children of migrant farm workers in a federally funded bilingual preschool program. She has written, co-authored, or edited more than 25 books, including *Early Childhood Language Arts, 6th edition, Creative Thinking and Arts-Based Learning, 6th edition, Exploring Your Role: An Introduction to Early Childhood Education, 4th edition*, and *Major Trends and Issues in Early Childhood Education: Challenges, Controversies, and Insights, 2nd edition*. In addition, she has written two books for NAEYC (*Learning to Listen, Listening to Learn* and *Young Children and Picture Books*, 2nd edition) and two for ACEI. Her writing has earned seven national awards for excellence that include two EDPRESS awards for Position Papers published by the Association for Childhood Education International. Since 1995, she has served as editor-in-chief of the Springer international publication, *Early Childhood Education Journal* and, since 2006, as series editor for Springer's edited book series, *Educating the Young Child: Advances in Theory and Research, Implications* *for Practice*. She has made presentations throughout the world on various aspects of early childhood education.

Aesha John is an Assistant Professor in the Department of Social Work at Northeastern State University, Broken Arrow, Oklahoma. She utilizes quantitative and qualitative approaches as well as Q methodology to examine wellbeing among families of children and adolescents with developmental disabilities in the US and India. She teaches social work classes on children and families, human behavior, social policy, and research. Aesha received her M.S.W from the Maharaja Sayajirao University, India and her PhD in Human Development & Family Science from the Oklahoma State University.

Linda Liebenberg, PhD, is Co-Director of the Resilience Research Centre (RRC), and Adjunct Professor, Faculty of Graduate Studies, Dalhousie University. She is a methodologist with an interest in image-based methods and mixed-methods designs. Linda's research examines the use of these methods in understanding the lives of children and youth living in challenging contexts. In addition to offering training in the use of elicitation and iterative use of methods, her work also includes the design of measurement instruments used with children and youth. She has published and presented internationally on resilience related themes relevant to the understanding of youth across cultures and contexts. Her publications include the two co-edited volumes (with Michael Ungar, PhD) *Researching Resilience* and *Resilience in Action*.

Paula McMurray-Schwarz received her PhD in Early Childhood Education and Child Development from The Ohio State University. She is an Associate Professor of Early Childhood Education in the Department of Teacher Education at Ohio University Eastern Campus. Her research interests include how teacher educators can assist early childhood teachers as they transition from pre-service to in-service status and technology use in early childhood teacher education. She actively presents at the national level on topics related to the preparation of early childhood professionals. Her work has been published in journals such as *Early Childhood Education Journal, Journal of Early Childhood Teacher Education, Early Childhood Research Quarterly, and International Journal of Qualitative Studies in Education*.

Ngaire Millar is engaged in case study research projects at the School of Education, University of South Australia. Her research interests are inquiry based learning and young children and cyber safety.

Diane Montgomery is Regents Professor of Educational Psychology at Oklahoma State University in the College of Education where she coordinates programs in educational psychology and gifted education. Her areas of research include Q methodology, creativity, transpersonal psychology, Native American Indian education, and teacher development. She has held positions on several editorial boards, such as *Operant Subjectivity: The International Journal for Q Methodology* and the *Journal of Human Subjectivity;* and boards of directors of national professional organizations, including The Association for the Gifted, a division of the Council for Exceptional Children and American Council on Rural Special Education.

David Oppenheim, PhD is Professor in the Department of Psychology and a member of the Center for the Study of Child Development at the University of Haifa, Israel. Dr. Oppenheim's research focuses on the central importance of caregiving relationships for children's social and emotional development. In particular, his research has examined the role of parental *Insightfulness* and *parent-child open communication* in the organization of attachment relationships throughout childhood. Dr. Oppenheim's studies on these questions involved longitudinal studies, and included typically developing children, children at high risk such as those in foster care, and children with atypical development such as Autism and Mental Retardation.

Lisa M. Perhamus is an Assistant Professor of Social Foundations of Education in Grand Valley State University's College of Education. She received her BA from William Smith College, her MA in Sociology from The New School for Social Research and her PhD in Curriculum Studies from the University of Rochester. Her research and teaching interests focus on the sociopolitical contexts of schooling, with particular attention to issues facing urban schools, families and neighborhoods. She specializes in the sociology of childhood and the sociology of curriculum.

Divya Peter is a graduate student in the Melbourne School of Psychological Sciences at the University of Melbourne, Australia. She received her Masters in Psychology in 2010 from the University of Mumbai, India. She is currently studying how self-compassion and self-criticism moderate the relation between childhood anxious solitude and depressive symptom trajectories.

Melinda Raab, PhD, is an Associate Research Scientist, Orelena Hawks Puckett Institute, Asheville and Morganton, North Carolina. Her research has focused on the characteristics and consequences of everyday child learning opportunities, the characteristics of early childhood classroom settings associated with positive child outcomes, and the extended benefits of response-contingent learning opportunities for children with significant developmental delays. Dr. Raab, along with Drs. Trivette and Dunst, has recently investigated the characteristics and consequences of effective professional development for use with early childhood educators.

Edna Runnels Ranck has worked in the early childhood education (ECE) field for over 40 years in volunteer and paid positions: church school kindergarten teacher and primary superintendent, preschool child care center director, child care resource and referral agency director, family child care network administrator, accreditation program observer, NJ state child care coordinator, director of public policy and research for a national nonprofit organization, senior researcher for military child care contracts, and accreditation facilitation project director for the nation's capital. She has published book chapters, journal articles, and online columns on ECE historical and administrative topics, and has presented at conferences throughout the United States and in 19 countries. In addition, she moderates the History Seminar at National Association for the Education of Young Children annual conferences; co-coordinates Our Proud Heritage, the history column for NAEYC's *Young Children* journal; and has served as OMEP-USA president. Her degrees are from Florida State University, Drew University, and Teachers College, Columbia University.

Beth Rous, is Professor and Chair of the Department of Educational Leadership Studies at the University of Kentucky. She serves as Director of the Kentucky Partnership for Early Childhood Services at the Human Development Institute at UK. Dr. Rous' primary interest is on the intersection between child care, early intervention, early childhood special education, Head Start and public pre-kindergarten programs. Her research and scholarship has focused on three major areas: 1) transition of young children between and among early childhood systems; 2) state standards and accountability systems; and 3) quality of workforce and service systems. She has served as a consultant and/or advisor on numerous national studies such as the State and Local Implementation of IDEA and Pre-Elementary Education Longitudinal Studies, and served as Principal Investigator for the National Early Childhood Transition Research Center.

António J. Santos is currently Associate Professor at ISPA-Instituto *Universitário de Ciências Psicológicas, Sociais e da Vida* where he teaches Research Methods. He received his Clinical Psychology Degree from ISPA-University Institute and his PhD in Developmental Psychology from the Université du Québec à Montréal, Canada. His main research on peer relationships embraces the fields of social ethology and child social development, focusing in particular on affiliative structures and social competence. He has coordinated several funded research projects and directed a large number of Masters and Phd Students.

Olivia N. Saracho is professor of education in the Department of Teaching, Learning, Policy, and Leadership at the University of Maryland. She has conducted research and written numerous articles on children's play. She is the author of *An Integrated Play-based Curriculum for Young Children* (Routledge/Taylor & Francis). She has also edited books on children's play such as *Contemporary Perspectives on Play in Early Childhood Education* (Information Age Publishing) and *Multiple Perspectives on Play in Early Childhood Education* (State University of New York Press). Olivia N. Saracho is coeditor, with Bernard Spodek, of the *Handbook of Research on the Education of Young Children*, 3/ed. (2013 Routledge/Taylor & Francis). She is also editor of the *Contemporary Perspectives in Early Childhood Education* series (Information Age).

Julie Sarama is the Kennedy Endowed Chair in Innovative Learning Technologies and Professor at the University of Denver. She conducts research on young children's development of mathematical concepts and competencies, implementation and scale-up of educational reform, professional development models and their influence on student learning, and implementation and effects of software environments (including those she has created) in mathematics classrooms. These studies have been published in more than 50 refereed articles, 4 books, 30 chapters, and 60 additional publications. She has been Principal or Co-Principal Investigator on seven projects funded by the National Science Foundation, including *Building Blocks—Foundations for Mathematical Thinking, Pre-kindergarten to Grade 2: Research-based Materials Development* and *Planning for Professional Development in Pre-School Mathematics: Meeting the Challenge of Standards 2000*. She is Principal Investigator on her latest NSF award, entitled, *"Early Childhood Education in the Context of Mathematics, Science, and Literacy."*

Dr. Sarama is also co-directing three large-scale studies funded by the U.S. Education Department's Institute of Educational Studies (IES). The first is entitled, *Scaling Up TRIAD: Teaching Early Mathematics for Understanding with Trajectories and Technologies*. The second is a longitudinal extension of that work, entitled, *Longitudinal Study of a Successful Scaling Up Project: Extending TRIAD*. The third, with Dr. Sarama as Principal Investigator, is an efficacy study, *Increasing the efficacy of an early mathematics curriculum with scaffolding designed to promote self-regulation*. Dr. Sarama was previously the lead co-PI at the Buffalo site on another IES-funded project, *A Longitudinal study of the Effects of a Pre-Kindergarten Mathematics Curriculum on Low-Income Children's Mathematical Knowledge* (IES; one of seven of a cohort of national projects conducted simultaneous local and national studies as part of the IES's *Preschool Curriculum Evaluation Research* project).

Dr. Sarama has taught secondary mathematics and computer science, gifted math at the middle school level, preschool and kindergarten mathematics enrichment classes, and mathematics methods and content courses for elementary to secondary teachers. In addition, she presenting is the Director of the Gifted Mathematics Program (GMP) at the University of Buffalo, SUNY. She designed and programmed over 50 published computer programs, including her version of Logo and Logo-based software activities (*Turtle Math*™, which was awarded *Technology & Learning* Software of the Year award, 1995, in the category "Math").

Ian Sinha is a pediatrician, researcher, and clinical educator. His research interests include the use of consensus techniques to standardize the design of clinical trials in children.

Catherine C. Smith is a doctoral student at the University of Tennessee-Knoxville, Department of Theory and Practice in Teacher Education, Special Education and Instructional Technology Instructional Program. Her research interests include the use of assistive, instructional and video technologies to support children and adolescents with intellectual disabilities and Autism.

Kylie Smith is a research fellow and senior lecturer in the Youth Research Centre at the Graduate School of Education, University of Melbourne. Kylie has extensive knowledge and experience of early childhood education policy and practice issues, built over 20 years in education as a teacher and, more recently, as a researcher. She has a passion for researching *with* people and particularly supporting young children participating as co-researchers. Kylie has drawn on action research as a participatory research methodology in 12 research projects working with children, families, educators, community leaders and policy makers.

John A. Sutterby is an associate professor of Early Childhood Education at the University of Texas at San Antonio. His research interests include bilingual education, family involvement, and outdoor play and play environments.

Robert Thornberg is Associate Professor of Education at Linköping University, Sweden, and an international research faculty member of the Center for Research on School Safety, School Climate and Classroom Management, at the College of Education, Georgia State University, Atlanta, U.S. His current research is on school bullying as social processes as well as from the perspectives of the students. His second line of research is on values education, morality and school rules in everyday school life. He is also a board member of the Nordic Educational Research Association (NERA) and a coordinator for the NERA Network of Value Issues and Social Relations in Education as well.

Amy Halliburton Tate is a Clinical Assistant Professor in the Department of Human Development & Family Science at OSU-Tulsa. She received her B.S. in Human & Organizational Development from Vanderbilt University, her M.Ed. in Sport & Exercise Psychology from the University of Virginia, and her PhD in Human Development & Family Science with an emphasis in early childhood education from the University of Missouri-Columbia. She teaches courses at both the graduate and undergraduate level in early childhood education, child development, and family science. Her research interests center around the developmental and family outcomes of children with and without disabilities, which drive her longitudinal research project with children, teachers, and families. Dr. Tate is a member of the Society for Research in Child Development (SRCD) and the National Association for the Education of Young Children (NAEYC); she also sits on the Oklahoma Partnership for School Readiness board as a designee.

Carol M. Trivette, PhD, is a Research Scientist, Orelena Hawks Puckett Institute, Morganton, North Carolina. Her research interests include the identification of evidence-based strategies that can be used by early childhood practitioners to build the capacity of parents to promote their children's learning and development. Her research interests have focused on the identification and use of implementation strategies that can be used to promote the adoption of evidence-based practices by early childhood intervention practitioners and parents to enhance the growth and development of young children. A focus of this research has been the importance of translating research into practices and strategies that have applicability for both home-based and classroom programs.

Michael Ungar, PhD currently holds a Killam Professorship in Social Work at Dalhousie University, is the Co-Director of the Resilience Research Centre (RRC) and Network Director for the Children and Youth in Challenging Contexts Network, a Networks of Centres of Excellence focused on sharing best practices related to working with vulnerable children and youth. Dr. Ungar is also a Clinical Supervisor with the American Association for Marriage and Family Therapy, Board Member of the American Family Therapy Academy, and a registered social worker. He has published over 100 peer-reviewed articles and book chapters on the topic of resilience and is the author of 11 books including *The Social Worker*, his first novel (Pottersfield Press, 2011). Among his books for professionals are *The Social Ecology of Resilience: A Handbook for Theory and Practice* (Springer USA, 2012); *Counseling in Challenging Contexts: Working with Individuals and Families Across Clinical and Community Settings* (Brooks/Cole, 2011); and *Strengths-based Counseling with At-risk Youth* (Corwin Press, 2006).

Brian E. Vaughn holds the position of Human Sciences Professor of Child Development in the *Department of Human Development & Family Studies* at Auburn University and has been on the Auburn Faculty since 1988. Prior to coming to Auburn, Dr. Vaughn held a faculty position at the University of Illinois at Chicago and Research Associate positions at the University of California, Berkeley, and the University of California, Los Angeles. He has maintained an active research program focused on the social behavior and social relationships of infants, toddlers, and young children for over 33 years.

Karen Winter is a lecturer in social work at Queens' University Belfast. She is a qualified social worker with over 16 years experience in working with children and families as a field social worker, team manager and a guardian ad litem. She has significant research experience in undertaking qualitative research with young children and engaging them through the use of participatory methods. She has written extensively on these matters in academic journals and most recently through a core text *Building Relationships and Communicating with Young Children: A Practical Guide for Social Workers* (London: Routledge, 2011).

Sue C. Wortham is a Professor Emerita at the University of Texas at San Antonio. She received a Bachelor of Science degree in elementary education with a minor in history from the University of Houston in 1964, a Master's degree in history with a minor in counseling and guidance from Southwest Texas State University in 1970, and a PhD in curriculum and instruction with concentrations in reading and early childhood education from the University of Texas at Austin in 1976. She taught in the public schools for 7 years, served as an administrator in Lockhart, Texas, for two years, and was an educational consultant at state and national levels before serving on the early childhood and elementary faculty at the University of Texas at San Antonio for 22 years. She has published 10 books, including *Early Childhood Curriculum: Developmental Bases for Learning and Teaching* (5th edition, 2010), *Play and Child Development* (4th edition, 20120, co-authored with Joe Frost and Stuart Reifel, and *Assessment in Early Childhood Education* (6th edition, 2012), all published by Pearson. Her most recent publication was as Editor of *Common Characteristics and Unique Qualities in Preschool Programs. Global Perspectives in Early Childhood Education,* published by Springer in 2013. She was a Fulbright Scholar in Chile in 1992 and was President of the Association for Childhood Education International from 1995 to 1997. Since retirement in 2000 she has conducted teacher training in Haiti, Guatemala, Senegal, Burkina Faso, and Sierra Leone.

Shira Yuval-Adler, MA is a Graduate student in the Department of Psychology and the Center for the Study of Child Development at the University of Haifa, Israel. Her research focuses on the roots of young children's story-stem narratives. In particular, in her dissertation she is examining the contribution of the early emotional climate of the family, including mother-father-child interactions and parental insightfulness, to children's emotion narratives.

CPSIA information can be obtained at www.ICGtesting.com
Printed in the USA
BVOW01*1319051114

373810BV00014B/175/P